American Journal of Archaeology • Archaeological Institute of America School of Oriental Research in Jer(American School of Classical Studies at Athens and American School of Classical Studies in Rome and American School for Oriental Study and Research in Palestine

Publisher's Note

The book descriptions we ask booksellers to display prominently warn that the book may have numerous typos, missing text, images and indexes.

We scanned this book using character recognition software that includes an automated spell check. Our software is 99 percent accurate if the book is in good condition. However, we do understand that even one percent can be a very annoying number of typos! And sometimes all or part of a page is missing from our copy of a book. Or the paper may be so discolored from age that you can no longer read the type. Please accept our sincere apologies.

After we re-typeset and design a book, the page numbers change so the old index and table of contents no longer work. Therefore, we often remove them.

We would like to manually proof read and fix the typos and indexes, manually scan and add any illustrations, and track down another copy of the book to add any missing text. But our books sell so few copies, you would have to pay up to a thousand dollars for the book as a result.

Therefore, whenever possible, we let our customers download a free copy of the original typo-free scanned book. Simply enter the barcode number from the back cover of the paperback in the Free Book form at www.general-books. net. You may also qualify for a free trial membership in our book club to download up to four books for free. Simply enter the barcode number from the back cover onto the membership form on the same page. The book club entitles you to select from more than a million books at no additional charge. Simply enter the title or subject onto the search form to find the books.

If you have any questions, could you please be so kind as to consult our Frequently Asked Questions page at www. general-books.net/faqs.cfm? You are also welcome to contact us there. General Books LLC®, Memphis, USA, 2012. ISBN: 9780217680400.

❧ ❧ ❧ ❧ ❧ ❧ ❧ ❧

FA 1.4-51.200
American Journal of Archaeology SECOND SERIES
The Journal Of The Archaeological Institute Of America
   Vol. XI, 1907 CEDttortaI Boaro
   Editor-in-Chief
   'HAROLD NORTH FOWLER,
Professor In Western Reserve University.
   Associate Editors
   J. R. S. STERRETT (for Vie American School at Athens),
Professor in Cornell University.
JOHN C. ROLFE (for the American School in Rome),
Professor in the University of Pennsylvania.
JOHN P. PETERS (for the American School in Palestine),
Rector of St. Michael's Church, New York.
ALLAN MARQUAND (for Mediaeval and Renaissance Archaeology),
Professor in Princeton University.
CHARLES PEABODY (for American Archaeology),
Cambridge, Mass.
   Honorary Editors THOMAS DAY SEYMOUR (President of the Institute),
Professor in Yale University.
JAMES R WHEELER (Chairman of the Managing Committee
of the School at A thens),
Professor In Columbia University.
ANDREW F. WEST (Chairman of the Managing Committee
of the School in Rome),
Professor In Princeton University.
CHARLES C. TORREY (Chairman of the Managing Committee
of the School in Palestine),
Professor in Yale University.
   Managing Editor JAMES MORTON PATON,
Cambridge, Mass.
   Miss Mary H. Buckingham, Classical Archaeology.
   Professor Harry E. Burton, Roman Archaeology.
   Mr. Harold R. Hastings, Classical Archaeology.
   Professor Elmer T. Merrill, Numismatics.
   EttitottsI Contributors
   Professor Frank G. Moore, Roman Archaeology.
   Mr. Charles R. Morey, Christian and Mediaeval Archaeology.
   Professor Lewis B. Paton, Oriental Archaeology.
   Dr. Arthur S. Pease, Classical Archaeology.
   Institute of America
THE TEMPLE AT MUSHENNEF, HAURAN, SYRIA plates I-IV

Through the kindness of Professor Howard Crosby Butler, who has lent me his notes and photographs, taken on the American Archaeological Expedition to Syria in 1900, I have been able to make a restoration of the temple found at Mushennef.

The site of Mushennef, which is that of ancient Nela (Waddington, *Inscriptions de la Syrie,* note on No. 2211), seems to have been an early place of worship, and there still remain the ruins of a temple surrounded by a paved court and its enclosing wall. On what appears to have been the lintel of a gateway in the north side of this wall, is an inscription of the time of Agrippa I (Waddington, *op. cit.,* No. 2211), which would lead us to believe that this wall enclosed a temple or shrine of Zeus as early as the first half of the first century. Another inscription near this, however, is of the time of Marcus Aurelius Antoninus, and it is possible that the wall may have been rebuilt during that Emperor's reign (Waddington, *op. cit.* No. 2212). The architectural details of the temple also seem to point to a period about the time of this last inscription, *i. e.* 171 A.d., and the style of the monument seems a little later than that of the temple at 'Atil, which is dated 151 A. d. These facts have been deduced from the material gathered by Professor William K. Prentice, another member of the expedition. For the photographs from which the greater part of the restoration has been made, see Butler, *Publications of an American Archaeological Expedition to Syria;* Part II, *Architecture in Northern Central Syria and the Djebel Hauran,* pp. 347-351. Plates III and IV, and Figs. 2 and 3, are reproduced from this work by the kind permission of Professor Butler and The Century Company.

-*Publications of an American Archaeological Expedition to Syria;* Part III, *Inscriptions,* Nos. 380, 380 *a*, 381.
American Journal of Archaeology, Second Series. Journal of the
Archaeological Institute of America, Vol. XI (1907), No, 1.

A considerable portion of the superstructure of the temple is still standing, and it is from photographs of these parts, and from measurements taken on the spot, that the restorations here presented were made. The plan is distyle *in antis* (Fig. 1), though at some time the front wall of the cella has been removed, and portions of it, together with fragments from other parts of the ruins, have been built into the spaces between the columns and antae. The cella was apparently crossed by a transverse arch, for portions of the piers still remain on the interior of the two side walls. The temple stands on a podium, 13.45 m. by 9.60 m. square, and is approached by a flight of steps which are still *in situ,* an unusual thing in Syrian temple ruins. The base of the podium is buried by debris so that its mouldings cannot be certainly known, but the cap is still visible, and consists of a cyma recta above a quarter round with its two fillets. Both of the columns are standing to about one third of their original height, and their plinth blocks rest on the second step from the top. Their base is of the ordinary Attic type with a scotia between two torus mouldings. The lower portions of

Figure 2.—Pilaster-cap, Architrave, And Frieze Of Southwest Angle Of Temple. their capitals, consisting of two rows of acanthus leaves, have been built into the rough east wall above what remains of the columns, and would seem to indicate that these columns were of the Corinthian order; but the upper part of one, found lying near by, consisted of a pair of small Ionic scrolls with an egg and dart echinus, thus proving them to have been of the Composite type.

Three of the angle pilasters are also *in situ,* and their height is 7.63 m. from the podium to the top of their caps. These caps are fine examples of the Corinthian style (Fig. 2) with rather salient angles, as the perspective shows (plate I). Their bases have a low plinth block surmounted by a scotia between two torus mouldings. These mouldings are beautifully carved in a manner characteristic only of a few Syrian bases. (*E.g.* Temples of Zeus and of Helios ? at Kanawat.) The lower torus is carved with the guilloche, the scotia with perpendicular reeds in groups of three, and the small torus with bay leaves.

The architrave and the frieze, with its egg and dart bedmould for the cornice, are still standing on parts of the walls, and have the forms and proportions shown in the elevation of the facade (plate II). No part of a broken or arcuated architrave between the two columns was found, but from the wide intercolumniation and the fact that this form of architrave was common in the Roman architecture of Syria (Serayil at Kanawat, remains of Propylaea at Damascus, South Temple at 'A til), it lias been assumed in the drawing. The architrave is two-stepped, and is carved with a meander with flowers and rosettes, probably of different patterns, in the alternate spaces. Its cymatium is carved with a band of egg and dart and a running foliate design. The frieze consists of a rinceau of acanthus crowned by an unusually heavy egg and dart moulding. Above the frieze, the cyma recta and slant of the roof are conjectural though there is evidence for both of them from ruins at other places in Syria. The roof of the so-called North Temple at 'Atil was of gable form, built on transverse arches. There are three special arguments to support the conjecture of the cymatium cornice. First: In none of the ruins in the Hauran, outside of Bosra, are there any remains of the Corinthian cornice with consols; but in all of them there are abundant remains of a rather salient cyma recta of such large scale that it could hardly have been anything but a cornice. Second: Buildings of this size were undoubtedly roofed with stone, and roofing slabs are found both at 'Atil and Mushennef with their ends carved in the form of a cyma recta. Third: In the front wall of a Roman basilica at Shakka, a niche, which may be taken to represent the facade of a temple, has both an arcuated architrave and a cymatium cornice.

Still more was assumed in drawing the front wall of the cella. Among the fragments in the present rough wall (Fig. 3) are

Figure 3. — Modern Wall Composed Of Ancient Fragments, Between Antae

And Columns Of Temple. parts of a lintel, ornamented with a grapevine, which from its size and form seems to have been the lintel of the main doorway, and has been used as such. A large broken consol is also present, and may have been one of a pair on either side of the door, though this has not been shown in the drawing. At 'Atil, a curved niche above a rectangular one was found on either side De Vogiie *Syria Centrale: Architecture Civile et Beliyieuse,* Pl. 15; Butler, *op. cit.* pp. 306, 367.

of the central entrance, and in this rough wall at Mushennef is an ornamental lintel, which from its size and style of ornament— a meander, like that of the architrave — would seem to have been the top of one of these rectangular niches. As for the curved niche, no parts remain, and it has been entirely assumed from examples at the North Temple at 'Atil and elsewhere. The arch over the doorway is a common expedient in Syria, both for admitting light and for discharging the pressure from the flat lintel, and therefore this feature lias been included.

The peribolos of the temple (plate III) is paved with flat stones of various sizes, smoothly cut and squared, and is surrounded by a colonnade and a temenos wall except behind the temple, where the colonnade is omitted (plate I). One column is still standing to the height of the necking, and shows a considerable entasis. Near it lies its capital of the Corinthian order, while in the rough front wall of the temple itself is a piece of an architrave which, from its rougher workmanship, and its inscription of the time of Alexander Severus (222-235 A. d.), would seem to have been part of the architrave of this colonnade, which is thus shown to have been of later date than the temple. Portions of the temenos wall are also *in situ,* and are of cut stones smoothed on all their faces, except in some of the lower stages along the shore of the little reservoir *(birkeK)* behind the temple, where there are some rusticated blocks (plate IV). This may be due to the fact that the wall was first built under Agrippa I, and then rebuilt at a later date, as stated earlier in this article.

The whole temple is built of black basalt in blocks of various sizes, and often of different heights, but finely cut and laid without mortar. All the ornaments are beautifully carved, and the mouldings are well denned. Altogether it is a very good example of the architecture of the Roman period in Syria during the second century of our era.

Clarence Ward.

Princeton University. Butler, *op. cit.* p. 346.

E.g. Kaisiriyeh at Shakka, De Vogite, *op. cit.* Pl. 0; Butler, *op. cit.* p. 371, and the Praetoriuin at Mousmyeh, G. Rey, *Voyage dans le Uaouran,* Pl. 3. Prentice, *op. cit.* No. 382.

American Journal Of Archaeology, Second Series Vol. XI (1907) Plate V

Institute of America

THE TECHNICAL HISTORY OF WHITE LECYTHI plate V

There is need of a scientific classification of white lecythi by shape, ornament, technique, and historical sequence of style. M. Pottier, in his *Etude sur leg lecythes blancs attiques,* pp. 91 ff., especially p. 103, and Professor Furtwiingler, in his *Beschreibung der Vagenmrnmlung im Antiquarium zu Berlin,* have attempted the task; but the material at Athens, at the time of his writing, was inadequate for the one, and the other based his very careful study on the limited collection in Berlin. M. Pottier remarks truly (p. 4) that Athens is the only place where a detailed study can be made. Many finds in Greece and many special articles have paved the way for a comprehensive survey.

The essential distinction to be made in such classification is between lecythi with designs in glaze paint and those in dull *(matt)* colors. The latter alone deserve the name of polychrome lecythi, though both classes are Attic. In the former class one must distinguish those vases with black glaze from those, more numerous and later, with a yellowish wash color. It was to the use of this wash that the first success of the white lecythi was due, and it led the way to the polychrome style with dull colors. These "golden glaze" lecythi, recently found *E.g.,* the "golden glaze" class lias largely increased even since Mr. Bosanquet wrote of them, *J.H.S.* 1899, p. 180. -Bibliography in Pottier, pp. 3 f. See also the works cited in this article. The failure to make this a primal distinction is the cause of much useless de'scription in catalogues; *e.g.* British Museum. No. I) 51, is said to have brown outlines, but brown wash for the hair; whence one might suppose the former was in dull paint, the other in glaze. Both are in wash of the glaze. Again, in the account of No. I) 57 the opposite blunder is made, —the outline is called brown glaze, the hair simple brown, though both are exactly the same, — wash color. Formerly only the lecythi with dull colors were called Attic. Pottier, p. 4.

American Journal of Archaeology, Second Scries. Journal of tbo 7

Archaeological Institute of America, Vol. XI (1907), No. 1.

in large numbers, deserve notice in a separate class because they bridge over the period (ca. 470-440 B.C.) between the severe red-figured vases and the later free style.

The matter of chronological sequence is also an important question that has not been adequately treated. Some lecythi are still loosely assigned to the fourth century B.C., as many red-figured vases used to be, whereas there is strong reason for believing that practically all the white lecythi belong to the fifth. I have important evidence on this point in the case of a lecythus found on the island of Rhenea. Apart from such external proof as fixes the date of the lecythus from Rhenea, internal proof is derived from the comparative study of artistic style in the last half of the fifth century; whereby Professor Furtwiingler *(Griech. Vcuenmalerei,* p. 39) was led to date the Meidias vase about 430 B.C., instead of in the fourth century.

It may be safely asserted that the dates generally assigned are from a score of years to a half century too late. However, as each style was invented, the old did not die out. The quality deteriorated; the class continued for a long time. A poor lecythus, made for the trade, cannot be dated accurately, since cheap productions of an older type long remained beside the newer styles.

The importance of the ornament (the form of the palmettes on the shoulder and the meander) and shape, as well as that of the technique, has not been recognized sufficiently. Rarely in Greek art does one find more experiment in detail than in the development of the lecythi, though they have been thought of as simple, conventional products by those who have seen only a few late and poor specimens in dull colors. These details alone See Pottier, p. 2, for the earlier view.

Cf. *infra,* p. 32, Group C. The analogies with sculpture, and sequence within the classes, are as useful for the chronology of the lecythi, as they have proved for that of the redfigured vases. Cf. *infra,* p. 35 n. 6. The various publications have not been of much aid to me in the matter of ornament, since their general descriptions are as vague as their accounts of the kind of color. Cf. *supra,* p. 7 n. 3. Only a study of the originals could assure me of the proper classification. My examples are almost entirely confined to the vases I have seen. It was by the kind permission of the American School at Athens that I was enabled to study the lecythi in the European museums during my year as Fellow of the School. give a clue to the course of development in technique, and enable us to understand the historical relation of the groups. The size of a vase determines its ornament.

To understand the evolution of the white lecythi, we must study briefly the formation of a canonical shape and ornamentation in the black-figured class on red or white ground, and in the red-figured class.

I. CLASSES PRECEDING WHITE LECYTHI PROPER

A. *Black-figured Lecythi with Red or White Ground.* — The general *shape* of early white lecythi — those with added white, etc., *infra,* p. 17 f.—had already been evolved in the severe red-figured class, *e.g.* No. 12394; but certain traditional forms of the black-figured style still persisted, especially on small vases of poor workmanship. A favorite shape for the body on black-figured lecythi with red ground is a more or less truncated cone (not a cylinder, as later), with a thin plaque for the foot; *e.g.* Nos. 1143, 1145. The lip is also low and spreading. This shape is carried over to the vases with black outline on white ground, but in a modified form; *i.e.* the body is longer in proportion to the greatest diameter, so that the angle of diminution is smaller than before. This elongated shape has several varieties, according as the angle is more or less great. With this occurs the common early form of the foot with an indentation at half the height of the side, not near the upper edge, as later. The small white lecythi with wash outlines continue this shape and foot for at least half a century, *e.g.* Nos. 2025, 2030, just as the small red-figured ones preserve the shape and ornament of the black-figured style, while the larger ones introduce such novelties as the meander and cross in place of the continuous meander (No. 1695). This elongated class has the black varnish reaching half way up the body, leaving a comparatively small space for the design. It also employs reserved or red bands on the glaze below the Where simple numbers of vases are given, they refer to those in the National Museum at Athens.

E.g. Nos. 1984, 1988, 1142, 1136, 12481 (the last two on white ground). *I.e.* a narrow band is left unpainted around the vase so that the red clay appears. The effect is the same as when red bands are painted over the glaze. design (No. 12749). Both peculiarities are borrowed by the later lecytlii with black outlines, *e.g.* Nos. 1984, 1988 (the latter with a red line). Other black-figured lecythi, though approaching the later shape, show rather heavy proportions and a convex outline of the body (No. 1124), and have their successors in the lecytlii with added white (No. 12771). The *lip,* in some instances *(e.g.* Nos. 1136, 1141), has a tulip form which recurs chiefly in very late white lecythi. The *neck* is usually undecorated, but rarely has perpendicular rays (No. 12776, black-figured on red ground), or ivy (No. 1129, white ground on neck and shoulder as well as on body). The small lecythi have both neck and handle unpainted. The transition between neck and shoulder is usually without prominent division.

Before the uniformity of the later meander pattern was attained, there was much tentative experimenting; either nothing was used (Xo. 1143), or a checker (No. 12841), or an ivy band (No. 12533), which degenerates into dots (No. 1158), or dots with connecting lines in zig-zag (No. 514), or denticulation (No. 513). A running meander was, however, the commonest form till the appearance of the class with added white, though a checker appears in the outline lecythus, No. 1972. Experiments were also made in putting the meander on white ground.

White was variously employed, foreshadowing the class with added white, as for the flesh of women (No. 1638, red-figured lecthyus earlier than 440 B. C.). This was an adaptation of the black-figured style. As on other red-figured vases, white is at times used for the hair of old men (Nos. 1301, 1641), and for various objects, as, for example, a ship's beak (No. 12769). White was also employed as a ground for the neck and shoulder, while the body remained red (Nos. 1142,1135), or for the neck, shoulder, and body together (Nos. 12481, 1129). The later use of white for the shoulder and body alone is very rare in earlier times, but is found on Nos. 12798 and 1973, which seem to be rather late in date. The class with added white was the first to have a white shoulder regularly, while before Also in hybrid varieties combined with the net pattern, as on the red-figured lecythus, No. 1194.

Nos. 1501, 1276, 1278 (small red-figured lecythi), 543 (black-figured). its appearance a red-figured shoulder was in vogue combined with a white body. In the same way three palmettes became canonical for the shoulder in place of five, or a lotus pattern.

The typical ornament on the *shoulder* for larger vases is five palmettes (sometimes four, six, or seven, as Wiirzburg,

No. 3756), which was continued in the group with black outline (No. 1972); for smaller ones, a double row of lines, the lower one of which is a degeneration of the lotus-bud pattern. These latter occur separately (No. 1136), or joined by intertwining lines (Nos. 12769, 1143). This lotus pattern is also found on the later lecythi with black outline. As the later canonical shape seems derived from red-figured lecythi, so the design with three palmettes on the shoulder apparently has the same origin, though the special form of the volute connecting the palmettes, and various details, were the invention of the potters of the white lecythi. Still one severe red-figured lecythus (No. 12893) shows a form very similar to that of the later ones. White lecythi with black outlines, however, employ the forms and ornament of the black-figured, as well as those of the redfigured style. Various peculiarities, such as the spreading form of the connecting lines about the palmettes seen in a later group with wash design *(infra,* p. 21), are found in the earlier style. Again the palmettes on the body of the vase limiting the design are common to both these early lecythi (Nos. 102, 12769, 1988) and those with black outlines. Above the palmette the egg pattern comes at the juncture of neck and shoulder in the better examples, but the usage is not fixed till the appearance of the class with added white; earlier, a row of lines commonly takes its place, as is the case also in the later small white lecythi.

One group, with black-figured designs on white ground, shows an attempt to elevate the lecythi above the vulgar products of the day, even as in the later class with added white. This is, perhaps, due to competition with the new red The earlier palmettes were placed vertically, and hence five were needed to rill the space around the shoulder. Later they were set horizontally, and, with the use of the flower, easily filled the space. Still later, in the canonical form, volutes were substituted for the flower.
Discussed by Miss Sellars in *J.H.8.* 1893, pp. 1 ff. pis. 1-3. figured lecythi, which still kept the high level of the other vases of this technique, and were successful by their fine shapes as well as by their elegant ornament. That this group belongs to the first quarter of the fifth century is clear from the style of the figures: as Circe (No. 1133), the Discobolus (No. 12533), the satyrs (No. 1129), which remind one of analogous sculptures of this date. The shoulder has five palmettes, but the pattern combining the meander and cross is borrowed from the red-figured lecythi (No. 1132), though at times there are only dots (No. 1130). The foot sometimes has the earlier form (No. 1133), or the later (No. 1130), or is concave (No. 1132). Added white is irregularly used for women's flesh; for while Circe is black on No. 1137, the siren on No. 1130 is white.

B. *Red-figured Lecythi.* — These need not delay us long, since we have already treated of some of their peculiarities in connection with the black-figured group. In one respect, however, they are of great importance in the history of the white lecythi, for the best examples show the canonical shape: a convex lip, marked division of neck and shoulder, well-proportioned cylindrical body curving abruptly to a foot, with a notch close to the upper edge. The decoration with three palmettes and a flower, usual in the red-figured style, also occurs sporadically later. The smaller and poorer specimens retain the shapes and ornaments of the earlier classes. The general technique is that of other red-figured vases.

Summing up, the earlier periods are times of experiment in form and ornament, while the later ones exhibit equal irregularities in technique and polychromy. The canonical shape occurs already in-the red-figured class, and the later ornament is worked out in detail in various earlier examples, but is not consistently accepted. There is the same distinction that is found later between large and small vases, — the former adopt new ideas, the latter cling to the old, *i.e.* the body in the shape of a truncated cone, the red neck and shoulder, the earlier foot, as well as the double lines or lotus buds on the shoulder. In No doubt it was the success of the red-figured style that made the potters imitate the funeral scenes of the white lecythi in the red-figured technique about the middle of the fifth century. Cf. Weisshaupl in *'Eip.'Apx*-1893, pp. 12 ff.

general, these early lecythi represent a comparatively poor grade of work. The exceptions in various series only prove the rule. II. THE TECHNIQUE OF WHITE LECYTHI

A. *The Meaning of the Outline Style.* — The black-figured style, whether on red or white ground, is based on the contrast of a solid color (black figures) with a uniform background. The red-figured style, on the contrary, is an anomaly. From the draughtsman's standpoint it is an exercise in line drawing; in effect it belongs to the same category as the black-figured style, — solid color (red) for figures, against a background (black) of a different color. The novelty of the outline technique in the lecythi is that the design appears as pure line. In the lecythi with black outlines we have the black and white technique; later, different colors are used for the lines.

In vase painting of the black-figured style, as in other fields of contemporary art, the idea of outline work was not an entire novelty; its importance in the case of white lecythi lay in its use as a standard, its consistent application. The new style is most clearly shown in the lecythi with black outlines, where, as a rule, no accessory color is employed, but only black lines on a white ground. In the application of the principle there is, however, already a compromise. Some vases use solid color for garments and details while the figures are in outline, others are consistent in limiting themselves throughout to pure line.

The limitation in the use of accessory color corresponds to the simplification of the black-and red-figured styles. There was even more reason for this sobriety in vases painted on red clay than in the case of white lecythi. The warm orange color of the Attic clay, whether for background or figures, was a compensation for the use of only two colors, since Cf. Pottier in *B.C.H.* 1800, pp. 376

ft, (the origin and development of the whiteground technique). Pure line work is seen both in the incised lines of black-figured vases and in the analogous art of incised bronzes.

This group, as well as that with added white, shows the tradition of the black-figured style in still clinging to the use of solid black for garments, which the later classes abandon. the red and the glistening black formed a striking contrast. There was a further reason in the practical purpose of the redfigured vases themselves, which were made for the hard usage of every-day life in the house. The black varnish was lasting, the red and white easily rubbed off. The white lecythi, however, as soon as they were limited to sepulchral use, did not need solidity as their first quality. Yet, in spite of the inferior wear of the white lecythi with black figures (which were made for domestic purposes), they had sufficient artistic charm in their novelty to be popular for some time beside the more usual red-figured technique. It was different with a simple black line on white ground. These pure outline lecythi looked thin, and did not have the warmth of color the Greeks always sought. Hence, the continued experiments with color. First "added white" was tried, — the ground was made cream color, the figures drawn in wash outline, and filled in with clear white. This was a compromise with the older series with solid color; for while the black outline appeared as line, the figure was in solid color. Unfortunately the result had the same fault as the black-figured style — lack of clearness of outline. The lines degenerated because they were to be filled in, and were not compelled to depend on their intrinsic value. The black-figured style with incised detail was better, for there the lines were added later, and stood out on their own merits; in the class with added white they were covered or disturbed by the filling of solid color.

The artistic quality of line work is that of pure drawing in contrast to general decoration. In the latter the eye is led That this was the reason of difference in technique may be seen in the few vases of other forms where white ground and outline drawing are used; as for example, the cyliees of the Euphronian school. On the cylix, Hartwig, *Meisterschalen,* pi. 51, the ephebe's cloak is solid brown. To be sure, experiments were made in the old style, as on the Orpheus cylix *J.U.S.* IX. pi. 6), where all is outline drawing, but the tendency was toward solid color for garments. In the twin cyliees of the Louvre, *Mon. Piot,* II. pis. 5, 0, one has solid color, the other outline. But it must be noted that both the Orpheus and the Louvre vases use warm wash for outlines, the lierlin cylix black. The painters of lecythi fluctuated some time between the consistent copying of the monochrome style of the red-figured vases and the legitimate changes that the new technique required. Hence, their irregular use of color, and even chary use of added white, for example on No. 1972 only for fillets. aside from what there is of line by color and accessories. Nevertheless, the few accessory colors in the class with added white (red and brown chiefly) were not pleasing enough to save the style. The only solution was in using color for the line as well as for the accessories. The new school of the day wished to show their *bravura* in technique, their firmness of hand; but they were not willing to sacrifice color. We have, in fact, the struggle between art and trade. It was fortunate that lecythi became popular at this time as funeral offerings, with the formation of distinctive scenes relating to the dead. The potter was at once released from the necessity of decorating chiefly with a view to solidity, and not artistic charm. He could now adopt the friable white *engobe* in place of the older, firmer, but less pure shade. The earlier black-and redfigured styles continued in use on cheap products for the home, the new became the field for experiment in a purely artistic direction. The sacred purpose only asked uniformity of ground (white), perhaps as a sign of purity or the like. The painter did not, however, immediately divorce the two classes of funeral and household lecythi. The scenes show this in their mixture of subjects. Lasting glaze paint was still used, but diluted till it became a beautiful golden color which had enough charm in itself to restrain the tendency to excessive polychromy. It was this modification of the paint that paved the way for a satisfactory artistic style. When color was given to the line its fineness and flow were accentuated, and with the addition of a simple scheme of accessory color, suitable to the relatively humble position of the lecythi, these vases reached their acme. The moving influence in these, as well as later changes, seems to have come from higher branches of art, and the probable sources have been studied elsewhere. The same impulse came over Kenaissance painters, who prefer finished outline drawings to the purely decorative work of the mediaeval artists. They also feel the added charm of color in line drawing, as did the Attic vase painters. So the degeneration of the colored drawings of the artists of the lecythi may be paralleled in the Renaissance. The careless but masterly strokes of the designs on the later lecythi remind one of the change from the careful sketches of the early Florentine painters to those of the Bolognese school. Cf. Girard, *La Peinture Antique,* pp. 152 ff.; Murray, *White Vases of the British Museum,* Introduction; Winter, *Jb. Arch. I.* 1897, p. 135.

B. *The White Ground.* — The white ground is at first a fairly solid basis for the painting. It does not flake off easily, as does the white added over the black varnish for women's flesh and details in black-figured vases. It varies in thickness, being at times applied thin like a translucent paint so as to show in places the clay beneath; but later, especially on good vases, forming a thick crust. The desire for a light background was satisfied in early times by the pale clays of Greece. There is little difference in effect between the early black-figured vases on the clay ground and the later black-figured ones with a white slip, which is not pure white itself and is half translucent. The potter was merely producing artificially from a red clay the light ground to which he had been accustomed. With the appearance of the class with added white, there was need of a distinction between the white of the figures and that of the background, and hence the use of two shades, one for the ground, the other for the flesh. The use of golden wash, however, necessitated a return to pure white for the ground, since any shade harmonizes better with a pure white. That this was felt as a simple artistic necessity is seen by the fact that it was adopted even on the small and poor lecythi of this technique. The later use of an extended polychromy still further required the pure white. We have already remarked how freedom was given to the technique *by* the exclusively sepulchral use of the later lecythi. We come to the dividing line, both in the admission of the water-color style of dull paints, and in the new friable white for ground, since the vase no longer feared the daily use. The dead enjoyed the gaudy but delicate toy.

III. EARLY WHITE LECYTHI

A. *Lecythi with Black Outlines.* — The first important change to note in this class is the appearance of the sharp incision, separating neck from shoulder, which characterizes the later classes, *e. g.* No. 12748. The neck is but rarely painted (Nos. 1791, 1792, 1804, 1906). One small group has palmettes on either side of a single figure (Nos.

Cf. the use of eyes to frame the design on cylices. Alabastra show the same usage. 12769, 1827, 1857, 1858, 2023, Munich, No. 245). These vases are chiefly severe in style, though the last mentioned is later, *ca.* 460 B.C. They seem to show Ionic influence in the Dionysiac subjects, the ornament, and the free use of color.

Solid black is sometimes employed for garments (Nos. 1906, 1792, 12588), or outlines with inner lines for folds *(Arch. Am.* 1902, p. 116), more rarely red (Nos. 1804, 1829). The subjects show the transition to the funeral type. The Nike flying to an altar or pouring a libation gives way to a man leaning on his staff, or a woman before a palmette stele (No. 1972) or an oval mound, or a bearded man pulling his hair before a mound (No. 12748). This class continues for some time beyond the severe into the freer style, *ca.* 480—160 B.C. Others with aXo?-naines, as No. 1806, are representative of the Euphronian school. Small vases keep the old shapes for a long time.

B. *Lecythi with Added White.* — The class with added white for the figures on a creamy ground is small, but important in the history of the lecythi. The best examples are inscribed with a «aXo?- name. One, with the name of Alcimachus, belongs to a series pointing both backward to the red-figured vases in the style of Euphronius and forward to the group with golden glaze. The shoulder is in the red-figured technique with a flower and palmette pattern, as one might expect in a vase inscribed with a name occurring also on a red-figured lecythus (Klein, *Q-r. Vasen mit Lieblingsinschriften,* p. 166, No. 5).

The shield design is white on the black varnish, though the rest of the design is entirely in outline style; cf. Six, *Gaz. Arch.* 1888, pp. 193 ff., 281 ff., pis. 28 ff., for early polychrome decoration on black ground. The name is Glaucon. The eye is *en face.* The clay has turned grayish from being badly burned; cf. Berlin, Nos. 2427, 24-13, as well as many examples in Athens. *Ath. Mitt.* 1890, pp. 41 ff. (Weisshaupl). Cf. my article on the vase in 'E. 'Apx-1905, pp. 38 ff. with colored plate. This is the first example of the name occurring on a lecythus with added white. A comparison with the other vases bearing the same name dates the class with added white shortly before the middle of the fifth century B.c. The name Glaucon, used by Euphronius, is also found on a lecythus with added white (Klein, pp. 156 f.). Cf. further Bosanquet, *J.H.S.* 1899, p. 179.

The series with the names Diphilus and Dromippus have the later conventional palmette and volutes on the shoulder, as well as the perfected shape. Almost all also have dots about the ornament, showing, with the stylistic likeness, that they all come from the same workshop. One of them (No. 12786) has the ornament first traced out with a dry point. In general, great care was taken with this group. The unsigned vases show more conservatism in using older forms and ornament, especially the red-figured shoulder with palmette and flower (Nos. 1897,12770), or black-figured with an older form of the palmette (Nos. 1953, 1826, Dummler in *Jb. Arch. I.* 1887, pp. 168 ff., pi. II). The old concave foot is seen on No. 1921. One vase (No. 1968) shows brown for the flesh of the figure of Athena. The outlines are drawn in wash color, and black and red are used for garments, brown for wood.

The class is really a survival of the technique in solid color, only in the choice of white the artist was almost necessarily confined to representing women, if he remained true to the tradition of the black-figured style. And in fact, this is almost always the case. In the rare instances where male figures Rosanquet, *J.H.S.* 1806, pp. 164 ff. Their number has increased largely since then by finds in Eretria (Klein catalogues only 5 with the former name, while I have seen 11). The two names mentioned above are with patronymics; other lecytbi have the simple name, as Timocrates, Acestorides, Hygiaenon, Lichas (No. 1913; Fig. 1); see Klein, s. p. for the list.

Of. Berlin, Inv. No. 3291, *infra,* p. 20. Cf. No. 1942, *infra,* p. 24.

Figure 1.—Athens, Museum, No. 1913. occur, they are drawn in outline only, as *Ath. Mitt.* 1890, pi. 1, Ashmolean (Oxford), No. 267, Athens, No. 1754. The result in the selection of scenes is that they are chiefly domestic, though the trays, lecythi, and fillets (Nos. 1845, 12770, etc.) seem to show preparations to visit the stele, and so foreshadow the beginning of the funeral cycle. A number also have holes in the sides, as if to let the offered liquid flow out when buried with the dead, though other vases show traces of burning and breaking. The sepulchral interpretation of such apparently domestic scenes is strengthened by clear cases, as No. 12748, where we see an ephebe worshipping at a grave mound decorated with fillets, No. 1982, a woman with a tray before a stele, also with fillets; both vases with the inscription (toXo?. So we must accept the double anomaly of a /taXo?-

name on vases chiefly domestic in scene and meant for the tomb. No doubt tha /taXo?-inscription had become a convention, and the women, as especially cultivating the worship of the dead, preempted the scenes. A lecythus with added white, in Vienna (Museum f. Kunst u. Industrie, No. 1090), has an Amazon; but with its red shoulder decorated with five palmettes, it rather belongs to the category of black-figured vases.

The transition to the class with golden glaze is seen in the Diphilus lecythus, No. 12789. It already has the palmette with quirks, and alternating leaves in red and black like the polychrome lecythi. In style it is also in agreement with Nos. 1959, 1815, etc. The scene is domestic; a woman with a *lecane,* another with a tray of pomegranates. It may be compared with the peculiar Glaucon fragment in Bonn *(J.H.S.* 189(3, pi. 4). Of still greater importance in connecting the series is Berlin, Inv. No. 3970, which, though signed with the name of Diphilus, is yet the first example of the name on a vase with the design in golden glaze.

IV. THE LECYTHI WITH GOLDEN GLAZE

A. *Wash Lecythi Transitional to the Clam with Golden Glaze.* — Before a regular class with a consistent style was formed, single lecythi or groups of two or three show experiments in the Cf. on this subject Weisshiiupl in *Festsehrift f. Benndorf,* pp. 80 f.

use of golden glaze. These are mostly contemporaneous with the class with added white; that is, *ca.* 470-460 B.C. A lecythus in Boston (No. 9069) has the palmette and flower pattern on the shoulder. A bearded man and ephebe are on either side of the stele. The stele has a pediment which contains black silhouettes of two boxers and two kneeling figures, while on the acroteria are nude ephebes in outline.

No. 1935, still with the black varnish only slightly thinned in places, is remarkable for its noble and extremely careful style, its large size, and its polychromy. The shoulder has no ornament and the meander is of a peculiar shape. A brownish yellow is used for the cloak of the ephebe and green for the leaves of the wreaths. Altogether it betrays a hand wont to paint other kinds of vases, or even a fresco painter, so noble is the drawing. No. 1932 is of similar style, but smaller and poorer in drawing. The palmettes are peculiar, set upside down, with buds attached and in outline only. Berlin, In v. No. 3291 has the same palmette. One figure, of a snub-nosed servant, is unusual in its realism, and paralleled only by the later Charon heads on the white lecythi. All three have scenes at the stele.

No. 1818 is another isolated vase of this period. The style A lecythus in Leyden (No. 22) in poor grayish glaze has, in addition to the usual three palmettes on the shoulder, two others, one on each side, behind them. The scene represents two ephebes before a stele.

For small figures in silhouette cf. the *eidola* on lecythi (Pottier, *filude,* pp. 75 ff. pi. 2), and various votive tablets shown on red-figured vases (British Museum, No. E 585). The nude ephebes correspond to other types on lecythi (No. 1822), and decorative statues on stelae are seen on the lecythi, *Bonner Studien,* pi. 10, and 'E. *'Ap-*1886, pi. 4. *J.H.8.* 1809, pi. 2. The illustration is deceptive in giving a brown shade to the lines of the figures, as if they were in dull colors. The style approaches that of the Berlin cylix of Kuphronius. A very rare omission except on the late and carelessly made lecythi with dull color (Nos. 1797, 1799, 1756, Leyden, No. 23, with wash design), and a few red-figured lecythi, as Nos. 12890, 1303, 1193, etc. Similarities in detail to later lecythi are the stele (No. 1959), round circles on the steps (No. 1958), lecythi on the steps (Nos. 12739, 12747).

» *J.H.8.* 1899, p. 172, Fig. 2.

"*Ibid.* pp. 173 and 178, pi. 3. The original sketch was made with the dry point, as on two lecythi in Athens, Nos. 1821, 1823. and on Berlin, Inv. No. 3171. *Bonner Stud.* pp. 156 ff. pi. 12. Six thinks of an influence from painting. Winter (*,7b. Arch. I.* 1887, p. 236) argues a relation to Myron's school, but probably wrongly. is extremely fine, but the proportions of the figures entirely different from those on No. 1935. It has the so-called Attic system of proportion, No. 1935 the Dorian. The polychromy is marked, red and saffron. The outlines are in fine wash color.

Nos. 1913 and 1945 have the same technique and colors and are of the same period as No. 1818, but differ in style; *e.g.* the figures have square chins, not rounded. The scenes are a simple preparation to visit the stele, and a libation.

Nos. 1821 and 1823 are also of the same technique and coloring, but peculiar in style. They show previous sketching of the design with a dry point. One has a stele scene.

B. *Groups of Related Lecythi.*—Nos. 1789,1790, 1958 (Fig. 2), 1959 (Fig. 3). This group is distinguished by the form of the palmette pattern. The lines bounding the central palmette are spreading, not enclosing a heart-shaped space as in the other classes. Nos. 1789 and 1790 have also quirks on either side, as in the class with golden glaze.

.. „ Figure 2.—Athens, Museum, *Iso. Woo.*

The meander is combined with the checker. The ornament and design are drawn in a wash varying from black to yellow, which in Nos. 1789 and The ephebe's proportions are related to those of figures on Nos. 1821, 12745, 1945.

Benndorf, *Gr. u. Sic. Vasenbihler,* pi. 20, 2. Very rare on the white lecythi. Cf. the contemporary No. 1953 and the later Nos. 1954, 1936, 12783, and the red-figured lecythus, No. 1695. 1790 has been discolored by breaking and burning the vase at the funeral. Nos. 1789 and 1958 are monochrome, while red for fillets and the ephebe's qloak occur on Nos. 1959 and 1790.

The early date of the class is shown by the heavy chin, which is somewhat angular, the upward line of the mouth, and the pouting lip which appear on the Alcimachus vase, No. 12771. The scenes depicted are unusual in type and transitional from the domestic to the funeral scenes. Three of the vases have sepulchral subjects, the fourth, No. 1789, a libation, which, as elsewhere, may bear a mortuary significance, the last libation of a departing warrior who was slain in battle. Nos. 12739, 12747, Berlin, x, Inv. No. 3262. This group

Figure 3. — Athess, Museum, No. 1059.. _,. _ » is also distinguished by the form of the pahnette pattern, which has the middle leaf in outline only. A flower is also added as on earlier red-figured lecythi and on a few white ones with red-figured shoulder.

The design is in a yellowish wash. The only additional color is red for the cloak on No. 12739. The style is very like that of the red-figured vases of the severe period, except that the eyes are correctly drawn in profile. The figures have an angular chin, as have those on No. 1815 ('E£. 'Ap%. 1886, pi. 4), which has, however, dull black for the shoulder and meander.

On all three vases of this class there is a three-stepped stele Cf. Nos. 12730, 1815, and the group including No. 12737.

Of the twin lecythi, Nos. 12745, 12740, one represents a stele scene, the other a domestic one, the preparation to visit the tomb. Likewise on another pair, Nos. 1943, 1045, one has a preparation, the other a libation. No. 1932 has all the palmette leaves in outline only. with lecythi and other vases on the steps; on the Berlin vase there are a lyre and a toilet box on top. On a wash lecythus in Vienna (Museum f. Kunst u. Industrie, No. 1088) a chair and a wool basket are on the stele. Berlin, No. 2252 *(Arch. Zeit.* 1880, pi. 11) has alternate outline and black leaves in the palmette, but is peculiar in the ornament above and below the design. Berlin, No. 2444 is related in style, but only the flower beside the central palmette is in outline. The scene shows a mother with a swaddled baby and a warrior. All these vases are spiritless survivals of older technique. A better work and early in date is the Charon lecythus, Munich, No. 209. It has the palmette and flower pattern on the shoulder and uses brown as an accessory color.

The small lecythi with glaze paint copy the new scenes while they keep the old shape, technique, and ornament, red shoulder and neck, with loosely joined palmette. The paint varies from almost black to golden. They rarely use more than one accessory color. Carlsruhe, No. B 2863 is an interesting example of this type with a representation of the dead in Charon's boat and an *eidolon* in the background.

C. *The Class with Golden Glaze.* — The class with golden glaze proper is distinguished by style and ornament. The foot has usually a notch near the upper edge, though Nos. 12790, 12791, 12794, 12795, and 12784 have none, and otherwise form a group by themselves. The shoulder ornament has quirks beside the central palmette. The meander is combined with the cross.

In agreement with the sober style and beauty of the lines and varnish, additional colors are little used; *e.g.* red on Nos. 12791, 12795, 1980, purple on British Museum, No. D 48. No. 1942 has unusual polychromy in the use of purple and green, while one face is in red silhouette. The paint for the outlines varies, 1 Benndorf, *Gr. u. Sic. Vasenbilder,* pi. 27, 1; *J.II.fi.* 1800, p. 18:2, shows Charon's head from a photograph.

Mr. Bosanquet gives a list of those he thinks related to the *Hi/giaenon* lecythi *(J.U.S.* 1800, pp. 170 f.). but he combines vases so far different in style and date as Nos. 1818 and 1866, which are at least thirty years apart in a period when styles were most rapidly changing. *J.H.8.* 1809, p. 179, Fig. 5. For similar examples, see *J.U.S.* 1899, p. 177; cf. *infra,* p. 35, n. 1 and 2. according to the firing and composition, from a slightly thinned black varnish or an almost lustreless gray wash to fine golden varnish of an orange shade, on No. 12794. The color also varies on the same vase as the paint is spread thinner or thicker, appearing black or yellow as the case may be. The date of this class is about the middle of the fifth century. The hole in the body shows the use for liquid offerings to the dead, as in the case of the class with added white, and few are broken or burnt. As in that class, the scenes rarely include the stele (Nos. 1822 plate V, 1980, 12746, Vienna, Mus. f. Kunst u. Industrie, No. 1088).

Male figures are also rather infrequent, as on Nos. 1980, 1740, 1838, 1822 (an ephebe softer in style than on No. 1818), *White Vases,* pi. 5 (British Museum, No. D 54, two ephebes). The scenes most frequently have two women. No. 1942 has a child seated on the stele steps. The monument is either a simple slab, an oval mound, or a slab with palmette capital. There is little attempt at characterizing the figures: the wrinkled old man on No. 1797, a vase with poor gray wash, is quite exceptional.

Nos. 1960 and 12792, of slightly later date, are related in having the leaves of their palmette ornaments drawn in dull black, though the bounding lines are in glaze. *White Vases,* pis. 1 (British Museum, No. D 57) and 3 *(Ibid.* No. D 51) are of the same style, yet use glaze for the ornament. British Museum, No. D 67 *(Catalogue* III, pi. 27) is remarkable for the realism in the design of the old man.

No. 1994 is a continuation of this style, but the paint is entirely dull black. The palmette ornament lacks the quirks on either side of the front palmette, which are a distinguishing mark of the previous group. It is also more developed in its polychrony, having purple, red, green, and yellow. The cap on one of the figures is like those on Nos. 1960, 1822, and 12784.

A further continuation of this group is seen in Nos. 1843 (a single ephebe beside a palmetted stele), 1813 (two ephebes), and 1928 (a "deposition" scene, where both Thanatos and Hypnos are beardless). The transition to the later style is shown in No. 12783, where the garments have purple borders, though the design seems to be wash. No. 1925 has the peculiar curved body of No. 12783, but uses red paint for the design, purple for the borders of the dress, and represents a " prothesis." No. 1951 is of similar style.

V. STYLES COMBINING GLAZE AND DULL COLORS

The glaze paints gradually gave way to the dull colors. One important element in the change was the custom, already found in the wash style, of using glaze paint only for the extremities of figures, the torso being covered by the colored drapery, *e.g.* No. 1860, *White Vases,* pi. 1 (British Museum, No. D 57). Advanced examples, where both design and ornament are dull black, but the lines of the head and arms are parti' in Also No. 1761 (Figs. 4 and 5), which has a peculiar meander with many involutions and uses blue as an accessory color *(J.H.S.* 1899, p. 182, 3).

wash, are two unnumbered lecythi in the Museum f. Kunst u. Industrie in Vienna.

A. *Glaze Ornament, Dull Design.*— The first transition is where the outlines are dull reddish (Nos. 1819, 1820, Berlin, Nos. 2449, 2450) or black, while the ornament is still in glaze. The purely decorative intention of the polychromy is manifest in the purplish hair given to the figures in harmony with the color of the outlines. In contrast to the previous class the stele is regularly represented. The date (ca. 440 B.C.) is shown to be later by the softer, more rounded outlines, which are almost effeminate for the male figures.

Nos. 1819 and 1820 are a pair, each having the same subject, an ephebe and woman at the stele, which has a palmette capital. By the same artist very likely are a lecythus in Palermo, and another in the Louvre. Nos. 1992 and 1965 are also a pair. No. 12747 is interesting because the two figures, a boy and woman, are on the same side of the stele, which here

Figure 6. — Athens, Museum, No. 1940. has not the conventional position in the centre of the scene. No. 1940 (Fig. 6) seems to be the earliest of the series, though These examples I owe to the kindness of Mr. Bosanquet.

No. 1966 has dull purplish ornament, but stylistically belongs here. Again No. 1949 has dull black for everything, but in style agrees with Nos. 1819, 1820. The scene shows two ephebes, one seated on the stele steps, and a bearded man. Purple is used. The same arrangement is found on No. 1957, one of the finer lecythi with dull paint *(infra,* p. 32, D). it is striking for its polychromy and water-color style. Yellow and reddish brown are used as accessor-colors. The

scene represents a woman and Hermes beside the funeral mound. *White Vases,* 9 (British Museum, No. D 59) probably belongs here, though peculiar in style. The ornament seems to have been in wash color, but is dull now; the outlines are dull black.

B. *Dull Ornament. Glaze Design.* — In another small group of medium-sized lecythi the opposite combination is tried; namely, wash for the outlines, and dull color for the ornament." Dull black is used on Nos. 1856 (Fig. 7), 19'28. 1993, and 12292, reddish on Nos. 1813,1832,1842, and 1843 (Fig. 8). In addition to red, green is used on No. 1813 and yellow on Hanover, No. 113. They all have the same type of ephebe in soft outlines, with curly hair, long, straight line of nose and forehead, and small, retreating chin. The style is for the most part verytine and careful. The type of ephebe riding past a stele (No. 1856) continues into the class employing entirely dull color, as Berlin, No. 2677, with dull black ornament and red outlines *(infra,* VI. C). British Museum, No. D 67 has the novel figure of a man mourning, with his hand pressed to his forehead; No. 1993 has an ephebe in like posture. Figure 8.-athens, Museum, No. 1843.

The class dates from *ca.* 440-430 B. C., though the Hanover vase is called fourth century on the label, — a good example of false ideas prevalent regarding the later lecythi.

VI. DULL TAINTS

A. *Description.* — With the coming in of dull paints tho white lecythi break up into many small groups, in addition to Other examples are in Cologne (Wallraf-Richartz Museum, no number), Vienna (Kunst, Hist. Mus. No. 621), anil the British Museum (*White Vases,* pi. 6, No. D 60, and *White Vases,* pi. 11, No. D 58). The last is of individual style, and apparently earlier than the others. This vase has also a technical novelty, the youth in three-quarters view, while Death is a portrait, if one may say so; cf. C. Robert, *Thanatos,* p. 20, pi. 2. An unnumbered lecythus at Munich and two other poor examples (Carlsnihe, No. 235 and Berlin. Inv. No. 3245) should

be added. Other examples of dull black ornament are given in *J.H.S.* 1899, p. 182, where, however, some corrections should be made; *e.g.* No. a has no shoulder ornament.

specimens isolated in technique. The new freedom in using several colors and shades for outlines with the half dozen colors common for garments, etc., enabled the artist to make each vase as a *unicum.* The possibility of combination was very large. Some of these single experiments are interesting as showing tendencies at earl' periods which were not followed out consecutively into regular classes. Among colors dull black is now used for both outline and ornament, *e.g.* British Museum, No. D 70, now for the one, while the other is in some variety of red or violet, or again both are red. There is considerable caprice in the choice of colors, so that clearly connected vases have a different technique. There is also wide variation in the amount of polychromy. Some take up the novelty of purple borders for garments, others still cling to the simpler use of solid red, or even confine themselves to mere outlines. Others, again, employ varied colors in great profusion, green for leaves or dresses, as on British Museum, No. D 70 (colored plates in Raoul Rochette, *Peintures ant. ined.* pis. 8-11), blue, as on the same vase for the egg ornament on the stele, purple, red in various shades, and yellow (most frequent on vases representing Charon). Tbe older styles are continued in more or less varied form. Along with large lecythi are made small and careless ones, like the degenerates of the red-figured vases. A number of lecythi of different styles show polychromy even on the shoulder, where the palmettes have alternate red and black leaves. Others use dull black for the leaves, while the bounding lines are colored (No. 1896). Various types of scenes also evolve characteristic styles. So the lecythi with Charon form a connected group, though the relation to other classes is clearly marked. Some vases may be considered to belong to one or another group as one regards one or another detail. The styles get mixed amid the many novelties. So an inconsistent use of the tulip-shaped lip is found on comparatively early vases. The stele, which in the previous class had a palinette capital, now has an acanthus or a combination of that with the palmette. Leyden, No. 34, "prothesis" scene. In the catalogue, published in 1905, the scene is said to be faded out, but a short inspection showed me a woman, the dead on a couch, and another figure. Cf. also Berlin, Inv. No. 3170; Boston, No. A P 456, which has a rare scene of two women with *Eros* in preparation to visit the stele.

The stele is frequently in the form of a shrine. The ornament is often omitted, *e.g.* Carlsruhe, No. B 2689. The dates range broadly from about 440-400 B.C.

B. *Related Groups, Mostly Early.* — Among early specimens of developed polyehromy in the dull technique is No. 12783, which has a lustreless black for the drawing. The shape is peculiar; a convex, not cylindrical body, like No. 1925, and a slightly convex shoulder. The drawing has a rare nobility. The date is fixed by the use of purple for the borders of garments, which appears about 440 B.C. This vase has a checker pattern like No. 1954. The scene is the "deposition" with Hermes.

Berlin, No. 2453, with red outline and ornament, is striking in drawing and agrees in date and style with the transitional lecythi with glaze shoulder and dull outline, yet the lip is tulip-shaped.

Nos. 1836, 1839, 1841, 1898, 1778, 12534, and 2012, for the most part of medium size or small, are closely related in style. The design is pinkish, the ornament dull black, except on No. 12534, which has a yellow design. Some have accessory colors, as blue and yellow on No. 1898. The group has alternate red and black palmette leaves for the shoulder. No. 1778 has an egg ornament in place of the usual meander. The first three have the same inner lines for the folds of the dress as Berlin, No. 2449 (Furtwangler, *Samml. Sab.* pi. 60, 1). Nos. 1836,1839, and 1898 use purple for the borders of garments.

The group is continued in style, but with the tulip lip, by Nos. 1831, 1832 (no ornament), 1755, 1796, 1907, and 1908. Poorer examples are Nos. 2011 and 1753, the latter only with the tulip lip.

Nos. 12135, 12136, and 12138 are distinguished by the form of the palmette. Dull black ornament and red design are used. The figures have a square chin. Accessory colors are red and yellow.

The vase is important as seriously invalidating the arguments of C. Robert, *Thanatos,* pp. 6 ff., that such scenes of the deposition were purely imaginary, and had no relation to the cult and popular belief, since Hermes never appeared in them, except in the very improbable example, p. 21, D. Here, however, is a lecythus with such a juxtaposition. ' This type of face is also seen on early lecythi, as No. 1815, etc.

Another group also has figures with square chins. The same technique is employed as in the last group, but No. 1890 has both outline and ornament in dull black.

Another group has usually a figure on the stele steps and includes Charon scenes. No. 1757 *(Ant. Denkm.* I, 33, 3) has brownish red outlines; No. 1758 *(Ant. Denkm.* I, 23, 1) is of like style.

C. *A Later Group, which can be closely dated.* — A number of vases, rather small, with dull black ornament and red varying to violet outlines, are important because one of them can be dated quite accurately.

This lecythus, now in the Museum at Myconus, was found in the excavations on the island of Rhenea, in a grave dating from the Peloponnesian War, when Delos was purified; in other words, it must date before 426-425 B.C. Of course, such lecythi may have been popular for some time longer, but their origin cannot be placed much earlier, because we have seen that the development of the decoration necessitates a considerable period for the lecythi with glaze and wash colors and the earlier dull vases that precede this group. And it is accepted that redfigured vases of the style of the white lecythus, No. 1935, date from about 470-460 B.C. Hence the space of not more than thirty years between this period and 440 B.C. is not too much for such technical and stylistic changes. This class may then have continued till the end of the fifth century, but must have originated about 440 B.C. The ephebe is of the type found on the vases with dull shoulder and glaze outlines, and resembles the knights on the Parthenon frieze. It is well known that sculpture follows the graphic arts at a considerable interval of time in respect to ripeness and novelty of style, and here we have another example of this fact.

D. *Fine Later Lecythi.* — Nos. 1936, 1937, 1954,1957,1977, Nos. 2019 (Benndorf, *Gr. und Sic. Vasenbilder,* pi. 18, 1), 2020 (Benndorf, *I.e.* pi. 16, 2), 1919, 1213", 1890, etc.

Others are Nos. 1950, 1951 (twin vases), and 1762 (large size and later). Nos. 1800, 1810, 1833, 1837, 1893, 1894, 1799 (no ornament), 2037, etc. The grave was that of a small child, and the *larnaz* was still intact when found, whereas other remains had been buried in heaps. This I learned by the kindness of the Ephor at Myconus. The much faded scene has the typical ephebe and woman before an oval mound; cf. the ephebe on No. 1843, Fig. 8. 1939, and Berlin, No. 2452. This group is distinguished externally by its meander and checker pattern (except No. 1939) and the peculiar form of the foot with an incision near the middle, not close to the upper edge, as earlier. The outlines are in a purplish red, varying in shade with the vase, and the ornament in dull black, though sometimes the meander is in the outline color (No. 1936). On No. 1954 the meander runs completely around the vase. Green and red are frequent, and purple is common for borders of garments and for details on the stele, which has a combined acanthus and palmette termination (as is usual in the later vases) and runs over on the shoulder. Another novelty is that the shoulder was painted after the design on the body, and not before, as earlier. This is shown by the distorted forms, adapted to the limited space left. The drawing is very fine and careful, as in the sketching of the hair and the naturalness of the various poses. There is also an attempt at making a real scene and not merely a conventional group; in one case the five figures make a frieze completely around the vase (No. 1954). The faces have the nose and forehead in the long straight line which is conventional from this time, the lips regularly turn down at the corners, the hair is sketched in lines and then filled in like a water-color. The scenes usually have a figure seated on the steps of the stele (No. 1936, a boy; No. 1939, a "deposition"). Nos. 1936 and 1954 are twin vases. The frequency of warriors in these scenes seems to point to the period of the Peloponnesian War.

Nos. 1955 and 1956 are closely related, having the usual foot, a continuous meander, and solid colors for garments. They both have one figure seated on the steps. No. 1891, in style like No. 1957, with dull black outlines and ornaments, represents Charon and a man.

Nos. 1950 and 1951 are also related, but use reddish brown for the ornament. No. 1799, of like style, has dull grayish outlines and purple and blue as accessory colors. These three have a slightly severer style than the previous lecythi and approach Nos. 1760 and 1949. Of these two vases, the former has dull black for the drawing, with accessories in red. The lines are fine and firm. The latter, No. 1949, uses dull black and is like No. 1814 (with Charon scene), which uses violet. Both have purple for the borders of garments. In No. 1814 we have a naturalistic treatment of a curly-haired, chubby baby, and No. 1947 shows another well-drawn baby in a "preparation" scene. Dull black is used for the drawing, with accessories in red.

Nos. 1817, 1818, perhaps the two most important lecythi extant from an artistic standpoint, seem to show the direct influence of contemporary painting. They have warm reddish brown for the outlines, and dull black for the ornament. Both design and ornament are drawn by the sjime hand, whereas earlier the latter was done by the potter. The ornament, however, is carelessly done, as by one inexperienced in this work and hasty, betraying thereby the artist accustomed to work on a larger scale, and impatient of conventional details. Blue, green, vermilion, and a creamy rose are the accessory colors. The figures have a unique largeness of style, and are more than worthy successors of No. 1935; only in place of a so-called Dorian ideal they give us that known as the Macedonian. On one we see the stern warrior angry with life and fate, as Achilles in Hades, on the other the same person in the sentimental melancholy of "the dying Alexander." In both there is a perfect example of Plutarch's picture of Alexander (yltez.IV), the warm, fiery nature tending to sentiment. It is no longer the pure Greek ideal of the ephebe, but the young man of Celtic type just come to early manhood. The work is such as one might expect from a successor of Polygnotus working in the early part of the Peloponnesian War. The hip of one of the men is foreshortened, a novelty found elsewhere only on a lecythus of the Louvre, which is of similar style, but by no means so fine. The freedom of the artist is shown in the masterly drawing of the hand holding the spear in No. 1817; his training in the fact that he does not hesitate to correct his sketch in places, differing from the vase-painters who draw once for all. The accessory figures are individual in style.

Collignon-Couve, plates. A discussion is to appear in 'Ej. 'Apx Other novelties in drawing on lecythi are foreshortening of the hand, Leyden, No. 30 (dull black ornament and red outline); Berlin, No. 2678, one figure in three-quarters face; lecythus in the Louvre (dull black for the drawing), the bottom of the foot seen foreshortened and one hand hidden behind the stele, the thumb only visible. Perspective of the stele step on Berlin, No. 2451 (Benndorf, *op. cit.* pi. 26). See *Mon. Piot,* XII, pp. 29 ff. (Collignon).

E. *Lecythi with Colored Outlines in Silhouette.* — The careful treatment of this group by Winter and Collignon makes more than a summary statement unnecessary. These vases follow Nos. 1817 and 1818 in largeness of style, but their relation to fresco or encaustic painting is still closer, as Winter points out. The transition between the two groups is seen in the vases published by Benndorf and Collignon *(l.c.),* where the figures are still in red outline, but the solid color of the garment is in the later style. The Berlin lecythus shows the compromise with previous styles: the woman has "added white" to represent flesh, while the man's skin is colored brown. There is some attempt at shading, as on the lecythus, *White Vases,* pi. 18 (British Museum, No. D 7). In spite of the advanced technique it seems probable that these vases belong to the fifth century.

Robert Cecil Mcmahon. *Berl. Winckelm. Progr.* 1895.

Mon. Piot, XII, pp. 29 ff., pis. 3-5. See also Girard, *La peinture* anf., pp. 215 ff. *Gr. u. Sic. Vasenbilder,* pi. 33 (Vienna, Museum f. Kunst u. Industrie, No. 351). For earlier examples cf. *supra,* p. 23 n. 4. On the Madrid lecythus *(Mon. Piot,* XII, pi. 5) the flesh of all the figures is brown. Cf. discussion in *Mon. Piot,* XII, p. 48. Furtwangler, *Gr. Vasenmalerei,* p. 200, referring to the Talos vase.

Enstitute of America

THE VISITATION BY LUCA DELLA ROBBIA AT PISTOIA plates VI-VII

A Recent pamphlet by Dr. Peleo Bacci of the Reale Galleria delle Belle Arti of Florence brings to light some interesting facts relating to the well-known group of the Visitation in the church of San Giovanni Fuoreivitas at Pistoia (plate VI). These facts are taken from the records kept by the Compagnia di S. Elisabetta, a religious association founded in the first half of the fifteenth century by Messer Lorenzo di Cristofano del Marruccia, prior of the church of San Giovanni.

The records inform us that as early as 1445 there existed in this church a group representing the Visitation. On October 11 of that year, Monna Bice, widow of Jacobo di Neri de' Fiorovanti, established a foundation to provide oil " *de quo voluit in perpetuam die noctuque ardere debeat unam lampadem ad onorem Dei et Virginia Marie coram fyuras Marie Sancte Eligabet visitationig earum in ecclesia sancti Joh. forcivitS*" The records show no further care for this group until September 22, 1507, when three *lire* were expended for six "braccie" of material to veil the statue of St. Elizabeth. On July 22, 1512, as many as twelve "braccie " of blue cloth were purchased to make a curtain for St. Elizabeth. The next entry of interest is that of May 9, 1513, when the Company, having learned that some devout person wished to have a tabernacle erected in honor of St. Elizabeth, contributed the sum of three large Pfcleo Bacci, *Il gruppo pistojese delta Visitazione, gia attribuito a Luca delta Robbia.* Firenze, Tipografla Domenicana, 1006.

Arch, del Patrim, eccl, di Pistoia. Compagnia de S. Elisabetta Testamenti, cod. C. n. 160, c. 5t.
American Journal of Archaeology, Second Series. Journal of the 30
Archaeological Institute of America, Vol. XI (1907), No. 1.
golden florins. The tabernacle appears to have been erected, for on April 24 and October 1 of the following year payments were amde to Giovanni Battista di Piero di Stefano, known also as Scalabrino, for having painted the tabernacle of the altar. On February 25, 1525, Nicolao di Giuliano Godemini, a member of the Company, presents 200 *lire* for the ornamentation of the chapel or tabernacle of St. Elizabeth, and accordingly on May 14 of the same year payment of 80 *lire* is made to Giuliano di maestro Bartolomeo, scarpellino da Firenze, for the ornamentation of this chapel. In 1546 and 1561 it was resolved to screen from public view the altar and the figures of the Virgin and St. Elizabeth except during Easter and other feast days. The altar of St. Elizabeth, including doubtless the tabernacle, was destroyed by the reforming Bishop Scipione de' Ricci, and the present altar, including perhaps the niche in which the group now stands, was rebuilt in September, 1790. This splendid group was itself, either by the reforming Bishop or by some one else, seriously damaged and put together again somewhat clumsily. Brogi's photograph indicates also that the Virgin's hair, the borders of her garments, and the neckerchief of St. Elizabeth were at some time very crudely "restored" with paint or gilding, which, as is indicated by Alinari's photographs, was afterward removed.

The use which Dr. Bacci makes of his discoveries is somewhat startling. It would have been absurd, he argues, for the Company of St. Elizabeth to have waited from 1446 until 1513 before making a tabernacle for this group which contained a statue of their patron saint. Hence there must have been two groups, the one piously worshipped by Monna Bice in 1445, which somehow has disappeared, and a second, the existing group, made at the end of the fifteenth or the beginning of the sixteenth century. The existing group, he argues, could not have been made by Luca della Robbia as early as 1445, for he considers it strikingly unlike Luca's Resurrection and Ascension Reliefs made in 1443 and 1446-50; and it could not have been made by him later than 1482, the year of his death. It represents St. Elizabeth on her knees, a composition which, Dr. Bacci believes, occurs for the first time in Ghirlandaio's picture of the Visitation (1491) now in the Louvre. In his view the Pistoia group is poorly glazed and crudely modelled, and is to be assigned to the period of the decadence of the Robbia school, when Benedetto Buglioni was one of its best representatives. He concludes, "Let art critics and connoisseurs bring forward whatever names they please; the history of art takes away from Luca that which does not belong to him."

The object of this paper is not only to disprove the assumption of Dr. Bacci that this group is a product of the decadence of the Robbia school, but to justify its attribution to Luca della Robbia. The assumption that the Company of St. Elizabeth was too pious and too wealthy to have allowed this group to have existed without a tabernacle for half a century does not carry with it convincing weight, when we consider the multitude of unappreciated and neglected treasures in the churches of Italy. Even in this case, the documents imply that the establishment of this tabernacle was due not to the Company itself, but to some devout person or persons, and that the contributions of the Company were applied only to its decoration. After the destruction of the tabernacle, has not this very group remained for more than a century without other framing than that of a very simple and commonplace niche? Nor can I agree with Dr. Bacci that this group was inspired by Ghirlandaio's Visitation of 1491, now in the Louvre. He is certainly in error in assuming that in this picture for the first time St. Elizabeth appears upon her knees. In the very museum with which Dr. Bacci is connected, a panel from the presses from the Sacristy of S. Croce, painted by some follower of Giotto (Alinari, No. 1490) represents the Visitation with St. Elizabeth on her knees. In the Baroncelli chapel of S. Croce is a more extensive treatment of the same composition (Alinari, No. 3901) executed by Taddeo Gaddi between the years 1352 and 13.56, a composition for which Giotto himself prepared the way in his representation of the Visitation in the Arena Chapel in Padua. One need only place before his eyes the three groups, Taddeo Gaddi's, the Pistoia group, and Ghirlandaio's, in order to see that the Pistoia group in all that concerns the My own recollection agrees with the statements of Dr. Bode and Miss Cruttwell that the glaze is of excellent quality and resembles that of Luca's other works.

pose both of the Virgin and of St. Elizabeth is derived from the earlier rather than from the later composition.

In spirit, too, the Pistoia group is closer to that of the Giottesques than to that of Ghirlandaio. The two women are here selected from the plain people of Italy. The attitude of St. Elizabeth is that of adoration toward the Mother of her Lord. Both figures are treated with the utmost simplicity and genuineness and in a religious spirit. In the Visitation of Ghirlandaio both the Virgin and St. Elizabeth are well dressed, aristocratic, refined, and posed with consummate art; in a manner, however, which impresses one with the beauty rather than the sincerity of the two women. Who would ever imagine that Ghirlandaio's Virgin would soon break forth with the grand song of the Magnificat?

Nor is it much easier to follow Professor Venturi *(IS Arte,* 1905, p. 151) and derive the Pistoia group from Albertinelli's well-known Visitation of 1503 now in the Uffizi. Albertinelli's Virgin and St. Elizabeth are, it is true, plain people, and his treatment of the theme is simple, sincere, and religious. But there is this difference: in the Pistoia group, St. Elizabeth adores the Virgin; in Albertinelli's picture, she rushes toward her, presses her hand and congratulates her as one woman would another woman. Albertinelli's painting was not without influence on the Robbia School. Giovanni della Robbia copied it, in 1525, in medallion form for the porch of the Ceppo Hospital at Pistoia, and again for a lunette now in the oratory of S. Ansano near Florence. But such copies are not for a moment'to be compared with the superb group in S. Giovanni Fuorcivitas. Nor is it likely that Andrea della Robbia would have been influenced by Albertinelli at this time. In 1503, Andrea was sixty-eight years of age, too accomplished and too conservative to be influenced by an inferior and much younger artist. In his works of this period, such as the lunette of the Cathedral at Pistoia (1505), there is an Umbrian sentimentality of which there is no trace in the Virgin of the Visitation.

If, therefore, the Pistoia Visitation does not reflect either the artistic overelaboration of Ghirlandaio nor the kind of religious emotion characteristic of Albertinelli, then it may be that Dr. Bacci is mistaken in assuming that there must have been two groups, one existing in the year 1445, and the other made not much earlier than 1513. Do the documents indicate that the group of 1445 was at any time destroyed or removed? Do they indicate the acquisition of a new group at any time near 1513? Is there, in fact, an atom of evidence in the documents to show that the group which we can see to-day in the church of S. Giovanni is not the same group as that for which Monna Bice provided the perpetual lamp?

Let us now assume that the statues of the Visitation of St. Elizabeth of 1445 were the same as those which we may see to-day, what consequences follow? In the first place, the attributions of the group to Fra Paolino (1488-1547) or to Andrea della Robbia (1435-1525) or, as Dr. Bacci would have it, to some still later member of the school like Benedetto Buglioni, fall to the ground. In the second place, the attribution to Luca della Robbia gains in definiteness. It cannot be assigned to the latest period of his life, as is done by Dr. Bode, but must be ranked with the earliest of his dated monuments. In an article on the Madonnas of Luca della Robbia, in *A.J. A.* (First Series), 1894, I attributed this group to Luca, and assigned it to the decade 1430-1440. The document recording Monna Bice's gift seems to prove that the group was in existence at least as early as October, 1445. That it might have been made by Luca della Robbia at this period is rendered almost certain by many analogies with his early works. The kerchief wound about the Virgin's head may be paralleled by that of one of the maidens of the Cantoria (1431-1438), Plate VII, 2, and by one of the heads from the bronze doors of the Sacristy (1446-1461), Plate VII, 3. Turbans for men and for boys occur also on Luca della Robbia's reliefs for the Campanile and for the Cantoria. Similar turbans for men and women abound in the works of Ghiberti, who exerted a formative influence on Luca's early works. This use of the kerchief for the Virgin is found in at least one other work by Luca della Robbia, — the unglazed, pointed arched relief in the Berlin Museum, — but would seem never to have been used by Andrea della Robbia, or by his sons, in any representation of the Virgin.
Florentiner Bildhaiter der Renaissance, 1902, p. 189.
The heavy drapery with its massive folds finds its closest analogues in that of the maidens of the Cantoria or that of the candelabra-bearing angels of the Sacristy (1448). It is far removed from the characteristic type of Andrea's draperies, which reveal more of the form beneath and a subtle arrangement of folds designed to charm the spectator.' Even the ruffle about the Virgin's neck occurs in one of Luca's earliest Madonnas, in the lunette from S. Piero Buonconsiglio; also in a second lunette recently acquired by the Berlin Museum (plate VII, 1). If we turn from the accidents of dress to the type of head, here again we find not only that shy, maidenly expression characteristic of Luca's early Madonnas, but the high forehead, the waving hair, the blue eyes, the high cheek bones, the strong mouth with the deep furrow on the upper lip.

For the kneeling St. Elizabeth, it is not to the Osservanza at Siena nor to La Verna that we must look for close parallels, but to the Resurrection relief in the Florence Cathedral. Here the Apostles adore their risen Lord at the end of His mission with the same absence of self-consciousness with which St. Elizabeth adores Him before His mission began. She is silent, but in a moment she will cry aloud, — " Blessed art thou among women, and blessed is the fruit of thy womb."

Allan Marquand.
Princeton University,
November, 1906.
Institute of Ameriea

UNUSUAL AND UNKNOWN POINTS IN PAJARITO PARK, NEW MEXICO plates VIII-IX

The scores of honeycombed cliffs, hundreds of stone houses, and thousands of cliff dwellings in and near the Pajarito Park section of the Jemez Forest Reserve, afford a field that would give the most zealous archaeologist months of unbounded pleasure and valuable returns for the time spent there. It is not the ruins as an entirety, however, that give me the most pleasure, although my months of continual riding in the discharge of my Forest Service work, almost continually in sight of some ruin, have only made me more enthusiastic in regard to the region; but it is the unusual and unknown points which arouse in me the greatest continual interest.

The district south of the Frijoles Canon is almost unknown, and Mr. Bandelier and other archaeologists who have been there have by no means exhausted the interest of this remote and not easily traversed region. There are large ruins and scores of points of interest that so far as I know have never even been mentioned.

In this region (which contains the famous painted cave, Plate VIII, and stone lions) is situated a large white bear, carved from the fairly soft stone (Fig. 1). This animal is certainly as plainly seen as the stone lions and, except for the fact that the head has been broken off and lies on the ground near, is in a state of excellent preservation. The figure was evidently at first well shaped and is even now in such condition that it cannot be mistaken. It is situated in the bottom of a small, almost hidden canon, and was discovered by the photographer Craycraft of Santa Fe, who took the photographs reproduced here. I have seen the animal from

American Journal of Archaeology, Second Series. Journal of the 42 Archaeological Institute of America, Vol. XI (1907), No. 1.

above the brink of the canon, and, as far as I have been able to learn, am the only person in addition to the discoverer who has had a view of it in modern days.

Southwest of Puye, at the end of a Mesa and near the only trail that passes through the ridge, is a huge head some six feet long and four feet wide with perfect eyes, nose, and mouth. I am not prepared to say, however, that this is not the work of time on the sandstone rather than the work of the cliff-dwellers. Situated as it is, however, surrounded by the homes of these people, it is an object of interest.

From the top of some of the Mesas many other honeycombed cliffs can be seen (plate IX). The openings almost without exception are toward the south, though among the first dwellings seen in the Las Alamos Canon is a small group, situated very high and in an almost inaccessible place, with a northern exposure. Strange to say, the timber originally used for the doorway in one of these dwellings is in better condition than any I have seen in the dwellings with the exposure to the balmy south. 'In the bottom of the Pajarito Canon, quite a distance from the large communal house of that name, is a circular pit sixty feet in diameter and at present at least ten feet deep. If this was a *Mva,* it is far larger than any others I have chanced upon.

Many of the cliff dwellings, sometimes called cavate dwellings, consist of a single room in the rock, although a large number have a room back of the original one. In the Las Alamos Canon there are several rooms, some of them several feet from each other, which are connected by openings (Fig. 2). The first series of this kind seen by me was in the Frijoles Cañon, where I sent my Indian cook into one room to see if it would protect us during the night, which promised to be stormy, and in a few seconds his head appeared in another doorway several yards further down the cliff.

At the head of the Sena Canon, in a small group of the cavate type, is a pillar of tufa some twenty feet long and ten feet thick, which rises several feet above the ledge on each side. In the centre of this, and two hundred feet from any other dwelling, is a cave. The owner evidently wished to enjoy his high and exclusive site to the fullest advantage, for he has cut a door on both the north and the south sides. This little peak standing alone with the hole in the centre, through which one can see to the other side, presents an unusual and strange appearance.

On the top of several of the commanding points are circular ruins of what were evidently watch towers. The watchers in the days gone past must have had a busy scene before them, while to-day one can sit on the ruins for days and never see a. human heing.

Above the Las Guahes Canon, and in a high semicircular ridge that rises from the Mesa and faces southeast, is a row of dwellings cut into much harder and darker colored rock than the thousands at other points. These dwellings also.appear to differ slightly in shape and construction from the ordinary type.

Generally speaking, the more inaccessible the house, the more care was spent in its construction and decoration. It is, therefore, the case that one is often repaid for a special effort to reach some doorway, by finding things much better preserved than where access is easy. The approaches to certain ridges, back of which were built the cliff dwellings, or to the top of some Mesa containing a communal house, were often well defended by walls, defiles in the rock, etc. These old paths are sometimes a number of feet deep, and so narrow that a full-grown man has difficulty in walking through without turning his shoulders sideways. They could, therefore, easily be defended against a foe. One of the best of these cut trails is seen at the main approach to Tsankawi Communal House.

At several points,mainly above the (larcia Canon, communal houses were situated on adjacent Mesa tops with ridges between. Frequently in these cases a well-worn path in the rock several inches deep shows how often the inhabitants of one of the houses visited the others.

The *Navas,* or hunting traps, are numerous. These consist of deep wells cut in the solid rock, in the middle of some trail across a Mesa. The situation of the valleys and Mesas is such, and so many of the canon walls are impassable, that it was an easy matter to drive the game across the selected trails. Deer and other animals naturally fell easy victims in these holes. The Pueblo Indians have used these traps in quite recent years.

On Laguna Mesa are the ruins of a house containing at least twenty rooms, and evidently only one story high. This is the I only ruin I have seen where every room can be seen plainly without excavation of any kind.

Some time since, while trailing a cougar, I chanced to find a small ledge back from what I, or any other passer in the Las Alamos Canon below, or the Mesa above, should have thought a solid wall, and around the ledge were over half a dozen unusually large cliff rooms. These rooms were at least a mile from any others, although the Mesa above did show signs of ruins. This was evidently a select colony, possibly some summer resort of the elite of the tribe.

These are only a few of the many special points of interest. When one can see so many similar sights, and when there are so many easily accessible ruins of interest, it is hard to realize that they are visited annually by comparatively few persons. The number of visitors this year, however, will far exceed that of any previous year. Every tourist in the West should make a point of visiting Santa Fe, where the proper arrangements can be made for seeing these wonders of a departed people.

Hugh H. Harris.

U. S. Forest Service. institute of America

. THE WORK OF THE INSTITUTE IN AMERICAN ARCHAEOLOGY

At the meeting in celebration of the incorporation of the Institute, held at Washington, D.C., on January 2, 1907, Mr. Charles P. Bowditch, Chairman of the Committee on American Archaeology, delivered an address of special interest on the undertakings of the Institute in this field. The part which presents the plan of the Committee for future work is here published.

The American work to which the Institute can look forward in the future has been admirably expressed by Miss Alice C. Fletcher, in her report to the Committee on American Archaeology, which I will now read:

"It is proposed that the basal plan for work under the American Committee of the Archaeological Institute of America shall be the preparation of a map of the culture-areas of the American continent, as a contribution to the world-study of the human race.

"Already much has been done toward the making of such a map, and all available work hitherto done by institutions, associations, or individuals will be duly credited and its bibliography given. It is believed that such a graphic tabulation will not only facilitate the task of correlating work already accomplished and now in progress, but will make it possible so to direct the efforts of the various Societies of the Institute which desire to support active field work in our own country, that all the archaeological research undertaken will fit into the broad plan proposed, and thus help toward the solution of some of the problems that confront the students of human culture.

. "A preparatory step toward the carrying out of this basal plan would be the appointment of an officer to be known as Director of American Archaeology, whose immediate duty would be to direct and coordinate all work undertaken by the affiliated societies of the Institute. This step should be followed by the establishment of a School of American Archaeology, in which graduate students should be received for instruction and employment in field research, and so fitted to be workers in the wide field opened by this basal plan.

"Since culture-areas do not correspond with political boundaries, international relationships and work will naturally follow."

This plan has been accepted by the Committee, and Mr. Edgar L. Hewett has been recommended to the Council as Director of American Archaeology.

It is hoped that the Western Societies of the Institute, inspired by the comprehensive plan which has been adopted, will join heartily in the effort to make such a plan successful by turning their local energy and local funds into work which will contribute toward the desired end.

The interest in the work of American Archaeology is increasing in all parts of the country, and the Committee has been informed that if a school of American Archaeology should be established in Santa Fe, the old Governor's palace would probably be placed at their disposal. While the Committee is not ready to take decisive action at the present time, it is hoped that in the near future such a school may be established, which shall be the centre of influence in the cause of American Archaeology throughout the West and Southwest.

Institute of America

GENERAL MEETING OF THE ARCHAEOLOGICAL

INSTITUTE OF AMERICA

FORMAL INCORPORATION OF THE INSTITUTE

JANUARY 2-4, 1907

The Archaeological Institute of America held its eighth general meeting for the reading and discussion of papers at the George Washington University, Washington, D.C., on Wednesday, Thursday, and Friday, January 2-4, 1907, in conjunction with the annual meeting of the American Philological Association.

A meeting of the incorporators of the Archaeological Institute of America, as named in an Act of Congress approved on May 26, 1906, was held at the George Washington University, on Wednesday, January 2, 1907, in accordance with a call dated October 9, 1906, signed by twelve of the incorporators.

Professor Seymour was elected Chairman, and Professor Carroll, Secretary of the meeting. The Chairman presented (1) a certified copy of the Act of incorporation; (2) the call for the meeting, signed by twelve of the incorporators; (3) the acknowledgment of each of the other (living) incorporators that he had received due notice of this meeting.

On motion of the Hon. John W. Foster it was unanimously resolved that the incorporators accept the Council of the voluntary association known as the Archaeological Institute of America, with its officers and its regulations, as the Council mentioned in the Act of Congress above referred to.

On Wednesday, January 2, at 4.30 P. m., the Institute and the American Philological Association held a Joint Session, with a celebration of the incorporation of the Institute.

Professor Thomas Day Seymour, President of the Institute, presided and read a brief account of the early organization of the Institute, and of the later development of its branches and enterprises.

The Hon. J. W. Foster, President of the Washington Society of the Institute, addressed the meeting on the work and aims of the Institute.

Brief addresses were made in behalf of the chief committees of the Institute, as follows: by Professor James R. Wheeler, for the School of Classical Studies at Athens; by Professor Andrew F. West, for the School of Classical Studies in Rome; by the Rev. Dr. John

P. Peters, for the School of Oriental Studies in Palestine; by Mr. Charles P. Bowditch, for the Committee on American Archaeology; and by Professor Allan Marquand, for the Committee on Mediaeval and Renaissance Studies.

The portion of the address by Mr. Bowditch, which presented the plan of the Committee for the American work of the Institute, is published on page 47 of the Journal.

By the courtesy of the George Washington University, the Archaeological Institute will have an office in the buildings of that University.

The Act of Congress which granted the incorporation of the Institute was published in this Journal, Vol. X, pp. 174, 175.

The Annual Meeting of the Council of the Institute was held on Friday, January 4, at 11 A.M. and 3 P.m.; a special meeting of the Council was held on Wednesday, January 2, at 10 A.m.; and the Annual Meeting of the Managing Committee of the American School of Classical Studies in Rome was held on Saturday, January 5, at 9.30 A.m.

The Council reelected all the officers of the Institute to serve for the year 1907-08, and chose also two additional Associate Secretaries, Professor F. W. Shipley, of Washington University, St. Louis, Mo., and Professor H. R. Fairclough of the Leland Stanford University, Cal. In accordance with the recommendation of the Committee on American Archaeology, Mr. Edgar L. Hewett was appointed Director of American Archaeology for the year 1907.

On Thursday afternoon the Hon. John W. Foster, President of the Washington Society of the Archaeological Institute of America, and Mrs. Foster gave a reception at their house to the members of the Institute and Association and their friends. On Wednesday evening, after the Joint Session, the Cosmos Club entertained informally the visiting members at their Club House, and on Thursday evening a Smoker was given by the Committee of the Washington Society at the University Club. Both the Cosmos and the University Clubs extended the privileges of their houses to all visiting members.

On Friday afternoon the visiting members and their friends were received at the White House by the President of the United States.

A resolution was passed thanking the President and members of the Washington Society of the Institute, the authorities of the George Washington University, the Cosmos and University Clubs for the hospitable reception given to the Institute, and for the excellent arrangements for the entertainment of the visiting members.

There were in all six sessions at which addresses and papers, many of them illustrated by the stereopticon, were presented. The abstracts of the papers which follow were, with few exceptions, furnished by the authors.

Wednesday, January 2. 10.30 A.m. 1. Professor Paul Baur, of Yale University, *Pre-Roman Antiquities of Spain.*

A discussion of discoveries of remains on Spanish soil, from the Bronze Age, co. 3000 B.c. to the Roman domination, *ca.* 200 B.c. The writer argued from architectural evidence, as well as from the sculpture, ceramics, and jewelry, that the ancient Iberians must have come into close contact first with the pre-Mycenaeans, then with the Mycenaeans, and from the seventh century B.c. onward with the Phocaeans, Massalians, Saniians, and Apulians, whereas the Phoenicians did not influence the art of Iberia. This paper will appear in a later number of the Joukxal. 2. Dr. Arthur Stoddard Cooley, of Auburndale, Mass., *Archaeological Notes.* 1. The American Excavations at Corinth. Private letters from Corinth state that in October last very heavy and long-continued rains washed much soil from the surrounding fields into the excavations. The Greek Archaeological Society with a large force of men began in November to remove this debris. The Society is also reelecting several prostrate columns of the temple of Apollo, which were discovered in 1898-99, and strengthening the broken architrave block on the south side. A part of the unfinished school-house, begun by Kapodistrias, which covered the east end of the temple, has been removed, and a new museum is to be built on the site to replace the present small one west of Plane Tree Square.
2. The British Excavations near Sparta. Two views were shown of the site of the sanctuary of Artemis Orthia, which is situated near the Eurotas, to the left of the road ascending from the second iron bridge over the river to the town. 3. The recent restoration of two columns of the Heraeum at Olympia by members of the German Institute at Athens was illustrated by three photographs.

Professor James R. Wheeler, Chairman of the Managing Committee of the American School at Athens, read portions of a letter from the Director of the School, giving further details of the situation at Corinth.

3. Professor William H. Goodyear, of the Museum of the Brooklyn Institute, *The Discocery, by Professor Gustavo Giovannoni, of Curves in Plan, Concave to the Exterior, in the Facade of the Temple at Cori.*

The Temple of Hercules at Cori (thirtysix miles southeast of Rome) is a well executed and well preserved monument, dating from the late period of the Roman Republic. Professor Gustavo Giovannoni, Assistant Professor in the Royal School of Engineering Architects at Rome, has recently announced the discovery of curves in plan concave to the exterior in the facade of this temple. Preliminary publication has been made in the annual Bulletin of the Roman Society of Architects, of which Professor Giovannoni is the VicePresident. Scaffoldings will be soon constructed by the Italian Government in order to isolate the temple from surrounding buildings, and this will offer occasion for measurements in detail of the upper members of the temple, following which, a special monograph on the subject will be published by Professor Giovannoni.

Meantime, the significance of the discovery iu relation to the existing knowledge of ancient horizontal curves is as follows:

First, it may tend to substantiate earlier observations for curves in plan, concave to the exterior, in the pediments of the Parthenon, which were made by Hoffer and Pennethorne. Penrose considered those curves to be accidental, and his opinion has been so far generally followed, perhaps with error.

Second, the Brooklyn Museum Survey of 1905, under direction of Mr. Goodyear, observed and photographed curves in plan concave to the exterior in the eastern pediment of the Temple of Neptune at Paestum. These curves are found in the cornice and in the line of abaci. These facts have recently been communicated to the Roman Society. The curve at Cori has a deflection of 10-12 cm. at the bases of the columns, but reaches the enormous extent of 35 cm. deflection in a length of 7.50 m. Such a curve could not be produced by accidental movement without extensive and visible shifts of the masonry of the entablature, gable, and cornice. Nor could it occur accidentally without very visible and considerable dislocations or inclinations of the columns of the facade. Thus, the curve at Cori is the first definitely established instance in ancient art, of constructive curves in plan which are concave to the exterior. Generally speaking, experts have only been familiar, in ancient art, with rising curves in elevation. Curves in plan convex to the exterior have been observed, but insufficiently considered. However, they would, in optical effect for the upper horizontal lines, also appear to be rising curves in vertical planes, and hence might be explained from the same point of view as the rising curves in elevation. On the other hand, a concave curve in plan produces the optical effect of a descending curve in a vertical plane.

Hence, the enormous importance of this discovery, for it has been widely supposed that the ancient curves in elevation were intended to correct an optical appearance of downward sagging, and thus to give the appearance of a straight line. Here is a curve which actually produces an effect of sagging in the upper horizontal line. It consequently cannot be intended to make the line appear straight.

The true purpose of the curves at Cori may possibly be the same as the purpose of the curve in plan concave to the exterior, and amounting to 10 inches, deflection, which is found in the facade of St. Mark's at Venice. Here again the curve begins at the foundation. The purpose of such a curve may possibly be conceived by considering its undoubted results. In the facade of St. Mark's the concave curve in plan, as seen below the level of the eye, appears to be a rising curve in a vertical plane. As seen above the level of the eye it appears to be a descending curve in a vertical plane. As regards the vertical lines at the angles of the faqade they are thrown forward of the optically assumed position, and perspective magnitude is much increased; but generally speaking the optical effects are contradictory and therefore vibratory in their results.

The question whether the results obtained in St. Mark's were intended at Cori may be left open at present.

In any case the discovery is epoch-making for the study of the ancient monuments, without reference to the possible relations between certain mediaeval deflections and those now observed in this Roman temple.

4. Mr. Edgar L. Hewett, Fellow of the Institute in American Archaeology, *The Preservation of American Antiquities: Progress in* 1906.

The year 1906 witnessed the successful consummation of many years of effort on the part of the Institute, and of many other scientific bodies looking toward the protection of American antiquities by law. A bill was enacted by the 59th Congress creating the Mesa Verde National Park in southwestern Colorado, for the purpose of preserving the remarkable remains of cliff dwellings in that region. This bill had been pending for several years, and much difficulty had been encountered in securing its passage owing to the fact that many of the most important of the ruins were situated upon the southern Ute Indian reservation.-The measure, as passed, arrives at a happy solution of the difficulty by creating the National Park, and including within the jurisdiction of its officers for administrative purposes, all ruins within five miles of its boundaries. This secures what had been so much desired by all, viz. the inclusion of *all* the great Mesa Verde and Mancos Canon ruins within the National Park. (See *A.J.A.* X, 1906, p. 376.)

The 59th Congress also passed the general archaeological measure, which was also warmly supported by the Institute, known as the Lacey Act, providing for the custodianship by the government of all archaeological remains situated on lands owned or controlled by the United States. This act makes it mandatory upon the various departments of government to protect from vandalism and unauthorized excavation all ruins within their respective jurisdictions. It also provides for the creation of National Monuments by act of the President of the United States. (See *A.J.A.* X, 1906, p. 175.)

The operation of this law has been prompt and effective beyond the most sanguine hopes of its supporters. All ruins on forest reserves, Indian reservations, public lands, military reservations, etc., have been placed under government protection, and the system of policing is being rapidly made effective. There is now almost no vandalism in the American ruins. Under the authority of this act, the President has designated as National Monuments the following: El Mono or Inscription Rock in New Mexico; Montezuma Castle in Arizona; the Petrified Forest in Arizona; Devil's Tower in Wyoming. Steps are being taken to secure at an early date a like action with reference to the famous ruins of Chaco Cafion, New Mexico.

Rules and regulations governing the granting of permits for excavation, etc., are in process of preparation by the departments, and will be announced at an early date. On the whole, the operations of the law seem eminently satisfactory.

Wednesday, January 2. 3 P.m. 1. Mr. Albert W. Van Buren, of Yale University, *The Temples at Ostia.*

The speaker proposed to identify the large temple at Ostia (F in plan) as the Capitolium, and the four small temples near the theatre (BCDE in plan; cf. *Not. Scav.* 1886, p. 162) as the temples of

Venus, Fortuna, Ceres, and Spes, on the basis of a fresh study of the remains and (for BCDE) of epigraphical evidence.

Temple F (the prominent brick temple, apparently of the second century A. d.) has at the back of the cella the remains of a large base for three cult statues; it is therefore to be identified as the temple of the Capitoline Triad, *i.e.* the *Capitolium* of the colony. This is confirmed by the fact that this temple is the largest one at Ostia, and is erected on a high podium. The Roman colonies, being in general modelled after Rome itself, adopted the Capitoline cult as their own principal state cult; and there is reason to think that when it was not possible to place the *Capiiolium* on a hilltop as at Rome the temple was artificially elevated by the construction of a high podium. This is rendered probable by the peculiarities of the *Capitolia &t* Pompeii, Lambaesis, and Thamugadi; cf. Pauly-Wissowa and Daremberg-Saglio, s.t. *Capiiolium;* also Mau-Kelsey, *Pompeii,* pp. 63-67; Gsell, *Man. Ant. de VAlgerie,* I, pp. 137,143, pi. XX, XXIII.

Temples BCDE, to judge from their style of construction, were built in the first century B.c. and restored in the second century A.d. They are identified with the four temples of Venus, Fortuna, Ceres, and Spes, which, according to *C. I.L.* XIV, 375 (= Dessau, 6147), P. Lucilius Gamala *constituit* about the middle of the second century A.d. Prom *C. I.L.* XIV, 376 it appears that this refers to a restoration. Temple P is identified by means of the altar inscribed *Veneri sacrum* found in it *(Xot. Seac.* 1886, p. 127; *C.I.L.* XIV, 4127) as one of the four temples of *C.I.L.* XIV, 375; as the latter inscription mentions the four temples in similar terms, and as BCDE form a homogeneous group, it is highly probable that the two groups are identical.

2. Mr. Oliver M. Washburn, of the University High School, Chicago, 111., *Sardis.*

After a brief survey of the importance of Sardis as the chief station on the ancient trade route from Mesopotamia to the coast districts of Asia Minor, the speaker described, with the aid of illustrations, the somewhat scanty remains now visible on this site.

Wednesday, January 2. 8 P.m.

Joint Meeting of the American Philological Association and the Institute. Professor Thomas Day Seymour, President of the Institute, presided.

President Charles W. Needham, of George Washington University, gave a brief address of welcome.

Professor Elmer T. Merrill, President of the Philological Association, delivered the annual address, *On Certain Roman Characteristics.*

The main part of the address consisted in the analysis of those elements of character and tendency that are usually defined by the epithet " classical," and the attempt to show, by the examination of a considerable number of details in the light of the foregoing analysis, that, whatever may be the case with the typical Athenian of the best days, the Roman was essentially "unclassical," but extremely like the American of to-day.

Thursday, January 3. 10 A.m. 1. Professor William N. Bates, of the University of Pennsylvania, *Notes on Greek Vases at the University of Pennsylvania.*

This paper was a discussion of three vases at the University of Pennsylvania: 1. A small amphora which the writer argued was to be classed with the Caeretan hydriae: 2. A Tyrrhenian amphora, on one side of which is represented Troilus and Polyxena at the fountain, and on the other side apparently two discus throwers: 3. A redfigured cylix upon which is represented an object which the writer identified with the horns of consecration such as have been found at Cnossus and at other sites in Crete. The paper will be published in full in the *Transactions of the Museum of Science and Art of the University of Pennsylvania.* 2. Professor Harold N. Fowler, of Western Reserve University, *The Beginnings of Greek Sculpture.*

The belief that early Greek works of sculpture show the influence of a previous school of sculpture in wood, from which sculpture in stone developed, has no sufficient foundation. Statements of ancient writers concerning *xoana* are inconclusive. The early Greeks saw about them remains of "Mycenaean" art and were acquainted with the art of Egypt and Asia. Hence they would naturally turn to sculpture in stone as soon as they began to practise sculpture at all. Comparison with monuments of other times and places shows that the qualities of early Greek sculpture are not seen in sculpture in wood and are found in sculpture in stone where no previous school of sculpture in wood is probable. 3. Mrs. Harriet Boyd Hawes, of New York City, *Minoans and Mycenaeans: A Working Hypothesis for the Solution of Certain Problems of Early Mediterranean Race and Culture* (read by Miss G. M. A. Richter, of the Metropolitan Museum of Art).

The autochthones of Greece and Crete were of one stock (Sergi's Mediterranean race), non-Aryan in speech and culture, perhaps of African origin. From the beginning of the Bronze Age they were subject to two opposite influences. Greece was constantly overrun by a pastoral folk, "Aryans" or "Aryanized," who came from the north and knew nothing of the sea. They had a rich spoken language without writing, a store of lays (basis for the Homeric epics), the patriarchal system, and a typical house form. This Achaean invasion was a gradual infiltration from a remote past of petty chieftains and their clansmen, never numerous. Crete in constant intercourse with Africa and the Levant developed steadily throughout the Bronze Age along non-Aryan lines, strong in art and letters (i.e. written language) and in religion, maritime from the first, retaining traces of the matriarchal system, and using for large buildings an Oriental form. In this development the Eteocretans of the highlands lagged behind the maritime Cretans, who were the true " Minoans." Minos *(ca.* 1500 B.c.) established a " sphere of influence" over the Cyclades and the Greek littoral. His artists carried the Cretan "Palace Style" to Argos, Mycenae, Attica, etc., — a peaceful invasion, — and in return learned new architectural ideas as seen in the latest palaces of Cnossus and Phaestus. The Achaeans becoming paramount in Greece, took to roving

(Trojan war), sacked the smaller towns of Crete (Gournia, Zakro, etc.) and finally Cnossus. The over-ripe Minoan art, declining *pari passu* in Crete and on the mainland, was spread far and wide in decadent form by the Achaean thalassocracy. In Greece, the primitive geometric principle under Minoan influence developed into the Dipylon style. Iron was introduced by the Dorians. They did not enter Attica, but their iron did by trade, and appears in Dipylon graves. Summing up, the Minoans were maritime Cretans, and their art was of native origin, although influenced by intercourse with the East, especially Egypt; the Mycenaeaus were a mixture of the native stock, akin to that of Crete, and Achaeans. In this mixture the native stock (Pelasgian) was more numerous, but the Achaeans furnished many leaders; the two elements lived together on friendly terms, the Achaeans finally gaining the upper hand. "Mycenaean Art" had its source in Crete; some "Mycenaean " objects are direct importations, but many were no doubt made in Greece after Cretan models. In Classical Greece we see the mingling of two unusually gifted races, the one contributing a highly advanced native civilization especially rich in art, the other its heritage of an Aryan culture and an all-conquering language.

4. Professor Allan Marquand, of Princeton University, *The Visitation of Luca delta Robbia at Pistoia.*

This paper is published in full in the present number of the Journal. 5. Professor Howard Crosby Butler, of Princeton University, *The Dome in the Architecture of Syria.*

That dome building was practised in Syria in very ancient times is shown by the sculptured reliefs of the Assyrians and Hittites; but little can be known about the actual construction of these early domes, since only the exterior forms are represented in the reliefs. The ancient domes that are still preserved intact, or in part, date from the second century A.d. and the four centuries following. These show that domes on every known form of ground plan and of every variety of material were built in Syria during these five centuries. The dome of a tomb near Bosra, in the Hau-rS,u, is an example of a dome of cut stone laid up with dry joints upon a circular substructure. It belongs to the second century. A concrete dome on a circular wall was found in the baths at Shehba, which was built in the third century. Christian domes of this plan existed in the Cathedral of Bosra, 512 A.d., and in the Church of the Archangels at Fa'lul, 526 A.d.

The central baths at Bosra present an example of a dome set above an octagonal plan; the dome itself is laid up in gores, like an umbrella, and is made of a concrete composed largely of light volcanic scoriae. It was built in the third century. Another type of a dome on a polygonal plan is to be seen in the church of St. George at Zor'a in the Hauran, dated 510 A.d. This type is, in section, an ellipse with its major axis vertical, giving a tall, conical effect. The spandrels of the eight supporting arches are curved slightly forward as they rise, and show the rudimentary principle of the pendentive.

The placing of a dome above a square compartment by means of pendentives was not a late invention of the Byzantine period, as is generally supposed; for this kind of dome construction is found in buildings of the Roman period in Syria that are not later than the third century, and are, probably, as early as the second century A.d. It is shown in a dome in the baths at Djerash and in a similar dome discovered by the Princeton expedition at Brad in Northern Syria. These two examples are built of highly finished blocks of stone laid without mortar, cement, or cramps of metal. Smaller domes of cut stone were set above square substructures by means of slabs laid across the angles of the square, and then cut to form quadrants. This kind of construction is found in late buildings, as well as in early structures, and is not to be considered as a stage in the evolution of the pendentive, but as a simpler mean's of accomplishing the same result in the smaller buildings. An example of this is found in the sixth century tomb of Bizzos at Ruweha. The largest and most ingeniously constructed of the Syrian domes is that of the church at Kasr Ibn Warden, dated about 560 A. d. The pendentives of this dome are enclosed within an octagon, and each pendentive is pierced with a window, a most unusual and difficult piece of construction. These Syrian domes, though smaller than some of those built by Roman and Byzantine architects, show greater variety and even greater technical skill.

6. Dr. David M. Robinson, of Johns Hopkins University, *New Inscriptions from Sinope.*

Views of the promontory of Boz-tepe', of the isthmus which connects it with the mainland, of the double harbor, and of the walls of Sinope were shown. Three new gravestones and a Roman milestone of Probus were discussed. These inscriptions are published in the *American Journal of Philology,* XXVII, 1906, pp. 447-450.

7. Professor G. Frederick Wright, of Oberlin College, *Recent Discoveries in the Mounds of Ohio.*

The Ohio Archaeological and Historical Society, which is now receiving aid from the state, has instituted a more thorough exploration of the mounds than has heretofore been attempted. During the past year the so-called Harness Mound in the Sciota Valley near Chillicothe has been thoroughly excavated with most encouraging results. In 1846 this mound was partially explored by Squier and Davis, who sunk a shaft in the centre of the mound and found what they supposed to be an altar with a few relics. Subsequently, Professor Putnam ran a trench from the south end half way through the mound, adding much to our knowledge of the work. Others also have carried on some explorations. In all, fifteen burial places have been found within its limits. The mound is 150 feet long, 40 feet wide, and 20 feet high. Upon thoroughly exploring it from end to end it was found that the most of the burials were near the circumference of the base of the mound, and no less than 130 were found by Professor W. C. Mills, who conducted the exploration. Much light was shed upon the habits of the moundbuilders, their method of burial, and the practice of cremation. A series of post holes were also found, showing that there was a wooden structure erected over the burials. Implements and ornamental articles were found in abundance, twelve hundred of them being of copper. These articles indicate a commerce which brought together copper from Lake Superior, obsidian from the Rocky Mountains, mica from the Alleghenies, and sea shells from the Gulf of Mexico. The implements also are believed to represent an earlier and higher culture than that which was found at Fort Ancient and in some of the other mounds. All together the work of the society is being amply rewarded, and further appropriations from the state are encouraged.

8. Dr. Oliver S. Tonks, of Princeton University, *An Interpretation of the so-called Harpy Tomb.*

The object of this paper was to identify, as far as possible, the figures decorating this monument, and to show that considerable Egyptian influence can be detected in the subjects of the reliefs. The four faces of the tomb were discussed in the following order:

Western side. In reference to the features on this face it was maintained that the lotus flower is borrowed from Egypt, where it is present in funeral scenes, and that in our monument, as in Egypt, it symbolizes rebirth; that the pomegranate, also used in Egyptian funeral scenes, possibly comes from Egypt, and here, on the Lycian tomb, is connected with the cult of the dead; that the egg suggests rebirth, and is in some way related in idea to the Orphic egg, which in turn is connected with the " Light " egg of Egyptian myth; that the group of a cow and calf, connected with the Isis-Hathor-Horus group, also connotes regeneration, and that the seated figure at the left is Demeter, her *vis-a-vis* Persephone, and the three standing figures the Fates.

Eastern side. The dog was shown to be of chthonic significance, and to suggest that the action is taking place in the presence of a god, the cock to be a bird associated with Hades and Persephone, and the seated figure to be Hades.

Northern side. The warrior giving up his arms was interpreted to mean that the scene was a " home-coming"; the pig was shown to mark the place of action as Hades; and the seated figure was identified with Minos.

Southern side. On this side the seated figure was identified with Rhadamanthus, and the human-headed birds, which also appear on the northern side, were shown, from their resemblance to the Babirds of Egypt, to represent the soul flying away with the "double" of the dead.

Thursday, January 3. 3 P.m.

Joint Session of the Institute and the American Philological Association. Professor Elmer Truesdell Merrill, President of the American Philological Association, presided.

1. Professor George H. Chase, of Harvard University, *Three Archaic Bronze Tripods in the Possession of James Loeb, Esq.*

This paper, in a slightly different form, is published in *B. Metr. Mus.* II, 1907, pp. 33-10.

2. Professor William N. Bates, of the University of Pennsylvania, *New Inscriptions from the Asclepieum at Athens.*

This paper was a discussion of four inscriptions carved upon a block of marble found in a mediaeval wall near the Asclepieum at Athens in the spring of 1906. The paper will be published in full in a later number of the Journal.

3. Professor Minton Warren, of Harvard University, *On the Stele Inscription in the Roman Forum.*

The Stele Inscription, published for the first time in the *Not. Save.* 1899, has called forth a flood of literature. No satisfactory interpretation has yet been reached, and possibly, owing to its fragmentary character, none ever will be reached, unless other early Latin inscriptions of a similar kind are found. Perhaps, however, some advance in the interpretation may be made by a comparison with Greek and Latin sacrificial inscriptions and the Iguvinian Tables. It has already been suggested that the Stele really contains two inscriptions, the first occupying lines 1-9, the second the remaining lines 10-16. Thurneyson and Hulsen read lines 11-15 in the reverse order, thus getting rid of the mysterious word *havetod*. This view was rejected, and it was proposed to supplement the second inscription so as to read

popliftigiOD IOvtf VXMEN
TA KAPIA DOT A *Vitulatione*
M Ifjoi'ei TERITom *viskesa*
kapitod keiviom QVOI HA
VELOD NEQVe *skelos estod*
sakrifikiOD IOVESTOD
LOIQVIOD

In the above text *kapia* was taken as a verbal adjective from *capio* (comparing *eximius* and *effugia,* both used in connection with sacrifice and *fili-us jUia)* and UXMENTA, which is separated by punctuation from 10, as meaning oxen, with the same root as Sanskrit *riksan,* and English *ox;* the whole phrase being supported by /JoC? 6 *KpLddi Ovtrat Zrjvl* To *TloXirji* and *rov* S« *KpiOivra rm Zrjvi,* which occur in the sacrificial calendar of Cos. Jupiter Territor (cf. Dessau, 3028, and Dionysius, vi, 90) was paralleled with *Turse Iovie, Ig. Tab.* VII, *a.* 53 (cf. Pais, *Ancient Legends of Roman History,* p. 280, n. 4). *Dota* was regarded as a mistake for *datod,* due to the boustrophedon order. For *vitulatio,* cf. Macrobius, 3, 2, 14. For *scelus esto,* cf. Livy, XXII, 10, and Cicero, *N.D.* II, 159. In *havelod, ha-haec, velod* is perhaps a mistake for *velid* or for *voted* = *volet,* frequent in Latin inscriptions. Cf. *totar pisi heriest, Ig. Tab.* VII, *a.* 52. *Loirptiod* is a verbal adjective ending in -*ion* like *capios,* showing the vocalism of Xoin-os. The sense of the concluding sentence would be, " Let whoever of the citizens wishes them, take the *viscera* and let it not be a sin provided a proper sacrifice be left.'' For *sacrificium iustum,* cf. Servius, *Aen.* Ill, 279.

The restoration of the first inscription is more difficult, but various supplements were suggested, as *e.g. quoi honke loukom (kipum) violasit* and *Soranoi ni redidesit extas porkiliasias* (or *porkas piakular sias*) based upon the Acts of the Arval Brethren. It was also proposed to read *regei loustratio estod komvorsoi ad levam, /cram* being re-

garded as the earlier form for *laivam* justified etymologically by Beraeker (*l. F.* X, 162). The paper will appear in full in the *American Journal of Philology.*
4. Professor Francis W. Kelsey, of the University of Michigan, *Codrus" Chiron (Jucenal 3, 20o) and a Painting from Herculaneum.*

The speaker pointed out difficulties in the current explanations of the reference to the Chiron in Juvenal's third satire, and advanced considerations in favor of the view that the name was applied to a diminutive copy of the group of Chiron and Achilles which, according to Pliny *(N.H.* 36, 29), stood in the Saepta at Rome, and is probably reproduced in the painting described in Helbig's *Wandgemulde,* No. 1291. The adjective *recubans* is humorously applied (cf. schol. in Jahn's edition of 1851, p. 209: Recubans: *enim el a posteriore parte recumbens).* The paper will be published with illustrations in a later number of the Journal. 5. Professor Charles C. Torrey, of Yale University, *Tracet of Portraiture in Old Semitic Art.*

Some undoubted specimens of portraiture are to be found among the pre-Christian Semitic monuments which have survived. A few of these are of remarkable interest, and all are deserving of more attention than they have received.

Old Babylonian art in its treatment of the human face is dominated by conventional modes to a remarkable degree; the eyes and eyebrows, especially, are conventional, so also is the manner of treating the hair and the beard. The persistence of these and other peculiarities of technique in West Asiatic art, from the earliest time down to the beginning of the Christian era, is remarkable.

Nevertheless, a high degree of excellence was reached by the Babylonians of the third millennium B.c. in their representations of the human head and face, whether in relief or in the round. Several sculptured heads of the latter class have the appearance of being true portraits. Among the earliest known portraits in relief are those of the kings Naram-Sin and Hammurabi.

In the Assyrian relief sculpture, the attempts at portraiture are very much obscured by conventional modes of treatment. As is well known, the Assyrian artists (like their predecessors in old Babylonia) often rendered race types in the faces of their figures; Jews, Arabs, Africans, Elamites, and others are more or less easily recognized. But they also achieved likenesses of individuals. Careful comparison of the monuments show that we have indeed a series of portraits of Assyrian and Neo-Babylonian kings which are on the whole trustworthy, so far as they go. With all their variety, they show essential agreement, and they can give us a fairly satisfactory idea of the profile, and especially of the nose and mouth, of each of these monarchs. The " royal personage " pictured in pi. XVI of the de Clercq catalogue is plainly Ashurbanapal.

From Phoenicia we have at least one excellent portrait executed in the native style, viz. that of the civil officer Baalyaton, found at Umm el-'Awamid. In the case of one or two anthropoid sarcophagi recently discovered, there is some evidence of an attempt at portraiture.

Friday, January 4. 9 A.m. 1. Dr. George D. Hadzsits, of the University of Pennsylvania, *Aphrodite and the Dione Myth.*

The Homeric and the Hesiodic legends, touching the story of Aphrodite's birth, are, in a sense, incompatible. This distinction rests upon the difference of locality in the two legends, since the Homeric account as clearly connects the goddess with Greek traditions as the Hesiodic does with Oriental.

The object of the paper was to show that in spite of external contradictions which are, perhaps, accentuated, the two legends possess a common, vital significance that makes them both expressions of a deep racial consciousness. For owing to certain prepossessions of the Greek mind, a motive must have led, originally, to the choice of *Dione,* as mother of Aphrodite, similar to that which resulted in the poetic fiction of her sea-birth.

It is very significant that there seem to be no ancient Greek traditions representing Aphrodite as earth-born or connecting her with iarents that are distinctly earth-divinities. Aphrodite's naturalization, as we find it in Homer, was undoubtedly the result of a long national religious and artistic reflection. But Oriental, *i.e.* Syrian, Phoenician, Cyprian traditions of her *birth,* renewed in the Theogony of Hesiod, and reenforced in Greek art, to which, besides, (ireek scientific speculation gave an intellectual justification, represent a combined force of religion, poetry, art, and reason that makes a departure in the case of the " Homeric " terminology most unlikely.

While admitting that the poet, following a popular impulse, may have represented Aphrodite as daughter of Zeus and Dione to introduce the goddess "into the Hellenic pantheon by a sort of legal adoption," the deeper reason for the particular choice of Dione seems to exist in Dione's strong attachment to rain, sea, and stream, to the element of moisture and the quickening of life that goes with it, since any other conception of Aphrodite's birth, taking her outside the circle of water-divinities, would have been alien to important premises in the matter.

Postponing to a later time a full discussion of this problem, with a citation of the evidence, suffice it to say that these two legends of Homer and of Hesiod seem to point to an ancient instinctive recognition of a great biological truth, and that *Diane,* in this relation, powerfully suggested the same direction of Greek thought, whereby, inevitably, the goddess of fertility in all departments of life owed her *birth* to. the *Sea.* 2. Professor Francis W. Kelsey, of the University of Michigan, *A Pompeian Illustration to Lucretius.*

The main part of the paper was devoted to an examination of the possible influence of the type familiar in the Venus Pompeiana upon the imagery of the proem of the *De rerum natura.* The paper will be published in full in a later number of the Journal. 3. Dr. James M. Paton, of Cambridge, Mass., *Two Representations of the Birth of Dionysus.*

The birth of Dionysus from the thigh of Zeus is rarely found on Greek vases. Two examples only were known to

Heydemann (*Diotiysos Geburt und Kindheit,* Halle, 188.5). One, a black-figured amphora in Paris, represents the little god standing on his father's knee with two torches in his hands. The other, preserved only in a drawing also in Paris, shows Dionysus emerging from the thigh of Zeus, and received by Eileithyia, in the presence of other divinities.

Two new representations can now be added. One is on a redfigured lecythus (ca. 460 B.c.) in the Boston Museum of Fine Arts. It shows Zeus seated on a rock, pressing with both hands his left leg, from which the head of Dionysus emerges. Before him stands Hermes, ready to carry the new-born god to the nymphs. The other is on a red-figured fragment in Bonn. Only enough is preserved to show the little god coming forth from the thigh of Zeus, and stretching out his arms toward a figure, of which only the arms holding a mantle are preserved, but which is certainly Eileithyia.

4. Professor G. Frederick Wright, of Obeiiin College, *Archaeological Treasures of the Crimea.*

A remarkable series of ruins of early Greek settlements is found along the border of the Crimea. At Chersonese near Sevastopol a Russian Society is making much progress in excavating the ruins of the Greek settlement, which for centuries flourished upon that peninsula, and the local museum is full of interest. At Theodosia on the eastern side of the Crimea much work has also been accomplished by a Russian Society, resulting in a local museum situated on a conspicuous hill overlooking the city. The most flourishing of all the Greek colonies was at Kertch on the Cimmerian Bosporus. The remains of its civilization have been very fully brought to light by excavations in charge of the Imperial Society. Mithradates Hill overlooking the city is crowned by a modern temple in imitation of the Parthenon, which was for a long time used as a museum. The most valuable of the discoveries have been taken to St. Petersburg, and form a centre of great attraction in the Museum of the Hermitage. In the neighborhood of the city are numerous *kourgana,* or large mounds of earth, which cover mausoleums constructed of stone. Outwardly these resemble the mounds of the Ohio Valley. But on their exploration in recent times elaborate stone mausoleums were discovered underneath resembling very closely the "Treasury of Atreus" at Mycenae. Beautiful frescoes are still in existence upon the walls, and many works of art of high order have been found.

Again, at the mouth of the river Don, about twenty-five miles from Rostoff, are extensive ruins of the ancient city of Tanis, founded 650 B.c, which are almost entirely unexplored. These ruins cover an area about a mile square, but present outwardly little but a series of low mounds and walls, which have been nearly levelled to the surface.

Thus it will be seen that all these Grecian centres of civilization were at commercial points, each one being where the roads from the interior converge upon a seaport. Apparently the Greek civilization never penetrated far from the coast, but numerous ruins of great interest are found in the interior, shedding light upon the life of the native races. Near Bakhtchi-Sarai, thirty miles northeast of Sevastopol, there is a large number of such ruins, the most conspicuous feature of which is a series of crypts dug into the face of the various lofty sandstone precipices, which have been exposed by the erosion of the streams. Many of these are now occupied by monks, but their construction and elaborate intercommunications carry us back to very early times when they were actually occupied as dwelling places much after the manner of the cliff dwellings of our western territory. There are literally thousands of these troglodyte dwelling places opening out upon the face of these cliffs. At Tchoufout-Kale a lofty promontory projecting between two streams is completely covered with ruins of stone structures upon the surface, while winding passages lead down through the rocky surface to numerous large excavations with windows opening out on the gorges below, making it one of the most interesting situations for defence that it is possible to conceive. For many centuries this place has been occupied by a colony of Karaite Jews, who, according to tradition, came into the country with the armies of Cyrus, Cambyses, and Darius, and have remained there ever since. In the Jewish cemetery near by there are inscriptions upon the tombstones which go back to 30 A.d. At the present time the site is entirely deserted except by the family of the Karaite Rabbi and a school of twenty pupils which he maintains in this picturesque situation looking off to Sevastopol on the southwest and Eupatoria on the northwest. Very valuable early manuscripts have recently been purchased from this school and transferred to St. Petersburg. Still more remains to be done. Classical scholars will do well to keep in closer touch with the work of the Russian archaeologists.

The following members of the Institute were registered as in attendance at the General Meeting:

Of the Baltimore Society:

Miss Alice C. Fletcher, Washington; Professor C. W. E. Miller, Johns Hopkins University; Professor Kirby F. Smith, Johns Hopkins University; Dr. David M. Robinson, Johns Hopkins University.

Of the Boston Society:

Mr. Charles-P. Bowditch, Boston; Dr. A. A. Bryant, Cambridge; Professor George H. Chase, Harvard University; Dr. Arthur S. Cooley, Auburndale; Professor William K. Denison, Tufts College; Mr. Francis G. Fitzpatrick, Cambridge; Professor W. F. Harris, Harvard University; Professor George E. Howes, Williams College; Professor John C. Kirtland, Jr., Phillips Exeter Academy; Mr. Charles S. Knox, St. Paul's School, Concord; Professor H. W. Magoun, Cambridge; Professor Clifford H. Moore, Harvard University; Dr. James M. Paton, Cambridge; Dr. Charles Peabody, Cambridge; Professor Alice Walton, Wellesley College; Professor Minton Warren, Harvard University.

Of the Chicago Society:

Professor Demarchus C. Brown, Butler College; Professor John A. Scott, Northwestern University.

Of the Cincinnati Society:

Professor J. E. Harry, University of Cincinnati.

Of the Cleveland Society:

Professor Harold N. Fowler, Western Reserve University; Mrs. Harold N. Fowler, Cleveland; Professor Samuel B. Platner, Western Reserve University; Professor George F. Wright, Oberlin College.

Of the Colorado Society:

Professor Edgar L. Hewett, Washington; Mrs. E. H. Thayer, Denver.

Of the Connecticut Society:

Professor Frank C. Babbitt, Trinity College; Professor Samuel E. Bassett, University of Vermont; Professor Paul Baur, Yale University; Professor Karl P. Harrington, Wesleyan University; Professor George D. Kellogg, Princeton University; Dr. George G. MacCurdy, Yale University; Professor Tracy Peck, Yale University; Professor B. Perrin, Yale University; Professor Louise F. Randolph, Mount Holyoke College; Professor Helen M. Searles, Mount Holyoke College; Professor Thomas D. Seymour, Yale University; Dr. Wilmot H. Thompson, Yale University; Professor Charles C. Torrey, Yale University; Mr. Albert W. Van Buren, Yale University; Dr. Mary C. Welles, Newington.

Of the Detroit Society:

Professor Francis W. Kelsey, University of Michigan.

Of the Iowa Society:

Miss Elizabeth D. Putnam, Davenport; Professor Charles H. Weller, Iowa State University.

Of the Kansas City Society:

Mr. James P. Richardson, The Prosso Preparatory School; Professor A. M. Wilcox, University of Kansas.

Of the New York Society:

Professor Hamilton F. Allen, Princeton University; Professor Sidney G. Ashmore, Union College; Professor Franz Boas, Columbia University; Professor Howard Crosby Butler, Princeton University; Professor William H. Goodyear, Museum of the Brooklyn Institute; Miss Bettina Kahnweiler, New York; Professor Allan Marquand,- Princeton University; Professor E. D. Perry, Columbia University; Rev. Dr. John P. Peters, New York; Dr. Edward Robinson, Metropolitan Museum of Art; Dr. Ida C. Thallon, Vassar College; Dr. Oliver S. Tonks, Princeton University; Professor A. F. West, Princeton University; Professor James R. Wheeler, Columbia University.

Of the Pennsylvania Society:

Professor William N. Bates, University of Pennsylvania; Professor Wilfred P. Mustard, Haverford College; Miss Caroline L. Ransom, Bryn Mawr College; Professor John C. Rolfe, University of Pennsylvania.

Of the Pittsburgh Society:

Professor W. A. Elliott, Allegheny College; Professor Robert B. English, Washington and Jefferson College; Mr. John B. Jackson, Pittsburgh; Professor Henry S. Scribner, Western University of Pennsylvania.

Of the St. Louis Society:

Dr. W J McGee, The Public Museum; Professor F. W. Shipley, Washington University; Mr. John M. Wulfing, St. Louis.

Of the San Francisco Society:

Dr. A. L. Kroeber, The Affiliated Colleges.

Of the Utah Society:

Professor Byron Cummings, University of Utah.

Of the Washington Society:

Dr. Cyrus Adler, Smithsonian Institution; Mr. William H. Baldwin, Washington; Professor George M. Boiling, Catholic University of America; Professor Mitchell Carroll, George Washington University; Professor George J. Cummings, Howard University; Hon. William E. Curtis, Washington; Professor Frank L. Day, George Washington University; Professor Thomas Fitz-Hugh, University of Virginia; Hon. John W. Foster, Washington; Professor W. H. Holmes, Smithsonian Institution; Professor Joseph Clark Hoppin, Washington; Rev. Dr. J. P. E. Kumler, Washington; Mr. John B. Lamer, Washington; Professor E. M. Pease, New York; Professor G. L. Raymond, George Washington University; Professor Charles S. Smith, George Washington University; Professor William R. Vance, George Washington University; Mr. T. W. Vaughan, Washington; Mrs. Thomas Wilson, Washington.

Of the Wisconsin Society:

Professor C. F. Smith, University of Wisconsin.

The sessions were attended also by many members of the Philological Association, of the Managing Committees of the Schools at Athens, in Rome, or in Palestine, by former members of the Schools, by members of the Faculty of the George Washington University, and by others, — not members of the Institute.

The next General Meeting of the Institute will be held at the University of Chicago on December 27, 28, and 30, 1907, upon invitation of the Chicago Society, and of the University. The Annual Meeting of the American Philological Association will be held in conjunction with the meeting of the Institute.

1906 July-December ARCHAEOLOGICAL NEWS NOTES ON RECENT EXCAVATIONS AND

DISCOVERIES; OTHER NEWS

James M. Paton, *Editor K5, Sparks St. , Cambridge, Mass.* GENERAL AND MISCELLANEOUS THE INTERNATIONAL ARCHAEOLOGICAL CONGRESS.—

In *Arch. Am.* 1906, pp. 270-272, is published the preliminary announcement of the International Archaeological Congress, which is to meet in Egypt in 1909. It is proposed to hold the sessions of the Congress at Alexandria, April 10-12, Cairo, April 13-18, and Thebes, April 19-21. Opportunities to visit other important sites will be afforded. All correspondence relating to the Congress should be addressed to the *Commission du Congres Arche'ologique International, Muse'e Jfgyptien, Caire.* ARCHAEOLOGICAL DISCOVERIES IN BELGIUM IN 1905.— In Belgium several archaeological societies are actively engaged in studying and collecting for their provincial museums the antiquities of the country, which are chiefly Belgo-Roman. Articles of glass and bronze have been found at F&cheron near Liege, sculptures and funeral vases near Tongres, also a stone belonging to an altar or base, which has Jupiter and Juno in relief on one side and the eagle and peacock on the other. For the museum at Namur there have been acquired a head of a divinity in cast bronze, a round drinking vessel with a Bacchic inscription in barbotine, a square flask of glass, and a beautiful cup of Roman enamelled bronze, probably the product of a local factory. Somewhat earlier finds are a very fine bronze statuette of Mercury, from the gates of Liege, and a huge cross beam of black oak from the ruins of the Roman bridge at Ombret, which was exposed by exceptionally low water in the Meuse. In Hainaut, the plans of two Belgo-Roman settlements now covered by forest have been ascertained, The departments of Archaeological News and Discussions and of Bibliography of Archaeological Books are conducted by Professor Paton, Editor-in-cliarge, assisted by Miss Mary H. Buckingham, Professor Hakby E. Burton, Mr. Harold R. Hastings, Professor Ei.mf.rt. Merrill, Professor Frank G. Moore, Mr. Charles R. Morey, Professor Lewis B. Paton, Dr. A. S. Pease, and the Editors, especially Professor Marquand.

No attempt is made to include in this number of the Journal material published after Jan nary 1, 1907.

For an explanation of the abbreviations, see pp. HO, 141.
and numerous small objects recovered. (L. Rknard-grenson, *Arch. Am.* 1906, pp. 183-187.) ARCHAEOLOGICAL DISCOVERIES IN SOUTHERN RUSSIA IN 1905. — In the region of the Kuban, ten or more tumuli, which were examined, had all been plundered in ancient times, but yielded a few gold ornaments such as were sewn on clothing, together with beads, amulets, and broken vessels of various kinds. Among these is a beautiful fiat bowl of light-colored bronze with an emblema of red copper, a fine Hellenistic work of the third or second century B.C., representing the Death-goddess and her victim. From Panticapaeum (Kertsch) came a large amount of Greek pottery, both black-and red-figured, also red glazed ware of the Roman epoch, gold objects, including a pendent in the form of a head of Hera, an elaborate decorated lead mirror, a large marble sarcophagus which contained a wooden coffin and a skeleton laid upon laurel leaves, and other wooden coffins, carved or painted. In the Crimea, graves of the third to the tenth century A.d. were found near Gursuf, and yielded some fine objects of the so-called Gothic style, and Roman graves were examined at Sebastopol. The city wall on the south side of Chersonesus is a fine piece of Greek work of the fifth century, through which a gate was cut in Roman times. Graves found here date from the fourth century B.C. to Byzantine and even Russian times, some of them having been used more than once. Among the terra-cottas are a figure of a woman entirely wrapped in a himation, and a bust in relief of a goddess on which are traces of color. In the settlement discovered on the island of Berezani, which belongs to the sixth and fifth centuries B.C., the pottery is chiefly Attic black-figured and Ionic ware. Of great importance is an old Swedish inscription, of the eleventh or twelfth century A.d., recording the death of a comrade in arms. At Olbia, the triangular terrace in the southerly quarter of the city is found to be the citadel, and to have been very strongly fortified, first in Greek times and then by repairs of the walls in Roman times. Among single finds are a fountain statue of a boy and a dedicatory inscription, both nearly perfect and both from the second or third century A.d. According to another inscription, Olbia seems to have belonged to the kingdom of Mithradates Eupator in the second and first centuries B.C. In the Government of Kiev, some remains of the eneolithic age show skeletons colored brown-red and buried in a crouching position. The mounds in which they were buried were surrounded by rows of stone slabs which must have been brought from a distance. In one large mound the grave was protected by a roof of oaken beams supported on pillars, and in another, the body was laid with no covering. (B. PhakmaKowsky, *Arch. Anz.* 1906, pp. 109-124; 9 figs.)

The caves about Bakhtchi-Saral *(supra,* p. 66) are described and illustrated by G. F. Wright in *Rec. Past,* VI, 1907, pp. 13-20 (10 figs.).

A fragmentary Latin epitaph from Sebastopol is published by R. CAonAt in *B. Soc. Ant. Fr.* 1906, p. 141.

THE FRENCH SCHOOLS AT ATHENS AND ROME. — The report on the works presented by the members of the French Schools at Athens and Rome for the years 1904-05 is published by E Chatklain in *C. R. Acad. Insc.* 1906, pp. 369-386. From the School at Athens four papers are summarized. L. Bizard reports on the exploration of the eastern wall of the temenos of Apollo at Delos. The most important result has been the discovery of a small monument dedicated to Dionysus, which has yielded a number of reliefs and statuettes. An inscription shows it was erected before 270 B. C. The house of the *Poseitloniastae* has been thoroughly cleared, and the results described by Bulard. The chief discovery was the group of Aphrodite, assisted by Eros, defending herself against Pan. E. C'avaignac has studied the monument of Aemilius Paullus at Delphi, with a view to its restoration, and E. Schulhof has edited a new inscription of the *UpoTTOLOi* of Delos recently found at Myconus, and important from its length (135 lines), its excellent preservation, and its information on the organization of the cults of the island. The only archaeological work from Koine is by Albertini, who has studied the history of the public works under Claudius.

WORK OP THE GERMAN ARCHAEOLOGICAL INSTITUTE IN 1905. — A. Conze, after nearly twenty years' service as General Secretary, has resigned the office, remaining, however, a member of the Central Committee. A bronze relief portrait of him has been made by Professor Briitt for the Institute. O. Ptichstein succeeds him. The Institute lost an unusually large number of members by death during the year. The *Jahrbuch* and *Anzeiger* have been published as usual, together with a sixth supplement on ancient magical apparatus from Pergainon, by R.Wiinsch. Progress was made on the index to Vols. XI-XX of the *Jahrbuch,* on Vol. II, pt. 5 of the *Anlike Denkmuler,* on Vol. Ill, pt. -i of the *Antilce Sarcophagreliefs,* and on parts 14 and 15 of the *Attische Grab-reliefs,* bringing this work down to the time of Demetrius of Phalerum. Work was also continued on the Grave Reliefs from Southern Russia, on the Grave Reliefs of Asia Minor, and on the Etruscan Urns. The Roman branch issued Vol. XX of its *Mitleilungen* and proceeded with the catalogue of the Vatican sculptures. The usual meetings and lectures were held. The Athenian branch published Vol. XXX of its *Mitleilungen,* and held the usual meetings and lectures. Dr. Dorpfeld, with the Rector of the University of Athens, conducted members of the International Archaeological Congress, in the spring of 1905, to the principal excavations of Greece and Asia Minor, and in the following autumn and spring the two secretaries took students to Pergamon, Olympia, Crete, Argolis, Corinth, and Delphi. Excavation work at Pergamon was devoted to the upper gymnasium, the house of the consul Attalus, the Greek theatre on the acropolis, and the burial mounds in the neighborhood. Lesser excavations were carried on at Kalyvia near Sparta and at the Heraeum at Olympia. The Roman-Germanic Commission made substantial progress toward the publication of the Roman Remains in Bavaria, the Roman Military Reliefs, the Roman Rings, and the Roman Brick-stamps. Excavations, often in conjunction with local societies, were undertaken in Haltern and Kneblinghausen (Westphalia), on the Friedberg, on the Buchenburg (Wetterau), in Monsheim, where the Worms society examined some neolithic habitations, in Dautenheim, where a Roman villa was uncovered, and at various places where there are ring-fortifications, especially in Franconia. *Arch. Anz.* 1900, pp. 89-95, Annual Report to the Prussian Academy of Sciences.) NORWAY.—A Bronze Statuette. — A tiny bronze figure of a woman, apparently the work of an Italian craftsman under Ionian influence, and not later than the last quarter of the sixth century B.C., has been found, together with three fibulae of a primitive type, in Norway. They are said to have been excavated in the neighborhood of Bergen, and if this is so, they are probably a relic of the very early amber trade between Jutland and Italy. (A. II. S. Ykames, *J. H.S.* XXVI, 1900, pp. 284-285;;j figs.) UNITED STATES. — Recent Archaeological Legislation. — The legislation for the incorporation of the Archaeological Institute, for the protection of American Antiquities, and for the creation of the Mesa Verde Xational Park, passed by Congress during May and June, 190G, is reported and discussed by F. W. Kelsey in *Rec. Past,* V, 1906. pp. 338-542. YEMEN. —Two Sabaean Inscriptions. — In *Z. Morgenl. Ges.* LX, 1906, pp. 662-665, E. Griffini publishes photographs and transcriptions of two squeezes of Sabaean inscriptions from an unknown locality in the interior of Yemen. They are brief votive inscriptions to certain unknown deities. NECROLOGY. — Henri Bouchot.—In *Athen.* October 20, 1906, W. Roberts publishes a short sketch of the life of Henri Bouchot, who in recent years was recognized as one of the greatest authorities on early French painters and miniaturists. He was born in 1849, and after completing his studies at the Ecole des Chartes, obtained an appointment in the Print Department of the Bibliotheque Xationale, of which he eventually became the Conservateur. His earlier publications dealt with books, their binding, illustration, etc., but since 1892 his writings have included works on early French artists, French costume, and especially an important guide to and catalogue of the Cabinet des Estampes. The success of the Exposition des Primitifs Francais in 1904 was chiefly due to his energy, and he prepared a large part of the exhaustive catalogue. EGYPT EXPLORATIONS AND DISCOVERIES IN 1905-1906. — The annual *Archaeological Report of the Egypt Exploration Fund,* 1905-06, contains a report of the work of the different branches of the society, as well as notices of other excavations and publications. E. Xaville and H. R. Hall describe their work at Deir el Bahari (pp. 1-7; 14 figs.), which was confined to clearing further the eleventh dynasty temple. The most important result was the discovery, in the western end, of a shrine containing a remarkably fine statue of the Hathor cow of natural size and in a perfect state of preservation (Fig. 1). This is the first time a shrine has been found with its goddess. The chapel was built by Thothmes III, and elaborately adorned with paintings and sculptures. It has been transferred entire to the Cairo Museum. For the Archaeological Survey X. De G. Da Vies continued his work on the rock tombs of el-Amarna (p. 8). For the (irecoRoman Branch, B. P. Grenfell and A. S. Hunt devoted a fifth season to Oxyrhynchus, with results even beyond those of the first campaign (pp. 8-16). The papyri, which fill 131 boxes, date from the second century B.C. to the sixth century A. D. Among the theological fragments is a vellum leaf containing 45 lines from a lost gospel. Two groups of literary papyri were found, but both were very fragmentary. Among the new pieces are about 200 lines from the paeans of Pindar, including poems for Delos. Delphi, Abdera, and Cos, and accompanied by elaborate scholia. There are also about 100 lines from a tragedy, apparently the *HypsipyU* of Euripides. In prose is part of a new history of Greece, dealing, in the o50 lines preserved, with events of the early fourth century. It is assigned tentatively to Cratippus. the continuator of Thueydides. Another new piece is a commentary on Thueydides, Book II, prolvably of the first century A.d. Lesser fragments include remains of Sappho and Bacchylides, as well as about 70 lines of the meliambi of Cercidas. The text of 11 out of about 80 ostraka are published, and some small objects of little importance are described.

The progress of Egyptology in Archaeology, Hieroglyphic studies, etc., chiefly as recorded in recent publications, is summarized by F. Ll. Griffith (pp. 17-52). In this summary are included (pp. 18-26) short reports on recent excavation and exploration furnished by various workers. A. E. P. Weigall has travelled through the region between the First and Second Cataracts, preparing a description of existing antiquities, and has collected much material on the " Pan graves." For the Liverpool Institute of Archaeology, Mr. Garstang reports the excavation of the cemetery at Esneh. which yielded a continuous series of antiquities from the twelfth dynasty to the middle of the eighteenth. The evidence suggests that the period between the twelfth and eighteenth was about two-thirds as long as the twelfth dynasty. In Nubia an undisturbed necropolis was found at Koatamneh. Its date is still uncertain, but it seems to afford evidence that the primitive Egyptian culture long survived in the more remote districts of Upper Egypt. Mr. Leorain describes his work of excavat ion and restoration at Karnak (see below), and J. E. QuiBell contributes a short notice of the results at Sakkarah.

The work of the British School of Archaeology is described by W. M. Flinders Petrie. In addition to the discoveries at Tell el-Yahudiyeh (see below), the history of the city at Tell el-Retabeh has been carried back to the ninth dynasty, and the Syrian foundation of the first fortress shown by the discovery of a child sacrifice under the wall. An inscription seems to mention the Israelites as "foreigners of Syria," who were here under a special governor. Less important excavations were carried on in several cemeteries. Recent work in Greco-Roman Egypt is summarized by F. G. Ken Yon (pp. 53-65), and in Christian Egypt by W. E. Crum (pp. 6680). An appendix (pp. 81-85) contains a report by Mr. ChA8SINAT on the work of the French Institute of Oriental Archaeology during the last two years. In 1904-05 the work was confined chiefly to the study of monuments of the Greco-Roman period. The inscriptions and paintings of the *mnmmisi* at Edfou were copied, and the architectural details drawn. A similar work was begun at Denderah. In 1905-06 excavations were carried on at two points in the Theban necropolis, but without important results beyond the collection of a series of sepulchral cones, which have yielded some new names.

Some of these discoveries are noticed in *Arch. Anz.* 1906, pp. 124-143 (13 figs.), by O. Rubensohn, who also reports on the following excavations. The Italians, working on the west bank near Thebes, found an untouched burial ground of the twentieth and twenty-first dynasties, with rich deposits. They excavated also at Antaeopolis and at Heliopolis. The Egyptian Department of Antiquities, at Karnak, collected the architectural meiubers of the temple of Aiuenophis I, and some fine reliefs. In the neighborhood of the Pyramids of Gizeh, the Americans have found an entire city, with streets and squares, underlying the mastaba field and affording means to study the development of the mastaba and the worship of the dead. The German Orient Society, which has undertaken to excavate the prehistoric cemetery at Abusir el-Malaq. opened about a thousand graves in the first season. The burials, which are in the crouching position, are too much injured by the salt earth to be satisfactorily studied as human types, but the furnishings are important for the study of costume and burial customs. Beside more ordinary objects, there are some unfamiliar types of pottery, some fine carvings in ivory, and a large limestone bowl in the form of a kneeling camel. Intruding among these prehistoric burials are others belonging to the Hyksos period, in which the bodies are mummified and laid at length. (See also *Bed. Phil. W.* 1906, pp. 1148-49, from *Mitt. Or. Ges.* No. 30.) At Elephantine, the temple, which was intact within the last century, has entirely disappeared, but something can yet be done with the remains of houses. These are of clay bricks and built literally in layers, often so placed that the older buried houses were used as cellars, sometimes for three or four stories, reached through holes made in their roofs. The papyrus finds here are rich, and some documents show the seals of very finely cut gems. An Egyptian tomb, showing Greek influence in the gaily painted floral decoration, has been found in the desert near Achmim. Another German undertaking is the excavation of the sanctuary of Saint Menas, comprising the magnificent basilica built by Arcadius, the older basilica, many tombs, crypts, inscriptions, etc., and the ovens where the bottles were made in which the healing waters of the place were exported. In Alexandria, blasting to level a hilly district is fast destroying the ancient tombs, but a few have been rescued and studied. These are in the form of underground chapels for the worship of the dead, with the burial chambers owning from them. The sarcophagus was usually carved in the rock in a niche above the funeral couch, but in one case the couch itself was fashioned into a sarcophagus. In the desert near the Serapeum. a number of sphinxes with fine female heads have been found, and with them funeral masks of marble to which hair and beards of stucco were attached. A rich find of gold objects and coins, accidentally made in the Delta, seems from the variety of articles to be the remains of a goldsmith's workshop. The coins date it in the third century u.c. Some bronzes found at Erment, south of Luxor, include a figure of a negro boy and two fine examples of the Greek execution of Egyptian types, — an Egyptian priest with bald head and hands hidden in his robe, and a swimming figure, with head thrown very far back, which was perhaps the handle of some object. From the Delta comes also a fine figure of Dionysus, 20 cm. high, of a type popular in Egypt and of Hellenistic origin.

WORK OF THE SERVICE DES ANTIQUITES. — A report of the work of the Service des Antiquites in Egypt during the past year is published by G. Maspero in *C. R. Acad. Insc.* 1906, pp. 495-499. As usual the chief work of this department has been in clearing and repairing the great ruins, leaving new discoveries to the foreign excavators. At Kamak, Mr. Legrain has completed the reerection of the columns which fell in 1899, and has continued clearing the court between the seventh and eighth pylons. He has found a gate with a row of cynocephalae. In all these works the blocks are replaced in their old positions, and the ground thoroughly excavated in order to examine the foundations and recover fragments. At Edfou, the condition of the temple has rendered necessary the removal and reerection of the west wall and eleven columns, which had to be done without removing the roof. At Deir el-Bahari, Mr. Baraize has strengthened some weak places in the temple and continued the systematic clearing of the Ramesseum. At Sakkarah, Mr. Quibell has excavated a corner of the necropolis belonging to the end of the sixth dynasty, and has found stelae with the name of one of the Heracleopolitau kings. At Toukh el-Garmous, Mr. Edgar has found some fine jewelry and goldsmith's work. At Kom-Ichgaou, G. Lefebvre has conducted two campaigns, which have yielded many papyri, among them a large number of well-preserved rolls containing Coptic texts of the seventh century. Of the greatest importance are seventeen fragments containing about twelve hundred verses of Menander. One leaf contains the *periocha, dramatis personae,* and 52 verses of an unknown comedy. Two leaves add 141 verses to the *UtpiKV.pop.tvi).* Seven leaves contain nearly five hundred verses from a comedy not yet identified, and seven more leaves, fortunately well preserved, contain five hundred verses from the *'EiiriTptirovTK,* so divided as to make possible a detailed reconstruction of this play, which resembled the *Hecyra* of Terence. A speedy publication of these fragments is probable. EXHIBITION OF THE EGYPT EXPLORATION FUND. — The annual exhibition of the Egypt Exploration Fund, held at King's College, London, is described in *Athen.* July 14, 1906. Most of the objects exhibited came from Deir el-Bahari, and included several representations of Mentuhotep, whose hawk-name was Neb-hapet-Ra, but unfortunately all too fragmentary to yield any long inscriptions. A new king of the eleventh dynasty is a Mentuhotep,. with the hawk-name Neb-hotep. Much of the sculpture is in high colored relief, and is frequently beautiful and carefully executed. Especially fine are some of the reliefs of animals. The fragments from the temple of the eighteenth dynasty also repay careful study. Interesting are also the tools of the workmen and many dolls, toy books of papyrus, and figures evidently intended to amuse children. There is also a fine set of palaeolithic flint implements and weapons. ABOUKIR. — A Treasure. — A list of the contents of the treasure discovered at Ahoukir (C'anopus) in March, 1902, with some indication of types and inscriptions, is given in *I. Num.* XIII, 1906, pp. 78-82, by Dr. Edde. who handled almost the whole of it. It contained about 600 Roman *aurei* of the third century, 2 Roman " medallions," 20 Greek " medallions," and 18 stamped bars of gold believed to be contemporaneous with the coins. Three of the bars are in the British Museum. The rest Dr. Edde was unable to buy, though they were offered him at bullion value, and the possessors straightway avoided embarrassment for themselves by melting them. LUXOR. — A Portrait of King Khuenaten.— In *S. BtW. Arch.* XXVIII, p. 156 (pi.), C. Campbell describes an inscribed slab with a portrait of the heretic king Khuenaten found by him in one of the courts of the temple of Luxor. NUBIA. — Explorations of the University of Chicago. — In *Bibl. World,* XXVII, 1906. pp. 68-71, J. H. Breasted describes the work of the expedition of the University of Chicago in the Nile valley, in the vicinity of the second cataract. In Lower Nubia there is a large number of beautiful temples with extensive inscriptions that are rapidly falling into ruin. Most of the inscriptions in these have never been published, and, unless they are now recorded, will soon be lost forever. The object of this expedition has been to secure photographic records of as many inscriptions as possible while they are still in position. Large inscriptions have been divided into rectangles and photographed in sections. The negatives have been developed on the spot and prints obtained. These have then been taken to a scaffolding and collated with the original and any deficiencies that the eye has been able to detect have been noted with colored ink upon the photographic print. By this means the most exact possible records have been secured, and these are to be published in a series of folio volumes which will serve in the future as standard sources for the monuments of t he Upper Nile. TELL EL-YAHUDIYEH.— A Hyksos Fort. — Near the temple of Onias (see.1 *.J. A.* 1906, p. 335) there has been discovered a large camp, over a quarter of a mile square, and surrounded by an embankment 100 to 200 feet thick, over 40 feet high, and with a slope 60 to 70 feet long. It is faced with white stucco. Later a stone wall was built at the foot of the slope, and the space between filled with earth. There was no gate, but a long ramp leading to the top of the wall. The construction indicates that the occupants depended on their archery. Graves were found inside the camp, and many Hyksos scarabsi It seems that this is the Hyksos city of Avaris. (W. M. Flindeks Petrie, *Man,* August, 1906; *Ree. Past,* V, 1906, pp. 286-288.) ASSYRIA, BABYLONIA, AND PERSIA THE GERMAN EXCAVATIONS. — At Babylon, the great wall between the north and south castles has been further excavated, and the quay walls of the canal Arachtu traced. At Assur, three periods have been clearly distinguished in the temple of Ann and Adad. A palace of Tukulti-Ninib has been excavated. Of especial interest are the private houses over the palace ruins. They are small but carefully drained. Within the houses are numerous graves, oriented according to the house walls, and apparently in use at the same time as the houses. The interments seem chiefly those of women, as weapons are lacking. There are clear traces in many cases of cremation in the grave. Among the objects found is a series of unbaked clay reliefs and figures. *(Berl. Phil. W.* 1900, pp. 1149-50, from *Mitt. Or. Ges.* No. 31.) BISMAYA.-The American Excavations. —In *Rec. Past,* V, 1906, pp. 227-230 (10 figs.), E. J. Banks describes his excavation of one of the highest mounds at Bismaya (see *A. J.A.* 1900, p. 96). The summit of the hill yielded bricks of 2750 B.C., and just below was found an inscription of Naram-Sin (3750 B.C.). A metre and half lower were bricks of about 4500 B.C., while

11 m. lower yet was a thick layer of wheel-made black pottery, which must belong to a very much earlier date. NINEVEH. —The British Excavations. — *Rec. Past,* V, 1906, p. 379, reprints from the *Antiquary,* London, a summary by Sir E. Maunde Thompson of the work at Nineveh which began in 1903, and ended in February, 1905. The mound of Kouyuujik has been fully explored by means of trial trenches. The principal recent discovery is the site of the temple of Nabu, the wav-god, which was found to have been so utterly destroyed, presumably by the Elamites, that it was impossible to make a complete plan. Indeed, so thorough was the destruction of the whole city by the conquerors, to judge from the condition of the remains, that the preservation of a portion of the great library of Sennacherib and Assurbanipal must be attributed to some accidental covering by debris, which thus saved it from the enemy. SUSA.—French Discoveries.—The results of the ninth campaign (1905-06) of the French expedition at Susa are summarized by J. De Morgan in *C. R. A carl. Insc.* 1906, pp. 275-281. The excavations were partly on a late level containing objects from the Persian to the Arabian period, and partly at a lower depth containing monuments destroyed at the sack of the city by Assurbanipal. Many reliefs, cuneiform inscriptions on brick and stone, and small objects have been found. A relief gives the name of a new Anzanite king, and a stele contains a long and important Anzanite inscription with many new words, names of divinities, and a valuable list of geographical names. Three inscriptions furnish new protoAnzanite characters. Three fragments of a second copy of the laws of Hammurabi have been recovered, and there seems reason to hope for more. Near Susa the remains of a brick Sassanide villa of about the fourth century A.d. have yielded much interesting architectural information.

Hebrew Alabastra. — In *C. R. Acad. Insc.* 1906, pp. 237-248 (3 figs.), Clermoxt-gaxxeau discusses two inscribed fragments of archaic Hebrew alabastra found at Susa, in a layer which was certainly earlier than the arrival of the Persians, though later than the destruction of the city by Assurbanipal. One is complete, and reads " 1 *kin* and J log and log," of the other only the end, "a fraction of a log" is preserved. The fragments seem to show that neither vase could have held 1 *kin* (6.074 l.), according to the common valuation. It is suggested that the *hin* was borrowed from the Egyptian *hen* (0.455 l.), and that its value underwent progressive changes.

SYRIA AND PALESTINE GREEK AND LATIN INSCRIPTIONS. — In *Mel. Fac. Or.,* I, 1906, pp. 132-188 (2 pis.), L. Jalabert publishes 61 inscriptions from various places in Syria. Of this number 17 are Latin, the rest Greek. Most of them are sepulchral or votive. No. 1 is the epitaph in elegiacs of a Otoaioti/s, who clothed the dead for burial. Under Xo. 16 are collected the Greek inscriptions of Syria referring to physicians. Xo. 22, the epitaph of a certain Tannelos, in five limping hexameters, reads like a *cento* from the Anthology. Xo. 31 is the circular inscription from Madaba, which is now almost wholly exposed. In addition to the inscriptions, pp. 141-143 contain an account of ancient remains at Oebeil, pp. 157-161 are devoted to the cult of Asclepius in Syria (4 inscriptions and 4 reliefs), and pp. 175-181 to a discussion of the few dedications to the Heliopolitan triad (see *C. R. Acad. Insc.* 1906, pp. 97-104; *A.J.A.* X, 1906, p. 336). ALEPPO.— A Jewish Aramaean Amulet. —In *J. Asiat.* VII, 1906, pp. 5-17 (2 pis.), M. Schwab describes a Jewish amulet found in a tomb in the neighborhood of Aleppo. It consists of a sheet of silver enclosed in a small bronze case, and bears thirty-seven lines of Hebrew writing hammered into the silver. It belongs, apparently, to the seventh century A.d., but may be older, and is of great interest on account of its antiquity, its curious vocabulary, and its type of writing. ER-RUMAM. — Ancient Sculpture. — In *Z. D. Pal. V.* XXIX, 1906, pp. 201-203 (2 figs.), G. Dalman describes a relief representing a bull with a fish over its head, discovered by him in the village of Er-Rumam on the route between Es-Salt and Jerash. He conjectures that the bull is a symbol of Hadad, the Syrian god, and the fish of Atargatis, his paredros. GEZER. — Results of the Latest Excavations. — In *Bill. World,* XXVIII, 1906, pp. 176-186 (3 figs.), E. W. Masterman summarizes the results of the latest excavations of the Palestine Exploration Fund at Gezer, as published in the last numbers of *Pal. Ex. Fund.* (See *A.J.A.* X, 1906, pp. 97, 98. 337.) JERUSALEM. — An Ancient Roman Prison. —In *Pal. Ex. Fund,* XXXVIII, 1900, pp. 225-231 (pi.; 5 figs.), J. E. Hanauer describes the clearing out by the Greek Catholics of certain subterranean chambers in the Via Dolorosa that seem to have been a dungeon in an ancient Roman prison. There are rock-cut benches for prisoners and guards, and holes for chaining captives. One device resembling stocks has lately been uncovered, and is claimed by the Greek Church as the prison in which Christ was confined, but according to Hanauer's observations these remains are open to the suspicion of having been tampered with by the ecclesiastical authorities.

Excavations on the Supposed Line of the Third Wall. — In *Jour. Bibl. Lit.* XXIV, 1905, pp. 196-211 (2 figs.), L. B. Patox discusses the evidence which shows that the third wall of Jerusalem on the north, constructed by Agrippa, is to be sought outside of the present city wall, and describes some excavations made in the side of a cistern north of the city which revealed stone cuttings which may be supposed to form part of the foundation of this wall. (See *A. J.A.* IX, 1905, pp. 81, 82.) MEROM. — A Phoenician Orave and the So-called Throne of the Messiah.—In *Z. D. Pal. V.* XXIX, 1906, pp. 195-199 (5 figs.). G. DalMan describes a remarkable megalithic tomb south of the waters of Merom on a steep hill near the village known as Khirbet Shana. The top of the tomb is built out of four huge stone blocks, and is covered with a single block of stone. The portico in front of it is made of four smaller blocks. The stone which covers the top is 2.4 m. broad, 3 m. long, and about 0.9 m. thick. No such remains are found anywhere else in Palestine. The socalled Grave of Hiram in Phoenicia bears some resemblance. The so-called Throne of the Messiah is a mass of rock eroded into a fantastic form in the neighborhood of the Phoenician tomb. It is regarded by the Jews as the throne on which the Messiah will seat himself when he appears.

RAKKA.-A Hittite Bronze Figure. —In *S. Bibl. Arch.* XXVIII, p. 228 (pi.), H. S. Cowper describes a bronze figure said to have come from Rakka, 150 miles northeast of llama, and 100 miles southeast of Jerabis. The place of finding and the type of art suggest a Hittite origin. TELL ELMTJTESELLIM. — Results of the Latest German Excavations.— In *Mitt. Pal. V.* 1906, pp. 17-70, G. Schumacher gives an account of his excavations at Tell el-Mutesellim in the spring, summer, and fall of 1905. In the neighborhood of the so-called treasury at a depth of from 8.5 to 10 m., he found two undisturbed sepulchral chambers built of stone with vaulted roofs, and provided with entrance shafts and sloping approaches. In one five skeletons were found, in the other twelve, with many objects left as burial deposits. Among these were a number of well-preserved clay vessels and dishes of different shapes, part of them filled with dry food, scarabs with figures of animals, some of them inlaid with gold, early clay lamps, fine flints, alabaster cruises, bronze knives, and bone implements. These graves must belong to the time from 1500-2000 B.C. The south edge of the hill was investigated, and a tower of hewn stone blocks was discovered. Here were found arrows, knives, rings, etc., of bronze. North of this was discovered the corner of a building, probably the palace, constructed of large, well-hewn blocks of limestone. This edifice was thoroughly excavated, and in it were found a number of smaller objects of archaeological interest. The report is richly illustrated with figures and photographs of the discoveries. URFA. — The Throne of Nimrod. —In *S. Bibl. Arch.* XXVIII, pp. 14155 (2 pis.; fig.), F. C. Buukitt describes the curious inscribed column known as the Throne of Nimrod at Urfa or Edessa. The character is a type of Estrangels earlier than our earliest manuscripts, and the inscription states that the column was erected by Aphtoha in honor of Shalmath, the queen. WADI-EL HAMAM. — Sculpture representing Lions. — In *Z. D. Pal. V.* XXIX, 1906, pp. 199-201 (2 figs.), G. Dalman describes certain caves in the Wadi-el Hamam that were perhaps the caves mentioned by Josephus as occupied by robbers in the time of Herod. In one of these is a relief, apparently of mediaeval Arabic origin, representing two lions disputing over the head of an ox. WADI-SUWEIL. — Roman Remains. — In /. *Bibl. Lit.* XXV, pp. 82-95 (11 pis.), N. Schmidt describes ruins of an aqueduct and houses discovered by him in Wadi-Suweil on the east side of the Dead Sea and believed by him to be of Roman origin. Traces of remains dating from the time when the Crusaders had sugar mills around the Head Sea were also recognizable. ASIA MINOR ALABANDA. — Further Discoveries. — The report of the second season's work (1905) at Alabanda is published by Edhem Bey in *C. R. Acad. Insc.* 1906, pp. 407—122 (13 figs.). Excavations in the neighborhood of the temple already cleared (see *A.J. A.* 1906, p. 99) led to no results. Better results were obtained in the lower city near a long wall previously discovered (Fig. 2). Here were found the foundations of a Byzantine church built of older material, and near by remains of an Hellenistic temple, which had been later altered into a structure which may have been the baptistery of the church. Still later a large building of uncertain plan and use had been placed upon this site. The peristasis of the temple was 34.53 x 21.66 m.; the cella 23.52 x 10.47 m. It is restored as pseudo-dipteros, with four columns before the pronaos, and 8 x 13 in the peristasis. It is perhaps the temple of Apollo mentioned by Vitruvius (III, 2, 6). Numerous fragments of a large Ionic order were found, including three more slabs of the frieze, representing an Amazonomachy. There were also remains of a small Ionic order, and of a Doric building, probably a portico. One of its columns contained a dedication of imperial times to the ©toi St/ Jarroi, Apollo Isotimos, and the Demos. APHRODISIAS. — Inscriptions. — The 221 inscriptions found by P. Gaudin at Aphrodisias in 1904 (*A.J.A.* 1905, p. 344) have been given to T. Reinach, who publishes 81 in *R. £t. Gr.* XIX, 1906, pp. 79-150. In the case of 28 texts already published only collations are given. The inscriptions are classified as follows: I Official documents, *a*. (1-6) Those issued by Roman authority. No. 4 mentions a new proconsul of Asia, Sulpicius Prisons. No. 6 is a Latin fragment of ch. 19 of the edict of Diocletian. *b*. (7-16) Decrees of Aphrodisias. No. 13, unfortunately very fragmentary, is in honor of a citizen who had contributed to the erection of two porticoes, and is interesting for the architectural terms employed, *c*. (17, 18) Police regulations. No. 17, from the facade of the baths, seems based on a Latin original. It reads Eav *Ti% lxwv yaXKov pr) irapaStiir*) »)Tt *iv ijovvSrl rfrt iv KafjtiTidTpw aijov aiTidatTai*. The bather who neglected to "declare" his money before undressing, was himself responsible, if it was stolen. No. 18 is Christian. II Dedications, *a*. (19—31) To gods, and emperors, *b*. (32) To another city. derhaps Ceretapa. *c*. (33-81) To individuals. These are partly from statue bases, and partly from sarcophagi. CORDELIO. — A Dedicatory Inscription. — In *11. £t. Anc.* VIII, 1906, pp. 285-286, A. Fontrier publishes a fragment of a dedication by the city of Smyrna to the river Hermus and the emperor Antoninus Pius. The stone is built into a stable in Cordelio. EPHESUS. — Progress of the Austrian Excavations. — At Ephesus the street from the theatre to the Magnesian Gate and the eastern portico of the Greek agora have been excavated. Among the finds are an inscription recording the work of Nero and Agrippina on this agora, an inscription showing that the Byzantine wall, which did not include the agora, was later than the Emperor IIeraclius, several reliefs from the monument for the Parthian wars, and some remains that may be those of the long-sought Auditorium. The

Church of the Virgin has been fully uncovered and is found to have an apse between square chambers at the west end,' a colonnade all around the inside, and a small building, possibly a baptistery, connected with the north side, and to have formed as a whole a decagon with four entrances, covered by a dome. Parts of the wall, when ruined, were incorporated into the city wall. The official publication of the results of these excavations has begun with a volume on the topography and history of the city, the bronze statues, and certain buildings. *(Arch. Anz.* 1906, pp. 95-97.)

The Honors of M. Nonius Macrinus. — In *Jh. Oest. Arch. I.* IX, 1906, Beiblatt, pp. 61-76 (fig.), R. Eg(jer publishes a Greek inscription, found at Ephesus in 1903, which contains the *cursus hnnornm* of a Macrinus, who is identified with *M. Nonius M. f. Fabia Macrinus*, legate of Pannonia. His life and offices, as recorded here and in other inscriptions, are discussed at length.

EUMENEIA. — Inscriptions. — In *B.S.A.* XI, 1904-05, pp. 27-31, M. N. Tod publishes four inscriptions from Eumeneia copied in 1903 by A. J. B. Wace, who also furnishes a brief description of the site. One inscription, a dedication to Apollo nptnruAuos, is engraved on either side of the relief of a double axe. Another is a sepulchral inscription in which Figrait 3. — Stati t the right of interment in the tomb is strictly limited Cape Phonias. figure of Chares of Teichiua to the family of the builder. The other two inscriptions are mere fragments. LINDUS (RHODES). —The Danish Excavations. — At Lindus Dr. Kinch reports the discovery of a very primitive temple on the Bukopia Place, where are many rock inscriptions. The long-sought necropolis of Lindus has been found, and the vase fragments indicate that it was used from the end of the geometric period until the fifth century B.C. Near Vrulia, at the southern end of the island, there has been found an ancient city of the time of the so-called Rhodian vases. *(Ath. Mitt.* XXXI, 1906, p. 368.) RHODES. — Votive Inscription. — In *R. £t. Gr.* XIX, 1906, p. 24, T. R. publishes an inscription from the citadel of Rhodes. It seems to be a dedication by a family of metics. New are the woman's name 'Xpunapiov and the abbreviation WE for *p.troiKo*. SAMOS. — Some Unpublished Sculptures. — At Cape Phonias near Tigani there was found in 1902 an archaic statue, now in the Museum at Vathy (Fig. 3). It is briefly described in *Ath. Mitt.* XXXI, 1906, pp. 86-87 (3 pis.), by T. Wiegand. The costume is the same as that of the seated ind the statue is the first known standing figure in the style of the older figures from Branchidae. The height is 1.79 m. *Ibid.* pp. 151-185 (3 pis.; 6 figs.), L. Curtius publishes with a full discussion twoother sculptures recently discovered on this island. The first is a seated marble figure somewhat over lifesize (Fig. 4). On the left side of the throne is the inscription KiaKrp avtOr)Ktv 6 Bpvawvos : os rrj "Hpr): rrlv (rvXriv : iirprlatv Kara 7Tlv imaTa.atv. 'EirprlGtv is interpreted as for *lirpamrt*, and *imoTamv* as referring to the office held by Aeaces, whose duty probably was to collect for Hera the tenth of all booty. The inscription seems to be of about the middle of the sixth century, and the statue probably represents the father of Polycrates. The name of the tyrant's brother, Syloson (-o-ai3v), "saviour of booty," may refer to his father's office. The style of the statue is closely analyzed in comparison with the figures from Branchidae, and contemporary works. It represents a later development of the same Ionic art. In this connection the marble statue published by Wiegand is discussed at length. A comparison with earlier Ionic work indicates that this statue and the Hera of Samoa show the effect of Egyptian art on Milesian artists after the founding of Naucratis. This influence and its modifications under Ionic tendencies are treated at length, and illustrated not only by marble statues and reliefs, but also by terra-cottas, including an alabastron from Rhodes, now in Munich, representing a kneeling figure. The pose is distinctly Egyptian; the treatment and style thoroughly Ionic. The second sculpture is a grave-relief, representing a child holding a bird by the wings. It is a work of the middle of the fifth century, and shows relationship with the relief from Paros in Brocklesby House *(Ant. Dent.* I, 54). The differences from the Attic work of that time are pointed out. In conclusion a sepulchral inscription of the second half of the sixth century is published. SARDIS. — A Representation of the Persian Artemis. — In *C. R. Acad. Insc.* 19015, pp. 282-285 (fig.), G. Radet publishes a brief summary of a paper on a terra-cotta plaque from Sardis in the Louvre, containing in a square field a representation of a winged goddess holding two lions by the tail. A similar field at the right, now broken, seems to have contained an archer. The plaque is of the end of the seventh or beginning of the sixth century n.c. The winged divinity in this attitude is due to Oriental or more specifically to Lydian influence. The name "Persian Artemis" is inappropriate for the early representations of the *irorvia Orfpwv*. It is better to designate this series by the name of the goddess of Sardis, Cybebe THRACE LEMNOS. — Archaeological Notes. —In *Ath. Mitt.* XXXI, 1906, pp. 60-86 (2 pis.: 24 figs.); 241-256 (7 figs.), U. Fredrich publishes the results of archaeological studies on Lemnos in 1901. The first article describes a number of small objects found near Myrina, and for the most part coming from a necropolis which seems to have been in use from the earliest times until the Roman period. Of the pottery there are some prehistoric pieces, resembling the Trojan and old Phrygian ware, but most of the vases are wheel-made, and resemble the *bncchero* vases of Etruria, though the form is peculiar. Among the terra-cottas a new group is formed by a series of plates (1 cm. thick), cut out like the Melian reliefs, but with a flat surface on which the design must have been painted. A group of reliefs seems to represent a seated woman with a lyre. There are also a number of heads distinguished by a lofty calathus. Most of these remains are attributed to the sixth century, before the Athenian conquest. Much of the article is given to a discussion of the worship of a great chthonic goddess,

Lemnos, in conjunction with the fire-daemon, Hephaestus, and the Cabiri, and a comparison of the Lemnian with the Samothracian, Theban, and other similar cults.

The second article is devoted to a more general trbiographical and archaeological description of the island, with special reference to the chief ancient sites, Myrina and Hephaestia. It also contains the brief record of a week's tour through the interior of the island, including a description of the old volcano, Moschylos, and the spot where the "Lesbian earth" is still dug for medicinal purposes.

THRACE. — Prehistoric Mounds. — In *B.C.H.* XXX, 1906, pp. 359432 (75 figs. ; 3 plans), G. Seure and A. Degrand describe the results of the excavation of certain mounds in Thrace. These mounds differ from the numerous *tumuli* in their size and shape, which is markedly oval, and resemble in so many ways the Asiatic "tells," that this name may be applied to them. Seven are known, of which four have been carefully explored, while three more have been plundered by peasants. The article contains a summary catalogue with many illustrations of all the objects known to have been found in Tell Ratcheff (624 numbers), the Tell of Metchkur (577 numbers), and the Tell of Costievo (88 numbers), as well as in the other and less productive mounds. It seems clear that these mounds were burial places. The bodies were burned, the ashes enveloped in layers of clay, surrounded by vases and offerings, and the whole covered with clay and again burned. The mounds are formed by successive strata of these tombs. The objects found are prehistoric, though some Roman and later graves occur near the surface. The discussion of the finds and their relation to discoveries in Asia Minor and Central Europe is reserved for a later article. GREECE ARCHAEOLOGICAL DISCOVERIES IN 1905. — Remains of the Mycenaean epoch have been found at Tiryna under the palace, at Thebes in graves containing skeletons and furnishings, and at Volo. In Laconia, the British School has explored various ancient sites as well as Sparta itself. (For the details, see *A.J.A.* X, 1906, p. 105, and *infra.*) The Greek Archaeological Society has been working especially at Epidaurus, where the architecture of the two temples and that of the building supposed to be the Abaton has been studied. Objects found now go to the local museum. The American School continued its work at Corinth. (See *A. J. A.* X, 1906, pp. 17-20.) Minor excavations were also made in the Asclepieum at Athens. At Delos, the French School has uncovered shops and other buildings near the Roman agora and a large building in its centre. This agora was not built over earlier constructions, but an early market-place is found to have been buried under the portico dedicated to Apollo by Philip V of Macedonia. The houses of Delos, unlike those of Priene, are entirely irregular in their grouping. They usually contain a peristyle around a central court. Their decoration is like that of the incrustation period at Pompeii. A figurine maker's workshop and four hordes of coin are among the finds. Among single objects discovered in Greece are five bronze helmets from the gymnasium at Olympia, found in the bed of the Cladeus, and articles of gold, said to come from Macedonia and Thrace. (,1 *rch. Anz.* 1906, pp. 100-102.) WORK OF THE GREEK EPHORS IN 1905-06. — Near Elatea. Soteriades has discovered pre-Myeenaean graves, with pottery, resembling the Kamares ware of Crete. Skias has determined the course of the walls of Lechaeum, and has thrown light on other points of Corinthian topography. On the Pagasaean Gulf, Arvanitopoullos has begun the excavation of the temple of Apollo Kopomubs. The peribolos wall has been partially cleared, and two dedicatory inscriptions found. Of the temple there are many fragments of poros architecture, and of the painted terracotta decorations. The vases include a mass of black-figured fragments. At Sepiada, the same Ephor has found the ruins of an archaic Doric temple, and nearby remains of early houses. (*Ath. Mitt.* XXXI, 1906, p. 369.) ARGOS. — Excavations in 1906. — In *C. R. Acad. lime.* 1906, pp. 493-494, W. Volloraff summarizes the results of excavations at Argos from June to September, 1906. At the east of the Larissa, near the theatre, the foundations of a small temple of tufa were found. A brick building higher up the hill proved to contain reservoirs supplied by the aqueduct from Belissi. The statue of the donor was found in a niche. It strongly resembles the statue of C. Ofelius Ferus found at Delos. Excavations within the citadel on the Larissa yielded many architectural fragments of Byzantine churches. South of the modern city the foundations of a prostyle temple 33 x 15.20 m. have been uncovered. Byzantine walls here have yielded many architectural fragments, and several stelae from the sanctuary of the Lycian Apollo. One contains a treaty made at Argos during the fifth century between the Cretan cities, Cnossus and Cylissus. Another is a decree of the third century in honor of the Rhodians, who had lent the Argives 100 talents to repair their walls and reorganize their cavalry. This work is also noted in *Ath. Mitt.* XXXI, 1906, pp. 365-366. ATHENS. — Marble Lecythus.— A beautiful but imperfect marble lecvthus, found beside the llissus in 1904, is published by S. M. Welsh in *J.H.S.* XXVI, 1906, pp. 229-234 (pi.). The relief, set between raised bands, contains four standing figures representing perhaps a young brother and sister who have died, and their surviving parents. Color and painted inscriptions, if there were any, have disappeared, but the words OPOS MNHMAT05 cut upon the neck suggest that the vase formed one of the memorials in a family burial lot which was not, as usual, surrounded by a wall. The figure of the older woman, who has the hair cut short, perhaps in token of mourning, resembles the well-known Mynno, and the younger woman suggests Hegeso. The figures as a whole closely resemble the Parthenon frieze and other work of the latter half of the fifth century, a period to which grave lecythi especially belong.

Boundary and Mortgage Stones. — In *B.S.A.* XI, 1901-05, pp. 63-71 (13 figs.), H. J. V. Tii.i.yard publishes for the first time 20 inscriptions in the Epigraphic

Museum at Athens. The first 17 are boundary stones, of which 5 are from graves. The last 3 are records of mortgaged property taken in default of payment *(irtirpaaOat iirl* Awrti).

Excavations at the Dipylon. — The ancient city wall at the Dipylon has been excavated for the German Archaeological Institute by F. Noack, who publishes a brief account of the results in *Ath. Milt.* XXXI. 1906, pp. 238, 239, 363. The oldest gateway and the Themistoclean wall near by were cleared, but to determine the line of the earlier wall from the old gate toward the Dipylon will require extensive excavations in the Pompeium. The wall near the boundary stone was certainly later. Several reliefs and two archaic inscriptions have been found built into the Themistoclean wall. One relief represents a standing youth, with a running Gorgon in the lower field. The style resembles that of the discus-bearer. Near the Piraeic gate a part of the old wall and a tower were found, showing three of the four periods of building which appear at the Dipylon.

Meetings of the German School. — At the open meetings of the German School in Athens the following papers were presented: 1905, December 20, H. Hepding, ' Minor Discoveries at Pergamon'; A. S. ArvanitopoulLos, 'A New Interpretation of Certain Figures on the Eastern Frieze of the Parthenon.' 1906, January 8, W. Dorpfeld, 'The Latest Excavations at Pergamon '; L. Curtius, 'New Sculptures from Samos.' January 17, G. Kaho, 'Egyptian and Mycenaean Ornaments'; W. Dorpfeld, 'New Excavations on Leucas-Ithaca.' January 81, G. Soterfades, 'Ethnology and Topography of Aetolia'; F. Noack, 'The Amazon of Polyclitus.' February 14, A. vox Salis, 'The Warrior of Delos'; W. Dorpfeld, 'Homer's Map and the Wanderings of Odysseus.' February 20, P. Steixer, 'On two Reliefs on the Old Metropolis'; G. Karo, 'The Oldest Gods in Greece.' March 14, R. Hkherdey, 'Excavations in Ephesus, 1906"; W. Dorpfeld, 'The Cretan Palaces.' March 28, F. Noack, 'On the Development of the Eleusinian Sanctuary before Pericles'; A. v. Premerstein, 'The Illustrated Medical Ms. of the Patrician Anicia Juliana'; W. DorpFeld, 'Brief Notice of the Excavations at Olympia.' *(Ath. Mitt.* XXXI, 1906, p. 240.) CARTHAEA (CEOS). — Accounts of the Temple of Apollo. — In *B.C.H.* XXX, 1906, pp. 433-452, P. Graindor continues his publication of inscriptions found during his excavations at Carthaea on Ceos *(see A.J.A.* 1905, p. 107; 1906, pp. 103, 343). The four stones discussed contain seven fragments of the accounts of the temple of Apollo, all of which belong to the categories already known at Carthaea *(F.G.* XII, v. i, 544 A, B, and C). The first and sixth are from the list of crowns offered to the god. The others are explained as from a list of tenants of the god, and this view is defended at length against the theory of Halbherr *(Museo Italiano,* I, pp. 211-214) that the names record the payment of a tithe on sales of property. The average rent is about that received by Delphi, and proves that the Apollo of Carthaea was relatively rich. Corrections to the inscriptions of Carthaea already published conclude the article.

CORONTA.— Inscriptions and Graves. — In *Ath. Mitt.* XXXI, 1906. pp. 94-96, E. Nachmaxson publishes four fragmentary sepulchral inscriptions from Coronta in Acarnania. He gives a more exact copy of *I.G.* XI, i, 441, and reports that No. 440 has been destroyed. *Ibid.* pp. 97-98, there is a note by E. Herkenrath on some graves recently discovered by peasants. They were apparently Hellenistic and contained little of value. One is said to have contained fourteen skulls, probably indicating repeated use. CRETE. — Archaeological Discoveries in 1905. — In *Arch. Am.,* 1906, pp. 97-99, is a summary of the discoveries during 1905, at Cnossus, Palaikastro, Phaestus, Hagia Triada, and Sitia. These results are reported below from other sources. CRETE. — CNOSSUS. — Excavations in 1905. — A provisional report by A. J. Evans on the excavations in and about the palace at Cnossus during 1905, appears in *B.S.A.* XI, 1904-05, pp. 1-26 (pi.; 12 figs.). The magazines along the Minoan road, which leads west from the " Theatral Area," were further explored and the course of the road traced beyond the modern highway. On the hill beyond the modern road was found a building reproducing on a reduced scale the leading features of the palace as it was remodelled about the beginning of the Late Minoan period. Some of the wooden columns had convex fluting in the Egyptian style. At a later time it seems to have been altered into a number of smaller dwellings. At this time a small balustraded space was walled up, and converted into a domestic shrine, in which were found fetish images, consisting of umvorked limestone concretions, of grotesque, quasi-human form. Among the fragmentary seals found here was one bearing the figure of a horse superposed on a ship with rowers. It evidently refers to the importation of horses to Crete, which apparently began early in the Late Minoan period. Excavations in the West Court of the palace confirmed the view that the whole western wing, while retaining earlier traditions, was a work of the Third Middle Minoan period. Owing to the damage caused by heavy winter rains, it became necessary to restore thoroughly the great staircase in the domestic quarter of the palace. During this work new light was thrown on the original structure. The roofing of the Throne Room has made it possible to arrange there a small reference museum of the less important fragments of pottery from the palace. CRETE. — PALAIKASTRO. — The Excavations of 1905.— The results of the final campaign at Palaikastro of the British School at Athens are described in *B.S.A.* XI, 1904-0,-), pp. 258-308. The first part (pp. 258-292; 7 pis.; 16 figs.) is by R. M. Dawkins. The work was chiefly in the temple area, though a block of Minoan houses on the opposite side of the street was cleared, the main street traced westward, and an ossuary found on the slopes of the Kastri. An important discovery was made at Magasa, about three hours from Palaikastro, where was found a neolithic settlement, consisting of a rock-shelter half shielded by a wall, and not far away the foundations of a house, the first yet discovered in Crete. The finds included hand-made gray potsherds, bone awls and pins, chips of obsidian, and thirtysix stone axes. The ossuary contained the usual mass of reinterred bones, with many fragments of Early Minoan III pottery. A comparison with the six other ossuaries shows that this form of reburial was in use from the early bronze age to the end of the Middle Minoan period. On the temple site the excavations showed below the Hellenic stratum a series of Minoan houses beginning in the Early Minoan period. At the end of Middle Minoan II a catastrophe seems to have occurred, and the reestablishment of the settlement occurred in Late Minoan I. This period (Late Minoan I and II) yielded some fine vases as well as those of degenerate styles, and in particular some carvings in ivory of excellent workmanship. The buildings of Late Minoan III were much damaged when the site was levelled for the Hellenic temple, which seems to have been the only building here in later times. The block of houses excavated showed four clearly separate strata of walls, extending from Middle Minoan to Late Minoan III. Much pottery was found, and about half way down, the indications of a place of sacrifice, white ashes, and remains of oxen. There were also fragments of bulls-heads of clay. Three sets of clay water-pipes were found in this section. Finally two burials in *larnalces* were found on a neighboring ridge. Evidently here also there was reburial of bones, for in and about the *larnak es* were no less thán twenty skulls. A series of /arnax-burials at Sarandari is described by C. H. Hawes (pp. 293-297; fig.). All belonged to Late Minoan III. The presence of skulls outside as well as inside the *larnax* is attributed to early plundering of these burials. The finds at the temple of Dictaean Zeus are described by R. C. Bosanquet (pp. 298-308; 2 pis.; 6 figs.). All remains of buildings were destroyed a generation ago, but the ground yielded many terra-eottas and bronzes. Of the former the most important are the remains of architectural decorations. From an early temple are numerous pieces of sima decorated with the recurrent group of a warrior mounting a chariot and followed by a second warrior on foot. From the same temple come antefixes in the form of a *gorgoneion*. From a later building are fragments of a conventional sima, as well as antefixes representing Medusa as a woman in Doric chiton, holding two snakes in her hands, while others spring from her shoulders. The same type is found at Praesus. Among the pottery lamps and torch holders are conspicuous, but there are few vases, figurines, or plaques. The bronzes include shields decorated with zones of animals, of the same type as those found in the Idaean cave, also miniature pieces of armor, and many fragments of small tripods. CRETE. — PHAESTUS. — The Italian Excavations. — In *Ath. Mitt.* XXXI. 1906, p. 366, is a summary of Pernier's work at Phaestus in 1906. On the slope to the south of the palace he found at the bottom the remains of houses of the older (Kamares) period, above these supporting walls of the later Mycenaean palace, and above these again the foundations of an archaic Greek temple. Numerous shafts have made clearer the relation between the earlier and later palaces. Below some magazines of the earlier palace was found a layer of primitive Kamares ware, and below this neolithic remains. CRETE. — PRINIA. — Recent Discoveries. — At Prinia, Pernier has found Hellenistic fortifications, a Mycenaean stele with a relief representing a standing figure in a long garment, and some rude idols around which twine snakes. The pottery includes many fragments of pithoi with decorations in relief. *(Ath. Mitt.* XXXI, 1906, p. 367.) CRETE. — SITIA. — An Early Dwelling. — *Ath. Mitt.* XXXI. 1906. pp. 367-368, reports some of the results of excavations by Xanthudides at Sitia *(Xafjuou£I)* east of Gortyn. Most important is the discovery of an elliptical walled enclosure (26 x 15 m.) divided into small chambers. Near the entrance was a small court with a well. One room was filled with pithoi, another contained a small altar and remains of ashes, and a third showed traces of a staircase. The pottery dates the settlement in the Kamares (Middle Minoan) period. The form of the building shows the transition between the large elliptical hut and the later palace, with its regular arrangement of rooms. DAULIB. — A Metrical Epitaph. —In *R. £t. Anc.* VIII, 1906, p. 284, A. E. Condolkon publishes the epitaph from Daulis of a certain Erato. It is in two elegiac couplets, which have for their theme that if money could purchase release from death, none of the rich would die. DELOS. — Recent Discoveries. — *Le Muse'e,* III, 1906, p. 360. reports the discovery at Delos of six large archaic marble lions. A statue of Polyhymnia resembles, but surpasses the statue of the Muse in Berlin. Another fine work is a head of Dionysus in the style of Scopas. (See *C. R. A cad. Insc.* 1906, p. 387.) Other finds include mosaics, jewellery, and a hoard of well-preserved coins. *Ibid.* p. 470, the discovery of a Mycenaean tomb is announced. X'o details are given. DELPHI. — The Treasury of the Athenians. — In *C. R. Acad. Insc.* 1906, pp. 531-533, J. Homolle reports the complete restoration of the Treasury of the Athenians at Delphi, undertaken at the expense of the city

Figure 5.—The Treasury Of The Athenians At Delphi. of Athens (Fig. 5). The work was begun in 1903. The duty of reconstructing the text of the numerous inscriptions on the antae and walls would alone have compelled the collection of the scattered stones of the building, and in fact the material is much more ample than was afforded for the restoration of the temple of Athena Nike or of the Erechtheum.

BPIDAURUS.—Recent Excavations. — Since 1903 Kavvadias has been excavating at Epidaurus, and the results are summarized in *Ath. Mitt.* XXXI. 1906, pp. lio'9-371. The base of a bronze statue near the ramp leading up to the temple has been found to be connected with a conduit, so that the water was carried through the right foot of the statue, and then by a series of basins to the Abatou and a neighboring room. Doubtless the water poured originally from a dish in the hand of the statue which must have represented the god, who thus furnished holy water to his worshippers. Xear the temple of Artemis a large building has been uncovered, which in its earliest form seems to have been a court surrounded by narrow passages. and before him, facing outward, a standing female. No snake or worshippers are present. The other relief (Fig. 6) shows the very unusual type of the worshipper standing alone. As no inscriptions were found, the name of the hero worshipped is unknown. The same writers describe (pp. 91-99; 4 figs.) the excavations at Geronthrae (Geraki). The search for the temples of Ares and Apollo mentioned by Pausanias proved fruitless, but the Acropolis showed everywhere traces of human habitations, and the bronzes, terracottas, stone implements, and pottery showed continuous occupation from neolithic times. Of some importance is the presence of Mycenaean ware

It is probably the early altar and Abaton where, as inscriptions show, Apollo and Asclepius were worshipped a hundred years before the temple of the latter was built. The later Abaton was in the long hall on the north wall of the temenos.

Figure 6. — Relief From Anc.ei.ona

L ACONIA. —Work of the British School in 1905. — A detailed report of the explorations in Laconia undertaken in 1905 by the British School at Athens (see *A. J.A.* X, 1906, p. 105), is given in *U.S.A.* XI, 1904-05, pp. 81-138. The discovery of the *heroon* at Kollyri, near Angelona. is described by A. J. B. Wace and F. VV. Hasldck (pp. 81-90; pi.; 8 figs.). The two reliefs are of sjecial interest. The one in terra-cotta represents the hero enthroned toward the left, holding a cantharus, with local peculiarities. Mr. Wace discusses (pp. 99-105; 6 figs.) four sculptures recently found here, to which is added the relief published by Schroder, *Ath. Mitt.* 1904, pp.47 ff. (see *A.J.A.* VIII, 1004, p. 380). He concludes that they are probably the product of a local school working in Laconia during the sixth and fifth centuries B.C. The inscriptions are treated by II. J. W. TillyArd (pp. 105-112). These are 11 in number, of which 5 are Christian. Most of the others are single names or small fragments. One, 10 lines in length, is part of a dedication by a victorious athlete, and seems to be somewhat earlier than the Damonon inscription, though later than 479 B.c. It seems to mention a festival 'ExaTd/x/Ja, perhaps the same as Strabo's 'EicaTcyi/3ua. No. 11 is from the base of a statue of Antigonus Uoson. This leads to a Historical Note (pp. 112-123) by Tillyaiu) and Wace in which are discussed the history of Demetrius the Fair (c. 295-247 B.c.) and the worship of the earlier Diadochi, who, it is maintained with Kornemann *(Klio,* I, p. 07), were not deified during their lifetime. G. Dickins describes the work at Thalamae (pp. 124-136; 7 figs.). Nothing of great importance was found, though the discovery of marble Doric capitals and pilasters seems to confirm the belief that here was the oracle of Ino-Pasiphae. The site seems to have been occupied since neolithic times, and the earth has been very thoroughly turned over in recent years. Among the six inscriptions is a dedication AavtK«i &vi$ijxt T5 AyAa7ricu, a form of the name Asclepius. The *'Kp/iux* on the northeast frontier of Laconia (Paus. II, 38, 7) are identified by K. Romaios (pp. 137138) with mounds at Vrrovs 4ov£/xcvous, which seem to have been tombs. A detailed discussion is withheld until after further excavation.

LEUCAS. — Progress of the Excavations. — During 1900 Professor Dorpfeld continued his excavations at Leucas, discovering a long settlement with simple walls, jxjttery with engraved ornament, and a few fragments of glazed ware. He considers this as the Homeric city of Ithaca. In the neighborhood has been found an archaic temple with old Doric columns outside, and Ionic columns within. The clearing of a cave has led to the discovery of prehistoric remains, including stone implements, monochrome potsherds such as are found in Troja II and Cnossos I, and also dull painted ware recalling the early Italian and Thessalian pottery. In Acarnania, opposite Leucas, Dorpfeld has also found a Greek temple and two sanctuaries with terra-cottas. *(Ath. Mitt.* XXXI, 1900, p. 364.) OLYMPIA. —The Age of the Sanctuary. — In *Ath. Mill.* XXXI, 1906, pp. 205-218 (8 figs.), W. Dorpfeld describes briefly some recent soundings in the Heraeum and Pelopion, undertaken primarily with a view to determining the nature of the earliest pottery. The excavations at Leucas had shown a settlement using monochrome geometric pottery, and also bronzes resembling the oldest found at Olympia. As this settlement was covered by a thick layer of gravel on which was a Greek settlement of the seventh century, the early date of these remains is clear. Similar pottery and bronzes were found at Olympia, but the results are of such importance that further excavations seem necessary. Dorpfeld argues that the geometric style of the early iron age represents the original art of the Achaeans, which was superseded at the courts of the princes by the Oriental "Mycenaean" art, whether this came from Crete or Phoenicia.

A Bronze Statuette. — The bronze statuette 23.7 cm. high, found beneath the opisthodomos of the Heraeum (Fig. 7), is described by P. Stkiner in *Ath. Milt.* XXXI, 190(5, pp. 219-227 (pi.). He compares it with a bronze from Delphi *(H. C.H.* XXI, 1897, pi. X), and one from the grotto of the Idaean Zeus. Among large figures the closest relationship is shown by the Apollo of Melos. There are marked divergencies from Mycenaean bronzes. All indications point to the Argolid as the probable place of origin. No sure date can be assigned, but it is certainly earlier than the sixth century B.C.

MOUNT PARNES. — The Cave of Pan. — A continuation of the account of the antiquities found in the excavation of the Cave of Pan (see *A.J.A.X,* 190G, p. 104) is published by K. Komaios in 'E£. 'A. 1906, pp. 89-116 (2 pis.; 11 figs.). Most noteworthy is a small gold clasp in the form of a *lellix.* It has archaic characteristics, and seems to be a specimen of the *tettiges* mentioned by Thueydides as worn in the hair before his time. The other articles described are a small gold model of a bedstead, four seal rings, a few bits of relief work in silver, an almost uninterrupted series of vases and vase fragments from prehistoric times down to the latest Attic styles, a few votive images in terra-cotta, and many lamps,

Figi'kf 7 Bronze Stat 'k, but nearly all Christian, which are

Ufttk From OiviipiA compared with those from Van published by

Bassett in *A.J.A. VII*, 1903, pp. 338-349. PHTHIOTIS. —Topography. —In *Ath. Mitt.* XXXI, 1906. pp. 1-37 (3 pis. : 13 figs.), F. Staehlin gives the results of topographical studies in the Phthiotis. The earlier maps are corrected in details, and the general features of the plain of Halmyros described. The ancient cities are then taken in order, and their situation, remains, and history briefly noted. The cities treated are Phthiotic Thebes, Pyrasos, Phylace, Ttonos, Eretria, Coronea, and Halos. There follows an account of unknown cities or forts near Tsurnati, Genitzek, Karatzadali, and Kokoti, and of remains of a temple not far from Genitzek. At Kokoti the walls are Hellenistic, but the objects found are of the stone age. The importance and ease of excavations in this region, which would throw light on the early civilization of Thessaly, are emphasized.

SCIATHUS AND PEPARETHUS (SCOPELOS).— Ancient Remains.— The topography and ruins on the islands of Sciathus and Peparethus (now called Scopelos) are described by C. Fredrioh in *Ath. Milt.* XXXI, 1906, pp. 99-128 (17 figs.). On Sciathus the modern city nearly corresponds with the ancient, of which but scanty remains exist. The site of the second ancient city is unidentified. The mediaeval town was on a cliff in the northern part of the island, now abandoned. There are ruins of one or more watch-towers at exposed points of the coast. On Peparethus were three cities, two, Peparethus and Selinus, in fruitful parts of the island, but with poor harbors, the third, Panormus, on the only good harbor. At the first and third sites the remains are scanty, chiefly traces of fortifications and terrace waiis. At Selinus there are more ancient walls and foundations visible than on any other of the Magnesian islands, and excavation would be easy. The remains seem to include a private house, public buildings, and a large terrace wall. On the island are also several ancient watch-towers. A. J. B. Wace contributes notes to this article, and *Ibid.* pp. 129-133 adds some results from his own visit to these islands. His article is concerned chiefly with the Christian remains, and includes an account of the Good Friday celebration at Sciathus, and a list of the carved screens (Tt/nirAa or tiKovoorafrtts) in the churches of Scopelos. SCYROS. — Ancient Remains. —In *Ath. Mitt.* XXXI, 1906, pp. 257278 (15 figs.), C. Fredrich describes in some detail the ruins of the ancient city of Scyros, including the walls and the Episkopi, built in 895 A.u. Other remains *on* the island, as seen during a brief visit in 1904, are also noted.

Archaeological Notes. —In *B.S.A.* XI, 1904-05, pp. 72-80 (3 figs.), R. M. Dawkixs publishes notes of a visit to Scyros in 1905. Section 1 gives a brief account of the Carnival masquerade characteristic of this island *(Ibid.* VI, 1899-1900, pp. 125-127). Section 2 contains a description and plan of the ruined church of the Episkopi, built in 895 A.o., according to an inscription originally on the facade. Its plan is almost exactly that of the Church of the Protaton on Mt. Athos. In section 3 is an account of late Mycenaean and geometric vases found in two recently discovered tombs. Both series show distinctly local characteristics indicating the isolation of the island during this period.

SPARTA. — The Shrine of Artemis Orthia. — The Managing Committee of the British School at Athens has issued an appeal for funds to enable the further prosecution of work at Sparta. The circular contains a summary of the results obtained in 1906, from which the following statement is abridged. Experimental and preliminary excavations were undertaken on the site of ancient Sparta. The discovery of the town walls proved that the city extended as far as the bank of the Eurotas. On the Acropolis part of the stage of the theatre was cleared as well as the foundations of the fortifications, and many inscriptions came to light. Of the Roman city a large bath was partly cleared. The most important results were obtained on the right bank of the Eurotas. Here a long narrow building has been fully cleared, and a small Hereon discovered which yielded stratified remains ranging from geometric to late Greek.

Not far from this on the bank of the river is the most interesting discovery yet made, and certainly the most important archaeological find of the year in Greece. This is the Shrine of Artemis Orthia, the savage goddess at whose altar the Spartan youths underwent the ordeal of scourging. Trial-trenches were sunk, and such rich remains of the archaic period of Greek art came to light, that the complete excavation promises to result in the discovery of a greater mass of such finds than has ever been found at any site in Greece, while, in view of the obscurity of the beginnings of art in Laconia, the interest of such objects can hardly be overstated. Thousands of votive offerings have already been found, comprising lead figurines (Fig. 8), carved ivories, pottery, bronze brooches and ornaments, and a remarkable series of clay masks, many of them painted and modelled with extraordinary freshness and vigor. As belonging to the archaic period of art their realism is without precedent. These may have been used in some ritual mystery play, and thus have important bearing on the earliest history of the drama in Greece. The almost innumerable lead figurines will present, when all the varieties have been recovered, the largest series of votive offerings ever found, and will shed much light on the cult of Orthia, and on Greek worship in general. In this same archaic stratum the trial-trench uncovered walls and roof-tiles, some of them painted, and the full excavation will possibly give the means of reconstructing in some measure the earliest temple on the site. Two archaic dedicatory inscriptions have been found, and it is probable that more remain. These results have been obtained from trial-trenches, which merely tap the archaic stratum, and there is no reason to suppose that the rest of the site will not prove equally rich. The stratum in question is partially covered by the foundations of a Roman arena, embedded in the masonry of which many archaistic inscriptions were found last year, and many others doubtless await discovery. This building has been partly cleared, and its peculiar form makes it a structure of great interest. It is a horseshoe-shaped arena which presumably enclosed the altar, at which the boys suffered, and it is built round the end of a temple, the foundation of which still remains.

A summary of these discoveries in *Ath. Mitt.* XXXI, l!)0(i, pp. 364—365, adds that fragments of Corinthian vases were found over a stratum belonging to the geometric period, as shown by the potsherds and bronze *fibulae,* which in turn rested on undisturbed ground. Of Mycenaean remains there was no trace.

STJNITJM. — Colossal Statues. — *A th. Mitt.* XXXI, 1906, pp. 363-364, contains a short account of the discovery by Stais, near the steps of the temple of Poseidon at Sunium, of a colossal archaic " Apollo " statue and of the torso of a second. Not only the size (en. 3. 50 m.), but also the careful rendering of the muscles, and the fine treatment of the hair render these statues far superior to the others of this type. The bases of the colossi were also found. It seems that here also after the Persian invasion the damaged votive offerings were used for building up the new terrace. TEGEA. —Inscriptions. —In *'Etj.* 'A. 1906,.pp. 23-66 (pi.; 2 figs.), A. S. Arvaxitopoullos publishes a number of inscriptions from Tegea. The list includes epitaphs, ephebic lists, a fragment of a decree containing a list of *irpocTTaTai* and generals, herms dedicated to various divinities, including Zeus 2Top7nuos and 'Ayu(?os ©tds, and an altar of Helios and Asclepius. THEBES. — Mycenaean Remains. — At Thebes, near the present Agora, Keramopoulos has found a burned Mycenaean building with fragments of frescoes and abundance of pottery, which he identifies with the ' House of Cadmus" (Paus. IX, 12,3-4). Above the Mycenaean strata there was absolutely nothing found from Greek or Roman time. The site seems first to have been occupied — after the destruction by fire of the Mycenaean building—in Christian times. Keramopoulos thinks he has here the chambers of Harmonia and Semele, of which Pausanias saw the ruins. (From a letter of B. H. Hill.)

Figure 8. — Lkai FigurIne From Shrine Of Artemis Orthia. TRICHONIUM. — Contents of a Burial Mound. — G. Soteriades publishes in "Ei£. 'Apx-1906, pp. 67-88 (pi.; 23 figs.), articles found by him in a great burial mound in the cemetery of the ancient Trichonium in Aetolia during 1903. The mound was made of earth and stones to cover a tomb formed of stone slabs, which was built over the ruins of an earlier tomb. In the later, undisturbed tomb, which dates from the first years of the second century B.C., were found an Aetolian silver didrachma of Demetrius II of Macedonia or Antiochus the Great of Syria, a crown of gold oak leaves, almost a score of small silver vessels, a bronze lamp-stand, and a seal ring with an intaglio representing Thalia with thyrsus and comic mask. In the earth of the mound and apparently from the earlier tomb were found a strip of silver, perhaps from a dagger-sheath, with an interesting relief representing a combat of horsemen against hoplites between a *tropaion* and a Nike, a pair of bronze spurs, two knitting needles of bronze, and two small silver reliefs representing Nike.

ITALY ARCHAEOLOGICAL DISCOVERIES IN 1905. —The principal discoveries in Italy, reported in the official publications during 1905, are summarized by G. Korte in *Arch. Anz.* 1906, pp. 102-109. Almost all have been noticed already in the Journal. Attention is called to the fact that the discovery in the foundations of the Campanile at Venice of an inscription of the time of Augustus bearing names known to belong to Este, shows whence were brought the stones for this building. BOLOGNA. — Excavations in the Necropolis. — The French School at Rome has been the first of the foreign schools to profit by the new Italian law permitting excavations. In *C. R. Acad. Insc.* 1906, pp. 315-325 (plan), A. Grenier reports on his first campaign at Bologna. He gives first a brief statement of the results of earlier excavations and of the importance of Bologna in the Etruscan question. His investigations were directed to finding (1) Villanova burials more archaic than those yet discovered, and (2) burials marking the transition from the Villanova period to the Etruscan. Neither object was attained. Between the Villanova necropolis outside Porta S. Isaia and the brook Ravone were found five skeletons, one surely Etruscan of about the middle of the fifth century, and four from the Villanova period, one hundred and fifty years earlier. Excavations near the Certosa led only to the discovery of Etruscan graves. The results confirm absolutely the conclusions of Brizio. The new excavations have shown the course of the ancient road along which the Etruscan graves are placed. It ran due west from the city gate. BOLSENA. — Recent Discoveries. — In *Not. Scac.* 1906, pp. 59-93 (32 figs.), E. Gabrici gives a report of recent discoveries near Bolsena. Excavation in the district of Barano in 1903 brought to light many chamber and trench tombs, containing fragments of vases, some crude, others with geometric decoration in white on a red ground. These are much earlier than the time to which the foundation of Bolsena has hitherto been assigned. In the district of Morone a tomb of two chambers was opened, containing vases of the seventh century B.C. At Pozzarello a rectangular area was found surrounded by an Etruscan wall. In this were many votive objects, including bronze figurines of the *Fortuna* type, coins, etc. The dates of the coins extend from the early part of the third century B.C. to the reign of Gordian IV. Near by are foundations, perhaps belonging to a temple of the Etruscan goddess, *Norlia.* On the road from Bolsena to Montefiascone were discovered the foundations of another temple. Remains of Roman houses were found in the district of Cividale and also in that of Mercatello. Excavation in the amphitheatre of Mercatello has brought to light the northwest entrance and also a subterranean passage. It is clear that there were two entrances at the extremities of the longer axis. From the wide passage extending around the building, inside the outer wall, stairways led to an upper passage; whether there was a third passage is doubtful; there certainly was not a fourth. Other discoveries of less importance have been made in the same locality. OSTIA. — Terra-cotta Stamps. — At Ostia about four hundred terracotta stamps have been found which represent theatrical and hunting scenes from the celebration of the public games. These were used to stamp the loaves of bread that were distributed to the people in connection with the public banquets provided during the games. *Mulsum* was also distributed with the loaves of bread, and many small measures, containing about threequarters of a litre, were found with the terra-cotta stamps. (S. B. P., *Nation,* July 26, 1006.) POMPEII. — Recent Excavations. — In *Not. Scav.* 1906, pp. 97-107 (7 figs.), A. Sogliaso gives the result of excavations at Pompeii, in 1902 at the Porta del Vesuvio, and in that year and the following years in the large theatre. The Porta del Vesuvio is approached by a broad passage with tufa walls, and a sidewalk on the. west side. Near the gate the passage is narrower, and there are blocks indicating the exact location of the gate; there are two altars here, of which the larger has painted decorations. Then the passage becomes wider again and has a sidewalk on both sides. At the end on either side are masses of masonry, which supported the vault covering the passage. That on the west is separated from the wall, indicating the existence of a narrow side-passage; that on the east is on the line of the wall.

Excavation outside the Theatre has shown that the east and west walls of the stage-building were once without openings and were decorated with five pilasters of tufa or limestone; later the three northern pilasters on each side were partly demolished. In the back wall there were originally five entrances. The level on the outside was then more than a metre below the present level. In the orchestra remains have been found of a circular basin, about 7 m. in diameter. Inside this was a smaller and later one, also circular. Further south in the orchestra are remains of small rectangular basins of various dates. The latest is a large rectangular basin, extending toward the north into the space occupied by the circular basins. These basins were covered by three successive pavements.

The Theatre. — The results of excavations conducted from 1902-190.") by W. Ddrpfeld and A. Man in the larger theatre at Pompeii are set forth at length by A. Mac in *Rom. Milt.* XXI, 1900, pp. 1-56 (pi.; 10 figs.). The history of the proscenium, stage, orchestra, and *cavea* is divided into six periods: (1) Of the first edifice *(ea.* 200 B.C.) we know only the *cavea,* which was smaller than the present *carea.* (2) In the second century B.C. the *cavea* was enlarged. (8) About 100 B.C. (or possibly 80) the present stagebuilding was erected in its earliest form. Its front had three doors on the level of the orchestra, and was enclosed by raking *parascenia;* behind was a hall with five doors; in the orchestra was a large round basin. (4) About SO B.c. (or possibly 40), the *parascenia* were removed, and a low stage introduced, with large side-entrances. The scene was a straight wall, with apparently five doors framed by columns. The floor of the hall behind the scene was raised, also the orchestra, so that the stage was about 0.70 m. above the latter; more basins were made in the orchestra. (5) About 1 B.C. came the alterations of the Holconii, including elaboration of the scene with ornate architecture in brick, and only three doors in the front. The floor of the hall was lowered somewhat. Marble replaced tufa in the seats of the *cavea.* tribunes were built over the *parmloi,* the orchestra was lowered to its original level, and a large basin constructed in the centre. (6) Later, but at an uucertain date, the basin was filled up. and the floor of the orchestra removed for a renewal which was never carried out. Mau concludes that in the early form of the theatre the actors stood on the level ground, but directly in front of the scene-wall, between the oblique side-walls, which can have had no other function than to frame in the scenes, with the least possible obstruction of vision.

ROME. — Changes at the American School. — Professor Richard Norton has resigned the Directorship of the American School of Classical Studies in Rome, and Professor Jesse Benedict Carter has been appointed in his place.

The Necropolis in the Forum. — In *Not. Scav.* 1906, pp. 5-46 (44 figs.), G. Boxi continues his detailed account of discoveries in the necropolis of the Roman Forum. At the time when the report was written, twenty-six tombs had l)een explored. These he divides into four groups: the first and second, — cremation and burial tombs respectively, — he calls *tombe preromulee;* the third, — burial tombs in trench form, like those of the second group. — he calls *lomhe romulee;* and the fourth, — two tombs of very young children, *suggrundaria,* — he calls *tombe post-romulee.* Five tombs of the first group are described in detail, the greater part of the report being devoted to the description of forty-six vases, including two hut-urns found in these tombs. The vases are all handmade and crude; they are generally without decoration. Many, however, are of graceful form, and some are decorated with projecting bosses or with simple incised geometric patterns. The only other objects found in these tombs were three bronze fibulae.

Ibid. pp. 46-54 (3 pis.; fig.), A. Mosso describes in detail the heads of four prehistoric skeletons found in the Roman Forum. One is that of the woman found near the *Equus Domitiam (A.J.A.* X, 1906, p. 35!i), the three others, those of a man and two children, were found near the temple of Antoninus and Faustina.

The *Tribunal Praetorium* in the Forum. — Part of an inscription, *Naevius L.f.* Hits, lias been found in the travertine pavement near the

Column of Phocas. This Naevius seems the same as the praetor whose name appears on the back of the relief of Mettius Curtius *C.l.L.* VI, 1408). The inscription of another praetor *C.l.L.* VI, 1278) was found on the steps of the column of Phocas in 1811. Hiilsen conjectures that these inscriptions were connected with the *tribunalpraelorium* which stood in front of the Basilica Julia. (T. Ashby, Jr., *Cl. R.* XX, 1906, pp. 378-379; S. B. P., *Nation,* July 26, 1906.)

The Column of Trajan. — In a notice of recent archaeological progress in Rome in the *Nation,* July 26, 1906, S. B. P(latner) reports the work of Commendatore Boni at the Column of Trajan. Investigation showed that a large excavation had been made under the pedestal of the column during the middle ages, and that a chamber in the pedestal itself had been filled up. This chamber has now been excavated. A small window opens into it on the southwest side, and along the northwest side something has been cut away which Boni thinks may have been a sarcophagus. Almost all the missing fragments of the great marble wreath that forms the base of the columns have been found, and are being replaced. A mould of this wreath is also to be made so that plaster casts may hereafter be procured. The architrave and the inscription are also to be restored. Under the concrete bed of the pavement of the Forum of Trajan has been found the pavement of a road belonging to the beginning of the first century A.d. It was flanked on both sides by buildings. It was evidently covered when the Forum of Trajan was built, and seems to disprove the removal of a ridge connecting the Quirinal and the Capitol to make room for the Forum. The work at the Column of Trajan is also discussed by T. Ashby, Jr., in *Cl. R.* XX, 1906, pp. 379-380.

A New Street. — Another name has been added to the list of Roman streets by the discovery of a marble altar dedicated to the Lares Augusti by the officials of the *Vicus Statae Matris,* on the Caelian. The inscription dates from 2 B.C., and gives the names of the consuls of that year, L. Caninius Gallus and C. Tufius Germinus, hitherto unknown in the *fasti.* This also indicates the date of the *lex Tufia Caninia,* relating to the manumission of slaves. (S. B. P., *Nation,* July 26, 1906.)

Minor Discoveries. — The following discoveries are reported from Rome: Near S. Croce in Gerusalemme, the pavement of an ancient street: near Porta Maggiore, marble architectural fragments; on the Via Labicana, about two kilometres from Porta Maggiore, an inscription relate ing to the Aqua Marcia, and the pavement of the ancient road which ran between the Aqua Marcia and the Aqua Claudia; on the Via Salaria, in the work on the new Corso di Porta Pinciana, various sepulchral inscriptions (G. Gatti, *Not. Scar.* 1905, pp. 405-408); near S. Croce in Gerusalemme a drum of a marble column, and fifteen terracotta amphorae; in the Via del Quirinale, near the building which was once the convent of S. Silvestro. drums of marble and granite columns; in the Via della Stamperia, the pavement of an ancient street; in the Via della Dogana Vecchia, late walls; in the Viale del Re, the pavement, of an ancient street, brick walls, and the floor of a room; in the Via Nomentana, between the Corso d' Italia and the Praetorian Camp, remains of two white marble pavements, one above the other, and below these a narrow passage lined with marble, slabs. Excavation in the Via di S. Sabina has brought to light a paved area on which rested the *carceres* of the Circus; also three rectangular bases, which probably held statues of horses. (G. Gatti and A. Valle, *ibid.* 1906, pp. 94-96.) In the Villa Colonna, on the Via del Quirinale, were found a wall of tufa and one of brick; in the Piazza dei Cinquecento, walls belonging to the large *piscina,* near the Baths of Diocletian; between the Vie del Tritone, dei Serviti, and dei Due Macelli, an ancient pavement running east and west, bordered by brick walls; also four white marble columns; in the Via Bocca della Verita, an ancient drain of tufa; on the Aventine, near S. Saba, ancient walls of brick and *npus reticulatum;* in the construction of the street leading from the Corso d' Italia to the new riding-school, several sepulchral inscriptions belonging to the late republican cemetery. (G. Gatti, *ibid.* 1906, pp. 119-122.) More inscriptions from the tombs on the Via Salaria are published by Hiilsen, *llrim. Mitt.* XXI, 1906, pp. 87-88.

SARDINIA. — A Prehistoric Settlement and Tombs. — At Ussana, on the hill called *Rruncu e sa Turre,* have been found several tombs of doubtful period; also, on the same hill, remains of a prehistoric settlement, including vase fragments and large blocks of stone, roughly cut. (A. TakAmki.li. *Not. Scar.* 1906', pp. 56-58.) SICILY. — Various Discoveries. — In *Not. Scav.* 1905, pp. 425-453 (16 figs.), F. Oitsi continues his account of recent explorations and discoveries in southeastern Sicily. Tombs of the Sicel, Christian, and Byzantine periods have been found in many places. At Pachino a marble portrait head of the fifth or fourth century B.C. was found; at Camarina a marble relief of a head, of the fifth century; at Buccheri a collection of coins, of Corinth, Thasos, and Macedonian kings; at Mineo, another collection, of Sicel and Greek coins. At Caltagirone were found evidences of a small Greek colony, established in the seventh or sixth century. At Maniace are remains of a small bathing establishment, with mosaic floors. At Mt. Bubonia are remains of a Sicel town, including a large rectangular structure and smaller houses; in the necropolis here were found native vases of the third and fourth Sicel periods, and Greek vases of the sixth and fifth centuries; also ornaments of bronze and silver. At S. Cataldo has been found a large sarcophagus with painted decorations, unlike anything hitherto found in Sicily or Greece. SICILY. — GIRGENTI." — A Greek House. — In *J.H.S.* XXVI, 1906, pp. 207-212 (plan), R. P. Jones and E. A. Gardner publish notes on a recently excavated house near Girgenti. It was originally a pre-Roman construction, but a bath and the smoothing over of fluted columns are Roman. The only capital found has the outlines of the best period of Doric. A peculiar feature is a square recess opening from the peristyle and containing a hearth. As there are two courts, this house corresponds better than any Greek house yet known with the type described by Vitruvius, which had one part for private life and another for entertainment. The excavation is not so complete as to make all points of the plan quite clear. TORRE NUOVA.— Sarcophagi. — In *Not. Scav.* 1905, pp. 408-121 (7 figs.), G. E. Rizzo gives a somewhat detailed description of the sarcophagi found in 1903 at Torre Nuova on the Via I.abicana *(A.J.A.* X, 1906, p. 3.-4). They date from the second century or the first part of the third. The most important lias sculpture on all sides, that of the principal side showing a style intentionally different from that of the three others. The principal side represents an initiation into the Eleusinian mysteries in a form much more complete than other representations of the same thing. It shows the initiation and purification of Heracles by Euinolpus, with sacrifice and libation to the three Eleusinian divinities, Demeter, Core, and Iacchus, in the presence of Dionysus and Hecate. The three other sides have scenes of mourning. A second sarcophagus is decorated with a relief illustrating the myth of Endymion and Selene. It is an ordinary subject, without noteworthy features. The cover of this sarcophagus, which, however, did not originally belong to it, is decorated with several small reliefs, chiefly of Bacchic subjects. A third sarcophagus has a representation of the myth of Dionysus and Ariadne; the most noteworthy feature is the figure of a female centaur with her small child. A fragment of a fourth sarcophagus shows the marriage of Aeneas and Lavinia; the scene includes a figure of Mars, on whose shield are the Lupercal, the *ficits RuminaHs,* and the wolf with Romulus and Remus. The cover of a missing sarcophagus is in the form of the upper part of a couch on which rests a youth with a small dog at his feet: the face is evidently a portrait and veryriifelike. VARIOUS DISCOVERIES. — Three Roman tombs have been found at Castenaso. In one was a white glass bottle, perfectly preserved, decorated with a complicated system of incised circles. (A. Negrioli, *Not. Scav.* 1906, pp. 113-116; fig.) At G-erace. in the neighborhood of ancient Locri, has been found a terra-cotta base with a relief representing a lion in the act of killing a deer. The style is that of the sixth century B.C. *(Ibid.* 1906, p. 55; fig.) At Lucca, in the demolition of the abandoned chapel of SS. Ippolito and Graziano, Roman substructures of tufa have been found, probably belonging to a small public building or temple. (L. Permier, *ibid.* 1906, pp. 117-119; 2 figs.) SPAIN AND PORTUGAL ARCHAEOLOGICAL DISCOVERIES IN 1905. — Many ship anchors of lead, found by sponge divers near Cape Palos. doubtless mark an important commercial port. They are of various weights and sizes, and have inscriptions in Greek or Latin characters, among these being a dedication to Zeus Casius which is reminiscent of the temples of that god in Corfu and on the borders of Egypt. A large marble statue of Apollo, of Augustan period and much mutilated, was also found in the sea, not far from Cadiz. The most interesting recent find, made by a peasant at Javea. in the northern part of the province of Alicante, on the eastern coast, is a gold diadem, gold chains with pendants, and other ornaments of gold and silver, found buried in an earthen pot. The workmanship, which is very fine, resembles that of similar ornaments found in Etruria and southern Russia, and appears to be genuine Greek, while the articles are like those worn by the Lady of Elche and the statues of Cerro de los Santos. Another accidental find is the Mithraenm at Merido, with inscriptions and statues, among the latter being the Mithraic Kronos, an erect nude figure with human head and surrounded by the coils of a snake. An altar commemorating the birth of Mithras has an inscription of 155 A.d. , giving the name of the founder of the shrine and his title of *Pater.* Two gentlemen of Seville, named Viera, have excavated a second underground megalithic structure in Andalusia, near the famous Cueva da Menga. It has a long corridor leading to a square chamber which is roofed by a single slab. A third dromos tomb, la Cueva de Romeral, has a circular chamber with dome-shaped roof, and is built of small stones. The native Iberian pottery with geometric curvilinear designs and of very ancient origin continues to be_ found in burial grounds, and some specimens are of great size and beauty. This style had a later development, influenced from the Orient, through floral and animal subjects to the human figure, and it continued in use down to Roman times. A rough heavy pottery of black clay is also found in Andalusia. Near Segobriga, in the province of Cuenca, is a grotto that was once inhabited, but no wall pictures have as yet been found. Remains in this region are chiefly Roman, but beneath the Roman are in many places older Iberian settlements. This is so at Numantia, where native pottery and sculpture comparable with that of southern and eastern Spain has been found. A cemetery at San Anton contains every sort of burial, partial and complete cremation, inhumation in terra-cotta jars, in slab graves, in trenches, under tumuli and cromlechs. At La Punta de Guixola are graves dug in the rock in regular rows and shaped like huge jars. They contain several tiers of ash-urns accompanied by vases of offerings. (P. Paris, *Arch. Anz.* 1906, pp. 168-181.) AUUSTREL.— Roman Regulations for a Mine. — In *C. R. Acad. Insc.* 1906, pp. 328-331, R. Cagnat publishes a provisional translation of the Latin text, recently found on a bronze tablet in the copper mine at Aljustrel in Portugal. It is of great length and contains detailed regulations for the development of the mine, the provisions under which contracts could be let for working the silver and copper veins, and the punishments for theft, for interfering with the supports or galleries, and for working outside of the allotted claims. ALMEDINILLA. — Excavations and Researches. — In *R. Arch.* VIII, 1906, pp. 49-92 (22 figs.), P. Paris and A. Engel describe excavations and researches at Almedinilla, in the province of Cordova, where excavations were carried on as early as 1866. The objects discovered in the excavations carried on by the present writers are, like those discovered previously, chiefly native pottery, with linear decoration, and bronze weapons. The date of some of these, at least in the necropolis of Cerro de la Cruz, is determined by the presence of a fragment of a red-figured Greek vase of the fourth century B.C. Still earlier primitive pottery was found at the hill of los Castillejos. The Roman village occupied only the site called Bergara. The two cemeteries, Cerro de la Cruz and Collados, are pre-Roman. SANTANDER. — Decorated Caves. — The Abbe Breuil has studied, in the province of Santander, six caves which are decorated with carvings or paintings of the same character as those found in other prehistoric caverns. Noteworthy in a cave at Hornos de la Peiia is an anthropoid figure with a tail, perhaps representing an ape. (C. R. Acad. In8c. 1906, pp. 480-481.) FRANCE ARCHAEOLOGICAL DISCOVERIES IN 1905. — No recent finds in Franee have been of great importance. Traces of the Ibero-Mycenaean pottery, already known in Narbonne, have been found also near Marseilles. A bronze vase filled with Roman coins of the middle of the third century A.d. was found near Jublains in northwestern France. On the neck of the vase, in sunken relief touched up with silver, are hunting scenes from the arena, including, besides a lion and a bear fight, some hares and a curious creature which may perhaps be the *arcoleo* mentioned by Capitolinus. Serious study of the Tropaeum of Augustus, set up in 7-6 B.c. among the Maritime Alps, which was blown up by one of the marshals of Louis XIV, has resulted in the finding of numerous fragments of sculpture, and there is a prospect of more complete recovery. (E. Miciion, *Arch. Anz.* 1906, pp. 181-181.) AGEN. — A *Mensa Ponderaria.*— In *B. Soc. Ant. Fr.* 1906, pp. 162166 (fig.). P. Lauzun describes an unpublished *mensaponderaria,* discovered about thirty years ago at Ageu. It contains ten cavities, some round and others rectangular, but the system of measures to which it belongs remains to be determined. With the possible exception of a stone from Maule, it is the only example of a *mensa ponderaria* found in Fiance. ALESIA. — The New Excavations.—In *C. R. Acad.*

Inst: 1906, pp. 251-252, A. Heron De Villefosse reports the discovery of the ancient theatre at Alesia, and the partial excavation of the substructures of the facade and hemicycle. The excavation of the centre is delayed by the state of the crops. *Ibid.* pp. 264-265, is a letter of Seymour De Ricci reporting the discovery of a well in a Roman house, which has yielded a number of well-preserved objects in iron, bronze, lead, leather, and wood. Among the latter is a Pan's pipe with eight tubes, hollowed in a block of wood. The only sculpture is a limestone group, representing two doves on either side of a mutilated human head. Possibly it may be connected with a Celtic god, *Moritasgits,* mentioned in a Latin inscription found in 1652 in the same field as the well. *Ibid.* pp. 389-393, is a further report by Commandant Esperandieu. It is chiefly concerned with the discovery, near the theatre, of the foundations of a large square structure, about 40-50 m. on a side, formed by two parallel walls, and with three apses, one on each of three sides. It is perhaps the *forum,* though its form seems peculiar. It is evident that the public buildings of Alesia were destroyed by fire not very long after its conquest, perhaps at the time of the revolt of Vindex. Noticeable is the large number of buildings erected by the Romans. It is clear that Alesia must have been not only an important mercantile community, but also a Gallic religious centre. *Ibid.* pp. 401-405 (4 figs.), the same writer reports the excavation of a temple between the theatre and the forum. Here have been found many fragments of a Celtic inscription in Greek characters, reliefs representing the Capitoline Triad, and a Dioscure, a torso of an Amazon, and of a seated Jupiter, as well as other fragments. Another trench yielded a small bronze representing a dead Gaul. *Ibid.* pp. 481-483 (fig.), more discoveries are reported. Among the sculptures are the torso of a Gallic warrior, with curious weapons and costume, and a singular relief of a horseman, whose saddle resembles that used by the Arabs. The excavations have shown that at Alesia the

Gallic huts were made of clay placed on a wicker frame, and then baked by fire on both sides, giving apparently a very durable structure. BATZ. —A Prehistoric Cemetery. — In *Le Muse'e,* III, 1906, pp. 424427 (2 figs.), G. Toudouze tells of the discovery of a prehistoric cemetery on the island of Hatz (Brittany) by G. Delasalle. Incineration seems to have been practised, and the ashes placed on a bed of sand accompanied by rude pottery. Large blocks of granite, arranged like small dolmens, surrounded the ashes. The graves surround a dolmen, at present surmounted by a crucifix. Excavations are to be continued during the present year.
"CAUCOURT. — A Bronze Vase. — In *B. Soc. Ant. Fr.* 1906, pp. 142144 (fig.). A. De Loisne publishes a small Gallo-Roman bronze vase found at Caucourt (Pas-de-Calais). He interprets it as representing a crouching shepherd with the *mulctra* between his knees. *Ibid.* pp. 308-309, J. Dkchelette argues that it is rather a young slave crouched on a doorstep with his lantern between his knees. See *R. Arch.* XL, 1902, pp. 392-397; *A.J.A.* VI, 1902, p. 480.
LA TERNE. — Gallo-Roman Statuettes. — In *R. £t. Anc.* VIII, 1906, pp. 2.13-259 (2 figs.), G. Chauvet describes two stone statuettes, found a number of years ago at La Terne (Charente) and recently secured for his collection. One seems to represent a seated Apollo, the other is a fully draped seated figure (probably female), whose left hand holds a large purse from which coins fall into her lap and are drawn to one side by the right hand. The type does not occur elsewhere, but has analogies with a seated god on an altar from Rheims. It is evidently a goddess who distributes wealth, but her identity is not established. As traces of polychromy on Gallo-Roman monuments are rare, it is noteworthy that the figure shows remains of brownish red color. LAVOYS-AUTRECOURT. — Coins in Graves. — In a cemetery at Lavoys-Autre'court (Meuse) a series of graves was excavated, none of which was earlier than the fourth century, in seventeen of which were found small bronzes, the earliest

of Gallienus, the latest of Constantius. A careful investigation of the position of each coin with reference to the skeleton showed that the coin in a number of instances had been placed at burial in one of the hands, but never in a single instance in the mouth. (Dr. Meunier, *B. Num.* XIII, 1906, pp. 73-77.) LISIEUX.— A Roman Balance.—In *B. Soc. Ant. Fr.* 1906, pp. 260261, F. De Mely describes a Roman balance found at Lisieux in 1S66. The weight is a bronze head with two faces representing a bearded old man. A curious analogy is found in a small glass vial in the shape of a double-faced head of the same size as the weight, and also found at Lisieux in 1866. LYON. — Medallions on Pottery. — In the part of the city called Trion wcrc found, twenty years ago, a series of pottery medallions bearing reliefs. They are now in the museum at Lyon, and have been published by Allmer and Dissard. Other specimens from the same locality which are now in the Musee Gnimet at Paris are published by A. Heron De VilleFosse in *R. £p.* No. 118 (1905-06), pp. 170-172. Two whole medallions and five fragments are described. One fragment represents part of a cock-fight, and shows a Syrian juggler in a crouching position with a knot of hair at the back of his shaven head, and an uncertain object in his right hand. Another fragment perhaps represents a sacrifice. MARTIGUES. — Three Inscriptions. —In *C. R. Acad. Insc.* 1906, pp. 358-363, Abbe A. D'agnel publishes three inscriptions from Martigues (Bouches-du-Rhone). The first is a dedication to Tiberius by *Sextus Aelianus Pisinus;* the second is sepulchral, but contains anew Celtic name, *Vebruius;* the third is a rock-cut inscription containing two names in Greek characters, probably later than the second century A.d. MONT CILDA (VELLICA).— Sepulchral Stelae. —In *R. £t. Anc.* VIII, 1906, p. 261 (pi.), C. J(ullian) publishes a note on some curious stelae from Mont Cilda, the ancient Vellica, in the extreme south of the country of the Cantabri. The decoration seems to resemble that on some of the Celtic monuments of Ireland. NIAUX. — Palaeolithic Drawings.

—In *C. R. Acad. Insc.* 1906, pp. 533-536, E. Cartailhac reports the discovery at Niaux in the Pyrenees of another cavern with paintings of the palaeolithic period. They are in a large chamber about 800 m. from the entrance, and are even found in crannies, where the artist must have lain on his back to work. Bisons predominate, but there are also horses, wild goats, and deer. The drawing is very good. In the galleries are a number of signs similar to those found at Marsoulas. Of special interest is the appearance on seven bisons of arrows conspicuously drawn. This seems to confirm the theory that these drawings are connected with primitive magic rites, designed to secure game. PARIS. — Discoveries at the Marche' aux Fleurs. — In *C. R.Acad. Iusc.* 1906, pp. 252-256, A. Heron Dk Villefosse reports interesting remains of Roman Paris discovered between the Hotel Dieu and the Tribunal du Commerce. Two walls have been found almost parallel to the Seine, and 6.50 m. apart, built of large blocks of stone laid without cement. Many architectural fragments, decorative sculptures, and inscribed funeral monuments have been recovered. Three inscriptions are published, all epitaphs. Among the sculptures the most important is the upper part of a pilaster with apparently remains of a procession on two faces. The other sculptures are from tombs, and belong to the class of professional reliefs. *Ibid.* p. 259, the same writer reports further discoveries, including a fine piece of decorative sculpture, and two more professional reliefs, and *ibid.* pp. 261-263, publishes the epitaph of *A urelius A Ibanus exarchus.* This is the tenth occurrence of this title, which seems to have been borne by the commander of a *numerus* or an *ala.* The walls found seem to belong to a Roman building inside the fortification, which apparently ran nearer the Seine. These discoveries are also very briefly noticed by C. Sellier in *B. Soc. Ant. Fr.* 1906. p. 267. The epitaphs are discussed with others in *R. £p.* 1905-06, pp. 162-168.
A Roman Vase. —In *B. Soc. Ant. Fr.* 1906, pp. 233-236 (2 figs.), A. Heron Dk Villefosse describes a vase found in

1904 in the Rue Gay-Lussac, Paris. It is covered with a red glaze, has three deep depressions on the sides and back, and in front a medallion decorated with reliefs representing offensive and defensive weapons.

Acquisitions of the Louvre. — Fragments of sarcophagi of the Asia Minor type, recently acquired by the Louvre, are briefly described by E. Michon in *B. Soc. Ant. Fr.* 1906, pp. 225-226.

The Department of Greek and Roman Antiquities received during 1905, by gift or purchase, the following objects, not including potter)-. *Marble.* Head of a woman with mural crown and elaborate headdress, from near Smyrna; upper part of funeral stele with siren, from Piraeus; inscribed grave lecythus from Athens with relief of a fainting woman supported upon a couch; relief of a funeral banquet from Rhodes, with inscription ONASANAPOY YAAAPIMEQS KAI TAS TYNAIKOS TTOTTOY5 KABAAISSA5; Greek inscription in honor of the emperor Gallienus, from Der'at; also *stoichedon* Greek inscription from Erythrae on a rectangular plate of gray stone containing a decree relating to the keepers of the marshes. *Bronze.* Small and rude seated figure from Olympia, with seal in curvilinear design cut on the bottom of the base; standing figure of Zeus, of fine archaic style, from Andritzena; two large fibulae from Sparta, the plates engraved with chariot fighters, heraldic horses, birds, fish, swastika; lamp ornament imitating in late Roman style the figure of a boy taking a thorn from his foot, from Calymnus; key with bust of a woman below the ring of the handle, from Cyzicus; statuette of partly nude woman, once gilded, from Smyrna; lower part of statue of Adonis, from Sidon, of which the other half was acquired in 1900; askos with richly ornamented handles, from near Beyrout; small dolphin and gold ring in the form of a coiled snake found in a tomb near Cnidus. *Terra-cotla.* Disk with figure of the saint Chnouti in relief, inscribed 0 ATIOC CIN801 ////, from Egypt. *(Arch. Anz.* 1906, pp. 241-244.) POMMIERS. — The Site of Noviodunum. — In *M. Soc. Ant. Fr.* LXV, 1904-05, pp.

45-90 (25 figs.), O. Vauville describes the results of excavations in the vicinity of Pommiers (Aisne). On a hill were found the remains of a strongly fortified Gallic *oppidum,* and to the north traces of a large Roman camp. It is claimed that here is the site of Noviodunum, the town of the Suessiones besieged by Caesar (cf. *B.G.* II, 12). A list is given of the Gallic (1945) and Roman (25) coins found here since 1860 by the author. In *B. Soc. Ant. Fr.* 1906, pp. 251-253 (4 figs.), the same writer describes four intaglios from the same place. The style and a Gallic inscription suggest that the Gauls may have been skilful in engraving gems as well as bronze.

PTJY-DE-DOME. — Recent Excavations. — In *R. £t. Anc.* VIII, 1906, pp. 341-342, H. Audollknt describes briefly the results of recent excavations at Puy-de-Dome. The foundations of a small temple have been laid bare, and near by has been found an interesting bronze statuette of Mercury. A trench near the Observatory has yielded a large mass of pottery of many varieties, as well as many coins, chiefly of the third and fourth centuries. C. J(ullian) notes that recent discoveries afford strong confirmation of Hettner's theory, that the square temple was a characteristic form of Gallic religious architecture.

The bronze Mercury is further discussed and illustrated by A. Audollent in *C. R. Acad. Insc.* 1906, pp. 393-399 (fig.). It is larger (18 cm. high) and of more careful workmanship than most statues of this god found in Gaul. The left hand held a purse, the right the caduceus. On the head were wings. It does not correspond exactly to any known type, but is certainly a Greco-Roman work of about the beginning of the second century A.d. It throws no light on the Gallic god here worshipped, who is called in an inscription *Mercurius Dumias.* RHEIMS.—A Relief represeutiug Attis. and a Sarcophagus. — In *B. Soc. Ant. Fr.* 1906, pp. 1287-289 (fig.), L. Demaison publishes a representation of Attis on a sepulchral monument now in the Musee Lapidaire at Rheims. The figure is almost life size and well preserved, but of very rude execution. Attis is a common figure elsewhere on sepulchral monuments, but this seems to be the only example of an Oriental cult found in the neighborhood of Rheims. *Ibid.* pp. 206-208, Demaison reports the discovery of a large sarcophagus. On the edge of one of the long sides are the letters A D, and on one of the short sides D A. Possibly these are stonecutters' marks. Similar signs on other sarcophagi are mentioned. It is also noted that the inscription *C.I.L.* XIII, 3309, should be omitted, as it appears correctly *ibid.* 10020, 1.

SAINTES. — Gallo-Roman Monuments. — Three monuments found near Saintes are described by C. Dauuibeaud in *It. £t. Anc.* VIII, 1906, pp. 260-261 (2 pis.). One is a cubical altar, having on each face a niche in which is a divinity, Mars, Minerva, Mercury, and Hercules. There is no inscription. This altar is now in private ownership at La Rochelle. The other two, both in the museum of Saintes, are a bronze statuette of Mercury, of unusual grace, and a small bronze head of good workmanship. It is hollow and was used as a box. SAINT-GENES-DE-LOMBAUD. — An Altar. — An ancient altar with branches carved in relief on one side now serves as a holy water basin in the parish church of Saint-Genes-de-Lombaud, near Bordeaux. The relief probably represents a sacred tree, perhaps the laurel. (A. Brutails, if. *E't. Anc.* VIII, 1906, pp. 261-262; fig.) TOURS.—Greek Sculpture. — In *R. Arch.* VIII, 1906, p. 322, S. R(einach) mentions a fragment (right leg, tree trunk, and boar's head) of a statue of Meleager, from Lesbos, and a bust of Demosthenes, with restorations, in the museum at Tours. VAROIS. —A Bronze Vase and Coins. —In *B. Soc. Ant. Fr.* 1906, pp. 229-230, Pallu Tr Lessert describes briefly a bronze oenochoe recently found at Varois (Cote-d'Or). The neck terminates in a human foot. In and about the vase were found 1034 coins, which are the subject of a note by A. Blanciiet *(Ibid.* pp. 214-246). They are *denarii* and *antoniniani,* from the time of Vitellius and Titus to that of Valerian and Gallienus. It is probable that the vase was hidden about 259 A.d. The importance of such hoards for determining the chronology of works of art is emphasized, and a partial list of similar discoveries is given. VARIOUS DISCOVERIES AND INSCRIPTIONS. — In *B. Soc. Ant. Fr.* 1906, pp. 200-203, A. Heron De Villefosse publishes a potter's stamp from Ambleny (Vie-sur-Aisne). and some notes and corrections to the stamps from Roman amphoras published in *C.I.L.* XIII, 10002. — *Ibid.* pp. 198-199, E. Esperandieu publishes, with brief comment, a Latin funerary inscription found in 1904 near Beziers. It contains two peculiarities: *Felix* as the surname of a female slave, and the designation of a *patronus* by his cognomen, *Dapsilis,* instead of the usual praenomen. — *Ibid.* pp. 311-312, A. Heron Dk Villefosse reports the discovery at Liglet (Vienne) of a well containing small objects in iron, bone, and terra-cotta, as well as many fragments of vases, one of which has the inscription SI IDIA probably for *Sidia(mis).* — In the collection Dassy at Meaux are two bronze statuettes representing Minerva and Dispater, which were probably found in the neighborhood.' (G. Gassies, *R. £t. Anc.* VIII, 1906, pp. 338-340; 2 tigs.) In *B. Soc. Ant. Fr.* 190(i, p. 233, A. Heron Dk Villefosse describes briefly two *ttyli* from Sacquenay (Cdte-d'Or). One is plain, the other bears engraved characters of uncertain meaning. It is possible that the latter is the beam of a balance, and that the marks have reference to weights. In the church at Salmaise (Cdte-d'Or) as a support for an altar is a large block containing a dedication to the *den Sequana.* The letters indicate the first century A.d. as the date. It seems probable that it has been brought from the Roman temple at the source of the Seine, some distance to the north. (A. Heron De Villefosse, *B. Soc. Ant. Fr.* 1906, pp. 309-311.) *Ibid.* p. 311, A. Heron De Villefosse reports the discovery at Vaison (Vancluse) of a Roman mosaic. The pattern is formed of a series of squares each of which contains the figure of an animal or bird. In the department of Vaucluse three altars have been found. One is dedicated to the *Matres,* but is otherwise very uncertain; another to Mercury; and the third to *Vasio,* perhaps the goddess of Vaison. (if. *£p.* 1905-06, pp. 161-162.) AUSTRIA-HUNGARY ARCHAEOLOGICAL DISCOVERIES IN 1905. — In Austria, the Limeskomission, working at Enns, has discovered the legionary camp of Lauriacum. and 5 km. eastward, the walls of a Roman fort. At Carnuntum, the *retentura* of the camp and a large building in the adjoining part of the civil settlement, also dwelling houses on the roads from Carnuntum to Scarabautia and Vindobona, have been found. A group of buildings in Pettau has yielded small articles, fragments of sculpture, reliefs, a bronze statue, and well-preserved wall paintings. At Virunum were found a Roman street, the foundations of a steam bath, and the usual small objects and fragments. A silver coin of the Celtic king Gesatorix, son of Eeritusirus, who may be Strabo's Kpiraoipos, defeated by the Dacian Burebista in 60 B.C., is of historical interest. Further excavations on the island of Brione Grande off Pola'and on the opposite coast show both shores to'have been thickly inhabited in Roman times. A wine-pressing establishment built on terraces resembles views seen in Pompeian wall-paintings. In Hungary, the finding of Roman remains at Temesvar has proved this to be, like other important towns in Hungary, on the site of a Roman settlement. The finds, both in Dacian and in Pannonian Hungary, are almost exclusively Roman, and include inscriptions, reliefs, coins, ornaments in gold and silver, graves, and the foundations of buildings, walls and streets. At Apulum (Dacia), silver coins have been found from Septimius Severus to Aurelian, 193-275 A.d.; at CsaJiberdny (Pannonia), they extend from Constantine to Valens. At Fenk, the shore is a mine of Roman coins. At Apulum, traces of the Roman water conduit which served as model for one built in the seventeenth century have been found. Two altars of Epona come from the same site, and altars of Silvanus from Csakbere'ny and Buda5rs (Pannonia). At Dunapentele are reliefs of Orpheus and Eurydice, Bacchus and the panther, and other subjects. (*Arch. Am.* 1906, pp. 188-192.) ANTHROPOLOGICAL DISCOVERIES IN 1905. —In *Mitt. A nth. Ges.* XXXVI, 1906, pp. 109-122, (4 figs.), is a report of discoveries in the Austrian Empire during 1905. For the most part these record the finding of neolithic and bronze age burial places or small settlements, and their interest is rather anthropological than archaeological. A detailed report is given of the contents of a grave, apparently of the Hallstatt period, at Jetzelsdorf, where the body, with the knees drawn up. lay on a mass of potsherds which belonged to nineteen different vessels. Apparently they had been broken before the interment, as pieces of the same pot were widely scattered. Of the discoveries elsewhere the reports are generally very brief.

GREAT BRITAIN ACQUISITIONS OF THE BRITISH MUSEUM IN 1905.—
Egyptian. — Among the important objects are a bronze figure of Harpocrates with parts inlaid in gold, silver, and enamel, dedicated to the wife of Amasis II, about 600 B.C., and part of the wall of the funeral chapel of the largest of the pyramids on the island of Meroe in the Soudan, which was built for one of the queens of Meroe called Candace, in the first or second century A.d. This has elaborate reliefs of funeral processions, sacrifices, etc., with the figures of the queen and her consort, but the cartouches for the names are left vacant. There are also collections of objects from the peninsula of Sinai, from Middle-Empire graves at Beni Hasan, from Deir el-Bahari, including a colossal Osiris statue and reliefs of Pharaohs of the eighteenth dynasty, and a cow's head from a statue of Hathor; also a bronze door plate from a temple at Thebes, with the name of Amenhetep III, co. 1450 B.C. Assyrian. Over six hundred tablets and fragments of tablets, chiefly from the first Babylonian dynasty, 2400 B.C. Greek and Roman. *Gold.* A bandeau with incrustation of granulated work; a necklace of beads with lunar pendant; a diadem with patterns in relief, victories, composite figures, and an Ionic column; a ring with an engraved design of a woman and a dolphin, like a type on coins of Histiaea; tiny stamped ornaments pierced for sewing; ear-rings from a tomb near Damascus. *Silcer.* A bangle of six coils, inscribed KAHTIOSt from Acarnania. *Bronze.* An archaic crouclmig Silenus; a dancing Silenus of the fifth century; Harpocrates with finger on lips and an asp coiled on his arm, Ptolemaic; a statuette of a fisherman with his basket, seated on a rock; an archaic "Apollo," of minute size and careful workmanship, from Arcadia; a clumsy figure of an armed warrior, early native art of Sardinia; a fully draped Gaulish Jupiter, Gallo-Romau art; a pair of hands joined by hinges and with sockets for handles; a bucket inscribed in Etruscan, *Suthina;* an Athenian jury ticket, inscribed E itIAOXAPHS AXAPNEYS. *Engraced Gems.* Four hematite. gems of the Mycenaean epoch, from a tomb near Mycenae; nine gems with intaglio designs, and one with a lion in relief. *Marble.* The head of a youth from an anthropoid sarcophagus, from Alexandria; the head of a youth in high relief, from a sepulchral monument, Attic, fourth century; a fragment of a stele with a unique scheme of decoration, three vases supported on an acanthus ornament and lion-gryphons, fourth century; a relief of an armed warrior leaning on his spear around which a snake is coiled, second century B.C., from Rhodes; a series of small figures of cats and a limestone base, inscribed TAAATEI A: 9EYA0T0Y BOYBASTI, said to be from Bubastis in Egypt, first and second centuries B.C. *Terracotta.* Three statuettes, a head of a goddess, and an inscribed whorl. *Pottery.* Three white lecythi with funeral subjects, and fragments of two others; a Boeotian plate with a border in pink, white, and black, and the representation of a woman holding yellow wreaths; a vase in the form of a lobster's claw, with a fox devouring a cock, and a dog running; a Greco-Phoenician bowl and covered jar from Cyprus, painted with girls holding flowers, sphinxes, rosettes, and flowers in red and black; a large wine jug with geometric and figure designs arranged in friezes, ProtoAttic ware of seventh century, from Athens; a black-figured

lecythus with pyxis-shaped body; a red-figured lecythus with Demeter before the car of Triptolemus, and the inscription *Aiotlfjuk* Koaos, a new KaAos-name, the missing fragment of a cup from Naucratis already in the museum. *Ivory.* Two plaques with designs in low relief, a lion devouring an ibex, and a reclining Silenus, rare examples of the Ionic art of the fifth century. The museum has also received by gift, archaic terra-cotta statuettes from Cyprus; objects found with papyri of the first to fifth centuries at Oxyrhynchus; a gold ring with a design in relief representing the temple of Aphrodite at Paphos; a steatite gem engraved with a wounded gazelle, from Cnossus, Crete. British and Mediaeval. Palaeolithic implements of porphyry and flint found in Herts and Kent; a large flint pounder, part of a flint knife, a vase with a band of bosses, perhaps neolithic, and a bronze spearhead, dredged from the Thames; an iron spearhead from River Lea; flint arrowheads and late Celtic bronze objects given by E. R. Yorks; bronze halbert blades from Denbigh and Cumberland; a late Celtic bronze bowl and an early British bronze embossed mount, found in London; late Celtic cinerary urns, one with a pedestal, from Rochester, Kent; a series of objects from the marsh village of Glastonbury; an iron sword of the La Tene type, from Essex; a late bronze-age knife from Denmark; a series of flint implements from Belgium, illustrating the change from eolithic to palaeolithic; a similar series from Thebes in Egypt; hammer-stones from Cnossus; flint flakes from central India; flint and other implements from mine heaps and ash heaps in the peninsula of Sinai; bronze brooches from Lincoln, an enamelled bronze brooch from Warwick, a bronze spoon handle from Suffolk, and an urn of gray ware, all belonging to the Romano-British period. *(Arch. Anz.* 1906, pp. 244-253.) ACQUISITIONS OF THE ASHMOLEAN MUSEUM IN 1905. — Many of the additions to the Museum at Oxford are for the very important Cretan collection, and come as gifts from the excavators or the Cretan government. From Cnossus are parts of frescoes showing fine decorative designs, and the figure of a female toreador, the earliest examples of the art of painting on European soil, and belonging to the late palace period, about 1500 B.C. The pottery includes beautiful naturalistic designs of plants and animals; egg-shell ware imitated from metallic vases, Middle Minoan, about 2500 B. C.; vases copied from various kinds of stone, including liparite from the Aeolian Islands; and a large jar, 4 ft. 7 in. high, decorated with raised medallions painted white on a purple ground. A part of a vase of black steatite with reliefs once covered with gold leaf, shows the origin of such work as the Vaphio cups. Two painted clay sarcophagi, one with floral ornament, the other with a hunting scene in which the Cretan wild goat is shown, are of the late palace period. Bronze votive offerings from the Dictaean cave are in the form of animals, double axes, and human figures, including one female figure which perhaps represents the mother of Zeus. From Zakro, eastern Crete, comes painted pottery showing a mixture of the Middle Minoan light-on-dark decoration with the brown-on-buff late Minoan or Mycenaean style. There are also two clay lamps of the primitive epoch, and seal impressions with winged monsters in a transitional style. For the Egyptian section there are various objects from the peninsula of Sinai, a Hathor-head capital from the temple of the goddess; a stele which gives the only known instance of the name of the god of the Ilyksos, Sutekh; fragments of glazed ware showing Rameses III in his harem, and a griffin hunting oxen and gazelles, in which the spirited drawing of the animals suggests possible Minoan influence; fragments of glazed votive offerings with cartouches of kings of the eighteenth and nineteenth dynasties; flint implements from Sinai, and others of the palaeolithic period, from Thebes. Four Hittite seals from near Caesarea, Cappadocia, include a bronze seal arranged for suspension, with a group of late quasi-cursive characters, one of red steatite, with late signs with a floral border, one of gray steatite, with floral decoration, signs, and a standing figure, and a scarab with two Hittite characters, an example of a hitherto unknown class. A Rhodian vase 1(3 in. high has in a panel on one side a shoemaker taking the pattern of a boy's foot for a sandal, and on the other, Hermes standing before a seated satyr who holds a writing tablet and is making the sign with finger and thumb that is still used in Naples to signify the concluding of a bargain. From Italy come nine votive terra-cottas from Veii. From Great Britain, a large neolithic axe from Shropshire, and a very thin bronze bowl found in a marsh at Barmouth, Wales, a relic of the Pre-Roman age, whether late Celtic or Italian in fabric. *(Arch. Anz.* 1006, pp. 254-257.) ABBRFBLDY. — A Stone Circle. — A megalithic monument near Aberfeldy in Perthshire is noted in *Reliq.* XIII, 1907, p. 47 (pi.). It consists of three circles of standing stones. The inner circle is 25 ft. 6 in. in diameter, the middle circle 41 ft. 3 in. , and the outer circle 58 ft. The largest stone is 6 ft. 6 in. high.

CAERWENT. — An Unusual Type of Roman House. — An unusual type of Roman house, in an excellent state of preservation, has been discovered at Caerwent. A departure from the conventional practice of the Romans in Britain, as revealed by previous excavations, is the provision of ixtra rooms abutting on the four sides of the courtyard. In the basements two completely perfect hypocausts were found, together with the peculiar blue tiles used for conducting the heat from the basement to the upper rooms of the dwelling. In the basement some exquisite specimens of Roman paving were also unearthed. *(Scientific American,* Oct. 27, 1900.)

COLCHESTER — Celtic and Roman Pottery. — Two late Celtic vessels of fine brown paste with a carefully smoothed surface, but almost devoid of decoration, are described by G. Wkioht in *Reliq.* XII, 1906, pp. 203-205 (2 figs.). The two pieces are a pot and a somewhat deep bowl which served as a lid. They were found near Colchester and are now in the Corporation Museum of that city. *Ibid.* p. 210 (fig.), the same writer describes a small Roman vase in the same museum. It has a hollow ring base on which stood three small cups. A curious feature is the arm-like support in the form of a human hand which springs from the base of each cup and rests on the side of its neighbor. LAKENHBATH. —A Late-Celtic Fibula. — In *Reliq.* XIII, 1907, pp. 62-63 (2 figs.), J. Romilly Allkn describes an S-shaped fibula found at Lakenheath, Suffolk. It shows no trace of Roman influence and is clearly Late-Celtic. Other examples of this typo are noted. LONDON.—The Collection of Lord Wemyss. — In *R. Arch.* VIII, 1900, pp. 821 f., S. R(einach) mentions the following works in the collection of Lord Wemyss in London (23, St. James Place): (1) Fine marble head of Dionysus or Ariadne; (2) good marble replica of the head of the Venus of the Capitol; (3) marble statue of Psyche(?), with some restorations; (4) two marble statuettes from Greece, a torso of Artemis running, and a draped Aphrodite; (5) an archaistic relief, analogous to that at Wilton House, representing the four great gods (ancient?): (6) bronze model (about 0.60 m. high) of the Borghese gladiator, perhaps ancient. Among Renaissance works are the St. Cecilia attributed to Donatello, a Dosso, two small paintings by Andrea del Sarto, a Previtale, and the profile of a woman attributed to the sculptor of the facade of the Certosa at Pavia. A later work is a group of two Bacchantes by Clodion. MANTON. — A Bronze-age Barrow. — The opening of a bronze-age barrow at Manton, near Marlborough, Wiltshire, is described by Mrs. M. E. Clnnington in *Reliq.* XIII, 1907, pp. 28-46 (16 figs.). Only one burial was found, apparently that of a woman. The skeleton lay on the left side, with the knees drawn up. No stones surrounded the body, and the clay showed distinctly the marks of the cloth in which it had been wrapped. A number of small objects were near the body, including a bronze dagger with an amber pommel, an amber disk in a gold setting, a " lancet" which had been set in a wooden handle plated with gold, 150 small jet beads, bronze awls, and two rude vases,

one a perfect specimen of "grape" cup. Of this type of vase only six specimens seem to have been previously known. Gold in bronze-age barrows is rare, the last recorded discovery in Wiltshire occurring one hundred years ago, though that county is the richest in these monuments. MELANDRA, — Late-Celtic Trade Weights. —In the *Derbyshire Archaeoloi/ical and Natural History Society's Journal* for 1903, Thomas May described and illustrated a double series of trade and coin weights from the Roman camp at Melandra near Glossop. In *Reliq.* XII, 1906. pp. 200-201 (cut), the same writer reports that seven of the lighter weights correspond to the Late-Celtic unit of 4770 grains. The Roman weights found with these give an average *libra* of 5115 grains. THORPE. — Various Antiquities. — In *Reliq.* XII, 1906, pp. 269-270 (colored pi.; 2 figs.), is a brief account of a cinerary urn of the bronze age found at Thorpe near Bridlington, and also of a fine Late-Celtic sword from the same place. The lower part of the hilt is of bronze, with circular settings of red and yellow enamel. These objects are now in the York Museum. AFRICA ARCHAEOLOGICAL DISCOVERIES IN 1905. —A summary of archaeological news, taken largely from published articles and books, is given by A. Schulten, in *Arch. Am.* 1900, pp. 143-108 (9 figs.).
Tunis. — P. Gauckler has resigned as head of the Archaeological work, after fourteen years of service, during which the Bardo Museum has increased from three to twenty-five rooms, the street plan and important public buildings of Carthage have been discovered, Thugga and Gigthis excavated, and the *limes Tripolitanus* studied in its course and details. In Tripolis, two sites have been discovered to correspond witli Ptolemy's inland and coast towns of Sabrata. Four more stations of the Itinerary between Thacapes and Leptis Magna have been identified, and the late Roman ruins of Ghirza, the finest in Tripolis, found. Here, in addition to the usual African type of tomb, a pyramid resting on several square basements, there is a very beautiful example of the temple

type, a small square tomb chamber surrounded by a colonnade, which in this instance is surmounted by an arcade. The reliefs of the Ghirza tombs are lifelike pictures of animals, including the camel. At Carthage, the dimensions and plan of the theatre with the elevation of the scene buildings have been ascertained, five houses near by with frescoes have been excavated, and old Punic painted pottery found in a lower stratum. At one corner of the Byrsa hill is an example of wall building with amphoras, which allowed water to drain through. Other finds are Greek terra-cottas of the fourth and third centuries B.C., some new specimens of the miniature "axes," one of them in a woman's grave, a wooden coffin of a priestess, and four sarcophagi with reliefs of the dead upon the covers. The representation of the dead as lying on the sarcophagus was originally a Punic idea, modified later under Greek influence to a representation of the figure as if standing. The fourth century reliefs closely resemble Attic grave reliefs of the same period. At Thugga, two temples of unusual outline were found. That of *Pielas A ugusta* has a semicircular cella, and that of *Mercurius Silvixu,* dedicated under Marcus Aurelius, has a large cella between two small ones. Beneath this temple are older remains, and a bilingual Libyan-Punic inscription says a temple of Massanissa was here. The columns of the temple of Caelestis have been set upright. A table of the winds found here measures 2 m. iu diameter, and gives a slightly novel selection of twelve names. At Hadrumetum, the Roman cemetery has yielded a quantity of rudely painted terra-cottas. The Christian cemetery and catacombs cut in the tufa rock have been excavated. The niches are cut in the walls of the passages in several rows one above another, and the inscriptions are painted or scratched. Mosaic sarcophagi from the seventh century A.d., mosaic floors in graves, one showing a gladiator scene, and other mosaics, including a comedy scene in the theatre and a picture of Neptune, are among the finds. Terracotta pipes are found in the cemetery.

The mercantile colony of Thyadrus was under the patronage of Mercury, according to an inscription found. At Segermes. the Capitol is on an unusual plan, being a square fortified building with three niches in the inner hall, perhaps for the Capitoline Triad. Capitals which may be from this building were used in the walls of a later basilica. At Thibaris have been found various votive tablets with religious subjects. In Thabraca, the floor of the basilica contains graves covered by mosaic slabs which have curious designs and inscriptions, among them the front and side views of a church, a scribe at his desk writing the lives of the martyrs, etc., an important source for early Christian art. In Uppena is a basilica built in the fourth century for sixteen martyrs, and the successive layers of graves give a series of mosaics from that time to the seventh century. Some portrait busts from Clupea belong to the time of the Republic. Several examples of the fortified country house called *turris* in Latin (Caes. *Bell. Afric.* 40) are found in the southern part of the province, which contained many large landed estates. The type is Carthaginian in origin. One such villa, belonging to the Manilii, was still occupied in the fourth century A. d. The Roman road along the south of the province, connecting Gabes and Theveste, the oldest African road, is found to have been built by the Proconsul L. Asprenas in 14-15 A.d., and the *cenlurialio* of the land dates from the same period. The territory of Punic Carthage, at least since the third century B.C., did not extend on the west beyond the basin of the Bagradas, and hence corresponded very nearly with the modern Tunis. For some distance beyond, Carthage had a predominant influence without real authority, and her art and language spread throughout the Libyan land.

Algeria. — At Timgad, eight bathing establishments are now known. The library building which has a square anteroom and side rooms, and a semicircular book room with niches for the books and a statue of Minerva, is now thoroughly understood. It most nearly resembles the library at Pompeii, but is to be compared also with those at Ephesus and Pergamon. Other objects here are a graffito of a victorious racing chariot, with the names of the driver and horses, a statue of a Dadophorus, belonging to the Mithras cult, which had its centre in the camp at Lambaesis, and a table of standard measures combining both wet and dry in one table. At Lambaesis, the barracks have been found in the northeast quarter of the camp, also the officers' houses, some clay sling balls, some exceptionally fine mosaics, one of them signed by a Greek artist, and bronze figures from the shrine of an Egyptian deity. At Cherchel, the scene buildings of the theatre are tolerably well preserved, though the material of the auditorium was removed in 1840 to build barracks. At Thibitis, in the house of an official of the time of Marcus Aurelius, an altar to the genius of the house, dedicated by a freedman, is standing under a canopy in the centre of the peristyle, being the Lararium. Near it are altars to Fortuna Redux and Victoria given by the same freedman on the occasion of his patron's absence in the Parthian war of Lucius Verus. At Thalnosicum Numidarum. the old forum with various public buildings about it has been excavated, and a table of standards found which has round hollows for solids and square ones for liquids. At Hippo Regius, the sanctuary of an old native divinity has been found on the summit of a hill. Frothingham's theory that triumphal arches marked the entrance to the *pomerium,* or city precinct outside the wall, is justified by all such arches found in Africa, and affords at times a means' of dating the foundation of a city. The third number of Gsell's Archaeological Atlas of Algeria shows among other tilings that the territory of Hippo Regius, at the mouth of the Rubricata, was thickly covered with settlements, and that the fortress of Rapidum had several enlargements, each addition being built on to the outside of the earlier enclosure. An inscription calls the inhabitants *ceteran! et pagani.* At Bogaz are many Libyan tombs of the truncated cone type like the Sardinian *nuraghi,* showing that this form was of African origin.

AIN-EL-HOUT. — A Roman Lantern. — To the three Roman lanterns from IIerculaneum, Pompeii, and Boscoreale (in Berlin), a fourth is now added. It was found in a tomb at Ain-el-Hout, in the province of Constantine, and is fully described and illustrated by the discoverer, Surgeon-Major Rouquktte in AT. *Soc. Ant. Fr.* LXV, 1904-1905, pp. 196-205 (4 figs.). Of special interest is the arrangement of chains for raising the cover, which is the same as is used in modern censers. BULLA REGIA.—New Excavations. — A letter by A. Merlin in *C. II. Actul. Innc.* 1906, pp. 217-223, contains a preliminary report of excavations by Captain Benet at Bulla Regia. lie has uncovered a paved area surrounded on three sides by a raised portico with columns and a mosaic pavement. The court and gallery were adorned with pedestals and statues, of which a number have been found. It is possible that this was the ancient *curia.* It was certainly a public building, and probably in close proximity to the Forum. Five inscriptions are published, one of which contains for the first time the name *Bulla Regia.* It shows that the town was a *colonia* in the fourth century. In front of a base bearing an inscription in honor of Minia Procuta was found the portrait statue of an aged woman. The head-dress is that of a *flaminica,* and Minia is so styled in the inscription. The other statues described are a draped female figure, perhaps Ceres, two male figures of the municipal type, a Jupiter with a cornucopia, and two Minervas, both originally with wings, and one a companion to the Jupiter, and also holding a cornucopia. *Ibid.* pp. 363-368, the same writer reports that three large rooms at the back of the court have been cleared, but no clue to the nature of the building has been found. One of the new inscriptions gives the full name of the city, *Colonia Aelia Hadriana Auguntia Bulla Regia,* showing that it was Hadrian who raised the *liberum oppidum* of the first century to the rank of a colony. Other statues have also been found, but the most striking discovery has been a lead collar for a slave with the inscription *Adultera meretrix tene quia fugivi de Bulla R(e)g(ia)*. It evidently had been placed on the neck of a female slave, perhaps the property of the town. *Adultera* is perhaps best interpreted as a proper name. CYRENAICA. — A Statuette of Aphrodite Anadyomene. — In *C. R. Acad. Insc.* 1906, pp. 387-388, is a note by G. Perrot on a marble statuette of Aphrodite Anadyomene, found in 1902 near Benghazi in the Cyrenaica, and now in Turin. It is of the same type as the statuettes in Munich and Rome, attributed by Furtwiingler to Euphranor, but differs from them in some important points of style, all of which point strongly to the influence of Praxiteles. TEBESSA. — Inscribed Boundary Stones. —In *C. R. Acad. Insc.* 1906, pp. 478-480, R. Caunat publishes three Latin inscriptions from the neighborhood of Tebessa. Two are dated in 104-105 A.d., and the' other in 116-117 A.d. They marked the boundary between the territory of the Musulami on one side, and the property of the Emperor or of an unknown community, the *Tiihenenses,* on the other. VARIOUS DISCOVERIES. — In *B. Soe. Ant. Fr.* 1906, pp. 182-183 (fig.), P. Moxceacx publishes the cursive inscription on a potsherd from Carthage. He reads Fiatenu8 *Tkecettinus _Jiijulus scri(p)si idibus sette(mhribus). Ibid.* pp. 190-192, A. Heron DE Villefosse publishes an inscription from Ghadames (Cidamus). The copy is the work of an Arab and unintelligible. Few inscriptions have as yet been copied at this place, which was a fortified post during the reign of Alexander Severus. *Ibid.* pp. 192-193, is a fragmentary Latin epitaph from Khsar-Soudan (Sainte Marie-du-Zit), communicated by Father Delattre. *Ibid.* pp. 199-200, Dr. L. Carton gives a very brief summary of recent discoveries in the neighborhood of Carthage. None are of special importance. *Ibid,* pp. 286-2H7, II. Bourbon reports the discovery of a mosaic at Byrsa. It is in a Byzantine building, but is certainly of earlier date. It is composed of a series of lozenges, in which are various animals, a satyr, and a lighted torch. UNITED STATES BOSTON. — Recent Appointments at the Museum of Fine Arts. —

Mr. Sidney N. Deane has been appointed Assistant Curator of the Classical Department, and Mr. Oric Bates has been appointed Temporary Assistant in Charge of the Department of Egyptian Art. (iJ. *Mus. F. A.* IV, 1906, pp. 34, 44.) NEW YORK. — METROPOLITAN MUSEUM. — A Statue of Eirene. — The Metropolitan Museum has recently bought a fragmentary replica (Fig. 9) of the Eirene of Cephisodotus. The statue was found in 1903 in Rome during excavations for building purposes in the Villa Patrizi. (See *Not. Scav.* 1903, p. 60; *B. Com. Rom.* 1903, p. 290.) In execution it is distinctly finer than the well-known Munich example. "The lines and folds of the drapery are carved with much greater sharpness and vigor.... The torso has about the same proportions, and is equally matronly in character, but the legs are nearly two inches longer, and make the figure as a whole less heavy and bulky in its general effect." It also differs from the Munich statue in having the space below the right armpit filled with drapery. It corroborates the recently expressed view *(R. Arch.* VII, 1906, pp. 111-138; cf. *A.J.A.* 1906. p. 44.-)) that the original belongs to the end of the fifth century B.C. (E. li ohinson, *B. Metr. Mus.* I, 1906, pp. 147-149; 3 figs.)

Greek Jewellery. — The Metropolitan Museum has recently purchased a number ' 9—»»« " '»of pieces of ancient Greek jewellery of great beauty and importance. They are said to have been found in the same grave and include a diadem (0.368 x 0.06 m.), a necklace (0.323 m. long), a pair of earrings (0.074 m. long), a finger ring, seven rosettes in the form of small flowers, and nineteen beads from a necklace, all of pure yellow gold. They are probably not later than the middle of the fourth century B.C. The *diadem* is decorated in repousse with carefully executed reliefs. In the middle are Dionysus and Ariadne, and on either side a series of large scrolls between which are five female figures playing on musical instruments or singing. The *necklace* consists of a closely woven braid of fine wire, from which three rows of pendants in the shape of amphorae are hung by chains and rosettes. The latter are shaped like flowers, and in the upper row alternate with exceedingly small protomes of winged griffins. The *earrings* consist of three parts. At the top is a disk, decorated with a rosette; from this is suspended a crescent, from which hang three rows of pendants like those of the necklace. The crescent is attached to the disk by two hooks which are masked by floral designs, and at the side of each stands an Eros. The floral design between the hooks forms a sort of bower within which is seated a Muse playing on a lyre. The other pieces are of less importance. (E. Robinson, *B. Metr. Mus.* I, 1906, pp. 118-120; 2 pis.)

A Greek Gravestone. — To the original sculptures in the Museum has been recently added a fine Attic grave relief of the fourth century B.C. It measures 1.14 m. in height by 0.68 m. in width at the bottom. The relief represents a seated young woman clasping the hand of a standing elderly woman. In the background between the two is a third woman holding a small box. On the entablature is the inscription *Awrurpd. Tr* (sic) *Tlava.Orrvati.* (E. Robinson, *B. Metr. Mus.* I, 1906, pp. 120-122; fig.)

Department of Egyptian Art. — On October 15 the Trustees of the Metropolitan Museum voted to establish a Department of Egyptian Art, and appointed Mr. Albert Morton Lythgoe as its Curator. Arrangements have been made for a campaign of excavation this winter under Mr. Lythgoe's direction, and every opportunity will be afforded for the systematic development of the Egyptian collection. The Museum will also endeavor to complete its collections by purchase as well as excavation, and a recent important contribution, made in behalf of the Museum to the Egypt Exploration Fund, makes probable increased additions from that source. *(B. Metr. Mus.* I, 1906, pp. 149-150.)

Architectural Fragments from Rome. — Five architectural fragments from the Forum of Trajan have recently been presented to the Metropolitan. Museum by Mr. J. P. Morgan. They are supposed to have formed part of the Basilica Ulpia. Two are parts of cornices, two belonged to friezes, and one in an ornamental block of architrave. (G. R., *B. Metr. Mus.* I, 1906, p. 162.) PHILADELPHIA. — A Collection of Greek Vases. — The Pennsylvania Museum and School of Industrial Art has long had a collection of about seven hundred Greek and Italian vases. These have been recently carefully examined and rearranged. All are genuine, though two cylices have been repaired and repainted. A large proportion of the collection is made up of Apulian vases, but there are examples of Cypriote, Corinthian, south Italian, and Bucchero ware, besides a number of Attic vases, including some good black-figured amphorae, and two white lecythi. The 7host valuable piece is an Attic red-figured *stamnos* (Fig. 10) containing on one side Heracles and the Nemean lion, and on the other Theseus and the Marathonian bull. On each side is the retrograde inscription Koaos tt. (Edith H. Hall, *Bulletin of the Pennsylvania Museum,* October, 1906, pp. 58-57; 9 figs.) EARLY CHRISTIAN, BYZANTINE, MEDIAEVAL, AND RENAISSANCE ART GENERAL AND MISCELLANEOUS BEERSHEBA (PALESTINE). — New Fragments of the Imperial Rescript. — Clermont-ganneau contributes to *C. R. Acad. Insc.* 1906, pp. 154-155, on behalf of Pere Lagrange, a new fragment of the Byzantine Imperial rescript of Beersheba, in which the contributions of the three, provinces of Palestine are listed, particularly those of Palestina Tertia. This fragment is the fifth to be recovered. It contains a number of names which add to our knowledge of the geography of Palestine and Arabia Petraea. and gives the key to the abbreviations in the decree. Hopes are entertained of the ultimate recovery of the whole of this important document, which throws much light on the *Notitia Dignitatum* and the mosaic of Madaba. The text will be published shortly by Clermont-Ganneau in *R. Bibl.* GALATA. —Late Inscriptions. — In *B.S.A.* XI, 1904-05, pp. 50-62 (pi.; 7 figs.), F. W. Hasluck publishes, with commentary, extracts relating to Galata from the Journals of Dr. Covel, chaplain to the British Embassy at Constantinople from 1669-1677. The notes are in Latin and perhaps derived from an earlier description. For the most part they are copies of unpublished Latin inscriptions of the fourteenth and fifteenth centuries. Twelve are given in full.

SAMARCAND. — Ancient Inscribed Grave Stones. — In *Or. Lit.* IX, 1906, pp. 233-240, 297-1504, 361-372, 421-431 (pi.), M. Hartmann discusses several ancient grave stones with Arabic inscriptions, dating from the seventh to the tenth century, that are found at present in the Russian museum at Samarcand. These are of historical interest and also of importance for the development of Arabic epigraphy. MEXICO. — TZINTZUNZAN. — A Painting by Titian. — According to A. De Ceuleneer there exists in the church of San Francisco in this town a Pietii by Titian, of large dimensions (4.40 x 2.80 m.), which was given by Charles V to the bishop Quiroga. (*R. Art Chre't.* 1906, pp. 266-267.) ASIA MINOR AND GREECE CILICIA AND LYCAONIA. — Byzantine Churches. — Notes on a Journey through Cilicia and Lycaonia.—In *R. Arch.* VIII, 1906, pp. 7-36 (29 tigs.), Gertrude Lowthian Bell publishes further notes (see *A.J.A.* 1906, p. 366), chiefly on Byzantine churches in Cilicia and Lycaonia. Four basilicas at Korghoz, the Corycian cave and chapel, the church at Olbia, and the church at Lira are described, with illustrations. Nearly all these churches have apses built within the edifice, with a room or passage between these inner apses and the rear (western) wall. *Ibid.* pp. 225-252 (26 figs.), the fifteen ruined churches at Daouleh, near Biubirklisse are described. In one (No. 3) was a long inscription, which gives the date of a restoration under Leo, metropolitan bishop of Iconium in 787 A.d. These churches are simpler than some of those described before. Most of them have a nave, two aisles, an apse, and a narthex. Five were smaller and simpler and were probably mausoleums. Several tombs were examined. The whole settlement was probably a monastic establishment. CYPRUS. — Byzantine Silver Dish. — A silver dish found at Cyrenia is published in *Byz. Z.* 1906, pp. 615-617 (fig-) by O. M. Dalton. Its decoration is confined to the centre of the inside, which is ornamented with two circular mouldings separated by foliate ornament. The presence of five official stamps shows that it belongs to the class of silver-work known as *apyvpov irtvTaaijpa.yiarov.* In the centre of the dish is a monogram which seems to read *(dtoSwpov.* The similarity of stamps and ornament shows that this plate belongs to the same set as a larger dish in the British Museum, published in *Archaeologia,* LVII, pi. 16, fig. 1.

A Treasure of Gold and Silver. — In *Le Muse'e,* III, 1906, pp. 121-129 (3 pis.), A. Samhon describes in some detail a number of gold and silver objects, found near Cyrenia (Cyprus) in 1899, and recently acquired by Mr. J. P. Morgan. There are five silver plaques decorated in reliefs with scenes from the life of David, a belt adorned with gold coins of Theodosius II, Justin and Justinian, and Maurice, and gold bracelets and necklaces. The work evidently belongs to the last part of the sixth or the early seventh century of our era. It w as perhaps part of a church treasure hidden at the time of the Arab invasions.

EPHESUS. — The Mosque of Isa Bey. — The ruined mosque at Ephesus, which was probably erected by Isa Bey about 1340 A.d., is briefly described by A. E. Henderson in *Rec. Past,* V, 1906, pp. 259-265 (8 figs.). It is a good example of Seljukian architecture, careful and exact in the details, but with no endeavor to develop a characteristic or ideal style. LACONIA.— Frankish Sculptures. — Sculptured monuments of the Frankish period iu Greece are rare, but some examples are published by A. J. B. Wack in *B.S.A.* XI, 1904-05. pp. 139-145 (4 figs.). At Parori, not far from Mistra, is a very rude relief of a warrior, represented *en face,* but with the legs and feet in profile. The long cloak and the shape of the shield mark it as Frankish. In the Frankish castle at Geraki are remains of several churches. Two of these show pointed arches and rude carvings much in the style of the relief just mentioned. In the church of St. George, which seems to have been the castle chapel, is a shrine with a remarkable frame, which in its clustered pillars and bands of interlaced tracery resembles neither Frankish nor Byzantine work, and is probably to be ascribed to Saracen artists in the service of the Frankish barons. All these sculptures were probably executed between 1209 and 1262 A.d. MISTRA. —Inscriptions. —In *B.C. II.* XXX, 1906, pp. 45.1-466 (4 figs.), (t. Millet publishes two new inscriptions from Mistra. The first is two monograms on a lintel, which read *£ap.irta vTt Xt£rlvavw, i.e. Isabelle de Lusii/nan.* She is known in the history of Morea in the fourteenth century, and seems to have been the second wife of Manuel Cantacuzene, or perhaps of his brother or of a nephew. The second is on a fragment of a large basin, called in the inscription *ayiaarpiov,* which here must denote either a receptacle for holy water or a font. In conclusion the monograms in the inscription *B.C.H.* 1899, pp. 97-156, No. 31, are resolved, and the term KafloXtKos pto-aw discussed. It denotes a general agent of the despot, as distinguished from local officers. NICABA.—The Existing Ruins. —In *Rec. Past,* V, 1906, pp. 323-331 (12 figs.), Isabel F. Dodd describes briefly the ruins of Nicaea in Bithynia as seen by her on three visits to this somewhat inaccessible place. The site seems likely to yield valuable results under scientific excavation. ITALY NEW DIRECTOR-GENERAL OF ANTIQUITIES. — Corrado Ricci has Ix-en appointed Director-general of Antiquities in the Kingdom of Italy. AREZZO. — Discovery of Frescoes by Piero della Francesca. — In *V Arte,* 1906, pp. 305-1106, U. Taranti reports that he has discovered in a building beside the church of S. Maria delle Grazie remains of the fresco of ' San Donato in episcopal robes with figures of children" mentioned by Vasari as painted by Piero della Francesca for a cloister belonging to that church. The fresco is nearly gone, but on a wall near by there are considerable remains of a frescoed frieze representing scenes from the life of the saint. The writer finds in these the characteristics of Piero.

Discovery of a Painting. — In a chapel adjoining the church of San Pier Piccolo has been found a picture by Fra Bartolomeo della Gatta. It is a portrait of Beato Jacopo Filippo, and seems to be the painting mentioned by Vasari, and believed to be lost. (£' *Arte,* 1906, p. 388.) BASSANO. — A Processional Cross by Filarete. — In view of the few works of Filarete preserved, interest attaches to the processional cross in the cathedral at Bassano Veneto. It was ordered by the municipality in 1449 and suffered repair from the *porno* down in 1622. The cross proper has a crucifix at the intersection, the vertical arm displaying a half figure of the Virgin; on the right arm is the Magdalen, on the left St. John, with the angel symbolical of Matthew in the field above the *porno.* The reverse has in the middle the Madonna and Child with the symbolical pelican above, and in the other fields the remaining evangelistic symbols. The flat surfaces on both sides are incised with ornament, symbols, saints, etc., and below the Madonna on the reverse is inscribed, *"Opus Antonii qui Rome Basilice Sancti Petri porta ereas fecit Eugenia I III pontijici hco* (sic) *factum sub anno Domini M.CCCC.XL Villi."* (G. Gerola, *V Arte,* 1906, pp. 291-296.) FLORENCE. — Discovery of a Fresco. — The removal of a curtain in the church of S. Maria in Campo brought to light a fresco which seems to represent an episode in the life of San Galgano. The composition is crescent shaped, and partly covered by a pilaster of the altar and a later wall. Competent critics have assigned the fresco to Filippo Lippi or his imitator Jacopo del Sellaio. (*Rass. a" Arte,* September, 1906, Cronaca.)

Discovery of a Fresco in the Belle Arti. — During the course of recent repairs in one of the rooms of the *Istituto delle Belle Arti* a fresco was discovered representing the Last Supper. The central part has been destroyed by the opening of a door. It is held to be the work of Stefano d'Antonio, a collaborator of Bicci di Lorenzo. Documents relative to the decoration of the church and hospital of San Matteo, which is now the seat of the Istituto, mention him among the painters employed on the building. (G. Carocci, *Arte e Storia,* 1906, p. 159.) MILAN. — Acquisitions of Milan Museums. — Sixteen frescoes by Luini from the Villa felucca near Monza have been presented by the king to the Brera. The Museo del Castello has added to its paintings two wings of a triptych by Defendente de Ferrari, representing donors; four pictures by Bonvicino, called *il Moretto,* a "Jeremiah," a "Saint John Baptist," a "St. Anthony of Padua," and a large "St. Ursula and her Companions"; a "Delilah" by Bernardo Strozzi, a "St. Helena" of the Venetian School, a " Madonna and two Saints" by Girolamo da Santa Croce, aud a "Salvator Mundi " by Rocco Marconi.

Loss of Documents relating to the Cathedral. — A fire at the Milan Exposition on the 20th of August consumed several ancient works of art in the Hungarian section, and in the Italian section, in addition to other objects, several plans, models, and documents relating to the building of the Milan cathedral. (*Chron. Arts,* 1906, p. 230.) PERUGIA. —Frescoes of the Thirteenth Century. — In the chapel of San Prospero near Perugia, frescoes have been discovered bearing the inscription, *In nomine Domini amen anno Domini AICCXXV indictione XIII tempore Honorii tertii et Domini Federici imperatoris hoc opus factum fuit tempore Domini Badaldi* (or *Rainalili* ?). *presliiteri S Prosperi mense Octobris Kyo Bonamicus pictor feci.* This artist cannot be Bonaiuico di Cristofano, called Buffalmacco, since his dates are certainly in the *trecento.* The frescoes antedate all other paint ings of Perugia (G. U., *V Arte,* 190G, pp. :S06-307).

PISA. — A New Madonna by Duccio. — A "Madonna and Child" belonging to the Contessa Tadini Buoninsegni is published for the first time in *V Arte,* 1906, pp. 372-373, by Pietro D" Achixrdi. It is assigned by him to Duccio di Buoninsegna on internal evidence, and is apparently part of a larger work, to be dated slightly before the great altarpiece preserved in the Museo dell' Opera at Siena, which was executed between 1308 and 1311. RIETI. — Discovery of a Fresco. — As a result of the recent removal of the altar-piece of the chapel of St. Ignatius in the Cathedral, a fresco of the fifteenth century has been found which is believed to be the work of Antoniazzo Romano. *(V Arte,* 1906, pp. 388-389.) ROME. — Examination of Relics in the Sancta Sanctorum.— The relics that have been kept in the private chapel of the Popes, the Sancta Sanctorum, since at least the twelfth century, have never been seen since the sixteenth century, under Leo X. The researches of the Jesuit Jubaru concerning the head of St. Agnes necessitated the examination of the relics, and in June last the altar was opened. The head of the saint was found in a silver box of the time of Honorius III. All the other relics and reliquaries were contained in a cypress coffer of the beginning of the ninth century, inscribed: *Leo indignus Dei famulus tertius episcopus fecit.* Among the objects found in it were a fragment of an ivory pyxis ornamented with a Bacchic scene of good workmanship; a cross in cloissonne-enamel, inclosing a piece of the true cross, which Grisar, who was in charge of the examination, assigns to the early sixth century; a jewelled cross containing the *caro circumeisionU;* a rectangular silver coffer ornamented with saints in relief, and Byzantine enamels on the cover, of the tenth or eleventh century; an oval coffer of silver with a rounded top, of a type similar to the well-known African coffer of the fifth century which was presented to Leo XIII by Cardinal Lavigerie; a small bas-relief in ivory representing the "Healing of the Blind Man," and belonging to the early Christian period; an ivory coffer of Moslem workmanship, assigned to the twelfth century; another of cylindrical form with a painted Cufic inscription; silk textiles of Byzantine or Sassanid origin which were wrapped around the relics or served as linings and cushions; two very old tunics, one of which passes for that of St. John Baptist, and a number of cedar boxes, ornamented with incised or relief designs or with paintings. Two of these have Byzantine painting on gold ground of the tenth and eleventh centuries (grisar gives a history of the reKcs in *Rom. Quart.* 1906, pp. 109-122, and a description in *Cirilta Cattolica,* June 2 and 16, 1906. They are also described by Lauer in *C. R. Acad. Insc.* 1906, pp. 223-226. D. Sant' Ambrogio in *Arte e Storia,* 1906, pp. 117-122, reviews Grisar's conclusions, contesting particularly the early date given to the enamelled *staurotlieca.* A complete publication of the relics will be made in several periodicals.

Excavations in the Cemetery of Priscilla. — The recent excavations, an account of which is given by O. MarucChI in *N. Bull. Arch. Crist.* 1906, pp. 1-65, have yielded no decisive proof that this cemetery was the "seat of St. Peter" (see *A.J.A.* 1904, pp. 328 and 497-498), but about twenty-seven inscriptions were found which are reproduced in the report. One of them mentions a *bisomum at Criscentioneni* and was found in the corridor opposite a cubiculum near the sepulchre of the Glabriones. This cubiculum was then the burial-place of the martyr Crescentio mentioned in the *itinerariiun Salisburgense,* as buried in *spelunca* under the basilica of San Silvestro. The *Liher Pontificalia* places the tomb of Pope Marcellinus near that of Crescentio, and Marucchi supposes it was in cubiculum M, adjoining the tomb of the Glabriones. A new plan accompanies the article.

The New Picture Gallery in the Vatican. — The *Nation,* July 26, 1906, reports rapid progress in the preparation of new quarters for the Vatican picture gallery: "The new gallery will occupy a part of the long wing on the west side of the Cortile del Belvedere, on the street leading to the entrance of the museum, and opposite the Vatican gardens. Each of the great masterpieces of the present collection—the Transfiguration, the Madonna di Foligno, and the Communion of St. Jerome — will have its own room, and in the new gallery will be placed all the pictures by the old masters that are now scattered in different parts of the palace, besides those in the present collection. No modern pictures will be hung here. The new gallery is to be equipped with all modern improvements in heating, lighting, and ventilating."

A New Painting by Luini. — A. Colasanti assigns to Luini on internal grounds a "St. Jerome Penitent" which exists in a private collection in Home and is published by him in *Ras.i. d' Arte,* 1906, pp. 102-101. On the back of the picture were found two seals, the smaller with an illegible inscription, the larger bearing the arms of the Medici surmounted by a cardinal's cap and surrounded by the name of Alessandio Medici, elevated to the sacred college in 1583 by Gregory XIII.

SARDINIA. — Byzantine Inscriptions. — In *Not. Scav.* 1906, pp. 123-138 (12 figs.), A. Takamklli publishes and discusses several Byzantine inscriptions preserved in various churches of Sardinia. They are of the tenth, eleventh, and twelfth centuries. SIENA. — Recovery of a Polyptych. — The polyptych by Luca di Tome which was once in the oratory of the *Muni.sterino* at Tolfe near Siena, but disappeared ten years ago, has been recovered and placed in the Accademia delle Belle Arti. The centre piece is a "Madonna and Child," the wings representing four saints. It is published with a reproduction in *Rass. d' Arte,* 1906, pp. 101-105, by E. Modioliaxi, who notes that it is the best and latest of the authentic works of this painter of the fourteenth century. SYRACUSE. — New Excavations in the Catacombs. — The results of new excavations in the catacombs at Syracuse are summarized by O. Marucchi in *N. Bull. Arch. Crist.* 1906, pp. 102-172. The excavations were made in the crypt of S. Marziano, and the chief discoveries were a cubiculum in which was found a closed loculus, with two *orantes* painted upon it, symbolizing the two infant occupants whose common name *Alexandria* appears in the Greek inscription bordering the figures, and an interesting fragment of a metrical inscription, with a consular date of 423 A.d. None of the tombs found antedate the fourth century. The excavations rather confirm the tradition that Martianus, first bishop of Syracuse, was buried in the crypt, but the little cemetery just discovered has no connection with the neighboring catacomb of S. Giovanni. URBINO.—A Fresco by Carnevale (?). — A fresco was recently discovered in the church of Santa Maria della Bella, representing the Crucifixion. The name of Fra Carnevale has been proposed as the author, but the superiority of the work over the known work of that master makes the attribution improbable. The influence of Piero della Francesca is manifest in the painting. (E. Calzini, *Russegna b'Miografica dell' urte italiana,* 1906, pp. 106-109.) SPAIN BURGOS. — New Symbolism on a Sarcophagus.— In *N. Bull. A rch. Crist.* 1906, pp. 93-95 (fig.), L. Huidobro describes a Christian sarcophagus (Fig. 11) from the convent of S. Francisco de Briviesca, now in the museum at Burgos. One side contains on the left an ' investiture " — a personage holding his hands toward another, who is dressed in a dalmatic — in the centre a ladder (flanked by two stare) which two Figure U._ Sahcophaous At Buncos, persons prepare to climb, and on the right the well-known Noah scene. The corners of the sarcophagus are decorated with a vine-ornament. The back shows the (iood Shepherd in the centre, to the right Adam and the Tree of Life, to the left the Sacrifice of Isaac. The writer considers the sarcophagus an example of Hispano-gothic work of the fifth century.

PALENCIA.—The Crypt of San Antolin. — Recent investigations have brought out the antiquity of the crypt of S. Antolin beneath the Cathedral of Palencia, which is an important connecting link between the classic and Moslem periods in Spanish architecture. The inner end of the crypt exhibits eight horseshoe arches of different proportions from the Moslem type, and the Visigothic capitals on the columns, together with other evidence, show that the style comes from the North rather than the South. The arcosolium of the saint and the constructions surrounding it are of the seventh century. Some difference of opinion exists regarding the date of the part of the crypt nearer the entrance, one critic assigning it to the classic period, while others regard it as a Romanesque work of the eleventh century. (F. Simon' Y Nieto, *Boletin de la Sociedad Expahola de Excuniones,* April, 1906, pp. 65-82, and E. Serrano Fatigati, *H. Art Chret.* 1906, p. 335.) VALENCIA. — Triptych by an Unknown Flemish Master. — A triptych, which is preserved in the College of Corpus Christi at Valencia and has never been exhibited save at the Columbian Exposition of Madrid in 1892, is published by E. Bertavx in *Gaz. B.-A.* XXXVI. 1906, pp. 219-222. The three compositions represent the Crucifixion, the Descent from the Cross, and the Resurrection. The artist seems most influenced by Roger van der AVeyden, but there are traces also of the influence of the "Maitre de Fle'malle" and Dirk Bouts. Four panels in the Prado, an "Annunciation," "Visitation," "Nativity," and "Adoration of the Magi," are assigned by Bertaux to the same master, because of similarity in particular figures, as well as in the inclosing arches, ornamented with small sculptured scenes. FRANCE AIX-EN-PROVENCE.— Identification of a New Early French Artist. — The "lietable de Boulbon" which made so great an impression on the students of the *Exposition iles Primitifs* was unsigned, but the small stork in one corner was held by some to be the monogram of the painter. This has been established by the discovery by F. De Mely at Aix-enProvence of a manuscript in which there occurs a miniature signed *Chugoinot,* old French for " little stork." The arms on the miniature are those of Pope Nicholas V (1447-1455), and both date and execution are consistent with the identification of its painter *Chugoinot* with the author of the Boulbon painting, which was originally made for a church in the same region. This identification gives us the name of a new French *primitif* of the first rank. (C. *11. Acad. Insc.* 1906, p. 145.) AVIGNON. — Discovery of Frescoes. — An interesting discovery has been made in the ancient Palace of the Popes at Avignon, which was for some time utilized as barracks. In a room which once served as the bedchamber of the Popes a series of interesting mural paintings has been revealed. These frescoes appear to date from the fourteenth century, and are admirably preserved. Only a portion has yet been recovered, but it is hoped to recover the whole. *(Athen.* Dec. 29,1906.) DIJON.— The Sculptor of the "Last Judgment "in St. Michel.— A document recently brought to light at Dijon records that this composition, which occupies the central tympanum of the grand entrance, was ordered in 1551 of Nicolas de la Court, native of Douai, and established at Dijon, who engaged himself to execute it after the "patron" which was furnished him, for the sum of seventy livres. (II. Chabeuf, *R. Art Chre't.* 1906, pp. 211-212.) PARIS. — Acquisitions of the Louvre. — The department of sculpture has recently received: a stone "St. Michael Slaying the Dragon," of the French Romanesque period; an early fifteenth century bust of St. Sebastian of French origin; and a polychrome "Virgin " of the fourteenth century. *(Chron. Arts,* 1906, pp. 196, 218.) New paintings are: a "Pieta" of the school of Avignon and four Spanish panels of the fourteenth century representing scenes from the life of St. George, all giveu by the Societe des Amis du Louvre; t he " Portrait of Mr. Hare" by Sir Joshua Reynolds; a " Parisian View " by Turner, the first picture by this artist to enter the Louvre; two portraits by Lawrence and a signed " Portrait of an Old Woman " by Hodgro. (J. Guiffrky, *V Arte,* 1906, pp. 456-458.) The Byzantine Section has recently received a small plaque in steatite, representing St. Michael, of the tenth or eleventh century. (J. J. Marguet De Vasselot in *B. Soc. Ant. Fr.* 1906, pp. 118-119.)

A Manuscript illustrated by Jean Fouquet. — Archives of the fifteenth century show that Jean Fouquet about 1474 illustrated a "Book of Hours" for Philippe de Commynes, the famous statesman and historian. Count P. Durrieu has found in the Bibliotheque Nationale a "Book of Hours" (Lat. no.

1417) which appears to be this work. It contains twenty badly damaged miniatures, in some of which the hand of Fouquet appears, and bears the arms of Commynes. *(C. R. Acad. Iusc.* 1906, p. 257.)

A Fourteenth Century Sketch Book. — Mr. Pierpont Morgan recently acquired in Paris a sketch book originally in a Roman collection, made of six thin panels of boxwood bound by thin strips of parchment. Each board was covered by a thin wash of gouache on which the drawings are done in silverpoint. The presence of a second and less skilful hand is noticed in some accessory sketches. The subjects are partly of the stereotyped religious sort, but also include scenes of forests, simple studies, and a *bal masque.* The costumes are of the end of the fourteenth century, and the *bal masque,* with courtiers disguised as *hommes sauvages,* may be a reminiscence of the famous masquerade of 1393, where the burning of some of the masquers brought on the madness of Charles VI. Coincidences in style point to the miniaturist Andre Beauneveu as the author. (roger Fry, *Burl. Mag.* X, 1906, pp. 31-38.) This attribution enables S. C. Cockerell *(Ibid.* X, 1906, pp. 130-131) to assign to Beauneveu the "Richard II" in Westminster Abbey, on internal evidence, chiefly the similarity in drapery and in the arrangement of the left hand to a "Virgin and Child" of the sketch book.

SASSANGY. — A Fifteenth Century Window. — A painted window in the possession of the Comtesse de Fleurieu at the Chateau de Sassangy, representing a gentleman and lady playing chess and dated by the costumes 1430-1440, adorned until 1840 a house in Villefranche in the Beaujolais. Tradition says that the window was placed in the house to commemorate the carrying-off of the daughter of the bourgeois Guyonnet de la Bessee, to whom the house belonged, by the last seigneur de Beaujeu, who was punished by the king with loss of his domains and died in 1400. The tradition with its attendant detail that the seigneur used the game as the pretext for his seductions, was probably attached to the window by a later age. The scene is a product of the genre painting introduced by the portraits of Jan Van Eyck, and is not, like the chess games on many contemporary ivory reliefs, inspired by a story of current minstrelsy. (L,. Bkgule and E. Bertaux in *Gaz. B.-A.* XXXVI, 1906, pp. 407-416.) SAUVEPLANTADE. — A Curious Church. — The little church at Sauveplantade was once the chapel of a Benedictine priory, and was built not later than the beginning of the twelfth century. It has a simple plan, but at the crossing of the nave and transepts instead of a dome there is an octagonal pyramid terminating in a truncated cone, which passes into a square belfry with two rows of windows. This arrangement is very rare and perhaps unique. Within the church are two ancient granite columns, with Byzantine capitals, probably from an earlier church. The abbey church of St. Orens at La Ruelle (Hautes-Pyrenees) has a similar curious construction, but here the pyramid is square, not octagonal. (Marquis De Vogue, *C. R. Acad. lnsc.* 1906, pp. 288, 486-492; 4 figs.; A. Brutails, *Ibid.* pp. 327-328; fig.) BELGIUM ANTWERP. — The Birthplace of Rubens. — It is announced from Antwerp that the birth in Germany of Rubens is now proved by a family tree of the painter, which, however, is unsigned. This document shows that Rubens was born at Cologne, and remained there until he was ten years old. *(Athen.* Dec. 29, 1906.) TOURNAI. — Discovery of a Tomb of the Fourteenth Century. — In the church of St. Quentin, the removal of wood-work on an altar of the last century has brought to light a tomb of the fourteenth century. The effigy, of which the head is last, is in the round, with the usual dog beneath the feet. The front of the tomb proper is adorned with eight.statuettes in the arches of an arcade. The inscription reads: *Chij gistJakemes Kaxtangnes ki tre.spassa Van mille ccc et xxvii.* (L. Cloquet, *R. Art ChrA.* 1900, pp. 212, 261-205.) GERMANY BERLIN. — Acquisitions of the Kaiser Friedrich Museum. — The Emperor has recently transferred from Potsdam to the Museum the following paintings: a " Magdalen" and " Venus and Adonis " by Rubens; an "Apostle's Head" by Van Dyck; a " Samson and Delilah" by Rembrandt; and a "Beheading of John the Baptist" by Romanino. By the bequest of Alfred Beit, the Museum receives Reynolds' "Portrait of Mrs. Boone and Daughter" and a bronze statuette of Hercules by Pollaiuolo. (H. V. Singer, *Jinrl. Mag. X.* 1006, p. 68.) Other paintings recently acquired are: "Four Monastic Saints" by Masaccio, part of the altar made for the Carmelites of Pisa in 1420; a predella, the "Miracle of an infant Saint" by Fra Filippo Lippi; a "Madonna" in the manner of Taddeo Gaddi; "Three Saints," forming the central part of the grand altar at Santa Croce in Florence, by Ugolino da Siena; a lunette of the Madonna with two angels by Luca della Robbia; a "Madonna and Child" of Giovanni Bellini; some pictures by Sassetta and Giovanni di Paolo; and two small allegorical paintings attributed to Pareutino (P. Schubhino in *V Arte,* 1906, pp. 386-387.) ' The *Nation,* Sept. 0, 1900, adds Rembrandt's sketch for the " Good Samaritan," in the Louvre, and " The Fainting Lady" by Metsu.

COLOGNE. — Frescoes of the Thirteenth and Fourteenth Centuries. — In the apses of the transept of St. Maria irn Capitol mural paintings have been discovered in two layers. The more recent belong to the fourteenth century and represent at the north "Christ enthroned among the Evangelists," at the south the ' Lamb with Evangelistic Symbols," and show traces of the influence of Wilhelm of Cologne. The earlier frescoes under these represent the Last Judgment and the Crucifixion. *(Chron. Arts,* 1906, p. 262.) FRANKFORT. — The Molinier Cranach. — The Museum at Frankfort recently acquired from the sale of the collection of Molinier, ex-director of the Louvre, a large triptych by Lucas Cranach the elder, of the beginning of the sixteenth century, which was found by its former possessor some years ago in a convent in southern Spain. *(Rass. a"Arte,* August, 1900, Cronaca.) STUTTGART. — Sixteenth Century

Views of Milan. — There are several drawings in the Museum at Stuttgart of architectural monuments in Milan, such as San Babila, Sta. Maria delle Grazie, Sta. Maria presso S. Celso, etc., which originally belonged to the sketch book of a Dutch artist, and date between 1508 and 1579. (C. vox Fabriczy. *Rass. a" Arte,* 1900, pp. 87-90; 4 figs.) GREAT BRITAIN MEETINGS OF ARCHAEOLOGICAL SOCIETIES. — The sixtyfourth annual meeting of the Royal Archaeological Institute, held at Worcester, July 24-31, and the sixty-third annual Congress of the British Archaeological Association, held at Nottingham, July 25-31, are described in *Allien.* Aug. 4 and 11, 19011. Both bodies devoted their time chiefly to visiting the various sites of archaeological interest in the neighborhood of the places of meeting, and these monuments are noticed in some detail in the reports. BLYTHBURG. — A Fifteenth Century Church. — Holy Trinity Church at Blythburg, Suffolk, is described by Charlotte Mason in *Reliq.* XII, 1906, pp. 217-228 (11 figs.). It was built during the fifteenth century by the monks of Blythburg Priory, almost wholly in the Perpendicular style. The stained glass has been destroyed, but the church still contains fine traceries and carvings. Noteworthy are the figures on the front of the choir-stalls and on the bench-ends. ECCLESFIELD.— An Early Cross Shaft.— In 1802 there were discovered in Ecclesfield churchyard the broken base and shaft of a stone cross. The shaft is decorated with incised crosses and circles and has a rolled edge. The base, which contains two sockets, has merely a roll moulding. It is possible that it belonged to a Saxon church destroyed at the time of the Conquest, but there are no other remains of either a Saxon or a Norman church. (E. Lloyd, *Reliq.* XII, 1900, p. 205; fig.) FOWNHOPE. — Sculptured Norman Tympanum. — In the west wall of the nave of Pownhope church, Herefordshire, is a Norman tympanum, sculptured in relief, with a representation of the Virgin and Child in the centre, and on either side the sacred vine, among the scrolls of which apiear the lion of St. Mark and the eagle of St. John. *(Reliq.* XII, 1906, p. 195; pi.) HARDWICK HALL. — Portrait of Mary Queen of Scots and Lord Darnley. — In *Burl. Mag.* X, 1906, pp.:?S—47, is a review by L. Cust of recent discussions concerning the portraits of Mary Queen of Scots, and particularly of Andrew Lang's recent book. He publishes a new portrait of the Queen and Lord Darnley in the collection of the Duke of Devonshire at Ilardwick, catalogued as the "Earl and Countess of Lenox," but shown by Miss M. K. Martin, on documentary evidence and by comparison with coins and the miniatures in the Rijks Museum at Amsterdam, to be really likenesses of the unfortunate Queen and her husband. This is, apart from coins, the ouly authentic portrait made during Mary's reign in Scotland. HOLKHAM HALL (NORFOLK). — Manuscripts. —The collection of 750 manuscripts at Holkham Hall has been studied and catalogued by L. Dorez, who reports briefly on the more important works in *C. R. Acad. Insc.* 1906, pp. 335—537. From Rome are a portfolio of drawings from the antique attributed to Raphael and an autograph manuscript of Leonardo da Vinci. From southern Germany, Flanders, and France are important illuminated manuscripts, several of which are from the library of the Dukes of Burgundy. LASTINGHAM. — A Pure Norman Crypt. — A unique example of a pure Norman crypt beneath the church of St. Mary at Lastingham is described in *Reliq.* XII, 1906, pp. 145-151 (6 figs.), by J. C. Wall. It consists of a nave, apsidal sanctuary and aisles, and was built by Stephen, Abbot of Whitby, in 1078-1088, to enshrine the body of St. Cedd, who had established a monastery at this place during the seventh century. *Ihid.* pp. 152-161 (28 figs.), the same writer describes a number of fragments of sculptured stones and wood in the Norman crypt. There are many fragments of stone crosses, bearing the interlaced patterns brought from Ireland to Iona and Lindisfarne, and thence spread through Northumbria. Other fragments belong to the Norman period and even later. LONDON. — Additions to the Morgan Collection at South Kensington. — The loan collection at South Kensington Museum was recently increased by the purchase on the part of Mr. J. Pierpont Morgan of the Baron Oppenheim collection of *ohjetn d'art.* The most interesting mediaeval specimens are: a seventh century Byzantine reliquary, a Carolingian ivory book-cover, a Franco-Arabian candlestick in silver-gilt and rock-crystal of the eleventh or twelfth century, the well-known Soltykoff reliquary, a reliquary in the form of the Madonna and Child, in gilt, copper and Limoges enamel, and a French ciborium in gilt and enamelled copper, the two last belonging to the thirteenth century. The Renaissance is represented by two fifteenth century busts of young women, one a French work of painted stone, the other in faience of Faenza, a salt-cellar in the rare " Henri II" ware, and a seventeenth century German glass beaker mounted in silver-gilt. *(Burl. Mag.* IX, 1906, pp. 227-234.)

Additions to the National Gallery. — Miss Eva Mackintosh has presented to the National Gallery Raphael's "Madonna of the Tower." The picture was formerly in the Orleans collection, and has since belonged to Messrs. Henry Hope, Samuel Rogers, and R. J. Mackintosh. Critics are not wholly agreed as to the value of the picture, which has suffered from unskilful cleaning, but the dominant feeling in the work is Raphaelesque. Another addition is " Christ preaching from St. Peter's Ship" by II. Saftleven, an artist hitherto unrepresented in this collection. It is the gift of Mr. C. L. Eastlake. *(Athen.* Aug. 11, 1906.)

A New Work by the " Maitre de Moulins." — In *Burl. Mag.* IX, 1906, p. 331, Roger Fry publishes an "Annunciation" in the possession of Messrs. Dowdeswell and Dowdeswell, which he attributes to the now famous ' Maitre de Moulins." He places the picture in the earlier part of his career, as it shows less power of composition and harmony of rhythm than the Moulins altar piece, and appears little removed from miniature painting, which we know was among the artist's pursuits. The early date is also borne out by the clumsy use of the classic forms in the architectural background, showing the painter's unfamiliarity with Italian renaissance designs.

Medals by Pastorino da Siena. — In *Burl. Mag.* IX, 1906, pp. 408-412, G. F. Hili. publishes some new medals by this sculptor, from the collection in the British Museum. He notes that the smaller medals without pearl borders are usually the earlier, and explains the inscription Cassan Ciaussi" found on the medal bearing the turbaned head of an Oriental, as equivalent to *Hassan Chawush*, the latter title being the Turkish for herald or pursuivant. This Hassan was perhaps the envoy who concluded the alliance between Paul IV and the Sultan in 1556, the date of the medal. The article includes further identifications and biographical notes regarding Pastorino's sitters.

ST. MARY BOURNE, HAMPSHIRE. —A Norman Font. —A fine Norman font of the twelfth century at St. Mary Bourne is described and illustrated by Ethel Mabey in *Reliq.* XII, 1906, pp. 279-281 (5 figs.). Among the decorations are doves drinking from a vase, vine branches with grapes, a sheaf of wheat, and an Anglo-Norman arcade. TISBURY. — A Mediaeval Grange. — At Place Farm, Tisbury, Wiltshire, is still to be seen an excellent example of a mediaeval farm, once the property of the Abbey of Shaftesbury. The gateways are but little changed since the fifteenth century. The house and stables have been adapted to modern conditions, but the great tithe barn has been scarcely altered save by adding four doorways. (E. Towry White, *Reliq.* XIII, 1907, pp. 5759; 3 figs.) YORK. — Romano-British Christian Burial. —In *Reliq.* XII, 1906, pp. 207-208 (fig.), is reprinted from the *Annual Report of the Council of the Yorkshire Philosophical Society for* 1901 an account of the discovery in 1901 at York of a Roman stone coffin, containing the bones of a young woman who had been buried with her ornaments. Among these was a bone slip, cut out so as to leave the letters (sor)O(r) AVE VIVAS IN DEO. The inscription proves that the girl was a Christian. The stone coffin was uninscribed and very rough. AFRICA CARTHAGE. — A Christian Cemetery. — At a place called Mcidfa, near Carthage, a Christian cemetery has been excavated by Father Delattre, whose report appears in *C. R. Acad. lnsc.* 1906, pp. 422-431. Nearly eighteen hundred epitaphs, chiefly fragmentary, have been found already, many of early date, and some engraved on the reverse of pagan *tituli.* Among the few sarcophagi is one of a child which bears a relief representing Erotes, one of whom is nearly concealed by a huge mask representing Silenus. In one inscription the words *eripuit pestis* may well refer to the great pestilence of 252 A.d. A. Heron De Villefosse, in presenting this report *(Ibid.* pp. 405-406), pointed out analogous representations, and commented on the pagan epitaph of *M. Yal(erius) Petao fS alae Gemellianae.* The letters IS perhaps stand for *immunis,* but it is very rare to find these privileged soldiers taken from auxiliary troops. *Ibid.* pp. 444-445, R. C agN at suggests that S stands for *sesquiplaris,* a soldier receiving one and one-half times the usual pay (Vegetius, TV, 7).

A Byzantine Seal. — In December, 1905, a Byzantine lead seal was discovered of the series belonging to the ex-prefect Paulus. One side presents a very complicated monogram of ©eord/t *BorjOti*; the other reads: + *HavXov* I *airoeirdpxwv-(B. Soc. Ant. Fr* 1906, p. 134.)

A Lead Seal of Bishop Fortunius. — A lead seal, recently found at Carthage, bears upon its two faces the inscriptions *Fortunio (pes* and *prima regio.* Fortunius was bishop of Carthage in the seventh century and took part in the council of 655 A.d. The words *prima regio* confirm the interpretation *regio sexta,* given to RG VI found on another seal of his, now lost. The *regiones* were divisions of the diocese, like those existing at Rome, and there were probably seven in Carthage as at Rome. Many of them are mentioned in the acts of councils and inscriptions, but hitherto no mention of the first region was known. (A. Heron De Villefosse, *C. R. Acad. Insc.* 1906, p 121.) HADRUMETUM. — The Christian Catacombs. — The report of the French exploration of the catacombs of Hadrumetum *(A.J.A.* 1906, pp. 123, 374) is continued by Abbe-Leynaud in *C. R. Acad. Insc.* 1906, pp. 298-303 (fig.). Numerous galleries have been opened containing about five hundred *loculi,* and yielding many fragmentary inscriptions painted or scratched on the limestone. Among other objects found is a small lamp with the image of a fish encircled by a palm branch. The most important discovery was a sarcophagus with a mosaic cover, bearing the inscription *T. E. D. qui et Evasius dor. in pace.* Two African saints bear this name. It is regarded by Father Delattre as the oldest sepulchral mosaic found in Africa. *Ibid.* pp. 433-481, A. Heron De Villefosse reports the discovery of a large and well-preserved gallery with branches and a light-well. A number of Greek and Latin inscriptions from lladrumetum are published by O. Marucchi in *N. Bull. Arch. Crist.* 1906, pp. 177-178.

LIBYA. — An Unusual Menas-Ampulla. — Among the discoveries made in 1905 by C. M. Kaufmaun on the site of the ancient sanctuary of St. Menas in the Libyan desert, as described by A. De Waal in *Rom. Quart.* 1906, pp. 82-86, is an ampulla with the usual figure of St. Menas between two camels on the front, while the reverse presents a female figure bound to a cross-shaped post, nude to the waist, with a bull on either side and a lion and a bear crouching at her feet. Wilpert, *ibid.* pp. 86—92. interprets the figure as St. Thecla bound to a stake, as was usual when Christians were condemned *ad hestias,* and surrounded by the beasts which, according to her *Acta,* when summoned by her persecutor, Alexander, to devour her, fawned upon her instead. SBEITLA. — A Lamp Manufactory. — M. Denian, of Sidi-NacemAllah, in the region of Sbeitla in Tunis, has found on his property the debris of a lamp-maker's establishment, consisting of fragments, Christian lamps in terra-cotta, and moulds for making them. The lamps found are nearly all defective and probably purposely cast aside. The moulds are in plaster, and of two types, for the upper and lower sides of the lamps. The subjects are not unusual. M. Denian is preparing a monograph on his discovery. (P. Monceaux, *B. Soc. Ant. Fr.* 1906, pp. 122-123.) UPPENNA. — Christian Inscriptions. — On the site of the Christian basilica four kilometers south of Uppenna, were found the following four inscriptions, published in *N. Bull. Arch. Crist.* 1906, pp. 175-178, by O. Marucchi. The first is in mosaic and surrounds a cross with a lamb and palm on either side: *Hec sunt nomina martirum Petru8 Pauhm Satttrninus presbyter* ! *idem* (a number of names follow) *passi die nonas Augustas Depositi VI idus Nobembres Gloria in escelsis Deo et in tera pacs omnibus.* It is a record of relics rather than of the actual burial of martyrs. The second is fragmentary, inscribed on a wall:... *tatis suae beatissimis, martyribus.* The third and fourth refer to local bishops: *Honorius episcopus ririt annis XC Deposifus sub die VI-II icus Augustas,* and *Iialeriolus episeo pus vixit annis LXXXII Depositus die VIII Kal Octobres.* Three other epitaphs of less interest are recorded. UNITED STATES CASSONE PANELS IN AMERICAN COLLECTIONS. — The publication of cassone panels by William Rankin and F. J. Mathek begins in *Burl. Mag.* IX, 1900, pp. 288-291, with a catalogue of the panels and salvers to be published, and a description and reproduction of the best of the series, the Botticelli "Lucretia," formerly in the Ashburnhain collection, now in the possession of Mrs. Gardner in Boston. The action takes place in an open piazza surrounded by colonades adorned with statues and sculptured scenes. In the colonade to the left, Tarquin threatens Lucretia with his sword, and in that to the right she is seen staggeriug forth from the palace. The central scene shows her lying on a couch in death, with Koman warriors swearing vengeance around her. Mather dates the panel about 1500. *Ibiil.* X, pp. 07-08, the two panels by Pesellino in Mrs. Gardner's collection are the subject of a description based on AVeisbach's "Francesco Pesellino und die Kornantik der Renaissance." The panels depict the six Petrarchan "Triumphs"; Love, Charity, and Death on one, and Fame, Time, and Eternity on the other. There is reason to suppose that they are copies of actual pageants. The panels date from slightly before 1450. BOSTON. — Acquisitions of the Museum of Fine Arts. — The Boston museum has recently acquired from the Ross Gift the "Apotheosis of a Poet" by G. B. Tiepolo and the "Portrait of Arnauld d'Andilly" by Philippe de Champaigne. *(B. Mus. F. A.* IV, 1906, pp. 35-36; 2 figs.) CAMBRIDGE. — Acquisitions of the Oermanic Museum. — The King of Saxony has presented to the Germanic Museum a cast of the pulpit in the church of Wechselburg, Saxony, an important example of German Romanesque work of the early thirteenth century. The Museum has bought casts of the large Crucifixion in the same church, and of the portal of the Cathedral of Augsburg. With these large pieces in place the available space in the Museum is entirely occupied, and the need of a new building becomes increasingly apparent. *(Boston Evening Transcript,* Dec. 29, 1906.) NEW YORK. — THE METROPOLITAN MUSEUM. — Recent Additions.— Among the paintings recently acquired by gift or purchase are the following: a "Portrait of a Man" by Hans Holbein (Fig. 12), dated 1517, and possibly representing the painter's brother, Ambrose (B. *Metr. Mus.* I, 1906, pp. 152-15;?; fig.; *Burl. Mag.* X, 190G, pp. 52-53; plate); a "Neptune" by Van Dyck, formerly ascribed to Rubens *(B. Metr. Mus.* I, 1906, p. 153). In *B. Metr. Mus.* I. 1906, pp. 164-165, R. E. F. describes: (1) A Madonna and Child, attributed to Pisanello, but more probably an example of the early Milanese school, and possibly not purely Italian: (2) A Madonna and Child, enthroned between St. John the Baptist and St..John the Evangelist by Francesco Pesellino. It shows strongly the influence of Masaccio. (3) A small picture by Giovanni di Paolo, representing blessed souls received by angels in Paradise. It is an exceedingly good example of his work, and like the similar painting in Siena, shows the influence of Fra Angelico. *Ibid.* pp. 162-103, R. E. F. discusses briefly the value of Rembrandt's Sybil, recently loaned to the Museum by Mr. Theodore Davis. A number of drawings of the Italian. Flemish, Dutch, French, and English Schools have been recently added. Noteworthy are a draw ing by Rembrandt, representing Tobias and Sara delivered from Asmodeus, and one by Jacob Jordaens, of which the subject is not clear, though it may be the Sacrifice

Figure 12. — Portrait By Holbein, Metropolitan Museum, New York. at Lystra. Both are characteristic works. *(Ibid.* pp. 160-I62; 2 figs.) A recent purchase includes four excellent specimens of gargoyles of the French Gothic period. Two are lions, one a variety of griffin, and the fourth seems to be a combination of ape and devil. (M. McL, *Ibid.* 1906, pp. 165-166.)

A Collection of Carved Wood-work. — The Metropolitan Museum has recently placed on exhibition an important collection of carved woodwork and furniture, divided into four groups, Gothic, Renaissance, German Renaissance, and French eighteenth century. The Gothic group includes buffets, chest fronts, a painted reredos and Pieta, a double choir-stall, and ten statues on pedestals and brackets. These latter works are of special interest from their beauty and excellent preservation. In the Renaissance groups are French cabinets and chests, two Italian marriage coffers, and two large German cabinets. The later French group includes eight pilaster fronts from designs by Salembier, formerly in the Lelong Collection, the gift of Mr. J. P. Morgan, and three large Louis XIV panels of French oak, formerly in the Bibliotheque Royal. *(B. Melr. Mus.* I, 1906, pp. 127-128.)

Flemish Tapestries. — In *B. Metr. Mus.* I, 1906, pp. 140-142 (fig.), C. H. describes briefly five large Brussels tapestries of the middle of the seventeenth century with scenes from the story of Antony and Cleopatra. It is known that Rubens furnished cartoons for tapestries on this subject, and these pieces bear evidence of being from his designs. They were formerly in the possession of the Barberini family, and later belonged to King Ludwig of Bavaria. With other tapestries they were bequeathed to the Museum in 1892 by Mrs. Elizabeth U. Coles in memory of her son.

Persian Enamelled Panels. — Three fine panels consisting of 112 enamelled tiles have been bought by the Metropolitan Museum. They were made under Shah Abbas I (1587-1628). They represent scenes of festivity in the open air, and in two of them Persian ladies receive men in European dress. While the style shows Chinese influence, the sentiment is clearly Persian, and drawn from the court life of the period. (B. B., *B. Metr. Mus.*

I, 1906, pp. 139-140; 3 figs.)
PHILADELPHIA. — Proposal for a Museum of Art. — Three wellknown collectors of Philadelphia, J. C. Johnson, W. M. Elkins, and P. A. B. Widener, have offered their galleries to the city on condition that a museum be built to receive them. All three collections contain works both of the Renaissance and of modern schools, the Johnson paintings being well known, and the Widener collection important for its Renaissance sculptures. *(Chron. Art3, 'l90C, p. 327.)*

New Pictures in the Johnson Collection. — Recent additions to the Johnson collection are described by F. J. Mather in *Burl, ag.* IX, 1906, pp. 351—363. The earliest is an " Annunciation " in the style of Taddeo Gaddi which Mather attributes to Michelino. Another attribution is that of an unfinished panel of " Adam and Eve with their two Sons," to Fra Bartolommeo. 'Siena is represented by a predella with a Pieta and saints, by Bartolo di Fredi. A "Madonna and Child" by Vincenzo Foppa and a "Madonna with Donors" by Andrea Salario are already known. The best of the Italian additions to the collection is a signed "Madonna and Child" by Giovanni Bellini with the emaciated hands and artless attitude of the Child which is seen in Dr. Frizzoni's Madonna. The picture is much repainted. Of the Spanish School there is a dramatic " Crucifixion " by El Greco and two companion portraits, by Goya, long separated, of the tragedian Maiquez and his wife. Among the northern schools noteworthy additions are an unidentified " Adoration of the Magi," the "Haybarn " (a peasant cutting hay in a barn, with his wife and boy near by), remarkable for its technical excellence in view of the fact that the signature ' G. Metsu, 1648," shows that Metsu was only eighteen years old when he painted the picture; a "Crucifixion" attributed to Bartholomaeus Bruyn, and a male portrait attributed to Holbein the Younger. The well-known panel of Hubert Van Eyck, " St. Francis receiving the Stigmata," is in this article reproduced for the first time in its original form, a recent cleaning having revealed a later addition above. Roger Fry *ibid.* p. 363) adds a note on the Bellini Madonna, dating it about 1460, and pointing out that the flaking off of paint shows that the sky had been altered by the painter to suit the temper of the picture, from a pure blue to a dull indigo and orange-gray. II. P. Horne *(ibid.* pp. 425-4:20) calls attention to an item in the deed of dissolution of partnership between Fra Bartolommeo and Mariotto Albertinelli, dated Jan. 5, 1512, which mentions "a little picture sketched out by the hand of Fra Bartolommeo in which is an Adam seated and an Eve standing upright, nearly half a braccio in height." This agrees with the height (12 in.) of Mr. Johnson's " Adam and Eve" (a braccio being about 23 in.), determines the date, and confirms Mather's attribution. C. IlrcKETTS *(ibid.* p. 420) believes that the " St. Francis receiving the Stigmata" is a copy of the Hubert Van Eyck in Turin, and that the Holbein portrait is a modern forgery. These criticisms are answered by Mather, *ibid.* X, 1906, p. 138.

AMERICAN ARCHAEOLOGY THE INTERNATIONAL CONGRESS OF AMERICANISTS.—

The fifteenth Congress of Americanists was held Sept. 10-15, 1900, at Quebec. Canada, under the Presidency of Dr. Robert Bell.

Among the papers presented were the following, dealing with the archaeological aspects of research in America. The numbers given correspond to those prefixed to the papers in the programme of the meetings.— (1) Rev. A. E. Jones, S.J., Archiviste, Montreal: 'The Topography of Huronia. Identification of the Sites of Huron and Petun Villages, at the Time of the Recollet and Jesuit Missions, 1615-50.' The author has made a study in detail of the topography of the Lake Simcoe Georgian Bay territory of Ontario, drained by the Severn River. — (12) Franz Boas, New York: 'Ethnological Problems in Canada.' As an aid to their solution "archaeological investigation is required in order to determine the ancient distribution of types of culture." Such inquiry is especially uecessary in the extreme northwestern Arctic region for fixing the influence of the Indian and Asiatic cultures upon the western Eskimo. There is need also of a study of the prehistoric culture of the northern part of the north Pacific coast, and an investigation of the limits in this direction of the distribution of pottery. — (Hi) Walter Hough, Washington: 'Distribution of the Ancient Population on the Gila-Salt River in NewMexico and Arizona.' The paper discusses the pueblos, caves, and cliffdwellings of the southern slope of the Pueblo Region, so-called, with special reference to the work of the Gates Expedition under the auspices of the United States National Museum at Washington. — (52) Leopoi.do Batres. City of Mexico: 'Excavations in Teotihuacan.' The paper was an account of the excavations undertaken in 1905 by the author under the initiative of General President Diaz. The work upon the " Pyramid of the Sun," and the stairways, walls, sculptures, and human remains from this pyramid were described. — (88) Edward Selkr, Berlin: 'Two Specimens from the Collection Sologuren, Oaxaca.' — (69) 'On the Monuments of Huilocintla, Vera Cruz.'—(70) 'Studies in the Ruins of Yucatan.'—(73) 'On the Reliefs of the Temple of Tepoztlan in the State of Morelos.' Illustrations of landscapes, ruins, and reliefs, including some representations of acts of self-tor-ture, were shown by Dr. Seler, who was on his way to Mexico to pursue further explorations. — (49) VV. Lehmann, Berlin: 'Die Altmexicanischen Mosaiken des Berliner Museums fur Volkerkunde.' Read by Dr. Seler. — (56) Miss A. Breton, England: 'A Note on Xochicalco.' — (62) 'The Wall-Paintings at Chichen Itza.' The papers were read and the reproductions of the paintings were exhibited by Dr. A. M. Tozzer of Harvard University. These reproductions, works both of skill and understanding, are now the property of the Peabody Museum at Cambridge, Mass. — (13) Alfred M. Tozzer, Cambridge: 'Some Survivals of Ancient Forms of Culture among the Mayas of Yucatan and the Lacandones of Chiapas.' The modern beliefs and customs in connection with certain vases, parts of vases, and figures, are clearly survivals of those mentioned by early travellers, and shed light on the part played by such objects in prehistoric times. — (51) George B. Gordon, Philadelphia: 'The Serpent Motive in the Ancient Art of Central America and of India.'—(36) George Grant Maccurdv, New Haven: 'The Armadillo in the Ancient Art of Chiriqui.' Both of these papers treated of the conventionalization of the representation of a typical animal; the progress from the realistic and obvious to the simplified and non-suggestive forms was in general assumed. — (68) Le6n Lejeal and Eric Boman, Paris: 'La Question Calchaquie.' Read by the former, the delegate of the French Government to the Congress. This paper was a long discussion leading to the conclusion that the common assumption of the independent origin of the Argentine Calchaqui culture is less likely to be true than the theory that this civilization is closely connected with that known as the " Ando-Peruvian." — (10) AlPhonse Gagnon, Quebec: 'Origine de la Civilisation de l'Amerique Precolombienne.' The author saw influences at work in this civilization which might be referred to India or to Chaldaea.— (17) Ales Hudlicka, Washington: 'A Resume, from the Standpoint of Physical Anthropology of the Various Skeletal Remains that suggest, or are claimed to represent an Early Man on this Continent.' A clear exposition, but quite negative in its presentation of any conclusive evidence of man's presence in America in glacial or pre-glacial times. The skull discovered in the autumn of 1906 in the Valley of the Missouri River, which is claimed to represent a very early stage in cranial development, was of course unknown to Dr. Hrdlicka. (45) George L. Konz, New York: 'On the Heber P. Bishop Collection of Jade and its Catalogue.' The paper (read by Dr. C. Peabody) also considered the question of the identity of jade and "chalchihuitl" in the Pueblo, Mexican, and Central American provinces. Among the publications distributed at the Congress special mention may be made of the Archaeological Report of Ontario for 1905 compiled under the direction of Air. David Boyle of the Provincial Museum at Toronto. It contains a noteworthy article by Mr. W. J. Wurtemberg on 'Bone and Horn Harpoon Heads of the Ontario Indians.' These furnish interesting comparisons with the well-known reindeer and stag-horn harpoons of the late palaeolithic and transitional periods in European prehistoric archaeology. The next meeting of the Congress is expected to take place in Vienna in 1908. (charles Peabody.) DOUGLAS COUNT'S", NEBRASKA. — Remains of Primitive Man. — Excavations by Mr. R. F. Gilder in a burial mound on a hill rising above the Missouri River in Douglas County, Nebraska, have brought to light very early human remains. The discoveries are discussed in *Putnam's Monthly,* January, 1907, by R. F. Gilder (pp. 407-409), II. B. Ward (pp. 410-413), and E. H. Barbour (pp. 413-415, 502-503). Before Nov. 17, 1906, portions of nine crania and skeletons were discovered, five being at a lower level and four at a higher. The cross-section of the mound shows: (1) vegetable mould, depth 6 in.; (2) loess, depth 3 ft. 6 in. in the middle; (3) earth and ashes, depth 4 ft. 5 in.; (4) loess, being the formation of the top of the hill on which the mound stands. The more primitive remains were found in this stratum. Professor Ward says: "All in all the skeletons of the lower layer show many points in common with primitive types of the human race.... The skulls of the upper layer are very likely from Indian tribes... but they carmot, without undue violence, be thrown into the same group with those of the lower layer." At the end of his postscript (p. 503) Professor Barbour writes: "there need be no hesitancy in pronouncing this Glacial or Loess Man." This discovery is also discussed in the *Century Magazine,* January, 1907, pp. 371-375, by H. F. Osborn. The type of cranium of the "Nebraska Man" is more recent by far than that of Neanderthal or possibly than that of the early neolithic man in Europe. It is certainly very primitive however, and "tends to increase, rather than diminish the probability of the early advent of Man in America." See also *Am. Anthr.*, VIII, 1906, p. 734, *Science,* Oct. 27, 1906, the *Omaha World-Herald,* Oct. 21, 1906. Professor Ward also presented the subject to the American Anthropological Association at its meeting in New York, Dec. 31, 1906.

GREEN LAKE, MINNESOTA. — Excavations of a Mound. —In *Rec. Past,* V, 1906, pp. 271-281 (12 figs.), Horatio Gates describes a group of mounds near Green Lake, Minnesota, and the excavation of one of them. In the centre were remains of a skeleton. The body had apparently been laid due north and south, with the face to the east. Some remains of stone weapons and fragments of coarse pottery were also found. JALAPA, VERA CRUZ.—An Ancient Megalith. — In *Am. Anthr.* VIII, 1906, pp. 633-639 (plate), J. Walter Fewkes describes an ancient megalith now in Jalapa, Vera Cruz, Mexico, but perhaps originally from Tuxpan. On it are carved two figures, one representing a priest performing a rite of blood-letting from the tongue, the other a zoomorphic personation of a supernatural being. Both represent the same god, for the priest is impersonating the great god, Quetzalcoatl. MONTEZUMA, ILLINOIS. — The McEvers Mounds. —In *Rec. Past,* VI, 1907, pp. 21-27 (2 figs.), Clara Kern Bayliss describes the excavation of eight mounds near Montezuma, Pike County, Illinois. No. 1 was 24 ft. high and 130 ft. in diameter. In Nos. 1 and 5 were found remains of large wooden cists 15 ft. by 7 ft. by 20 in. and 14 ft. by 12 ft. by 2J ft. respectively, built on the original surface of the ground. On a portion of the floor of the cist of No. 1 lay 1259 leaf-shaped blades of chert,-and upon this a burial had been made. Other promiscuous burials in the same cist were accompanied by numerous bone perforators. The cist in No. 5 contained few objects. In all the mounds human remains were found, sometimes accompanied by shells, bone implements, and potsherds. Secondary burial is suggested as accounting for the bundled and disconnected remains found in these mounds. (See also *A.J.A.* IX, 1905, p. 388.) PAJARITO PARK.— The Cliffdwellings. — The ruins in Pajarito Park (see *supra,* pp. 42-46) are also briefly described, and their growing accessibility emphasized by H. II. Harris in *Rec. Past,* V, 1906, pp. 291-295 (4 figs.). ROSS COUNTY, OHIO. — A Prehistoric Village. — In *Rec. Past,* V, 1906, pp. 303-313, 342-352 (18 figs.), William C. Mills describes in detail the results of three campaigns in the Baum Prehistoric Village, near Bourneville, Ross County, Ohio. The excavations brought to light 49 tepee sites, 127 burials, and 234 subterranean storehouses, which were also used as refuse pits. The burials of each family were made close to its tepee, and in general the bodies were simply placed in open graves with their implements and ornaments. The people of the village were agricultural, but secured the meat by hunting, as was shown by the great number of bones from deer and wild turkeys. The culture is essentially identical with that found at Gartner Village on the Scioto, and at Fort Ancient on the Miami. The presence of copper, ocean shells, and mica shows the existence of inter-tribal trade. Nothing was found showing acquaintance with Europeans. *Abh.:* Abhandlungen. *Allg. Ztg.:* Miiichener Allgemeine Zeitung. *Alt. Or.:* Der alte Orient. *Am. Ant.:* American Antiquarian. *Am. Anthr.:* American Anthropologist. *Am. Archit.:* American Architect. *A.J.A.:* American Journal of Archaeology. *A. J. Num.:* American Journal of Numismatics. *A. J. Sem. Lang.:* American Journal of Semitic Languages and Literature. *Ami d. Mon.:* Ami des Monuments. *Ant. Denk.:* Antike Denkmaler. *Am. Schw. Alt.:* Anzeiger fur Schweizerische Altertumskunde. *Arch. Ael.:* Archaeologia Aeliana. *Arch. Am.* :Archaologischer Anzeiger. *Arch. Bee.:* Architectural Record. *Arch. Bel.:* Archiv fur Religionswissenschaft. *Arch. Miss.:* Archives de Missions Scientifiques et Litteraires. *Arch. Stor. Art.:* Archivio Storico dell Arte. *Arch. Stor. Lomb.:* Archivio Storico Lombardo. *Arch. Stor. Nap.:* Archivio Storico Provincie Napolitane. *Arch. Stor. Patr.:* Archivio della r. societa romana di storia patria. *Athen.:* Athenaeum (of London). *Ath. Mitt.:* Mitteilungen d. k. d. Archaeol. Instituts, Athen. Abt. *Beitr. Assyr.:* Beitrage zur Assyriologie. *Birl. Akad.:* Preussische Akademie der Wissenschaften zu Berlin. *Berl. Phil. W.:* Berliner Philologische Wochenschrift. *Bibl. Stud.:* Riblische Studien. *Bibl. World:* The Biblical World. *B. Ac. Hist.:* Boletin de la real Academiade la Historia. *Boll. Art.:* Bolletino d' Arte. *Boll. Num.:* Bollettino di Numismatica. *Bonn. Jb.:* Bonner Jahrblicher: Jahrbilcher des Vereins von Altertumsfreunden im Rheinlande. *B.S. A.:* Annual of the British School at Athens. *B.S.B.:* Papers of the British School at Rome. *B. Arch. M.:* Bulletin Archeol. du Ministere. *B. Arch. C. T.:* Bulletin Archeologique du Comite des Travaux hist, et scient. *B.C.H.:* Bulletin de Correspondance Hellenique. *B. Hist. Lyon:* Bulletin historique du Diocese de Lyon. *B. Inst. Eg.:* Bulletin de l'Institut Egyptien (Cairo). *B. Metr. Mus.:* Bulletin of the Metropolitan Museum of Art, New York. *B. Mus. F. A.:* Museum of Fine Arts Bulletin, Boston. *B. Num.:* Bulletin de Numismatique. *B. Soc. Ant. Fi::* Bulletin de la Society des Antiquaires de France. *B. Soc. Anth.:* Bulletin de la Soci£t£ d'Anthropologic de Paris. *B. Soc. Yonne:* Bulletin de la Soci£t6 des Sciences historiques et naturelles de l'Yonne. *B. Mon.:* Bulletin Monumental. *B. Arch. Stor. Dal.:* Bullettino di Archeologia e Storia Dalmata. *B. Com. Bom.:* Bullettino d. Commissione Archeologica Comunale di Roma. *B. Arch. Crist.:* Bullettino di Archeologia Cristiana. *B. Pal. It.:* Bullettino di Paletnologia Italiana. *Burl. (Inz.:* Burlington Gazette. *Burl. Mag.:* Burlington Magazine. *Byz. Z.:* Byzantinische Zeitsehrift. *Chron. Arts:* Chronique des Arts. *Cl. Phil.:* Classical Philology. *Cl. B.:* Classical Review. *C. B. Acad. Insc.:* Comptes Rendus de l'Acadmie des Inscriptions et Belles-Lettres. *C.I.A.:* Corpus Inscriptionum Atticarum. *C. I.G.:* Corpus Inscriptionum Graecarum. *C.I.L.:* Corpus Inscriptionum Latinarum. *C.I.S.:* Corpus Inscriptionum Semiticarum. 'E0. 'Apx-'*Etrnupls* 'a/xhoxo7oct). *Eph. Ep.:* Ephenieris Epigraphica. *Eph. Sem. Ep.:* Ephenieris fiir Semitische Epigraphik. *Exp. Times:* The Expository Times. *Fundh. Schwab.:* Fundberichte aus Schwaben, herausgegeben vom wiirttembergischen anthropologischen Verein. *Gaz. B.-A.:* Gazette des Beaux-Arts. *G. D.I.:* Sammlung der griechischen Dialekt-Inschriften. *I.G.:* Inscriptiones Graecae (for contents and numbering of volumes, cf. *A.J.A.* IX, 1905, pp. 90-97). *I.G.A.:* Inscriptiones Graecae Antiquissimae, ed. Roehl. *I.G.Arg.:* Inscriptiones Graecae Argolidis. /. *G. Ins.:* Inscriptiones Graecarum Insularum. *I. G. Sept.:* Inscriptiones Graeciae Septentrionalis. /. *G. Sic. It.:* Inscriptiones Graecae Siciliae et Italiae. *Jb. Arch. I.:* Jahrbuch d. k. d. Archaol. Instituts. *Jb. Kl. AIL:* Neue Jahrbiicher fiir das klassische Altertum, Geschichte und deutsche Litteratur und fiir Piidagogik. *Jb. Kunsth. Samm.:* Jahrbuch der Kunsthistorischen Sammlungen des allerhochsten Kaiserhauses. *Jb. Phil. Pad.* : Neue Jahrbiicher fiir Philologie und Padagogik (Fleckeisen's Jahrbiicher). *Jb. Preuss. Kunsts.:* Jahrbuch d. k. Preuss. Kunstsaniiulungen. *Jh. Oesl. Arch. I.:* Jahreshefte des oesterreichischen Archiiologischen Instituts. *J. Asiat.:* Journal Asiatique. *J.A.O.S.:* Journal of American Oriental Society. *J. Anth. Inst.:* Journal of the Anthropological Institute of Great Britain and Ireland. *J. B.*

Archaeol.: 140 Journal of the British Archaeological Association../. *B. Archil.:* Journal of the Royal Institute of British Architects. *J. Bibl. Lit.:* Journal of Biblical Literature. *J.H.S.:* Journal of Hellenic Studies. *J. Int. Arch. Num.:* Aiffnjs 'E/wpls Tjjs nfuanartufis Apxuooylas, Journal international d'archeologie numismatique (Athens). *J. T. Vict. Inst.:* Journal of Transactions of the Victoria Institute. *Kb. Gesammtcer.:* Korrespondenzblatt des Gesammtvereins der deutschen Geschichts-and Altertumsvereine. *Kb. Wd. Z. Ges. K.:* Korrespondenzblatt der Westdeutschen Zeitschrift fur Geschichte und Kunst. *Klio:* Klio: Beitrage zur alten Geschichte. *Kunstehr.:* Kunstchronik. *Mel. Arch. Hist.:* Melanges d'Arch6ologie et d'Histoire (of French School in Rome). *Mil. Fae. Or.:* Mélanges de la Faculte Orientale, Beirut. *M. Acc. Modena:* Memorie della Regia Accademia di scienze, lettere ed arti in Modena.-V. *Inst. Gen.:* Memoires de l'Institut Genevois. 31. *Soc. Ant. Fr.:* Mmoires de la Socie des Antiquaires de France. *Mitt. Anth. Gen.:* Mitteilungen der anthropologischen Gesellschaft in Wien. *Mitt. 0.-Comm.:* Mitteilungen der koniglich-kaiserlichen Central-Commission fiir Erforschung und Erhaltung der Kunst-und historischen Denkmale. *Mitt. Or. Ges.:* Mitteilungen der deutschen Orient-Gesellschaft. *Mitt. Pal. V.:* Mitteilungen und Nachrichten des deutschen Palestina Vereins. *Mitt. Nassau:* Mitteilungen des Vereins fiir nassauische Altertumskunde und Geschichtsforsehung. *Mitt. Vorderas. Ges.:* Mitteilungen der vorderasiatischen Gesellschaft. *Mon. Ant.:* Monumenti Antichi (of Accad. d. Lincei). *Mon. Piot:* Monuments et Mémoires pub. par l'Acad. des Inscriptions, etc. (Fondation Piot). *Mun. Akad.:* Koniglich Bayerische Akademie der Wissenschaften, Miinchen. *N. D. Alt.:* Nachrichten iiber deutsche Altertumsfunde. *Not. Scav.:* Notizie degli Scavi di Antichita. *Num. Chron.:* Numismatic Chronicle. *Num. Z.:* Numismatische Zeitschrift. *N. Areh. Ven.:* Nuovo Archivio Veneto. *N. Bull. Arch. Crist.:* Nuova Bullettino di Archeologia cristiana. *Or. Lit.:* i trientalistische Literal urzeitung. *Or. Lux:* Ex. Oriente Lux. *Pal. Ex. Fund:* Quarterly Statement of the Palestine Exploration Fund. ΠpaκTi/d: llpavTiKd rijs iv A0j)rais dpxatooyiKijs iraiptlas. *Proc. SoC. Ant.:* Proceedings of the Society of Antiquaries. *Ross, d' Arte:* Rassegna d' Arte. *Bec. Past:* Records of the Past. *ll. Tr. Eg. Assyr.:* Recneil de travaux relatifs a la philologie et a l'archeologie egyptiennes et assyriennes. *Reliq.:* Reliquary and Illustrated Archaeologist. *Rend. Acc. Lincei:* Rendiconti d. r. Accademia dei Lincei. *Rep. f. K.:* Repertorium fiir Kunstwisscnschaft. *R. Assoc. Bare.:* Revista de la Associacion artisticoarqueologico Barcelonesa. *R. Arch. Hibl. Mus.:* Revista di Archivos, Bibliotecas, y Museos. *R. Areh.:* Revue Archeologique. *R. Art Ane. Mod.:* Revue de l'Art ancien et moderne. *R. Art Chret.:* Revue de l'Art Chretien. *R. Beige Num.:* Revue Beige de Numismatique. *R. Hibl.:* Revue Biblique Internationale. *R. Hp.:* Revue Epigraphique. *ll. Et.Anc.:* Revue des Etudes Anciennes. *R. £t. Gr.:* Revue des Etudes Grecques. *R. £t. J.:* Revue dea Etudes Juives. *R. Hist. Bel.:* Revue de l'Histoire des Religions. *R. Num.:* Revue Numismatique. *R. Or. iMt.:* Revue de l'Orient Latin. *R. Sent.:* Revue Se'mitique. *R. Suisse Num.:* Revue Suisse de Numismatique. *Rh. Mus.:* Rheinisches Museum fiir Philologie, Neue Folge. *R. Abruzz.:* Rivista Abruzzesa di Scienze, Lettere ed Arte. *R. Ital. Num.:* Rivista Italiana Numismatic. *R. Stor. Ant.:* Rivista di Storia Antica. *R. Stor. Calabr.:* Rivista StoricaCalabrese. *R. Stor. Ital.:* Rivista Storica Italiana. *Rum.-Germ. Forsch.:* Bericht iiber die Fortschritte der Romisch-Germanischen Forschung. *Rom. Mitt.:* Mitteilungen d. k. d. Archaol. Institute, Rom. Abt. *Rom. Quart.:* Romische Quartalschrift fiir christliche Altertumskunde und ftir Kirchengeschichte. *Saehs. Ges.:* Sachsische Gesellschaft (Leipsic). *Sitzb.:* Sitzungsberichte. *S. Bibl. Arch.:* Society of Biblical Archaeology, Proceedings. *Voss. Ztg.:* Vossische Zeitung. *W. Icl. Phil.:* Wochenschrift fiir klassische Philologie. *Z. D. Pal. V.:* Zeitschrift des Deutschen Palestina Vereins. *Z. Aeg. Sp. Alt.:* Zeitschrift fiir Aegyptische Sprache und Altertumskunde. *Z. Alttcst. Wiss.:* Zeitschrift fiir alttestamentliche Wissenschaft. *Z. Assur.:* Zeitschrift fiir Assyriologie. *Z. Bild. K.:* Zeitschrift fiir Bildende Kunst. *Z. Ethn.:* Zeitschrift fiir Ethnologie. *Z. Morgenl.:* Wiener Zeitschrift fiir die Kunde des Morgenlands. *Z. Morgenl. Ges.:* Zeitschrift der deutschen Morgenlandschen Gesellschaft. *Z. Miin. Alt.-:* Zeitschrift des Miinchener Alterthumsvereins. *Z. Num.:* Zeitschrift fiir Numismatik.

Institute of America

THE "ARMING OF AN EPHEBE" ON A PRINCETON VASE

Notwithstanding the apparent antiquity of the Athenian *efTf3eia,* descriptions of it or allusions to it in Greek writers, or illustrations of it on Greek monuments rarely antedate the middle of the fourth century. This is especially true of the literary sources. Our present guide with reference to the ephebic discipline is the lately recovered *Constitution of Athens* of Aristotle, written between 328 and 325 B.C. The very word *ef)T)/3o;,* if we are to believe Girard's article on *ephebi* in *D. S., Diet. Ant.,* is not used by writers of the fifth century, the concept apparently being expressed by *veanaroi* in Thucydides and Aristophanes.

The monumental material is also almost entirely later than the fifth century. Our earliest inscriptions referring to ephebes fall in the latter half of the fourth century, unless we include in that category the epitaph on the stele of Dexileos, the twentyyear-old knight who fell at Corinth in. 394 B.C. There are, however, two vases of the black-figured and red-figured style respectively, which form exceptions to the generally late date of ephebic monuments and help to illustrate the institution as it was in the fifth, and even the sixth century. The first is an early black-figured Attic amphora, and the second a redfigured vase in the Hermitage at St. Petersburg, both described and reproduced by Conze. The black-figured amphora represents a young man facing to the right, clad in crested helmet and himation, with his shield behind him, resting against his Ed. Sandys; Introd. p. xxxix. *Ann. d. 1st.* 1808, pp. 264-207, pla. H and I.

legs. He is pouring a libation over an altar-fire in the presence of an old man who wears the long chiton and himation, and stands with right hand raised, grasping a sceptre in his left. Brunn and Conze saw in the scene an ephebe taking the oath in the sanctuary of Aglauros, the formula of which is preserved to us by Pollux and Stobaeus. The red-figured vase in St. Petersburg is reproduced in Girard's article (Fig. 2677). It should date, according to the description of it given by Conze, about 450 B.C. An ephebe, facing left, equipped with spear and shield, and draped with the himation, extends his right hand over an altar. An old man on the left of the altar holds out his right hand toward the youth in similar fashion, administering the oath. Behind the ephebe, to the right, stands a Victory holding his helmet. The old man, according to Girard, personifies the /sovxtj, before whom or whose representatives the oath was taken.

We have no literary evidence for the ephebic discipline in the period represented by these vases, but in the descriptions of later writers elements may doubtless be found which belonged to the epheby in its earliest stage. Aristotle's description occupies chapter 42 of the *Constitution of Athens*. We learn from this that the appearance of the ephebes before their respective *Snpdrai* was merely for the purpose of registration, and was attended with no ceremony. This was followed by the *hoKifiaaia,* or examination before the Council. After the ephebes had passed this test, their fathers, voting by tribes, chose three tribesmen over forty years of age, from whom the people selected a *aaxfrpoviGTrf; ipr)/3av* for each tribe, and then from the whole body of citizens there was elected the general director of all the ephebes or *KoafivTi*. Under the leadership of *aaxppoviarai* and *KoapvTrp* the youths made the rounds of the sanctuaries *(ra Upa irepirjXdov),* at which time they probably took the oath in the cave of Aglauros, and then departed for the Peiraeus, where they acted as garrisons, some in Munichia, Pollux, VIII. 105. Stobaeus, *Florileg.* 43, 48. Girard doubts the correctness of this interpretation, but gives no reasons, and the scene seems to me to be an earlier version of the oath-taking pictured on the red-figured vase.

Conze says chlamys, but the garment has the oblong shape of the himation and is draped like it, while it does not in the least suggest a chlamys. others in Acte. Their garrison duty, however, was in the nature of a training school rather than real military service, and this passage in the description is followed immediately by a list of their instructors and of their military exercises, and a description of their mode of living. The formal presentation of arms to the ephebes did not occur until their year in the Peiraeus was finished. At this time, "after having displayed," says Aristotle, "at a public assembly in the theatre, their prowess in arms, and after having received from the city a shield and a spear, they patrol the country and spend their time in the fortified posts. For two years they do guard duty, costumed in the chlamys and exempt from all public obligations." At the end of the second year, at the age of twenty, the ephebe took his place among the citizens.

We see from the above account that as the oath preceded the ephebe's first year, so the formal presentation of arms opened the second; consequently, the helmet, shield, and spear which form the accoutrement of the ephebes who are taking the oath in our two vase-paintings are either put in for artistic effect, or are the arms used by the ephebe in his lessons in warfare. We must remember, however, that a different arrangement may have existed a hundred or a hundred and fifty years before Aristotle. This suggests the query: how old is the epheby, and how much of Aristotle's description may be regarded as true for its earliest period?

The first question has never been definitely answered. Girard, who is disposed to be conservative, admits that it may have arisen before 500 B.C., and in fact there is no evidence against so early a date, while the military training of the youth, in some form or other, was obviously one of the first needs of an early state. The divinities invoked in the ephebic oath are of remote antiquity, and the black-figured amphora published by Conze may be regarded, it seems to me, as evidence of the existence of the ephebic discipline at least as early as 550 B.C. Now, of the customs recorded by Aristotle, the oath certainly belongs to the epheby in its earliest form. The other ceremony which seems to stand out in the description as an original element, is the public presentation of arms to the ephebe, with which his second year commenced. It is, in fact, the obvious culmination of the training of young soldiers for the state service, and is probably to be classed with the oath as one of the ceremonies which always attended the transformation of the Athenian youth into the Athenian citizen.

In the Princeton Art Museum there is an early black-figured Attic amphora (Fig. I), which is decorated with a scene portraying, in my opinion, this arming ceremony as it existed in the sixth century. On the front (plate X) we see an ephebe, facing right, with left shoulder draped in himation, standing between two old men dressed in long tunic and himation, each holding a spear, while the one facing the youth holds out the spear in his right hand toward him. To the right a youth, perhaps the ephebe's squire, reins the horse on which he is mounted into position before a third old man, who also holds a spear in his right hand, but rests it on the ground instead of presenting it. He, too, is dressed in long tunic and himation, and is accompanied by another old man in similar but somewhat plainer costume. The back of the vase (plate XI) is decorated with one of those representations of the "Departure of Warriors" which are very common on these amphorae. It is possible to see the ephebe and his squire in the two young men in the centre of the picture, but inasmuch as there is no necessary connection between the front and back of a vase, the complementary character of the departure scene is hardly to be insisted upon.

The inscriptions were blurred in the burning of the vase, and are illegible. They are scarcely of importance in determining the meaning of the scene, as in most representations of this kind on black-figured vases the names written beside

Figure 1.

The panel is 10 in. by 14 in. In the reproduction, hatchings denote purple. The early date of the vase is shown by its shape, and the absence of any indication of folds in the draperies. The spear in the hand of the old man behind the youth was intended by the artist to rest on the ground, but the lower part was blurred in burning. the characters are meaningless decorative imitations. Thus all the inscriptions on the "departure" or "arming" scenes given by Gerhard *(Amerlesene Vasenbilder,* IV, pis. cclxiv, cclxvii, cclxx) are meaningless. Apparently the only inscribed black-figured vase in the British Museum which contains one of these representations is No. 306 in the Catalogue of Vases, Vol. II, and the inscription is there described as an imitation. Even if our letters originally spelled intelligible names, we may gather what they would have been from the individual names in No. 1657 of Furtwangler's Catalogue of the Vases in the Antiquarium at Berlin: *'Aydvap,* At-t7ra? (?), *Xopp,* Eu/iaov, 3af0o? (written beside a horse). This is the only scene of the kind which I have been able to find, whose inscriptions spelled real names, and in this case they are chosen at random, and do not affect the interpretation.

The inscriptions out of the way, the scene is readily interpreted. We *have* the arming of an ephebe before us, which lacks entirely the domestic atmosphere ordinarily surrounding such scenes, and usually emphasized by the presence of women. The dog is scarcely an argument to the contrary, since a dog often appears on black-figured vases in situations where he is not only not needed, but scarcely desirable, as in mythological scenes, and occasionally in representations of a public character, *e.g.* a chariot race.

The ceremonial attitude of the figures, especially of the filleted old man to the right of the ephebe, indicates a public occasion, and I am therefore led to regard our painting as a representation of the public arming of the ephebes as it existed in the sixth century. The old man who hands the spear to the standing youth, represents the official delegated to perform the ceremony, the ephebe standing for the college as a whole.

The subject is almost unique in vases, but some paintings reproduced by Gerhard may be compared with it. One black-figured scene, representing three fully armed young hop Furtwilngler, *Vasensammlung im Antiquarium,* Noe. 1685 B, 1688 A, 1691 A, 1903.

Auserl. Vasenbilder, IV, pi. cclxii. lites, facing whom, to the left, stands an old man, with another old man to the right of the warriors, may refer, as Gerhard says, to the arming ceremony. Gerhard's No. cclxiii represents a filleted old man facing right, and addressing two hoplites, behind whom stand two ephebes, with a third behind the old man, all in the attitude of spectators or auditors. The age of these hoplites, however, is uncertain, their faces being concealed by their shields.

The mounted youth to the right in our scene is, perhaps, better interpreted as the squire of the ephebe. The old man to the right, it will be noted, is not handing his spear to the squire, but rests it on the ground. We have, then, an ephebe cavalryman receiving his two spears, with his squire mounted on and holding his horse. We are nowhere expressly told that the corps of ephebes included cavalry, but indirect evidence shows that it did, the horsemen apparently being recruited from young men of wealth. Aristophanes speaks of the good work done by the cavalry of the *veayraroi* at Solygia. The relief on the stele of Dexileos, who Girard thinks was still an ephebe when he fell, depicts him as a horseman. It is interesting to note that the knights who pass in review before the committee of the *fiovkr)* on the Orvieto cylix are all youths, and also that the petasos and chlamys, the characteristic dress of ephebes in the fourth century, is not only used on red-figured vases to costume Hermes, Theseus, travellers, and huntsmen, but regularly as the dress of horsemen. The ephebic uniform may thus have been generalized from the costume of the mounted members of the college.

The earliest monument which uses the petasos and chlamys distinctively as the ephebic costume seems to be the stele of Dexileos. The red-figured vase with the ephebe taking the oath drapes him in the himation, agreeing thus with the *Knights,* 604 ft. *l.c.* p. 630, note 182. *Arrk. Zeit.* 1880, pi. xv.

The existence of a corps of cavalry in the college seems to be shown by the references to training in horsemanship in the ephebic inscriptions. Cf. *C.I. A.* II, 478, fragm. a. 1. 20: "rijs *re iv Srois xal IrriKijt* dr(C7(crewj *ToKvtppovrltrtm"* fragm. c. 1. 8: "r flxXois *yvumaiav* «rol *Tv repl ri.* iinrucA *tpiXoTovlar,"* II, 479, 1. 29: "ts *Iv roll Ittikou lyvfj.naalat',"* 11,482, 1. 21: "ris *rur Xttuv yvurajlas."* sixth century monuments, like our vase, and Conze's Attic amphora, where the ephebe is given the himation. The youthful cavalrymen in the long procession of warriors on the black-figured Castellani cylix, now in the British Museum, have all the appearance of ephebes, and wear the himation without head-covering. Altogether, it seems that the distinctive use of the petasos and chlamys arose in the fourth century, and that the *i(fr)fie(a* was not distinguished by a particular costume in the earlier period.

Aristotle says: XaySo'in-e? *aairiha KaX hopv iraph* rr/s *iroXew.* No shield appears in our painting, inasmuch as the shield, at least in the fourth and fifth centuries, and doubtless earlier, was not a regular part of the cavalry equipment. This accounts for the use of *aa-rrtBe:* to distinguish hoplites from the cavalry.

It is to be regretted that the interpretation of so interesting a monument cannot be supported with literary evidence, showing the existence of the arming ceremony in the period of the early black-figured vases. In my opinion, however, the scene itself is ample proof. It is certainly the arming of a youth, and it differs vastly in its formal tone from the ordinary arming scenes, whose domestic character is felt at once. The vase should be classed, I think, with that other blackfigured amphora published by Conze, as well as the vase in Gerhard's *Auserl. Vasenbilder,* which was cited above, as illustrating, in their sixth century aspect, two elements, the ceremonies of the oath and of the arming, which reappear in the ephebic discipline of the fourth century.

C. R. Morey.

Princeton University. *Cat. Vases Brit. Mus.,* II, No. 426. Figured in *Mon. d. 1st.* IX, pis. 9-11.

Martin in *D. & S'., Diet. Ant.,* Ill, p. 766.

Institute of America

AN UNPUBLISHED AMPHORA AND AN EYE CYLIX SIGNED BY AMASIS, IN THE BOSTON MUSEUM plates XII, XIII

The unpublished amphora signed by Amasis, which was acquired by the Boston Museum of Fine Arts in 1901 from the Bourguignon collection, presents striking characteristics of that master's work, showing his skill in technique, and especially in composition and movement. In these respects it must be placed at the head of his known works, and proves that Amasis was not merely a clever draughtsman following traditional types, but a painter who possessed both originality and artistic ability.

The vase (Fig. 1) is 30.5 cm. high, with a diameter of 20.5 cm., and has the same general shape as the other signed amphorae. The height of the greatest diameter and its large ratio to the height of the vase give a bold outline that conveys an impression of solidity and compactness rather than grace. Lip, neck, and foot are sharply defined, but the transitions are Twenty-sixth Annual Report of the Trustees, 1901, p. 32, No. 5. Mentioned by Hauser in *Jb. Arch. I.* 1896, p. 178, note 1. For kind permission to publish this vase, I am much indebted to the authorities of the Boston Museum of Fine Arts.

-There are in all eight signed vases:— three amphorae: Paris, Cabinet des Mdailles, Klein, *Die griechisehen Vasen mit Meistersignaturen,* p. 43, No. 1; Boston, Museum of Fine Arts, Klein, No. 3; Boston, Museum of Fine Arts, hitherto unpublished: — two olpae: London, British Museum, B 471, Klein, No. 4; Klein, No. 6:—two oenochoae: Paris, Louvre, Klein, No. 5; Wurzburg 384, Klein, No. 7:— one eye cylix, Boston. Museum of Fine Arts, hitherto unpublished. All except those treated in this paper are published in the *Wiener Vorlegeblatter,* 1889, pis. Ill and IV. It has been clearly proved that the amphora in the British Museum, B 209, Klein, No. 2, is not the work of Amasis. For a full bibliography of the discussion, see *Catalogue of Vases in the British Museum,* II.

American Journal of Archfteology, Second Series. Journal of the 150 Archaeological Institute of America, Vol. XI (1907). No. 2.

American Journal Of Archaeology, Second Series Vol. XI (1907) Plate XII

I

American Journal Of Archaeology. Second Series Vol. XI (1907) Plate XIII made by tiny curved fillets. The handles are of triple form, and the profile of the foot is angular, in which details it resembles the other amphora in Boston. The effect of the vase is brilliant, both in color and draughtsmanship. The black glaze has a peculiarly metallic lustre, in which the thread-like incisions are extraordinarily clear. There are traces of white pigment which was used to emphasize the incisions, a device noted on a fragment in Athens, also ascribed to Amasis, and not infrequent elsewhere, especially on Ionic ware.

Purple and white give variety of color, as on the other vases of Amasis. The former is freely used for the Figure 1. — Amphora Of Amasis. linings and folds of drapery, where it is contrasted with an overlapping black surface, for details of muscles of animals, the neck of the stag, fillets, the body of the tripod, bands and patches on the quivers, helmet, shield, and boots. In decorative designs it is applied with lavish hand to alternate with black, as in the lion's mane and in the diaper pattern, and rows of purple dots, frequently encircled by white dots, ornament the long folds of drapery. Certain details of the minor decorations are picked out in purple, as for example the centres and alternate lobes of palmettes, the central leaf of the lotus, and the transverse lines between links of the palmette-and-lotus band; and two purple lines are found over the black glaze of the interior of the neck. White is more sparingly used, never in masses, except for the flesh of Thetis, the teeth of the lion, and por i Studniczka, 'E£. 'Ap. 1886, p. 124; Duramler, *Horn. Mitt.* 1888, p. 161; cf. Benndorf, 'Zur Vasentechnik,' *Arch. Zeitung,* 1881, 1. Slight traces of white are visible on the other amphora in Boston.

tions of the scabbard; but minute dots of it follow the lines of other patterns, as on the crest of the helmet, the body of the serpent, around larger purple dots, and bordering one side of the favorite step pattern.

While Amasis has spared no pains in ornamenting his work wherever a pattern could be placed, he has been careful not to disturb the effect of the large masses of color, nor to distract the eye from the centre of interest. There are no abrupt transitions, but the lines flow naturally, following the profile of the vase from one part to another. The general scheme of decoration is the usual one on Attic red-bodied amphorae, but with certain details which show the utmost delicacy of feeling, and an endeavor to modify inherited conventional types. The palmette-and-lotus band of the neck differs from those of the other amphorae in the connecting elements, having a single link while the others have respectively a double link and a scroll pattern. A bit of step pattern bordered with white dots is introduced on the stem of the three-pronged lotus. The scroll pattern which forms the transition between the neck and shoulder is not of the conventional form, but is broken at intervals, while an elaborate palmette-and-lotus volute connects and separates the main pictures below the handles, which are graduated by a toothed pattern at their juncture with the body. Above the slender double rays is the step pattern, as on the other amphora in Boston, where the Paris amphora has a lotusbud chain and a zigzag pattern. The use of purely decorative elements for transitions is of more artistic value than the introduction of human figures, as they set in greater relief the pictorial designs of the vase. Our artist seems to have worked out in his amphorae this principle, which was so well known to Attic vase painters of the best period, and it may be that our vase represents his latest as well as his best developed work.

The side bearing the signature (plate XII) represents the Rape of the Tripod in the presence of Hermes, and on the reverse (plate XIII) is the Delivery of Arms to Achilles by Thetis in the presence of Phoenix. The names are inscribed in curves following the lines of the heads, and the signature AMA£I£ MErOIESEN is doubly curved to fit the volute and the head of Hermes. The placing of the inscriptions, as well as the accuracy in forms, shows that they were regarded as an integral part of the decorative scheme and thought worthy of the same painstaking attention as the other ornamental details.

Reference to the plates will obviate the necessity of the detailed description of the main designs which otherwise might be needed for comparison with other work of Amasis. I shall therefore consider only those features which have special interest in relation to the style of the master. Beginning at the left of the obverse, Apollo bends forward to the right to grasp the legs of the tripod. He wears a leather cuirass of the Ionic type with *pteryges* and shoulder-pieces over a plaited chiton. The form and decoration of the cuirass are almost duplicated by that worn by Achilles and, with slight variation in pattern, by one of the warriors on the other amphora in Boston. The palmette behind the shoulder is like those ornamenting the tripod. This is the usual form of the cuirasses of Amasis, but the chiton is variously treated, scant and straight on the circle of warriors on the Paris amphora, in rigid plaits on the olpe, Klein, No. 6, and on an unsigned Berlin amphora. His open quiver with its four feathered arrows is like that of his opponent Heracles here and on the Paris oenochoe, and of a bowman on the Paris amphora. Apollo's flowing hair is bound with fillets in a manner repeatedly found on these vases, with two locks in front of the ear, and two behind it, which escape in front of the shoulder, while the rest falls in a curly mass behind. Were the vase not broken across Apollo's face, we should see that the locks ended in hooks, which pointed forward like those of Achilles. Such forward-pointing hooks with locks drawn either separately, as on our vase, or in pairs, are a mannerism Of the other signatures only two have surely no M before EPOIEEN, the cylix and one of the olpae, Klein, No. 6. On the Würzburg oenochoe only 01EN remains. The M was probably written on the obverse of Klein, No. 3, where the vase is broken before E, as it appears in the intact signature of the reverse side. This signature on the reverse is omitted by Klein.

I am greatly indebted to Miss Harriet Whitaker for her willingness to undertake the task of preparing the drawings for this paper. Her accuracy of observation has aided me materially in my own work. Adamek, *Unsignierte Vasen d. Amasis,* pi. I. *E.g.* Athena, Poseidon, and Dionysus on the Paris amphora; a warrior and the old man on the other Boston amphora. of Amasis. The short front hair is waved across the forehead in a unique manner and, like that of Achilles, shows the background underneath the lock at the top of the head. The arrangement of the hair of Hermes, however, is common in works of Amasis and elsewhere. Hermes wears a purple petasus of a form differing from the straight-brimmed caps on the other vases. Curiously enough it is secured by strings, represented by fine incisions, one of which passes across the fillet to the back of the head, while the other passes in front of the ears and below the chin, where a knot is tied.

The ear of Hermes is large and drawn with a double lobe toward the front. This is the form of the ear of the Gorgon and of most male figures of Amasis, and is found in other blackfigured work, but seldom so clearly marked as here. The nose with its well-defined nostril and the straight line of moustache placed high above protruding lips are features of the other bearded figures. But variation in profile is noticeable, and the energetic lines of Heracles and Hermes are in marked contrast to the more delicate drawing of nose and mouth, which gives repose to the faces of Achilles and Thetis. Hermes wears his chlamys over both arms as on the Paris oenochoe, and below his dotted chiton appears a nebris minutely incised like the skins of animals elsewhere. The boot was decorated with There is a striking example of this treatment on a fragment in the style, if not from the hand, of Amasis, published by Hauser in *Jb. Arch. I.* 1896, p. 179, fig. 6. The Gorgoneion which forms the shield device wears carefully hooked locks, but they point outward, which probably was intended to give the monster a more ferocious aspect. The hooks are greatly exaggerated on the amphora in the British Museum, B 209, which may be a point in favor of the suggestion that the manner of Amasis was here consciously imitated, as undue emphasis upon unessential details is characteristic of imitative work.

While on red-figured vases the strings are frequently found, especially to fasten a *petasus* hanging at the back of the neck, I have been able to find but two undoubted examples of this usage represented on publications of black-figured vases, — a Corinthian amphora published in *Monumenti Inediti,* X, pi. LII, on which the hat is fastened under the chin by two parallel lines, and an oenochoe formerly in the Sabouroff collection (pi. L, 2), on which the petasus and its string are purplo. On a red-figured cylix of Brygos in Corneto, *Monumenti Inediti,* XI, pi. XX, the arrangement is identical with ours. For other examples see *Monumenti Inediti,* VIII, pi. XXVII; *Bom. Mitt.* 1890, p. 332; *li. Arch.* 1898, p. 156; *J.U.S.* 1904, pi. VIII;

Monuments Grecs, I, pls. I and IV; Hartwig, *Die grieckischen Meislerschalen,* pls. LIII and LIV. *E.g.* lion and stag on the shield of Thetis; lion's skin of Heracles here and purple like those of Hermes on Klein, No. 5, and of all three figures on Klein, No. 4. The caduceus is very slender, as well as the shafts of all spears, the sceptre, and the trident, and on all of these shafts one or more knobs are drawn below the point. Heracles is clothed in a splendid example of conventionalized lion's skin and mask, and carries a bow, quiver, and sword. The sword in form and ornament, even to the corresponding use of purple and white and the baldric attachments, is the counterpart of those on Klein, Nos. 3, 5, and 6.

On the reverse, Phoenix wears such a chiton as the other elderly men, but instead of wearing his himation shawl fashion, tucks it under his bare right arm and over the left shoulder, as Poseidon does on Klein, No. 5, except that Poseidon discreetly covers his right elbow in his chiton. His bald and wrinkled forehead is an interesting indication of the realism of the artist, who represented his hoary locks by incisions, not by the more usual method of white pigment. Nowhere else does Amasis show his love for finished detail more than in the extremities, for the feet, though unduly long, are well shaped and minutely treated, while the finger nails are incised. The figure of Achilles presents no features not already mentioned, and the last figure is that of Thetis, who stands almost covered by the round shield. Her hair is arranged in six prim waves like the woman on the Wiirzburg oenochoe. The ear with its large lobe is unfortunately blurred, but the huge earring resembles that on the Berlin amphora, or those on the Paris amphora, and the wavy necklace is like that of all the women on these vases, except of Athena on the Paris amphora, who wears a plain band. The flesh is white, in the Attic manner, and details are incised into the black, except in the outline on Klein, No. 6; fawn and panther, Klein, No. 1; goats on the shield on Klein, No. 3.

These projections are not common except on vases in the manner of Amasis, where they are the rule. On red-figured vases the shafts are frequently supplied with one or more transverse lines at the corresponding point. Cf. Gerhard, *Etruskische und Kampanische Vasenbilder,* pl. VI; Hartwig, *Die grieehisehen Meistersehalen,* pls. IX, XII, XIII, LXXI, *etc.* Apulian vases elaborate these into a ribbon twisted around the shaft. Adamek, *op. cit.* pl. I. of the eye and the nostril, where the white surface appears merely to be indented. Strangely, too, the white of the eye and of the face are now differently discolored, suggesting that the paint may have been differently treated in these places. The surface of the cheek appears to have received an extra coat of paint, as it is perceptibly higher than that of the eye, the whiteness of which is therefore better preserved; possibly the two surfaces were never alike in color. The iris consists of a purple ring enclosing a dot which may once have been white but is now discolored. Thetis wears a straight plaided chiton, closely resembling that of Athena, on Klein, No. 3. A lion tearing a stag is not common as a shield device, though a warrior on the Paris amphora has a stag alone in the same position on his shield. The subject of a lion tearing a stag or other animal is too familiar in Greek decorative work to need comment, were it not that a new scheme of composition is used by our artist. The lion usually stands with but three paws on his victim, which makes the horizontal axis longer than the vertical. Here the lion stands fully on the back of the stag, thus practically equalizing the axes, and so adapting the type to the circular space to be filled. A characteristic touch is the single line of the lion's tail, which is curved to fit the circle of the shield. The lion generally bites the neck from the side nearer the spectator; but Amasis taxes his ingenuity to the utmost in drawing the lion's head behind the stag, as is shown by the delicately branching antlers incised in the mane and above it, and by the position of the white tooth which tears the slender neck. The centre of interest on this side is the princely helmet of elegant proportions, decorated with a sweeping crest supported by a bearded serpent. This unusual detail is paralleled only by the fox which decorates the amphora in the British Museum which bears the name of Dr. Chase notes only two others, the composition of which is less compact than ours. Cf. Shield devices among the Greeks.' *Harvard Studies in Classical Philology,* vol. XIII. -On a gem in the British Museum figured in Imhoof-Blumer u. O. Keller, *Tier-u. Pflanzenhilder auf Munzen u. Gemmen,* pl. XIV, 30, the lion's head is behind, but the composition is oblong. On coins of Velia (Head, *Histnria Numorum,* fig. 50) not earlier than the fourth century B. c., the composition is adapted to the circle, but the lion bites from the side nearer the spectator.

Amasis (Klein, No. 2). A black-figured cantharus with elaborate decorations has a crest supported with curves, in form similar to ours, but without the head of the serpent. A redfigured pelike in the British Museum, E 363, has two crests supported by serpents, drawn, however, with far less feeling, and without fineness of detail. A fragmentary hydria of late fine style, in the same museum, E 252, has a support in the same form. The support, in form of a swan's neck and head, was common in archaic art, and may be seen both on bronzes and vase paintings. It seems to have suggested the support which terminates in a hook distinct from the crest. The cheek piece of our helmet is ornamented with an incised ram's head, like the one at the top of the sceptre on Klein, No. 6. Rams' heads in relief form the cheek pieces on a helmet in the British Museum, and are represented in the same way on a red-figured cylix, E 3, in the same museum. Facility and delicacy in the use of ornament are the most striking characteristics of our artist, and it is surprising to note that, with all the wealth of detail, he does not lose interest in his work and treat his designs conventionally. In spite of the ever-recurrent step pattern, the fringed and dotted draperies, there is real feeling for new effects, and the very contrast produced *by* so archaic a feature as a foldless chiton placed near elaborate drapery, proves less the witless art of a mechanic than the skill of a designer who, by infinite variety, carries his point. Amasis makes the impression of having been open-minded and sensitive to influence, but with a power of invention which puts the stamp of his personality upon all his work.

In action and composition the vase is more interesting. On the reverse, the type of the Delivery of Arms is far less common on black-figured vases than the one in which Achilles puts on his greaves. Probably the accessory figure was regularly an old man in this type as in the other published black-figured From the Acropolis. *B.C.H.* XX, pi. VII. Swan's head on statuette in the Acropolis Museum, Catalogue 796, 'Ei£. *'Kpx*188", pi. 7: on vases, Timonidas vase in Athens, National Museum, Catalogue 620, *Wiener Vorlegeblatter,* 1888, pi. I; early black-figured vase from Caere, *Monumenti Inediti,* VII, pi. LXXVIII: curved hook support, black-figured lecythus in Dresden, *Arch. Anz.* 1900, p. 112. *Catalogue of Bronzes,* 2830. vase, while the other type has warriors or Nereid figures, only once an old man inscribed *Peleus,* on a pinax in Athens somewhat resembling the work of Amasis.

The vertical composition is somewhat lifeless, although the figures are not unrelated, but the lines of hands, helmet, and sword and the direction of the faces lead the eye from the two sides of the design to the front of the helmet, which is at the centre of action, in such a way as to indicate that the action passes toward Achilles. As the helmet is not at the mathematical centre, balance is maintained by opposing the heavy shield to the broad surface of the draperies of Phoenix.

There are three types of the Rape of the Tripod; the tripod stands on the ground, it is pulled in both directions as here, or it is carried by Heracles followed by Apollo. Here, again, the least common type is followed. On one other vase of the type Hermes is placed between the contestants, but usually Athena or Artemis witnesses the scene. Tlie composition is more lifelike than the reverse, being pyramidal, and there is a tine decorative effect in the balance of black and red patches of color. The lines of the legs interlock in natural poses, and skeleton lines of legs, arms, bodies, and the tripod compel the eye to rest at the point of interest, the top of the tripod, where converge also the quiver of Apollo and the sword of Heracles. The unity is further aided by the direction of the faces of the figures. The attitudes are full of life, the subtle curve of Apollo's back suggesting the strategic movement of the athlete, while the greater mass of Heracles is full of muscular strength. The muscles and articulations are variously treated, as if Amasis tried to follow the natural movements of the body, and understood the value of a single line rightly placed. In action and rhythm the composition, at least of this side, surpasses most black-figured work and proves that Amasis was an artist of striking individuality, in spite of much lifeless work which passed from his brush.

The fragmentary eye cylix of the Bartlett collection (Fig. 2) shows the same careful drawing and use of accessory colors.
Overbeck, *Gnllerie heroUcher Bildwerke,* p. 442, No. 83; of. Micali, *Mmmmenti,* pi. 82, 1, 2. National Museum, No. 671.

Its diameter is 17.5 cm., which allows room between the eyes for a single figure, probably a Dionysus, as hinted by the ivy and the bit of drapery; a figure like those under the handles

Figure 2. — Fragments Of F.ve Cylix Of Amasis. of the amphora in Boston, Klein, No. 3. Its only points of interest lie in the inscription, in which M is not written before ErOIE£EN,and in the form of vase, which is not known to have been used elsewhere by Amasis.

Alice Avalton.

Wellesley College. Amasis signs his vases only as maker *itrol-qaev),* not as decorator *iypayf/ev).* In this paper it has been assumed that the maker was also the decorator, an assumption which is justified in the case of Amasis by the identity of style in the decoration of the vases that bear his name.

Institute of America

THE DISCOVERY, BY PROFESSOR GUSTAVO GIOVANNONI, OF CURVES IN PLAN, CONCAVE TO THE EXTERIOR, IN THE FACADE OF THE TEMPLE AT CORI

The object of this paper is to call attention to the recent remarkable observations of curvilinear refinements in the Temple at Cori (plate XIV) by Professor Gustavo Giovannoni, Assistant Professor in the Royal School of Engineering Architects at Rome.

The announcement regarding these curves was originally made by Professor Giovannoni before a meeting of the Roman Society of Architects which was held on the 6th of February, 1905. It was first published in the *Annuario* of the Society for that year. The additional facts to be related were then obtained through personal correspondence with Professor Giovannoni, who has also allowed me to describe and publish them. I am advised by his letter of December 8, 1906, that the isolation of the Temple at Cori from adjacent buildings will be shortly undertaken by the Italian Government and that this opportunity will be used for the construction of scaffolds which will enable him to take measurements in detail of the upper portions of the facade. Meantime I quote from an earlier letter, of July 2, 1906, the following information:

"The temple of Hercules at Cori belongs to the late epoch of the Roman Republic and is one of the finest specimens of Of the illustrations. Plates XV and XVII are from drawings by John W. McKecknie, Plates XVIII-XXI are from photographs of the Brooklyn Museum Survey of 1895, and Plate XXII from a photograph of the same survey in 1905. The adjacent buildings interfere with a view of the curve. Its character is shown in Plate XXI.

American Journal of Archaeology, Second Series. Journal of the lflO
Archaeological Institute of America, Vol. XI (1907), No. 2.

this period of transition from the Greco-Etruscan style to the Roman. The pronaos and the great door are still in almost perfect preservation and show splendid execution, both from the artistic and from the constructive point of view.... The suspicion of accident (in regard to the curves) cannot be entertained.

"No one, however, as far as I am aware, has previously observed or measured the curve of the façade. This curve exists notwithstanding, and is very clearly defined. The concavity (in plan) which is small at the columnar bases, where it measures 10 or 12 cm. deflection, increases to nearly 35 cm in a length of 7.50 m. at the cornice. The gable follows the same line, and the regularity of the joints gives assurance that neither (original) accident nor subsequent movements have produced this remarkable deflection. There are no curves on the flanks."

As regards the measurements just quoted it is to be observed that the curve of 10-12-cm. quoted for the line of the bases is one of unusually large deflection for the given length of 7.50 m., as compared with other classic curves; and that the curve at the cornice, of 14 inches or 35 cm., is far greater than any curve previously recorded for the ancient monuments, both as regards the actual measurement and still more as regards the relation of other deflections to the greater widths or greater lengths of the given buildings.

Aside from the remarkable amount of the curve, its still more remarkable feature is the concavity in plan, and I need hardly "Le Temple d'Hercule à Cori appartient à la dernière époque de la République, et il est un des plus beaux spécimens de cette période de transition du style grec-étrusque au romain. Le pronaos et la grande porte sont encore presque entièrement conservés et montrent encore une exécution splendide du côté artistique et constructif. Cette perfection d'ouvrage nous assure que les courbures qui nous pouvons y constater sont vraiment voulues par l'artiste; ce sont en effet des 'refinements.' La doute qu'il peuve s'agir d'un hasard ne vaut pas ici.

"Personne, cependant, que je sache, n'a remarqué ni mesuré avant moi la courbure du temple. Toutefois cette courbure existe et est très sensible. La concavité, qui est très petite à la base des colonnes, où elle mesure dix ou douze centimètres de flèche, rejoint presque 35 cm. en horizontale (sur une largeur de m. 7.50) dans la corniche, un peu en retraite du soubassement au milieu. Le fronton aussi suit ce tracé et la régularité des joints nous assure que ni le hasard ni des modifications ultérieures ont produit cette singuliere anomalie. Les flancs n'ont pas de courbe." add that this feature constitutes its astounding and novel characteristic. It is further to be noticed that no other Roman temple has been so far announced as showing any curves whatever, with the exception of the Maison Carree at Nimes (plate XV), which has curves in the cornices of the flanks which are convex to the exterior.

Aside from the assurances given by Professor Giovannoni as to constructive intention there are two evidences of such intention which speak for themselves, even to those who have not examined the temple; viz., that the curve is found at the bases of the columns and that a concave curved deflection in plan, of the cornice and gable, to the extent of 14 inches, could not have been the result of accidental movements, without the appearance in the connected structure of very visible and palpable dislocations, which must also have visibly affected the supporting columns, either at the angles or near the centre, one or both.

As regards the theories which have been advanced to explain the ancient curves, the discovery of curves at Cori, concave in plan to the exterior, lias a revolutionary and far-reaching significance. The optical effect above the level of the eye of a curve concave in plan is that of a curve in elevation (that is, of a curve in a vertical plane) which descends towards the centre. Consequently the explanation which has been so widely quoted and credited, that the ancient curves were intended to correct optical effects of sagging downward, is immediately and decisively thrown out of court in the case of the temple at Cori, for it is exactly an effect of sagging downward which is actually produced by this curve, so far as the upper horizontal lines are concerned.

So conclusive an argument leads us to examine the previous standing of the widely spread impression that the Greek curvilinear refinements were intended universally to correct optical effects of sagging and thus cause the lines to appear straight.

The upper dotted line suggests the optical effect of the curves in plan, convex to the exterior, which are found on the flanks of this temple. The constructive existence of these curves has been verified by the official architect of the city of Nimes and also by his predecessor in the same position. See Smithsonian Reports for 1894 (published in 1896). 'A Discovery of Horizontal Curves in Plan in the Maison Carrie at Nimes.' Under the same title see also *A.J.A.*, First Series, X, 1895, pp. 1 ft., and *Arch,* fiec, IV, 1895, No. 4.

This explanation is frequently quoted for the rising curves in elevation, such as are found in the Parthenon and some other Greek temples; and these are the curves which have so far generally received attention. It is true that different curves may have been employed in different ancient buildings for different reasons. It would be establishing a very important fact, if this fact alone were proved by the instance at Cori, but the opportunity is a convenient one to point out that the widely quoted explanation is essentially a popular misapprehension of an entirely different proposition and has never been mentioned by any of the optical experts who have made special publications on the Greek curves.

It is a popular modern prejudice that architectural lines ought to *be* straight. Consequently the suggestion appeals to the popular mind that the Greeks curved their architectural lines in order that they might *appear* straight. Hence, probably, the widely quoted but really mistaken statement that all horizontal architectural lines tend to sag optically at the centre. This impression among architects may be due to the occasional practice of cambering interior flat ceilings or tie beams under a gabled roof, but the problem of optical effects in such interiors has no relation to the general, but mistaken, proposition.

It is an elementary proposition in perspective that horizontal lines above the level of the eye, on near approach, curve downward toward the extremities. This is most easily realized by assuming the position of the spectator to be opposite the centre of a building of such dimensions that the head has to be turned first in one direction and then in the other in order to take in the entire upper line. As the really horizontal upper line to the left of the spectator will descend optically in perspective towards the left, and as the really horizontal upper line to the right of the spectator will descend optically towards the right, it is manifest that the eye in passing from left to right, or from right to left, must see the whole horizontal line optically as a curve descending towards the extremities and highest in the middle. It is equally true that all lines which descend in perspective in a single direction must descend in a curve, optically speaking, because the line which is really straight and horizontal descends in gradually increasing amount according to the distance from the eye. Consequently an actually horizontal straight line which, optically speaking, changes direction from point to point must necessarily change direction, optically speaking, in a curve. It is only the mental knowledge that the line is really straight and horizontal which interferes with the perception that the line is really seen as a curve.

The interference of a mental conviction, based on general positive knowledge, with an actual optical appearance is a wellestablished fact. This interference of the brain with the true facts of vision has been ably described by Professor Guido Hauck in a publication to be presently quoted. Professor Hauck found that the ability to see the rising curves which optically exist in all horizontal lines above the level of the eye (unless interfered with by other lines) was strongest in women and in the persons whom he calls "Naturmenschen," among whom he includes artists, whereas persons with mathematical and scientific training were frequently unable to see the curves at all. He also found in his own experience a progressive improvement in his ability to distinguish the curves as actually seen by the eye. He also found that optical curves in lines really straight and horizontal could be seen in a line of separated lights illuminating an architectural line at night, when they could not be seen in the same architectural line by daylight. The mental conviction had an effect on the continuous line which it did not have on separate points of artificial light, not visibly connected by the architectural line. The mental corrections of optical appearances which are described by Professor Hauck have a curious analogy in the experience of Mr. John W. Beatty, M.A., Director of Fine Arts in the Carnegie Institute at Pittsburg, Pennsylvania. The following extract from his letter to me on this subject is published by his permission: —

"Briefly put, my experience was this: When I first put on glasses for astigmatism, perpendicular lines appeared not parallel, being wide at top; in the size of a newspaper page, about one and one-half inches wider than normal. When I had worn the glasses for several months, lines seemed again parallel. Now, when I take the glasses off, lines are again not parallel, but *wider at the bottom.* Dr. Lippincott's theory was that I had always made mental correction, and lines recorded on the retina out of parallel were made to appear parallel by virtue of mental correction. This seems to be absolutely proven by the history of the case, as above briefly outlined. When I take the glasses off now, I see lines imperfectly at the instant of time, because the brain is not given time to correct the defect. The fact that the greater width is now at the bottom

All these facts assist us to understand why lines which are optically seen as curves are not generally recognized as curves by the everyday human being. They also enable us to understand that the perception of the curves which are optically present in the facts of vision varies according to temperament and according to training. As a matter of fact there is no perspective which is not curvilinear, but as these perspective curves are too delicate to be generally represented in the dimensions of pictures, instruction in perspective, as regards draughtsmen and painters, generally ignores them and hence does not tend to counteract the average human indifference to their existence, which is due to mental correction.

All these points bear on the popular error that there is a natural sagging effect in architectural horizontal lines above the level of the eye; but no optical expert who has made a special study of the Greek curves has ever suggested that such a general sagging effect exists.

Thus the first investigator who made publication on the subject supposed that the Parthenon curves were intended to accent and increase perspective effect, because they develop and accent a form of curve which already exists in the normal optical appearance. This investigator was Hoffer, whose observations, measurements, and publications were made in 1838, and thus anticipated the earliest observations of Penrose by seven years and his publication by thirteen years.

Hoffer's publications were made in the *Wiener Bauzeitung* for 1838, whereas Penrose did not visit Athens till 1845 and did not publish his *Principles of Athenian Architecture* until 1851. The discovery of the Parthenon curves by Pennethorne in 1837 is generally supposed to have preceded the observations of Hoffer, but the publication of Hoffer long preceded that of Pennethorne, which appeared in 1878.

It will be observed that I am not advocating at present the explanation of Hoffer; I am simply pointing out that he was the first expert who made a special publication on the Greek curves and that, so far from suggesting that these curves were without glasses, whereas it was at the top with glasses when they were first used, is significant. You will find the reference to my case in the *Archices of Ophthalmology,* Vol. XVIII (1889), p. 18, and more particularly p. 28." intended to correct an effect of sagging, he supposed that they were intended to enhance and exaggerate a curve of exactly contrary character, and that this curve was mentioned by him as the ordinary optical appearance due to perspective.

The popular impression that the rising curves were intended to correct an effect of sagging, popularly said to be inherent in horizontal lines generally, is probably simply a misapprehension of the theory of Penrose, who never, however, suggested any such appearance in horizontal lines as a general rule. Penrose rested liis theory of correction on the optical tendency of a horizontal cornice to curve downward under a gable, because the lower acute angles of the gable tend to appear wider than they actually are; therefore the bottom line appears depressed at the angles, and as the effect of depression gradually decreases according to the distance from the angles, therefore the depressed line appears as a downward curve. According to Penrose the rising curve under the gable was to counteract and correct this effect. But as far as the flanks are concerned Penrose supposed the curves to be explained by the sentiment of beauty and the appearance of strength, but to have been originally suggested by the application of the curve as an optical correction under the gable. Thus we are led next to ascertain the present standing of the gable theory of Penrose, which appears to be the original form of the debated popular impression, although it is really a wholly distinct proposition.

This leads us to consider what other authorities later than Penrose have had to say about his gable theory. This gable theory has never, to my knowledge, been accepted or even favorably mentioned by any German optical authority. On the contrary, it has been vigorously and successfully contested by the two greatest German authorities who have subsequently discussed the curves from the standpoint of the expert in optics. First, Thiersch added to a variety of solid arguments one which must appeal to every understanding, whether that of an expert or not. The argument is, namely, this: If Penrose was correct in believing that the curves of the entablature and cornice at the ends of the temple were in 'Optische Tauschungen auf dem Gebiete der Architecture *Zeitsehrift fur Bautcesen,* XXIII, Berlin, 1873. tended as an optical correction under the gable, and to make the lines appear straight, how does it then happen that the stylobate is curved also, for which no such gable effect exists? This argument is unanswerable. Its only weakness is that it is so simple, so conclusive, and must be so briefly stated, that it falls short of effect from sheer simplicity. It is not necessary here to rehearse the special theory of Thiersch, who thus and otherwise contested the gable theory of Penrose, because it has also been thrown out of court by two subsequent publications. One of these publications was that of Guido Hauck. Although Hauck abandoned the new explanation of Thiersch, he approved, rehearsed, and elaborated the arguments which led Thiersch to reject the theory of Penrose, especially dwelling on the point that the stylobate need not have been curved if the object of the curve was to correct an apparent deflection under the gable. Both Thiersch and Hauck also urge the sensible view that to consider the curves of the entablature on the flanks of a temple as purely an afterthought is a far-fetched and wholly unsupported hypothesis. Let it be also observed that the theories of Thiersch and Hauck which proposed to supplant the theory of Penrose make no reference to a general sagging effect in horizontal lines, and Hauck expressly develops the fact that horizontal lines above the level of the eye tend normally to curve downward toward the extremities instead of curving upward toward the extremities, as they would if they had a sagging effect. Thiersch alludes to the same fact as holding for near approach.

The publication of Hauck is undoubtedly the most valuable and far-reaching contribution to the optics of rising curves in elevation which has ever been made. But as an explanation of the subject of curvilinear refinements, viewed as a whole, it has also been thrown out of court, and therefore needs no detailed description. It is sufficient to say that it is based, like the theory of Thiersch, on the form of the Greek temple and on the idea that the Curves were invented by the Greeks and that these curves were always rising curves in elevation.

Neither Thiersch nor Hauck was acquainted with the *curves* Dr. Guido Hauck, *Die Subjective Perspektive und die Horizontalen Curvaturen des Dorischen Styls.* Stuttgart, Conrad Wittwer, 1879.
in plan of the cornice, convex to the centre of the court, in the second Temple Court of Medinet Habou (plate XVI). These curves were discovered by Pennethorne in 1832, but he did not publish them until 1878. This was only a year before Hauek's publication, and the Egyptian curves were still unknown to Hauck in 1879. If the gable theory of Penrose required a final death blow, it would be furnished by the curves in plan of the second Temple Court of Medinet Habou, where there are naturally no gables. But the curves in plan at Medinet Habou also fall outside of the special theories of both Thiersch and Hauck, and this is why I have not explained the latter's view. It will not be overlooked, however, that the optical effect in the cornices at Medinet Habou is that of a rising curve in a vertical plane. At the angle of 45 degrees the spectator has the effect of a rising curve in elevation of an amount equal to that of the curve in plan (plate XVII). At points farther removed the curve appears less. At nearer points the effect is greater and increases enormously on close approach. Thus on close approach the normal perspective curve is much exaggerated. The upper dotted lines show the optical effect of the curves in plan. The theory of Thiersch, briefly stated, starts from the illusion which tends to affect the appearance of two lines meeting at an angle. These effects were cited by Penrose for acute angles, as calling for a correction under the gable. Thiersch, however, points out that, whereas acute angles appear larger than they really are, obtuse angles appear smaller. His arguments contend

that the direction of Vitruvius regarding the construction of the curves was limited to those temples which stand on an elevated platform above the level of the eye. Thus the Parthenon, as seen by a spectator *looking toward one of the angles,* would exhibit obtuse angles both in the stylobate and in the entablature (with the apex of the angle turned toward the spectator). These angles would appear smaller than they are, and as this effect decreases with the distance from the angle, the lines would appear to curve downward away from the angle. This effect would be corrected by a rising curve in elevation. Hauck contested this explanation on the ground that the optical deflection of the obtuse angle was so inconsiderable that a correction would not be needed, but more particularly because such a correction would, in any circumstance, only be needed for the spectator looking toward the angle of the building, and would not be needed in views facing the front or sides. Hauck based his own theory on the fact that the intercolumniations of the Parthenon are smaller at the angles, by about two feet, in order to admit of placing the corner triglyphs at the angles of the building, instead of placing them over the centre of the abacus, where they normally appear. This diminution of spacing gives an increase of perspective from the

Still another argument against the gable theory of Penrose is furnished by the Brooklyn Museum surveys of 1895. The point of view facing any side of the temple from positions nearly opposite the centre. Hence according to Hauck, if the perspective rising curves in elevation were not also correspondingly increased, the perspective effect of the columns would be out of harmony with the perspective effect of the horizontal lines. Thus Hauck in a sense returned to the explanation of Hoffer. For although he held that perspective exaggeration, for its own sake, would not have been in line with Greek feeling, he also held that this perspective exaggeration was properly sought in view of the contradictory effects otherwise produced by the necessary narrowing of the angle intercolumniations.

As the title of Professor Hauck's monograph indicates, he supposed that the Greek curves were confined to the Doric style, in which style alone the angle intercolumniations were reduced, in order to allow the triglyphs to be placed at the angles of the temple. Since that date the discovery of curves in the Ionic temple at Pergamon would have vitiated his theory, but it is also wholly unavailable for the curves at Medinet Habou. So far as the theory of Thiersch is concerned the openings of the obtuse angles in the interior of the court at Medinet Habou are turned toward the spectator, not away from him (as in the exterior of a Greek temple). The angle illusion, if any were produced, would, therefore, be a rising curve in elevation and would thus need no correction.

Although the theories of Thiersch and Hauck are no longer tenable, their publications still have great interest and importance as critiques of the theory of Penrose, and otherwise.

It ought perhaps to be added that the theory of Thiersch is the only one which has ever even been offered, to explain the account of Vitruvius. Although the explanation of Vitruvius has been otherwise universally discarded, or (more generally) ignored, it ought to be possible to determine his reasons, even if his explanation be not correct. Vitruvius directs that the stylobate of the temple shall be built with a rising curve in elevation, lest it appear "alveolated" (like the bed of a channel) and the curves of the entablature are considered as a mere outcome or logical sequence of the stylobate curve. Thiersch moves from the fact that Vitruvius is speaking of temples resting on a *podium,* that is, above the level of the eye of the exterior spectator, and that the effect of sagging from the exterior point of view was to be counteracted by the curve. I will venture to suggest that Vitruvius is speaking of an effect of "alveolation" for the spectator standing on the platform. It is a logical result of the laws of curvilinear perspective that all plane surfaces below the level of the eye must tend optically to " dish"; that is, to appear like a dish or bowl. Aeronauts find this appearance in the earth's surface when raised above it in a balloon, for the same optical reason. The same optical laws explain the dome-shaped appearance of the sky. Thus, although the explanation of Vitruvius is certainly insufficient to cover the known facts, it appears to be a common-sense and practical explanation, which deserves recognition and mention, among the many which have been offered. It is additionally interesting from the fact that it is not simply the outer porticos of the Parthenon which have the stylobate curves. The entire platform of the temple is delicately hemispherical; or, as the French would say, *bombe.* photographs, taken under my direction, of the Temple of Concord at Girgenti, show that there are rising curves in elevation on the flanks (plate XVIII), but no curves under the gable (plate XIX). Hence the curves of the flanks could not well be an afterthought derived from the curves under the gables, since the latter do not occur in this temple. This very important argument against the gable theory of Penrose has never been adequately published.

Penrose had based his argument for the derivation of curves on the flanks of a temple from the curves under the gable, on the high antiquity of the Temple of Poseidon at Paestum and on the supposed fact that this temple had curves under the gable, but none on the flanks. Thus, for Penrose, the Temple of Poseidon represented the primitive type of the Greek curves, but he was ignorant that Jacob Burckhardt in his " Cicerone had announced constructive curves in plan convex to the exterior on the flanks of the Temple of Poseidon. These curves were photographed for the first time by the Brooklyn Museum surveys of 1895 (plate XX).

From the preceding summary two results are fairly well established. First, the popular impression that the Greek curves were intended to make the lines look straight, and to correct effects of sagging supposed to be inherent in straight lines above the eye, is without authority, so far as the quoted experts are concerned, and the theory of Burnouf, in the *Revue GstiSrale de VArchitecture* for 1875, is too fanciful to require more than passing mention here. The second result is this. So far Straight lines have been drawn on the negative, in order to show the rising curves in elevation of the stylobate and entablature. Even the briefest mention of Burnouf ought not, however, to oinit to give him credit for having, alone among modern authors, given the correct explanation of the *scamilli imparts* of Vitruvius. Penrose supposed that the *scamilli impares* were the drums of the columns which rested on the stylobate. These drums, in the Parthenon, are of unequal height on opposing sides. Otherwise the columns resting on the curved and sloping surface, would lean away from the centre of the temple. This interesting proof of the intended construction of the curves is not, however, the true explanation of the *scamilli impares,* by means of which the curves were to be constructed. Even in the second edition of his *Principles of Athenian Architecture,* published in 1888, Penrose was still ignorant of the obviously correct explanation offered by Burnouf in 1875. It is significant of the general neglect by archaeologists of the subject of as Penrose is concerned, he only suggested a sagging effect under the gables at the ends of a temple as the explanation of the curves. Against this theory the following points may be urged. It has not been accepted or favorably mentioned by any French or German expert. It has been vigorously opposed by two distinguished experts in optics, and the theory of Hoffer is also opposed to it in principle. It is finally thrown out of court by known facts in Egypt and at Girgenti.

We are now able to return to the discovery of Professor Giovannoni at Cori, which disposes of the gable theory of Penrose for all time, as a general or universal explanation of the classic curves, for the simple reason that the curve at Cori produces a sagging effect in the upper horizontal line and therefore could not counteract one.

But the discovery does far more than this; it forces a revision of most of the other theories on Greek curves and widens our views regarding them to a very remarkable extent. And before I take up this phase of the subject I wish to point out the possibility that the curves at Cori may not be the only ones which are concave to the exterior, even in existing classic monuments.

Pennethorne observed curves *in plan* concave to the exterior in the entablatures at the ends of the Parthenon. Hoffer explicitly described the same curves and measured them. The plan of these concave curves, with measurements, is published in the *Wiener Bauzeitung* of 1838. Hoffer described these curves in plan as beginning in the capitals, as continuing in the entablature and sloping cornice, but as not being found in the face of the tympanum. They amount to about two inches only, at the cornice. Penrose quotes the observation of Pennethorne

Greek curves that Burnouf's explanation has not even been alluded to by any other authority.

Burnouf points out that *seamillus* is a diminutive of *axiiimv,* and may be translated as "a little stool" (Burnouf says *un petit bane).* These little stools were the small pyramid-shaped sighting blocks which are still used in France for levelling a line of steps or a masonry platform. If placed in graded unequal sizes, gradually increasing in height from the centre toward the extremities of the line of steps, such *scamilli* could be used for constructing a curve, and, as Burnouf says, it was as easy in antiquity to construct a curve with these implements, as it now is to build to a level. He also points out that such *scamilli imparts* must have been used for building curves in plan.

and gives his reasons for believing the curves to be accidental. In deference to Penrose, Pennethorne, in 1878, adopted his view that these curves were accidental. The argument of Pen- rose is that the gaps between joints were greater in the rear than in the front. Hoffer's observation that the tympanum surface is without curve would appear to suggest that the curves above and below it could hardly be due to accidental movement. No decision on such a head can be reached, or even suggested, in this paper, and the explosion which ruined the Parthenon is not to be forgotten, but it is surely worth remembering, in face of the concave curves at Cori, that concave curves in the Parthenon gable fronts were observed, measured, and published in 1838, by Hoffer, as constructive.

There is another observation on this head which is attested by the photograph herewith published. In 1895, I observed curves in plan concave to the exterior in the eastern pediment of the Temple of Poseidon at Paestum, and they were photographed at that time. This photograph (plate XXI) shows the concave curve in the line of abaci as well as in the cornice. I have never previously published these facts, for lack of time and opportunity, but I was moved by the observation at Cori to make them known to Professor Giovannoni and to send him a photograph. This observation has been laid before the Roman Society by Professor Giovannoni at their session of November 6, 1906, and the President of the Society has been kind enough to write me a congratulatory letter on this subject. It appears to me of high importance that the curve in plan at Paestum, concave to the exterior, should be carefully examined by experts, on the site. Whatever the result at Paestum might be, the curves at Cori still remain the first conclusively demonstrated constructive curves in plan, concave to the exterior, which have ever been found in a classic monument.

This is the proper point at which to close this paper, for it is not my purpose to explain these concave curves. So long as it appears certain that the facts now known are sufficient to compel new explanations it seems hardly worth while to figure as a theorizer. It is mainly my wish to show that previous explanations of the classic curves are insufficient to cover the facts now known. I may, however, add that Professor Giovannoni's announcement of the curves at Cori was made to the Roman Society of Architects in a report of a favorable nature regarding my own observations of mediaeval asymmetries and deflections. Therefore, I may also add that the closest mediaeval analogy to the facade at Cori is that offered by the lower facade of St. Mark's at Venice, which curves concave to the exterior, from the foundations up, with a deflection of 10 inches at the foundations (plate XXII).

It appears highly improbable that the facade of St. Mark's was curved for the effects of concavity in the upper line. It is rather probable that the entire surface of the facade was considered. As regards line effects the curves would, below the level of the eye, produce the optical effect of rising curves in vertical planes. Above the level of the eye they would produce the optical effect of descending curves in vertical planes. These line effects are optically contradictory and therefore optically illusive. They must, therefore, give to the facade an effect of "life " or of optical mystery and vibration.

As regards views slanting along the facade of St. Mark's from left to right, or *vice versa,* the perspective effect is enhanced very considerably in the way of magnitude, if the terminal upright lines, rather than the upper horizontal lines, be considered. But here again it appears more likely that an effect of optical mystery and vibration, rather than a direct increase of size in perspective, was considered. It may be that the delicately varied effects of light and shadow, which are involved in a curved surface, were the dominant consideration.

As regards the facade of St. Mark's, it should be remembered that only the lower facade is in question, and not the upper facade, which stands back of a wide platform, bounded by the cornice of the lower facade. Although this cornice has not been levelled or plumbed, it appears to rise from the extremities toward the centre so as to correct the effect of concavity at the cornice line. (In the upper facade the pinnacles are arranged in descending heights from the centre toward the extremities.) The deflection is best seen on the outer line of the paving slabs in front of the church. And especially so for the reason mentioned later, that the cornice line appears to the eye to be built with slight obliquities rising from each end toward the centre, so as to correct the effect of concavity.

In simple language, and aside from optical explanations, the facade of St. Mark's, in my opinion, gains vastly in artistic charm by its delicately and imperceptibly curvilinear surface, as well as by its subtle variations in the dimensions of the arcades. If mediaeval curves be admitted to have been constructed at all, it must be conceded that the lively effect of the curved line or surface was held to be superior to the rigidity and greater formalism of the straight or plane surface, and that no other universal explanation can be offered. Whether or no this lively effect is physiologically due to optical mystery, which is again due to an optical vibration between the contradictory optical effects which must always be found in delicately distorted architectural surfaces or lines, or whether it is due to varied effects of shadow, is hardly worth debating. It may be that both explanations have to be considered. I offer the suggestions for what they are worth, with the remark that the concave curve in plan at Cori demands some kind of explanation.

If mediaeval analogies be excluded, it is still evident that some explanation similar to those which have just been offered for them must now be sought for such ancient curves as are found at Cori. This involves farther reference to the concave curves in the Parthenon, if for no other reason than the one that other experts than Hoffer have already been inclined to admit their constructive existence. Thus Reber considers the concave curves of the Parthenon to be constructive. His explanation is significant in view of the fact that the optical effect, in front view, is that of a descending curve in a vertical plane, which equals the amount of the curve in plan at the angle of 45 degrees, which decreases in amount from farther points of view, and which increases in amount on nearer approach. Reber holds that the concave curve was intended to contradict and decrease the excessive curve in elevation due to the combination of the optical perspective effect in elevation, on close approach, with the constructive curve in elevation. The interesting feature of this explanation (although it cannot be applied to Cori) is that it realizes the two effects as being contradictory. Ilauck quotes the explanation *Kunstyeschichte den Alterthiims.* p. 207. of Reber with tentative approval and expressly affirms the principle that the effects of a rising curve in elevation and of a concave curve in plan are contradictory, and that the optical effect of the concave curve is that of a descending curve in a vertical plane..It is, of course, understood, as Hauck points out, that the contradictory effect is insignificant from distant points, and then almost disappears. It is also understood that whereas the rising curve in elevation has its greatest relative effect from a distance, the optical perspective curve is far the greater on close approach, so much so, that on close approach the constructed curve in elevation is not an important addition to its amount. Neither Reber nor Hauck has considered the possibility that the concave curve might have been considered desirable for its effects from the slanting side view, and Hoffer is at a loss for any explanation.

Although the constructive facts in the Parthenon may be held to be doubtful, the above explanations are of value as showing the difficulties which have hitherto surrounded the explanations of concave curves in plan, and also as showing that the effects of concave curves in plan above the level of the eye are recognized by optical experts as being those of descending curves in elevation for the front view.

The concave curves at Paestum do not appear to be exposed to suspicion on the score of constructive existence, and here again there are also rising curves in elevation at each end of the temple.

For the Temple of Cori the question is not complicated by the existence of curves with contradictory effects, but it still remains to be debated whether the side effect was not considered as much as the front view. The Temple of Cori stands on a high elevation, and the front view from below would, on near approach, much increase the optically descending effect toward the centre of the curve. For such points of view it could only, be presumed that the curve was considered more agreeable than the straight line, without reference to the question whether it was a rising or a descending curve. For the *Op. cit.,* pp. 109,144.

It would, disappear entirely when the eye is on the level of the concave curve. Here the concave curve appears as a straight line. side view the effects would be optically contradictory as regards perspective, an effect of increase if the vertical terminal lines be considered, and an effect of decrease if the upper horizontal lines'be considered.

It is a natural result of our interest in the surviving ancient monuments, that we tend to overlook their actually very small number and the enormous number of those which have utterly disappeared. The discovery at Cori makes it probable that curves were employed in ancient art to a much greater extent and in much greater variety than has hitherto been supposed. The same conclusion would inevitably be suggested by the possibility that the mediaeval curves are historically related to the classic; because the mediaeval curves exhibit a variety of character and use far surpassing that which has been hitherto presumed to exist in antiquity.

In a paper which I published in this Journal, Vol. VI, 1902, pp. 166 ff., 'Architectural Refinements in Italian Churches,' I discussed the optical effects of the cloister curves, convex to the centre of the court, at Verona and Bologna. I pointed out that the line effects were contradictory above and below the level of the eye inside the corridors, and that they were again contradictory, but in the reverse sense, as observed on the exterior, *i.e.* from the interior of the court. From this I argued that the curve must have been preferred for its own sake and independent of any definite particular perspective effect. It has since occurred to me that an effect of vibration or of optical mystery in such curved lines or surfaces, must result from the shifting of the eye to different lines or planes of sight or from the inclusion, at points more distant from the eye, of such contradictory effects within the limits of fixed vision in a single direction. In churches like S. Apollinare Nuovo at Ravenna, which have true parallel curves in plan in the alignment of columns, continuing in the walls of the clerestory, it is evident that the optical effects must again be contradictory on the two sides of the nave, because the columns and wall surfaces are concave to the nave on one side and convex on the other.

In the Pisa Cathedral, moreover, where the gallery parapets are built in parallel curves in plan (which continue in the walls above) the same parapets also have constructive rising bends in elevation *(Arch. Ilec.* VI, No. 4).

Thus, from the pavement below, the curve in plan increases the effect of the bend in elevation on the south side, where it is convex to the nave, and decreases it on the north side, where it is concave to the nave. (For the north side of the nave, the facts are analogous to those in the Temple of Poseidon at Paestum, and in the Parthenon, where contradictory effects are found in the cornice.) It may also be pointed out that, wholly aside from curves, I have always contended that effects of optical mystery were studied at Pisa. The explanation is offered for what it is worth, and any others would be equally satisfactory to me which cover all the constructive facts.

Finally, as regards relationship in feeling, if not in continuity of historic practice, as between Antiquity and the Byzantine and Romanesque monuments of Italy, the authority of Jacob Burckhardt may be cited. Ernst Foerster, in his *Handbuch fur Jleisende in Italien,* I, pp. 364-365, was apparently the first to announce intentional irregularities of line in the Pisa Cathedral. He held them to be "die unbeholfensten Aeusserungen des romantischen Kunstgeistes." Jacob Burckhardt's footnote to the account of the Leaning Tower in his " Cicerone" quotes Foerster's idea as follows:

"For the history of art Foerster's opinion about the relation of the Leaning Tower to the irregularities of measurement, oblique and bent lines, irregular intervals, etc., would be much more important than his opinion about the Tower itself; in all these things he sees a dislike of mathematical regularity and of exact symmetry; these are said to be the clumsy expression of Romanesque endeavor' (Die unbeholfensten Aeusserungen romantischer Bestrebungen). *Since we must unconditionally admit something of the kind in Greek temples, this view has something cery attractive.* I believe, however, that the given phenomena must be otherwise explained, and, namely, not by want of dexterity, — which could not be suggested for the noble Pisan buildings,— but by an indifference to mathematical accuracy, which was peculiar to the earlier Middle Age."

Burckhardt then proceeds to give examples of this indiffer This footnote appears only in the first three editions. ence (which certainly also existed). The footnote just quoted inspired me to make a personal call on Jacob Burckhardt at Basel in 1870. I showed him the measurements and drawings which I had just brought from Pisa. He advised immediate publication, and professed his previous ignorance of the facts thus brought to his notice. Thus my own contact with Burckhardt showed that he was not familiar with the constructive facts at Pisa, whereas to him belongs the original suggestion that, if the constructive facts exist, they would be analogous in feeling to the deflections and asymmetries of Greek temples. (Burckhardt's matter on the Temple of Poseidon at Paestum to which he refers in this footnote has been retained in later editions.) To Foerster, on the other hand, belongs the original suggestion that obliquities and bends were intentionally constructed at Pisa. He can hardly, however, have noted the true and delicate curves which are also found in the cathedral, for these certainly cannot be called "unbeholfen" or clumsy.

As a final suggestion for fagades like

those of St. Mark's and Cori it appears that the varying effects of light and shadow may have been the important consideration. Since these varying effects of light and shadow were notoriously studied with the greatest care in the profiles of classic architecture, why may they not have been considered for the surface of the facade at Cori? The same explanation may be sufficient for the concave curves of Paestum and of the Parthenon.

William H. Goodyear. of Classical Stunics in ftomr AN INSCRIPTION OF THE CHARIOTEER
MENANDER

This inscription (Fig. 1) is on a slab of white marble, 0.105 x 0.205 x 0.037 m., and was obtained by the Director of the American School in Rome in December, 1905, from a dealer who stated that it was found near the new Corso di Porta Pinciana. The two iron nails by which the stone was attached are still in For some time I have been preparing for publication a catalogue of the inscriptions at the American School in Rome. The stone, however, which is the subject of this paper, is of such exceptional interest as to warrant its immediate publication in a separate article.

Outside the Aurelian Wall, between the Porta Pinciana and the Porta Salaria. On the ancient cemetery between the Via Salaria and Via Pinciana see Jordan-Hiilsen, *Topographic der Stadt Horn*, I, 3, p. 437. In the course of the extensive improvements and construction of new streets there during recent years, numerous *columbaria* and inscriptions have been found; see *Not. Srav.* 1901, p. 891; 1905, pp. 13, 19, 38, 71, 81, 100, 142, 200, 270, 364, 375, 407; 1900, pp. 96, 121, 143, 181, 211, 251, 299, 336, 357. Our School has a number of other inscriptions from that region.

American Journal of Arctaaeolofry, Second Series. Journal of the 179
Archaeological Institute of America. Vol. XI (1907), No. 2.

place. The minium in the letters is fairly well preserved. The inscription — an admirable example of Roman calligraphy—is in the *scriptura actuaria*. The first three lines are more monumental in style; in the last four, the hand is more documentary, especially toward the end. Note the forms of A, P, R. The height of the letters is: 1.1, 0.013-0.015 m.; 1.2, 0.009-0.012 m.; 1. 3, 0.009 m.; 11. 4, 5, 0.007 m.; 11. 6, 7, 0.006-0.007 m.

Druso Caesare co« *C. Norbano Flacco Menander C. Comini Maori et C. Cornell Crispi bigarius uincit 5 ludis Mart(i) q(nos) ffecerunt) co(nsule)s eq(uis) Basilisco Rustico, Iwlis uictor(iae) Caesar(is) q(uos) /(ecerunt) P. Cornelius Scip(io), Q. Pompeius Macer priaetores), eq(uis) Histro Corace.*
Lines 1, 2: the date is 15 A.d. This is the earliest dated inscription of a Roman charioteer known. *C.I.L.* VI, 10051, mentions games in A.d. 13 ff., but is itself somewhat later. *C.I.L.* VI, 10046, is probably of the time of Augustus; see below. *Line 3: Menander:* the *agitator* Menander of *C.I.L.* VI, 10046,1. 8, is perhaps the same person. *C.I.L.* VI, 10075, is perhaps his tombstone; but the name is not uncommon. *C. Comini Macri:* cf. Tac.-tl/M. 4, 31 (24 A.d.):.. . *C. Cominium, equitem Romanum, probrosi in se carminis conuictum, Caesar precibns fratris, qui senator erat, concessit.* He is not mentioned elsewhere; we learn his *cognomen* from this inscription. *Line 4: C. Corneli Crispi:* he is not mentioned elsewhere, unless he is the Cornelius spoken of in Tac. *Ann.* 6, 29 (34 A.d.): *Verum ah Seruilio et Cornelio accusatoribus adulterium Liuiae, magorum sacra obiectabantur. ... 30: Ac tamen accusatores, si famltas incideret, poenis adficiebantnr, tit Seruilius Corneliusque perdito Scauro famosi, quia- pecuniam a Vario Ligure omittendae delationis ceperant, in insulas interdkto igni atque aqua demoti sunt. bigarius:* on the *hnli circenses,* see *C.I.L.* I, 1, *index rocab. s.v. ludus;* VI, 10044-10082, 33937-33958; *I.G.* XIV, 1474, 1503, 1604, 1628; Friedlander, *Sittengeschichte*, (1889), II, pp. 325 ff. 498 ff. *Line 5: ludis Mart(i):* May 12, see *C.I.L.* P, 1, p. 318 (Mommsen). *q(uos) /(ecerunt):* so in 1. 6. Cagnat, in his table of abbreviations in *Epigr. Lat.',* does not record this use of Q.F. *eq(uis):* so in 1. 7. Cagnat does not record this use of EQ. *Line 6: ludis uictor(iae) Caesar(is);* July 20-30, cf. *C.I.L.* I, 1, p. 322. There were also presumably special games this year in connection with the celebration of military victories; cf. Tac. *Ann.* 1. 55: *Druso Caesare C. Norbano consulibus decemitur Germanico triumphns manente hello ... 72: Decreta eo anno triumphalia insignia A. Caecinae, L. Apronio, C. Silio ob res cum Germanico gestas. P. Cornelius Sci1no:* it is hardly likely, although barely possible chronologically, that he is the person mentioned in Velleius, 2, 100, 5: *Quintiusque Crispinus, singularein nequitiam supercilio truci protegens, et Appius Claudius et Sempronius Gracchus ac Scipio aliique minoris nomiuis utriusque ordinis uiri, quasi cuiuslibet uxore uiolata, poenas pependere, cum Caesaris Jiliam et Neronis uiolassent coniugem* (2 B.C.). *C.I.L.* VI, 1G203 may refer to him. *Line 7: Q. Pom1eius Macer:* see *Prosopogr. Imp. Rom.* His *praenomen* occurs here only. *Corace:* this name for a horse occurs also in Pausanias, 6, 10, 7; Pliny, *N.H.* 8, 65, 160; on an archaic vase from Caere (Cerveteri), *Annali deW Inst.* 1848, p. 354; and on a lamp, *C.I.L.* XV, 6250 (CORACINIC). There remains the question as to the purpose of this inscription, and the occasion of its erection. It is obviously not a burial inscription, and can hardly be an honorary inscription; its form is not what one would have expected on, *e.g.,* the base of a herm of the charioteer himself. It reads almost like a section from some *fasti.* One might perhaps suggest that it was set up, as a memorial tablet of Menander's successes in the year 15 A.d., in the training school or stables to which he was attached. On this question, however, the inscription itself sheds little light; and in the absence of accurate information concerning the circumstances of its finding — in the absence as well of other similar inscriptions — a definite conclusion on the subject can hardly be reached.

Albert W. Van Buren. *C.I.L.* VI, 10054, 10055, cannot be adduced as parallels.
institute of America
PRE-ROMAN ANTIQUITIES OF SPAIN

In order to become familiar with the pre-Roman antiquities of Spain, it is necessary to visit almost every province of the peninsula. A wealth of material has already been collected in public and private museums, but until one makes a careful study of this material, it is hard to realize what interesting problems have been suggested concerning the early inhabitants of Iberia. To be sure, the work is still in its infancy, and it is too early to try to answer many questions which naturally arise. Were the Iberians the aboriginal people of Spain? Under what conditions and when did they reach the acme of their civilization? Are the Basques of to-day the lineal descendants of the Iberians? These are problems still unsolved, but another question, which will ultimately throw light on the entire subject, can be answered. How far were the Iberians influenced by foreigners, and who were these foreigners? That they were the Phoenicians, as was formerly supposed, can no longer be held in the light of recent investigations. That the Phoenicians were mere traders with only a few stations on the Spanish coast, and that the inhabitants of Tartessus (the Tarshish of the Bible) were not Phoenicians but Iberians has been proved beyond doubt by Eduard Meyer, *Geschichte des Alterthums,* II, pp. 141-154, 683-694.

One is forced to admit after a careful study of the antiquities that first pre-Mycenaean or Cretan, then Mycenaean, and finally Greek influence was all-powerful in the development of Spanish art. But at the same time it is easy to see that Iberian art in The only scientific treatment of the subject known to me is the invaluable book of Pierre Paris, *Exsai stir Vart el vIndustrie de vEspayne primitive,* vol. I (1903), vol. II (1904). The results of the excavations are published with good illustrations in the *lievista de. Archivos, Bibliotecas y Museos* (Madrid). The illustrations in this paper, except Figure 9, are taken partly from the former and partly from the latter work. See also P. Paris. *Arch. A)iz.* 1900, pp. 168-181.

American Journal of Archaeology. Second Scries. Journal of the 182 Archaeological Institute of America, Vol. XI (1901), No. 2.
all its phases had a decided local color. I purposely refrain from a discussion of the Palaeolithic period, the age of cavedwellers, which is identical with that of France, and also of the Neolithic period, and begin with the Bronze Age.

The first illustration (Fig. 1) takes us back to the Mycenaean period. We have before us a beehive grave found at Antequera, north of Malaga, in southern Spain. It was published in the *Revista de Archivos* by Senor Bosco, who very correctly compares it, as his illustration shows, with Mycenaean tholos tombs of continental Greece. The construction is no longer

Figure 1. — (1) Plans Of Mycenaean Tombs Op Greece. (2) Section And Plan Op Beehive Tomb At Antequera. *(ReviMa de Archivos,* XII, pi. 19.)
megalithic, but the walls are formed of rough limestone slabs, bonded with mud, like the later and poorer tombs of Mycenae. The cupola is only 4 in. high. Unfortunately the tomb was robbed, and so its exact date cannot be fixed.

Figure 2 is a section and ground plan of a similar tomb found at Cintra, west of Lisbon, Portugal. Further excavations will doubtless bring to light a large number of such tombs on the east as well as on the south and west coasts of the peninsula.

For a report on the finds in the palaeolithic grotto at Altamira, see *A.J.A.* VI-II, 1904, p. 323, and *Arch. Anz.* 1906, pp. 173-175, where the literature is given.

At Tarragona, for example, good specimens of Cyclopean masonry of the Mycenaean style can still be seen in the lower courses of the city wall.

The small votive offerings of priests, priestesses, and deities in bronze, reproduced in Figure 3, are from the rich collection of Sefior Vives, who showed me much courtesy last summer in Madrid. Similar types of bronze statuettes are found everywhere in Spain. Mr. Horace Sandars found quantities of them at Despenaperros in the Sierra Morena, where they were no doubt manufactured. One half of his collection he donated to

Figure 2.— Section And Plan Of Beehive Tomb At Cintra. (P. *Paris,* I, p. 39.) the British Museum, where, thanks to the director Mr. Cecil Smith, I had the opportunity last June to study them, although at that time they were not yet exhibited. The other half, Mr. Sandars gave to Sehor Vives, who has lent the most important specimens to the Archaeological Museum at Madrid. They date from the early Bronze Age *(ea.* 3000 B.C.) to the sixth century B.C., and many of them show decided influence of Mycenaean or Cretan art.

Fig. 3, Nos. 19 and 20 (P. Paris, II, pp. 18.3, 184, Figs. 280, 281) are probably priests. The former is 97 mm. high, aud was found in

Santisteban del Puerto (Jan); the latter is 89 mm. high, and was acquired at Granada.

No. 21 (P. Paris, II, p. 194, Fig. 311) is probably a priestess. Height 98 mm. From Linares (Jae-n).

No. 7 (P. Paris, II, p. 159, Fig. 231). A nude male figure called Mars or Neton by Me-lida. P. Paris justly doubts this name, because it is not at all certain that the figure wears a helmet. It seems to be a caricature. Height 81 mm. From Linares (Jaen).

Nos. 26, 25, 27 (P. Paris, II, p. 189, Figs. 303, 304, 305). Veiled female figures. The body of the first is reduced almost to a plaque.

Figlre 3.—Bronze Votitk Offerings. *(Revista de Arehivos,* IV, pi. 6.)

Height 52 mm. Provenance unknown. The second wears a peaked cap and a veil. Height 68 mm. From Castellar de Santisteban (Jaen). The body of No. 27 is reduced to a rectangular plaque, but the head, as in all these types, is worked out plastically, a process which reminds one of the prehistoric terracottas from the Argive Heraeum and elsewhere. In front of the body the hands, with the indication of fingers, and the borders of the mantle are visible. Height 58 mm. From Castellar de Santisteban (Jaen).

No. 12 (P. Paris, II, p. 169, Fig. 252). Probably a god of war, because the figure wears a helmet. It is extremely difficult to date this type, because it was retained for centuries after its first invention. Similar types are found not only in the early Bronze Age, but also in the early Iron Age. Height 61 mm. From Palencia.

No. 10 (P. Paris, II, p. 171, Pig. 258). Male figure with plaquelike body. The curve of the nose, which gives the face a Semitic appearance, is merely accidental. There is no Phoenician influence here. Height 56 mm. Bought at Granada.

No. 4 (P. Paris, II, p. 171, Fig. 257). We have here a neolithic type of female idol, such as is found in the second city of Troy (ca. 2500-2000 B.c), but translated into bronze, a most remarkable example of the early Bronze Age. Height 70 mm. From PuenteGenil (Cdrdoba). The same type in stone and terracotta occurs also

FIGCRE 4. — Samian Bronze Statuette. Archaeological Museum, Madrid. *(P. Paris,* I, p. 108.) in Spain, and can be seen in the Museo Proto-Historico Iberico at Madrid, Calle de Alcald 86.

No. 30 (P. Paris, II, p. 159, Fig.-233). Not a gladiator holding a sword, as Melida surmises, but more probably a commander holding a rod or baton, symbolic of power, as P. Paris suggests. Height 67 mm. Bought at Granada.

The most interesting of these bronzes is the mask (Fig. 3, No. 35) with the peculiarly arranged hair. It is early archaic Greek work, and may be more specifically assigned to the school of Phocaea, because a Phoeaean vase, now in the British Museum (C 268) has exactly the same kind of mask painted on either side. It is not surprising to find Phoeaean influence in Spain, because the earliest Greek colonies in Iberia were founded either from Phocaea itself or from the Phoeaean colony Massalia. The Iberians even received their alphabet from Phocaea (Eduard Meyer, *op. cit.* II, p. 691). As early as the seventh century B.C. Phoeaean merchants came to Tartessus,

Figure 5. —Bull With Human Head From Balazote. *P. Paris,* I, pi. 4.) and soon outbid the Phoenician traders (Ed. Meyer, *op. cit.* II, pp. 692-693).

Samos, too, had dealings with Tartessus in the seventh century B.C. (Ed. Meyer, *op. cit.* II, pp. 692, 533-534), and so it is only natural to find in Spain a genuine Samian bronze statuette (Fig. 4) of the archaic period. It closely resembles the Samian terracottas and the Samian statue dedicated by Cheramyes to Hera.

Reproduced in *J.H.S.* II, p. 304. I do not agree with Walters, *History of Ancient Pottery,* I, p. 264, who calls it Cypriote. On p. 64 of the same volume Walters expresses himself more guardedly and with less assurance regarding its fabric. A curious bull with human head (Fig. 5), found at Balazote near Albacete in southeastern Spain, shows decided influence of Oriental, *i.e.* Asiatic, art. Heuzey points out various details of technique recalling monuments of Babylonia and Persia. Similar animals have been found elsewhere in Spain.

Figure 6 reproduces three bronze heads of bulls of the Mycenaean period, in technique much like those from Crete. They were found at Costig in Majorca, an island with many traces of Cyclopean masonry. Indeed, I am inclined to believe that the bull-fights of Spain may go back to the influence

Figure 6.—Bronze Heads Of Bills From Majorca. *(P. Paris,* I, pi. 0.) of the Minoan Cretans, who are now known to have been very fond of the sport of bull-baiting.

Figures 7-9 reproduce representative specimens of local Iberian pottery. The pieces in Figure 7 are incised prehistoric black ware from Andalusia and belong to Mr. Bonsor's collection. I saw even earlier ware than this in the Museo ProtoHistorico Iberico at Madrid, vases which are identical with Quoted by P. Paris, *Essai,* I, pp. 118-121.

The resemblance is more marked between the Cretan type illustrated in *P.S.A.* VI, p. 62, and the Iberian type pictured in P. Paris, *Essai,* I, p. 147, Fig. 112. The horns of the bull on the Cretan agate intaglio (.B. *S.A.* IX, p. 114, Fig. 70) are identical with those from Costig. » *B.S.A.* VIII, p. 74.

those of the second city of Troy (ca. 2500-2000 B.C.). They are hand-made, and the incised lines were filled with chalk. Primitive stone idols similar to those of Parian marble found on the Aegean Islands can also be seen in the same collection. In fact, the art of primitive Spain is identical with that of the entire Mediterranean basin. There must have been much livelier intercourse between those countries in early days than has usually been admitted. From the Mycenaean period down to the Roman domination in the second century B.C. the pottery shows strong Mycenaean influence (Fig. 8), though local peculiarities are apparent. The earliest pieces have curvilinear types of ornamentation; later come vegetable and floral types, and finally animal types (Fig. 9). The latter are much like those of the sub-Mycenaean pottery of Cyprus. Furthermore, the Messapian ware of Apulia influenced the latest Iberian styles of pottery. Thus an askos of local Apulian fabric in the British Museum (Walters, *History of Ancient Pottery,* II, 320, Fig. 185) is decorated with designs that occur frequently on local Spanish pottery. It may be, however, that the Messa The mask on the askos is also seen on a fragment from Elche (P. Paris, II, p. 99, Fig. 197); the fish is similar to the one on another fragment from Elche pian ware and that of the Peucetians go back to the same source from which the Iberians drew. The local Apulian pottery was supplanted by the Athenian red-figured ware in the fourth century B.C., but the local Spanish pottery remained free from Athenian influence, and continued without interruption down to the period of Roman domination. E. Albertini, a member of the French School at Rome, who has been working at Elche with P. Paris, has begun to publish in the *Bulletin hispanique* (1906, pp. 333-362; 1907, pp. 1-17) a thorough account Figure 7. — Ikciskm Pottery From Andalusia. (P. Paris, II, p. 43.) of indigenous Spanish ceramics, and much light will also be thrown on the whole subject by the investigations of the German archaeologists Schulteu and Koenen, who are making (P. Paris, II, p. 95, Fig. 184); the S-shaped designs occur on a fragment from Meca (P. Paris, II. p. 100, Fig. 200); the wave pattern occurs also on a fragment from Meca (P. Paris, II. p. 8(i, Fig. 173); the ivy decoration occurs on a vase from Klche (P. Paris, II, p. 69, Fig. 102); and the star is similar to the star on a fragment from Amarejo (P. Paris, II, p. 54, Fig. 50).

It is noteworthy that the tongue pattern *(Stnbornament)*, which first makes its appearance in Attic ceramics in the sixth century B.C., does not occur on Iberian pottery.

Figure 0.—Painted Shards From Elche. systematic excavations at Numantia in the northern part of central Spain. It is interesting to note that this Ibero-Mycenaean pottery, as it is now called, has been found in southern France, brought there most probably by Massaliote traders.

In the Archaeological Museum at Madrid there is a considerable collection of limestone statuary, found for the most part at Cerro de los Santos, near Murcia, in southeastern Spain. This is usually called Graeco-Phoenician; but since this term is now applied — without good reason, however— to Cypriote statuary, and since there is a decided difference between the art of Cyprus and that of Iberia, I prefer the term Graeco-Iberian. The general style of these sculptures — they belong to the sixth, fifth, and fourth centuries B.C. — is Greek, but there are decided local peculiarities in the drapery and jewellery. The statue reproduced in Figure 10 still belongs to the archaic period. It represents a veiled woman, probably a priestess, holding a sacrificial cup and laden with gold jewellery such as has actually been found in Spain. That the Spanish and Moorish women of to-day are just as fond as were their ancestors of veils, mantillas, and jewellery is seen in Figure 11.

...,... Figure 10. —Graeco-ibe

Une ot the richest discoveries ot ,,

Man Statue. *(P. Paris,* the last decade is the famous gold i pi, 7.) and silver jeweller', found in a field 4 km. from Javea, in the province of Alicante. The masterpiece of this treasure, now in the Archaeological Museum at Madrid, is a diadem of gold, 37 cm. long and weighing 133 grammes (Fig. 12). It is much like the jewellery from Cerro de los Santos, as Melida, the Director of the Museum, correctly noticed, but he certainly erred in assigning it to a native Iberian artist. Pierre Paris is right in calling it purely Greek, and in comparing it with the Greek jewellery of Etruria and southern Russia. But that it is the work of an Attic goldsmith, as he claims, seems doubtful to me. It is more probably the work of an

Figure 11. — Moorish Woman. *(Sevista de Archivos,* IX, pi. 6.)

Figure 12. — Gold Jewellery From Javea. *(Revista de Archivox,* XIII, pi. 18.)

Ionian of Asia Minor, who very successfully combined Attic *Arch. Am.* 1906, pp. 169-171. *R. Arch.* VIII, 1906, pp. 424-436, pi. VII.

Figure 13. — Bust From Elche (P. *Paris,* I, pi. I.) delicacy with Ionic sumptuousness.

I have withheld to the last the finest monument ever found on Spanish soil, the much admired bust from Elche (Fig. 13), now in the Louvre. It is a queenly figure, worthy of the hand of a Phidias, during whose lifetime it seems to have been made. The artist no doubt lived among the Tartessians and knew their customs; otherwise he could not have added all that wealth of detail, and all those eccentricities of dress which give his work so foreign an appearance. Such are the peaked cap, the golden diadem, the peculiar disks of gold on either side of her head. The artist must furthermore have been personally acquainted with this queenly beauty, for he has given us a very faithful portrait. Her features are not Greek nor are they Semitic. This is probably the best and the truest likeness of a typical Iberian woman that we may ever hope to find.

Figure 14 is a portrait of a modern Spanish woman in Valencian costume. The peculiar coiffure is especially interesting, and has often been cited in explanation of the remarkable headdress of the Queen of Elche.

_ Figure 14. — Modern Spanish 1 AUL liAUR. Woman. *(Revista de Arckivos,* Yai.e University. IX, pi. 6.) of CIassieaI Stuotes in Horne COINS FROM ASIA MINOR plate XXIII

The coins described in this paper were collected in Asia Minor during the spring of 1904.

1. Tarsus, Cilicia. *M* 1.4. *Obv.* Head of Caracalla r. laureate. AVKAM AVPCG VHPO CANTDNEINOC CGB. In field, TT TT. *Rev.* Female figure wearing calathus, standing 1. In 1., cornucopiae. In r., Nike holding wreath. AAPCEVH-PANTnNEIOVTTOA. To 1., KOIN OBOV AION. Below TAPCOVMH TPOTT. In field to 1., (".

To r., B.

2. Tarsus, Cilicia. *JE* .7. Variety of No. 99 in *Cat. Gr. Coins in Brit. Mus. Obv.* Head of city, turreted and veiled. Fillet border.

Rev. Sandan on honied animal. In 1., bipennis. To r., TAPSEQN. Border of dots.

3. Adana, Cilicia. JE.85. *Obv.* Bust of Athena. Crested Corinthian helmet and aegis. *Rev.* AAANEQN. Nike advancing r. In 1., palm. In extended r., wreath. To 1., SP MA KA. 4. Ephesus, Ionia. *JE* .5. *Obv.* Eit. Bee. Laurel border. *Rev.* Stag standing r. Head turned to 1. Magistrate's name, AIONYCIOV. 5. Soli, Cilicia. *JE* .5. Similar to *Cat. Or. Coins in Brit. Mus.,* No. 34.

American Journal of Archaeology, Second Series. Journal of the J94 Archaeological Institute of America, Vol. XI (1W7), No. 2.

Obv. Head of Athena, r. Crested Athenian helmet. *Rev.* Bunch of grapes. Below, SOAEQN. In field to 1., K. To r., AA.

6. Soli, Cilieia. *M* .8. Like *Cat. Gr. Coins in Brit. Mus.,* No. 39, but with the position of the letters reversed. *Obv.* Head of Artemis r. Behind, /t. Border of dots. *Rev.* Athena fighting, to r. In 1., shield. In r., bolt. To 1., down» wards, SOAEfiN. To r., monograms, A, and another now illegible. 7. Soli, Cilieia. *M* . 65. *Obv.* Head of Artemis r., with bow and quiver. Border of dots. *Rev.* Cup in shape of Mycenaean cylix, with handle and trace of lip. On either side, branch. Above, KY. To r. and 1., *S Q I A 0 S* 8. Soli, Cilieia. *M* .5. *Obv.* Eagle,

border of dots.
Rev. Bunch of grapes. To r., K. Above, SJOAEfiN. 9. Side, Pamphylia. *M* .75. *Obv.* Bust of Hadrian, r. AVKAITPAI AAPIANOC. *Rev.* CIAH TUUN. Athena advancing l., with crested helmet and long chiton. In r., pomegranate and spear. On l. arm, shield. Before her, l., snake. See *Cat. Or. Coins in Brit. Mm.,* No. 83. 10. Clazomenae, Ionia. *M* .7. *Obv.* Head of Athena, with Corinthian helmet. Countermark, star. *Rev.* Ram walking. Countermark, prow, r. Above, PAPMIS. 11. Apamea, Phrygia. *M* .75. *Obv.* Head of Zeus, r., wearing oak wreath. *Rev.* Cultus statue of Artemis. To r., downwards, ATTAMEJ2N. To l., downwards, HPAKAE *V.* 12. Cremna, Pisidia. t M. B. Similar to Cohen, IV, No. 298. *Obv.* Bust of Geta, to r. P SEP GETA PON CAES *Rev.* Nemesis with small griffon at feet, l. VLTRI (to l.). COL. CR. (to r.).

C. Densmore Curtis. 1906 July — December ARCHAEOLOGICAL DISCUSSIONS SUMMARIES OF ORIGINAL ARTICLES CHIEFLY IN CURRENT PERIODICALS

James M. Paton, *Editor 65, Sparks St. , Cambridge, Mass.* GENERAL AND MISCELLANEOUS

Photography of Manuscripts. — In *Jb. Kl. Alt.* XVII, 1906, pp. 601658 (15 pis.), K. Krumbacher discusses in detail the value of photography, and the methods by which it can be economically employed in philological and archaeological studies. He urges students to photograph manuscripts upon paper films, and emphasizes the superiority of this method to collation. It is also relatively cheaper. *Ibid.* p. 727, he adds a few notes.

Materials for the History of Prehistoric Archaeology. — An Unpublished Memoir of Montfaucou on the Arms of the Ancient Gauls and the Neighboring Peoples. — In *R. Arch.* VIII, 1906, pp. 37-48, E. T. Hamy publishes, with introduction, an essay by Bernard De MontfauCon, written in 1734. In this the theory that the stone and the bronze arms belonged to different contemporary races is maintained.

The Evolution of Culture. — The earliest systematic attempt to apply the theory of evolution to the products of human handiwork was made by Lt.-Gen. A. Lane-Fox Pitt-Rivers, who gathered and arranged the large ethnological collection now at Oxford. His principles of arrangement and his theories of development were set forth in various addresses. These have now been collected with an introduction in which some of the main principles of the author are discussed. The essays are: I, The Principles of Classification, adopted in the arrangement of the author's collection (1874): The departments of Archaeological News and Discussions and of Bibliography of Archaeological Books are conducted by Professor Paton, Editor-in-charge, assisted by Miss Mary H. Buckingham, Professor Harry E. Burton, Mr. Harold R. Hastings, Professor Elmkrt. Merrill, Professor Frank G. Moore, Mr. Charles R. Morey, Professor Lewis B. Paton, Dr. A. S. Pease, and the Editors, especially Professor Marquand and Dr. Peabody.

No attempt is made to include in this number of the Journal material published after January 1, 1907.

For an explanation of the abbreviations, see pp. 140, 141.

II, On the Evolution of Culture (1878); III-V, Primitive Warfare (18671869); VI, Early Modes of Navigation (1874). (Lt.-Gen. A. Lank-fox Pitt-rivers, *The Evolution of Culture and Other Essays,* edited by J. L. Mykes, with an Introduction by Henry Balfour. Oxford, 1906, The Clarendon Press, xx, 232 pp.; 21 pis. 8vo. 7s. 6rf.; $2.50 net.)

The Origin of Spiral Decoration. — In *Z. Ethn.* XXXVIII, 1906, pp. 1-33 (76 rigs.), A. G. Wilke discusses the origin and spread of the spiral maeander and similar systems of decoration. He argues that they developed from the shifting of concentric half-circles. Concentric circles are found in the late neolithic and early bronze ages in northern Europe, and the whole varied system of spiral decoration appears in southern Hungary, especially in Transylvania and Butmir. From this region it spread by trade to the north and west, and by invasion to'the Aegean region. The true spiral developed from the spiral maeander. The angular decorations of the same character are also due to shifting of other geometric figures. This origin explains the appearance of the maeander and spiral as decorations among widely separated peoples.

Prehistoric Oriental Influence in Northern Europe. —In *Mitt. Anth. Ges.* XXXVI, 1906, pp. 57-91 (11 figs.), M. Much examines the evidence for Oriental influence in the arts and customs of northern Europe during the neolithic and early bronze ages, with special reference to the views of Sophus Miiller, who holds that almost all the northern civilization is of Oriental origin. He concludes that this influence is as yet not proved, and that the growth of civilization in Europe shows an independent character, varying according to the natural features of the regions in which it developed.

The Origin of Mythological Monsters. — In *Z. Ethn.* XXXVIII, 1906, pp. 269-311 (26 figs.), II. Bab argues that mythological monsters owe their existence in great measure to abnormal or monstrous human births. This thesis is discussed at length with special reference to the phantastic creations of Asiatic mythology.

The Pumpelly Expedition of 1904. — In *Z. Ethn.* XXXVIII, 1906, pp. 385-390, H. Schmidt reports briefly the results of the Pumpelly Expedition to Turkestan in 1904. Excavations were conducted at two large mounds, near Anau. They showed long occupation in which four periods could be distinguished; three of the bronze, and one of the iron age. The last bronze age period seems to have reached its height about 1500 B.C. The fourth period seems to belong early in the first millennium B.C. Trial excavations were also made at old Merv.

The Names of the Letters of the Alphabet. — In *Eph. Sem. Ep.* II, 1906, pp. 125-139, M. Lidzbarhki discusses the origin of the names of the letters of the Semitic alphabet, and comes to the conclusion that these names are of genuine Semitic origin and that the alphabet must have been invented by a Semitic people. It is possible, however, that it is based upon some foreign phonetic or acrophonetic system. This may have been one of the varieties that have lately been discovered in the eastern Mediterranean. It is impossible that the Greek alphabet was original, and that the Semitic was borrowed from it.

Aramaic Texts on Stone, Clay, and Papyrus. — In *Eph. Sem. Ep.* II, 1906, pp. 200-250, M. Lidzbarski summarizes the discoveries and publications of Aramaic texts from bilingual cuneiform inscriptions, Egyptian papyri, ostraka, and stone inscriptions from Egypt and various parts of Syria.

Himyaritic Inscriptions. — In *S. Bibl. Arch.* XXVIII, pp. 143-148 (pi.; fig.), D. H. Muller discusses the Himyaritic inscriptions discovered by G. U. Yule and published *Ibid.* XXVII, 1905, pp. 153-155. He reviews previous discussions and translations, and gives a corrected edition of the text in transcription, a translation, and commentary.

South Arabian Temple Codes. — In *Or. Lit.* IX, 1906, cols. 256-262, 324-330, 395-398, H. Grimme describes a number of Sabaean inscriptions which contain regulations in regard to the entering of sacred precincts, the protection of consecrated property, and offerings of atonement in case of violation of sanctity. These texts are of peculiar interest on account of the light which they throw upon the ancient Semitic conception of holiness, and their parallels to the old Hebrew and other ancient religious conceptions.

The Friezes from Bum. — In *M. Soc. Ant. Fr.* LXV, 1904-1905, pp. 3244, H. A. Vasnier criticises the restoration of the friezes from Susa in the Louvre. No mortar should appear between the joints of the face. The bricks are slightly wedge-shaped, in order that the mortar at the back may not interfere with the exact contact of the enamelled surfaces in front. This method of construction is found in Turkestan on the tomb of Timur, the work of Persian artists, and its employment in the Louvre would add much to the beauty of the reconstruction.

Notes on Old Persian Inscriptions. — In *J.A.O.S.* XXVIII, pp. 190194, A. V. W. Jackson publishes an important list of corrections of old Persian inscriptions, collated by him during a recent trip through Persia.

In *Or. Lit.* IX, 1906, cols. 481-488, A. Hoffmann-kutschke discusses the text and interpretation of several passages in the Achaemenid inscriptions.

Parthian Coins with Beardless Faces. — In *Num. Chron.* 1906, pp. 221231, H. H. Haworth reiterates, as against Mr. Wroth, his previous doubts about the accuracy of the classification of the coins with a beardless face on the obverse, generally placed at the head of the Parthian series, and repeats his suggestion that they may be attributed to the Arsacidan rulers of Armenia.

The Earliest History of Cyprus. — In *Milt. Vorderas. Ges.* XI, 1906, pp. 1-78 (10 pi.), R. vox Lichtenbero gathers information concerning Cyprus from the Egyptian and Assyrian inscriptions, the principal historic remains in the island itself, and the statements of Greek writers, and constructs from them a sketch of the earliest history of the island. He concludes that there was a homogeneous civilization in Cyprus, Troy, and Phrygia, whose roots are to be sought in the direction of Thrace, and which perhaps can be traced as far as southern Hungary. With this conclusion the ancient traditions agree which represent the Trojans and Phrygians as migrating from Thrace to Asia Minor. The earliest inhabitants of Cyprus are to be regarded as nearly related to these races. As early as the third millennium B.C. they came by land to the southern coast of Asia Minor, whence they were attracted to Cyprus by the fertility of the island.

Ancient Ships.—In *Jh. Areh. I.* XXI, 1906, pp. 107-115 (3 figs.), E. Assmann criticises rather unfavorably P. Gauckler's article on the ship mosaic discovered in 1896 at Althiburus (C. *R. Acad. Insc.* 1898) and Schiff's discussion of the ship graffiti in Alexandrian tombs. The ignorant maker of the mosaic seems to have applied names to types of vessels quite at random; hence nothing can be safely inferred as to the meaning or even the correct form of the names used. Among the names that are clearly misapplied are *actuaria* and *tchedia*. The large single vessel on the floor of another room of the same villa, marked APAEOXA LIBURNI, is not a Liburnian type of vessel, but a ship called *Apaeona* or *Apafona*, probably a Phoenician name, which belonged to Liburnius, the owner of the house. The supposed discovery, in the Alexandrian sketches, of a lateen sail, is a mistake.

Survival of Pagan Cults in Thrace. — In *J.II.S.* XXVI, 1906, pp. 191206 (9 figs.), R. M. Dawkins gives an account, partly from personal observation, partly from an earlier native writer, of a village masquerading festival which is celebrated at Carnival time in the district of Vigo, the ancient Thracian capital, between Constantinople and Adrianople. Some features are evidently survivals of the ancient spring festival of the Spirit of Vegetation, and are akin to the ceremonies of the Curetes and the Roman Salii, while others belong more directly to the cult of Dionysus. The little drama includes planting and sowing, animal disguises with a mock slaying and resurrection, phallic features, prophylactic bells, etc. Somewhat similar ceremonies in the island of Scyros, together with a resemblance of dialects, suggest that after the inhabitants of that island were removed to Corfu by the Venetians in the seventeenth century, it was repopulated from this part of Thrace.

The Shoe in Primitive Ceremonies. — At the May meeting of the Berlin Arch. Society, E. Samter spoke on the shoe in primitive marriage and funeral ceremonies, and traced the custom of throwing an old shoe after a newly married pair, or some one starting on a journey, to the wish to sacrifice a part of one's clothing to propitiate evil spirits, and to the placing of shoes in the grave for use on the journey of the soul. Marriage ceremonies were in origin a form of service to the dead. *Arch. Anz.* 1906, cols. 191-195.)

The Origin of the Taurobolium. — The paper by C. IT. Moore, presented at the General Meeting of the Archaeological Institute in Boston *A.J. A.* IX, 1905, p. 71), is published in full in *Harvard Studies in Classical Philology*, XVII, 1906, pp. 48-48.

Angariae. —The Persian postal system (αγγαπρjιον) is described by Herodotus, and in the fourth century A. d., *angarium* denotes the state transport of burdens, and *angariae* the animals and wagons pressed into this service. The period between Herodotus and Diocletian is studied in *Klio,* VI, 1906, pp. 249-258, by M. Rostowzew, who shows that the custom of pressing animals and men into public service continued unbroken through Hellenistic and Roman times, and increased with the institution of the imperial fast post, until it was placed on a legal basis by the later emperors. The custom is best known in Judaea and Egypt. The verb used is regularly *ayyapixx.iv.*

Jugglers. — The feats of jugglers in ancient and mediaeval times, as shown on works of art or mentioned in literature, are discussed by A. Warren in *Keliq.* XIII, 1907, pp. 1-16 (11 figs.). A list of representations of such feats is given in an appendix.

Horse Brasses. — The ornamental brasses used to decorate horses were originally amulets, and are still so regarded in some European countries. Their origin, use, and meaning are discussed, and 165 forms illustrated by Lina Eckenstein in *Reliq.* XII, 1906, pp. 247-262 (13 figs.).

EGYPT

The Oldest Fixed Date in History. — In *Bibl. World,* XXVIII, 1906, pp. 108-112, J. II. Breasted discusses the Egyptian calendar and the information that it gives in regard to the antiquity of Egyptian civilization. The Egyptian year consisted of 365 days, so that every four years the New Year was celebrated one day too soon. In the course of 1460 years New Year's day thus made a complete circuit of the year and came back to the day from which it had set out. This circuit is known as the Sothic period. The beginning of such a period is recorded 2780 B.C., and it is impossible to suppose, in view of the high culture of this age, that the calendar was first introduced at this time. Moreover, the year of 365 days is mentioned in Pyramid texts. We must go back, therefore, another 1460 years to 4241 B.C. to find the beginning of the Egyptian era.

Totemism in Egypt. — In a lecture at the Musee Guimet, V. Loret argued that the gods of the Egyptians were the totems of the different Egyptian clans before they were worshipped as gods. In spite of some difficulties, the theory has much to recommend it, and would certainly explain the worship of animals, which has formed one of the standing puzzles of Egyptian religion. *(Alhen.* Sept. 15, 1906, p. 310.)

The Prehistoric Kings of Abydos. — In *J. Asiat.* VII, 1906, pp. 233272, E. Amelineau reviews his former discussion of the historical character of the first kings of Abydos named in the Palermo stone, and shows how his conclusions have been confirmed by recently published Egyptian and Ethiopian records and by archaeological discoveries, which prove the persistence of the cults of these early Pharaohs down to a comparatively late time.

A Statuette of the Goddess Buto. — In *S. Bibl. Arch.* XXVIII, pp. 201-202 (pi.), V. Schmidt discusses the pedestal of an Egyptian statuette in the Civic Museum at Mantua, which bears an inscription, stating that it was erected by Rameses II, in honor of the goddess Buto.

The Title "Father of the God." — In *Sitzb. Sachs. Ges.* 1905, pp. 254270, L. Borchardt finds that the title " Father of the God" designates the king's father-in-law, during the Old and Middle Kingdoms. In the New Empire the title has the same meaning, and in later times it designates the king's father. Since the service of the gods imitated that of the kings, the same title designates the " father-in-law " of a god.

The Stele of the Excommunication. — The stele of the excommunication from Napata is translated and discussed in *Klio,* VI. 1906, pp. 287-296 (fig.), by H. Schafer, who argues, against Maspero, that it is a royal decree excluding all members of a certain family from the temple of Amon at Napata, because some of them had planned a murder in the temple, for which crime they had been burned to death. The edict closes with a curse upon all prophets and priests who do evil in the temples.

The Nubian king's name has been erased, but the language indicates a date not later than the end of the seventh century n.c.

The Arrival of the Statue by Bryaxis at Alexandria. — In *R. Arch.* VIH, 1906, pp. 322 f., is a summary by G. Dattari of a paper presented by him at the Antiquarian and Numismatic Society of Montreal, in which, on the evidence of coins, he fixes the date at which the statue of Serapis, by Bryaxis, reached Alexandria in 214-213 B.C.

Two Statuettes of Serapis. — In *Ath. Mitt.* XXXI, 1906, pp. 55-59 (2 pis.; fig.), F. W. Von Bissixg publishes two statuettes of Serapis from Cairo in his collection. One is a limestone figure (height 0.19 m.), of good workmanship, and clearly a copy of a statue, which can scarcely be other than the work of Bryaxis. The other figure is of bronze, and also repeats the motive of the great statue, but emphasizes the drawing back of the left leg and extension of the right.

Ancient Dice. — In *B. Soc. Ant. Fr.* 1906, pp. 158-159, E. Michon describes two steatite dice from Egypt. One is a regular icosahedron, having a letter of the Greek alphabet, from A to Y, on each face. The other is a dodecahedron, having the first twelve Greek numerals on its faces.

Two Bronze Portraits from Egypt. — There is in the British Museum a pair of statuettes representing a male and a female figure, in the guise of Olympian deities but with portrait faces and certain attributes which belong to Ptolemy Philadelphus and Arsinoe II. The figures, which measure a few inches over a foot in height, are wholly Greek in conception and workmanship, although from Egypt. They are interesting as giving an idea of the appearance of statues of the 6iol d&Xoi. (C. C. Edgar, *J.H.S.* XXVI, 1906, pp. 281-282; pi.)

Public Works under Ptolemy Philadelphus. — In *C. R. Acad. Insc.* 1906, pp. 433-441, P. Jouguet and J. Lesquiek publish a papyrus fragment relating to works of irrigation undertaken in the twenty-seventh year of Ptolemy Philadelphus (259 B.C.). It contains a plan of the proposed canals, with specifications as to dimensions, and estimates of the cost, varying according to the season when the work is carried on. The fragment shows that the *naubion* was at this time a cube, measuring two royal cubits on each side and therefore equal to the *aiolion*.

"Chiselled" Coins. — Dr. Edde, in *B. Num.* XIII, 1906, pp. 7-9, argues, on the basis of a small hoard of coins acquired by him in Egypt, in behalf of the theory examined and rejected by Babelon *(Traite,* I, pp. 644 f.), that the coins gouged by a chisel were thus cut by the casual possessors in order to determine whether they were of the proper metal throughout, or were merely plated.

Roman and Egyptian Legal Formulae. — The relation of the written instructions given by the magistrate in Roman Egypt to a subordinate *(index pedaneus)* to the *formulae* used in similar cases in Roman law has been studied by L. Boulard. He considers the scope and optional characters of these instructions, and reaches the conclusion that they do not agree with the *formulae* in essential points, and that their origin is to be sought in the Egyptian procedure under the Ptolemies, and not in the Roman law. (Louis Boui,ARn, *Les Instructions ccrites du Magistral au Juge-commissaire dans l'£gypte Romaine,* Paris, 1906, E. Leroux. Pp. viii, 127. 8vo.)

BABYLONIA AND ASSYRIA

A Babylonian Map of the World. — In *Exp. Times,* XVIII, 1905, pp. 68-73, A. H. Sayck describes a map which is at least as old as the Hammurabi period and probably a good deal older. It is published in *Cuneiform Texts,* Vol. XXII, and represents the world as a disk surrounded by the ocean which is named the "Salt Kiver." On the map the location of a number of cities of Babylonia and of Assyria, and the Euphrates and the Persian Gulf are clearly shown. The text is of interest for the interpretation of the Gilgamesh epic and for the Hebrew conception of the garden of Eden. See also *Am. Ant.* XXVIII, 1906, pp. 334-338 (fig.).

Date and Place of the Code of Hammurabi. — In *J.A.O.S.* XXVIII, pp. 123-134, D. G. Lyon inquires into the year when and the place where the Code of Hammurabi was first promulgated. The text discovered in Elam could not have been written before the thirtieth or thirty-first year of his reign, but the promulgation of the code is older. The prologue suggests that the code was published at the beginning of the king's reign, and a chronological table which gives the name of his second year as the year in which righteousness was established, would suggest that this was the year in which the code was promulgated. As to the place, the author maintains that a correct interpretation of the text shows that it was erected in Babylon and not in Sippar.

Did the Babylonian Temples have Libraries? —In *J.A.O.S.* XXVIII, pp. 146-189, M. Jastrow, Jr., discusses the question of the existence of Babylonian temple libraries. Three important mounds have thus far been pretty thoroughly explored; namely, Telloh, Abu Habba, and Nippur; and a fourth site, Babylon, has been under investigation since 1899. In none of these mounds has anything that can properly be called a temple library been discovered. All that has been found in connection with the temple has been either records connected with the temple administration, or business documents of a private character, stored there for safety, or tablets for use in the temple schools. Among the latter, mythological and ritual texts, which served as writing exercises for the children, have occasionally been discovered, but nothing which indicates the preservation of literature in the narrower sense. The Babylonian temples were halls of record rather than libraries, and the only library which has yet been discovered is that found in the palace of Assurhanipal at Nineveh.

The Participation of the Babylonians in the Destruction of Nineveh. — In *Or. Lit.* IX, 1906, cols. 444-447, B. Mkissner calls attention to passages in the recently published *Cuneiform Texts in the British Museum,* XXII. which favor the view that the Babylonians shared with the Medes in the destruction of the Assyrian empire, in spite of the assertion of Nabonidus, that they had not destroyed the sanctuaries of the Assyrian gods.

Babylonian War Gods. —In S. *BiU. Arch.* XXVIII, pp. 203-218, T. G. Pinches discusses the names and attributes of Nergal and of the gods who are equated with Ninib, or, as the author thinks it should be read, Nirig, in the so-called monotheistic cuneiform tablet. He appends also a transcription and translation of two hymns to Nergal from the city of Cutha.

The Etana Myth in Babylonian Art. — In *Or. Lit.* IX, 190C, cols. 431432, 477-481 (fig.), A. Hermann-describes and discusses a number of Babylonian representations of the myth of Etana and the eagle.

A Chaldaean Dragon.— Among the German discoveries at Babylon is a curious monster with a serpent's head, which was represented on the enamelled bricks of the walls of Nebuchadnezzar. The type is much older, occurring on a stone vase and on a seal of Gudea, discovered by de Sarzec. This early dragon was sacred to the Chaldaean god, Nin-ghis-zida, and the type can be traced through various transformations to the Babylonian period, when the sacred dragons form a pair of fantastic creatures, dedicated to Marduk and Nebo. (L. Heuzey, *C. R. Acad. Imc.* 1906, p. 540.)

The Technique of Cuneiform Writing on Clay. — In *Or. Lit.* IX, 1906, cols. 304-312, 372-1380 (5 figs.), L. Messerschmidt makes a careful study of the way in which cuneiform writing on clay was produced. He comes to the conclusion that the writing instrument was a stylus made of a segment of bamboo reed formed by two cuts, one passing through the centre of the reed, the other tangential to the inner circumference. By this means an instrument was produced by which all the lines, curves, and angles that are found in cuneiform inscriptions could be executed.

A Sumerian Incantation.—In the *Recueil de Travaux, V.* Brummer publishes a unique incantation tablet in Sumerian, which he thinks may be as old as 3500 B.C. It confirms the view that the spells in Assurbanipal's library were copied from much earlier documents. The article also discusses the importance of the temple of Ea at Eridu as the chief holy place of the Sumerian religion. *(Athen.* Sept. 15, 1906, p. 309.)

The Chedorlaomer Tablets. — In *S. Bibl. Arch.* XXVIII, pp. 193-200, A. H. Sayce subjects the famous tablets published by Pinches in 1895, to a detailed examination, and concludes that Pinches was correct in reading the name written KU-KU-KU-MAK or KU-KU-KU-KU-MAR as Ku-durlakh-kha-mar. He brings fresh evidence to establish the correctness of this reading, and gives a new transcription and translation of the first thirty-four lines of the tablet.

Documents from the Time of the First Dynasty of Babylon.—In the *Publications of the Babylonian Expedition of the University of Pennsylvania,* Series A, Vol. VI, Part I, H. Ranke publishes a collection of 119 tablets belonging to the period of the first dynasty of Babylon. These tablets come 'for the most part from Sippar, a few perhaps from Babylon. All the tablets which belong to the reigns preceding that of Hammurabi, that are found in the University of Pennsylvania collections, are given in full. From the time of Hammurabi onward only specimens of the more interesting tablets are given. All the rulers of the first dynasty of Babylon except Sumuabum are represented. The tablets consist of contracts concerning the purchase of slaves, exchange of houses, hiring of servants, lease of fields, loans, donations, and divisions of inheritances, also decisions of the courts in contested cases, memoranda, lists, etc. The proper names of the period show that two races were living side by side in Babylon at this time, one the old Babylonians who were amalgamated with the Sumerians, the other the new Babylonians, or Amorites, to which the ruling dynasty belonged. The fact that names were compounded with that of the goddess Lagamal is interesting because of its bearing on the Chedorlaomer controversy. The texts are published in seventy-one plates of autography and thirteen plates of photographs. The volume is provided with complete indices of all the proper names, and a list of the signs that were in use during this period.

Seal Inscriptions on an Early Babylonian Contract. — In *J.A.O.S.* XXVIII, pp. 133-141 (3 pls.; 2 figs.), D. G. Lyon describes a "case" tablet in the Harvard Semitic Museum, containing an unusual number of interesting seal inscriptions, and shows the importance that such seal tablets as these have for the dating of seals whose origin is otherwise unknown.

A Babylonian Adoption Contract. — In *Or. Lit.* IX, 1906, cols. 534-5:18, A. Unonad translates and comments upon a tablet of the Kassite period. Vol. XIV, No. 40, of the University of Pennsylvania texts. A certain woman adopts a daughter upon payment of seven shekels of gold with the stipulation that the latter shall care for her during her life, and after her death shall make libations of water for the repose of her soul. A breach of the contract exposes the mother to pecuniary loss; the daughter, to degradation to the condition of a slave.

Documents of the Kassite Period. — In the *Publications of the Babylonian Expedition of the University of Pennsylvania,* Series A, Vols. XIV-XV, A. T. Clay publishes a collection of tablets bearing (1) complete dates, and (2) incomplete dates, from the period of the Kassite dynasty of Babylon. Nearly all of these tablets were discovered in the second expedition to Nippur under the directorship of J. P. Peters. The documents are contracts, deeds, and similar business records and belong to the reign of every one of the Kassite rulers except Kadashman-Burish. The tablets allow us to reach some conclusions in regard to the length of the reigns of successive monarchs, and these are hard to bring into accord with the famous Babylonian list of kings. The proper names found in the tablets are important for the history of migrations into Babylonia. They exhibit three main types, the old Babylonian, the Amorite, and the Kassite. Most interesting, perhaps, are a number of names compounded with Ya-a-u, which has been supposed to be Yahweh, God of the Hebrews. For instance, Ya-u-bani is formed like Ea-bani, and Ya-u-a seems to be the same as Jehu. There is also a goddess Yautum, corresponding with the masculine divinity. The work is provided with translations of specimens of the different classes of tablets, and with an elaborate index of names of persons, places, and deities. A list of signs that occur in the text is also given, transcriptions of 168 tablets in 72 plates, and photographic reproductions of these same tablets in 15 plates. See also *Rec. Past,* V, 1906, pp. 213-224 (14 figs.).

The "Koudourrou." — In *C. R. Acad. Insc.* 1906, pp. 308-319, E. Cuq discusses a class of Chaldean monuments, the *Koudourrous,* containing records of the ownership of land, with an exact indication of the boundaries. Their principal object is to place the property under the protection of the gods, and they are marked by two characteristic features, — reliefs containing the emblems of divinities, and a series of imprecations against those who may dispute the ownership or shift the boundaries of the piece of land. The form of the documents indicates a time when the authority of the law was insufficient to protect the owner. The series recently brought to the Louvre from Susa belongs to the Kassite period (1330-1117 B.C.), and refers to lands bought by the king from a tribe or city, and bestowed by him on some individual. The documents throw much light on the nature of landed property, and on the decadence of civilization in the Kassite period, as contrasted with the time of Naram-Sin or Hammurabi.

Mitanni Names from Nippur. —In Or. *Lit.* IX, 1906, cols. 588-591, F. Bork discusses a number of proper names in the documents recently published by Clay for the University of Pennsylvania. These are compounded with Teshup and Tarku, which are well-known names of divinities of the land of Mitanni. Another name, A-ga-ab-ta-ha, is mentioned in an Elamitic inscription as that of a refugee from the land of Mitanni. The collection of proper names that can be made from these documents throws not a little light upon the language and commercial relations of the

Mitanni people.

An Assyrian Grammatical Treatise. — In *J.A.O.S.* XXVII, 1900, pp. 88-103, S. Langdon discusses a tablet, published in the second volume of Rawlinson's Inscriptions, which has hitherto been supposed to be a list of synonyms, but which he maintains is a chronological treatise based upon an omen tablet as a specimen. The text is published in full with transcription and translation.

Assyrian Incantations against Ghosts. — In *S. Bibl. Arch.* XXVIII. pp. 219-227, R. C. Thompson publishes a transliteration and translation of a remarkable tablet published in *Cuneiform Texts*, Vol. XXIII. The contents are largely new, and describe the Assyrian method of laying a ghost.

Meaning of the Names of the Rulers of Shirgulla. — In *Or. Lit.* IX, 1906, cols. 312-315, 380-385, V. Brummek discusses the names of the earliest rulers of the Babylonian kingdom of Shirgulla (Shirpurla). He starts with the name Akurgal, which means " son of the great mountain," and maintains that this must be a title of a deity, and that the king's name is an abbreviation due to the omission of servant or son before the name of the god. On this basis lie attempts to explain the names of the remaining rulers of this dynasty as similar *hypokoristika*.

The Babylonian"Chronicle. —In *Abh. Sachs. Ges.* XXV, No. 1 (46 pp.), F. Df.litzscii republishes in transcription and translation the *Babylonian Chronicle* of 745-668 n.c. with commentary. An appendix (pp. 41-46) contains the *Synchronistic History P.* in transcription, with notes.

Babylonian Astrology in Late Jewish Tradition. — In *Or. Lux*, II, 1906, pp. 113-168, A. Wunschk maintains that numerous traces of Babylonian cosmology and astrology are to be found in the Talmud, the midrashes, and the cabalistic writings. As an illustration of this he takes the descriptions of Solomon's throne and hippodrome in the different recensions of the Agada. The numerous animal forms which stand upon the steps of the throue are not the creations of Jewish fancy, but Babylonian astrological figures. The throne itself represents the Babylonian conception of the sky, and the hippodrome represents the Babylonian myth of the course of the seasons.

SYRIA AND PALESTINE

The Old Hebrew Calendar. —In *Z. Morgenl. Ges.* LX, 1906, pp. 605644. E. Konio gives a thorough discussion of all the material bearing on the nature of the old Hebrew calendar, and conies to the conclusion that in the earliest times the day began with the dawn and that the custom of beginning the day with the evening is found only in later strata of Old Testament literature. The change cannot be attributed to Babylonian influence, since, according to Pliny, the Babylonians began the day with sunrise. It is due rather to observation of the moon for the purpose of determining the beginning of feasts. The new moon can be observed only in the evening, and hence arose a tendency to begin the day when the new moon first appeared. The months were known originally by the Canaanitish names Abib, Ziw, Ethanim, Bui, etc. Not until after the Exile did the Babylonian names Nisan, Iyyar, etc. , appear. This was due to direct borrowing from the Babylonians. The method of numbering the months instead of naming them is found in all periods. The month was originally a lunar one, but the year was solar, so that the insertion of an occasional intercalary month was necessary. The year originally began in the autumn. The beginning of the year in the spring with the month Nisan cannot be traced before 600 B.C., and is probably due to Babylonian influence.

Origin of the Hebrew Alphabet. —In *Am. Ant.* XXVIII, 1906, pp. 329-334, H. Proctor argues that the Hebrew square characters were derived directly from hieroglyphics, and not from the Phoenician, and that they probably formed from the earliest times a sacred system of writing.

Palestine before the Hebrew Conquest. — In *Bibl. World*, XXVIII, 1906, pp. 360-373 (3 figs.), G. A. Barton summarizes the results of the latest archaeological discoveries for the history and civilization of Palestine before the arrival of the Hebrews. He accepts the views that the aborigines of the country were non-Semitic, that the earliest Semitic immigrants were the Amorites, and that the Canaanites were a second wave of Semitic migration, contemporaneous with the Kassite conquest of Babylonia and the Hyksos conquest of Egypt.

Topography of Jerusalem. In *Pal. Ex. Fund*, XXXVIII, pp. 206212, 278-286, J. C. Nevin discusses the location of the Acra, Millo, the King's Gardens, the Rock Zoheleth, Silla, Gihon, the King's Pool, Enrogel, the Lower Pool, the Upper Pool, the Broad Wall, the Furnace Tower, and other points in the topography of Jerusalem.

The Location of Golgotha. —In *Pat. Ex. Fund*. Vol. XXXVIII, 1906, pp. 269-274, A. W. Crowley-boevey discusses C. Wilson's ' Notes on Golgotha and the Holy Sepulchre' in the preceding volume, with a result unfavorable to the genuineness of the traditional location of the Holy Sepulchre.

The Meaning of the Expression "Between the Two Walls." — In /. *Bibl. Lit.* XXV, 1906, L. B. Paton discusses the location of the two walls mentioned in Jer. xxxix, 2-5; lxii, 5-8; 2 Kings xxv, 2-5; Isa. xxii, 9-11, and holds that they can only have been the walls on either side of the mouth of the Tyropoeon Valley, near the pool of Siloam; that is, the west wall on the east hill and the east wall on the west hill. The use of this expression as early as Isa. xxii, 9-11 shows that the second wall on the south, which enclosed the southern end of the western hill and joined it to the eastern hill, was in existence as early as the time of Hezekiah, and suggests that it was the wall mentioned in 2 Chron. xxxii, 5, and that it was built by Hezekiah.

The Siloam Tunnel. —In *Bibl. World*, XXVII, 1906, pp. 467-472, T. F. Wright gives a history of the exploration of the Siloam Tunnel at Jerusalem, and compares the methods used by the constructors of this tunnel with those employed by the engineers of the Simplon.

Weights found in Jerusalem. — In *Pal. Ex. Fund*, XXXVIII, 1906, pp. 182-

189, 259-267, C. Warren discusses a number of weights found in Jerusalem, and after a general review of ancient weights and measures, reaches the conclusion that the old Troy grain, which was one per cent heavier than the present Troy grain, was a general unit of weight throughout the ancient world, and that these Jerusalem weights, as well as various Babylonian and Egyptian weights, are multiples of this standard.

Notes on Semitic Incriptions. — In *Eph. Sem. Ep.* II, 1906, pp. 140119, M. Lidzbarski discusses all the seals and weights with Semitic inscriptions discovered within the last two years, including the seal of Sheina, the servant of Jeroboam, from Tell el-Mutesellim, that of Joshua, the son of Asayahu *J. A.O.S.* XXIV, 1903, pp. 205-226), and that of Hanan, son of Yedayahu *Mitt. Pal. V.* 1903, p. 30). *Ibid.* pp. 150-152, the same writer reviews recent discussions of the genuineness of the Mesha Inscription, and concludes that there Is no sound reason for doubting its authenticity. *Ibid.* pp. 153-171, the same writer publishes and discusses all the Phoenician inscriptions which have been discovered during the last three years. *Ibid.* pp. 190-199, he discusses the date of the Siloam inscription, and concludes from a comparison with the earliest gems that it cannot be brought down to post-exilic times, but belongs to the first period of Hebrew epigraphy. He also describes the inscriptions on ossuaries found at Jerusalem and Gaza during the past three years. *Ibid.* pp. 251-316, he reports the Nabataean and Palmyrene inscriptions discovered or published within the past three years.

Some Aramaean Inscriptions.—In *J. Asiat.* VII, 1906, pp. 281-304. (1 pi.), J. B. CnABOT discusses a number of recently published Aramaic inscriptions. The first is a mosaic at Edessa with a Syriac inscription, naming Aftoha the son of Garmo. The second is an inscription published in *Z. Morgenl. Ges.* XIV, as old Indian. A new examination of the squeeze preserved in the Louvre shows that this is a Syriac inscription from Sinai. There are also Palmyrean sepulchral inscriptions from the collection of Mr. Jacobsen at Copenhagen.

Notes on Some Phoenician Inscriptions. — In *Z. Morgenl. Ges.* LX, 1906, pp. 165-168, F. Praetorius discusses expressions in the Marseilles Inscription, the Inscription of Eshmunazar and the inscription, *C.I.S.* I, pp. 29 ff.

Palmyrene Inscriptions. — In *R. Arch.* VIII, 1906, pp. 253-267, Ch. Clermont-ganneau discusses ten Palmyrene epitaphs published by Chabot (*/. Asiat.* 1906, T, pp. 293-304) and publishes (2 figs.) two inscribed reliefs representing, one a woman, the other a man. Both were in the collection of the Countess de Beam, and the first is now the property of Mr. A. Dutens. A reading of the epitaphs is given. A translation (in pious memory to him whose name is blessed for eternity, the good and the pitiful! Invoking the holy god, X son of Y, and Z son of...) of the inscription discussed by the same writer *(Recueil d'Arch. Orient.* VII, p. 36, No. 11) and others is given.

The Inscription of Namara.— In *Or. Lit.* IX, 1906, cola 573-584, M. Hartmann discusses the inscription published by Dussaud in *R. Arch.* 1902, pp. 409-421 (see *A J.A.* VII, p. 235). This inscription states that the building on which it stands is the mausoleum of the king of all the Arabs, Maralqais Ibn 'Amr, and mentions the day of his death, the 7th of Kislul 223; that is, the 7th of December, 328 A.d.

The Temple of Bel at Palmyra. — The plan and architecture of the temple of Bel or Helios at Palmyra were discussed by O. Puchstein at the May meeting of the Berlin Arch. Society. The great court was surrounded by colonnades, double on three sides, and single but higher on the fourth. The temple pro1er was Corinthian, with the entrance at the west end. The cella had windows and an adyton at either end. The style points to the time of Augustus or Tiberius, and to a Greek or Greco-Roman architect, who sought a perspective effect in the decorative reliefs. *(Arch. A nz.* 1906, cols. 193-194.)

Meaning of Baal in Sabaean. —In *Or. Lit.* IX, 1906, cols. 251-256, H. Winckler defends the view that Baal in Sabaean denotes an inhabitant of a place, not a deity of that place.

The Dating of Samaritan Manuscripts. — In *J. Bibl. Lit.* XXV, pp. 29-48 (2 pis.), R. Gottheil discusses the date of a Samaritan Hebrew text of the Pentateuch that was recently offered for sale in New York. It is claimed to be the oldest dated Hebrew codex in existence and to belong to the year 734 A.d. The author maintains that it is some 785 years younger than has been supposed, and in support of this gives an elaborate discussion of the way in which Samaritan manuscripts are dated.

A Portrait of Antiochus VII.— In *Le Muse'e,* III, 1906, pp. 75-78 (pi.), A. Sambon publishes a silver "emblema" on which is a head wearing the Phrygian cap, while behind the shoulders appear the horns of the crescent. From a comparison with the coins of Antiochus VII of Syria, he concludes that it is a portrait of that king with the attributes of the god Men, and a fine example of Syrian art in the second century B.C.

A Weight from Seleucia.—In *B. Soc. Ant. Fr.* 1906, pp. 193-198, E. Michon publishes a double mina of Seleucia recently acquired by the Louvre. It is a square lead plate with the figure of an elephant in relief, and weighs 1143 grammes. It bears the inscription 5ΕΛΕΥΚΕΙΟΝ ΛΙΜΝΟΥΝ ΕΤΤΙΑΕΛΙΩΝΟΣ (the agoranomos) and also the numerals CKP, *i.e.* 126 of the Seleucid era (186 B.C.).

The Architecture of Baalbek. — Architectural members from Baalbek have been brought to Berlin, sufficient to show the details of the architecture and ornament as well as the technical structure of the various temples and colonnades of Heliopolis. Baalbek represents the Syrian type of Roman architecture under the Emperors, and shows an astonishingly rich and beautiful variety of decoration. The buildings represented are as follows: I. The small round building over a water basin at some distance from the town, erected in the first century A.d. It has column bases of an elaborate floral design —an ancient Oriental idea worked out in the Hellenistic spirit — spiral-fluted shafts and classical

Corinthian capitals. II. The colossal temple of Heliopolitan Zeus. The frieze here consists of consols decorated by the fore parts of bulls and lions alternately, and connected by garlands in relief. Traces of color are found. The acanthus and palmettes on the sima and elsewhere are very free in design, with lilies on branching stems. Certain differences of style in the decorative members point to an alteration of taste during the extended time occupied by the building. III. The two courts in front of the temple, begun in the latter half of the second century and finished under Caracalla. They show the later tendency to striking and picturesque ornament, and a beautiful polychromy of material in the monolithic shafts of polished pink granite contrasting with the pure white limestone, now golden with age. A column base from one of these halls, as well as a bit of the podium of the stage wall of the theatre, shows that round members were first cut in plane surfaces with the forms of the mouldings indicated at an edge, to be worked out after the stones were in place. IV. From the temple of Bacchus there is only a piece of an abacus, which has a figure of Pan in place of the usual acanthus flower, and from the round building in late Roman style, only small fragments. The only representation of the Heliopolitan Zeus, a cippus found in the round fountain house, remains at Baalbek, but three small reliefs of the Heliopolitan Triad are in Berlin. A characteristic type of monument, with a baldaquin supported on four columns over a statue, is represented by parts taken from a grave monument and a fountain. There are smaller articles of terra-cotta, glass, faience, and mosaic, of Arabic origin. (O. Puchstein, 4rcA. *Anz.* 1906, cols. 225-240; 2 figs.)

The Fortress of Masada. — The fortress of Masada, built by Herod the Great, and the last stronghold held by the Jews after the destruction of Jerusalem, is briefly described by F. B. Wright in *Rec. Past,* V, 1906, pp. 368-372 (4 figs.).

The Rock Sculptures of Kab Elias. — The rock sculptures near Kab Elias *(Sunday School Times,* 1902, p. 546; cf. *AJ.A.* VII, 1903, pp. 107, 366) are discussed by S. Ronzevalle, in *Mel. Fac. Or.* I, 1906, pp. 223-238 (2 pls.). The first relief represents only a bull, near whose head in three niches are badly mutilated reliefs of divinities, apparently a local triad similar to that of Heliopolis. It seems to belong to Roman times. The second relief is much earlier, and represents an eagle-headed man, wearing a long garment and holding a sceptre. The style suggests Babylonian origin, but no exact parallel can be cited.

ASIA MINOR

Hittite Inscriptions. —In *S. Bibl. Arch.* XXVIII, pp. 133-137 (3 figs.), A. H. Sayce proposes several emendations of the Ardistama and Ivriz inscriptions published by him in Vol. XXVII; and describes, with a tentative translation, some Hittite seals in the Ashmolean Museum.

The Ancient Harbor of Chalcedon. — The remains of the ancient moles at Chalcedon were traced in 1882, and show that the Kauotos Ai/xijv (Appian, *Bell. Mith.* 71, p. 380) was formed by a long mole extending toward the northwest, and a shorter mole running northeast from the point near the English cemetery. (I. Miliopulos, *Ath. Mitt.* XXXI, 1906, pp. 53-54; fig.)

The Lion-Group from Cyzicus. — In *B.S.A.* XI, 1904-05, pp. 151-152. F. W. Hasluck suggests that the relief from Cyzicus representing two lions standing over two bulls *(B.S.A.* VIII, p. 192; "see *AJ.A.* VIII, p. 101) may have formed part of the decoration on the base of a throne for a statue of Cybele. Several possible restorations of the statue as standing or seated are suggested.

Ancient Sinope. — The articles on the history of Ancient Sinope, its inscriptions, and Prosopographia by D. M. Robinson *(American Journal of Philology,* XXVII, pp. 125-153, 245-279; *AJ.A.* IX. 1905, pp. 294-233) have been bound in one volume, with title-page and corrigenda. (david M. Robinson, *Ancient Sinope.* An historical account with a Prosopographia Sinopensis, and an Appendix of Inscriptions. Baltimore, 1906, The Johns Hopkins Press. 8vo. i 1.00.)

Votive Reliefs in the Louvre.—In *R. £t. Anc.* VIII, 1906, pp. 181-190 (2 pls.), E. Michon discusses some reliefs from Asia Minor, illustrating the syncretism prevalent among the partially Hellenized natives. From Philadelphia is a dedication to Marvijvi/, seemingly a local form of the *irorvia BripSiv.* A dedication from Acmonia mentions Artemis *'Aa-rtXtam1,* apparently referring to the nature goddess, commonly called Anaitis. A more comprehensive syncretism appears on a stele from Ouchak in Phrygia, representing Cybele, with Hermes and a draped figure on either side. Above is a mounted warrior, with an eagle and Victory in front, and a winged genius behind. *Ibid.* pp. 281-283, F. Cumont interprets the relief from Ouchak as showing the *Mtfrr1p Ottav,* as the goddess of the earth, while above rides through the heavens *Myjv Oipavios.* Hermes frequently appears on Oriental monuments as an intermediary between earth and heaven.

A Decree of Outlawry from Miletus. — In *C. R. Acad. Insc.* 1906, pp. 511-523, G. Glotz studies in detail an inscription from Miletus *(Sitzb. Berl. Akad.* 1906, pp. 252 ff.; *Arch. Anz.* 1906, p. 17). The nature of the penalties shows that the crime for which Nympharetus, Stratonax, and their sons were proscribed was political, though by a legal fiction it is classed as murder. A comparison with Nicolaus of Damascus, Frag. 54, which refers to a banishment of the Neleidae in the sixth century, leads to the conclusion that this decree of the fifth century was engraved on the lower part of the stele on which the earlier degree had been inscribed, and that it refers to a second banishment of the family, probably about 449 B.C., as a result of oligarchical disturbances.

Inscription from Rhodes.— In *Jh. Oest. Arch. I.* IX, 1906, Beiblatt, pp. 85-88, F. Hiller Von Gaertringen discusses a Rhodian inscription in the Evangelical School at Smyrna. It refers to honors bestowed by To *Kchvov* To *'Epfiaiorav* AYTQN. The last word is explained as a stonecutter's error for *avrovoptov,* which is found as an epithet of Rhodian

'Eppdioral in *I.G.* XII, 1, 101; *S.G.D.I.* 3829.

The Edict of the Emperor Valens. — Schulten's interpretation of the edict of Valens addressed to Eutropius (see *AJ. A.* X, p. 443) is discussed by R. Heberdey in *Jh. Oest. Arch. I.* IX, 1906, pp. 182-192. He argues that about 365 A.d. Valens had allotted to certain cities of the province of Asia through the *adores rei privatae* portions of the income of the *fundi rei publicae* for rebuilding their walls. Irregularities crept in and the governor, Eutropius, asked that the cities be placed in control of the funds. This was first tried at Ephesus, and by the new edict the division of the funds and the *res privatae* are intrusted to the governor.

GREECE ARCHITECTURE

Cretan Palaces and Aegean Civilization. — In *B.S.A.* XI, 1904-05, pp. 181-223 (3 pis.; 4 figs.), D. Mackenzie publishes the first of a series of articles in criticism of Dorpfeld's theory of Achaean palaces in Crete *(Ath. Mill.* XXX, pp. 257-296; see *AJ.A.* X, p. 188). He argues from a close analysis of the remains at Phaestus and Cnossus, that no Achaean megaron ever existed at the former place, and that at the latter Dorpfeld's view of the stratification is wholly erroneous. The architecture of the palaces is homogeneous in style and the only changes are due to development. The first invaders from the mainland, Mycenaeans, *i.e.* Pelasgians, of the same stock as the Cretans, destroyed the palaces at Cnossus and Phaestus, but the Achaeans did not arrive till long after both palaces were in ruins, near the end of Late Minoan III, and form a mere prelude to Hellenic invasions in general. All evidence as to Achaean settlement in the Aegean is of too late a character to assist Dorpfeld's theory as to Achaean builders of the later palaces in Crete.

Ionic Terra-cotta Friezes.— At the July meeting of the Berlin Arch. Soc, L. Kjki.lbkkg spoke on the terra-cotta friezes, eight in number, discovered at Aeolic Larissa, near Smyrna, and compared them with terracotta architectural members in Sicilian and Italian buildings. Those of Larissa include, beside purely ornamental designs, also figure scenes, for which there is no counterpart in this material in western Greek art. They represent races, a combat of centaurs, and a symposium, and, as excellent examples of Ionic art at about 500 B.C., furnish a basis for comparison of the genuine work with the Etruscan imitations. *(Arch. Am.* 1906, col. 205.)

In *Rom. Mitt.* XXI, 1906, pp. 64-82 (pi.; 6 figs.), L. Savigno.vi compares certain Ionic fragments from Palaikastro in Crete with similar specimens in Ktruria and elsewhere. These fragments belonged to a terra-cotta frieze with reliefs of warriors and chariots. Savignoni's study is largely devoted to the form and use of the frieze placed above the cornice, as on the "Sarcophagus of the mourners" from Sidon. The subsequent history of this Ionic feature, rare in Ionia itself, is traced in the attica of the Roman triumphal arch.

The Date of the Temple of Athena Nike at Athens. — An examination of the north wall of the bastion of the temple of Athena Nike, which is as a whole an integral part of the Cimonian wall of the Acropolis, has disclosed the fact that it originally made a right angle with the west front. Thus restored, the lines of the bastion all run either parallel with or at right angles to the numerous old walls which are found about and under the Propylaea and which belong to the time of Cimon. After the Propylaea of Mnesieles was started, the north wall of the bastion was moved to correspond, and later the small stairway leading to the terrace above was constructed, the temple was built, the balustrade around the terrace was erected, and the ground level lowered. The decree of 450 B.C. , directing that a temple and altar be erected in the precinct of Athena Nike, was the work of the party opposed to Pericles, for such an erection was inconsistent with the plans for the new Propylaea of Mnesieles. For a time Pericles and his party were strong enough to go on with their work as planned; but when their influence waned, the demand for the use of the precinct compelled the curtailing of the south wing of the Propylaea, and the temple was at last built. Although this was just before the Peloponnesian War, the design of the temple in many wavsbetravs its earlier origin. (A. Roster, *Arch. I.* XXI, 1906, pp. 129-147; 5 figs.)

The Corinthian Capital at Phigalia. —In *Jh. Oest. Arch. I.* IX, 1906, pp. 287-294 (7 figs.), J. Durm discusses the lost Corinthian capital from the temple at Phigalia. The unpublished journal of Haller von Hallerstein shows that Cockerell's drawing is trustworthy. Similar capitals with a double row of acanthus leaves have been found at Delphi, and an architectural connection between the temple at Phigalia and the Tholos in the Marmoria seems probable.

The Temples represented ob Certain Reliefs of Apollo Citharoedus. — Four replicas of a relief of Apollo with the lyre, about to offer a libation as a victor, are discussed by F. Studniczka in *Jb. Arch. I.* XXI, 1906, pp. 77-89 (5 figs.), with reference to the spot represented. This he concludes to be the Pythion on the Ilissus at Athens, where there was no temple, but an ancient *agalma,a.* tripod, and an altar, while a wall separated it from the Olympieum. All these details are shown in the best examples of the relief, the temple being Corinthian, as completed by Hadrian, and the other details being consistent with a late date. On the frieze of the temple is a chariot race, the pediment figures suggest a conflict of gods and giants, and the acroteria are Victories in the attitude of the Nike of Paeonius. These decorations are suitable to the Olympieum. It is suggested that the octostyle Corinthian temple on a relief at the Villa Medici, once interpreted by Petersen as the temple of Mars Ultor, is probably the temple of Divus Hadriauus, with the figure of the emperor in the centre of the pediment.

SCULPTURE

A Handbook of Greek Sculpture. — A welcome addition to the handbooks published by the Royal Museums in Berlin is the volume on Greek Sculpture by R. Kekule Von Stradoxitz. It is a brief history of this branch of Greek art, in which each period is first discussed in its general aspects and with reference to its typical productions, and then illustrated further by an account of representative works in the Berlin collections. This method of treatment and the large number of illustrations render the work useful also to those at a distance from Berlin. There is no discussion of disputed points, and the subject is naturally presented from the standpoint of the author, who has little sympathy with some recent hypotheses and identifications in this field. *(Die Griechische Skulptur, von R. Kekule Von Stradoxitz, Handbiic/ier ler Konigtichen Musee.n zu Berlin,* Vol. XI. Berlin, 1906, G. Reimer, 383 pp.; loo figs. 8vo; Mk. 4.50, paper, 5. bound.)

An Imitation of Ancient Clay. — The *Scientific American,* October 27, 1906, describes an artificial clay invented by a Norwegian sculptor, C. D. Magelssen, which is characterized by plasticity and ability to withstand intense heat without shrinking or cracking. It is possible to mould figures of large size on iron frames and bake them without detaching the clay from the supports. The discoverer believes that to the use of a clay possessing these properties, which depend on the absence of organic impurities, the Greek artists owed the perfection of their large statues and small figurines of terra-cotta.

Some Sculptures at Turin. — Five pieces of sculpture at Turin are described by A. J. B. Wace in *J.H.S.* XXVI, 1906, pp. 235-242 (3 pis.). They are: (1) Head of an athlete, a copy of a bronze original belonging in the latter half of the fifth century, and perhaps by an Athenian artist who came under Argive influence. The hair is Polyclitan, the flesh rather Athenian in style. (2) Torso of Athena, a good copy of a type of the school of Praxiteles. Fifteen replicas are known, including the fine bronze at Florence. (3) Youthful male torso, in a dancing or rising attitude, slender and graceful and with excellent drapery. Copy of a bronze of the later fourth century, which may be classed with the Ganymede of the Vatican attributed to Leochares and the bronze dancing satyr at Naples. (4) Head of an athlete, of a type which may be placed with the so-called Jason, between the Apoxyomenus and the Borghese warrior, about 200 B.C. (5) Statuette of a priestess of Isis, with long flowing draperies and head thrown back. It is Graeco-Egyptian work of the late third century B.C., and shows to a marked degree the *morbidezza* characteristic of Greek work of that period.

Ancient Sculptures in the Church of the Panagia Gtorgoepikoos at Athena. — The fragments of ancient reliefs which are built into the outer walls of the church of the Panagia Gorgoepikoos ("Little Metropolitan") at Athens are described in some detail by P. Stf.iner in *Ath. Milt.* XXXI. 1906, pp. 325-341 (2 figs.), as a supplement to the account of the church by Michel and Struck (see *infra,* p. 234). Fourteen pieces are described, but the discussion is concentrated on two reliefs representing Nikes handing prizes to female figures, who represent the victorious tribes; an archaistic relief, representing a warrior apparently following the body of a friend; a graverelief, representing two women in an aedicula, which leads to a brief discussion of typical figures appearing in late grave-reliefs, but evidently drawn from earlier statues; and the frieze with cult objects, which seem to point to a connection with the Eleusinium. The calendar frieze has already received adequate discussion elsewhere, and the reliefs representing Roman military decorations are treated in *Bonn. Jb.* 114, pp. 1-98.

Terra-cotta Plaques from Praesus.— In *U.S.A.* XI, 1904-05, pp. 243257 (20 figs.), E. S. Forster continues his discussion of the terra-cottas from Praesus (see *A J. A.* VIII, p. 314) by publishing the series of plaques, containing some thirty types. Seventeen varieties had been published by Halbherr, *A.J.A.* V, 1901, pp. 371-392. The plaques fall into an archaic group, a middle group corresponding roughly to the fifth and fourth centuries, and a Hellenistic group. In the first period the types seem connected with the Eteocretan religion, and show relations with Egypt, Cyprus, and Sardinia; in the second period the types are less hieratic, and show an art far behind that of the mainland; in the third period Hellenistic Greek art is completely dominant.

The Group of Harmodius and Aristogeiton. — In *Jb. Kl. All.* XVII, 1906, pp. 544-549 (2 pis.), F. Studniczka discusses the group of the Tyrannicides by Critios and Nesiotes, and its relation to the earlier group by Antenor. He accepts the Boston fragment (see *A J.A.* X, p. 471), as conclusive evidence that the Naples statues represent the later group, but argues that it resembled closely the earlier work for which the best authority is the Skaramangd lecythus in Vienna (Masner, Catalogue. No. 264, Fig. 19).

"The Birth of Venus." —In *Rec. Past,* VI, 1906, pp. 204-213 (2 figs.), S. A. Jeffers discusses the relief representing the birth of Aphrodite now in the National Museum at Rome, and Botticelli's painting of the birth of Venus in the Uffizi, as typifying the ideals of Greek art in the early fifth century, and those of the Renaissance.

A New Replica of the Choiseul-Gouffier Type. — The right leg of a statue of Greek marble in the style of the middle of the fifth century is now. in the Terme Museum at Rome. It corresponds in all details with the Choiseul-Gouffier statue in London and the "Apollo on the Omphalus" in Athens, and represents a very fine replica of the type. A quiver hanging on the supporting tree trunk corroborates the usual interpretation as an Apollo. (G. Dickins, *J.H.S.* XXVI, 1906, pp. 278-280; 3 figs.)

An Apollo by Paeonius. — A definite idea of Paeonius of Mende's representation of a god may be gained by a comparison of the youthful Apollo at Ince Blundell Hall with the Nike and with the Hertz head *(Rom. Mitt.* IX, p. 162) which is a copy of that of the Nike. This comparison reveals such close and striking resemblances in detail as to prove conclusively that the originals were from the same hand. The Hertz head is a.good copy from marble, the Apollo statue an inferior copy from bronze. The attitude of the statue has many analogies among the reliefs of northern Greece, but none in the round.

It shows the attempt of the sculptor to modify the stiff conventionality of the archaic standing position, and cannot be later than the middle of the fifth century. This fixes also the disputed date of the Nike, as the resemblances are too strong to admit of any considerable interval between the two works. (B. Sauer, *Jb. Arch. I.* XXI, 1906, pp. 163176; 10 figs.)

Leto with her Children. —In *R. Arch.* VIII, 1906, pp. 290-296, A. Mahler discusses the bronze statuette of Leto and her children in the Capitoline Museum (Reinach, *Repertoire de la statuaire*, II, 417, 7) and its replicas. Following Arndt, he compares it with a statue in Copenhagen *(Glyptotheque Ny-Carlsberg,* pis. 38-40, *Repertoire,* II, 419, 2), and indirectly with Calamis. He thinks it may be the work of Praxiteles mentioned by Pausanias (I, 44, 2), in which case it must be by the elder Praxiteles, whom he regards as a pupil of Calamis and father of Cephisodotus. This accounts for the resemblance between the Leto and the Eirene and Plutus.

Splanchnoptes.—In *Jb. Arch. I.* 1893, pp. 224 ff., M. Mayer interpreted a marble statue from the Olympieum in Athens (Kawadias, *τχvirra,* No. 248), as a *anrXayxyoTm,* a youth holding the flesh of an offering on a fork over the altar. In confirmation of this view, A. Von Salis publishes in *A then. Mitt.* XXXI, 1906, pp. 352-358 (pi.), a small bronze statuette from Dodona representing a youth holding a three-pronged fork, and in style very similar to the Athenian statue. Analysis of the forms leads to the conclusion that the original was a product of the transitional period, which preceded the Parthenon sculptures, and of which the boy extracting a thorn from his foot is one of the best examples.

The East Frieze of the Parthenon. — Quite independently K. WeissMann and A. S. Arvanitopoullos have identified the ten standing figures on either side of the gods-on the east frieze of the Parthenon (Michaelis, *Parthenon,* Nos. 18-23, 4;1-46) with the eponymous heroes of the ten tribes. The former *(Hermes,* XLI, 1906, pp. 619-623) identifies Nos. 43-46 with Oeneus, Acamas, Aegeus, and Pandion, Nos. 18, 20, and 23 with Cecrops, Erechtheus, and Leos, while the other three members must include Ajax,

Antiochus, and Hippothoon. The latter *(Ath. Milt.* XXXI, 1906, pp. 3849; 2 pis.; 2 figs.), suggests that Nos. 43-46 are Erechtheus, Aegeus, Pandion, and Leos, and Nos. 18-23, Acanias, Oeneus, Cecrops, Hippothoon, Ajax, and Antiochus. He also uses the parody of the Panathenaic procession iii Aristophanes, *Eecles.* 728 ff., to explain some details in other portions of the frieze.

Apollo or Athlete?—In *Jh. Oest. Arch. I.* IX, 1906, pp. 279-287, F. Hauskr defends his view *ibid.* VIII, pp. 42 ff.; *A J.A.* IX, p. 468), that the Diaduinenus of Polyclitus was originally an Apollo against Lowy *(ibid.* pp. 269 ff., *A J.A.* X, p. 445). It must be proved that so marked an attribute as the quiver is ever used thoughtlessly. The Deliau artist would not have transformed a short-haired athlete into an Apollo, for the typical

Figure 1. — Marble Head Of Figure 2.—Bronze Statuette Op Alexander. Alexander.

Apollo after Praxiteles was not an athlete; he must therefore have known that the original represented Apollo. A definite school of Greek art uses the same types for gods and men. Several details in Lowy's argument are also discussed.

Calamis. —The literary evidence as to the date and works of Calamis is examined in detail in *Jh. best. Arch. I.* IX, 1906, pp. 199-268 (4 figs.) by E. Reisch. Praxias, a pupil of Calamis, made the sculptures in the east pediment of the temple of Apollo at Delphi (Pans. X, 19, 4). This can only refer to the new temple, and Praxias, who is also known from inscriptions of about 360 B.C., must have finished his work not later than 340 B.C. His master then was active in the early part of the fourth century, and this agrees with the passages which refer to works of Calamis in connection with those of Praxiteles and Scopas. A Calamis also made, with Onatas, the group ordered by Hiero and dedicated at Olympia by Deinoinenes in 467466 B.C. To the same artist must belong the offering of Acragas at Olympia, the statue of Amnion dedicated at Thebes by Pindar, and the colossal Apollo at Apollonia. Thus literary evidence points to two artists named Calamis, living nearly a century apart, and a study of the statements about the statues of Calamis shows that they naturally fall into two groups, of which one seems to contain works characteristic of the fourth century. The elder Calamis worked exclusively in bronze. To the younger are ascribed chryselephantine and marble statues, and his name is mentioned as a worker in precious metals by Pliny, *H.N.* 33, 156.

Two New Portraits of Alexander.— In *R. Arch.* VIII, 1906, pp. 1-6 (2 pis.; 6 figs.), S. Reinach publishes and discusses the marble head and the bronze statuette — both portraits of Alexander — in the Uattaricollection inCairo(Figs. 1 and 2). See *Arch. An:.* 1905, pp. 67 f.; *A.J.A.* 1906, p. 63.

Pannyohis. — The bronze group of statues by Euthycrates, son of Lysippus, mentioned by Tatian is discussed by E. Ma Ass in *Jb. Arch. I.* XXI, 1906, pp. 77-107 (2 figs.). He interprets Tatian's words to mean, "The wooing at the night festival of the Pannychis"; and with the aid of the "Auge and Heracles "in the house of the Vettii at Pompeii, and the " Heracles and Telephus before Arcadia" from Herculaneum, he gains an idea of the appearance of the group. The wide-winged figure in thePompeian Fjgcrk 3. —votive Relief To Asclepius. fresco is the personified Pannychis, and the winged woman in the Herculanean painting is Themis, while the eagle and lion, king of birds and king of beasts, indicate the power of the heaven-born child over the fierce passions of nature.

A Votive Relief to Asclepius. — The votive relief to Asclepius (Fig. 3) recently discovered in Athens (see *A.J.A.* IX, p 108) is discussed in *B.S.A.* XI, 1904-05, pp. 146-150 (2 figs.) by G. B. Byzantinos. He regards it as a work of the early third century B.C. It is possible that Silon dedicated the sandal as a memorial of his journey to the shrine, but it is also possible that the sandal had saved its wearer's foot from injury. A shoe which had saved its owner from the bite of a snake was seen by the author among the votive offerings in a Greek church.

A Head connected with Damophon. — The Vatican contains a head in *rosso antico* (Catalogue, Xo. 293»; Helbig, Fiihrer, I, p. 144, No 242) a replica of which in the same material is in the Ny Carlsberg Glyptotek at Copenhagen. The head seems to represent a satyr and bears a striking resemblance to the head of Anytus by Damophon. The stylistic forerunner of these heads is the Zeus of Otricoli, and two derivatives of this head, in Naples and Parma, correspond in their variations with the heads of Anytus and the satyr. The satyr head seems to represent an early work of Damophon, or perhaps of his master, and to belong to the period of reaction which falls in the first half of the third century B.C. (G. Dickins, *B.S.A.* XI, 1904 1905, pp. 173-180; pi.)

The Aphrodite of Polycharmua. — In *C. R. Acad Insc.* 1906, p. 306, S. Reinach proposes to read in Pliny, *H. N.* XXXVI, 36, *Venerem lacantem sese Daedalm, stanlem pede in* uno *Polycharmus*. The statue of Polycharmus is therefore represented by the numerous figures of Venus standing on one foot while adjusting her sandal on the other. The original was probably at Aphrodisias.

Ganymede. — A fragmentary statue from Ephesus, now in Vienna, represents Ganymede seized by the eagle. The boy has-sunk on his left knee, while the right leg is stretched out. A replica of this statue is in Madrid, and the same version of the scene is found on a relief in Florence and mosaics from Baccano and Sousse. The statue from Subiaco and the Ilioneus also probably represent Ganymede alarmed by the eagle. The mosaics and relief seem derived from a painting, which also influenced the sculptor, who may have known the work of Leochares. (H. Lucas, *Jh. Oest. Arch. I.* IX, 1906, pp. 269-277; pi.; 3 figs.)

The LaocoSn in Prance. — The discovery of the right arm of Laocoon by L. Pollak (cf. *AJ.A.* X, 1906, p. 352) leads E. Michon in *B. Soc. Ant. Fr.* 1906, pp. 271-280, to a discussion of the restorations made during the sojourn of the group in France. The earlier restorations were removed before the group was taken from Rome, and replaced in plaster on its arrival in Paris. At this time the right arm of Laocoon was modelled from a restoration of the group by Girardon. The restorations were still in place on the return of the group to Italy, and do not seem to have been removed since.

A Pseudo-Praxitelean Group. — The Louvre contains a Graeco-Roman group of Aphrodite and Eros, the plinth of which bears the name of Praxiteles (Loewy, *Inschr. griech. Bildh.* No. 502). It is commonly stated that during the last century this base was removed. In *B. Soc. A nt. Fr.* 1906, pp. 120-122, Ch. Ravaisson-mollien argues that this removal never took place. *Ibid.* pp. 125-133, E. MicnoN gives a full account of the history of the group and its inscription. While the authenticity of the inscription is not beyond question, it has never been removed from the group. When the group was first exhibited in the Louvre it was provided with a square base, which concealed the inscribed oval plinth. This border has since been removed, and the inscription is now plainly visible. A portion of the forged inscription on the statue of the Procurator Caninius has also become visible by the removal of a modern border. *Ibid.* p. 134, Ravaisson-molmen claims that the figure of Eros is in a Roman style, inferior to that of the Aphrodite. The head and part of the bust of the goddess are modern and taken from a statue of the seventeenth century.

VASES AND PAINTING

Cretan Decorative Art. —In *Transactions of the Department of Archaeology* (University of Pennsylvania), II, 1906, pp. 5-50 (3 pis.; 68 figs.), Edith H. Hall examines the designs on Cretan vases of the bronze age. She classifies the designs as (1) *Imitative,* including (a) pure naturalistic designs, (6) conventional naturalistic designs, in which natural objects are represented in conventional forms, (c) conventionalized naturalistic designs, in which natural objects are represented in stereotyped forms due to mechanical copying, and *(d)* sacral designs; and (2) *Non-Imitative,* including (a) simple, and (6) complicated patterns. An elaborate chronological table, gives the Cretan vases, and other decorated objects, with their provenience and place of publication, as well as some non-Cretan parallels. Before the Kamares ware (Middle Minoan II) only non-imitative designs are found, though tendencies toward conventional naturalistic decorations are found in Early Minoan III and Middle Minoan I. In Middle Minoan III a purely naturalistic type is achieved, and sacral patterns appear. The marine designs appear in Late Minoan I. In Late Minoan II all classes of design, except the complex non-imitative, are represented. Late Minoan III contains the " Mycenaean" vases, which are characterized by a large use of conventionalized naturalistic designs, due to unintelligent copying.

Middle Minoan Pottery. — In *J.H. S.* XXVI, 1906, pp. 243-267 (5 pis.), D. Mackenzie supplements his earlier study of Cnossian pottery *(ibid.* XXIII, pp. 157 ff.; *AJ.A.* VII, p. 468) from the larger material now at hand. The dark-on-light and light-on-dark techniques he again finds coexisting from the beginning to the end, as two sides of the decorative principle of contrast. The Early Minoan age inherited simple geometric forms and colors from the neolithic age and used chiefly white, red, and black. Here began the tendency to curvilinear forms which was developed in the succeeding first period of Middle Minoan. In this period, with an increase in forms, new colors also appear, having a general tendency toward lighter and yellowish shades. The Kamares period brought polychrome decoration to its height, with the most successful synthesis of dark-on-light and light-on-dark in harmonious design. With a growing appreciation of the relation between shape and decoration, the main design tended to usurp the space on the shoulder of a vase, leaving the less conspicuous parts for simpler and more primitive ornament. The principle of decorating in horizontal bands, which maintained a successful rivalry with that of vertical panelling and a symmetric arrangement, and survived into classic times, had its origin quite as much in this sense of fitness as in the conveniences of the wheel. The third period, which saw the rapid decay of polychrome ornament, is characterized by the growth of a naturalistic tendency and a return to monochrome technique, the last as a natural consequence of the first, because the polychrome scheme of the earlier period could not represent natural objects in their proper color. Here wall-painting and ceramic art, so long parallel, may have taken different ways. This period saw the perfection of the free, broad use of naturalistic design, especially in the pottery of the temple repositories. Each of the last two periods ended with some widespread calamity which hastened the already latent tendency to decay. The art known as Mycenaean or Achaean in Greece, Italy, Asia Minor, and elsewhere belongs to the outskirts of the Minoan culture of which Crete was the centre, and is wholly southern and not European in origin.

A Proto-Corinthian Lecythus in Berlin. — A class of very small lecythi with plastic decoration imitated from metal, of which there is a very fine specimen at Berlin, is discussed by O. Washburn in *Jb. Arch. I.* XXI, 1906, pp. 116-127 (pi.; 4 figs.). The Berlin example, 7 cm. high, has a lion's head as a mouth, a lion for a handle, and other plastic as well as painted decoration. The influence of Mycenaean art is clear, but there are indications of another origin, perhaps geometric and contemporary with the Dipylon and Boeotian styles, in the ninth century. Probably none are so late as 600 B.C., though the Berlin vase is one of the latest. The inscriptions on several indicate an Aeolic or Doric origin, probably in Asia Minor, for the single example with an Ionic inscription, that at Boston, is exceptional. Proto-Corinthian ware remained in use during the early Corinthian period, and some of it may have been made at Corinth.

Fragments from Eleusis. — In *Ath. Mitt.* XXXI, 1906, pp. 186-204 (pi.; 3 figs.), K. Rhomaios publishes two vase-fragments from Eleusis of especial interest because of their technique, as the decorations are applied in color on a black ground. The more important fragment is part of the inner picture of a cylix. A full discussion leads to the conclusion that the scene represents Pluto with Demeter and Cora, and that the style and technique indicate the work of an Ionian artist settled in, Attica about 530 B.c. The polychrome decoration on a black ground is claimed as Ionian in origin. The other fragment, in similar technique, is a head of Athena from an omphalos cylix. It is Attic work.

The Cacus Vase in the Ashmolean Museum. — The interpretation of E. Pernice *(Jb. Arch. I.* XVI, 1906, pp. 45 ff.; see *AJ.A.* X, p. 449), that this vase represented Hermes seizing Paris, is rejected by P. Gardner in *J.H.S.* XXVI, 1906, pp. 226-228 (fig.). The inconsistencies in the drawing are perhaps due to an unskilful workman, who adapted a group from another scene to the Heracles and Cacus story.

Distribution of Attic Vases. — The distribution of Attic vases throughout the ancient world is discussed by Miss (J. M. A. Richter in *B.S.A.* XI. 1904-05, pp. 224-242 (4 figs.), on the basis of a study of the number of examples of each form in the Athens Museum in comparison with those from Etruria and Campania in the British Museum, the Berlin Museum, and the Hermitage. A classified table shows that the chief demand from Italy was for amphorae, hydriae, cylices, oenochoae, and to a less extent for lecythi, crateres, and cups. Loutrophori, lebetes, ovm, white lecythi, redfigured aryballi and pyxides are not found in Italy. In Athens itself the vases are chiefly such as were used for the toilet or for special purposes, as funerals and weddings. These vases, manufactured for the home market, are studied in detail. In two appendices are published a red-figured loutrophoros with the death of Penthesilea, and a fragment of a pyxis showing apparently a bride surrounded by vases received as gifts.

An Amphora in the Boston Museum. — In *Harvard Studies in Classical Philology,* XVII, 1906, pp. 143-148 (pi.), G. H. Chase publishes in a modified form a paper presented at the General Meeting of the Archaeological Institute at Princeton *(AJ.A.* VII, 1903, p. 96), in which he describes a redfigured amphora in the Boston Museum of Fine Arts, bearing the inscriptions *YliOoiv Koxt)* and Ni'10/ *Koxtl.*

Two White Lecythi from Eretria. — In E£. *'h.p.* 1906, pp. 1-22 (2 pis.; 7 figs.), K. Kourouniotks publishes two Attic white lecythi from a tomb at Eretria, both inscribed Ai'tAos Koaos, and evidently from the same workshop. Lecythi bearing the same KaAot-name, published by Bosanquet, *J.H.S.* 1896, pp. 164 ff., while contemporary, seem from a different pottery. The writer describes the construction of the Attic lecythi, differing from Pottier on several points. He interprets the scenes on his two specimens as representing the deceased woman seated and receiving offerings from the living woman who stands before her.

INSCRIPTIONS

The Oldest Greek Alphabet. — The origin and development of the Greek alphabet is discussed by A. Gercke in *Hermes,* XLI, 1906, pp. 540561. After considering many details, he concludes that the supplementary signs were developed before the foundation of Cumae *(ca.* 730 B.C.), and that the origin of the Greek alphabet cannot be placed much later than the beginning of the ninth century, as the Lycian and Carian alphabets, which imply the Greek, originated before the end of that century. In any case the invention of the alphabet is later than the Dorian occupation of the islands.

Tsade and Sampi. — In *J.H.S.* XXV, 1906, pp. 338-365, F. W. G. Foat discusses in detail the history of the sign for 900 in Greek numeration, including the question of the relation of the Phoenician and Milesian alphabets, and the Greek and Hebrew numerical systems. He concludes that Greek M, not T, represents the Semitic Tsade, and that the name Sampi as applied to the sign "9 lias no ancient authority. *Ibid.* XXVI, 1906, pp. 286287, he calls attention to the discovery of the forms TcTapts and TcTapaOoyTa in an early Ionic inscription from the Artemisium at Ephesus. This confirms the view that the character represented a dental sibilant. It seems to have been confined to the Ionic coast of Mysia and Lydia, and the Pontic coast of Thrace.

An Epitaph from Megara. —In *Ath. Mitt.* XXXI, 1906, pp. 89-93, 229230 (pi.), A. Wilhelm publishes the earliest known epitaph from Megara, consisting of an elegiac couplet, with remains of a preceding line. The forms of the letters indicate a date in the early fifth century. The couplet reads Aa *KkrjrovwpoK* AcoaraiScnriSe *(TaiTCKaaXrj: Kwlk aX-qdtalirivTrj&erp* oirot7roXios. Though the lines are practically complete, the interpretation is difficult. Wilhelm regards it as expressing the grief of a wife or mother for the dead. F. Solmsen *(ibid.* pp. 342-348) criticises Wilhelm's readings in detail. He thinks the inscription was on a cenotaph. In *Nachrichten von der Gesellschaft der Wissenschaften zu Gottingen,* 1906, pp. 231-239, B. Keil accepts Wilhelm's interpretation, but reads the text very differently. *Ibid.* pp. 240-241, E. Schwartz argues that it is from a cenotaph. In *Philologus,* LXV, 1906, pp. 474-475, J. Bacnack adds a note on the text.

Notes on Attic Inscriptions. — In *Rh. Mm.* LXI, 1906, pp. 344-351, J. E. Kirchner publishes notes on Attic inscriptions. He treats first the priests of Asclepius, in connection with Sundwall's and Ferguson's discovery that the annual priests were chosen in the official order of the tribes. He gives a table of archons, tribes, and priests, so far as they are known, from 350-318 B.C., based chiefly on *I.G.* II, 766 and 835. The priest Aij/uov AjjjioptAovt LTouavttvs *(I.G.* II, 1654) is placed in 350-49 B.C., and identified with the cousin of Demosthenes. The article also discusses the deme of the *Tiordfuoi* Aeipaotumu, who appear in the fourth century. It belonged to the tribe Antigonis, and its members sometimes appear under the double name, and sometimes under each name singly.

Attic Accounts of the Fifth Century. — In *Rh. Mus.* LXI, 1906, pp. 202-231, W. Bannier discusses the formulae employed in the Attic inscriptions containing official accounts. He concludes that the older documents were all arranged by the year, that changes in detail soon appear, and that probably between 423 and 418 B.C. the accounts were arranged by prytanies with further variations in the details.

The Walls built by Conon. —In *Ath. Milt.* XXXI, 1906, p. 372, E. Nachmanson reports that the inscription relating to the rebuilding of the walls of Athens by Conon *(Ath. Mitt.* 1905, pp. 391 ff.; *A.J.A.* X, p. 450) is now in the Musees Royaux du Cinquantenaire, in Brussels, and gives some minor corrections furnished by J. de Mot.

The Erection of a Tripod. —In *Ath. Mitt.* XXXI, 1906, pp. 134-144 (fig.), M. Holleaux publishes with a detailed commentary an inscription recently found near Athens, containing specifications for the erection of tripods at Cynosarges. *Ibid.* pp. 145-150 (fig.), W. Dorpfeld reconstructs the monument. Underground was a foundation of rough stone, on which was erected an *orthostates,* a square pillar, covered by a large flat stone, on which the tripod was placed and secured by lead. Under the bowl of the tripod was placed a marble column. *Ibid.* pp. 359-362, H. Lattermann suggests corrections to the text.

An Inscription from Carystus. — The inscription *I.G.* Ill, 1306, containing a list of *Bouleutai* is shown by a copy made by Mionnet to come from Carystus in Euboea. It thus gains greatly in value, as throwing light on the organization of this important place in the second century A.d. (F. Hiller Von Gaertringen, *Ath. Mitt.* XXXI, 1906, pp. 349-351.)

The Report of an Agonothetes. — In *B.C.H.* XXV, pp. 365 ff. *(AJ.A.* VII, p. 373) W. Vollgraff published the *airoKayla* of an Agonothetes of the *Basileia* at Lebadia. This has been again studied by M. Holleaux, *ibid.* XXX, 1906, pp. 469-481 (fig-), who gives a new text of one face of the stele, and argues at length that the inscription must be dated at the end of the second or beginning of the first century B.C.

Inscriptions from Delphi. — In *Hermes,* XLI, 1906, pp. 356-377, II. Pomtow discusses the fragments from Delphi of the list of honors bestowed on Cassander, son of Menestheus of Alexandria Troas, a fragment of which was published by Kaibel, *ibid.* VIII, pp. 417 ff. Recent discoveries show that it was probably engraved on the Treasury of the Cnidians. The article also contains corrections to the six other Delphian inscriptions published by Kaibel.

An Inscription from Cumae. — In *Not. Scav.* 1905, p. 377, A. Sogliano published an archaic inscription from Cumae, reading Ov *Oifwt* Tvtova» *Ktuto at* fit roe *BtBtvnt vov.* In *B. Phil. W.* 1906, pp. 957-958, R. ExGelmann interprets *px.* as *faj,* and the inscription as a prohibition against burying the uninitiated in a certain place.

Notes on Dialectic Inscriptions. — In *Sitzb. Sticks. Ges.* LVII, 1905, pp. 272-286, R. Meister continues his studies in Greek epigraphy. (1) The inscription MENETY5EAYYA on coins of Aspendus is read MeVtrvs tX(X)vra(v); in Attic ot MtVirros *tyXvpa.v.* (2) The inscription from Laconia *(B.S.A.* X, p. 188, No. 15) is corrected and interpreted. It is in the old Doric dialect, which is scarcely known outside of Sparta. The examples of this dialect from Laconia are given. (3) Corrections and notes on the dialect of Boeotian inscriptions from Thespiae, Acraephia, and Thebes.

"ApxiarpAs Ta 8'. — In *Jh. Oest. Arch. I.* IX, 1906, pp. 295-297, P. WolTers discusses the phrase *apuxTpos* To 8', which appears in a list of victors in the *aywv Tsv iarpwv* at Ephesus *(ibid.* VIII, pp. 119 ff.; *A.J.A.* IX, p. 346). It does not refer to a fourtli election as city physician, for this was a life appointment, but to a fourth choice as Agonothetes.

'Attpowxa. — In *Rh. Mus.* LXI, 1906, pp. 472-473, F. B. discusses the meaning of *aKpoyva,* as it appears in the phrase *lv rt rots dKpovuots tai rfj TavpoSiSaita,* in an inscription from Miletus *(Sitzb. Bert. Akad.* 1906, p. 258). The word refers to the firm grip on the hoof or horn of the animal, and is probably a technical term with trainers.

Epigraphic Notes. — In 'Ei£. 'Ap. 1906, pp. 115-116, S. Bases suggests corrections to the Thessalian inscriptions published by G. Zekides, *ibid.* 1905, pp. 189 ff. In *B.C.H.* XXX, 1906, p. 466, are brief notes by A. Jarde on Thessalian inscriptions in "Eip. 'Ap. 1905, pp. 187 ff. *(AJ.A.* X, p. 349.) In *B.C.H.* XXX, p. 468, M. Holleaux confirms a suggestion of Meister as to the Thespian inscription, *ibid.* XXI, p. 5o4. *Ibid.* pp. 467468, A. D. Keramopoullos gives a revised text of the dedication of Philetaerus and epigram of Honestus from Thespiae, published by P. Jamot, *ibid.* XXVI, p. 155 *(AJ.A.* VII, 380). In *Alh. Mitt.* XXXI, 1906, pp. 228-229, A. Wilhelm gives a revised text of the archaic inscription from Tegea, published by G. Mendel, *B.C.H.* XXV, p. 267. In *Klio,* VI, 1906, p. 331, H. Lattermann publishes a revised text of the Eleusinian inscription, *I.G.* II, 1054, lines 52-57, which confirms some important restorations suggested by him, *Klio,* VI, pp. 140-168. In *Ath. Mitt.* XXXI, p. 236, S. N. Dragoumes suggests a restoration of the dedication to Aphrodite Pandemus recently discussed by Weilbach and Kawerau (see *AJ.A.* X, 1906, p. 194).

Epigraphic Bulletin. — The articles on Greek epigraphy, which appeared in fifty-seven periodicals during 1903 and 1904, are summarized with annotations and occasional publication of the inscriptions, by £. Bourgcet in *R. kt. Or.* XIX, 1906, pp. 25-55.

Greek Epigraphy in Europe. —In *R. Arch.* VIII, 1906, pp. 97-119, S. Chabert concludes his history of the study of Greek epigraphy in Europe (see *AJ.A.* 1906, p. 197) with a brief description of the present condition of that study and the work carried on by the scholars of the various nations.

COINS

Signatures of Engravers on Greek Coins. — In *R. Beige Num.* LXII, 1906, pp. 5-38, 117-153 (many cuts), L. Forrer completes his descriptive catalogue of Greek coins, with signatures of engravers. He also mentions a number of inscriptions that cannot with certainty be interpreted as the signatures of the artists, and others that, though formerly accepted as such, must now be rejected.

Asiatic Influences in Cumae. — The coinage of the Italian Cumae shows connection in artistic and religious types with the Graeco-Asiatic east, thus proving that others than settlers from the Aeolic Cyme had a share in founding the Italian city. (ettore Gabrici, *R. Ital. Num.* XIX, 19(16, pp. 317-328, plate; 3 figs.)

GENERAL, AND MISCELLANEOUS

Cretan Fencing. — In *Athen.* July 21, 1906, A. Lang calls attention to the long bronze rapiers found in the graves at Cnossus. Such weapons for thrusting must have been useless against the great shields, and seem to indicate a school of fencing with rapier and dagger or cloak, such as prevailed in Europe at the end of the sixteenth century.

The Vaphio Cups. — In *Jh. Oest. Arch. I.* IX, 1906, pp. 294-295, A. Korte following a suggestion of the late Professor Lipschitz, argues that on the second Vaphio cup, the affectionate attitude of the two animals is best explained if the smaller one in the background is a cow.

Scylla in Mycenaean Art. —In *Ath. Mitt.* XXXI, 1906, pp. 50-52 (2 figs.), F. Studniczka compares a seal from Cnossus *(B.S.A.* IX, p. 58) representing a boatman attacked by a sea-monster, with a fragment of fresco from Mycenae *('Ef.* 'Ap. 1887, pi. 11). These designs point to a legend similar to that of Scylla in the Odyssey. This early Scylla is also briefly discussed by O. Crusius in *Philologus, LX V,* 1906, p. 320.

An Homeric Burial Custom.— In *Hermes,* XLI, 1906, pp. 378-388, W. Helbig calls attention to the Greek custom of enveloping the remains of the dead, after burning, in wrappings, and then interring them in a coffer or urn. In Italy this method is first found in the later *tombe a pozzo* at Corneto, and may have been introduced by Greeks. In the Odyssey, XXIV, vss. 7!—79, the remains of Achilles and Patroclus are placed in one covering, those of Antilochus in another, and thus kept separate, though in the same urn.

Topography of Early Athens. —In *Philologus,* LXV, 1906, pp. 128-141, W. Dorpfeld discusses certain points in early Athenian topography, in reply to E. Drerup's article, *ibid.* LXIV, 1905, pp. 66 ff. He considers the Pelargikon, the Pnyx, and the oldest city, controverting sharply Drerup's theories, and restating his own well-known views.

A Note on the Enneacrunus. — In *Cl. R.* XX, 1906, p. 330, J. R. Wheeler points out that Guillet's (or the Capuchin) map of Athens scarcely affords proof that in the seventeenth century there were remains of the Enneacrunus, where Dorpfeld would place it, as is stated by Miss Harrison in her recent work, *Primitive Athens as described by Thucydides,* p. 131.

The Social Position of Athenian Officials in the Fourth Century. — A careful examination of the literary and epigraphic evidence has led J. Sundwall to conclude that in the time of Demosthenes the government of Athens was by no means so completely in the hands of the proletariat as is commonly supposed. A study of the lists of officials of all kinds shows everywhere a disproportionate number of names from wealthy families. The annual priests of Asclepius are shown to have been chosen according to the official order of the tribes. (J. Sundwall, *Epigraphische Beitrage zur sozial-politischen Geschichte Athens im Zeitalter des Demosthenes.* Leipzig, 1906, G. Kreysing. vi, 92 pp. 8vo).

The Attic "Teniae." — In *Jh. Oest. Arch. 1.* IX, 1906, Beiblatt, pp. 7786, E. Petersen discusses in detail Hauser's article on the Athenian Tettix (see *A.J.A.* X, p. 457). He argues that the literary evidence, when properly interpreted, is directly opposed to Hauser's view, and that the monuments lend themselves much more easily to the theory of Studniczka.

Triremes. — In *Cl. R.* XX, 1906, pp. 324-325, C. Tork replies to Newman's view of the Athenian trireme as represented on the Acropolis relief (see *A.J. A.* X, p. 457). The Athenian docks show that the triremes were not more than 20 ft. wide; hence if there was a gallery "of some amplitude," the hull would be so narrow as to afford neither room for the crew nor sufficient displacement to float its weight.

The Myth of Erichthoniua. — The myth of Erichthonius and the three daughters of Cecrops is the subject of an investigation by the late BenjaMin Powell. He reaches the conclusion that "the whole myth is a confusion of Olympian divinities with chthonic or primitive cults, and Eastern influences, which it is well nigh impossible to unravel completely and to tabulate." An appendix contains the text of the literary sources. *Cornell Studies in Classical Philology,* No. XVII. *Erichthonitis and the Three Daughters of Cecrops,* by Benjamin Powell. New York, 1906, The Macmillian Co. 86 pp.; 12 pis. 8vo. Price 60 cents.)

The Cave at Vari and Plato. — In *Harvard Studies in Classical Philology,* XVII, 1906, pp. 131-142 (fig.), J. H. Wright suggests that in the allegory of the Cave *(Rep.* VII, 514a-516c), Plato was influenced by recollections of the cave at Vari *(A.J.A.* VII, 1903, pp. 263-349), which in its natural features corresponds very closely to the philosopher's description.

Notes on the Prosopographia Attica. — In *Klio,* VI, 1906, pp. 330-331, J. Sundwall gives the family tree of 'AvTcpaxos Qvdwopjov Mapaflwvios, whose name he supplies in *I.G.* II, 269. From *I.G.* II, 2516, he reconstructs in part the list of Sophronistae for 306-305 B.C. The *Prosopographia Attica* mentions neither Lysiades of Athens (Cic. *Phil.* V, 131), who seems to have been archon in 51-50 B.C., nor Heraclitus, general in 133 B.C.

The Sanctuary at Eleusis. — At the July (1906) meeting of the Berlin Arch. Society, F. Noack described the growth of the Sanctuary at Eleusis. A small natural terrace was, in the second millennium B.C., surrounded by a double wall, for support and for defence, and used as a place of worship and sacrifice. Here were the temple and altar mentioned in the Homeric Hymn. The area was enlarged by Pisistratus, by Pericles, and in the fourth century. The old terrace form was lost under Pericles, and the altar was moved eastward with each enlargement of the space, but the position of the entrance fjate remained substantially the same, because determined by the path from the cave which was the seat of the most ancient worship. The chief building always retained, more than other temples, the domestic character of a megaron, as the home of the goddess and of her family of worshippers. *(Arch. Anz.* 1906, cols. 266-268.)

The Site of Delium. — In *B.S.A.* XI, 1904-1905, pp. 153-172 (2 figs.), R. M. Burrows discusses the site of Delium, and concludes that, while there may have been a village near the modern Dilisi, the evidence points to the neighborhood of the chapel of Hagios Demetrios, where there is a fragmentary inscription (... v'AiroWuvi r6v vaov). Excavations here have yielded no further evidence, but there is no trace of the temple elsewhere.

Delphica. —In *Berl. Phil. W.* 1906, pp. 1165-1184, H. Pomtow describes conditions at Delphi, as studied by him during the spring of 1906. While praising the general work of the French, and especially their liberality to other scholars, he criticises sharply many details. Among the results of Pomtow's visit are a large number of topographical notes, new attributions of foundations, and new arrangements of many monuments. Homolle's Treasury of the Cnidians is assigned to the Siphnians. On the lower terrace, south of the temple, there were no anathemata, but the old sanctuary of Ge, and the sacred grove of laurel and myrtle. At the Marmoria the two temples of the *ivaytU* lay between the two temples of Athena. An appendix contains the translation of a letter by a Greek archaeologist, which appeared in the'Aoru, March 19, 1905, complaining of the delay in the publication of the results of the excavations.

An account of the ruins at Delphi, with some discussion of the topography and the sculpture, by P. Ducati is published in *Atene e Rama,* 1906, pp. 198-212.

Olympiaca. — In *Jb. Arch. I.* XXI, 1906, pp. 147-163 (3 figs.), E. Pfiihl reaches the following conclusions: The elliptical foundation which lies before the east front of the Pelopium represents the House of Oenomaus, while the Great Altar of Zeus lay in the narrow space between the Pelopium and the Heraeum. The double temple of Sosipolis and Eileithyia, the small building behind the Exedra of Herodes Atticus, was divided across the middle of the cella by a fixed screen, traces of which are preserved. In the east pediment of the temple of Zeus, leaving unchanged the five standing figures, the chariots and their drivers, and the reclining river gods, a new disposition of the other four figures is desirable. The two narrow, half-kneeling figures should be placed in front of the horses, as Sterope's maid and Pelops' groom; while the two broader, half-reclining figures belong behind the charioteers, the one with a staff on the left side, and the one without a staff on the right.

Honorary Statues in Ancient Greece. —In *B.S.A.* XI, 1904-1905, pp. 32-49, Miss M. K. Welsh discusses the erection of honorary statues in Greek times. Honorary statues are defined as " portrait-statues set up by the authorization of a public body out of regard for the person represented." They were erected in sacred or public places, and the expense was frequently borne by the person honored. The erection of such statues became a custom in the fourth century B.C. The history of the custom is traced in Athens, the rest of Greece, and finally in Asia Minor, with special reference to the Hellenistic period.

The Centaur in Art. — The development of the type of the Centaur in ancient art, and the scenes in which these monsters appear, are briefly discussed by A. Sambon, *Le Musee,* III. 1906, pp. 4-13 (pi.; 12 figs.).

Negroes in Ancient Art. —In *Jh. Oe8t. Arch. I.* IX, 1906, pp. 321-324 (2 pis.; 2 figs.), R. Von Schneider publishes two new representations of negroes.

The first is a vase in the form of a negro's head from Anthedon, belonging to the early third century and offering an instructive contrast to the vase with the name of Leagros in Athens. The other is a bronze statuette from Carnuntum, representing a negro boy in a violent dance. It probably formed part of a lamp or candelabrum.

Alexander's Funeral Car. —In *Rh. MuS.* LXI, 1906, pp. 408-413, F. Reuss continues the discussion of the funeral car of Alexander (see *A J.A.* X, 1906, pp. 199, 458). He argues that the *iafmpa* denotes a space covered by a vaulted roof, above which was the royal standard *(iftoivudt)*. The irdAos (Diod. XXVII, 4) was a pivot cotinecting the floor of the *Kapdpa* with the axles so that the latter could be turned without disturbing the body of the car. Other details are also considered.

Savings Banks in the Form of Beehives. — In *Ath. Mitt.* XXXI, 1906, pp. 231-235 (fig.), L. Deubner collects some evidence to show that Greeks as well as Romans (see *AJ.A.* VI, 1902, p. 455) had savings banks in the form of beehives, and that their existence explains *aip/3Xo xPr)* Aristophanes, *Vesp.* 241.

Greek Boxing. —In *J.H.S.* XXVI, 1906, pp. 213-225 (2 pis.; 2 figs.), K. T. Frost discusses Greek boxing as known through literary allusions and vase paintings. The sport early attained a high development, and remained substantially the same for several centuries. It differed essentially from the modern form in using round arm rather than straight blows, and in making little use of foot-work. The use of hard hand coverings, with or without weights, was universal. As there was no handicap, only the heaviest men tended to compete at the great festivals, and the sport was dangerous as well as painful.

Glass Goblets as Prizes. — Small glass goblets decorated with crowns and palms, and inscribed Xa/St ryv vtutrlv, or tiatXolov Aa/Jt rqv Viktlv, are discussed in *M. Soc. Ant. Fr.* LXV (1904-05), pp. 291-300 (fig.), by P. Perdrizet, who concludes that they were made in Phoenicia, and were prizes at some of the Greek contests under the empire.

Archaeological Notes — In *Le Musee,* III, 1906, A. Sambon describes briefly a number of works of Greek art. Pp. 54-60 (10 figs.) he publishes five scenes from Greek vases, including the sale of an amphora, and the stratagem of Rhea, and a group of monuments representing a seated child holding a bunch of grapes which he tries to defend from a bird. Pp. 106107 (2 pis.; fig.) he describes a red-figured lecythus with the inscription Xdxos and a picture of Dolon creeping past a tree, a marble head resembling the Aeginetan sculptures) and a terra-cotta group of a young girl playing with a dog. Pp. 263-266 (3 pis.; fig.) contain a description of four archaic Greek bronzes. Pp. 428-432 (4 pis.; 5 figs.) he publishes (1) A very primitive bronze group of a small centaur before a tall man; (2) A Roman bronze statuette of Mars; (3) The bronze statuettes from a Lararium near Boscoreale; (4) A bronze vase in the form of a woman's head, probably Egyptian work of the time of Constantine; (5) A fragment of a vase signed by Nicosthenes; (6) A fine red-figured amphora from Capua; (7) A red-figured hydria from Italy with a curious representation of the finding of Erichthonius, in which the author suspects Etruscan contamination.

Archaeological Bulletin. —In *R. tt. Gr.* XIX, 1906, pp. 151-174 (19 figs.), A. De Ridder publishes a 'Bulletin archeologique,' in which he summarizes with comments five articles on Greek architecture and excavations, fifteen on sculpture, five on frescoes and vases, five on bronzes and terra-cottas, and two on a silver mirror and a glass bust. The articles have been already summarized in the Journal.

Strabo's Travels in Greece. — The paper on 'The Extent of Strabo's Travels in Greece,' read by C. II. Weller at the General Meeting of the Archaeological Institute at Ithaca *(A.J.A.* X, p. 84) is published in *Cl. Phil.* I, 1906, pp. 339-356.

ITALY ARCHITECTURE

Vitruvius and his Work. — In *R. Arch.* VIII, 1906, pp. 268-283 (cf. *ibid.* XLI, 1902, pp. 39-81, III, 1904, pp. 222-223, 382-393, IV, 1904, pp. 265-266; *A J. A.* 1904, p. 491), V. Mortet discusses the limitations of the work of Vitruvius and finds that the term *architectura* was ordinarily restricted to the construction and decoration of public and private edifices properly so called. Other matters are treated by Vitruvius only as subordinate.

The Rostra. — In *Bert. Phil. W.* 1906, pp. 1119-1120, F. Brunswick points out that in determining the date of the Rostra it is important to discover the relation of the structure to the recently discovered subterranean passage near by. An irregularity in a portion of the foundations of the front wall seems connected with a continuation of this gallery, but also indicates that the wall was built after the passage was abandoned and forgotten. In *Cl. R.* XX, 1906, p. 379, T. Ashby, Jr., discusses with approval Mau's paper on the Rostra *(Rom. Mitt.* 1905, pp. 230-266; see *A J.A.* X, p. 459). Minute details which throw light on the relation of the Rostra of Caesar and those of Trajan, together with the various alterations of both, are briefly discussed by E. Petersen in *Rom. Mitt.* XXI, 1906, pp. 57-63.

SCULPTURE

The Arch of Titus. — In *Pal. Ex. Fund,* XXXVIII, 1906, pp. 306-315, W. S. Cai. oecott gives the exact measurements of the golden candlestick and table of shew-bread on the Arch of Titus, and compares them with the figures given in the Old Testament and Josephus. He finds that the candlestick corresponds with these figures, but the table is larger. This increase in size is attributed to aesthetic considerations.

INSCRIPTIONS

The Eituns Inscriptions. — In *Cl. Phil.* I, 1906, pp. 414-415, N. W. DeWitt interprets the *Eituns* inscriptions at Pompeii as indicating the places at which the Oscan citizens were allowed access to the city wall for purposes of promenade. *Eituns = liceto ire.* according to this interpretation.

The Calendar of Verrius Flaccus. — The new fragment of the calendar of Verrius Flaccus from Praeneste *(Not.*

Scav. 1904, p. 393; *A.J.A.* 1906, p. 109) is discussed in *Atene t. Roma,* 1906, pp. 212-214. by C. Pascal. He gives a tentative restoration of the text, accepting Marucchi's *stultor urn feriae* in the last line, but differing in other details.

Oculists' Stamps. — Most of the stamps used by Roman oculists to mark the pastilles employed in their treatment of the eyes have been found in Gaul, some in Germany and Britain, but very few elsewhere. None are from Greece, where eye-salves were sold in jars, not as pastilles. The inscriptions on these stamps, originally edited by E. Esperandieu in *C.I.L.* XIII, pp. 559-610, have been reprinted in a separate volume, with plates, a bibliography, full indices, and a brief discussion of the forms and uses of the stamps. *(Signacula Medieorum Oculariorum reeensuit Aemilius EspeRandieu. Paris, 1905, E. Leroux. 175 pp.; 68 pis. 8vo.)*

In *B. Soc. Ant. Fr.* 1906, pp. 147-149, E. Esperandieu publishes four inscriptions from the cachet of an oculist, recently found near Reimersheim.

Epigraphio Bulletin. — In *R. Arch.* VIII, 1906, pp. 206-224, R. Cagnat and M. Besnier, in their review of epigraphical publications relating to Roman antiquity for the period March-June, 1906, give the text of sixtyeight inscriptions and notes on publications relating to epigraphy.

VASES

The Primitive Italian Urn. — At the May meeting of the Berlin Arch. Society M. Mayer discussed the primitive Italian urn, calling attention to a form resembling the Villanova type, but simpler, which was used for secular purposes only, and is found chiefly in southern Italy. The decoration of the Villanova urns shows northeastern and continental rather than Greek or Aegean affinities. It is doubtful whether Mycenaean influenced geometric art to the extent commonly supposed. *(Arch. An:.* 1906, col. 193.)

COINS

The 'oPods in Polybius. — In *C. R. Acad. Insc.* 1906, pp. 458-470, E. Babelon argues that Polybius, when speaking of Roman money, uses *6fioX6s* to denote the *as libralis* of 327 gr. This gives a more reasonable value to the prices mentioned in II, 15 and VI, 39, 12, where the Greek value for the o/3oAos is absurd.

The Type of Three Monetae. — The three standing female figures on certain Roman coins, each figure holding a pair of balances and a cornucopia, represent the coinage in the three metals. The middle figure occupies the place of dignity and represents Gold. The figure to her right represents Silver, as occupying the place next in dignity, that to her left, Bronze or Copper; cf. the position of the Capitoline group of Jupiter, Juno, and Minerva. (fr. Gnecchi, *R. Ital. Num.* XIX, 1906, pp. 311-316; 3 figs.)

Countermarks on Roman Coins. — G. Pans A writes in the *R. Ital. Num.* XIX, 1906, pp. 397-417 (pi.), on the countermarks found on Roman bronzes of the imperial period. He claims that these marks were designed not merely to legitimatize, upon the accession of a new ruler, or the assumption of a new title, the coins of the preceding period, pending the issue of the new types, but sometimes also to mark coins intended for public donatives. The countermarks are due to the authority of the Senate, and consequently are found generally on bronze coins only. Exceptionally silver coins are also thus stamped, when an emperor, by *damnatio memoriae,* lost also the right of coinage. Sometimes the existence of more than one stamp on the same coin is to be interpreted as due to the act of the emperor's own official, thus approving, by his supreme authority, the previous act of the Senate. The much-discussed stamp NCAPR is to be interpreted *Neronis Caesaris Auctoritate Probatum.*

Roman Contorniates. — In *Num. Chron.* 1906, pp. 232-266 (2 pis.), Katharine A. Mcdowall argues in support of the claim that the socalled contorniates are properly denominated *calculi* and were used as counters in the games of the *tabulae lusoriae.* The article classifies the various types, and offers new interpretations of some unexplained or disputed types, and accurate reproductions of others which, though easy of interpretation, are of archaeological or mythological interest.

Roman Medallions. — Francesco Gnecchi (who projects a corpus of medallions) argues that under medallions should be included all those pieces, of whatever size, that were issued by authority of the emperor, and not S-C, even before Hadrian's time. From the period of Gallienus, fabric and style must furnish the basis for decision. The classification should be into *maximi moduli* (the pieces now usually called medallions), *magni moduli* (large, or first, bronzes), *medii moduli* (middle, or second, bronzes), and *minimi moduli* (small, or third, bronzes — otherwise quinarii), thus retaining the time-honored designation M. M. *(R. Ital. Num.* XIX, 1906, pp. 295-810.)

Coinage of Hadrian. — In *R. Ital. Num.* XIX, 1906, pp. 329-374 (2 pis.), L. Laffranchi presents a systematic classification, year by year, of the issues of Roman coins under Hadrian, — a task that neither Eckhel nor Cohen essayed.

Coin Portraits of the Third Century. — A bronze sheet with three coinportraits of the third century A.d. in the Museo Kircheriano is discussed by F. Staehlin in *Rom. Mitt.* XXI, 1906, pp. 85-86 (fig.).

Coinage System of Diocletian and Constantino. — G. Dattari presents in *R. Ital. Num.* XIX, 1906, pp. 75-396, a new theory of the system of Roman coinage introduced among the reforms of Diocletian, and continued, with modifications, into the time of Constantine. The history of each move is set forth, and the whole made clear by classified tables.

Birthday Coins. —In *B. Soc. Ant. Fr.* 1906, pp. 184-185, J. Maurice discusses the formula PLURA NATAL("i) FEL(ic('a), which occurs on some small bronzes of Maximianus and Constantine. He argues that this refers to the *diet natales,* and that the coins were struck for the celebrations of February 27 or July 21, 307, or February 27, 308 A.d.

GENERAL AND MISCELLANEOUS

The Ara Pacis Augustae. —In *Jk. Oest. Arch. I.* IX, 1906, pp. 298-315 (3 figs.), E. Petersen discusses the Ara Pacis in the light of the recent excavations on its site. The enclosure had openings on both the east and west, though only on the latter side are there remains of steps. The procession advancing toward the wast occupied the two long sides. The smaller slabs were placed on either side of the openings. At one end were the relief of Tellus and the relief representing a libation, in which the two figures personify the Senate and People. At the other end were the two sacrificial reliefs, which represent rites performed at the Lupercal and before the Ara Pacis. It seems better to place the latter pair on either side of the entrance, but there are some reasons for believing that this position was occupied by the former pair. The large altars recently discovered in Asia Minor are helpful in the restoration of the Ara Pacis. The two openings seem suggested by the shrine of Janus, with which this monument is contrasted by Ovid (*Fasti*, I, 121 ff.).

The Pine-Cone as Fountain. — In *Rh. Mus.* LXI, 1906, p. 311, K. TitTel corrects a misunderstanding of his discussion of the use of the pinecone as the monumental mouth of a fountain. The Vatican cone was probably placed on a low base, not on a column. It cannot, however, be regarded as the first example of such a use of this ornament.

The *Solea*. — In *B. Soc. Ant. Fr.* 1906, pp. 266-267, Commandant Lefebvre Dks No'ettes reports on some experiments with the *solea*. He claims that it was a shoe, but that the animal provided with it could only move at a walk. It was therefore of use only to veterinaries, as it enabled horses to be treated while on the march.

The Suburbs of Pompeii. — *Le Muse'e*, III, 1906, pp. 159-212 (8 pis.; 40 figs.), contains a description of recent discoveries in the neighborhood of Pompeii. The paintings of the villas at Boscoreale are described by Geor«es Tocdouze, the furniture by J. De Foville, and the silverware by A. Sambon. Two unsigned chapters give a brief account of the discoveries of G. Matrone at Boscotrecase near the ancient mouth of the Sarno, and especially of the dispersion of part of the jewellery there found.

FRANCE

A Bronze Plaque from a Girdle. — In a tumulus at Belignat (Ain) were found, in 1895, some human bones, a plaque with ornament in *repousse*, a large ring or collar, and thirty-two bracelets, of which seven only were preserved. All are of bronze. The plaque, which doubtless formed part of a girdle, is rectangular, 0.468 m. long by 0.157 m. wide. The thickness is hardly 0.001 m. The decoration consists of bands of straight lines, and in the bands are geometrical patterns. A number of knobs is added. The decoration resembles closely that of the plaque from Corveissiat (E. Chantre, *Album du premier age de fer*, pis. XXIV and XXIV *bis*), and the two plaques are evidently of the same period, the end of the Bronze Age and the beginning of the Iron Age. (E. Chanel, *R. Arch.* VIII, 1906, pp. 120-125; fig.)

Alesia. — The commencement of systematic explorations at Alesia (AliseSainte-Reine, cf. *A J.A.* X, pp. 116, 355) has led A. Heron De Villefosse to give, in *M. Soc. Ant. Fr.* LXV, 1904-1905, pp. 207-272 (pi.; 3 figs.), a summary of the results of the irregular excavations on the site since the seventeenth century. After a historical sketch, he comments on *C.I.L.* XIII, 2885, 2876, 2877, and 2878, and publishes some fragments consisting of single letters, a tombstone, and a fragment, mentioning a priest of Rome and Augustus. The cantharus of Alesia (cf. *A.J.A.* VIII, p. 323) and its puzzling inscription are discussed, and the article closes with a chronological catalogue of the monuments from Alesia preserved in the Museum at Dijon.

The Greeks in Southern Gaul. —In *Jh. Oest. Arch. I.* IX, 1906, pp. 165-182 (3 figs.), E. Maass continues his study of the survival of Greek influence in southern Gaul. La Tarasque and her conqueror St. Martha (perhaps a *Mrjrnp*) are a survival of the personified miasma overcome by a god or hero. Similar influences are traced in the legend of St. Aegidius whose city, St. Gilles, occupies the site of the Doric Heraclea in the Rhone delta.

The Temper of Gallic Swords.— Polybius declares that the Gallic swords were so poorly tempered that they bent or broke on the Roman armor. In *C. R. Acad. Insc.* 1906, p. 260, is a summary of a paper by S. Reinach, who argues that this statement rests on the discovery in Gallic graves of swords, which had been broken, according to the Gallic custom, before burial. The Gallic swords in modern museums are of good quality. The paper is published in full in *L'Anthropologie*, XVII, 1906, pp. 343-358.

Gallo-Roman Chronicle. — In his 'Chronique Gallo-Romaine' (*R. iZt. Anc.* VIII, 1906, pp. 263-271, 343-349; fig.), C..titlman notes briefly numerous books and articles on Gallo-Roman topics, giving special attention to Alesia. He also discusses unfavorably the study of the Greeks in southern Gaul by Maass (cf. *A.J.A.* X, p. 467).

The "Cabinet de Prance." — *Le Muse'e*, III, 1906, pp. 309-358 (8 pis. ; 33 figs.), contains an account of the more important works of art in the Cabinet de France in the Bibliotheque Rationale. The sculpture, bronzes (a collection of exceptional value), terra-cottas, and vases (including the valuable collection of the Due de Luynes) are described by N. De Rome; the silver by A. Sambon; the engraved gems by A. Moriani; the coins and medals by J. De Foville; and the furniture, arms, ivories, etc., by Georges Toudouze.

Epigraphic Notes. — In *B. Snc. Ant. Fr.* 1906, pp. 255-257, A. Heron De Villekosse discusses the inscription from Frolois (see *A.J.A.* X, p. 356). He reads *D.M. Munimentum Ripcicnus Du*-*nai*u or *Dxmau/*. Ripcus occurs on an inscription from Autun. In *It.* 2?/. 118, 1905-06, pp. 168-169, the same writer proposes a new interpretation for part of an inscription from Orange recording a grant of land, published in *C. R. Acad. Insc.* 1904, pp. 497-502; *R. Bp.* 114, pp. 97-99.

GERMANY

Neolithic Settlements in Southwestern Germany. — In *Z. Ethn.* XXXVIII, 1906, pp. 312-345 (map; 12 figs.), A. Schliz discusses the neolithic settlements in southwestern Germany, basing his arguments largely on the decorations of the pottery. The pottery decorated with string patterns *(Schnurkerajnik)* belongs to a race of hunters living on the wooded hills, while that decorated with bands *(Banrfkeramik)* belongs to an agricultural people, whose settlements are found on the loess, which furnished the only land which could be cultivated with stone tools. These people were of the same race as the hunters, whom they seem to have found in the land when they arrived from the Danube valley, and to whom they seem to have submitted. Later they withdrew southward, for their villages were abandoned, not destroyed. The dwellers in the Lake villages were of another race and civilization, though all these people seem to have influenced each other. All seem to have been overcome by invaders in the early Bronze Age.

Terra Sigillata Ware in Northern Germany. —In *Z. Ethn.* XXXVIII, 1906, pp. 369-377, H. Draoendori'f discusses the discoveries of *terra sigillata* in northern Germany. The vases usually belong to the second or even third century 'a.d., and, with the Roman glass and bronzes, bear important testimony as to Gallic trade with the coasts of the North Sea and the Baltic. Their evidence confirms the view that this trade was largely carried on by water from Nymegen.

AUSTRIA-HUNGARY

A New Group of Neolithic Pottery. — In *Z. Ethn.* XXXVIII, 1906, pp. 221-227 (15 figs.), £. Von Majewski describes a group of neolithic pottery with string patterns arranged in waving lines *(Schnuricellenornament)* found in southern Poland. The ornament seems unknown elsewhere in pottery of this period, but strongly resembles the decoration found on Slavic pottery of Christian times.

The Survival of Neolithic Ornamentation. — In *Mitt. A nth. Ges.* XXXVI, pp. 98-100, K. FuChS notes a number of examples showing that neolithic systems of spiral decoration, discussed by Wilke *(ibid.* XXXV, pp. 249-269; *A.J.A.* 1906, p. 437), have survived until recent times in Transylvania.

A *Beiixio Amatoria.*— ln *Jh. Oest. Arch. I.* IX, 1906, pp. 192-198, A. Von Pkemerstein publishes with a facsimile a lead tablet found at the Roman colony Poetovio (Pettau). The inscription reads *Paulina acersa sit a viris omnibus et ileficsa sit, ne quid possit malifacere. Firminam* c/orf«s *ah o mnibus humanis.* It is apparently of the second century A. d., and is the first example of a *defixio* found in Pannonia. This form of curse originated in the Greek Orient, and examples are rare in those provinces which were but little reached by Greek influence.

A Roman Sarcophagus. — In *Jh. Oest. Arch. I.* IX, 1906, Beiblatt, col. 87 (fig.), W. Kubitschek publishes a Latin inscription from a large sarcophagus found in 1905 at Doclea. It is the epitaph of P. Cornelius Julius, dedicated by his daughters Julia and Irene.

AFRICA

Bronze Maces from Cheliff and La Chiffa (Algeria). — In *R. Arch.* VIII, 1906, pp. 284-289 (3 figs.), E. T. Hamy comes to the conclusion that some cylindrical bronze maces from Cheliff and La Chiffa, in Algeria, similar to maces found in Germany, were probably the weapons of some band of northern invaders in the fifth century after Christ.

The Ancient Lamp. — The evolution in the form of the ancient clay lamp is traced in *Reliq.* XII, 1906, pp. 263-268 (18 figs.), by Sophia Beale, chiefly on the evidence afforded by the collections in the museums at Carthage and Tunis.

New Punic Inscriptions. — In *Eph. Sern. Ep.* II, 1906, pp. 171-190, M. Lidzbahski reviews the publications and discussions of Punic inscriptions that have been discovered within the last three years.

An Inscription in Honor of Sextus Appuleius.— In *C. R. Acad.Inse.* 1906, pp. 470-478 (fig-), R. Caijnat discusses a fragmentary inscription from Carthage, which seems to contain an *elngium* of Sextus Appuleius. The writing indicates the Augustan age, and it is probabl% that the persou honored by the Carthagiuians was the husband of Octavia the elder, sister of Augustus, and father of the consul of 29 B.C. He is also known from a Greek inscription of Pergamon.

Senatus Consultum Beguense. — The text of the *senatus consultum de nundinis saltus Beguensis (C.T.L.* VIII, 270, 11451), after careful revision before the originals in the museum of the Bardo, is published in *C. R. Acad. Insc.* 1906, pp. 448-456 (fig.) by A. Merlin. In addition to numerous minor corrections, lines 5-7, containing the date (October 15, 138 A.d.) and the names of four senators, are given for the first time. They are: *Idibus Oct. in Comitio* Rvm *in Curia ltd. scribundo adfuerunt Q. Gargilius Q. f. Quir. Antiqus, Ti.* CI. *Ti.f. Pal. Quartinus, C. Oppius C.f. Vel. Secerns, C. Herennius C.f. Pal. Caecilianus, M. Iul. M.f. Quir. Clarus.* In line five the letters Rvm are distinct but inexplicable.

A Latin Metrical Inscription. — In *Berl. Phil. W.* 1906, cols. 1118-1119, R. Engelmann points out that the inscription *C. R. Acad. Insc.* 1904, p. 697, is an African hexameter, *bide* (for *vide), Diote, bide, poss(id)as plurima, bide,* which is appropriate for the landowner contemplating his possessions, who is represented on the monument.

EARLY CHRISTIAN, BYZANTINE, AND MEDIAEVAL ART GENERAL AND MISCELLANEOUS

The "Virgin" in the Inscription of Abercius. — In *R. Arch.* VHI, 1906, pp. 93-96, W. R. Paton explains the *mpdevos* aytij, of line 14 of the inscription of Abercius, as Faith, who is mentioned in line 12. The use of the word pjrros as an indication of Christianity is noted.

The Meaning of XMI. —The discussion of the abbreviation XMT (see *A.J. A.* X, p. 471) is continued in *Berl. Phil. W.* 1906, cols. 1082-1088, by J. J. Smirnoff, who argues that in the numerical value (643) of the letters is the key to their meaning, and suggests possible interpretations. The Copts seem to have considered the letters as a symbol of the Trinity. The interpretation of the letters as initials is an early endeavor to explain the meaning of a forgotten symbol. Perhaps the origin is to be found in a Hebrew symbol written in Greek letters.

The Church of the Panagia Oorgoepikoob in Athens. — In *Ath. Mitt.* XXXI, 1906, pp. 279-1524 (2 pls.; 30 figs.'), K. Michel and A. Struck begin a study of the churches in Athens belonging to the Middle Byzantine period (eighth and ninth centuries) by a detailed discussion of the church of the Panagia Gorgoepikoos, or the "little Metropolitan." After a full bibliography, they analyze the architecture of the building, which belonged to the cloister of St. Nicholas, and describe fully the Christian sculptures which decorate the exterior. The frescoes of the interior have almost wholly disappeared. The question of the date is difficult, but a long argument leads to the conclusion that it was built about the beginning of the ninth century at the instance of the Kmpress Irene, and with the picture of the Panagia Gorgoepikoos took this name, which had previously belonged to the Parthenon. The building replaced an earlier church, which had superseded the temples of Isis and Eileithyia, and was dedicated to Hagios Eleutherios, who in more than one locality has succeeded to the cult of Eileith via. The architectural influence of the church may be traced in other Athenian churches of this time, and seems to have been felt in the church at Skripu (874 A.d.). For the ancient sculptures in this church, see *supra*, p. 214.

The Dome of SS. Sergius and Bacchus at Constantinople. — The discussion of the dome of this church by Allan Marquand presented at the General Meeting of the Archaeological Institute at Ithaca (see *A.J.A.* 1906, p. 77) appears in *Rec. Past,* V, 1906, pp. 355-362 (5 figs.).

Byzantine Sculptures in Constantinople. — In *N. Bull. Arch. Crist.* 1906, pp. 107-121, A MuKOZ cites two sarcophagi from Asia Minor, showing the same characteristics as a group in Europe for which he had already claimed Asiatic origin. The series now contains twenty-one sarcophagi or fragments. He also describes some Byzantine sculptures in the Museum and elsewhere in Constantinople, including two reliefs of the "Youths in the Fiery Furnace," a "Raising of Lazarus," a relief representing two warriors, an arch from a ciborium now used to decorate a wall, a Madonna with Saints, and a Hellenistic relief, Christianized by a cross carved on the drapery of one of the figures.

A Seal of the Emperor Leontius. — A circular seal bearing the inscription: *Deus aiuta. Leontii* and on the reverse: *Aug. Romion* is published by Mordtmann in *Byz. Z.* 1906, p. 614. The avoidance of a type is natural for an iconoclastic emperor. Noteworthy are the already Italian *aiuta* and the genitive plural *Romion.*

"Resurrection" in Early Christian Art. — In *Rom. Quart.* 1906, pp. 2848, A. De Waal discusses six "Resurrection" scenes occurring in paintings or on sarcophagi: the "Vision of Ezechiel," the Raising of Lazarus, the Raising of the Youth of Nain, the Raising of the Daughter of Jairus, the Risen Christ, and the Raising of Tabitha. The "Vision of Ezechiel" is merely a representation of the resurrection at the Last Day. An interesting group of monuments depicts the Raising of Lazarus in an unusual manner, the grave being horizontal and not vertical. A reproduction is given of the only Pre-Constantinian representation of this scene, on a sarcophagus iu the Late ran.

Christian Sarcophagi and Inscriptions. — In *Ri'nn. Quart.* 1906, pp. 126, A. Wilpert discusses, first, the interpretation of reliefs on sarcophagi. He maintains that the relation between the reliefs and the deceased must always be considered. He thus interprets a Perugia sarcophagus as a sculptured rendering of the catacomb type of Judgment, with Christ as Judge, the deceased as defendant, and five saints as advocates. The two *orantes* on a sarcophagus of St. Cannat in France, personify the soul of the deceased, doubled for the sake of symmetry. The lay figure added to Biblical scenes in many reliefs is also a representation of the deceased. The second part of the article discusses the development and characteristics of formulae in the inscriptions of the first and second levels of the catacomb of S. Priscilla, with corrections of previous publications.

The "Crown of Thorns" in Art. — Commenting upon a statement of E. Male in a recent article in the *Revue de deux Mondes* to the effect that the crown of thorns does not appear in art before the beginning of the fourteenth century, F. De Mely shows that its first appearance is in the twelfth century. He adds some observations on the skull depicted at the foot of the Cross, symbolical of Calvary and on the meaning of the latter word *(B. Soc. Ant. Fr.* 1906, pp. 215-221).

A Font at Gumlose. Sweden. — A fine sculptured font in Gumlose church, Skane, south Sweden, is briefly described in *Reliq.* XII, 1906, pp. 276-278 (2 figs.). The carving in its high finish suggests the hand of a worker in ivory. On the base are four lions, each holding a dragon between his teeth. On the bowl, under a series of arches, are represented The Adoration of the Magi, The Annunciation, and The Baptism of Christ. The scenes are accompanied by inscriptions.

ITALY

Iconography in Sta. Maria Antiqua. — W. Von Gruneisen in *Arch. Stor. Pair.* 1906, pp. 85-95, after a careful examination of the fresco of St. Anne with the infant Virgin in her arms, in the central chapel of Sta. Maria Antiqua, reports that it belongs to the rare type in which the Virgin holds the cross in her hands. There is no doubt that a nimbus encircles her head. He also argues, in opposition to Wilpert's theory of the origin of the quadrate nimbus (see *A.J.A.* X, p. 206), that the heads of Theodotus and Pope Zaccharias were not painted on canvas, but on small plaster surfaces which were fastened by means of nails over heads already existing, but without change in the figures below.

Byzantine Coinage at Syracuse. — With the advance of the Lombards in the sixth century, communication between Ravenna and southern Italy became difficult, and under Maurice Tiberius a Byzantine mint was established in Syracuse, which continued in operation until 726 a.d. The chief issues are briefly described and illustrated in

Le Musee, III, 1906, pp. 267273 (24 figs.) by A. Sambon.

A Romanesque Pulpit at Arcetri. — The Romanesque pulpit in San Leonardo at Arcetri near Florence stood originally in the church of San Piero Scheraggio in Florence. The reliefs, which represent the Tree of Jesse, the Nativity, the Adoration of the Magi, the Deposition, the Presentation at the Temple, and the Baptism, are not by the same sculptor, but show four separate hands. Two reliefs have been lost. They are in the realistic narrative style of the North contrasting with the southern symbolism as seen, for example, in the pulpit at Ravello. (O. H. Giglioli, *VArte,* 1906, pp. 278-291.)

The Miniatures of the Codex Gertrudianus. — D. Roche contributes to *B. Soc. A rtl. Fr.* 1906, pp. 216-251, a resume of Kondakoff's recent study of the miniatures of the Codex Gertrudianus in the archives of the cathedral at Cividale. The codex is a psalter written for Archbishop Egbert of Trier (97!-993), but afterward the property of Gertrude, wife of Grand Duke Iziaslav Iaroslavitch of Poland and mother of his third son, Iaropolk IziasleVitch. The miniatures were added at this time. The first miniature shows Iarapolk and his wife Irene adoring St. Peter, while the princess, Gertrude, kneeling, seizes one of the apostle's feet in such a way that Kondakoff thinks that the ceremony of kissing the toe of the statue of St. Peter in Rome must have been usual at this time. In the " Nativity of Christ," two lions are added at the bottom of the picture, of so plastic a character as to suggest that the artist was a sculptor. The "Crucifixion " is not rigorously Byzantine. The " Virgin Enthroned" corresponds to the eleventh-century mosaics. As a whole, the miniatures offer an example of a translation of Byzantine types by a non-Greek artist, whose nationality Kondakoff does not venture to determine.

Lombard Fragments at Ferentillo. — In *Rom. Quart.* 1906, pp. 49-81, E. Iikuzig publishes architectural and other Lombard fragments in the Abbey of S. Pietro at Ferentillo, which dates from 575. The most interesting is a slab, with incised ornaments and two *orantes,* inscribed *Hildericus Dagileopa* -f *in honore Sci Petri et amore Sci Leo(nin) et Sci Grigorii (p)ro remedin n(nimae) m(eae)* + *Ursus Magester fecit.* It was probably sketched out and never finished. The Hilderic who was the donor became Duke of Spoleto in 739. The article contains a reconstruction of the chancel-screen and illustrations of several sculptures. Further investigations are urged in order to ascertain the extent of the earliest church and the contents of the five sarcophagi still in the abbey/

SPAIN

Three Castles in Spain. — The castle at Loarre is not a homogeneous building of the last quarter of the eleventh century, as Spanish writers have claimed, but was worked upon from time to time in the twelfth. The castle of Metfina del Campo is interesting in the adaptation, by the sixteenthcentury architect who remodelled it, of the old fortifications to the demands of artillery. The castle of Coca is modelled upon that of Medina del Campo, but shows much originality in its decorative battlements. (E. LefkvrePontalis, *C. R. Acad. Insc.* 1906, pp. 199-200.)

The Cloister of Santo Domingo. — The cloister of the abbey at Silos in Castile was commenced in the middle of the eleventh century by the abbot, St. Dominic the elder, whose epitaph is preserved on the capital of one of the columns. This capital and others show fantastic motives which have no counterpart in Europe and are the work no doubt of Mussulman slaves. The reliefs on the pillars at the corners of the colonnade are of the twelfth century and show analogies to the school of Toulouse. Others belong to the thirteenth century, like the Tree of Jesse and the Annunciation in the southwest corner. To the same century belongs the upper cloister, whose capitals show a curious persistence of archaic traditions. Toward the end of the fourteenth century, the lower cloister was decorated with a wooden coffered ceiling with painted groups in each compartment, among which is the earliest representation of a bull-fight in Spain. The ceiling is perhaps the work of a Mussulman carver working with a Christian painter. (E. Bertaux, *Gaz. B.-A.* XXXVI, 1906, pp. 27-44.)

FRANCE

The Motive of a Thirteenth-century Fresco. — The representation of the Virgin kissing the hand of the infant in a thirteenth-century lunette in the church of Notre Dame at Montmorillon has been regarded as a genre conception. P. Perdrizet in *R. Art Chrtt.* 1906, pp. 289-294, derives the motive from Byzantine sources, comparing an ikon published by Kondakoff in his *Monuments de I'art chre'tien a I'Athos,* in which the same gesture is reproduced. The writer regards it as symbolic, referring to the wounds of the Cross.

The Door of the Abbey at Vezelay.— In *R. Art Chre't.* 1906, pp. 253257, L. E. Lefevre, while accepting G. Sanoner's interpretation of the sculptures on the lintel of the door of the abbey at Vezelay (see *A J.A.* IX, p. 488), suggests an interpretation for the eight compartments bordering the tympanum, in which is depicted Christ sending forth his'Disciples to preach the Word (Fig. 4). The group in the lower left-hand compartment represents Christ and St. John; the others are allegorical representations of the seven churches of Asia, following the description of the Apocalypse.

The Church of Issoire. — The church of St Austremoine and St. Paul at Issoire in Auvergne, dating probably from the eleventh century, and an exceedingly fine example of the Romanesque architecture of Auvergne, which contains Byzantine elements, is described in some detail by E. D'hauterive in *Le Mu. ie'e,* III, 1906, pp. 383-388 (2 pis.). In the outer wall of the north transept are two fine early reliefs, and four of the capitals in the choir are decorated with subjects from the New Testament. The building was originally the chapel of a Benedictine abbey, but since the Revolution has been the parish church.

Architectural Refinements at Amiens. — In./. *B. Archil.* 1906. pp. 397—117 (7 figs.), J. Bilson discusses the views of W. H. Goodyear as to the irregularities in mediaeval buildings, lie denies that these are intentional refinements, and illustrates his argument by a detailed examination of the cathedral at Amiens. He concludes that the deviations from the normal at Amiens are merely the accidental results of movements which have taken place in the structure, as is proved by the recorded history and present condition of the building. In fact, the only surprising thing is that they are not much greater.

GREAT BRITAIN

Pre-Norman Crosses in Staffordshire. — In *Reliq.* XII, 1906, pp. 229246 (11 figs.), G. Lk Blanc Smith continues his discussion of pre-Norman crosses in Staffordshire (see *A.J.A.* IX, p. 229), describing first a fragment at Ham and two at Checkley, which belong to the Dovedale Sub-group. At Leek are the remains of three crosses, one cylindrical, with the upper part hewn flat on four sides, and two rectangular. The decorations are chiefly knots and interfacings, but No. 3 has on one side a cross-bearing figure, with discs and worms in the field, and above the lower part of another figure. As there is no nimbus, the figure may be merely a pilgrim.

A Fragment of Pre-Norman Sculpture. — In *Reliq.* XII, 1906, pp. 270-273 (2 figs.), J. Romilly Allen shows that a fragment of pre-Norman sculpture in the museum at York originally formed part of an altar-tomb at St. Andrew's, whence it seems to have been brought by Dibdin about 1838.

AFRICA

Christian Inscriptions of Africa. — In *R. Arch.* VIII, 1906, pp. 126142, P. Monceaux publishes, with notes, twenty-one further metrical Christian inscriptions, all of which have been published in the *C.I.L.* or elsewhere (see *A J.A.* 1906, p. 477). *Ibid.* pp. 297-310, thirteen inscriptions (Nos. 215-227) are published and discussed.

Christian Carthage. — In *Reliq.* XII, 1906, pp. 162-170 (8 figs.) Sophia Beai.e gives a brief description of the remains of the great Christian basilica at Carthage, and of a number of the Christian relics in the museum. In conclusion some terra-cotta statuettes, the bronze cover of a mirror case, and an engraved razor recently found in Punic graves are described.

RENAISSANCE ART GENERAL, AND MISCELLANEOUS

Laocoon in the Middle Ages and the Renaissance. — The most ancient representations of the fate of Laocoon are found iu Cod. Riccardianus No. 881, of the fourteenth century, in Vat. Lat. No. 2761, of the fifteenth century, and in the Riccardianus Virgil No. 492, whose miniatures show the hand of Gozzoli. One of Filippino Lippi's drawings in the Uffizi (No. 109) shows the influence of Servius' commentary on the Virgilian passage. The discovery of the marble group (1506) gave a new form to the representations in painting, but did not stereotype them, and they finally became entirely different, as in the fresco of Gaudenzio Ferrari. Marco Dente's print is drawn both from the Vatican Virgil and the group, but Fontana's prints, the frescoes of N. Abati, and of Giulio Romano, and the painting by El Greco in the gallery of San Telmo at Seville are all independent of the classic sources. (R. Forster, *Jb. Preuss. Kunsts.* XXVII, pp. 149-178.)

Attributions to Pier Francesco Fiorentino. — The following pictures are added to Berenson's list in a note signed X. in *Rass. d'Arte,* 1906, p. 136: a Madonna with the Child and infant St. John, recently assigned to Neri v di Bicci by A. Colosanti; a Madonna with the Child, St. John, and an Angel, in the Collegiata of Sinalunga, also hitherto given to Neri di Bicci, a Madonna and Child with the infant St. John in the museum at Dijon; a Madonna in the Houghton collection at Florence; a large altar-piece in the Cathedral at Empoli; a Madonna and Child with the infant St. John in the Fogg Museum at Cambridge; and a Virgin adoring the Child with Angels in the collection of Mr. Herbert Home.

Hispano-Moresque Ware. — The processes used in making the HispanoMoresque ware, and the characteristic shapes and decorations, are briefly described with illustrations from the collections of the Boston Museum, in *B. Mus. F. A.* 1906, pp. 37-38 (fig.).

Rembrandt. — Rembrandt's relation to the art of his time has been studied by T. Neal, who in his little book discusses the works and personality of the artist, the Rembrandt exhibition at Amsterdam in 1898, an unrecognized painting by Rembrandt, and the painting of the seventeenth century. He regards Rembrandt as the greatest exponent of tendencies influencing many contemporary artists. The new painting is in a private collection at Florence, and represents an old woman holding a book against her breast. The face appears in at least six other works of Rembrandt. This picture is a thoroughly characteristic work. (T. Neal, *Rembrandt e V Arte del suo Tempo.* Florence, 1906, B. Seeber. 119 pp.; plate; 8vo.)

Claus Sluter, Jan van Eyck, and Rembrandt. — F. SchmidtDegener in *Gaz. Ji.-A.* XXXVI, 1906, pp. 89-108, brings evidence to show that the ten statuettes in bronze in the Museum of Amsterdam are not the original work of Jacques de Gerines, but cast by him after models furnished by a pupil of Claus Sluter and by Jan van Eyck. He rejects the names of historical persons now applied to the figures and believes seven of them (those inspired by van Eyck) to be representations of the Virtues, while two others, with characteristics of Sluter, are interpreted as Philip the Good invested as Count of Holland by the Emperor. The tenth statuette is rejected as not belonging to either artist. The figure of the Duke of Burgundy reappears in many of Rembrandt's pictures, and that of the Emperor in at least two. All seven of the Virtues were also borrowed by Rembrandt. The writer also identifies the "Head of an Old Man, by van Eyck" which appears in the inventory of Rembrandt's possessions with the "Man with the Carnations," and finds that the painter copied the portrait in several works between 1641 and 1642, as well as in-his own portrait in Vienna, which is dated in 1658.

Rembrandt as an Etcher. —In *Burl. Mag.* IX, 1906, pp. 245-253, 313323, 383-390, C. J. Holmes continues his studies of Rembrandt as an etcher (see *A.J.A.* X, 479). After settling in Amsterdam in 1631, the artist made many studies from life, but was only partially successful in freeing himself from his model. Of this period is the first " Raising of Lazarus," which is theatrical and lacks the subtle " ghostliness " of which he was master later, and which first appears in the " Descent from the Cross" of 1633. A desire to obtain simplicity led him to imitate Rubens and the. Venetians. All his earlier etchings show countless experiments. The over-completeness of the "Triumph of Mordecai" is remedied in the second "Raising of Lazarus," where the unessential is resolutely suppressed. Growing technical capacity, shown in the series of portraits (1646-1648), enabled him to deal with his favorite mystery with greater success, a fine example being the "Christ appearing to His Disciples," which is the earliest example of " impressionism," being a wonderful realization of the iuvisible. Rembrandt's tendency in his last period (1650-1661) toward the simplest forms of expression is shown by the changes made in the plates for " Christ presented to the People" and the "Three Crosses." The earlier proofs are filled with figures, while the later show large unfilled spaces, and simple contrasts of darkness and light. His failing sight is shown by certain loose touches in "Christ and the Samaritan Woman," but before the end came he was able to produce the later series of portraits, remarkable for their psychological insight, and fine studies of the nude, like the "Negress," the " Woman at the Bath," and the "Phoenix." In his early period conscientiousness fettered imagination, and even when complete mastery over his medium arrived, his early training asserted itself; the invisible, which he craved to depict, is made substantial.

Rembrandt at the Latin School.— For seven years before commencing his career as a painter, Rembrandt frequented the Latin School at Leyden, and these early studies are often reflected in his works. Many drawings and paintings show acquaintance with Ovid, and several are based on episodes of Roman history. Purely Greek themes are less frequent, but an example is the "Achilles and Briseis." (W. R. Valentiner, *Jb. Preuss. Kunsts.* XXVII. pp. 118-128.) ITALY

Florentine Drawings of the Trecento. — In *Jb. Preuss Kunsts.* XXVII, pp. 208-223, Osvald Siren attributes to Giovanni da Milano a drawing of the Crucifixion in the Kupferstichkabinett at Berlin; to Agnolo Gaddi a folio with drawings of heads in the Museo del Costello at Milan; to Spinello Aretino a folio in the Louvre and to Niccold di Pietro Gerini another folio in the same collection. A drawing in the Albertina, "A Saint, the Madonna and Child and a donor," is assigned to Pietro di Domenico da Montepulciano, a painter of the beginning of the fifteenth century, who signed a picture now in private possession at Naples, and who is identified with the artist whom the author previously designated *Il maestro del bambino vispo* (see *A.J.A.* 1905, p. 491).

Allegretto Nucci da Fabriano and Francescuccio di Cecco.— Anselmo Anselmi publishes in *V Arte,* 1906, pp. 381-383, from the archives of Fabriano in the Marches, documents which show that Allegretto Nucci da Fabriano died between September 26, 1373, and September 28, 1374, and was buried in or near the church of San Nicolo in Fabriano, although the chroniclers say that he died in 1385, while his place of burial is variously given. An article on the painting of Nucci and Francescuccio di Cecco is contributed to *V Arte,* 1906, pp. 241-254, by A. Colosanti.

Ambrogio de Predis and Leonardo. — In *Jb. Kunsth. Sarnm.* XXVI, pp. 1-48. W. Von Seidlitz discusses very carefully certain disputed paintings of the Lombard school, — the two portraits in the Ambrosiana, the "Pala Sforzesca" in the Brera, and the Litta Madonna, — and assigns them all to Ambrogio de Predis. Documents show that he was at Innsbruck in 1493, at Milan in 1494, that he was a designer of tapestries in 1498, and that at some time between 1484 and 1494 he collaborated with Leonardo in painting for the monks of San Francesco in Milan the "Madonna delle Rocce" and the two Angels in the National Gallery in London. These last and the male portrait in the Ambrosiana are assigned to the period between 1491 and 1494; the Sforza altar-piece to 1495; the female portrait to about 1502, the time of the portrait of the Emperor Maximilian at Vienna. Drawings attributed wrongly to Leonardo are fully discussed. The Louvre "Madonna delle Rocce" is the original, while the Loudon picture is a copy by Ambrogio. To the same painter are assigned the "Chastity" in the Galleria Czartorizky and the "Resurrection " at Berlin. (See also *A J. A.* VIII, pp. 332-333, 504-505; IX, p. 493.)

Antonio di Chellino. — In *U Arte,* 1906, pp. 442-445, C. De Fabriczy reconstitutes the life and works of Antonio di Chellino, a follower of Donatello. An uncolored terra-cotta relief of the Madonna and Child, recently acquired by the Museo Nazionale in Florence, is of Paduan origin, and shows the influence of Donatello. To the same artist belong four other terra-cotta reliefs, — a Madonna and Child belonging to Conte Camerini at Piazzola near Padua, the Madonna in the tabernacle on the Via Pietrapiana at Florence, the " Madonna del Perdono " in the transept of the cathedral of Siena, and a Madonna in the Palazzo Saracini in Siena. Among Donatello's assistants at Padua, Antonio di Chellino best answers the requirements of the maker of these works. Traces of his hand may be found in Donatello's altar in the Santo at Padua.

The Interpretation of Botticelli's "Spring." — The motive for the "Spring" is found in the description in the *Mythologicon* of Fulgentius, of the wedding of the Poet and Satyra. The Graces are present as in Fulgentius; Calliope in the centre points out to the bridegroom the bride, who advances, accompanied by Urania scattering flowers, and Philosophia, who is depicted as a divinity of the air. In default of a description in Fulgentius, the bridegroom, represented as Mercury, is drawn from Martianus Capella's " Marriage of Mercury and Philology," which also inspired another "Wedding " of Botticelli's, the frescoes from Villa Tornabuoni in the Louvre. In another nuptial painting, the " Birth of Venus," the painter drew from the *Pervigilium Veneris.* That the Codex Salmasianus, which contains the *Pervigilium,* was known in Florence in Botticelli's time, is proved by the use of a poem of Responsianus, which is contained only in this Codex, in Botticelli's " Mars and Venus" in London, and in the similar picture by Piero di Cosimo. (F. Wickhoff, *Jb. Preuss Kunsts.* XXVII, pp. 198-207.)

New Facts regarding VIttorio and Oiacomo Crivelli. — C. Grigioni in *Rass. bibl. dell' Arte ital.* 1906, pp. 109-119, contributes some new facts about Vittorio Crivelli. He finds references to six works executed or begun by Vittorio, of which one only remains, a triptych of 1481 in the church of Sta. Maria Novella at Montelparo. A document of 1502 appears to show that Giacomo Crivelli did not follow his father's profession, since in it he contracts for the completion of a polyptych of his father by a Venetian painter, living in Fermo, Antonio de Soleriis. The writer identifies this master with Antonio Solario, called *lo Zingaro.*

Lorenzo Leombruno. — A life of Lorenzo Leombruno of Mantua is given iu *Rass. d' Arte,* 1906, pp. 65-70, 91-96, by Carlo Gamba. He was born in 1489, and after 1537 nothing more is heard of him. He was lacking in originality, but technically clever and especially gifted with the decorative sense. A list of his works is also given.

Macrino d' Alba and the Umbrian School. — Starting with the "Madonna and Saints " in the Capitol at Rome, which is now attributed to Macrino d' Alba, Lisetta Ciaccio contributes to *Rans, d' Arte,* 1906, pp.

Figure 5. —Santa Barhara. (By Palma Vecchio.j The Magdalen. (By Bergamasco.) 145-153, a minute examination of the artist's characteristics, from which she concludes that his art is really dependent on the Umbrians, and particularly on Pinturicchio and Luca Signorelli. He probably visited Rome between 1481 and 1483, when the Umbrian artists were working in the Sistine chapel.

New Light on Palma Vecohio.—The uncertainty surrounding the life and works of Palma Vecchio is somewhat lifted by an article by G. Frizzoni in *Rans. d' Arte,* 1906, pp. 113-121. An interesting comparison is made between the famous Sta. Barbara in Sta. Maria Formosa and the statue of the Magdalen by Guglielmo Bergamasco, which stands in the central niche of the altar in the Magdalen chapel of SS. Giovanni e Paolo at Venice (Fig. 5). The sculptor very plainly drew from the painter. To the list of Palma's works are added a St. Jerome and an Adoration of the Child Jesus in the Pinacoteca Borronieo at Milan, a Risen Christ in the Crespi collection, a Resurrection of Lazarus in the possession of the author, and a Madonna and Child in the Visconti-Venosta Gallery. The restoration by Carnaghi of the altar-piece at Peghera, is praised. There is a curious resemblance between Palma's Holy Family in the Venice Gallery and Titian's in the Louvre.

Pietro de Saliba.--The life and works of Pietro de Saliba are carefully studied by E. Bruxelli in *V Arte,* 1900, pp. 357-371. He was the nephew of Antonello da Messina senior, brother of Antonello junior, for a long time confused with Pino da Messina, but now properly identified with the painter signing himself *Petrus Metsanetu.* His conception is vulgar, his drawing incorrect, and his style impersonal, showing servile imitations of the great Antonello and the influence of Cima da Conegliano. To his four signed works Brunelli adds a Madonna and Child of the Museo Civico in Padua, the Madonna of the Rospigliosi Gallery, there ascribed to Gian Bellini, and the St. Sebastian of the Hertz collection in Rome.

Vincenzo Foppa and a Print of Fra Giovanni Maria da Brescia. — W. Suida publishes in *Ross. d'Arte,* 1906, pp. 135-136, a print of 1502, by Fra Giovanni Maria da Brescia representing Trajan and the poor widow. He believes the print to be executed from a painting by Vincenzo Foppa, and suggests that the original was perhaps the fresco painted by Foppa about 1490 in the Loggia of the Old Palace at Brescia, the subject of which is unknown.

Giovanni Bartolo of Siena. — S. J. A. Churchill writes in *Burl. Mng.* X, 1906, pp. 120-125, of Giovanni Bartolo of Siena, goldsmith to the papal court of Rome and Avignon (1364-1385). His chief works were the busts of St. Peter and St. Paul in the Lateran, known only through descriptions, and a reliquary bust of St. Agatha preserved in the cathedral at Catania, made in Avignon for the Bishop Marziale, who took the reliquary with him to Catania in 1377.

Giovanni dal Ponte. — In *Burl. Mag.* 1906, pp. 332-337, H. P. Horxe has untangled the error which made Vasari place Giovanni dal Ponte in the middle of the fourteenth instead of the fifteenth century. He also publishes evidence from several Florentine census reports, which throw much light on the life of the painter, and on that of his partner, Smeraldodi Giovanni, and confirm Vasari's characterization of Giovanni as a spendthrift.

An Unknown Work of Sanaovino. — In the church of Sta. Margherita at Montici ndar Florence is a small marble ciborium with ornamental carvings and two adoring angels, which, by comparison with other works of Sansovino, is shown to be an early work of that master by C. vox Fabriczy in *Jb. Preuss. Kunsts.* XXVII, pp. 79-105. The writer adds a number of documents recently discovered, on the basis of which he forms a chronological table of the life and works of the artist.

The Palazzo Mansi at Lucca. — The Palazzo Mansi at Lucca is a fine example of late Renaissance architecture, but is of special interest for its valuable tapestries and paintings from the Low Countries. These are chiefly of the seventeenth century, though a triptych is perhaps by Lucas van Leyden. The gallery also contains a Holy Family attributed to Pierino del Vaga, and a charming Madonna by Francia. (J. De Foville, *Le Muse'e,* III, 1906, pp. 439-445; 3 pis.)

A Picture by Vincenzo Pagani. — The "Coronation of the Virgin " in the

Brera was recently proved to be by Vincenzo Pagani by Centanni and Ricci. Cari.o Grigioni in *Arte e Storia.* 1906, pp. 87-88, corrects the previous descriptions, proves that the picture was painted in 1518, and expresses the opinion that Vincenzo's father, Giovanni Pagani, collaborated with him in the picture..

A Painting by Monte di Giovanni. — P. Toesca recognizes in the anonymous Annunciation of the Galleria Estense at Modena a work of the miniaturist Monte di Giovanni, who with his brother Gherardo illuminated several existing manuscripts of the early sixteenth century. The hand of a miniaturist of northern Italy is also claimed for a small triptych representing the Nativity, flanked by the angel and Virgin of an Annunciation in the Museo Kircheriauo at Rome. (£' *Arte,* 1906, pp. 373-377.)

Two Tombs in the Cathedral of Reggio Emilia. — A curious instance of the use by pupils of designs of the master is communicated to *Rass. d' Arte,* 1906, pp. 156-158, by A. Balletti. In the Florence galleries is a pen-drawing for a tomb by Prospero Clementi, which was apparently his first conception of the monument which he afterwards made in much simpler form for the Canon Fossa, in the cathedral of Reggio. The original drawing, however, was faithfully copied in its essential points by his pupils, who carved the monument of Orazio Malaguzzi in the same cathedral.

A New Interpretation of Titian's "Amore Sacro e Profano." — A new reading of the riddle of the picture in the Borghese fiallery is presented by L. Ozzola in *V Arte,* 1906, pp. 298-302. He believes the principal figures represent Venus persuading Helen to fly with Paris, and relies for his proof mainly upon the reliefs pictured on the sarcophagus. The horse is the Trojan horse, and the group on the right end of the sarcophagus represents Menelaus slaying Deiphobus with the connivance of Helen. The figures on each side of and behind the horse make up a group depicting Venus saving Paris from Menelaus in battle.

ROME. — Pictures in the Museo Cristiano. — Osvald Siren contributes some critical notes on the paintings preserved in the *Museo Cristiano* of the Vatican library to *V Arte,* 1906, pp. 321-335. Most interesting are some new identifications, including a Birth of the Virgin, attributed, with reservations, to Andrea Buonaiuti (*ca.* 1370); the series of Scenes from the Life of St. Stephen, assigned to an unknown artist between Ambrogio Lorenzetti and Bernardo Daddi; three *predelle* with scenes from the life of Sant' Antonio Abate, by Giovanni dal Ponte, and the predella of the altar-piece, recently reconstructed by Herbert P. Horne, which Gentile da Fabriano made for the church of San Niccold alia Porta San Miniato in Florence. The predella contains scenes from the life of St Nicholas of Bari. The four saints of the wings are in the Uffizi, the central Madonna is in the collection of the King of England. Notes on the same museum are contributed to *Rass. a" Arte,* 1906, pp. 106-108 and 121-123, by F. Mason Perkins, who gives a number of new attributions, but agrees with Siren in assigning the St. Stephen series to a contemporary of Bernado Daddi, to whom he also assigns a Madonna and Saints in the Accademia delle Belle Arti at Siena, and the Deposition in Sala III of the Museo Cristiano.

The Date of Guido da Siena. — R. Davidsohn in *Rep. f. K.* 1906, pp. 262-267, follows the opinion of Milanesi and Wickhoff that the date on the Madonna and Child signed by Guido, in the Palazzo Pubblico in Siena is MCCLXXXI and not MCCXXX. There is no other evidence for, an early Guido, while at the end of the thirteenth century, an artist Guido is frequently mentioned in the Sienese archives. Davidsohn is inclined to rate Guido higher than this one picture would place him, because the commission for a Madonna with St. Peter and St. Paul, in the Palazzo Pubblico, important for its connection with contemporary politics, was given to him instead of to Duccio.

The Chapel of S. Biagio in SS. Nazaro e Celso. — The history of the chapel of S. Biagio in the church of SS. Nazaro e Celso in Verona is worked out with the aid of new documentary evidence by G. Biadego in jV. *Arch. Ven.* 1906, pp. 91-134. Among the new facts about the sculpture and paintings in the chapel, the most noteworthy are the additions to the biography of Francesco Morone.

FRANCE

Simone Martini and Cardinal Stefaneschi. — In a study of Simone Martini's work at Avignon in *L' Arte,* 1906, pp. 330-344, G. De Nicola publishes from the Vatican library a group of drawings which were doubtless those sent by Suarez to Cardinal Barberini from Avignon between 1633 and 1666. One of them, representing St. George killing the dragon, is probably a copy of Simone's fresco on the facade of Avignon cathedral. The verses which were inscribed above the maiden's head in the fresco are attributed to Petrarch, by Valladier, but appear in the *Life of St. George,* by Cardinal Jacopo Stefaneschi, as his own. It was therefore he who ordered the fresco from Siinone Martini at Avignon, and it was a pupil of Simone's who illustrated the cardinal's *Life of St. George.* Stefaneschi is probably the cardinal, mentioned by Tizio the Sienese historian, who took Simone from his work at Camollia to France, in 1335. Good tradition and the evidence of Suarez's drawing show that Petrarch's Laura was the model for the virgin in the Avignon fresco.

The Betrothal of St. Catherine at Lyons. — E. Bertaux recently published a marble relief in the Aynard collection at Lyons, which he interpreted as a "Betrothal of St. Catherine," and assigned to Agostino di Duccio. This position is disputed by E. Buunelli in *V Arte,* 1906, pp. 379381. There is no parallel to this conception of the betrothal, the technique is too weak for Agostino, and the sphinx with a coat-of-arms hung about its neck, seated beside the saint, is not consonant with the taste of the fifteenth century. The work is by an imitator, and is probably a modern forgery, *Ibid,* pp. 454-455, Brunelli suggests that the relief is imitated from a representation of Christ taking leave of his mother.

Attributions in the Louvre. —In *V*

Arte, 1906, pp. 401-422, G. FrizZoni criticises some of the attributions given to Italian pictures in the Louvre. Among others he discusses a Madonna and Child with Saints and Angels labelled "attributed to Cosimo Rosselli or the school of A. Verrocchio," but now generally recognized as a work of Botticini; a Madonna and Child, which is taken from Ghirlandaio and restored to Piero di Cosimo; an unattributed tondo representing the Marriage of Peleus and Thetis, which he gives to Girolamo di Benvenuto; the portrait of a Young Man in the Salon Carre, also unattributed, but assigned to Franciabigio; the "Vierge aux balances" and the "Bacchus," both given to Cesare da Sesto; the ancient copy of Leonardo's "Cenacolo," given to the Lombard, Marco d' Oggiono; a Madonna and Child signed *Johannes Bellinus,* but relegated to his school; the Apollo and Marsyas, catalogued " Raphael," which is restored to Perugino; and two pictures placed among the French *primiti/s* which are ascribed to Defendente dei Ferrari.

Signatures on the "Entombment" at Solesmes. — After a reexamination of the casts of the "Entombment," the sculptural group of the end of the fifteenth century on the church of the abbey of Solesmes, F. De Mely found on the Virgin's veil, what he considers to be the signatures of the artists in the letters VASORDY ET FABERTI. The names suggest an Italian origin, and the writer claims Italian influence in the figures of an angel and of Joseph of Arimathea. *(Gaz. B.-A.* XXXVI, 1906, pp. 315322.) GERMANY

Painting on the Upper Rhine. — D. Burckhardt in *Jb. Preuss. Kuntto.* XXVII, pp. 179-197, demonstrates on the basis of a painting from the church of St. Dominic at Basel that about 1385 the upper valley of the Rhine was under Italian influences which came by way of France. A drawing in the Museum at Basel proves even closer relations with France, and it is noted that the father of Eonrad Witz (1398?-l447) was court painter of the Dukes of Burgundy. Two of his pictures in private possession at Basel show relations with the school of the van Eycks.

A Gerard David in Berlin. — The Eaiser Friedrich Museum in Berlin has recently acquired a Madonna nursing the Child, with a landscape background, by Gerard David. The motive, often repeated in the fifteenth century, is derived from Roger van der Weyden's " St. Luke." David here imitates somewhat Hugo van der Goes, from whom he seems to have copied in his Adoration of the Magi in Munich. Comparison with the Louvre Madonna dates this picture about 1495. (M. I. Friedlander, *Jb. Preuss. Kunsts.* XXVII, pp. 143-148.)

Italian Trecento Painting in Minor German Galleries. — Osvald Siren in *Rass. il' Arte,* 1906, pp. 81-87, contributes notes on Italian paintings of the fourteenth century in the Museums of Strassburg, Hanover, Brunswick, and Frankfort. To Taddeo Gaddi he attributes a small altarpiece in the Museum of Strassburg, and to Bernardo Daddi, with some hesitation, a St. Catherine and St. Agatha in the same museum. Giovanni dal Ponte is given a Madonna in the Stadel Institute, and a wing of a triptych in the Hanover Museum, while a series of Episodes in the Life of St. Francis in the same collection is assigned to Taddeo di Bartolo. Works by Lorenzo di Niccol6 Gerini, Bicci di Lorenzo, and Lorenzo Monaco are identified In the Museum at Brunswick.

GREAT BRITAIN AND IRELAND

The New Raphael in the National Gallery. — A note in *Burl. Mag.* X, 1906, pp. 29-150, gives the history of the " Madonna of the Tower" recently presented to the nation by Miss Mackintosh. A product of Raphael's early Roman period, it was a prolific subject of copies, by Domenico Alfani, one of Raphael's own pupils, by Sassoferrato, by Ceresa, and others. Its authentic history begins with its appearance in the Orleans gallery, from which it was purchased by Mr. Willett for £150, then by the poet Rogers, at whose death in 1856 it was bought by Mr. Mackintosh for 480 guineas.

Early German Art at the Burlington Fine Arts Club. — In *Burl. Mag.* IX, 1906, p. 254, Lionel Ctst describes a panel lent to the recent exhibition of the Burlington Art Club by the King. It represents a Madonna and Child of Byzantine aspect in a frame decorated with eight compositions from the lives of Christ and the Virgin, the latter being superior in execution to the main picture. It is interesting as an example of the rarely found early Bohemian School. Aymeb Valla.vce *(ibid.* pp. 254-264) discusses German art before Diirer as illustrated by works in the exhibition. He finds, among other qualities, a, fantastic variableness in architectural ornament, and redundance and rigidity, particularly in draperies. Five paintings by Diirer and his successors are discussed by Charles Ricketts *(ibid.* pp. 264-208), the most interesting being a "Christ taking leave of his Mother," by Altdorfer, which well illustrates his characteristic fantastic landscape.

The Majolica Roundels at South Kensington. — W. R. Lethaby in *Burl. Mag.* IX, 1906, pp. 404-407, reopens the question whether Luca della Robbia was the author of the painted majolica tondos, representing the months of the year, in the Victoria and Albert Museum. He finds that the curvature of the panels shows that they were made for the vaulted ceiling of a small room, such as that which Luca decorated in Cosimo dei Medici's palace, according to Filarete and Vasari. The borders and figures can be paralleled in other works of the sculptor, and the difficulties as to style are met by assigning the roundels to Luca's early period.

The Subject of the Newgass Rembrandt. — In an article on the Rembrandt tercentenary and exhibition at Leyden in *Gaz. B.-A.* XXXVI, 1906, pp. 265-280 (pi.), F. Sciimidt-degeneu describes as of special importance the recently discovered painting owned by Mr. Newgass of London. It represents a mounted Roman consul at the head of his troops, accosted by an old man who has just dismounted from his horse. It has been called the "Triumph of Scipio." In *Chron. Arts,* 1906, p. 290, the same writer cites Valerius Maximus (II, 2, 4) to show that the painting represents Fabius Maximus doing homage to

Rubens or Frans Pourbus the Younger? — H. Hymaxb in *Chron. A rtt,* 1906, pp. 198-199, defends his opinion that the so-called "Marie de Medicis" belonging to Mrs. Alfred Morrison is by Rubens. He points out that the sitter wears French not Flemish costume, and that the similarity to the likeness of Charlotte de Montmorency, princess of Conde which is preserved in the Musee Coude at Chantilly, proves that the latter was the subject of the London portrait. The princess was carried off to Brussels by her husband in 1609, and it was in that year that Rubens became the court painter at the Flemish capital. The internal evidence confirms this attribution.

A New Venetian Painter. — The signature *Alesander Oliceriu s V* on the-'Portrait of a Gentleman" recently acquired by the National Gallery of Ireland was supposed to be the name of the sitter until Ludwig proved the existence of Alessandro Oliviero, pupil of Alvise, living in Venice before 1539. Another picture is now claimed for him on internal evidence — a "Madonna with Angels" in the Dublin Gallery — by Sir Walter ArmStrong in *Burl. Mag.* X, 1906, p. 126.

AMERICAN ARCHAEOLOGY

The Origin of American Civilizations. — A review of the theories as to the origin of American races and their civilizations is published in *Mitt. Anth. Ges.* XXXVI, 1906, pp. 87-98, by R. Andre'e. He regards it as certain that man in America was autochthonous, and that American civilization is an independent development, unaffected by early Asiatic or European influences.

The Remains of Prehistoric Man in the Dakotas. — In *Am. Anth:* VIII, 1906, pp. 640-651 (5 pis.), Henry Montgomery describes the remains of prehistoric man in the Dakotas. He distinguishes Burial Mounds, Ceremonial or Feast Mounds aud Beacon Mounds. Burials were made in a crouching posture, but in some places the skeletons are defective and the bones scattered. The illustrations show good pottery of a somewhat primitive type, points for spears in stone and bone, carved animal figures on catlinite, pipes of stone, antler or clay ornaments, etc. The author concludes that, "both in their pottery and in their mode of burial, the prehistoric Mound Builders of the Dakotas differed very widely from the prehistoric people of Utah and the Southwest. That they were akin in culture to the Mound Builders of the Mississippi Valley there can be no doubt; yet they differed from them in some respects."

Mound Builders of the Mississippi Valley. — The Mound Builders of the Mississippi Valley are discussed in *Rec. Past,* V, 1906, pp. 236-239, 365-367 (7 figs.), by R. Herrmann. He argues that burial in mounds was practised by the Muskwakies of the Foxes as late as the arrival of the first white settlers in the neighborhood of Dubuque. The chiefs seem to have been buried in their tepees, which were usually placed on high ground, and hence chiefs' burial mounds are found on prominent cliffs and other points commanding a wide view. A Pueblo Indian pot with a representation of a village of tepees inclosed by a stockade is also described.

The Department of Archaeology at Phillips Academy. Andover. — *Bulletin III,* 1906, issued by the Department of Archaeology, Phillips Academy, Andover, Massachusetts, contains 'A Narrative of Explorations in New Mexico, Arizona, Indiana, etc., together with a Brief History of the Department,' by Warren K. Moohehead. The paper narrates the explorations by which the collections at Andover have been formed. Some of these were earlier than the establishment of the Museum in 1901, while others, were undertaken later. The investigations at Hopkinsville, Illinois, here receive their first official publication. Of special interest is the discussion of the pictographs on birch-bark from Fairfield, Iowa. The author regards them as authentic, but leaves the decipherment of the characters to the future.

The Shell Heaps of Florida. — The coasts, lakes, and rivers of Florida are bordered by numerous large heaps of shells, mingled with bones of fish and animals, pottery, flint and bone implements, and occasionally glass, or even metal. Sometimes the mounds conceal remains of buildings, as the small stone fort at New Smyrna. Their age probably varies greatly, though the high antiquity of some deposits is shown by the large trees now growing on the mounds. (C. De W. Brower, *Bee. Past,* V, 1906, pp. 331338; 6 figs.)

An Engraved Bone from Ohio. — In *Transactions of the Department of Archaeology* (University of Pennsylvania), II, 1906, pp. 103-105 (3 pis.), G. B. Gordon republishes from an old engraving four views of a fragment of engraved bone found near Cincinnati in 1801. The principal feature of the design is the highly conventionalized head of an animal, apparently a puma.

The Mandana.— In *Peabody Museum Papers,* III, 1906, pp. 148-187, G. F. Will and N. J. Spinden discuss the archaeology of the Mandan tribe, collecting most of their material from the Burgois site, 14 miles northwest of Bismarck, North Dakota. An excellent plan is followed by a description of the mounds, "cache pits," and house sites. Articles in stone include hammers, celts, discoidal mullers, elliptical blades, knives, arrowheads, spearheads, scrapers, chippers, and decorated stones. The stone counters (?) are interesting. Shell objects are not numerous, either as ornaments or implements, and copper only occurs twice. Bone hoes, grainers, straighteners, scrapers, digging implements, awls, needles, fishhooks, gorgets, beads, buckles, and bracelets were found. The pottery is an excellent ware, thin, well made, and with a characteristic development of form and ornament Two skeletons were found, one in a flexed position, the other as a " bundle" burial. The former was buried in a manner apparently foreign to Mandan custom, the latter more or less in consonance with it.

The Ancient Mexican Calendar. —In *Z. Eihn.* XXXVIII, 1906, pp. 485-512 (4 figs.; 2 tables), E. De Joughe presents his view of the present state of the discussion of the complicated calendar of ancient Mexico. He treats of the two periods, of 260 and 365 days respectively, by which time was reckoned, of the eighteen monthly festivals, and of the relation of the Mexican to the solar and the European year.

Xochicalco. — In *Transactions of the Department of Archaeology* (University of Pennsylvania), II, 1906, pp. 51-68 (5 pis.; 14 figs.), Adela Breton discusses the sculptures on the building at Xochicalco, Mexico. Her notes correct in details the plates published by Penafiel, *Monumentos del Arte Mexicano Antiguo,* and describe especially the sculptures on the lowest stage. Stress is laid on the differences in detail in repetitions of the same general theme, and on the need of further study and excavation at this important site.

A Zapotecan Manuscript from Santiago Guevea, Mexico. — In *Z. Ethn.* XXXVIII, 1906, pp. 121-155 (29 figs.), E. Seler describes in detail a sheet containing a hieroglyphic record.of 1540 from Santiago Guevea. The upper part contains a representation of the village with nineteen surrounding points, which are said to mark boundaries but seem also connected with heathen observances. The lower portion shows the warriors of the village bringing tribute to the kings of the land. These kings seem to be the great king, Cocijoeza, and his sons and successors, especially Cocijopij, king of Tehuantepec. Such records were prepared by the Indians after the Spanish conquest, especially under Mendoza, 1535-1549, to fix the boundaries of the communities, and are still jealously guarded in many Indian villages.

The Mayas and the Lacandones. — In his Report as Fellow in American Archaeology of the Archaeological Institute of America for 1902-05, Dr. A. M. Tozzer has given a comparative study of the Mayas of Yucatan, who have been subject to Spanish influences since the Conquest, and the Lacandones of Chiapas, Mexico, who are practically unchanged and untrammelled by Spanish contact. He discusses the history, personal and social characteristics, industrial and artistic activity, and religion of both peoples. The religion of the Lacandones occupies a large space, and a full description is given of the complicated ceremonial connected with the incense burners, or *braseros,* for here much seems little changed from the preSpanish times. Among the Mayas also there are many survivals of ancient rites. Fifty-one Lacandone chants are given with translations, and a full bibliography. *(Archaeological Institute of America, Report of the Fellow in American Archaeology. A Comparative Study of the Mayas and the Lacandones,* by Alfred M. Tozzer. New York, 1906, The Macmillan Co., xx, 195 pp.; 29 pis. ; 49 figs. 8vo. $ 1.25.) BIBLIOGRAPHY OF ARCHAEOLOGICAL BOOKS 1906

James M. Paton, *Editor-in-charge Books, pamphlets, and other matter/or the Bibliography should be addressed to* James M. Paton, *65, Sparks Street, Cambridge, Mass.* GENERAL AND MISCELLANEOUS

Fr. Adler. Zur Ktmstgeschichte. Vortriige, Abhandlungen und Festreden. Berlin, 1906, E. S. Mittler & Sohn. vi, 217 pp. 8vo. M.4. Allge meines Kinstler-Lexikon. 3d cd. revised and enlarged by H. W. Singer. Frankfurt am Main, 1906,

Liter. Anstalt. 295,5 pp. 8vo.

O. Almgren, " Kung Bjorns Hog" och andra Fornlamningar vid Hàga. Mit einem deutschen Auszugc. (Arkeologiska Monografler utgifna af Kungl. Vitterhets Historié och Antikvitets Akademien Nr. 1). Stockholm, 1905, K. H. Beckmans Boktrykkeri. 59 pp.; 3 pis.; 33 flgs. 4to. H. d'Arbois de Jubainville,

Les druides et les dieux celtiques à forme d'animaux. Paris, 1905, Champion. 8vo. Archaeological Institute of America. Report of the Fellow in American Archaeology, 1902-1905. A Comparative Study of the Mayas and the Laeandones. By Alfred M. Tozzer, Ph. D. New York, 1906. The Macmillan Co. xxii. 196 pp.; 29 pis.; 49 tigs. 8vo. $1. 25. L'Architecte, Revue mensuelle de l'art architectural, publiée sons les auspices de la Société des architectes diplomés par le gouvernement. January, 1906. Paris, 252

Libr. Cent, des Beaux-Arts. 8 pp.; 6 pis. Folio. Architektur des

Auslandes. I Série, Belgien und Holland. Vienna, 1906, F. Wolf rum & Co. 60 pl. in portfolio. M. 50.

Art. An illustrated quarterly of ancient and modern art. New series. Vol. I, no. 1. London, 1906,

H. Grevel. 76 pp.; ill. 4to.

L'Artiste, Revue bi-mcnsuelle d'art ancien et moderne. March, 1906.

Paris, 80 Rue Taitbout. 111. 4to.

Ateneo. Revista mensual. January, 1906. Madrid, 21 Prado, 129 pp.

8vo. Atlas archéologique de la Tunisie. Fasc. 10 (Aïne-Djeloula, Moknine, Kairouan, Kerkez). Paris, 1906, Leroux. 4 maps. Ausgra bungen in Numantia. see A. Schul ten. Augusta Perusia, Rivista di Topograila, Arte e Costumi dell' Umbria, diretta da Ciro Trabalza. January. 1906. Perugia, Unione tipog. cooper. 16 pp.: ûgs. 4to. . Baedeker, Unteritalien, SizUien, Sardlnlen, Malta, Tuuis, Corfu. Handbuch fiir Reisende. 14te Ausg. Leipsic, 1906, K. Baedeker, liv, 492 pp.; 30 maps; 28 plans. 8vo. M. 6. E. R. Ball, Rome. A practical guide to Rome and its environs. London, 1906, Black, viii, 256 pp.; 3 maps; 8 flgs. 8vo. 2s. fid.

Barre et Bertrand, Relations des fouilles faites a Chantenay (Nifcvre) en 1903. Moulins, 1906. 23 pp. 8vo.

E. Bassermann-Jordan, Die Kunstsammlung des Kgl. Professors Dr. Wilhelm v. Miller in Milnchen. Munich, 1906, F. Bruckmann. vll, 78 pp.: 39 pis. 4to. M. 30.

M. Berthelot, Archeologie et histoire des Sciences. Paris, 1906, Gauthier-Villars. 337 pp.; 8 flgs.

4to. R. Blomfield, Studies in Architecture. London, 1906, Maemillan & Co. 220 pp.; 36 pis.; 14 figs. 8vo. J. H. Bloom, Seals.

London, 1906, Methuen. xvi, 274 pp. ; 3 pis.; 274 flgs. 8vo. K. Boetticher, Zur Kenntnis antiker Gottesverehrnng. Aufsiitze. Eine Gabe zur 100 Wiederkehr seines Geburtstages. (Deutsche Biicherei, Vol. 62.) Berlin, 1906, Expedition der deutschen Bticherei. 86 pp. 8vo.

A. Bohnemann, Grundriss der Kunstgeschichte. 2te Ausg. Leipzig, 1906, Hirt & Sohn. viii, 320 pp.; plate; 197 flgs. 8vo. M. 4. E. L. Borrel, Les

Ceutrons pendant les temps pré-historiques et l'epoque gallo-romaine. Mofltiers, 1905. 8vo. G. B. Brown, The Care of Ancient Monuments. An account of the legislative and other measures adopted in European countries for protecting ancient monuments. Cambridge, 1906, University Press, xii, 260 pp. 8vo. Heinr.

Brunn, Kleine Schriften. Gesammelt von Herm. Brunn und H. Bulle. Bd. 3: Interpretation. Zur Kritik der Schriftquellen. Allgcmeines. Zur neueren Kunstgeschichte. Nachtrag. Verzeichnis samtlicher Schriften. Leipzig and Berlin, 1906, B. G. Teubner. viii, 356 pp.; portrait; 53 tigs. 8vo. M. 14.

Bulletin de la SociGte d'histoire et d'archeologie du 7 arrondissement de Paris. March, 1906. 116 Rue de Crenelle. 32 pp.; ill. 8vo. J. Burgess, The Mohammedan Architecture of Ahmndabad. Part II. (Archaeological Survey of Western India.) London, Quaritch. 109 pp.; 8 pis. Folio. 31. x. 6d. Catalogo della Collezione di oggetti di scavo del fu Prof. Prospero Sarti. Sculture in marmo e bronzo, terrecotte, oreflcerie, etc. Roma, 1906, Tipogratla dell' unione cooperativa editrice. 96 pp.; 31 pis. 4to.

Catalogue des antiquites composant la Collection Hakky-Bey. Paris, 1906. 52 pp.; 12 pis. 4to.

Catalogue of Photographs of Paintings, Sculptures, Bronzes, Terracottas, Ceramics, Textiles, Wood Carvings, Gems, Jewellery, Coins, Casts, and Miscellaneous Objects ln the Museum of Fine Arts, Boston, Mass., U.S.A. Boston, 1906, B. Coolidge. 20 pp. 8vo. Catalogue of a series of Photographs from the collections of the British Museum. Part V: Greek, Etruscan, and Roman Series. Section I. Sculpture, Vases, etc. London, 1906, Mansell & Co. 38 pp.; 17 pis. 8vo. Ph. Champault, Pheniciens et Grecs en Italie d'apres l'Odyssée. Etude géographique, historique et sociale par une methode nouvelle. Paris, 1906, E. Leroux. 602 pp. 8vo. L. Claremont, The GemCutter's Craft. New York, 1906, Macmillan. xv, 296 pp.; ill. 4to. $5.00.

Collection de Clercq, Tome IV: Les marbres, les vases peints et les ivoires par A. de Ridden Paris, 1906, E. Leroux. 232 pp.; 41 pis. 4 to. Comptes rendus du congres international d'archeologie. Session 1. Athenes, 1906, Beck & Barth. 400 pp. 8vo.

M. 7. Congres archeologique de France, LXXP session tenue au Puy en 1904. Paris, 1906. hi, 599 pp.; 146 pis. and flgs. 8vo. Contains: J. Dcchelette, Sur les bas-reliefs gallo-romains du Musee de la cathC drale du Puy. Corolla numis matica, Numismatic Essays in Honor of Barclay V. Head. Oxford and London, 1906, H. Frowde. 386 pp.; 18 pis. 8vo G. Cousin, Etudes de geographie ancienne. Nancy, 1906, Berger-Levrault & Cie. xviii, 572 pp. 8vo. R. A. Cram, Impressions of Japanese Architecture and the Allied Arts. London, 1906, Lane. 240 pp. 8vo. F. Cramer, Uber dieUrzeit Eschweilers und seiner Umgebung. Festschrift zur Anerkennung des Gymnasiums zu Eschweiler. Eschweiler, 1905. L. F. Day, Alte und neue Alphabete fiir den praktischen Gebrauch, nebst einer Eloleitnng iiber die Kunst im Alphabet. Leipzig, 1906, Hiersemann. 74 pp.; 175 pis. 8vo. M. 5. M. Dessoir, Aesthetik und allgcmeinc Kunstwissenschaft. Stuttgart, 1906, Euke. xii, 476 pp; 19 pis.; 16 tigs. 8vo. M. 14.

Documenti per servire alia storia di Sicilia. Series 4, Vol. X. Palermo, 1906, Reber.

P. Eudel, Dictionnaire des bijoux de l'Afrique du Nord, Maroc, Algerie, Tunesle, Tripolitaine. (Bibliotheque d'archeologie africaine, Vol. 8.) Paris, 1906, E. Leroux. 242 pp.; ill. 8vo.

Festschrift zur Feier des 50jahrigen Bestehens des Romisch-Germauischen Zentralmuscums zu Mainz. Mainz, 1902, Ph. v. Zabern. vi. 109. pp.; 7 pis. ; 23 flgs. 4to. Contents: 1. I... Lindenschmit, Beitrage zur Geschichte des R6misch-Germanischen Zentralmuseums zu Mainz. 2. L. Beck, Der Eintiuss der romischen Herrschaft auf die deutsche Eisenindustrie. 3. K. Schumacher, Zur Besiedelungsgcschichte des rechtsseitigen Rheintals zwischen Basel und Mainz. 4. V. Reeb, Elne flgiirliche Darstcllung der illyrischthrakischen Gotten! reiheit Silvanus. Diana, Apollo? 5. P. Reinecke, Zur Kenntnis der La Tene-Deukmiiler der Zone nord warts der Alpen.

L. Forrer, Biographical Dictionary of medallists, coin-, gem-, and sealengravers, mint-masters, etc., ancient and modern, with references to their works. B.C. 500-a.d. 1900. Vol. I. London, 1906, Spink, xlviii, 691 pp.; ill. 8vo. R. Forrer,

Les antiqultes, les tableaux et les objets d'art de la collection Alfred Ritleng a Strasbourg. Strasburg, 1906, Revue Alsacienne. 76 pp.; 41 pis. 4to. — Von alter und iiltester Bauernkuust. Esslingen, 1906, P. Neff. Plate; 32 tigs. 8vo. M. 1.

J. G. Frazer, Adonis, Attis, Osiris. Studies in the history of oriental religion. London, 1906, Macmillan & Co. xvi, 339 pp. 8vo. 10s. E. Friedlein, Tempera und Tempera-Teehnik (Sammlung maltechnischer Schriften). Munich. 1906, Callwey. 107 pp. 8vo.

Geographic g£nerale du departement de l'Htrault. Publióe par la Sociéte' Languedocicnne de. geographie. Tome 5, fasc. 2: Antlquites et monuments du département. Montpellier, 1906. 199-754 pp.; 12 pis.; 72 tigs. R. Glazier, A Manual of Historic Ornament. 2d rev. ed. New York, 1906, Scribncrs. 168 pp.; ill. 8vo. $3.00. W.

Goble and A. van Millingen, Constantinople. New York, 1906, Macmillan. ix, 282 pp.; 63 colored plates. 8vo. 86.00. P.Graindor.

Histoire de l'lle de Skyros jusqn'en 1538. (Bibliotheqne de la Faculte de philosophie et lettres de l'Universite de Liege. Fasc. 17.) Liege. 1906, 11. Vallant-Carmanne. 89 pp.

8vo. R. Graul, Ostasiatische Kunst und ihr Eintiuss auf Europa. Leipzig, 1906, Teubner. vi, 88 pp.; plate; 49 figs. 8vo. H. Gre goire. Saints jumeanx et dieux cavaliers. l'aris. 1905, Picard &

Fils. iii, 76 pp. 8vo. Grie chenland und Kleinasien. (Meyers Reisebucher) fite Autl. Vienna and Leipzig, 1906, Bibliographisches Institut. x, 336 pp.; 23 maps; 23 plans; 3 tigs. 8vo. G. B.

Grundy, Mare Aegaeum. 3 maps and 9 plans of cities on one sheet. (Murray's Handy Classical Maps.) London, 1905,. 1. Murray. 8 pp.; 1 sheet. 49 x 63 cm. 4to. Th.

Gsell-Fels. Rom und die Campagna. (Meyers ReisebUcher) 6te Autl. Vienna and Leipzig, 1906, Bibliographisches Institut. xvi pp.; 1146 cols.; 6 maps; 53-plans; 61 tigs. 8vo. M. 12.50.

A. Hackmann, Die iiltere Eisenzeit in Finnland. I. Die Fnnde aus den fOnf ersten Jahrhunderten. Helsingfors, 1906. Finn. Altertumsgesellschaft. iii, 377 pp. ; map; 22 pis.; figs. 8vo. M. 16. Handbook of the Museum of Fine Arts in Boston. Boston, 1906. 204 pp.; ill. 16mo. C. Gasquoine Hartley, Moorish Cities in Spain (I.angham series). London, 1906, Stegle, Hill, & Co. viii, 100 pp.; 8 pis.; figs.; 16mo. J. Heierli, Die archiiologische Karte des Kantons Solothurn nebst Erliluterungen und Fundregister. Solothurn, 1906, Th. Petri. 92 pp.; 9 pis. : map. 8vo. — Vindonissa. 1. Qnellen und Literatur. Im Auftrage der VindonissaKommission z u s a in m e u gestellt. Aarau, 1906, H. R. Sauerlander & Co. 112 pp.: 9 pis.; map. 8vo.

M. 3.80. K. Henrici. Abhand lungen aus der Gebiete der Architektur. Munich, 1906, Callwey, 278 pp.; ill. 8vo. A. Houl£, Notice-etude sur une stature découverte dans une sépulture du cimetiere franc de Bury (Oise).

Beauvais, 1905. 8vo. A. M.

Hyamson, A Dictionary of artists and art terms. London, 1906, Routledge. 178 pp.; 48mo.

P. Hamilton Jackson, The Shores of the Adriatic. London, 1906, Murray. 111.; 8vo. T. G. Jackson, Season in Architecture. Lectures before the Royal Academy. London, 1906.

Murray. 111.; 8vo. E. Jacobs, see Zangemeister. C. Jacobsen,

Ny Carlsberg. Glyptoteks Tilblivelse. Copenhagen, 1906, Ny Carlsberg. 76 pp. 4to. P. Jobard,

Les Enceintes defensives antiques dans la Cote d'Or. Essai de Nomenclature. Paris, 1906, Picard. 8vo.

H. Joly. Meisterwerke der Bau kunst u. des Kunstgewerbes aller Lander u. Zeiten. Alphabetisch nach Orten herausg. Spanien. Vol. I. Alcola de Henares, Archena, Argentina. Avila, Barcelona, Burgos. Leipzig, 1906, H. F. Koehler. x pp. text; 113 pp. flgs. 8vo. M. 5.

O. Kaemmel, Rom und die Campagna. 2d ed. (Land und I.eute, Vol. 12). Bielefeld and Leipzig, 1906, Velhagen & Klasing. 194 pp.; plate; 156 flgs. 8vo.— E. Kalinka, Antike Denkmaler In Btilgarien, unter Mitwirkung von Fachgenossen bearbeitet. Vienna. 1906, Holder.

Map; 162 flgs. 4to. M. 20. O. Kern, Goethe, Biicklin, Mommsen. 4 Vortriige iiber die Antike. Berlin, 1906, Weidmann. 101 pp. 8vo. M.

I. 80. H. Kiepert, Formae orbis antiqui. 36 Karten im Format von 52: 64 cm. mit kritischem Text und Quellenangabe zu jeder Karte, hrsg. v. R. Kiepert. Nr. 13: Peloponnesus cum Attica. 6 pp. text. Nr. 14: Phocis. Boeotia. Attica. Athenae. 8 pp. text. Berlin. 1906, 1). Reimer. M. 6.

R. Kiepert, Karte von Kleinasien in 24 Blatt. 1: 400.000. Blatt B. I: Alvalyk. 48.5x63 cm. Berlin, 1906, I). Reimer. M. 6. H.

Knackfuss and M. G. Zimmermann, Allgemeine Kanstgeschichte, Vol. II. Kunstgcschichte der (Jotik und Renaissance. Bielefeld, 1906, Velhagen and Klasing. viii, 688 pp.; 5521 flgs. 8vo. M. 12. T.Koch,

Anfange der Kunst im LTrwald. Indianer-Handzeichnungeu. auf seinen Reiseu in Brasilieu gesam melt. Berlin, 1906. viii, xv, 70 pp.; 63pis.; 2maps; tigs. 8vo. M. 15.

R. de Lasteyrie and A. Vidier, Bibliographic generale des travaux historiques et archeologiques publies par les societes savantes de la France. T. V, fasc. 1. Paris, 1906,

Leroux. 200 pp. 4to. WLiibke,

Die Kunst des Altertums. 13. And., vollstandig neu bearbeitet von M. Semrau. (Ltibke, Grundriss der Kunstgeschichte I.) Stuttgart, 1904, P. Neff. viii, 381 pp.; 5 pis.; 411 flgs. 8vo.

G. Macdonald. Coin types. Their origin and development. Being the Rhind lectures for 1904. Glasgow, 1905, Maclehose and Sons, x, 275 pp.; many ill. 8vo.-R. S. Maffei,

Volterra. Melfl, 1906, G. Gricco. — L. Magne, Lecons sur l'histoire de l'art. I. L'art dans l'antiquite. Paris, 1906, Levy. 241 pp.; 175 flgs.

8vo. E. Manceri, Siracusa (Monografle Siciliane.) Palermo, 1906, Pedone Lauriel. 38 pp.; flgs. 16mo. C. Marcais, L'Art em

Algerie. Paris, 1906, Libr. afric. et coloniale. 166 pp.; flgs. 8vo.

W. Marcais. sec Musees et collections. Mare Aegeum, see

Grundy. Masterpieces selected from the Korin school, with biog. sketches of the artists and descriptions by Shichi Tajima. Vol. IV. Tokio. 1906, Shimbi Shoim. 3 pp.; pis. 93-122. Folio. Ch. Matthis,

Die Wascnbhrg. Eine elsassische Ritterburg im 14. Jahrhundert und e'tn romischer Merkurtempel. Strassburg, 1906, J. H. E. Heitz. 32 pp.; 2 pis.; 2 plans. 8vo. M. 1.

J. R. Melida, Les esculturas del Cerro de los Santos. Cuestion de autenticidad. Madrid, 1906. 112 pp.; 10 pis. 8vo.— Mexican and Central American Antiquities. Calendar systems and History. 94 papers by Ed. Seler, E. Forstemann, P. Schellhas, C. Sapper, and E. P. Dieseldorff. Trans, from the German under the supervision of C. P. Bowditch. Washington, 1906, Gov't Printing Office. 682 pp.; ill. 8vo.

A. G. Meyer. Gcsammcltc

Reden und Aufsiitze. Berlin, 1906, Meyer, v, 212 pp.; ill. 8vo.

A. Michaelis. Die archaologischen Entdeckungen des neunzehnten Jahrhunderts. Leipzig, 1906, E. A. Scemann. viii, 325 pp. 8vo.

G. Migeon, Le Caire, le Nil et I Memphis. (Villes d'art celebres.) Paris, 1906, Laurens. 100 pp.; 133 tigs. 4to. O. Miller, Von Stoff zu Form. Essays. Frauenfeld, 1906, Huber & Co. 168 pp. 8vo.

M. 3.20. Th. Mommsen, Gesammelte. Schriften. Bd. 4: Historische Schriften Bd. 1. Berlin, 1906, vveidmannsche Bnchh. vii, 566 pp.

8vo. M. 12. J. de Morgan, Les recherches arch6ologiques, leur but, leurs procedfis. l'aris, 1905, Librairie de la "Revue des idees," 84 pp. 8vo. W. A. Miller,

Nacktheit und Entbliissung in der altorientalischen und iilteren griechischen Kunst. Leipzig, 1906. 6 pis. 8vo. M. 4. A Miiveszetek tortenete. History of Art, edited by Z. von Beothy. Vol. I. Antiquity (F. Sebestyn, Prehistoric Art. — E. Mahler, Ancient Oriental Art. — F. Lang. Greek Art.—J. Zsamboki, Roman Art. — V. Kuzsinszky, Monuments of Roman Art in Hungary.) Budapest, 1906, Lampelsche Buchhandlung A.-G. xi, 565 pp.; 29 pis.; 688 figs. 4to. Hungarian. Musees et collections archeologiques de I'Algerie et de la Tunisie. Tome 13: Musee de Tlemcen par W. Marijais. Paris, 1905, E.

Leroux. 14 pis. 4to. Musees et monuments de France. Revue mensuelle d'art ancienet moderne publiee sous la direction de Paul Vitry. Paris, 1906, Laurens. 16 pp.; 4 pis.

4to. Musees royaux du cin quantenaire. Antiquit6s orientates, grecques et romaines. Guide sommaire. 2d ed. Brussels, 1906. 64 pp. 8vo.

G. von Neumayer, Anleitung zu wissenschaftlichen Beobachtungen auf Reisen. 3. Aufl. Hanover, 1905. Contains: F. von Luschan, Urgeschiclite und Technik von Ausgrabungen. H. Nissen, Orientation. Studien zur Geschichte der Religion. Heft 1. Berlin, 1906, Weidmann. iv, 108 pp. 8vo. M. 2. 80.

H. v. Pernull, and A. Rivela, Siziliens antike Denkmaler. Palermo, 1905, ir/.i. 156 pp. 8vo. L. 4.

J. L. Pic, Le Hradtscht de Stradonitz en Bohemc. Ouvrage traduit dn tcheque par J. Dtchclctte. Leipzig, 1906, K. V. Hlersemann. 58 pis.; 15 figs. 4to. M. 4H. Lt.

Gen. A. Lane-Fox Pitt-Rivers, The Evolution of Culture and other Essays. Edited by J. L. Myres. With an Introduction by Henry Balfour. Oxford, 1906, Clarendon Press, xx. 232 pp.; 21 pis. 8vo.

S. Reinach, Apollo: storia generale delle art! plastiche. Bergamo, 1906, Istituto d' arti graflche. x, 357 pp.; 649 figs. 8vo. L. 7.50. — Cultes, mythes et religions. Tome II. Paris, 1906, Leroux. xviii, 467 pp.; 30 tigs. 8vo. Resultate der wls senschaftlichen Erforschung des Balatonsees. Bd. 3, Toil 1, Sektion 1: Archilologische Spuren aus der Urzeit und dem Altertum bei Veszprem von G. Rh6. Vienna, 1906. E. Holzel. 33 pp.; plate; 20 figs. 4to.

A. de Ridder, see Collection De Clercq. C. Robert.Zum Gediicht nis von Ludwlg Ross. Rede bei Antritt des Rectorats der Universitiit Halle-Wittenerg am 12. Juli 1906 gchalten. Nebst dem Bikinis von Ludvvig Ross. Berlin, 1906, Weidmannsche Buchh. 28 pp. M. 1.

A. Rusconi, La Villa, il Museo e la Gallerla Borghese. Bergamo, 1906, Istit. ital. d'arti graf. 196 pp.; plate; 157 tigs. 8vo.

Sammlung F. Sarre, Erzeugnisse Islamischer Kunst. Bearb. v. F. Sarre, mit epigraph. Bcitritgen v. E. Mittwocli. Leipzig, 1906, Hiersemann. viii, 82 pp.; 10 pis.; 54 figs.

4to. M. 12. A. Schiller, Zeit tafeln der Baustile. Stuttgart, 1906, H. Enderlen. 13 pp. 8vo. M. 0.50.

Guilelmus Schmidt, De die natali apud veteres celebrato quaestiones selectae. Giessen, 1905. 36 pp. 8vo. Dissertation. K. E.

Schmidt, Der perfekte Kunstkenner. Vademecum f. Kenner und solche, die es werden wollen. Stuttgart, 1906, Spemann. 128 pp. 8vo.

M. 2.40. C. Schuchhardt. Die Uberreste der Eroberung Nordwestdeutschlands (lurch die Romer, Sachsen und Franken. Vortrag vor dem Provinzialverein des hiiheren

Lehrerstandes. A. Schulten, Ausgrabunsen in Numantia. Berlin, 1906, H. Feyl & Co. 8 pp. 8vo.

H. H. Graf von Schweinitz, In Kleinasien. Ein Keitausmig (lurch das innere Kleinasien i. Jahrc 1905. Berlin, 1906. D. Reimer. xiv, 204 pp.; 8 pis.; 86 figs, from Photographs by the Author; 1 map; 2 outline maps. 8vo. M. 6.

H. Semper, Das Fortleben der Antike in der Kunst des Abendlandes (Fiihrer zur Kunst. Bd. 3). Esslingen, 1906, P. Neff. 105 pp.; 3 pis.; 30 figs. 8vo. M. Semrau, see W.

Liibke. F. M. Simpson, A History of Architectural Development. Vol. I. London, 1906, Longmans. 276 pp.; 24 pis.; 156 tigs. 8vo. 12s.

6d. H. Sobrmann, Die altin disclie Siiule. Ein Beitrag zur Saulenkunde. Dresden, 1906, Kiihtmann. vii, 79 pp.; 57 llgs. 8vo.

E. v. Stern, Das Museum tier kais. Odessaer Gesellschaf t ftir Geschichte- und Alterutuinskunde. Lfg. 3: Theodosia und seine Keramik. Frankfurt a. M., 1906, Baer & Co.

91 pp.; 10 pis. Folio. Ad. Struck, Makedonische Fahrten. 1. Chalkidike. (Zur Kunde der Balkanlialbinsel. Keisen und Beobachtungen hrsg. v. 0. Patsch. Heft 4.) Vienna & Leipzig, 1906, A. Hartlebens Verl. 4 sheets; 83 pp.; 15 tigs.; map. 8vo. M. 2.20. T. Strunz.

Scheroatische Leitfaden der Kunstgeschichte bis zum Beginne des 19 Jahrhunderts. Vienna, 1906, Deu ticke. xi, 152 pp. 8vo. Russell

Sturgis, A History of Architecture. In 3 vols. Vol. I: Antiquity. New York, 1906, Baker and Taylor. 423 pp.; ill. 8vo. Complete §15.00.

L v. Sybel, Die klassische Archaologie und die altchristliche Kunst. Rektoratsrede. Marburg, 190G, N. G. Elwert. 18 pp. 8vo. Also published as Marburger aka demische Heden. No. 16. J. A.

Symonds, Sketches and Studies in Italy and Greece. Third series. New ed. London, 1905, Smith, Elder

& Co. 386 pp.; plate. 8vo. E. Szanto, Ausgewahlte Abhandlungen. Hrsg. von H. Swoboda. Tiibingen, 1906, J. C. B. Mohr. xxiv, 419pp.; portrait; plate; tigs. 8vo. M. 9.

A. M. Tozzer. see Archaeological Institute of America.

C. Uhde. Die Konstruktionen u. die Kunstformen der Architektur. Vol. IV, 1: Der Steinbau in klinstl. Stein, die geschichtl. Entwickelung der Gesimse in den verschiedenen Baustilen. Berlin, 1905, Wasmuth. xiii, 79 pp.; 91 figs. 4to. M. 6.50. University of

Pennsylvania. Department of Archaeology. Pachacamac. Report of the William Pepper Peruvian Expedition of 1895-1897. By Dr. Max Uhle. xi, 103 pp.; map; 21 pis.; ill. Folio. 9 10.00 — Transactions of the Department of Archaeology, Free Museum of Science and Art. Vol. II, Part 1. Philadelphia, 1906, Edith H. Hall, The Decorative Art of Crete in the Bronze Age. pp. 550; 3 pis.; 68 figs. — Adela Breton, Some Notes on Xochicalco. pp. 5168; 6 pis.; 13 tigs. —G. B. Gordon, Notes on the Western Eskimo, pp. 69-102; 18 pis.; 23' tigs. — G. B. Gordon, An Engraved Bone from Ohio. pp. 103-105; 3 pis.— P. Grafin von Uwarow, Collections for the Archaeology of the Caucasus, Part 10. Moscow, 1905. 4to. Russian.

G. Vallette, Promenades clans le passed Rome, Corse, Grece. Geneva, 1906,

Jullien. 8vo. Verhandlungen der 48. Versammlung deutscher Philologen und Schulmilnner in Hamburg vom 3. bis 6. X. 1905. Im Auftrage des Presidiums zusaromengestellt von K. Dissel und G. Rosenhagen. Leipzig, 1906, B. G. Tenbner. vllL 229 pp. 8vo. M. 6.

J. Vinycomb, Fictitious and

Symbolic Creatures in Art. With specal reference to their use in British Heraldry. London, 1906, Chapman & Hall. 288 pp.; ill. 8vo.

T. Volbehr, Gibt es Kunst gesetze? (Fiihrer zur Kunst) Esslingen, 1906. P. Netf. 54 pp.; 8 llgs. 8vo.. M. 1.

E. Wagner, Uber Museen und (iber die grossherzoglichen Staatssammlungen ftir Altertums-und Vblkerkunde in Karlsruhe. 2 Vortriige. Carlsmhe, 1906, G. Braun. 32 pp.; 8vo. M. 6. E. Wickenhagen,

Kurzgefasste Gesehiehte der Kunst. der Baukunst, Bildnerei, Malerei u. Musik. 11th ed. Esslingen, 1906. P. Neff. vi, 322 pp.; 4 pis.; 302 figs. 8vo. M. 5. H. Windel.

Bericht fiber eine Sttidienreise nach Italien. Herford. 1906. Programme. E. Wurz, Plastische

Dekoration des Stiitzwcrkes in Baukunst und Kunstgewerbe des Altertums. (Zur Kunstgesch. des Auslandes. Heft 43.) Strassburg, 1906. 83 figs. 8vo.

M. 8.

K. Zangemeister, Theodor Mommsen als Schriftsteller. Ein Verzeichnis seiner Schriften, fortgesetzt von E. Jacobs. Berlin, 1905, Weidmann. xi, 188 pp.; 8vo. Zeitschrift fur Asthetik und allgemeine Kunstwissenschaft. Herausg. v. Max Dessoir. Quarterly. Stuttgart. 1906, Enke. Each fasc. M. 5. J.

Ziehen, Kunstgeschichtliches AnschauuDgsmaterial zu Goethes Italienischer Reise. Bielefeld and Leipzig, 1906. Velhagen & Klasing. 62 pp. 8vo.

EGYPTIAN ARCHAEOLOGY

Ahmed Bey Kamal. see Catalogue general.

Fr. W. Frhr. von Bissing, Denkmiller iigyptischer Skulptur. Hrsg. u. mit erlauternden Texten versehen. Lfg. 1-4. Miincheu, F. Bruckmaim, 1906. Each 12 pis. and text. Folio. Each M. 20. Fr. W. Frhr. von Bissing and L. Borchardt, Das Re-Heiligtum des Konigs Ne-Woser-Re. Vol. I. Der Bau, von L. Borchardt, Berlin, 1905, Duncker. vi, 89 pp. ; 6 pis.; 62 figs. Folio. —-P. A. A.

Boeser, see A. E. J. Holwerda.

A. Bouche Leclercq, Histoire des Lagides. Vol. III. Les Institutions de l'Egypte Ptolemai'que. Pt. I. Paris, 1906, E. Leroux. 8vo. 10 fr. L. Boulard, Les instructions ecrites du magistrat au juge commissaire dans l'Egypte Roraaiue. Paris, 1906, E. Leroux. 8vo. 5 fr. J. H. Breasted, Ancient Records of Egypt. Historical documents from the earliest times to the Fersian conquest. Vol. I. The First to the Seventeenth Dynasties. 344 pp. Vol. II. The Eighteenth Dynasty. 427 pp. Vol. III. The Nineteenth Dynasty. 279 pp. Vol. IV. The Twentieth to the Twenty-sixth Dynasties. 520 pp. Chicago, 1906, University of Chicago Press. 8vo.

Capart, Recueil de monuments égyptiens. 2 sOrie. 50 planches phototypiques avec texte explicatif. Bruxelles, 1905, Vromant & Cie. 4to. 40 fr. — Primitive Art in Egypt, translated from the specially revised original edition bv A. S. Griffith. London, 1906, H. Grcvel & Co.

213 ill. 8vo. 16s. H. Carter, see Theodore M. Davis' Excavations. Catalogue General des antiquitCs egyptlennes du musee du Caire. XIX: Oraeco-Egyptiau glass. By C. C. Edgar, v, 92 pp. XX: Steles PtolCmalques et Romames. Far Ahmed Bey Kamal. Tome 1. 2. XXI: Archaic objects. By J. E. Qulbell. Tome 1. 2. Le Caire, 1905, Institut Frangais d'archeologie orientale.

Theodore M. Davis' Excavations, Biban el Moluk. The Tomb of Hatshopsttu. Introduction by Th. M. Davis. The Life and Monuments of the Queen, by Ed. Naville. Description of the Finding and Excavation of the Tomb by H. Carter. London, 1906, A. Constable & Co. xv, 112 pp. 4to.

Agyptische Grabsteine und Denksteine, aus verschiedenen Sammlungeu. Hrsg. v. V. Spiegelberg. III. Bonn, Darmstadt, Frankfurt a. M., Genf, NeuchStel. Bearbeitet v. A. Wiedemann u. B. Portner. Strassburg, 1906, Schlesier & Schweikhardt. v, 52 pp.; 11 pis.

4to. M. 12. B. P. Grenfell, see

Hibeh Papyri.

H. Hartleben, Champollion, sein Leben und sein Werk. 2 Bde. Berlin, 1906, Weidmanusche Buchh. xxxii, 593, 636 pp.; plate; 19 figs. 8vo. M. 30. The Hibeh

Papyri, edited with translations and notes by B. P. Grenfell and A. S. Hunt. Part I. London, 1906. Egypt Exploration Fund, xiv, 410 pp.; 10 pis. 4to. 45s A. E. J. Holwerda, P. A. A. Boeser and J. H. Holwerda, Die Denkmiller des alten Reichs (Beschrcibung der ilgyptischen Sammlung des Niederlandischen Reichsmuseums ln Leiden, No. 1). Text, Atlas. Leiden, 1905, E. J. Brill. 4to. and Folio.

J. H. Holwerda, see A. E. J.

Holwerda. A. S. Hunt, see

Hibeh Papyri.

W. Max Miiller, Egyptological researches. Results of a journey in 1904. (Carnegie Institution of Washington. Publication No. 53.) AVashingtou, 1906, Carnegie Institution. 62 pp.: 106 pis. 4to.

Papiri Greco-Egizii pubblicati dalla r. Accademia dei Lincei sotto la direzlone di 1). Comparetti e G. Vitelli. (Supplement! fllologlcostorici ai Mini. Ant.)

Vol. I. Papiri Fiorentini, Fasc. 1. Nos. 1-35. Florence, 1905. 64 pp.; 6 pis. L. 23. Fasc. 2. Nos. 36-105. Milan, 1906, L. Hoepli. Pp. 65-257; pis. 7-15. 4to. M. 27. W. M. Flinders Petrie, Researches in Sinai. With chapters by C. T. Currelly. London, 1906, J. Murray, xxiv, 280 pp. ; 4 maps; 186 photographs. 8vo. 21. B. Portner, see Wiedemann. W. Schmidt, Choix de monuments egyptiens faisant partie de la Glyptotheque Ny-Carlsberg, fondee par

M. Carl Jacob-sen. Copenhagen, 1906, Hoest & Fils. 2 pp.; 6 pis. 4to. G. Steindorff, The Religion of the Ancient Egyptians (American Lectures on the History of Religions. Series 5). New York, 1905, G. P. Putnam's Sons, xi, 178 pp. 8vo.

A... Wiedemann and B. Portner, Agyptische Grabreliefs aus der Grossherzogl. Altertlimer-Sammlung zu Karlsruhe. Strassburg i. E., 1906, Schlesier & Schweikhardt. 32 pp.; 7 pis. 4to.

ORIENTAL ARCHAEOLOGY

R. Dussaud, Notes de mythologie syrienne, II-IX et Index. Paris, 1905, E. Leroux. Pp. 67-188; 42 flgs. 8vo.

The Babylonian Expedition of the University of Pennsylvania. Series A. Cuneiform Texts, edited by H. V. Hilprecht. Vol. XIV and XV. Documents from the Temple Archives of Nippur, by Albert T. Clay. Philadelphia, 1906, published by the Department of Archaeology, University of Pennsylvania, xii, 74, 12 pp.; 72, xv pis. in Vol. XIV; xii, 68 pp.; 72, xii pis. in Vol. XV. 4to.

M. Moore, Carthage of the Phoenicians in the light of modern excavation. London, 1905, Heinemann. 176 pp.; plates. 8vo. 6s.

Orientalische Studien, Theodor Noldeke zum 70. Geburtstag gewidmet von Freunden und Schiilern. Bd. I, II. Giessen, 1906, A. Topelmann. M. 40. Partial contents of Vol. II: W. W. Graf Baudissin, Esmun-Asklepios. Pp. 729-755. — V. Gardthausen, Die Farther in griechtsch-romischen Inschriften. Pp. 838-859. —A. v. Domaszewski, Virgo Caelestis. Pp. 861-863.—J. Oestrup, Smintheus. Pp. 863-870. — C. F. Lehmann-Haupt, BijXiTai-af und Berrripat. Pp. 997-1014.

L. Venetianer, Ezekiels Vision und die Salomonischen Wasserbecken. Budapest, 1906, F. Kilian Nachfolger. 40 pp. 8vo.

CLASSICAL Af GREEK AND ROMAN (Works treating of the monuments of the Greeks and Romans, but not exclusively of those of either.)

Ausstellung von Fundstiicken aus Ephesos im unteren Belvedere. Vienna, 1906, Gerold & Sohn. viii, 32 pp.; ill. 8vo. M. 1.50.

G. Colin, Rome et la Grece de 200 a 146 ayant Jesus-Christ (Bibliotheque des Ecoles franchises d'Athenes et de Rome. Fasc. 94). Paris, 1905, A. Fontemoing. 683 pp. 8vo.

Denkmaler Griechischer und Romischer Skulptur. Parts 117-120. Miinchen, 1906, F. Bruckmann.

Each M. 20. Denkmaler der Malerei des Altertums. Ed. Paul Herrmann. Munich, 1906, F. Bruckmann. Series I, Pt. I. (Complete I in 3 series of 20 parts each.) 12 pp. text; 2 figs. 4to.; 10 pis.

Folio. M. 20. D. Detlefsen, Ur sprung, Einrichtung und Bedeutung der Erdkartc Agrippas. (Quellen und Forschungen zur alten Geschichte und Geographie. Heft 13.) Berlin, 1906,Weidmann. vi, 118 pp.

8vo. M. 4. F.von Duhn, Pom peji. eine hellenistisehe Stadt in Italien. (Aus Natur und Geisteswelt.Vol. 114.) Leipzig, 1906, B. G. Teubner. 115 pp.; plate; 62 flgs. 8vo. M. 1.

H. d'Espouy, Fragments d'archltecture antique d'apres les releves et restitutions des anciens penslonnaires de l'Academie de France a Rome. T. II sera complet en 10 fascicules, fasc. 1-5. Paris, 1905-06, Schmid. 50 pis. 4to.

Forschungen in Ephesos, veroffentlicht vom Osterreichischen archaologischen Institut. Bd. 1. Wten, 1906, Holder. 285 pp.; 9 pis. in Heliogravure; map; 206 figs. Folio.

Harvard Studies in Classical Philology. Vol. XVII. Cambridge, 1906, Harvard University. 185 pp.; 4 figs. 8vo. Partial contents: M. H. Morgan, Notes on Vitruvius. — C. H. Moore, On the Origin of the Taurobolium. — V. W. Goodwin, The Battle of Salamis. —J. H. Wright. The Origin of Plato's Cave. — G. H. Chase, An Amphora with a New KaXit-Name in the Boston Museum of Fine Arts. — P. Herrmann, see Denkmaler der Malerei.

Inscriptiones Graecae ad res Romanes pertinentes III 5. Curavit R. Cagnat. auxiliante G. Lafaxe. Paris, 1906, Leroux. Pp. 489-560. 8vo.

P. Larizza, Rhegium chalcidense (Reggio di Calabria). La storia e la nuraismatica dai tempi preistorici flno alia cittadinanza romana. Rome, 1906. 118 pp.; 14 pis. 8vo.

L. 20. F. Lehner. Homerische Gottergestalten in der antiken Plastik. III. Linz, 1906. 21 pp.; 5 pis. 8vo. Programme.

Meisterwerke antiker Plastik. 30 Reproduktionen nach anttken Bildwerken. (1) Neapel. (2) Rom. Berlin, 1906, Globus-Verlag. Each 30 pp. 4to. Each M. 1.50.

J. Nicole, Un catalogue d'oeuvres d'art conserves a Rome a l'fipoque impeYiale. Texte du papyrus latin VII de Geneve transcrit et comments. Geneva & Basel, 1906, Georg & Co. 34 pp. Facsimile. 4to. 5 fr.

Griechische und rdmische Portrats, Parts 71-74. Munich, 1906, F. Bruckmann. Folio. Each M. 20.

W. Rappensberger, Classical Antiquities of Sicily. Magyar6va, 1905. 45 pp. 8vo. Hungarian. Programme. S. Reinach, Repertoire de la statualre grecque et romaine. Vol. I. Clarac de poche. 2«6d. Paris, 1906. Leroux. lxv,661 pp. 16mo. 5fr. E. Rizzo, Scul ture antiche del Palazzo Giustiniani. Rome, 1906. 129 pp.; 9 pis. 8vo.

Max Schmidt, Kulturhistorische Beitrage znr Kenntnis des griechischen und romischen Altertums. Heft 1. Leipzig, 1906, Diirr. 8vo.

GREEK (Including also titles of works relating to pre-Hellenic inhabitants of Greece and to kindred peoples, and to monuments of Greek art wherever found.)

I. GENERAL AND MISCELLANEOUS

Philosophische Abhandlungen, Max Heinze zura 70. Geburtstage gewidmet. Contains, O...Ktilpe, Anfange psychologischer Asthetik bei den Griechen. Berlin, 1906, E. S.

Mittler & Sohn. A. G. Amatucci, Hellas. Disegno storico della cultura greca. Vol. I. Dai tempi piu antichi al secolo V a. C. Bari 1906.
330 pp.; 30 figs. 8vo. 3 fr.

The Annual of the British School at Athens. No. XI, session 1904-05. London, 1906, Macmillan & Co. xii, 346 pp.; 16 pis.; 106 figs. 4to. 21s. A. J. Evans, The Palace of Knossos and its Dependencies.— M. N. Tod, Inscriptions from Eumeneia. M. K. Welsh, Honorary Statues in Ancient Greece.— F. W. Hasluck, Dr. Covel's Notes on Galata. —H. J. W. Tillyard, Boundary aud Mortgage Stones from Attica. — R. M. Dawkins, A Visit to Skyros.

— A. J. B. Wace, F. W. Hasluck. H. J. W. Tillyard, G. Dickens, and K. Romaios, Excavations in Laconia. —G. P. Byzantinos, A Votive Relief to Asclepius. — F. W. Hasluck, Note on the Lion-Group from Cyzicus. — R. M. Burrows, An Apollo Inscription from the District of Delium. — G. Dickens, A Head in Connexion with Damophon.

— D. Mackenzie, Cretan Palaces and Aegean Civilization. —G. M. A. Richter, The Distribution of Attic Vases. — E. S. Forster, Terracotta Plaques from Praesos. — R. M. Dawkins, C. H. Hawes, and R. C. Bosanquet, Excavations at Palaikastro. — Annual Meeting, Reports, Lists, etc. — Athenes et ses Environs, Extrait du Guide de Grece rfidigS par G. Fougeres. Paris, 1906, Hachette. 227 pp.; 2 maps; 16 plans; 6 figs. 8vo. G. d'Azambuja, La Grece ancienne (avec prfcface par E. Demolins), Paris, 1906, Bibliotheque de la Science Sociale. 8vo. 6 fr.

G. Cardinali, II regno di Pergamo. Kicerche di storia e di diritto pubblico. (Studi di storia antica. Fasc. 5.) Rome, 1906, E. Loescher & Co. xiv, 303 pp.

W. Dorpfeld, Zweiter Brief tiber Leukas-Ithaka: die Ergebnisse der Ausgrabungen von 1905. Athen, Buchdruckerei Hestia. 20 pp.; 8vo.

A. Pick, Vorgriechische Ortsnauien als Quelle fur die Vorgeschichte Griechenlands verwertet. Gottingen, 1905, Vandenhoeck & Rup precht. viii, 173 pp.; 8vo. G.

Fougeres, see Athenes. —-A. Furtwangler, Aegina. Das Heiligtum der Aphaia. Unter Mitwirkung von E. R. Fiechter und H. Thiersch. I. Textband. xii, 504 pp.; 7 pis.; map; 413 flgs. II. Tafelbd. xx pp.; 130 pis. Munich, 1906, Verlag der Kgl. Bayer. Akademie der Wissenschaften. 4to. Die

Bedeutung der Gymnastik in der griechischen Kunst. Leipzig, 1905, B. G. Teubner. 15 pp.; 8 flgs. 8vo. M. 0.80. Reprint from "Der Saemann, Monatsschrift ftir p&dagogische Reform."

G. Glotz, Etudes sociales et juridiques sur l'antiquite grecque. Paris, 1906, Hachette et Cie. iii, 303 pp. 8vo. O. Gruppe, Griechische Mythologie und Religionsgeschichte. Bd. 2. Handbuch der klassischen Altertumswissenschaft. Bd. 5, Abt. 2. Munich, 1906, C. H. Beck'sche Verlagsbuchh. Pp. 719-1923. 8vo. M. 15.

J. E. Harrison, Primitive Athens as described by Thncydides. Cambridge, 1906, University Press, xii, 168 pp.; 8vo. 6s. L. Heide mann, Die territoriale Entwicklung Lacedamons und Messeniens bis auf Alexander (§ 1 A Die dorische Wandernng). Berlin, 1904. 53 pp.
8vo. Dissertation. G. Held,

The Altar of Zeus at Pergamon. Reval, 1905. Russian. F.

Frhr. Hiller von Gaertringen, Geschichte und Erforschung von Priene. (Heprinted from the " Inschriften von Priene.") Berlin, 1906, G. Reimer. G. Hock,.Griechische Weihegebrauche. YVlirzburg, 1905, H. Stiirtz. 134 pp.
8vo. N. Hohlwein, La Papy rologie grecque. Liiwen, 1905, Peeters. 178 pp. 8vo. Fr. 3.

V. Inama, Antichita greche pubbliche, sacree private. Milan, 1906, Hoepli. xv, 230 pp.; 19 pis.; 16 flgs. 2. 50 fr.

A. Lang, Homer and his Age. London, 1906, Longmans, Green & Co. 6 flgs. 8vo. 12s. 61. F.Lang, The Exploration of the Seats of Greek Civilization. Budapest, 1906. 30 pp.

8vo. Hungarian. Programme. E. Lassel, Delphi.

Brass6 (Kronstadt), 1906. 14 pp.; 3 pis. 4to. Programme.

J. P. Mahaffy, The Silver Age of the Greek World. Chicago, 1906, The University of Chicago Press, vii, 482 pp. 8vo. «3.00. R. Maisch,

Griechische Altertumskunde. Neu bearbeitet von Fr. Pohlhammer. Leipzig, 1905, G. J. Goschen. (Sammlung Goschen, No. 16.) 220 pp.; 9 pis. 8vo. M. 0»80. A.

Malinin. Hat Dorpfeld die Enneakrunos-Episode bei Pausanias tatsachlich geliist oder auf welchem Wege kann diese geliist werden? Einige Bemerkungen zu Judeichs Topographie von Athen. Wien.
1906, A. Holder. 35 pp. 8vo.

K. Meischke, Zur Geschichte des Konigs Eumenes II von Pergamon. Pirna, 1905. Programme. Dr.

Mollet, La medecine chez les Grecs avant Hippocrate. Paris, 1906, Maloine. Konigl. Museen zu Berlin. Milet. Ergebnisse der Ausgrabungen und Untersuchungen seit dem jalire 1899 hrsg. v. Th. Wiegand. Berlin, 1906, G. Reimer. Heft i: Karte der milesischen Halbinsel (1: 50,000). Mit erlauterndem Text von P. Wilski. 1 sheet, 24 pp.; 3 rigs.; map. 4to. M. 5. — Altertiimer von Pergamon. Bd. Ill, 1: Der grosse Altar. Der obere Markt von Jac. Schrammen. Text. 128 pp.; 57 flgs. 4to. Atlas, 34 pis.; Berlin, 1906, G. Reimer. M. 180.

M. P. Nilsson, Griechische Feste von religioser Bedeutung mit Ausschluss der attischen. Leipzig, 1906, B. G. Teubner. v, 490 pp. 8vo. M. 12.

J. Oehler, Zum griechischen Vereinswesen. Vienna, 1905. Programme.

D. Philios, Eleusis. Her mysteries, ruins, and museum. Translated by H. Catliff. London, 1906, Appleton. 8vo. 5s. R. Pohl, De Graeco rum medicis publicis. Berlin, 1905. 86 pp. 8vo. Dissertation.

F. Pohlhammer, see Maisch.

K. Riezler, Uber Finanzen und Monopole im alten Griechenland. Berlin, 1906, Puttkammer & Muhlbrecht. 98 pp. 8vo. A. Romaides,

Delphi im Bilde. Photographien und Lichtdrucke. Athens, 1906, Beck & Barth. 53 BL 22 x 29 cm. Complete M. 36 or 28; single prints 0.80 or 0.70.

J. Schrammen, see Kdnigl. Museen zu Berlin. Frh. v. Schwarz,

Alexanders des Grossen Feldztige in Turkestan. Kommentar zu den Geschichtswerken des Flavius Arrianus und Q. Curtius Rufus auf Grund vieljahriger Reisen im russischen Turkestan und den angrenzenden Landcrn. 2. Aufl. Stuttgart, 1906, F. Gruh. iv, 103 pp.; 2 pis.; 6 plans; map. 8vo. M. 2. J.

Sods, Pausanlas' Description of the Acropolis, with Commentary. Kisujszallas, 1905. 40 pp. 8vo. Hungarian. Programme.

M. N. Tod and A. J. B. Wace, A Catalogue of the Sparta Museum. Oxford, 1906, Clarendon Press, viii, 249 pp.; 8 figs. 8vo. $3.40.

B. Warnecke, The Woman Question on the Attic Stage. Kazan, 1906. Russian. Oration. Th. Wie gand, see Kdnigl. Museen zu Berlin.

P. Wilski, see Kdnigl. Museen zu Berlin.

II. GREEK ARCHITECTURE

L. Bolle, Die Btthne des Aschylus. Wismar, 1906. 18 pp. 4to. Programme.

E. R. Fiechter, Der Tempel der Aphaia auf Agina. Miinchen, 1906, Technische Hochschule. 57 pp.; 6 pis.; 16 figs. Dissertation.

A. Koester, Das Stadlon von Athen. Berlin, 1906, Albrecht Dtirer-Haus. 30 pp. 8vo. M. 0.80.

M. Schmidt. The Erechtheum and the Temple of Nike. Budapest, I, 1905. 15 pp.; 4 tigs. 8vo. Hungarian. Programme. O. Skerling,

De vocis *axirf* quantum ad theatrum graecum pertineat signiflcatione. Marburg, 1906. 45 pp. 8vo. Dissertation.

III. GREEK SCULPTURE

W. Deonna, Les Statues de terre-cuite en Grece. Paris, 1906, Fontemoing. 73 pp. 8vo.

A. Furtwangler, Die Agineten der Glyptothek Ludwigs I nach den Resultaten der neuen bayerischen Ausgrabung. Munich, 1906, A. Buchholz. 58 pp.; 14 pis. 8vo. M. 3.

E. A. Gardner, Appendix to the Handbook of Greek Sculpture. London, 1906, Macmillan. Pp. 523-588; flgs. 8vo. Die attischen Grabreliefs,

Hrsg. im Anftrage der K. Akademie der Wissenschaften zu Wien von A. Conze unter Mitwirkung von Ad. Michaelis, A. Postolakkas, R, v. Schneider, E. Loewy, A. Brueckner, P. Wolters. Lfg. 16; ix and 353-370 pp.; 25 pis. Berlin, 1906, G. Reimer. M. 65.

R. Kekule von Stradonitz, Die griechische Skulptur. (Handbficher der Koniglichen Museen zu Berlin). Berlin, 1906, G. Reimer. iv, 383 pp. 8vo.

H. Lechat, Phidias et la sculpture grecque au V« siecle. Paris, 1906, Librairie de l'art ancien et moderne. 176 pp.; 27 flgs. 8vo. W. Ler mann, Attgriechische Plastik; eine Einf Uhrung in die griechische Kunst des archalschen und gereinigten Stils. Munich, 1906, C. H. Becksche Verlagsbuchhandlung. xiii, 231 pp.; 25 colored plates; 80 flgs. 4to. M. 25.

J. N. Svoronos, Das Athener Nationalmuseum. Phototypische Wiedergabe seiner Schatze. Deutsche Ausgabe besorgt von W. Barth. Athen, 1906, Beck & Barth. Nos. 78. Pp. 183-238; pis. 61-80. M. 14.40.

IV. GREEK VASES AND PAINTING

M. F. E. Angles d'Auriac, Catalogue des vases fitrusques et des vases grecs (Ioniens, Cojinthiens, Attiques) appartenant a la ville de Grenoble. Grenoble, 1905, Allien 24 pp. 8vo.

E. Fdlzer, Die Hydria. Ein Beitrag zur griechischen Vasenkunde. (Beitrage zur Kunstgeschichte, N. F. XXXIII). Leipzig 1906. viii, 120 pp.; 10 pis. 8vo. A. Furtwangler and K. Reichhold, Griechische Vasenmalerei. Auswahl hervorragender Vasenbllder. 2te Serie. Lfg. 2, pp. 63-109; 10 pis. Munich, 1906, Bruckmann. 4to. Subscription price, M. 40.

E. Pottier, Catalogue des vases antiques de terre cuite du Mus6e du Louvre. 3 partie: L'ecole attique. P. 601-1133. Paris, 1906, Motteroz. 8vo.

V. GREEK INSCRIPTIONS

A. Brinck, De choregla quaestiones epigraphicae. Kiel, 1906. 36 pp. 4to. Programme. B. Bursy,

Unedited Stamps on the Handles of Greek Amphorae. Niezin, 1905. Russian.

W. Janell. Ausgewahlte Inschriften. Grlechlsch und deutsch. Berlin, 1906, Weidmannsche Buchh. vi, 148 pp.; 4 tigs. 8v o. M. 4.

J. Sundwall, Epigraphische Beitrage zur sozial-politischen Geschichte Athens im Zeitalter des Demosthenes. Leipzig, 1906, Dleterich. vii, 94 pp. 8vo.

Ad. Wilhelm, Urkunden dramatischer Aufl'iihriingen in Athen. Mit einem Beitrage von G. Kaibel. (Sonderschriften des osterreichischen archaologischen Instituts in Wien. VoL 6). Vienna, 1906, A. Holder. 28 pp.; 68 figs. 4to. M. 16.

VI. GREEK COINS

B. V. Head, Catalogue of the Greek Coins of Phrygia. (A Catalogue of the Greek Coins in the British Museum, Vol. 25.) London, 1906, British Museum. cvi, 491 pp.; 53 pis.; map. 8vo. G. F. Hill,

Historical Greek Coins. London, 1906, A. Constable & Co. six, 108 pp.; 13 pis. 8vo.

F. Imhoof-Blumer, Die Antiken Mtinzen Nord-Griechenlands. Bd. III. Makedonia und Pannonia. Abt. 1. Die Makedonlschen Landesmiinzen, u. s. w. bearb. v. H. Gaebler. Berlin. 1906, G. Keimer. 5 pis. 4to. M. 19.

G. Macdonald, Catalogue of Greek Coins in the Hunterian Collection, University of Glasgow. Vol. 3: Further Asia, Northern Africa, Western Europe. Glasgow, 1905. J. Maclehose & Sons, vi, 799 pp.; pis. LXVII-CII. 4to.

K. Regling, Die Griechischen Mtlnzen der Sammlung Warren. Berlin, 1906, G. Reimer. viii, 264 pp.; 37 pis. 4to. M. 40.

ROMAN (Including also titles of works relating to the monuments of the Etruscans and other peoples who inhabited Italy before or contempo raneously with the Romans, as well as to Roman monuments outside of Italy.) *L* GENERAL AND MISCELLANEOUS

W. Amelung and H. Holtzinger,

The Museums and Ruins of Rome. The English Edition revised by the authors and Mrs. S. A. Strong. London,

1906, Duckworth. 2 vols. 350 and 296 pp.; map; plans; 268 ills. 8vo. 10s. J. Assmann, De coloniis oppidisque Romanis, quibus imperatoria nomina vel cognomina imposita sunt. Jena, 1905. 152 pp. 8vo. Dissertation.

M. Bang, Die Germanen im romlschen Dienst bis zum Regierungsantritt Constantins I. Berlin, 1906, Weidmannsche Buchh. 116 pp. 8vo.

M. 4.80. Bertrand, Decouverte des ruines d'un grand edifice galloromain sur le point-culminant du bourg de Chatel-Deneuvre (Allier).

12 pp. 8vo. L. Bloch, Romische Altertumskunde. 3d revised ed. (Sammlung Giischen, No. 45), Leipzig. 1906, G. J. Goschen. 173 pp.; 8 pis. M. 0.80. T. Blume, Der Hildesheimer Silberfund. Hildesheim, 190G. 46 figs. M. 2.

J. Carcopino, see Huelsen. J. B. Carter, The Religion of Numa and other Essays on the Religion of Ancient Rome. London and New

York, 190C. 8vo. 3s. 6d. Carton, La colonisation romaine dans le pays de Dougga. Tunis, 1906. 198 pp.; ill. 8vo. G. Colasanti, Fregellae.

Storia e topografia. Rome, 1906, Loescher. 225 pp.; 2 pis. 8vo. Er. 6.

V. Forot. Etude sur les ruines galloromaines de Tintignac, commune de Naves. Tulle, 1905, Crauffon. 8vo.

G. F. Gamurrini. Bibliografla dell' Italia antica. Vol. I. Parte generale. Arezzo, 1905. 8vo. 10 fr.

E. G. Hardy. Studies in Roman History. London, 1906. Swan Sonnenschein & Co. ix, 349 pp.; 12mo.

F. J. Haverfield, The Romani sation of Roman Britain. London, 1906, Frowde. E. Hesselmeyer,

Hannibals Alpentibergang im Lichte der neueren Kriegsgeschichte. Tubingen, lDOfi. J. C. B. Mohr. 48 pp. 8vo. M. 0.80. H. Holtzinger, see Amelung. Ch. Huelsen, Le Forum romain, son histoire et ses monuments. Traduction francaise par J. Carcopino. Rome, 1906, Loscher. 2 plans; 143 tigs. 8vo.

E. Kalinka. Das romische Kriegswesen in Casars gallischen Kilmpfen (Anhang zu Prammers Ausgabe des bellum gallicum). Vienna, 1906, F. Tempsky. 51 pp.; 39 tigs. 8vo.

P. Kiraly, The Forum Roma num. Erzsebetvaros, 1906. 95 pp. 8vo. Hungarian. Programme.

R. Lanciani, La villa Adriana: Guida e descrizione. Roma, 1906. 40 pp.; plan; 16 tigs. 8vo. L. 1.50.

A. Lank6, The Roman Cities during the First Two Centuries of the Empire. Erzsebetvaros, 1950. 68 pp. 8vo. Hungarian. Programme.

Limes, Der obergermanisch raetische, des Riimerreiches. Lfg. 26. No. 72. Das Kastell Weissenburg. Untersucht von W. Kohl und J. Troltsch. Unter Mitwirkung von J. Troltsch, Joh. Jacobs und W. Barthel bearbeitet von E. Kabricius. Pp. 1-59; 15 pis.; 9 figs. —Lfg. 27 (1906). No. 12. Das Kastell Kapersburg (Jacobi). 57 pp.; 10 pis.; 6 figs.

P. Manfrin, La dominazione romana nella Gran Bretagna. Rome, 1906.

Vol. II. +05 pp. 8vo. 5 fr.

P. Marciano. Ricerche storlche ed archcologiche intorno all' accademia Ercolanese per la ripresa degli scavi di Ercolano. Napoli, 1906, Lanciano, Veraldi & Co. 43 pp. 8vo.

A. Martow, On the Honorary Offices of the Roman Emperor in the Cities of the Empire during the first three Centuries A.d. Niezin, 1905. Ill pp. 8vo. Russian.

A. Merlin, L'Aventin dans l'antiquité (Bibliotheque des Ecoles franoaises d'Athenes et de Rome. Fasc. 97.) Paris, 1906. A. Fontemoing. 476 pp.; map; 2 figs. 12 fr.

Monumenta Pompeiana. Nos. 47-50. Leipzig, 1906, G. Hedeler. 12 M. each.

Papers of the British School at Rome, Vol. III. London, 1906, Macmillan &Co. xii, 314 pp.; 32 pis.; 2 maps: 15 figs. 4to. 308. T. Ashby, Jr., The Classical Topography of the Roman Campagna. — H. Stuart Jones, Notes on Roman Historical Sculptures. — A. J. B. Wace. Fragments of Roman Historical Reliefs

In the Vatican and Lateran Museums. — G. F. Hill, Some Drawings from the Antique, attributed to Pisanello.

— Miss K. A. McDowell, A Portrait of Pythagoras. V. Parvan,

Cateva euvinte cu privire la organizatia provinciei Dacla Traiana. Bucharest, 1906, Gobi. 64 pp. 8vo.

G. Pinza, II comizio romauo nella eta repubblicana ed i suoi monumeuti. Roma, 1906. 58 pp.; 2 pis.; 4 tigs. 8vo. 2. 50 fr.

A. Pirro, Le origini di Napoli. Studio storico-topografico. Parte 1: Falero e Napoli. Salerno, 1905, Fratelli Jovane. 57 pp.; plate. 8vo.

O. Prein, Aliso bei Oberaden. Neue Forschungen und Vermutuugeu. Miiuster, 1906, AschendorfF. vll, 79 pp.; plate; map. 8vo.

Fr. Richter, De deorum barbarorum interpretatione Romana quaestiones selectae. Halle, 1906. 58 pp. 8vo. Dissertation.

C. Schuchhardt. Aliso. Fiihrerdurch die Ausgrabungeu bei Haltern. 3. Aufl. Herausgegeben vom Altertumsverein zu Haltern. Haltern, 1906. 56 pp.; 38 tigs. 8vo. E.

Schulze. Die romischen Grenzanlagen in Deutschland und das Limeskastell Saalburg. (GymuasialBibliothek. Heft 36.) 2. verb. Aufl. Giitersloh, 1906, E. Bertelsmann, vlll, 115 pp. ; 4 maps: 23 figs. 8vo. A. Sogliano, Dei la vori eseguiti in Pompei. Relazione a S. E. il Ministro della Istruzione Pubblica. Napoli. 1906. 14 pp.; 8vo. S. A. Strong, see Ame lung.

H. Thedenat, Pompei. —Vol. I. Histoire; Vie privee. 164 pp.; 123 figs.; plan. Vol. II. Vie publique. 140 pp.; 77 figs.; plan. Paris, 1906,

Laurens. 8vo. R. Thiele. Das Forum Romanum mit besonderer Beriicksichtigung der neuesten Ausgrabungeu. 2. Aufl. Erfurt, 1906, K. Villaret.

G. Veith, Geschichte der Feldztige C. Julius Caesars. Vienna, 1906, L. W. Seidel & Sohn. xx, 552 pp.; portrait; 46 maps. 8vo. M. 25.

W. Wagner. Rom. Geschichte des romischen Volkes und seiner Kultur. 8. Autl. bcarb. v. O. E. Schmidt. Leipzig, 1905. O. Spamer. xlv, 846 pp.; 322 tigs. ; 2 maps. 8vo.

M. 10. P. Werner, De incendiis urbis Romae aetate impcratorum. Leipzig,

1906. 87 pp. 8vo. Dissertation.

II. ROMAN ARCHITECTURE

W. Altmann, Die Itallschen Rundbauteu. Berlin, 1906, Weidmannsche Buchhandlung. 101 pp.; 20 iigs. 8vo. M. 3.

G. Dietrich, Qraestionum Vitruvianarum specimen. Meissen (Leipzig), 1906. 84 pp. 8vo.

H. Holtzinger. Timgad und die romi-! sche Provinzialarchitektur in Nordafrika. (Die Baukunst hrsg. v. R. Bormanu u. R. Graul. 3. Serie? Heft I.) Stuttgart, 1906, V. Spemann. 24 pp.; 6 pis. 4to. M. 4.

H. Wurz, Zur Charakteristik der klassichen Basllika. (ZurKunstgeschichte des Anslandes. Heft 40.) Strassburg, 1906, J. H. E. Heitz. 61 pp.; 5 pis.; 12 tigs. 8vo.

III. ROMAN SCULPTURE

J. Hampel. Die altesten pannonischen Grabsteine des National-Museums. (Abhandlungen d. histor. Klasse der Ungar. Akademie d. Wissenschaften, xxi, Bd. I.) Budapest, 1906, Akademle-Verlag. 74 pp.; 23 pis. 8vo. 2 Kr.

IV. ROMAN, ETC., VASES AND PAINTINGS

G. v. Cube, Uber die romische " scenae f rons" in den Pompejanischen Wandbildern 4. Stils. Hannover, 1906. 43 pp. ; 10 pis.; 7 tigs. 4to. Inaugural Dissertation. Also Beitriige zur Bauwissenschaft, Heft 6. Berlin. 1906, E. Wasmuth.

O. Engelhardt, Die IUustrationen der Terenzhandschriften. Ein Beitrag zur Geschichte des Buchschmucks. Jena, 1905. 97 pp. 8vo. Dissertation.

R. Knorr. Die verzierten Terra sigillata-Gefiisse von Cannstatt und Kongen-Grinario. Hrsg. von der Wtirttembergischen Korumission ftir Laudesgeschichte. Stuttgart, 1905, W. Kohlbammer. 49 pp.; 47 pis. 8vo.

Mestverdt, Die romischen Tongefasse der Altertumssamlung in Cleve, II. Cleve, 1906. 23 pp. 8vo. Programme.

V. ROMAN INSCRIPTIONS

Corpus Inscriptionum Latinarum. Vol. 13: Inscriptiones trium Galliarum et Germaniarum latinae. Partis 3: Instrumentum domesticum fasc. 2: Insunt signacula medicornm oculariorum ed. E. Espérandieu. Berlin, 1906, G. Reimer. Pp. 431-773. Folio. M. 32. H. Dessau, Inscriptiones latinae selectae. Vol. 2, pars 2. Berlin, 1906, Weidmanu. iv, 137-1040 pp. 8vo.

E. Esp£randieu, see Corpus Inscriptionum Latinarum.

G. Fregni, Delle iscrizioni die si leggono nell' arco di Fl. Costantino Massimo a Roma: studi storici e fllologici. Modena, 1906. 24 pp.; plate. 8vo. L. 1.

W. Ludowici, Stempelbikler romischer Topfer. Aus meinen Ausgrabungen in Rheinzabern nebst dem 2. Teil der Stempelnamen, 1901-1905. Munich, 1906, Meisenbach, Rifl'arth & Co. 4to. M. 50.

E. de Ruggiero, Dizionario epigraflco tli antichiti Romane. Fasc. 86-87: Continentia-Corsica. Roma, 1906, Pasqualucci. Pp. 1185-1248. Fasc. 88: Genius. Fasc. 89: GeniusGermania. Pp. 449-512. M. 2.40. Fasc. 90-93: Corsica-Curator. Pp. 1249-1376.

VI. ROMAN COINS .. Sambon, Les monnais antiques de lTtalie (Etrurie, Ombrle, Picenum, Samnium, Campanie). Fasc. 5. Angers, 1905, Burdin. Pp. 341-445; pi. 8vo.

CHRISTIAN ART

I. GENERAL AND MISCELLANEOUS

Julia de Wolf Addison, The Art of the National Gallery. London. 1906. Bell, x, 389 pp.; plan; 48 tigs. 8vo.

Bau-und Kunstdenkmaler des Herzogtums Braunschweig, herausg. u. P. J. Meier. Bd. III. Kreis Wolfenbuttel. 2 Abtlg. Die Ortschaften des Kreises mit Ausschluss der Kreisstadt. Mit Beitragen v. K. Steinacker. Wolfenbuttel, 1906. J. Zwissler. xviti, 448 pp.; 23 pis. ; 205 figs. 8vo. M. 15. Bau-und Kunstdenkmaler der freien u. Hansestadt Liibeck. Vol. II. Fetrikirche, Marienkirche, Hell. GeistHospital. By F. Hirsch, G. Sehaumann, and F. Bruns. Liibeck, 1906, B. Nohring. xi, 511 pp. ; 111. 8vo. M. 12. Bau-und Kunstdenkmaler Thiiringens. Bearb. v. F. Lehfeldt u. G. Voss. Fasc. 32: Herzogt. Sachsen-Coburg u. Gotha, Landratsamt Coburg; Amtsgerichtsbez. Coburg. Jena, 1906, G. Fisher, viii, 153-474 pp.; 42 pis.; 84 flgs. 8vo. M. 12. Bau-und Kunstdenkmaler der Frov. Westpreussen, bearb. v. B. Schmid. Fasc. xii, Kreis Rosenberg. Danzig, 1906, I,. Saunier. viii, 113-234 pp.; 22 pi.; 92 tigs. 8vo. M. 6. A.

Beaunier, L'Art de regarder les tableaux. Paris, 1906. Lib. cent, des Beaux-Arts. 280 pp.; 69 pis.

8vo H. Bergner, Handbuch der biirgerlichen Kunstaltertlimer in Deutschland. 2 vols. Leipzig. 1906. Seeraann. viii, 644 pp.; 790 flgs. 8vo. P. Bergner, Verzeichnis der Graflich Nostizschen GemaldeGallerie zu Prag. Prague, 1905, C. Bellmann. 66 pp.; 5(5 flgs. M. 2.40. Berner Kunstdenkmaler. Ill Bd. Fasc. 1. Bern, 190!, Wyss. 0 pp.; 4 pis. 4to. Be schreibende Darstellung der alteren Bau-und Kunstdenkmaler des Kiingreichs Sachsen. Fasc. 26: H. Bergner: Beschr. Darst. des Krcises Naumburg (Land). Halle, 1906. O. Hendei. viii, 252 pp.; 159 flgs.; map. 8vo. Fasc. 29: Amtshauptmannschaft Zittau. Part I. Land. Dresden, 1900, Meinhold & Siihne. ii, 268 pp.; 7 pis.; flgs. 8vo. R. Bosselt. Ueber die Kunst der Medaille. Darmstadt, 1S1CK5. Kiistler. 39 pp.; 18 flgs. 8vo. Bourelly, La France militaire monumentale. l'aris, 1900, Combet. viii, 232 pp.; 41 flgs. 8vo. B. Brand. Bau ilenkmaler, Bischdfc und Landesherreu, KUnstler und Wappen, welche flir die Bau-und Kunstgeschichte Wiirzburgs besoiulers in Betraclit kommen. VViirzburg, 1906. Selbstverlag. 42 pp.; flgs. 8vo.

R. Bruck, Die Malereien in den Handschriften des Kiinigr. Sachsen. Dresden, 1900, Meinhold & Siihne. vii, 469 pp.; 1 pi.; 283 flgs. 8vo.

M. 25. H. Bulle, Einfuhrung in die Kgl. Gemalde-galerie Erlangen. Erlangen, 1906, Fr. Junge. 42 pp.

C. H. Caffin, How to Study Pictures. New York, 1906, The Centurv Co. xv, 513 pp.; 56 flgs. 8vo. 82.00.

G. Caprin, Trieste (Italia ar tistica). Triest, 1906, F. H. Schimpfl. 148 pp.; 139 flgs. 8vo.

M. 4. G. Carocci, II Valdarno da Firenze al Mare (Italia artistica). Bergamo. 1906, Istit. ital. d' arti graflche. 146 pp.; 138 flgs. 8vo. ——Catalogue de la Collection des portraits francais et Strangers conservee au Department des Estampes de la Bibliotheque Nationale. Commence par G. Duplessis, continue par G. Rlat. Vols. VI-VII (complete in 8 vols.). Paris, 1906-07, Rapilly. 8vo. Catalogue rai sonne de la collection Martin Le Roy (Moyen Sge et Renaissance), publie sous la direction de J. J. Marquet de Vasselot. Fasc. II: Ivoires et sculptures par R. Koechlln. Paris, 1906, Foulard. 134 pp.; 38 pis. 4to. A. Colasanti,

L' Aniene (Italia artistica). Bergamo, 1906, Istit. ital. d' arti graflche. 128 pp.; 105 flgs. 8vo.

P. Corberon, Auxerre: sa cathedrale, ses monuments. Guide du touriste. Auxerre. 1906, Lanier. 96 pp.; 23 flgs. 8vo. G. Cri vellari, Milano e dintorni: profllo storico con carta topographica delle epoche pre-romana, romana, medioevale e moderna. Milan, 1906,

Sacchi e flgli. H. H. Cunyng hame, European Enamels. London, 1906, Methuen. 204 pp. 8vo. — On the Theory and Practice of ArtEnamelling upon Metals. 3d ed. New York. 1900, Macmillan. xxlv, 188 pp.; ill. 12mo. $2.00.

G. Dehio, Handbuch der deutschen Kunstdenkmaler. I Bd. Mitteldeutschland. Berlin, 1906, Was muth. ix, 360 pp.; map. 8vo.

G. Dehio and G. Bezold. Die Denkmiiler der deutschen Bildhauerkunst. 1st series. Fasc. 2. Berlin, 1906,

Wasmuth. 20 pis. 4to.-J. De stree, Tapisseries et sculptures bruxelloiscs a l'exposition d'art ancien bruxellois organisee ft Bruxelles au cercle artistique et litteraire de julllet a octobre 1905. Brussels, 1906, G. van Oest et Cie. 93 pp.; 50 pi.; figs. Folio. 75 f r.

Documents classes de l'art dans les Pays-Bas du X an XIX" siecle. recueillis par A. Weissmann. architecte, formant suite a l'ouvrage de feu J. J. van Ysendyck, Fasc.V-VIII. (Complete in 144 pis.) Haarlem, 1906, Kleinmann. Pis. 25 48. Folio. Each fasc. 3 fr. O.

Doering, Braunschweig (Beriihmte Kunststatten). Leipzig, 1906, E. A. Seemann. 136 pp.; 118 figs. 8vo.

B. Ebhardt, Deutsche Burgen. Fasc. 8. Berlin, 1906, Wasmuth. Pp. 837-384; 4 pis.; flgs. 4to.

J. Fogolari, Cividale del Friull (Italia artistica). Bergamo, 1906, 1st. ital. d'artigraf. 138 pp.; 143 figs. 8vo.

A. Forestier and G. W. T. Omond, Bruges and West Flanders. New York, 1906, Macmillan. x, 187 pp.; 37 colored plates. 8vo. $3.00.

E. Fritze, Dorfbilder. (Neue Beitrfige zur Gesch. Deutschen Altertums.) Meiningen, 1906, Brtickner & Renner. 101 pp.; map; 50 flgs. 8vo. M. 2.50.

Fiihrer durcli die k. Staatssammlung vaterlandischerKunst-u. Altertumsdenkmfiler in Stuttgart. 2d ed. Stuttgart, 1906, H. Lindemann. xi, 126 pp.; plan; 25 flgs. 8vo. 70 pf.

Die Galerien Europas, Farbige Nachbildungen alter Meister. Fasc. 1-5 (complete in 25 fasc). Leipzig, 1906, Seemann. Each fasc. 9 pp.; 8 pis. 4to. C. Garces y Vera,

Guia ilustrada Toledo publicada por le Touriste. Madrid, 1906, Marzo. 45 pp.; flgs.; map. 4to. 2 pesetas.

Die Gemalde-Galerie der konlgl. Museen zu Berlin. With expl. text by J. Meyer, W. Bode, H. von Tschudi, and others. Berlin, 1906, Grote. 22 fasc. each 20 pp.; flgs., and 6 pis. M. 30. Die GemaldeGalerie des Prado in Madrid. Text by K. Voll. (Complete in 14 fasc.) Munich, 1906, Hanfstaengl. Each fasc. 84 pis. w. text. 4to. Each fasc. M. 40. Gemalde alter

Meister im Besitze Sr. Maj. des deutschen Kaisers u. Konigs von Preussen. Unter Mitwirkung von W. Bode, und M. J. Friedlander heraugs. von P. Seidel. In 24 fasc. with 200 figs. Fasc. 1-12. Berlin, 1906, K. Bong. M. 5 each. A.

Genewein, Vom Romanischen bis zum Empire. Eine Wanderung durch die Kunstformen dieser Stile. Leipzig, 1906, Rothbarth. 140 pp.; 295 flgs. 8vo. O. H. Giglioli,

Empoll artistica. (La Toscana Illustrata.) Florence, 1906, Lumachi. 304 pp.; 30 flgs. 16mo.

T. Guedy. Manuel pratique du collectioneur de tableaux comprenant: les principales ventes des XVIII, XIX siecles jusqu'a nos jours des oauvres des peintres de toutes les ecoles. Signatures et monogrammes. Paris, 1906, Laurens, 164 pp. 8vo.

A. Hallays, Nancy. Paris, 1906, Laurens. 144 pp.; 118 flgs. 8vo.

Hauptwerke der Bibliothek des Kunstgewerbe-Museums (Berlin). Fasc. 1: Mobel und Holzarbeiten. 3d ed. Berlin, 1906, G. Reimer.

29 pp. 8vo. 35 pf. A. Haus mann and E. Polaczek, Denkmaler der Baukunst in Elsass vom Mittelalter bis zum 18. Jahrh. Fasc. 15-20 (last), each 5 pis. and text. Strasburg, 1906, Heinrlch. viii, 123 pp.; 6 pis.; flgs. 4to. J.

Helbig, L'art mosan depuis l'introduction du christianisme jusqu'a la fln du XVIII" siecle. Pub. par les soins de P. Brassinne. T. I. Des origines a la fln du XV siecle. Brussels, 1906, G. van Oest. 147 pp.; 36 pis.; flgs. 4to. E.

Hintze, Die Breslauer Goldschmiede. Eine archival. Studie. Leipzig, 1906, K. W. Hiersemann. viii, 215 pp.; 6 pi.; 40 flgs. 4to.

M. 20. A. von Holder, Die Reichenauer Handschriften, beschrieben u. erlfiutert. I Bd. Die Pergamenthandschriften (Handschr. der grossherzogl. badischen Hof-u. Landsbibliothek in Karlsruhe). Leipzig, 1906, Teubner. ix, 642 pp. 8vo. M. 20. C. Holland, Wessex. London, 1906, A. & C. Black. xii. 280 pp.: 75 pis.

8vo. G. Home, Normandy. London, 1906, Dent. xvi. 248 pp.; 25 pis.; flgs. 4to. E. Hutton,

The Cities of Spain. London, 1906, Methuen. xvi, 324 pp.; 44 pis. 8vo.

Italienische Forschungen. herausg. von dem Kunsthistorischen Institut in Florenz. Vol. I. Berlin, 1906, Casstrer. xiii, 388 pp.; 3 pis.; flgs. 8vo. M. 16.

A. Jacquot, Essai de repertoire des artistes lorrains. Les orfevres, les joalliers, les argentiers, les potiers detain lorrains. Paris, 1906, Libr. de l'art anc. et mod. 33 pp.; flgs.

8vo. Mrs. Henry Jenner, Christ in Art. London, 1906. Methuen. xii, 186 pp.; 39 pis. 16mo. G. Kahn, Das Weib in der Karikatur Frankreichs. Fasc. 1 (complete in 20 fasc). Stuttgart, 1906, H. Schmidt. 24 pp.; 5 pis. 8vo. M.l.

Katalog der Kunst-Sammlung des Herrn von Niesewand. Gemfilde, Minaturen, Mobel, etc. Bonn, 1906, M. Lempertz. vii, 38 pp.; 15 pis.; llgs. M. 5. F. Kopera, Miniatures of Polish origin. Cracow, 1906. 28 pp.; ill. Polish. L. von Kunowski, Durch Kunst zum Leben. V. Bd.: Licht und Helligkeit. Mit 8 rythm. Studien von Gertr. von Kunowski. Jena, 1906,

Diederichs. 390 pp.; ill. 8vo.

Kunst-und AHertumsdenkmale Wiirttembergs. Vol. I. Neckarkreis. v. E. Paulus. Iv, 624 pp.; HI. 8vo. M. 18. — Ergitnzungs-Atlas. Fasc. 13-15. Esslingen, 1906, P. Neff.

4 to. Kunstdenkmaler des Gross herzogthums Baden. Vol. IV. Kreis Mosbach. Part 4. A. von Oechelhauser: Die Kunstdenkmaler der Amtsbezz. Mosbach u. Eberbach. Tubingen, 1906, J. C. B. Mohr. il, 231 pp.; 21 pis.; map; 144 flgs. 8vo. SI. 6.50. Kunstdenkmaler des kbnigr. Bayerns. II. Bd.: Reg.-Bez. Oberpfalz u. Regensburg. Herausg. v. G. Hager. Fasc. 1-5. Munich, 1906, R. Oldenbourg. xxxii, 844 pp.; pis.; flgs. 8vo. Kunstdenkmaler der Prov. Hannover. Herausg. v. Carl Wolfl. III.: Reg.-Bez. Liineburg. Bearb. v. F. Kriiger u. W. Reinecke. Hanover, 1900, Th. Schulze. xvi, 435 pp.; 12 pis.; 190 flgs. 8vo. M. 12.

Die Kunstdenkmaler der

Rheinprovinz. Herausg. von Paul Clemen. V. Bd. 3 Abt.: Die Kunstdenkmaler der Stadt und des Kreises Bonn, v. P. Clemen, vii, 403 pp.; 29 pis. ; 367 flgs. VIII. Bd. 3 Abt.: Die Kunstdenkmaler des Kreises Heinsberg, von K. Franck u. E. Kenard. vi, 171 pp.; 8 pis.; 116 flgs. Dtisseldorf, 1906, Schwann.

8vo. Das alte Kunsthandwerk,

Verzeichnis v. den ausgestellten Gegenstiinden auf der 8. deutschen Kunstgewerbe Ausstellung, Dresden 1906. Dresden, 1906, W. Baensch. xii, 228 pp. ; 8 pis. 8vo. M.l.

Kurzer Fiihrer durch das Reichsmuseum zu Amsterdam. Nach der Bearbeitung von W. P. Brons. Amsterdam, 1906, von Holkema & Warendorf. 124 pp.; 2 plans.

8vo. Kurzgefasste geschicht liche Darstellung der Malerei, Portrait und Lebenslauf der bertihmtesten Meister.

Namenverzeichnis hervorrag. Klinstler aller Zeiten. Berlin, 1906, Wichmann-Riesenburg. 51 pp.; 11 pis.; flgs. 4to. !. Lacher, Altsteirische Wohnraume im Landesmuseum zu Graz. Leipzig, 1906, Hiersemann. 32 pis. with text. Folio, xi. 40. M. Lang lois, Le Musee de Chartres. Chartres, 1906, Soc. arch. d'Eure-etLoire. 71 pp.; map.; 28 flgs. 16mo.

G. de Lorenzo, Venosa e la regione de Vulture (Italia artistica). Bergamo, 1906, Istit. ital. d' arti graf. 116 pp.; 120 flgs. 8vo.

;. von Mach, Outlines of the History of Painting from 1200 to 1900 A.d. New York, 1906, Ginn & Co. 186 pp. 4to. 81. 65. F. Malaguzzi

Valeri, Milano (Italia artistica). Bergamo, 1906. Istit. ital. d'arti graf. 170 pp. ; 155 flgs. 8vo. — Bergamo (Italia artistica). Bergamo, 1906, Istit. ital. d' arti graf. 162 pp.; 140 flgs. 8vo.-H. Martin,

Les Miniaturistes francais. Paris, 1906, Leclerc. viii, 246 pp.; 35 flgs. 8vo H. J. and L. J. Masse, Oxford. (Langham Series.) London, 1906, Siegle, Hill & Co. viii, 112 pp.; 11 pis. 16mo.—
—-A. Maurel, Petites villes d'ltalie (Toscane, Venetie). Paris. 1905, Hachette.

307 pp. lfimo. P. J. Meier and

K. Steinacker, Die Bau-und Kunstdenkmaler der Stadt Braunschweig (mit Ausschluss der Sammlungen). Herausg. vom Geschichtsverein f. das Herzogt. Braunschweig. Wolfenbuttel, 1906, J. Zwissler. iii, 150 pp.; flgs. 8vo. M. 1.20.

Meisterwerke alter Kunst aus dem Besitz von Mitgliedern des Kaiser-Friedrich-Museum-Vereln8 in Berlin. Berlin, 1906, Photogr. Gesellschaft. 29 pis. 8vo. Meisterwerke der fiirstl. Lieclitensteinischen GemSldegalerie in Wien. Berlin, 1906, Photogr. Gesellschaft. 48 pis. with text. Folio.

Meisterwerke der Kunst aus

Sachsen u. Thliringen. Herausg. von O. Doering and G. Voss. Magdeburg, 1906, Bacnsch jun. 118 pp.; 129 pis.; figs. M. 60.

Moderner Cicerone, Berlin 1:

Das Kaiser-Friedrich-Museum. Stuttgart, 1906, Union, xli, 407 pp.; 2 plans; 276 figs. 16mo.

K. Moklowski and M. Sokolowski,

On the History of religious Architecture in Ked Russia. Cracow, 1906. 30 pp.; ill. Folio. Russian.

P. Molmenti, La Storia di

Venezia nella vita privata. Part II. La Splendore. Bergamo, 1906. Istit. Ital. d' arti graf. 656 pp.; 44 pis.; ligs. 8vo. P. de Mont, Le

Musee des Enluminures. Fasc. II-V. (Fasc. IV-V. Livre d'heures d'Hennessy.) Haarlem, 1906, Kleinmann. Each fasc. 20 pis.

with text. Folio. A. MuHoz,

Monument! d' arte mediaevale e moderna. Rome, April, 1906, Danesi. 4 pis. 4to. Monthly.

Le Music d'Amsterdam, Fasc.

1-9 (complete in 15 fasc). Buiksloot, 1906, J. M. Schalekamp. Each fasc. 4 pis. Folio.

Nieubarn, Die Verherrlichung des hi. Dominikus in der Kunst. Gladbach, 1906, B. Kuhlen. 39 pp.; 32 pi. in portf. 4to. M. 20. Ella

Noyes, The Casentino and its Story. London, 1906, Dent, xii, 330 pp.; 25 pis.; figs. 4to.

G. W. T. Omont, see A. Forestier.

A. M. Pachinger, Die Mutterschaft in der Malerei u. Graphik. Introd. by G. Klein. Munich, 1906, G. Miiller. 212 pp.; 130 figs. 8vo.

M. 8. A. Palmieri, Gil antichi castelli comunali dell' Appenino bolognese. Bologna, 1906, Beltrami. 40 pp.; ill. 8vo. N.

Pelicelli, Guida storica artistica e monumentale della citta di Parma. Parma, 1906, Battel, xxv, 279 pp.; plan; figs. 16mo. P. Pert zow, Venezia. St. Petersburg, 1906.

90 pp.; 25 pis. 8vo. O. Piper,

Burgenkunde. Bauwesen und Geschichte der Burgen zuniichst innerhalb des deutschen Sprachgebietes. 2d rev. ed. Part II. Fasc. VXI. Munich, 1906, R. Piper & Co. pp. 383-755; ill. 8vo. M. 14. — Oesterreichische Burgen. 4 Teil. Vienna, 1906, Holder, vi. 252 pp.; 260 figs. 8vo.

J. J. Raven, The Bells of England. London, 1906, Methuen. 354 pp. 8vo. J. Ross, Florentine Pal aces and their Stories. London, 1906, Dent. 426 pp.; 30 figs. 8vo.

W. Rothes, Die Madonna in ihrer Verherrlichung durch die bildende Kunst. Cologne, 1906, Bachem. xv, 160 pp.; 128 figs. 8vo. The Royal Collection of Paintings at Buckingham Palace and Windsor Castle. With introd. and text by L. Cust. Vol. I. Buckingham Palace. Vol. II. Windsor Castle. London, 1906, Heinemann. 92; 180 pis. Folio.

Schweizerisches Kiinstler Lexikon. herausg. v. (I. Brun. Fasc. 2-5. Frauenfcld, 1906, Hubei. 8vo.

H. Sepp, Bibliographic der bayerischen Kunstgeschichte bis Ende 1905. Strassburg, 1906, Heitz. ix, 345 pp. 8vo. M. Sokolowski,

K. Worobjew, and J. Zubozyck. Churches and fortified cemeteries in Poland. Cracow, 1906. 48 pp.; 28 figs. Folio. Polish. P. Sos son and J. Nickers, La trfisor de l'6glise cathedrale de Saint-Aubin *h* Namur. Namur, 1906, V. Delvaux. viii. 119 pp.; ill. 18mo. 1.50 fr.

W. S. Sparrow, Apostles in Art. New York, 1906, Stechert. Folio. 91.25. E. Staley, The Guilds of Florence. London, 1906, Methuen. xxvi. 626 pp.; 75 pis. 8vo. W.

S. Stoughton, The Old Testament in Art, from the Creation of the World to the Death of Moses. London, 1906, Hodder & Stoughton. 252 pp.; 22 pis.; figs. 4to. C.

W. Stubbs. Cambridge and its Story. London, 1906, Dent, xviii, 302 pp.; 24 pis.; 30 figs. 4to. R. Sturgis,

The Appreciation of Pictures. London, 1906, Batsford. 308 pp. 8vo.

W. Suida, Genua (BerUhmte Kunststatten). Leipzig, 1906, Seemann. xii, 205 pp.; 148 figs. 8vo.

M. 4. I. B. Supino, GH albori dell' arte fiorentina. Architettura. Florence, 1906, Alinari. 180 pp.; 37 pis.; 17 tigs. 8vo.

L. Testi, Parma (Italia artistica). Bergamo, 1906, Istit. ital. d' arti graf. 134 pp.; 130 figs. 8vo

Margaret Thomas, How to judge Pictures. London, 1906, Treherne. 190 pp. 8vo.

Von nordischer Volkskunst, Beitrage zur Erforschg. der volkstuml. Kunst in Skandinavien, Schleswig-Holstein, in den Klistengebieten der Ost-u. Nordsee sowie in Holland. Gesammelte Aufsitze, heransg. v. Karl Miihlke. Berlin, 1906. W. Ernst & Sohn. vl, 252 pp.; 336 flgs. 8vo. M. 5.schreibendes Verzeichniss seiner Gemiilde mit Nachbildungen. Geschichte seines Lebens und seiner Kunst, miter Mitwirkung von B. Hopstcde deGroot. VIII Bd. (end). Also in French and English editions. Paris, 1906, Sedelmeyer. vi, 340 pp.; (il pl. Folio. — Rembrandt und seine Zeitgenossen. Charakterbilder der grossen Meister der hollilndischen und vlamischen Malerschule in siebzehnten Jahrhundert. Leipzig, 1906, E. A. Seemann. ii,

W. G. Waton, Five Italian Shrines. With an Essay on Early Tuscan Sculpture. London, 1906, Murray.

ill. 8vo. A. Weese, MUnchen (Beruhmte Kunststatten). Leipzig, 1906, Seemann. viii, 248 pp.; 160 flgs. 8vo. Werke alter Meister, 500 Reproduktionen nach Originalen aus europ. Galerien. Berlin, 1906,

Globus-Verlag. 504 pp. 4to.

T. A. Wigram, Northern Spain. London, 1906, A. & C. Black, xvi, 311 pp.; 75 pis. 8vo. M. G.

Wildeman. Itineraire archeologique de Delft. 2d rev. ed. Delft, 1906, J. Vis, Jr. 97 pp.; ill. 8vo. 0.7511.

A. von Wiirzbach, Niederlan disches KUnstler-Lexikon. Mit mehr ais 3000 Monogrammen. Vol. I. Vienna, 1906, Halm and Goldmann. viii, 778 pp. 8vo. M. 40.

E. Zabel, St. Petersburg. (BerBhmte Kunststatten.) Leipzig, 1906, E. A. Seemann. viii, 126 pp.; 105 flgs. 8vo.

n. EARLY CHRISTIAN, BYZANTINE, AND MEDIAEVAL

D. Ajnalow, Monuments of the Christian Chersonese. Pt. 1: Ruins of Churches. Moscow, 1906. 4to. 4 rbls. Russian.

C. Barreca, Le catacombe di S. Giovanni in Siracusa. Syracuse, 1906, tip. del Tamturo. A.

Baudot and A. Perrault Dabot, Les Cathfidrales de France. Fasc. 3. Paris, 1906, Laurens. 25 pis. Folio.

A. Bauer and J. Strzygowski, Eine Alexandrinische Weltchronik: Text u. Miniaturen eines griechischen Papyrus der Sammlung W. Goleniscer. Vienna, 1906, Gerold. 204 pp.; 8 pis.; 36 flgs. Folio.

F. Baumgarten, Das Freiburger Minster beschrieben u. knnstgeschichtlich gewlirdigt Stuttgart, 1906, Seifert. vii, 59 pp.; 9 pis.; plan. 8vo. M. 0.75.-A. Baumstark,

Abendliindische Palastinapilger des ersten Jahrtausends und ihre Berichte. Eine kulturgeschichtliche Skizze. Cologne, 1906, Bachem. xii, 88 pp. 8vo. J. de Baye,

Quelques emaux occidentaux conserves au Musee imperial historique de Moscou. Paris. 1906, Nilsson. 187 pp.; ill. 8vo. D. Beljaew,

Byzantina. Vol. 3: The Processions of the Byzantine Emperors to the City and Suburban Churches of Constantinople. St. Petersburg, 1906. 2 pis.; 27 flgs. Russian.

M. Bendiner, Das Strassburger Miinster, seine Baugeschichte u. Beschreibung. Stuttgart, 1906, W. Seifert. 40 pp.; 17 pis. 8vo. 75 pf.

R. Bernoulli, Die romanische Portalarchitektur in der Provence. (Zur Kunstgeschichte des Auslandes.) Strassburg, 1906, Heitz. viii, 87 pp.; map; 19 flgs. 8vo. M. 4. F. Bond, Gothic Architecture in England. New York, 1906, Scribner. 804 pp.; ill. 8vo. $ 12.00. R. Borrmann, Aufnah men mittelalterlicher Wand-und Deckenmalereien in Deutschland. Unter Mitwirkung von H. Kolb und 0. Vorlaender heransg. II. Bd. 1. Lfg. Berlin, 1906. Wasmuth. 6 pp.; 7 pis.; flgs. Folio. H.

Bouvier, Histoire de lVglise et de l'ancien archidiocese de Sens. T. I: Des origines a l'an 1122. Paris, 1906,

Picard. xix, 475 pp. 8vo. L.

Brehier, Les Basiliques chr£tiennes. Paris, 1906, Blond & Cie. 65 pp.; ill. 16mo. — Les Eglises byzantines. Paris, 1906, Blond & Cie. 64 pp.; ill. 16mo. — Les Eglises gothiques. Paris, 1906, Blond & Cie. 64 pp.; ill. 16mo. — Les Eglises romanes. Paris, 1906, Blond & Cie. 61 pp.; ill. 16mo. A.

E. Brinckmann, Baumstilisierungen in der mittelalterlichen Malerei. Strassburg, 1906, Heitz. vii, 54 pp.; 9 pis. 8vo.

W. Brockhoff, Studien zur Geschichte der Stadt Ephesos vom IV. nachchristlichen Jahrhundert bis zu ihrem Untergang in der ersten Halfte des XV. Jahrhunderts. Jena, 1905. 78 pp. 8vo.

Dissertation. G. Baldwin Brown, The Arts in Early England. Vol. Ill: The Decorative Arts of the Anglo-Saxon Period. London. 1906, Murray. 8vo. Edith A.

Browne, Gothic Architecture. New York, 1906, Macniillan. xvi, 125 pp.; 48 flgs. 8vo. 81.75.

F. Cabrol, Dictionnaire d'archeologie chretienne et de Iiturgie. T. I. Fasc. 9-11 (Antiphone — Azymes). Paris, 1906. Letonzey et Ane Cols. 2465-3274; 6 pis. ; flgs. 8vo.

D. C. Calthrop, English Costume. Vol. 1, Early English. London, 1906, A. & C. Black, xiv, 80 pp.; figs. 8vo. E. Calvi, Bibliografla generate dl Roma. Vol. 1: Bibliografla di Roma nel medio evo (4761499). Rome, 1906, E. Loescher &

Co. xxiii, 175 pp. 8vo. M. C.

Catalano, L' Arte cristiana primltiva. Vol. II. Naples, 1906, D'Auria.

1. Cledat, Le Monastere et la

Necropole de Baouit. Fasc. 2. Cairo, 1006. 73 pis. Folio. 130 fr. G. H. Clerambault, Les Donjons romanes de la Touraine et de ses frontieres. Paris, 1906, Picard.

55 pp.; 4 pis. 4tO. Codices e

Vaticanis select! phototypice expressi, iussu Pii PP. X consilio et opera curatorum bibliothecae Vaticanae. Milan, 1906, Hoepli. Vol. IV. Bibl. SS. Graec. Cod. Vat. 1209 (Cod. B): Pars. I. Testam. vetus Tom. II-III. Pp. 395-1234. 4to. M. 256. —Vol. V. Cod. Vat. Pal. Graec. 431. 39 pp.; 31 pis. Folio. M. 128.—Vol. VII. M. Cornelii Frontonis aliorumque reliquiae quae codice Vat. 5250 rescripto continentur. 31 pp.; 286 pis.

Folio. Collezione paleografica Vaticana. Fasc. I: Le Miniature della Bibbia, Codice Regniense Greco I, e del Salterio, codice Palatlno Greco 381. Milan, 1906, Hoepli. 28 pp.; 22 pis. 4to. 55 fr.

C. Diehl, Figures byzantines. Paris, 1906, A. Colin. 343 pp. 8vo. 3.50 fr.

G. Gerola, L' Arte veneta a Creta. Rome, 1906. vii, 117 pp.; 135 flgs. 8vo.

E. Happel, Romanische Bauwerke in Niederhessen. Kassel, 1906, C. Vietor. 110 pp.; 24 drawings. 8vo.

M. 1.50. A. Haseloff, Die Kaiserinnengraber in Andria; ein Beitrag zur apulischen Kunstgeschichte unter Friedrich II. Rome, 1905, Loescher. viii, 61 pp.; 9 pis. 8vo.

E. Herzig, Die longobardischen Fragmente in der Abtei S. Pletro in Ferentillo (Umbrien). Rome, 1906. 37 pp.; 7 figs. 8vo. A. Holtmeyer, Cisterzienserkirchen Thtiringens (Beitrage zur Kunstgeschichte Thtiringens). Jena, 1906, G. Fischer, viii, 407 pp.; table; 177 figs. 8vo. M. 8. Homeri

Iliad is plctae fragmenta Ambrosiana phototypice edita cura doctorum Ant. M. Ceriani et Ach. Ratti.

Milan, 1906, U. Hoepli. 44 pp.; 104 pis.; oblong 8vo.

O. Jozzi, Roma sotterranea. II cimetero di S. Castolo M. sulla via Labicana a un miglio da Porta Maggiore descritto ed illustrato. Rome, 1905. plan; 20 pis. Folio. 20 fr.

C. M. Kaufmann, Die Ausgrabung der Menas-Heiligtiimer in der Mareotiswiiste. I Periode: November, 1905-June, 1906. Cairo, 1906, Diemer. 107 pp.; 54 figs. 8vo. M.7.50.

F. Kempe and K. Schuster,

Das Freiburger Monster. Ein Fiihrer fiir Einheimische und Fremde. Freiburg i. Br., 1906, Herder. 232 pp.; 93 figs.; plan. P. Kondakoff, Representations of the Russian Knias family in miniatures of the XI century. St. Petersburg, 1906. 6pis.; 13figs. 2rbl. Russian. A. Kriicke, Der Nimbus und verwandte Attribute in der frdhchristlichen Kunst (Zur Kunstgeschichte des Auslandes). Heft 35. Strassburg, 1905, J. H. E. Heitz. 145 pp. ; 7 pis. 8vo. K. Kunstle, Die

Kunst des Klosters Reichenau im IX. und X. Jahrh. und der neuentdeckte karolingische Gemaldezykhis zu Goldbach bei Ueberlingen. Freiburg i. B., 1906, Herder, viii, 62 pp.; 4 pis. 4to. M. 20.

Graf Karl Lanckoronski, Der Dom von Aquileja, sein Bau u. seine Geschichte. Unter Mitwirkung von G. Niemann u. H. Swoboda. Vienna, 1906, Gerlach & Wiedling. xiii, 162 pp.; 22 pis.; 97 flgs. M. 2.50.

H. Lehmann, Zur Geschichte der Glasmalerei in der Schweiz. Part I: Ihre Entwicklung bis zum Schlusse des 14. Jahrh. (Mitt, der antiq. Gesellschaft in Zurich.) Zurich, 1906, Fftsi & Berr. 56 pp.; 8 pis.; 32 flgs. 4to. M. 4. O. von Leixner, Lehrbuch der Baustile. Mit besonderer Berucksichtigung des architektonischen und technischen Details. II. Bd.: Die Baukunst des Mittelalters. Leipzig, 1906. vi, 227 pp.; 32 pis.; 56 flgs. 4to. Lemaire, Les origines du style gothique en Brabant. Part I: L'architecture romane. Brussels, 1906, Vromant. xi, 312 pp.; 199 tigs. 4to. A. Lindner, Der Dom zu KOln und seine Kunstschatze. Introd. by M. C. Nieuwbarn. Haarlem, 1906, Kleinmann. vii, v, 50 pp.; 50 pis. Folio.

J. Mantuani, see Premerstein.

A. Michel, Histoire de l'art depuis les premiers temps Chretiens jusqu'a nos jours. Vol. I, Part II: Des debuts de l'art Chretien a la lln de la periode romane: Vol. II, Part I: Formation, expansion et evolution lie l'art gothique. Paris, 1906, Colin. Vol. I, Part II, pp. 443957; pis. vi-xii; figs. 208-171. Vol. II, Part I, pp. 1-520; pis. i-v; figs. 1-333. 4to. F. Miltoun,

The Cathedrals of the Hhine. London, 1906, Johnson & Ince. 388 pp.; 111. 8vo. K. Mohrmann and F.

Eichwede, Germanische Fruhkunst. Fasc. 9. Leipzig, 1906, Tauchnitz. 10 pis. with text. 4to. A. Mu

Doz, L'Art byzantin a l'exposition de Grottaferrata. Rome, 1906, Danesi. 195 pp.; 3 pis.; 146 tigs. — I codici greci miniati delle minori biblioteche di Koma. Leipzig, 1905, Brockhaus. 100 pp.; ill. 8vo. M.4.

P. Perdrizet, La peinture religieuse en Italic jusqu'a la fin du XIV» siecle. Lemons professees a l'universitfi de Nancy. Nancy. 1906, Imp. de l'Est.

Louise Pillon, Les Soubassements des portails lateraux a la cathedrale de Kouen. Paris, 1906, Laurens. 150 pp.; 40 figs. 8vo. 5 fr. —— A. de Premerstein, C. Wessely, J. Mantuani, De codicis Dioscuridei Aniciae Julianae, nunc Vindobonensis Med. Gr. I historia forma plcturis moderante J. de Karabacek scripserunt. Levden. 1906, Sijthoff. 491 pp.; 3 pis.; 6 figs. 4to. M. 17. E.J. Prior, The Cathedral Builders of England. London, 1906, Seeley. 112 pp.; ill. 8vo.

C. Romussi, II duomo di Milano nella storia e nell' arte. Milan, 1906, Sonzogno. 245 pp.; figs. 16mo.

H. Rousseau, Esquisses d'art monumental. Le moyen age. Brussels, 1906, O. Schepens & Cie. 842 pp.; ill. 8vo. 3. 50 fr.

H. Schetelig, The Cruciform Brooches of Norway. Bergen, 1906, Cani meyer. 162 pp.; 194 tigs. 3 kr.

F. Schmidt, Ueber den Ursprung des romanlschen Baustile. Munich, 1906. 83 pp.; ill. 8vo.Dissertation.

A. Seyler, Die mittelalterliche Plastikin Regcnsburg. Munich, 1906. 115 pp. Dissertation. R. Stet tiner, Die lllustrierten PrudentlusHandschriften. Berliu, 1905, G.

Grote. 22 pp.; 200 pis. 4to. J. Strzygowski, Die Miniaturen des serbisclien Psalters der kiinigl. Hof-und Staatsbibliothek in Mfinchen. Einleitung v. V. Jagic (Denkschriften der k. Akademie der Wisscnschaften). Vienna, 1906. lxxxvii, 139 pp.; 62 pis.; 43 figs. 4to. M. 42. Studien iiber christliche Denkmaler. herausg. v. J. Ficker. III. Dasgeographische Mosaik von Madaba von A. Jacoby. Leipzig, 1905. ix, 110 pp.; map; 4 figs. M. 4. L. von Sybel, Christliche Antike. Einfiihrung in die altchr. Kunst. I Bd. Einleitendes. Katakomben. Marburg, 1906, Elwet. vi-ii. 308 pp.; 4 pis.; 55 figs. 8vo. M. 7. A. Venturi, Storia dell' arte italiana. Vol. V: La pittura del trecento e le sue origini. Milan. 1900, Hoepli. xxxvi, 1073 pp. ; 818 figs. 4to. M. 30.

C. Wessely, see Premerstein.

Jos. Wittig, Die altchristlichen Skulpturen im Museum der deutschen Nationalstiftung am Campo Santo in Rom. Festschrift zur Silberhochzeit des deutschen Kaiserpaares. (Supplement der *R'om. Quart.)* Rome, lifOO, Typographia Polyglotta. 144 pp.; 0 pis.; 68 figs. 4to. M. 15.

J. Zeiller, Les origines chrfetiennes dans la province romaine de Dalmatie. (Bihliotheque de l'Ecole des Hautes fctmles. Sciences historiques et philologiques. Fasc. 156). Paris, 1900, E. Champion, xviii, 188 pp. 8vo. 289 pp. 8vo. P. de Bonchaud, Tableau de la sculpture italienne au xvi' siècle, Jean de Bologne (15241608). Fin de la Renaissance. Paris, 1906, Lemerre, 348 pp.

16mo. Das Breviarium Gri mani in der Bibliothek von S. Marco in Venedig. Vollstandige Reproduktion herausg. v. Scato de Vries u. S. Morperrgo. I-V Bd Leipzig, 1906, Hiersemann. Complete in 12 vols, containing 1568 pis. M. 2400.

Julia Cartwright, Raphael. London, 1906, Duttou. 229 pp.; ill. 24mo. $0.75. A. Christian, Études sur le Paris d'autrefois. III. Ecrivains et Miniaturistes: Les Primitifs de la peinture; Les Origines de l'imprimerie; La Décoration du Livre. Paris, 1906, Champion. 269 pp. 8vo. G. Clausse, Les Farnèse peints par Titien. New York, 1906, Bouton. 15 flgs. 8vo. $3.00.

G. Clinch, St. Paul's Cathedral, London. London, 1906, Methuen. 246 pp. 12mo. H. Cochin, Le Bienheureux Fra Giovanni Angelico de Fiesole (Les Saints). Paris, 1906, Lecoffre. x, 285 pp.; 2 figs.

16mo. Codex Escurialensis. Ein Skizzenbuch aus der Werkstatt Domenico Ghirlandaios. Unter Mitwirkung von C. Huelsen u. A. Michaelis hrsg. v. H. Egger (Sonderschriften des ôsterreichischen archilogischen Institutes in Wien, Bd. 4). Vienna, 1906, A. Holder. 2 vols. I. 174 pp.; 70 flgs.; 4 pis. II. 143 pp.; 137 flgs. 4to. M. 38. L. Coletti, Arte senese. Treviso, 1906, Zoppelli.

125 pp.; 10 pis.; flgs. 8vo. S. Colvin, Early Engraving and Engravers in England (1545-1695). A critical and historical Essay. London, 1906, Quaritch. 170 pp.; 41 pis.; 46 flgs. Folio. Kenyon

Cox, Old Masters and New. Essays in Art Criticism. New York, 1906, Dufflled. $1.50 R. H. Hobart Cust, Giovanni Antonio Bazzi (hitherto usually styled "Sodoma"). The Man and the Painter, 1477-1549. London, 1906, Murray.

xviii, 442 pp.; 60 tigs. 8vo. 21n. . R. D'Allemagne, Les Cartes à jouer du XIV au XX siecle. 2 vols. Paris, 1906, Hachette, xv, 504 and 640 pp.; 37 pis.; flgs. -4to.

B. Daun, Veit Stoss (Kunstler Monographien). Bielefeld, 1906, Velhagen & Klasing. 94 pp.; 100 flgs. 8vo. M. 3. —M. Deri, Das Rollwerk in der deutschen Ornamentik des 16 u. 17 Jahrh. Berlin, 1906, Schuster & Beifleb. 97 pp. 8vo. M. 2.—-Dessins anciens des écoles hollandaise et flamande conserves au Cabinet des estampes du Musée de l'Etat à Amsterdam; classes par E. W. Moes. Fasc. 6 and 7. The Hague, 1906, Nijhoff. Paris, Rapilly. Each fasc. 10 pis.

Folio. Ch. Diehl, Botticelli (Les Maîtres de l'art). Paris, 1906, Libr. de l'art anc. et mod. 176 pp.; 24 flgs. 8vo. Drawings from the

Old Masters. First Series. 60 reproductions of drawings in the Albertina, Vienna. London &

Glasgow, 1906, Gowans & Gray.

P. Duhem, Études sur Léonard de Vinci, ceux qu'il a lus et ceux qui l'ont lu. Paris, 1906, Hermann, vii, 359 pp. 8vo.

H. Egger, see Codex Escurialensis. Einblattdrucke des 15 Jahrh.

Herausg. v. P. Heitz. Kolorierte Friihdrucke aus der Stif tsbibliothek in St. Gallen. Introd. by A. Fah. Strassburg, 1906, Heitz. 13 pp.; 43 pis. 4to. M. 80.

Bettina Feistel-Rohmeder, Frauenbilder in der venezianischen Renaissance. Leipzig, 1906, Roth bart. 77 pp.; 10 pis. 8vo.

Fierens-Gevaert, Études sur l'art flamand. La Renaissance septentrionale et les premiers maîtres des Flandres. Brussels, 1906, G. van Oest & Cie. 224 pp.; 106 flgs. 4to. A. Franklin, Dictionnaire historique des arts, metiers et professions exercées dans Paris depuis le XIIP-siecle. Pref. by E. Levassent Paris, 1906, Welter, xxvi, 856 pp. 8vo. W. Fred, Ben venuto Cellini (Die Kunst). Berlin, 1906, Bard, Marquardt & Co. 66 pp.; 16 flgs. 16mo.

P. Gauthiez, Luini (Les grands artistes). Paris, 1906, Laurens. 128 pp.; 24 flgs. 8vo M. Geisberg,

Das iil teste gestochene deutsche Kartenspiel vom Meister der Spielkarten (1446). Strassburg, 1906, Heitz. 56 pp.; 33 pis. 8vo. O. Gerst feldt, Hochzeitsfeste der Henaissance in Itallen (Ftihrer zur Kunst). Esslingen, 1906, Neff. ii, 51 pp.; 3 pis.; 6 flgs. M. 1. H. von

Geymiiller, Das Problem des Heidelberger Schlosses u. seine Gefahren. Baden-Baden, 1906, C. Wild, lit, 77 pp. 8vo. M. 1.50. T. G. T.

Graesse and F. Jaennicke, Guide de l'amateur de porcelaines et de faiences (y compris gres et terrecuites). 2d ed. enlarged. Leipzig, 1906, R. C. Schmidt & Co. ill, 262 pp. 8vo. M. 8. R. Graul, Funfzig Zeichnungen von Rembrandt. Leipzig, 1906, E. A. Seemann. 18 pp.—Rembrandt. Eine Skizze. Leipzig, 1906, E. A. See mann. 41 pp.; 14 flgs. Great

Masters, 100 Reproductions in photogravure of the great masters' masterpieces, selected mainly from private collections. Text by'M. Conway. London, 1906, Heine mann. 100, pis. with text. 4to.

K. Grossmann, Der Gemaldezyklus der Galerie der Maria v. Medici v. Peter Paul Rubens (Zur Kunstgeschlchte des Auslandes). Strassburg, 1906, Heitz. vii, 114 pp.; 9 pis. 8vo. M. 8. G. Guillot, Les Moines precurseurs de Gutenberg. Etude sur l'invention de la gravure sur bois et de l'illustration des livres. Paris, 1906, Blond. 62 pp.; 3 flgs. 16rao.

K. E. Hackenberg, Rembrandt als Germane und Protestant. Leipzig, 1906, J. Baedeker. 48 pp. 8vo.

M. 1.20. R. Hamann, Rem brandts Radierungen. Berlin, 1906, Cassirer. vi-ii, 329 pp.; 2 pis.; 137 flgs. 8vo. M. 12. Handzeich nungen alter Meister aus der Albertina und anderen Sammlungen. Herausg. v. Jos. Meder. XI Bd. Ease. 1-6. Vienna, 1906, F. Schonck.

Each fase. 5 pis. 4to. Hand zeichnungen alter Meister der vUVmischen Schule. XIV, XV, XVI Jahrhundert. Series I, Case. 1-2 (eacli 8 pis). Haarlem, 1906, Klein mann. Folio. Handzeichnungen schweizerischer Meister des XVXVIII Jahrhunderten. Herausg. unter mitw. v. D. Burckhardt u.

H. A. Schmid von P. Ganz. Series I, fasc. 3-4. Series II, fasc. 1. Basel, 1906, Helbing & Lichtenhahn. Each 15 pis. in folio; text in 4to.

C. R. Hartmann, Formenlehre der Renaissance. Ein Lchrbuch f iir das architekton. Zeichnen. 2. Teil. Leipzig, 1906, Gebhardt. viii, 150 pp. 8vo. M. 4.50. Hausschatz deutscher Kunst der Vergangenheit. 2. Aus Rembrandts Radierungen. Introd. by Severin RUttgers. Berlin, 1906, Fischer & Franke. iv pp.; 20 pis. 4to. M. 1. E. Heidrich,

Geschlchte des Diirerschen Marienblldes (Kunstgesch. Monographien). Leipzig, 1906, Hiersemann. xiv, 209 pp. ; 26 flgs. 8vo. M. 11.

Marie Herzfeld, Leonardo da Vinci. Der Denker, Forscher u. Poet. Nach den vcroffentlichten Handschriften. 2d enlarged ed. Jena, 1906, E. Diederichs. clix, 316 pp.; 4 pis. 8vo. M. 10. C. Lewis

Hind, Days with Velasquez. New York, 1906, Macmillan. xii, 160 pp.; 24 flgs. 8vo. $3.00. T. Hoffmann, Bauten des Herzogs Federigo di Montefeltro als Erstwerke der Hochrenaissance. Leipzig, 1906.

220 pp.; 451 flgs. oblong 4to.

C. Hofstede de Groot, Die Urkunden ttber Rembrandt (1575-1721) (Quellenstudien zur hollandischen Kunstgeschichte.) The Hague, 1906, Nijhoff. viii, 524 pp.; 4 pis. 8vo. M. 10. — Dessins originaux par Rembrandt Harmensz van Rljn, reproduits dans les couleurs des originaux. 3d series, vol. II. The Hague, 1906, Nijhofl. 50 pis. Folio.

F. M. Hueffer, Hans Holbein the Younger. London, 1906, Duckworth. 190 pp.; ill. 12mo. C.

Huelsen, see Codex Escurialensis.

G. Imbert, La vita florentina nel seicento secondo memorie sincrone. (1644-1670). Florence, 1906. viii, 307 pp. 8vo.

B. Jacobi, Rembrandt. Ein Verzeichnis der durch Photographie u. Kunstdruck reproduzierten Arbeiten des Meisters. Berlin, 1906, Gesellschaft zur Verbreitung klass. Kunst.

iv, 39 pp. 8vo. M. 1.50. E. Jacobsen, Die "Madonna piccola Gonzaga" (Zur Kunstgeschichte des Anslandes). Strassburg, 1906, J. H. E. Heitz. 21 pp.; 3 pis. 8vo. M. 2.50.

L. Kainzbauer, Holbein der "Verbesserte." Eine neue Untersuchung der beiden Madonnen des Biirgermeisters Meyer in Basel. Munich, 1906, Bruckmann. 28 pp.; 2 pis.

8vo. M. 1. H. v. Kilenyi, Ein wiedergefundenes Bikl des Tizian. Budapest, 1906, F. Kilians Nachf. 81 pp; 7 pis. 8vo. M. 6. E.

Kiihnel, Francesco Botticini (Zur Knnstgescliichte des Anslandes). Strassburg, 1906, Heitz. vi, 70 pp.; 15 pis.; 40 flgs. 8vo. M. 7.

A. Lang, Portraits and Jewels of Mary Stuart. New York, 1906, Macmillan. xiii, 107 pp.; 17 flgs. 8vo. $2.75.

Leonardo da Vinci, Thoughts on Art and Life. Ed. by L. Einstein. Trans, by M. Baring (The Humanists' Library). Boston, 1906,

Merryinount Press. 8vo. $6.00.

G. Ludwig and P. Molmenti, Life and Works of Vittorio Carpaccio. Translated by R. H. Hobart Cnst. London, 1906, Murray. 111. Folio.

£2 12s. 6(7. J. Lydgate, The Assemble of GodUes. Facsimile reproduction of the edition of 1500. Cambridge, 1906, University Press. 90 pp. 8vo. 17s. Gd.

Caret van Mander, Das Leben der niederliindischen und deutschen Maler (Kunstgeschichtliche Studien). Trans, and annot. by H. Floerke. Munich, 1906, G. Miiller.

460 pp.; 20 flgs. M. 15. P. Marcel, Inventaire des papiers manuscrits du cabinet de Robert de Cotte, premier architecte du Roi (1656-1735) et de Jules-Robert de Cotte (1083-1767), conserves a la BibliothequeNationale. Paris, 1906,

Champion, xxx, 268 pp. 8vo.

Masterpieces of Early Flemish Painters; of Rubens; of Reynolds; of Teniers the Younger; of Titian; of van Dyck. Each 1 vol. London, 1906, Go wans & Gray. Each 64 pp.; 60 pis. 16rno. E. von Mayer,

Die Seelc Tizians. Zur Psychologic der Renaissance (Fiihrer zur Kunst). Esslingen, 1906, Nell", iii. 74 pp.; 4 pis. ; 1 fig. 8vo. M. I,

E. McCurdy, The Note-books of Leonardo da Vinci. London, 1906, Duckworth, xiv, 289 pp.; 13 figs. '8vo. Meisterwerke der

Malerei, Alte Meister. 2. Samm lnng. Pref. and text bv W. Bode. Fasc. 12-20. Berlin, 1900. Bong. Each fasc. 6 pis. u. 1 p. text. 4to. Hans Memling, Cent reproductions d'apres les tableaux les plus eminents du maitre. Fasc. 10 (last). Haarlem, 1906, Kleinmann. 10 pis. Folio. 15 fl. E. Meynell, Giovanni Bellini (Newnes Art Library). New York, 1906, Bouton.
64 pis. 4to. $ 1.00. A. Michaelis. see Codex Escurialensis. E.

Michel, Les Chefs-d'ceuvre de Rembrandt. Paris, 1006, Hachette. Eng. ed. London, 1906, Heinemann. 75 pis. (30 colored)..Folio.
40 fr. Michelangelo, Des Meis ters Werke in 166 Abbildungen (Die Klassiker der Kunst). Introd. by F. Knapp. Stnttgart, 1906, Deutsche Verlagsanstalt. xiv, 181 pp.; 166 flgs. 8vo. H. Miles, Titian's

Later Works. (Newnes Art Library.) New York, 1906, Bouton. 111. 4to. $1.00. P. de Mont, Pieter

Brueghel dit le Vieux. L'homme et son ceuvre. Fasc. V-X (last). Haarlem, 1906, Kleinmann. Each fasc. 5 pis. Folio. T. Sturge

Moore. Correggio. London, 1906, Duckworth. 276 pp.; 55 flgs. 4to.

R. Muther, Goya (Langham

Series). London, 1006, Siegle. viii, 64 pp.; 12 flgs. lOmo. — Rembrandt (Die Kunst). Berlin, 1906, Bard, Marquardt & Co. 50 pp.; 15 flgs. 16mo.

The National Gallery, London: The Flemish School, with introd. by F. Wedmore (The Art Galleries of Europe). New York, 1906, Bouton.
65 pis. 8vo. SI.25. T. Neal,

Rembrandt e 1' arte del suo tempo. Colla riproduzione di un quadro di Rembrandt tinora inedito e sconosciuto. Florence, 1906, Seeber. 119 pp.; pi. 16ino.

W. Pastor, Donatello (Die Kunst). Berlin, 1906, Bard. Marquardt & Co. 100 pp.; 16 flgs. lOmo. J. W.

Pattison, The World's Painters since Leonardo. New York. 1906, Dnffleld. $4.00. Peintures ecclSsiastiques du Moyen &ge de lVpoque d'art de Jan von Scorel et P. von Oostzaanen, 1490-1560, pnbliees sous les auspices de G. v. Kalcken et accompagnees de notices de M. le chevalier Dr. J. Six. Fasc. I-XI. Haarlem, 1906, Kleinmann. 14 pp. ; 54 pis. Folio. E. Picot, Les Franeais italianisants an XVI« siecle. T. I. Paris. 1906. Champion, xi, 381 pp. 8vo. Marie K. Potter. The Art of the

Venice Academy. New York, 1906, Stechert. 372 pp. 8vo. $1.50. E. Raehlmann. Ueber die Technlk der alten Meuter der klass. Zeit, bearteilt nach mikroskopischen Untersuchungen von Bruchstficken Ihrer Gemalde. Munich. 1906.
Reiahardt. Raphael (Klassiker tier Knnst). Introd. by A. Rosenberg. 3d ed. Stuttgart, 1906, Deutsche Verlagsanstalt. xxxvi, 168 pp.; 203 flgs. 8vo. M. 5.

Hope Rea, Rubens (Great Masters). London, 1906, Bell, xiv, 138 pp.; 33 pis. 8vo. Rembrandt-Alma nach, 1906-1907. Eine Erinnerungsgabe zu des Meisters 300. Geburtstage. Stuttgart, 1906. Deutsche Verlagsanstalt. 64 pp.; 10 pis.; flgs. 8vo. M. 1. Rembrandt in It lei und Wort. Herausg. v. VV. Bode unter Mitwirkung v. W. Valentiner. In 20 fasc. Fasc. 1-10. Berlin, 1906, R. Bong. 4to. M. 1.50 each. Des Meisters Radierungcn ln 402 Abbildungen (Klassiker der Kimst). Herausg. v. H. W. Singer. Stuttgart, 1906, Deutsche Verlagsanstalt. xxlv, 285 pp.; 402 tigs. 8vo. M. 8. — Quatorze planches en couleurs accompagnees de notices. et precedees d'une biographie du maitre, par A. Moreau. Paris. 1906. Laurens. 15 pp.; 14 pis., each with 2 pp. of text. 4to. M. Rey mond, Michel-Ange (Les grands artistes). Paris. 1906, Laurens. 111. 8vo. $0.50. — Verrocchio (I,es Mattres d'Art). Paris, 1906. Lit. de I'art anc. et mod. 168 pp.; 24 flgs. 8vo. Sir Joshua Reynolds, Discourses delivered to the Students of the Royal Academy. Introd. and Notes by Roger Fry. London, 1906, Seeley. 478 pp. 8vo.——-G. Riat, Ruysdaul. (Les grands artistes). Paris, 1906. Laurens.
128 pp.; 24 flgs. 8vo. C. Ricci,

Cento vedute di FIrenze antica. Florence, 1906, Alinari. 18 pp.; 81 pis. 4to. L. Riotor, Car peaux (Les grands artistes). Paris, 1906, Laurens. 8vo. $0. 50.,

E. Rodocanachi, La Femme Itallenne pendant la Renaissance. New York, 1906, Bouton. 76 pis. I 4to. $6.00. M. Rooses, Jor-1 daens' leven eu werken. Fasc.

I-V. Antwerp. 1906. Xederlandsche boekhandeL 317 pp.; 33 pis.: 140 flgs. 4to. Rubens Meister bilder. Leipzig, 1906, Weicher. 172 pp.; 60 *tiss.* 16mo. . Sanpere y Miquel. Los Cuatrocentistas Catalanes. Historia de la Pintura en el siglo XV. Tomo 1: Primera mitad del siglo XV. Tomo II: Seguuda mitad del siglo XV. Barcelona, 1906, Lib. L'Aveuc. 319: ciii. 284 pp.; tigs. 8vo. M.54.

H. Schmerber. Betrachtungen tiber italienische Malerei im 17. Jahrhundert. Strassburg, 1906,

Heitz. vii, 232 pp. 8vo. W.

L. Schreiber. Holzschnitte u. Schrotblatter aus der kgl. I'niversitats-Bibliothek in Tiibingen (Einblattdrucke des 15. Jahrh.). Strassburg, 1906, J. HV E. Heitz.
16 pp.; 15 pis. 4to. M. 40. See lengartlein. Hortulus animae. Codex Ms. 2706 der K. K. Hofbibliothek in Wicn. Herausg. mit Einl. v. F. Dornhoffer. (Complete in 11 fasc.) Leipzig. 1907, Hiersemauu. 514 pis. with text. M. 660. M. Sie bert, Die Madonnendarstellung in der altnicderlandischen Kunst von Jan van Eyck bis zu den Mauieristen. Heidelberg, 1906. 36 pp. 4to.

Dissertation. E. Sinigaglia,

De' Vivarini. pittori da Murauo. Bergamo, 1906. 1st. Hal. d'arti graflche. 68 pp.: 24 pis. 8vo.

G. Sortais, Le Maitre et l'Eleve. Kra Angelico et Benozzo Gozzoli. Paris, 1906. Desclee, de Brouer 4. Cie. 275 pp.; 4 pis.; 48 flgs.
4to. 15 fr. A. Speltz. Das i)rua nient der Renaissance, des Barock und Rococo,

iies Louis XVI = and Empirestiles, sowie des klassiziereudeu unglischen Stiles (Der Ornamentstil). Berlin, 1906. pp. 261 504; 150 pis.; tigs. 8vo. M. 6.

F. Stahl, Wie sah Rembrandt aus? Berlin, 1906, Gose & Tetzlaff. 54 pp.; 28 pis. E. Staley, Fra Angelico.

Paris, 1906, Laurens. 64 figs. $1.25. K. Statsman, Zur Ge schichte der deutschen Frtihrenaissance in Strassburg. Strassburg, 1906, Beust. 88 pp.; 77 flgs. 4to.

C. Stegmann and H. von Gey miiller, Die Architektur der Renaissance in Toscana. Allgemeine Ausgabe. 44 fasc. Munich. 1906, Bruckmann. Each fasc. vili, 16, 17. 1 pp.; 6 pis. Folio. E. Steinmann, Das Geheimnis der Medicigraber Michel Angelos (Kunstgeschichtliche Monographien). Leipzig, 1907, Hiersemann. 127 pp.; 15 pis.; 33 tigs. 8vo. — Die sixtinische Kapelle. II Bd. Michelangelo. Munich, 1906, Bruckmann. xx, 812 pp.; figs. 8vo. with album of 70 pis. and viii pp. of text.

E. C. Strutt, Fra Fllippo Lippi. New ed. New York, 1906, Macmillan. xxiii, 202 pp. j 56 figs.

8vo. $2.50. A. Sturdza, Michel Ange poete et epistolier. Paris, 1906, Renouard. 45 pp. 18mo.

Theophil Thor6 (W. Buerger), Jan V'ermeer van Delft. German by P. Prina. Leipzig, 1006, J. Zeitler. 83 pp.; 4 pis. 8vo. H. Inigo

Triggs, The Art of Garden Design in Italy. New York, 1900, Bouton. 128 pis. ; 150 flgs. Folio. 820.00.

H. von Tschudi, Das Portrat.

Fasc. I. C. Gurlitt, Das Englische PortrSt im XVIII Jahrh. (Complete in 20 fasc.) Berlin, 1900, Cassirer. 7 pp.; 5 pis.; 5 flgs. Each fasc. 7s.

H. Uhde-Bernays, Albrecht DurerHeft. Eine Einfiihrung in Albrecht Diirers Leben u. Werk. Stuttgart, 1906, K. A. E. Miiller. 32 pp; 54 flgs. 4to. M. 25. W. Unger.

Rembrandt van Rijn. Twintig etsen. Introd. by H. Coopman. Brussels, 1906, L. J. Kryn. 6 flgs.; 20 pis. Folio. 30 fr. G. Urbini,

Disegno storico dell' arte italiana. Part II (XV and XVI centuries).

Turin. 1906, Paravia. O. Uzanne,

Les Deux Canaletto (I.es grands artistes). Paris, 1906, Laurens. 8vo. $0.60.

W. R. Valentiner and J. G. Veldheer, Rembrandt Kalenderbook voor 1906. Introd. by C. Hofstede de Groot. Amsterdam, 1900, Meulenhoff & Co. 48 pp.; 14 pis.; flgs. Folio.

Van Dyck, Etchings. Introd. by F. Nevvbolt. New York, 1906, Scrib ners. 33 pis. 4to. $2.50. Van

Dyck Meisterbilder. Leipzig, 1906, Weicher. 71 pp.; 00 flgs. 16mo.

Giorgio Vasari, Die Lebens beschreibungen der beriihmtesten Architekteu, Bildhauer u. Maler. Deutsch herausg. v. A. Gottschewski u. G. Gronau. Ill Bd. Die italienischen Architekten u. Bildhauer des 15 Jahrh. Uebers u. angemerkt v. A. Gottschewski.

Strassburg, 1906, Heitz. viii, 360 pp. 8vo. M. 10.50. Diego

Velasquez, 50 planches d'apres ses osuvres les plus cfilebres. Introd. by Paul Lafond. Paris, 1906, Manzi, Joy ant & Cie. 11 pp.; 50 pis.

Folio. Jan Vermeer von Delft und Karel Fabritius. Photogravuren nach ihren bekannten Gemalden, mit biogr. u. beschreibendem. Text v. C. Hofstede de Groot. Leipzig, 1906, Hiersemann. Complete in 4 fasc, each with 9-10 pis. 4to. A. de Vesme, Le peintre graveur italien. Leipzig, 1906, Brockhaus. ii, 542 pp. 4to. M. 25. K. Voll, Die altniederliind ische Malerel von Jan van Eyck bis Memling. Ein entwicklungsgeschichtl. Versuch. Leipzig, 1906, Poeschel & Krippenberg. v, 328 pp.; 57 pis. 8vo. M. 13. A. Walcher Ritter von Maltheim, Bunte Hafnerkeramik der Renaissance in den oesterrelchisc'hen Landern. Vienna, 1906, Gilhofer & Ranschburg. viii, 121 pp.; 25 pis.; 140 flgs. 4to. M. 125. H. Wal lis, Italian Ceramic Art. Figure design and other forms of ornamentation in XVth century Italian majolica. London. 1906, Quaritch. xxxii, 103 pp.; 4 pis.; 101 flgs. 4to. A. Weese, Renaissance

Probleme. Bern, 1906, A. Francke. 76 pp. 8vo. M. 1. W. Weisbach,

Der junge DUrer. Drei studien. Leipzig, 1906, K. W. Hiersemann. vii, 108 pp.: 1 pi.; 31 flgs. 4to.

M. 16. H. Willich, Giacomo

Barozzi da Vignola (Zur Kunstgeschichte des Auslandes). Strassburg, 1906, J. H. E. Heitz. viii, 174 pp.; 22 pis.; 38 flgs. 8v o. M. 12. — Die Kirchenbauten des Giacomo Barozzi da Vignola. Ein Beitrag zurEiitwicklnngsgeschichte des Barockstils. Munich, 1906. 64 pp.; 40 flgs. 8vo. Dissertation.

Max Wingenroth, Angelico da Fiesole (Kiinstler-Monographien). Bielefeld, 1900. Velhagen & Klasing. 124 pp.; 109 flgs. 8vo. M. 4.

H. Wolffiin, Die Kunst Albrecht Diirers. Munich, 1906, Bruckmann. viii, 316 pp.; 132 flgs. 8vo. K.

Woermann. Die italienische Bildnismalerei der Renaissance (Fiilirer zur Kunst). Esslingen, 1906, P. Neff. iv, 96 pp.; pi.; 58 flgs. 8vo. M. 1. L. Woltmann, Die Germanen und die Renaissance in Italien. Leipzig, 1906. viii, 150, 48 pp. 8vo. R. Wuitminn,

Albrecht Dfirer. Leipzig, 1906, Teubner. vl, 100 pp.; 33 figs. 8vo.

M. 1. Kate Wyatt and M. R. Gloag, A Book of English Gardens. London, 1906, Methnen. 335 pp.; 24 pis. 8vo.

Zeichnungen alter Meister im Kupfcrstichkabinet zu Berlin. Herausg. v. F. Lippmann. Fasc. 15-17. Berlin, 1906, Grote. Each fasc. 10 pis.

Folio. A. Zeller, Das Heidel berger Schloss. Werden, Zerfall und Zukunft. Karlsruhe, 1906. xvi, 143 pp.; 34 pis.; tigs. 4to.

American Journal Of Archaeology, Second Series Vol. XI (1907) Plate XXIV American Journal Of Archaeology, Second Series Vol. XI (1907) Plate XXV ANTONIAZZO ROMANO plates XXIV-XXVII

The history of the native school of art in Rome during the fifteenth century will probably never be satisfactorily elucidated. Although recently discovered documents have given us a number of names of hitherto unknown artists, their connection with existing works is difficult to establish, and must be open to discussion.

If we may trust Platina's description of Rome when Martin V took up his residence there in 1421, after the conclusion of the great schism, there could have been nothing in the conditions of the city life capable of creating or maintaining such a product of high civilization as a school of art; though Platina, perhaps, was influenced by the natural tendency of the historian and chronicler of all ages to heighten his picture with dramatic contrasts, and to dwell on the extremes of misery as well as of happiness.

With all the disorder and lawlessness, churches and convents flourished, and doubtless groups of artisans carried on the traditions of cutting and laying stone, and of decorating with mosaic and fresco. Apparently, however, their resources were small, for the pope brought into the city Gentile da Fabriano and other artists from more favored regions, especially from Umbria and Tuscany, to carry out his enterprises.

As painters from outside continued to be called in to decorate the structures inaugurated by the popes of the fifteenth century, it is evident that the group of native artists in Rome must have remained small and unimportant. Vasari hardly mentions the Roman painters of this period. In his life of Filippino Lippi he does tell us, incidentally, that Antoniazzo Romano and Ladislao di Padova, "among the best painters

American Journal of Archaeology, Second Series. Journal of the 279 Archaeological Institute of America, Vol. XI (1907), No. 8.

then in Rome" (pittori ambedue de' migliori che fossero allora in Roma), were called in, according to the liberal custom of the time, to estimate the value of Filippino's frescoes in the chapel of Cardinal Oliviero Caraffa in the church of S. Maria sopra Minerva. Antoniazzo's name does not occur again, and as late as the year 1857, a note of the editor in Lemonnier's edition of Vasari says that nothing further is known of these two painters.

In 1869 Costantino Corvisieri published in *Tl Buonarroti,* a Roman review long since discontinued, a short article on Antoniazzo based on documents found in the various archives of the city. This is of the highest value, as it gives us records of important works executed by him, and proves conclusively that such a painter really existed, a fact which, until then, some historians of art were disposed to consider as at least doubtful. But Corvisieri had so little knowledge of Antoniazzo's works, that he knew of only one authentic example, the picture in San Clemente at Velletri, signed and dated 1483. Crowe and Cavalcaselle had, however, already mentioned Antoniazzo in their first English edition of 1864, and had referred to a number of signed works; but they seem to have fallen into the mistake of imagining the existence of two or three generations of equal artistic importance, — a mistake surely excusable in regard to a name which was recorded with delightful impartiality as Antonasso, Antonazzo, Antoniazzo, Antonaccio, Antonello, Antonuccio, etc.

In 1883 Sig. S. A. Bertolotti published many additional facts about Antoniazzo derived from his exhaustive study of documents, and E. Miintz, in *Les Arts d la Cour des Papes,* has recorded further interesting documents, so that from all this material it is not difficult to reconstruct something of the history of the man, and to know the scope of his larger artistic undertakings, although with uncommon perversity the documents almost invariably refer to works.now lost, or known to Signor Venturi considers this a mistaken reading of the date which he found almost obliterated. *Le Gallerie Raliane,* III, 1897, pp. 252-254.

Rep. f. K. VI, 1883, Heft 8. The same commentary appeared in Italian, with a few slight changes in the *Archivio della citta e provincia di Roma,* V, 1883, Fasc. 1. have been destroyed, and we are obliged to depend largely on internal evidence in order to demonstrate that he is the author of the numerous works which modern criticism has attached to his name.

The history and enumeration of lost works of art easily degenerates into mere pedantry or useless juggling of names and dates; but in studying this painter, who is still but little known, we are justified in noting whatever may establish his connection with more famous artists, and with the great art movements of his day, or anything that will offer a suggestion toward the solution of the more important problems of his artistic education, and the influences which helped to form him.

That his family name was Aquilio we may consider as certain, but the date of his birth has never been discovered. Even his father's name and occupation are hypothetical, though he is assumed to have been a painter named Benedetto, of the *rione* Colonna. This *rione,* which is near the Piazza Colonna, we at least know to have been the residence of the Aquilio family and of Antoniazzo himself.

The first appearance of Antoniazzo's name on the public records of his native city is somewhat inauspicious, though a modern investigator may hardly regard it entirely as a misfortune that on February 14, 1452, he was condemned to pay a fine for "excesses committed against Mancino Ogliararo."

A signed picture at Rieti bears the date 1464, and in the same year Antoniazzo contracted to decorate, for Cardinal Bessarion, the chapel of Sant' Eugenia in the church of SS. Apostoli. As this is the earliest date to be found in connection with any of his works, and as it occurs more than once, we may conjecture, in the absence of anything more definite, that the young artist was at that time just beginning to be known as a capable painter. The date is also of some assistance in helping us to an approximate estimate of his age. As he died before 1512, and possibly a few days or weeks after making his will in 1508, this contract was executed at least forty The text of his contract is given by Muntz, *Les Arts a la Cour des Papes,* I, p. 82.

Bertolotti, *op. cit.* four years before his death. If we consider that the fine of 1452 would hardly have been imposed on a youth under fifteen years of age, it will be safe to assume that he must have been at least twenty-seven years old at this time. The exact date of the contract is September 14, 1464, and the work was to be finished August 25, 1465. In

October, 1464, Antoniazzo, along with other painters, was paid for painting banners and decorations used in the coronation ceremonies of Paul II.

Antoniazzo's work in the SS. Apostoli, as well as that of Melozzo da Forli in the dome of the tribune, was destroyed when the church was enlarged in 1711, but there still remains there a memorial of the connection between Antoniazzo and his patron, although it seems to have escaped the notice of students heretofore. Over the altar in the first chapel on the right is a life-sized picture of the Madonna and Child, and underneath is the following inscription: *Vetustissima deiparae imago, quam ven. Bessario a Constantino, hue trastulit.* This picture, which is in perfect preservation, is certainly a work by Antoniazzo, though evidently a free copy from that Greek painting, the tradition of which is preserved in the inscription quoted. That Antoniazzo was reputed to be singularly happy in his copies from the old pictures of the Greek school is attested by an epigram, discovered by Corvisieri, which celebrates his success in a similar undertaking and reveals the name of another distinguished patron, Alesandro Sforza of Pesaro.

A second epigram also attributed by Corvisieri to Martino Filetico, a dependent of the Sforzas, is similar in form and spirit to the first, and commemorates a similar triumph of Melozzo, whose name is thus in a shadowy sort of way brought for the iblioteca Angelica, Cod. F. 6. 16.

Ad Mariain Maiorem
Virginia est Roma quam Lucas pinxit imago
Tam sancta: errorem quis putet esse suam
Hanc? Antonatius pictor romanus ab ilia
Duxit. Alexander Sfortia solvet opus.
Ad Mariam de Popolo
Hanc divus Lucas vivo de Virfrinis ore
Pinxerat; haec propria est Virginia effigies.
Sfortia Alexander iussit. Melotius ipsam
Effixit. Lucas diceret esse suam.
first time into association with that of Antoniazzo, long before their actual partnership in carrying out the decoration of the Vatican library.

Judging from the papal accounts, Antoniazzo was employed chiefly on purely commercial work by Paul II, who was rather a patron of architects, sculptors, and goldsmiths than of painters. But the diary of Infessura records that in 1470 the interior and facade of S. Maria della Consolazione were decorated by Antoniazzo. This church was a small structure built as a shelter for a miracle-working picture of the Madonna. It was afterwards completely demolished to make way for the larger present building.

Antoniazzo was undoubtedly an important figure in.the group of painters who worked for Sixtus IV after 1471. His talent by this time must have reached its highest development, and as one of the best of the native Roman artists he must have enjoyed the advantages which the man on the spot, who knows the conditions, always has over outside competitors.

In 1478 he was appointed by the pope one of three artists to draw up the statutes of the newly founded Academy of St. Luke, a fraternity of Roman painters. This indicates that the pope considered him one of the chief masters of his craft, that he was respected by his coworkers and endowed with common sense and practical organizing ability.

Details as to his personality are so entirely lacking that we are grateful for anything that admits a possible inference. Even the uncomplimentary suffix by which his family and friends changed the original name of Antonio to Antoniazzo is not without its value for us, as it implies a personal appearance more than usually unattractive, or perhaps some especially marked defect.

Probably the most important commission Antoniazzo ever received was that in which he was associated with Melozzo da Forli and Domenico Ghirlandaio, to decorate the Vatican library under the direction of the celebrated historian Platina. Nothing of Antoniazzo's work on the library remains, but a "precious fragment by Melozzo is in the Vatican picture gallery, where the figure of Platina is represented kneeling before his patron, Sixtus IV.

Platina's expense account of the work on the library mentions payments to Melozzo and Antoniazzo together, in June, 1480, and to Antoniazzo alone on April 10, 1481.

Antoniazzo was always successful in getting a large share of the decorative painting which was required at each new papal coronation. This work was very remunerative, and we find that after the coronation of Innocent VIII in 1484, Antoniazzo, along with one Petrus de Perusia, was paid 310 florins for various items, including twenty-five figures of St. Anthony. Miintz and others assume this Petrus to have been no other than the great Perugino, who is known to have been in Rome shortly before, working on the Sixtine Chapel for Sixtus IV. It would be nothing extraordinary for a man of Perugino's acutely developed commercial instincts to have undertaken such an humble commission.

The papal receipts from 1484 to 1492 show that during that time our painter was paid for a large amount of unimportant work, including flags, banners, doors, windows, coats of arms, etc. 1489 is the date on the signed picture at Capua which Antoniazzo painted for Bishop Girolamo Gaetani. In 1491 we find him arranging with Gentil Virginio Orsini to carry out extensive decorations in fresco at the castle of Bracciano, which was then being constructed under the direction of the famous military architect, Francesco di Giorgio di Martini, of Siena. On January 1, 1491, Antoniazzo wrote to Orsini the following letter, which puts us for a moment on almost intimate terms with the painter, showing him as the head of an extensive organized business, buying his colors in the best market, and solicitous that his "turba" of workmen shall not lose time waiting for scaffolds to be built:

Sioxor Mio

A questo. *di* passati Maestro Francesco me venne ad trovare et mi disse che era tomato da Venetia perche haveva comprato tutti quelli colori li haveva importo la Vostra Illustris» S. dovessi comprare. Et me sollecitava grandemente dovessi venir ad incomenzare el lavoro. Io li risposi che era paratissimo; et che non desiderava altro uocte et di si non de venire ad servire la vostra Illustris" S.

Bertolotti, *op. cit. II Castello di Bracciano,* Luigi Borsari, Rome, 1895.

Si che pertanto adviso quella si voglia dignare de far fare un ponte allarco et un altro in nella sala che tenga tutta una faccia del la gala. Perche impendendomi li fredi et giacci grandissimi che sono adesso, la colla et opera che io facessi in nello arco se veneria ad giacciar. Et la vostra 111TM Signnoria non veneria ad esser ben servita da me. Per la qual cosa io ho deliberate quando serranno li tempi dolci et che la colla non se possa venir ad giacciar di lavorare in esso arco et dipinger piu presto larco che la sala concedendome questo el tempo. Aduncha donde che la S. V. Ill" ha inteso el bisogno, prego quella se degni de far spacciar li poni in essi lochi de copra nominati quanto piu presto meglio, et facti che serranno questi se degni farme scrivere una piccola letteruza overo de mandarine un piccolo messo et subito io me ne venero colla mia turba de lavoranti che io menassi con mi veneriamo a perder tempo, et ad me incurreria non piccolo danno.

Non altro. Si non che mi riccomando alia vostra Illustriss"" S. la quale conserci sempre Idio in prospero et felice stato. Vale. Rome die prima mensio Januarii 1491.

Vester humillimus servus,
Antonatius Pictor.

The frescoes under the arch and several others in the castle still exist in a damaged condition at Bracciano, but judging Mr Most Illustrious Lord:

Yesterday Master Francesco came to find me and to tell me that he had returned from Venice where he had bought all the colors which your most illustrious lordship had ordered him to purchase. And he also urged me strongly to come and begin work. I replied that I was most ready, and that I desired nothing better, night and day, than to serve your most illustrious lordship.

Will you, therefore, deign to have a scaffold made in the arch, and another which shall extend along one entire wall in the room? This I ask, because if I should work on the arch now I should be impeded by the very great frosts and cold we are having, which would freeze the sizing and the work itself. So that I should not be serving your illustrious lordship well. Therefore I have decided to paint in the room when there may be frosts, and when the weather becomes mild, so that the sizing will not turn to ice, to paint the arch, finishing it before I do the room, if the weather will allow. Since your most illustrious lordship understands the necessity, I beg that you will condescend to have the scaffold hurried along in the places named above, as soon as possible, and when they are done, to deign to write a little letter or send me a small message, and 7 shall come immediately with my crowd of workmen. But if the scaffolds are not built, all my workmen which I shall bring will lose time, and I shall suffer no little loss.

I have nothing more to say except that I commend myself to your most illustrious lordship, and may God preserve you ever in a prosperous and happy condition. Farewell.

Your most humble servant,
Aktonius Pictor.
Rome, January 1, 1491.

from the photographs of those under the arch, Antoniazzo must have left the entire execution to the "turba " of workmen.

This same year Antoniazzo contracted to paint an altar-piece at the church of S. Maria della Pace. The work is no longer in place, but it may possibly be identified with the St. Sebastian now exhibited at the Corsini Gallery, and there attributed to Melozzo da Forli.

The performance of all this important work quite justifies Vasari's estimate of Antoniazzo, casually given in the passage already quoted, in connection with the valuation of Filippino's work in the Caraffa chapel in 1493.

One of the vagaries of history has transmitted to us the fact that a work of Antoniazzo at Campagnano, dated 1497, was struck by lightning some three centuries later. Even a description of this unfortunate picture is not lacking. This date is the latest which has yet been discovered on a work of our artist.

The details of his immediate family connection have been very clearly worked out by Bertolotti and show us a group of relatives and fellow-craftsmen living and working together in the houses owned by Antoniazzo in the Piazza Cerusa, now known as the Piazza Rondinini. The little square, very near the Pantheon, is dull enough to-day, and there is nothing to indicate that it was once the abode of the most distinguished Roman painter of the fifteenth century. Just around the corner is the church of S. Luigi de' Francesi, where Antoniazzo was buried in the chapel of the Aquilio family, which, according to the epitaph, must have contained an altar-piece by his own hand. Neither picture nor tombstone is now to be found, though the text of the epitaph with its unqualified eulogy of the "incomparabilis pictor" has been preserved.

The wills of Antoniazzo and of his second wife give incidentally some insight into the family relations. The lady, whose name was Girolama, was a rich widow, who kept her property quite separate from her husband's, even taking five ounces of pearls as security when Antoniazzo borrowed twenty-five ducats For the text of the contract, which is evidently in the painter's own handwriting, see Corvisieri, *op. cit.* Corvisieri, *op. cit.* Corvisieri, *up. cit.* from her; but her business sense must have been tempered with affection, for she left him a life interest in her estate when she died. Among her children by her first husband was a daughter Diana, who married Marcantonio, the son of her second husband. He also was a painter, and one example of his art is to be found in the sacristy of the church of Santa Chiara at Rieti with the inscription, *Marcus Antonius magistri Antonatii romanus depinxit M D XI.*

Marcantonio is mentioned in his father's will as having received fifty ducats from the commune of Rieti for a portrait of the gonfalonier, while he, the father, only received twenty-five ducats. For that reason, he explains, Marcantonio shall not inherit anything from him.

From a notary's deed it appears that in Antoniazzo's house of three floors, there lived, in addition to himself and his family, Evangelista *"magister Nardi pictoris"* probably a nephew of Antoniazzo, the painter Pietro Antonio di Lorenzo Vessecchia, the brother of Antoniazzo's first wife, the sculptors Maestro Bartolomeo di Luca of Florence, Pietro di Antonio of Ancona, and the painter Sebastiano di maestro Lorenzo di Cimena; quite enough to create that intangible something which modern artists call " an art atmosphere," for the sake of which they still segregate themselves into colonies.

Bernardino, Antoniazzo's youngest son, became a painter, and it is on record that in 1549 he painted a chapel in the church of St. Andrew at Carrara. The ruins of this work were covered over with colored marble in 1856. By the end of the sixteenth century the name Antoniazzo had become a surname.

Perhaps the best-known work by Antoniazzo is the Virgin and Child with St. Paul and St. Francis, in the Corsini Gallery at Rome (Fig. 1, Anderson, No. 4048). This picture, which is signed *Anthonatius Romanus pinzit*, was discovered a few years ago in the convent of S. Paolo at Poggio Native As its authenticity is undisputed, a study of its characteristics will supply us with the best possible means for the identification of other examples. The composition is of the simplest description. The Virgin, seated on a throne in the centre, supports with both hands the standing figure of the Child. A Bertolotti, *op. eit.* male saint stands on either side nearer the foreground. There is a striking absence of small accessories. The background is gilded. The throne, which is designed with a semicircular niche at the back, has a simple moulded cornice supported by slightly ornamented pilasters and capitals. Rosettes fill the spandrils and a crown is suspended above the Virgin's head. A narrow expanse of brocade on the lower step of the throne is almost concealed by the Virgin's robe, and this is the only attempt, except the throne itself, to vary the monotony of the surroundings. The figures are well proportioned and stand well on their feet. The drawing of the nude Child shows a genuine feeling for action and for childish character. But the types of the heads, the modelling of the flesh, and the drawing of the hands are the most characteristic features, and they will help us most in studying other works.

In the three adults the eyes have dense, unlighted pupils and. heavy, fevered lids. The eyebrows are arched and represented by a single firm, dark, tapering stroke, and without blending at either edge. All the heads are characterized by high prominent cheek-bones, and the male heads are represented with a sharp hollow in the lower part of the cheek. The Madonna's head is reminiscent of the Byzantine type, with the nose long, the small mouth with thin lips almost peevish, and the expression pensive. The Child has a full, round face with slight modelling and a rather silly, doll-like expression. The modelling of the flesh is everywhere somewhat defective. Lights and shadows are blended and fused so gradually that only rudimentary structure is expressed, and in the Madonna and Child the shadows are weak and pale in value. Those on the faces of the saints are stronger, but still very indefinite and unstudied as to the shape of the shadow, and consequently very insufficient in the expression of form.

One of Antoniazzo's most characteristic mannerisms is in the treatment of hands, of which the right hand of the Virgin in this picture offers us an excellent illustration. The two middle fingers are pressed tightly together with a slight suggestion of crossing; the little finger is curved out strongly, with the end bent in again to touch the next finger; the forefinger is similarly curved out and the end drawn in figain to touch the middle finger. This mannerism often amounts to a distortion, especially when, as in this case, the hand is foreshortened. Both hands of the St. Francis show something of the same treatment. The sinewy structure of the hands and feet is carefully rendered. The general characteristics of the figure of St. Francis hardly vary from the type which had already become almost stereotyped in Umbrian painting. The ample draperies of St. Paul's mantle are somewhat over-artificial and arranged with angular folds and a peculiar double notch in the termination of some of the depressions. A certain flatness of outline is noticeable at the top of the head of St. Paul, and this mannerism occurs frequently in other works.

These characteristics give us a working basis for a comparison with numerous unsigned examples, easily accessible in Rome, that are now generally acknowledged as works of Antoniazzo, such as the "Madonna della Ruota," the frescoes in the chapel of St. Catherine at the Minerva, and the Annunciation in the same place. From a study of all these we can arrive at a fairly definite idea of his style and attainments.

It is scarcely necessary to assert that the general impression made by the group of works now attributed to Antoniazzo is that they are the productions of a follower of the Umbrian school. But it may as well be confessed that Antoniazzo's work shows that while he was technically well equipped as a painter of the human figure, he was unfortunately somewhat devoid of inventive or imaginative powers, working over the ideas of greater men or faithfully following traditional compositions, repeating types and arrangements with a fidelity notable even in an age when there was no premium on originality for its own sake, when art was rather a refining and perfecting of traditional forms. We must, however, place him on a higher plane than Crowe and Cavalcaselle, with their limited knowledge of his work, were willing to accord to him. In their day his known works were so few and of so inferior a quality that, although they recognized traces of his manner in the frescoes at Santa Croce in Gerusalemme, they were unable to believe him the author of work so good.

His general understanding of the proportions and construction of the human figure was up to the average of his time, and his figures stand firmly on their feet with a well-defined and consistent movement. His visualization of the nude figure is largely a matter of outline, which he renders with vigorous ease. In his modelling of flesh he shows himself timid and conventional, particularly in the treatment of the Madonna and Child. There his shadows are weak and pale in tone, and undefined in shape. This is what we might expect from a man of feeble imagination, who clings to a traditional treatment as well as type of the Madonna, displaying his higher technical attainments in portraits, and in such accessories as draperies, which can be studied from the objects themselves.

In the beginning, Antoniazzo often regarded this motive of the Virgin and Child as hardly more than a religious symbol. Whatever personal artistic feeling he may have had was here carefully suppressed. The wonderful power over the devotional mood of the old Byzantine symbolistic treatment of this subject is due largely to the elimination of the personal quality. The very abstraction and unreality, the absence of any striking artistic interest, concentrates the attention and induces a sentiment of awe. There are several reasons for supposing that Antoniazzo's first efforts were made in the manufacture of such rude religious symbols, which were steadily in demand in Italy all through those centuries when painting as an art was producing for another stratum of society its great masterpieces. Probably his father's trade may have been in just such wares, and his continued use of the type was as much a matter of business principle as of habit, for his patrons for many years were small country churches in the Sabina, where the conservative provincial taste would be for a devotional picture rather than for the latest thing in the art movement of the day. It is notorious that all miracle-working pictures have been those of an archaic type and three at least of Antoniazzo's Madonnas — that at the church of Santa Maria del Buon Aiuto near Santa Croce in Rome, the "Madonna of Constantinople" at the SS. Apostoli, and the one at San Salvatore in Lauro—attained distinction as workers of miracles, and as a number of others have been disfigured by crosses, earrings, and other ex-votos, they were evidently considered to possess special power.

It would be wrong to imply that Antoniazzo never conceived the Madonna in a more human and attractive form. As early as 1467, in the signed and dated picture of S. Francesco, at Subiaco, the Madonna is represented with the characteristic high cheek-bones, but with few traces of the Byzantine type of the Corsini example, which is reported to have borne the date of 1487, though no traces of it are now visible.

In the example at Harvard University (plate XXIV) and in the Annunciation at the Minerva (Fig. 3, Anderson, No. 3726), the Madonnas are of great beauty and sweetness and are evidently derived from Umbrian sources, the first from Pinturicchio and the second from Perugino.

As there are no documents to show the actual artistic paternity of Antoniazzo, the most the student can do is to point out what possibilities he had in Rome for contact with the great art movements of his day, and then to seek in his works characteristics directly suggestive of such contact. The excessive use of the "theory of influences," so much ridiculed by Morelli, is certainly capable of being pushed to an absurdity, but Morelli himself depended on this theory and used it, as all students must. To understand how sensitive artists of every age are to influences, one need only cite the influence of Monet, of Whistler, or of Rodin, which any unpractised eye must have felt dominating in varying degrees every important exhibition of painting and sculpture of recent years.

Aside from the reminiscences of Byzantine character, the strongest and most constant influence which appears in Antoniazzo's work is that of Melozzo da Forli. It is hardly possible that the relation of master and pupil, as usually understood, ever existed between them, judging from what we know of their relative ages. Melozzo was born in 1438, and in 1452, the year in which Antoniazzo was fined for disturbing the peace, would have been fourteen years' old, while Antoniazzo must have attained that age at least, and was probably older. It is more likely that they were both pupils of some Umbrian painter working in Rome between 1450 and 1460. Vasari, in his life of Benozzo Gozzoli, warns his readers not to confuse that painter with Melozzo, and his warning seems to have been due to personal experience, as in his first edition he considered the work of Melozzo in the SS. Apostoli to be by Benozzo. Only in his second edition does he mention Melozzo, giving a meagre account of his works and calling him a pupil of Piero della Francesca. Vasari also tells us that Piero worked for Nicholas V at the Vatican, and from the dates of Piero's presence in other localities it has been reckoned that he was in Rome from 1447 to 1450 or thereabouts. Antoniazzo, who was at least twelve or fourteen years old at that time, may very well have been put to work under him, as he had probably already shown some promise in his father's workshop.

The two Latin epigrams already quoted were found by Corvisieri in the Biblioteca Angelica without date, but the dates before and after them on the same page led him to assign their composition to the year 1460. There is certainly something more than chance in the association of these two young men in such similar fashion. But after all it is not important to establish the exact relationship. The only thing of real value in studying the genesis of a painter is to know the derivation of his habits of mind and of his methods of expression, and these may have been received from an associate as well as from a master.

The influence of Melozzo is most apparent in the treatment of heads, and specially in details such as the eye with its heavy lid and dense unlighted pupil, imparting an austere look to the sacred personages depicted. This characteristic occurs, though not invariably, in works of Piero. Its presence in the head of Christ in the famous Resurrection at Borgo San Sepolcro helps to create the impression of power which that figure has always inspired. It is to be found in Melozzo's head of Christ in the Ascension at the Quirinal, and in the heads of the Apostles "among the fragments at St. Peter's. Antoniazzo invariably expresses the eyebrow by a sharp cleancut line with no blending of the edges. This type occurs in Melozzo, but he also treats it in a less summary fashion, carefully rendering the transition from the flesh of the forehead to the different color and texture of the eyebrow — a treatment that is never found in works by Antoniazzo. Perhaps the greatest power of our painter is shown in his drawing of the nude figure of the Christ Child. In the upright figures of this subject in the picture at the Corsini and in the "Madonna della Ruota" the pose is strong and decided, and the action very consistently expressed, and the reclining form of the Infant in the Harvard example (plate XXIV) is most charming and unhackneyed in conception, and exceptionally skilful in drawing, the foreshortening of the face being especially well rendered. With all this feeling for movement, proportion, and contour we are disappointed by the modelling, which is weak and slight, and as a rule deficient in precision.

His treatment of drapery is distinctly superior to that of Piero evidently inherited it from his master Domenico Veneziano. The heavy lids and weary expression of the eyes are very noticeable in Domenico's signed altar-piece in the Uffizi.

flesh. The folds are graceful, and there is a feeling of dignity and of amplitude, while the arrangement shows him enough of a true figure painter to wish to express the form and movement underneath. The draperies are carefully modelled, too, and reflected lights are closely observed.

Considering Pinturicchio's popularity in Rome, and the extensive undertakings he was carrying out there toward the end of the fifteenth century, it is strange not to find more evidence of his influence on Antoniazzo. It is most apparent in his landscapes, as would be natural, and where we find Antoniazzo departing from his Byzantine type of Madonna, he gives us a version strongly imbued with the characteristics of Pinturicchio, as in the Harvard example and in certain heads of Sibyls at Tivoli. As Pinturicchio is not known to have painted in Rome before 1480, we may fairly consider those works of Antoniazzo which show his influence to have been executed after that date.

In a recent review of a book on Fiorenzo di Lorenzo, Mr. F. Mason Perkins speaks of Antoniazzo as one of Fiorenzo's pupils. There is at present no positive proof that Fiorenzo ever worked at Rome, so we cannot conjecture under what circumstances Antoniazzo came under his influence. But there are certain characteristics in Antoniazzo that could hardly have been derived from any one else, and most prominent is the peculiar hand already described. This occurs in one of Antoniazzo's earliest known works, that of 1467 at Subiaco, and persistently reappears throughout his career. It is true that a similar hand occurs in works of the other Umbrian painters besides Fiorenzo.-Pinturicchio has used it as well, but infrequently. It seems to have been originally derived from early Sienese art, as one can see such a hand in the signed work of Meo di Siena in the Municipal Gallery at Perugia, and also in a picture in the same gallery by Taddeo di Bartolo (Sala E N. 10), who is supposed to have had so much influence in forming the school of Perugia. With Fiorenzo it is a fixed characteristic, and we may suppose that Antoniazzo came strongly under his influence at some time in the beginning of Although it is not found in Giotto, the "cramped hand" appears in the work of almost every one of his successors in the fourteenth century in Florence. his career. The two men were probably of about the same age, Fiorenzo having been born in 1440.

Another feature of Antoniazzo's work which recalls Fiorenzo, though not so strikingly, is the character of the folds of drapery, particularly in the observation of reflected lights, though Antoniazzo never carries this so far as does Fiorenzo, whose draperies are too often open to the charge of suggesting polished metal rather than soft fabrics.

In none of his best authenticated works in Rome is there a landscape background, and it seems quite in character with his lack; of invention and his predilection for Byzantine types that he should ha.ve persisted in the use of gold grounds long after they had become obsolete in the art centres of Italy. These backgrounds are usually patterned with a large repeat of the ogee type similar to that used on brocades. As a colorist, Antoniazzo follows the traditions of the Umbrian school, and his panel pictures have a rich, mellow tone, but in fresco, if we may judge from works which have been so much repainted, there is crudeness and lack of harmony.

So little critical attention has been paid to Antoniazzo that no complete list of his works has to my knowledge been attempted since that of Crowe and Cavalcaselle.

Lafenestre, in his *catalogue raisonni* of paintings in the galleries and churches of Rome, included nearly all that can now be ascribed to Antoniazzo in that city. Sig. Diego Angeli of all the Italian critics has studied Antoniazzo most carefully, and in his book, *Le Chiese di Roma,* agrees with most of Lafenestre's attributions to Antoniazzo of works in churches. He has also added considerably to the number of the painter's works through his researches in the small towns of the Sabina. In none of these lists, however, have I found any reference to the painting at the SS. Apostoli already referred to, which is known, under the title of the " Madonna of Constantinople," as a famous miracle-working picture. Its authorship, in spite of the tradition of its origin, offers little difficulty to the student of Antoniazzo's works. The general type of the Virgin, the In the Adoration of the Magi of the Barberini Gallery, recently attributed to Antoniazzo though formerly considered to be by Ghirlandaio, the landscape is clearly derived from Pinturicchio.

treatment of the flesh almost without light and shade, are all his, and more convincing is the hand, where his mannerism is clearly seen in the curving out of the forefinger and little finger, with the two middle fingers pressed closely together and held straight. The pattern of the gold background is identical in every detail with that on the "Madonna della Ruota" (Anderson, No. 4499).

The picture of St. Sebastian with the two kneeling churchmen, catalogued at the Corsini as a work of Melozzo da Forli (plate XXV, Alinari, No. 17489), has been so ruined by overcleaning that hardly more than the outlines remain. Fortunately the reproduction of the portrait heads from a photograph taken before the cleaning gives us some idea of its original appearance, which to my mind could never have borne much resemblance to the style of Melozzo. The statement has sometimes been made that we have no right to say that a picture cannot be the work of a certain painter on the ground that it is not *good* enough in quality; that the business of the connoisseur is only to determine if it is *characteristic*. Without arguing the merits of this statement, it may be said that the attribution to Melozzo has been received with general incredulity by critics who know his work, precisely on the ground that it contained none of the known characteristics of that painter. When we add to this the general opinion that neither is its quality up to the level of Melozzo's achievement, we have at least prepared the ground for considering it rather the work of his associate Antoniazzo, with whose characteristics and whose quality it coincides perfectly. In all known works of Melozzo the modelling is very strong and sure; the solidity of the forms and the variety of surfaces of the flesh are really represented and not merely suggested as in this picture. On the other hand, there are many details which connect it with the style of Antoniazzo. The head, for example, is very similar to a head of the Saviour on the ceiling at S. Giovanni Evangelista at Tivoli, while the pose of the body is precisely the reverse of that of the St. Sebastian at S. Vito e Modesto (Moscioni 4448), which is generally acknowledged to be a genuine work of the Roman painter. Even such a detail as the loin cloth is repeated without alteration. Both these figures resemble quite closely in action and pose the St. Sebastian of Piero della Francesca at the church of the Hospital at Borgo San Sepolcro, even the loin cloth being the same; but Piero's figure is far more powerfully modelled. After recognizing the characteristics of Antoniazzo in this panel, I was struck by a certain coincidence in the documentary evidence. For this picture came originally from the church of S. Maria della Pace, where, in 1491, Antoniazzo contracted to paint an altar-piece for a certain chapel which, in a seventeenth-century document, is referred to as having been formerly called the chapel of St. Sebastian.

The most extensive and important piece of work in Rome which has been associated with Antoniazzo's name is the fresco on the dome of the apse at Santa Croce in Gerusalemme (plate XXVI, Alinari, Nos. 20130, 20131, 20132). No one seems to have been prepared to make a positive statement about it, but both Lafenestre and Angeli think it may possibly be of the school of Antoniazzo. In the last edition of Burckhardt's *Cicerone* it is attributed to the school of Pinturicchio. It is certainly difficult to judge now what its original appearance was, it has been so crudely and thoroughly repainted. At the first glance it is difficult to connect this picture, with its variety of action, pose, and incident, its fantastic and varied landscape, with the hieratic treatment and gold ground of Antoniazzo as we have first known him. A closer inspection, however, discloses here and there features which even in its present state betray the style of Antoniazzo.

The general cast of the drapery and the treatment of the individual folds of all the principal figures are in Antoniazzo's manner. On the right the head of the second old man (Alinari, No. 20131), behind the mounted figure bearing the cross, has the exaggerated hollow in the cheek, the dense eyes, and all the traits with which Antoniazzo endows his heads of aged saints in his altar-pieces. Farther to the left the figure of the empress (plate XXVI, Alinari, No. 20130) in type, pose, and treatment of details betrays our painter's habitual manner, the Corvisieri, *op. cit.* In an article published after this paper was written, the St. Sebastian is likewise attributed to Antoniazzo by E. Jacobson in *Rep. f. K.* XXIX, 1906, pp. 104-107. See *A. J.A.* X, 1006, p. 482.

lower hand laid against the cross being unmistakable. The same characteristics are to be seen in the figure of the kneeling churchman on the other side of the cross, whose costume is identical with that of the members of the tribunal of the Ruota in the picture at the Vatican. The head of the old man farther to the left is one which we meet often in Antoniazzo. The flatness of the top of the head, where the line sinks, instead of curving up as it should, is characteristic. There are other smaller details which are significant, but enough has been indicated to show that all the most important figures in the foreground of this fresco are by Antoniazzo, so we must conclude it to have been carried out by his "turba" of workmen with his aid and direction. The landscape in breadth, in charm, and in fancy is far beyond what we should expect from a painter who is ordinarily so sparing in decorative accessories of all kinds. The principal features of the landscape, it is evident, are those with which Pinturicchio has made us familiar in his works in Rome, but I find no single figure or face here which suggests that either he or Perugino was the author, though both names have been suggested as possible.

Crowe and Cavalcaselle, after observing reminiscences of Antoniazzo, Caporali, Piero della Francesca, Signorelli, Alunno, and Pinturicchio in this fresco, conclude that it is possibly the work of Bonfigli.

Over the second altar on the left, in the Church of S. Salvatore in Lauro, is a life-sized picture of the Virgin with the Child seated in her lap. Lafenestre and Angeli say of it, that it is attributed to Pollaiuolo. It was recognized recently by Mr. Richard Norton as a work of Antoniazzo. The style of the Madonna is similar to that at S. Paolo, that is, reminiscent of Pinturicchio. The Child has the type of face, the proportions, and drawing which are characteristic of Antoniazzo. The inscription in Roman letters on the step of the throne follows also a habit of the artist. Worked into the meaningless hieroglyphics of the gold-patterned hem of the robe on its lower edge is the inscription *Antonio pinxit*. This signature is

'Signor Angeli, in *Le, Chiene U Roma*, says that this church was restored in 1492. Some years after, Cardinal Bernardino Carvejol ordered the vault of the tribune to be painted with frescoes, probably between 1490 and 1500. apparently the only foundation for the astonishing attribution to Pollaiuolo and would serve equally well to make out a case for Antoniazzo, did not a close inspection arouse some suspicion that it was not a part of the original work. The enclosing border lines of gold widen in an awkward way where they enclose the lettering, which is a trifle wider than the other motives of the band, and it all gives an impression of being inserted later than the original painting. The picture, which is poorly lighted and almost ruined by varnishes, must have been one of Antoniazzo's most attractive works.

Signor Angeli has suggested that the altar-piece of the little church of S. Omobono in Rome is by Antoniazzo, but I fail to discover in it any of his characteristics. The types, the color, and modelling all suggest a painter much nearer to the school of Perugino. Nor can I find anything in the ruined fresco over the tombs of the Pollaiuoli at S. Pietro in Vincoli at all reminiscent of what we know of Antoniazzo, though Herr Steinmann has put forth the suggestion that this might be a work of his.

The paintings on the tabernacle at S. Giovanni Laterano (plate XXVII) are still attributed to Barna di Siena (d. 1387), according to some old tradition, and their lack of conformity to fifteenth-century art is explained by their free restoration in 1851. But wherever the restoration is less drastic, the handiwork of Antoniazzo is clearly betrayed.

A small triptych has recently been removed from the Institute of Fine Arts in Ravenna to the Uffizi Gallery in Florence, where it is exhibited as a probable work of Fiorenzo di Lorenzo (Fig. 2, Alinari, No. 18260). This picture seems to me undoubtedly by Antoniazzo. The one characteristic which recalls Fiorenzo is the cramped hand of the Virgin and of St. Peter, but this is quite as characteristic of Antoniazzo, and the hands are far inferior in firmness of drawing and modelling to those of Fiorenzo. Indeed, the strongest argument against this being by Fiorenzo, is that in quality, that most important of all the attributes of painting, it is much inferior to any known work of Fiorenzo, and both the Virgin and the Child are types quite foreign to his style.

This also is attributed to Antoniazzo by E. Jacobson, *op. cit.*

Signor Ricci is inclined to see the handiwork of Fiorenzo di Lorenzo in the small Madonna and Child in the National Gallery, there catalogued as a work of Pinturicchio, and in the replica in the Municipal Gallery at Trevi. The hand of the

Madonna certainly suggests Fiorenzo, but is even more characteristic of Antoniazzo, and the quality of the whole seems inferior to either Fiorenzo or Pinturicchio. From the proportions, action, modelling, and type of the Child, and from numerous other considerations, I would suggest Antoniazzo rather than Fiorenzo as the author of these panels.

Dr. Bode, in the latest edition of the *Cicerone*, calls the Annunciation at the Minerva Antoniazzo's masterpiece (Fig. 3). It is the most charming of his works in Rome, and before its mutilation the composition must have been much finer. The background, now of plain gold, shows traces of having been once richly patterned with a design similar to that on the Madonna della Ruota, and the original position of the Almighty is still indicated, directly above the Angel, by the imperfect patching of the rectangular space left when the picture was

Figure 3. — Annunciation In S. Maria Sopra Minerva, Rome. enlarged to fit its present frame. The original shape was evidently almost square.

Certainly Antoniazzo never produced anything better than this. The idea is unusual, for the Virgin is represented as receiving the Divine message just as she is in the act of distributing dowries to a group of three orphan maidens, who are presented to her by a churchman said to be Cardinal Turrecremata, the founder of the charity of the Santissima Annunziata. The Virgin, whose head is very lovely, kneels gracefully, with a sweet and pensive expression, and turning from her reading desk, presents a purse to the maidens.. These are drawn to a smaller scale and kneel on a lower level, with upturned eyes and graceful poses. The angel moves swiftly in with spread wings and an action as if about to kneel. The Cardinal is drawn in profile, with a mild and beneficent expression. The Almighty above with raised hands is more conventional in conception and pose. The color is deep, rich, and mellow; the drawing satisfactory, and the modelling, if still a little uncertain on the Madonna's face, is on the figures of the kneeling maidens stronger and more expressive than is usual with Antoniazzo.

Other works of interest by Antoniazzo might be cited, but the examples referred to are sufficient to give an adequate idea of his style and of his position in the history of art. As one of the more interesting of the minor painters of the fifteenth century in Italy, and especially as the one known native Roman artist of that period, his name deserves to be rescued from the oblivion in which it has remained so long.

Any list of the works of a painter so little known, whose style has been so often confused with that of more famous artists, must be incomplete for some time to come. In the following are included all the works whose attribution to Antoniazzo the author has been able to discover.

List Of Works By Antoniazzo Romano

A. Signed Works

Rieti. Municipal Library. Formerly in S. Antonio del Monte. Madonna and Child with SS. Francis and Anthony on side panels. Signed: ANTONIUS DE ROMA MCCCCLXIV EPINXIT.

Subiaco. S. Francesco. Triptych. Virgin and Child between SS. Francis and Anthony. Signed: A.D.M.CCCCLXVII ANTONIUS DE ROMA ME PINXIT DIE. II. OCTOBRIS.

Rome. Corsini Gallery, No. 2371. Virgin, Child, and SS. Paul and Francis. Signed: ANTON AT1US ROMANUS PINXIT MCCCCLXXXVI1I. Height, 1.60 m.; width, 1.25 m. On wood. From convent of S. Paolo at Poggio Nativo.

Ponticelli. Franciscan Convent. Altar piece with SS. Anthony and Francis.

Capua. Cathedral; Cappella Gaetano. Virgin and Child between SS. Stephen and Lucy. Signed: ANTONIATUS ROMANUS M. FOR. P. MCCCCLXXXIX. Venturi speaks of another work of Antoniazzo in the Cathedral of Capua attributed to Silvestro de' Buoni.

Velletri. S. Clemente. Virgin and Child. Signed: ANTONATIUS ROM ANUS ME PINXIT ANNO MCC... According to Venturi the date which has been interpreted as 1483 is undecipherable beyond this point.

B. Unsigned Works Generally Accepted

Bracciano. Castello. Fresco. Cavalry Procession with portrait of Gentil Virginio Orsini.

Castelnuovo. Church of the Pagani family on the road from Rignano to Rome. Christ Blessing; a long inscription ends with the date 1501. St. John Baptist, St. John Evangelist.

Rome. S. Maria sopra Minerva. Fourth chapel on right. Annunciation with Cardinal Turrecremata and maidens receiving dowries. Figures life size. Chapel of S. Catherine. Frescoes formerly in the transept; life size. Crucifixion. Four male saints. SS. Lucia and Appollonia. Pieta. Bishop with kneeling donor. SS. Onofrio and Jerome. Annunciation. 'Rome. S. Paolo fuori le Mura. Sacristy. Madonna and Child with SS. Paul, Benedict, Peter, and Giustina.

Rome. S. Pietro in Montorio. Third Chapel: Frescoes. Altar; Holy Family. Semidome; The Eternal. Right; David. Left; Solomon. Centre; Escutcheon of Spain. Figures life size.

Rome. Vatican, Picture Gallery. "Madonna della Ruota." Virgin Enthroned with SS. Peter and Paul and twelve members of the Tribunal of the Ruota kneeling in the foreground. Presented to the Tribunal by the president Mgr. Brancodoro, whose arms are on the pedestal of the throne. Height, 2.50 m.; width, 2.30 m. In tempera, on wood. Figures threequarters life size.

C. Attributions For Which The Author Alone Is Responsible

Florence. Uffizi, No. 1558. Triptych; Madonna and Child between St. Peter and St. Paul. Above; the Eternal: the Annunciation. Back; St. Sebastian, St. Anthony Abbot. Dated 1485.

London. National Gallery. Madonna and Child, attributed to Pinturicchio.

Palombara. S. Francesco in Organtella. Annunciation. Rome. SS. Apostoli. "Madonna of Constantinople," 1464 (?). Life size. On wood.

Rome. Corsini Gallery. St. Sebastian with two kneeling Churchmen, attributed to Melozzo da Forli. Canvas stretched on a panel. Figures life size. From S. Maria della Pace, Rome (?), 1491 (?).

Rome. Santa Croce in G-rusalemme. Semidome over apse; Discovery of the Cross. 1495-1500 (Y).

Rome. S. John Lateran. Tabernacle. Front, central panel, Crucifixion; right panel, SS. Peter and Andrew; left panel, SS. Paul and James. Right, central panel, Virgin enthroned with donor; right panel, SS. Stephen and John Evangelist; left panel, SS. Lawrence and John Baptist. Left, central panel, Christ feeding lambs; right panel, SS. Jerome and Ambrose (?); left panel, SS. Gregory and Augustine (?). Back, central panel, Coronation of the Virgin; right panel, SS. Catherine and Anthony Hermit; left panel, Annunciation.

Trkvi. Municipal Gallery, Madonna and Child; attributed to Pinturicchio.

D. Recent Attributions Still Under Discussion

Altenburg. Madonna and Child. (Schmarsow.)

Brussels. Christ with two saints. (Venturi.)

Cambridge, U.S.A. Harvard University. Fogg Art Museum. Tabernacle, Madonna and Child with St. John and angels; above Almighty. (Norton.)

Campagnano. S. Maria del Prato, altar-piece. (Angeli.)

Farfa. Abbey, two portraits of Abbots. (Angeli.)

New York, U.S.A. Fischof Collection, Madonna and Child. (Perkins.)

Philadelphia, U.S.A. Johnson Collection, Madonna and Child. (Perkins). Weidner Collection, Madonna and Child. (Perkins.)

Poggio Nativo. S. Annunziata, Triptych with Christ Blessing between St. Michael and St. Sebastian. (Angeli.)

Rome. S. Maria del Buon Aiuto. Madonna and Child. Fresco, life size. (Angeli.)

Rome. Barberini Gallery, Epiphany. (Perkins.)

Rome. S. Pietro, Ante-chamber of the treasury; St. Veronica with St. Peter and St. Paul. (Burckhardt)

Rome. S. Salvatore in Lauro. Madonna enthroned. Figures life size, on canvas. Signed in hem of robe, ANTONIO PINXIT. (Norton.)

Rome. S. Vito e Modesto. Fresco. Lunette, Madonna enthroned with SS. Crescentia and Modesto. Panels below, St. Sebastian, S. Vito, St. Margaret. (Angeli.)

Rome. Capitoline Gallery, Sala VI, Madonna and Angels. Fresco. (Jacobson.)

Rome. Corsini Gallery. Madonna enthroned with SS. Peter and Paul. Not exhibited. (Jacobson.)

Rome. Pantheon. Chapel R. of hfgh altar, Madonna with SS. John and Francis. (Jacobson.)

Rome. Vatican Gallery. Madonna with SS. Peter and Paul; attributed to Melozzo da Forll. (Jacobson.)

Tivoli. S. Giovanni Evangelista. Frescoes. Left wall, Assumption of the Virgin. Right, Birth and Naming of John the Baptist. Arch, Twelve Sibyls.

Vault, Four Evangelists and Four Doctors. (Rossi.) All these frescoes were attributed to A. by Jacobson, *op. eit.,* after the above was written.

Bibliography *Archivio della città e provincia di Roma,* V, 1883, Fase. I. A. Bertolotti, 'H pittore Romano Antoniazzo e la sua famiglia.' The most complete and authoritative account based on documents. Practically the same article in German in *Rep.f. K.* VI, 1883, Heft 3, 'Der Maler Antoniazzo von Rom und seine Familie.' *Arch. Stor. Art.* II, 1889, p. 478. E. Muntz, 'Nuovi documenti.' Article on Antoniazzo with documents.
, VII, 1894, p. 154. Illustration of Madonna with Leo IX and Angel.
Short reference in article on ' Le Esposizioni d' Arte Italiana a Londra,' by Constance Jocelyn Ffoulkes.

Basilio Magni, *Arte Italiana,* Rome, 1901, II, p. 139. Short account, with list of works.

E. Muntz, *Let Arts ala Cour des Papes,* Paris, 1878. Documents relating to various works executed by Antoniazzo for the popes.
, *Les Arts a la Cour des Papes Innocent VIII, Alexandre VI, Pie III,* 1482-1503. Paris, 1898. Additional documents. *V Arte,* I, 1898, p. 374. A short letter with comment by A. Venturi concerning a picture attributed to Antoniazzo, taken from Rome to the Brussels Museum and there exhibited as of the school of Mantegna. , V, 1902, p. 333, Diego Angeli, ' Un Affresco inedito di Antoniazzo Romano in Roma.' Illustrated. Refers to work at S. Vito e Modesto.
, p. 374. Paolo D' Ancona, ' Le Rappresentazioni Allegoriche dell'

Arte liberale.' Refers to work of Antoniazzo at Bracciano.
, VI, 1903, pp. 102-105. Refers to picture in the Uffizi at Florence and to work at Capua. , VII, 1904, p. 89. Suggestion by E. Stkinmann that the fresco over the tomb of the Poliamoli at S. Pietro in Vincoli is by Antoniazzo. From *Kunstchronik,* XIV, p. 33. , pp. 146 ff., 9, Attilio Rossi, ' Opere d' Arte a Tivoli.' Illustrated.
Deals with frescoes in the church of S. Giovanni Evangelista.
Il Buonarroti, Rome, June and July, 1869. 'Antonazzo Aquilio romano, pittore del secolo XV. Commentario di Costantino Corvisieri.' A careful sketch of Antoniazzo's life based on documents. *Bullettino della Società filologica romana,* N. 3, Rome, 1902, p. 57. Short article by F. Hermanin on triptych by Antoniazzo in the church of S. Francesco, near Subiaco; mentioned also in *Memorie di Subiaco* by G. Innucelli.

Luigi Borsari, *Il Castello di Bracciano,* Rome, 1895, pp. 60 ff. Description of fresco at Bracciano.

Diego Angeli, *Le Chiese di Roma,* Roma, 1903. Locates Antoniazzo's works in the Roman churches.
Le Gallerie Nazionali Italiane, Rome, 1902, p. 188. Gino Fogolari, 'Cristoforo Scacco da Verona, pittore.' Discusses Antoniazzo's works at Capua and attributes pictures formerly considered to be by him, to Ssacco. , pp. 252-254. A. Venturi, ' La Galleria Nazionale in Roma.' Short résumé of Antoniazzo's life, with references to his work in the Sabina. *Gaz. B.-A.,* September, 1897. August Schmarsow, 'Maitres Italiens a la Galdrie d'Altenburg.' Illustration and description of a picture attributed to Antoniazzo.
Crowe and Cavalcaselle, *A New History of Painting in Italy.* London, 1864. Vol. III, p. 168.
Rass. a" Arte, May, 1905. 'Pitture Italiaue nel Fogg Museum a Cambridge.' , August, 1905. F. Mason Perkins, ' Pitture Italians nella Raccolta
Johnson a Filadelfta, U.S.A.' , August, 1907. A picture of SS. Vincenzo, Catarina, and Niccolo at

Montefalco is reproduced, and other works of Antoniazzo are mentioned.
Rep.f.K. XXIX, 1906, pp. 104-107. E. Jacobson, 'Neue Werke von Antoniazzo Romano.' Suggests Antoniazzo as the author of a number of works in Rome, including the St. Sebastian at the Corsini Gallery and all the frescoes on the tabernacle at the Lateran.
Herbert E. Everett. of Classical Stuotes at atijens NEW INSCRIPTIONS FROM THE ASCLEPIEUM AT ATHENS

In February, 1906, while I was examining the walls of the Asclepieum on the south side of the Acropolis at Athens with Professor Dorpfeld, we noticed some letters on the end of a piece of marble built into a low mediaval wall. This wall lies directly south of the temple of Asclepius and forms the northern side of a small fountain which stood there in mediaeval times. The stone was at the eastern end of the wall. So few of the letters were visible that nothing could be made of the inscription while the stone was still in position, but as Professor Dorpfeld with his usual courtesy withdrew any claim he might have to the discovery, I made application to the authorities and was granted permission to remove the stone. It proved to have on it four inscriptions, three on one side and one on the other, all clearly cut and perfectly legible. All were more or less broken, but fortunately in such a way that three of them can be restored with certainty and the fourth with a high degree of probability. The stone had originally stood upright and supported a votive offering in honor of Asclepius, as appears from the inscriptions on one side, but there is no indication of what that offering was. At a later time a moulding was cut lengthwise upon the other side and the stone used to form part of the pedestal which supported the statue of a certain Menander. It is now lying in the precinct of Asclepius near the piece of wall in which it was found.

The stone is of Pentelic marble 72. 7 cm. long, 17 cm. wide, except where the edge is broken away, and 16.6 cm. thick. On the flat side are three inscriptions, one below the other, running across the stone, but in the middle there is a cutting which seems to have been made for the insertion of a clamp probably at the time when the moulding was cut upon the reverse side. This cutting is 37 cm. from the top of the stone, 34 cm. from the bottom, 7.8 cm. from one side, and 5 cm. from the other. It is 7.9 cm. long, 3.5 cm.

The second inscription (Fig. 1) is evidently the oldest on the stone. It reads:

KJaWiat
KJaAAtbv
EAioia/Atiis
avtOr)Ktv. Callias ton of Qalliat of Euonymon dedicated (this offering') to Atclepiut. The letters are those of the Ionic alphabet as it appears at Athens in the second half of the fourth century.
They are regular in shape, clearly cut with a slight thickening at the ends of the strokes where the apices later appear, and show very little difference in height, varying only from 1.1 cm. to 1.2 cm. They were filled with stucco at the time the stone was found, but showed no trace of color. Upon epigraphical grounds the date of this inscription may be placed in the second half of the fourth century B.C. Nothing definite is known of wide at its widest part, and has the shape of two small rectangles connected by a narrow bar.
this Callias. In the archonship of Glaucippus, 410 B.C., a Callias of the deme of Euonymon was *'EWrlvorafiia,* and he may well have been a member of the same family, perhaps the grandfather of this man, but nothing more is known of him. The name Callias was, of course, common at Athens, and there is mention in inscriptions of two other men called Callias son of Callias, but there is nothing to connect either of-them with the man mentioned here. The inscription unfortunately does not help to locate the deme Euonymon, the site of which is still doubtful.
In the course of time the offering of Callias disappeared, and in the next century the letters were filled with stucco so that no trace of them was visible, and then two new inscriptions were cut upon the stone and it was made to serve as the base for another offering. These new inscriptions are the first and third on the stone. The first (Fig. 2) reads: *Apollodorus son of Aristomenes of Sypalettus* (anrf) *Lysandrides son of Lysanias of Peleces dedicated (this offering) to Asclepius*. There can be no question as to the certainty of the restorations proposed. At the end of the first line the *iota* is broken off, but a trace of it is still visible. The letters vary in size. The 0 is 1 cm. high; the others vary from 1.8 cm. to 2.2 cm. They are typical letters of the third century B.C.

There is no other mention of Apollodorus son of Aristomenes so far as known, although the name Apollodorus is a common one. In the archonship of Eupolemus, 185 B.C., a certain Apollodorus was To/iwtv *rwv Trpmdveeov,* and in the list of prytanes occurs the name 'ApJto-TO/teVfjj?, but this is probably merely a coincidence. Again, in the archonship of Nicocrates, 333 B.C., there is reference to Antidotus son of Apollodorus of Sypalettus. Here there does seem to be some connection, as both men come from the same deme, but what the relationship was can only be conjectured.

In regard to Lysandrides the case is somewhat different, for although he is not mentioned elsewhere, there are two other references to his father. In *G.I.A.* II, 316, there is recorded a decree passed in the archonship of Nicias, 281 B.C., in which it is proposed to praise and to crown with a golden crown the *ephebi* for their conduct while the city was engaged in war during the archonship of Menecles, 282 B.C. In the list of *ephebi* which follows the decree there occurs (11. 53, 54) the following:

Amrams Avray8pi'8ou.

Lysanias the father was, therefore, *ephebus* in 282 B.C., which means that he was born about 300 B.C. Our inscription, then, must date considerably after 282 B.C., for Lysanias must become old enough to marry and his son must grow to manhood. This could hardly take less than forty years, so that our inscription cannot be safely dated earlier than 240 B.C.

Lysanias is also mentioned in *C.I.A.* II, 1040, where we find in a list of names:

Avcnmas Ajvcrai'8pi8ou
C.I.A. n, 440.

Our inscription makes possible the restoration of the father's name *Avaav8piBr):* in each of these inscriptions. According to Sundwall a Lysanias of Melete was priest of Asclepius in 257 B.C., but he is not likely to have been the same as Lysanias of Peleces.

The site of neither of the demes mentioned in the inscription is known. Each is classed as *Landtrittys* by Pauly-Wissowa, but that is about all that can be said of them. It has been suggested that Sypalettus was the modern Sepolia.

The third inscription (Fig. 3), which is the shortest, is in some respects the most interesting. It reads: *In the priesthood of Philiua of Phalerum.* The letters vary from 1.3 cm. to 1.8 cm. in height and resemble those of the inscription just discussed. This inscription, then, gives the date when Apollodorus and Lysandrides made their offering to Asclepius. For it certainly is not contemporary with the Callias inscription, and it is not at all likely that it was added at a subsequent time. The restoration cannot be regarded as absolutely certain, but is, at least, very probable. The break in the stone comes across the first E in *lepei'w*; and at the beginning of the second line the Y is placed below the space between the E and the P. 4 IA10 would, therefore, just fill up the vacant space. Philius of Phalerum is known as a priest of Asclepius from another *Epigraphische Iieitrage zur Ceschiehte Athens,* p. 78.

Real-Encyclopadie, II, p. 2214; cf. Loper, *Alh. Mitth.* XVII, pp. 411 and 383 ff. P. Kastroinenos, *Die Demen von Attica,* p. 99. Or *M Uptlm* ; cf. *C.I.A.* II, 1491. inscription *(C.I.A.* II, 1505) preserved in the Epigraphical Museum at Athens. It reads:

Xtmj A7κAip«p

An examination of this stone revealed the fact that the letters correspond very closely with those of our inscription. In fact, the resemblance is so strong that we must conclude that both inscriptions were carved by the same man. If my restoration is accepted, we have an approximate date for Philius.

If it is true, as it seems to be, that the priests of Asclepius were chosen each year in regular rotation from the different tribes, the names of these priests furnish a system of chronology for dating historical events, and it is, therefore, of the utmost importance that the year in which each priest served should be definitely ascertained. J. Sundwall, arguing upon epigraphical grounds, makes

Philius priest in the year 211-10 B.C. The deme of Phalerum belonged to the tribe Aeantis and a priest from that tribe would have been in office in the years 236-5 and 224-3, as well as in 211-10 B.C. The priest is not known for any of these years. We have already shown reasons for dating our inscription after 240 B.C. Philius must, therefore, be dated in one of these years. The date suggested by Sundwall is possible, but the year 224-23 B.C. is perhaps more probable. Lysandrides would probably have been about fifty years old at that time.

In this inscription attention might be called to the spelling tepewB? instead of *tepeoK*. The form in « occurs elsewhere, especially in inscriptions of the fourth and third centuries B.C.

The fourth inscription is cut lengthwise on the opposite side of the stone in letters 3.5 cm. high, with the exception of 0, which is 3 cm. high. A moulding, an outline of which is given 1 am indebted to Professor Leonardos, Curator of the Epigraphical Museum, for a squeeze of this inscription. *Op. cit.* pp. 75 ff.
I regret that I have been unable to see W. S. Ferguson's *ffie Priests of Asklepios*, but I understand that the edition printed was almost entirely destroyed in the San Francisco Are. Cf. Meisterhans, *Grammatik der Attischen Inschriften,* 3d ed., pp. 45 f.; also *C.I.A.* II, 706, lS. in Figure 4, runs the length of the stone. The inscription (Fig. 5) reads: 6 8/ios rafavTos *rov* fool Mjei'arSpai *XtiTOvpyif.*
Hie people, at the command of the god, to Menander, public servant.
The restoration must he regarded as certain. In later times,
then, the stone had formed part of the pedestal which supported a statue set up in honor of a man named Menander. The letters are regularly cut and such as are found in inscriptions of the middle of the first century A.D. The only peculiarity to be noted is that the I of MENANAPftl was omitted, evidently by accident, when the inscription was cut and afterwards inserted. When the stone was found, traces of red paint could be seen on the E, 0, and 5 of *rdtjavTos,* and on the T of *rov.* At the ends, along the upper moulding, were also traces of green paint. At the left end this runs down between the second and third letters preserved in the first line, and across the first and second in the line below.
It is not easy to determine who this Menander was. The solution of the problem must depend largely upon the interpre 1. 5 cm.
2.4 cm.
Figure 4.— Profile Of Moulding.
Figure 5. — Inscription From The Asclepieum., tation given to the words, ra'f euro? *rov 9eov.* At first sight one would naturally refer them to the Delphic oracle, and such an interpretation would fit in well with the fact that the statue Cf., for example, *C.I.A.* III, 1, 456; Loewy, *Insch. Gr. Bildhauer,* p. 231.
was erected by the people. In that case it would be necessary to suppose that the Menander thus honored was a man well known in Greece; but such an interpretation meets with a difficulty in *XeirovpyK.* This word, which is not found in any Attic writer, is rare even in inscriptions, and seems to mean in late Greek times a public servant or one who performed some service for a god. That an Athenian in this station in life should be honored with a public statue by command of Apollo at Delphi is hard to imagine. Therefore either *Xeirovpyos* must have another meaning, or a new explanation must be sought for rafairo? *Tov deov;* and as there is not sufficient evidence to establish the former alternative, we must turn to the latter for our solution.
In *C.I.A.* II, 1491 we find, 'AaitXr)irip 'PoSr) irpoardi-avTos *rov deov.* 'etti iepeay; 'OXvpirfyov Kviadr)vaieoy;. In other words, Asclepius orders Rhode, probably by means of a dream, to make some unnamed offering to him. In this place *deov* must refer to Asclepius, and here, I think, we have a hint as to the true interpretation of our inscription. The 0eo? referred to would then be Asclepius, and this would suit *Xeirovpyot* very well. That is, we imagine that Menander was an attendant in the precinct of Asclepius, who had perhaps held his office for many years and performed many services for the patients who frequented the temple, and that finally the people at the command of the god honored him with a statue. The fact that the statue was erected by popular vote need not be a difficulty, for if some influential citizen while sleeping in the holy precinct of Asclepius dreamed that the god ordered the people to erect the statue, the people might easily be persuaded to vote to do so.

Nothing further is known of this Menander; but from the place where the stone was found it seems likely that the statue was set up within the precinct of Asclepius close to the way leading up to the theatre.

William N. Bates. of Oriental ftcscarcft. m Palestine

A NEW INSCRIPTION FROM UPPER GALILEE

On Wednesday, April 4, 1906, as the pupils of the American School of Archaeology, on their tour through northern Palestine under my direction, were approaching the bridge over the Hasbani, near its junction with the Leddan and Banias sources to form the Jordan, in the midst of a furious storm which had threatened the complete arrest of our expedition, I was halted at the head of the line of march by a shout from my son, B. Selden Bacon, at its other extremity, that he saw traces of lettering on a stone by the roadside. We were then less than half a mile west of the bridge Gisr el-Ghajar, on our way to Banias, having left Abil (Abel of Beth-Maacah) less than an hour behind us to the west, and looking directly east over Tell el-Khadi (Dan) to the splendid castle of Subebeh (Belfort) towering above Banias (Caesarea Philippi). We were following the immemorial track of commerce from Tyre, Sidon, and the Phoenician coast to Damascus by the south side of Hermon over Dan (Laish "which belongeth to the Sidonians") and Caesarea Philippi. In the pelting storm photography and squeeze impression were equally impossible. Even a notebook copy was a matter of hours, owing to the extreme faintness of the lettering, but for which, however, the inscription in so public and well travelled a spot must long since have been reported. Under the circumstances the only practical course appeared to be to permit the party to continue, remaining behind with my son to make the copy, and returning under more favorable conditions if the inscription proved unknown and of sufficient importance.

In spite of numbed fingers and dripping note-book, the copy of the faint, almost undecipherable letters was at last complete, yielding a Greek inscription of 304-305 A.D. in thirteen lines

American Journal of Archaeology, Second Series. Journal of the 316 Archaeological Institute of America, Vol. XI (1907), No. S.

with letters averaging 1£ inches in height. The stone was a basalt boulder similar to those which completely cover the fields at no great distance, but of unusual size, and doubtless chosen for its purpose (the marking of a boundary) because of its convenient shape. About 5 feet in total length, the upper part, measuring about 2 feet by 1£, and about 9 inches thick, presents on one side a fairly smooth and uniform surface for the lettering which covers it. This appears to be due to careful selection of the block rather than to artificial shaping. The lower part, probably once sunk in the ground, though the stone lay prostrate on the surface when discovered, was about 3£ feet in length, broader and thicker than the upper third, and less even in surface. Minute and careful examination revealed no trace of lettering on it. The copy of the inscription follows: AIOKAHTIANOC
KAIMA5IMIANOC
CGBKKAI
KUINCTANTIOC
6. KAIMA5IMIANOC
KeCAPGCAIOONA!
OPIZONTAArPOY
GTTOIKIOYXPHCIM!
ANOYCTHPIX0H
10. NeeKGAGYCAN
PONTIAIGAI.
CTATOYTOYTOYAI
AKHM.

The opening formula, "Diocletian and Maximian, august Caesars, and Constantius and Maximian, Caesars," is supported by a Latin inscription from Palmyra which uses the equivalent style, *D. et M. invictissimi imperatores, et C. et M. nobilissimi Caesare8.* The rest of the inscription scarcely admits of doubt as to the reading, except in the case of what would seem to be two proper names. Sublinear points in the copy above indicate the doubtful letters. It may be possible, however, to Lebas-Waddington, No. 2626.

obtain some further light from the excellent photographs (Figs. 1 and 2), which were taken after the removal of the stone to a position of security against defacement.

With the exception of the doubtful letters of the name in line 8 the translation leaves little to be desired in point of clearness as far as line 11. The emperors named "have ordered (this) stone to be set up to define the boundary of the farm adjoining the villa of Chresimianos (?) (placing the work) under the care of..." Lines 12 and 13 can also be read with practical certainty by the aid of an almost exactly parallel inscription on a boundary stone of the same emperors, the same date, and the same region found at Namara (Namr) in the Hauran, and published in the *Recueil cTArchiologie Orientale* (Tome I, 1888, p. 4) as follows:

C6B KWN..
KAIMA2IMIAN0CeTTI«t
KAICA... AI0ONAIOPIZON
TAOPOYCKUUMHCrA...
MGACKAINAMAP?..
WN(C)THPIXOHNAieteA
eYCAN«tPONTI( )MAP( )
I0Y4.. TTTTKHMCeiTO
POC

The last word is obviously a transliteration of the Latin "censitor," the functionary charged in this case with fixing the boundary. In the inscription from Abil either the word is abbreviated or the letters following have been obliterated. It seems to be preceded by the preposition *Sid*. Thus only the perplexing letters at the end of line 11 remain to be elucidated. *SpovriSi emarwov Tov-tov Sia KilfiaiTopot* might possibly be rendered "under charge of the officer appointed for this purpose through the assessor "; but aside from questions of grammar, it is difficult to find a TT under the pretty distinct A near the end of line 11, and there are traces of one or more letters following.

The two photographs are taken from slightly different angles with the main object in Fig. 2 of bringing the lower lines (scarcely visible in Fig. 1) into better view.

Professor Clermont-Ganneau, to whom I owe the reference to two similar inscriptions recently discovered by Dussaud in the Hauran, accepts also that author's suggestion as the most important clew to the meaning. Two fragments found on the road between 'Atil and es-Souwaida, in the Hauran (No. 23, p. 247) give the names of the emperors Diocletian and Maxiniian as fixing the boundaries (Spot) of Dionysias (es-Souwaida) and Athelene ('Atil). A larger inscription of sixteen lines (No. 175, p. 208) found at 'Aqraba in almost perfect condition gives the following: Dussaud, *Mission dans les Regions Desertiques de la Syrie Moyenne,* 1903, pp. 247 and 298.

Figure 2.—Lower Part Of The Inscription. *AeaTTOTat r)fimv iOKXrTiavK MatpiavK aefta/TTOt Kai KtovffTairreio? xal lalipiavK itaUrape; Xl8ov Siopcoma opow p.i)Tpo/tai/xt'a? 'A'epa/Sij? Kai 'Aafyw aTi)piy8t)vai etteXevaav, ippovTiSi Aovkwv Kata/itoi/ KT)vaiTopo;.*

The stone, accordingly, like that of Namr first mentioned, marked the boundary between the mother village Akrabe ('Aqraba) and Asichon ('(Jsidj). Dussaud infers from the number of boundary stones of this date and type the probability of some vast *operation cadastrale,* with relation to the establishment of a taxable unit, the *iugum* or *caput,* consisting of lands of differing character and unequal extent, whose total would represent an equal value. He refers to M. van Berchem, *La proprisU territoriale et Vimpot fonder sous les premiers Califes,* Geneva, 1886, pp. 46-47, and calls attention to the mention of the *censitor* whose function was the registration of imposts. I have not been able to consult the work of van Berchem, but it would appear to be a confirmation of Dussaud's conjecture that the new inscription from Abil, unlike those previously discovered, records the boundaries, not of a village or district, but of a country estate *(aypov eiroLiclov)*. It would seem not unreasonable to connect these evidences of a fixation of land values by the " censitor," with the edicts of Diocletian for the fixation of prices of goods sold in the markets.

B. W. Bacon. See the articles by Mommsen in *Hermes,* XXV, 1890, 'Diocletian's Edict De pretiis rerum venalium' and by Bluemner in *Philologus,* LIX, 1900, on newly discovered fragments.

Institute of America

AN INTERPRETATION OF THE SO-CALLED HARPY TOMB

Since the discovery of the so-called Harpy tomb by Fellows in 1838 many interpretations of its sculptures have been offered. But, while most of the figures in the reliefs have received various explanations more or less satisfactory, the meaning of the human-headed birds has remained unsolved. The different interpretations of the reliefs that have appeared are arranged by A. H. Smith, in three groups.

In the first are the interpretations of those who have believed that the subject represented is the rape of the daughters of Pandareus by the Harpies. As Mr. Smith notes, such a subject is inappropriate for a tomb, and moreover, these " Harpies" are not objects of terror to the persons whom they carry.

According to the second group of interpreters the seated figures are infernal divinities to whom the souls of the dead pay reverence. Thus on the west side Demeter sits at the left and Persephone at the right, the standing figures are worshippers carrying symbols of life, while the door of the tomb signifies death, and the cow suckling her calf over it is symbolic of the renewal of life. The three seated figures that remain represent then either Zeus, on the south side, Poseidon, on the east, and Hades, on the north, or Zeus shown under his triple aspect. Curtius, who advanced this last view, went even farther in elaborating his explanation, and saw a suggestion of the egg, as the symbol of life, in the form of the "Harpy" body. Conze, however, shows the futility of such an inter I am much indebted to Professor W. Max Miiller for suggestions in regard to the Egyptian material in this paper, but he is in no wise responsible for any errors into which I may have fallen. *British Museum Cat. of Archaic Greek Sculpture,* 1802, pp. 58-59. Braun, *Annali delf 1st.* 1844, p. 161. *Arch. Zeit.* 1855, p. 10. *Arch. Zeit.* 1869, p. 78. American Journal of Archaeology, Second Series. Journal of the 321 Archaeolo.rical Institute uf America, Vol. XI (1907), No. 8.

pretation by citing other birds that have the same form. Other parallel instances are cited below.

The third group of commentators believes that the seated figures represent the heroized dead, and the persons with offerings the surviving members of their families. The difficulty with this explanation, according to Mr. Smith, is that the subject of a youth giving up his arms to an heroized ancestor is without parallel. Mr. Smith himself thinks that it is best "to suppose that we have on this tomb scenes connected with death, though we cannot attempt, for want of knowledge of Lycian mythology, to assign names to the personages represented."

Such a view as the last appears unnecessary, for, even if some of the figures may remain unidentified, it seems that others admit a reasonable explanation. Moreover, it appears that Curtius came the nearest to the solution when he saw in the Harpies, so-called, a resemblance to the "Ba-birds" on a monument of Ptolemy Euergetes III. His mistake, however, was in trying to see in the form of the Harpies a resemblance to an egg, and hence to infer a relationship with the Orphic egg, and so to find there a symbol of life. As a matter of fact the eggshaped body and fan-shaped tail are found in other birds in Egyptian art, notably in the representation of vultures. On the other hand, the identity of the Harpies with the Egyptian birds in the method of attaching the tail to the body and in the outline of the body does point to Egypt. For that reason the evidence is valuable, when taken with other proofs, in turning us toward Egypt as the source of some of the motives in the Xanthus reliefs.

From an early time Egyptian influence was felt in the Mediterranean and in Asia. The relations between Egypt and Greece and the Greek Islands are too well known to need comment. As to Asia, the brilliant campaigns of Thothmes III Milchhofer, *Arch. Zeit.* 1881, p. 58; Friedericha-Wolters, *Gipsabyusse,* p. 76. *Arch. Zeit.* 18f!9, pp. 10-17.

Maspero, *Hixtoire Ancienne des Petiplen de V Orient,* I,"p. 415; Champollion. I, pi. xciv; III, pi. ccxvii (flying hawk); Prisse D'Avenues, *Atlas,* II, Necropole de Thebes, AmounOph II et sa gouvemante = de la Faye (text) *peinture,* pi. vii (duck or poose). For Egyptian objects at Mycenae, see Schuchhardt. *Schliemann's Excavations,* pp. 207, 213, 294, 310, 352; for interrelation of Egypt and Crete, see (ea. 1500 B.C.) had brought this country under Egyptian control, and, under Amenhotep III (car. 1400 B.C.), the Amarna letters show all the powers—Babylonia, Assyria, Mitanni, and Alasa, that is, Cyprus — courting the friendship of Egypt. As early even as this (XVIII Dyn.) the Lycians came in contact with Egypt. Their relations, however, hardly redound to their credit, for it was as roving bands of pirates that they descended on the coasts of the Delta and of Cyprus. At a much later date, and at one more important for our thesis, namely, under Amasis (596525 B.C.), Egypt was in close friendly relations with Greece. Granting that this intercourse made possible the presence of Egyptian elements in the sculptures of the Harpy tomb, it now remains to show that these sculptures are Greek, and not specifically Lycian, in conception. This seems to me to be established not only by the fact that from time immemorial the Lycians participated in Greek life, as, for instance, in their campaign against Egypt in company with the Akaiuasha (Achaeans), in their presence in the league of the Ionic cities in the sixth century B.C. (about the time of our monument), and later in their membership in the Attic-Delian confederacy, but it is also established by the style of the work, which is Ionic Greek, and by the fact that another Lycian relief on the heroum of Gjolbaschi contains scenes from Greek legends. It will also be recalled that Apollo bore an epithet which suggests a relation with Lycia.

The Harpy tomb consisted of a square shaft seventeen feet in height, placed on a base which rose on one side to a height of six feet, and on the other was little above the present level of the ground. Within the top of the shaft was hollowed out the sepul B.S.A. 1899-1900, pp. 1-93 *passim;* of Egypt and Cyprus, Myres and Richter, *Cat. of the Cyprus Mus.* pp. 99, 19, 29; for a juneral discussion of the relations of the Egyptians and the Mediterranean peoples, Hall, ' Keftiu and the Peoples of the Sea,' B.S.A. 1901-1902, pp. 157 ff.; and Muller, *Asienu. Europa,* pp. 336 ff.; *Mitt. Vorderas. Ges.* 1904, p. 125; *Gaz. B.-A.* 1907, p. 95, where a faience plaque from Cnossus is given showing a goat standing on a ground line of Egyptian leaf pattern and suckling a kid.
For traces of Egyptian influences in Asia Minor see sculptures of Boghaz Koi. Breasted, *A History of Egypt,* p. 332. Breasted, *op. cit.* p. 424; Muller, *Asien u. Europa,* pp. 354 ff. This description is abridged from the *Catalogue of Archaic Greek Sculpture in the British Museum,* pp. 54 ff. chral chamber, with the entrance on the west side, while on each of the faces of the monument, at the top, was a relief in white marble. These reliefs measure 3 feet 3 inches in height, 8 feet 2 inches in length on the east and west sides, and 7 feet (3 inches on the north and south sides. The decorations are as follows:
West Side (Fig. 1). Near the left side of the relief is a small doorway over which is a cow suckling a calf. At the extremes of the relief sit two female figures, the one at the left holding a phiale, the other a lotus and a pomegranate. Toward the figure at the right advance three female figures.
East Side (Fig. 2). In the centre a bearded figure sits facing the right, with a sceptre against his left shoulder, and a flower in his right hand. Behind him stand two male figures, the first of whom holds a flower (?) and a pomegranate. Before the seated figure stands a boy offering a cock and a pomegranate, while at the extreme right stands a youth accompanied by a dog.
North Side (Fig. 3). A bearded figure sits facing the left on a seat under which is a pig, while before him stands a youth (?) fully armed. At each end of this relief a humanheaded bird flies away from the central group, bearing a diminutive figure held by its arms and claws. In the lower right-hand corner crouches a figure looking up in despair.
South Side (Fig. 4). In the centre sits a male (bearded?) figure with a staff, pomegranate, and apple (?). Before him Smith, *Brit. Mus. Cat. of Archaic Greek Sculpture,* p. 56, and Friederichs Wolters, *Gipsabgilsse,* p. 71, call the animal a bear. Professor Fowler writes me that Wolters once said that he half believed the beast a pig.
stands a male figure with a dove (?). At the right and left ends of the relief a "Harpy" flies off with its burden, as on the north side.

Inasmuch as the western side seems to be the chief one, — for it has two seated figures, — it may be well to begin here the discussion of the details of the monument. The seated figure at the right and the second standing figure hold a lotus flower in their right and left hands respectively. This flower, which is not a native of Greece, in fact never grew north of Egypt, makes its appearance continuously in the funeral monuments of the latter country. It was, we learn, placed in the hands of guests at Egyptian funerals. The other connections in which the flower may have been used are aside from the question here at issue. It is enough for us that it was distinctly a funeral flower.

In view of this it is reasonable to suppose that when this flower was taken over from the Egyptians by the Greeks (there is no reason to look for any intermediary) and introduced into their funeral scenes, it had some funerary meaning. What that meaning may be I shall endeavor to develop later.

The second symbol that appears (twice) on this western side is the pomegranate. It is held both by the seated figure at the right and by the second adorant. This fruit, which according to Greek mythology was the especial attribute of Persephone, was the one eaten unwittingly by her, and the one that prevented her complete return to the upper day. It also appears, though rarely, in Egyptian funeral scenes. From the Greek story it is clear that it is connected with the cult of the dead, and from its appearance on the Theban monument it may be that this symbol, too, came from Egypt.

The third symbol that is on this same relief is the egg. This recalls, of course, the familiar Greek story of the Orphic egg Goodyear, *Grammar of the Lotus,* p. 4, who quotes from Osburn, *Monumental History of Egypt,* I, p. 63.
P. Gardner, *J.S.S.* 1884, p. 130; Preller, *Grieeh. Myth.* I, 492.
'Prisse D'Avennes, II, *Offrande de fleus et de fruits* = de la Faye (text), *peinture,* pi. xxvi.
Milchhofer, *Ath. Mitt.* 1877, p. 464, Note 3, notes that the pomegranate was the attribute of Zeus, Hera, Hades, Demeter, Kore, and Aphrodite. For a clay pomegranate found in a tomb see Millin and Millingen, II, 78. from which sprang Phanes, the primordial being, who created heaven and earth; and it is natural to suppose that in this symbol appears again the suggestion of the creative power of nature, and, to carry it a step farther, of rebirth. There is, moreover, some reason to believe that the Orphic mysteries were of Egyptian origin, for it was a widely spread view in antiquity that Orpheus introduced these rites from Egypt.

The next symbol on this relief that demands explanation is the group of the cow and calf that stands over the doorway. Such a group has already been recognized as symbolic of fecundity, or of the life-giving power of nature often connected with the Asiatic nature goddess, whom the Greeks as a rule identified with Hera or Artemis. Both these interpretations are correct in general. But it seems possible to get a yet closer definition of the meaning of this group.

We have already seen that the lotus and the pomegranate appear on Egyptian monuments, and that the egg appears in Egyptian legend. Bearing this in mind, it is natural to look to Egypt for an explanation of the cow and calf on this monument. A parallel, in fact, seems to lie in the Egyptian group of Hathor-Isis and Horus. In the Egyptian myth the sun *Prod, in Tim.* B. § 130, p. 307, ed. Schneider, *xal dmjs)* irp&ura diri Too irpti)T07fwCf (ioC, *iv if art-piULTtndt T6* fyoy *iariv.* Roscher, *Lexikon,* s.v. Orpheus, p. 1105.

The following note I do not offer as a demonstration. It suggests, however, some interesting Egyptian parallels with the Greek story. According to one Egyptian doctrine (Brugsch, *Religion u. Mythol. l. Allen Aegypter,* p. 161), Chnum, the maker, potter, and architect, modelled on his wheel the egg which concealed in itself the light and germ of the world to be. Again Egyptian legend has it (Maspero, *Hist. anc.* I, p. 88.) that Ra is the luminous egg, hatched in the east by the celestial goose, from which the sun breaks forth every day. This last belief bears a close resemblance to the Greek story of the sun-god, Apollo, if we recognize that the name Leda is often associated with Leto, and that the goddess was looked upon as Night, the mother of the gods of light (Roscher, *Lex.* p. 1924). The likeness is made even clearer if Stephani *Compte-Rendu,* 1863, pp. 23 ff.) is right in thinking that in the original legend Leda was not a swan, but a goose.

Rayet, *Monuments de VArt antique,* I, p. 4; Curtius, *Arch. Leit.* 1855, p. 3. Head, *Historic. Numorum,* p. 276. See also p. 303, where this group is the "type" of the coins of Carystus in Euboea, and is taken as symbolic of Hera. On p. 572 the cow suckling a calf is given as a type of a Lycian coin dating 480-450 B.c. (Horus) is described as a "sucking calf of pure mouth," while his mother, Isis, has the form of a cow. Originally the cow (or bull) was the concept for the heaven. But if Isis (the cow) had this meaning at first, by the time of Herodotus, at least, she was recognized as the same #s Demeter—that is, she had become the earth goddess. This same conception of the goddess remained down to the time of the first century A.d.; and her character as an earth goddess is made clear by such descriptions as "creatress of the green crop, the green one, whose greenness is like the greenness of the earth," and "mistress of bread." Since this character of an earth goddess remained so long attached to Isis, and since it was fully known as early as 450 B.C., the time of Herodotus, it is reasonable to think that it was also the character of the goddess seventyfive or one hundred years before, at the time of our monument. Egyptian religion was very stable; and the inference from Herodotus, who does not speak of the likeness of Demeter to Isis as a new one, is that the likeness had existed for some time. Since, then, it is possible that the Greeks of the time of our monument knew Isis as an earth mother, it was also possible for them, when they wished to represent the earth goddess, Demeter, in the capacity of an all-nourishing mother goddess, to borrow the original cow form of the goddess, and introduce it, together with the calf as a symbol of the nourished, into their monument. In this way it seems reasonable to interpret the group as suggestive of resurrection.

An explanation has thus far been suggested for all the symbols that appear on the western side of the Xanthus monument, except the patera held by the figure seated at the left. In this, owing to its general use in worship, it seems impossible to see any definite meaning beyond its suggestion of the performance of a religious ceremony.

Of the two figures, both of whom are heavily draped and Maspero, *Hint. anr.* p. 89; and for Horns as a calf, Bnijrsch. *op. cit.* I, 100.

For a discussion of the primitive idea of the heaven as a cow or bull, see Iluller, *Mitt. Vorderas. Ges.* 1904, pp. 108 ff. Herod. II, 59. ITM *Si irn Kara Ttjv* 'exxtjcwi' *yutr(rav ATjTrjp.* Frazer, *Golden Bough,* I, p. 310, and Bmgsch, *op. cit.* p. 64".

Patera-shaped dishes appear in Egypt as early as the XVIIIth Dyn. See Maspero, *Manual of Egyptian Archaeology,* p. 314. sit upon thrones furnished with arms and footstools, the one at the left is of a fuller, more mature form, and seems to have a somewhat more elaborate diadem. If there is any particular meaning in this, and any relation is to be seen between the two figures, it is a natural suggestion that the one on the left is the mother, and the other the daughter. With this step taken it is easy to surmise the names Demeter and Persephone. But it remains to adduce further proof before such designations can be accepted.

In the first place the pomegranate would point to Persephone, but, as noted above, this fruit appears as the attribute of other divinities, and so by itself is not decisive. It is possible to get more definite information, however, if we turn to the Spartan reliefs. Their relationship in spirit with the Xanthus monument has been from time to time noted by archaeologists. Furtwangler, in discussing one of these reliefs (Fig. 5), calls

'Overbeck, *Griech. Plast,* p. 226, suggests two goddesses, the one with the patera the goddess of death, the other of life. Rayet, *Mon. de V Art Ant.* I, p. 4 (Harpy tomb), thinks the figures those of goddesses; Braun, *Ann. d. 1st.* 1844, pp. 133 ff., and Murray, *Hist, of Greek Sculpt.* I, p. 120, both name the figures Demeter and Persephone.

Ath. Mitt. 1877, pis. xx, xxii, xxiv. *Sammluny Sabouroff,* pi. i; also Milchhofer, *Ath. Mitt.* 1877, p. 460. Note 1. attention to the fact that the woman wears shoes with curving toes, and adds that they are of an Eastern type. This is confirmed by the fact that on the Xanthus monument the figure of Persephone—to grant the name for designation—and the seated figure on the south side appear to wear the same kind of shoe. This offers us some reason for looking to the Spartan reliefs for an explanation of the seated figure.

On one of the reliefs (Fig. 6) Hades and Persephone are seated on a throne that has the back, as on the throne of the scene, for their temple was found near that of Demeter and Persephone at Corinth, the three goddesses were grouped near Demeter, Persephone, and Hades on the Hyacinthus altar, and they appeared with Zeus Moiragetes on a relief in a stoa on the way to the temple of Despoina at Lycosura. The Fates, Graces, and Hours are also associated with Persephone in a Shoes with curved toes are common in Hittite sculpture, and appear elsewhere in Asia. But, to my knowledge, we have no evidence of interrelations between Greeks and Hittites. Details of costumes would be likely to be familiar to the Greeks only from the coast peoples of the Mediterranean; and since there are reasons to believe in a kinship between the Spartan reliefs and the Xanthus monument in other respects, it is fair to see a kinship in the matter of costume.

Annali, 1847, pi. F. Muller-Wieseler, *Denkmdler,* II, Text to pi. lxviii, No. 856. Pau8. II, 4, 7. *Ibid.* Ill, 19, 4. *Ibid.* VIII, 37, 1. dance in Orphic Hymn 43. That the goddesses appear on the Xanthus tomb without attributes is no cause for doubt. They are shown in the same manner on the Francois vase, which is somewhat earlier in date than the tomb.

Of the seated figures on the other sides of the monument, only that on the east sits on a throne with arms and a footstool, like that on the west side. One may assume, then, that this figure equals in dignity those seated on the side diametrically opposite, and for that reason it may appropriately be considered next. Rayet suggested that the seated personage was Asclepius, and the two figures standing behind him his daughters, Hygieia and Panacea. The cock, held by the figure before the throne, might be an offering to Asclepius — witness the dying words of Socrates—but the other identifications are wrong, because the figures behind the throne are male. It may be well to leave the naming of the enthroned person until the questions raised by the other elements in the relief are settled.

To start at the right, the first object to give us pause is the dog that stands looking up at his master, the youthful figure at the extreme right. On one of the Chrysapha reliefs (Fig. 7) is a man seated on a chair, with a dog fawning upon his knees. On yet another relief from Sparta, a dog sits beside the throne of an enthroned male and female pair. According to Furtwiingler the dog was sacred to Hecate and offered to her in sacrifice. It was, he goes on to say, peculiarly a hero animal, that is to say, associated with the dead. Moreover, if we are to Roscher, *Lex.* p. 3092.

Furtwangler and Reichhold, *Griech. Vasenm.* I, Taf. 1-2. *Monuments,* I, p. 7. For Asclepius as a chthonic god, see Walton, *The Cult of Asclepius,* p. 17. *Ath. Mitt.* 1882, pi. vii. « *Ibid.* 1877, pi. xxii. *Ibid.* 1882, pp. 160-173. For the dog grouped with a heroized youth see Millin and Millingen, II, pp. 32, 33.

Figure 7. — Relief From Chry9apha. see in the last cited relief from Sparta, and in still another with the same subject, a representation of an enthroned god and goddess, then we must believe that the dog appears in scenes with chthonic gods, and to focus our attention, that the dog on the east side of the Xanthus monument offers one bit of evidence that we are in the presence of a god. In the hands of the next figure (apparently a child) is a cock. This bird, I have already suggested, might be appropriately offered to Asclepius. The cock, however, finds a place among the offerings to other chthonic deities. Thus, on a terra-cotta relief from Epizephyrian Locri (Fig. 8) Persephone clasps two cocks in her left arm as she is snatched away, while again on a relief already cited, the enthroned goddess holds the same kind of a bird. That the cock is also associated as a funeral symbol with mortals is shown by the grave stele of a youth from Larissa. But, as we have seen, the bird does occur in Figures.— Hades And Pkksephone. association with Hades and Persephone, and it may have some such use here. The lotus (?) held by the seated figure and by the one standing behind him, and the pomegranate in the hand of the standing figure, have both been shown to belong to chthonic deities and burial rites. To summarize, then, there is on this side a series of symbols all associated with the dead. More than that, of these symbols the cock, the lotus, and the pomegranate have been associated with Persephone, and, in all probability, the hound was introduced at least once in a *Ath. Milt.* 1877, p. 444. *Arch. Zeit.* 1870, p. 77. *Ann. d. Inst.* 1847, pi. F. *Ath. Mitt.* 1882, p. 78. Weicker, *Ath. Mitt.* 1005, pp. 207-212, explains the cock on grave stelae as a symbolic representation of the soul of the deceased. It is interesting to note that in Egypt (Wilkinson, III, p. 319) white and saffron colored cocks were sacrificed to Anubis, who became identified with the Hermes psychopompus of the Greeks. Certain Boeotian terra-cottas show Hermes carrying a cock. relief of Hades and Persephone. All this added to the fact that the seated figure on this east side is enthroned with the same dignity as the seated figures on the west, makes it more than likely that he is to he associated with these goddesses. The only deity that could well be associated with Persephone (for she is the chief figure on the western side), and the only one to whom the symbols already mentioned could fittingly be given, must be a chthonic god, and that god is Hades.

On the north side is a scene in which a warrior offers his arms to a seated bearded figure who holds a sceptre. That the act is one of offering on the part of the warrior is shown not only by the fact that it would be natural for a man to remove a helmet from his head by the front, but that it seems to have been the manner of holding a Corinthian helmet (Fig. 9), and of extending it toward another person. The scene, then, is not a departure, but rather an arrival home, as it were. The warrior is laying aside his arms. The question is to whom he offers them. The other features of the frieze show that *tevvvpiwyvywwWP-PVl* the scene is not an ordinary home-Figure 9.— Method Of Holding coming." Under the chair of CoTMTM" Helmet. the seated figure, who seems to be marked as a deity by his sceptre, stands a pig. We find this animal offered to Aphrodite, Dionysus, and Demeter, who, in some of their characteristics, are chthonic divinities. Besides this one need hardly emphasize the slaughter of pigs at the Thesmophoria, where the deities concerned are—to say nothing of Hades — Demeter and Persephone. It probably suggested, as at Eleusis, the Gerhard, *Ans. Vasenb.* pi. cxci.

Ibid. pi. cclxviii, 2; Furtwangler und Reichhold, *Or. Vas.* II, 66 a. *Aus. Vasenb.*, pi. clxxxviii, where Hekate holds a helmet as does our figure. Furtwangler, *Ath. Mitt.* 1882, p. 164, Note 1, says that the arms appearing in hero reliefs, especially In later times, belong to heroes in general. Schcimann, *Qriech. Alterthlimer*, II, p. 240. idea of purification. At all events, the creature is decidedly associated with chthonic gods. So, too, in Egypt we find the pig entering into the worship of the preeminently chthonic god, Osiris. We may or may not accept Mr. Frazer's very convincing argument that Osiris was originally the " personification of the great yearly vicissitudes of nature, especially of the corn," wherein it is easy to imagine lurked the idea of resurrection; at all events, the god was from early times connected with the idea of immortality, and as early as the fifth dynasty had become the judge and god of the dead. Whether there is any relation between the immolation of the pig in the worship of Osiris and in the Thesmophoria I do not venture to say. There is no doubt, however, that in the latter case the sacrifice was in honor of deities of vegetation, and particularly of corn, and in the case of the offering to Osiris, I think Mr. Frazer has made it very clear that originally, at least, the pig was offered to Osiris as a corn-god. While we may not say that this resemblance is proof of Greek borrowing from Egypt, at least the parallelism is very close, and suggests the possibility that there might have been a borrowing.

The pig, then, in this relief, being a chthonic offering, would seem to connote a scene in Hades. If this is so, the seated figure must be some deity or important personage in that realm. That the figure represents Hades himself is unlikely if that god is the occupant of the throne on the east side. The less elaborate nature of the throne points to some subordinate. Of such characters the most likely to be enthroned in Hades are Minos and Rhadamanthus, the judges of the dead. Such an identification Miss J. E. Harrison, *Prolegomena to the Study of Greek Religion,* p. 153. Herod. II, 47. Whether Herodotus was right or not in associating Osiris with Dionysus is of little moment here. He does tell us that the pig was an offering to an infernal god. Frazer, *Golden Bough,* II, p. 69, would make the pig originally a representative of the corn spirit. Frazer, *Adonis. Attis, Osiris,* p. 211. Budge, *The Gods of the Egyptians,* I, p. 147. It may be argued, of course, that the idea of the sacrifice of the pig to chthonic gods was native to Greece, or, if borrowed, may have come from some other quarter. It may have been indigenous, no one can gainsay that, but the intimate intercourse between Egypt and Greece, and the greater antiquity of the former country, would seem to lend plausibility to the argument for borrowing on the part of the Greeks. fits well here, for the corresponding side, on the south, shows a figure similarly seated on a like throne. It does not seem farfetched therefore to name these two figures Minos and Rhadamanthus, and inasmuch as the north side seems to have more detail, namely, the pig and the mourning figure, as well as the warrior and "Harpies," perhaps one may hazard the name Minos for the seated figure now under discussion.

With such an interpretation one of course thinks of naming the figure seated on the east side Minos, and those on the north and south Rhadamanthus and Aeacus. But in addition to the fact that the east side is so intimately connected with the west, the late introduction of Aeacus prevents such an identification.

Finally — to leave the flying figures and their burdens to be treated with those on the south side—it remains to consider on this northern relief only the crouching figure in the right-hand lower corner. Two possibilities present themselves. In the first place it may be that the figure represents a personage who is soon to be carried away by the human-headed birds, secondly it may represent one of the living relatives mourning the dead. If the former supposition is true, the small size of the bird demands that the figure be diminutive; if the latter, the mourner would be made smaller to distinguish him from the heroized dead. The identification of the figure as that of a mourner seems precluded by the fact that in no other part of the reliefs do we have such a figure of a living person introduced.

On the south side, before the seated figure, who is perhaps Rhadamanthus, stands a worshipper holding in his left hand a bird which possibly may be a dove. Its presence here is probably to be explained by the chthonic character that attached to it. It was an appropriate offering to Aphrodite and Astarte (who were more or less related, and were in some characteristics chthonic goddesses) and to Adonis, who so closely resembled Osiris (an earth god) as to be confused with him.

In the right hand of Rhadamanthus is a spherical object which may be an apple. Why it is shown here is hard to say. The pomegranate, on the other hand, also held by the figure, has already been shown to be of chthonic significance. Frazer, *Attis, Adonis, Osiris.* p. 19. *Ibid.* p. 64. *Ibid.* p. 18. For a clay apple found in a tomb, see Millin and Millingen, II, 78. l'iguhe 10.—Ba-bird Revisiting The Mummy.

It now remains to explain the two human-headed birds that appear on both the north and the south sides. Mention has already been made of the attempt on the part of Curtius to find in the shape of the body the symbolism of the egg. While that was seen to be wrong, this shape did help in showing where to look for the original. It is, in fact, the common form given to the vulture, and even to other birds in Egypt. Having, therefore, turned our eyes to Egypt, it is hard not to see in the birds on the Harpy tomb a kinship with the Ba-birds of the Egyptian tombs. There we find these soul-birds revisiting the mummy, seated on the edge of the funeral couch (Fig. 10), hovering over the mummy on the couch, or standing on a grave tablet.

Moreover, the Ba-birds and the Double are often represented together. Thus the Double, receiving the homage of the living, clasps his soul, in the form of a bird, to his breast, or rides with his soul, or Ba-bird, on the back of the Hathor-cow" (Fig. 11). Sometimes the man is represented together with his Double.

To these Ba-birds of Egyptian monuments the so-called Harpies on the Xanthus tomb bear too striking a resemblance not to have been inspired by them. This curious human-headed bird evidently caught the attention of other dwellers within the Mediterranean i Maspero, *op. cit.* pp. 135, 239, vulture; p. 192, duck, s Maspero, *Hist. Arte.* I, p. 198. 8 *Ibid.* p. 199.
Wilkinson, *op. cit.* III, pi. xxxv. Konigl. Mus. zu Berlin, *Aegypt u. Vorderasiat. Altherthumer,* Taf. 128. Maspero, *op. cit.* pp. 183, 187. '*Ibid.* p. 187. *Ibid.* p. 259.
Figure 11. — The Ba-bird And Double ON ThE BACK OF ThE Hathok-cow-. periphery, for such a creature has been found, cut in stone, in Cyprus. But here, as in the Harpy tomb, the artist has misunderstood the original meaning of the creature. The Cypriote statuette (as is often the case with the Ba-bird in Egypt)' wears what appears to be a false beard, and is represented as playing on a syrinx. In this way the Ba-bird has been modified into a male siren.

On the Xanthian monument the artist has not changed the character of the Ba-bird as did his Cypriote brother. But he did make use of the figure in a manner differing from that of the Egyptian sculptors. This change, as I have just stated, was probably due to a misunderstanding of the Egptian monuments. What the artist means by the figures on the Harpy tomb I shall try to show presently.

It must be noted first, however, that the Greeks did not think of a man as divisible into the elements which the Egyptians attributed to him. They did, nevertheless, conceive the dead man in the other world as a spiritual projection, so to speak, of the physical being. As a rule the soul was represented, at least as it left the body, as a fluttering, winged manikin *(eidolon),* as we learn from the vase paintings. But, at times (even as was the practice with their Egyptian neighbors), the Greeks gave the soul the form of a human headed bird. AVe need therefore feel no shock at finding the soul shown as a Ba-bird on our monument. This, in fact, is what I believe we have on the tomb. But instead of showing the Ba-bird in the arms of the Double, as on the Egyptian monuments, the artist has reversed the arrangement, in a measure, by representing the soul, or "Ba," flying away with the man himself. That the figure carried is not the soul is demonstrated by the absence of wings. This reversal of relationship between soul and Double, as I have tried to emphasize, was probably due to a misunderstanding of the Egyptian sources.

One further observation may strengthen the evidence for the Perrot and Chipiez, III, p. 600, %. 410.
Ann. d. 1st. 1845, p. 10, where de Luynes cites, first, a vase showing the death of Procris, where the soul of the heroine is represented as a human-headed bin!, and, secondly, another vase where the soul of the Cretan bull appears also as a " siren." relation which I have attempted to establish between the different faces of our monument. On the north side the seated figure faces to the left, while on the south the corresponding figure faces to the right. In other words, if we imagine the monument transparent, the artist thought of the two figures as face to face. This arrangement also occurs on the east and the west sides. For, granting that Persephone, who sits at the right on the west, is the chief figure on that side, then she and the chief figure on the east face are vis-a-vis.

Oliver S. Tonks.

Princeton University. 1907 January— Jane ARCHAEOLOGICAL NEWS NOTES ON RECENT EXCAVATIONS AND DISCOVERIES; OTHER NEWS

James M. Paton, *Editor 65, Sparks St.*, *Cambridge, Mass.* GENERAL AND MISCELLANEOUS

A NEW JOURNAL OF ANCIENT ORIENTAL ART. — In April, 1907, appeared the first number of *Memnon,* edited by R. von Lichtenberg. The field of the new journal is the Aegean Islands, Asia Minor, the Semitic countries and Egypt, with special reference to the art and civilization of these regions rather than the languages and archaeology. It is finely printed and richly illustrated, and promises to be an important addition to the literature of Oriental studies. A special feature is the full classified bibliography.

ADULIS AND GABAZA. — Preliminary Investigation of the Ruins. — In *Z. Assyr.* XX, 1907, pp. 171-182 (2 pis.), R. Sundstrom reports the results of a preliminary survey of the ruins of Adulis, the seaport of the Aksumate kingdom in Abyssinia, and the neighboring port of Gabaza, undertaken for the Princeton University Expedition. Little remains above ground except a few low piles of small black porous stones, but excavations made by the natives disclosed parts of beautiful columns and large slabs. Fragments of marble, two slabs with reliefs of grapes and vines, and other marble ornaments, parts of a thin copper chain, nails and spikes of copper, and pieces of painted glass, together with a number of gold and silver coins, were found near the surface. Excavations would probably yield rich results both in antiquities and in inscriptions, including possibly fragments of the Monumentum Adulitanum copied by Cosmas Indicopleustes. AKSUM. — The Ancient Monuments. — The antiquities of Aksum, in northern Abyssinia, and of the surrounding country have been studied by a l The departments of Archaeological News and Discussions and of Bibliography of Archaeological Books are conducted by Professor Paton, Editor-in-chargc, assisted by Miss Mary H. Buckingham, Mr. Harold R. Hastings, Professor Elmkr T. Merrill, Professor Frank G. Moore, Mr. Charles R. Morey, Professor Lewis B. Paton, Dr. A. 8. Pease, and the Editors. No attempt is made to include in this number of the Journal material published after July 1, 1!«7.

For an explanation of the abbreviations, see pp. 140, 141.
frerrnan expedition, and a portion of the report of D. Kkencker is given in *Arch. Anz.* 1907, cols. 35-63 (5 figs.). Aksum was the capital of a kingdom founded by a Semitic trading colony from southern Arabia, and the early monuments and inscriptions are of Sabaean and Aethiopian origin, but not Egyptian. Greek influence entered in the first century A.d. The kingdom became Christian in the fourth century and was overcome by the Mohammedans in the sixteenth, but Aksum still remains the centre of Ethiopian Christianity, and has a highly venerated sanctuary. The characteristic remains from pagan times are funeral monuments in the form of monolithic stelae or obelisks, and honorary thrones of stone with inscribed slabs. The early Christian art is of Byzantine character. The monolithic stelae and obelisks, some of which are standing while others lie overthrown, are of many tyles and sizes and include one which is taller than the tallest known Egyptian obelisk (Fig. 1). This belongs to a group of monuments which are carved in relief to represent towers of several stories with windows and doors and an exact imitation of the peculiar native architecture combining stone and wood. This technique, in which wooden beams are run through the stone work to give it stability, still survives in the church of the monastery of l)ebra Damo, which is built on an isolated rock accessible only by a rope, and which perhaps dates from the fifth century. Thischurch contains the oldest timber rafters that are known to exist. A peculiar ground plan, in which the middle portions of the four sides of a square recede behind the corner sections, is shown in these relief stelae and in certain ancient buildings here. It is of southern Arabian origin and occurs again in Moslem architecture. BULGARIA. — The Burial Place of the Emperor Decius. — Professor K. Skori'il of Varna identifies the ancient Abrytus, where the emperor Decius died in 251 A.d.,

with Abtat Kalessi in Bulgaria. The ancient walls and towers are still partly preserved, and the coins show that the settlement dates from the time of Trajan. After the Gothic invasion it seems to have been abandoned. (*W. kl. Phil.*, March 13, 1907.) CONSTANTINOPLE. — Inscriptions. — In *Ath. Mitt.* XXXI, 1906, pp. 430-433, F. Hiller Von Gaertrinoex publishes two inscriptions recently found in Galata. The first is an epitaph below a "Funeral Feast"; the Becond is a decree voting Diocles a golden crown and a bronze statue, to be erected *iv* Tu /aecrooruAiu *Tov Bov. tvrnpiov.* The decree is not Byzantine, as it is not Doric Greek, but nothing shows its source. The *fuaoarvXav* may be a court with columns, such as is found before the Bouleuterion at Miletus. NECROLOGY. — Otto Benndorf. — Archaeological science has met with a heavy loss in the death, January 2, 1907, of Otto Benndorf, Director of the Austrian Archaeological Institute. After completing his studies at Bonn, he travelled in Greece and Italy, and in 1868 published with R Schone the catalogue of the Lateran Museum. He was Professor at Zurich, Munich, Prague, and Vienna, retiring in 1898 in order to give his whole time, to the new Austrian Institute. He took part in four great archaeological enterprises, — the excavations at Samothrace, the expedition to Lycia, which discovered the sculptures at Gjolbaschi, the examination of the monument at Adam-Klissi, and the excavations at Ephesus, — and had a prominent place in the publication of the results of these labors. Important also are his works on the sculptures from Selinus, on funeral masks and helmets, and on the Greek and Sicilian vases. He was also the founder of the Archaeological Seminary in the University of Vienna. (S. Reinach, *Citron. Arts,* 1907, p. 15.) See also *R. Arch.* IX, 1907, pp. 170-172 (fig.), and *Jh. Oest. Arch. I.* X, 1907, Beiblatt, cols. 1-6 (fig.).
Frank Sherman Benson.—The numismatist Frank Sherman Benson died on February 28,1907. Soon after his graduation from Yale University in 1876, he devoted himself to the study of early

Greek coins, and gathered a valuable collection, which was especially rich in specimens of the best Syracusan works. *(A. J. Num.* XLI, 1907, pp. 79-80.)

Friedrich Blass. — Friedrich Blass was born at Osnabriick in 1843, and died at Halle in March, 1907. His contributions to the study of the Greek language and literature were many and important, comprising editions, monographs, books (among them his *Atlische Reredsamkeit* in three volumes), and articles. Many readings of papyri are due to his learning and acumen. *(R. Arch.* IX, 1907, pp. 338 f.) See also notices of the life and works of Professor Blass by J. P. M., *Athen.* March 16, 1907, and by T. D. Seymour, *Nation,* April 4, 1907, and *Cl. Phil.* II, 1907, p. 334.

Louis fenile Bournouf. — On January 15,1907, there died in Paris, at the age of eighty-five, Louis Emile Bournouf, Honorary Director of the French School at Athens. Appointed Director in 1867, he secured in 1873 the establishment of an auxiliary school at Home, under the direction of A. Dumont. He also secured at Athens the concession of land on which was erected the present home of the French School. Under his direction excavations were made on the Acropolis, at Delos, and at Thera. He was the author of numerous works on Athenian archaeology. *(Citron. Arts,* 1907, pp. 23-24.) See also *R. Arch.* IX, 1907, pp. 172-173.

Edoardo Brizio. — Edoardo Brizio died at Bologna, May 5, 1907. He was born at Turin, March 3, 1846, and after completing his studies assisted at the excavations in Pompeii and Rome. In 1876 he became Professor of Archaeology at the University and Director of the Museum at Bologna. He was best known for his admirable arrangement of the Museum and his careful studies in the antiquities of the Emilia. He early became convinced and maintained to the end that the civilization of the caves and the *terramare* was Ligurian, that of the Villanova type Umbrian or Italian, and that of the Certosa and later strata Etruscan, Gallic, or Roman. *Boll. Arte,* I, 1907, v, p. 36.)

Paul G-uiraud.— The death of Paul

Guiraud, which took place February 26, 1906, in the fifty-eighth year of his life, removed a conscientious and accurate scholar. His chief works were: *Assemblies procinciales dans VEmpire romain, La propricte fonciire en Gr'ece,* and *iStwles e'conomiques sur Vantiquite.* (S. R., *R. Arch.* IX, 1907, p. 333.)

Albert Harkness. — Albert Harkness, Professor Emeritus of Greek at Brown University, died on May 27, 1907. He was born in 1822, and was a graduate of Brown University. In 1845 he received the degree of Ph.D. from the University of Bonn. On his return from Europe he was appointed professor at Brown University, where he remained until his death. He was one of the founders of the American Philological Association, a member of the Boston Society of the Archaeological Institute, and one of the committee which founded the American School of Classical Studies at Athens. He was the author of a Latin Grammar, and many other text-books, chiefly for the study of Latin.

Wilhelm von Hartel. — Wilhelm von Hartel, who died on January 14, 1907, was Professor at the University of Vienna, and twice Minister of Public Instruction in Austria. He was the author of important studies on the times of Demosthenes and on the formulae in Attic inscriptions. With Mommsen he contributed largely to the association of the European Academies. (S. R., *R. Arch.* IX, 1907, p. 173.) See also *Jh. Oest. Arch. I.* X, 1907, Beiblatt, cols. 6-8.

Henry Pelham. — Henry Pelham, Camden Professor of Ancient History, and President of Trinity College, Oxford, died February 12,1907. His special work lay in the field of Roman history, but he wrote little, though as a lecturer he exercised a powerful influence, and to him more than to any other man is due the growth of the newer historical school and also of archaeological study at Oxford. The Hellenic Society and the British School at Athens owed much to his aid, and the British School at Rome was almost his own creation. He was also one of the founders of the British Academy. (F. Havekfield, *Athen.* February 16, 1907.)

Colonel Stoffel. — Colonel Eugene Georges Henri Celeste Stoffel, who was born at Paris March 14, 1821, and died there April 5, 1907, was a distinguished officer. Napoleon III left him his material for the completion of the *Life of Julius Caesar,* and Colonel Stoffel's work, *Histoire de Jules Cesar: Guerre civile,* in two volumes, appeared in 18S7. In 1862 Colonel Stoffel was in charge of excavations at Alesia, and he was interested in the new excavations at that place. *(R. Arch.* IX, 1907, pp. 329-332; fig.) PERSEPOLIS. — The Ancient Palaces. — A brief account of the ancient palace at Persepolis and its remains is given in *Rec. Past,* VI, 1907, pp. 131-137 (5 figs.), by T. F. Nelson, who urges the importance of a thorough excavation of the site.

SWITZERLAND. — Various Discoveries. — Near Altstetten there has been found a fine golden bowl, richly decorated. The animal figures recall those of the Hallstatt period, but the work seems unique.— In the amphitheatre at Avenches (Aventicum) excavations have brought to light a mass of fragments of the old building, all of great size. — At Kaiseraugst (Castrum Rauracense), near Basel, excavations have been carried on in the » late Roman fort, leading to the discovery of the western gate, fragments of architecture, and a drain. The fort was abandoned on the invasions of the Alemanni (354 and 357 A.d.), but was refortified under Julian and Valentinian I, and finally abandoned by Stilicho in 402 A.d. *(W. Id. Phil.* March 6, 1907.) Excavations at a point marked "Tempel" in an old plan of Roman Augst have led to the discovery of bronze reliefs, vases, fragments of marble slabs, ete. These works seem to belong to the early imperial period. *(Ibid.* June 19, 1907.) —In *Z. Ethn.* XXXVIII, 1906, pp. 996-998 (fig.), II. Gross reports the partial excavation of a large cemetery of the La Tene period at Milnsingen between Bern and Thun. Already 211 graves have been opened, yielding many armlets, spiral fibulae, girdles, necklaces, etc. On the skeleton of an old woman were found 28 fibulae, 4 armlets, a chain girdle, 7 rings on the fingers, and 4 on the toes. Some of the graves have yielded weapons. Among the skulls two are of special interest, as showing traces of trepanning. EGYPT EXCAVATIONS BY THE BRITISH SCHOOL OF ARCHAEOLOGY. — In a lecture at University College, London, May 9, 1907, Professor Flinders Petrie described the excavations of the British School in Egypt and the Egyptian Research Account during 1907. At Qizeh objects were found of the first, second, and third dynasties, showing that the first occupation of the site goes back further than the fourth dynasty, to which it had hitherto been ascribed. At Assiut, a large cemetery was discovered, with hundreds of tombs from the sixth to the twelfth dynasty. Among the objects found were offerings for the dead (miniature representations of houses with tanks, as well as boats with masts, oars, and cabins), the head of a fine coffin with gold foil and one shrouded in silver foil. In a tomb of the nineteenth dynasty was found the first certain representation of a camel. Though there is evidence from the earliest times of the existence and use of this animal, no actual representation had hitherto been known. *(Nation,* June 13, 1907; London *Times,* May 10, 1907.) GERMAN EXCAVATIONS IN 1906. — In *Klio,* VII, 1907, pp. 138142, L. Borchardt describes the German excavations in Egypt in 1906. Most of the results have been reported, *A.J.A.* XI, p. 76. At EschmunSn the finds were chiefly papyri, including parts of two poems by Corinna, an unknown epic, and a gigantomachy. At Elephantine the papyri included a bundle containing carefully sealed original documents and copies, all dating from the time of Ptolemy I. At Gizeh the ground between the two cemeteries excavated in earlier years was cleared, and fifty-two mastabas opened. The most important discovery was a ramp leading to the roof of a mastaba, by means of which the body and the other contents of the grave were introduced. EXCAVATIONS IN 1907. — In the *Nation,* April 4, 1907, H. F. O. gives a brief account of present methods of investigation in Egypt, and of the principal places where excavations were in progress during the past season. ASSUAN. — The Aramaic Papyri. — In *Bibl. World,* XXIX, 1907, pp. 305-310, R. II. Mode gives a thorough account of the Aramaic Papyri recently discovered near Assuan, which contain the records of a Jewish family HviDg at this place during the reigns of Xerxes, Artaxerxes, and Darius Nothus. In *R. Bill.* XIV, 1907, pp. 258-271 (fig.), M. J. Lagrange describes and discusses these papyri, as published by A. II. Sayce and A. E. Cowley. In *Z. Assyr.* XX, 1907, pp. 130-150, T. Xoldkke subjects the published papyri to an elaborate philological and historical investigation. BTJBASTIS. — Egyptian Plate. — In the *Journal des Dcbats,* January 5, 1907, G. Maspero reports the discovery at Bubastis of a number of vessels of gold and silver, richly chiselled and decorated, bracelets of gold and lapis lazuli with the name of Rameses II, and two gold necklaces set witli precious stones. With these objects was found a mass of cheap jewellery of the late Roman or early Arab period. A goldsmith of that time seems to have had in his shop this ancient treasure. *(Chron. Arts,* 1907, pp. 2(i-27, 30.) CAIRO. —Greek Bronzes. —In *Ath. Mitt.* XXXII, 1907, pp. 71-79 (2 pis.; 2 figs.), F. W. Von Bissing publishes some small bronzes from Cairo in his collection. One is a silvered bronze statuette of Aphrodite, wearing the cestus, and arranging her hair with her right hand. It is apparently of the second or first century B.c. The others are-eight small grotesque figures, said to have been found at Naucratis, and perhaps originally part of the decoration of candelabra. They are of about the second century A.d. DEIR EL-BAHARI. — Recent Excavations. — In the London *Times,* April 9, 1907, E. Naville reports, on the work of the Egypt Exploration Fund at Deir el-Bahari during the past season. The temple of Mentuhetep, of the eleventh dynasty, was further excavated. Back of a pyramid base rising in a columned hall, an open court with a colonnade was found, and then a hypostyle hall, not yet completely excavated. In the open court, discovered last year, a sloping subterranean passage, 150 m. long, was cleared. It ends in a room, built of large granite blocks, in which is a large alabaster shrine, devoid of inscription or ornament except a cornice and moulding. The shrine was empty, but seems to have been regarded as the abode of the *Ka* of the king, represented by a statue now lost. There are evidences of offerings before it, and a stele at the entrance of the passage refers to the daily provision of food and drink for the cave of Mentuhetep. LISHT. — Excavations of the Metropolitan Museum. — In *B. Metr. Mus.* II, 1907, pp. 61-63 (5 figs.), 118-117 (7 figs.), A. M. Lythgoe reports on the excavations undertaken by him for the Metropolitan Museum of New York at Lisht, where are the pyramids of Amenemhat I and Usertesen I of the twelfth dynasty. The work has been concentrated on the east front of the former pyramid. After the removal of a layer of remains of the Roman period, the remains of the pyramid temple have been partially uncovered, and also the mastaba of Antef-aker, an important official of the period. Among single discoveries the most important is the " false door " or offering-stele of the temple, which is the only royal stele yet found. The temple altar has also been recovered, and many architectural remains and inscriptions. The temple was evidently reconstructed at a later time, and part of the earlier material was used in the new foundations. The report on the excavation of a contemporary necropolis is to appear later. THEBES. — The Tomb of Queen Thyi. —In *S. Bibl. Arch.* XXIX, 1907, pp. 85-SG, E. R. Avrton gives an account of the discovery by Mr. Davis and himself of the tomb of Queen Thyi, the wife of Amenhotep III. It is situated in the valley of the tombs of the kings at Thebes in the same hill as the tomb of Rameses IX. A flight of steps leads to a corridor which opens into a large room with a small side chamber. This room was originally covered with white stucco and left uupainted. Fragments of a large wooden coffin lay on the floor, while on one side was the royal mummy in a case of exquisite workmanship, inlaid with precious stones set in gold. The whole of the woodwork is so fragile that it was impossible to move it, but the contents of the tomb were photographed before any attempt was made to handle them. The doors of the room were covered with gold leaf and decorated like the coffin with scenes of Aten worship. Accounts in the *Nation,* February 14, 1907, and *W. kl. Phil.* March 20, 1907, add that buried with the queen were solid gold plates and jewellery. On her head was the royal gold crown, representing a vulture with a signet ring in each talon. Of special beauty and interest are several portrait busts of the queen in alabaster set with obsidian and lapis lazuli. The mummy had been damaged by water, and fell to pieces when uncovered. The name of her son, the heretic king, Khuenaten, had been everywhere erased from the inscriptions, but otherwise the tomb was not damaged. WAD Y HALFA. — A Temple of the Eighteenth Dynasty. — In *S. Bibl. Arch.* XXIX, 1907, pp. 39-46 (5 pis.), P. Scott-moxcriekf describes the excavation for the Soudan government of a temple on the west bank of the Nile opposite the village of Wady Haifa. It was built by Thotmes II and continued by Thotmes III. Rameses III and Itameses IX also made additions to it. The position of the stones throws some light upon the disputed question of the relations of the reigns of Thotmes II and Thotmes III. An inscription of Thotmes III is given in transcription and translation. BABYLONIA AND ASSYRIA ASSYRIOLOGY IN THE YEAR 1904. — In *J. Asiat.* VIII, 1906, pp. 4:19-490; IX, 1907, pp. 1—18, C. Fossf.y gives an elaborate survey of the work done in the field of Assyriology during the year 1904, grouping the material under the heads of "exploration and excavation," " Sumerian and Assyrian languages," "literature," " geography," "history," "religion and mythology," "public and private law," "mathematics," "metrology," "archaeology," and "Babylonian influence upon other countries." LATEST RESEARCHES IN BABYLONIAN-ASSYRIAN RELIGION. —In *Arch. Rel.* X, 1907, pp. 104-128, C. Bezold records the discoveries bearing on religion that have been made in Babylonia and Assyria in the course of the last three years and the books and treatises on the Babylonian religion which have been published within the same period. THE" GERMAN EXCAVATIONS. — The excavations at Babylon have been chiefly along the two brick walls between the south and north castles of Nebuchadnezzar. A Persian building on one of the hills has yielded many fragments of enamel. Below the brick walls has been found the continuation of quay walls of Nabopolassar and of Sargon. At Assur a plan of the northwestern part of the excavations has been prepared. The fortifications have been found well preserved. Private houses containing many tablets have been found, built against the walls, leaving only the gates free. The Gugurri gate has been cleared, and shown by inscriptions to be the work of Salmanassar II, but altered by the Parthians. The new inscriptions have made it possible to complete in great measure the gap in the list of rulers. *(Berl. Phil. W.* 1907, cols. 319-320, from *Mil. Or. Ges.* No. 32.) SYRIA AND PALESTINE ANCIENT PALESTINE. — In *Pal. Ex. Fund,* XXXIX, 1907, pp. 5663, 152-157, S. A. Cook gathers up the results of the latest archaeological research for the first period of Palestinian history. ALEPPO. —A Hittite Cuneiform Tablet. —In *S. Bibl. Arch.* XXIX, 1907, pp. 90-100, A. H. Sayce describes a cuneiform tablet recently brought from Aleppo. It was written by a Hittite who was acquainted with Assyrian, but a number of words are Hittite and have the same forms as the Yuzzat tablet recently published by Pinches and Sayce. Mixed with Hittite words are many Assyrian words that are provided with Hittite grammatical inflections. Several new deities are mentioned. GEZER. — Resumption of Excavations. — In *Pal. Ex. Fund,* XXXIX, 1907, p. 81, announcement is made that a new firman has been granted for the continuation of excavations at Gezer and that work will be begun again at once under the directorship of R. A. S. Macallister. JERUSALEM.—A New Holy Place. —In *R. Bibl.* XIV, 1907, pp. 113-123 (4 figs.), M. R. Savionac discusses a cavern recently shown by the Greek Church in Jerusalem as the "prison of Christ." From a comparison with the description and plans of Clerrnont-Ganneau in 1873-1874, he shows that it has been extensively modified. Cuttings have been made in the rock and iron rings have been inserted, giving it the semblance of a prison. In reality, he thinks, it is nothing more than an ancient tomb, and every feature that suggests its use as a prison has been recently added.

A Creek Inscription found near the Church of St. Stephen. — In *Pal. Ex. Fund,* XXXIX, 1907, pp. 137-139, C. K. Spyridonidis describes a Greek inscription which seems to indicate the site of the original church of St. Stephen on the supposed place of the saint's martyrdom outside of the Damascus gate in Jerusalem. This inscription is also described by H. VinCent, *R. Bibl.* XIV, 1907, pp. 276-277.

PALMYRA. — Tesserae. — In *J.A.O.S.* XXVII, 1907, pp. 397-399 (pi.), H. H. Spoer publishes eight small Palmyrene tesserae bearing each a single name and containing various figures and ornamental devices. SCYTHOPOLIS. — Present State of the Ruins. — In *Pal. Ex. Fund,* XXXIX, pp. 100-101, R. A. S. Macallister describes the advantages that Beisan or Scythopolis offers as a place for excavation. At present the tombs are being plundered by the natives and the ruins are rapidly being destroyed. ASIA MINOR ANATOLIA. — Report of a Journey in the Summer of 1906.—

In *Memnon*, I, 1907, pp. 19-40 (32 figs.), E. Brandenburg records the results of an archaeological investigation of Anatolia. A large number of prehistoric grottoes were discovered, and many of these contained evidences of having been used for religious purposes. The Hittite remains on Mt. Sipylus known as Niobe, the grave of Tantalus, Sesostris, etc., were revisited and new photographs were taken. An investigation of the remains leads to the conclusion that Sipylus was a main point of contact between the IIittite and the Mycenaean civilizations.

APHRODISIAS. — Inscriptions. — In *R. £t. Gr.* XIX, 1906, pp. 205298, T. Rkinach continues his publication of the inscriptions from Aphrodisias (see *AJ. A.* XI, p. 82). Nos. 82-121 continue the dedications to individuals. No. 84 is metrical. Most of these inscriptions are very fragmentary. III. Monumental Inscriptions (122-137). These record the dedication of columns, or parts of buildings by various donors, many of whom are known from other inscriptions. It is argued that Aphrodisias was not known as Tauropolis, but as Stauropolis in Christian times. IV. Gifts for Religious Purposes (138-142). These deal with large donations by Attalus Adrastus to Aphrodite for a festival hall, the investment of the funds, gifts by others, and the will of Attalus. V. Agonistic Inscriptions (143-148). VI. Sepulchral Inscriptions (149-189). These are chiefly from sarcophagi, and frequently contain long documents, reserving the rights of burial with heavy fines for violators. One sarcophagus bears the name of M. Aur. Glycon, a sculptor. VII. Uncertain Fragments (190-202). VIII. Christian Inscriptions (203-221). These are chiefly sepulchral. No. 203 is a long epitaph, with detailed dates in the reign of Justinian. BOGHAZ-KOI.—Excavations in the Summer of 1906.— In *Or. Lit.* IX, cols. 621-634, H. Winckler describes the excavations made by him at Boghaz-koi, the site of the ancient Hittite capital in Asia Minor. Two trial trenches from the foot and the summit of the mound resulted in the discovery of fragments of 2500 tablets, written partly in Babylonian and partly in cuneiform, in the same language as that found in the so-called Arzawa letters of the Tell el-Amarna collection. In a number of these tablets Arzawa is mentioned as a tributary province, which shows that the theory is inadmissible that Arzawa was the name of the Hittite capital. On the other hand, these tablets show that the ancient name of Boghaz-koi was Hatti, so that it must have been the capital of the Hittite empire. The language of the non-Babylonian tablets, accordingly, which is the same as the language of Arzawa, must be Hittite. How this language is related to the language of the pictorial Hittite hieroglyphs still remains uncertain. The two may be simply different ways of writing the same tongue, or they may be different languages. An inscription in the pictorial hieroglyphs was discovered here on a wall of rock. Many of these tablets belong to the time of the Tell el-Amarna letters and the period immediately succeeding. Some of them are from the time of Rameses II and his contemporary Hattusil, who is the same as Hattusir of the Egyptian inscriptions. All of the names of Hittite kings mentioned by the Egyptians are found here. There is also a cuneiform translation of the treaty between the Hittite and Egyptian kings that is inscribed upon the temple wall at Karnak. The finds are of extraordinary interest, and show that archaeology has still a great deal to learn from Asia Minor. CHIRISHLI TEFE. —A Primitive Shrine. —In *Rec. Past,* VI, 1907, pp. 99-102 (3 figs.), G. E. White describes a primitive shrine on the hill, Chirishli Tepe, about 25 miles from Samsoun. The hill is surrounded by three walls, and on the summit are traces of buildings. Near the surface are many terra-cottas, chiefly heads of oxen. Similar figures but in smaller numbers have been found on the neighboring hill of Arab 'Oghlou. CYZICTJS.— New Inscriptions. — In *J.H.S.* XXVII, 1907, pp. 61-67, F. W. Hasluck publishes fourteen inscriptions found in the region of Cyzicus in 1906. Dedications to Zeus Brontaeus and to Dionysus occur. An honorary dedication to Pompey the Great, belonging to the time of the passing of the Manilian law, 66 B.C. , seems to imply his personal presence at Miletopolis. The inscribed and sculptured epistyle from a shrine of the Tyche of the Miletopolitans has now been recovered in fragments. Other Roman architectural remains exist at the site from which this is supposed to have come, and have evidently been drawn upon for building a mosque in the district. A curious collection of aphorisms, twenty-five in number, beginning *fiut; SorjOti,* seems epigraphically to date from about 300 B.C. In *Bert. Phil. W.* 1907, cols. 765-768, O. Hexse discusses this inscription, which has been identified by Bucheler with Sosiades' collection of the sayings of the Seven Wise Men (Stobaeus III, 1, 173, p. 125, 8 Hense). PERGAMON. — Progress of the German Excavations. — At the December (1906) meeting of the Berlin Arch. Soc, A. Conv.e reported on the work of the year at Pergamon. The discoveries included the architrave inscription of a temple of Hera Basileia dedicated by Attalus II, some wall paintings similar to those of the first style at Pompeii and others resembling those from Prima Porta, and the grave of a warrior outside of the town in which was a superb golden oak-leaf crown with a figure of Nike. The bridge over the Selinus, leading to the Roman buildings, is found to have been originally a Greek structure dating from the kingly period. The city water supply has been traced back to the sources of the Ca'icus. The ancient highroad from Pergamon to the valley of the Hermus is found to lie on the route still followed by camels, at least in the summer. *(Arch. Am.* 1906, cols. 326-328.) SAMOS. —Hybla. —In *Ath. Mitt.* XXXI, 1906, pp. 115-420, 568 (fig.), R. Jacoiisthal publishes a sepulchral inscription from Samos, 'Hy-qaayop-qi 'ybkt)tlo(v). The name Hyblesios is not rare on Samos. It seems to show that Hybla, the seat of an oracle of Apollo (Athen. XV, 672 a), was on the island of Samos. GREECE THE WORK OF THE GREEK ARCHAEOLOGICAL SOCIETY.— The YlpaKTiKCL for 1905 (Athens, 1906) contain reports of the work of the Greek Archaeological Society for that year. P. Kavvadias furnishes a general report (pp. 13-27) of the work, from which it appears that the recrection of the temple at Bassae has been nearly completed; a museum, chiefly for inscriptions, has been opened at Thebes; at Epidaurus the new museum is expected to be chiefly architectural and epigraphic; small excavations have been conducted by B. Leonardos at the Amphiareum at Oropus; at Volo, K. Kourouniotes has excavated a beehive tomb containing about twenty bodies, as well as Mycenaean pottery and gold ornaments. The same writer gives (pp. 44-89; 6 pis.; 22 figs.) a detailed report of his discoveries at Epidaurus, already reported in *A J. A.* XI, p. 92. The sacred spring and the early building identified with the great altar are fully described, but the most space is given to the description and reconstruction (Fig. 2) of the later Abaton, a stoa 4.30 m. to the north of the temple, 70.92 m. long and 9.42 m. broad. At the eastern end was a sacred well. The stoa, on the level of the temple, seems to have been built in the fourth century B.C., and later, probably in Roman times, the two-storied extension was constructed. ATHENS.— A Hoplitodromos on a Lead Token. — In /. *Int. Arch. Num.* IX, 1906, pp. 55-60 (2 figs.), Anna E. Apostolaki publishes a lead token *(avfifSoXov)* recently found in Athens, on which is represented a hoplitodromos running to the right. Another token in the Numismatic Museum at Athens shows a young warrior running, but it is not clear that he is a racer. Both works are of the late fifth or early fourth century B.c.

Inscriptions from the Acropolis. — In 'Ep. 'Apx-1906, pp. 189-196, (fig.), K. Romaio8 publishes four inscriptions from a pile of rubbish on the north side of the Acropolis: a signature of the well-known sculptor of the second century B. C., Evttp *Ev/3ovXt* Sov *KpunriSip;* an agonistic inscription of about 30 B.c.; an inscription on the base of a statue of a priestess of Demeter and Kore, of the third century B.c.; and a koAds-name on a roof tile, Kapi5orros (or 2aftwrros) Koaos.

The Wall of Themistooles. — In *Ath. Mitt.* XXXII, 1907, pp. 123-160 (4 pis.; 16 figs.), F. Noack begins the account of his excavations near the Uipylon (see *A.J.A.* XI, p. 87). The wall by the inscribed boundary stone was found to be later than the Themistoclean wall, which was only found near the old course of the Eridanus (see Fig. 3). Its foundations were on a lower level than had previously been cleared, and traces of three later walls were above it. The building of this wall had led to the construction of restraining walls for the Eridanus, and of a gate (I). Later the level of the road was raised and a new gate

(II) built. To this period belongs the polygonal wall (S'S.) previously ascribed to Themistocles. The Dipylon belongs to the third period. All attempts to trace the course of the Themistoclean wall beyond the bank of the Eridanus have proved unsuccessful. The article describes in great detail the complex of walls and the evidence as to their order and purpose.

CRETE.— Excavations in 1906. —In *Ausonia,* I, 1906, pp. 109-120 (10 figs.), L. Pkrnier describes the excavations in Crete in 1906. At Palaikastro, R. M. Dawkins discovered a natural cave containing many fragments of vases and three *larnaltes.* The vases seem to belong to a period of transition between Late Minoan II and III. At Vasiliki, R. B. Seager (see *A.J.A.* X, p. 344) has excavated a series of small houses of the Early Minoan or Cycladic period, with many specimens of the distinctive local pottery, and two rock-hewn Mycenaean tombs with larnax burials and many Mycenaean vases. On the deserted island of Pseiras in the gulf of Mirabello the same excavator has discovered a Mycenaean village, and many fine examples of the best style of Mycenaean pottery. S. Xanthoudides has worked near Koumaaa. where he has completed the excavation of four tholos-tombs of the Early Minoan period. Before the door is always a square vestibule, and near is an open place in which were found charred human bones and charcoal. The dead seem to have been partially burned before burial. There were also some carefully paved circular areas, which are believed to be for funeral ceremonies. Near by has been found a settlement of the same period, near the centre of which is a carefully built shrine of several rooms. In it were found a table for libations and four aniconic clay idols. At another point in this region two more *tholoi* have been cleared which were in use even in the Mycenaean period. Not far from Kandila Mr. Xanthoudides found another *tholos* of the same period, containing a layer of partially burned human bones, about half a metre thick. Part of the pottery showed the beginnings of polychrome decoration. The article also describes in detail the Italian work at Phaestus and Prinia, already reported briefly in *A.J.A.* XI, p. 90.

The Prehistoric House at Sitia. —In "E£. '*Apx*-1906, pp. 117-156 (5 pis.; 8 figs.), S. A. Xanthoudides describes in detail the house (Fig. 4) excavated by him near Sitia, Crete *AJ.A.* XI, p. 90). It occupies like a small fortress the carefully levelled summit of a hill. It is probable that an upper story was accessible by ladders, and that the closed room (13) was entered from above. The objects found in it indicate a date at the end of the Early or the beginning of the Middle Minoan period.

A Bronze Mitra. — In *A th. Mitt.* XXXI, 1906,' pp. 373-391 (pi.; fig.), F. Poulsen publishes a bronze *mitra* now in the Museum of Candia. Two men in the centre hold a crown over a *tropaion,* consisting of a palm tree upon which is a cuirass. Behind them are two other men. Six unpublished *mitrae* found at Axos by the Italians are closely related to this work. All are Cretan products of the seventh century B.C., showing in technique Phoenician influence, but in style purely national. Crete, like Byzantium in the Middle Ages, handed down the traditions of an earlier art, while the new Hellenic art developed in Ionia.

DELOS.—Excavations in 1904. —In *B. C.H.* XXX, 1906, pp. 483672, is a detailed account of the results of the excavations at Delos, conducted by the French School at Athens at the expense of the Due de Loubat (see *AJ.A.* IX, p. 353). The excavations in the quarter by the theatre are described (pp. 485-606; 3 pis.; 52 figs.) by J. Chamouard. The most important discovery was a large house (House of Dionysus) near the middle of the street running from the sanctuary toward the theatre. This house is described in detail. The walls are of granite and schist, the door frames of marble. There are no windows on the outside. In one room was a well-preserved stone stairway, and, judging from the fragments found

Figure 4. — Hodse At Sitia. in the debris, the upper story had mosaic floors and other decorations. On the lower floor the stuccoed walls imitated incrustation. In the impluvium is a very fine mosaic representing Dionysus riding on a tiger. On the walls are graffiti, chiefly drawings of ships. Among the objects found were marble statuettes of Poseidon and Cybele, a rehef representing an omphalos surrounded by a serpent, and some remains of furniture. The street of the theatre (Fig. 5) was paved with irregular blocks of schist, beneath which was a sewer. In' general only the rooms bordering on the street were cleared, and it has been found that many of these were shops, in some cases with a room behind. Numerous wells were also found. The buildings bordering the street are described in great detail, and there is an inventory of the objects found. W. Deonna adds a note (pp. 607-609) on a small apotropaeic relief, which was found in a shop. A group in marble representing Aphrodite assisted by Eros defending herself against Pan, found in the building of the Poseidoniastae of Berytus, is discussed (pp. 610-631; 4 pis.; 3 figs) by M. Bulard. It was dedicated by a certain Dionysius of Berytus to the *Oeol iraTpioi.* It is probably a work of the second half of the second century B.C., not based on any literary tradition. Such a group seems to be the origin of the numerous statuettes of Aphrodite holding a sandal in her raised right hand. The excavations in the mercantile quarter are reported (pp. 632-664; pi.; 8 figs.) by A. Jarde, who describes the streets, quays, and some of the warehouses in detail. Finally part of the inscriptions are published (pp. 665-672) by L. Bizard. Eleven honorary decrees are given, two of which are votes of the league of the islands, the others of the senate and people of Delos.

Progress of the French Excavations. — At Delos during 1906 the French excavated the large north portico of the sanctuary, which seems to have been erected by Antigonus Gonatas. Near by were found a Mycenaean tomb and a mass of pottery containing all known archaic varieties. Two new blocks of houses were cleared in the quarter by the theatre. An inscription fixes the building of this quarter in the middle of the second century B.C. Many interesting statues, including the Muse Polyhymnia, were found in these houses. South of the sanctuary was discovered a circular monument dedicated to the hero archagetes of an Athenian family. On a rocky terrace in this neighborhood stood five colossal lions of Naxian marble, valuable examples of archaic island sculpture of the seventh or sixth century. Among the inscriptions is one giving a list of the priests under the second period of Athenian rule. Many deposits of coins have been found. (C. *R. Acad. Insc.* 1906, p. 546; summary of a report by M. Holleaux.) At a meeting at the French School in Athens, Mr. Leroux described the marble lions and showed that one of the four lions at the Arsenal of Venice came from Delos. *(Chrnn. Arts,* 1907, p. 74.)

Two Hellenistic Potters. — The excavations at Delos have yielded a number of lamps from the potteries of Asclepiades and Ariston. Both names also appear on Greek vases decorated with reliefs. A comparison of the lamps and vases show that they come from the same potteries, and that Ariston is the younger potter. He seems to have had his factory at Delos. (W. Deonna, *R. tit. Gr.* XX, 1907, pp. 1-9.) EPIRTJS. —An Inscription from Photice. — In *B.CH.* XXXI, 1907, pp. 38-45, H. Gregoire publishes the first Greek inscription from Limboni, the ancient Photice. It is of the late third or early fourth century A. d., and records the *cursus honorum* of Aelius Aelianus, who is honored by the *(TVVt&plOV $tiTtKT)TldV.* LEUCAS. — The Excavations of 1906. — In a third " Letter," dated in March, 1907 (19 pp.), W. Dorpeeld reports in some detail the excavations at Leucas in 1906 (see *A J. A.* XI, p. 93). The settlement in the plain of Nidri is 2 km. long. Its pottery closely resembles the dark Villanova and the Hallstatt ware. The same pottery appears below the Heraeum at Olympia. The search for the royal palace was unsuccessful, unless a large wall found at the end of the season proves to belong to this building. The caves in the neighborhood also yielded monochrome and a few Mycenaean potsherds. In the cave Choirospilia, identified with the home of Eumaeus, a large quantity of prehistoric objects was found, for the most part earlier than those from Nidri. Near the cloister of St. John Bodakis the foundations of a large Doric temple were discovered. Excavations were also carried on in grottoes on the bay of Sybota, the Homeric harbor of Phorkys. The letter also describes discoveries of ancient remains at various points in the neighborhood, and discusses briefly some of the recent literature on the Ithaca-Leucas question.

LOCRIS. — Manumission Inscriptions. — In *Ath. Mitt.* XXXII, 1907, pp. 1-70 (2 pis.; 2 figs.), E. Nachmanson publishes with a full discussion the Greek manumission inscriptions from the sanctuary of Asclepius *iv KpowoK* not far from Naupactus. Nine inscriptions are published *I.G.* IX, i, 379-387. These and sixteen others, all on a column and anta, are published from Nachmanson's copies, and nine others are added from a Bussian article by Nikitsky. The texts throw light on the Aetolian calendar, and on the relation of Naupactus to the Aetolian League. The dates seem to lie between 170 and 143 B.C. LOCRIS AND PHOCIS. — Recent Excavations. — In *Ath. Mitt.* XXXI, 1906, pp. 392-404, G. Sotiriadis describes briefly his recent excavations in the western part of Ozolian Locris, and in Phocis. In Locris he excavated near a fortified summit not far from Soule, which he identifies with Oeneum. Shaft and chamber graves of classical times were found. The former always contained a small silver coin. In the neighborhood a Mycenaean grave has been found by the natives. The results here are of importance for the interpretation of Thuc. III, 96 ff. In Phocis two more prehistoric settlements near Elatea (see *A.J.A.* X, p. 103)-were excavated. A considerable quantity of primitive pottery of various types was found, but the problems connected with these pre-Mycenaean settlements are still unsolved. A pre-Mycenaean grave, containing fragments of early Kamares ware, was excavated near Drachmanl. PELOPONNESUS. — German Excavations in 1907. — la *Ath. Mitt.* XXXII, 1907, pp. i-xvi (map), W. Dorpfeld gives a summary account of excavations undertaken in the spring of 1907 by the German Archaeological Institute at Athens. At Tiryns remains of an earlier palace were found, including a well-preserved gate beneath the later propylaea. Two periods of construction were found in the fortifications. Below the palace were found walls and early graves. Similar results were obtained by shafts on the middle terrace. On the lower terrace a gate was cleared and much Mycenaean pottery found. Outside the upper terrace a large deposit of post-Mycenaean terra-cottas was found, and between the hill and the railway station the necropolis was discovered. At Olympia further excavations in the Pelopium and the Heraeum showed the same strata already recognized (see *A. J.A.* XI, p. 93). In the Heraeum the discoveries indicated that the temple was built over an earlier altar. Most important was the discovery near Zacharo in Triphylia of the remains of three large beehive tombs and near by an ancient fortress. The pottery was partly the monochrome Leucadian ware, but Mycenaean vases and many small objects of amber, gold, bronze, and ivory were found in the only tomb excavated. Dorpfeld argues that the place is probably the site of the Homeric Pylus, and that the finds confirm the theory that the monochrome ware is the native Achaean pottery. All these excavations are to be continued. SPARTA. — Excavations of the British School.— The site of the temple of Athena Chalkioikos at Sparta has been discovered by the British School. The identification is proved by three roof tiles stamped 'Atfjjjras XaA(«otKov, and confirmed by the discovery of bronze nails and fragments of bronze plates. Ten bronze statuettes have been found, of which the finest is a fifth century representation of a trumpeter, 13 cm. high. There are also eight bronze bells with votive inscriptions to Athena, and two archaic inscriptions, one containing fifty-two lines referring to athletic victories. Excavations were continued on the site of the Agora and of the temple of Artemis Orthia. About half the circuit of the town wall has also been traced. North of Sparta a Heroum has been unearthed, containing about ten thousand small vases, but little else of importance. (F. H. Mar8hall, (7. *R.* XXI, 1907, p. 126; London *Times,* April 10 and 29, 1907.) SYRUS.-Pre-Mycenaean Tombs. — At Syrus, K. Stephanos has excavated about fifty tombs, which, from the quantity of bronze, he attributes to the A morgan period of the pie-Mycenaean civilization. The bodies were lying on one side with the knees drawn up. *(Ausonia,* I, 1906, p. 1(19.) TENOS. — Excavation of the Temple of Poseidon. — The temple of Poseidon at Tenos and the surrounding precinct have been excavated by the Belgian, P. Graindor. He has found a stoa, an exedra, remains of sculpture, and many inscriptions, one of which contains the names of several early artists. A large block contains a sundial and also the direction of the wind, the course of the sun, and the seasons. An inscription states that it was modelled after the work of Andronicus Cyrrhestes, who it now appears was a native of Macedonia, and an interpreter of the works of Aratus. *(Nation,* February 14, 1907, from *Muse'e Beh1e.)* VATHY. —An Inscription. — Near Vathy (northeast of Tanagra) has been found the inscription Ejkaisus, Ovtov *iOatj/av Tv aovvOovrr) Tv 'Api*(rriaaTj/ Kt) *'AippoSurtaaTri Ktl Tv fyapaTpiTr.* The dialect is the usual Boeotian of the third and second centuries B.C. Interesting is the evidence for Ariste as a goddess. She was previously known at Athens and Metapontum. (E. Hkkkknrath, *Ath. Milt.* XXXI, 1906, pp. 434-43(1.) VOLO.—Excavation of a Beehive Tomb. — In "Eif. "Ap. 1906, pp. 211-240 (4 pis.; 15 figs.), K. KouhouNiotes describes a beehive tomb in Volo which he excavated in 1905. It is of the same period and type as the tomb at Menidi. It was built in a hole excavated in level ground, its upper half, which projected, having been covered with a mound of earth. The twenty skeletons found on its floor had no separate burial compartments. The offerings included many pieces of jewellery and ornaments of gold, a few bits of ivory, bronze, and silver, a piece of iron 0.02 m. square, vase fragments, and a few whole Figure 6. —Gold Relief From Volo. specimens of Mycenaean and pre-Mycenaean ware. Most interesting of all was a low relief in gold (Fig. 6) representing a house front of two stories with a large central door and acroteria, the first representation of a Mycenaean house found outside of Crete. ITALY

A NEW ARCHAEOLOGICAL, SOCIETY. — A new archaeological society, the *Societa Italiana di Archeologia e di Storia dell' Arte,* was formed on January 29, 1906, with its headquarters in Rome. The president is Professor D. Comparetti, and the secretary, Professor L. Mariani. The society has published the first volume of its periodical, entitled *A usonia,* containing twelve articles, reports on recent discoveries, summaries of periodicals, reviews, and notes. Summaries of the articles and reports will appear elsewhere in the Journal. (.1 *usonia, Rivitta delta Societa Italiana di Archeologia e Storia dell' Arte,* I, 1906. Rome, 1907, E. Loescher & Co. Pp. xiii, 203; 4 pis.; figs. 4to.) ANTITTM. — Purchase of a Statue. — The Italian Government has bought for 450.000 L. the statue of a maiden, found at Antium in 1878, and kept by the Aldobrandini family in their villa at Porto d' Anzio. it has been discussed by Alt maun (see *A J. A.* VIII, p. 304) and others. *(Chron. Arts,* 1907, p. 174.) See also Brunn-Bruckmann, *Denkmider,* II, 583,584; Reinach, *Repertoire,* III, 193, 6.

AQUILA. — A Sacred Treasure. — Near Aquila about two hundred coins were found in April, 1906. Most of them were scattered. A few are published by G. Pansa, *B. Com. Roma,* XXXVI, 1906, pp. 224-234 (pi., fig.). Among them are didrachms of Naples of the period preceding the First Punic War. Of unique interest among the Roman *asses sextantarii* is one with the inscription, DIOVIS ST IP E, showing that the treasure consisted of offerings to Jupiter. Pausa holds that the legend was impressed by the priests upon the coins to render them useless for circulation, and in this view he is supported by Serafini. CAPENA. — Excavations of Tombs. — In *Mon. Ant.* XVI, cols. 277490 (3 pis.; 81 figs.), R. Pakibeni describes excavations conducted in 1904 and 1906 in the territory of the ancient Capena, near the hill of Civitucola,, identified by some with Capena, by others with Lucus Feroniae. He describes in great detail the necropolis of the Contrada di S. Martino (tombs 1-70), then that of Monte Cornazzano (71-103), and then earlier excavations at Civitucola. Another chapter examines all this material chronologically. Nothitig found has determined the ancient name. The early tombs at Civitucola are of the Villanova type, without trace of Greek influence. A later group, chiefly of the seventh century, contains Greek vases, and native vases and bronzes showing Greek and Phoenician influence. A third necropolis was in use from the fifth to the second centuries, though there is little from the early part of this period. In general the finds show closer connections with the Sabines and Umbrians than with the Faliscans or Etruscans. The excavations at Monte Cornazzano are briefly reported *Not. Scav.* 1906, pp. 178-179. CASTEL PORZIANO. — A Replica of the Discobolus and Other Antiquities. — In *Mon. Ant.* XVI, cols. 241-274 (3 pis.; 10 figs.), R. LanCiani describes in some detail the results of excavations on the royal estate at Castel Porziano and in the neighborhood. At Castel Porziano on the coast near the ancient Via Severiana was found a villa built about 142 A.d. on the site of a villa of the Augustan age. It was not large, but admirably planned, and throws much light on the Roman summer dwellings. In the adjoining garden were found the fragments of a fine replica of Myron's Discobolus. The article gives an account of the discovery of the other replicas of this statue, and of earlier excavations in thisregion. AtCapocotta on the Via Lavinata, recent excavations have shown the presence of a settlement, and yielded some inscriptions, of which the most important is a fragmentary record of the action of the local community of Jews, who bestowed upon a Gerusiarch a small plot of ground for a family tomb. In *Not.*

Scav. 1906, pp. 403-415 (pi.; 3 figs.), G. E. Rizzo describes briefly the Discobolus, and E. Ghillanzonj the brick stamps and other inscriptions. His restoration of the Jewish inscription differs in details from Lanciani's. The objects found have been presented by the king to the National Museum in Rome, where the Discobolus has been restored (Fig. 7). The statue is fully described in *Boll. Arte,* I, 1907, i, pp. 3-14 (3 pis.; 7 figs.), by G. E. Rizzo, who thinks that in fidelity to the original and in execution this seems to be the best copy of Myron's work. CER VETRI. — Examination of the Regolini-Galassi Tomb. — In *Not. Scav.* 1906, pp. 331-333, G. Pinza reports the results of a new excavation in the RegoliniGalassi tomb at Cervetri. The plans of Canina were corrected in several particulars. Some fragments of bronze, iron, and vases were found. Among the latter are six proto-Corinthian *scyphi,* and possibly remains of a Rhodian and a Corinthian vase. A neighboring tomb yielded little of importance. See also *Ausonia,* I, 1906, pp. 121122, where the new results are given, and it is added that all the objects found have been secured for the Museo Gregoriano in the Vatican. COMO. — Additions to the Museo Civioo. — The Museo Civico at Como has received by bequest the antiquities collected by A. Garovaglio. The larger part of the collection consists of Roman and pre-Roman antiquities from Lombardy, but there are bronzes, vases, and glass from Etruria and Greece, as well as objects from Egypt, Assyria, and Babylon. (.4 *usonia,* I, 1906, pp. 200-201.) ESTE. — Discovery of Roman Remains. — At Este in 1905 there w-ere discovered beneath the *Teatro sociale* the remains of a Roman building with a mosaic pavement supported on a series of low arches to protect it from moisture. In the *Giardino Pellesina* a Roman street, walls, pavements, and fragments of vases and other objects have been found, including a small plate of bone, which, from the scale marked on one edge, seems part of a Roman rule. (A. Pkosdocimi, *Not. Scav.* 1906, pp. 171-175; fig.) NAPLES.—The Greek City Wall. — In *Not. Scav.* 1906, pp. 448-465 (2 plans; 16 figs.), E. Gabrici describes in detail the discovery of the remains of the old Greek city wall of Naples at the comer of the Via Forcella and the Vico Egiziaca (see *A.J.A.* X, p. 350). The discussion of the historical and topographical questions will appear later.

Figure 7. — Disconou-s From Castel PORZIANO.

OSTIA. — Terra-cotta Moulds. —In *Not. Scae.* 1906, pp. 367-373 (20 figs.), A. Pasqui describes in detail the moulds recently found at Ostia (.4 *.J. A.* XI, p. 98). In a shop, forming part of a small house, were thirty-five large jars, in which were found about four hundred double moulds. There is no record of a similar discovery elsewhere, but in the *Magazzino archeologico communale* at Home are two fragments which seem to belong to similar moulds. The large moulds are thin, and the smaller moulds thick, so that the cakes pressed in them would all have about the same weight, and experiment shows that this weight was about a Roman pound. In the house were also found many jugs, all holding the same quantity. Near the house was a *pvttrinum.* POMPEII. — Progress of the Excavations. — In *Not. Scat:* III, 1906, A. Sogliano continues his account of the excavations at Pompeii from December, 1902, to March, 1905 (see *A.J.A.* XI, p. 98). They were confined to Reg. VI, Ins. XVI, south of the Porta Vesuviana. Between the gate and the Insula is an open square. The Via Stabiana was cleared along the east of the Insula, and is now open its entire length. Its width varies decidedly. The trapezoidal shape of Ins. XIV and XVI shows that the *piano regolalare* of the Etruscans was based upon the preservation of the main streets of the older town. Some inscriptions and small objects were found during the excavation of the street (pp. 148-161; 8 figs.). The side street bounding Ins. XVI on the west has been cleared. It was much worn by traffic. A number of inscriptions and some small objects were found (pp. 318-32:?; 2 figs.). Excavation of the Insula began at the south, and continued along the Via Stabiana. On the southern street was a small house and *thermopolium;* on the southeast corner a *fulionica;* on the Via Stabiana two small houses, one of which is scarcely more than a side entrance to the large house, No. 7 (pp. 345-351; 2 figs.). This house, called that of the *Amorini ilorati,* has been fully excavated, but only the entrance, *atrium,* and *tablinum* are described. In a room opening from the atrium were found bronze vases inlaid with silver and a herm of Parian marble, with yellow hair adorned with a red band. Among the paintings is a mutilated replica of the unexplained picture, Sogliano, No. 627, with the name Phoenix beneath one of the standing figures (pp. 374-383; 6 figs.). RAVENNA. — A Greco-Roman Sarcophagus.— In *Boll. A rte,* 1,1907, iv, pp. 1-9 (2 pis.; 5 figs.), P. Amaducci publishes a Greco-Roman sarcophagus of the late third or early fourth century, recently found in S. Vittore at Ravenna. On one side is a seated woman (inscription, *Memphi);* on the other, apparently the same woman in a doctor's office (inscription, *Memphi Glegori).* On the front, flanking the funerary inscription, are on the right a seated figure reading from a scroll; on the left a similar figure playing on a stringed instrument. Above each figure is a Greek inscription in Roman characters. The Latin inscription on the front, repeated on the back, shows that the sarcophagus was the grave of Sosia Juliana and Tetratia Isiade, daughter and wife of C. Sosius Julianus. The meaning of the scenes and inscriptions is briefly discussed. ROME. — The Necropolis in the Forum. — In *Not. Sent:* 1906, pp. 253-294 (38 figs.), G. Boni publishes his sixth report on the excavation of the necropolis (see *A J. A.* XI. p. 99). He describes with great care a trench tomb (B) containing a burial, and three pit tombs (V, X, Y) containing cremations. The vases were of the types found in the other graves. Tomb Y contained a hut urn, and a stand for coals or incense *(acerra).* The human remains are described by Professor Tkdksciii of Padua.

Discoveries on the Palatine. — In an attempt to ascertain the position of the entrance to the early fortification on the

Palatine, a circular ditch was found similar to one close to the Forum. It is believed to be a tomb, belonging to the time of the earliest settlement on the Palatine (London *Times*, April 22, 1907). Under walls long considered as belonging to *Ruma quadrata* D. Vaglieri has discovered tombs like those in the Forum. In one was a vase which can scarcely be earlier than the end of the fifth century. This seems favorable to the view that until after the Gallic invasion only the Capitol was fortified. *(Chron. Arts,* 1907, p. 174.)

The Sacred Grove of the Nymph Furrina.— In July, 1906, workmen in the Villa Sciarra on the Jauiculum discovered fragments of architecture, sculptures, and inscriptions in a semicircular hollow. These discoveries, first communicated to W. St. Clair Baddeley, are published by P. GAucKleR in *C. R. Acad. Insc.* 1907, pp. 135-159 (2 figs.). The inscriptions are chiefly dedications to Syrian gods, including *Adadus, Jupiter lUaleeiabrudis* (hitherto unknown), and others. A richly carved altar was erected by Artemis of Cyprus to Zeus Ceraunius and the *Nymphae Furrinae*. This then was originally the grove of the old Roman nymph Furrina, later identified with the Furiesand pluralized. In the second century A.d. it became the sanctuary of many foreign gods. Two Greek pentameters show that a certain Gaiouas built a fountain to supply water for the sacred rites. Partial reports are given by W. St. Clair Baddeley, London *Times,* March 15, 1907, and *A then.* April 6, 1907, and by G. Gatti, *Not. Scav.* 1906, pp. 248 and 433.

A New Statue of a Daughter of Niobe. — In *B. Com. Rom.* XXXIV, 190R, pp. 157-185 (3 pis.; fig.), It. Lantiani discusses the Niobid group of the Gardens of Sallust, where was found, June 13, 190ti, a perfectly preserved statue in Greek marble of one of the Figure 8. — Statie Of Daughter Of daughters of Niobe (Fig. 8).-The Niohe. statue had been carefully concealed in an underground gallery at the southeast of the Nympheum (Piazza Sallustiana), close to the northern angle of the Servian Wall. Lanciani's article deals chiefly with the history of excavations in the Gardens of Sallust, and the previous evidence for the existence of this group. In *Not. Scan.* 1906, pp. 434-436 (4 figs.), G. E. Rizzo discusses the new statue, concluding that it probably belongs with the Niobids in Copenhagen *(A.J.A.* V, p. 232; VIII, p. 474), but that it is not a Greek original of the fifth century, but the work of an eclectic sculptor of about the first century B.C., who affects archaistic traits. Much in the treatment suggests the so-called Venus of the Esquiline. The statue is also published in *C. R. Acad. Insc.* 1907, pp. 104-113 (pi.), by P. GaucKler, who tentatively suggests that it is the work of a Hellenistic sculptor in Asia Minor, and recalls the group brought from Syria by C. Sosius (Plin. *H.N.* 36. 5. 28). The figure has no connection with the Florentine group. In *Allg. Ztg.* December 12, 1906 (Beilage) A. Furtwangler points out the value of this figure and its connection with the Copenhagen statues.

The Via Triumphalis and Sarcophagi. — A short distance north of the Vatican Palace a piece of the Via Triumphalis has been found in an excellent state of preservation. Near the same spot a large marble sarcophagus of the fourth century has been discovered. The decoration of the front is extraordinary in the attempt to adapt to this purpose the grandiose arabesques of a temple frieze. The inscription on another sarcophagus shows that the senate still had its *scribae* in the fourth century. Tombs and inscriptions of older date have also been found by the Via Triumphalis. (G. Gatti, *R. Com. Rom.* XXXVI, 1906, pp. 321-326; 2 pis.; *Not. Scav.* 1906, pp. 300-304; 3 figs.) Another section of the Via Triumphalis has been found on the Via Famagosta. Near the place where the sarcophagi were found are remains of columbaria with inscriptions of the family Socconia. (G. Gatti, *Not. Scav.* 1906, pp. 336-338.)

Excavations on the Via Appia. — In *Not. Scav.* 1906, pp. 338-344 (plan), G. Pinza describes excavations on the Via Appia five miles from the Porta Capena at the *ustrinum* or " Grave of the Horatii." To the north were found walls of buildings, which probably belonged to a posting station, and remains of two early tombs, to avoid which the road makes a curve. Probably these are the traditional tombs of the brothers. The so-called *ustrinum* occupied an earlier enclosure, possibly a station for the Ambivarlia. Here, too, was the *sacer campus Horatiorum,* and apparently a *Fossa Cluilia.*

Minor Discoveries. — In *Not. Scav.* 1906, Nos. 4-12, G. Gatti and D. Vaglieri record a number of minor discoveries at various points in Rome. For the most part these consist of foundations, fragments of sculpture and architecture, lead pipes, bricks, and fragmentary inscriptions. On the Via Quirinale, near the Villa Colonna and the former convent of S. Silvestro, many ancient remains have come to light, the most important of which is a relief representing a country scene. On the left Pan is seated in a cave; at the right is an *aedicula* containing a statue of Diana as huntress with a garlanded altar in front; in the foreground is a herd of cattle and sheep with dogs (pp. 245-247; fig.; see also pp. 180, 356). Near S. Croce in Gerusalemme have been found the upper part of a sarcophagus, with traces of two busts in a medallion, and an inscription giving the exact age of *Cassia Pisonis,* who died September 16, 346 A. d. (pp. 334-335; fig.), and also several inscriptions, including part of a list of Roman nobles of the beginning of the fourth century A.d., each of whom had subscribed 400,000 sesterces for some unknown purpose (pp. 430-431). Building operations on the Via Flaminia, Via Salaria, and Via Nomentana have led to the discovery of columbaria and tombs yielding a number of inscriptions (pp. 143-148 (fig.), 181-182, 211-213, 249-252, 299-300, 335-336, 356-357, 431433). On the Via Labicana by Tor Pignattura have been found sixteen new inscriptions from the cemetery of the *equitessingulares* (G. Tomassetti, pp. 208-211). On the Via S. Martino ai Monti has been found a deep well of the republican period, lined in the lower part with rings of tufa formed by joining four blocks, and in the upper with *opus reticulatum* (A. Valle, pp. 838-884).

SARDINIA.—Minor Discoveries.—In *Not. Scav.* 1906, A. TaraMelli reports discoveries at several places in Sardinia. Near Assemini are the remains of a Roman villa, much damaged by the peasants, though part of a bath is traceable (pp. 200-202). Near Cagliari, a tomb has been found containing five vases of the eneolithic period, with no traoe of Phoenician or Punic influence (pp. 162-167; 4 figs.). At Zeppara is an inscription of 62 A.d., apparently referring to the erection of a public building at the expense of certain Sardinians, whose names are hard to parallel in Roman inscriptions (pp. 198-200; fig.). SICILY. — SYRACUSE. — Acquisitions of the Archaeological Museum. — In *Boll. Arte,* I, 1907, iii, pp. 7-13 (12 figs.), P. Orsi records the more important additions to the Archaeological Museum at Syracuse. Among the terra-cottas is an equestrian figure of the early fifth century which was probably part of an acroteriou, a flying Nike of the later fifth century, and a curious *xoanon*; the two latter are unique among Sicilian terracottas. Of the vases the most important is a black-figured cylix, with youths on foot and on horseback, and a sphinx to whom clings a man in the position of Odysseus escaping from the cave of Polyphemus. Some bronzes, jewellery, glass, coins, and gems are briefly noticed, as well as two pieces of Sicilian majolica, and a German painting of the fifteenth century. TTVOLI. — Survey of the Villa Hadrian. — In *Not. Scav.* 1906, pp. 313-317 (4 plans), V. Reina describes the careful survey of the Villa Hadriana at Tivoli by students of the Engineering School at Rome, giving the position of the base line, and the methods and formulae employed in the triangulation and levelling. MINOR DISCOVERIES. — Among the minor discoveries reported in *Not. Scae.* 1906, Nos. 4-12, are the following: At Arqua Petrarca, relics of the neolithic age, including rude pottery and stone weapons (A. Alfonsi, pp. 353-355). At Canova di Puglia, the funeral urn of L. Abuccius Salvius, with richly sculptured ornaments, including fruits, flowers, and emblems; and a statue of Jupiter, the work of a native artist inspired by a Greek model. (Q. Quagliati, pp. 323-328; 6 figs.) At Cantalupo, a new example of the rare stamp, *C.I.It.* XV, 1441. (D. Vaolieri, p. 384.) At Castel d'Agogna, a votive tablet on which the name of the divinity is indicated only by the letter M, and some Gallo-Roman pottery and glass. (G. Patroni, pp. 169-170.) At Migliadino S. Fidenzio, in repairing the old church, a number of fragmentary Latin inscriptions, and two mediaeval sarcophagi, one inscvibed. As no ancient foundations were found, the material is believed to have been brought from Este. (A. Prosdocimi, pp. 417— 422.) At Milan, two sepulchral inscriptions, and from the Via Oriani two fragments of a richly carved cornice, seemingly from an important Roman building. (A. De Marchi, pp. 385-388.) At Maruggio, a hoard of 48 silver coins of Magna Graecia, including coins dating from the sixth century (Sybaris) to the early years of the fourth. (Q. Quagliati, pp. 215-217.) At Monterotondo, near the Via Salaria, remains of a Roman villa, and an architrave inscribed *Herculi sacrum P. Aelius Hieron Aug. lib. ab culmissione.* (G. Tomassetti, pp. 213-214.) At Padua, a silver ring set with a carnelian. The ring is inscribed *veltneip: vesie: am. hi: al;* the bezel, /. *ikeinu.* (A. Moschetti, pp. 329-330; fig.) At Palestrina, a new dedication to Fortuna Primigenia. (G. Gatti, p. 344.) At Pavia, in searching for the pre-Roman necropolis, a Roman cemetery, which was in use from the first to the fourth century A.d. (G. Patroni, pp. 389-393.) At Pernumia, four pre-Roman vases, which are the first early remains from this neighborhood. (A. Prosdocimi, pp. 175-176.) At Posta, a dedication to the old Sabine goddess Vacuna, by P. Flavidius Septuminus, *praefeclus classis,* which indicates that there was a shrine of the goddess in the valley as well as on the mountain near Laculo. (N. Persichetti, pp. 465—466.) Remains at Rocca di Gioia, which show that this mediaeval castle occupies the site of a prehistoric as well as Roman settlement. (A. De Nino, pp. 467-468; fig.) At S. Oiacomo di Portogruaro, near the ancient Concordia, Roman urns, fragmentary inscriptions, a grave relief, and coins of the first century A.d., and in the neighborhood two bronze hatchets of the pre-Roman period. (G. C. Bertolini, pp. 422-429; 5 figs.) At S. Polo di Pieve, a hoard of 587 Roman bronze coins, dating from 5-248 A.d. (pp. 140-141.) Near S. Vittorino (Amiternum) a portion of the Via Salaria, which supports the view that this road followed a straight line from Amiternum to Foruli; remains of Roman buildings, a fountain, and fragmentary inscriptions. (N. Persichetti, pp. 183-185.) Near Tarentum, Q. Qi-agliati reports (pp. 468-474; 5 figs.) the examination of a Greek tomb consisting of two rockcut chambers, each with its own door and stairway. Each contained a stuccoed funeral couch. The tombs had been already plundered. At Teolo, trial pits near Monte Rosso have revealed a settlement of the eneolithic period, with pottery bearing characteristic terra-mare decorations, stone implements, fragments of bronze, carved wood, nuts, shells, etc. (A. Moschetti and F. Cordenons, pp. 393-400; 6 figs.) In Cattolica Eraclea, in Sicily, the foundation walls of a magnificent theatre, dating from the classical age, have been uncovered. In Ancona a number of Roman tombs, probably of the third century B.C., have been found, containing, among other things, two beautiful silver vases, a number of urns, with ashes of cremated persons, and gold earrings with smaragd stones. *(Nation,* April 18, 1907.) SPAIN COTO FORTUNA. — Ingots of Lead. — An ingot of lead, with the inscription *Societ. Mont. Argent. Ilucro,* has teen found at Coto Fortuna, 7 km. west of Mazaron, province of Murcia. Several other ingots without inscriptions were found at the same place, where are considerable remains of ancient mines. The ancient working of these mines began about 200 B.c. and stopped soon after 400 A.d. (H. Jecquier, *It. Arch.* IX, 1907, pp. 5862). An ingot from the same mines, with the inscription *Societ. Argent. Fod. Mont. Ilucr. Galena,* was found at Koine in 1887. Ancient mines in Spain were well

known and important. In the Louvre is an ingot with the inscription *M. P. Roscieis M. F. Maic,* which was found about 1840. Other similar ingots are in other museums. (heron De Villefosse, *Ibid.* pp. 63-68; fig.) NUMANTIA. — Discovery of Scipio's Works. — In *Arch. Anz.* 1907, cols. 3-35 (plan; 7 figs.) A. Schvlten gives the results of the work in 1906 around Numantia. As the first campaign had proved the existence of an Iberian city, the second was devoted to the evidences of Scipio's blockade. Five of the seven forts mentioned by Appian have been found, as well as several larger camps and parts of the wall of circumvallation. The positions were chosen and strongly fortified for defensive rather than offensive purposes, and all the barracks and other buildings were made of stone. No other such military structures are known before the great permanent camps of imperial times at Novaesium and Carnuntum. FRANCE ALESIA. —A Pan's Pipe. —In *C. R. Acad. Insc.* 1907, pp. 100-103, T. Reinach describes a Pan's pipe recently found at Alesia. It is a rectangular block of wood in which are seven holes of varying depth and remains of an eighth. The small size of the holes makes the tone very shrill. Calculation and experiment indicate that the scale was the Hypophrygian. ARRAS. — A Gallo-Roman Settlement. — During the construction of new boulevards at Arras (Pas-de-Calais) numerous Gallo-Roman antiquities have been found, including rings, buckles, fibulae, styli, coins of the first and second centuries A.d., lamps, and many fragments of stamped pottery. The potters' stamps number 36, of which six are new. (Count A. De Loisne, *B. Soc. Ant. Fr.* 1906, pp. 403-409.) BIOT. —A Roman Monument. — In if. *fit. Anc.* IX, 1907, pp. 48-68 (5 pis. ; 14 figs.), R. Laurent and C. Dugas describe the results of excavations in 1906 at a hillock between Antibes and Nice near the station Biot. The hill in Roman times lay between the Via Aurelia and the sea and commanded the bridge over the Brague. The finds included sculptured stones forming apparently part of a gateway, pottery, and a few coins of the first, third, and fourth centuries A. d. A careful comparison of the Gallic arms on these sculptures with those on other monuments and on coins leads to the conclusion that the monument was erected in the reign of Augustus. LTEVIN. — A Gallo-Roman and Merovingian Cemetery. — At Lievin (Pas-de-Calais), six hundred and sixty tombs ranging in date from the GalloRoman to the Merovingian periods have been discovered. A description of the finds, which are particularly important in the Frankish section, is given by Count A. De Loisne in *B. Sue. Ant. Fr.* 1906, pp. 358-364; 2 figs. NICE. —An Attic Relief. —In *B. Soc. Ant. Fr.* 1906, pp. 336-337 (pi.), fi. Esperandieu publishes the grave relief of a young athlete now in the Museum at Nice. The inscription *(C.I.A.* II, 1344) shows that it came from the Piraeus. It is a work of the second century B.c., and not without merit. PARIS. — Acquisitions of the Louvre in 1906.—In *B. Soc. Ant. Fr.* 1906, pp. 417-423, A. H£ron De Villefosse and E. Miciion report the acquisitions of the department of Greek and Roman Antiquities of the Louvre during 1906. Seventeen marble statues and busts are described, including a child's head of Praxitelean style. Among the eight reliefs are fragments of two Attic stelae and a lutrophorus. Seventeen ancient glass vessels have been obtained from tombs at Cyzicus. Inscriptions and objects of bronze, wood, and ivory are eleven in number, among them the carved ivory hilt of a dagger in fine Mycenaean style from Egypt.
Fragment of a Sarcophagus. — In *B. Soc. Ant. Fr.* 1906, pp. 392-394 (fig.), E. Michon publishes the fragment of a sarcophagus containing an Amazonomachy in the Louvre. Its source is unknown, and it is badly mutilated, but clearly belongs to the fourth group of the second class of these representations (robert, *Antike Sarkophagreliefs,* II, p. 77).

Discoveries at the Marche' aux Fleurs. — In *B. Soc. Ant. Fr.* 1906, pp. 409-416, A. Heron De Villefosse summarizes the discoveries at the Marehe aux Fleurs (see *A.J.A.* XI, p. 106), describing the professional reliefs, and discussing the five epitaphs already found. In August, 1906, another inscription was found, the epitaph of a certain Fortunatus, described as *cexsillarius exercitus.* This is the fifth monument of a Roman soldier discovered in Paris. PEYRIEU. '— Minor Discoveries. — In *B. Soc. Ant. Fr.* 1906, pp. 337338, £. Chanel reports the discovery at Peyrieu (Ain) of three graves, and two potters' furnaces, which have yielded numerous fragments of pottery, and some small objects. SAINTB COLOMBE. — Roman Baths. —In *C. R. Acad.* 7n.se. 1907, pp. 60-92 (12 figs.), A. Heron De Villefosse describes the Roman remains found at Sainte Colombe near Vienne in a group of ruins long known as the "Palais de Miroir." Haphazard excavations have brought to light mosaics, architectural fragments, and statues, the best of which is the crouching Venus now in the Louvre. More systematic excavations begun in 1906 by T. Chaumartin have shown that the remains belong to extensive and handsome Thermae. The *calailarium, tepidarium,* and *frigidarium* can be identified. The latter was richly decorated with statues. In the debris from earlier excavations has been found part of the left foot of the Venus. In *B. Sue. Ant. Fr.* 1906, pp. 343-344, the same writer publishes three graffiti from pottery belonging to F. Chaumartin.

BELGIUM AND HOLLAND NAMUR. — Discovery of a Bronze Head. — At the Roman villa of Mettet near Namur a curious bronze head has been recently discovered. It represents a man with a curled beard and the ears of a he-goat, one of which is turned toward the face. It is considered Gallo-Roman work of the second or third century A.d. It is perhaps the only male Roman head with long hair. Similar heads are at Spires (a centaur) and at St. Germain-en-Laye. *(Athen.* April 27, 1907.) THE HAGUE.— A Collection of Greek Coins. —The *Cabinet des me'daillet* at the Hague has recently acquired a large number of ancient coins from the collection of the late Mr. Six. In *R. Beige Num.* 1907, pp. 113-147 (2 pis.); 277-303 (2 pis.),

De Dompierre De Chaufbpie begins the publication of a selection from this acquisition. A short sketch of the collection of Mr. Six is followed by a description of 317 Greek coins, chiefly from the cities of Asia Minor and the adjacent islands. The plates contain eighty-seven reproductions. GERMANY THE WORK OP THE ROMANO-OERMAN COMMISSION. — In *Rom. Germ. Forsch.* 1905 (Frankfort, 1906) is given a summary of the year's work in the study of early Germany. In all the reports the literature is summarized and discussed, and the field work described. A short outline (pp. 1-4) of the activity of the Romisch-Germanische Kommission is given by H. Dragendorff, the Director. K. Schumacher discusses (pp. 5-26) the prehistoric discoveries, especially in western Germany. There is little of significance to report for the earlier periods. A Hallstatt settlement has been found on the Lorelei. The report is chiefly concerned with recent publications. Pp. 26-48 (2 figs.), E. Anthes discusses the investigation of the early fortifications *(Ringwdlle),* treating first the present state of their study. The remains date from neolithic to the Carolingian times, and differ widely in form, and probably in use. The scientific study is only begun, and much is still unsettled. Excavations are described on the Kastelberg near Kdstlach (Hallstatt), on the Britzgyberg near Illfurt (probably Hallstatt), on the Lorelei (later bronze age and Hallstatt), and on the Altenburg near Niedenstein (La Tene). The remains of the Roman occupation are discussed (pp. 48-69; 2 figs.) by H. Dragendorff. A second Roman fortress on the Lippe has been found, at Oberaden, and has led to renewed discussion whether here or at Haltern is the site of Aliso. H here, then at Haltern was the *caslellum Lupiae Jlumini adpositum.* Further excavation is needed to decide the question. At Haltern the gates of the large fort have been found in irregular positions, and the outline of a large intrenched camp traced. Many minor excavations are reported, and a longer account is given by G. Wolff of the excavations at Heddernheim, where four successive fortifications can be traced, extending from a provisional camp to a walled town. Pp. 69-82 (map), G. Wolff discusses the settlements in the southern Wetterau in prehistoric and Roman times. Neolithic and Hallstatt remains do not occur on the same sites. La Tene settlements coincide often with each of the earlier periods.-Roman settlements are often found on neolithic and La Tene sites. During the Roman period single villas or farms were more common than villages. With the Frankish occupation comes a gathering of the population into villages. Numerous new discoveries in Roman Germany are briefly noted (pp. 82-90) by H. Dragendorff, who also notices (pp. 90-97) the recent discussions of provincial ceramics. II. Schuchhardt adds (pp. 97-99) a brief mention of Frankish and Saxon remains.

BONN. — Excavations of the Provincial Museum. — In *Bonn. Jb.* 1906, pp. 204-343 (14 pis.; 11 figs.), is published a report on the excavations and discoveries of the Provincial Museum at Bonn from 1903-1906. The work was chiefly at Remagen and the "Alteburg" near Cologne. Both were *castella,* built under Tiberius, with a palisaded earth wall and trenches, and rebuilt in stone about 70 A.d. About 270 A.d. the Alteburg was abandoned and the fort at Remagen included in a larger stone wall. These forts belong to a system of defensive works, while the earlier forts of Drusus are obviously offensive and temporary. An introduction by H. Lehner (pp. 204-213) is followed (pp. 213-244) by a detailed account by the same writer of the work at Remagen. He also describes the excavations at the Alteburg (pp. 244-266), while the objects discovered are treated (pp. 266318) by J. Hagen. Excavations on the Fiirstenburg near Xanten, described (pp. 318-330) by II. Lehner, led to the discovery of part of the defences of a Roman fort, like those at Haltern and Remagen. The grave of a Gallic warrior at L'rmitz of the La Tene period is described (pp. 330-339) by C. Koenen, who also discusses briefly (pp. 339-343) a Gothic pottery of about 1200 A.D., which is important for the history of mediaeval ceramics in Germany.

COLOGNE. — Roman Graves. — The Roman graves discovered in Cologne during the last ten years are described in *Bonn. Jb.* 1906, pp. 344378 (6 pis.; 9 figs.), by J. Foppki.ueuteh. The finds show that during the first century A. d. the pottery and other art is distinctly classic, then follows a period of decline, and at the end of the second century a marked revival in ceramics, glass, and metal. It is possible that this new Hellenic influence came up the Rhine, rather than by way of Marseilles. It seems probable that by the middle of the third century there was a strong Christian element in Cologne. Toward the end of the fourth century there is a complete cessation of the art products. *Ibid.* pp. 379-434, J. Hagen gives a minute inventory of the contents of seventy-three graves.

A Roman Weight. — In *Bonn. Jb.* 1906, pp. 435-441 (fig.), E. Pernice publishes a stone ball, recently found at Cologne. It weighs 39,500 gr., originally had an iron handle, and is marked by nine vertical lines crossed by a horizontal line. It is a weight containing ninety units, which, allowing for the handle, must correspond to ninety Attic minae. Many examples of the use of the Attic standard in the Roman Empire are given.

KLEIN-KUHNAU.-A La Tene Cemetery. —In *Z. Ethn.* XXXIX, 1907, pp. 186-192 (36 figs.), Mr. Seelmann reports the discovery of a cemetery of the La Tene period at Klein-Kiihnau (Dessau). A number of urns, in which the ashes had been buried with ornaments, are described with their contents in detail. The most interesting object is the fragment of a Pan's pipe, with traces of five reeds set in resin. XANTEN. — Discovery of a Roman Amphitheatre. — In *Bonn. Jb.* 1906, pp. 447-453 (2 figs.), J. Steiner describes the Roman Amphitheatre at Colonia Traiana near Xanten. Its excavation was completed in 1901. Only the foundations remain, but the plan is clear. The axes of the elliptical building are 100 m. and 90 m., of the arena, 58. 50 m. and 49 m. It is argued that this was the scene of the martyrdom of St. Victor and the "Theban Legion." AUSTRIA-HUNGARY CASTELVENERE. — Recent Discoveries. — In *Mitt. Anth. Ges.* XXXVI, 1906, pp. 141-143 (fig.), L. K. Moser describes discoveries at Castelveuere in Istria. They include potsherds and other objects from the neolithic period, with some remains of Roman and Venetian times. LAURIACUM. — A Bronze Tablet. —In *Jh. Oest. Arch. I.* IX, 1906, pp. 315-321 (pi. ; fig-), E. Bormann discu&ses a fragment of a bronze tablet containing five lines of a Latin inscription from the legionary camp of Lauriacum near Enns. A comparison with the bronze tablets of Salpensa *(C.I.L.* II, 1963) leads to the conclusion that the fragment was part of the constitution given to a *municipium* at Lauriacum in the time of Caracalla. A fragmentary inscription on stone is also published containing the titles of Septimius Severus and Caracalla. TOMAJ. — Prehistoric Discoveries. — In *Mitt. Anth. Ges.* XXXVI, 1906, pp. 140-lil (2 figs.), L. K. Moser reports excavations at the Gradisce and the Tabor near Tomaj. At the latter point strata were found containing objects of the middle ages, Roman times, and the bronze age; at the former three graves containing skeletons with bronze ornaments of the La Tene period. GREAT BRITAIN CIRENCESTER. — A Romano-British Village. — In *A then.* May 11, 1907, St. Clair Baddeley describes the excavation, about four miles south of Cirencester on the estate of Lord Biddulph, of a number of small houses and a shallow pit, which the pottery shows must belong to a Romano-British village. Nothing Saxon has been found, nor any " Samian " ware. LONDON. — BRITISH MUSEUM. — Bust of Agrippina the Elder. — In *Burl. Mag.* XI, 1907, pp. 99-100 (pi.), Cecil Smith describes a small plasma bust, recently given to the British Museum, which is evidently a portrait of Agrippina, the wife of Germanicus. The material is rarely used for anything but small intaglios. The portrait is a remarkably fine work, especially impressive for quiet dignity and largeness of style, and clearly the work of a master hand. As a characteristic portrait it is distinctly superior to the bust in the Capitoline Museum.

Illustrations of Greek and Roman Life. —The authorities of the British Museum have placed in the former Etruscan room a collection of objects illustrative of Greek and Roman life, both private and public. The exhibition includes specimens of children's toys and games, surgical instruments, illustrations and models of industrial processes, dress, furniture, weights and measures, building materials, ships, burial customs, the drama, religion, politics, games, and war. A somewhat detailed account of the objects and their arrangement is given in the London *Times,* May 13, 1907. NEWSTEAD. — The Roman Camp.—In *The Builder,* February 2, 1907, the excavations conducted since 1895 by the Scottish Society of Antiquaries at the Roman camp at Newstead, near Melrose, are described. The central fort was built in the time of Agricola. The *praetorium,* the *via principalis,* various storehouses, lodgings for soldiers, etc., have been identified, and weapons, pottery, and other small objects have been found. The excavations are to be continued. *(R. Arch.* IX, 1907, p. 335.) STOKE COURCY. — Excavation of the Wick Barrow.—The excavations at the Wick Barrow in Stoke Courcy, Somerset, which were begun during the middle of April by the Somersetshire Archaeological Society, have been discontinued for the present. The result so far is said to show that the mound belongs to the early bronze age, as it contains two fairly perfect interments with characteristic pottery of that date. Below these in the unexplored portion is a curious wall, the use of which is not yet apparent. There was also at least one interment apparently unconnected with those already mentioned. It is certain that the mound is not the burial place of the Danish chieftain, Hubba. *(A then.* May 4, 1907.) AFRICA BULLA REGIA. — Progress of the Excavations. — In *C. R. Acad. Inne.* 1906, pp. 547-563 (3 figs.), A. Merlin reports the results of further excavations at Bulla Regia (see *A.J.A.* XI, p. 116). In the three rooms at the back of the court have been found colossal marble statues of Apollo, Ceres, and Aesculapius. Many fragments of inscriptions have

been found, of which eight are published. They show that Apollo was worshipped as *Genius coloniae,* and that the other gods were associated with him as *Dii Augusli.* Other fragments mention the *rostra,* the *tabularium,* and a temple of Diana. CARTHAGE. — Punic Inscriptions. — In *C. R. Acad. Insc.* 1907, pp. 180-185 (2 figs.), P. Berger discusses three Punic inscriptions recently found in the necropolis of Bordj-Djedid. One is the epitaph of Batbaal, a high priestess, whose husband belonged to a family that had held the office of *suffet* for four generations. The priestess bears the title *Rab Cohanim* (chief of the priests), which may be compared with the *Mater Sacrorum* of a Carthaginian inscription (C. *R. Acad. Insc.* 1899, p. 160), and seems to show that a woman was president of a college of priests. The other inscriptions are unimportant epitaphs. A Latin Inscription. — In *B. Soc. Ant. Fr.* 1906, pp. 373-377, A. MerLin reports the discovery at Carthage (Ouled-l'Agha) of the epitaph of a soldier of the first *cokors Urbana,* from Emerita (Merida) in Lusitania. It is the first example of a native of Spain in this cohort, but it is probable that a fragmentary list of soldiers from Spain and Italy (C. *R. Acad. Insc.* 1891, pp. 29-31) also refers to this body.

TIMOAD. — Recent Discoveries. — The house of a Roman Flamen, Corfidius Crementius, has been found with an inscription in which the owner praises the decoration of his house. In the house was found a quantity of scorched wheat and other grain, showing that this part of the city was destroyed suddenly. Elsewhere an industrial quarter has been found, including the workshop of a bronze caster, with the furnace still filled with fuel, and a pottery. A new forum, a small temple of Mercury, and the twelfth basilica were also discovered. *(W. Id. Phil.,* April 10, 1907.) UCHI MAIUS. — A Dedication to Carthage. — In *C. R. Acad. Insc.* 1907, pp. 94-95, R. Cagnat publishes a Latin inscription recently found on the site of Uchi Maius. It is a dedication *ex testamento* of Q. Apronius Vitalis *Karthagini Augustae.* It is the first dedication found to

the deified city. UNITED STATES BALTIMORE. — Egyptian Antiquities at Johns Hopkins University. — The Johns Hopkins University has received a collection of Egyptian antiquities from Deir el-Bahari. The most interesting object is the relief of a crocodile with a fish in its mouth. The pottery includes 31 vessels of various kinds. *Rec. Past,* VI, 1907, p. 95 from the *Washington Herald.)* BOSTON. —The Administration of the Museum of Fine Arts.—
Mr. Gardiner M. Lane lias been chosen President of the Museum of Fine Arts in place of Mr. Samuel D. Warren, who declined a reelection. *(B. Mus. F. A.* V, 1907, p. 1.) For the assistance of visitors who may desire special guidance in the Museum, Mr. G. M. Borden of the Museum staff has been appointed Docent. *(Ibid.* p. 9.) Professor Arthur Fairbanks of the University of Michigan has been elected Director of the Museum.

Accessions of the Museum of Fine Arts. — In the *Thirty-first Annual Report* (1906) of the Boston Museum of Fine Arts, pp. 55-01, S. N. Deane gives a detailed account of the accessions during the year to the Department of Classical Art. The most important is a fine marble head of Augustus given by Mr. E. W. Forbes (Fig. 9). A large part of the upper left side of the head has been lost. It is an unusually characteristic portrait. The realistic modelling of the face is in contrast with the more idealized head of Augustus from the Despuig collection already in the Museum (see also *B. Mus. F. A.* V, 1907, pp. 1-3; 4 figs.). Among the vases is a Nolan amphora, a bequest of Mrs. Martin Brimmer, with a representation of Oedipus and the sphinx. The terra-cottas include a whistle attached to the image of a crouching cat The Museum has also purchased 131 Byzantine lead seals. In *B. Mus. F. A.* V, 1907 p. 12 (2 figs.), S. N. Dean'k reports that Mrs. W. Scott Fitz has given the Museum a number of unusually beautiful examples of Graeco-Syrian glass from the neighborhood of Damascus.

In the *Thirty-first Annual Report,* pp. 74-78, O. Bates gives a description of eighteen objects received from the excavations at Gizeh in 1905-06 (see *A J. A.* X, p. 364). Some of these objects are also discussed in *B. Mus. F. A.* V, 1907, pp. 20-21 (six figs.). The most important is a portrait head (Fig. 10) in limestone of the fourth dynasty. It belongs to a very small group of sculptures, and is a fine example of the early art of the Old Empire. It is in almost perfect condition, but part of the upper lip was repaired in plaster by the sculptor. Other interesting specimens are three limestone groups in good preservation from mastabas of the fifth dynasty. From the estate of Airs. Martin Brimmer has been received an unusually large (11.3x7.8 cm.) and fine scarab in greenish blue faience, bearing the cartouche of Seti I (Fig. 11). Unusual features are the curious bands of electrum which seem to have served for suspension, and the elevation of the body of the beetle from the base (see also *B. Mus. F. A.* V, 1907, p. 3; 3 figs.).

CHICAGO. — Inscriptions in the Field Columbian Museum.—Ia *Cl. Phil.* II, 1907, pp. 277-280 (4 figs.), E. J. Goodspeed publishes four inscriptions, which form part of a collection of Egyptian antiquities recently given to the Field Columbian Museum of Chicago by Mr. S. L. James.

Figure 10. — Limestone Head.
Figure 11
Akar Of Seti I.
Three of the inscriptions are apparently fragments of Greek gravestones. The fourth is a Roman brick stamp (see *C.I.L.* XV, i, 169 a), and was possibly purchased in Rome.

NEW YORK —METROPOLITAN MUSEUM. — Acquisitions of Greek and Roman Antiquities. — The principal additions to the Greek and Roman antiquities of the Metropolitan Museum are described in *B.Metr. Mus.* II, 1907. Pp. 5-9 (16 figs.) E. Robinbon comments on the seventytwo terra-cottas, of which sixty-seven are statuettes, chiefly from Tanagra. Important is the fragment of a large female statue (45 cm. high), which reflects the qualities of Attic sculpture of the age of Phidias. Pp. 122-125 (6 figs.) the same writer describes in detail fifteen objects in precious metals and gems. Among these are a pair of electrum spirals of unusual shape, probably Phoenician work of the eighth or seventh century B.C.; a Greek gold ring of the fifth century bearing the figure of a nude dancing girl; a gold ornament from the back of a fibula of pediment shape, surmounted by an acroterion and ending at the corners in the fore parts of winged horses, modelled in the round; a fragment of a cameo representing a Nereid riding on a Triton, a work of great beauty; a flying Xike of chalcedony, lacking the head, arms, and wings, but finely executed; a large silver handle, probably of the first century A.D., cast solid and weighing 1438.536 gr. It is decorated in relief with hunting scenes and ornamental motives. Pp. 17-20 (7 figs.). Miss G. M. A. Richtkr describes seventeen bronzes, which include four minor handles of the sixth and fifth centuries, statuettes of a youth carrying a pig (archaic), Poseidon (fourth century) and Mercury (Gallic-Roman), two mirrorcases with decoration in relief, and two *emblemata* representing satyrs' heads. Pp. 82-83 (2 figs.) the same writer publishes a white lecythus of the early fifth century (Fig. Figure 12. — Perseus And Medusa. 12) with a representation of the flight of Perseus. The figures of Perseus and Pegasus are in dark brown with incised details, that of Medusa is wholly in outline. Various details are in vermilion.

Department of Egyptian Art. —In *B. Metr. Mus.* II, 1907, p. 22, is reported the receipt of a number of fragmentary reliefs from the temple of King Mentuhetep at Deir el-Bahari. They consist principally of representations of birds and plants, are well preserved, and are almost unique examples of Egyptian temple sculpture of the eleventh dynasty. From the same site comes a statue in gray granite of the scribe Netjem, a characteristic work of the nineteenth dynasty. All these objects are the gift of the Egypt Exploration Fund. For the excavations undertaken by the Museum in Egypt, see p. 314.

Two Bronze Tripods. —In *B. Metr. Mus.* II, 1907, pp. 33-40 (11 figs.), G. II. Chase publishes a description of the two bronze tripods recently lent the Mu-

seum by Mr. James Loeb (*A.J.A.* XI, p. 61). As a detailed study of these tripods by the same author will appear in *A.J.A.* XII, a summary of this article is omitted.
EARLY CHRISTIAN, BYZANTINE, MEDIAEVAL, AND RENAISSANCE ART GENERAL AND MISCELLANEOUS APHRODITO. — Arabian Papyri. —In *Z. Assyr.* XX, 1907, pp. 68104, C. H. Becker publishes and translates seventeen Arabic papyri from the first century of Islam that were found at Aphrodito in Egypt. These are governmental and police records of the most varying character. ATHENS. — Byzantine Lead Seals. — In *J. Int. Arch. Num.* IX, 1906, pp. 61-146, K. M. Konstantopoulos begins the publication of a supplement to the catalogue of Byzantine lead seals in the National Numismatic Museum at Athens. The present article describes 448 siecimens. *Ibid.* pp. 49-54 (2 figs.), N. A. Vkes publishes three Byzantine lead seals of the eleventh or twelfth century. BULGARIA. — Melnic and Rossno. —In *B. C.H.* XXXI, 1907, pp. 20-37 (5 figs.), P. Perdrizet describes some of the more important early churches, treasures, and frescoes at Melnic, which boasts 64 churches, of which 57 are still standing. The most space is given to the little monastery of St. Charalambos. A short notice of the monastery of Rossno is added. CILICIA AND LYCAONIA. — Byzantine Churches. — Notes on a Journey through Cilicia and Lycaonia. — In *R. Arch.* VIII, 1906, pp. 390-401 (11 figs.), Gertrude Lowthian Bei.l continues (see *AJ.A.* XI, p. 120) her description of churches and other buildings at Daouleh. Two of these were large buildings of several rooms, undoubtedly monasteries, and in one of them was a chapel resembling in form the mausoleum of Galla Placidia at Ravenna. *Ibid.* IX, 1907, pp. 18-30 (14 figs.), a twostoried building at Daouleh, the domed cruciform basilicas of St. Michel at Silleh and St. Eustathius at Miram, and a rock-cut church, the Kyriacon, near Silleh, are described. CYPRUS. — The Treasure from Cyrenia. —In *Le Muse'e,* IV, 1907, pp. 157-160 (pi.), A. Sambox publishes another piece of the treasure from Cyrenia (see *AJ.A.* XI, p. 120), purchased by J. P. Morgan. It is a large silver plaque richly decorated with scenes from David's combat with Goliath, arranged in three compartments. Three other plaques are in the Cyprus Museum. The history of this treasure and the objects in the Morgan collection are treated in *Burl. Mag.* X. 1907, pp. 355-362 (pis.), by O. M. Dai.ton. The silver dishes with the story of David are probably Syrian work not later than the third quarter of the sixth century, and continue the series begun in the fourth century by such works as the shield of Theodosius at Madrid and the shield of Aspar at Florence. The scenes are probably from miniatures. KERM ABUM. — New Finds in the Sanctuary of St. Menas.—
C. M. Kaufmaxj) publishes the results of his excavations in 1906 on the site of the sanctuary of St. Menas at Kerm Abum in the Libyan desert in *Rom. Quart.* 1906, pp. 189-204 (plan). The most important discoveries were the baptistery and the "burial basilica" of the north cemetery. The excavation of the baptistery made possible a general plan of the sanctuary (120 m. x 50 m.). Among the finds are the niche which probably held the effigy of St. Menas between two camels, described by an Arab traveller, and imitated in a small relief in the Museum at Alexandria. See also *Klio,* VII, 1907, pp. 141-142.
SWITZERLAND. — Plaster Ornaments. — At Disentis (Grisons) excavations on the site of one of the churches of the monastery of Desertina, founded in 612 A.d., have brought to light interesting fragments of plaster ornament. They date from the seventh or eighth century. At Miinster there exists in the monastery a plaster statue of Charlemagne, probably of the latter half of the twelfth century. Fixed in the wall of the monastery church is a plaster Baptism representing Christ, the Baptist, and an angel holding the Saviour's garments. (E. A. Stuckelberg, *B. Soc. Ant. Fr.* 1906, pp. 324-329.)" AN UNPUBLISHED DRAWING BY DURER.—S. Scheikevitch publishes in *Gaz. B.-A.* XXXVII, 1907, pp". 331-336, a drawing by Albrecht Durer, signed with his monogram and the date 1515, representing an owl perched upon a branch, wings outspread, with a vulture (?) at either side. This drawing was used by the author of a popular wood-cut, illustrating a verse upon Envy and Hate by Hans Sachs. The latter was included by Passavant among the wood-cuts of Durer, but was rejected by Valentin Scherer; rightly, as Scheikevitch believes, from a comparison with the newly discovered drawing.
ITALY ACQUISITIONS OF ITALIAN MUSEUMS. — The Uffizi will shortly acquire the collection of drawings belonging to Baron Geymuller, important for its architectural designs. The Galleria Nazionale at Rome is to have the works of art now kept in the hospitals of Rome, among them a Madonna by Mino da Fiesole and the Madonna signed *Opus Andreae,* now on a stairway in San Giacomo. The Museo Nazionale of Florence has acquired a fragment of a Delia Robbia figure, a relief in terracotta of the fifteenth century, another terra-cotta in high relief of the Madonna, and a wooden Virgin and Child, Umbrian work of the fifteenth century (£' *Arte,* 1907, p. 156). G. Frizzoni in *Russ. d' Arte,* 1907, pp. 65-67, notes three additions to the gallery of the Museo Municipale at Milan: a St. Francis, which he attributes to Francesco Mazzuchelli, called Morazzone (1576-1626), and two pictures by Pellegrino, a St. Victor and a St. Margaret. A number of drawings have also been added both to this gallery and to the collection in the Castello Sforzesco. BORGO A MOZZANO. — An Annunciation. — In the church of S. Jacopo at Borga a Mozzano, in a dark niche, were two statues of painted terra-cotta representing the Annunciation. They have recently been removed, cleaned, and replaced in a better light. They are clearly in the style of Giovanni della Robbia. *(Boll. Arte,* I, 1907, i, p. 27; fig.) BURLIGO. — A Borgognone. — A Virgin and Child now in the church of Burligo (Bergamo) is published by L. Angelino in *Rass. d' Arte,* 1907, pp. 76-77. He attributes it to Borgognone. The motive is unusual; the Madonna stands looking down at the Child, who, moving gently to the right,

holds up an apple in his left hand to his mother. FIESOLE. — Additions to the Museum. — The contents of the Oratorio of San Ansano, Fiesole, have been acquired by the Italian Government and will soon be placed in the little museum on the Piazza Mino. The sculptures include the head of a boy in unglazed terra-cotta, by Luca della Robbia — pne of his most beautiful works; a round of the Virgin in Adoration, by Andrea della Robbia, with a notable frame of flowers and fruit; besides interesting fragments of Byzantine wood carving. The pictures

Figure 13. — Fresco Ix The Istituto Delle Belle Arti. number about fifty of the fourteenth and fifteenth centuries— mostly of small size and importance. *(Nation,* January 21, 1907.) FLORENCE. — Discovery of Frescoes in the Belle Arti. — The fresco of the Last Supper recently found in a room on the ground floor of the *Istituto delle Belle Arti* in Florence *(A.J.A.* XI, p. 122) is described by D. B. Marrai in *Boll. Arte,* 1,1907, i, pp. 25-26 (2 figs.). At the left enters the head of the Hospital of St. Matthew, with attendants, and at the right is a youth reading aloud (Fig. 13). The figures of Christ and four apostles were destroyed by a door opened in 1783. *Ibid,* ii, p. 34, it is reported that on the opposite wall has been found a fresco of the Crucifixion, evidently the work of a different artist.

A Michelangelo Room in the Accademia. — Corrado Ricci's plan of substituting real works by Michelangelo for the casts which are now grouped around the "David " in the Accademia is finally to be carried out. The " River-god " is already there, and the king has recently permitted the removal of the "Slaves" from the Boboli gardens. It is hoped that the "Adonis" and "Victory" of the Bargello, and the "St. Matthew" in the court of the Accademia will also be transferred. *(Chron. Arts,* 1907, p. 94.)

Acquisitions of the National Museum.—In *Boll. Arte,* I, 1907, i, pp. 20-22 (8 figs.), I. B. Supino describes briefly some objects recently exhibited in the National Museum at Florence. A bronze plate inlaid with gold and silver contains a hunting scene in a style suggestive of the third century A.d. The article also reproduces some bronze profiles, Florentine and Ferrarese work of the fifteenth century, and a fine carved wooden triptych of the Bolognese school of the same period.

Acquisitions of the Uffizi. — In *Boll. Arte,* 1,1907, ii, pp. 25-29 (2 pis.; 5 figs.), C. Gamba describes some of the Venetian paintings recently added to the Gallery of the Uffizi. Among them are S. Louis of Toulouse, by Bartolomeo Vivarini, and a Holy Family by Cariani. The other paintings are of the eighteenth century. *Ibid.* p. 33, there is noted the acquisition of a tabernacle of the sixteenth century, containing a painting of the Madonna and Child, and above, a Crucifixion with St. Francis and St. Jerome. It seems to be of the school of Filippo Lippi.

An Annunciation by Nicola Gallucci di Guardiagrele. — The National Museum in Florence has recently acquired a stone group representing the Annunciation formerly in a garden at Tocco Casauria in the Abruzzi. In *Boll. Arte,* I, 1907, iii, pp. 1-6 (3 pis.; 3 figs.), A. ColaSanti points out the importance of this work for the history of art in the Abruzzi during the Renaissance, analyzes its style, and attributes it to Nicola Gallucci di Guardiagrele, who made the silver *paliotto* of the Cathedral at Teramo.

A New Painting by Filippo Lippi. — A Madonna formerly in the Villa Pucci, later in the monastery of S. Salvi and now belonging to the *Deputazione provinciate,* has been recognized as an important work by Filippo Lippi. On the back of the picture is a drawing representing the penitent St. Jerome. *(Rass. a" Arte,* 1906, December, Cronaca.) See also *Nation,* January 31, 1907. The picture is to be exhibited in the Hall of Luca Giordano in the Riccardi Palace. The composition resembles that of the Madonna with Four Saints in the Accademia, but the Child stands on the Virgin's left.

MILAN. — The Last Supper of Leonardo da Vinci. — *Boll. Arte,* I, 1907, i, pp. 15-19 (pi.; fig.), contains the report of the commission on the preservation of the Last Supper of Leonardo da Vinci. The report describes previous attempts at restoration, and shows the present dangerous condition of the painting, which is due partly to the original materials, partly to unskilful repairs, and partly to natural causes. As the experiments of L.Cavenaghi have proved successful, he is to undertake the work of preservation. After the most careful cleaning the painting is to be fastened to the wall with a preparation of resin, which will exclude the moisture. MONZA. — The Frescoes of Luini in La Pelucca. — A careful examination has been made of the country house called La Pelucca near Monza, where were the frescoes by Luini now in the Brera at Milan. The size of the original rooms and the arrangement of the paintings, especially in the

Figure 14. — Head By Gcido Mazzoni. chapel, have been determined, and as the king has given the Brera such of the frescoes as are in the palace, it will be possible to rearrange them in their original order, provided additional rooms can be obtained in the Brera. *Doll. Arte,* 1,1907, v, pp. 27-28; fig.) PADUA. — A Masterpiece by Guido Mazzoni. — The remains of the terra-cotta Pieta which Guido Mazzoni made for Sant' Antonio in Venice, are now in the museum at Padua, having been acquired from the *Fondazione Breda,to* which they passed at the death of Senator Breda. These remains include only the busts of the Virgin, St. John, and the Magdalen, and a magnificent recumbent head of Christ (Pig-14). The history of the group is traced with the aid of documents by A. Moschetti in *L' Arte,* 1907, pp. 112 (4 figs.).

PALESTRINA.— A New Pieta by Michelangelo.— In *Gaz. B.-A.* 1907, XXXVII, pp. 177-194, A. Gkenieu describes the Pieta (Pig. 15) carved in the rock at Palestrina, which serves as altarpiece in one of the chapels in the oratory of Sta. Rosalia, belonging to the Palazzo Barberini. The work is unfinished, except for the legs of the Christ, and the motive is the one peculiar to Michelangelo, the Virgin raising with an effort the limp body of her Son, while to the right kneels the Magdalen, assisting to support the Saviour. The powerful use of disproportions and contrasts, the fact that the motive is peculiar to the master, and the resemblance to the Rondanini Pieta and to the unfinished Deposition in the National Gallery, are the chief points in favor of attributing the work to Michelangelo. It is mentioned neither in his biographies nor his correspondence, and only one of the local histories refers to it as his work; but as his patrons the Famese occupied Palestrina from 1541 to 1550, this work could have been executed at Figure 16. — Pietx At Palestrina. that time. In *Chron. Arts,* 1907, p. 107, H. Vasnier recalls the fact that Du Pays, in an old edition of the *Guide Joanne,* speaks of the work as attributed to Michelangelo. PARMA. — Acquisitions of the Picture Gallery. — Among the recent acquisitions of the Picture Gallery at Parma, are the fresco of the *Vergine delta Misericordia,* by Pier Antonio Bernabei, formerly over the outer door of the Orphanage for Girls, and a painting by Battista di Dosso, representing St. Michael overcoming the devil in a splendid landscape; in clouds above is the Virgin surrounded by angels. It seems to have been painted about 1524. (L. Testi, *Boll. Arte,* I, 1907, iv, pp. 19-22; pi.; 2 figs.) PERUGIA. — The Exhibition of Umbrian Art. — In the *Nation,* June 20,1907, M. describes the exhibition of early Umbrian art then open at Perugia. It includes works in Umbria, whether by native artists or not, and thus shows clearly the generally imitative character of the Umbrian artists, who do not form a true school, but borrow usually from Siena, or the Marches, or Florence. Among the notable works are a bishop's crozier of the fourteenth century arid an altar front of the twelfth from Citta di Castello, and numerous fine textiles and embroideries. The pictures and other objects have been often gathered from inaccessible towns or monasteries, and their arrangement makes it possible to study the development of many of the local schools and artists. The value of this exhibition is also noticed by B. Berexson, *Chron. Arts,* 1907, p. 136, and London *Times,* April 25, 1907. See also *Boll. Arte,* I, 1907, v, pp. 34-35, and London *Times,* May 22, 1907. RADICENA. — Discovery of a Drawing by Raphael. — In the village of Radicena there was recently discovered the sketch made by Raphael for the "Battle of Constantine " in the Stanze of the Vatican. The sketch was formerly in the collection of the *Castello reale* at Naples. (*Chron. Arts,* 1907, p. 75.) REATI. — An Unpublished Presepio. — In *Rass. d' Arte,* 1906, pp. 190-192 (fig.), G. Petrini publishes a description of an important sixteenth century picture in the gallery at Reati representing the Virgin and Joseph adoring the infant, with the Magi in the distance. Angels play above the hut, and God the Father appears surrounded by cherubs in the sky above. The painting shows the influence of Lorenzo di Credi. RIPATRANSONE. — Frescoes in the Church of Sta. Maria Magna. — The frescoes in the church of Sta. Maria Magna at Ripatransone in the Marches are described in *Rass. d' Arte,* 1907, pp. 7-10, by C. Grigioni, who ascribes to the same artist the frescoes of the church of Santa Vittoria in Mantenano and a diptych in the Palazzo Comunale at Ripatransone. There is no clew to the artist's name unless the reference in a document of 1461 to Giacomo di Campli, as the "painter already here," refers to the author of the frescoes. ROME. — Excavations in the Catacombs. — In *Not. Scav.* Ill, 1906, pp. 304-312, O. Marucchi reports on the excavations in the catacombs during 1905 and 1906. In the cemetery of Sta. Priscilla (cf. *AJ.A.* XI, p. 123) excavations were continued near the ancient baptistery. It was surrounded by a mass of galleries before the stairway was built from the surface. The rock here is full of water, and as such a region is otherwise avoided by the ancient excavators, it is clear this site had a special importance. This confirms the view that this is the *coemeterium ad nymphas B. Petri,* where the apostle Peter baptized. Part of the old basilica of S. Silvestro, abandoned in the ninth century, has been excavated. Excavations were also conducted between the Via Appia and the Via Ardeatina, in search of the basilica of the Pope Marcus, and the cemetery of Balbina. The results are not yet conclusive, but the remains found may belong to the basilica.

Acquisitions of the Cabinet of Prints. — In *Boll. Arte,* I, 1907, v, pp. 7-18 (pi.; 5 figs.), F. Hermanin describes a number of drawings recently acquired by the Cabinet of Prints in Rome. Three of these are by Polidoro da Caravaggio, of whose works the Cabinet now has an important series, which is discussed in detail. Another, representing Hercules fighting, is attributed to the school of Antonio Pollaiuolo. A study in drapery belongs to the school of Andrea Verrocchio. Others show the style of Pierino del Vaga, Rosso Fiorentino, and Pietro da Cortona.

A Relief of the Renaissance. — In the Palazzo della Scimia in Rome is a fine relief, hitherto unpublished, representing the Virgin seated with the Child on her lap between St. Peter and St. Paul. The former seems to commend to her protection a tower, evidently the one now known as the Torre della Scimia. Below are the arms of the Scapucci family, and the date MCIII, probably an error for 1503. The style indicates a work of the Lombard School, in which Andrea Breguo probably had a share. (V. LEoxarDI, *Boll. Arte,* I, 1907, iii, pp. 19-22; fig.) SANTA VITTORIA. — Works of Art in a Country Church. — In the church belonging to a confraternity of St. Francis, near the village of Santa Vittoria in Piedmont, there are to be found a painting of the school of Macrino d' Alba and important frescoes from the hand of some Piedmontese paiuter of the *quattrocento.* (E. Milano, *Arte e Storia,* 1906, pp. 179-184.) SARDINIA. — Churches and Works of Art. —In *Boll. Arte,* I, 1907, ii, pp.:J—16 (3 pis.; 22 figs.), D. Scano describes a number of old churches in Sardinia, and the works of art in the Cathedral at Cagliari. The churches discussed are the recently restored S. Gavino at Portotorres, of the eleventh century; Sta. (iiusta at Sta. Giusta, one of the earliest Romanesque churches on the island; S. Pantaleo at Dolianova, which shows a puzzling combination of Romanesque and Gothic elements, and the churches of the Cappuccini and of Sta. Chiara at Iglesias, both belonging to the transitional period between Romanesque and Gothic. Of the plate in the cathedral the most important piece is a large silver crucifix, which rests on a base in the form of a richly decorated Gothic shrine, and is itself adorned on both sides with numerous figures in relief. It is assigned to the fifteenth century. In *V Arte,* 1907, pp. 47-52 (3 figs.), E. Bruneli.i describes a plate and ewer, and a *pianeta* preserved in the same treasury. The decorations of the latter are in the Spanish style of the sixteenth century. The plate and ewer are probably the work of local artists. There is no trace of the art of Cellini, the traditional maker. Sardinian work generally preserves Gothic traditions until the introduction of Spanish baroque, but there is a brief interval, in which these works belong, when the influence of the Italian renaissance is felt.

SICILY. — Catacombs near Priolo. — The excavation of Christian catacombs and tombs near Priolo is described in *Not. Scar.* 1906, pp. 185-198 (8 figs.), 218-243 (21 figs.), by P. Orsi. A southern group is about the catacomb of Manomozza and the early church of S. Foca (cf. *Byz. Z.* 1809, pp. 636-642). The catacomb consists of an atrium and a neighboring chamber, both containing *arcotolia* and apparently pre-Constantinian. Later another chamber was added in which were two tombs under baldachins, and above a cupola terminating in an opening for light. Fragmentary painted Greek inscriptions and some small objects of clay and glass were found. At Riuzzo is a northern group of tombs, and two catacombs. The smaller of these is perhaps that of a family and its dependants. Nothing was found to fix the date. The larger seems formed by the later union of two secret burial places. In one chamber was a large tomb carefully protected by a stone screen. In this catacomb were found marble masks and heads of the Roman period, which had apparently been introduced when the catacomb was plundered by Vandals or Arabs.

TURIN. — Reliefs in Wood. —The Royal Gallery at Turin has received three reliefs in wood. A triptych is Flemish work of the fifteenth century. A panel, with four Franciscan saints above, kneeling Franciscans, men and women, in the middle, and below a fawn, seems to be Piedmontese work of the fifteenth century. The third, a polyptych with painted wings, and a relief of the Madonna and Child, is also Piedmontese, but of the early sixteenth century. (A. Vesme, *Boll. Arte,* IV, 1907, iv, pp. 16-18; 3 figs.) VENICE. —A Portrait by Lorenzo Lotto. — The Royal Gallery at Venice has lately secured a fine portrait by Lorenzo Lotto, representing in halflength a bearded man, wearing the black cap of a scholar of the fifteenth century. It is a good example of Lotto's early work, at the tran- sition from his first to his second style. (G. Foooi.ari, *Boll. Arte,* I, 1907, i, pp. 23-24; fig.) VERONA. —A Gothic Burial. —In *Madonna Verona,* 1907, pp. 1-9 (2 figs.), C. Cipoi.la describes the discovery in a court of the Palazzo Miniscalchi of a grave of the Gothic or early Lombard period. Among the contents were a gold pectoral cross, earrings, and a ring, all of rich workmanship. The absence of weapons makes it probable that the tomb was that of a woman. FRANCE AVIGNON. — Discovery of Frescoes. — In the course of investigations in the Palace of the Popes at Avignon the painter Yperman has discovered at the end of the chapel called the " Consistory Hall " the traces of a large Crucifixion in fresco, dating from the middle ages. The coloring is gone, but the drawing, of a remarkable purity, remains. Similar traces have been found on the right wall of the same chapel. (*Citron. Ails,* 1907, p. 150.)

Statuette of a Kneeling Monk. —In *Le Muse'e,* IV, 1907, p. 228 (pi.), E. Bailly publishes a marble statuette recently found in the walls of an old house at Avignon and now in the collection of Mme. P. Biollay. It represents a kneeling monk, looking upward, and seems to have formed part of a group, probably on a tomb. It is a good example of local art at the time of the Papal residence.

AZAY-LE-RIDEAU. — A New Museum of Renaissance Art. — Gifts by Mme. Louis Stern, the Rothschilds, Fernand Halphen, and Charles Stern, together with contributions from the *Administration des Beaux-Arts,* have rendered possible the formation at Azay-le-Rideau of a museum devoted to the art of the Renaissance. (*Chron. Arts,* 1907, p. 18.) *Ibid.* p. 93 are announced additional gifts. DAUMAZAN. — A Mediaeval Inscription. — In *B. Soc. A nt. Fr.* 1906, pp. 340-342, C. Eslart publishes four Latin hexameters, referring to the capture of Jerusalem by the Crusaders, July 15, 1099. They were recently discovered in the south wall of the transept of the parish church at Dauuiazan. Above the verses is carved an alphabet, and below is the date, 1156, which probably refers to the consecration of the church, when an alphabet was often traced on the building. PARIS. — Acquisitions of the Bibliotheque Nationale. — Among the recent additions to the department of manuscripts in the Bibliotheque Xationale are a missal of the Premonstratensian use, with miniatures, bequeathed by Mme. Clery, and the second volume of Josephus' *A ntiquities* with the miniatures by Jean Foucquet, presented by the King of England (see *A. J. A.* X, p. 372). A detailed list of the accessions is given in *Bill. Ec. Charles,* 1907, pp. 1-74, by H. Omont.

Acquisitions of the Louvre. — Recent additions to the Louvre collections include two fourteenth century statues, the effigies of Charles IV and his wife Jeanne d'Evreux, by Jean de Liege; a fourteenth century angel; a Virgin of the fifteenth century; a kneeling donor of the sixteenth century, — all from the abbey of Maubuisson, and presented by the *Socie'te des Amis du Louvre.* (*Burl. Mag.* XI, 1907, pp. 55-56.) In *B. Soc. Ant. Fr.* 1906, pp. 394-400, Marquet De Vasselot describes a copper basin of the middle of the twelfth century recently acquired. It is decorated with an inscription in leonine verse and several scenes in outline from the life of the apostle Thomas. Similar basins are found in the museums of western Germany, and are supposed to be of Westphalian origin. See also *Citron. Arts,* 1907, p. 42. Other additions are an ivory Virgin of the fourteenth century, from the Adolphe Rothschild fund, and a bronze group representing a Peasant leading a Cow, a realistic Flemish work of the early seventeenth century, presented by M. Radzersdorfer. *(Chron. Arts,* 1907, pp. 114-115.) Cointe Potocki has lent Rembrandt's Portrait of his Brother *(cu.* 1650). which he intends to bequeath to the Louvre. *(Chron. Arts,* 1907, pp. 85-86.)

Additions to the Trocade'ro.— The *Muse'e de Sculpture comparee du Trocade'ro* has added casts of the following objects: the Romanesque capitals of the abbey church of Dommartin at Amiens; a double figured capital from the cloister of Corbie in the same city; the twelfth century censer in the Lille museum; and two fragments of statues from the old cathedral of Cambrai; from the thirteenth century, the sepulchral figure of Ste. Ozanne in the crypt of Jouarre, a small bas-relief of the Coronation of the Virgin, at Metz, a female head from Reims, and the sarcophagus of John of Salisbury, bishop of Chartres, discovered during the excavations in the abbey of Josaphat; from the fourteenth century, the four statuettes of the collegiate church at Mantes; from the fifteenth century, four figures in the Amiens museum and a bust of the "Virgin of Pity"; from the sixteenth century, the altarpiece of Ilattonchatel (Meuse), the sepulchral figure of Philippe de Gueldres, the marble medallion of Antoine de Lannoy, governor of Genoa, in the Museum of Amiens, and two purely Italian reliefs in the same museum. A new catalogue, including a bibliography, will soon appear. *(Chron. Arts,* 1907, pp. 174-175.) VALENCIENNES. — A Fourteenth Century Tapestry. — A description of a tapestry preserved in the museum at Valenciennes is given in *Chron. Arts,* 1907, p. 36, by M. Henault. It represents a fifteenth century tourney, which includes among the participants such famous persons as Charles VIII, Philippe le Beau, his wife Jeanne la Folle, and the young Maximilian, together with many secondary personages who appear in other tapestries. The tapestry belonged to an unknown family of the fifteenth century, from whom it passed to the house of Saxony, whose arms appear upon the border. At the time of the Revolution, it was preserved in a room of the Hotel de Ville at Valenciennes.

GERMANY ITALIAN MINIATURES IN GERMANY. —In *V Arte,* 1907, pp. 25-32 (6 figs.), P. D' Ancona describes five manuscripts containing miniatures by Italian artists. The first is a fifteenth century manuscript of Boccaccio's *Filocalo* now in Cassel, with miniatures by a Neapolitan, as is shown by the love of minute detail and the peculiar treatment of water and mountains. Another codex in the same library contains Aretino's compilation of the *Rime, Trionfi,* and *Vita del Petrarca,* and was decorated by Marmitta, a sixteenth century painter mentioned by Vasari, as appears from some verses inserted by way of introduction. The artist shows the influence of Mantegna. The third manuscript is Cod. 277, A. Extr. at Wolfenbiittel, which contains verses, probably by some imitator of Giusto. Its two miniatures of Apollo and Daphne, and Apollo and the Muses, are plainly the work of Liberale da Verona. The article concludes with a description of two small manuscripts of Petrarch's *Trionfi,* one in the Royal Library at Dresden, the other in the Imperial Library at Vienna.
BERLIN. — Acquisitions of the Kaiser Friedrich Museum. — Recent additions to the Kaiser Friedrich Museum include: from the Hainauer collection, by gift: a small clay " Thorn extractor," probably by the Paduan Bellano, a Venetian bronze statuette of St. Peter (the companion piece, St. Paul, has recently been bought), a Gothic ivory statuette of the Madonna, two late sixteenth century bronze chandeliers from the Strozzi palace, a Madonna adoring the Child by Domenico di Paris, a marble bust *oi* Luca Mini by Mino da Fiesole, a small bronze relief of the Madonna with angel musicians by Donatello, a polychrome relief of the Madonna by Rossellino, four panels of Saints, parts of an altarpiece by Martin Schaffner, and a Decapitation of St. John by Herri Met de Bles. These two painters were not heretofore represented in the Berlin Gallery. Other acquisitions are: Three Musicians with an Ape by Velasquez, an Adoration of the Shepherds by Murillo, a Portrait of a Lady by Joos van Cleve, and Anthonio Mor's Por, trait of the Duchess Margaret of Parma. *(Burl. Mag.* X, 1906, p. 199.) To the collection of mediaeval and Renaissance sculpture have been added: an Apostle by Tilman Riemenschneider; a polychrome Baptism in relief by Hans Leinberger of Landshut; a group of figures for a Mount Calvary, South German carving of about 1500; a French thirteenth century Madonna enthroned; and a Burgundian stone statuette of "Pharaoh's Daughter finding Moses" of the end of the fifteenth century. *(Burl. Mag.* X, 1907, pp. 399-400.) BRLANGEN.—A New Museum. — The catalogue of the new gallery of paintings at Erlangen shows that the collection includes seventy-four pictures taken from the stock of the Alte Pinakothek at Munich, twentyfour from Augsburg, and twenty-three from Schleissheim. The museum was opened by the government in response to a request from the University of Erlangen to facilitate studies in the history of the fine arts, and for this purpose characteristic examples of the old German, Dutch, Flemish, and Italian schools were selected and sent to the museum. *(Burl. Mag.* X, 1907, p. 399.) AUSTRIA-HUNGARY GRATZ. — A Crucifix of the Nuremberg School. — The very beautiful Christ on the Cross in the church of the Brothers of Mercy at Grata was recently identified by Professor Brandstetter as a work of the Nuremberg school. He detached the body from the cross and after a careful cleaning discovered upon the drapery the inscription: *Georg Schweigger in Nilrnherg anno 1633.'* *(Chron. Arts,* 1907, p. 85.) VID'DI NARENTA. —A Fifth or Sixth Century Relief. —Fr. BuLid publishes in *N. Bull. Arch. Crist.* XII, 1906, pp. 207-214 (2 figs.), a relief representing two peacocks facing a bowl, a well-

known motive with eucharistic meaning. The relief, which is of the fifth or sixth century, is important only as confirming the author's opinion that Narenta. the ancient *Narona,* was not destroyed in the third or fourth century A.D., but continued in existence until the disappearance of Roman authority in Dalmatia. GREAT BRITAIN DISCOVERY OF A PAINTING BY VELASQUEZ. — A picture belonging to Sir George Donaldson is identified by H. Cook in *Burl. yig.* X, 1906, pp. 171-172, as Velasquez's missing portrait of Calabacas, a fool of the court of Philip IV. The subject is a laughing clown, standing before a folding stool, holding in his right hand a lady's portrait, and in his left a paper windmill on the end of a stick. The clown is identified with the subject of the *Bobo ile Carta* in the Madrid Gallery. HEXHAM.— The Abbey Church. —In the London *Times,* April 1, 1907, E. S. Savage reports discoveries at Hexham in clearing the ground for the erection of a nave for the old abbey church. These include the remains of a late Gothic nave, and of the earlier Saxon church *(ca.* 674 A.i.), as well as fragments from the neighboring Roman town, Corstopituni. Among the latter are a bust of an emperor, and more of the inscription in the north passage of the crypt. It named Severus and his sons, but Geta's name had been erased. IXWORTH. —An Ornamental Metal Disk. —In *Reliq.* XIII, 1907, pp. 133-134 (2 figs.), is published a metal disk with zoomorphic designs found at Ixworth, Suffolk. It is Anglian work, and originally formed the head of a pin. LONDON. — Acquisitions of the National Gallery. — By the legacy of Miss Cohen, the National Gallery has become the possessor of twenty-six paintings, the most important of which are three portraits by Romanino, Alvise Vivarini, and Costa. They are described, with reproductions of the Romanino and Vivarini, by Herbert Cook in *V Arte,* 1907, p. 152. See also *Chron. Arts,* 1906, p. 342.

Old Masters at the Royal Academy. — The exhibition of Old Masters at the Royal Academy is discussed by H. Cook in *V Arte,* 1907, pp. 150-152. Among the pictures which the exhibition first made generally known is a large Circumcision by Bartolomeo Veneto, signed and dated 1506. Other noteworthy pictures are a Holy Family by Andrea del Sarto, a Venus or Lady at her Toilet, which may be a copy of the Bellini in Vienna, and a much discussed Portrait of a Lady by Ambrogio de Predis, from Lord Roden's collection at Tullymore Park in Ireland. The identification of the lady in this picture is attempted by Miss Hewett in *Burl. Mag.* X, 1907, pp. 309-313 (2 pis.), who considers that she is Lucrezia Crivelli. Mr. Cook, however, believes that the letters L. O. and the Moor's head on the clasp she wears are an allusion to Ludovico il Moro, and that she is Cecilia Gallerani, his mistress.

New Italian Medals in the British Museum. — G. F. Hill in *Burl. Mag.* X, 1907, pp. 384-387, describes and reproduces some Italian medals recently acquired by the British Museum. One is a lead proof of Pisanello's medal of Vittorino da Feltre, another the same artist's medal of Pier Candido Decembrio, formerly in the Piot collection, and the rest belong to the more common work of Pastorino da Siena.

A Wax Model attributed to Michelangelo. — Two small models have been recently brought to light by the Keeper of Mediaeval Antiquities of the British Museum, one of which is an upright male torso, apparently by Baccio Bandinelli, while the other, a recumbent torso, recalls the figures on the Medici tombs so closely so as to suggest the attribution to Michelangelo. There is a lack of finish about the figure, and nothing of the heroic or superhuman in the proportions, but the first objection is removed by comparing the model for a Hercules and Cacus in the Victoria and Albert Museum, and the latter disappears when we find that the master's preliminary studies are almost invariably naturalistic, in spite of the disproportions of his finished work. (C. J. Holmes, *Burl. Mag.* XI, 1907, pp. 189-190.)

The "Madonna del Divino Amore." — The picture called the "Madonna del Divino Amore," recently offered in London as a Raphael, was submitted to Messrs. Holmes and Fry for examination, with the result that they have found it a genuine product of Raphael's immediate entourage, probably executed by Baldassare Peruzzi after a drawing by Raphael himself. *(Ross, a" Arte,* May, 1907, Cronaca.) ROWLSTONE. — A Sculptured Norman Tympanum. — The Norman tympanum over the south doorway of the church of St. Peter at Rowlstone, Herefordshire, bears a representation of Christ in Glory, within an oval aureole supported by four angels. The nimbus is cruciform, but without the enclosing circle. *(Reliq.* XIII, 1907, pp. 135; fig.) STIIiLINGFLEET. — A Viking Ship on a Norman Door The door of the church at Stillingfleet, Yorkshire, is adorned with two horizontal hinge straps of iron, with ends terminating in beasts' heads. On the upper part of the door are iron ornaments, including figures of men, a device of fleur-de-lys, and a Viking ship. The whole design is intensely Scandinavian in character. Another boat is represented on the ironwork of a church door at Stapleford, Kent. *(Reliq.* XIII, 1907, pp. 127-128; 2 figs.) AFRICA CARTHAGE. — The Cemetery at Mcidfa. — Father Delattre publishes in *C. R. Acad. Insc.* 1907, pp. 118-127 (2 figs.), a report on the continuation of his excavations at Mcidfa (see *A.J.A.* XI, p. 131). Of the basilica only the foundation and some architectural fragments remain, but beside the church is a large rectangular area filled with tombs. Many fragments, including part of a concave sun-dial, lamps, and slabs decorated with Christian symbols have been recovered, but the chief result is the discovery of 3963 fragments of Latin inscriptions, chiefly Christian. *Ibid.* pp. 176-177, A. Heron De Villefosse reports that Father Delattre has discovered in fragments a slab from a tomb bearing the names of the martyrs Perpetua, Felicitas, and their companions.

Seals and Inscriptions. — In *B. Soc. A nt. Fr.* 1906, pp. 322-324 (3 figs.), P. Monceaux publishes two lead amulets, in the form of the seal of Solomon, and a lead tablet containing remains of a magical inscription. All were found at Carthage by Father Delattre. *Ibid.* pp. 351-353, he describes two Byzantine lead seals, and two coins from the same source. *Ibid.* pp. 372-373 (2 figs.), he publishes an abraxas gem, and a fragment of a Christian lamp, on which is represented a ship with four passengers, and in front of the prow a swan.

HENCHIR CHORAB — A Dedication. — The following dedication has been recently found inscribed upon a pilaster of an early Christian basilica at Henchir Chorab: *ad hanc domum Dei tribunal basilicae Dominae Caslae sanctae ac cenerande martiri* (palm) *Sabinianus una cum con iuge et Jilis votumperfecit* (two palms). The martyr Casta is mentioned in the *martyrologium Hieronymianum.* The *tribunal basilicae* is interesting as a phrase transferred from the terminology of the pagan basilica to denote the elevated presbyterium. (O. Marucchi, *N. Bull. Arch Crist.* 1906, pp. 315-316.) HENCHIR KEMABLEL. — Christian Inscriptions. — Upon the arch of a basilica at Henchir Kemablel the following inscription was recently found: MER ARMIGERORVM BOTVM COMPLEBIT DOGS. The first words refer to the *numerus* with its epithet *armigeri.* The abbreviation completing the inscription is the famous *Deo gratias* adopted by the Catholics as counter cry to the schismatic Donatists. The same formula is found in another inscription on a basilica in the neighborhood. (O. Marucchi, *N. Bull. Arch. Crist.* 1906. pp. 314-315.) THABRAKA. — Mosaics. — Among the mosaics in the pavement of a basilica discovered in Thabraka, one was found which outlined the plan and elevation of a church, the *ecclenia mater* according to the accompanying inscription. Another depicts a scribe at his desk, busily copying a *martyrum vita.* (O. Marucchi, *N. Bull. Arch. Crist.* 1906, pp. 316-317.) UNITED STATES BROOKLYN. —A Triptych by Sano di Pietro. —The Brooklyn Museum of Arts and Sciences has received from Mr. A. A. Healy a triptych by Sano di Pietro (1406-1481), representing the Virgin seated between two Evangelists. It belonged for several generations to a family living near Siena and was shown in the Sienese exposition of 1904. The only other painting by Sano in the United States is that in the Jarvis Collection at New Haven. *(Chron. Arts,* 1907, p. 77.) CLEVELAND. — Italian Pictures in the Hollenden Gallery. — The gallery of Mr. L. E. Holden contains a number of Italian paintings which were bought, in 1867, from the Jarvis collection. The most important of them are described and reproduced by Mary Logan Berenson in *Rass. d'Arte,* 1907, pp. 1-5. Those reproduced are: a Madonna suckling the Child, of the Sienese school; a Madonna adoring the Child, ascribed to Domenico Ghirlandaio in the gallery but probably by Botticini; a Virgin suckling the Child, by Lorenzo di Credi; a portrait of Giuliano de' Medici, drawn from Michelangelo's statue, probably by Salviati; an excellent Madonna and Saints, by Lorenzo da San Severino, the only representation of the Umbrians in the collection; an Adoration of the Shepherds, possibly of Bramantino's school; an interesting Leonardesque Madonna which is already well known; and a Portrait of a Gentleman and his Wife, by G. B. Moroni. NEW YORK. — Acquisitions of the Metropolitan Museum.—In *B. Metr. Mus.* 1907, p. 27 (tig.), the acquisition is reported of a Nativity by Fiorenzo di Lorenzo, a small but good example of this Umbrian master. *Ibid.* pp. 40-45 (5 figs.), Bashford Dean describes a series of Burgundian tapestries of the fourteenth century representing the Seven Sacraments, recently presented by Mr. J. P. Morgan. Nothing is known of their history, and their origin and date are determined by internal evidence. *Ibid.* pp. 7780(3 figs.), R. E. Fry describes a large altarpiece dedicated to St. Andrew, formerly in the church of Perpignan. It is probably the work of Luis Borrassa, and is an admirable example of the recently discovered Catalan school, which flourished near Barcelona in the early fifteenth century. *Ibid.* pp. 108-109 (fig.), L. M. P. describes four Renaissance objects: a small marble statue of Temperance, a work of the Pisan school of the late fourteenth century; a terra-cotta relief of the Virgin and Child, by Jacopo della Quercia; a *cas.ione* panel of about 1420, representing the capture of Salerno by Robert Guiscard; a tabernacle with painted wings enclosing a relief of the Madonna, attributed to Rossi. *Ibid.* pp. 93-99 (5 figs.), E. Robinson announces that Mr. J. P. Morgan has presented to the museum the objects in the eighteenthcentury section of the Hoentschel collection, and made an indefinite loan of the Gothic section. These objects will be exhibited in a new section of the building, and a detailed description is deferred. PHILADELPHIA. — The Future Picture Gallery. — F.j.mather, in *Burl. Mag.* X, 1907, pp. 269-271, gives an estimate of the value of the gallery which it is said will be formed in Philadelphia from the collections of W. L, Elkins, J. G. Johnson, and P. A. B. Widener (see *A. J.A.* XI, p. 135). Two-thirds of the 1400 pictures are earlier than the nineteenth century. The Flemish and Dutch schools will be most completely represented by fine pictures. The Italian and Spanish painters will appear in less numbers, but some of the canvases are very important. English art of the eighteenth century and the landscape-painters from Gainsborough and Wilson to Turner will be "splendidly in evidence." French painting prior to 1800 will be the weakest portion, but the list includes some primitives, Clouet, and a remarkable Watteau. Early German painting is adequately represented, although most of the attributions to Durer and Holbein are questionable. The gallery will rank with European museums of the second class, being " fairly on a par with the Cassel gallery, for instance, or with that of Glasgow, while being more comprehensive than either."

Publications of the Institute Proper

Annual Reports

Reports I-XVII. (1881-1896.) Each. $0.50.

First Annual Report, with accompanying papers. I. A Study of the Houses of the American Aborigines, with a Scheme of Exploration of the Ruins in New Mexico and elsewhere. By Lewis

H. Morgan. II. Ancient Walls of Monte Leone, in the Province of Grosseto, Italy. By W. J. Stillman. III. Archaeological Notes on Greek Shores. Part I. By Joseph Thacheb Clarke. (1880.) In red cloth. Pp.163. Illustrated. *(Out of Print.)* Papers—Classical Series

Vol. I. (1882.) Report on the Investigations at Assos, 1881. By Joseph Th Acheb Clarke, with an Appendix containing Inscriptions from Assos and Lesbos, and Papers by W. C. Lawton and J. 8. Dillbr. 8vo. Pp.215. Boards. Illustrated. $3.50. Vol. II. (1897.) Report on the Investigations at Assos, 1882, 1883. By Joseph Thachef Clarke. With an Appendix on the Relations of Modern to Ancient Life. 8vo. Pp. 330. Boards. Illustrated. $3.50. Vol. IIL No. 1. (1890.) Telegraphing among the Ancients. By A. C. Merriam. 8vo. Pp. 32. $0.50. Papers — American Series

Vol. I. (1881.) 1. Historical Introduction to Studies among the Sedentary Indians of New Mexico. 2. Report on the Ruins of the Pueblo of Pecos. By A. F. Bandelier. 8vo. Pp. 135. Boards. 111. *Second Edition.* $1.00.

Vol. II. (1884.) Report of an Archaeological Tour in Mexico in 1881. By A. F. Bandelier. 8vo. Pp. 326. Boards. Illustrated. *(Out of Print.)*

Vol. III. Part I. (1890.) Final Report of Investigations among the Indians of the Southwestern United States, carried on mainly in the years from 1880 to 1885. By A. F. Bandelier. 8vo. Pp. 218. Boards. Illustrated. $3.00.

Vol. IV. fl892.) Part II. of above Report. 8vo. Pp.591. Boards. Illustrated. $3.00.

Vol. V. (1890.) Contributions to the History of the Southwestern Portion of the United States. By A. F. Bandelier. 8vo. Pp. 206. Boards. Map. $2.00. Bulletin, Report, Index

Bulletin I, January, 1883. I. The work of the Institute in 1882. II. Report of A. F. Bandelier on his Investigations in New Mexico in the Spring and Summer of 1882. III. Note on a Terra-cotta Figurine from Cyprus of a Centaur with human forelegs in the Metropolitan Museum of Art, New York. With a plate. By Thomas W. Ludlow. Pp. 40. Paper. $0. 50.

Report on the Wolfe Expedition to Babylonia in 1884, 1885. By William Hayes Ward. (1886.) Pp. 33. Paper. $0. 50.

Index to Publications of the Institute and of the School at Athens, 1879-89. Br W. S. Merrill. (1891.) Pp. 89. Boards. $1.00. Journal of the Institute

American Journal Of Archaeology, *Second Series.* Vols. I-X. (1897-1906.)

Each 85.00. For special rates to members of the Institute and libraries, see advertising pages.

The Argive Heraeum. Published for the Institute and the School at Athens.

The Argive Heraeum. By Charles Waldstein, with the cooperation of G. H. Chase, H. F. De Cou, T. W. Hbermanck, J. C. Hoppin, A. M. Lythooe, R. Norton, R. B. Richardson, E. L. Tilton, H. S. Washington, and J. R. Wheeler. In two volumes. Large quarto. Boston and New York: Houghton, Mifflin & Co. Vol. I., 1902: Vol. II., 1905. $30. 00 for the two volumes, in cloth; 860. 00, in full morocco ($20.00, in cloth, for members of the Institute and of the Managing Committee; $44.00, in full morocco).

The Codex Venetus of Aristophanes. Published by the Institute and the Society for the Promotion of Hellenic Studies. Api2to«a.noys KOMniAiAi. Facsimile of the Codex Venetus Marcianus 474. With a preface by John Williams White, and an Introduction by T. W. Allen. Pp. 23 + 344. London and Boston. 1903. $155.00, in portfolio; $36.75, in halfmorocco.

»» All the publications of the Institute and of the School at Athens, except *The Argive Heraettm* and *The Facsimile of the Codex Venetus of Aristophanes,* mav be procured through Macmillan & Co. , 64-66, Fifth Avenue, New York City. *The Argive Heraeum* may be procured through Professor T. D. Seymour, Yale University, New Haven, Conn., or through the Publishers. *The Facsimile of the Codex Venetus of Aristophanes* may be procured through Professor John Williams White, Harvard University, Cambridge, Mass.

Publications of the American School of Classical Studies at Athens

Annual Reports

Reports I-XV. (1881-96.) The first three Reports are bound in one pamphlet; the fifth and sixth also are published together. Each, $0.25.

Papers of the School

Vol. L (For 1882-83.) 1. Inscriptions of Assos. By J. R. S. Sterrett. 2. Inscriptions of Tralleis. By the same Author. 3. The Theatre of Dionysus. By James R. Wheeler. 4. The Olympieion at Athens. By Louis Bevibr. 5. The Erechtheion at Athens. By Harold N. Fowler. 6. The Battle of Salamis. By W. W. Goodwin. Published in 1885. 8vo. Pp. viii 262. Boards. Illustrated. 82.00.

Vol. II. (For 1883-84.) An Epigraphical Journey in Asia Minor in 1884. By J. R. 8itlington Sterrett, with Inscriptions, and two new Maps by H. Kiepert. Published in 1888. 8vo. Pp. 344. Boards. 82.50.

Vol. HI. (For 1884-85.) The Wolfe Expedition to Asia Minor in 1885. By J. R. SitLington Sterrett, with Inscriptions mostly hitherto unpublished, and two new Maps by H. Kiepert. Published in 1888. 8vo. Pp. 448. Boards. 82m

Vol. IV. (For 1885-86.) 1. The Theatre of Thoricus, Preliminary Report. By WalTer Miller. 2. The Theatre of Thoricus, Supplementary Report. By William L. Cushinq. 3. On Greek Versification in Inscriptions. By Frederic D. Allen. 4. The Athenian Pnyx. By John M. Crow; with a Survey of the Pnyx, and Notes, by Joseph Thacheb Clarke. 5. Notes on Attic Vocalism. By J. Mckeen Lewis. Published in 1888. 8vo. Pp. 277. Illustrated. Boards. 82.00.

Vol. V. (For 1886-90.) 1. Excavations at the Theatre of Sikyon. By W. J. Mcmurtry and M. L. Earle. 2. Discoveries in the Attic Deme of Ikaria. By C. D. Buck. 3. Greek Sculptured Crowns and Crown Inscriptions. By George B. Hussey. 4. The Newly Discovered Head of Iris from the Frieze of the Parthenon. By Charles Waldstein. 5. The Decrees of the Demotionidai. By F. B. Tarbell. 6. Report on Excavations near Stamata in Attika. By C. Waldstein and F. B. Tarbell. 7. Discoveries at Anthedon in 1889. By J. C. Rolfe, C. D. Buck, and F. B. Tarbell. 8. Discoveries at Thisbe in 1889. By J. C. Rolfe and F. B. Tarbell. 9. Discoveries in Plataia in 1889. By same. 10. An Inscribed Tombstone from Boiotia. By J. C. Rolfe. 11. Discoveries at Plataia in 1890. By C. Waldstein, H. S. Washington, and W. I. Hunt. 12. The Mantineian Reliefs. By Charles Waldstein. 13. A Greek Fragment of the Edict of Diocletian from Plataia. By Professor Theodor Mommsen. 14. Appendix. By A. C. Merriam. Published 1892. 8vo. Pp. 314. Boards. Illustrated. $2.50.

Vol. VI. (For 1890-97.) 1. Papers supplementary to Vol. V. *a* Excavations in the Theatre at Sicyon in 1891. By MORTIMER Lamson Earle. *b* Further Excavations in the Theatre at Sicyon in 1891. By Carleton L. BrownSon and Clarence H. Young, *c* Discoveries at Plataea in 1890: Votive Inscription. By R. B. Richardson, *d* Discoveries at Plataea in 1891: A Temple of Archaic Plan. By Henry S. Washington. 2. Excavations and Discoveries at Eretria, 1891-1895. *a* Introductory Note. By Charles Waldstein. *b* Eretria: A Historical Sketch. By R. B. Richardson, *c* Inscriptions, 1891. By R. B. Richardson, *d* The Theatre, 1891: The Stage Building. By Andrew Fossum. Cavea, Orchestra, and Underground Passage. By Carleton L. Brownson. *e* Eretria: A Topographical Study. By John Pickard. / A Temple in Eretria (1894). By R. B. Richardson, *g* The Theatre, 1894. By Edward Capps. *h* The Theatre, 1895. By T. W. Hbermance, *i* Fragment of a Dated Pana then ale Amphora. By T. W. Hbermance. The Gymnasium, 1895. By R. B. Richardson. / Inscriptions, 1895. By R. B. Richardson and T. W. Hbermance. 3. Excavations at Sparta, 1893. Reports. By Charles Waldstein and C. L. Meader. 4. Excavations and Discoveries at the Argive Heraeum, 1892-1895. *a* Excavations in 1892. By Carleton L. Brownson. *b* Sculptures. By Charles Waldstein. *c* A Head of Polycletan Style (1894). By Charles Waldstein. *d* Stamped Tiles. By R. B. Richardson. *e* Inscriptions. By J. R. Wheeler and R. B. Richardson. 5. Miscellaneous Papers, *o* The Relation of the Archaic Pediment-Reliefs of the Acropolis to Vase Painting. By Carleton L. Brownson. *b* The Frieze of the Choragic Monument of Lysicrates at Athens. By Herbert F. De Cou. *c* Dionysus *ir* Aiva«. By John Pickard. *d* A Sepulchral Inscription from Athens. By William Carey Poland. *e* A Torso from Daphne. By R. B. Richardson. / A Sacrificial Calendar from the Epakria. By R. B. Richardson, *g* The Chorus In the Later Greek Drama, with Reference to the Stage-Question. By Edward Capps. *h* Grave-Monuments from Athens. By Thomas Dwioht Goodell and T. W. Heermance. Published in 1897. 8vo. Pp. viii, 446. Boards. Illustrated. $3.00. Note. —The Papers In Vols. V and VI had previously appeared In the *American Journal qf Archaeology, First Series,* Vols. V-XI.

Bulletins and Other Reports

Bulletin I. Report of Professor W. W. Goodwin, Director of the School in 1882 83. (1883.) $0.25.

Bulletin H. Memoir of Professor Lewis R. Packard, Director of the School in 1883 84, with the Resolutions of the Committee and a Report for 1883-84. (1885.) $0.25.

Bulletin HI. Excavations at the Heraion of Argos. By Dr. Charles Waldstein. 8 Plates. (1892.) $3.00.

Bulletin IV. Report of Professor John Williams White, Professor of the Greek Language and Literature at the School in 1893-94. $0.25.

Bulletin V. The First Twenty Years of the School at Athens. By Professor Thomas Day Seymour. (1902.) Illustrated. With Appendix. $0.25.

Preliminary Report of an Archaeological Journey made through Asia Minor during the Summer of 1884. By Dr. J. R. S. Sterrett. $0.25.

Annual Reports and Papers of the School

Since 1897 these have been printed in the Journal of the Archaeological Institute of America *(American Journal of Archaeology, Second Series).*

Publications of the American School of Classical Studies in Rome

The *Annual Reports* and *Papers* of this School have been published in the Journal of the Archaeological Institute of America *(American Journal of Archaeology, Second Series).*

Supplementary Papers of the School in Rome

Vol. I was published in 1905. For contents see advertising pages.

THE MACMILLAN COMPANY 64-66, FIFTH AVENUE, NEW YORK

Life in Ancient Athens THE SOCIAL AND PUBLIC LIFE OF A CLASSICAL ATHENIAN OF THE TIME OF PERICLES

By T. G. TUCKER, *Professor of Classical Philology in the University of Melbourne* 315 Pages and Index. Cloth, Illustrated, $1.25

A surprising number of details recovered from historic monuments, literary allusions, artistic sources, are woven together into pictures of the daily social life of a typical citizen; it should be in the hands of every student, for there is no question of his reading it with ease and interest, and it will throw constant light on everything he reads or hears of the classic age of Greece.

The following are earlier issues in the notable series edited by

Professor Percy Gardner, *University of Oxford,* and

Professor Francis W. Kelsev, *University of Michigan.*

A Handbook of Greek Sculpture. By Ernest Arthur Gardner, formerly Director of the British School of Archaeology at Athens.
i2mo, cloth, $2.50 *net.*

A Grammar of Greek Art. By Percy Gardner, Litt.D., Professor of Classical Archaeology at Oxford. Illustrated. Extra crown 8vo, $1.75 *net.*

A Handbook of Greek Constitutional History. By A. H. J. Greexidge, Lecturer in Ancient History at Oxford. i2mo, cloth, $1.25 *net.*

Roman Public Life. By Professor A. H. J. Greenidge, Oxford.
i2mo, cloth, $2.50 *net.*

The Roman Festivals of the Period of the Republic. By W. Warde Fowler, M. A., Fellow of Lincoln College, Oxford. i2mo, cloth, $1.25 *net.*

A Handbook of Greek and Roman Coins. By G. F. Hill, Department of Coins and Medals, British Museum.

With 15 collotype plates. i2mo. cloth. $2.40 *net.*

The Destruction of Ancient Rome. By Rodolfo Laxciani. Professor of Ancient Topography in the University of Rome. i2mo, cloth, $1.50 *net.*

Monuments of the Early Church. By Walter Lowkie, of the American School of Classical Studies in Rome. i2mo, cloth, $1.75 *net.* THE MACMILLAN COMPANY, Publishers 64-66 FIFTH AVENUE, NEW YORK PERSIA PAST AND PRESENT

By A. V. WILLIAMS JACKSON

Professor of Indo-Iranian Languages, and Sometime Adjunct Professor of the English Language and Literature in Columbia University

A book of travel and research, suggestive because of the light it throws upon certain historical points which were not previously clear or even known; and because in regard to matters already familiar it is an entirely new presentation.

Professor Stanley Lane-poole says in the *Tribune:* "It is a blessing to come across a traveller who is also a scholar. ... He went to Persia to see the remains of the Zoroastrian ages, and to trace out everything that bore upon his special study of the Avesta. He knew the Persian language, old, middle, and modern, and was fully equipped by careful study of his predecessors' works. The result is not merely a description of some of the most interesting historical monuments in the world—Ecbatana, Behistan, Pasargada?, Persepolis, among the sites are names which indicate the absorbing subjects of the volume — but a scholarly collection of previous accounts and of published inscriptions.... As a study of the Achaemenian and Sasanian sculptures and monuments Professor Jackson's book will be welcome to every student of Persian antiquities. It is scholarly from beginning to end, without ever being dull.... The volume is splendidly illustrated by over two hundred photographs and reproductions of old prints, which really illustrate the text, and there is a very detailed index."
THE MACMILLAN COMPANY, Publishers 64-66 FIFTH AVENUE, NEW YORK

Institute of America

THE TEMPLE OF HELIOS (?) AT KANAWAT plates XXVIII-XXXI

Kanawat, the ancient Kanatha, is a site of great antiquity and contains ruins covering many periods, among which are those of two temples belonging to the latter half of the second century A. d. The one dedicated to Zeus is situated in the upper part of the town near the southern wall, and its plan, and photographs of its present condition, may be found in Professor Butler's *Architecture in Northern Central Syria and the Djebel Haurdn.* The second large temple at Kanawat is situated outside of the walls and far to the north on lower ground. This is the so-called Temple of Helios, the restoration of which I have attempted.

Its attribution to Helios rests upon the rather uncertain evidence of an inscription cut upon the east face of the die of the pedestal of the first column standing at the south end of the outer row of columns on the east side of the temple. This inscription has been several times copied, and as restored by Professor Prentice reads:

®e/?df77S 2i'0pov Tov vJaoK 'HAt'ov ex *Tuv* 1S1W *ciaefitov avfdrjKtv. Tliebaties, son of Sithros, in devout service, erected at his own expense the temple o f Helios.* As in the case of a former article on Mushennef *(A.J.A.,* XI, pp. 1-0), I am largely indebted to Professor Howard Crosby Butler and Professor William Kelly Prentice, two of the members of the American expedition to Syria in 1900, for the photographs, notes, and inscriptions from which the restorations shown in this article have been made.
Part II of the *Publications of an American Archaeological Expedition to Syria in* 1890-1900, pp. 352-354. *American Archaeological Expedition to Syria,* 1899-1900, Part III, No. 407.
American Journal of Archaeology, Second Series. Journal of the 387 Archaeological Institute of America, Vol. XI (1907), No. 4.

If this is the correct reading, and it is practically the one which was adopted by Berggren, who probably saw the inscription when it was in better condition than in the time of his successors, it would indicate that the temple was dedicated to Helios, and for the present at least such an attribution is the most plausible.

The temple is peripteral (Fig. 1) and faces toward the east, with a double row of six columns on the front, single rows of nine on the sides, and a single row of seven in the rear, the latter being a very unusual arrangement, probably adopted to regulate the intercolumniation. Seven of these columns are still standing to their full height (plate XXVIII). Only the plan of the exterior wall of the cella can be traced, but this shows a series of pilasters corresponding to the columns with only a narrow pteroma between. The whole temple stood on a podium, paved with large slabs of stone which formed the ceiling of a basement within the podium, and was approached by a flight of steps between two parotids on the east front of the temple. Originally there was probably a large paved court surrounding the whole building, and this has been shown in the plan (Fig. 1) though no data either for its existence or extent were found, other than the paved courts that surround many temples of the same period in the Haur&n.

In explaining the method used in the accompanying restorations (plates XXIX-XXXI), I shall describe the parts of the temple in detail, beginning from the base, and showing what authority there is for the various forms, mouldings, etc. , employed.

One half of the western wall of the podium, together with two small sections of it below the two standing columns on the southern side, and a quarter of its eastern wall below the two standing columns adjoining the steps were still standing in May, 1900. Some of the north wall was also *in situ,* but a part had been torn down to furnish an entrance to the arched basement which is now used as a shelter for cattle. The northern half of the podium on the west facade (plate XXVIII) is free from debris for its entire height. Its base mouldings were thus found and consist of a plinth, surmounted by a cyma reversa with its two fillets. The total height is 2.50 m., and the cap is composed of a cyma recta above the conventional quarterround, beneath which is a broad flat-band above three small fillets. A portion of the steps and the cap of the podium at the point where it breaks out to crown one of the parotids are in place (Fig. 2), though the number of steps and their exact dimensions cannot be obtained and have been merely conjectured.

Below each of the pedestals on which the columns of the peristyle rest, the wall of the podium is slightly broken out, as is shown in Plates XXIX-XXXI. These pedestals are a little less than two diameters high, and consist of a plinth in two stages, a base composed of a cyma recta above a torus, a die 0.55 m. high, and a cap consisting of two fillets, an ovolo, a cavetto, and a fillet. Above this and belonging to the same block as these mouldings, though cut back from the edge, is a broad band of such a size that it forms a sort of plinth for the base of the column.

The bases are of the Attic type with two toruses separated by a scotia and these mouldings are richly carved. Above the bases, an ovolo and a narrow fillet take the place of the usual cincture and apophyge in accomplishing the transition from the base to the shaft proper. The shafts themselves are about eight diameters high, though with the base and capital added their height is increased to practically ten diameters, and thus, with the pedestals on which they stand, the columns have a very slender and graceful outline. There is considerable entasis (Fig. 2), which seems to have its greatest extent about midway up the shaft. The capitals are of the Corinthian type, and although all ti'e volutes have been more or less broken, enough remains to render their reconstruction possible.

Unfortunately, as may be seen from the photographs, nothing is standing above the columns, and all this portion had to be assumed from other examples in the country. No parts of the architrave or cornice were found even upon the surrounding ground, and in fact from the systematic demolition and removal of all the parts of the structure which were of squared blocks, it would seem that the entablature and cella walls were undoubtedly removed to some other locality to furnish material for the construction of later, perhaps mediaeval or modern, buildings. Even portions of the podium were re-' moved, and it is probable that' . FIGURE 3. — Lntaui. atire At Bosra. the only reason why it was not totally destroyed was the fear lest the huge columns should fall. It was therefore necessary, as I have said, to supply an entablature, and the one surmounting a column in front of the so-called Nymphaeum at Bosra (Fig. 3) was chosen. To be sure, it is the only known example of an entablature with consoles in this part of Syria, but it is from a building of nearly the same date as the temple of Helios and it seems probable that this feature should have been employed at both places. I have again used the arcuated architrave over the central pair of columns on the eastern facade (plate XXIX) as in the case of Mushennef *(A.J.A.,* XI, Pl. II), for the width of the intercolumniation and the general use of this feature in the Hauran seemed to me sufficient indications of its employment here. The gable form of the roof can also be only conjectured, but it is found with the arcuated architrave in many of the buildings of the country, including the so-called triumphal arch at Damascus, where the same form of entablature is also employed (Fig. 4).

The four inner columns of the second row at the east end are interesting from the fact that they are set upon octagonal instead of square pedestals, as is shown in the one at the left of the steps in the perspective (plate XXXI). As I have remarked, the use of seven columns in the rear, or west, elevation of the temple is unusual, and it is to show the effect of such an arrangement that Plate XXX has been drawn. If as few as six or as many as eight columns had been used, the intercolumniation would have been so changed as to have left no columns opposite the ends of the cella walls and the spacings would have been quite different from those of the other sides of the building, whereas they are now almost the same, though slightly narrower.

In the elevation of the cella wall of course everything was assumed, for it has been levelled to within 0.30 m. of the pavement and only its position was obtainable. The doorway with its relieving arch is of the type most common in the country and was used at 'Atil, in the Kaisariyeh at Shakka, and many other places.

The perspective (plate XXXI) has been drawn directly from the measured drawings of the facade and plan, and nothing new has been assumed except the tile roof, and as tiles were frequently used in the Hauran, they have been adopted here. The paved court is no longer to be seen, but there are courts at Mushenef and else-Fmure 5.—Restored Base Of Column. where, and in all probability it still exists here, covered by soil and debris, unless it has been carried away for the sake of its squared blocks.

The details and ornamentation of the temple are most interesting, and in order to show the mouldings and carvings of the pedestal and base of one of the columns, I have made a drawing of this detail (Fig. 5) on a larger scale than was possible in either of the elevations. In this drawing, I made use of a photograph of one of the pedestals (Fig. (5) and also of the fragment of a column base which may be seen, half hidden in the grass, in the foreground of Fig. 2. It will be seen how elaborately the mouldings of the base were carved, the torus having a guilloche of an interesting type with little circular knobs between the braids, while the scotia has the reeded ornament found in the Temple of Zeus at Kanawat, the Temple at Mushennef, and elsewhere, with groups of three perpendicular reeds in high relief at equal intervals around the columns. Above this, the small torus is carved with the bay leaf pattern in which the berries are shown in various places between the leaves, thus adding a considerable realism and charm to the effect. The little curved fillet above this torus is carved with a miniature reproduction of the guilloche of the large torus and completes the elaborate decoration of the base. The base shown in the photograph seems to have its lower moulding carved with a braid ornament, and it is probable, therefore, that the bases were somewhat varied in their treatment. The pedestals and their mouldings are uncarved, but show very interesting profiles and well-proportioned forms. Inscriptions occur on many of them, sometimes, as shown in the photograph, on the crowning bands, and sometimes across the die itself, but these contain no archaeological information further than the designation of the person who erected the columns. (Prentice, *op. cit,* Nos. 407-411.)

Situated as it was, outside of the city but high above the plain and with a superb view across the low lands toward the snow-clad peaks of the Anti-Lebanon, this temple must have produced a striking effect with the light, airy appearance of its many slender columns and the grace and charm of its proportions. Professor Butler has called it the "most beautiful and impressive of all the ruins of the Hauran," and it is greatly to be regretted that it is impossible to make an absolutely correct restoration of this appropriately dedicated Temple of the Sun.

Clarence Wakd.
Pkincetox, N.J.
Institute of Ameriea

LYSIPPUS AS A WORKER IN MARBLE

With the discovery at Delphi, in 1897, of the group of statues dedicated by Daochus, a new impetus was given to the . study of Lysippus. When Preuner found the same metrical inscription which was on the base of 'the best preserved statue of the group — the Agias — in the travelling journal of Stackelberg, copied from a base in Pharsalus, the home of Daochus, with the added words that Lysippus of Sicyon was the sculptor of the statue, our views of Lysippus had to undergo revision. For this discovery brought the Agias (Fig. 1) — if not the others in the group — into direct connection with Lysippus by documentary evidence, while the easily recognized Lysippian characteristics of the statue confirmed this connection on stylistic grounds. It was clear that Daochus had set up a series of statues in honor of his ancestors both at Pharsalus and at Delphi. Whether the Thessalian group was of bronze, as is generally held owing Fioure 1. — Statue Of Agias. i widespread belief that Lysippus worked only in metal, and the group at Delphi was composed of marble replicas of these original bronze statues, will *Ein Delpkisches Weihgeschenck.* Leipzig, 1900.

American Journal of Archaeology, Second Series. Journal of the 396 Archaeological Institute of America, Vol. XI (1907). No. 4.

be discussed later. If the marble statues were copies, the inference is that they reproduced the originals, if not mechanically (as in later Roman days was the custom) at least faithfully; for having employed noted artists like Lysippus in the one case, the dedicator would have wished careful and accurate reproductions in the other. In any case it is safe to assume that the Agias represents the style and characteristics of Lysippus himself, and we are justified in making this statue the centre of our treatment of this artist.

But another statue, the so-called Apoxyomenus (Fig. 2), had, ever since its discovery in 1849, held this honored position. The words of Pliny (XXXIV, 62) describing one of Lysippus' best known works as an athlete "*destringens* «e," and recording that this artist introduced a new canon into art, "*capita minora faciendo quam antiqui, corpora graciliora siccioraque, per quae proceritas signorum major videretur*" seemed to have their best illustration in this statue, which, though admittedly a late Roman work, has been looked npon as a copy of an original by Lysippus, and as faithfully representing his style in detail. When, however, the Apoxyomenus and the Agias were compared, despite certain marked similarities of pose, slender body and limbs, and small head increasing the apparent height (characteristics not exclusively Lysippian, as we see them quite as prominently in some other works, *e.g.* the warriors of the Mausoleum frieze), nevertheless the differences were seen to be so striking that it seemed futile to some to attempt to keep both statues as examples of the work of the same artist, even if they were assigned to different periods of his career.

These differences are most obvious in the surface modelling and facial expression of the two works: in the Agias the muscles are not overemphasized in detail, but show the simple directness of observation of artists who worked before the critical study of anatomy in the Alexandrian schools had reacted upon sculpture; in the Apoxyomenus, however, we see an intentional display of the results of this study in the drawn and labored muscular treatment, showing the artist's correct knowledge of the human form, a knowledge which characterized the sculptors of later Hellenistic times, when technique was learned and well nigh perfect, but freshness and vigor were wanting. Such academic work — which culminates later in realistic works like the Laocoon— hardly antedates the beginning of the third century, and there is absolutely no trace of it in the Agias. Furthermore, the face of the Agias has the intense expression, elsewhere seen only in works supposed to show the influence of Scopas, which recalls what the ancient critics, notably Plutarch, said of Lysippus' portraits of Alexander as reproducing his manly and leonine air. A comparison of this face with that of the Apoxyomenus, which exhibits the utter lack of vigor and expression common in early Hellenistic works, makes it still more clear that we should no longer regard both these statues as examples of the style of one and the same artist.

Many critics have had their doubts about the Apoxjomenus, as its Hellenistic character has become more and more apparent, and have offered various explanations, not wishing to give the statue up as evidence. So far back as 1877 Kohler, admitting these later characteristics, still thought the Roman copyist had preserved the general type of the original statue of Lysippus, though he had modernized the anatomical treatment. In a recent book, Professor

Michaelis expresses the opinion that the Agias is an early work of Lysippus, who was at that time under the influence of Scopas and Polyclitus, but whose style changed in his later years to that seen in the Apoxyomenus. But the Agias is no youthful work of Lysippus, nor can the influence of Scopas upon this artist For ancient criticisms of Lysippus see Overbeck's *Schriftquellen,* pp. 28" ff. *Ath. Mitt.* 1877, p. 57. *Arch. Enldeckungen d. 1J" Jahrh.* p. 276. have been that of master upon pupil, as is generally assumed; but rather that of one great artist upon an independent contemporary. These points will be discussed later in this paper. The differences between the two statues seem too great to be reconciled on any such principle—their style and workmanship seem manifestly of two different periods. By separating them entirely, as P. Gardner in his illuminating discussion of this whole question has done, we can rightly assign to Lysippus the early date which other evidence requires, and remove the Apoxyomenus from the fourth century altogether, thus explaining its later modelling, its expressionless features, and the build of the figure, which shows the use of three instead of two planes; and doubtless we should see with Gardner in the original a work not by Lysippus at all, but by some pupil or later member of his school. After thus eliminating the Apoxyomenus, we are justified in using the Agias as the centre of our future treatment of this artist, as furnishing the truest indication of his style, and best supported by circumstantial evidence.

As the Agias is the statue of a victor, we can form from it an idea of the manner in whieh Lysippus represented his athletes; in giving up the Apoxyomenus, we must also give up statues of athletes, which have hitherto, on the basis of their *iJ.H.S.* 1905, pp. 234 ff.

As, *e.g.,* those ascribed to Lysippus by Furtwangler, *Masterpieces,* p. 364 anil n. 2. resemblance to it, been assigned to this artist, and future ascriptions of this class of statues must be based on stylistic resemblance to the Agias. Impressed by its remarkable likeness to the head of the Agias, I, some time ago, hazarded the opinion that the much discussed marble head (Figs. 3 and 4) from Olympia was Lysippian, and attempted to bring it into

At first this head was ascribed with surprising unanimity to the school of Praxiteles, and later, after the discovery of the Tegean heads, with almost equal unanimity to that of Scopas. Treu, who first published the head, pointed out its near relationship to the Hermes, which appeared to him to be obvious, notwithstanding the injured condition of chin, nose, mouth, and Such a statue in Copenhagen (Ny-Carlsberg, no. 240) is ascribed to Lysippus by Mahler, *Polyk-lH u. seine Schule,* p. 153, n. 1.

In *De Olympionicarum Statute,* Halle, 1902, and enlarged 1903, pp. 27 ff. *Ausgr. v. Olympia,* V (1881), Taf. XX; also *Ergebnisse* III. Taf. LIV, 3-4. The head is still exhibited at Olympia in the same room as the Hermes. *Arch. Zeit.* 1880, p. 114, and *Ausgr ». Ol.* V, pp. 13-14. relation with the statue of the Acarnanian boxer (whose name I restored as Philandridas) which Pausanias (VI, 2, 1) says was the work of Lysippus. Since then, after a careful study of the evidence, my original opinion has become conviction, and I now have no hesitancj in expressing the belief that in this beautiful marble head we have to do with an original work by Lysippus himself. It will be the purpose of the present paper to examine the reasons which lead me, in spite of serious and weighty objections, to maintain this view. brows. He found the general proportions, the shape of the cranium and forehead, and the form of the cheeks and mouth the same, while the differences, the deeper cut and wider opened eyes, with their *yopyov* expression, the hair, and the fact that the whole head is harder, leaner, and bonier than that of the Hermes, were all explained on account of the different character given the statue of a victor. Many other archaeologists, like Botticher, Laloux and Monceaux, and Furtwingler, have seen sure signs of the hand of Praxiteles or his school in the graceful attitude, delicate chiselling and finish of the work. Still others, however, found every characteristic of Scopas in this head. Even Treu later found the head more Scopaic than Praxitelian, and yet, by a careful analysis, he conclusively shows that the formation of the eyes, opening of the mouth, and treatment of the hair are so different in the heads from Tegea (and especially in that of Heracles) as to preclude the possibility of assigning them and the head from Olympia to the same sculptor, and so he declares for some independent sculptor among the contemporaries of Scopas. But he does not see Lysippus in this allied but independent sculptor, though he admits the resemblance of the head in question to that of the Agias, as do Homolle, Mahler, and other critics.

A detailed comparison of this head with that of the Agias (Fig.

Olympia, p. 343. *Restauration d'Olympie,* p. 137. Roscher, *Lexikon,* s. V. *Herakles,* p. 2106. *E.g.* Graf, *Rom. Mitt.* 1889, pp. 189-226, and v. Sybel, *LMzow's Zeitsch.* N. F. II, pp. 253 ff. *Olympia, Ergebnisse,* III, 1897, pp. 208-209, and n. 1 to p. 209. *B.C.H.* XXIII, p. 456. 0?. *cit.* p. 149.

Figure 6. — Head or Agias. 5) will show wherein the wonderful resemblance — so striking at first glance — consists, and will prove its Lysippian character. Neither head is a portrait, nor even individualized; the Agias could be no portrait, for Agias was the great-grandfather of Daochus, who enlisted the services of his contemporary, Lysippus, in erecting the dedication, and he won his victory in the pancratium over a century before these statues were set up. A glance at the head from Olympia also clearly discloses its ideal character; for it is no portrait of Philandridas, but the victor *Kot zxv* the pancratium. The small head of the Agias — under life size — first arrests attention as the chief characteristic of the whole statue, and, taken with the other proportions of the body, the chief mark of its Lysippian origin. As Homolle says, it is not that small heads are not found outside the school of Lysippus or before his day, — for Myron can furnish examples of them, — but it is only with Lysippus and after him that we see a conscious intention of having the proportions thus reduced. Now the head from Olympia is also less than life size, but as the head alone is preserved, we can only assume the proportions it bore to the body to be similar to those we see in the Agias. The conformation of both crania is, as in Attic works, round, with small only slightly projecting occiputs, as opposed to the squareness of Polyclitan heads, which are longer from front to back and flatter on top, — showing how Lysippus in this respect departed from the Doryphorus. This cranial conformation is almost identical in both heads, as is clearly shown in the accompanying diagram (Fig. (3), where one is drawn in profile over the other.

The head of the Agias is turned slightly upward and to the left. Treu found traces of the use of a file on the back of the neck of the head from Olympia, which show from their position, what also was clear from the muscles of the throat, that this head also was inclined somewhat to the left and upward, pos Premier *(op. cit.* p. 12) dates the dedication 339—331 *B.C.* Homolle *(op. cit.* p. 440) more closely, 338-334. Preuner dates Arias' victory about 450 B.c. Treu, *Arch. Zeit.* 18K0, p. 114, gives these measurements:

Height with neck.... 0.270 m.
Height of head alone.. 0.21") m.
Breadth of head.... 0.170 m.
   Breadth of face.... 0.127 in.
Height of face.... 0.150 m.
sibly more than that of the Agias. The outlines of the face — lean and bony in both — are oval, in the head from Olympia somewhat broader, rounder, and fleshier toward the chin. In both the forehead is remarkably low, with a low depression or crease in the middle and with a very prominently projecting superciliary arcade, which breaks the continuous line from forehead to nose very perceptibly. This line is concave above and

Figure 6. — Profiles Of Aoias And Philanliridas. below, but convex at the projection itself, though this is less prominent in the Agias. The powerful framing of the eyes, which are deep set and thrown into heavy shadows by the projecting bony structure of the brows and the overhanging masses of flesh, the eyeballs slightly raised and peering eagerly into the far distance, the slight upward inclination of the head, and the prominent forehead drawn together, all combine to give both heads, though young and vigorous, a pensive, even a sad look of heroic dignity, a look seemingly of one who takes no joy nor pleasure in victory, though it is not profoundly mournful. This humid and pensive expression was doubtless a characteristic of works of Lysippus (it was, as we know, present in his portraits of Alexander), though he did not treat it with the intensity of Scopas.

The eyeballs in both heads are strongly arched, though the inner angles are not so deep as in Scopaic heads: the raised upper lids form a symmetrically narrow and sharply defined border over the eyeball, and in neither head is this lid covered by a fold of skin at the outer corners, as in the Tegean heads; the mass of flesh at. the outer corners is heavier in the head from Olympia, and the expression of the eyes is more free and defiant than in the more meditative Agias. In both the cheek bones are high and prominent. The elegant contour of the lips of the Agias is wholly wanting in the head from Olympia, as the lips are broken off, like the nose and the chin, but it is clear that they too were slightly parted, just showing the teeth, not, however, as in the Tegean examples, as if the breath were being drawn with great effort. The look of pensiveness is also increased by the open lips. The contour of the jaw bone is not so visible as in the Agias, where it is clearly discernible beneath the closely drawn skin, giving the face a look of greater leanness, as of an athlete in perfect training.

In both heads the swollen and battered ears, though small, are prominent, and in both the hair is closely cropped, as becomes the athlete. The hair of the Agias does not show so much expression as is displayed in that of some Lysippian heads, nor the nice detail we should expect from Pliny's statement that Lysippus excelled in the treatment of hair — for it is in great measure only sketched out. In Lysippian portraits of Alexander the hair is generally expressively treated, and this is often the case in early Hellenistic heads. However, we should not expect an elaborate treatment of the hair in the statue of a pancratiast. The head from Olympia also shows great simplicity in this regard. As in Scopaic heads, the hair is fashioned into little ringlets ruffled straight up from the forehead in flat relief, though the curls are shorter and more tense. It covers the temples and surrounds the ears as in the Agias, though it is not, as there, bounded by a round floating line across the forehead nor divided into little tufts modelled in relief radiating in concentric circles from the top of the head. Though lacking in detail, the hair of the Agias is treated carefully and with the greatest variety. Narrow bands, perhaps the insignia of victory despite their small size, encircle both The hair, however, of the Apoxyomenus is an exception, for, even if worked out with some care, it is devoid of expression.

heads: in the Agias the band is dextrously used to heighten the effect of variety in the hair by alternately flattening and swelling it here and there. In neither head is there any.sign of the use of the drill to work out the tufts of the hair; only the chisel was used.

Finally, the whole expression of these two ideal heads is one of force and energy, of heroic dignity tempered by a humid pensiveness and pathos, which is even, in the head from Olympia at least, a little dramatic. The fierce, almost barbarous look of this head may well be explained by its representing a victor from Acarnania, a country noted among the other Greek states for anything but culture and refinement. Both heads, though ideal, show close observation of nature in modelling and expression; and both show Lysippus' predilection for types in which force and energy predominate, and his indifference to the softer and more delicate types of manly beauty so characteristic of his contemporary, Praxiteles.

In the foregoing comparison, I have assumed that this marble head is from an athlete statue and moreover, like the

Agias, represents a victor in boxing, though many have seen in it no victor but a youthful Heracles. The swollen ears and the band in the hair might pass equally well for either, just as the fact that it was unearthed in the ruins of the gymnasium (if it were necessary to assume that the statue once stood there) might be adduced as evidence for either interpretation; for statues of athletes as well as those of Heracles (who like Hermes was a patron of athletic exercises) adorned palaestras and gymnasia. That the head is of marble and slightly under life size seems to lend some support also to the belief that it is a fragment of a statue of Heracles, on the assumption that statues of victors in the Altis were uniformly of bronze, an assumption, however, not supported by facts, as will be shown later. So some have seen the heroic features of the youthful hero in the *yopyov* of the eyes, the energetic forehead, closely cropped hair, muscular neck, and almost challenging inclination of the head seemingly corresponding to an energetic raising of the left shoulder.

The use of the drill is seen in the Praxitelian Hermes, but is not seen in the Tegean heads, nor is it common in the first half of the fourth century. Cf. Furtwangler, *Masterpieces,* p. 309.

In determining whether a given head belongs to a statue of a victor or of Heracles, we are aided but little by the swollen ears; for as Reisch has pointed out, though these may in early times have played a role as the characteristic of a boxer, later they served just as well as a characteristic of pancratiasts and even athletes in general. Boxers were sufficiently characterized by the thongs which they carried in the hand, as in the case of the statue of Acusilaus, or wound around the forearm. Many statues besides those of boxers had swollen ears, *e.g.* the Borghese warrior, the Munich Diomedes, various statues of Ares, Heracles, and the Dioscuri. So they are no personal characteristic, only a professional one common to athletes and gods alike, if these latter have practised athletic exercises. Where personal attributes are absent it is therefore often difficult to determine whether an ideal athlete or a Heracles is intended, for it may be the hero in the guise of an athlete or an athlete in the guise of the hero. And many statues of athletes were more or less assimilated to those of Heracles, for this hero was especially honored by victors in the *TraXy* and *Tray/tpdriov.* Pausanias (V, 8, 4), as well as other writers, mentions his mythical victories in these contests, and in another passage the periegete says that beginning with the 142d Olympiad, whoever won on the same day in both these events, was called *irpSroi, Sevrepos, K.t.x.* ai*f* 'HpaκXe'ov;.

So it is not surprising that some have regarded the head under discussion as that of a youthful Heracles. Yet this view is manifestly wrong; for, apart from all considerations of identifying it with the Acarnanian pancratiast, and in the absence of distinguishing attributes, if it be compared with another Lysippian head from a statue universally recognized as that of a Heracles, — the famous one in Lansdowne House, — we can at once see how fundamentally different is the whole spiritual conception and how differently an athlete — even if highly idealized — and a hero are treated by the same artist. And if we once recognize in it a victor, then the swollen ears, fierce, almost barbarous look of the eyes, and half-painful expression of the mouth all concur in convinc *Grieehische Weihgeseh.* pp. 42—43.

The thonjs are mentioned in Schol. to Pindar, *Ol.* VII, p. 156 B. ing us that we here have to do with a victor in boxing, the most brutal and dangerous of contests.

Having established the Lysippian character of the head, and the fact that it is from a statue of a victor in boxing (or the pancratium), we will next see what is the evidence for identifying it with one of the statues mentioned by Pausanias in his periegesis of the Altis. He names only five statues of victors by Lysippus: those of Troilus (VI, 1, 4), victor in the chariot race, Philandridas (VI, 2, 1) and Polydamas (VI, 5, 1) in the pancratium, Chilon (VI, 4, 6) in wrestling, and Callicrates (VI, 17, 3) in the heavy armed race. Of these the only two which could come into consideration are those of the two pancratiasts, and one of these, that of Polydamas, can at once be eliminated, for this small head can have nothing to do with the pretentious monument mentioned by Pausanias in these words: 6 Se *eirl Tu /3d6pai* Tg *vyjrtXq Avafairov fiev ianv epyov, p.eyiaro'; 8e airavrav iyevero avOpamcav K.t.x.* Fragments of the basis of this monument have been found, and it stood in a part of the Altis too far removed from the spot where the Philandridas stood or that where the marble head was found. Our choice then is limited to the statue of Philandridas, the tenth in the series of 169 named by Pausanias in his first " victor ephodus."

We can determine very closely the position of these first few statues in the Altis. Pausanias (VI, 1, 3) begins his enumeration *ev Seia Tov vaov* Tt)? *"Hpai;,* in the northwest of the sacred enclosure. I have elsewhere shown that these words must be taken of the temple *', 'pro persona"* and so must refer to the southern side of the Heraeum. Pausanias is often loose in his employment of words to denote position, and especially in that of the terms *ev Seia* and *ev apiarepa,* which must be interpreted sometimes from the point of view of the spectator and at others from that of a given monument. Now we have no idea where Pausanias was just before he commenced his victor periegesis at the beginning of his sixth book; for at the end of the fifth book (27, 11) he is manifestly in the centre of the Altis, but in the next paragraph (27, 12), which seems to have been added as a transition to his account of the statues of victors, he speaks of the trophy of the Mendaeans, which, he says, he nearly mis East of the Temple of Zeus. See *De Olymp. Stat.* p. 66.-*Ibid.* p. 64.

took for a pentathlete, as it stood near the statue of the Elean wrestler Anauchidas, a statue which must have stood somewhere between the eastern front of the Temple of Zeus and the Echo Hall and so far away from the centre of the Altis. It is, therefore, impossible to accept the theory of Dorpfeld that Pausanias approached the Heraeum from this point to begin the athlete periegesis, and that the words *iv Beia* mean the space before the eastern front of the temple. So we are left entirely dependent upon the meaning of the words *iv Sefcia* as to whence Pausanias started. Now the eastern end of a temple is always the front, if no special part is mentioned, as *e.g.* in V, 24, 3: *rov vaov Be iariv iv Segia Tov /xeydXov Zeti? 71750? avaroXas f)(ov.* The marble head was found in this neighborhood, in the wall of a late Byzantine hut behind the southern end of the stadium hall of the great gymnasium, 23.50 m. north of its southeastern corner and 5 m. east of its back wall, and therefore very near the Heraeum. Inasmuch as the inscribed tablet from the base of the statue of Troilus (VI, 1, 4), the sixth statue mentioned by Pausanias, and the inscribed base of the monument of Cynisca (VI, 1, 6), the seventh, were both found near by in the Prytaneum, and the basis of the statue of Sophius (VI, 1, 3), the twenty-second in the series, was found also in this part of the Altis in the bed of the Cladeus, we can conclude that all four monuments originally stood near together and in the order named by Pausanias, along the southern side of the Heraeum. *Ve Olt/mp-Stat.* p. 07. *Olympia, Ergebnisse,* I, p. 87. Blümner, reviewing my monograph *De Olymp. Stat. (Berl. Phil. W.* 1904, col. 1382), objects to my interpretation of *iv iefip*, and admits not one but three possibilities; *a)* of the temple *pro persona, i.e.* south side; *b)* of a spectator facing the eastern front, *i.e.* the northern half of the space before the eastern front; *c)* of a spectator with his back to this front, *i.e.* the southern half of this space. But if Pausanias had meant either of the two latter, he would have said, not *iv Sefcp Tov vaov* but *irp6 Tov vaov* or *iiravTiKpv rov vaov* as in V, 27, 1. There is no need of making him out more ambiguous than he is. In other passages he seems clear enough when speaking of temples: cf. V, 20, 2 and VIII, 38, 2 (the latter cited by Blümner himself), where Mt. Lycosura is *iv apiorep? Tov Upov rijt Aeirirofnjs, i.e.* to the north of the temple. In V, 21, 2 it is also clear which side is meant. *Olympia, Ergebnisse,* III, p. 209. See *Inschr. v. Ol* nos. 100 (Troilus), 100 (Cynisca), 172 (Sophius).

There are traces of the use of the file on the back of the neck of the marble head, and the hair is merely blocked out behind, especially near the left ear, so that not even the contours of the locks are marked out. This unfinished condition of the head, the remarkably good preservation of the surface, and the fact that it was found in the gymnasium led Treu and others to suppose that it once adorned an inner room of the exercise place of the athletes. The Praxitelian Hermes also shows an unfinished treatment of the hair at the back of the head, due, as Furtwangler conjectures *(Masterpieces,* p. 308, n. 7), to the fact that it was made to be placed against the inner wall of the Heraeum. Just so, without doubt, the statue of Philandridas was intended to be set up against a solid background. It seems most probable that it, as well as some of the other statues just mentioned, was placed along the southern steps of the temple, doubtless against a column and so more or less sheltered.

The date of the victory of this Philandridas is not recorded, but it is clear that it must lie within the years of the activity of Lysippus who made his statue. On the principle, which has been sufficiently demonstrated in my monograph *De Olympionicarum Statuis,* that statues of nearly contemporaneous victors were grouped together in the Altis, as well as those of the same family or state, or those who had been victorious in the same contest, I already *(ibid.* p. 27) have proposed Ol. 102 or 103 (372 or 368 B.C.) as the probable date of his victory, as his statue stands among those of victors, none of whom can have won later than Ol. 104. The first six mentioned are all Eleans and the dates of their victories fall between Ols. 94-104; the sixth, Troilus, certainly won in Ol.102, as Pausanias records, while none of the following seven Spartans, among whom was placed the statue of Philandridas, can be later than Ol. 97, and most of them belong to the close of the fifth century. Sostratus (VI, 4, 1) won in the same contest as Philandridas in Ol. 104, and doubtless his two other victories should be assigned to the two succeeding Olympiades, and to bring Philandridas down as far as Ol. 107 is unwarranted, since no statue of so late a date stood in this vicinity. On the other hand, to place his victory earlier than Ol. 102 is also out of the question, owing to the inexpediency of dating Lysippus so early. So doubtless his statue was placed in the Spartan group at about the same time as that of Troilus, by the same sculptor, was placed among the Eleans. This is an independent argument then for so early a date for Lysippus.

P. Gardner, in the discussion of the date of this artist, has shown how flimsy is the evidence for any date later than 320 B.C., the probable date of Chilon's statue (Paus. VI, 4, 6-7), and that the wish not to separate him from the Apoxyomenus has been the real reason that influenced so many archaeologists to extend his activity to the end of the fourth century, and to explain away the evidence for an earlier date offered by the statue of Troilus. If we once for all give up the Apoxyomenus, the difficulty in an early dating disappears, as does also the theory that Scopas could have strongly influenced the youthful Lysippus as a master would a pupil, and it becomes clear that this influence must have been mutual, that of one great contemporary artist upon another. Though Lysippus worked longer, as is attested by his work for Alexander and his generals, he could have been but little younger than either Scopas or Praxiteles, from both of whom he learned. As Homolle says, an analysis of the style of the Agias shows the mixed influences of Praxiteles and Scopas as well as the independent work of Lysippus, in the pose, proportions, and whole type of the figure.

Lysippus was a great reformer in art, breaking away from Argive and Polyclitan traditions, even though he called the Doryphorus as well as Nature his master, and though the influence of

Polyclitus is visible in the body of the Agias and that of Scopas in the treatment of forehead, eyes, and mouth and in the intensity of expression. Evidently he was strongly affected by the work of his great predecessors and contemporaries, but developed at the same time new and For the early dating of Lysippus, cf. Winter, *Jb. Arch. I.* VII, 1892, p. 169; Treu, *Olympin, Ergebnisse*, III, p. 211, and Milchhofer, *Arch. Slud.Jur H. Brunn*, p. n. 2.

Op. cit. pp. 245-249. *B.C.H.* XXIII, p. 422. The Agias is but slightly later than the Hermes if we accept Furtwansler's dating for the latter, about 343 B.C. (*Masterpieces*. pp. 307-308). independent tendencies. Thus the Philandridas must have been—like the lost statue of Troilus—an early work of the master, whereas the Agias was the work of his mature genius. The difference between the two can thus be explained by the lapse of time between them and by the early influences that surrounded the youthful artist; but the similarities between them are striking, and there is little resemblance in either to the Apoxyomenus, another link in the chain of evidence that the latter could not have been produced by the same artist, for artists do not radically change their style after many years of work, and Lysippus must have been well over fifty years old when he created the Agias.

The identification of this marble head with that of the victor statue of the Acarnanian pancratiast by Lysippus, raises two important questions which I shall briefly examine; whether these statues in the Altis were ever of marble, and whether Lysippus ever worked in that material. Pausanias throughout his whole victor periegesis (and he enumerates 192 monuments) makes no mention of the material of which statues of victors were made, except in the case of the first two set up at Olympia, those of Praxidamas and Rhexibius, who won in 01. 59 and 01. 57 respectively (VI, 18, 7); and it is evident that he mentions these two because of their antiquity, their special position in the Altis apart from the others (near the column of Oenomaus), and their material, for they were of wood and consequently badly weatherbeaten. In his book on Achaia, in speaking of the statue of the victor Promachus, set up in the gymnasium of Pellene, he says (VII, 27, 5): /cat avrov Kal etVeoVa? iroitfaavTe; ol TleWrjv- el'; rrjv fiev e? 'OXvfnriav aveOeaav, Tt)v Se iv Ts yvfivcurup (6ov Tavrrjv Kal ov %aicov. Many archaeologists have inferred from these words that, although Pausanias says nothing about the material of statues of victors in the Altis, they were all of bronze, — an argument *ex silentio*. Other writers furnish no evidence concerning the material used in these statues. Moreover, all the artists mentioned by Pausanias in his victor periegesis are known to us — if known at all — as bronze workers *icar eoijv*, and none is known exclusively as a sculptor in marble. Furthermore, all the bases excavated and identified show clear marks that the statues upon them were of metal, and there are even bronze fragments of these statues, identified through inscriptions. Thus at first sight it Avould seem that the case for metal statues was well made out; and doubtless the belief that the statues of victors, as well as the other statues in the Altis, were usually of metal is well founded. The fact that so few fragments of these monuments have survived, is in itself a proof of this, as bronze was eagerly sought by the barbarian plunderers of Olympia, and on *a priori* grounds as well we should have assumed metal to be the material for monuments standing in the open air and subject to all kinds of weathering; besides, the later Peloponnesian schools of athletic sculpture, characterized by their predilection for bronze founding, would nowhere be more prominently in evidence than at Olympia.

But that there were many exceptions to this general rule can be not only conjectured but proved from actual discoveries at the excavations. The silence of Pausanias as to the material used in these statues is in accordance with his general custom, for he rarely mentions the materials of monuments and only where bronze and stone stand closely together in a circumscribed area, as when he enumerates the various monuments in the Heraeum (V, 17, 3). In introducing the statue of the Trat? *avaSov/ j.evo;* of Phidias (VI, 4, 5) — whatever this statue may have been — between the statues of Leontiscus and Satyrus, though manifestly it must have been of marble, he makes no mention of the fact. The words quoted above which specify bronze as the material of the statue of Promachus at Olympia must be intended to distinguish that from the stone one at Pellene, and we are not justified in drawing from them any wider inference. Other stone statues of victors are men Cf. *Inschr. v. 01.* V, pp. 234-235. Also a bronze foot ascribed by Furtwangler (*Olympia, Ergebnissc*, IV, Taf. II, III, p. 11) to one of the statues of Caper (VI, 16, 10).

Furtwangler (*Masterpieces*, p. 40, n. 1) and others look upon it as a votive offering; however, the possibility of its being an unknown boy victor cannot be excluded; in several instances Pausanias does not know the victor's name, *e.g.* the Samian boxer (VI, 2, 9) and the Arcadian boxer (VI, 8, 6), whose statue by Myron a century later was used for Philip of Pellene (for the curious difficulty of Pausanias in regard to the latter statue see my explanation, *De Olymp. Stat.* p. 39). Other examples of unnamed statues are VI, 15, 7 and VI, 3, 1. tioned outside of Olympia, *e.g.,* that of Arrachion at Phigaleia (VIII, 40, 1); why then should we not believe that there were statues of stone at Olympia, even if Pausanias does not mention them? Besides, he mentions only a few of the great number of statues of victors there, as he himself (VI, 1, 2) says. Pliny (XXXIV, 16) says that it was the custom for all victors to set up their statues in the Altis, and though this merely refers to the privilege, of which many victors could not or did not avail themselves on account of poverty, early death, or for other reasons (Pausanias, VI, 1, 1, says that not all victors set up statues), still the number of such statues in the Altis must have been very great. Not one-fifth of those mentioned by Pausanias are known to us through the recovered inscriptions, and doubtless many of the number not mentioned would not be of the usual material. Just as many victors, owing to the expense involved, contented themselves Avith small bronze statues, — several such statuettes have been recovered at Olympia, and that they were common elsewhere is shown by the many athlete statuettes, especially Discoboli, in European museums, — so others would use a cheaper material than bronze, just as was done elsewhere, *e.g.* in the cases of Promachus and Arrachion mentioned above. Treu mentions marble fragments of several life-size statues of victors as well as of others which were made smaller (three-fifths size) for the sake of economy, and also of several statues of boy victors. So the objection to assigning the marble head under discussion to the statue of Philandridas, on the ground that statues of victors were uniformly of metal, is shown to be groundless.

But to regard a marble work as an original work of Lysippus, who has almost universally been looked upon as a worker in bronze exclusively, seems much more objectionable.

Gurlitt *(Uber Pausanias,* p. 414), less correctly, one-sixth. From corrected lists in *De Olijmp. Stat.* I find there are 188 victors with 192 monuments mentioned by Pausanias in his victor periegesis; 40 inscriptions found at Olympia can be referred to these monuments, while about (iO additional ones have not been identified. This gives a ratio 40: 192:: 60: x (288), yielding a total of 480 statues on the basis of the small number mentioned by Pausanias; a small fraction of the whole number. Forster *(Olymp. Sieger,* II, p. 30) enumerates 034 victors from all sources — manifestly only a fraction of the whole. *Olympia, Ergebnisse,* IV, p. 21, nos. 57, 59, 63. *Ibid.* Ill, p. 210.

Pliny certainly classed Lysippus among bronze workers, for in the preface to his account of bronze sculptors (XXXIV, 37) he tells us that this artist produced fifteen hundred statues, and doubtless we are to infer that he looked upon them as being of « metal. He further (XXXIV, 61) speaks of this artist's contributions to the "*statuariae arti*" where it seems clear that the term is used in its narrow sense of sculpture in bronze as opposed to "*sculptura,*" that in marble. How firmly the belief that Lysippus worked only in bronze is established can be seen in these very strong words of Overbeck: "*Zu beginnen i»t mit wiederholter Hervorhebung der durchaus umweifelhaften und wichtigen Thatsaehe, dass Lysippus ausschliesslich Erzgiesser war.*" That Lysippus was preeminently a bronze worker and that his reputation was due to his bronze works cannot be doubted; but to say that he never essayed to produce works in marble (as so many other Greek artists did, who worked in both materials) is, as one lately has termed it, a "*kindisches Vorurteil.*" That marble work was done in his studio is well attested by the reliefs from the basis of the statue of Polydamas mentioned above, which have generally been referred to his pupils. They are so damaged as to be almost worthless as evidence of his style; still the legs of Polydamas himself, in the central relief, so far as they can be made out, are thin and sinewy as in Lysippian work, and doubtless would have been regarded as the work of the master himself, if it had not been taken for granted that he worked only in bronze. But for the same assumption, doubtless some critics would have seen an original from the hand of Lysippus in the statue of Agias at least, if not in the others of the group at Delphi.

It has been generally assumed that the original group of statues in Pharsalus was of bronze, though we have no proof that it may not have been of marble, while the one at Delphi was copied almost simultaneously in marble, so faithfully that even the

» So contrasted also in XXXV, 156 and XXXVI, 15.

Oesch. d. gr. PL II, p. 150. Among recent writers opposing the view are to be noted: Kopp, *Ueher d. Bildnits Alex. d. Or.* p. 29; and Premier, who, *Dclph. Weihgtsch.* pp. 46-47, clearly shows his doubts. Fr. Spiro, *W. kl. Phil.* 1904, col. 702. Illustrations: *Olympia, Ergebnisse,* III, Taf. LV, 1-3. This is practically Premier's opinion, *op. cit.* p. 46-4" and 39-40. proper marble support to the figure of the Agias was omitted. The inexact modelling of the hair of this statue, inasmuch as hair cannot be rendered so perfectly in marble as in bronze, has also been brought forward as a sign that the marble figure was a copy from a bronze original, and the omission of the artist's signature on the base of the marble Agias has been taken to mean that some pupil—Lysistratus has been named — did the work of transference in the master's studio, under his supervision and doubtless from his very model. The slight and sketchy treatment of the hair of the Praxitelian Hermes — for the most part only blocked out — might, on such grounds, be used as evidence that this statue is only a copy, especially as we know that Praxiteles also worked in bronze; and if one started with the premise that an artist worked only in metal, it would be easy to find in any marble work showing elements of his style, reasons for pronouncing it a copy. Now if the original work at Pharsalus was of bronze, why would it not have been easier to have reproduced it in that material, from the model preserved in the master's studio, than to have transferred it to marble? Nor does it seem reasonable that Daochus would have had the statue by a great sculptor like Lysippus almost simultaneously (and most authorities think the marble copy was made almost simultaneously with the original) copied in another material by an inferior artist who was free to indulge his individual taste in details, — mechanically exact copies being unknown in the fourth century,—especially as it was to be placed in so prominent a spot as Delphi. It would seem more reasonable to give the orders for the two statues at the same time. I think we should have ascribed the Agias on stylistic grounds to Lysippus as an original work — even if all the details are not so perfect as we should expect from ancient criticisms of his statues — had we known this artist as a worker in marble as well as in bronze. And if the belief once gains ground that Lysippus also produced works in marble, the number of such works to be ascribed to him will not be small. Such monuments as the Lansdowne Heracles, the Vatican Meleager, the beautiful funeral relief from the Ilissus, and other allied works, now for the most part ascribed to the influence of Scopas, will doubtless with justice be looked upon as Lysippian. It seems there is good evidence for adding at least one more work to the list, this marble head of the Acarnanian pancratiast.

In closing this paper it ma,y be well to sum up briefly the various points discussed. In the first place, it was contended that our conception of the style of Lysippus had been revolutionized by the recent discovery of the marble statue of Agias at Delphi, a work which henceforth should replace the Apoxyomenus, the original of which is now justly referred to a period later than Lysippus, as the centre of our treatment of this artist. Secondly, the Lysippian character of a marble head from Olympia was demonstrated by pointing out its striking resemblance to that of the Agias; and by comparing it with another work in the Lysippian style, the Lansdowne Heracles, it was shown that it could not be the head of that youthful hero, as many have maintained, but must belong to the statue of a victor in the pancratium or the boxing match. Thirdly, this head was assigned to the statue of a certain Acarnanian pancratiast named Philandridas which is mentioned by Pau-, sanias as the work of Lysippus, — the only statue by this artist mentioned in the victor periegesis to which it could be referred, t— and it was shown that the head was excavated not far from the spot where the statue of this Acarnanian must have stood, and near which the bases of neighboring statues have been found. The objection that the statues of victors at Olympia were exclusively of bronze has been shown to be ill-founded, as likewise the assumption that Lysippus worked only in metal. The date assigned by circumstantial evidence to the victory of Philandridas — quite independently of other dates in the career of Lysippus — adds another piece of evidence that this artist's activity began earlier than many writers have maintained, at a date which would have been accepted but for the later style of the Apoxyomenus, which they regarded as his work. All this evidence agrees in demonstrating that this beautiful head is an original work from the youthful hand of the great art reformer of the fourth century.

Walter Woodburn Hyde.
Princeton. *May,* 1907.
Institute of America

THREE VASES IN THE METROPOLITAN MUSEUM, ILLUSTRATING WOMEN'S LIFE IN ATHENS

The daily life of Athenian women during the years that intervened between the rule of Pisistratus and the end of the Peloponnesian war is rendered familiar by countless representations on Attic vases. That it was not so monotonous as might be inferred from Xenophon's *Oeconomicue* is attested by the diverse activities illustrated by the Greek potter. H. B. Walters, in his *History of Ancient Pottery,* II, pp. 172 ff., enumerates no less than thirty women's occupations depicted in vase-paintings. Household, toilet, and bridal scenes are in the majority, but women are also seen indulging in games and music, and, in a few instances, taking part in religious ceremonies. To Walters' list of games two may be added. The game of kottabos was played by women as well as by men, as is shown by scenes on vases in the British and Berlin Museums. The finger game "*alia morra*" was also one of their pastimes, and is illustrated on a hydria in the Berlin Museum.

In our attempt to reconstruct the life of the past, each new representation of a scene from that life is important either in verifying our present knowledge or in supplementing it by fresh facts. For this reason I take the opportunity of discussing three unpublished vases dealing with the life of the Athenian woman, all of which are now in the Metropolitan Museum, New York. On one is depicted a household scene, — women conversing and working wool, a favorite subject with Greek vase-painters, but one that never grows monotonous, the scenes being always variously composed and illustrative of different *Catalogue of Greek and Etruscan Vases in the British Museum,* III, E 813; *Vasensammlung im Antiquarium,* 2410.

Vasensammlung im Antiquarium, 2177.
American Journal of Archaeology. Second Series. Journal of the 417 Archaeological Institute of America, Vol. XI (1907), No. 4.

aspects of the same occupation. On another are represented two women spinning tops. On the third is a scene which will, no douht, be variously explained. The interpretation I shall suggest connects it with an important religious festival, and, if correct, would be of peculiar interest, since we are much in want of direct illustrations of the manifold literary evidence for the active part which women took in religious celebrations.

Pyxis. 06.1117 (Figs. 1, 2, and 3). Height without lid 3J in. (8.2 cm.); with lid to the top of the button 4f in. (12.1cm.). Greatest diameter 3 in. (9.2 cm.). On the lid, a pattern of enclosed palmettes. The design forms a frieze around the body. The execution is of extreme delicacy and grace, and belongs to the period of about 460-440 B.C. Beneath the desigu is a band of tonguepattern. Except for a few small chips which were broken from the base and replaced the vase is intact and in an admirable state of preservation.

The locality of the scene is indicated as the interior of a house by a fluted Ionic column on a plinth. To the right of this a woman, clothed in a short-sleeved chiton and mantle, and wearing a fillet in her hair, is conversing with another woman, who is clothed in a long-sleeved chiton, mantle, and *sakkos,* and is seated in a chair with a *kalathos* beside her. The first woman holds a long fillet in her extended hands, as if offering it to the other, who holds up a flower in her right hand. The two women are evidently exchanging pres ents; the one nearest the column we may suppose to have just entered the apartment (note that she does not wear the *sakkos* as do the other women in the scene), and to he bringing her friend a small present, while the hostess is offering a flower in return, as a mark of welcome. The woman on the right, who is hurrying away from this group, also holds a flower in her right hand, while her left is raised as if in surprise. She is probably hastening to the other women to tell them of the arrival of their friend or to leave the two by themselves. With her back to this group a woman in a long-sleeved chiton, mantle, and *sakkos* is seated in a chair, holding in both hands a string of beads of the shape that often occurs on Greek vases. In front of her stands a woman, similarly clothed, engaged in spinning. In the accustomed way she holds up in her left hand the distaff (Xa/taTi;) with a hank of wool wound around it, to twist from it the thread between the thumb and first finger of her right hand. She is represented at the moment when she has drawn out a sufficient length of yarn, and is twisting it still more completely by twirling the spindle (aTpa/tTO?), which she is holding over a *kalathos* filled with unworked wool. It is interesting to notice how clearly the several parts of the spindle are indicated. Above is the slit or catch *(ayKtarpov)* with the thread securely fixed in it; then comes the stick or spindle proper, and into the lower extremity of this is inserted a whorl (cr-coVsuXo?), of which so many specimens have survived from antiquity.

The scene is completed by the figure of another woman, clothed in a long-sleeved chiton and a *sakkos,* and seated in a chair. Her occupation is not so obvious as that of her companions. Her right leg is raised and supported upon a high foot-rest; she bends slightly forward and her expression indicates that she is devoting her entire attention to her task. This seems to be the winding of the wool into a skein. The lump of spun wool is on the ground; by passing the thread alternately between the second and third fingers, first of her right hand and then of her left, she is undoing the bobbin *Qirrfviov)* she had formed on the spindle, and winding the thread into a skein. Her dress is tucked up above her knee, leaving bare the lower part of her leg, over which she is drawing the thread to prevent it from snarling. Just such another representation does not, to my knowledge, occur on Greek vases or elsewhere. The several processes of actual spinning are common enough; but the treatment of the wool, when once it is spun, is not often shown, though we know that it was eventually wound into a ball *(raXvrr), KXtoar-qp),* and balls of wool occur not infrequently in interior scenes.

Lecythus, G.R. 538, with bulbous body (Fig. 4). Height 6 in. (17.3 cm.). Greatest diameter 4 in. (10.2cm.). Between the neck and shoulder a strip of tongue-pattern; below the design egg-pattern. No white or purple is used in the design, which is of the period about 450-430 B.C. The vase is in a good state of preservation, except the glaze, which is much injured and has in places almost entirely disappeared.

Two women, each clothed in a long chiton of soft material and a himation of heavier texture, are engaged in spinning tops. The stick of the whip held by the woman on the left is clearly indicated; the lash (or lashes?) have disappeared. The stick of the other woman is mostly hidden by her body; Cf. Schliemann, *Troja,* p. 203. For the operation of spinning in antiquity cf. Yates in *Smith's Diet. Ant. s.v.* "fusus"; Bltimner, *Techn. u. Term, der Gewerbe und Kiinste bei den Oriechen und Romern,* I, p. 107, and H. Lafaye in *Daremberg and flnglio, Diet. Ant. s.v.* "fusus." For representations of the subject see the list of references mentioned by Hartwig in his *Meisterschalen,* p. 340, note 1, and Walters, *History of Ancient Pottery,* II, p. 173, note 5.

part of it is still visible near the curve of her shoulder, and it clearly extended a little farther, as is shown by some indistinct traces; the lashes attached to it have wholly disappeared, the surface being much injured just at this point. The woman oh the left wears a *mkkos.* Though the drawing of these figures is somewhat hasty and not carried out with the minute care which characterizes many vases of this period, it is very spirited. The intensity and physical exertion which both women bring to bear on their occupation are admirably expressed. Each woman places her left foot forward, letting her weight rest firmly on it, while the right foot is drawn back, ready at any time to change _. position, according to the movements of the top; with one hand each gathers up her himation, to keep its voluminous folds from getting in the way; in the other each holds the whip, dealing vigorous blows at the tops which are spinning between them. The lively effect of the scene is further increased by the concentrated look with which each woman watches her own top.

Representations of this game are comparatively rare. In addition to the vase just described, I know of but three other instances in which the scene occurs. In one of these it is again a woman who is so occupied. This is the cylix in the van Branteghem Collection (Frohner, *Catalogue,* No. 167, pi. 42) signed by Hegesiboulos. Here the woman is similarly clothed in chiton, himation, and *sakkos,* and holds a whip with two lashes. The design, which is painted in diluted glaze on a white ground, is lifelike, but there is none of the dash and vigor that we find in the figures of our lecythus. A bearded man spinning a top occurs on a cylix in Baltimore, and a youth evidently thus occupied, on a cylix in Berlin.

It is noteworthy that while this game is with us played only by children, with the Greeks it seems to have been practised by grown-up people. The fact that we find women engaged in it is especially interesting and shows us that Greek women did by no means abstain from games requiring active physical exercise.

We possess a number of ancient tops found in the Kabeirion near Thebes, presumably placed there as votive offerings, since the word *arpoiXov* occurs in a list of dedicatory offerings found on that site. These tops are mostly of terracotta; some, of very small dimensions, are of bronze.

Cotyle. 06.1021.181 (Figs. 5 and 7). Height 7 in. Greatest diameter, without handles 7 in. (10.3 cm.), with handles 12j5 in. (32 cm.). A raised gilt surface is used for jewelry and for the object on the lap of the seated woman. Round the lip, egg-pattern; leneath the handles, pattern of palmettes and scrolls. The design belongs to an advanced stage of the "graceful period," probably about 430-420 B.C., when the drawing is minute and delicate, with very thin inner markings in diluted glaze, and when gilt is used freely for accessories, but washes of white have not yet been introduced.

On one side (Fig. 5) is represented in the centre a woman seated on a four-legged stool; she is clothed in a thin chiton, which has fallen from her right shoulder, leaving the upper part of her body nude; on her head she has a *sphendone;* she also wears earrings, necklace, and bracelet. With both hands she holds on her lap an object which is occupying her whole attention; its special significance will be discussed later. In front of her stands another woman, clothed in chiton and himation, and wearing a bracelet, necklace, and earrings as well as a fillet in her hair. She is holding her himation with her left hand; her right is raised over the object on her companion's lap. It is unfortunate that just beneath her hand are several breaks, various fragments having been pieced together; thus part of the surface has been chipped away and afterwards filled in with black by the restorer. Whether, P. Hartwig, *Die Griechiscken Meisterschalen,* pi. lxxvii, 2.

Hartwig, *op. cit.,* pi. xxvii. *Ath. Milt.* 1888. pp. 426-427. therefore, there were originally any further indications of what her raised hand was doing, cannot he ascertained. Close behind this woman stands a satyr, his right hand raised, his left lowered. He is nude and wears a gilt band in his hair. Behind the woman in the centre is the figure of a nude winged Eros, leaning with his left elbow on her shoulder; he also wears a gilt band in his hair. Approaching the central group from the left is a young woman, clothed in a chiton with diploidion, and wearing earrings and a necklace; she is looking toward the central group.

The interest of the scene is evidently centred in the object on the seated woman's lap. The exact use and meaning of objects of this kind have long been a puzzle to archaeologists. They do not appear frequently, but the explanations offered by those who have discussed the vases on which they do occur have been most varied. It may be of advantage to collect the evidence supplied by the other vases, and see whether this does not suggest a satisfactory explanation.

Besides the cotyle just described, there are to my knowledge six vases on which this object occurs.

(1) An aryballus in the British Museum (E 697), representing "Aphrodite and her following." Here a woman, inscribed Peitho, is occupied with putting sprigs of olive into the uprights of such an object. Mr. Cecil Smith, in the *Catalogue of Greek and Etruscan Vase»* in the *British Museum,* III, calls it "an open-work basket of fruits (?)" Stackelberg, in his *Gräber der Hellenen,* pi. xxix, called it "*ein bacchischer Dreifuss ohne Lebes.*" Furtwängler, *Griechische Vasenmalerei,* pi. 78, 2, speaks of it as "*ein Gerät das im Aphroditekultus eine Holle spielte und wahrscheinlich ein Kohlenbecken zum Räuchern ist.*" (2) A lecane from Kertsch in the Hermitage, St. Petersburg, on which are represented various scenes from the gynaeceum. Here such an object, entirely gilt, is seen standing on the

Figure (5. — Oenochoe Is Bkhi.in. ground. Stephani, *Compte Rendu,* 1860, pi. 1, p. 38, and in his catalogue of the Hermitage vases, No. 1791, calls it *"ein eigentümliches, reich vergoldetes Geräth, dessen Bestimmung sich nochinkeiner Weise feststellen lässt.*" In his *Griechische Vasenmalerei,* II, pl. 68, Furtwängler recognizes its similarity to the object on the British Museum aryballus and gives the same explanation of its use, *i.e.* calls it a *"Kohlenbecken zum Räuchern,"* a brazier for burning incense.

(3) An oenochoe in the Berlin Museum (Fig. 6), where three girls are represented, one carrying a similar object on her head. Furtwängler, *Vasensammlung im Antiuarium,* No. 2189, calls the whole subject "*Zug dreier Madchen (zu mcraler Handlung.*)," and speaks of the object itself as *ein durchbrochenes Stabgestell mit drei Lb'wenklauen als Fuss.* In the *Museo Chiusino,* pi. 68, it is called a "*eista che racchiudeva oggetti sacri di mistica rappresentanza, non visibile ad ogni profano.*" In the *Elite Ceramographique,YV,* pi. 28, p. 160, the suggestion is made that the subject may represent three Arrhephori in the Panathenaic procession, and the object is called "wne *espece degrande corbeille.*" In this vase a part of the mouth, including the upper part of the object in question, is wrongly restored and the latter does not, therefore, closely correspond in shape with the other stands. The lower part, however, which is original, is exactly the same as in the other instances and leaves no doubt of the identity of the object. Both in the *Elite Ceramographique* and in the *Museo Chiusino* the reproduction of this scene, which was made from a drawing, is so poor and inexact that the vase has been reproduced here from a photograph. (4) A lecane published by Dumont and Chaplain, *Ceram. de la Grece propre,* pis. xxxviii-xxxix, where the same object, profusely gilt, occurs on the lap of a woman. Its use here is left unexplained. (5) A small loutrophorus, published in Stackelberg, *Graber der Hellenen,* pi. xxx. Here, what perhaps is the same object again occurs on the lap of a woman. The latter is described as occupied "*mit der Bereitung eines Korbes aus goldenen Zweigen.*" (6) A lekane recently found at Kertsch and published by B. Pharmakowsky, *Arch. Am.,* 1907, cols. 134 ff., Figs. 3-7. He calls the representation "*eine bekannte Scene der Frauentoilette.*" In the centre is seated a female figure surrounded by Erotes, and from both sides approach women carrying vases, garments, taenia, and so forth. One of these women is holding the object in question. Pharmakowsky does not attempt to explain it, and only says ',',die Bedeutung des Gerates ist nicht klar.*"

It will be seen from the above that the interpretations hitherto offered for the use of this object show a great variety. The object, which might be described as a framework of broad bands joined by crossing strings or narrower bands For the photographs I am indebted to Dr. R. Zahn.

and resting on a bottom with three feet, must have been intimately connected with some occupation practised by women, since it is among them that it always occurs. Moreover, it is noteworthy that in all the instances cited it is invariably handled by well-born women, not handmaids. It must have been of gold or gilt, since it always appears so whenever gilt accessories are used. It could be placed on the ground, held on the lap, or carried on the head. The fact that it was carried on the head in what seems to be a procession on the Berlin vase (No. 3, above) suggests the idea that it was used in some women's ritual. Furtwiingler, as we have seen, thought it was connected with the cult of Aphrodite, basing his opinion chiefly on the scene on the aryballus in the British Museum (No. 1, above). The scene on our cotyle, however, throws new light on the subject. Here, in a scene which is ostensibly in a woman's apartment, is introduced the figure of a satyr. The natural explanation of his presence is that the scene in question is connected with a cult in which satyrs played an important part; in fact, it suggests that we have here women preparing for the Dionysia, one of the most important festivals celebrated in Athens. This possibility is strengthened when we recall the words of the scholiast on Aristophanes, *Acharnians*, 242: Kara Tt)v T£v Aiovvai'wv eopTtjv irapa rot? 'AOrjvaioK at evyevefc irapdevoi iicavt)(pdpovv. rp) Be ix % pvcrov ireTroirjfieva ra /cava, ep' &v rax cnapxa; dvdvrcov erlBeaav, (" At the Dionysiac festival in Athens the well-born maidens carried baskets made of gold, in which they placed first-fruits of all kinds.") The reference here is to the *Aiovvaia To iv acnei*, celebrated in the city itself in the month Elaphebolion (March—April). One of the chief features of this celebration was the procession which accompanied the image of Dionysus to a small temple situated outside the city. The *Kavrjp6poi*, mentioned by the scholiast, formed part of this procession, which we know to have been fitted out with great pomp. The selection of the maidens for this *trop.irr* was one of the archon's duties.

We have already seen that during the period when gilt accessories were in use the objects on the vases discussed are always gilded; also that they are invariably handled by Cf. Momrasen, *Feste der Sladt Atken,* pp. 436 ff.

evyeveU irapOevoi, and that, at least in one case, a woman appears actually carrying one on her head. It may be argued that the object is unlike the ordinary *itapovv,* or basket, which occurs on Greek vases. But if, indeed, it was used for carrying first-fruits in a procession, the fact that the sides were left open made it more appropriate, since then the offerings could be seen by all. In the scene on the British Museum aryballus we actually see some fruits placed in this object, which has made Mr. Cecil Smith suggest that it was "a basket of fruits." A few choice products, placed in a beautiful receptacle and carried so that all could behold them and be grateful for the bountiful goodness of the gods, was what the occasion demanded. Into the uprights of the stands we may suppose were put branches, as indicated by the fact that on the British Museum aryballus Peitho is engaged in sticking branches into the uprights of the "basket." The appropriateness of her occupation is clear if the object was used for carrying first-fruits; but how could we explain her action, if, with Professor Furtwangler, we took it to be a "*Kohlenbecken zum Rsuchern*" 1

On the vase recently found at Kertsch (No. 6, above) we may suppose that the figure in the centre is one of the girls who is to join the procession. Her friends assist her in her toilet, and bring her the various requisites needed for the occasion. Or, if we accept A. Brueckner's interpretation of such scenes, this may be a representation of the festival of Aphrodite when the newly married women went up to the goddess to bring gifts as thank-offerings. We know that on that occasion a bride would dedicate the girdle she had worn last when still a maiden, as well as other appropriate articles. Is it not possible that the gold basket she had carried in "the procession of maidens" was also deemed a suitable offering?

In the scene on the cotyle in the Metropolitan Museum it would seem that the basket is being prepared for the procession. As has already been pointed out, the surface around the right hand of the woman standing before the object has been restored, and we cannot, therefore, say exactly what she is doing. She is perhaps occupied in decking out the basket, or may be in the act of placing something in it.

Ath. Mitt. 1907, p. 112.

The scene on the back of our vase (Fig. 7) is evidently subsidiary, but its connection with the principal picture is shown by the satyr who is seated on the extreme right, holding a thyrsus in his left hand and leaning his weight on his right. He is looking toward the group in the centre. This consists of a seated woman, clothed in chiton and himation, and wearing a necklace, earrings, bracelets, and diadem, conversing with an attendant who stands in front of her. The latter is clothed in a long-sleeved, dotted garment and a tightfitting cap; like her mistress she wears a necklace, bracelet, and earrings. It is interesting to notice, by the way, that the woman in the centre is seated on a square box of the shape which occurs not infrequently on Attic vases and is also identical with the seats of the so-called Demeter and Kore of the Eastern pediment of the Parthenon.

GISELA M. A. RICHTER.

Metropolitan Museum Of Art,
New York, N. Y.

The identity of the seats of the " Demeter and Kore" of the Parthenon with the square boxes which occur on Attic fifth-century vases was first pointed out by Furtwangler(Gr'riecA!«c/ie *Vasenmalerei,* I, p. 215). Studniczka's assertion *(Jb. Arch. 1.* 1904, pp. 1 ff.) that these were identical with the round cistae of Demeter and, therefore, prove the statues to be Demeter and Kore, has been opposed by Furtwiingler *(Aegina,* p. 332, note 1).

Instttute of Ameriea

A TYRRHENIAN AMPHORA IN PHILADELPHIA

In 1896 the Free Museum of Science and Art of the University of Pennsylvania acquired a small number of Greek vases which had once formed part of the collection of Tewfik Pasha, Khedive of Egypt. Among these was a vase of the type known as Tyrrhenian amphorae which is interesting because of two of the scenes depicted upon it. The vase has the usual shape of the Tyrrhenian amphora; that is, it is rather slender, with handles extending from the body of the vase half way up the neck. It has the echinusshaped lip and the style of decoration in zones typical of vases of this class (Fig. 1). The height of this specimen is 38.5 cm.; the diameter of the top 15 cm., and that of the base 11. 7 cm. Below the lip, which is painted black, there is a complicated ornament of a palmette pattern similar to one represented by Thiersch, but not quite identical. The outline is the same, but in the vase in Philadelphia the pattern is scratched in upon a black background, whereas in *Tyrrhenische Vasen,* p. 83.

American Journaf of Archaeoloiiry, Second Series. Journal of the 429 Archaeological Institute of America, Vol. XI (1907), No. 4.

Figure 1.—Ami'hora In Philadelphia. the example just mentioned red was used to bring out the design. Thiersch has pointed out that a mixture of the palmette cross of the Chalcidian style and the lotus cross of the Corinthian style is typical of vases of this kind; and they all have some ornament similar to this on the neck. Below this is a band of tongue-pattern 2.5 cm. high such as is found on all Tyrrhenian amphorae, and below this three zones of painted decoration. Again, below these zones is a band of ray ornament 6.8 cm. high, also characteristic of this style of vase, and still farther down the usual black foot.

The three bands of figures put this vase into Thiersch's third class, which, he has shown, does not go so far back nor last so long as the class with two zones. The size, too, corresponds well with the size established for this class, which varies from 38 to 44 cm. in height. If lack of skill on the part of the artist is a token of age in Tyrrhenian amphorae our vase must be regarded as one of the earlier examples. Its decoration is crude, no other color than black is used, and the detail is scratched in. The clay is soft and rather coarse, without glaze, and is light pink in color, and the figures project slightly from the background as though it had been scraped away after the paint had been applied. This may have been done in part at least in modern times.

The most interesting of the three zones of figures is the one at the top, which is 8 cm. wide. This has on one side a representation of the Troilus story (Fig. 2). To the left is Achilles concealed by the vine which grows about the fountain. He is on the point of starting forward. In his right hand he brandishes a spear, only part of which is seen, while on his left arm he carries a large round shield, the usual form on vases of this style. He wears a helmet with a crest, and likewise greaves, which is exceptional. The fountain is represented, as on other vases upon which this scene appears, as a sort of column with a spout on one side from which the water is supposed to flow. In some examples the water is actually depicted flowing from the spout (cf. Fig. 3). In front of the fountain is a stand, upon which the water jars were rested while they were being filled, and through which the waste water probably passed. On a vase in Vienna (Fig. 3) published in the *Annali del Insti tuto,* 1866, Tav. d'agg. R., there is a stand of almost identical form. In front of the stand and approaching it is Polyxena. She holds in her two hands what is evidently intended for a hydria adorned with bands. The absence of handles on the jar must be due to the crude ness of the drawing. At first one might imagine that the artist wished to represent some kind of covered vessel, but it is more likely that the broad band is merely intended for decoration. Polyxena has one hand on the mouth or neck of the jar and the other under the base. She has a sort of kerchief about her forehead and coming down over her neck. Part of the chiton is indicated, and below there is an elaborate border on the skirt. This Cf. Masner, *Die Sammlunff anliker Vasen mid Terracotten im oesterreichisehen Museum,* No. 221.

consists of two rows of rather large dots, a kind of ornamentation found on other Tyrrhenian vases, but not elsewhere, I think, as a border for a garment. Behind Polyxena is Troilus, represented as a nude youth on horseback. He has his hair tied up in a bunch at the back of his head (cf. Fig. 3), perhaps in the

Figure 3. — Fkom A Vase In Vienna. KpcoftvXos. The horse has a rather elaborate bridle. Behind Troilus are two warriors armed with helmets, shields, and greaves. The identification of this scene is made certain by comparing it with the plate in the *Annali del Institute* just referred to, where, beneath the figure on horseback, is the name "'O'lloIT. It is needless to discuss the drawing. Its defects are apparent and are the same which are found on other vases of this class. The crouching Achilles is nearly twice as tall as the other figures, horse and all. The artist, too, has not succeeded in keeping all his figures within bounds, for the handle of the spear of Achilles, the head of Troilus, part of the head of the horse, and part of the helmets of the warriors project into the border above.

The scene depicted here is not an uncommon one in Greek vase painting. Schneider enumerates twelve vases upon which it occurs, and according to Baumeister there are as many as sixteen. Three of these are Tyrrhenian amphorae. More numerous still are the vases upon which the pursuit and death of Troilus are represented. This story formed one of the episodes in the *Cypria,* but almost nothing of it has *Der troische Sapenkreis,* p. 114.

Denkmaler des klass. Altertums, p. 1000. come down in the literature. Sophocles wrote a tragedy called *Troilus,* but nothing more is known about it than that in it he told how Troilus while exercising his horses was ambushed by Achilles and killed near the temple of Thymbrian Apollo. In the *Iliad* Priam refers to his son Troilus *lirrnoXap/j.T)*';, *delighting in horses,* as having died in battle, and the other references in ancient literature give us little more information. But the whole story may be reconstructed from the vases. It was apparently this: Polyxena goes to the fountain outside the walls to fill her water jar. The boy Troilus goes along, too, partially as an escort, though hardly as a protection, for he is unarmed, and partially to water his horse. Achilles, who is lying in wait behind the fountain, rushes out and pursues Troilus to the temple of Apollo, where he slays him before Hector and his other brothers can come to the rescue. There are variants at almost every step in the story, but this must have been essentially the form in which the story appeared in the *Cypria*. One might perhaps ask whether the artist who painted uui" vase had any definite heroes in mind for the two warriors at the right, and whether it is possible to identify them. On the vase in Vienna (Fig. 3) there is a warrior who has his name, Phocus, beside him; and on another two old men are standing by, one of whom is named Priam. But it seems more likely that the artist had no particular heroes in mind and that these warriors are part of the escort of Troilus and Polyxena. The representation of Troilus as a boy accords with most of the other vases, though sometimes he appears bearded. One feature which does not appear on the vase in Philadelphia is the bird sent by Apollo, which is sometimes perched on the fountain, and sometimes flying towards Troilus Schol. to *Tl.* XXIV, 257, quoted by Nauck, *Trag. Graec. Frag.* p. 212, ir- rtv8ev SooitX$i iv TpolXip pi)rli ain-bv XoxfuSrai (Klein; codd. *dxcvSijyai*) inr & 'AxiXMws firirous *yvuvdfarra rapi. ri 6vp.ppa.toi ol irodaveiv.* Kustathius, 77. p. 1348, 23, says, &v *(paaiv trrovs (v Tif QvpfSpaitp yvprdfovra XiyxV reaeir vb* 'Ax'xxws.

Arch. Zeit. 1863, pi. 175; cf. also Reinach, *Repertoire des vases prints,* I, p. 394.

'Brit. Mus. hydria B 324; Gerhard, *Auserl. gr. Vasenbild.* pi. xcii; also a vase in Athens mentioned in the preceding note.

as if to warn him of the impending danger. The Troilus story is not found elsewhere exactly as it is painted here.

On the other side of the vase, in the same zone, is a peculiar group consisting of two human figures standing between two sirens and apparently engaged in some sort of contest (Fig. 4). The figure at the right wears a short chiton and evidently a cap of some sort. It is impossible to say what the sex of the figure is, but the artist presumably intended it for a man. He is advancing to the left as if at a run, with one hand in the air, while the other holds a circular object below and behind him. At first sight the hand in the air seems to be the right hand, but it is more likely that this is the left and that the hand holding the circular object is the right. Lack of skill on the part of the artist prevented him from distinguishing clearly right from left. The other figure seems to be nude. The line near the top of the head may indicate a cap, or may be intended by the artist for a band about the hair. The detail just below must be intended for the ear. This man also is advancing to the left, but looking back at the other man. He is gesticulating with his left hand, which is raised, while in his right hand he, too, holds a circular object. Between the two men, in the middle of the field, is another round object with a decoration consisting of four lines crossing in the middle.

No such scene as this occurs elsewhere on a Greek vase, so far as I have been able to discover, and one may well speculate as to what the artist wished to portray. At first sight one might think of some kind of boxing contest in which the figure at the right is about to deal the other a furious blow. But this interpretation is impossible because on another amphora of this style there is a boxing matcli represented and the contestants have their hands tied up and are standing in the traditional manner. Again, one might think of some kind of ball game or tennis match in which the object between the two men would be the ball, but this, too, seems unlikely. Rosettes are common in the field in vases of this class, and it seems natural to regard this as such a rosette. One very similar appears at the end of the sphinx's tail in the zone below. Again, one Cf. Thiersch, *op. cit.* No. 19, and pi. ii.

might think of some kind of dance, but this would not explain the circular objects held by the two men. The true explanation is, I believe, that we have here two discus throwers about to engage in a contest. The man at the right is just starting at a run to get what momentum he can for the throw. The man at the left is looking back, watching him and waiting for his turn. It is true that neither of the figures has the traditional attitude of the discus thrower, but it may be that the artist meant to make the man at the right hold the discus in the usual » way but was prevented by lack of skill from doing so. If this interpretation is correct, this must be regarded as one of the earliest representations of the discus throw. On either side of this group is a siren apparently with raised wings, although it is not easy to decide which the artist wishes us to con This is the opinion of Professor Furtwiingler. who saw the vase in 1904; cf. *Sitzb. MUn. Akad.* 1905, II, p. 206.

Professor Marquand has suggested that this figure may be changing the discus from one hand to the other. sider wings and which tail. The head of the siren at the right has heen painted over, but this seems to be the only place on the vase which has been so treated.

Below this zone of figures comes a band of animals 7.2 cm. high arranged in two groups of three figures each, as is often the case in vases of this class. The group beneath the Troilus scene consists of two sirens between which is a bearded and winged sphinx (Fig. 5). There is nothing particularly remarkable about the sirens. The one at the right has its wings painted in the recurved fashion usual in early art and often found on these vases. The fact that the wings of the other siren and of the sphinx are not so painted shows that the artist knew better, but perhaps in this case preferred the older style for the sake of variety. The figure in the middle is quite exceptional. The sphinx is a common figure on Tyrrhenian amphorae, but not a bearded sphinx. Yet in this case there can be no doubt that the artist wished to depict a sphinx with a beard. The nearest analogy to this that I can find is a bearded siren on a Tyrrhenian amphora in Munich; Thiersch, *op. cit.* No. 47. but the artist may perhaps have had some knowledge of the bearded sphinx of Egypt. The creature is also winged and has its wings extended, as frequently happens. Then the artist to give him additional beauty made his tail end in a rosette. This figure could not keep within bounds, as its hind legs encroach upon the zone below, and even its fore feet come a little below the line.

The other three animals are also interesting. There are two panthers moving in opposite directions and between them a bull facing to the right (Fig. 6). The panther is a very common animal on Tyrrhenian vases, in fact it is more frequently represented than any other animal and usually in the same elongated form as here. The bull is unusual. Thiersch can cite only one example, an amphora in Berlin. There can be no question, I think, that the artist intended this animal for a bull. The tail of the panther at the left extends into the zone above.

The third zone, 6 cm. wide, also has two sets of animals. On what may be called the front of the vase are a ram and a panther face to face (Fig. 7a); and on the other side what seems to be a ram charging a panther (Fig. 7J). Like the panther the ram is often found on vases of this class. Neither of these groups deserves special comment. The panther in the first pair has a rather surprised expression, but the ram is perfectly stolid. In the second group the head of the charging ram is far from being true to nature.

The Tyrrhenian amphorae are an interesting class of vases. Their place of manufacture is still unknown, and unfortunately not enough information has been preserved about the vase in Philadelphia to throw any light upon this problem. The little group of vases of which it was one was said to have come from Samos and Chios, — a statement too uncertain to be of much value. All the extant specimens of which the history is known were found in Italy, chiefly at Caere and Vulci; but it is clear that they are not Etruscan. They have been called Attic; Attic influenced by Corinthian; or by Boeotian; old Cf. *Monument! del Inst.* IX, pi. 55, and Thiersch, *op. cit.* p. 107.

Studniczka, *Jb. Areh. I.* 1886, p. 00, n. 17. Pottier in Dumont and Chaplain, *Les ceramiques,* etc., I, pp. 328 ff.; also Walters, *Cat. Gr. and Etr. Vases in Rr. Mus.* II, p. 35. Hauser, *Jb. Arch. I.* 1803, p. 03, pi. I.

Doric; or Attic Ionic. But Thiersch points out that the alphabet used in the inscriptions on these vases is not Corinthian, and that the shape of the vase, the type of decoration, the frequency of the Troilus myth, and a few other minor points all suggest Ionia as the place of manufacture. This conclusion may be safely accepted, although there is not sufficient evidence available at present to locate them more exactly. There are between seventy and eighty of these vases known. They are all closely connected, and Thiersch even argues that they are not merely the product of a single shop, but the work of one man. This, I think, is going too far. If the extant specimens form, as is likely, only a small proportion of the vases made, the original number must have been far more numerous than one man or one shop is likely to have turned out. But that they were made somewhere in Ionia within a comparatively short space of time is, I think, reasonably certain.

William N. Bates. Wissowa, *Lexicon,* I, p. 1773. s. v. Amazones.
De Ridder, *De ectypis quibusdam aeneis,* pp. 39 and 52.
8 *Op. cit.* pp. 19 fi.
Institute of Ameriea

GREEK OSTRACA IN THE HASKELL MUSEUM

Thk Greek and other ostraca in the Haskell Oriental Museum, as well as those in the Field Museum, were brought to Chicago from Egypt by Mr. Edward E. Ayer, in 1900. Fifteen of the Haskell ostraca were published in *The American Journal of Philology,* XXV, 1904, pp. 45-50. These with the ten further texts here presented constitute about one-fourth of the Haskell Greek collection. The texts that follow are arranged in general in chronological order. They come for the most part from Thebes, and belong, with one exception, to the Roman period.

Ostracon Haskell 16. cm. 4.5 x 7. From Crocodilopolis. Ptolemaic times.
'etovs t $atoi£i.. Tt'(Ta»rai) tiri Tt)v iv Kpo(Ko8tXov) ird(Xei) Tpd(irt£av) .

The missing part of the ostracon may have contained two further short lines, like the last in Wilcken, *Gr. Ostr.* II, No. 1617, which has some affinities with this document.
2. We should expect *eft fp,* etc., but the last letter cannot be e. It may be *fi* or *a.*
Institute of America

ANNOUNCEMENT

During the past season the Committee on American Archaeology of the Archaeological Institute of America offered properly qualified students the privilege of joining the field expeditions of the Institute in Colorado, Utah, and New Mexico. A number of students availed themselves of the opportunity to participate in the practical work of exploration, mapping, and excavation of ruins in the San Juan and Rio Grande basins. These expeditions closed October 1.

Through the courtesy of the Secretary of the Smithsonian Institution the Committee is authorized to announce that the Government excavations at Casa Grande in the Gila Valley, Arizona, will be resumed about November 1, under the direction of Dr. J. Walter Fewkes, to continue during the fall and winter, and that students may arrange through the Archaeological Institute to participate in the work at this site. As Government institutions are not permitted to accept volunteer services, Dr. Fewkes is authorized to pay a limited number of students (not to exceed ten) for their services in connection with the work a nominal salary of ten dollars per month, it being understood that they provide for their own travelling expenses and subsistence. This nominal salary will about cover field subsistence at Casa Grande.

Students desiring to avail themselves

of this opportunity should correspond with the undersigned as early as convenient. Applications should be accompanied by the recommendation of the professor under whom the applicant has studied.

EDGAR L. HEWETT, *Director of American Archaeology of the Archaeological Institute of America, 1333, F Street, Washington, D.C.*

Oct. 21, 1907.

CORRECTIONS TO *A.J.A.* IX, 1905, PP. 319 AND 328

I am now able to give a better copy of the second inscription published in this Journal, Vol. IX, 1905, p. 328, No. 75. The inscription should be read and restored substantially as follows: *DD. NN. Imperatori Caes.*
Fl. Val. Constantino
P. F. M. Vietori
5 *Ac Triumfatori*
Semper Aug. Ef
Fl. Cl. Co(n)stimtino
Et Fl. /«/. ConstantTM
Et Fl. (Iul.) Co(n)sta(nti) Nobb. Caess.
10 *Fl. Iul. Leontius V. P.*
Penes. /V. Ilelenop.
D. N. M. Q. Eprum
MAC

The restoration of the first six lines might take any one of several different forms, but the general sense is given by that here adopted. For lines 7-9, cf. *AJ.A.* X, 1906, p. 431. In line 10 there are distinct traces of the first two letters of Leontius, who was already known as i?(ir) *pierfectissimus) praes(es) pr(orinciae) Helenop(onti) d(evotus) n(umini) m(ajestati)-q(ue) eorum* from *C.I.L.* Ill, 14184 (where the form *Costantino* also occurs), and 14181. MAG, if a correct restoration, stands for *w(ilia)* XXXV.

With regard to *AJ.A.* IX, 1905, p. 319, No. 57, I failed to'state that the inscription is 2.til m. high, 0.55 m. wide, and 0.24 m. thick. The letters are 0.015 'n. high. The stone, used for years as one of the jambs of a gateway, is so large that it is almost certain that it was not transported all the way from Tarsus to Sinope, as Wilamowitz and Ziebarth say *(Berl. Phil.* IV., 1907, col. 334). *Tapo-os* seems an unlikely restoration in line 2.

DAVID M. ROBINSON.

American Journal of Archaeology, Second Series. Journal of the Archaeological Institute of America, Vol. IX (1907), No. 4.

1907 January —Jane ARCHAEOLOGICAL DISCUSSIONS SUMMARIES OF ORIGINAL ARTICLES CHIEFLY IN CURRENT PERIODICALS

James M. Paton, *Editor 65, Sparks St. , Cambridge, Mass.* GENERAL AND MISCELLANEOUS

The Decoration of Neolithic Pottery. —In *Z. Ethn.* XXXIX, 1907, pp. 108-120 (7 figs.), J. Teutsch, in answer to criticisms by H. Schmidt, maintains that on certain painted pottery from Bnrgenlandin Transylvania white is used as background while the ornament is in red outlined with black. He also argues that this type of decoration is derived from the Aegean vases. *Ibid.* pp. 121-136, H. Schmidt replies, modifying in some details his earlier views. He still believes that white is originally applied as decoration, and that this is generally its use. It is possible that in some cases there may be a secondary use of the original clay or colored background as decoration. The spiral decoration, the white incrusted, and white painted pottery were characteristic of the late neolithic period in central Europe and were brought to the Mediterranean by emigrants from that region.

The Earliest Ships. —In *Z. Ethn.* XXXIX, 1907, pp. 42-56, E. Hahn discusses the construction of the earliest sea-going ships. Por transport by water, primitive races have used inflated bladders, skins, reed boats, rafts or catamarans, hollowed logs, and especially sewed bark. Sea-going ships, which must have existed in very early times, have developed from the boat of logs tied together, though the earliest form was probably like the Malay proa with an outrigger.

Painting of the Body and Tattooing. — In *R. Arch.* IX, 1907, The departments of Archaeological News and Discussions and of Bibliography of Archaeological Bonks are conducted by Professor Paton, Editor-in-charge, assisted by Miss Mary H. Buckingham, Mr. Harold R. Hastings, Professor Elmer T. Mkrrill, Professor Frank G. MooRk.Mr. Charles R. Morey, Professor Lewis B. Patox, Dr. A. S. Pease, and the Editors, especially Professor Marqi And and Dr. Peabody.

No attempt is made to include in this number of the Journal material published after July 1,1007.

For an explanation of the abbreviations, see pp. 140, 141.

pp. 38-50 (4 figs.), J. Dechklette shows that the Europeans of the stone age and early part of the bronze age decorated their persons with painting, tattooing, or both. This was the case in the eastern and western Mediterranean regions, as well as in France and more northern parts of Europe.

Pictorial Art and Oriental Research. — In *Memnon,* I, 1907, pp. 918, J. Strzygowkki pleads for the emancipation of the history of Oriental art from the study of philology and epigraphy. He claims that at present inscriptions are the only objects that interest Orientalists, and that sculpture and painting are passed over as mere accessories of written texts. In reality, however, the art of the various west-Oriental peoples throws as important a light upon their ideas and the history of their civilization as do their inscriptions. The history of Oriental art should be constituted a distinct discipline in the universities, and should devote itself to the investigation of material, technique, object, figure, form, and content. Scarcely a beginning has been made in determining the deeper spiritual ideas that underlie the varying forms of art in the chief centres of ancient Oriental civilization.

The Origin of the Himyaritic Script. —In *S.Bibl. Arch.* XXIX, 1907, pp. 123-132 (2 pis.), E. J. Pilcher argues that the Himyaritic script was not of ancient Semitic origin, but was derived from Greek colonists in Egypt. Letters which are distinguished in Phoenician have not separate signs in Himyaritic, but only slightly modified forms of the same sign, as would be the case if they had been derived from a non-Semitic people. Himyaritic is written *boustrophe-*

don like ancient Greek. In Himyaritic the words are marked off from one another by a perpendicular stroke, which is also an early Greek custom. Several of the most puzzling characters of the Himyaritic are explained most readily from Dorian Greek forms.

Katabanian Inscriptions. — In *Milt. Vorderas. Ges.* XI, 190(i, pp. 1-48, D. Nilsen publishes two new inscriptions of the Glaser collection, one recording how a certain *mukarrib* of Kataban constructed a new road through the mountains and rebuilt the temple; the other recording how a king of Kataban sacrificed a she-camel to 'Athtar, 'Amni, and Shamash.

Tarshiah and the Jonah Legend. — In *Memnon,* I, 1907, pp. 70-79 (3 figs.), G. Husing contests the current view that Tarshish is to be identified with Tartessus in Spain. The two passages on which this view rests are Gen. x. 4 and Jonah i. 3. In the first, TarshLsh is mentioned in connection with Cyprus, Crete, and Rhodes and is, therefore, to be regarded as a textual corruption for Turshim, the Tursha of the Egyptians which constantly appears in connection with Crete and Cyprus. In Jonah a different division of the letters changes " he went down to Joppa " to " and he (Yahweh) pursued him," thus removing the indication that Joppa was on the way to Tarshish. In 1 Kings and 2 Chron. it is declared that Ezion-Geber was the port for Tarshish, which indicates that Tarshish lay in the east. It is to be identified with the coast of ancient Elam, and the story of Jonah is a modified form of an ancient Elamitic myth which is widely prevalent in the Orient and throughout the classical world. See also *Or. Lit.* X, 1907, col. 26.

The New Testament in the Light of Recent Archaeology. — In *Exp. Times,* XVIII, 1907, pp. 202-211, A. Deissmann discusses the bearing of recently discovered papyri and inscriptions on the interpretation of the New Testament religion. The classical literature gives a distorted conception of the scepticism of the world into which Christianity came. Inscriptions and papyri show us that in general people were deeply religious and were thus prepared to receive the new teaching. They show also an uncertainty in regard to immortality that prepared the way for the positive message of Christianity on this subject. The inscriptions also throw light upon the current meaning of many New Testament terms.

Ancient Glass. — In *Le Musee,* III, 1906, pp. 477-524 (3 pis.; 102 figs), A. Sambon gives an account of ancient glass. The material is arranged by countries and periods, and the characteristic products of each group are noticed and illustrated by typical specimens.

The Roll in Ancient Art. — The representations of the papyrus roll in ancient art have been collected and fully discussed by T. Bikt. In an introduction he treats briefly the roll in ancient Egypt, and the use of papyrus rolls and parchment among the Greeks and Romans. The use of a *codex* is scarcely represented before the fourth century A. d. Parchment was used for school books, as more durable and apparently cheaper in the time of Martial, and perhaps for reference books, but not for ordinary editions. The chapters treat in detail of the closed roll, the open roll and reading, writing, the character of the roll and its preservation, the illustrated book, which is held to have inspired the form of the sculptures on the columns of Trajan and Marcus Aurelius, and the representation of rolls in the Middle Ages. (T. Birt, *Die Buchrolle in der Kunst. Archnoior/ischantiquarische Untersuchungen zum Antiken Buchwesen.* Leipzig, 1907, B. G. Teubner. x, 352 pp.; 191 figs. 8vo. M. 12.)

Roman Fortified Boundaries in Germany and Britain. — In *Rec. Past,* VI, 1907, pp. 9-13, 50-57, 83-89 (11 figs.), G. II. Allen describes the development of the Roman system of fortifications along the boundaries of Germany and Britain, the character of the remains, and in particular the restored fort at the Saalburg.

The Date of the Ruins in Rhodesia. — In his report of a journey in South Africa *(Z. Ethn.* XXXVIII, 1906, pp. 863-895; 17 figs.), F. Von Ltschan discusses the age of the ruins at Simbabwe and other points in Rhodesia. He examines the arguments in detail, and agrees with Randall MacIver that the ruins are of comparatively recent date, and probably of native origin. The figure of Egyptian porcelain is declared a modern forgery, but even if genuine, it proves nothing, for many Egyptian antiquities are now brought into South Africa by Greeks. *Ibid.* pp. 896-904 (3 pis.; 12 figs.), H. Schafek gives at length the grounds for declaring the porcelain figure one of a series of modern forgeries made in Thebes. *Ibid.* pp. 916-923 (fig.) is published a discussion of von Luschan's views, in which a greater antiquity is claimed for the ruins and the objects found there by Staudinger, Fritsch, and Oppert.

Persian Numismatics. — In *J. Asiat.* VIII, 1906, pp. 517-532, Allotte De La Fuye discusses a series of coins with Aramaic legends containing the titles *Prtkra* and *Malka,* and bearing the names of certain Persian monarchs. He comes to the conclusion that all Persian coins are later than the reign of Antiochus II. They are probably contemporary with the reigns of Mithridates I, king of Parthia, and his successors. Arsacid influence is unmistakable in these coins.

Hindu Architecture in the Par East. — The Hindu architecture in the Far East has been studied by General L. De Beylie. He reviews briefly the architectural styles of India, and the influences received or exercised by Hindu art before the Mahonimedan invasion, and then considers the special characteristics of the architecture in the neighboring countries, treating successively Cambodia and Annam, Siam and Laos, Burmah, Java, and Ceylon. He concludes that Hindu architecture is composed of indigenous elements strongly modified by Persian and Greek influence; that it does not generally employ brick and stone before the second century B.C.; that Indian art reached Indo-China and the islands during the first two centuries of our era, but that in all these countries it was modified by strong local tendencies; that the stone and brick monuments of these regions are not earlier than the sixth century A. n.; and that later the so-called Chinese style became more and more prevalent. (General L. De Beylie, ᴠArchitecture Hindoue en Extreme-Orient. Paris, 1007, E. Leroux. 416 pp.; 360 figs, large 8vo.)

The Monuments of Cambodia. — The second volume of the *Inventaire Descriptif des Monuments du Cambodge*, by E. Lunet De Lajonquiere (Paris, 1907, E. Leroux. xlv, 355 pp.; 2 pis.; 112 figs, large 8vo.), is published by the *Ecole Francaise d'Extreme-Orient*. In the brief Introduction a general account of the diffusion of early Cambodian civilization in the valleys of the Menam and the Mekong is followed by notes on the monuments, their construction and decoration, supplementary to the introduction in the first volume *(A. J.A. VII, p. 454)*. The monuments (Xos. 291-470) are then described in detail according to their geographical distribution in provinces recently added to Cambodia, French Laos, eastern Siamese Laos, western Siamese Laos, and the valley of the Menam.

EGYPT

Babylonian Influence in Egyptian Art. — In *Memnon*, I, 1907, pp. 8085 (4 figs.), F. Hommel claims that the bark of the sun in Egyptian art is derived from the floating shrine of the sun-god in Babylonian art, and that the eight Igigi of Babylonia are the prototypes of the eight genii who in Egypt accompany the sun-god with music.

Egyptian and Assyrian Standards. — Tn *Klio*, VI, 1906, pp. 393-399 (4 figs.), H. Schafkk points out that Egyptian and Assyrian standards, which consist of a pole bearing the symbol of a god, are carried on a warchariot, and enjoy a special cult in the camp. They are not merely standards, but indicate the actual presence of the gods. The custom seems to have originated in Egypt, whence it was borrowed by the Assyrians.

The Writing and Language of the Egyptians. — In *Alt. Or.* VIII, 1907, part II, pp. 1-32, V. Spieloelberg gives an account of the development of the Egyptian script from the pictures of the earliest period through the hieroglyphic, hieratic, and demotic to the Coptic, and adds a brief history of the decipherment of the monuments and of the development of the Egyptian language.

The Tablets of Negadah and Abydos. — The excavations at Negadah and Abydos have disclosed a number of small inscribed pieces of wood or ivory which belong to the earliest Egyptian dynasty. These are discussed by F. Leoge in *S. Bibl. Arch.* XXVIII, 1906, pp. 252-263 (2 pis.); XXIX, 1907, pp. 18-24, 70-73 (pi.), 101-106 (pi.). One tablet records the celebration of the so-called Sed festival at the tomb of King Aha, another the foundation of the temple of Neith at the funeral of the same king, another names King Zer.

An Egyptian Bust in the Louvre. — In *Mon. Pint*, XIII, 1906, pp. 527 (2 pis. ; 6 figs.), O. Benkdite argues that in Egyptian art it is necessary to distinguish the stereotyped hieratic style, common in temples and tombs, from a much freer naturalistic style shown in early mastabas and later in furniture and household ornaments and utensils. The articles made for the living are a truer measure of Egyptian art than those intended for the gods or the dead. A fine limestone bust of Amenophis IV in the Louvre shows clearly how this king broke with the official art as well as the official religion.

An Egyptian Head in BrusselB. — In *Mon. Pint,* XIII, 1906, pp. 29-34 (pi.; fig.), J. C'apakt publishes a fine Egyptian portrait now in Brussels. It belongs apparently to the early years of the nineteenth dynasty, and shows the freedom and delicacy characteristic of Egyptian art under the influence of Amenophis IV. The author argues that the change from the realism of the early sculpture to the later ideal type is due in great part to a change in the belief as to the nature of the " Double," in consequence of which the need of accurate portraiture was no longer felt.

A Pendant on Statues of Usertesen III. — In *S. Bill. Arch.* XXVIII, 1906, pp. 268-209 (pi.), V. Schmidt describes the representation of a pendant on three statues of Usertesen III, and concludes that it is an amulet consisting of a linen cord tied with peculiar loops.

The State Post under the Ptolemies. — In *Klio,* VII, 1907. pp. 241277, F. Preisioke examines the *verso* of *Hibeh Papyri*, I, 110, which contains the records of a postmaster at some place in the Fayum. Analysis shows that the post left this place for the north and south, probably every six hours, that it was used only for state despatches requiring speed, and that it was a liturgy performed probably by colonists holding lands from the king. There are indications of other arrangements when speed was not needed. Private letters do not seem to have been forwarded by the state.

Ptolemaic Metrology. — In *11. El. Gr.* XIX, 1900, pp. 389-393, T. R. discusses the *naubion* and the *staler* in Ptolemaic Egypt. For the former he accepts the conclusions of Jouguet and Lesquier *(A.J.A.* XI, p. 202). The same document fixes the *staler* as equivalent to the silver tetradrachm, and this seems its value in Herondas, VII, 99.

The Gold Medallions of Abukir. — A brief account of the large gold medallions found at Abukir *(A.J.A.* VIII, p. 468), the suspicions regarding the alleged discovery, the purchase of four by the Berlin Museum, and the disappearance of the other Seciiuens is given in *Burl. Mag.* XI, 1907, pp. 162-163 (pi.) by A. Koester.

BABYLONIA AND ASSYRIA

The First Babylonian Dynasty.— In *S. Bibl. Arch.* XXIX, 1907, pp. 107-111, C. II. W. Johns discusses the lists of names of the years in the period of the first dynasty of Babylon. The Babylonian custom was to name each year after some important event which occurred in it. A number of chronological lists of these names of the years have come down to us in a fragmentary condition. The author seeks from a study of contract tablets of the period to fill up the gaps in these lists and supplies a large number of new year-names for the reigns of the first dynasty.

Old Babylonian Chronology. — In *Or. Lit.* X, 1907, cols. 169-181, L. Mksserschmidt publishes a new collation of the chronological table of the first dynasty preserved in the museum at Constantinople.

Mathematical, Metrological, and Chronological Tablets from Nippur. — In the *Publications of tlie Babylonian Expedition of the University of Pennsylvania,* Vol. XX. Part I, 1906 (30 pis., 15 photos), II. V. Hli.iitEtHT publishes forty-seven tablets in transcription and seventeen in photograph from the excavations of the so-called temple library of Nippur. These consist of tables of multiplication and of division, in all of which the number 12,960,000 is taken as the basis of the calculations. The multiplication tables are tables of the factors of this quantity, and the division tables are for the most part tables of quotients obtained by dividing 12,960,000. The explanation of this fact is that 12,960,000 (=60 = 3600) is a sacred number representing the number of days in the sacred cycle of 36,000 years which played so important a part in Babylonian cosmological speculations and was known to the Greeks through Pythagoras and Plato. There are also tables of squares from one to fifty and of square roots, and tables of measures of capacity and of weights. From these tables it appears that the Babylonian scribes of the third millennium n. c. were familiar with the computation of the areas of rectangles, squares, right triangles, and trapezoids and the volumes of rectangular parallelopipeds and of cubes. If the vessel whose contents were measured was a cylinder, we shall have to assume that they were also familiar with the approximate ratio of the circumference of a circle to its diameter. More important than all these mathematical tables is a list of early Babylonian kings containing originally about 180 names of rulers. It shows that at least 135 kings who reigned before the time of Hammurabi were known to the Babylonians. That is, that Babylonian history could be written for as many years before Hammurabi as elapsed from Hammurabi to the fall of Babylon. By means of this list the chronological relations of the dynasties of Ur and of Isin are established, and the exact number of years of each king's reign is recorded. The texts are provided with an elaborate introduction describing their characteristics and their historical significance.

In *Or. Lit.* X, 1907, cols. 109-113, IT. Ranke discusses this list of early Babylonian kings and agrees with Hilprecht that the downfall of the dynasty of Isin is to be identified with the capture of Isin by Rim-Sim recorded in the seventeenth year of Sin-muballit. This view is supported by a tablet which mentions the year in which Amurum drove out Libit-Ishtar, who is probably identical with the last king of Isin. Amurum denotes the West Semitic people who overran Babylonia in the time of the first dynasty of Babylon. *Ibid.* cols. 114 ff., B. Mf.issner disputes the identity of Libit-Ishtar with the last king of the dynasty of Isin, and holds that he was a governor of the city of Sippar. *Ibid.* cols. 207-210, II. Ranke disputes Hilprecht's identification of Immerum with Xur-(ilu)im of Larsa.

The Chronology of Ashurbanipal's Reign.—In *S. Bill. Arch.* XXIX, 1907, pp. 74-84, C. II. W. Johns publishes the fifth of his important investigations into the chronology of the reign of Ashurbanipal. The eponyin list is defective during this reign, but by an elaborate study of business documents of the period the author succeeds in restoring with a high degree of probability the names of all the eponyms for the years between 671 and 660 B.C.

The Alabaster Relief of King Ashurnasirpal IT. — In *Or. Lit.* X, 1007, cols. 115-126, A. Hermann discusses the significance from the point of view of the history of civilization of the armor, dress, ornaments, and other details on the alabaster relief from the northwest palace of Ashur-nasirpal II.

The Archaeology of the Cuneiform Inscriptions. — In the Rhind Lectures for 1906 Professor A. II. Sayce discussed the archaeology of Babylonia and Assyria, chiefly from the evidence of the inscriptions, as the excavations have not as a rule been conducted with sufficient scientific accuracy to make possible a classification of the pottery and other objects. The volume containing these lectures, with an article from the *Contemporary Review* for August, 1905, treats of the decipherment of the cuneiform inscriptions, the archeological records, which are best known at Susa, the Sumei ians, the relation of Babylonian civilization to Egypt, Palestine, and Asia Minor, and the condition of Canaan in the century before the Exodus. (A. II. Sayce, *The Archaeology of the Cuneiform Inscriptions.* London, 1907, Society for Promoting Christian Knowledge. 220 pp.; 19 pis. 8vo. *5s.)*

Aramaean Tribes in Babylonia. — In *Milt. Vorderas. Ges.* XI, 1906, pp. 203-246, M. Streck discusses information gained from Babylonian and Assyrian sources in regard to the nomadic tribes that dwelt in Babylonia and the adjacent regions. The cuneiform records afford no evidence that the Aramaean migration had occurred before the fifteenth century B.C., and there is no trace of Aramaean settlements in Babylonia before the tenth century. The main sources of information in regard to these tribes are described and discussed in chronological order, and this is followed with an alphabetical index of Aramaean tribal names with references to all the passages in the cuneiform literature where these tribes are mentioned.

Chedorlaomer Tablets. —In S. *Bihl. Arch.* XXVIII, 1906, pp. 241251; XXIX, 1907, pp. 7-17, A. II. Sayce continues the translation and discussion of the socalled Chedorlaomer tablets *(A.J.A.* XI, p. 204).

The Meaning of the Title Bur-G-ul. — In *Or. Lit.* X, 1907, cols. 175-181, A. Poebel shows that the *bur-gul,* who occurs in numerous tablets from Nippur, was a functionary who performed the duties of a notary-public in witnessing signatures and attesting seals.

Signs for the Liver in Babylonian Inscriptions. — In *Z. Assyr.* XX, 1907, pp. 105-129, M. Jastrow, Jr., discusses the signs used for the liver in Babylonian tablets. The ideogram commonly read H A R, which is known to denote the liver, he holds should be read U R. Four other signs are also used for the liver, showing the unique importance that was attached to this organ in Babylonian haruspicy. The liver was regarded as the genuine seat of the soul and it was the only organ inspected in sacrificial victims. This fact gives a new meaning to a number of Babylonian omen tablets and especially to the famous series of omens of Sargon and Naram-Sin, which instead of being astrological, as was formerly supposed, are in reality all liver omens.

The Historical Topography of the Region of the Tigris. — In *Memnon*, I, 1907, pp. 89-143 (pi.; 9 figs.), E. Hekzkeld discusses the modern geography of the region occupied by ancient Assyria, and then the relics that survive at various points from the Assyrian, Persian, Greek, Parthian, and Sassanian epochs. The article also contains a collection of all the passages in the classical writers descriptive of this region.

Dilmun. —In *Exp. Times*, XVIII, 1907, p. 234, A. H. Sayce claims that Dilmun of the cuneiform inscriptions is not the island of Bahrein, as has been commonly supposed on the basis of the Annals of Sargon, 309-370, but is really a district of northeastern Arabia.

Karduniash. — In *Or. Lit.* IX, cols. 663-065, G. HUsing argues that there is no evidence in support of the view that Duniash is the Kaasite name for Babylonia. Karduniash is the name of a divinity, and cannot mean "the fortress of Duniash." The word must be explained from K assite-Elamitic.

The Four Sacred Rivers. — In *Or. Lit.* IX, cols. 558-663, F. Hommel shows that the conception of four sacred rivers is common in Babylonia, and compares the four rivers of Paradise in Genesis ii. These rivers were originally located in eastern Arabia west of the Euphrates, but subsequently the names were transferred to the region east of the Tigris in the vicinity of Dur-ilu.

Babylonian Parellels to the Genealogy of Abraham. — In *Exp. Times*, XVIII, 1907, pp. 322-333, A. II. Sayce argues that the ancestors of Abraham in Genesis xi are Babylonian names of cities and tribes, so that this chapter contains an historical reminiscence of the migrations of the forefathers of Abraham from Ur of the Chaldees to Mesopotamia.

The Tree of Truth and the Tree of Life. —In *R. Bibl.* XIV, 1907, pp. 271-274, P. Uiiorme discusses the Babylonian beliefs concerning the "tree of truth " and the "tree of life," which are the counterparts of the "tree of the knowledge of good and evil" and the "tree of life " in Genesis. The "tree of truth " in the Babylonian conception was planted at the east and was guarded by the rising sun. It stood at the entrance of heaven. The " tree, of life " was also a mythological conception, but had its counterpart on earth in a tree in the garden of the temple at Eridu. Both trees are frequently mentioned in early Babylonian texts.

The Dove with the Olive-leaf. — In *Exp. Times,* XVIII, 1907, pp. 377-378, W. O. E. Oestkhi.ey discusses the meaning of the olive-leaf brought back by the dove in the story of the flood. He holds that both the dove and the olive-twig were originally sacred to Ishtar, and that in the original Babylonian version of this story the dove appeared as the messenger of Ishtar to Noah, bringing him assurance of the cessation of the deluge.

The Ark of Yahweh.—In *Exp. Times,* XVIII, 1907, pp. 155-15S, F. Hommel points out the analogies to the Ark of the Covenant and the tables of the law in the Babylonian "tablets of fate." and "chamber of fate." The latter was a kind of portable chest in which the "tablets of fate" were kept, and which was carried on the Babylonian New Year festival from the temple of Marduk to the house of sacrifice. These analogies seem to show that the connection of the tallies of the law with the ark is very ancient and that the statements of the Hebrew Priestly Code on this subject are trustworthy.

SYRIA AND PALESTINE

The Origin of the Semitic Alphabet. — In *Z. Assyr.* XX, 1907, pp. 49-58, H. Grimme discusses the origin of the Semitic alphabet. He rejects the theory of Egyptian origin and holds that the Babylonian origin is antecedently most probable. Both *'Ayin* and *Teth* are represented by a circle in the old Semitic alphabet, and the same sign, a circle, represents *hi* or'» and *ti* in old Babylonian script. This suggests that these two letters at least have been derived from the Babylonian character. Later *Teth* was discriminated from *'Ayin* by the insertion of a cross *(Tau)* in the middle of the circle. The same process of discrimination by combination with another letter is traced through the South Arabian alphabet and the Ethiopic, The Aramaeans are the most probable originators of the alphabet on account of the absence of distinction between *He* and *Heth* in their language. The Semitic alphabet knows nothing of this distinction.

The Cities of the El-Amarna Letters. — In *Z. D. Pal. V.* XXX, 1907, pp. 1-79, II. Ci.auss publishes an elaborate study of the names of towns and districts in the Amarna letters in comparison with their equivalents in the Bible and in modern times. One hundred and fifteen names are arranged in alphabetical order, and all the passages in which these names occur are brought together under each head. At the end of the article a table is given of the Amarna names and their later equivalents.

The Archaeological History of Jerusalem. — n *Bibl. World,* XXIX, 1907, pp. 7-22; 86-96; 168-182; 247-2.19; 327-333, L. B. Paton discusses a number of the archaeological problems of ancient Jerusalem, taking up in the successive articles the following topics: (I) The Location of the Temple; (II) The Valleys of Ancient Jerusalem; (III) The Springs and Pools of Ancient Jerusalem; (IV) The City of David; (V) Zion, Ophel, and Moriah.

The Location of Golgotha. —In *Pal. Ex. Fund,* XXXIX. 1907, pp. 7-5-76, 140-147, F. W. Bikcii presents anew his theory that Golgotha was situated on Mount Zion. The evidence is derived from the interpretation of Old Testament literature and prophecy, rather than from history or archaeology.

The Isaiah Inscription. — In *Bibl. World.* XXIX, 1907, pp. 338-390, T. F. Wright discusses the inscription found by Schick in 1889 in the village of Silwan near Jerusalem, where it was placed on a sort of chapel in honor of the Prophet Isaiah. lie compares the copies made by Schick and Petrie and concludes that Schick's is more accurate. The meaning is, " For the bas-relief and shrine of Isaiah the prophet."

Small Antiquities at Jerusalem. — In *J.A.O.S.* XXIX, 1907. pp. 400401, (i. A. Barton describes three objects in the Clark collection at Jerusalem. The first is a weight in the form of a turtle inscribed with the word "five" in old Hebrew letters. Its weight is 58 grains, and it is evidently meant to be the fifth of a shekel. The second is a head resembling the Hittite type, with inscribed characters on the back which may be Hittite. The third is a small stone duck designed, perhaps, for a weight.

Sites on the Sea of Galilee. — In *Pal. Ex. Fund,* XXXIX, 1907, pp. 107-125, R. A. S. MACALi.iSTER describes certain sites on the Sea of Galilee and discusses their probable identification with places mentioned in the Gospels.

The Site of Syohar. —In *Pal. Ex. Fund,* XXXIX, 1907, pp. 92-94, R. A. S. Macallistkk disputes the common identification of Sychar with Askar, and proposes a mound nearer Nablus which shows traces of Jewish occupation.

Jewish Aramaean Tablets. — In *J. Asiat.* IX, 1907, pp. 150-152, R. Gotthf. il describes eight amulets now in New York, similar to the one described by Schwab, *ibid.* VIII, 1906, pp. 5 f. With one exception these were found at Irbid near Tiberias in rock-hewn tombs, and were probably interred with the persons who had worn them during life.

The Phoenician Inscriptions. — In *Alt. Or.* VIII, 1907, Part III, pp. 127, W. Von Landau describes the discovery of the Phoenician inscriptions and the history of their decipherment. He then gives an account of the principal Phoenician cities in Syria and in other lands adjacent to the Mediterranean, with translations of the most important inscriptions from each place.

The Zenjirli Inscriptions. — In *Z. Assyr.* XX, 1907, pp. 59-67, C. Sarauw proposes readings for certain gaps in the inscriptions of Panammu and Hadad, and discusses the dialect of these inscriptions. He holds that this is predominantly Aramaean and that there is no reason to suspect Canaanitish, but some grounds for belief in Assyrian, influence.

ASIA MINOR

The Hittite Relief at Ibriz. —In *B. El. Anc.* IX, 1907, pp. 109-113 (2 pis.; fig.), J. Db Nettancourt publishes new photographs of the Hittite relief at Ibriz, with a brief description of the place, and of the new details which appear in these views.

The Date of the Battle of Halys. — In *Or. Lit.* X, 1907, col. 23, G. HUsing discusses the cuneiform evidence which shows that the battle of Halys coincided with the eclipse of the sun on either May 19, 557 B.C., or November 1, 556 B.C.

The Asclepieum at Cos. —In *Arch. Bel.* X, 1907, pp. 201-228 (pi.), R. Herzog discusses Ilerondas IV in the light of his excavations at the Asclepieum of Cos, seeking to identify the various objects mentioned by Heiondas with the objects disclosed by the excavations.

The Rhodian Fireships. — In *Bert. Phil. W.* 1907, cols. 28-32 (fig.), R. Schneider calls attention to a painting in an Alexandrian tomb, which explains the construction of the Rhodian fireships in 190 B.C. On the forecastle is a tower, from which projects a beam with an iron basket full of coals at the end. The ships seem to have been effective because of the terror they caused, for in actual combat they must have been as dangerous to their own crews as to the enemy.

The Topography of Smyrna. —In *B. Et. Anc.* IX, 1907, pp. 114-120 (plan), A. Foutrier publishes notes on the topography of Smyrna with special reference to the position of fountains, and brief mention of many ancient remains. The fountain of Sidrivan-Djami corresponds to the KAAEfiN, which appears on coins of the Roman Empire.

Ex-votos to Apollo KrateanoB. — In *B. El. Gr.* XIX, 1906, pp. 304317 (fig.), IS. MicnoN discusses, with full references to the earlier literature, ten dedications to Apollo Krateanos, of which one just added to the Louvre is new. It reads *'attowosottk 'aitkxjltt8ov* "attoaadvi *KpartaviS apiarypiov.* In the accompanying relief, representing a sacrifice to Apollo, the victim is a bull instead of the usual ram. The word *xPiar)P* indicates that this is a thank-offering rather than a propitiation. This inscription is also noticed, *B. Soc. Ant. Fr.* 1906, p. 302.

Zeus Askraios. — In *Cl. R.* XXI, 1907, pp. 47-48, W. R. Paton publishes a dedication from Myndus by certain Halicarnassians Au 'Attpaup. This suggests that the Zeus Askraios of Halicarnassus (Apollonius in Westermann, *Paradox. Gr.* p. 109) should be Zeus Akraios. The same correction of 'AKpuos for 'AoKpatos is probable in other passages.

Life in Ancient Cities. — In No. 131 of the series *Aus Natur und Oeisleswelt,* E. Ziebarth gives a picture of life in the ancient cities as shown by recent excavations, and the study of inscriptions and papyri. In the first chapter the nature of the ancient archives and their value is discussed, and then Thera, Pergamon, Priene, Miletus, the temple of Apollo at Didyma, and the Greek cities in Egypt are described. The book contains brief accounts of discoveries hitherto accessible only in large publications or in scattered reports. (E. ZlEBarTh, *Kullurbilder aus griechischen Stndten.* Leipzig, 1907, P. G. Teubner. 120 pp.; pi.; 22 figs. 12mo. M. 1.25.) GREECE

ARCHITECTURE

The Origin of the Greek Temple. — In *Z. Ethn.* XXXIX, 1907, pp. 5779 (15 figs.), P. Sarasin traces the development of the Greek temple from a primitive house raised on piles, such as is common in the Celebes. The peripteros represents the outer row of piles. The naos is formed by walling up the inner columns, as is often done by the Malays. The entablature and pediment are the original dwelling, which has shrunk to a merely ornamental element. The triglyphs occupy the place of windows. The theory is developed in detail for all the architectural elements.

Parthenon and Opisthodomos. — The double meanings of these two words are discussed by E, Petersen in *Jb. A rch. I.* XXII, 1907, pp. 8-18. He finds that

Parthenon, in addition to its application to the whole building, was used specifically of the western enclosed room, and that Opisthodomos, 'rear building,' was used both for the entire western division of the temple, including enclosed room and open portico, and also for the open western portico alone, when the adjoining room was called Parthenon. The restricted meanings belonged to official language, the less definite uses were popular. Similar uses of the word Ttoais are also differentiated.

Building Material at Delphi. —In *Philolngus*. LXVI, 1907, pp. 260-286, H. Pomtow and R. Lepsius publish the results of the examination of 160 specimens of stone from the buildings and monuments of Delphi. Excluded are the local varieties, *i.e.* limestone from Parnassus and the quarries of St. Elias and a breccia. Lepsius distinguishes five varieties of poros, all from Corinth and Sicyon, three of limestone, and five of marble. Pomtow adds a detailed list, arranged topographically, of the monuments from which the specimens were taken.

SCULPTURE

Primitive Terra cottas. — In *J.H.S.* XXVII, 1907, pp. 68-74 (5 figs.). E. S. Forster publishes five early terra-cottas, two standing and one seated figure from Boeotia and two equestrian groups from Crete, each of which is noteworthy for some peculiarity. It is evident that religious conservatism required the most primitive type of figure to be used, even after the skill of the artist, as seen in the head and face, was capable of something much more advanced.

Early Types of Greek Sculpture. — The representation of the human form in pre-Hellenic and early Hellenic art is discussed by F. Poulsen, in *Jb. Arch. I.* XXI, 1906, pp. 177-21'1 (12 figs.). To the first childish conception of a body with arms, legs, and head, there was added, in the desire for realism, the expression of sex and later that of clothing, either by color or plastically, and the wish not to omit either of these details led to strange inconsistencies and perhaps to the effect of transparent drapery. The cylindrical idols, representing women with long robes, belong to the third stage. After the artistic retrogression due to the Dorian migration, the samb development took place again, and once more numerous inconsistencies occurred. When the progress toward realism for the second time reached the point of clothing the figure, the artistic appreciation of the superior beauty of the natural form had also developed, and then there came, instead of the childish, unconscious nudity, one that was intentional and artistic. This stage was of course reached at different times by different communities, and tradition had much to do with prolonging the life of the primitive nudity, especially for divinities. Bronze, b?ing less susceptible to color than wood or stone, had to omit or express by graving or raised surfaces what was painted upon the other materials; otherwise material had not much influence on expression. Large plane surfaces with sharp angles, when found in stone, show not an imitation of wood technique but the blocking out of the figure, — a stage beyond which the skilled artist would go to the more perfect roundness, and at which the unskilled artist, whether early or provincial, would stop. As to the position of the hands, after the lifeless hanging at the sides was outgrown, they were shown as held in front of the body because this was the most natural way to dispose of them. The earliest expression of the action of the person on the drapery is perhaps found in a female torso in high relief from the Acropolis, where the ends of the sash are parted in front by a hand held before the stomach. The holding up of the skirt at one side by the Acropolis maidens and many other figures was due to the same desire for expression of personality.

The Frieze of the Hecatompedon. — In *Sitzb. MUn. Akad.* 1906, pp. 143-150, A. Fcrtwangleb criticises Schrader's theory *(A.J.A.* X, p. 414) of the Ionic frieze on the Pisistratean Hecatompedon. He argues that there is no evidence for an Ionic frieze on a Doric temple of the sixth century, and that in any case the slabs in the Acropolis Museum are too large for the building. They may have decorated the great altar of Athena. He also combats briefly Jacobsthal's view that the attributes held by two of the Tritopatores (or Typhon) are thunderbolts.

The Group of the Tyrannicides. — A new restoration of the group of Harmodius and Aristogiton has been made in plaster at the Ducal Museum in Brunswick, under the direction of P. J. Meier, who describes and justifies it in *Rom. Mitt.* XX, 1905, pp. 330-347 (pi.; 2 figs.).

The Charioteer of Delphi. —In *Ath. Mitt.* XXXI, 1906, pp. 421-42!), F. Von Duhn suggests that if Washburn's reading of the erased inscription on the base of the charioteer at Delphi *(A.J.A.* X, pp. 153, 194) is correct, it is probable that the group was originally ordered by Anaxilas of Rhegium, and after his death paid for and dedicated by Polyzalus, brother of Hiero. If this is right, it is almost certain that it is the work of Pythagoras of Rhegium.

A Terra-cotta Statue at Catania. — In *R. £t. Anc.* IX, 1907, pp. 121131 (2 pis.), W. Deonna publishes the terra-cotta statue of a woman in the museum at Catania. Its origin is uncertain, but it is probably an original work of the first quarter of the fifth century B.C. It derives additional importance from the rarity of large terra-cotta statues of this period, though specimens from the sixth and fourth centuries are fairly numerous.

Calamis. — The elder and younger Calamis are discussed in *Ahh. Sachs. Ges.* XXV, No. 4, by F. Studniczka, who accepts in general Reisch's view *(A.J. A.* XI, p. 216), but differs widely from him in the distribution of the recorded works between the two sculptors. To the younger Calamis are assigned the Erinys at Athens, possibly the Asclepius at Sicyon, and certainly the Sosandra. This famous statue is probably the original of the numerous statuettes and reliefs representing a dancer wrapped in a mantle which also covers her head. The elder sculptor was probably a Boeotian, a pupil of Onatas, and active from about 470-440 n.c. To him are assigned, in addition to the works given by Reisch, the Nike at Olympia, the statues of Hermione and Alcmene, the Aphrodite dedicated on the Acropolis by Callias, the quadriga, whose driver was probably by the elder Praxiteles, and which seems to have been later placed on the great pedestal before the Propylaea in honor of Agrippa, the Apollo Alexicacus in Athens, whose surname only is due to the plague, and the Hermes and Dionysus at Tanagra. Extant works by him cannot with certainty be identified. Possibly the Apollo in the Museo delle Therme at Rome is a copy of the Alexicacus, and if so the "Demeter " of Cherchel may be the Aphrodite. (E. Studniczka, *Kalamis, ein lieitrag zur griechischen Kunstgeschichte.* Leipzig, 1907, B. G. Teubner. 104 pp.;" 13 pis.; 19 figs. 8vo. M 7.20.)

Leda and the Swan. —In *B. Mus. F. A.* V, 1907, p. 15 (fig.). S. N. D(eane) publishes with brief comment the marble group of Leda and the Swan in the Boston Museum of Fine Arts (*A.J.A.* IX, p. 367). It is a work of the end of the fifth century by a somewhat unskilful sculptor.

The Pseliumene of Praxiteles. — In *R. Arch.* IX, 1907, pp. 69-74, F. Poulsev explains that a *iptiov* is a single ring, whether large or small, and more especially a bracelet, while a necklace is ordinarily a οΤpem-ov, composed of several *KpUoi.* The Pseliumene of Praxiteles was therefore probably putting on a bracelet, not a necklace. In the " Venus Montalvo" (published by Milani, *Strena Ifelbigiana,* p. 188; now in America, see *A J.A.* IX, p. 375), Poulsen sees a later adaptation of the motive of the Pseliumene, though the "Venus Montalvo" is taking off, not putting on, her bracelet.

The Tegean Sculptures of Scopas. — In *Sitzb. Miin. Akad.* 1906. pp. 383-388, A. Fuktwangler agrees with E. Gardner that the female head and torso at Tegea (see *A J.A.* X, pp. 445-446) belong to the Atalanta of Scopas. The figures of the east pediment, except the boar, seem to have been of Parian, those of the west, to which the heads in Athens belong, of Doliana marble. The style of the head agrees with the female heads assigned to Scopas in *Meistervoerke der griech. Plaslik,* p. 639.

The Statue from Subiaco and the Niobid Chiaramonti. — In *Ausonia,* I, 1906, pp. 21-32 (3 figs.), E. Brizio argues that the statue of the kneeling youth from Nero's villa at Subiaco represents a Niobid. The base represents rocky ground such as is found on the base of one of the Florentine figures. The moulding on the base is a later addition, made when the statue was separated from the group. A similar treatment of the base is found in the Niobid Chiaramonti. The evidence that this statue was discovered in the Villa Hadriana is very weak, and it is more probable that it came from Subiaco. Both statues are original works of the fourth century, and apparently by Scopas.

A Terra-cotta Head in the Antiquarium in Berlin. — In *R. Arch.* VIII, 1906, pp. 402-408 (pi.), W. Deonna publishes and discusses a large (height 0.25 m.) terra-cotta head from Tarentum, now in the Antiquarium in Berlin. It resembles in many respects the "Praying Boy" in Berlin, and is modelled entirely by hand. Its date is the end of the fourth or early in the third century B.C. Other statues of terra-cotta are mentioned, and the group from Civita Vecchia, now in the Villa Giulia, at Rome, is described. These are of the same date. At that time some real artists made terra-cotta statues, as they had also done in the sixth century.

The Maiden from Antium. — The statue of a maiden bearing a tray which was found at Antium in 1878 (*A J.A.* VI-II, p. 307) has been bought by the Italian government and placed in the Museo Nazionale at Rome. The statue is discussed in *Boll. Arte,* I, 1907, v, pp. 19-23 (2 pis.; 2 figs.), by A. Della Seta, who argues that it is probably a temple servant of Apollo, intent upon the care of some sacred objects. The working of the marble shows that it was to be seen from the side. It is probably au early Hellenistic work.

In *Nuova Anlolnt/ia,* May 16, 1907, F. Peli.ati suggests that the statue represents a Thespiad, and may be the work of Cleomenes, if it is not one of the statues by Praxiteles brought from Corinth by Mummius. It could have been brought to Antium by Claudius or Nero after the burning of the temple of Felicitas. The statue is published by W. Amelung, in BrunnBruckmann, *DenkmSler,* II, 583-4, and by Reinach, *Repertoire,* III, 193, 6.

The Hero iirl BXa«T. — Light is thrown on the various statements about the word BXaiVij (slipper), as the name of a goddess or heroine (*C.I.A.* Ill, 411), of a place in Athens (Hesychius s.c), and as a designation for a hero (pws 'AOrlvrlaiv 6 iirl HXavry, Pollux, *Onnm. Z,* 87) by the discovery on the south slope of the Acropolis of the votive stele with a sandal in relief. (*AJ.A.* IX, p. 108; XI, p. 217.) It seems likely that there was at this point the shrine of a hero, whose name gave rise to the use of a slipper as his symbol. This would explain the name in Pollux, and also his statement about a shoemaker who dedicated the stone image of a slipper. (C. Tsoi'ntas, "Ei/. 'Apx-1906, pp. 243-248; fig.)

The Dionysus of the Great Frieze at Pergamon. — In *R. Arch.* VIII. 1906, pp. 409-112, P. Ducati discusses the figure of Dionysus in the frieze of the Great Altar at Pergamon, and, by comparing it with the figure on the vase from Kertsch, on which Dionysus is a witness of the strife between Athena and Poseidon, and with other monuments, he reaches the conclusion that it was derived from a representation of the battle of the gods and giants, dating probably from the latter part of the fourth century.

The Trial of Orestes. — The various reliefs representing the trial of Orestes are compared by W. Ameluno in *RSm. Milt.* XX, 1905, pp. 289-309 (2 pis.; 4 figs.), with fresh evidence from a New Attic relief, a fragment of which is in the Antiquarium at Rome. Special prominence is given to the interpretation of the Corsini silver cup.

The Reliefs of Apollo Citharoedus. — In considering for a second time (see *A J.A.* XI, p. 213) the backgrounds of the reliefs representing Apollo Citharoedus, F. Stcdniczka admits that the scene, which he interpreted as a view of the

Pythium and Olympieum at Athens, may also represent the sanctuary at Delphi; for although the great temple of Apollo was always Doric, it does appear on coins at least as Corinthian, and the reliefs may have used the same liberty. *(Jb. Arch. I.* XXII, 1907, pp. 6-8; fig.)

A Sarcophagus of the Sidamara Type. — Nine fragments of a very beautiful sarcophagus of Greek marble, now at Doughty Hall, Richmond, England, are published and discussed by J. Strzygowski in *J.II.S.* XXVII, 1907, pp. 99-122 (5 pis.; 16 figs.). Single figures of pure fourth century and Praxitelean type stand before niches which are flanked by columns and have the tympanum ornamented with a shell. Such niches, in groups of five, occur notably on the Sidamara and Selefkah sarcophagi at Constantinople, also in Pompeian wall paintings of the fourth style, on the throne of St. Maximian at Ravenna, and in various examples of Christian art. They were originally imitated from the facade of the stage of a theatre, and the earlier examples, especially the sarcophagi, are Syrian. The idea may have originated in Antioch. In *Burl. Mag.* XI, 1907, pp. 109-111, E. Strong points out that these sarcophagi and the ivories show a creative power inconsistent with Straygowski's theory that Hellenism succumbed to Oriental art, which tends to substitute ornament for the human figure.

VASES AND PAINTING

Vases from Crete in the Louvre. —In *B.C.H.* XXXI, 1907, pp. 115-138 (pi.; 4 figs.), E. Pottier begins the publication of important additions to the collection in the Louvre since the appearance of his *Vases Antiques du Louvre*. This article describes four vases from a tomb near Ligortyno in Crete. The first is a rhyton in the form of a bull's head. The others are craters, one decorated with a design of wild goats on either side of a palm (?) tree with a fish below, another with a large polyp, the third with curved lines. All belong to the later Cretan or Mycenaean period. Much of the article is given to a discussion of the significance of these decorations. The bull, goat, polyp, and fish have originally religious significance, and are reproduced with magical intent. The artistic forms, but not the religious value, are influenced by the Orient. The tendency of these designs is to become decorative, with a reminiscence of the good results such representations may bring to the owners. No extended religious symbolism is to be found in the groupings or decorative developments of these simple elements.

Catalogues of Cypriote Vases. — In 1899 the Athenian National Museum acquired at Alexandria a collection of Cypriote antiquities, including vases, terra-cottas, glass, and bronze weapons and tools. A catalogue of these vases is published in *Bulletin de VInstitut genevois,* XXXVII, 1907, pp. 405-442 (also separately, Geneva, 1907, Librairie Kiindig; 3 fr.), by G. Nicole. After a brief account of the collection and of a few noteworthy pieces, he describes 318 vases, using the classification adopted by Myres and Ilichter in their *Catalogue of the Cyprus Museum. Ibid.* pp. 443-481 (also separately, 3.50 fr.), the same author publishes a similar catalogue of the Cypriote vases (857 numbers) in the museum at Constantinople. They came to the museum in 1873, along with terra-cottas and sculptures from the Cesnola collection.

Athenian Wedding Gifts. —In *Ath. Mitt.* XXXII, 1907, pp. 79-122 (5 pis.; 18 figs.), A. Brueknkr discusses the vases given as presents to the Athenian bride, and their decoration. After considering a vase representing the entrance of the bride into her new home, and others referring to the wedding-night, he takes up the Kpaulia, or gifts brought to the bride by her friends on the day after the wedding. This presentation, or sometimes the marriage procession, is regularly represented on the yofiucos or *w/xtfiiKos tB-ns,* which seems to have been a common present, and to have been used for bringing a warm breakfast to the newly married pair. Many of these vases are published and fully discussed. As presents, judging from their pictures, were also given hydriae, lecythi, pyxides, and other vases. Unlike the loutrophoros, which appears as wedding gift, and also as vase for the dead, the lebes was connected only with the wedding. The wedding gifts, preserved as ornaments in the house, were buried with the wife at her death. A comparison of such vases with funeral vases in the same grave would give evidence for the length of the married life. It is also argued that in Athens weddings were regularly celebrated at the end of Gamelion, and that the brides all offered to Aphrodite on the fourth of Anthesterion. This scene is shown on many of the small vases with gilded decoration.

The Use of the «vos or fcrlvirrpov. — In *Berl. Phil. W.* 1907, cols. 286-287, R. Engklmann argues that the oios or *lirlvryrpov* was used in preparing the thread for weaving. The woman rolled the thread on the ovos to remove uneven places which might have arisen in the spinning.

The Tablet of Ni(i)nion. — In E£. 'Ap. 1906, pp. 197-212, D. Philios examines anew the interpretation of the much-discussed Eleusinian tablet dedicated by Ni(i)nion, which was first published by Skias *Ibid.* 1901, pp. 1-39 and 163-174. (See *A.J.A.* VI, pp. 207, 471.)

An Attic Vase from the Crimea. — Fragments of a large Attic vase *(ca.* 450 B.C.) found in the Crimea about 1877, and now in the Hermitage at St. Petersburg, are discussed by P. Dccati in *Riim. Mitt.* XXI, 1906, pp. 98-141 (2 pis.; fig.), who explains the scene as the slaying of Argos, and makes many comparisons, in particular with the hydria belonging to J. C. Iloppin. *(Harvard Studies in Classical Philology,.* XII, pp. 335 ft.; *A. J.A.* V, p. 469.)

Heracles and the Hydra. — In *Ausonia,* I, 1906, pp. 33-35 (pi.), G. Patisoni discusses a hydria with a representation of Heracles killing the Hydra. The monster is concealed in great part by an alter, on which is a sort of platter containing a boy's head. This is interpreted as the remains of a human sacrifice, offered to the Hydra as to other monsters. The vase is the one published by Sambon in *Le Musee,* III, 1906, p. 431, *A.J. A.* XI, p. 227, as the finding of Erichthonius.

Heracles and Linus. —In *R. Arch.* IX, 1!07, pp. 84-93 (pi.; 4 figs.), R. Engelmann discusses a vase painting in the Bibliotheque Nationale (De Ridder, *Vases de la Bibl. nat.* II, p. 470, No. 811), in which a youth is striking an old man with a stool. A diptych hung on the wall indicates that the scene is a schoolroom. Three other vases and a relief on a sarcophagus in the Museo Pio-Clementino prove that the killing of Linus by Heracles is represented. Literary allusions show that the story was familiar in the fourth century and later.

An Aryballus in Berlin. —In *Ausonia*, I, 1906, pp. 36-50 (6 figs.), P. Ducati publishes a small aryballus, with scenes from a centauromachia. It is Attic work of about 370-360 B.C., and is a good example of the somewhat decadent style of the fourth century. The characteristics of the later Attic vases are analyzed at some length and the examples grouped, with differences in detail from the classification and chronology of Furtwiingler.

The Birth of Dionysus. — In *"Earla*, February 15 (28), 1907 (fig.), Dr. K. Lambros points out that the legendary births of Dionysus and Asclepius are the earliest examples of the Caesarian operation. He publishes from a vase in the British Museum a group which he interprets as Zeus seated on an altar with the bandage about his thigh, and holding the little Dionysus in his arms.

The Fight over Temesa. — The picture described by Pausanias (VI, 6, 11) of the Locrian hero Euthymus in combat with a monster named Alybas, has been reconstructed by E. Maass and made the occasion for a series of essays on subjects connected with the Iapygian peninsula, — Hera Lacinia, the spring of Leuce, and the relation of pagan and Christian myths, the myth of Temesa and its embodiment in poetry and painting. *(Jb. A rch. I.* XXII, 1907, pp. 18-53.)

Nealces.—J. Six, in *Jb. Arch. I.* XXII, 1907 (pp. 1-6; fig.) discusses a new reading of Fronto's line, *Quid si Parrhasium cersicolora pingere iuberet... out Nenlcen magnifica.. .,* making the deduction that Nealces painted on a small scale, but not necessarily small pictures. (See *ibid.* XXIII, pp. 34 ff.; *A J. A.* VII, p. 475.) INSCRIPTIONS

Corrections to Attic Inscriptions. — In *Cl. Phil.* II, 1907, p. 100. D. M. Robinson makes a few corrections to the inscriptions on Kiovutkot near the Dipylon, published by Mylonas, "Ei£. 'Ap. 1893, pp. 221-224.

Researches in Athenian and Delian Documents. — In *Klio,* VII, 1907, pp. 213-240, W. S. Ferguson publishes some results of his study of Athenian and Delian inscriptions. It is probable that the Athenian priests of Artemis were chosen according to the official order of the tribes, and that the same tribe held the priesthoods of Asclepius and Artemis in successive years. The same rule seems to have prevailed at Delos in the period 166/5-103/2 B.C. for the choice of the priests of the Great Deities, Serapis, and Aphrodite. The following dates for Athenian archons are suggested: Aristaechmus, 159/8; Meton. 144/3; Dionysius, 141/0; Xenon, 121/0; Sosicrates, 111/0; Heracleides, 108/7; Demochares, 94/3 or much later. The history of the sanctuaries of the Foreign Gods on the Inopus at Delos is traced in detail. The Athenian cleruchy was established in 167/6 B.C., but the decrees of the cleruchs cease in 131 B.C., and later honorary statues are set up by Athenians, Romans, Greeks, and others. It is probable that this revolution was connected with the servile disturbances of about 131 B.C.

A Dedication by Antigonus Doson. — In *B.C.H.* XXXI, 1907, pp. 94114 (fig.), M. Hollkacx publishes the inscription *A.J.A.* X, p. 104) from a dedication to Apollo by Antigonus Doson and the Macedonians after the battle of Sellasia, 222 B.C. As Antigonus died near the end of 221 B.C., the date of the dedication is closely fixed. A full discussion leads to the conclusion that after the battle of Andros Egyptian rule ceased in most of the Cyclades, but that Antigonus established Macedonian suzerainty only over a few, including Delos. The rest remained independent or under Rhodian protection until in 202 B.C. Philip V converted the Aegean into a "Macedonian lake."

A Delian Law. —In *B.C.H.* XXXI, 1907, pp. 40-93 (3 pis.), E. SchulHof and P. Huvklin publish with a detailed discussion the Delian law regulating the sale of wood and charcoal *A J.A.* X, p. 104) by importers. It requires the sole use of public weights, the sale at exactly the price set in the declaration made at the custom house, and the immediate delivery of the goods. Heavy penalties are fixed, but these are much lightened for the aTtXtls. The provisions show curious analogies to various mediaeval laws. The article also gives some account of an unpublished Delian *upa. rvyypafr),* regulating the leases of sacred lands.

A Delian Decree. — In *Herinea,* XI.II, 1907, pp. 330-333, A. Wilrelm argues that the inscription from Delos, *B.C.H.* XXVIII, p. 138. No. 34, is the second part of the inscription *ibid.* p. 281, No. 9. The object of the decree is to free the property of Hegestratus, or Herostratus, from liability to seizure by creditors of the community of Delos. but not from the claims of his private creditors. The end of the second inscription and the beginning of the first should be read: *prjSk Tsv* 7rpos *rrjp iroiv* o-w77AXax *Tiav fir/ St lav* Tis *va-rtpov* awaAAa£i;i, *iav prj* Tts *ISlai rvp.fiaXrn irpb%* H.. *arparov.*

The Revolution of 363 B.C., at Delphi. — In *Klio,* VI, 1906, pp. 400-419 (fig.), II. Pomtow publishes corrections to the text of the documents in Delphi relating to the property of the exiles of 363 and 346 B.C. These confirm his earlier views *Klio,* VI, pp. 89 ff.) and add some details. He argues that between the Tholos and the eastern temple of Athena in the Marmoria were two temples of the later sixth century, one Doric, the other Ionic. These were surrounded on three sides by the slabs containing the records of banishment and of the disposal of confiscated property.

The Pythian Stadium and the Law concerning Wine. — In 'E£. 'Apx 1906, pp. 157-186 (8 figs.), A. D. Keramopoullos discusses the law inscribed on the southern retaining wall of the stadium at Delphi, forbidding the bringing of wine into the stadium. He criticises the interpretations of Frazer *(Pausanias,* V, pp. 394 and 200) and of Homolle *(B.C.H.* XXIII, p. (ill) and reads ts *Tov Spo/xov* (=cts To. *Tov* oraoYov *piprf)* instead of ts To E *vSpopov,* a reading which is not justified by the stone, and introduces an unknown hero *Ev&popos.* The terrace below the stadium at this point was apparently occupied by dressing rooni6 for the contestants, which were replaced by others at a higher level when the stadium was remodelled, probably at a time previous to the reconstruction by Herodes Atticus.

Inscriptions from Heraclea. — In *Philologus,* IX, 1854, pp. 392 f., A. Baumeister published four inscriptions said to have been found by Gabras on the little island of Heraclea near Naxos. In *Ath. Mitt.* XXXI, 1906, pp. 565-567, F. Hillek von Gaertringen points out that all seem to be from Perinthus, called Heraclea during the later empire. A genuine inscription from the island Heraclea was published by J. Delamarre in *Recue de Philologie,* XXVI, 1902, pp. 291 ff.

An Archaic Inscription from Cumae. — The inscription from Cumae. published by Sogliano *(Not. Scav.* 1905, p. 377) is further examined by D. Comparetti in *Ausonia,* I, 1906, pp. 13-20 (fig.). He reads: Oi *Offus ivTovOa KtiaOai* (t)i *fir) Tov /3tf3a.xxtvfitvov.* It certainly contains the prohibition of a Bacchic 0tao-os against profane interments in its ground. Such exclusiveness in burial has hitherto been known in antiquity only among the Jews and early Christians. The fifth century, to which the inscription belongs, was the time when Dionysiac worship flourished. The Bacchic elements in the Orphic mysteries, and their prevalence in Magna Graecia are also discussed.

Epigraphic Bulletin. — In *R. £t. Or.* XX, 1907, pp. 38-96, A. J. Reinach notices the contributions to the study of Greek inscriptions which appeared in 1905 and 1906, either as separate works or in ninety-one periodicals.

COINS

The Corpus Nummorum Graecorum. — In *Klio,* VII, 1907, pp. 1-18, H. Von Fritze describes the preliminary studies, which are necessary if the *Corpus Nummorum Graecorum* is to make the material really available to the historian and archaeologist. The valuable results of these methods are shown in the treatment of the Macedonian and Paeonian coinage by II. Gabler in Vol. III, 1 of *Die antiken Miinzen Nord-Griechenlands* (Berlin, 1906), published by the Berlin Academy.

Early Greek Money. — In *J. Int. Arch. Num.* IX, 1906, pp. 153-236 (11 pis.; 23 figs.), I. N. Svoronos publishes part of his lectures on Numismatics at the University of Athens in 1906-07. After a brief sketch of the history of the Athenian collection of coins, he considers early Greek money, treating first briefly various non-metallic standards of value, and then considering the metallic money. The names for the early forms are derived from the shapes given to the masses of metal, and do not necessarily indicate fixed weights. The Homeric Ittxtktis (851) are identified with the masses of bronze in the shape of double axe-heads found in Sardinia, Cyprus, Mycenae, Phaestus, and in the sea off Euboea. The weight varies from 37 kg. to 23 J kg. Similar masses of metal are borne by tributaries on Egyptian monuments. The signs on these pieces probably indicate the weight. The tus-tXt/tKa have not been found. In the same way the Homeric raXavTov of gold is not a weight but denotes a piece of metal in the form of the pan of a pair of scales, like the gold disks from Mycenae. The iron *Ttixiivoi* of Lycurgns were money of the same kind. The iron ojStAot retired by Pheidon are represented by the bars of iron, slightly pointed like oxgoads, which were found at the Argive Heraeum, and of which six make a handful *(Spaxfiij).* The large iron bar found with the *of3tXoi* is the same length (1.20 m.) and is probably the standard for determining the length. Such metal masses were also the Cyprian *iyicupai.* The "fish " of Olbia, and the coins of Nemausus which end in a pig's leg, owe their shape to the use as currency of fish among the Scythians and hams in Gaul. The Cretan TpiVoSts and *XtB-nrts* are not named from objects used as money, but from stamps on the reverse of didrachms coined in twelve Cretan cities.

Coinage of Peparethus. — A group of silver coins, having a bunch of grapes as the design of the obverse and connected by identities of die, is discussed by W. Wroth in *J.H.S.* XXVII, 1907, pp. 90-98 (pi.; 3 figs.), and tentatively assigned to Peparethus. They belong to the period before 470 B.C. With them he publishes a silver coin with grapes and dolphins, as yet unidentified, and three small bronze coins of Peparethus which are of considerably later dates.

Eccentricities of Coin Engraving. — In *Le Musee, TV,* 1907, pp. 14-'144 (pi-), L. Forhkr calls attention to some eccentricities in the engraving of Greek coins. On a bronze coin of Athens (second century A.d.) the helmet of Athena shows the profile of a man. On two tetradrachms of Agrigentum (fifth century B.C.) the body of the crab resembles respectively the face of a lion and a bucranium.

The NfiE Coins of Apamea. —In *Z. Alttest. Wins.* XXVII, 1907, pp. 73-74, J. B. Selbst discusses the correctness of published representations of coins of Apamea bearing the legend NfiE.

Heracles and Eros. —In *B. Hoc. Ant. Fr.* 1906, pp. 385-388 (fig.), A. Dieudonne discusses the reverse of a bronze coin of Temenothyrae (Head, *Catalogue of Coins in British Museum: Phri1gia,* p. 410, 12). It represents Heracles, holding a torch in his extended right hand, before a column on which is a statue of Athena. Behind the column a small Eros flees from Heracles. The representation of Heracles pursuing Eros with a lighted torch, as if to singe his wings, seems unique.

An Attic Coin Weight. — In */. Int. Arch. Num.* IX, 1907, pp. 237-244 (fig.), I. N. Svoronos describes a copper disk, with a wreathed head and the inscription *TtTpdSpaxhy* obverse, and on the reverse a galloping horse. It is not a coin, and as the weight (17.50 gr.) agrees with that of the Attic tetradrachm, it is probably a piece used to test the weight of the silver coins. The head with the wreath suggests a connection with the

Spaxfuil 2,T«(lavr)il6pov, which were probably issued from a mint in the heroutn of Stephanephorns.

GENERAL AND MISCELLANEOUS

Primitive Shield-Devices and Coin Types. — In /. *Int. Arch. Num.* IX, 1906, pp. 5-45 (pi.), C. Gerojannis discusses the earliest shield-devices as known from the literature or works of art, and points out their similarity to designs on early coins. He argues that the Gorgoneion in these devices is not connected with the myth of the Gorgon or with Oriental human masks, but is derived from hideous heads of animals considered as demons and representing the idea of *ip6Bos*. The animal and monstrous representations on shields and coins alike have no mythological or astronomical meaning, but are purely apotropaeic.

The Excavations in Crete. —In *R. Bill.* XIV, 1907, pp. 1-64, 163206 (6 pis. ; 22 figs.), M. J. Lagrange gives a detailed account of the excavations in various parts of Crete during the last seven years. No new material is published, but a valuable summary of the reports up to date.

In *Gaz. B.-A.* XXXVII, 1907, pp. 89-113 (17 figs.), R. Dussaud reports those discoveries in Crete which throw light on pre-Hellenic art and architecture. He describes the more important objects in the museum at Candia, and the remains at Cnossus and Phaestus.

East Asiatic Ornaments and Cretan Art. — In *Metnnon,* I, 1907, pp. 44-69 (7 figs.), A. Reichel points out that the conventional Cretan representations of earth by ragged patches scattered over the surface of the decorated object are analogous to the forms seen in the earliest Chinese and Japanese art. The Shang dynasty in China was contemporary with Mycenaean civilization, and the art of its period was characterized by the frequent use of the so-called "cloud," which is really the same as the irregular patches scattered over the background of Mycenaean vases and bronzes. These "clouds " are combined in the same way with men and animals, and are used to fill up vacant places between figures. In both arts they serve purely ornamental purposes. It is not likely that these conventions reached China from Europe, but it is probable that they came to Europe from China, especially as there is ancient evidence of the importation of silk and other East Asiatic commodities. Possibly both countries were influenced by the primitive civilization that had its seat in the Tarim basin of Central Asia.

The Land of Odysseus. — The identity of the Homeric and the modern Ithaca is maintained in a recent book by N. K. Pavlatos, a native of the island. His own discussion (pp. 1-179) is a detailed examination of the evidence, and a somewhat polemical denial of Dorpfeld's conclusions. To this he adds a translation of a portion of *Wintertagen auf Ithaka* by the Archduke Ludwig Salvator (pp. 180-209), and of the chapters in G. Lang's *Untersuchungen zur Geographie. der Odyssee* (pp. 210-306), which treat of Leucas, Dulichium, Asteris, and Ithaca. (X. K. Pavlatos, 'H *Harpls Tov* '08t)crrc(o9. Athens, 1907. 308 pp.; map. 8vo.)

In *Hermes,* XL11, 1907, pp. 326-327, E. Bethf. points out that in the Alcmaeonis Penelope had two brothers, Alyzeus and Leucadios, and in *II.* IV, 421, Odysseus avenges a companion Aevxos. The authors of these passages had no suspicion that Leucas had ever been named Ithaca.

TA dpxeuiTjpa Aiovwia. — In *CI. Phil.* II, 1907, pp. 25-42, E. Capps discusses the meaning of Ta *apxP Aiovvcria* in Thucydides II, 15. The phrase refers to the Anthesteria, and distinguishes this festival from the other apx"" *Aiovvaux,* the Lenaea. As all the ancient sanctuaries outside of the Acropolis are grouped by Thucydides in the same part of the city, the Lenaeum must be sought near the temple e'y Aii/cus. The latter is identified with the temple discovered by Dorpfeld within the Dionysium, in which the *Xrjvos* is actually preserved.

Topographical and Epigraphical Notes on Cephissia.—In 'E£.'Apx1900. pp. 187-190, S. X. Dragocmes calls attention to ancient remains and an inscription showing that the villa of Herodes Atticus at Cephissia had a greater extent than hitherto supposed.

The Heracleum of the Battle of Salamis. — In "E«p. 'Apx-1906, pp. 239-244 (fig.), P. H. Rediades identifies as the Heracleum mentioned by Diodorus and Plutarch in their accounts of the battle of Salamis an enclosure 230 ft. square, formed by large blocks of stone set in the ground at regular intervals, and situated at the inner end of the bay of Keratsinion, near the straits of Salamis. The determination of the location of this heroum helps greatly in understanding the different accounts of the battle.

The Topography of Argoa.— In *B. C.H.* XXXI, 1907, pp. 139-184 (I pis.; 11 figs.), W. Vollgrafk first describes the remains of prehistoric houses on the Aspis of Argos *AJ.A.* X, p. 342), and then discusses in detail the topography of the ancient city. Few remains are left above ground, as the site has been continually inhabited since ancient times. The article treats of the Larissa, the Aspis, the city walls, the temples of the Pythian Apollo and Athena, the Stadium, the Agora, the Gymnasium of Cylarabis, the temples of Artemis, and the temple of Ares and Aphrodite. In each case the literary evidence is given and also a careful description of the remains and of the results of recent trial excavations.

The Topography and Monuments of Delphi. — In *Ath. Mitt.* XXXI, 1906, pp. 437-504 (4 pis.; 32 figs.), II. Pomtow begins the publication of a study of the monuments and topography of Delphi, based on a careful examination of the existing remains and the literature. The studies follow the course of the Sacred Way, and show that Pausanias never leaves this road, and describes only such monuments as are on it or visible from it. This is also true of Plutarch. The present article discusses: (1) The chief entrance, its steps, and the basins for holy water (pp. 441-443); (2) The statue of Phayllus of Croton (pp. 444-450), which stood on a large circular basis *(ca.* 2.37 m. in diameter) at the left inside the entrance. A note (p. 504) gives Dorpfeld's view that this basis is far too large to have supported only a single figure; (3) The Bull of Corcyra (pp. 450-400), which stood on the right inside the entrance: (4) The Monument of the Arcadians (pp. 461-491), which occupied a long base beyond the Hull; (5) The Monument of Lysander erected after the battle of Aegospotami (pp. 492563), which was placed in the large niche behind and above the statues of the Arcadians.

In the case of each monument all the stones which can be identified are exactly described, the inscriptions given, and a reconstruction of the bases attempted, while for the last three monuments the arrangement of the statues is discussed in detail by II. Bullr. The extremely minute character of these important studies precludes a brief summary of the results.

The Date of the Heraeum at Olympia. — In *Sitzb. Miln. Akad.* 1906, pp. 467-484, A. Furtwangler discusses the recent discoveries in the Heraeum at Olympia *AJ.A.* XI, p. 93). The bronze statuette belongs to a clearly defined group which certainly belongs to the seventh century B.C. The Heraeum was therefore built after the middle of the seventh century, as was to lie inferred from all other archaeological evidence. The pottery recently found is like some discovered in the earlier excavations and is certainly postMycenaean, as iron was found in considerable quantities in the lowest stratum. The bronzes from Chortata on Leucas are contemporary with the Olympian bronze, and the pottery from Nidri may well belong to the same period.

The Topography of Olympia.— In *Klin,* VI. 1906. pp. 380-392 (plan), L. Weniger discusses the Hippodamium at Olympia. The cult and temenos of Hippodamia are older than those of Pelops. The temenos was probably in the northeast corner of the Altis, between the Metroum and the Echo Hall, though the evidence is scanty. In this neighborhood many fragments of bronze votive offerings were found. As Kara *rqv irofiiriKrlv* trroSov (Paus. VI, 20, 7) can only refer to the gate at the southwest corner of the Altis, where there is no room for the Hippodamium, it is best to read *Spoautrni* for *irofiirutrjv. Ibid.* VII,

1907, pp. 145-182 (3 figs.), the same writer discusses the cult of the Mother of the Gods and kindred deities. The stone altar at the west of the Metroum is contemporary with the temple. The original altar was at the southwest corner of the temple, and partly covered by its walls. The altar near the treasury of the Sicyoniang, originally circular, belonged to the Cure tea. The small sanctuary north of it is the chapel of Eileithyia and Sosipolis, and probably occupies the site of the artificial Idaean cave (Pindar, *Ol.* V, 17 ff.). This article is a discussion of mythological rather than archaeological questions.

Cyriacus of Ancona at Samothrace. — In September, 1444, Cyriacus of Ancona visited Samothrace and copied some of the inscriptions and sculptures. The accounts of this visit in his letters and journal, together with the drawings and the text of the unpublished inscriptions, are edited in *Ath. Mitt.* XXXI, 1!)06, pp. 405-414 (3 figs.), by E. Zierarth.

The Canal of Xerxes. —In *Jb. Kl. Alt.* XIX, 1907, pp. 115-130 (pi.), A. Struck gives the results of a measured survey of the course of Xerxes' canal across the peninsula of Mt. Athos. The canal can be traced in a series of shallow ditches and low banks, which follow a somewhat irregular line across the isthmus. The length agrees very closely with the statements of Herodotus. The article also contains a summary of the ancient statements and of the narratives of modern travellers.

An Onyx Cameo. —In if. *Arch.* VIII, 1906, p. 449 (2 figs.), Andrew Lang publishes a white onyx cameo on the front of which are two lions and a pillar, resembling the relief over the Lions' Gate at Mycenae. The back is carved in imitation of masonry. The cameo is probably antique.

Throwing the Discus. —In *J.H.S.* XXVII, 1907, pp. 1-36 (3 pis.; 24 figs.)E. Normav Gardiner discusses the Homeric o-dAos, perhaps originally a round stone on the seashore, and its successor the metal discus, with the ancient manner of throwing the latter. The whole action, like the modern golf stroke, was a

swing of the whole body, rather than of the arm, and was pivoted on the right foot. The standing Discobolus of the Vatican is measuring his distance from the front line of the /3aA/Jis; Myron's Discobolus is just at the end of the backward swing of the discus which came between the preliminary forward movement in the left hand and the final throw with the right. All the intervening and following positions, which show some variation in the method, are illustrated in vase paintings and statuettes.

Heron's " Cheiroballistra." — For the model of the supposed *cheiroballistra* of Heron, as restored by the French engineer, Victor Prou, and preserved in the museum at St. Germain-en-Laye, all textual foundation has been destroyed by Rudolf Schneider's discovery *(Riim. Mitt.* XXI, 1906, pp. 142-168; 11 figs.) that the manuscripts with which Prou operated really contain a fragment of a Greek manual for engineers and mechanics, and have little or nothing to do with artillery. The obscure fragment was wrongly labelled by some Byzantine scholar, and thus brought into false connection with the name of Heron.

Archaeological Notes. — In *Le Musc'e,* IV, 1907, A. Sambon describes a number of works of Greek art. Pp. 26-27 (pi.) he discusses the bronze statuette of a young dancing satyr in the Walters collection. It is a fine Hellenistic work of the second or first century B. C. On p. 81 (fig.) he publishes an Attic vase, bearing in black outlines on a white ground a representation of Peleus giving the little Achilles to Chiron. A vase from Sicily with a comic scene — an actor with an amphora on his shoulder, and a Paniscus riding a goat — is published, pp. 174-175 (fig-), and a Hellenistic ivory relief with the background out away, representing a young satyr with a girdle of ivy leaves, is described, p. 176 (pi.). On p. 141 (pi.) I. M. describes a Hellenistic bronze statuette of a standing Zeus now in the Morgan collection.

ITALY

ARCHITECTURE

Roman Imperial Architecture. — The development of arcaded and zigzag friezes from rows of wall niches or aediculae with arched or pointed tops is illustrated by B. Schulz in *Jb. Arch. I.* XXI, 1906, pp. 221-230 (8 pls.; 7 figs.). The best examples of Roman architecture of the middle and later Imperial times, in which such wall decoration is especially important, are found in Syria, as there has been less wholesale destruction there than in Europe.

The Temples in the Forum Holitorium. — The group of temples in the Forum Holitorium at Home is discussed by Ch. Hulsen in *Rum. Mitt.* XXI, 1906, pp. 169-192 (pl.; 9 figs.), with special reference to the Doric temple, and the drawings and restorations of the same by Peruzzi, Antonio da Sangallo the Younger, and other Renaissance architects. Hulsen takes issue with It. Delbrtick, and is inclined to identify this temple with that of Juno Sospita, dating in its first form from 197-194 B.C., but restored, with extensive use of travertine, in the time of Sulla. The article also contains a valuable discussion of the probable date at which *lapis Tiburtinus* began to be used for building purposes and inscriptions.

The Ionic Temple near Ponte Rotto. — The Ionic temple by the Tiber near Ponte Rotto has received a thorough examination at the hands of E. K. Fiechter, who publishes his results in *Rom. Milt.* XXI, 1906, pp. 220-279 (7 pls.; 13 figs.). After a careful comparison of details and constructive methods with those of other republican monuments, he assigns the building to the middle of the first century B.C.

The Large Theatre at Pompeii. — In *Arch. Am.* 1906, cols. 301-314 (4 figs.), O. Puchstein discusses and sums up the successive forms of the large theatre at Pompeii, especially those of the stage buildings. He presents some points of difference from the opinions of Mau (*Riim. itt.* XXI, 1906, pp. 1-56; *AJ.A.* XI, p. 99).

SCULPTURE

Unpublished Ancient Statues in Turin. — In *R. Arch.* VIIT, 1907. pp. 872-389 (49 figs.), Seymour Ie Ricci describes seventy-one, and publishes forty-nine, hitherto unpublished statues in the museum at Turin. The cuts are, with three exceptions, very small drawings from photographs. Nearly all the statues are described by Diitschke, *Antilte Bildwerke in Italien,* Vol. IV.

A Roman Tradesman's Sign. — A Roman sign in the Vatican is interpreted by J. Sieveking in *lliim. Mitt.* XXI, 1906, pp. 89-97 (2 figs.). The edifice represented is a nymphaeum at Rome, while the great basin in front, shown in plan instead of perspective for greater emphasis, indicates that fountain basins were furnished by the dealer.

Bronze Decorations on Roman Ships. — In *Ausonia* I, 1906, pp. 103108 (8 figs.), E. Ghislanzoni describes some bronze reliefs, in the form of animals' heads with rings in their jaws, from the sunken ships in the Lake of Nemi, now in the Museo Nazionale at Rome. They probably decorated posts, and the ends of cross-beams, which projected along the gunwale. Similar ornaments are represented on reliefs of ships. The rings held by the animals could not have borne any strain without breaking.

The Ficoroni Cista. — The Ficoroni cista is fully discussed in a dissertation by F. Behn. The inscription shows that the cista was engraved by a Campanian during the first twenty years of the fourth century B.C. The feet and the handle, though derived from Greek models, are Etruscan work and probably somewhat earlier in date. A careful examination of the principal scene leads to the conclusion that the engraver used a Tarentine pattern which in turn was derived from M icon's painting in the Anaceum at Athens. The hunting scenes on the cover also show the influence of Polvgnotan art. (F. Behn, *Die Ficoroninclte Cista, archaeologische Studie.* Leipzig, 1907, B. G. Teubner. 80 pp.; 2 pis. Svo. M. 3.)

Hadrian and Sabina. —In *B. Soc. Ant. Fr.* 1906, pp. 365-366, C. RaVaissonmollien argues that the group in the Louvre (Clarac, *Muse'e,* pl. 326, 1431) probably represents Hadrian and Sabina. The female head does not belong to the statue, and perhaps is a portrait of Faustina.

INSCRIPTIONS

The Date of the Lex Fufia Caninia. — An altar, discovered April, 1906 (see *A. J.A.* XI, p. 100), on the Caelian, near the Via Claudia, has at last settled the long controverted date of the *Lex FuJia Caninia,* and established the correctness of the form *FuJia.* The altar bears on both faces the names of the consuls L. Caninius Gallus and C. Fufius Geminus, *suffecti* in 2 B.C., as we now learn. From this altar we further gain a new street-name, the *View Statae Motrin,* — a divinity believed to stay the progress of a fire. (G. Gatti, *B. Com. Rom.* XXXIV, 1906, pp. 185-208, 2 pls.; and *Not. Scav.* Ill, 1906, pp. 179-180.)

Roman Milestones. — In *Sitzb. Bed. Ak.* 1907, pp. 165-201,0. HntschFei.d discusses the Roman milestones, of which about four thousand are known. The erection of the stones became general in Italy in the time of C. Gracchus, though the earliest example dates from the First Punic War. The earliest provincial stones are also from the time of the Gracchi, though the great development of road-building took place under the empire. The expenses were generally borne by the local authorities and the name of the emperor was placed on the stone to show the imperial character of the road. Under Trajan the Gallic *leuga* replaces the Roman mile in Gallia Celtica, Germania, and the borders of Gallia Belgica. In an appendix it is argued that under Constantine the Gallic *c'witates* were replaced by the cities as governmental units, often with a transference to the city of the old communal name.

Autobiography in Roman Inscriptions. — The autobiographic element in Roman inscriptions is discussed in *Rec. Past,* VI, 1907, pp. 111-110, 141— 145 (5 figs.), by II. H. Armstrong. It appears in metrical dedications, epitaphs, — especially those in verse, — autobiographic records like the socalled milestone of Publius Popilius, and *graffiti.* The autobiographic feeling was strong among the Romans, but in the inscriptions its expression is restricted by a tendency to formulae.

Religious Syncretism and Epigraphy. — The prevalence of syncretism under the Roman empire is exaggerated in literature, which reflects either the views of the cultivated and intellectual pagans or of Christians. Inscriptions offer the only trustworthy information on the subject, and these show that the Greco-Roman and Roman deities were worshiped as individuals distinct from the various foreign deities. Statistics of inscriptions from southern Italy, Sicily, and Sardinia show the prevalence of such worship, its relation to definite centres of cult, and its tendency to overcome the worship of foreign divinities even among foreigners. The statistics are given in tabular form. (V. Macchioko, *R. Arch.* IX, 1907, pp. 141-157 and 258-281.)

A Forged Military Diploma. — In *B. Soc. Ant. Fr.* 1906, pp. 355-357, A. Iikkon De Villefosse describes a military diploma, said to have been found in Palestine. It is a forgery on an antique bronze plate, apparently made in Palestine before 1897, and is copied from the diploma in the Louvre, *C.I.L.* Ill, p. 2328, 70.

Inscriptions relating to Roman Antiquity. — In *R. A rch.* VIII, 1906, pp. 469195, R. Cagnat and M. Besnier give text or references for ninety inscriptions, besides a brief statement of the contents of articles dealing with Roman epigraphy and of epigraphic publications relating to Roman antiquity, published in 1905, June-December. Several of the inscriptions are in Greek. Indices are added, pp. 490-505. *Ibid.* IX, 1907, pp. 347-368, the publications of the first third (January-April) of 1906 are reviewed. Sixty-four texts are published.

COINS

The Early Coinage of Italy. —In *Le Musc'e,* IV, 1907, pp. 105-114 (14 figs.), A. Sambon discusses the early Italian ingots of copper with various stamps, and also the early examples of the *aes grave*. He disputes the Capuan origin of these types, considering them Etruscan, Umbrian, or Sabellian, and dwelling on the importance of Cales, Suessa, and Beneventum. He thinks it better for the present to be guided in the classification by the places where these coins are discovered, and emphasizes the need of further scientific study.

Early Roman and Italian Coinage. — In *Klio,* VI, 1906, pp. 489-524, K. Regling discusses the standard units in the early Roman and Italian coinage. He accepts in general the results obtained by E. J. Hüberlin, *Zum corpus numorum aeris grat is: die Sgstematik des iilteren rbmischen Miinzwesens* (Berlin, 1905), which differ widely from Mommsen's system. Three periods are distinguished after the introduction of the *aes grave,* ca. 335-312, 312-290, 290-268 B.c. In the first period the silver didrachm (7.58 g.) is worth 3 *asses* (272.87 g.) In the second period the didrachm (0.82 g.) corresponds to the *tressis,* or the *as = 2 scriptula*. In this period begin a gold coinage and the appearance of regular series of heavy copper money corresponding to the issues of silver. Iu the third period the *as* becomes semi-libral and equal to the sestertius in value. The weight of the *uncia* and other fractions of the *as,* if the latter was 136.4 g., were decimal and no longer duodecimal. Regling believes that they remained duodecimal and that the *as* was half of a new pound of 327.45, and that the ratio of silver to copper was fixed at 144:1. The older Italian standard (vd/tos) was a didrachm of 8.32 or 8.37 g., which was gradually reduced to about *1* g. When the Romano-Campanian stater was reduced to 6.82 g., Tarentum and other Greek cities were forced to follow. Tables are given of the weights of Italian staters and distaters and a complete list of staters weighing more than 8 g. In an excursus (pp. 525-528), C. F. Lehmann-iiaupt argues that the Roman ounce of 27 g. represents an early copper unit, also used for gold and silver.

The Aminei near Sybaris. — Three incused staters from Magna Graecia, bearing a bull looking backward, and an inscription read MA = 'Art, have been attributed to a city Asia in Bruttium. In reality the inscription is WA = 'A/u, and the coins belong to the Aminei. As the coins resemble those of Sybaris and Siris, it seems these Thessalian colonists were settled near those cities, while their rarity points to only a short period of independence. (E. Pais, *Rend. Acc. Lincei,* XI, 1907, pp. 8-23; fig.)

GENERAL AND MISCELLANEOUS

Aegean Civilization in Sicily. — In *Ausonia,* 1,1906, pp. 1-12 (4 figs.), P. Oust describes certain objects showing intercourse between Sicily and the Aegean lands during pre-Mycenaean and Mycenaean times. Bone sheaths with carved bosses found at Castelluccio and Cava Lazzaro are like others found in the second city at Troy. A small Mycenaean amphora from the shore near Girgenti is an important witness to trading along the open southern coast of Sicily, as well as in the sheltered harbors of the east. A gold ring from Pantalica is decorated with an interlaced pattern of distinctly Mycenaean type.

Weapons of the Villanova Population North of the Apennines. —

In *R. Arch.* IX, 1907, pp. 1-17 (12 figs.), A. Ghenikr, after commenting upon the small number of swords, daggers, spearheads, etc., found among the remains of the Villanova civilization north of the Apennines concludes that the chief offensive weapon of the people was the palstab-axe, which he identifies with the Celtic *caleia*. Defensive arms, helmets, shields, and breastplates seem not to have been used.

Archaeology and the Origin of Rome. — In *R. Slor. Ant.* XT, 1907, pp. 81-99, E. Gabrici discusses the bearing of recent archaeological discoveries on the early history of Rome. He concludes that these discoveries show that the traditions have a basis of truth, however exaggerated and distorted by later writers.

The Rostra and the Comitium. — The controversy in regard to the relation of the rostra to the "tomb of Romulus," and the comitium is continued by E. Petersen in *Riim. Mitt.* XXI, 1906, pp. 193-210, with particular reference to the objections of HUlsen and the theory of Pinza.

The Grove of Anna Perenna. — The grove of Anna Perenna, mentioned by Martial in the famous epigram on the view from the villa of Julius Martialis on Monte Mario, forms the subject of a paper by H. Schknkl in *Riim. Mill.* XXI, 1900, pp. 211-219. The well-known crux, *virgineo cruore gaudet* (IV, 64, 10), is treated at length. A note on the topography of the grove is added by Ch. Iiulsen.

Porta Fontinalis.— In *B. Com. Rom.* XXXVI, 1906, 209-223, L. MorPurgo advances the theory that the Porta Fontinalis in the Servian Wall was at the foot of the Caelian, *i.e.* near S. Stefano Rotoudo. He also holds that the open ground without the gate was known as *Campus minor,* or, where there could be no ambiguity, *Campus.*

Trajan's Column. — At the meeting of the British Academy, May 29, 1907, G. Boxr described his discoveries at Trajan's Column *(A.J.A.* XI, p. 100). It was certainly a sepulchral monument. Excavations in the neighborhood revealed early imperial and republican works, including a tufa wall. It is therefore certain that no great mass of earth was removed to make a place for Trajan's Forum, and the inscription on the column simply refers to the buildings in the Forum and on the surrounding hills, which the column overlooked. The column itself was exactly 100 Roman feet in height. *(A then.* June 1, 1907.)

The Castle of Sant' Angelo. — Colonel Borgatti's researches in Castel Sant' Angelo, as reported in the *Tribuna,* have led him to the following conclusions: The building was begun by Hadrian as a conical pyramid. Antoninus changed and greatly enlarged the plan, choosing the form of a drum upon a square basement, and providing a place of burial for all the Imperial family and their descendants. During the Renaissance it was greatly enlarged as a fortress, and is one of the most remarkable examples of an Italian fortification in use from the fourteenth to the nineteenth century. *Nation,* January 31, 1907.)

The Villa and Tomb of the Furii. — In *Ausonia,* I, 1906, pp. 56-59, F. Grossi-gondi describes the discovery near Tusculum in 1665 of the tomb with inscriptions of the Furii *(C.I.L.* XIV, 2700-2707), and later of votive inscriptions and remains of buildings. The buildings are later than the inscriptions, but seem to show that the villa as well as the tomb of the Furii was in or near the grounds of the Cainaldolese monastery.

Excavations at Herculaneum. — Past excavations at Herculaneum and the objects therein discovered, especially the important bronzes, are described by Ethel R. Barker. *Burl. Mag.* XI, 1907, pp. 144-156 (5 pis.).

Selinus. — In *Le Mu.iee,* IV, 1907, pp. 201-227 (3 pis.; 8figs.), J. Hulot describes briefly a series of drawings in which he has attempted a complete restoration of the city of Selinus, including the houses, public buildings, temples, especially those of the Acropolis, and the harbor. An appreciation of the metopes from Selinus by G. Toudouze, and a description of the coinage by L. Forrer are added.

Notes on Sardinian Archaeology. — At a meeting of the British School at Rome. March 23, 1907, the Director, T. Ashby, Jr., discussed some points in Sardinian archaeology. The "nuraghi" were fortified habitations rather than tombs, which are represented in the prehistoric period by the *sepolture dei Giganti,* resembling cromlechs, and by rock-cut chambers. The remains of the system of Roman roads, and the fine mediaeval churches were also described briefly. *Athen.* April 13, 1907.)

Representations of the Liver. — An Etruscan bronze sheep's liver (for the use of the *haruspices)* found near Piacenza in 1877, and preserved in the local museum, is discussed at length by G. Korte in *Rom. Mill.* XX, 1905, pp. 348-379 (3 pis.; 5 figs.), with interpretation, so far as possible, of the inscriptions. The specimen is absolutely unique.

In *Memnon,* I, 1907, pp. 86-88 (4 figs.), F. Hommel claims that certain objects found in Etruria and at Troy, and often described as representations of a temple with its orientation, are really representations of a liver such as was used for prophetic purposes, and are similar to the stone livers found in Babylonia.

The So-called Byblis from Tor Marancia. — The five pictures of Greek heroines discovered at Tor Marancia, in 1817, are identified by inscriptions. With them is exhibited a sixth painting, commonly known as Byblis or Medea, and said to come from the same excavations. In reality this painting was probably found at San Basilio in 1810, and examination shows marked differences from the others in size and style. It seems to be a portrait, and owes its present place and name to an error of Biondi. (B. Nogaua, *Ausonia,* I, 1906, pp. 51-55; pi.)

Weavers Weights. — In *R. Arch.* VIII, 1906, p. 453 (3 figs.), R. EngelMaxn publishes three further (cf. *R. A rch.* II, 1903, p. 122) weavers' weights on which are owls in relief.-The owls have human arms. One has a basket below his arms, and the object held by another rests on a column. Many such weights are found at Ruvo.

The Origin of the Pilum.—In *R. Arch.* IX, 1907, pp. 243-252, A. J. Reinach argues that the word *pilanus* is derived from *pilus,* not from *pilum.* He believes that the pilum was not introduced into the Roman army before the fourth century B.C.

The Hasta Pura. — In *Rend. Acc. Lincei,* XVI, 1907, pp. 3-4, W. Helbig argues that the *hasta pura,* the most ancient of the *dona militaria,* is really the primitive wooden spear, with the point sharpened and hardened in the fire. Such a spear was used by the *pater patratus* in declaring war. The *hasta* is the symbol of the *imperium,* and the *dona militaria* bring emancipation from the *imperium.*

The Milites Frumentarii. — That the *milites frumentarii* were originated by Hadrian, not for the purpose of the military commissariat, but for the victualling of the court, is maintained by R. Parjbeni in *Rom. Mitt.* XX, 1905. pp. 310-320.

The Imperial Body-Guard. — The imperial body-guard is the subject of a study by R. Paribeni in *Rom. Mill.* XX, 1905, pp. 321-329. He argues that the *Germani corporis custodes* were at first slaves, not soldiers (Augustus, Tiberius); but later (Claudius, Nero) were freedmen and *indites.*

Vitruvius and his Work: Roman Hydraulics. — In *R. A rch.* IX, 1907, pp.

75-83, V. Mortet continues his 'recherches critiques' on Vitruvius. He discusses Book VIII, 7, the description of aqueducts, and concludes that the *cnlliciaria* or *colluviaria* (not *columnaria, colliquiaria,* nor *colliciaria*) mentioned were an arrangement for the cleaning of the channels.

The Roman Limes. —In *Klio,* VII, 1907, pp. 73-121, E. Kornemanx discusses very fully the results of recent studies on the boundaries of the Roman empire, with special reference to the evidence afforded by the defences as to the policy of the emperors. He distinguishes five periods: I. Under Augustus and Tiberius, there was in general a preference for river valleys as boundaries, or as bases for further advance, though the policy was in general defensive. II. From Claudius until Trajan there is evident a spirit of expansion. Along the new boundaries roads were built, defended by forts. The whole system was controlled by military considerations. III. From Hadrian until the end of the second century another policy is apparent. Hadrian seems to have marked the frontier by a *vallum* of earth, sometimes with a trench and palisades, and defended by forts and towers. This boundary was not fixed for military reasons, but was simply a barrier to limit intercourse in time of peace, though under Hadrian's successors it became a line of defence, for which it was often ill adapted. IV. In the third and fourth centuries there was some expansion in Arabia and Africa, but elsewhere a withdrawal to river frontiers and, where these failed, the erection of strong stone walls. V. In the Byzantine period this use of "Chinese walls " on the frontier was continued, as in the great wall of Anastasius west of Constantinople.

A Mosaic representing Gallia. — In *Revue Celtique,* XXXVIII, 1907, pp. *1- 3* (pi.), S. Keinach discusses a mosaic from Mesopotamia, now in Berlin, which represents Gallia as a powerful woman crowned with towers like Cybele, and like a bronze statuette found in Paris, which probably represents Lutetia. This medallion formed part of a large mosaic representing the emperor surrounded by twelve provinces. In *B. Soc. Ant. Fr.* 1906, pp. 380-384 (2 figs.), E. Michon also discusses this unique representation of Gallia. The mosaic is from Biredjik where the highway from Edessa crossed the Euphrates *(Arch. Am.* 1900, p. 109). The twenty-seven fragments known are divided between Berlin, Rome, St. Petersburg, and Dresden, and a new fragment, representing Eros holding a rod in a border of foliage, is now in the Louvre. It is a work of the third century A.d. SPAIN AND PORTUGAL

The Regulations for the Mines at Aljustrel. — In *C. R. Acad. Insc.* 1907, pp. 95-99, E. Cuo. discusses those portions of the law relating to the working of the mines at Aljustrel *(A.J.A.* XI, p. 103), which concern the occupation of abandoned or forfeited shafts and the formation of companies to develop them. A summary account of this law drawn from the *Journal des Savants* is given in *B. Com. Rom.* XXXVI, 1906, pp. 341-346, by L. Cantarklli.

Ampurias. —In *Jb. Kl. Alt.* XIX, 1907, pp. 334-346 (3 pis.), A. SchulTkn describes the ancient remains at S. Martin de Ampurias, north of Barcelona, the site of the ancient Emporion. The Greek colony was on the island, now a peninsula, of S. Martin de Ampurias, the Iberian city covered the hill on the mainland, and the Roman colony occupied a small square on this hill. The course of the walls of these cities and of a great mole can be easily traced. The most important object of the Roman period is a mosaic representing the sacrifice of Iphigenia *(Arch. Zeit.* 1869). The necropolis has yielded Punic, Egyptian, and old Corinthian objects of the seventh century, black-figured and red-figured vases from Boeotia and Athens, and much that shows an active trade with Campania and Sicily. Extensive plundering of the necropolis has been in progress for many years, but little scientific exploration has been undertaken.

The Treasure of JAvea. — In *R. Arch.* VIII, 1806, pp. 424-435 (pL), P. Paris discusses the treasure of gold and silver ornaments found near Javea, in 1904, and published by Jose Ramon Melida, in *R. Arch. Bibl. Mug.* 1905, i, p. 360 (2 pis.). The ornaments resemble in style some of those found in Etruria, but are really Attic work, made for the Spanish trade. The manner of wearing the gold chains, pendants, necklaces, and diadems is seen in the sculptures from Cerro de los Santos, now in Madrid.

FRANCE

The Moreau Collection. — In *R. Arch.* VIII, 1906, pp. 337-371 (figs. 37-73), II. Hubert continues his description of the Moreau collection at Saint Germain (cf. *ibid.* 1902, ii, pp. 167-206). The cemetery of Sablonnieres is described and a catalogue of the contents of thirty-two tombs of the La Tene period is given. The contents of one of five tombs at the chateau of Fere-en-Tardenois are similarly described.

Ancient Establishments in the Upper Basin of the Garonne. — In *R. Arch.* IX, 1907, pp. 94-118 (fig.), Leon Joulin describes the numerous remains of ancient settlements in the upper basin of the Garonne, the region about Toulouse. Some tombs are earlier than the fourth century li.c. Indigenous pottery is followed in the fourth century by wares showing strong Greek influence and by imported wares, after which Roman and Gallo-Roman ware prevails. The earliest coins found were struck in the third century B.c. The Hallstatt and La Tene periods are represented also by bronze arms, fibulae, spiral silver rings, and other small objects. *I hid.* pp. 226-242, further details are given, and the characteristics of the civilization of this region at various periods are pointed out. See also *C. R. Acad. Insc.* 1906, pp. 723-724, where these results are summarized.

The Reliefs of the Altar of the Nautae Parisiaci. — In *R. Arch.* IX, 1907, pp. 31-37 (3 figs.), A. T. Vercoutre argues that the fragmentary reliefs on the altar in the Cluny Museum with inscription *Tib(erio) Caesare Aug(usto) Iovi Optumo Maxsumo Nautae Parisiaci (pu)blice posierun(l)* represent (1) *nautae,* who were formed into cohorts as military auxiliaries, (2) *fabri tignarii,* and (3) *exoneratores,* associated with the *nautae.*

The Discoveries at the Marche'-aux-Fleurs. — In *B. Soc. Ant. Ft:* 1906, pp. 313-1314, Ch. Sellier discusses briefly the two parallel walls recently uncovered near the *Quni de la Cite.* They belong to the Merovingian period, and were probably built after the fire of 585 A.D. With this fire may be connected the name of the neighboring church, St. Pierre des Arsis.

The Situation of Alesia. —In *C. R. Acad. Insc.* 1906, pp. 724-725, A. Berard gives a summary of the reasons why he places the site of Alesia on the plateau of Izernore (Ain) rather than at Alise-Sainte-Reine.

The Mosaic of Vaison. — The mosaic of Vaison *(A.J.A.* XI, p. 109) is an important fragment of the mosaic of Narcissus in the Musee Calvert at Avignon. It has been known since 1858, and shows how freely and badly the portion in Avignon has been restored. (L. H. Labande, *B. Soc. Ant. Fr.* 1906, pp. 377-379; fig.)

A Correction to *C.I.L.* XIII, 5451 a. —The little inscription *C.I.L.* XIII, 5451 a, was found at Saveux. It is not the base of a statuette, but one of a series of weights bearing inscriptions to show that they have been officially tested. (A. Heron Dk Villefosse, *B. Soc. Ant. Fr.* 1906, pp. 329-333.)

Divinities with Horns in Gaul. —In *R. fit. Anc.* IX. 1907, pp. 184186 (2 figs.), G. Gassiks publishes a statuette at Clermont-Ferrand, representing a seated goddess with the horns of a deer, and a fragmentary relief at Melun of a goddess with many breasts. These confirm his view of the existence of the cult in Gaul of the Terra Mater and a feminine equivalent of Cernunnos. C. Jullian regards these deities as local manifestations of Terra Mater and Dis Pater considered as divinities of streams or fountains.

The Celtic Table Knife. —In *R. fit. Anc.* IX, 1907, pp. 181-183, A. Blanchet discusses a passage of Posidonius *(Frg. Hist. (Jraec.* Ill, p. 260, No. 25), and concludes that the ancient Celts carried a small knife in a sheath attached to the scabbard of the great sword. Small knives have been found in Celtic graves in positions which favor this view.

Gallo-Roman Chronicle. — In the 'Chronique Gallo-Roinaiue' in *R. fit. Anc.* IX, 1907, pp. 8:5-92 (2 figs.), C. Jullian mentions briefly numerous recent publications dealing with Gaul, including discoveries at Alesia and Vdsone, Hannibal's passage of the Alps, and the discoveries at Paris, near Notre Dame, in 1711. He publishes two sculptures from Alesia showing a bust with birds perched on the shoulders. *Ibid.* pp. 189-192, these notes are continued. The name Mycenaean ought not to be used in discussing Iberian pottery, which is very much later.

The Museum at Avignon.— In *Le Mnse'e,* IV, 1907, pp. 51-70 (3 pis.; 9 figs.), fe. Bailly describes some of the more important works in the Musee Calvet at Avignon. Among the Greek works is the upper part of a fine Attic grave-relief from the Nani collection. Later works include a relief of Jupiter Helipolitanus, one of Sucellus in an *aedicuia,* and two fine statues of Gallic warriors. There are numerous Romanesque, Gothic, and Renaissance works, including statues and paintings, among the latter works attributed to Nicolas Froment, Corneille de Lyon, and the brothers Le Nain.

GERMANY

The Roman Bronze Industry in Lower Germany. — In *Rh. Mus.* LXII, 1907, pp. 133-150 (6 figs.), H. Willeks discusses the Roman bronze industry, as shown by discoveries in northern Germany and southern Scandinavia. During the first century A.d. the demand for fine bronzes was supplied by manufacturers at Capua. In the second and third centuries there appears in the north a metal closely resembling brass, which seems to have been manufactured at Stolberg, and exported to free Germany and Scandanavia by way of Xymwegen.

A Gallo Roman Monument at Trier. — In *Revue Celtique,* XXXVIIT, 1907, pp. 41-42 (pi.), H. D'arbois De Jubainville publishes a GalloRonian relief at Trier, which combines two scenes on an altar in the Musee de Cluny *(Ibid.* XVIII, pp. 253-256). Above a man cutting a tree are a bull head and two cranes. The representation refers to a Gallic myth's preserved in the Irish Tain bd Ciialnge. The man is Cuchulainn, the bull the divine Donn, and the cranes the triple goddess, Bodb, Morrigan, and Nemain, who in bird-form warns the bull of the danger of capture.

AFRICA

Roman North Africa. —In *Rec. Past,* VI, 1907, pp. 67-76 (8 figs.), C. D. Curtis gives a brief description of some of the more characteristic sites in Roman North Africa, mentioning more particularly Dougga, Khremissa, Timgad, and adding some particulars of the modern life in Tunis and Algeria.

A College of Tubicines. — In *Klio,* VII, 1907, pp. 183-187, R. Cagnat publishes an inscription from Lambaesis containing the regulations of the college of *tubicines* of *Legio III Augusta.* It furnishes a close parallel to the regulations of the *cornicines C.I.L.* VIII, 2557), and is of about the same date (203 A.d.).

The "Lex Hadriana de rudibus agris." — In *Klio,* VII, 1907, pp. 188212 (map), A. Schultex discusses an *Ara* recently found near Thignica containing a *sermo procuralorum Hadriani,* apparently an extract from the *lex Hadriana de rudibus agris* with its application to a special case. It thus resembles the inscription from Ain Wassel *Hermes,* 1894, p. 204), and the two documents complete each other in many points. It appears that the *lex Hadriana* extended the operation of the *lex Manciana* of the time of Trajan, in that it not only provided for the occupation of open land by the colonists, but also for the occupation of leased land where the lessee had left it uncultivated for ten years.

The Metrical Inscription from Ouled l'Agha. — The Latin metrical inscription from Ouled l'Agha *A.J.A.* XI, p. 234) is discussed in *Rh. Mus.* LXII, 1907, pp. 157-159, by G. Guxderman, who thinks the inscription refers to the wine, olives, and other riches shown on mosaics in the neighboring rooms. *Ibid.* p. 328, C. Hulsen compares another African inscription, *C.I.L.* VIII, 11,083, which was also engraved on a threshold. In *Bed. Phil. W.* 1907, cols. 478—479 (fig.), R. Engelmann publishes a new collation, by Gauckler, which reads *Bide, oive et) bide, possas plurima, bide.* The inscription probably refers to the man represented below.

EARLY CHRISTIAN, BYZANTINE, AND MEDIAEVAL ART GENERAL AND MISCELLANEOUS

St. Menas of Alexandria. — In *S. Bibl. Arch.* XXIX, 1907, pp. 25-30, 51-60, 112-122 (8 pis.), Miss M. A. Murray discusses the legend of St. Menas of Alexandria, the representations of scenes from the life of the Saint on shrines and reliquaries, the location of his church at Tel Abumna, and the numerous oil-flasks bearing the name of the Saint that are found in Egypt and in adjacent countries.

The Mosaic Map at Medeba. — In *Bibl. World,* XXIX, 1907, pp. 370375 (3 figs.), H. H. Nelson describes anew the finding of the Medeba mosaic map. and its present condition as seen by him during a recent visit.

The Tychalon at Is-Sanamen. — In *R. Arch.* VIII, pp. 413-423 (7 figs.) Howard Crosby Butler discusses the temple of Tyche, built in 192 A.d., at Is-Sanamen, in Central Syria. This has at one end an apse, at each side of which is a room. This is exactly the arrangement of several early Christian churches in Syria. The plan of the Christian churches was probably derived from the pagan temples, and it is "not proven that the Western Church did not derive its visible and temporal expression from the Eastern Church."

Origin of Knotted Ornamentation. — The peculiar form of "returning knot" which appears in Byzantine ornament in the sixth century, in Syria in the fifth or sixth century, in Celtic and English illuminations of the seventh and eighth centuries, seems to have originated as a means of treating the ends of the ribbons which tie garlands in classic art. W. R. LethAby (*Burl. Mag.* X, 1907, p. 256) who has found the prototype in Coptic textiles of Baouit of the fifth and sixth centuries suggests that the Arab conquest caused the dispersion of Coptic artisans throughout Europe, and hence the wide diffusion of this pattern.

A Byzantine Lead Seal. — In *J. Int. Arch. Num.* IX, 1906, pp. 46-48 (fig.), C. M. Constantopoulos discusses a Byzantine lead seal, on one face of which are two standing saints. Their costume is that of the warrior saints, and as they are bearded it seems certain that they are the two Theodores. The reverse bears an inscription in two trimeters showing that it was an amulet.

Paintings with Byzantine Types in Arab Manuscripts. — In *R. A rch.* IX, 1907, pp. 193-223 (10 figs.), E. Blochet discusses three manuscripts of the *Malamat* of Hariri, now in the Bibliotheque Nationale at Paris. Illustrated Arab manuscripts are very rare. These date from the thirteenth century. They were probably executed in Syria, and the paintings show strong Byzantine influence. Some signs of the influence of ancient Egyptian monuments are also detected, and this influence is much stronger in the paintings of a manuscript from St. Sophia, Constantinople, of the fourteenth century.

The Dome of SS. Sergius and Bacchus. — In *Rec. Past,* VI, 1907, p. 64, is a note by H. C. Butler, in which, as the result of a recent examination, he corrects certain details in the description given by W. R. Lethaby of the dome of SS. Sergius and Bacchus in Constantinople. See *A. J.A.* X, p. 77; XI, p. 235.

Byzantine Frescoes at Nereditsl. — The church of the Saviour at Nereditsi near Novgorod was built by laroslav Vladimirovitch in 1198 and 1199. It is still well preserved and has suffered little by restoration. The frescoes, probably by Greek painters, are described in detail in *Mon. Plot,* XIII, 1906, pp. 35-55 (2 pis.; 6 figs.), by J. Ebersolt, who points out their connection with the great works of the eleventh century, such as those at the monastery of St. Luke and at Daphni. While they follow the tradition of the mosaics, they show some promise of the greater freedom which appears in the fourteenth century at Mistra.

The Age of Recently Discovered Tapestries. —In *Arte e Sloria,* 1907, pp. 1-6, D. Sant' Ambrooio argues against a Byzantine origin and a date prior to 1000 A.d. for the textiles found in the Sancta Sanctorum of the Lateran (*A.J. A.* XI, pp. 123, 482), and in the tomb of St. Cunibert at Cologne in 1898. He believes that the latter do not antedate the work of the *ouvriert Sarrazinois,* who settled in France in the eleventh and twelfth centuries, and that the former belong to the same period. The vestments recently found in the tomb of Charlemagne at Aachen are also probably the product of the factories established by Frederick II.

The Life of Christ on Sculptured Portals. —In *R. Art Chre't.* 1907, pp. 17-25, appears the last of eight articles by G. Sanoner (commenced *ibid.* 1905, p. 217) on sculptured scenes from the Saviour's life, the examples being chiefly French and Flemish. In this article he considers " Christ before Pilate," the " Flagellation," the "Crowning with Thorns," the " Ecce Homo," "Christ carrying his Cross," and the "Nailing to the Cross."

The Origin of "Rioe-grain" Technique. — In the British Museum is a bowl of creamy white semi-translucent ware, with an animal drawn in colors and spotted with points of translucent glaze in the "rice-grain " technique. The bowl belongs in the group of early pottery found in Persia and Syria, and probably of Egyptian origin, as translucent ware with lustrous decorations was seen at Cairo in 1012 A.d. by Naslr i Khusran. The bowl settles the question as to the origin of the "rice-grain " technique, as it is far earlier than the examples from the Far East. (R. L. Hobson, *Burl. Mag.* XI, 1907, pp. 83-89.)

Lustrous Oriental Pottery in the Louvre. — In *Mon. Piot,* XIII, 1906, pp. 77-84 (pi.; 6 figs.), G. Migeon publishes three tine specimens of Oriental faience decorated in lustrous gold. One, a cup of creamy enamel, is Syro-Egyptian work of the twelfth century, another is a bottle with a crackled white ground from Rhages in Persia, a work of the thirteenth century, and the third is a fourteenth-century vase of blue enamel belonging to the group commonly called Siculo-Arabian, but really Syro-Egyptian, and probably from potteries at Da-

ITALY

Byzantine Inscriptions from Sardinia. — In *N.Bull. Arch. Crist.* 1906, pp. 305-306, E. Josi comments upon the Byzantine inscriptions of Sardinia, published by Taramelli in *Not. Scav.* 1906, pp. 123-138. The principal interest of the inscriptions, which are of the tenth or eleventh century, lies in the twice occurring mention of an *iLpw* SapSvtas. Taramelli's interpretation of some of the abbreviations is corrected.

The Sarcophagus from Via della Lungara. — The sarcophagus found on the Via della Lungara three years ago, and now in the Museo delle Terme, is discussed by O. MarucchI in *N. Bull. Areh. Crist.* 1906, pp. 199205. The sculpture is confined to three panels in front and the two ends. The central panel represents an Orans, surrounded by the doves symbolizing the elect. The panel on the left shows a fisherman with rod and basket, probably referring to Christ's words, "I will make you fishers of men." The adjoining scene on the small end is a baptism, but it lacks the usual dove and must therefore be referred to the liturgical sacrament. The juxtaposition of the two scenes appears to epitomize the Christian pastor's function of conversion. The panel on the right has the Good Shepherd, and the sheep of His flock are on the adjoining end.

The Meaning of a Graffito. — The following graffito was discovered during recent excavations in the cemetery of Commodilla: non *dicere ille secrita ah boce,* i.e. *non dicere ille secreta ab voce.* In *N. Bull. Arch. Crist.* 1906, pp. 239-252, the word *secrita* is referred to the mass, particularly the Canon, in mediaeval use called *secreta.* The sentence would then take the form of an admonition "not to speak the secrets, or Canon, of the mass with a loud voice."

The Relics in the Sancta Sanctorum. — In *Mon. Piot,* XV, 1906, pp. 1-142 (18 pis.; 35 figs.), P. Laukk publishes a detailed description of the objects recently discovered in the Sancta Sanctorum at Rome *(A.J.A.* XI, p. 123). The enamelled cross, which once enclosed a piece of the true cross, is perhaps the one found by Sergius I (687-701). It is a work of primitive Byzantine art possibly of the end of the fifth century. The silver box which contained it is of the seventh century, though the cover is about a century later. In it was a piece of silk which is clearly sixth-century Persian work. The gold cross set with jewels seems to be the one given by Charlemagne to Hadrian I (772-795). It is Carolingian in style, and was enclosed in a silver-gilt cruciform coffer, which bears an inscription of Pope Pascal, probably Pascal I (817-824). In addition to the detailed discussion of the contents of the altar, the chapel is fully described, and the frescoes published for the first time. They are of the late thirteenth century, but have been several times restored. The chapel also contains the painting of Christ "made without hands," which is enclosed in elaborately wrought silver, part of which is of the thirteenth century. The author points out that the discovery has raised questions which call for much further study before a final answer can be given.

The Frescoes in S. Clemente in Rome. — The results of the study by J. Wilpeht of the frescoes in the lower church of S. Clemente in Rome are published in *R. A rt Chnt.* 1907, pp. 69-70. The "Scenes from the Martyrdom of St. Catherine" and the "Council of St. Zosimus" in the right aisle really form one composition representing the Last Judgment, as is shown by the inscriptions. The fresco known as "St. Cyril before the Emperor" represents Esther before Ahasuerus, a mediaeval symbol of the intercession of the Virgin. On the left in the narthex is a fresco representing St. Cyril accompanied by St. Clement and the archangel Gabriel before Christ, on whose left stand St. Methodius, St. Andrew, and the archangel Michael. The inscription on this fresco shows that the tomb of St. Cyril was below it.

The Churches of St. Pantaleon. — The three churches in Rome dedicated to St. Pantaleon are the subject of a topographical and diplomatic study by P Spezi, in *B. Com. Rom.* XXXVI, 1906, pp. 270-307.

The Guild of Marble Workers in Rome. — The history of the guild of marble workers, *Unicerritas marmorariorum,* has been investigated by G. Tomassetti in *B. Com. Rom.* XXXVI, 1906, pp. 235-269. The guild celebrated its fifth centenary last October, and its history is of interest to all who concern themselves with the mediaeval Cnsmati ornamentation.

The Reconstruction of the Cathedral of Bari. — F. Carabellese contributes to *VArte,* 1907. pp. 65-70. the documentary history of the reconstruction of the Duomo at Bari after its destruction in 1156 during the siege by Guglielmo I.

Barbaric Ornaments at Lucca. — In *Ausonia,* I. 1906. pp. 60-67 (2 figs.), P. Toesca describes some metal objects now in the Pinacoteca of Lucca, where they are ascribed to the twelfth century. They are, however, Lombard work of about the seventh century and important for the history of barbaric art. The most interesting piece is a plate of gilded metal, representing a warrior, wearing a long tunic and the "scramasax," and holding a staff, which ends in a cross on which is perched a dove.

Minor Examples of Lombard Ornament. — G. Pacchioxi, in *L'Arte,* 1907, pp. 124-130, discusses variations in Lombard ornamental motives in Emilia, as seen in S. Lorenzo di Panico at Bologna, the oratory of S. Michele near Livizzano, the oratory of Denzano near Castelvetro, Modena, S. Michele di Pievepelago, the Pieve del Trebbio, and the Pieve di Reno. He finds the motives in these churches influenced by the great Lombard buildings of Bologna, Piacenza, and Modena. Three classes are distinguished: poor imitations of work in the great cathedrals; variations due to the caprice or ignorance of the artist; and motives wherein all tradition is forgotten and the artist is guided only by his observation of nature or his imagination.

The First Roman Work of Arnolfo di Cambio. — In *Cod. barb. Int.* 4423 of the Vatican library is a seventeenth-century sketch (Fig. 1) of a funeral monument which still exists in St. John Lateran. It represents a prelate lying in death upon his couch, and in the background a procession of six clerics bearing the symbols of his rank. The slab containing the procession (Fig. 2) is now on the east wall of the cloister, while the reclining figure is at the end of the left nave of the church. Panvinio (1502) describes it as the tomb of Cardinal Riccardo Annibaldi and gives the date as 1273, which can be corrected to 1276, the year of the cardinal's death. The style is that of Arnolfo di Cambio, and the date marks it as his earliest work in Rome. (G. De Nicola, *L'Arte,* 1907, pp. 97-104; 4 figs.)

Rome, belonging to the end of the fourteenth and beginning of the fifteenth century. The monuments described are: (1) The tomb of Cardinal Vulcani in S. Francesca Romana (1394 or 1403). (2) The fragment from the tomb of Caracciolo in S. Maria del Priorato. (3) The tomb of Cardinal d' Alencon in S. Maria in Trastevere, now separated, since the baldachin has been used for an altar. (4) A fragment in the cloister of the Lateran, representing a procession (see preceding article). (5) The tomb of Cardinal Adam of Hartford in S. Cecilia in Trastevere. (6) and (7) Two statues of Boniface IX, one in the round in S. Paolo fuori, the other in relief in the right transept of the Lateran. Some of these have been wrongly attributed to Magister Paulus (see below), three of whose works (8-10) are discussed. To an unknown tomb belongs (11) two angels holding back curtains in S. Cesareo. Other tombs of this period are those of (12) Cardinal Pietro di Fonseca in the Grotte Vaticane; (13) Cardinal Lando formerly in S. Maria Maggiore; and (14) Cardinal della Porta in the Grotte Vaticane, dating from 1434 and the last of this style.

Magister Paulus.—There are two monuments in Rome signed by a *Afayister Paulus,* the tomb of Bartolomeo Carafa and that of Cardinal Stefaneschi. Other works of his are discussed in *L'Arte,* 1907, pp. 116-123, by Laura Filippini, who assigns to him as an early work the tomb of the brothers Anguillara in the church of S. Francesco at Capranica di Sutri, two figures of angels in the Capella della Pieta at St. Peter's, and an angel holding a scroll in S. Maria sopra Minerva. He probably worked between 1380 and 1417. His faces are summary, his drapery hard and with fewfolds, but he obtains tetter success with reclining than with erect figures.

Eight Statues of the Virtues. —In *Boll. Arte,* I, 1907. v, pp. 1-6 (8 figs.), V. Spinazzola discusses eight small marble statues belonging to Baron Mazzoccolo of Teano. They seem to have formed part of funeral monuments. Five, representing *Fortitudo, Temperancia, Charitan, lusticia,* and *Fides,* belong to the end of the thirteenth century, and are among the earliest of the series of Neapolitan supports for sarcophagi. Two others, of about the same period but somewhat smaller, represent Charity and Justice. The eighth, representing Prudence, is not earlier than the beginning of the fourteenth century.

Maestro Cicogna. — In 1899 some damaged frescoes were discovered in the Romanesque church of S. Martino di Corrubio on the hill of Castelrotto di Valpolicella. An inscription showed that they were finished by *Magister Cicogna,* May 31, 1300. Other frescoes of his seem to exist in S. Felice di Cazzano (1322). the Castello Scaligero at Soave (a condottiere and his soldiers), and probably in the Museo Civico from the old Palazzo del Comune in Verona, dated perhaps in 1326. These works show that Cicogna, uninfluenced by Giotto, adhered closely to the old Byzantine traditions. (L. Simeomi, *Madonna Verona,* I, 1907, pp. 11-17.)

FRANCE

The Codex Purpureus Sinopensis. — In *N. Bull. Arch. Crist.* 1906, pp. 215-237, A. Munoz examines the Codex Purpureus Sinopensis in the Bibliotheque Nationale from the iconographic and stylistic points of view. He finds that in comparison with the Codex Rossanensis, it shows a more purely illustrative intention on the part of the artist, the miniatures being more closely connected with the text. In technique it is much inferior to the Rossanensis. Many peculiarities are shared with the Vienna Genesis, and the three manuscripts form a group with many affinities to Syrian art, but some Hellenic elements. The provenience of the Sinopensis shows that they are products of a school in Asia Minor.

The Sculptured Tympanum at Autun. — The early sculptured representation of the Last Judgment in the tympanum of the west doorway of Autun Cathedral is published with a brief description in *Reliq.* XIII, 1907, p. 121 (pi.).

Abbot Suger. —In *Le Muse'e,* IV, 1907, pp. 160-173 (3 pis.; fig.), J. Robiquet writes of Suger, the great Abbot of St. Denis, as a lover of art. He describes briefly his activity at St. Denis, the great works in precious metals executed by his order, and the few smaller treasures which are now in the Louvre and the Cabinet des M6dailles.'

The Church of Saint Sulpice at Favieres.— In *Le Muste,* IV, 1907, pp. 28-37 (2 pis.; 2 figs.), L. Riotor describes in detail the interesting Gothic church of St. Sulpice at Favieres. Commenced about 1250 and completed about 1335, it has suffered by fire and by the Revolution, but in the tympanum of the main portal still remain early reliefs of the Resurrection and Last Judgment. There are also two good windows of the thirteenth century and some interesting tombs.

The South Portal of Chartrea Cathedral. — In *R. Art Chre't.* 1907, pp. 100-107, L. E. Lefevre discusses the sculptures in the left bay of the south portal of Chartres Cathedral. The lintel is decorated with the stoning of St. Stephen; in the tympanum is Christ with adoring angels; on the voussoirs are martyrs. The author, who considers that the sculptures on mediaeval portals are often inspired by the Apocalypse, separates the tympanum from the lintel, and interprets it as the apocalyptic Agnus Dei, surrounded by angels and saints. On the keystone of the second order of voussoirs is a ram's head. From a wound in the throat pour streams of blood, represented by undulations which border the first and second rows of voussoirs, and in which the saints of the second row seem to dip their garments.

A Relief representing St. Matthew (?) and an Angel. — The Louvre has recently received from Chartres a relief of the thirteenth century, representing St. Matthew (?) writing from the dictation of an angel. The history of the relief is uncertain, but in *Man. Plot,* XIII, 1906, pp. 57-66 (pi.: 6 figs.), A. Michel points out its close resemblance to the sculptures of the Cathedral of Chartres, and particularly to the fragments of the jube destroyed in 1763. It is possible that it once formed part of this monument.

Ivory Altar-pieces of the Fourteenth Century. — In *Mm. Plot,* XIII, 1906, pp. 67-75 (pi.; 4 figs.), R. Koechlin discusses several ivory reliefs of the fourteenth century, containing scenes from the Passion, which he believes formed parts of large ivory altar-pieces. He attributes these to two schools, both Parisian, of the early and late fourteenth century. The same schools probably produced some of the small triptychs and polyptychs, from which the appearance of the large altar-pieces may be imagined.

GREAT BRITAIN

The Early Stained Glass in Canterbury Cathedral. — The important question of the historical relation of the stained windows of Canterbury, Sens, and Chartres is discussed in *Burl. Mag.* XI, 1907, pp. 172-180, by Clement Heaton, who concludes that the glass at Canterbury was the work of a French artist who commenced it soon after the fire of 1175. Soon after 1185, he left for Sens. Here he labored until 1206, when he went to Chartres and made the first thirteenth-century windows in that cathedral, leaving a school, which completed his work. His style, originating in the earlier Romanesque which lies behind the windows of St. Denis, afterward spread to Rouen, Bourges, and many other places.

Some Devon Churches.—In *Relvj.* XIII, 1907, pp. 73-96 (17 figs.), G. Le Blanc Smith describes a number of churches in the Teign Valley, Devon. Most of these are perpendicular, but have little architectural interest. They usually contain old painted oak screens, carved bench ends, and other decorations, many of which are described and illustrated with considerable detail.

The Church of St. George. Southacre. — In *Reliq.* XIII, 1907, pp. 121126 (2 figs.), A. C. Fryer describes the church of St. George at Southacre, Norfolk. It possesses a fragment of a finely carved wooden screen, and an interesting Norman font with an elaborate cover, now badly damaged.

RENAISSANCE ART GENERAL AND MISCELLANEOUS

The Grimani and Morgan Breviaries. — A number of illustrated manuscripts show more or less affinity to the famous Breviarium Grimani, but its nearest relative is the breviary belonging to Mr. J. P. Morgan. The latter antedates the Grimani breviary, as appears from the fact that in the Grimani the text illustrations of the Morgan manuscript have been in some cases broken up and used as border decorations without relation to the text. (V. Gr. Simkhovitch, *Burl. Mag.* X, 1907, pp. 400-405.)

The Biblia Pauperum. — The illustrated manuscript known as the Biblia Pauperum in now in private possession in the United States. At the instance of the owner, Campbell Dodoson prepared a description of which fifty copies were printed for private circulation. An outline of this work is given by the author in *Rep. f. K.* 1907, pp. 168-172. He denies the attribution to Konrad Avitz of Basel, proposed by Schmarsow *(ibid.* XXVIII, p. 340).

An Art Patron of the Fifteenth Century. — T. Leclere in *Gaz. B.-A.* XXXVII, 1907, pp. 132-146, discusses the Challant family of the valley of Aosta, and the works of art due to their encouragement. The most conspicuous of the family as an art patron was George of Challant, to whom are due the stalls of the cathedral of Aosta, executed by local artists and by others from Savoy and Geneva; the castle of Issogne and the frescoes which adorn its walls; and finally an illuminated missal (1499) now in the possession of the Comte Passerin d'Entreves. The frescoes and illuminations were probably the work of Lyonese artists, though local artists may have executed the frescoes.

The Virgin with the Club. — A small number of paintings, chiefly Umbrian, of the fifteenth and early sixteenth centuries represent the Airgin armed with a club chasing a demon from a child. This weapon is due to the double sense of the epithet *clavigera,* which is applied to the Virgin as bearer of the key of Heaven, but might mean "club-bearer." In art the key is reserved for St. Peter. *Claviger* is an epithet of Janus and of Hercules. (S. Reinach, *C. if. Acad. Inxc.* 1907, pp. 43-45.)

The Van Eyck Technique. — In *Rep. f. K.* 1906, pp. 425-440, is an exhaustive analysis by A. Eibner of the passages in Vasari relative to the discovery of oil technique by Jan Van Eyck. He concludes that Van Eyck was searching for a quick-drying varnish with which to finish tempera painting, and that the mixture mentioned by Vasari was an oil-lacquer, which he then found to be available as a direct medium. Berger's theories are fully discussed and rejected.

New Pictures by Gerolamo da Cremona. — In *Rass. d'Arte,* 1907. pp. 33-35, B. Berenson publishes a " Poppaea giving alms to St. Peter" in the collection of Lady Henry Somerset. The painting was attributed to Liberale da Verona, but must be given to his companion miniaturist, Gerolamo da Cremona. Sienese influences are seen in his painting, and his own impress appears in the works of Neroccio and Fraucesco di Giorgio. The influence of Liberale and Gerolamo upon Sienese masters may explain certain pictures which are given now a Sienese, now a Veronese, origin. *Ibid.* 1907, p. 78, G. Cagnola reproduces a Nativity in the possession of the antiquaries Grandi in Milan, which he assigns to Gerolamo.

New Pictures by (Man Francesco de' Maineri. — In *vArte,* 1907, pp. 33-40, A. Venturi adds a number of pictures to those by Gian Francesco de' Maineri. The first is a Holy Family, formerly in the collection of Ettore Testa at Ferrara, on which Maineri's signature has been found. Replicas are in the Kaiser Friedrich Museum in Berlin, and in the Prado. The Madonna in the Accademia Albertina in Turin, attributed to Maineri by Venturi in 1890, is shown to be his by the discovery of the signature. Another Madonna, probably by Maineri, is in the ducal gallery at Gotha. On internal evidence, Maineri is given four pictures of Christ bearing the cross, in the Galleria Estense at Modena, the Doria collection, the Uflizi, and the collection of the late Sig. Mazocchi in Rome.

The Life of Torrigiani. — Pietro Torrigiani's quarrel with Michelangelo seems to have clouded all his later career. It led to his flight from Florence, and a wandering life, at first with Valentino and then with the condottiere Paolo Vitelli. To this period belong the stucco ornaments on the Torre Borgia, and his sculptures on the Piccolomini altar in Siena. He then went to England, where in 1512 he executed the monument of Henry VII and Elizabeth of York in Westminster Abbey. Other works in England are the tomb of John Young (1515) now in the Public Record Office, a bronze medallion of Sir Thomas Lovell in Westminster Abbey, and a marble head of Christ in relief now in the Wallace Collection. In 1519 he left England and went to Spain, where he made the St. Jerome, and perhaps the terracotta Madonna and Child, in Seville cathedral, as vi?Tl as a lost bust of the Empress Isabella. Vasari's story that he starved himself to death in 1528 to escape the Inquisition has not been disproved. (C. Justi, *Jb. Pretus. Kututs.* XXVII, 1906, pp. 249-281.)

Pictures by Palma Vecchio. — The Piping Faun in the Alte Pinakothek in Munich was ascribed by Miindler to Pahna Vecchio. This attribution is supported on internal evidence by Claude Phillips in *Burl Mag.* X, 1907, pp. 213-252, who finds the poetic quality of the picture unusual for Palma Vecchio, and suggests that such works may be explained by assuming that Palma derived his art, not directly from Giovanni Bellini, but through the more fanciful Cima da Conegliano. This assumption leads the writer to accept Vasari's ascription to him of the " Tempesta al Mare " in the Venice Academy, and he supports this thesis with many comparisons of details in Palma's authenticated works. *Ibid.* X, 1907, pp. 315—1517, the same writer reproduces and criticises Palma Vecchio's " Two Nymphs," which he regards as a work done under the influence of Giorgione and even showing imitation of the "Concert ChampOtre," with the consequent date 1510-1515. *Ibid.* XI, 1907, pp. 188, C. J. Holmes publishes a new "Shepherd and Nymphs," which must be attributed to Palma Vecchio. It is quite in the same character as the "Two Nymphs," and even more reminiscent of Giorgione. The picture is in the possession of Mr. Phillips.

IT ALY

The Rucellai Madonna. — In *VArte,* 1907, pp. 55-59, A. Chiappelli points out resemblances between the busts of saints in the medallions of the frame which encloses the Rucellai Madonna in S. Maria Novella, and pictures by Cimabue, notably his Madonna in the Belle Arti at Florence and some figures in his Crucifixion at Assisi. These resemblances are strongly opposed to the attribution of this Madonna to Duccio.

Frescoes in the Cathedral of Atri. — In *Boll. Arte,* 1907, iii, pp. 14-18 (3 figs.), L. Canevaghi calls attention to the importance of the frescoes and other works of art at Atri. Especially noteworthy are the frescoes in the old church beneath the cathedral. Some of these are by followers of Giotto, but others are apparently by local artists of the early fourteenth century, and show an harmonious combination of Tuscan art with that of La Marcha and Umbria.

A Triptych by Allegretto Nuzi. — In *VArte,* 1907, pp. 143-144, A. Munoz disputes Suida's view that the triptych in the Museo Cristiano of the Vatican, representing the Madonna and Child with saints and donors, though signed by Allegretto Nuzi, differs so much from his other signed works that it must be by another hand. He points out that in 1674 Alveri describes the picture in San Leonardo alia Lungara, and gives the signature and date, 1365.

The Date of Masolino. — In the *Nation,* May 2, 1907, P. J. Gentner points out that the date, 1428, on the church at Castiglione d'Olona refers to a restoration and not to the dedication; while the date 1435, in the baptistery, is in its present form modern. Records of the Branda family show that the church was ready for consecration in 1422, and it is therefore probable that though the baptistery frescoes are later than those in the church, Masolino executed all this work before his paintings at Rome and Florence. *Ibid.* June 13, 1907, W. Rankin, accepting this date, points out that in the paintings of S. Clemente some of the scenes show the hand of Masaccio, who seems to have helped Masolino. He also doubts whether Masolino had any part in the painting of the Brancacci Chapel at Florence.

Donatello and the Antique. — Donatello's use of the antique is described by F. Burger in *Ilep.f. K.* 1907, pp. 1-13, as both eclectic and imitative. In the Flagellation of the Berlin Museum, the movement of the figure of Christ is studied from one of the Dioscuri. Many examples of the use of the Meleager sarcophagus in Pisa can be cited, and one of the executioners in the Crucifixion of the Museo Nazionale in Florence is drawn from the sarcophagus group of Hercules and the hydra, the resemblance extending even to the club which the executioner uses to drive the nail into the foot of one of the two thieves. The sculptor used the reliefs of the column of Trajan more than any other ancient monument, and it is to his study of them that his freer later style in relief is due.

Sculptures by Isaia da Pisa in Rome. — In *Jb. Preuss. Kunsts.* XXVII, 1906, pp. 228-244, F. Burger discusses the work of Isaia da Pisa in Rome, and assigns to him lunette No. 224 of the tabernacle of S. Andrea in the Grotte Vaticane (the other two lunettes are by Paolo Romano), the Virtues on the Acquaviva and Chiaves monuments in the Lateran, the relief in the Chapel of Sixtus V in S. Maria Maggiore, and parts of relief No. 204 of the Grotte Vaticane, which the writer considers the tomb of Cardinal Latino Orsini. The attributions are based on a comparison of these monuments with a known work of Isaia, the tomb of Eugenius IV in S. Salvatore in Lauro. Other sculptures assigned to Isaia are: the statuette of the Madonna in the *Pregnantinus* chapel of the Grotte Vaticane, the St. Mark in a niche in the Lateran, another St. Mark in the doorway of the church of the same name, and the tombstone of Fra Angelico in the Minerva.

New Fragments of the Tomb of Paul II. — In *Jb. Preuss. Kunsts.* XXVII, 1906, pp. 129-141, F. Burger publishes a number of fragments which he attributes to the tomb of Paul II. They consist of some pieces in the left wall of the Cappella della Pieta in St. Peter's, and several figures of angels and two pilaster faces with papal crests by Mino da Fiesole and Giovanni Dalmata, which are preserved in the Grotte Vaticane. These fragments suggest a new reconstruction, which adds a cornice to the tomb as it appears in Ciacconio's print.

Antonio Carpenino. — The life of Antonio Carpenino, the Ligurian painter of the first half of the fifteenth century, is reconstructed by U. MazZini in *Rass. bibl. arte ital.* 1907, pp. 1-9. A list of his works is given, together with two documents regarding him from the archives of Genoa.

Two Wooden Statues. — In *VArte,* 1907, pp. 131-133, Lisetta CiacCio points out the common authorship of two wooden statues, one representing a monastic saint, in the baptistery of the Collegiata in Empoli, the other an angel (or Salome) carrying the head of St. John Baptist, in the baptistery of Pistoia. The breadth of handling and nobility of the figures betokens an artist of the first rank, but there is no clue to his identity. His style indicates Florentine rather than Pisan or Sienese influence.

An Early Work of Leonardo. — In the *Nation,* May 16, 1907, AV. RanKin points out that in the Annunciation in the Uffizi, although the design may le due to Verrocchio, to whom the picture is often ascribed, the landscape shows a beauty and power which suggest that the painting is an early work of Leonardo da Vinci.

Pietro Summonte's Letter to Miohiel. — The letter of Pietro Summonte (1463-1526), the Neapolitan scholar, to Marcantonio Michiel of Venice, a document important for the history of early painting in Naples, is published in a critical edition with notes in *Rep./. K.* 1907, pp. 143-168, by C. Von Fabriczy.

A Miniature by Gentile Bellini. — The peculiar Turkish name " Ibn Muezzin" on the miniature from Constantinople (*A.J.A.* X, p. 366) has been explained by H. Brockhaus, who points out that Bellini is in Turkish Ibn Bellin (son of Bellin). In Greek letters of the fifteenth century *ir* and v, and X and £, are easily confused; hence *furtWiv* could be misread *fivt££iv.* and this mistake seems to have been made in translating into Turkish a Greek inscription, lost in cutting down the picture for a Turkish owner. (F. R. Martin, *Burl. Mag.* IX, 1906, p. 148.) In *Jb. Preuss. Kunsts.* XXVII, pp. 302-306 (pi.), F. Sarre accepts this explanation, and suggests that the blonde hair and facial type of the youth indicate that he was one of the pages chosen for the Sultan from his Christian subjects.

Paintings by Antonello da Messina. — The Madonna Annunziata in the Academy at Venice, though signed *Antonellu8 Messanius,* has been considered a copy of an original in Munich. In *vArte,* 1907, pp. 13-17, E. Brunelli argues that the Venetian picture displays an archaic rigidity of line unlike the Munich painting, and is probably a copy of an earlier work of Antonello, which he finds in the Madonna of the Palermo Museum. The Palermo painting is also published in *Boll. Arte,* 1907, ii, pp. 30-31 (pi.), by A. Salinas, who regards it as a contemporary replica of the Venetian picture, and suggests that the artist is Antonio de Saliba, who was from Messina. In *Rass. d'Arte,* 1907, pp. 75-76, E. Manceri publishes a picture of St. Zosimus in the cathedral of Syracuse, which he ascribes to Antonello.

Documents concerning Michelangelo. — In *Rep. f. K.* 1906, pp. 387424,485-516, is published a collection of documents concerning Michelangelo formed by E. Steinmann and H. Pooatscher. These include: (1) unedited documents, consisting of three memoranda of Michelangelo, two letters of the artist's father to his sons Giovan Simone and Michelangelo, data on the Sixtine and Pauline frescoes, two briefs of Paul III and Julius III directed to Michelangelo, and documents concerning Michelangelo's monument at Santa Croce in Florence; (2) poems and dedications to Michelangelo; (8) correspondence between Michelangelo and Pietro Aretiiio, and letters of the latter to Enea Vico and Allessandro Corvino concerning the master's Last Judgment; (4) the Cavalieri documents.

A New Master. — Pietro Toesca in *L'Arte,* 1907, pp. 18-24, attacks the attribution to Leonardo Scarletta of the Madonna, Saints and Angels in the Pinacoteca Civica at Faenza. This is an early work of an unknown artist steeped in Ferrarese traditions, who afterward painted the San Bernardino and Donor in the same gallery and shows his fullest development in another Madonna, Saints and Angels in the collection of Mr. Claude Phillips in London. This unknown artist may be called the Maestro Emiliano.

Unpublished Documents of the Sixteenth Century. — In *A usonia,* I, 1906, pp. 9—102, R. Laxciani publishes new documents relating to artists of the sixteenth century. The first shows that the mausoleum of Nicolas IV in the choir of Santa Maria Maggiore was erected in 1576 by Cardinal Peretti, later Sixtus V. The work was executed by Alessandro Ciuli of Florence, while the statue of the deceased and two other figures were by Leonardo Sormani da Savona. The second is the contract for the tomb of Cardinal Gambara in S. Maria delle Grazie at Brescia. The third shows Pirro Ligorio as a painter of grotesques in 1542 for the Archbishop of Beneventum, Francesco della Rovere.

The History of the Villa Papa Giullo. — P. Giordani contributes to *L'Arte,* 1907, pp. 133-138, an account of the construction of the Villa Papa Giulio from its designing by Vasari to the final entry in the expense account of Julius III of payment for gilding to Giovanni Giacomo da Parma.

Notes on the Museo Civico of Verona. — In *Madonna Verona,* I, 1907, pp. 49-52 (pi.), A. Venturi attributes to Bernardo Parenzano a small painting in the Museo Civico of Verona representing the Conversion of St. Paul, and remarkable for its endeavor to render the Oriental surroundings. He also argues that the terra-cotta reliefs in the Cappella Pellegrini of S. Anastasia and fragments of an altar in the Museo Civico indicate that Bode's " Maestro della Cappella Pellegrino" was probably a Veronese.

Cecilia Brusasorci.— In *Madonna Verona,* I, 1907, pp. 26-31, Lilian Priijlibon collects some facts about Cecilia Brusasorci, daughter of Domenico Riccio called Brusasorci, and sister of Felice Brusasorci. She was born in 1549, and her will is dated in 1593. As a painter she was praised for her portraits, but her works have not been identified with the probable exception of seven female saints, forming the lower part of a painting (No. 448) in the gallery at Verona.

FRANCE

The Miniaturists of Avignon. —In *Gaz. B.-A.* XXXVII, 1907, pp. 213-240, 289-305, L. II. Labande studies the miniatures of Avignon and their painters. Few of the latter were natives of Avignon. The majority were from the north of France, but some were from Italy and their influence is very apparent. Five periods are distinguished, beginning in the thirteenth century with a very Byzantine Crucifixion in MS. 176 of the Avignon Library, and continuing through the fifteenth century. The Italian influence appears under John XXII, but the French school prevails until toward the end of the fourteenth century, when Italian styles again appear. After the departure of the popes French methods prevailed, but the cosmopolitan character of Avignon prevented the development of a distinct local school.

The Altar-piece from Boulbon. — In *Mon. Piot,* XIII, 1906, pp. 85-105 (pi.; 4 figs.), F. Ie Mei.y discusses in detail the early French altar-piece from Boulbon, now in the Louvre. He concludes that it was painted for the church of St. Agricola at Avignon, and that a little stork *(cicogne)* is the cipher of the artist. The same bird appears in miniatures executed at Avignon between 1447 and 1455 in a Book of Hours now at Aix by an artist who signs himself T. Chugoinot. The Picard *Chugoinot* is in French *Cicoignot,* and in old French *cieoineau* means *petit cicogne.* The miniaturist therefore was probably the painter of the altar-piece.

Gtodefredus Batavus. — The miniatures of the *Commentaires des Guerres Gatlii/ues,* having been ordered by Francis I, have been assigned, together with some preliminary drawings, to the court painter Jean Clouet. This attribution is vigorously contested by A. De Mely in *Gaz. B.-A.* XXXVII, 1907, pp. 403-417, who cites the signature of the miniatures, *Godefroy,* and argues that there is no good reason to suppose that original designs by Clouet were executed by Godefroy..Other signatures prove that Godefroy's family name began with R and that he used at times a lizard as his symbol.

Portraits in the Bibliotheque Natiouale. — In *Le Musee,* IV, 1907, pp. 127-140 (3 pis.), J. Guibkrt notices the recent exhibition of portraits in colored crayon belonging to the Bibliotheque Nationale at Paris. The collection began with the acquisition of the drawings and engravings of the Abbe Marolles in 1667, was further increased by the Gagnieres collection in 1715, and now numbers over 800. The drawings, frequently studies for larger portraits, are the work of the Clouets, Corneille de Lyon, Dumonstier, Le Mannier, and others.

The "Vierge aux Rochers." — In the "Vierge aux Rochers" in the Louvre the angel points toward St. John Baptist, a gesture of special significance for Florentines. It is probable that this picture was painted by Leonardo before leaving Florence, while the London copy, in which this gesture of the angel is lacking, was executed at Milan with the assistance of Ambrogio da Predis. (S. Reixach, *C. R. Acad. Insc.* 1907, pp. 16-17.)

The Marmion Family. — In *R. Arch.* IX, 1907, pp. 119-140, Mauisice Henault begins an account of the Marmion family (Jehan, Simon, Mille, and Colinet). Jehan, first mentioned in 1426, at Amiens, painted decorations there until 1444, but in 1465 was living at Valenciennes, where he was a person of some importance in 1473. He died certainly before 1489. His children were Mille (not Wille or Guillaume), Simon, and a daughter. Mille was a painter of some importance. In 1464 he executed paintings for the city hall at Amiens, in 1466 he was settled at Tournai, where he was in 1473, but in 1499 he lived at Abbeville. There is no record of his living at Valenciennes. Simon was born, apparently at Amiens, about 1425, where he painted for the city between 1449 and 1454. In 1458 he acquired property at Valenciennes, where he became an important and evidently wealthy man. He already had two sons by a previous marriage. In 1464 or 1465 he married Jeanne de Quarouble. In 1468 he was made a member of the guild of painters at Tournai. He died in 1489, at Valenciennes, leaving a daughter Marie or Marion, who died before 1505. The property of Simon Mavmion passed, on the death of his widow, who had married again, to the children of his sister, Michel, Jeanne, and Isabeau Clauwet. No certainly identified work of Simon Marmion now exists, though several works are known, chiefly through the records of Amiens and Valenciennes. The discussion *(ibid.* pp. 282-297; bibliography, pp. 297304) of the works attributed to Simon Marmion leads to the conclusion that no work of this artist has been identified with certainty and that it is not even certain that he was a great or original artist.

The "Man with the Wine-glass." — In *Gaz. B.-A.* XXXVII, 1907, pp. 1-24, P. Leprieur in a discussion of new pictures in the Louvre rejects the attribution of the "Man with the Wine-glass" *(A J. A.* X, p. 371) to Jean Fouquet, because the artist shows Flemish training rather than the Italian leanings of Fouquet, uses broader brush work, and differs in detail and arrangement. He makes no attempt to name the author, however, calling him simply the "Maitre de 1456."

Attributions in the Museum of Dijon. — In *Bass. d'Arte,* 1906, pp. 186-189, G. Frizzoni discusses two Italian pictures in the museum at Dijon. A Portrait of a Woman, catalogued under the name of Hans Holbein the Younger, he ascribes to Lotto. A Resurrection is assigned to Francesco Ubertini, called il Bacchiacca (1490-1557). It shows the influence of the painter's master, Perugino.

The Tournament at Sandricourt. — The "Pas des armes de Sandricourt" was a celebrated tourney held in 1493 by Louis d'Hedonville, in his chateau of Sandricourt, near Pointoise. Among the Louvre drawings is a series of sixteenth-century sketches illustrating this tourney and signed "Baullery." This name belongs to two artists, father and son, but it is impossible to tell which was the author of the drawings, as the work of both is practically unknown. (P. Marcel and J. Guiffrev, *Gaz. B.-A.* XXXVII, 1907, pp. 277-288).

A Portrait by Brescianino. — The attractive Portrait of a Young Man in the Montpellier Museum, once attributed to Raphael, is now given to Brescianino on internal evidence by Bernhard Berenson. He compares its details with those of the Madonna with St. Dominic and Angels in the Uffizi, and the Madonna with St. John Baptist and St. Jerome in the church of San Lorenzo at Babbiano. *(Gaz. B.-A.* XXXVII, 1907, pp. 208-212.)

The Aynard Relief again. — The discussion of the authenticity of the Betrothal of St. Catherine in the Aynard collection, opened in *L'Arte* by E. Bertaux and E. Bkunelli *(A.J.A.* XI, p. 246), is continued by the same writers, *ibid.* 1907, pp. 144-148.

The Gobelin Factory. — A sketch of the famous Gobelin factory by Lady St. John appears in *Burl. Mag.* X, 1907, pp. 279-289. The family was founded by Jehan Gobelin, the discoverer of a fine crimson dye, who lived in Paris in 1450. The tapestry works were established under the patronage of Henry IV in 1603, and made a royal manufactory by Louis XIV in 1662. The history of the Gobelin tapestries falls into four periods: (1) prior to 1662, when the cartoons were often designed by Rubens and other great artists; (2) the reign of Louis XIV; (3) the eighteenth century, in general a time of brilliant achievement; (4) the period of decadence which followed the Revolution.

The Fountain of St. Jean du Doigt. — In *Le Mwee,* IV, 1907, p. 118 (pi.), O. Theatks describes the fountain of St. Jean du Doigt, near Morlaix, which is probably by an Italian artist of the early sixteenth century. It consists of three superposed basins, each surrounded by cherubs' heads; above is a half-length figure of God the Father, and a little below, a group representing the Baptism.

The Bronze Copy of the Borghese Dancers. — In *Mon. Piot,* XIII, 1900, pp. 107-116 (2 figs.), £. Michon states that in the former house of Gouthiere in Paris there is a cast of the Borghese Dancers in the Louvre. Probably the bronze reliefs in London and the Louvre *(A.J.A.* X, p. 210) were made, as Bode has suggested, by Gouthiere at the end of the eighteenth century. The writer corrects errors in Visconti's account of the Borghese collection, and points out that a lost relief, formerly in the Villa Negroni, was a companion to the maidens decking a candelabrum in the Louvre.

BELGIUM

Attributions in the Gallery at Brussels. — In *Gaz. B.-A.* XXXVI, 1900, pp. 281-300, and XXXVII, 1907, pp. 54-68, 418-435, E. Jacobsen discusses the attributions of German and Flemish pictures in the Brussels Gallery. He first takes up Barend van Orley, reviews the painter's characteristics, and points out that his earlier art shows the influence of Giulio Romano's frescoes at Mantua, which the northern painter must have visited before 1521, in view of the use he makes of Mantegna's Triumph of Caesar. A Pieta (No. 559) is selected as typical of his middle period, although it has been refused to Van Orley by other writers. The Holy Family (Xo. 338), which shows Raphael's influence, and three portraits represent the last period of the artist's activity. A number of other pictures are also assigned to Van Orley or his school. The chief attributions to Jan van Coninxlo are two triptych wings with scenes from the life of St. Benedict, which Jacobsen regards as a youthful work of the master. To Cornelis van Coninxlo he gives a Madonna and Holy Women. Several new attributions are made in the case of Herri Met de Bles and the "Maitre de Flcmalle," while the well-known Sforza triptych is described as a product of the atelier of Rogier van der Weyden, very probably executed in conjunction with his pupil Mending. The discussion of the Oultremont altar-piece is prefaced by a valuable list of thirty-five recent attributions to Jan Mostaert (or to the "Maitre d'Oultremont"). Gliick's attribution of the Oultremont picture to Mostaert is rejected by Jacobsen, who identifies the Descent from the Cross on the central panel with the painting mentioned by Van Mander in his life of Jacob Cornelisz. Admitting, however, the possibility of a mistake by Van Mander, Jacobsen merely reviews the evidence for and against assigning the triptych to Cornelisz. The third article contains a number of attributions in the Cologne School and a discussion of other remarkable pictures in the collection.

GERMANY

Botticelli's St. Sebastian at Berlin. — The painting of St. Sebastian, considered a youthful work of Botticelli, and now in the Kaiser Friedrich Museum in Berlin, was originally designed for a pilaster of S. Maria Maggiore in Florence. (dktlev Freih. Von Hadeln, *Jb. Preuss. Kunsls* XXVII, 1906, pp. 282-284.)

The Altar-piece in St. John's, Nuremberg. — In *Burl. Mag.* X, 1907, pp. 257-258, S. Montagu Peartree reproduces two panels of Lucas Moser's altar-piece in Tiefenbronn in Baden and the Crucifixion previously discussed by him *(ibid.* p. Ill), in the Church of St. John in Nuremburg. A comparison of the two leads to the conclusion that the Crucifixion is also by Moser. The power of realization shown by the artist, remarkable in so early a work (dated 1431), is due to Italian influence, which appears particularly in the architecture and in the group of the Virgin and her attendants at the foot of the Cross.

The Master N. H. — The initials N. II. appear on a German wood-cut published by Camprell Dodgson in *Burl. Mag.* X, 1908, pp. 309-322. The scene is a "Battle of Naked Men and Peasants, in Utopia," as we learn from the verses which accompany one of the copies. The engraver signs himself *Hanns. Leuczellburger. Furmschnider* 1522, and is the same craftsman who made the blocks for Holbein's Dance of Death. The designer "N. II." is certainly the author of the first thirty-seven woodcuts in Weissenhorn's edition of Apuleius of 1538. His drawings were made earlier, however, at a date nearer his other works, Maximilianus Transilvanus' *Legalio ad sacratissunum Caesarem Carolum* (1519-1520), a signed set of thirtyseven woodcuts in a book on the Passion with verses by Chelidonius (Cologne, 1526), and others. The verses accompanying the "Battle of Naked Men," make it plain that the artist and Lutzelburger are represented in the two non-combatants to the left.

Veronese Paintings in Stuttgart. — In *Madonna Verona*, I, 1907, pp. 7-10 (pi.), C. Von Fabriczy describes briefly twenty-three paintings of the Veronese school in the gallery at Stuttgart. The list includes four paintings by Bonifacio de' Pitati, one each by Torbido, Paolo Veronese, and Zelotti, and three by Alessandro Turchi.

Augustus and the Sibyl. —In the Museum at Stuttgart is a painting, probably by Paolo Veneziano, representing Augustus and the sibyl of Tibur, with the Madonna and Child above. In the lower right-hand corner are represented the falling idols in the temple of Peace. Scrolls bear inscriptions abridged from the Golden Legend of Jacopo da Voragine. (L. VenTuri, *Ausonia*, I, 1906, pp. 93-95; pi.) ENGLAND

The Italian Drawings at Oxford. — In *L'Arle,* 1907, pp. 81-95, G. Frizzoni comments on the drawings by Italian masters in the fifth portfolio of the Oxford Collection. The first drawing, a female profile by Pisanello, is a study for the princess in Pisanello's St. George in Sant' Anastasia at Verona. Colvin's discovery of a study by Leonardo for the angel's sleeve in the Uffizi Annunciation is not conclusive as to the authorship of that picture, which is probably the product of collaboration in the studio of Verrocchio. Colvin's doubts regarding the authenticity of a sketch of two figures supposed to be studies for Raphael's School of Athens, are scouted by Frizzoni, who also differs from Colvin in assigning a drawing of two figures, to Sebastiano del Piombo, rather than to Giorgione's school, pointing out that reminiscences of Giorgione appear in some of Sebastiaho's work.

A Forgery Proved. — The " Enthronement of Thomas a Becket," lent by the Duke of Devonshire to the Guildhall exhibition of 1906, bears the inscription *Johes de Eyck fecit — ano.*MC-CCC ZI-30. *Oetnbris.* The date 1421 is remarkably early for a work by Jan Van Eyck, and the picture shows nothing of his hand. Alfred Marks, *Burl. Mag.* X, 1907, pp. 383— 384, proves that the signature is a forgery, being copied, with modifications, from the signature on the Portrait of a Man, No. 222, in the National Gallery, dated 1433, 21 *Octobris.* W. II. J. Wkale, *ibid.* XI, 1907, p. 45, suggests that the painter of the disputed picture may have been Dirk Bareutz (Theodore Bernardi) of Amsterdam, who came to England in 1519 and worked for churches in Sussex and Hampshire.

A Lost Painting by Jan Van Eyok. — In *Burl. Mag.* X, 1907, p. 325, A. G. B. Russell calls attention to a picture in the painting by Haecht (1628) representing a picture gallery. It represents a young woman assisted at her bath by an attendant dressed in red. In the window hangs a mirror in which both are reflected. From a close resemblance in the figures and details with Jan Van Eyck's other works the author concludes this a copy of a lost painting by that artist. In *Chron. Arts,* 1907, pp. 99-100, H. Hymans analyzes Haecht's painting, which represents a visit of the Archduke Albert and the Archduchess Isabelle to the gallery of Cornille van der Geest in 1615. He identifies many of the pictures represented in the gallery, and suggests that the "Woman Bathing," may be a copy of the painting by Van Eyck which once belonged to Cardinal Ottaviani. See also *A then.* January 26, and February 9, 1907.

The Baptism of Christ, in the National Gallery. — In 1894 the National Gallery acquired a small picture representing the Baptism of Christ ascribed in the last catalogue to the school of Perugino. The genuineness of this painting was attacked by R. C. Fisher and M. W. Brockwell and defended by Sir E. J. Poynter in a series of letters in *A then.* January 26, February 29, and 16, and the Loudon *Times,* March 30, April 1, 4, and 8. In *Chron. Arts,* 1907, pp. 167-168, 177, and London *Times,* April 13, E. Durand-greville argues that the picture is a copy by Raphael of Perugino's picture in Rouen. In the three little compositions in Rouen from the predella of Perugino's Ascension, the figures indicate the collaboration of Raphael.

A Crucifixion by Konrad Witz of Basel. — A Crucifixion, belonging to the Rev. Lewis Gilbertson, is reproduced by Claude Phillips in *Burl. Mag.* XI, 1907, pp. 103-109, and assigned to Konrad Witz on internal evidence. The painter of this work was influenced by contemporary Flemings, and yet in the group of holy women shows the Italo-French modes as practised by Netherlanders in France. The lake in the background resembles so strongly a study of an inlet on the Lake of Geneva that the picture probably dates from 1444, the year of Witz's residence in Geneva.

Correction of a Date. — The Crucifixion by Marco Palmezzano, now in the collection of Canon Raymond Pelly, when shown at the Exposition of Ancient Masters at Burlington House bore the restored date MCCCCLXXX. C. Jocelyn Foulkes in *Rass. bihl. arte ital.* 1907, pp. 16-19, states after examination that it should have been MCCCC-CXXXI. This date agrees better with the developed style of the picture than 1480, which would have made it the earliest known work of the artist.

Early Works of Velasquez iu England. — *Burl. Mag.* X, 1906, pp. 172-183, contains an appreciation and critique by Sir J. C. Robinson of four early works of Velasquez in English Collections: the "Beggar with the Wine-bottle" and the "Omelette Woman" in Sir Frederick Cook's collection, the "Mary and Martha" in the National Gallery and the "Steward" in his own collection. These are all of the *boihgon* class, a species of genre painting of which Velasquez is the first great exponent. The "Mary and Martha" is probably the earliest Velasquez now known. *Ibid.* XI, 1907, pp. 394, the same writer discusses two other pieces of the same class, the "Kitchen" in the collection of Sir Frederick Cook, and the "Fight at the Fair" in his own gallery, both of which he ascribes to the culmination of Velasquez's *bndegon* period. The latter shows the collaboration of an inferior hand, perhaps that of Pacheco.

UNITED STATES

Cassone Panels in American Collections. — The publication of the Cassone panels in American collections (*A..I.A.* X, p. 133) is continued in *Burl. Mag.* X, 1906, pp. 205-206, where F. J. Mather describes three panels by Jacopo del Sellaio; the "Actaeon" in the Jarves Collection in New Haven, and "Nostagio's Feast" and the "Battle of Romans and Sabines" in the Johnson Collection of Philadelphia. The "Actaeon" shows many reminiscences of Uccello, but the landscape is strikingly suggestive of Alessio Baldovinetti, the whole composition dating about 1475, when Jacopo had passed out of Fra Filippo's influence and was not yet the follower of Botticelli and Filippino. "Nostagio's Feast" is a characteristic copy of the panel in the Spiridon Collection, attributed by Berenson to Bartolommeo di Giovanni or Alunno di Domenico. The "Battle of Romans and Sabines" is very Filippinesque and might date anywhere between 1484 and 1493. *Ibid.* pp. 332-335, W. Rankin describes two panels by Piero di Cosimo, representing a Hunt and Return from the Hunt, now in the Metropolitan Museum. He classes them among Piero's earlier works and finds the influence of Filippino in the landscape. A note by F. J. Mather calls attention to an intentional striving after bizarre effect, which contains in it the seeds of decadence. *Ibid.* XI, 1907, pp. 131-132 (2 pis.), W. Rankin publishes two panels with scenes from the Aeneid and the Visit of the Queen of Sheba to Solomon, in the Jarves Collection at New Haven. They are ascribed to Uccello, but the writer hesitates to assign a name to the painter, stating only that the same artist made the panels lent by the Earl of Crawford to the Exhibition of Early Italian Art, held at London in the winter of 1893-1894.

The St. Francis in the Johnson Collection. — In *Burl. Mag.* XI, 1907, pp. 46-48, A. F. Jaccacci defends the authenticity of Hubert Van Eyck's painting of St. Francis receiving the Stigmata in the Johnson Collection in Philadelphia (cf. *AJ.A.* XI, pp. 136-137), holding that the Turin picture bears all the marks of a copy. As between the brothers Van Eyck, he prefers Hubert, on account of the depth of feeling displayed. If this attribution is correct, the view of Assisi and the Alps would indicate that Hubert also had travelled beyond the Low Countries.

AMERICAN ARCHAEOLOGY

Prehistoric Man in America.— The discovery of human remains in undisturbed loess in Nebraska (*A.J.A.* XI, p. 138) is further reported in *Rec. Past,* VI, 1907, pp. 85-39 (5 figs.), by R. F. Gilder, who describies his first excavations at Long's hill, and pp. 40-40 (5 figs.), by E. II. Barbour, who gives the results of his examination of Mr. Gilder's work and discusses the geological stratification. *Ibid.* pp. 70-78, E. E. Bi.ackman calls attention to certain earlier discoveries which point to the presence of man in the West in glacial or possibly pre-glacial times. *Ibid.* pp. 115-157, 163-181 (17 figs.), N. II. Winchkll examines briefly all the scattered evidence for the presence of early man in America, and concludes that man existed in the Pleistocene period, and that the recurring periods of glacial action caused extensive migrations. As the close of the Wisconsin ice-epoch occurred about 7000 to 8000 years ago, the last movement northward may be comparatively recent.

Mound Builders of the Mississippi Valley. — In *Rec. Past,* VI, 1907, pp. 79-82 (4 figs.), R. Herrmann continues his discussion of the Mound Builders of the Mississippi Valley (*A J.A.* XI, p. 249). lie considers battle mounds, Indian cremation, and tribal or national mounds, arguing that the effigy mounds were erected by tribes, whose names they represent, as memorials of some great event.

The Antiquities of the Jemez Plateau, New Mexico. — The Bureau of American Ethnology has begun the publication of a series of bulletins describing briefly the antiquities on the public domain of the United States. The first bulletin contains an account by E. L. Hewf.tt of the antiquities of the Jemez Plateau in Xew Mexico. The region was inhabited in prehistoric times by an agricultural people, who lived in excavated cliff-dwellings or in pueblos. Rock pictures are common in this region. The early inhabitants seem to have gradually abandoned the region about six or eight hundred years ago in consequence of climatic changes, though some of their descendants are doubtless living among the Pueblo Indians, who are partly of another race. The report describes in detail the ruins in three groups: those of the Pajarito plateau, of the Chama drainage, and of the Jemez valley. In all forty-nine sites are noted. (*Smithsonian Institution, Bureau of American Ethnology, Bulletin 32. Antiquities of the Jemez Plateau, New Mexico,* by Edgar L. Hewett. Washington, 1900, Government Printing Office. 55 pp.; 10 pis.; map. 8vo.)

Mexican Myths. —In *Z. Ethn.* XXXIX, 1907, pp. 1-il (15 figs.), E. Seler examines the basis in natural phenomena of various Mexican myths. He argues that many of the divinities of the earth and harvest are really lunar, such as the *pulque* gods, Tlacolteotl, the old goddess, Xipe Totec, the god of spring, and the goddess of love, Xochiguetzal. The ballground, which appears in connection with these gods, is a symbolical representation of the conflict between sun and moon, or between light and darkness. The lunar nature of Te/.catlipoca and Quetzalcouatl is discussed in connection with the legend of the early wanderings of the Aztecs, and the importance of the moon in early religions is emphasized.

THE BORROWER WILL BE CHARGED AN OVERDUE FEE IF THIS BOOK IS NOT RETURNED TO THE LIBRARY ON OR BEFORE THE LAST DATE STAMPED BELOW. NON-RECEIPT OF OVERDUE NOTICES DOES NOT EXEMPT THE BORROWER FROM OVERDUE FEES.

Revolutions and nationalities

PUBLISHED BY THE PRESS SYNDICATE OF THE UNIVERSITY OF CAMBRIDGE
The Pitt Building, Trumpington Street, Cambridge, United Kingdom

CAMBRIDGE UNIVERSITY PRESS
The Edinburgh Building, Cambridge CB2 2RU, UK   http://www.cup.cam.ac.uk
40 West 20th Street, New York, NY 10011-4211, USA   http://www.cup.org
10 Stamford Road, Oakleigh, Melbourne 3166, Australia
Ruiz de Alarcón 13, 28014 Madrid, Spain

© Cambridge University Press 2000

This book is in copyright. Subject to statutory exception and to the provisions of relevant collective licensing agreements, no reproduction of any part may take place without the written permission of Cambridge University Press.

First published 2000

Printed in the United Kingdom at the University Press, Cambridge

Text design by Newton Harris Design Partnership
Map artwork by Kathy Baxendale

Typeface 10.5pt Minion   *System* QuarkXPress®

A catalogue record for this book is available from the British Library

ISBN 0 521 78607 X   paperback

The cover painting of Giuseppe Garibaldi (1807–82), Italian patriot and hero of the Risorgimento, by Silvestro Lega (1826–95) is reproduced courtesy of the Art Archive/Museo Civico Modigliana, Italy/Dagli Orti.

ACKNOWLEDGEMENTS
AKG London: pp. 39, 91*b*, 168; Archivio del Museo Centrale del Risorgimento, Rome: pp 58*l&r*; Bibliothèque nationale de France: pp. 5, 67; Bildarchiv Preussischer Kulturbesitz, Berlin: p. 147; *Liberty Leading the People,* 28 July 1830 (oil on canvas), by Delacroix (Ferdinand Victor) Eugène (1798–1863), Louvre, Paris, France/Peter Willi/Bridgeman Art Library: p. 19; *Industry of the Tyne: Iron and Coal,* 1861 (oil on canvas), by William Bell Scott (1811–90), Wallington Hall, Northumberland, UK/Bridgeman Art Library: p. 175; Civica Raccolta della Stampe Achille Bertarelli, Milan: pp. 55, 193; Deutsches Historisches-Bildarchiv bzw: pp. 87, 169; Mary Evans Picture Library: pp. 47, 113; Hulton Getty Picture Collection: pp. 30, 91*t*, 120, 157, 178; International Institute of Social History, Netherlands: p. 119; David King Collection: p. 129; Musée d'Unterlinden, Colmar, Reproduction Christian Kempf: p. 70; Muzeum Wojska Polskiego, Warsaw, *The Battle,* by Artur Grottger: p. 183; NOVOSTI (London): p. 122; Popperfoto: pp. 93*t*, 152, 164; Société de Géographie: p. 103; Roger-Viollet Agency Photographique: p. 93*b*.

We have been unable to trace the copyright holder of the photograph on page 16, and would be grateful for any information that would enable us to do so.

Picture Research by Sandie Huskinson-Rolfe of PHOTOSEEKERS.

We are grateful to Macmillan Ltd for permission to reproduce extracts from *The making of Italy, 1796–1866* by Denis Mack Smith.

Every effort has been made to reach copyright holders. The publisher would be pleased to hear from anyone whose rights have been unwittingly infringed.

Contents

1 The 'short nineteenth century' — 1
Forces for change — 4
Forces for continuity — 9
Europe, 1825–90: reaction, conflict and reform — 11

2 Europe during the 1820s — 14
Country and town — 14
Industry and trade — 16
Romanticism and nationalism — 18
Reaction and revolt — 20

3 Changing the face of Europe: Italy, 1830–70 — 24
How united was Italy between 1830 and 1847? — 25
What impact did the revolutions of 1848 to 1849 have on efforts to create a united Italy? — 32
How and why was Italy united in 1861? — 37
How far did the system of government established in 1861 help to unify Italy? — 52
How united and how Italian was Italy by 1871? — 54
What was the relationship between the unification of Italy and the Risorgimento? — 58
Historical sources — 59

4 Continuing to change: France, 1848–75 — 62
Why did the Second Republic replace the July Monarchy? — 64
Why did the Second Empire replace the Second Republic? — 66
What problems did Napoleon III face in governing France, and how far did he solve them? — 76
What were the main aims of Napoleon III's foreign policy and how far did he achieve them? — 81
Why did the Second Empire end? — 86
Why did the Third Republic take the form that it did by 1875? — 89
Historical sources — 97

5 Having to change: Russia, 1825–81 — 99
What were the main features of tsarist Russia in 1825? — 101
How successfully did Nicholas I govern Russia? — 106
How significant were the main forms of oppositional thought? — 114
How successfully did Alexander II govern Russia? — 120
How and how far did Russia change between 1825 and 1881? — 131
Historical sources — 132

6 Changing the face of Europe: Germany, 1862–90   **135**

What different forms of German unification were being considered in 1862?   137
What were the main forces working for and against German unification in 1862?   140
Who or what was responsible for the creation of the German Empire in 1871?   145
What problems did Germany face between 1871 and 1890, both at home and abroad, and how successfully were they overcome?   154
How can Bismarck's leadership of Prussia and Germany be assessed?   169
Historical sources   *171*

7 Towards collectivism: Europe during the 1880s   **174**

Urban growth and rural decline   174
Technical innovation and economic depression   176
Socialism and nationalism   177
Conservatism and reform   180

8 Revolutions and nationalities: Europe, 1825–90   **182**

Nationalism and liberalism   183
The absence of revolutions   184
Nationalism and revolutionary change   185

Document study: Italian unification, 1848–71   **187**

Why was Italy not united in 1848–49?   188
How important to the unification of Italy were foreign circumstances and assistance?   190
How important to the unification of Italy were the efforts of Italians?   193

Appendix A   European states, 1825 and 1890   197
Appendix B   The use of military force by type, 1825–90   198
Appendix C   The use of military force by great powers, 1825–90   199
Appendix D   Bismarck's alliance system, 1879–90   200
Appendix E   The British system of government in the nineteenth century   201

Further reading   203
Index   207

1 The 'short nineteenth century'

To the historian of modern Europe two features of the nineteenth century stand out particularly clearly. Firstly, the 'nineteenth century' may be better described as the 99 years from 1815 to 1914, for there is a coherence to the 1815–1914 period that the period 1801–1900 lacks. In 1815 one general European war ended, in 1914 another started; there was no war on such a scale between these two dates. Secondly, the period between 1815 and 1914 was an era of relative political calm which separated two stormier periods. Nothing in the nineteenth century matches the French Revolution and the rise of Napoleon on the one side and the First World War, the Russian Revolution and the rise of fascism on the other. One cannot compare the Crimean War with Napoleon's Moscow campaign, the revolutions of 1848 with the 1917 October Revolution, Napoleon III with Napoleon Bonaparte or Bismarck with Hitler. If the 1820s to the 1880s, a period that is the essence of the nineteenth century, is considered its relative insignificance appears to be reinforced. This was the era when middle-class politicians, such as Thiers and Cavour, triumphed over such popular revolutionaries as the Paris communards and Garibaldi, when such revolutionaries as Mazzini and Marx failed to put their ideas into practice. It was the age of the bourgeoisie, of bankers, industrialists and government administrators who lack the interest and impact of figures like Napoleon, Lenin and Hitler.

And yet the 'short nineteenth century', as the period between the 1830s and the 1880s is sometimes called, should not be written off so quickly. It was a time of great importance in the history of Europe. During the 65 years from 1825 to 1890, Europe underwent a series of transformations. Consider just three contrasts:

- In 1825 there was just one railway track in Europe on which a steam engine ran: from Stockton to Darlington in north-eastern England. By 1890 there were almost 200,000 kilometres of railway lines across Europe. This contrast is important not just in itself but because of the impact the building of so much track had on European societies and economies.

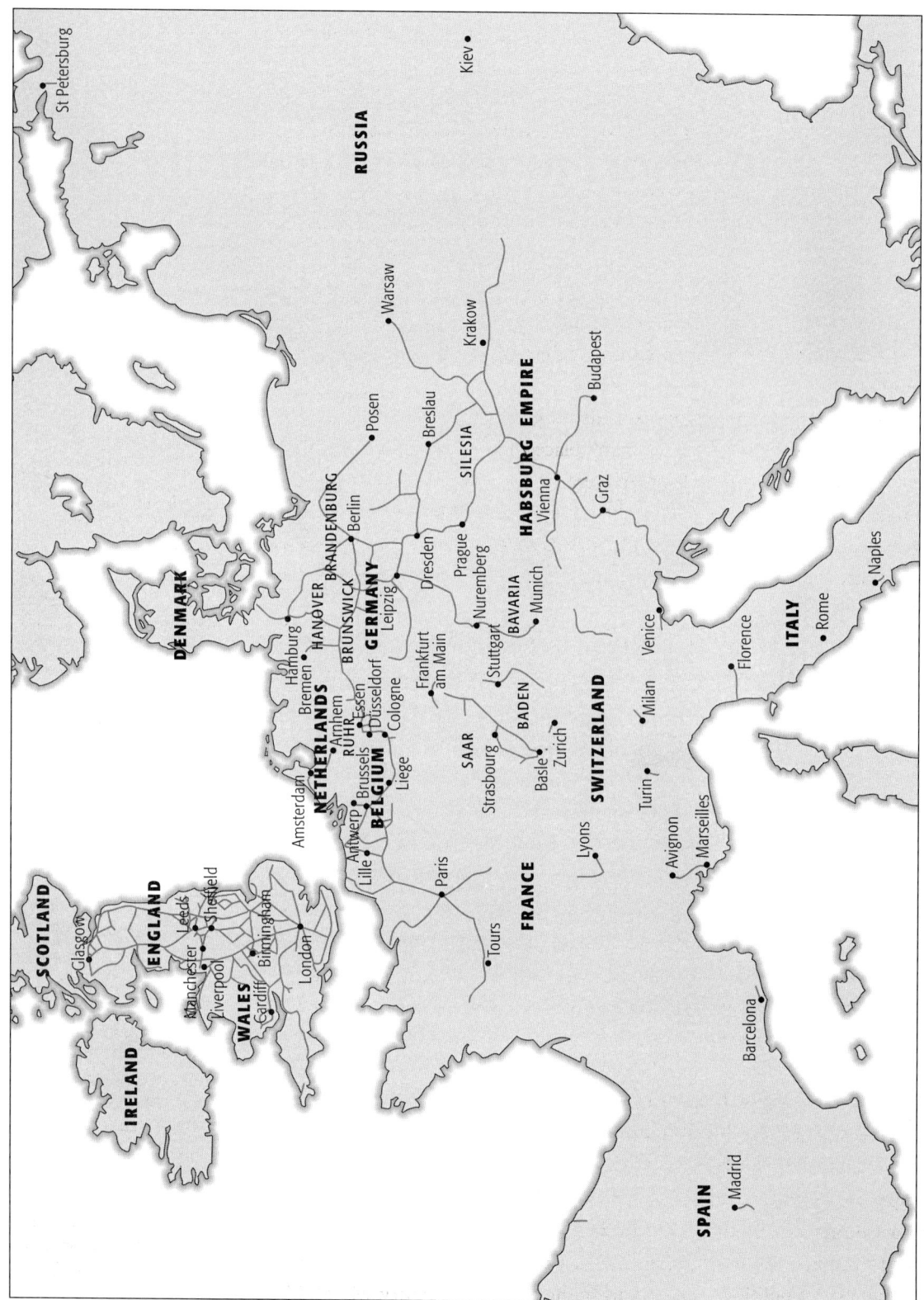

The European railway system in 1850. The degree to which a country had industrialised can be gauged from the extent of its railways.

- In 1825 Europe was divided into around 60 states, the rulers of which were hereditary rulers. These individuals were sovereign in both senses of the word. Some, such as the king of Prussia, ruled over geographically separate territories; others, like the duke of Lucca in Italy, governed states that were only a few square kilometres in size, while some, such as the Austrian Habsburgs and the Russian Romanovs, were sovereign over huge areas. By 1890, however, Europe was in the process of being formed into fewer than 30 states, most based on the concept of common national identity (see Appendix A). The nation state was becoming the norm. By 1890 all European states had given the vote to adult males, a few to all adult males. The sovereignty of the monarch was giving way to the sovereignty of the people.

  Hardly anyone at the time considered giving the vote to women. The conventional view was that a woman's place and role was different, that her very nature was different. Women were seen as dependent on and subordinate to men, almost as part of the natural order of things. Some women were starting to challenge this view, for example by fighting for the right to university education. A collective and more effective challenge did not emerge until after 1890.
- In 1825 most people in Europe lived in the countryside, working in agricultural and related occupations, often in a traditional form of subsistence farming. By 1890 many people lived in towns and cities, working in factories producing industrial goods. (Only in Britain and Germany did *most* of the population live in towns in 1890.) These towns and cities grew with great speed: in 1850 400,000 people lived in Berlin, by 1890 1,900,000. This great shift from countryside to town, repeated in all parts of Europe, had huge social consequences.

This period furthermore saw the emergence of two sets of ideas that would revolutionise the ways in which people across the globe viewed themselves:
- In 1831 a 22-year-old English scientist set sail for the Pacific, where he spent five years. In 1859 he published the conclusions that he had drawn from his journey in a book that shocked contemporary society. He was **Charles Darwin**, the book was *The origin of species*. The idea that shocked was the theory of evolution. It forced people to view the relationship between humans and animals, between humans and God, in a new light.
- In 1848 a 30-year-old German journalist published a short book which began: 'A spectre is haunting Europe – the spectre of communism'. Its publication went unnoticed at the time. However, *The communist manifesto* was to become the best-known of the writings of **Karl Marx**. As well as having a great political impact during the twentieth century, Marx's ideas

Charles Darwin (1809–82), one of the great figures of natural science, developed the theory of natural selection to explain how animal life had evolved. His ideas are often summarised by the phrase 'the survival of the fittest', though it was a term he did not invent. His theories, when applied by others to human life, became known as Social Darwinism and were sometimes used to justify racist beliefs.

Karl Marx (1818–83) was a German journalist and philosopher whose writings have had a profound impact on modern history. Best known for *The communist manifesto* (1848), which he co-authored with Frederick Engels, he also wrote prolifically on such contemporary events as Louis Napoleon's *coup* of 1851. For most of his adult life Marx lived in exile in London.

also had a wider intellectual effect. They made people rethink the place of economics. In a broad sense we are all Marxists now. Today economics is the social science that lies at the heart of government policy and public life.

The 'short nineteenth century' of European history was therefore a time of great importance to the modern world. The period was furthermore perhaps more significant in terms of its impact on ordinary people's lives than the era that preceded it. An incomplete list of important innovations of the time includes electro-magnetism, telephony, cheap newspapers, trade unions, state social insurance, mass education, the breech-loading gun, antiseptics, postal services and photography. Someone born in 1810 who lived until 1890 would have seen a transformation in their lives greater than their parents had experienced, especially if they were male, even if they were female. So what helped to bring about this transformation?

Forces for change
Demographic change

The population of Europe grew very rapidly during the nineteenth century: it is estimated that it more than doubled to 400 million by 1900. In addition, around 21 million Europeans emigrated, mainly to the Americas, during the last 30 years of the century alone. This sustained population increase, which occurred at a rate never experienced before or since, was bound to have great economic and social consequences. In the short term the living conditions of the labouring classes, the vast majority of people, was made worst. Many who had always been poor, struggling to survive, now became paupers, completely dependent upon the charity of others. This economic and social degradation helps explain elements of the revolutions of 1848–49. In the longer term, however, continued economic growth meant that enough job opportunities were provided, either in Europe or overseas, to avoid the many dangers of mass pauperism.

Yet because this demographic growth was concentrated among the poor, the ruling classes feared revolt by the uneducated masses, especially when they were congregated in towns. When this fear became reality in 1848, European governments eventually learnt their lesson and took various steps to prevent it from happening again.

Economic change

One reason why the doubling of Europe's population did not lead to the major problems predicted by **Thomas Malthus** was the ability of many companies to benefit from new technologies. The new railways not only brought

The Reverend **Thomas Malthus** (1766–1834) was the author of *An essay on population* (1798), which asserted that the growth in population would outstrip the growth in food supply; the two would be balanced only when famine, disease and war reduced the number of people. So far his ideas have proved mistaken on a global scale.

A new railway viaduct and engine at Chantilly, France, photographed in 1855. The picture illustrates the ability of the Second Empire to cross natural obstacles to progress.

supplies of perishable foodstuffs to new towns more quickly than drovers or carters, they also stimulated demand for other industrial products, such as iron and steel. These industries in turn needed more workers to meet the new demand. Distance now ceased to protect isolated economies as they were opened up by railways and steamships. Even Marx, writing in *The communist manifesto*, could not but admire these developments:

> The bourgeoisie, during its rule of scarce one hundred years, has created more massive and more colossal productive forces than have all the preceding generations together. Subjection of nature's forces to man, machinery, application of chemistry to industry and agriculture, steam navigation, railways, electric telegraphs, clearing of whole continents for cultivation, canalisation of rivers, whole populations conjured out of the ground – what earlier century had even a presentiment that such productive forces slumbered in the lap of social labour?

Social change

The economic change of industrialisation brought with it enormous social change. People seeking work moved from the countryside to towns in their hundreds of thousands. They worked in factories that were badly lit, poorly ventilated and dangerous, lived in houses that were overcrowded and walked unsanitary streets. It was several decades before governments did anything to improve these conditions. Meanwhile the workers, forced together, developed a shared sense of interest and identity. They were called the working class. Another term applied to them at the time, especially by Marx, was the proletariat. All they had was their labour.

On the outskirts of town, in larger, more comfortable houses, lived the workers' bosses, the middle class – or, in Marxist terms, the bourgeoisie. They owned the factories and machines, the property and capital. A class-based, industrial society was replacing the old, status-based, agrarian society. Marxists predicted that the conflict between the two classes would become so great that it would result in revolution. Others believed that the different class interests were not as important as common national or material interests and that they could thus be reconciled. Whichever was right, the growth of a class-based society was a major force for change.

Political change

Here the change was less the development of new ideas and more the working out of those which had emerged in the French Revolution. 'Liberty, equality, fraternity' were the watchwords of the French revolutionaries. Napoleonic armies had spread these ideas across most of Europe. The defeat of Napoleon between 1813 and 1815 gave the old order the chance to suppress them, but it could not eradicate them. Such repressive attempts only caused some to support them all the more, however, especially once the memories of the French Revolution began to fade.

Liberty

The concept of liberty usually took two forms: firstly, the freedom to do things, such as speak or write whatever you wanted to say, and, secondly, freedom from arbitrary government, from officials who ordered you around. The two forms were usually combined in demands for **constitutional government**. Such ideas appealed particularly to the new middle classes.

> **Constitutional government** can be defined as government that is limited by a set of rules stating what it can do and to whom it is accountable. It usually includes a statement of the rights of the people that is often written down in a single document, like that in the USA in 1787 which became the model for many European liberals.

Equality

At this time equality usually meant political equality, although some argued for economic equality as well. Political equality envisaged everyone (or every adult male) having the same political rights. The right to vote was the most obvious form of political equality. It meant democracy, rule by the people rather than by monarchy or aristocracy. The idea alarmed Europe's kings and nobles. Most people were poor and ignorant. Those who considered themselves superior to the poor often thought that they were stupid, too, and therefore incapable of deciding how the country should be governed. Democracy was a dangerous idea for most of the nineteenth century.

Fraternity

The concept of fraternity took one of two forms: national or social. The brotherhood of nationalism was the unity gained from a shared history, usually strengthened by a sense of separation from neighbouring nationalities.

One significant statement of nationalism was made in 1807 by Johann Fichte, who wrote in his *Address to the German nation*:

> It is only by means of the common characteristic of being German that we can avert the downfall of our nation which is threatened by its fusion with foreign peoples and win back again an individuality that is self-supporting and quite incapable of any dependence upon others.

A later example of nationalist sentiment was contained in Vincenzo Gioberti's *On the civil and moral primacy of Italians*, published in 1843:

> What more beautiful image can be fed to an Italian soul than one of his homeland unified, strong, powerful, devoted to God, calm, confident in itself, respected and admired by other peoples? What more radiant future can be imagined for her? What bliss more desirable?

Nationalism took different forms as it appealed to different groups across Europe. Irish nationalism gained support from an essentially agrarian society, in part because of the religious differences between Catholic Ireland and Protestant Britain. In Greece, where the Orthodox Greeks were ruled by the Muslim Turks, religious factors were also predominant in creating feelings of national fraternity. For the Poles, a people without their own nation state, nationalism was primarily a movement of the landed gentry. In Germany it was mainly the middle classes, professional and business people, who were attracted to nationalism. Yet whatever its basis of support, nationalism would prove a very powerful force for change, both during the nineteenth century and later.

The other form of fraternity was socialism. The word was first used during the 1820s, when Robert Owen in England and Charles Fourier in France became critical of the reality of the emerging industrial society and argued that self-governing communities should be established. Within these – at least for Owen – it was envisaged that everyone would be equal, contributing to and benefiting from the work of the commune. Socialism thus combined fraternity with economic equality. Such a way of life soon received another label: communism. Although these early socialists were called Utopian because their ideas were seen as being unrealistic, by the 1840s Marx was developing a form of socialism or communism that he claimed was more scientific. As with nationalism, socialism was to prove a significant force in European history over the next century and beyond. Indeed, some politicians claimed to combine nationalism and socialism, one with devastating effect.

Military change

The 'long nineteenth century' (1789 to 1914) is often regarded as a time of peace. This view distorts the reality. Europeans continued to fight wars. It was just that – with one brief exception – they managed to avoid waging a war involving more than two states. There was no general European war throughout the entire nineteenth century; Europeans instead fought short wars and brief campaigns. The number of such campaigns reaches a surprisingly high total (see Appendices B and C). This continual warfare encouraged innovation, the new technologies and methods of the industrial economy contributing to some significant changes in how wars were fought. Indeed, it can be argued that the nineteenth century witnessed a military revolution that was as significant as the Industrial Revolution. Four innovations were particularly important:

- Railways replaced horse and foot as the main means of transport. They enabled troops to be brought to the battlefield more quickly. The French were the first to use railways in this way, during the 1859 campaign in northern Italy. Travelling by railway, French forces reached the theatre of war in eleven days instead of the two months that it would previously have taken. The size of armies on the battlefield became larger. The army of 1,200,000 men that was raised by Prussia against France in 1870, for example, was twice the size of the army with which Napoleon had invaded Russia in 1812.
- The breech-loading rifle replaced the front-loading musket. Breech-loading meant that bullets were loaded at the base of the gun, not down the barrel. This allowed soldiers to reload without standing up. They were less vulnerable. They could reload more quickly. A breech-loader fired three shots to the musket's one. Furthermore, the development of the cylindrical bullet made better use of the rifled barrel than did the round musket ball, with the result that enemy soldiers could be killed even when they were up to 1 kilometre away. The same principles were applied to artillery cannon, too. And mass-production techniques ensured that these guns could be produced in huge quantities.
- The development of railways required changes in the organisation and tactics of armies. The rapid movement of large numbers of troops – and their supplies – required careful co-ordination in order to be effective; individual armies could not be given too much freedom. The idea of a general staff, a group of army generals responsible for co-ordinating military campaigns, became important. Members of the general staff did not need to be physically present on the battlefield. In 1866, for example, the Prussian general staff organised the first stages of the war against Austria from Berlin. In 1870, the French general staff failed to co-ordinate its various armies effectively, thereby putting their forces at a great disadvantage against Prussia. The result was a significant shift in the balance of national power in Europe.

- Larger armies equipped with weapons that were both easier to use and more sophisticated required disciplined and better-trained troops. **Conscription**, a feature of the Napoleonic wars, became increasingly essential. Some states began to insist that all adult males had to join the army for a few years to learn military skills and then had to spend some years in the reserves maintaining those skills. During the 1860s Prussia was the first to introduce such reforms and other states soon copied its example. States created national armies that in turn helped to create nation states.

Conscription is the policy that requires some or all adult males, usually aged around 18, to serve in a country's armed forces for several years, even in times of peace. Conscription was first introduced by France after 1789 and was applied by most continental powers during the nineteenth century (Britain, however, preferred to rely on volunteers).

Forces for continuity

It is important to appreciate that features which ensured continuity with the past – and the future – co-existed with forces for change within nineteenth-century Europe. Among such forces for continuity were state governments, the Catholic Church, the land-owning class and memories of the French Revolution.

State governments

The various state governments of Europe all worked to prevent change from overwhelming their countries. They were less concerned with economic change than with political change – that is, a shift in the distribution of power – although even economic developments eventually forced governments to act. In order to weaken the attraction of socialism, for example, they had to reduce the worst effects of industrialisation. Controls on factory conditions had therefore become commonplace by the late nineteenth century. Some states even began to provide welfare benefits for workers, Germany leading the way during the 1880s.

Sometimes governments opposed all political change, as was the case during the years immediately following the defeat of Napoleon. At other times they accepted lesser forms of change in order to avert greater upheavals, as was the case during the 1850s, when some governments introduced limited constitutions with the aim of preventing democratic government. Only once did the governments of Europe seem to lose their nerve, and that was in the spring of 1848, when they backed down in the face of demonstrations in the streets. They soon recovered their confidence, however, withdrawing the concessions that they had made and restoring order. Only rarely did a government encourage change; France under Napoleon III was one such country, and in 1870 both state and emperor paid the price for doing so.

Governments were powerless to prevent political change when it was instigated by other, more powerful governments. Although the small states of Germany did not want to surrender their independence to a united Germany

The 'short nineteenth century'

from 1866 to 1871, they had to give way to the superior force of Prussia. Similarly, from 1858 to 1860 the small states of Italy had to concede to Piedmont, which was backed by France.

The Catholic Church

Of the **three Christian churches** in Europe it was the Catholic Church that did the most to prevent change. It was a powerful religious force throughout much of southern and central Europe. Until 1860 it was also a considerable political force within Italy because it governed much of the centre of the country. In both respects the Catholic Church was on the side of order. When in the process of losing its power in Italy it declared itself against many forces for change in *The syllabus of errors* of 1864, in which 80 contemporary 'errors' were identified. The Catholic Church was not always against change, however: Pope Pius IX, who introduced *The syllabus of errors*, had supported some liberal reforms on becoming pope (see Chapter 3). Yet for all but a few years the papacy was a powerful force for conservatism.

The land-owning class

Although Europe was beginning to industrialise, it remained predominately agrarian. A small minority of individuals owned the majority of the land in each country, usually in the form of large estates. (France was the only major exception.) This land-owning group, which included the nobility or aristocracy, had a great influence on government, both national and local. It used its position to prevent change or, if change was unavoidable, to ensure that it took account of the interests of the landed class. The emancipation of Russian serfs is a classic example of this process in action. The landowners acted as a brake on change throughout the nineteenth century.

Memories of the French Revolution

It might seem strange to class the French Revolution as a force for continuity, but the stories and images associated with the French Revolution cast a long shadow over the nineteenth century. For the landed and propertied classes the French Revolution was a reminder of how dangerous radical ideas could be. Liberty had become the freedom to execute the king of France; equality had caused peasants to seize private property; fraternity had resulted in the guillotining of those whom the state declared to be the enemies of the people. The people of the French Revolution came to be regarded as a mob – emotional, irrational and dangerous.

The persistence of such images and perceptions did much to strengthen the will of governments against popular demands. Although governments on occasions initially gave in to protests on the streets, they did not do so for

---

Catholicism, Orthodoxy and Protestantism are **the three main Christian churches**. 'Catholic' means 'universal', and the Catholic Church in Rome was the first to be established. The Orthodox Church was based in Byzantium (Constantinople, or today's Istanbul) and became the predominant church for most of eastern Europe. The Protestant churches split with Catholicism at the time of the Reformation and became strongest in northern Europe.

The syllabus of errors (1864)
[It is not true that]:
15 Every man is free to embrace and profess the religion he shall believe is true, guided by the light of reason.
18 Protestantism is nothing more than another form of the same true Christian religion, in which it is possible to be equally pleasing to God as in the Catholic Church.
23 The Roman Pontiffs and Ecumenical Councils have exceeded the limits of their power, have usurped the rights of princes and even committed errors in defining matters of faith and morals.
80 The Roman Pontiff can and ought to reconcile himself to, and agree with, progress, liberalism, and civilisation as lately introduced.

long. After the 1790s the propertied middle classes in western and central Europe supported demands for limited reforms only, and rarely supported popular revolution. Once the barricades went up they usually aligned themselves with the government. Such was the case in 1848.

The balance of the forces for and against change shifted over the 65 years after 1825. Sometimes the need for stability prevailed, sometimes the desire for change. The interplay of reform and conservatism, of people and events, resulted in several distinct phases in the history of the 'short nineteenth century'.

Europe, 1825–90: reaction, conflict and reform

This period can be divided in many different ways. Probably the most useful is the following division into three eras of roughly equal lengths: reaction and peace, 1825–47; revolution and wars, 1848–71; and from liberalism to collectivism, 1871–90.

Reaction and peace, 1825–47

This era was one of general peace interrupted only by one brief period of political upheaval between 1830 and 1831, when a revolution in France encouraged revolts in Belgium, Italy and Poland. Despite overthrowing the Bourbon monarch, the revolution in France in 1830 proved to be more moderate than many had feared. The revolts in central Europe were defeated by Austria and Russia. Only the Belgian revolt was successful, with Belgium breaking away from the Netherlands. Although there were frequent conflicts in the Balkans and the Near East as a result of the weakness of the **Ottoman Empire**, these regions were on the edge of Europe. Europe 'proper' remained quiet.

The governments of the time crushed popular revolutions. After a few upheavals between 1819 and 1821 in Italy, Spain and Germany, repression became the order of the day. **Metternich** established a spy network in the Habsburg lands and beyond that appears to have been reasonably effective.

These were reactionary times, there was little economic change and Europe remained quiet for the greater part of these 22 years.

Revolutions and wars, 1848–71

The calm of Europe was shattered by the revolutions of 1848. France, Germany and Italy all experienced large-scale upheavals. The popular call was for constitutions and/or national unity. The spring of 1848 was called the 'springtime of the peoples', but by the summer of 1849 that springtime had turned into autumn and the old order was largely restored.

The **Ottoman Empire** comprised lands ruled by the Turkish Ottoman dynasty, including lands in the Balkans, the Middle East and North Africa. The Ottomans were Muslim, but their European subjects were Christian. The declining power of the Ottomans was a major international problem of the nineteenth century that is usually termed the 'Eastern question'.

Prince Klemens von **Metternich** (1773–1859) was the Habsburg Empire's foreign minister from 1809 to 1848 and its chancellor from 1821 to 1848. The 1815–48 period is sometimes called the 'Age of Metternich' because Metternich used Austrian power to do all that he could to stop the spread of revolutionary ideas. His downfall, which came in 1848, was both a consequence and cause of the 1848 revolutions.

The 1850s were similar to the 1820s in being another period of relative political quiet. They were, however, a time of rapid economic growth, with the expansion of the railways stimulating industrial growth. Liberalism in its economic form – free trade and minimal government intervention – became acceptable to more governments.

The restoration of the old order after 1848 was incomplete, with France changing from a monarchy to a republic and then to an empire, all within four years. Its emperor, Napoleon III, was less orthodox than most leaders. He wanted to redraw the map of Europe, associating its boundaries with the defeat of his uncle, Napoleon Bonaparte. Within a space of 17 years he therefore took part in no fewer than three European wars, as well as several overseas campaigns. Another great power war, between Austria and Prussia, took place without his direct involvement, although he had encouraged its outbreak. As a result of these wars Napoleon got his way: the map of Europe was redrawn and a united Italy was formed. The only trouble was that the redrawing was ultimately at Napoleon's expense. In 1870, Prussia defeated France. Napoleon had to abdicate. Furthermore, while it was occupying France, Prussia announced the formation of the German Empire. France's star was on the wane and Germany's in the ascendant.

From liberalism to collectivism, 1871–90

After 23 years of conflict and political change there were no wars between the European great powers until 1914. The year 1890 is a rather artificial finishing point to the period. The most significant event of that year was the fall from power of the German chancellor, Otto von Bismarck, who had held office in Prussia and Germany since 1862. Although his departure was seen as the end of an era, in most respects it was not: Bismarck's successors made only a few changes to German policy, while his enforced withdrawal from public life did not make much difference to the rest of Europe. The key features of the 1880s were still in evidence during the 1890s.

If there was a more significant turning point in the post-1871 era it came in around 1879. Then the liberal policies that had been pursued by most governments since the 1850s began to be replaced by more **collectivist** policies, ones that affected whole groups of people. The best examples of these were Germany's social insurance policies of the 1880s, by which Bismarck made employers and workers contribute to a state insurance scheme as protection against sickness and disability, accidents and old age. Other countries soon followed suit. In addition, free trade was replaced by customs duties, or tariffs, which protected national economies against foreign competition.

There were two reasons for this change of direction. One was economic. Following the boom of the 1850s and 1860s Europe experienced a setback to

Collectivist ideas or policies, like socialism and nationalism, put the group before the individual, unlike liberalism. Collectivism came to prevail with the rise of mass societies during the late nineteenth century.

economic growth during the 1870s that lasted until the mid-1890s. Although this so-called **'Great Depression'** hit profits, prices and employment more than it did production and living standards, it nevertheless caused problems for workers and bosses alike, who consequently demanded government action. The results were tariffs and social welfarism. The other reason was political. The working classes were growing rapidly in numbers and were starting to organise themselves into either socialist parties or trade unions (or both). In 1875 the Social Democratic Party was established in Germany, and during the 1880s several workers' parties were set up in France. Strikes became more commonplace. Socialists were elected to national assemblies. After several decades free from anxiety, the ruling classes again began to develop a fear of popular revolution, one that would now be class-based. They were therefore forced to introduce limited social reforms in order to prevent more radical social – and political – upheaval.

There was another significant development in the 1880s: various governments discovered the attraction of acquiring overseas colonies. Although their exact reasons – diplomatic, economic or political – for doing so were not always clear, the decade marked the beginning of the age of imperialism.

By 1890 Europe was well on the way to becoming a mass society. Domestic politics were being increasingly centred on the needs of the people, foreign policies on the self-interest of democratic nation states. Technological innovations and economic growth encouraged the emergence of the consumer society. The Europe of the 1890s was closer to the Europe of the early twentieth century than that of the early nineteenth century. The 1820s were a different world, more akin to the eighteenth century.

'Great Depression', 1873–96
A depression is a long period during which economic growth either slows down or reverses. From 1873 prices and profits in most industrial countries fell and unemployment became a major problem. In relation to the period between 1873 and 1896 the term is usually placed within quotation marks because historians question whether the economic downturn was a depression of the severity of the Great Depression of the 1930s.

2 Europe during the 1820s

Although by 1825 the most extensive wars that Europe had experienced for many years were 10 years in the past, their impact was still great. The wars had been revolutionary, fought by the French as much to spread the revolutionary ideas that they believed in as to gain territory. The two decades during which France occupied parts of Germany and Italy ensured that such new ideas took root in these parts of Europe: some Germans and Italians believed in democracy and freedom. While the wars alarmed the ruling classes of Europe, the practical application of these ideas before 1815 frightened many more. Despite Napoleon's exile to St Helena, where he died in 1821, fear of both revolution and of France was still widespread. Many governments wanted to restore and maintain as much of the pre-revolutionary order as possible. The 1820s are thus often seen as a time of restoration. Yet the old order had been smashed by the French and could not be fully restored. It is therefore more appropriate to regard the 1820s as a reactionary age, when the rulers of Europe tried to undo what they perceived to be the damage of the previous 30 years. How far did they succeed?

Country and town

From one end of Europe to the other during the 1820s the majority of people lived in villages and hamlets in the countryside and rarely travelled further than the local market towns. Most people were either peasants or **serfs**. Peasants usually rented, sometimes owned, their small plots, which produced food enough to feed their families. Serfs could be bought and sold as if they were cattle or pieces of furniture. Peasants had some rights, serfs none. One of the key differences between western and eastern Europe was that by 1830 peasants were found in the west and serfs in the east. For both groups life was tough: they lived in poverty for most of their lives, a situation that was often made harder by failures of crops, by disease, by rising – or falling – prices and by government taxes. Many people ended up either as paupers dependent upon state hand-outs or as beggars.

Serfs were peasants who were literally and legally the property of their landowners. The term is usually applied to Russia, where serfdom was introduced during the sixteenth and seventeenth centuries in order to help to establish the power of the tsar.

Few peasants were able to read or write. Providing accurate literacy figures for the 1820s is impossible: there is just no information for most countries. France, however, can provide some: the number of army recruits during the 1830s who could sign their name was around 50 per cent. However, being able to sign your name does not necessarily mean that you can read and write. This figure probably exaggerates the extent of male literacy, and Olwen Hutton, in *The prospect before her* (1995), suggests that the level of literacy among women was lower than that among men. Lacking even a basic education, most peasants relied for information on those in their communities whom they could expect to be educated, such as landowners, doctors and priests (not that all of them necessarily were).

The societies of the 1820s were thus very unequal. Despite the hardships, however, more people were surviving the many diseases that the young are prone to. Although no one is certain why this change in life expectancy happened its consequences were great: because a family's plot of land could not provide a living for its growing number of children, many had to leave their homes. Most moved to the towns, but some went further afield, leaving the country for the Americas, Africa, Asia and Australia.

Most towns were small, although a few were very large. Each country had one or two such huge cities, one of which was usually the capital: Paris and Marseilles in France, Berlin and Hamburg in Germany, Moscow and St Petersburg in Russia. Even so, in comparison with their modern counterparts such cities were not that large. In 1800 there were just 21 towns across Europe with a population of more than 100,000. The population of the largest city of the time, London, passed the 1 million mark only in 1850, when that of the second largest, Paris, numbered just over 500,000.

People moved into these towns in increasing numbers during the early nineteenth century, seeing them as places where fortunes could be made and where they might have the chance to become 'civilised'. Yet such opportunities were given to only a few and people had to make their own way, receiving little help from either the public authorities or private charities. Cities were furthermore dangerous, unhealthy places for both individuals and governments. Revolutions usually began in towns: the French revolutions of 1789, 1830 and 1848, for example, all broke out in Paris. Although most people lived, worked and died in the countryside, towns were more important to a country's history. This contrast became even greater during the early nineteenth century as industrial towns became a new feature of European life.

With their town houses and country estates the wealthy landowners had the best of both worlds. They governed the state at both local and national level, controlling both the countryside and cities. They helped to maintain the traditions that had been established by their forefathers. They saw themselves as born to rule. Yet by the 1820s their birthright was being challenged in the more 'advanced' parts of western Europe by new political ideas and economic forces. The ruling class, often labelled the *ancien régime* (old regime), reacted by stopping people from supporting these new ideas, closing down radical newspapers, banning political associations and throwing the ringleaders into jail – or onto boats bound for the other side of the world. They wanted to preserve the old world by suppressing those aspects of the new that they did not like. Their attempts at social control came into conflict with the economic reality, however.

Industry and trade

The markets for both agricultural and industrial products were local; most goods were produced in workshops and sold nearby. Before 1830 there were very few factories in which products were made in great quantities. Almost all of the few that existed were in Britain, mainly because it had an overseas

An early photograph of Parisian workers, necessarily posed because of the limitations of the technology. The news sheet at the bottom right is an example of a very early advertisement (for the photographer).

empire that provided both cheap raw materials and a large market, especially for the cotton industry of Lancashire. The population of Manchester, the main cotton town, grew from 17,000 in 1760 to 180,000 in 1830. France, the only other European state with a large colonial empire, had perhaps been the economic equal of Britain during the mid eighteenth century but later fell behind, probably as a result of the upheavals of the French Revolution. Although north-eastern France (and Belgium) had some new factories, they were the exception: in the rest of Europe the traditional, centuries-old methods of producing goods survived into the 1820s.

There were sound reasons for this. There were still many obstacles to gaining access to larger markets and thus to increased trade. Guilds were one such obstacle: as organisations of masters and workers in certain industries, they restricted access to markets and recruitment of labour while also discouraging new methods of production. Despite their position having been weakened by the French Revolution, in many countries they fought to protect the status of their trades well into the nineteenth century.

Nor did customs duties make trade any easier. Whether they were on roads or rivers, customs barriers were still common and in regions that consisted of many small states, like Germany or Italy, trade suffered many obstacles. Along the river Weser, between Minden and Bremen in north-western Germany – a distance of just over 100 kilometres – there were 22 tolls at which vessels would be stopped and goods examined. Even within countries, there were often trade barriers. Although one such country, Prussia, removed such internal duties in 1818, it continued to maintain customs duties when trading with all of the other German states until 1834, when it established a German customs union (see Chapter 6). Even then, some cities, such as Hamburg, did not join this customs union until the 1880s.

During the 1820s the idea of free trade was still too radical for most people. Proposed by **Adam Smith** in his book *The wealth of nations* (1776), the idea came to be crucial to the unprecedented economic growth of modern times. Although British politicians began to reduce tariffs during the 1820s and again during the 1840s, they mainly did so because Britain, as the leading industrial economy, did not suffer from doing so. Other countries were much more cautious, however, and free trade's time was not to come until the mid nineteenth century – and even then not for long.

The major hindrance to trade, however, was communications, which were almost invariably poor. Roads, the main means of overland travel, were inadequate in many places, being little more than cart tracks. It was often quicker to travel by water, whether by river or sea, despite the tolls. The one significant innovation in transport made during the 50 years before 1830 was the canal, which enabled bulk goods to be more reliably transported over greater dis-

Adam Smith (1723–90), a Scottish professor, was a leading figure in the development of economic thought. In some respects he may be considered to be the founder of economics as an academic discipline. In *The wealth of nations* (1776) he argued the case for the benefits of an unrestricted market economy. His ideas have had a great impact on governments, both then and now.

tances, yet even canals had major limitations. The poor state of Europe's roads, rivers and canals was one reason why the railways had such a great impact, but, again not until later in the century. In the 1820s, George Stephenson and others like him were still grappling with the technical problem of how to put a steam engine on wheels.

Although these many obstacles to industry and trade certainly held back their development, they could not stop them and the new industrial society increased in size and strength until by the early nineteenth century it was hard to ignore.

Romanticism and nationalism

Many of the educated classes disliked what they saw of the new industrial society and instead looked to previous times, to the Middle Ages and even earlier. They escaped the towns and the farmed countryside to explore nature, especially mountains and lakes like the Alps, the Lake District and the mountains of southern Germany. Rather than accept either the rational, but inhuman, beat of the factory machine or the irrational violence of the 'mob' they preferred to trust their own emotions. Such people formed part of a large, sprawling movement known as romanticism.

Based on feeling rather than reason, romanticism was first and foremost a reaction to the **Enlightenment** of the mid eighteenth century. As both political and economic revolutions occurred in France and Britain so romanticism gained new inspiration and took new forms. The romanticism of the 1820s was different from that of the 1780s.

During the first half of the 1820s the leading romantic figures were the British poets Shelley and Byron, both of whom died early, 'romantic' deaths, Shelley in 1822, aged 30, and Byron in 1824, aged 36. Byron died as a result of an illness contracted while he was in Greece, trying to help the Greeks to gain their independence from the Ottoman Empire. Romanticism became linked with nationalism. This pattern was repeated to a certain degree in Russia, whose own romantic hero was Alexander Pushkin. Pushkin died in 1837, at the age of 38, when he was killed in a duel. By the mid nineteenth century the idea of the romantic hero had therefore been firmly re-established as one of the central myths of European culture. The political form of romanticism promoted by writers such as Byron was sustained by the new generation of French romantics. During the late 1820s Victor Hugo reacted against the humdrum nature of restoration France by glorifying Napoleon. Another leading French romantic, the artist Eugène Delacroix, painted revolutionary ideas in romantic form, as is best seen in his image of the 1830 French revolution: *Liberty leading the people* (1830).

The **Enlightenment** was a movement based on a belief in the superiority of reasoned thought and scientific method over tradition and superstition. It was strongest in France (where Voltaire and Montesquieu were key figures), Britain and the USA. The ideas of the Enlightenment were one of the main intellectual causes of the French Revolution.

Liberty leading the people. A romantic image of the revolution of 1830 by Eugène Delacroix, one of the great artists of the time; it has been used as the basis of cartoons ever since

Romanticism became linked with nationalism during the 1820s because nationalist beliefs had to be expressed in indirect ways rather than openly. Poems and plays were more acceptable to the authorities than marches and demonstrations. Indeed, the governments that had defeated Napoleon repressed the revolutionary ideas that France had exported to the rest of Europe and restricted freedom of speech and freedom of association. For most of Europe in the nineteenth century, the 1820s were the height of political repression.

One nationalist revolt was tolerated, and even supported, by the rulers of Europe during the 1820s, however: the **Greek War of Independence** (1821–30). The revolt of the Greeks was tolerated mainly because Greece was on the edge of Europe and relatively isolated. The rest of Europe regarded the Orthodox Christian Greeks as fellow Europeans and the Muslim Turks as infi-

Greek War of Independence, 1821–30
When some Greeks rose in revolt against Ottoman rule in 1821 they received the sympathy of the European public and also of the British and Russian governments. As a result of these two great powers attacking the Ottoman Empire the Greeks were freed from their allegiance to the Ottoman Empire.

Europe during the 1820s

dels or unbelievers. Greece, or, more precisely, the city state of Athens, had furthermore been the place where democracy had first been established. A mixture of sentiment and self-interest thus caused much of western Europe to support the Greeks. A similar combination – although the sentiment had more of a religious element – caused Russia to do the same, uniting Europe against the Ottoman Empire. In 1827, without bothering to declare war, Britain, France and Russia sank the Turkish fleet at Navarino. By 1832 Greece had become an independent nation state.

In Europe 'proper', however, nationalist groups made little or no mark during the 1820s. A study of popular protest in Germany during the 1820s, for example, identified only 29 recorded small-scale incidents, of which 13 were instigated by students (which is usually regarded as evidence of a lack of seriousness) and just 4 had a political objective. Yet this evidence of minimal political activity does not mean that there was little belief in nationalism, rather that circumstances did not encourage the expression of such beliefs. The forces of reaction were too strong.

Reaction and revolt

In 1815 the new order associated with Napoleon was defeated and the old order regained control. It did not reinstate the order that had existed in 1789, however, for to do so would have been impossible. Even restoring all of the states that had existed in 1789 was impractical: too much had changed and too many people had benefited from the revolution. Instead, the old order used its power to prevent further change. Governments claimed the principle of legitimacy for their decisions in order to justify the new order. Legitimacy – the concept that authority is derived from a hereditary line of succession – was the only possible justification they could use: nationalism, democracy and liberalism were too revolutionary. Yet many people in 1815 did not regard their new rulers as being legitimate. The foundations of the **1815 settlement** were not that sound.

The **1815 settlement** was the settlement that stipulated how Europe should be ordered following the final defeat of Napoleon. In 1815 European statesmen met at Vienna and established governments and borders that were designed to contain the twin dangers of France and revolution. The 1815 settlement is often favourably compared with the 1919 settlement of Europe.

As well as political legitimacy, religious conformity helped to maintain the new order. During the early nineteenth century there was something of a revival in organised religious worship as those who rejected the rationalism of the Enlightenment and anti-religious aspects of the French Revolution often discovered (or rediscovered) the Christian faith. This revival, which involved Protestant, Catholic and Orthodox believers, was not brought about simply by the churches' leaders. Rather, it was a widespread response to the uncertainties of the time.

The churches themselves had suffered from the reforms of the French Revolution. The Catholic Church, in particular, was determined to do all that

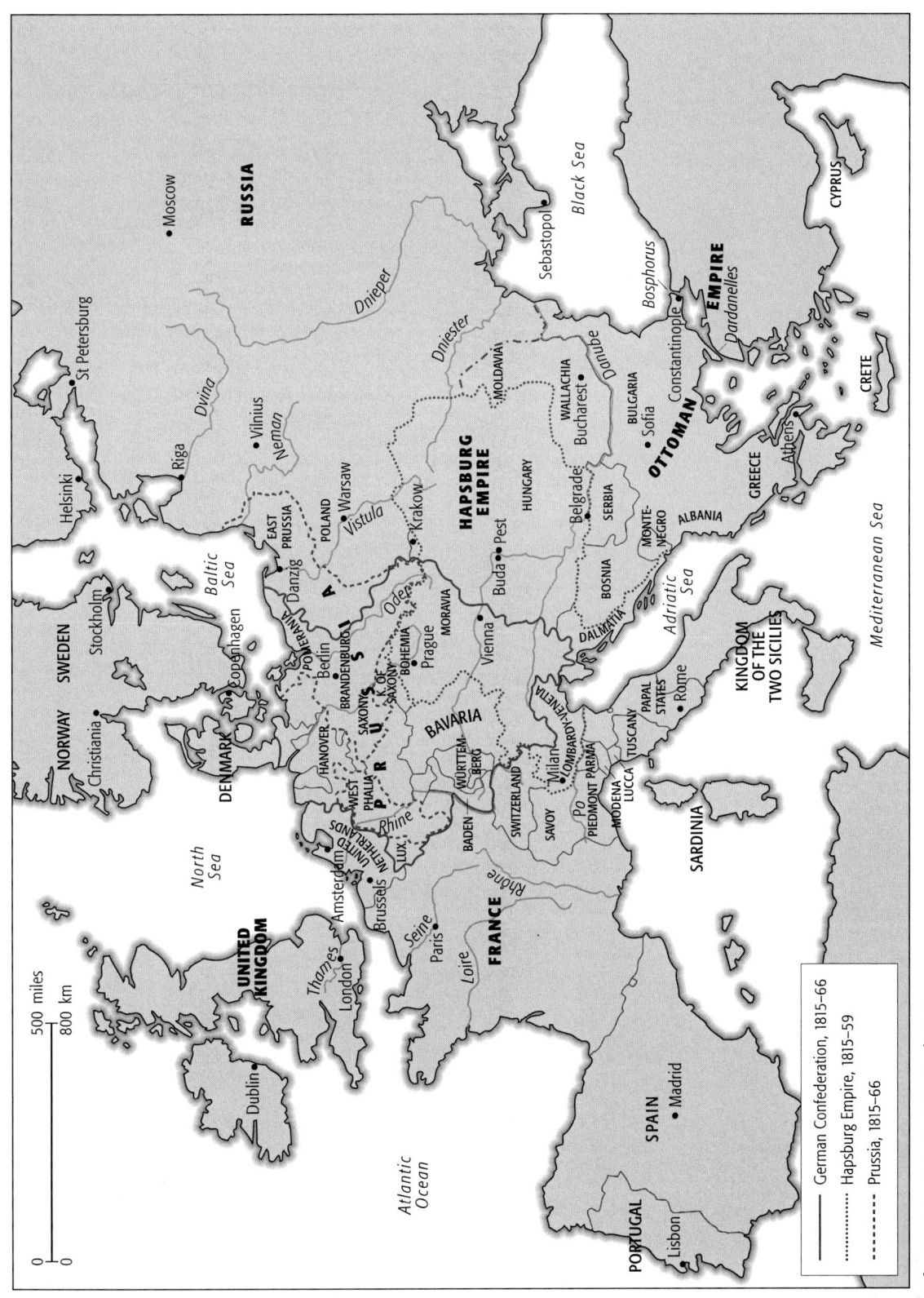

The European states system after 1815.

The Society of Jesus, or **Jesuits**, is a Catholic order established in 1534 that helped to rebuild support for Catholicism during the sixteenth and seventeenth centuries. Historically, it has been perceived as an arm of the Catholic Church and was therefore mistrusted by many governments.

it could to regain its former position after 1815. The Catholic Society of Jesus, more commonly known as the **Jesuits**, had been revived in 1814 after having been abolished in 1773, even before the outbreak of the French Revolution. It sometimes worked in partnership with the state in an alliance of throne and altar – this was especially noticeable in restoration France. The churches, both Catholic and Protestant, also often rebuilt their position by providing more church schools to educate increasing numbers of children in the ways of their faiths.

The key power in restoring order in Europe was one of the Catholic powers, the Habsburg Empire. The key figure was the Habsburg foreign minister from 1809 to 1848, Metternich. He made sure that the 1815 settlement gave the Habsburg Empire influence in both Germany and Italy, the two regions closest to France. When unrest occurred in either region he took action to crush it: in Germany student societies were closed down in 1819, while Austrian troops in Italy acted to defeat revolts in Naples and Piedmont between 1820 and 1821. Repression became the order of the day. With the restored French monarchy anxious to become one of the accepted great powers again, and thus on its best behaviour, there were few obvious threats to the political order. Europe was unusually quiet during the 1820s.

It was not wholly peaceful, however. Apart from the exceptional case of the Greek revolt against the Ottoman Empire there was one other threat to the new order, which came from unusual source: a section of the Russian cavalry. When Nicholas I was controversially nominated tsar instead of his brother in 1825 the cavalry in several parts of Russia revolted against his rule (see Chapter 5). The revolt was quickly crushed, however, and the old tsarist order remained intact. For the rest of the 1820s there was barely a sound of political protest from one end of Europe to the other.

The 1820s are perhaps best seen as an 'in-between' decade, a time of transition. All periods are times of transition in one sense or other, but that change often takes the form of significant events. During the 1820s such events were few and far between, however. Although there was admittedly the revolt in Greece and the brief attempt at revolt in Russia the significant developments that occurred during these 10 years concerned social and economic matters, such as the growth in population and the emergence of an industrial society. During the period between 1825 and 1830 there was only one such development of any great importance for the history of Europe over the next few decades: what could be called the 'war' of the three German customs unions. Prussia won this battle quickly, forming the *Zollverein* (customs union) of 18 states in 1834. Although this relatively undramatic change may have had only a limited impact at the time, it had considerable consequences in the longer term. Yet the 1820s had hardly passed before the authority of the French king,

Charles X, was challenged by the people of Paris. As a result he swiftly decided to abdicate, thus setting in motion the wider revolutionary events of the next two years. France, Italy and Poland were all seriously affected.

The calm of the 1820s was never to return. During the next 60 years Europe would undergo a series of changes, both political and economic, which together can be described as revolutionary. At the forefront of the political upheaval was the rise of nationalism, a development that became more noticeable during the 1830s. Leading the way against the old order was a handful of Italians who provided an example from which other nationalities took heart a few years later.

3 Changing the face of Europe: Italy, 1830–70

> **Focus questions**
>
> ◆ How united was Italy between 1830 and 1847?
> ◆ What impact did the revolutions of 1848 to 1849 have on efforts to establish a united Italy?
> ◆ How and why was Italy united in 1861?
> ◆ How far did the system of government established in 1861 help to unify Italy?
> ◆ How united and how Italian was Italy in 1871?
> ◆ What was the relationship between the unification of Italy and the *Risorgimento*?

Significant dates

- **1831** Revolts in Parma, Modena and part of the Papal States around Bologna; Young Italy formed by Mazzini
- **1848–49** Revolutions throughout Italy: in Sicily, Piedmont, the Papal States, Tuscany, Lombardy and Venetia; Piedmont goes to war against Austria but is defeated at Custoza
- **1849** A republic is declared in Rome; Piedmont goes to war against Austria but is defeated at Novara; the Roman Republic defeated by France and the Venetian Republic by Austria
- **1859–60** Piedmont and France defeat Austria at Magenta and Solferino; the armistice signed at Villafranca; Lombardy annexed by Piedmont; revolt in Tuscany
- **1860** Tuscany and Emilia vote to join Piedmont, and Nice and Savoy to join France; revolt in Sicily; Garibaldi conquers Sicily and then Naples and transfers them to Victor Emmanuel; plebiscites held in Sicily, Umbria and Marches result in their joining Piedmont
- **1861** Italy-wide elections held; Victor Emmanuel proclaimed king of Italy
- **1866** The Italian army is defeated by Austria at Custoza and its navy at Lissa; Austria hands Venice to Napoleon III, who transfers it to Italy
- **1870** French troops withdraw from Rome; Italian forces occupy Rome; the papacy is established in the Vatican City

Overview

The Italian word for the movement that worked towards the achievement of an Italian nation state during the late eighteenth and nineteenth centuries is *Risorgimento*. The word has been variously translated as 'resurrection', 'revival', 'resurgence' and 'renewal', all similar but with different shades of meaning. The one element that they have in common is the idea of returning, of creating once more the key features of a former, more glorious state.

As they considered their present position in Europe in 1830, some Italians would have noted a world in which the divided states of Italy suffered by comparison with the united nation states of France and Britain. Even Germany in 1815 had its *Bund* (see Chapter 6). Italy, had no equivalent. It had the papacy, but the papacy was the Catholic, or 'universal', church, more European than Italian. Popes were always Italian, but their main responsibility was to Catholics in Europe and beyond. A few Italians determined to change this situation and to create an Italian state that was united and free.

In 1861 a united Italy indeed came into existence. To be more precise Italy was only partly united, partly free. By 1870, however, Italy also included Venice and Rome and was free of Austrian and French armies. Yet this Italian nation was not really a 'renewal' of a former state because an Italian nation state had never existed before. During the 40 years from 1830 there was a revival of a kind, one which gradually gained support, both within Italy and from other parts of Europe. That support was enough to overcome opposition to the cause – eventually.

How united was Italy between 1830 and 1847?

Italy had been divided for centuries. It was a region that included city states, of which Venice and Florence were the best known, and larger states, such as Naples. Local rivalries were intense and deep-rooted. The disunity of Italy allowed greater powers, such as France, Austria or Spain, to occupy and control large parts of the peninsula. During the Napoleonic era (1796–1814) France controlled Italy and its reforming zeal changed many features of Italian government. A united Italy of sorts was formed, first as a republic and then as a kingdom, but it was far from independent. On Napoleon's final defeat the great powers agreed that Austria should replace France in controlling Italy. The predominance of Austria over Italy was to be of central importance to Italy's development during the following half century.

The forces against unity

The states system was a major obstacle to change. After 1815 the Italian peninsula contained seven separate states (see the map on page 50). It is important to have some understanding of those states in order to understand the events of the *Risorgimento*.

One state was part of the **Habsburg Empire**, usually called Austria, which ruled two provinces in north-eastern Italy, Lombardy and Venetia. These were usually paired together as one state, Lombardy-Venetia. Austria had acquired Lombardy during the early eighteenth century. Its capital was Milan, a city that was second only to Vienna within the Habsburg Empire. Venetia, or Venice, once an independent republic that had dominated trade in the eastern Mediterranean, was a more recent acquisition as a result of the Napoleonic wars. Located in the Po valley, these two provinces were the most prosperous parts of Italy in 1830.

To the west of Lombardy-Venetia was a state which was called either Piedmont or Sardinia, or also, although less frequently by the nineteenth century, Savoy. Savoy was a province in the Alps which gradually expanded into the upper Po valley and became known as Piedmont. When the duke of Savoy gained the island of Sardinia in 1720 he also gained the title of king. In 1815 Piedmont was given Genoa, a port that had also been a republic, in order to strengthen its position as a front-line bulwark against France. Acquiring Genoa made Piedmont more Italian than it had been in the past. Just as importantly, it was the only state in the peninsula which had no formal ties to Austria. However, the suppression of the 1821 revolutions in Piedmont had required intervention by Austrian troops. In 1830 Charles Felix was king of Piedmont. He discouraged the development of liberal policies, whether economic or political. He was the classic reactionary ruler of the time.

South of Lombardy-Venetia were two small states, Parma and Modena. Together with the larger state of Tuscany, which was on the other side of the Apennines, Italy's central chain of mountains, they are usually called the central duchies. (There was also a fourth duchy, Lucca, which was absorbed by Tuscany in 1847.) In reality there was just one thing that the three states had in common: they were all ruled by junior members of the Habsburg royal family, which helped to reinforce Austrian predominance. In an age of reaction the government of Tuscany was quite tolerant, certainly the most tolerant in Italy, while Parma's ruler until 1830, Napoleon's second wife, Marie Louise, also tolerated different ideas. Modena, however, insisted on conformity to the values of the time, punishing those who disobeyed.

Alongside, and to the south of, Tuscany lay the Papal States. These lands were unusual in that they were ruled by clerics, with the pope as head of state. Because the pope's status was far greater than that of the heads of the other

---

The **Habsburg Empire** comprised the lands ruled by the Austrian Habsburg dynasty, one of the greatest dynasties in European history. By 1815 the Habsburgs ruled over lands in south-eastern Europe, as well as Austria, while also dominating Italy and Germany. A conservative, multinational state, the Habsburg Empire was threatened by the growth of liberal and national ideas.

Italian states the papacy was to have an important influence on the *Risorgimento*, at least for a time. Based in Rome, the pope ruled over the region of Umbria, directly to the north of Rome. Further north (and on the other side of the Apennines) was the state of Romagna, also known as the Legations, while to the east of Rome and Umbria were the Marches. These states had little in common except that they were all badly governed. Indeed, the situation was so bad that the papacy occasionally came under foreign pressure to improve matters; nothing really changed, however. Between 1829 and 1831 there were three popes in quick succession. Pope Gregory XVI took over in 1831, just as revolutions broke out in the Marches. This experience ensured that papal government would be reactionary for the next 15 years.

Occupying the whole of southern Italy was the kingdom of the Two Sicilies, a title that neatly summarises the fact that the kingdom consisted of two elements: the mainland and the island of Sicily. Relations between the two were usually tense and often hostile. The state was also often known as the kingdom of Naples, after its capital city, which in 1830 was the third-largest city in Europe after London and Paris. Naples was ruled by a branch of the Spanish Bourbons, rarely an enlightened or progressive set of rulers. If the government of the papacy was bad that of Naples was even worse: the country was very poor and the regime brutal. There were revolutions in 1799 and 1820, the latter being defeated only with the help of Austrian troops.

Although the seven states varied greatly in size, all were governed by rulers who wanted to maintain the status quo. In terms of national links, these seven states had no equivalent of the German *Bund* or *Zollverein* (see Chapter 6). Austria dominated Italy, and her chancellor, Metternich, was prepared to take any necessary step to maintain the new order of 1815. The last thing that the Habsburgs wanted was a united Italy on its southern borders.

Italy's culture and society was also divided. The experiences of many centuries had reinforced a sense of separatism in most parts of Italy. There was no single Italian language that was spoken and understood by one and all; instead different dialects meant that someone from Milan found it difficult to understand someone from Naples. French was more often spoken in Piedmont, Spanish in Naples, while the official language in the Papal States was Latin. The first edition of the most important novel of the *Risorgimento*, **The betrothed**, by Alessandro Manzoni, was published in 1827. It was written in Milanese. Thirteen years later it was republished in what became the 'official' Italian dialect, that of Tuscany. Slowly a fragmented Italy was beginning to acquire a single language.

Italian society was also fragmented. An essentially agrarian society, most of the land in Italy was owned by the nobility or by the Catholic Church. The majority of Italians were peasants. There was great inequality. Although

The betrothed, by Alessandro Manzoni, is a novel set in northern Italy during the early seventeenth century, at the time of the Thirty Years' War (1618–48), when Italy was under foreign domination.

feudalism had been abolished by Napoleon, the nineteenth century brought no improvement in the peasants' lot: the rapid growth in population made their situation just as bad as it had always been. Neither was the situation much better in Italy's many towns and cities. They were controlled by wealthy nobles and merchants. The urban poor lived in overcrowded slums. There were occasional revolts against the poor economic and social conditions, but these revolts had no national goal. Italy's deep social divisions made national unity harder to achieve.

Although the one institution that was common to all of Italy was the papacy, or Catholic Church, the fact that this religious organisation was one of the seven states of Italy weakened its national appeal and thus its potential as a force for unity. Given the confusion caused by the combination of religious and secular roles, the other states regarded papal policies with suspicion. The Catholic Church's economic and social power also made it a force for order (with one brief exception, as will be explained later).

The forces for unity

After 1815 the main groups that identified the most with the concept of a unified Italy were the secret societies that were scattered across the peninsula. Formed during the Napoleonic period in order to expel foreigners from Italy and restore Italian independence, many persisted in their aims after 1815, the Austrians and various junior Habsburgs now becoming the focus of their attentions. Societies of **freemasons** were prominent in the north, while in the south those of the *Carbonari* (charcoal-burners) predominated. The *Carbonari* were both better known and more important to the Italian cause than the freemasons. Estimates of the number of *Carbonari* in the south during this period vary from 60,000 to 150,000 (the latter figure equating to roughly 1 in 20 of the population of the whole of Italy). There were also many members of the *Carbonari* in central and northern Italy. These numbers never achieved much because they were disorganised and lacking in clear and agreed aims. Although they believed in revolution, they were not sure to what end: unity or independence. Their greatest success came during the 1820 revolution in Naples, but lasted for only a few months before Austrian troops arrived and restored the old order.

In 1830 the odds therefore seemed heavily against Italy being united in the foreseeable future. The **July Revolution** in France had no immediate effect in Italy, but in 1831 two developments set events in motion that would lead to a united Italy being formed exactly thirty years later.

Significant developments in Italy between 1831 and 1847

Although the period between 1831 and 1847 was one of relative peace in Italy,

---

> What, in the period 1815–30, were the main forces working for and against the unification of Italy?

freemasons
Freemasonry is a secret brotherhood that is dedicated to good works and the power of reason. It emerged in France during the second half of the eighteenth century and spread rapidly. The freemasons' policy of secrecy meant that they were – and still are – regarded with suspicion by many. Garibaldi was a freemason.

July Revolution
In July 1830 the Bourbon king of France, Charles X, was overthrown in favour of the Orléanist Louis-Philippe. The event encouraged unrest in Belgium, Germany and Poland.

there were some significant developments, two of which occurred in 1831: Charles Albert's accession to the throne of Piedmont and the formation of the Young Italy organisation.

Charles Albert's accession and rule

Limited revolutions broke out in central Italy in 1831 when members of various secret societies in Modena, Parma and Romagna revolted against their reactionary rulers, encouraged by the example of France in 1830. (One of the conspirators was the future Napoleon III.) They also incited popular insurrection in other parts of the Papal States. The revolutionaries were divided, however, and Austrian forces quickly moved in to restore order, occupying the key papal city of Bologna, while France ordered its troops to the papal town of Ancona. Both forces remained in these towns for seven years.

These limited revolts were not the most significant events of 1831, however. The first important event was Charles Albert's accession to the throne of Piedmont-Sardinia. At the time his accession did not encourage Italy's nationalists. He was as politically reactionary as his father, Charles Felix. Furthermore, in the confused situation of the 1821 revolution in Piedmont he had flirted with liberalism only to back down later. The new king maintained political censorship and supported the Catholic Church, both within Piedmont and elsewhere. His response to an appeal from the former *Carbonaro* **Giuseppe Mazzini** in 1831 to lead Italian efforts to remove Austria from Italy was to order his arrest should Mazzini enter Piedmont again. He furthermore suppressed a Mazzini-inspired conspiracy of army officers with considerable brutality in 1833.

Charles Albert did, however, begin to modernise Piedmont. Laws were codified, tariffs reduced, roads improved and railways introduced, while feudalism was abolished on the island of Sardinia. In addition, Piedmont's government became less corrupt than those in the rest of Italy and trade and industry grew. As a result, those nationalists who believed that the creation of Italian unity required an Italian state to lead the movement for independence began to look to Piedmont, which was both reasonably independent and reasonably progressive in economic matters. During the 1840s Charles Albert himself became more openly anti-Austrian, and in 1848 was to act in ways that were at odds with his policies over the preceding 17 years.

The establishment of Young Italy

The second event of 1831 that would be of significance to the *Risorgimento* did not occur in Italy but in the French port of Marseilles, where Mazzini had gone after spending three months in a Piedmontese prison in 1830–31. There Mazzini announced the formation of a nationalist organisation called Young

Giuseppe Mazzini (1805–72) was one of the leading figures of the *Risorgimento* and, indeed, of nineteenth-century European history. He was the leading exponent of democratic nationalism, which he regarded as a progressive, God-given faith. He formed the Young Italy organisation in 1831. He spent most of his life in exile, mainly in England and always wore black in mourning for Italy. He was viewed as something of a failure because his attempts to incite national revolts in Italy never succeeded.

A portrait of Mazzini, dressed in black, as a young man, undated but probably from the 1830s. Why do you think the artist has painted Mazzini in this pose?

Italy, so-called because Mazzini did not want anyone older than 40 to join it, believing that people over 40 were too old and too cynical. (Young Italy's main ideas are set out in the extract on pages 59–60.)

Mazzini gave the cause of Italian unity a sense of purpose and strategy that it had never had before. He tried to achieve his aims through education and insurrection. The main form of education that he used was the movement's newspaper, *Young Italy*, which his supporters smuggled into Italy. A talented journalist, Mazzini's writings inspired young Italians to join his cause. As a result the movement gained considerable support in central and northern Italy. Although estimating the extent of that support is hard, by the mid-1830s members of Young Italy certainly numbered thousands, if not tens of thousands.

Mazzini did not wait long before attempting insurrection. A native of Genoa, he chose Piedmont as the focus of his efforts and in 1834 presided over plans to invade Piedmont from Switzerland and France. The Swiss group, consisting of some 200 Mazzinians, argued amongst themselves and never reached Piedmont, while the French group was easily defeated by the Piedmontese *Carabinieri* (a semi-military police force). Mazzini's insurrection therefore had to be postponed. In 1844 there was another attempt to provoke insurrection when the Bandiera brothers and 19 of their supporters landed on the eastern coast of Italy. Having been easily defeated by the Neapolitan authorities, nine were executed. They became martyrs to the nationalist cause.

Despite these setbacks Mazzini continued his policy of education, writing from exile in Switzerland and England. In 1834 he set up Young Europe, hoping that the brotherhood of nationalities would lead to some kind of European unity. He was 120 years ahead of his time.

The changing face of the old order

Although Mazzini had achieved none of his goals by 1847, in those reactionary times he had kept the cause of Italian unity alive and had developed the idea of Italian nationalism. Perhaps just as importantly, his lack of success, together with his extreme views and methods, encouraged more moderate nationalists to develop different ideas about how to unify Italy.

One such Italian nationalist was Vincenzo Gioberti, a Piedmontese priest and former Mazzinian, who published his influential work *On the moral and civil primacy of Italians* in 1843. Gioberti's **neo-Guelph** ideas gained considerable support during the mid-1840s, especially from the Piedmontese middle classes. They initially seemed to stand little chance of being implemented as the Papal States were notorious for their bad government and the pope for his reactionary policies. When Pope Gregory XVI died in 1846 his successor was Pius IX (also known by the Italian version of his name, Pio Nono). For two years Pius IX did not fully conform to the traditions of his post. He was a liberal pope. He introduced an amnesty for all political prisoners in the Papal States (some 2,000 in total). He transferred the role of censoring the press from the Catholic Church to a commission that mainly consisted of non-clerics and set up similar commissions to reform various aspects of government policy. He established a civic guard. He protested when Austria occupied the papal town of Ferrara in 1847. Pius IX's actions raised the hopes of the neo-Guelphs, becoming something of a hero to liberals and nationalists alike.

Neo-Guelphs were a new form of the Guelphs, who had been supporters of the papacy during its struggle with the Holy Roman Empire during the fourteenth century.

Thus the Italy of 1847 was different from the Italy of 1831, despite the efforts of Austria and its allies to prevent change. Piedmont was modernising itself, and even the Papal States were changing. Different forms of Italian unification were being proposed and different methods for achieving this aim advocated. There was evidence of growing support for nationalist ideas: the operas of Giuseppe Verdi, for example, were sometimes given a nationalist interpretation, as was the case with *Nabucco* (1842) and *I Lombardi* (1843), which were very popular across Italy. In 1846 press censorship was relaxed in Piedmont. The establishment of a customs union was even agreed between the papacy, Tuscany and Piedmont, partly in response to the Austrian

> Explain the different forms of a united Italy that were proposed during the 1840s and how their supporters thought that they would be achieved.

occupation of Ferrara. By 1847 it was clear that the old order was beginning to change. In the new year it was all but swept away.

What impact did the revolutions of 1848 to 1849 have on efforts to create a united Italy?

The first of the many European revolutions of 1848 occurred in Italy, in January, when the people of Palermo, in Sicily, revolted against rule by Naples. Almost the final revolution of all to be crushed was that in Venice, which did not submit until August 1849. The events of these 20 months can be divided into two roughly equal halves, the autumn of 1848 being the dividing line.

During the first phase popular revolutions broke out in two states at opposite ends of Italy, Naples and Lombardy-Venetia, but were defeated (apart from the revolts in the island of Sicily and the city of Venice). A national war against Austria, led by Piedmont, was also defeated. During the second phase further popular revolutions occurred, this time in central Italy, in Tuscany and Rome. Piedmont made a second unsuccessful attack on Austria. The Habsburgs were able to reassert their control over Tuscany and Venice, while the French defeated the Roman Republic and the Bourbons eventually regained control of Sicily without foreign help. By the autumn of 1849 the revolutions had been defeated and a form of order had been restored. It was not the pre-revolutionary order, however: the Italy of the 1850s was different from that of the 1830s and 1840s.

Three elements of these revolutions are important in analysing the strength of Italian nationalism:
- the aims of revolutionaries and how far they achieved them;
- the amount of support for a united Italy;
- the impact of the 1848–49 revolutions on the process of Italian unification.

The aims and successes of the revolutionaries

In Sicily the revolutionaries demanded the return of the constitution that they had been granted in 1812: political autonomy and freedom from Naples rather than unity with Italy. When the Sicilians declared that the Bourbon monarch was no longer their ruler they did not announce that they would become part of a united Italy, but that another Italian prince would govern them. The revolutionaries in Naples itself demanded both a constitution and that Naples support the northern war against Austria. Although a constitution was soon granted, it covered the whole kingdom of Sicily. Troops were briefly sent to the north to support the nationalist cause. A few weeks later, however, clashes in the streets of Naples enabled the king to reassert his control, even though he dared not remove the constitution.

Milan and Venice followed the lead of Palermo. The fall of Metternich in March 1848 encouraged both cities to rise in revolt against Austrian rule. There were 'five days' of street-fighting in Milan, when the people opposed the Austrians and caused the Habsburg troops to abandon the city. There was less fighting in Venice, from which the Habsburgs also withdrew, prompting Venice to declare itself a republic once again. The people of both states wanted a union with Piedmont in order to protect them against what they regarded as an inevitable Austrian attack.

In Tuscany, the ruling duke granted the people a constitution and sent troops north to assist in the effort against the Austrians; Parma and Modena did the same. The people of the central duchies also decided by means of plebiscites that that the duchies should join forces with Piedmont.

In the spring of 1848 Piedmont, because of its independence, and the Papal States, because of Pope Pius IX, seemed to hold the key to achieving greater unity. Initial signs suggested that the pope was still liberal. In March he granted a constitution. In early April some papal forces joined the war in the north, although not with the pope's consent, revolutionary enthusiasm proving stronger than obedience to the pope. Then, on 29 April, Pius issued what became known as the Papal Allocution (see page 189). In it Pius stated that he had no wish to lead the nationalist cause. (He did not reject liberalism, however, and he appointed a reformist ministry in the summer.) The hopes of the neo-Guelph movement were dashed by the pope's announcement, and moderate nationalists now had to look elsewhere. Piedmont seemed the best, the only prospect.

By the spring of 1848 Charles Albert of Piedmont was prepared to put himself at the head of the movement to eject the Austrians from northern Italy. He feared that if he did not support the uprisings in Lombardy and Venetia then Piedmont might suffer similar revolts, with untold consequences. Although his motives were essentially conservative and dynastic, the reasons that he gave in his proclamation of 23 March for sending Piedmontese troops into Lombardy were rather different (see page 189).

The war with Austria began promisingly for Piedmont. Then the Austrians defeated a Piedmontese attempt to take Venetia at the Battle of Custoza. An armistice was signed by which the Austrians regained Venetia (except for Venice, which was still controlled by the revolutionaries) and Lombardy. Piedmont had quickly lost control of the two states that it had joined forces with just a few weeks earlier.

By the autumn of 1848 the nationalists appeared to have been defeated and the old order restored. However, two more attempts to establish a new political order were made. The first occurred when Piedmont once again went to war with Austria, in March 1849. This time the war lasted for only three days,

Victor Emmanuel II (1820–78) was the last king of Piedmont and the first king of Italy. Blunt, coarse and lecherous by nature, he was regarded as something of a buffoon. He threatened to abolish the 1849 constitution, but never did. He was not quite the buffoon that he seemed, however, for he shrewdly recognised Cavour's ability and won Garibaldi's support.

Giuseppe Garibaldi (1807–82) was one of the leading figures of the *Risorgimento*. Born in Nice (then part of Piedmont), he initially worked as a sailor. He joined Young Italy in 1833 and was involved in the 1834 uprising. Condemned to death in his absence, he escaped to South America, where he led guerrilla groups. These became the basis for the Italian Legion that he formed in 1843; its members wore red shirts, which became their trademark.

ending when the Piedmontese were defeated at Novara, in Lombardy. This defeat caused Charles Albert to abdicate in favour of his son, **Victor Emmanuel**. Austrian control of northern Italy, apart from Venice, was now fully restored. The second attempt was centred on Rome. When the pope's chief minister, Count Pellegrino Rossi, was stabbed to death in late 1848 the pope left Rome for the safety of Gaeta, a few miles down the coast in Naples. In January 1849 Rome elected its representatives to an Italian constituent assembly (that is, one that would decide on the new government for Italy). Shortly afterwards Tuscany elected representatives to this assembly, too. When the Romans then declared a Roman republic, in February 1849, the pope appealed to Catholic states to overthrow the new regime. The rift between the papacy and Italian nationalism was now complete.

It was at this point that Mazzini returned to Italy once more, travelling to Rome for the first time (he had briefly returned to Piedmont in 1848). Such was his reputation that he was chosen to be a member of the triumvirate governing Rome. For the only time in his long career Mazzini became a practising politician. Another Italian nationalist, **Giuseppe Garibaldi**, joined Mazzini in Rome. Garibaldi had returned to Piedmont in 1848 after 14 years in exile and had offered his services to Charles Albert, who had turned him down. He had then raised a small force and had fought the Austrians in Lombardy after Piedmont's defeat at Custoza. Garibaldi arrived in Rome in February 1849 and was soon elected to the new constituent assembly. He brought with him some 500 irregular troops.

Two days before Garibaldi's forces arrived in Rome a French army of 6,000 troops entered the Papal States to restore the rule of Pius IX. (Louis Napoleon had two reasons for taking this step: firstly, he needed to gain the support of Catholics in France and, secondly, he wanted to reassert French power in Italy at the expense of Austria.) Following their victory at Novara, Austrian troops had occupied central Italy, while Neapolitan forces had moved up from the south. There was even a Spanish force to the west of Rome. The Roman Republic, now surrounded by enemy troops, decided to resist them. The siege that resulted lasted for just over two months during the summer of 1849. It took the French forces, now numbering 20,000, four weeks to gain control of the city. The Romans fought fiercely, especially when they were led by Garibaldi. Even after the Roman Republic was defeated Garibaldi remained defiant. Reports of what he said to the crowd in St Peter's Square differ. One version has him saying:

> I am leaving Rome. Whoever is willing to follow me will be received among my people. I ask nothing of them but a heart filled with love for our country. They will have no pay, no provisions and no rest. I offer hunger, cold, forced marches, battles and death. Whoever is not

satisfied with such a life must remain behind. He who has the name of
Italy not only on his lips but in his heart, let him follow me.

Several thousand did so, although their numbers dwindled rapidly as Garibaldi led his troops across the Apennines to the Adriatic Sea. Several small boats set sail for Venice, but were stopped by Austrian forces. Garibaldi himself headed back inland, trying to evade capture. While on the run, his wife died in his arms. Garibaldi could not risk staying with the body, which was buried in an unmarked grave. Two months after leaving Rome Garibaldi left Tuscany for Piedmont, where he was arrested and exiled. Mazzini, who had fallen out with Garibaldi during the siege of Rome, also went into exile once more. The Roman Republic had lasted for some five months.

When he left Rome, Garibaldi's intended destination, Venice, was the last surviving centre of resistance. Under Danieli Manin's leadership it held out against an Austrian bombardment, supplemented by starvation and cholera, for four months until August 1849. By then the revolutions of 1848 had finally been defeated. The revolutionaries had not managed to create a united Italy.

> Summarise the key developments of the 1848–49 revolutions in (a) the Papal States and (b) Piedmont.

Support for a united Italy

The universal demand for constitutional government from within the Italian states shows that there was considerable support for freedom from autocratic rule and for political liberty. The widespread demand in 1848 that other state governments assist Piedmont's attempt to evict Austria from the peninsula suggests that there was much support for an independent Italy, one that was free of foreign interference. However, there is not a lot of evidence of popular support for a single Italian state.

In Italy, there was no government in embryo (as there was in Germany at the same time) which would have provided a focus for Italian unification. Furthermore, although there were certainly many who wanted a united Italy, they disagreed over the form that such an Italian state might take. The great divide, in terms of goals, was between the republicans and the monarchists. The division over aims was reinforced by disagreements between moderates and revolutionaries over methods. This disunity was evident in 1849, when the republicans in Rome and the monarchists in Piedmont could not join forces in the name of a united Italy. If anything, the republicans were more willing to work with the monarchists than the monarchists were to co-operate with the republicans, the monarchists fearing revolution more than they feared the Austrians.

Yet if support for Italian unification was not widespread it was certainly intense among the nationalists who joined Mazzini and Garibaldi in Rome, who believed that they were fighting for a greater Italian cause, not just for a Roman republic.

The impact of the 1848–49 revolutions on Italian unity

The 1848–49 revolutions did not help the cause of Italian unity in three significant respects:

- With one significant exception that will be explored later, the old order had been restored. In some cases the restored regimes were as repressive as any before 1848 (this was particularly true of the Papal States and Lombardy). The hereditary rulers had returned and all but one of the constitutions had been withdrawn. The forces of order had triumphed – at least in the short term.
- The forces of reaction had been reinforced. French troops now occupied Rome and Austria troops northern Italy. Having been a supporter of reform from 1846 to 1848, Pius IX had returned to the papacy's traditionally reactionary role. Once regarded as a potential leader of a united Italy, the pope was now one of its leading opponents.
- The 1848–49 revolutions had revealed the weakness of the nationalist cause. There was a lack of popular enthusiasm for Italian unification, the aim of the revolutionaries more often being to obtain local freedom; only in Rome, in 1849, did people fight and die for the Italian cause in any significant numbers. The events of these years showed that Mazzini's theory that insurrection would lead to a national revolution was just that – a theory. Furthermore, they also revealed the deep divisions among the nationalists. It was not just a question of republicans against monarchists, or revolutionaries against moderates: the republicans disagreed among themselves, as was shown by the rift between Garibaldi and Mazzini in Rome over how best to further the cause of a united Italy. The moderate nationalists also argued about strategies and tactics, as well as about whether to react to events or to push for change. Finally, Italian nationalism lacked a physical force strong enough to eject the non-Italian powers from the peninsula. Piedmontese troops had twice tried, and failed, to do so, being humiliated on their second attempt. As he prepared for war in 1848 the Piedmontese king, Charles Albert, promised that 'Italy will do it on her own'. Yet on the evidence of 1848 to 1849 it could not.

Italian nationalists clearly needed some assistance if they were to achieve their aim of a united Italy. The events of 1848 to 1849 themselves saw developments that strengthened the cause of Italian nationalism. Some were evident at the time; others became apparent only later. In the first category were the events in Rome and, to a lesser extent, in Venice, in 1849. Their resistance to the French forces (which were then regarded as being the most powerful in

Europe) and readiness to die for a united Italy won the Roman revolutionaries admiration in Italy and beyond. Garibaldi, in particular, inspired many to support his cause. Here his personal qualities were significant. Neither a politician nor an abstract revolutionary thinker, he remained unaffected by the adulation that he began to receive wherever he went. When not at war he lived an ordinary life, returning to sea to earn his living after 1848 before retiring to the small island of Caprera, off the western coast of Italy. The combination of his great military exploits and plain lifestyle made Garibaldi a heroic figure.

One of the potentially unifying factors that became more significant only as the 1850s progressed was the constitution that Piedmont retained after the events of 1848 to 1849. Although the *Statuto*, as it was called, was a far from perfect document, it provided a basis for some kind of constitutional government that was exceptional in Italy. Attracted by this, many liberals and nationalists moved to Piedmont from the rest of Italy. Now that the papacy had changed sides, the nationalists also increasingly focused on Piedmont, despite its military failures of 1848 to 1849. Furthermore, during the 1850s Piedmont found a political leader who could identify with nationalist aspirations: **Count Camillo di Cavour**.

Another significant force emerged during 1848 to 1849 that would eventually help the Italian cause. It was the support of the new leader of France, Louis Napoleon, who had used his army to defeat the Roman Republic and Italian nationalism in 1849. Nine years later, his army would assist Italian nationalists. Since his days as a *Carbonaro* in 1831 Louis Napoleon had retained his sympathy for the Italian cause, but it would take some years and a strange combination of events before his sympathy turned into practical support.

There is one final point worth making about Italy between 1848 and 1849: the revolutions in northern and central Italy were defeated by the military intervention of Austria and France (although Naples was a different matter). The Italian rulers were not strong enough on their own to defeat the revolutionaries' demands for freedom and unity. Although Italian liberalism and nationalism lacked the strength to defeat the forces of the two great powers, they were not as weak as is sometimes thought.

How and why was Italy united in 1861?

There are no simple answers to these questions. The first Italian parliament met in February 1861, less than 12 years after the final defeat of the revolutions of 1848 to 1849, when hopes for Italian unification had crumbled in the face of nationalist division, popular indifference and great-power opposition.

Intelligent, ambitious and unscrupulous, **Count Camillo di Cavour** (1810–61) was one of the three great leaders of the process of Italian unification. The son of a Piedmontese landowner, after an army career he travelled to France and Britain where he gained ideas for the modernisation of Piedmont, before running his family's estate for 13 years. In 1847 he founded and edited the liberal newspaper *Il Risorgimento*.

Identify three ways in which the revolutions of 1848–49 helped the cause of Italian unification.

How was Italy united in 1861?

Before we can really explain why this amazing reversal of fortunes occurred, we need to consider how it happened. In order to give some cohesion to the complex, fast-changing years between 1849 and 1861, the period is best divided into three. This subdivision centred on the developments in Piedmont, which became the focus of the hopes of increasing numbers of Italian nationalists.

Peace and reform, 1849–55

Under two prime ministers, **Massimo d'Azelgio** and Cavour, Piedmont became a progressive, liberal state during the 1850s. Although Cavour is the better known of the two, d'Azelgio began the process of reform. Under d'Azelgio the privileged status of the Catholic Church was greatly reduced, a process that Cavour later continued. Not only did this action antagonise Pius IX and Austria, but it also attracted liberals who supported the policy of 'a free church in a free state', in other words the ending of the privileged position of the Catholic Church. Many such liberals were also nationalists who regarded Piedmont as having the best chance of achieving their goal of a unified Italy. Under d'Azelgio's premiership, too, the Piedmontese constitution survived the uncertain months following the setbacks of 1848 to 1849. The Piedmontese electorate initially voted for deputies who refused to accept the peace with Austria (which indicates some nationalist sentiments among these middle-class voters). It took three elections in 1849 before a pro-government majority was returned, Victor Emmanuel having threatened to withdraw the constitution if voters did not vote the 'right' way. Although constitutional government survived, and with it Piedmont's position as the most advanced state in Italy, it had been a close-run thing.

D'Azelgio was supported in his policies by Cavour, who was appointed minister of the navy, commerce and agriculture in October 1850. Within a year he had signed trade treaties with France, Britain, Belgium and Austria and was promoted to the cabinet position of minister of finance in 1851. From then on he began to outmanoeuvre his leader, d'Azelgio. The best example of his skill was the deal that Cavour himself regarded as his finest achievement: in 1852, while still in government, Cavour secretly agreed to work with Urbano Rattazzi, the leader of the centre-left group in parliament. This link between the moderate-right and moderate-left politicians excluded the extreme republicans on one side and members of Piedmont's clerical party on the other, giving Cavour a broad base of support that would subsequently enable him to govern without too much fear of opposition. It became known as the *Connubio*, or marriage, and lasted for five years, until Cavour was forced to transfer his support to the political right as the clerical party

---

Massimo d'Azelgio (1798–1866) was a Piedmontese aristocrat, artist, novelist and politician. A moderate nationalist, in 1846 he wrote the work *On the recent events in the Romagna,* which argued that the evolution of public opinion would result in Italian unity. He was appointed prime minister of Piedmont in May 1849.

A close-up photograph of Cavour looking straight into the camera, undated but probably from the 1850s. Compare the impression of Cavour given by this photograph with the impression of Mazzini given by the painting on page 30.

gained increasing support. D'Azelgio initially knew nothing of this agreement, but once he realised what was going on he could no longer trust Cavour and relations between the two men became so bad that Cavour left the government. However, his skills and ambition were such that within six months he was back in office, this time as prime minister. From 1852 to 1861 his premiership would prove of great importance in the history of Italy.

What sort of man was Cavour? A close friend of his, Michaelangelo Castelli, later gave this description:

> His easy manners, his joviality, his genuine interest in new acquaintances... his readiness to listen to serious men or any enterprising project made him popular with all acquaintances as well as intimates. He was respected and loved by his juniors and servants... His perceptiveness, his benevolence, his instinctive understanding of our times made him a believer in political and civic equality. Yet deep down you could sometimes find traces... of a less progressive man.
>
> From the outset I had set myself to study his real character and to clarify the distrust in which he was held. More than once I showed him the apparent contradictions between what he said and what he did. He would be taken aback for a moment and usually ended up by turning

the matter into a friendly joke, realising he was in the wrong. His activity was ceaseless; if he was not doing something, he was thinking; hence his occasionally abstracted manner, his odd forms of posture, his constant need to be at work.

What did Cavour believe in? Consider this letter that he wrote in 1835, when he was in Paris:

> The more I observe the course of events and the behaviour of men, the more I am persuaded that the *juste-milieu* [middle way] is the only policy right in the circumstances, capable of saving society from the two rocks which threaten to break it – anarchy and despotism. When I say *juste-milieu* I am thinking not of the special system of any particular man, but rather of the policy which consists in according to the demands of the time everything that reason can justify, while refusing anything which is founded merely on party clamour or the violence of destructive passions.

One example of Cavour's flexibility can be seen during the first crisis that he faced as prime minister when, in early 1853, Mazzini tried to incite another revolt in Milan, hoping that it would spark a nationwide revolution. The badly organised revolt conformed to the pattern of those that had preceded it, however, and was a total failure. Although Cavour supported Austria in crushing the revolt, when Austria also seized the property of those who had left Lombardy, whether or not they were revolutionaries, Cavour broke off relations between Piedmont and Austria. He had thus shown his opposition to the 'anarchy' of extreme republicanism while also playing the nationalist card against the despotism of the Austrians.

In continuing d'Azelgio's process of modernisation Cavour concentrated on the Piedmontese economy. **Free-trade** treaties started to take effect and Cavour borrowed money to invest in Piedmont's infrastructure, its railways, roads and irrigation schemes. Piedmont's economy did develop, though it was on a limited scale when compared to the German *Zollverein*. The fact that economic success was only partial was not as important to the issue of Italian unification as the fact that Piedmont was being seen to be modernising, and on all fronts. No longer a reactionary, repressive state, Piedmont was now the only realistic means of achieving the goal of an independent, united Italy.

Did the Piedmontese government want to lead a united Italy? Almost certainly not. In the early 1850s national unity was still too revolutionary an idea, associated with rule by the people, with the revolutions of 1848. The new King, Victor Emmanuel II was neither a democrat nor a nationalist. He greatly mistrusted leading nationalists such as Mazzini, even though Mazzini had

---

Free trade requires the removal of customs duties (also known as tariffs) from imports, thereby allowing goods to move more freely and more efficient producers to be gained at the expense of less efficient ones. Free trade is a key aspect of economic liberalism and is also an important force for change in modern history. Many people opposed free trade because they wanted local industries to be protected.

> Explain four ways in which Piedmont was modernised in the first decade of the reign of Victor Emmanuel.

come to accept that a united Italy would occur only with leadership from Piedmont. But Victor Emmanuel's views soon counted for less than those of his indispensable Prime Minister, Cavour.

What of Cavour? Did he want a united Italy? Almost certainly not, as will be discussed later. He did want an independent Italy, however, with Piedmont as its leading power. Cavour recognised that Italian independence would require the eviction of Austria from northern Italy, and the events of 1848 to 1849 had shown that the help of foreign powers – probably Britain and perhaps France – would be needed to achieve this aim. In 1854 the crisis emerged which might allow this to happen. In what soon became known as the Crimean War, Britain and France declared war on Russia. Austria seemed likely to support Russia. (In 1849 Russia had sent its troops into Hungary to help the Habsburgs defeat the revolution there and restore order; Austria was now expected to return the favour.) It was possible to imagine Piedmont joining Britain and France in a western alliance against the conservative forces of Russia and Austria. As so often happens, events did not turn out as imagined.

The Crimean War and its aftermath, 1855–57

Although Piedmont did join forces with Britain and France it did so only after the war was already a year old and against Russia alone; far from siding with Russia, Austria sympathised with Anglo-French attempts to curb its power. How Piedmont became involved is a complicated story that also illustrates how historical explanations can change.

The traditional explanation for Piedmont's participation in the Crimean War focuses on Cavour. It argues that he took Piedmont into the war because he recognised the benefits of being an ally of Britain and France. As well as raising Piedmont's international reputation, the advocates of this theory continue, Piedmont's assistance would cause Britain and France to support Piedmont in its struggle against Austria. Indeed this did happen a few years later, with France providing military support and Britain diplomatic assistance. This interpretation reinforces the reputation of Cavour as a skilful, far-sighted and nationalist politician.

If the evidence of more recent historical research is to be believed, however, the reality was very different: Cavour was wary of committing Piedmont to war because he was aware of two significant problems that he would face if he did so. Firstly, there was little domestic support for the war, especially since it was against Russia rather than Austria. Secondly, despite putting pressure on Piedmont to fight alongside them, Britain and France were unwilling to make any promises regarding Italy. Victor Emmanuel, who was keen on sending Piedmontese troops to the Crimea, became impatient with Cavour and considered replacing him with a more aggressive, right-wing government. In response Cavour changed tack and came out in favour of participating in the war, winning over Rattazzi by introducing further anti-clerical reforms. Eventually, in March 1855, a year after Britain and France had declared war on Russia, Piedmont did so too. In April 1855 15,000 Piedmontese troops travelled to the Crimea, where they fought one battle and lost 2,000 men to cholera. Within a year the war was over and a peace treaty had been signed.

The direct benefits of the Crimean War to Piedmont were very limited: Piedmont had made no territorial gains from the peace negotiations in Paris and Cavour had to work hard to persuade the great powers even to consider the Italian question. It had, however, gained status and prestige, now being recognised as the leading Italian state by Britain and France. Within Italy, some moderate republicans, such as Manin, turned to Piedmont for leadership when they formed the National Society in 1857, while yet another failed Mazzinian revolution – this time in Naples – indicated that popular insurrection was unlikely to be effective.

The indirect benefits of the war to Piedmont were great, however, even if they were not apparent at the time. Austrian neutrality during the war had smashed the conservative alliance between Austria and Russia that had existed in one form or other since 1815. The result was that Austria was now the only power that still defended the status quo of 1815. The Crimean War showed that Piedmont was too cautious to risk removing Austria from Italy without foreign help. Of all the great powers France was now the most likely to provide that assistance: Napoleon III wanted to dismantle the 1815 settlement and part of that settlement was Austria's control of Lombardy-Venetia. Cavour realised this. He tried to gain Napoleon's support by using both orthodox and unorthodox methods. In 1857 he sent his cousin, 18 years old and by all accounts very attractive, to seduce Napoleon. She did so, after having had sex with Victor Emmanuel before leaving Piedmont. There is no evidence that the tactic worked. What, then, would it take to persuade Napoleon III to support the cause of Italian unity?

> How did the Crimean War affect the political situation in Italy?

Plots, wars and revolts, 1858–59

The first of the several plots that were hatched between 1858 and 1861 was the most important. It involved Napoleon III and Cavour, who, in July 1858, met secretly in the village of Plombières, in the French Alps, to plot war against Austria. The meeting led directly to the unification of Italy less than three years later.

The event that pushed the French president into action was Felice Orsini's appeal to Napoleon III to help the Italian cause. An Italian nationalist, Orsini had tried to assassinate Napoleon III early in 1858, killing 10 people and wounding 150 in the process. This was not the first time that an Italian nationalist had tried to assassinate the French president, and Napoleon demanded that Piedmont take some action against its republican revolutionaries. Cavour did so. When Orsini later repented and urged Napoleon III to assist the Italian cause Napoleon had Orsini's speech printed in France and urged Cavour to do the same in Piedmont. Giving publicity to Orsini was giving publicity to his cause. Napoleon went further. He approached Cavour through intermediaries, an approach that resulted in their secret meeting in Plombières. So secret was the meeting that Cavour travelled on a false passport. The only documentation that we have of the meeting are two reports that Cavour sent to Victor Emmanuel, one short, the other long (see pages 190–91 for key sections of the latter, which is worth reading in its entirety in Denis Mack Smith's *The making of Italy, 1796–1866*, pages 238–47). Here were two men deciding on the spoils of war, trying to think of plausible reasons to go to war, taking a break by going for a ride in the Alps and then discussing the marriage of Victor Emmanuel's 18-year-old daughter to Napoleon's 36-year-old cousin, the dissolute Joseph. Much of Cavour's dispatch is taken up with attempts to persuade the presumably reluctant Victor Emmanuel to accept the idea. It is hard to think of other occasions in modern European history when the political heads of two countries supposedly committed to maintaining peace discussed preparations for war in quite such a way and in quite such an unusual setting. The meeting at Plombières led to a formal treaty between Piedmont and France in January 1859 by which they agreed to join forces in the event of Austrian aggression (see page 191 for the terms of the treaty).

Cavour now prepared for war, working with the Italian National Society to try to create a pretext for conflict in central Italy. In December 1858 he met Garibaldi, told him of the terms of the agreement reached at Plombières (although he did not mention **Nice**) and asked him to join the Piedmontese army. Garibaldi's agreement helped to make the planned war appear less Piedmontese and more Italian. Cavour even secretly supplied Hungary and Romania with weapons to ensure widespread anti-Austrian action.

Nice was Garibaldi's birthplace. The 1859 treaty conceded it to France.

As Cavour plotted, however, Napoleon's enthusiasm waned. Diplomatic pressure from Britain and Russia forced him to agree to a congress on the Italian question. Just when it seemed that Cavour would not be going to war after all, in one of the many ironies of history his intended enemy came to the rescue. Austria gave Piedmont an ultimatum to disarm immediately. Piedmont refused to comply. On 26 April 1859 Austria declared war on Piedmont; a week later, after Austria had invaded Piedmont, France declared war on Austria.

The so-called 'Third War of Italian Independence' lasted for two months. Many French troops were brought to the war zone by train, making it the first war of the railway age. There were two major battles, Magenta and Solferino, in which 40,000 troops were either killed or wounded. At Magenta, just within Lombardy, the Austrians were defeated by the French (the Piedmontese troops arrived after the battle was over). Milan fell to the allies. One month later the combined French and Piedmontese forces defeated the Austrians at Solferino, in eastern Lombardy. (One businessman who saw the horrors of the battlefield for himself went away and formed the Red Cross.) Despite these victories the Austrian forces were still in Lombardy and still in good shape, making a long and bloody war seem probable. Less than two weeks after the Battle of Solferino, however, Napoleon wrote to Franz Joseph, the Austrian emperor, offering a truce. (Prussia was starting to mobilise its troops on the Rhine and the last thing that Napoleon wanted was to have to fight a war on two fronts.) Within two days Franz Joseph had agreed and three days later, at Villafranca, Austria and France agreed peace terms (see pages 191–92). Cavour knew nothing about the truce.

On the same day that the Villafranca treaty was agreed Cavour resigned. On hearing the news of the treaty he had a huge row with Victor Emmanuel after the king refused to continue the war against Austria without France as an ally. (On this occasion the king was more realistic than his first minister.) Cavour did nothing for six weeks and then began to yearn to be in office once more so that he could influence developments that followed the war and peace with Austria.

> Identify and explain the aims of Cavour in 1858–59.

For the war against Austria had sparked nationalist revolts in parts of central Italy. The duke of Tuscany had to flee soon after the outbreak of war and the rulers of Parma and Modena not long after. The people of Romagna, the northern part of the Papal States, rose in revolt and Austria withdrew its troops from the area after Magenta, Parma, Modena and Romagna came together to establish the short-lived state of Emilia.

According to the terms of Villafranca (see pages 191–92), the pre-war status quo should have been restored. Piedmont still controlled the region that it had gained during the confusion of war, however. Tuscany and Emilia looked to Piedmont for protection, encouraged by Piedmontese agents. Napoleon III was committed to defending the papacy and to implementing the agreement reached at Villafranca. He changed his mind in December 1859 when, in an anonymous pamphlet written on his behalf, he accepted that the papacy should rule a smaller territory, which in effect meant losing the Romagna. His change of heart was due in part to the fact that many people in France were demanding greater gains from the war with Austria. The British government also used its influence. In June 1859 a Liberal government, led by Lord Palmerston, had been formed. It was sympathetic to the Italian cause. Britain, an ally of France, not only helped to persuade Napoleon to allow the Italians to sort out their own affairs but also put pressure on Victor Emmanuel. In

January 1860 the king reappointed Cavour prime minister once more, even though he could not stand him, expecting him to do a deal with Napoleon III. In March 1860 the deal was done.

By the Treaty of Turin, Piedmont would gain Tuscany and Emilia. In return France would receive Nice and Savoy. (If the terms of France's alliance with Piedmont had been honoured the latter provinces would have gone to France after the Austrian war.) **Plebiscites** were held in both areas and in each case the people voted overwhelmingly in favour of the proposals agreed by France and Piedmont. The loss of Romagna infuriated the pope. He excommunicated those involved, including Victor Emmanuel and Cavour. The loss of Nice infuriated Garibaldi, who never forgave Cavour.

Thus it was that Piedmont acquired Tuscany and Emilia to add to the province of Lombardy that it had gained the previous summer. The plots, war and revolts of 1858 to 1859 had led to the unification of most of northern and central Italy, which was more than the Italian nationalists could have hoped for even two years earlier. The next six months would prove even more dramatic than the preceding two-and-a-half years, however.

> A **plebiscite** (more usually called a referendum today) is a direct vote by the electorate on a single issue, although the result of the vote need not be binding on the government. Plebiscites strengthen direct democracy at the expense of indirect, or representative, democracy. Under Louis Napoleon France was the first state to make regular use of this device.

> How did the 1859 war with Austria affect the political situation in Italy?

Plots, revolts, wars and unity, 1860–61

The next stage of Italian unification involved a second round of plots, revolts and wars, eventually leading to the unification of northern and southern Italy. This time the sequence was a little different. In the south a revolt in Sicily, as well as a nationalist plot, led to a war between the nationalists and Naples. In the north Cavour plotted revolts in Naples and the Papal States before ordering the invasion of the latter by Piedmontese troops. Two wars were therefore fought during these few months, and to a certain extent both were civil wars.

The Sicilian revolt occurred in April 1860. Mazzini had already been preparing to send a group of revolutionaries to Sicily to foment a revolution in southern Italy. Garibaldi became convinced that it would be better to support the revolt in the south than to launch an attack on Nice he was planning. He spent a month in Piedmont equipping a force to invade Sicily.

Historians, greatly intrigued by Cavour's attitudes to Garibaldi's plans, have asked many questions. Did Cavour publicly oppose Garibaldi while privately helping him to succeed? Or was the only help he provided that of not interfering with Garibaldi's plans? Did Cavour allow Garibaldi to go to Sicily because he thought his scheme a crackpot one and doomed to failure? (On the evidence of previous Mazzinian expeditions his plan stood no chance of success.) Finally, would Cavour have liked to stop Garibaldi but could not risk doing so for fear of upsetting the voters of Piedmont? It is hard to answer such questions, especially given Cavour's ability to make contradictory statements. Four points can be stated with some confidence, however:

- Cavour did nothing to help Garibaldi, refusing to provide him with the rifles that he wanted.
- Cavour was unpopular at the time and elections were imminent. Preventing Garibaldi from sailing to Sicily would have added to Cavour's unpopularity. Cavour had to let him leave.
- Cavour did not know exactly where Garibaldi was heading when his two paddle steamers set sail; there was talk of an attack on the Papal States, which would have caused great international problems.
- Victor Emmanuel seemed intent on forming a new government, as well as supporting Garibaldi.

Garibaldi had just one thousand men under his command. It was a volunteer force that included people from all walks of life, many of whom were middle-class professionals like doctors and lawyers. After Garibaldi had left the port of Genoa, Cavour ordered the Piedmontese fleet to arrest him, but it failed to do so. Once at sea Garibaldi announced that his cause was Italy and Victor Emmanuel – until then it had been uncertain which form of Italian unity he would support, republican or monarchist, Mazzinian or Piedmontese. It was still not clear how far he planned to go, however. Garibaldi talked of advancing through Naples to Rome, but such a plan seemed very far-fetched; a thousand untrained volunteers could never defeat the Neapolitan army. But people could never be sure of what Garibaldi might manage. He could achieve the seemingly impossible. In the summer of 1860 he did so.

Garibaldi's conquest of Sicily is one of the great events of nineteenth-century history. His army of a thousand men were untrained and badly equipped and faced with a disciplined Neapolitan force of 25,000 men. Yet within a month of landing at Marsala (see pages 192–95) Garibaldi had gained control of the island. The key battle was at Calatafimi, which was a very close-run thing. One of his men later described Garibaldi in the heat of the fighting:

> The plain was quickly crossed and the first enemy line was broken but when we came to the slopes of the opposite hill it was not pleasant to look upwards. I saw Garibaldi there on foot with his sheathed sword over his right shoulder, walking slowly forward, keeping the whole action in view. Our men were falling down all around him and it seemed that those who wore the red shirt were the most numerous. Someone came up at a gallop to offer shelter with his horse and he pulled the general behind his animal, calling out, 'General, is this the way you want to die?' 'And how could I die better than for my country?' replied the general and freeing himself from a restraining hand walked forward with a frown.

One of the many reconstructions of the landing at Marsala. Compare it with another version on page 193.

Despite his triumph at Calatafimi, Garibaldi's victory was still not assured and further fierce fighting followed before Sicily's capital, Palermo, fell. Once Garibaldi had gained control of the island and had become its dictator the next question was whether he would cross the Straits of Messina to the mainland. He certainly intended to do so. He wanted to enter Rome. Since having to leave the city in 1849, Garibaldi's rallying cry had been 'Rome or death'. Although Cavour tried to stop him because the international consequences would be so great, he could not afford publicly to oppose Garibaldi. Instead, he continued to plot, trying to encourage revolts in mainland Naples to give Piedmont a pretext to intervene. He failed in this plan, however. Reinforced by the arrival of forces from northern Italy, Garibaldi and his men crossed the straits and advanced northwards, towards the city of Naples. Here the combination of Garibaldi's troops and peasant revolts proved all-conquering, and by September 1860 Naples had fallen to Garibaldi, whose forces now numbered 40,000.

Garibaldi's success horrified Cavour, for the possibility of Garibaldi advancing on Rome was now very real. In addition, it was conceivable that Garibaldi might make southern Italy a Mazzinian republic that presented a direct challenge to Piedmont in the north. He therefore believed that Garibaldi had to be stopped, even at the risk of civil war. Cavour faced two

Changing the face of Europe: Italy, 1830–70

major obstacles in doing so. The first was the Papal States, which Piedmontese troops would have to cross to reach Naples; a reason would have to be found to justify doing so. The second was Napoleon III, the defender of the papacy: the Papal States still hosted a French army, the practical manifestation of France's guarantee to protect the pope. Yet Napoleon remained sympathetic to the aims of moderate Italian nationalism and Cavour was able to persuade him to accept a Piedmontese invasion of the Papal States as long as Piedmont's forces stayed clear of Rome and the French troops. For the third time in just over two years the two men had come to an agreement that enabled Cavour to manipulate events. Before the event Cavour tried to justify Piedmont's intervention by fomenting popular revolts in the Papal States. He was using methods very similar to those of Mazzini. Four days after Garibaldi entered Naples 30,000 Piedmontese troops invaded the Papal States, defeating a cosmopolitan papal force led by a French general at Castelfidardo. As a result, Piedmont acquired two more papal territories: the Marches and Umbria; only the area around Rome remained outside Piedmontese control.

Cavour's justification for Piedmont's actions, as he explained to the Piedmontese Senate in October 1860, is worth careful consideration:

> How should we have reacted to recent events in Naples? Clearly the Neapolitan government was unable to withstand a handful of volunteers and so lacked the essential conditions for political existence ... As the Bourbon government had recognised its own powerlessness by surrendering the town of Naples without a fight, morally it was dead. What were we to do? Should we have left that noble part of Italy helpless before events? Should we have allowed the germs of revolution which we had destroyed in northern Italy to multiply elsewhere? No, we could not.
>
> By resolutely seizing the direction of political events in southern Italy, the king and his government prevented our wonderful Italian movement from degenerating; they prevented the factions which did us so much harm in 1848 from exploiting the emergency conditions in Naples after its conquest by Garibaldi. We intervened not to impose a preconceived system on southern Italy but to allow the people there to decide freely on their fate. This, gentlemen, was to be not revolutionary but essentially conservative.
>
> In the Roman [Papal] States, too, our presence can be equally justified. Even those most considerate of papal rights cannot surely believe that these states under the pope could go on existing once they found themselves caught between liberal northern Italy and revolutionary Italy in the south ... The pope's temporal power in the

Marches and Umbria was doomed from the day that the rest of Italy, from the Po river to the Gulf of Messina, had become free.

No doubt he could have gone on fighting for a while but the final outcome was certain, and this was a fact with which we had to reckon. We had to stop any conflict which might divert our national movement or arouse revolutionary passions. We had to carry out a great act of justice and remove that blemish in central Italy where Italian provinces were bent under an iron yoke by the force of foreign mercenaries. Perhaps the means we adopted to carry out this great act have not been entirely regular; but I do know the cause is holy and the ends will perhaps justify any irregularities in the means. (Signs of approval.)

Even in these provinces, gentlemen, we have not brought revolution and disorder. We are there to establish good government, legality and morality. Whatever people may say, I proclaim with certainty – and this will be confirmed by the impartial voice of enlightened, liberal Europe – that no war has ever been fought with greater generosity, magnanimity or justice.

As the Piedmontese forces moved south, the Neapolitan government decided to return to Naples before they arrived. Garibaldi's army stood in its way. A battle was consequently fought around the Volturno river. Neither side won a clear-cut victory – the Neapolitans failing to advance towards Naples and Garibaldi realising that he would not be able to march on Rome. The Piedmontese troops then entered the kingdom of Naples. Garibaldi now decided to hand his conquests over to Victor Emmanuel. On 26 October 1860 the Piedmontese king met Garibaldi at Teano, on the border between the Papal States and the Kingdom of the Two Sicilies. The guerrilla fighter greeted Victor Emmanuel as the king of Italy. The new state of Italy was formed, if not fully formed. Venice and Rome were not yet part of the new state.

> Identify and explain the aims of Cavour in 1860.

Why was Italy united in 1861?

If the 'how' of Italian unification has been described, what of the 'why'? Trying to explain why Italy came to be formed in 1861 requires very careful analysis. The short – and obvious – answer is that the forces in favour of unification were stronger than those against. In 1830 the situation in both Italy and Europe had prevented the idea of a united Italy becoming a reality. By the 1850s much had changed. Within Italy, one of the seven states was building itself up as a modern and more liberal state, a state that could provide the basis of an Italian nation state. In addition, Piedmont wanted to assert itself more forcefully, at least in northern Italy. The two wars of 1848 to 1849 had made Piedmont's intentions clear, and in Victor Emmanuel and Cavour it now had an ambitious leadership, even if they were sometimes at loggerheads.

Italy in the nineteenth century. The dates below each state refer to the date when that state joined Piedmont and/or Italy.

There was also greater support for the nationalist cause, as was shown by the growth of the Italian National Society and by the willingness of some people to fight for the cause in 1860. By the late 1850s that support was less divided than it had been before: nationalists of all kinds had accepted that the only way of achieving their goal in the short term was to support an Italian monarchy led by Piedmont. Since 1848 the nationalists had ruled the papacy out, while the various attempts to establish a republic had come to naught. Even Mazzini had come to accept the need to support Piedmont. Mazzini could stand neither Cavour nor Napoleon III and opposed the 1859 war because the campaign to eject Austria was too dependent on France. He argued that if the war was won Italy might be free, but it would not be independent. Yet he did concede the necessity of rallying behind Piedmont, and although he did not abandon the tactic of popular revolution he ceased to advocate the formation of a republic as an immediate goal. Originally a Mazzinian, Garibaldi was impressed by Victor Emmanuel when he first met him in 1858 and believed that he should become the first leader of Italy. By the 1850s it was clear that the only practical means of unifying Italy was under Piedmont's leadership.

Yet there was still not a lot of active popular support for the idea of a single Italy if the evidence of the failure of the attempts to incite revolts by both Mazzini and Cavour is anything to go by. Although the various plebiscites of 1859 to 1860 seem to indicate the contrary, these were more a passive vote after the event. Furthermore, the size of the majorities in favour of joining with Piedmont was so overwhelming that it raises doubts about the validity of the poll. Possible evidence of popular support can be seen in the peasant revolts in Sicily and Naples, but these were more of a protest against the government than a call for unity. The people did not to unify Italy; politicians and revolutionaries did.

In addition, the forces within Italy that were trying to maintain the status quo were weak and becoming weaker. The key factor was the declining position of Austria, which was not the force that it had once been. After 1848 its attentions were focused on other parts of its empire, especially Hungary and Germany, while the Crimean War spelled the end of its conservative partnership with Russia. Austria was now isolated. On its own it lacked the military and diplomatic power to prevent change, especially now that more effective leadership within Italy, as well as significant support from other European great powers, backed that change.

The sympathetic attitude of the French emperor, Napoleon III, towards the Italian nationalist cause was of primary significance, especially since at crucial moments his sympathy was manifested by military or diplomatic support. In sending an army to attack Austria in 1859 he provided a major stimulus for the process of unification, Piedmont's subsequent acquisition of Lombardy representing the first significant political change in the settlement of Italy since 1815. In early 1860 Napoleon accepted Piedmont's absorption of Tuscany and Emilia. Later in the same year he agreed to Piedmont's invasion of the Papal States. Had he opposed either move Cavour, who was a political gambler, might have hedged his bets. During the 1850s the Italian cause was therefore greatly helped by Napoleon III's leadership of France. Britain, too, had sympathy for, and occasionally acted to assist, the Italian nationalists. The Liberal government that was appointed in 1859 helped to persuade Napoleon to allow Piedmont's acquisition of the central duchies, while its navy assisted Garibaldi, especially during his crossing from Sicily to mainland Italy, by preventing any attempts to stop him from doing so.

The reasons for the unification of Italy are therefore complex. The extent to which the various individuals and groups involved contributed to Italian unity has been a source of continuing historical debate. Although the roles of Mazzini, Garibaldi and Cavour were originally regarded as having complemented each other – Mazzini providing the ideology of nationalism, Garibaldi military and popular leadership and Cavour political leadership – such a neat view is hard to sustain today. A general point worth remembering is that few people wanted unification, at least in the form that it took, but that they had to modify their aims in response to the rapidly changing circumstances. The creation of Italy in 1861, which had not been planned, is a nice example of the law of unintended consequences.

> Summarise the main contributions of (a) Mazzini, (b) Garibaldi and (c) Cavour to the unification of Italy by 1861.

How far did the system of government established in 1861 help to unify Italy?

Because the new state of Italy had been created in something of a rush its unity could not be taken for granted. There had been little time to consider what form the system of government should take, or even how it should be agreed upon. Yet how Italy was governed in its early years would affect whether it became more or less united.

> A **constituent assembly** is one of two main types of national assembly. A constituent assembly is formed to decide on the system of government, while a national assembly is chosen to represent key groups within the state and to approve laws and policies. The British national assembly is parliament. Most assemblies are bicameral, that is they have two chambers, one representing the people, the other various groups or states. It is important to distinguish assemblies from governments.

The democratic ideal was that there should be a **constituent assembly**, composed of delegates from all parts of Italy, which would decide on the form of Italy's government (which is what had happened in the USA in 1787). Such an assembly had been expected in Lombardy in 1859 and proposed by Garibaldi for Naples in 1860. Indeed, the statement made by Cavour in October 1860 (see pages 48–49) suggests that he intended to give the people of Naples freedom of choice when it came to their system of government. The reality was rather different, however. Garibaldi was uncertain as to whether or not Naples should have a constituent assembly. The alternative was to hold an immediate plebiscite on whether Naples should join Piedmont. Unsurprisingly, Piedmont's representatives argued for the plebiscite. Garibaldi leant first one way and then the other until he eventually agreed to the plebiscite. In October 1860 the Neapolitans voted in a ratio of 99 to 1 to join 'Italy one and indivisible under our constitutional sovereign Victor Emmanuel'. Yet just as there had been no constituent assembly for Lombardy, the central duchies or the Papal States so there was none for Naples. Following unification the laws and government of Piedmont were simply extended to the other states (with the limited exception of Tuscany) and the *Statuto* of 1848 became the Italian constitution.

It is therefore possible to regard the creation of the new state in 1861 more as the expansion of Piedmont than the unification of Italy. This view is further supported by the fact that the new king of Italy was still known by his Piedmontese title, Victor Emmanuel II, instead of the more logical and more diplomatic Victor Emmanuel I. Furthermore Piedmont's capital, Turin, became the capital of Italy.

Although Cavour continued to reaffirm his intention to introduce regional government he never did so. As a result Italy became a unitary state rather than a federal one (in contrast to the new state of Germany that was formed 10 years later, see Chapter 6). The electoral franchise that had been introduced by the 1848 *Statuto* was very restricted, and because those restrictions were not lifted in 1861 less than 2 per cent of Italy's adult males had the vote (and an even smaller percentage actually voted). Although the system of government was representative it was thus far from being fully democratic, the government being accountable only to the national assembly and a small proportion of the Italian people.

The unitary state was reinforced by the Piedmontese model of administration, which, based on the example of France, was very centralised. The national government appointed prefects to run local affairs and there was little local democracy. In a country that had a long history of local autonomy this went against the grain. Yet had this tradition of local independence been allowed to continue there was a danger that the new state would have broken up. This was especially true during the 1860s, when localism seemed a more powerful force than nationalism. There was furthermore a desire to raise national standards of government to levels that had so far been established only in Piedmont. Corruptible administrators existed in many parts of Italy, making centralised government a preferable option.

Yet centralisation made the creation of a sense of national unity even more difficult. This was especially the case in the south, where few people could identify with the people and rule from the north. They preferred Garibaldi, but he had returned to his island retreat of Caprera. If anything the new government wanted to erase the people's memories of him, which only made matters worse. In addition, Piedmont's policies often had a harmful effect on the south, as when tariffs were reduced and local goods began to lose out to imports from the rest of Italy. Joined by poor peasants, demobilised soldiers took to the hills, both on the mainland and in Sicily, using their training and weapons to terrify local towns and villages. The so-called 'brigands war', a series of large-scale local insurrections, had begun. (The insurrections did not conform to Mazzini's ideal because they had no clear – or progressive – political ideology and had negative, rather than positive, aims.) The government sent an army against the brigands that at its peak totalled some 100,000 troops. Brutal means were used to crush the brigands and it is estimated that more people were killed in these wars during the 1860s than in the wars of independence between 1848 and 1861.

While this low-intensity civil war dragged on in the south, the rest of Italy struggled to cope with the imposition of the Piedmontese system of government. Things might have worked out differently had Cavour not died in June 1861, aged 51, probably of malaria. After Cavour's death Victor Emmanuel appointed various of Cavour's followers in quick succession to the position of prime minister between 1861 and 1870: Ricasoli, Rattazzi, Farini, Minghetti, Lamarmora, Ricasoli (again), Rattazzi (again), Menabrea and Lanza. None had the skill of Cavour. The new state had many complex problems to face and this ministerial instability made things worse.

> Give three reasons why Italy was established as a unitary state rather than as a federal state.

How united and how Italian was Italy by 1871?

By 1871 the reality of the new Italian state did not measure up to the hopes of Italian nationalists, whether republicans or monarchists, revolutionaries or moderates. Not only were the longstanding divisions between the north and south as great as ever, but if anything the events of the 1860s had made them worse. The new political system, with its limited franchise, meant that the brotherhood of Italians was far from established. Most Italians still identified with their local province. Indeed, it would take many decades before people regarded themselves as being first and foremost Italian.

The nine years between 1861 and 1870 represented something of an anticlimax after the heady three years that preceded them, although the most important issue of this period continued to be that which had dominated the previous 30 years: a united and free Italy. While the Austrians occupied Venetia, and the papacy, supported by France, remained in Rome, Italy could be neither united nor free. At least two leading Italian nationalists, Garibaldi and Mazzini, therefore tried to complete the process that they had started.

With the option of Venice or Rome to concentrate on, two nationalist leaders who did not get on and a monarch and his governments who were committed to intrigue (often against each other), there were many plots and plans in the next few years. In 1861, for example, while Mazzini was planning a petition with 500,000 signatures with which to put pressure on Italy to occupy Rome, Garibaldi was involved in various government schemes to attack Austria in the Balkans. Both plans were impractical.

Aspromonte, 1862

In the event Garibaldi opted for Rome rather than the Balkans. In 1862, after revisiting the scenes of his earlier triumphs in Sicily, he gathered a force of some 3,000 men around him. 'Rome or death' was their inevitable slogan. They crossed the Straits of Messina and then headed north. Although many believed that Victor Emmanuel was playing his old game of opposing Garibaldi in public and supporting him in private, 1862 was not 1860, Rome was not Naples and there was no longer a Cavour to deal with Napoleon III. France and Austria demanded that Garibaldi be stopped, and so the Italian

Garibaldi wounded at Aspromonte. A romantic reconstruction of what must have been a more turbulent scene. The figure with his head bowed is the commander of the Italian troops which attacked Garibaldi's force.

army was ordered to do so. The two forces clashed at Aspromonte. Although Garibaldi refused to shoot at his fellow Italians his fellow Italians had no such scruples. He was wounded in the foot and then arrested – though never tried.

The state imposed the death sentence on some of Garibaldi's fellow conspirators and produced forged documents that blamed Mazzini for Aspromonte. As a result, Mazzini decided to return to the politics of insurrection. Working from London, he continued to try to educate the Italian people on the need to fight to eject the foreigners from their country, but the people did not pay much attention to him. Unwilling to become involved in any Mazzinian schemes, Garibaldi returned to Caprera. Victor Emmanuel talked secretly and separately to both of them. He also talked to Napoleon III, and in the autumn of 1864 reached an agreement with the French emperor that caused the nationalists to despair.

The September Convention, 1864

By the terms of the September Convention Napoleon III agreed to withdraw his troops from Rome within two years, Victor Emmanuel promising to defend the Papal States in return. It was furthermore decided that the Italian capital would be moved from Turin to Florence. Either Victor Emmanuel had abandoned the idea of Rome becoming the capital of Italy or he did not intend to honour the terms of the September Convention. Whichever the true reason, the decision did nothing for Victor Emmanuel's popularity and reputation, and 50 people were killed in riots in Turin. The French troops did withdraw from Rome in 1866 – by which time Italy had acquired Venice.

The war with Austria, 1866

Venice was acquired by Italy as a result of the struggle for supremacy over Germany between Austria and Prussia (see Chapter 6). By 1865 the Prussian chancellor, Bismarck, was willing to risk war with Austria and calculated that the risk to Prussia would be greatly reduced if Austria were to face a war on two fronts. Prussia therefore proposed to Italy an anti-Austrian military alliance.

Italy had sought other ways of gaining Venice: it had offered Austria 100 million lire for the province and had also suggested that Austria might gain Romania in compensation for the loss of Venice. Both proposals had been turned down, however, and it therefore seemed that there was no alternative to Prussia's offer. In April 1866 Italy and Prussia signed an alliance by which it was agreed that Italy would fight Austria if Austria and Prussia went to war with each other within the next three months. When war broke out just over two months later Italy (or Piedmont) went to war with Austria for the fourth time in less than 20 years. By this time Austria had already agreed with France that France would receive Venice.

The war went badly for Italy. Despite its numerical superiority its army was defeated at Custoza and its newly formed navy at Lissa, in the Adriatic. Although Garibaldi led a small force that achieved a minor victory its impact was minimal. Prussia ended the war quickly, before Italy could make any gains. Italy was even unable to occupy Venice because it had been handed over to the French. A plebiscite was held in Venice, with the usual, one-sided result. Venice had at last become part of Italy, but only thanks to the Prussian army. Although Napoleon III had ensured that Italy received Venice, his role was the lesser one. In the words of Mazzini, Venice had been 'tossed to Italy as a penny might be thrown to a beggar'.

Mentana, 1867

With the acquisition of Venice, only Rome remained to be incorporated into the new Italy. (Some nationalists also laid claim to such areas as the south Tyrol and Trieste, but without much support from within Italy and certainly not from outside.) Mazzini immediately began to plan an uprising in Rome, as did Victor Emmanuel. Impatient as ever, Garibaldi raised another force of 3,000 men and marched on Rome, causing Napoleon to order French troops back to the city. In November 1867 Garibaldi's forces suffered a heavy defeat at Mentana, thanks mainly to the new breech-loading rifles with which the French were equipped. Garibaldi was arrested and sent back to Caprera to endure a kind of internal exile. The French army remained in Rome and Rome remained part of the Papal States, separate from Italy.

Into Rome, 1870

Within three years, though, the French troops had withdrawn from Rome to take part in the more urgent struggle against Prussia. The government prepared to fill the vacuum that the French forces had left. Mazzini was arrested in Sicily and Garibaldi was confined to Caprera (although his military career was not yet over; his last campaign was on behalf of the new French Republic). The government then tried to stir the inhabitants of Rome into revolt, but without success. When it sent the Italian army into Rome to defeat a non-existent revolutionary threat to order, Pius IX objected (and later excommunicated all involved), but after only a few hours of fighting the army prevailed. Another plebiscite was held with the usual result. Rome became the capital of Italy.

Having gained Rome, the Italian state accepted the extra-territorial status of the Vatican City and guaranteed diplomatic freedom to the pope. Pius IX refused to accept these terms, however, and it was not until 1929 that a formal agreement was reached between the Italian state and the papacy.

> Compare the process by which Italy gained Venice in 1866 with the process of gaining Rome in 1870.

Left: A drawing of Garibaldi to make him look like Christ, even down to the stigmata on his hands. This parallel was frequently made in the 1860s, when the picture was probably drawn. To many, nationalism was the new, secular faith and an alternative to religion.
Right: A print showing Garibaldi welcomed into the pantheon of national heroes on his death in 1882 by Mazzini, Victor Emmanuel and Cavour.

What was the relationship between the unification of Italy and the Risorgimento?

The state of Italy was finally established in 1870. The outcome of some 40 years of history, it could be variously described as either a great achievement or a minor tragedy, as a fluke of international circumstances or the just reward of a few dedicated nationalists' commitment to their cause. Not only do opinions on Italian unification differ, but they have also changed over the years. At one time most historians, certainly in Italy and Britain, regarded Cavour, Mazzini and Garibaldi as heroes. Today, however, only Garibaldi's reputation remains relatively unblemished, although even he has become something of a forgotten historical figure (**Garibaldi biscuits** are still sold in Britain, for example, but few people now know why they got their name).

Can the establishment of the state of Italy be equated with the *Risorgimento*? To take the briefest definition of the term, did it mark the resurrection of the Italian people? It is hard to regard it as such, since the majority of the Italian people remained indifferent to the unification of Italy. To cite the results of the many plebiscites that were held as evidence of widespread support for a unified Italy is to misunderstand the nature of the evidence. A few Piedmontese, Venetians or Tuscans had come to believe in the unique qualities of Italy, in its claim to the loyalty of the people and in its moral superiority. It is among this minority that the *Risorgimento* can be found. Yet their beliefs would never have brought about a united Italy had it not been for the support of less nationalistic political leaders, both inside and outside Italy.

Garibaldi became a great hero of the British people in the early 1860s. They wrote a musical about him, named streets after him and gave his name to a type of blouse and a type of biscuit. It seems that the first **Garibaldi biscuit** was produced in 1861, though the evidence is hazy. Did Garibaldi ever eat one of the 'squashed flies' biscuits named after him? No one seems to know.

58 *Changing the face of Europe: Italy, 1830–70*

The unification of Italy does, however, illustrate a key feature of modern nationalism: the difference between its political and cultural forms, which never really fused within the Italian nationalist movement. Although a single nation state had been formed, the people of Italy remained disunited, and their disunity would be an important cause of many of Italy's problems over the following decades. Had the unification of Italy been based on the growth of a widespread identity with the idea of Italy, then those later problems might have been avoided. Perhaps Mazzini, for all his impracticalities, was right after all.

> Summarise the main features of the *Risorgimento* under the following headings: political, social, economic, cultural.

Historical sources

Perspectives on Italian unification, 1831–47

1 Mazzini's statement of principles, 1831

Young Italy is a brotherhood of Italians who believe in a law of Progress and Duty and are convinced that Italy is destined to become one nation – convinced also that she possesses sufficient strength within herself to become one, and that the ill success of her former efforts is to be attributed not to the weakness but to the misdirection of the revolutionary elements within her – that the secret of force lies in constancy and unity of effort. They join this association in the firm intent of consecrating both thought and action to the great aim of reconstituting Italy as one independent sovereign nation of free men and equals.

Young Italy is Republican and Unitarian. Republican – Because theoretically every nation is destined, by the law of God and humanity, to form a free and equal community of brothers; and the republican is the only form of government that ensures this future . . . Because the monarchical element being incapable of sustaining itself alone by the side of the popular element, it necessarily involves the existence of the intermediate element of an aristocracy – the source of inequality and corruption to the whole nation.

Young Italy is Unitarian – Because without unity there is no true nation. Because without unity there is no real strength; and Italy, surrounded as she is by powerful, united and jealous nations, has the need for strength before all things. Because federalism, by reducing her to the political impotence of Switzerland, would necessarily place her under the influence of one of the neighbouring nations.

The means by which Young Italy proposes to reach its aims are – education and insurrection, to be adopted simultaneously and made to harmonise with each other. Education must ever be directed to teach by example, word and pen, the necessity of insurrection. Education, though of necessity secret in Italy, will be public out of Italy.

Insurrection – by means of guerrilla bands – is the true method of warfare for all nations desirous of emancipating themselves from a foreign yoke . . . It forms the military education of the people and consecrates every foot of native soil by the memory of some warlike deed. It is invincible, indestructible.

Source: extracts from Giuseppe Mazzini's *General instructions for members of Young Italy*, 1831

2 A priest hopes for papal leadership of Italy, 1843

The Papacy is supremely ours and our nation's because it created the nation and has been rooted here for eighteen centuries; it is concrete, living, real . . . not an abstraction or a chimera but an institution, an oracle and person. It is also ideal because it expresses the greatest concept that can be found in the world.

That the Papacy is naturally, and should be effectively, the civil head of Italy is a truth forecast in the nature of things, confirmed by many centuries of history, recognised on past occasions by the peoples and princes of our lands and only thrown into doubt by those commentators who drank at foreign springs and diverted their poison to the motherland.

The benefits Italy would gain from a political confederation under the moderating authority of the pontiff are beyond enumeration. For such a co-operative association would increase the strength of the various princes without damaging their independence and would put the strength of each at the disposal of all: it would remove the causes of disruptive wars and revolutions at home and make foreign invasion impossible; it would give us an honour we had in bygone times by placing Italy again in the first rank of the Powers.

Source: Abbé Gioberti, *On the moral and civil primacy of Italians*, 1843

3 The views of a Piedmontese journalist, 1846

The movements organised after 1830 . . . were easily suppressed before they had even broken out. Inevitably so; for these movements, relying solely on republican ideas and demagogic passions, were sterile.

The subversive doctrines of Young Italy are taking little hold among those who have an interest in maintaining social order. Excepting the young, whose experience has not yet modified the doctrines imbibed in the exciting atmosphere of schools, only a tiny number of Italians exist who are seriously disposed to apply the exalted principles of that unfortunate and embittered sect.

Thank heaven, the stormy passions aroused by the July Revolution have now calmed down and their traces almost effaced . . . Everything now points towards a better future.

This future, which we desire with all our prayers, will be the triumph of our national independence. Here is a supreme good which Italy can obtain only by the combined effort of all her children. Without independence, Italy cannot hope for any durable political improvement or be confident of any real progress.

Source: Count Camillo di Cavour, writing in *Il Risorgimento*, 1 May 1846

4 The view of the Austrian chancellor

The word 'Italy' is a geographical expression. Though it is a term that slides easily off the tongue, it has none of the political implications which the revolutionary ideologists are trying to attach to it – implications which would threaten the very existence of the individual states which make up the Italian peninsula.

Source: a letter from the Austrian chancellor, Klemens von Metternich, to the Austrian ambassador in Paris, 12 April 1847

Historical-source questions

1. Study source 4. From this source and your own knowledge, explain what is meant by 'the political implications which the revolutionary ideologists are trying to attach to it'.
2. How useful is source 3 as a statement of the situation in Italy in 1846?
3. Study sources 1 and 2. Compare and contrast the aims and methods advocated by the two authors.
4. Using all these sources and your own knowledge, consider the view that Italy was no more than a 'geographical expression' between 1830 and 1848.

Summary questions

1. Identify and explain any *two* factors that explain why a united Italy was not established in 1848–49.
2. Compare the importance of at least *three* reasons for the union of northern and southern Italy in 1861.
3. How united was Italy by 1870?

4 Continuing to change: France, 1848–75

Focus questions

- Why did the Second Republic replace the July Monarchy?
- Why did the Second Empire replace the Second Republic?
- What problems did Napoleon III face in governing France, and how far did he solve them?
- What were the main aims of Napoleon III's foreign policy and how far did he achieve them?
- Why did the Second Empire end?
- Why did the Third Republic take the form that it did by 1875?

Significant dates

1848	The February Revolution; fall of Louis-Philippe; Second Republic declared; 'June Days'; presidential elections: Louis Napoleon elected
1851	*Coup d'état* by Louis Napoleon
1852	Second Empire established
1854–56	Crimean War
1859	War with Austria in Italy; Napoleon III agrees peace with Austria
1860	Free-trade treaty with Britain; liberalisation of the political system
1862–67	Mexico expedition
1870	'Liberal Empire' established; war with Prussia; Sedan; Napoleon III abdicates; Third Republic; Siege of Paris
1871	Peace with Prussia; Paris Commune; Thiers becomes president (until 1873)
1875	The constitution of the Third Republic agreed by the National Assembly

Overview

To misquote the poet T. S. Eliot, this period of French history starts with a bang and finishes with a whimper. In February 1848 a popular revolution in

Paris established the Second Republic; four months later the new government used force to crush working-class opposition to it in Paris, killing around 2,500 people in doing so. By contrast, in 1875 a series of undramatic constitutional laws were passed that became the basis for the Third Republic.

The period between these two dates was as turbulent in France as the better-remembered era of the French Revolution and Napoleon. 1875 was a postscript to the much more dramatic events of 1870 to 1871. In 1870 the people of Paris helped to establish the Third Republic; in 1871 the new government used force to kill around 20,000 people in one 'bloody week' and to crush the Paris Commune. There are obvious parallels between the events of 1848 and 1870 to 1871. The years in between were less bloody, even though the Second Republic was ended in all but name by a **coup d'état** led by its president, Louis Napoleon (who soon styled himself Napoleon III). His Second Empire provided a period of relative stability for the French until it collapsed in 1870, unable to stand the shock of a military defeat by Prussia.

During the 27 years between 1848 and 1875 France experienced three systems of government. This was not unusual, as the French Revolution of 1789 had brought an instability to French government that lasted until the 1870s. Between 1789 and 1848 France was a monarchy (three times), an empire (once) and a republic (once). The mid nineteenth century marked the final stage in the resolution of the political consequences of the French Revolution. Ordinary people had overthrown the state in 1789, and from the 1820s they often tried to repeat their success. They demonstrated, put up barricades and sometimes even succeeded in bringing down the system. They used the ideas of the French Revolution to justify taking power: the slogan 'Liberty, fraternity, equality' inspired many people to challenge the government. The revolutionary practices of the early 1790s, as exemplified by the use of the guillotine, frightened almost as many people, however. They wanted the authorities to pull down the barricades and forcibly deal with those behind them, hence the 'June Days' of 1848 and the 'bloody week' of 1871. The latter would be the last of its kind, however, for after that barricades went out of fashion.

If the French Revolution had caused great internal conflict, it had also established France's position as the greatest of the Continental powers. Aiming to apply their ideas to other countries, as well as to their own, the revolutionaries chose an outstanding general, Napoleon Bonaparte, to lead them. Under Napoleon, France ruled most of Europe for the first decade of the nineteenth century. Although the other European powers eventually defeated Napoleon and forced France to retreat behind its traditional borders, thereafter France was regarded as a threat to the peace of Europe. Not until the rule of Bonaparte's nephew, Napoleon III, did that view finally change. The

The translation of the French term *coup d'état* literally means a blow of, or by, the state. A *coup d'état* involves actions taken by a state institution, usually the government and/or the army, to overthrow the constitution and to strengthen its own power. The *coup d'état* of December 1851 was a classic model for the seizure of government power.

emergence of Bismarck's German Empire was ultimately at France's expense, and France ceased to be Europe's greatest military power.

The 1848–75 period can thus be seen as the end of the revolutionary era that began in 1789. The period started with the overthrow of the **Orléanist** monarch, Louis-Philippe, who had himself come to power as a consequence of the revolution against the **Bourbon** monarch, Charles X, in 1830. Why, after proclaiming himself king of the French, did Louis-Philippe, who had fought on the side of revolution, suffer the same fate as Charles X?

Why did the Second Republic replace the July Monarchy?

This apparently simple question is properly two separate, if interrelated, questions: firstly, 'Why did the July Monarchy collapse?' and, secondly, 'Why was a republic established in its place?'

Why did the July Monarchy collapse?

The July Monarchy was the label given to the Orléanist monarchy that was established in 1830. Louis-Philippe's acceptance of the crown in 1830 after Charles X's abdication in July 1830 caused a rift with the Bourbon branch of the French royal family. The Bourbons had been restored to power by the great powers of Europe between 1814 and 1815 and had been overthrown by the people of Paris in 1830. To the supporters of the Bourbons Louis-Philippe was an illegitimate ruler. He was certainly an unusual ruler, in that he was a monarch who had come to power as the result of a popular revolution and who had accepted the flag of the revolution, the tricolour, instead of that of his royal family. He was seen by many people as a suitable compromise between two extremes: a republic and an absolutist monarchy.

In 1848 Louis-Philippe followed his Bourbon predecessor into exile. How far was he to blame for his own inglorious departure, and how far was he the victim of circumstances? An analysis of the immediate events of the February Revolution of 1848 that led to the end of the July Monarchy provides a suitable framework within which one can consider other revolutions of this era:

- *21 February*: A ban on a political banquet planned for 22 February in Paris is published by the authorities.
- *22 February*: Students and workers hold demonstrations, shouting the slogan 'Long live reform, down with Guizot!'
- *23 February*: Barricades are erected in many parts of Paris; **Guizot** falls; most members of the **National Guard** support the protesters; troops are called in and clash with the demonstrators, killing about 40 people.

The **Bourbons** and **Orléanists** were the two branches of the French royal family. The Bourbons provided the monarchs of France from 1589 to 1792 and from 1815 to 1830. The Orléanists were descendants of the younger brother of Louis XIV (1643–1715).

François Guizot was the conservative prime minister in February 1848, having been the foreign minister between 1840 and 1847.

The **National Guard** was a citizen's militia, a part-time police and defence force. Founded in 1789, the National Guard played an important part in the events of 1830, 1848 and 1870–71 in Paris. Although it was usually controlled by the Parisian middle class, in times of crisis it was expanded to include the city's working class.

- *24 February*: The town hall and royal palace in Paris are occupied by demonstrators; the army withdraws; Louis-Philippe abdicates in favour of his young grandson; the Second Republic is proclaimed.

These immediate events suggest that short-term political events explain why revolutions occur: people demonstrate, they clash with the police, people are killed, the protests grow, the government abdicates, and a revolutionary government is established. However, most accounts of revolutions usually include longer-term factors, especially economic ones. In the case of the February Revolution there are two. Firstly, there was an economic depression between 1846 and 1847 which was caused by food shortages and a financial crisis and led to working-class unemployment and middle-class bankruptcies. The government was blamed for doing nothing about the first and for causing the second and demonstrations began to be held across the country. Secondly, two scandals (one financial, the other sexual) involving former government ministers and a peer symbolised for many the corruption at the heart of government. The government showed little concern about either crisis because the 1846 elections had given it a majority in the assembly for the first time. As a result, dissatisfaction with the government began to grow. In order to escape the government's ban on political meetings, in 1847 some middle-class reformers hit on the idea of holding a political banquet. This could be described as a private, not a political, meeting. It was a great success and so more were held in late 1847. The government's attempt to deal with the problem of the political banquets was the direct cause of the events of February 1848.

> Identify three main causes of the French revolution of February 1848.

Why was a republic established in its place?

Explaining why the July Monarchy collapsed does not explain why it was replaced with a republic. There were alternatives; indeed, several gained considerable support before 1875. The Bourbons were close to being restored during the 1870s, so why was this not the case in 1848? An empire was reintroduced in 1852, so why had this not happened four years earlier? Why did the new government have to be a republic? The short answer is because the people of Paris wanted a republic. They had also wanted a republic in July 1830, but had been outwitted by middle-class politicians into agreeing a compromise with Louis-Philippe, the so-called 'citizen king'. In 1848, however, the politicians had to accept a republic that they hoped would avoid the excesses of 1793 to 1794. In 1848, as in 1830, 1792 and 1789, the people of Paris decided on the government of France, confidently proclaiming in February a new government with the following statement:

> In the name of the French people:
>
> A reactionary and oligarchical government has just been overthrown by the heroism of the people of Paris. The government has fled, leaving behind a trail of blood that forbids it ever to retrace its steps.
>
> The blood of the people has flowed, as in July; but this time the people will not be deceived. It has won a national and popular government in accord with the rights, the progress and the will of this great and generous nation.
>
> A provisional government is for the moment invested with the task of assuring and organising the national victory. With the capital of France on fire, the justification for the present provisional government must be sought in the public safety. All France will understand this and will lend it the support of its patriotism.
>
> The provisional government wishes to establish a republic – subject, however, to ratification by the people, who shall be immediately consulted.
>
> The unity of the nation (formed henceforth of all the classes of citizens); the government of the nation by itself; liberty, equality and fraternity as fundamental principles and 'the people' as our watchword: these constitute the democratic government which France owes to itself and which our efforts shall secure for it.

Securing democracy would prove much harder than any of its supporters in 1848 could possibly have imagined, however. Although no one knew it at the time, the ascendancy of Paris would last for only a few months more.

Why did the Second Empire replace the Second Republic?
The 'June Days'

As is the case with most revolutions, the initial response of the majority of the people to the overthrow of the old order was one of excitement and enthusiasm: they felt united, liberated and optimistic. These feelings would not last long. By the end of June 1848 the revolutionaries were deeply divided.

The cause of this division can be quickly explained. Committed to the idea of the right to work, the new government set up a scheme known as the National Workshops to help the unemployed in Paris. Benefit levels were generous, and taxpayers had to pay an additional 45 per cent levy to fund them. As a result there were protests throughout France, especially because little work was required of the claimants and the numbers claiming benefit grew rapidly. When the government decided to close down the National Workshops those who were benefiting from them resisted. The government

One of the barricades of February 1848. An artist's reconstruction of one incident of the revolution of 1848 and thus more symbolic than representative. What points are there to note about the details of the drawing and especially the group of revolutionaries on the barricades?

sent in the troops, led by General Cavaignac. The 'June Days' were the result. Alexander Herzen, a Russian exile in Paris, reported on events:

> On 23 [June] I was walking along the Seine towards the Hôtel de Ville; the shops were being shut, detachments of the National Guard, looking menacing, were marching in various directions. I stopped at the Pont Neuf. The measured sound of the tocsin [warning bell] rang out. The proletariat, betrayed again, was calling its brothers to arms. One could hear the drums on all sides; the artillery was moving slowly from the Place du Carrousel.
>
> On the other side of the river barricades were being raised in all the streets and alleys. I can still see the gloomy faces of the men dragging stones; women and children were helping them. The tocsin was still tolling. Meanwhile the artillery clattered across the bridge.
>
> On the evening of 26 June we heard the sound of gunfire at short, regular intervals. 'The firing squads', we all said with one voice and turned away from each other. Moments like this make me hate for a whole decade, seek revenge all one's life. Woe to those that forgive such moments.
>
> After the slaughter, which lasted four days, silence descended – the calm of the siege. The arrogant National Guard, with an expression of savage, dull cruelty, protected its shops, threatening passers-by with

butt and bayonet. Boys of sixteen and seventeen boasted of the blood of their brothers which had dried on their hands; they were thrown flowers by shop girls who ran out from behind their counters to greet the victors. The bourgeoisie was triumphant. Paris had not seen this, even in 1814.

Cavaignac's forces killed about 500 people during the fighting and shot some 2,000 immediately afterwards (about 1,000 soldiers were also killed.) Around 12,000 people were arrested, many of whom were then deported to Algeria.

The 'June Days' had profound consequences. The revolutionary government that had been established by the people had used force against the people. The republic had proved itself to be more reactionary than revolutionary, for at the first sign of crisis it had sided with the propertied classes. Now Paris, having dictated the events of February as it had during previous revolutions, was being dictated to. This was a significant change that deepened the divisions between the moderate and radical republicans. The effects of the 'June Days' would last for many years to come.

The elections of 1848

There were two elections held during 1848: one to elect members of the constituent assembly and the other to elect the president. One of the first acts of the Second Republic had been to introduce **universal male suffrage** (the male deputies who made the decision assuming that the French woman's place was in the home). This decision increased the electorate from 250,000 to 9 million. It was a bold step: no other major European power had given the vote to all men equally, whatever their wealth and education.

The elections for the constituent assembly resulted in a massive turnout, around 85 per cent, of the electorate. With no significant support given to the radical republicans, the first democratic election in France resulted in an assembly that was composed of moderate republican and conservative deputies. The constituent assembly decided that a single-chamber assembly should make the laws and that the government should be led by a democratically elected president chosen by the people who would govern for one term of four years and no more. (Some deputies had had doubts about a single-person executive, preferring a more democratic, collective **presidency**.) Although they debated at length whether any candidates should be excluded from standing for the presidency, they eventually decided that there should be no restrictions. This would prove a decision of great consequence.

The presidential elections were held in December 1848. One candidate, Louis Napoleon Bonaparte, the nephew of the great Napoleon Bonaparte, gained a massive majority of almost 75 per cent of the total vote. Why was he

---

Universal male suffrage is the right of all males to vote, irrespective of differences in their income, wealth and status. It was a radical idea during most of the nineteenth century, but was gradually accepted by governments as they realised that most voters did not want revolution.

A **presidency** is similar to a monarchy in that both a president and a monarch are types of heads of state, the former chosen by election and the other by birth (an elected monarch is possible, but rare). Some heads of states are also heads of governments, as in the USA, but most countries separate the two functions.

able to win so comfortably? The reasons are not hard to find. Above all, Louis Napoleon won because he was a Bonaparte: no other candidate had the advantage of such an instantly recognisable name. By 1848 the Napoleonic myth had come to mean different things to different groups of people. The monarchists, for example, saw in Louis Napoleon a substitute monarch who would restore order, while the poor believed that he wanted improve their condition. He was also backed by many politicians and businessmen, who thought that they would be able to control a man of his limited experience. In addition, he was helped by the speed with which the election was held following the revolution: Louis Napoleon was a new face who had played no part in the events of 1848. He furthermore refused to be identified with any political party and also spent a lot of money on publicity, using such direct methods as posters and songs to make sure that everyone knew about his campaign. The other candidates stood no chance.

> Identify the main stages by which the July Monarchy became the Second Republic.

The new president

Why Louis Napoleon Bonaparte won the presidential election is, however, a less important issue than who he was. In order to help us to assess his leadership of France over the following 22 years we therefore need to make an initial assessment of the man himself.

Louis Napoleon was 40 years old when he became president. Until then he had spent the greater part of his life either exiled from France or in prison in France. Both were the consequences of his being a Bonaparte. Exile is easily explained; the name of Bonaparte was too great a threat to the new monarchies. Prison resulted from the second of two attempts that he made to invade France in order to provoke a revolt against the government. He spent almost six years in jail before escaping to England in 1846. When the February Revolution occurred he was cautious about returning to France, but finally did so after being elected to the assembly in a by-election held in September 1848. He did not cut an impressive figure as a deputy, both his physique and speaking voice (he spoke with a German accent) letting him down. What did he believe in? Let his election manifesto of November 1848 speak for him:

> In order to recall me from exile you have elected me a representative of the people; on the eve of choosing a president for the republic my name presents itself to you as a symbol of order and security.
>
> Those proofs of so honourable a confidence are, I am well aware, addressed to my name rather than myself. As yet I have done nothing for my country but the more the memory of the emperor protects me and inspires your votes, the more I feel compelled to acquaint you with my sentiments and principles. There must be no misunderstanding between us.

I am moved by no ambition which dreams one day of empire and war, the next of applying subversive theories. Brought up in free countries, disciplined in the school of misfortune, I shall ever remain faithful to the duties which your votes and the will of the assembly impose on me.

If elected president, I shall shrink from no danger, from no sacrifice in the defence of society which has been so outrageously assailed. I shall devote myself without reservation to the consolidation of the republic so that it may be wise in its laws, honest in its aims, great and strong in its deeds. My greatest honour would be to hand on to my successor, after four years in office, the republic consolidated, its liberties intact and genuine, progress assured.

LOUIS NAPOLEON BONAPARTE.

> Summarise briefly the main points of Louis Napoleon's election manifesto of November 1848.

Assessing Louis Napoleon's personal qualities is much harder to do than describing his early career or public statements (which were not the same as his true beliefs). As Theodore Zeldin asked in his book *The political system of Napoleon III* (1958), 'How can one hope to understand a man who spoke so little and wrote even less?' As a result, some people called him a sphinx, a mysterious figure, hard to understand. Bismarck was more cynical, however, calling Louis Napoleon a 'sphinx without a riddle'.

Napoleon III, reputedly on his fiftieth birthday, posing for his equestrian portrait. Presumably the photograph was published only after the emperor's death.

Louis Napoleon's early career might provide some clues. His attempts to enter France and stir up revolution demonstrated both romantic (albeit unrealistic) ambition and a commitment to the Napoleonic legend. He saw himself as a 'man of destiny', a belief strengthened by the events of 1848. However, he did not want to return to the situation prior to 1815, when his uncle had been in power, knowing that turning the clock back would have been impossible. Although the fact that he tried to adapt the Bonaparte legend to mid-nineteenth-century conditions suggests some ability, Louis Napoleon is sometimes regarded as having been unintelligent. In comparison with Bismarck, his great rival during his last few years in power, perhaps he was. Yet his electoral victory suggests that he was no fool. So what can we learn about Louis Napoleon from his rule as France's prince-president?

Louis Napoleon and the Second Republic, 1848–51

On becoming president Louis Napoleon took an oath that he would maintain the constitution of the Second Republic. Almost exactly three years later he broke that oath by leading the *coup d'état* of December 1851. Why did he do so? His public proclamation on seizing power can be used as a start in developing an explanation:

> Frenchmen! The present situation can no longer continue. Each day that passes increases the country's dangers. The assembly, which should be a bastion of order, has become a centre of conspiracies. The patriotism of three hundred of its members has not been able to stop these fatal tendencies. Instead of making laws in the general interest it is forging arms for civil war. It is encroaching on the authority I hold directly from the people. It encourages every unhealthy discontent. It compromises the tranquillity of France. I have dissolved it and I make the people supreme judge between it and me. The constitution, as you know, has been drawn up with a view to weakening, from the start, the power which you had given to me. Six million votes were a striking protest against it. Nevertheless I obeyed it faithfully. But now that fundamental pact is no longer respected by the same people who unceasingly invoke it. [Now] the men who have already brought down two monarchies want to tie my hands in order to overthrow the republic. My duty is to thwart their treacherous schemes, to maintain the republic and to save the country by invoking the solemn judgement of the only people I recognise in France, the People.

> Explain in your own words, taking no more than three lines, Louis Napoleon's justification for seizing power in December 1851.

Louis Napoleon's statement shows that his quarrel was with the legislative assembly, the directly elected parliament of the Second Republic. The assembly's members had been elected in May 1849, when the political right, known

Continuing to change: France, 1848–75

as the Party of Order, won around two-thirds of the 700 seats in the assembly. The government ministers whom Louis Napoleon appointed when he became president were members of that party. Although there should therefore have been no great disagreement between the government and the assembly, there were several. Three, in particular, brought their relationship to breaking point.

Louis Napoleon's tactics
As the months passed, Louis Napoleon took greater personal control of all aspects of government. In October 1849 he dismissed the Party of Order ministers, replacing them with less experienced, non-party men, whom he could more easily dominate. In January 1851 he dismissed the leader of the army and National Guard in Paris, later appointing someone who was loyal to Louis Napoleon himself to command all of the French forces.

The assembly's decision to limit the franchise
The members of the assembly's right-wing majority were alarmed by by-elections that returned left-wing candidates, as happened between 1849 and 1850. In provincial France the left wing was developing links with the rural poor and deputies feared the return of a more radical republic – or even a popular revolution – when elections were held in 1852. They therefore decided to limit the franchise in May 1850, imposing a three-year residential qualification on the right to vote, among other limitations, all of which hit the working class and thus the radicals hard. Some 3 million voters were disenfranchised by this measure – Karl Marx called the law the 'bourgeoisie's *coup d'état*'. Although Louis Napoleon announced in October 1851 that he would restore universal suffrage, the assembly refused to change its mind.

The assembly's refusal to amend the constitution
Louis Napoleon was unable to gain the three-quarters majority that he needed to change the law that stipulated that presidents could serve for only one term. He consequently mobilised public support, over 1.4 million voters signing petitions in support of a change in the constitution that would enable him to stand for a second term. In July 1851 a majority of deputies voted in favour of this reform. It was not enough, however, and by mid-1851 Louis Napoleon had accepted that if he was going to remain in power he would have to carry out a *coup d'état*.

His planning was meticulous. He continued to tour the provinces and occasionally made hints about the future, as in a speech that he made in Bordeaux (see pages 73–74). His trusted advisers drew up detailed plans of army movements and of whom to arrest. But planning is not the same as doing, and Louis Napoleon still hoped that he could reach an agreement with the assembly. A reluctant conspirator, he eventually decided to act, choosing 2 December – the anniversary of Napoleon's coronation in 1804 and of his victory over Russia and Austria at Austerlitz – as the date for his *coup d'état*.

The *coup d'état* of December 1851

The immediate aims of the *coup d'état* were quickly accomplished. Troops occupied key positions in Paris, including the assembly building, and 14 deputies, among them **Adolphe Thiers**, were arrested. The legislative assembly was dissolved and universal suffrage was restored. Although a few deputies, including **Victor Hugo**, tried to organise resistance, they were unsuccessful, only around 1,000 people manning the barricades that went up in Paris. (At least 20 people were killed as the troops removed the barricades, but rather than being rebels they were mainly onlookers.)

The greatest resistance to the *coup d'état* came not from Paris, but from the provinces. The close links between the radical left and the rural poor resulted in quite extensive revolts, especially in the south-east of France. Indeed, for a week Louis Napoleon faced the largest rural rebellion of the century. Approximately 100,000 people took part in the revolt, of which 26,000 were arrested and 10,000 were deported (there seem to have been few, if any, deaths). In trying to make an assessment of Louis Napoleon it is worth realising that he intervened to stop some of the sentences being imposed on the rebels and remained unhappy about the consequences of the *coup d'état* for the rest of his life. If he was an autocrat he was therefore something of a compassionate one.

Three weeks later Louis Napoleon held a plebiscite asking the people to approve the changes to the constitution that he planned to make. Although 7 million voters did so, just over 600,000 did not. Despite the abstention of up to 2 million voters it was a triumph for Louis Napoleon: the new constitution that was accordingly introduced in January 1852 both strengthened his power and enabled him to rule for 10 years. From then on the Second Republic was a republic in name only. Louis Napoleon now toured the country preparing the people for the introduction of an empire, as can be seen in the speech that he made in Bordeaux in October 1852:

> The purpose of this journey was to see for myself our beautiful provinces of the south and familiarise myself with their needs. It has, however, given rise to a much more important result. Indeed, never has a people testified in a manner more direct and unanimous the longing to be freed from anxiety as to the future by concentrating in a single person an authority which shall accord with their desires. They realise now both the false hopes with which they have been deluded and the dangers which threaten them.

Adolphe Thiers (1797–1877) was a moderate liberal politician who was involved in French national politics from 1830 until his death. Before becoming a moderate republican he was an Orléanist. He is best known for saying 'The republic is of all the governments that which divides us least' (1850). Although he was exiled between 1851 and 1863, he played a crucial and controversial role in French politics between 1870 and 1871 and led the Third Republic during its early years (1871 to 1873).

Victor Hugo (1802–85) was a French poet and novelist who is best known today as the author of *Les Misérables* (1862). This great figure of nineteenth-century French literature was also involved in national politics. Having taken part in the 'June Days' of 1848 he initially supported Louis Napoleon, but later turned against him, writing *Napoléon le petit* in 1852. After living in exile between 1851 and 1870 he was involved in the Siege of Paris (1870–71). During the 1870s and 1880s he was regarded as the grand old man of French culture.

Continuing to change: France, 1848–75

France today encompasses me with her sympathies because I do not belong to the group of dreamers. In order to benefit the country it is necessary not to resort to new systems but to establish confidence in the present and security for the future. That is why France seems to wish to revert to the empire.

There is, however, one apprehension and that I shall set at rest. A spirit of distrust leads certain persons to say that the empire means war. I say the empire means peace. France longs for peace and if France is satisfied the world is tranquil. Glory is a right handed down by heredity, not by war.

I concede, nevertheless, that, like the emperor, I have many conquests to make. Like him, I would conquer the warring parties and bring into the greater popular currents the wasteful and conflicting eddies. For the sake of religion, morality and material ease, I would conquer that portion of the people which, in a country of faith and belief, hardly knows the precepts of Christ; which in the midst of the most fertile country of the world, is hardly able to enjoy the basic necessities of life. We have numerous uncultivated districts to open, harbours to construct, rivers to make navigable, canals to finish and our network of railways to complete.

This is what I understand by the empire, if the empire is to be re-established. These are the conquests which I contemplate and all of you who surround me, who, like myself, wish the good of our common country – you are my soldiers.

In November 1852 Louis Napoleon held a second plebiscite, this time asking for the people's approval of the re-establishment of the empire. This time some 8 million voters agreed. In December 1852, on the first anniversary of his *coup d'état*, Louis Napoleon announced the establishment of the Second Empire. He was proclaimed Emperor Napoleon III as a reminder of the link with his uncle. Instead of ruling for 10 years he would now be emperor for life. Few lamented the passing of the Second Republic, which, of the many constitutional systems that France adopted between 1789 and 1875, was the briefest.

> Identify Louis Napoleon's goals for France as set out in his Bordeaux speech.

Why did the Second Empire replace the Second Republic?

When a similar question was asked of February 1848 it was divided into two further questions. It is much harder to do so when considering the events of December 1852. The Second Empire collapsed because its president destroyed it. Louis Napoleon was the cuckoo in the nest, the enemy within. Not only did he have imperial ambitions that were by definition anti-republican, but he also made no secret of them. The *coup* of 1851 had been talked about for months before it happened. The more interesting question is why the Second Republic failed to prevent Louis Napoleon from establishing the Second Empire.

Although the legislative assembly should have been the first bulwark against the ambitions of the president, most of the deputies were more anti-republican than anti-imperial, preferring strong to democratic government. The rising that had led to the 'June Days' reinforced memories of 1794, many deputies fearing that a more extreme revolution would break out in 1852. The assembly was furthermore deeply divided and never presented a united front against Louis Napoleon. The deputies argued among themselves; this only strengthened Louis Napoleon's contention that he was the only true representative of all the people.

The second bulwark against Louis Napoleon might have been the people themselves. But when they were given the vote Frenchmen voted time after time for Louis Napoleon, even after he had acted unconstitutionally. The people supported his establishment of a dictatorship. Indeed, Louis Napoleon was a new phenomenon: a democratically elected emperor.

Finally, as a result of the 'June Days' the mob power wielded by the people of Paris, which had been so impressive in 1789, 1830 and February 1848, and which might have stalled Louis Napoleon, no longer existed. And manhood suffrage had dealt the final blow to the claim of Paris to speak for France.

History's view of Louis Napoleon's *coup d'état* has been critical. It has been reinforced by two very different writers of the time who immediately attacked his actions. From exile in England Karl Marx wrote a pamphlet called *The eighteenth Brumaire of Louis Bonaparte* (1852). (The eighteenth *Brumaire* was the date in the French revolutionary calendar on which Napoleon Bonaparte launched his *coup* against the First French Republic.) It opens with the oft-repeated – and usually misquoted – remark about history repeating itself. What Marx actually wrote was: 'Hegel [a great German philosopher] remarks somewhere that all the great events and characters of the world occur, so to speak, twice. He forgot to add: the first time as tragedy, the second as farce.' He then made several comparisons between the minor figures of 1789–94 and 1848–51 before continuing: '. . . the nephew in place of the uncle. And we can perceive the same caricature in the circumstances surrounding the second edition of the eighteenth Brumaire.' Marx's words have helped to reinforce the view that Napoleon III was something of a comic figure.

Then from exile in Jersey, Victor Hugo published a book in the same year called *Napoléon le petit*. The title alone is enough to confirm the unfavourable view of the nephew when compared with his uncle. The following extract from the book gives a flavour of Victor Hugo's style and arguments:

Louis Napoleon is a man of middle height, cold, pale, slow in his movements, having the air of a person not quite awake. He is a good horseman. He speaks with a drawl and a slight German accent.

The great talent of M. Bonaparte is silence. Before 2 December he had a council of ministers. The president presided. Never or scarcely ever did he take part in their discussion. While [a minister] was speaking, he occupied himself, says one of these ministers, in constructing, with great earnestness, in drawing men's heads on the documents before him.

To feign death, that is his art.

This silence of his, Louis Bonaparte sometimes breaks but then he does not speak, he lies. This man lies as other men breathe. He announces an honest intention; be on your guard. He affirms; distrust him. He takes an oath; tremble for your safety.

Machiavelli has made small men. Louis Napoleon is one of them.

> Summarise (a) the weaknesses of the Second Republic and (b) the strengths of Louis Napoleon that led to the end of the Second Republic.

Although the historical reputation of Napoleon III has never really recovered from these early attacks by two great writers, in 1852, for the French people at least, his reputation seemed as secure as the great power that he had acquired. He claimed that he would use his unparalleled power in the interests of France. How far did he do so?

What problems did Napoleon III face in governing France, and how far did he solve them?

The eighteen years of the Second Empire can be subdivided into three discrete periods: from 1852 to 1860, the 1860s and 1870. The Second Empire's first eight years represented a period of success for Napoleon III: there was unprecedented prosperity at home, while France fought and beat Russian and Austrian forces in two separate wars abroad. By 1860 Napoleon III dominated both French and European affairs. The 1860s brought only setbacks, however. France's economic growth slowed and domestic opposition to Napoleon grew. Napoleon found himself being left behind in Europe as Prussia took control of events, while his involvement in the complex affairs of Mexico ended in failure. In 1870, in what turned out to be the final year of the Second Empire, Napoleon changed his political direction at home, replacing his authoritarian rule with a parliamentary system. This action might have saved the Second Empire had Napoleon not allowed himself to be drawn into a war with Prussia. Following France's swift defeat by Prussia Napoleon had to abdicate, becoming the latest in a line of ex-rulers of France who crossed the Channel to exile in England.

The new regime

The only figure of any significance in the new regime of 1852 was the emperor, who had enormous power. Although two assemblies – the legislative body and the senate, which were respectively elected and appointed – were established, both had only an advisory function. The ministers were individually responsible to the emperor, not collectively to the assemblies. The emperor himself was responsible only 'to the French people, to whom he always has the right to appeal', which effectively meant that he would use plebiscites whenever he thought them necessary. As emperor for life he no longer needed the people's direct approval for his actions.

If Napoleon III's personal power was great, in whose interests did he intend to use it? He never identified himself with any one political group or party, saying that he wanted to govern in the interests of all of the French people, to be a 'people's emperor'. He believed that his destiny was to lead the French nation towards greater prosperity and success, as well as to maintain order and security. Whether he meant what he said was another matter. There was one specific national interest that he knew that he had to fulfil: ensuring the continuation of the Napoleonic dynasty. In 1853, at the age of 45, he therefore abandoned his English mistress and married Eugénie, a 27-year-old Spanish noblewoman whom he had known for only a few weeks. When Eugénie had a son in 1856 the succession seemed secure. During the 1860s, especially after Napoleon III became ill, Eugénie found a new role for herself as she gained political influence over her husband.

How did Napoleon III rule? He listened to his ministers, many of whom were experienced businessmen and former Orléanists. Although a small number were Bonapartists they had few positive qualities. He made most of the appointments to both central and local government in order to ensure that the state was run by people who accepted the Second Empire. He cultivated the Catholic Church. He used the police and the courts to maintain order, especially during the 1850s when the empire was new and memories of the Second Republic were still fresh. The press was censored. The Second Empire was not a police state, however, at least not in the twentieth-century sense. During the 1850s, in particular, he continued to tour the country, listening to people and picking up ideas.

Finally, what values and beliefs influenced Napoleon III's exercise of power? The example of Napoleon I was obviously a key factor. However, realising that the world had moved on, Napoleon III did not try to re-create the policies of his uncle. At home, he argued that the government should do more for the poor in the face of the rapid economic and social changes. Some historians argue that he was influenced by the ideas of the **Comte de Saint-Simon**. There is no direct evidence that he was, although he did appoint

The ideas of the **Comte de Saint-Simon** (1760–1825) were the basis of an influential mid-nineteenth-century school of thought. His beliefs included the need to reform society in order to help its poorest members, with the state leading the way by spending more. His followers held government office during the Second Empire. Napoleon III was sometimes called 'Saint-Simon on horseback'.

some of Saint-Simon's followers to key governmental posts. Believing that economic prosperity was the foundation of social and political order, he gave economic matters more attention than his predecessors had done. Abroad, he wanted to undo the 1815 settlement that was linked to the defeat of Napoleon I. The revision of the settlement would be accomplished by building a Europe based on nationalism, a force which the peacemakers of 1815 had ignored and which, Napoleon III believed, had been the undoing of his uncle. Napoleon III therefore took a radical, reforming approach to both domestic and foreign affairs. His sense of destiny meant that he believed that he had gained his almost unlimited power for a purpose, and now that he was emperor for life he had to act.

Domestic affairs

After the political turmoil of the Second Republic, the Second Empire was quiet during the 1850s. There was little public debate or discussion of political matters. Although there was some criticism of the regime, it was implied, indirect and expressed through the medium of the arts, as is usual in authoritarian states. The persecutions of 1852 had been a warning, and those who might openly have challenged the new regime usually kept quiet. During the 1857 election to the legislative body (which was admittedly closely controlled by state officials), only six of the hundred republican candidates who stood were elected. More people voted for, and fewer against, the Second Empire than in the 1852 elections. Perhaps the most significant figure was the proportion of abstentions, which remained little changed, with just over a third of the voters choosing not to vote. As always with high abstention rates, such figures can be seen as evidence of either satisfaction or dissatisfaction with the government.

The growth of the French economy

If French politics were quiet during the 1850s the same cannot be said of the economy: France prospered during this decade. External circumstances helped. The discovery of gold in California in 1849 provided the basis for expanding the supply of money. All of Europe benefited from this development. The French government played a part in encouraging growth in three important ways.

The development of the banking system
Before the Second Empire French banks had been very conservative in their lending policy. In 1852 the government supported the formation of three banks, of which the Crédit Mobilier became the most significant. These banks attracted the small saver. The banks lent the funds that they raised to

companies, thus helping to stimulate economic growth. Eventually speculation grew, investments ran out of control and the inevitable economic crash followed. That happened in the 1860s. During the 1850s the new banks did much to contribute to French economic growth. In one sense the Second Empire was built on easy credit.

The development of the railways
Before the Second Empire the growth of the railways in France had been haphazard and slow. Now the government encouraged a more co-ordinated policy to create a national network by connecting different parts of the railways. It also subsidised the building of lines to remoter regions. By 1870 the amount of track in France was 10 times greater than it had been in 1848 and the French railways matched those of Britain and Germany. Such a rapid rate of railway growth was a major stimulus to greater economic activity.

The redevelopment of Paris
Although many French towns were redeveloped during the 1850s and 1860s, the redevelopment of Paris was by far the greatest and most significant. Under Baron Haussmann, the prefect of the Paris region from 1853 to 1869, 85 miles of new roads were laid in the centre of Paris, with new houses built to standard specifications alongside. The economic and social benefits of this redevelopment was not the only reason for such a massive project. It added to the prestige of France: the new Paris was intended to symbolise the success, strength and glamour of the Second Empire. (The Suez Canal, which was opened in 1869, was another such symbol of French leadership.) A further reason, according to some historians, was the benefit to social order: the old streets had been well suited to the erection of barricades and ill suited to troop manoeuvres. The new streets were broad and wide and working-class residents were moved to the outskirts of Paris. Mobilising a mob in support of revolution would be harder, crushing it easier.

The government's motives for encouraging economic growth should be explored. It is generally accepted that its aim was to modernise rather than to industrialise. Because the government feared that industrialisation would create a new, more class-based society, with its associated problems, funds were not channelled into new industries. The government's aim was instead to encourage economic activity so that current society would benefit. Even with this limited goal, the form of intervention practised by the Second Empire set it apart from its contemporaries. Some have even described it as an early form of state socialism.

In his economic relations with other countries, however, Napoleon III began to follow a policy of liberalism. Accepting the benefits of free trade – as argued by such people as Richard Cobden, the great British advocate of economic liberalism – he signed nine free-trade treaties between 1860 and 1865, the most significant ones being with Britain and Prussia. The economic consequences of these reforms are hard to determine. Their political effects are more obvious. Napoleon used his presidential power to achieve the reforms in the face of strong opposition from both French businessmen and Catholic groups (the 1860 Cobden treaty with Britain was called an 'economic *coup d'état*'). Many people blamed the free-trade treaties for the economic downturn that occurred from the mid-1860s, and when Crédit Mobilier crashed in 1867 amidst stories of corruption, the bright hopes of the Second Empire came to an end. By then economic and financial problems were being accompanied by growing political opposition to the government.

> Identify three policies of the French government in the 1850s that helped modernise the French economy.

Growing political dissent

During the 1860s voices critical of the government began to be heard. There was an interplay between Napoleon III's liberal reforms, the state of France and election results. In 1860 Napoleon granted limited concessions to the legislative body, partly as a result of which the 1863 election campaign was livelier than that of 1857. Not only did more people vote, but more voted for non-government deputies. Although the opposition deputies numbered only 32, the result was a clear setback for the government. Napoleon resisted further liberalisation of politics for a few more years, although in 1864 he did allow workers the right to strike. In 1867, however, as the situation at home and abroad got worse, Napoleon introduced a second set of limited reforms, including the relaxation of controls on the press. Despite – or because of – these reforms, the 1869 election was a disaster for the government, the total votes cast for the government falling by almost 1 million, while the opposition's rose by more than 1 million.

Napoleon responded to this electoral setback by making further, more radical, concessions. He drastically modified the 1852 constitution by introducing a parliamentary system. Ministers would now be chosen from the largest party in the legislative body, to which they would also be accountable. He chose Emile Ollivier, one of the six republican deputies who had been elected in 1857 and a leader of the opposition, to head his new government. Napoleon's reforms were the basis of another plebiscite in 1870, in which the government won a clear majority on a scale similar to its victory of 1852. The new system became known as the 'liberal empire'.

Why had Napoleon made such a remarkable U-turn? Although it is not possible to give a precise answer to this question because he never explained his motives – either privately or in public – several reasons can be put forward: firstly, because he had to and, secondly, because he wanted to.

According to one argument, Napoleon had to make some political concessions in order to try to contain the rapid growth of opposition to the government, both within the legislative body and in the country at large. It was not possible simply to try to repress that opposition: the Second Empire was not a twentieth-century police state and Napoleon's reaction to the repression of 1852 also showed that he was no ruthless dictator. In addition, time was running out for Napoleon, who was over 60 year of age. He was diagnosed as having gallstones in 1865, a painful condition which he either refused to have, or could not have, treated. He therefore had to establish a broader base of support for the Second Empire so that it would outlive him.

Another argument claims that after having restored order during the 1850s Napoleon was prepared to relax state controls during the 1860s, hence his reforms of 1860, 1864, 1867–68 and 1869–70. The 'liberal empire' thus represented the continuation of his earlier policies. It did not mean the abandonment of the use of measures of control when necessary, however, as was shown by the action that was taken against strikers and socialists in 1870. Napoleon's use of the plebiscite further strengthened the position of an emperor who had not surrendered his power, either to the legislative body or the people.

We do not know whether the 'liberal empire' would have succeeded. Within four months of the 1870 plebiscite the Second Empire had gone. Military defeat following a failure of foreign policy had brought it down. It is to Napoleon's foreign policy that we must turn.

> Trace the changing policies of Napoleon III towards opponents of the Second Empire.

What were the main aims of Napoleon III's foreign policy and how far did he achieve them?

Having another Napoleon leading France caused alarm across Europe during the early 1850s, especially given Louis Napoleon's belief that he was a 'man of destiny', fated to restore France to the pre-eminent position in Europe that it had enjoyed under his uncle. Napoleon III said on several occasions that 'the empire means peace', in an attempt to reassure the leaders of other European countries of his intentions. Although he certainly wanted to change the map of Europe, he preferred to do so using peaceful, political means rather than waging war. It is therefore ironic that French forces under Louis Napoleon/Napoleon III fought eight campaigns over twenty-two years, four of them in Europe. This may suggest that Napoleon III talked peace but waged war. Yet one of these European campaigns took place during the Second Republic, when French troops were sent to Rome. Furthermore, of the three European wars fought under the Second Empire – against Russia (1854–56), Austria (1859) and Prussia (1870) – in only one – that against Austria – did Napoleon III actually plan the outbreak of war, and even then he quickly began to have doubts. In this respect Napoleon III was not a chip off the old Napoleonic block.

Although Napoleon III relied on diplomacy to change the map of Europe, he did not have a clear idea of how exactly he would do so. He thought that he needed the support of Britain to help him to revise the 1815 treaties. Not only was Britain the world's leading power, but it was the state which had defeated Napoleon and which now supported liberal nationalism. He also decided details of his foreign policy with one eye on their domestic consequences, hoping that success abroad would increase his support at home. These two aims – Napoleon's desire for partnership with Britain and to win over the Catholics at home – began a chain of events that resulted in the only war between 1815 and 1914 to involve more than two great powers: the Crimean War.

The Crimean War, 1854–56

1852: French demands regarding the holy places are granted; Russia makes counterdemands on the Ottoman Empire in Turkey.

1853: The Ottoman Empire declares war on Russia after Russia occupies the principalities of Moldavia and Wallachia (part of the Ottoman Empire) at the mouth of the river Danube; British and French navies sail to the Bosphorus; the Russians destroy the Ottoman fleet at Sinope.

1854: France and Britain declare war on Russia; Russia withdraws from the Principalities; the allies decide to capture Sebastopol, the headquarters of the Russian Black Sea fleet, in the Crimea.

1855: Alexander II becomes the Russian tsar in March; the allies take Sebastopol in September.

1856: Congress of Paris: the Black Sea is neutralised and the Principalities are given autonomy.

The Crimean War, 1854–56

The fact that the participation of three European powers in the Crimean War was exceptional does not mean that it was significant (although it would have significant consequences), for none of the three's national interests were directly or immediately threatened. France started the crisis by reasserting its right to look after the holy places in Jerusalem (which was then controlled by the Islamic Ottoman Empire) on behalf of Catholic Christians. The sultan of the Ottoman Empire's agreement to this arrangement upset Russia, which also had a right to look after the holy places, although on behalf of Orthodox Christians. In addition, the Russian tsar, Nicholas I, could not stand the French emperor, whom he regarded as an upstart. This minor squall blew up into a major international storm in a matter of months. As soon as war seemed probable Napoleon III blew hot and cold, but mainly cold. He had not intended to provoke a war, and there was no evidence that the French people wanted it, but he had to follow the lead of the more aggressive British, whose anti-Russian fears were heightened by the sinking of the Turkish fleet at Sinope.

The allied forces soon became bogged down in the inhospitable Crimean peninsula, where they remained for 18 months. Only the French army came out of the war with an improved reputation, being both larger and better organised than the British army. It also suffered greater casualties, over

100,000 Frenchmen being killed. Once Sebastopol had been taken in 1855 Napoleon III was keen to make peace, the consequent peace congress being held in Paris, a further sign of France's importance. By the mid-1850s France had thus been restored to the centre of European cultural and political life, a success for which Napoleon III took the credit and enjoyed the glory.

The effects of the Crimean War were certainly greater than its causes. The war shattered the longstanding partnership of Russia, Austria and Prussia that had maintained the 1815 settlement for 40 years. Though their policies towards Russia during the war had differed, neither Austria nor Prussia had given Russia any effective support. Prussian neutrality meant that Russia felt more antagonism towards Austria, which had sided with Britain and France. Russia resented the 1856 settlement and wanted to change it. As a result she was not prepared to support either Prussia or Austria in any attempt to uphold the existing state system. At around the same time developments in Germany were putting the Austro-Prussian alliance under great strain.

By 1856 the only power that was fully committed to upholding the settlements of 1815 and 1856 was Austria. Seeing an opportunity to alter the European status quo, Napoleon III now looked to Italy. The way in which he became drawn into Italian affairs was most unusual, the Orsini affair demonstrating just how unpredictable Napoleon could be.

> In what ways did the Crimean War help to strengthen the position of Napoleon III?

The war against Austria, 1859

In January 1858 Felice Orsini, an Italian nationalist, threw a bomb at Napoleon and Eugénie as they were going to the Paris Opera. The bomb killed 10 people and wounded 150 more. Napoleon and his wife escaped unhurt. Orsini had decided to try to assassinate the French emperor because he had become disillusioned by Napoleon's failure to help the cause of Italian independence. He thought that the death of the emperor would lead to a French republic which would assist the Italian cause. This relatively minor incident had considerable international consequences after Orsini wrote a letter to Napoleon pleading the case for a united Italy. It seems strange that Napoleon should have been impressed by the letter rather than dismissing it out of hand; maybe it awakened memories of his conspiratorial youth, when he had tried to help the cause of Italian nationalism. Whatever the reason, he decided to act, secretly meeting the prime minister of Piedmont, Cavour, at the French Alpine resort of Plombières a few months later (see page 43). Together the two men hatched a plan to provoke a war against Austria, a war that broke out less than a year later, in May 1859. Between the meeting at Plombières and the outbreak of war, however, the French emperor had yet again blown hot and cold. Cavour tried to manipulate events to ensure that war broke out. The Austrians saved the day.

The two main battles of the war against Austria were those at Magenta and Solferino. Napoleon III, who was leading the French troops, was shocked by the scale of the casualties. The fact that no clear victory over the Austrians had been achieved only made his distress worse, and he worried about the possible intervention of the other great powers. Much to Cavour's anger, Napoleon therefore quickly made peace with Franz Joseph, the Austria emperor, at Villafranca. With events in Italy now running out of control, Cavour agreed that the Piedmontese provinces of Nice and Savoy could become French if their populations agreed, which they did. The acquisition of these provinces expanded France's borders, further revising the 1815 settlement. Yet if the war with Austria had seemed to emphasise Napoleon's role as the leader of Europe, that role would not last much longer.

Dilemmas and blunders: the early and mid 1860s

During the early to mid 1860s Napoleon III's foreign policy upset almost every other European country, as well as many people in France. Either he tried to pursue impractical schemes or he made the 'wrong' decisions when faced with tough choices.

One of the impractical schemes that Napoleon promoted was the proposal that a congress should revise the 1815 settlement to take account of the power of nationalism. The reason for proposing such a congress was the Polish revolt of 1863. Although both Napoleon and the French people wanted to help the Poles, in practice France could provide no direct assistance to them. It became clear that the Poles' position could only be improved if the Polish question became part of a Europe-wide discussion. When France put the idea to the other great powers, however, Britain completely rejected the idea and it was therefore dropped. The Poles had been abandoned and their supporters in France were angry. The other impractical scheme concerned Mexico. In order to ensure that European interests in Mexico were properly looked after following a financial crisis in 1861, Napoleon III proposed establishing Maximilian, the brother of the Habsburg emperor, as the emperor of Mexico. By the mid-1860s 30,000 French troops were required to maintain Maximilian's position. Napoleon could not afford to provide these troops so he abandoned Maximilian, who was shot by a firing squad in 1867. The Mexican episode meant continual criticism of Napoleon III from many quarters throughout the mid-1860s.

One set of hard choices that faced Napoleon concerned Italy: he had to decide whether to support the nationalists or the Catholics. The papacy had refused to recognise the new Italian state, which wanted to gain control of Rome. Since 1849 the pope had been protected by French troops. Reaching a solution that was satisfactory to all parties concerned proved impossible, and

Napoleon eventually allowed Piedmont to gain part of the Papal States, keeping his troops in Rome until, in 1864, he agreed to withdraw them within two years. His actions in Italy upset both the Italian nationalists and the Catholic Church's supporters, resulting in criticism of Napoleon from all sides.

The German question: the mid and late 1860s

Another series of tough choices confronted Napoleon after Bismarck came to power in Prussia. Although Napoleon tried to intervene in the Danish crisis in 1864, no other great power would support him. The German question began to take up more of Napoleon's time. He made several decisions over Germany that would ultimately contribute to the collapse of the Second Empire. Although he was sympathetic to the idea of a reconstructed Germany in principle, it was its practical form that caused him problems. Whether *grossdeutsch* or *kleindeutsch* (see Chapter 6), a unified Germany would be a stronger Germany, which would change the European balance of power and pose a direct threat to France.

Napoleon responded to the growing war of words between Austria and Prussia after 1864 by trying to persuade both sides to give him what he wanted, namely the Austrian province of Venetia so that he could then hand it over to Italy. In October 1865 Napoleon met Bismarck at Biarritz. During the meeting it seems likely that Bismarck hinted at the possibility of Italy receiving Venetia, as well as France gaining land in Belgium, if Napoleon supported a Germany reorganised around Prussia. Then, in June 1866, France and Austria signed a treaty by which France would receive Venetia if it did not participate in the imminent war between Austria and Prussia.

Having negotiated with both sides, Napoleon III seemed to be in a strong position and expected to be able to influence, if not dictate, the peace settlement after the war had broken out. Although the French government did consider intervening once the war had actually started, Napoleon decided against the idea, and by the time that he had changed his mind the war was over. France had been caught out by the speed with which Prussia had won the war and made peace. Following the war Venetia was ceded to France, which in turn gave it to Italy. But, in the space of a summer, a Prussian-led Germany had come into existence on France's eastern borders. France demanded territorial compensation in return for accepting the new German order. This issue would bedevil Franco-Prussian relations for the next four years. A draft proposal submitted in 1866 by the French ambassador to Berlin for France's acquisition of territory on the left bank of the Rhine was ignored (Bismarck published it in 1870 to devastating effect).

Then, in 1867, came the Luxembourg crisis (see Chapter 6). As talk of a Franco-Prussian war became increasingly widespread, Napoleon sought allies, but neither Austria–Hungary (as the Austrian Empire became in 1867) nor Russia wanted to commit themselves to such an alliance. France could therefore do nothing but reorganise its army and wait. When news of the Hohenzollern candidature to the throne of Spain (see Chapter 6) leaked out prematurely during the summer of 1870 the 'liberal empire' expressed its outrage: this was one Prussian move too far. Napoleon found himself unable to resist French demands to humiliate Prussia, demands that Bismarck was able to turn to Prussia's advantage by means of the **Ems telegram** (see page 150). In July 1870 France went to war, a united country convinced that it was going to win. Six weeks later Napoleon III surrendered to the Prussians at Sedan. The Second Empire was finished.

> Identify the main elements of Napoleon III's foreign policy towards (a) Piedmont and Italy and (b) Prussia and Germany.

Why did the Second Empire end?

It was clearly military defeat that brought the Second Empire down. However, the French army had built up a formidable reputation over the previous years, so why did France lose so quickly and so dramatically? And why did the French not rally behind the Second Empire? Only one French army had been defeated at Sedan; others had been mobilised. The capture of Napoleon III should not necessarily have meant the collapse of the Second Empire. Indeed, France continued to resist Prussia for a further four months. Why did it prefer to do so under the banner of a republic rather than that of the Second Empire?

Napoleon III had realised the military importance of the Austro-Prussian War. The French government calculated shortly afterwards that Prussia could raise an army at least four times the size of that of the French. It was clear that something had to be done, and quickly. During the late 1860s the French government did indeed try to modernise its army, just as Prussia had done after 1859 (see Chapter 6). There is a fascinating parallel between the two countries: whereas Prussia, under Bismarck, was able to push through reforms, despite the opposition of the national assembly, France, under Napoleon III, was not. Napoleon had tried to reform the army just as the legislative body had been given more power and the opposition parties were gaining increasing support. The government had had to compromise, with the result that the reforms were not as thorough as Napoleon would have liked. In addition, they had been only partly implemented by the time that war broke out. Part of the problem was national complacency: many army officers thought that the position of France as the leading military power of Europe had been restored under the Second Empire, so why did it need to reform its army? The French army was just not ready for war with Prussia in 1870.

The French army's defeat at Sedan was the complete opposite of what the French had expected to happen and therefore came as a great shock. No one

Because Napoleon III was suffering from gallstones, riding a horse caused him great physical pain. The outcome of the battle of Sedan caused him great mental anguish. It is claimed that he rode round the battlefield, trying to be shot and killed.

had imagined Napoleon III surrendering to the Prussians. And Napoleon's surrender helps to explain why Sedan brought down the Second Empire: the Second Empire was Louis Napoleon's own creation. Although the French had accepted it in 1852 because there was no practical alternative, by the 1860s the old alternatives were starting to resurface: the republicans began to desire a republic once more and the monarchists a proper monarchy. Napoleon III lost control of events during the summer of 1870 (perhaps because he was ill) and allowed France to wage war on Prussia. Having suffered a military defeat as shocking as Sedan, the Second Empire was doomed. Had Napoleon III avoided war, had his empire truly stood for peace, then he might have survived. Instead Napoleon III was brought down by military defeat, just as his uncle had been before him.

Continuing to change: France, 1848–75

Assessing the Second Empire

It is hard to assess the Second Empire. One reason for this difficulty is that the Second Empire of 1852 was different in nature from the Second Empire of 1869. Another is that our view is affected by how the Second Empire ended: the military defeat and national humiliation that was experienced by France between 1870 and 1871 reflect badly on the regime that had brought them about. And yet the Second Empire can be credited with much. It provided greater material prosperity for most of its people (although it was greatly helped in this by the Europe-wide economic boom of the 1850s and early 1860s). It had the support of the people, as expressed in a plebiscite in 1869 (although the freer election of 1867 gave a different picture). Its foreign policy had also improved France's international standing (although events in Mexico and Rome proved embarrassing). It had provided order, too. The Second Empire had been a qualified success.

Any assessment of the Second Empire has to be combined with an assessment of the emperor, however, and it is even harder to summarise Napoleon III. He was a bundle of contradictions: conservative and radical, authoritarian and liberal. At times he was skilful, at other times inept: although he was skilful in gaining presidential power, he was particularly inept at times of crisis. He was a man of Napoleonic destiny who lost his way, developing the forms of imperial authority without ever developing the substance. Indeed, there is something of the twentieth-century Italian dictator Mussolini about him – not the buffoonery, but the bombast: he was a little man who was trying to be bigger than he was. And he was trying to develop one-man rule in a country which, by the mid nineteenth century, was turning away from such rule towards democracy, however imperfect.

Napoleon III was a figure of some significance in the history of Europe, however. He showed that democracy and order could be reconciled, that universal male suffrage could lead to a kind of popular quasi-dictatorship. He demonstrated that democracy was not inevitably revolutionary, that the people were often conservative in attitude. (In this respect he probably taught Bismarck a thing or two.) He developed new techniques for the new era of mass politics that others later used, the plebiscite being the main innovation. And in his desire to revise the 1815 settlement he allowed the formation of a national Italy and a national Germany, without really realising what he was doing. He therefore encouraged the development of the nationalism that eventually brought him down: the clash between French and German nationalism during the late 1860s was a conflict that he could not control. He was overwhelmed by the forces that he had helped to unleash.

> Identify three achievements of the French Second Empire.

Why did the Third Republic take the form that it did by 1875?

The five years following Napoleon III's downfall in 1870 is another historical period that is perhaps best divided into three stages, as military defeat and civil war gave way to the search for a settlement. By 1875, the end of this period, France's various political groups had declared an uneasy peace with each other as they absorbed the implications of 1870–71.

Wars and sieges, 1870–71

September 1870 was almost a rerun of February 1848 as the people of Paris forced the proclamation of a republic. The government that had been chosen by the people preferred to call itself the Government of National Defence, hoping thereby to win the support of all of the French people, whatever their political views. Although they believed that a republic could defeat the Prussians where an empire had failed, the new politicians had reckoned without the Prussians' determination to inflict an even greater defeat and loss of territory on France. It took them four months to recognise Prussia's ambition, during which time Paris was isolated and besieged by German troops. The only way in which it was possible to travel in and out of Paris without the permission of the Germans was by balloon, a means most famously used by **Léon Gambetta**. In January 1871 the siege became a bombardment, which lasted for three weeks and resulted in some 100 people being killed and 300 wounded. This first example of a military attack on civilians in modern European history failed to achieve its goals, however, for it did not cause Paris to submit more quickly. Indeed, Paris's surrender came about as a result of a traditional battle when the National Guard tried to break out of Paris and was soundly beaten. As a result, the national government sued for peace and a three-week-long armistice was agreed.

The armistice gave the French government the chance to hold a general election. Almost two-thirds of the deputies that were elected to the National Assembly were monarchists, either Bourbon or Orléanist. The French voters

> **The Franco-Prussian War and the Paris Commune, 1870–71**
>
> *September 1870:* The Battle of Sedan; German armies surround Paris; the Siege of Paris begins.
> *October 1870:* The last of Napoleon III's armies surrenders as Metz is taken by the Prussians.
> *January 1871:* The Prussian bombardment of Paris begins; the formation of the German Empire is declared at Versailles; an armistice is agreed and the Siege of Paris ends.
> *February 1871:* Elections for a national assembly result in a royalist majority; Thiers becomes the government's chief executive; peace terms are provisionally agreed by Thiers and Bismarck.
> *March 1871:* A revolt breaks out in Paris; the Paris Commune is established.
> *April 1871:* Government troops besiege Paris.
> *May 1871:* The Treaty of Frankfurt is signed, ending the Franco-Prussian War; 'bloody week' in Paris.
> *August 1871:* Thiers is appointed president of the Third Republic by the national assembly.

Léon Gambetta (1838–82) was a radical republican deputy and minister who organised French resistance to Prussia outside Paris in 1870. He resigned in January 1871, but helped to establish the Third Republic between 1873 and 1875. He became prime minister in 1881, but his government lasted only until 1882.

had turned away from those who were linked with the war, whether Bonapartists or radical republicans. The people of Paris, who regarded themselves as the only true defenders of the republican cause, consequently found themselves at odds with the new national government. When Adolphe Thiers (who was appointed president of France in 1871) sent troops to disarm Paris, fighting broke out and two generals were lynched (see illustration on page 91). Paris was in revolt once more and the government withdrew to Versailles. At this stage it appeared that Paris had avoided a repeat of the 'June Days': this time Paris had won, not the government.

The people of Paris now elected their own government, which called itself the **Paris Commune**, a name that took people back to 1792 rather than 1848. To the communards there were many parallels – though presumably they overlooked the eventual fate of the first Paris Commune. Thiers was not prepared to accept a revolutionary state within France. Paris was therefore besieged for the second time in a few months, this time by its own government rather than the national enemy. At the end of May 1871 Thiers sent an army of 140,000 men into Paris from the south and west; because the German army was still stationed to the north and east of Paris the communards could not escape (Bismarck had actually offered Thiers the use of German troops against the Paris Commune). The French troops moved slowly across the city, killing and wounding as they went. No one knows the exact number of people who died. Although the death toll has been calculated as being a minimum of 10,000 people, some estimates double or triple that figure. In addition, some 40,000 people were arrested, of whom a quarter were convicted. Parisians in 1871 suffered the same fate as their predecessors during the 'June Days' of 1848, but they did so on a much greater scale. Not only did Frenchmen kill many of their fellow citizens in 1871, but radical republicans were put to death on the orders of moderate republicans.

The Paris Commune of 1871 can be said to have been the last in a series of direct revolutionary interventions in national politics by the people of Paris that stretched back to the 1790s. The barricades went up in 1871 for the last time until 1944 (in rather different circumstances). Although many communists regarded the Paris Commune as a model for the future, in many respects it was more of an attempt to restore a model of politics that had disappeared in 1848. Paris no longer ruled France.

The Paris Commune has been the focus of much controversy and debate ever since 1871. Karl Marx published his study of the event, entitled *The civil war in France*, within a month of the end of the Paris Commune. Communists regarded it as the prototype of working-class government and the communards as working-class heroes. Republicans argued that the Paris Commune was the true republican government as opposed to the conservative republic

Paris Commune of 1792
At a time when the revolution was in danger from foreign invasion, the Paris Commune seized power, overthrew the monarchy and organised a defence of the revolution against both foreign invaders and its enemies within France. The Paris Commune was linked with the Reign of Terror, during which several thousand people were guillotined, and which ended with the execution of Robespierre in 1794.

The lynching by firing squad of two generals in 1871, one of the first photographic reconstructions of a historical event. 'General Thomas was dragged out into the little garden [by the mob]. No proper execution squad was formed and after a first ragged volley of shots, the general still stood there. Shot after shot was fired until he finally fell, with a bullet through the eye, insulting his executioners to the last breath. Lecomte was then dispatched with one shot in the back' (commentary from Alistair Horne, *The fall of Paris* (1965)).

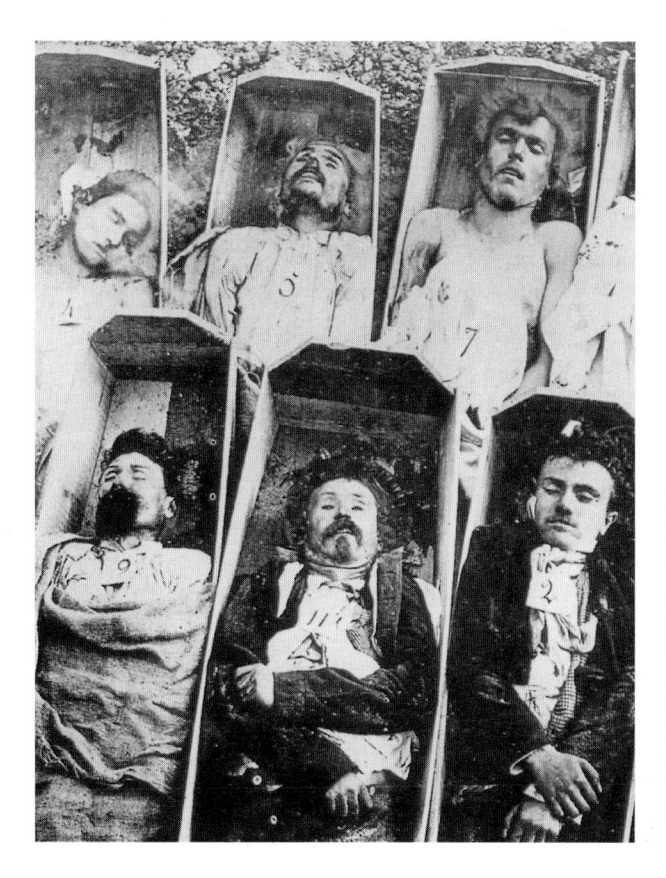

A photograph showing the corpses of some of the Paris communards. As far as we know, this is not a reconstruction. What does this photograph tell us about (a) the communards who died in March 1871 and (b) the attitude of the authorities towards them?

Continuing to change: France, 1848–75 91

that developed during the 1870s. By contrast, members of the political right have used the events of 1871 as evidence of the danger of democracy leading to anarchy and thus of the need to maintain order at all costs. Although the debate is perhaps less heated in today's non-ideological times, the Paris Commune will always be reconsidered in the light of the latest historical concerns. An event of such intensity, with so many individual tragedies, should not be forgotten.

The 'republic of Monsieur Thiers', 1871–73

Having defeated the radical republicans of Paris and gained control of France's capital city, Thiers' main aim during this period was to pay off as quickly as possible the war indemnity of 5,000 million francs that had been imposed on France by the newly united Germany. Under the terms of the Treaty of Frankfurt of 1871 the German army of occupation would remain in France for three years, or until the indemnity was paid off. This massive sum was the equivalent of the entire French budget for at least the next two years. It was to Thiers' great credit that the government was able to raise the sum by means of two massive loans in 1871 and 1872. By September 1873 the last German soldiers had returned home.

There was a second withdrawal at this time, too, when, in May 1873, Thiers resigned from his position as president. He had been so indispensable to the well-being of the Third Republic in its first few years that some called it the 'republic of Monsieur Thiers'. Although his rule was very controversial – not least in ordering that the Paris Commune should be crushed – he was the only French politician that Bismarck was prepared to work with. In terms of French politics, he was acceptable to both the moderate left and, as a former Orléanist, the moderate right. He was never trusted, however, especially by the right. Once the consequences of war had been all but dealt with he became dispensable. In May 1873 the right voted against what it believed was his growing republicanism. Although Thiers resigned the presidency he remained a deputy and continued to work towards establishing the new conservative republic. By the time of his death in 1877 that republic was just about secure.

Compromises and laws, 1873–75

Thiers' successor was named as General Patrice MacMahon. A right-wing figure, he claimed that he would lead a government of moral order, in contrast to the immorality and disorder of the Second Republic and Second Empire. The restoration of the monarchy seemed possible at this stage, and would probably have happened – at least in the short term – had Comte Henri de Chambord, the Bourbon claimant to the throne, accepted the revolutionary flag, the tricolour. Instead, he insisted on the restoration of the monarchist

A painting by a German artist of Bismarck (left) negotiating the terms of the peace treaty of 1871 with the two French politicians, Favre (centre) and Thiers (right), this illustrates the new relationship between Germany and France.

A cartoon by a French illustrator which gives an unusual and rather shocking view of the relationship between Bismarck and Thiers. Compare it with the other painting of Bismarck and Thiers on this page. Does this cartoon have any historical value?

white flag, which infuriated all but the staunchest royalists. As a result, the Bourbons and Orléanists fell out. The moderate monarchists began to work with the moderate republicans in an attempt to achieve a form of government that would be acceptable to a majority of deputies in the national assembly. Eventually, after many months of discussion, this alliance edged towards a compromise acceptable to both sides.

The key resolution was the famous 'Walloon amendment' of January 1875 (named after the deputy who introduced it). The majority in favour of the resolution was the narrowest possible – one vote. The amendment simply stated: 'The president of the republic is elected by an absolute majority vote of the senate and the chamber of deputies meeting as the national assembly. He is elected for seven years and is re-eligible.'

This apparently insignificant resolution was, in fact, very significant, and requires further explanation. The key points include the following:

- The naming of the post of president put the emphasis on the office rather than the individual holding the office. Until then, individuals had been named as president – Thiers and MacMahon. Referring to the post made the presidency seem less personalised, more institutionalised and therefore more permanent.
- The election of the president by the national assembly meant that the president would no longer be directly elected by the voters, thus avoiding the danger of the people electing another Napoleon III. This was an important consideration for republicans.
- The reference to the senate in the amendment was significant. The republicans had always opposed the idea of a second chamber because they believed that it would undermine the authority of the chamber of deputies and give too much patronage to the government. The inclusion of a senate was important to members of the political right, who saw it as a barrier against radical populist reforms made by the directly elected chamber. That role was strengthened when the assembly agreed on the form that the electoral college that would chose most of the senators would take, ensuring that the interests of rural France were properly represented in the new senate.

The vote also broke the stalemate that had existed for the past two years. Further laws were passed in February and July 1875 that clarified the powers of the president and the relationship between the government and the assembly. The senate – whose members were partly chosen, partly elected – was intended to be the equal of the chamber of deputies. All three elements of the government – the presidency, senate and chamber of deputies – had a part to play in making laws (see the diagram opposite).

Although the political parties now had agreed rules by which they could work, the settlement was an unsatisfactory compromise in some respects. It contained gaps which would cause problems over the next few years. There was no formal constitutional document, no grand statement of rights and no mention of the judiciary. The reforms were pragmatic, cautious and as much as both sides could agree to in 1875. Everyone apart from the extreme monarchists and the extreme republicans had got something. France's politicians had therefore agreed on a mongrel system of government in 1875 that had many contradictions. It was a republic that was based in theory on the

> Explain the role in the French Third Republic of (a) the national assembly and (b) the senate.

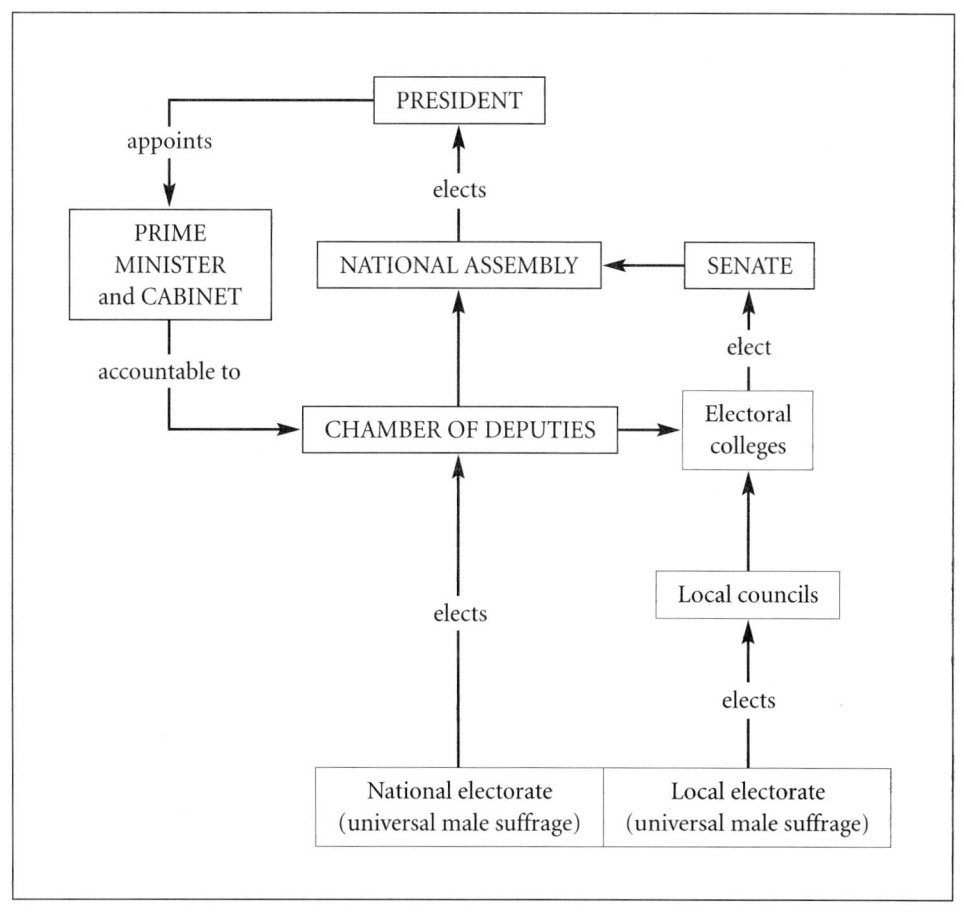

The constitution of the French Third Republic. The arrows show how authority is given by one body to another, the direction of the arrows symbolising the direction of the transfer.

sovereignty of the people and in practice on the sovereignty of parliament. It was a democratic system agreed by politicians and never put to the people for their approval. It was a republic that had been introduced only because it had the support of a large group of monarchists. Moderate politicians of both sides had come to accept that a durable system of government needed both republican and monarchical elements, ending up with a republic that was closer to the British parliamentary system than the American federal government.

For once – and just briefly – French politicians had put the interests of national government before those of their parties, for the experience of the previous five years (and even the previous thirty years) had shown what could happen to France if they did not. Although nobody expected the new system to last, following the crisis of the late 1870s it did, and for much longer than could have been imagined at the time.

> Compare the main features of the Third Republic's system of government, as had been agreed by 1875, with those of the Second Empire.

Continuing to change: France, 1848–75

France, 1848–75

It is hard to regard the turbulent years between 1848 and 1875 as a great era in the history of France (in contrast to a period of similar length and turbulence, from 1789 to 1815). Between 1848 and 1875 France tried all types of government before settling on a very cautious and uncertain compromise. It had experienced a military defeat as great as any in its history, and one that was all the harder to come to terms with for a nation that remembered the exploits of Napoleon Bonaparte. The rule of his nephew, Napoleon III, which took up most of this period, was seen as a very unsatisfactory attempt to build a new empire. Although Napoleon III may have been judged a little harshly, he suffers by comparison with his uncle. Here was a man who spent his whole life trying to fulfil his destiny as a Bonaparte, yet proved unequal to this self-imposed task.

If Napoleon III was obsessed by the past, he was not alone. There is a sense in which French politics at this time was determined by differing views of France's recent history. Some wanted to re-create the glories of the past, like the Paris communards of 1871 (who even revived the revolutionary calendar of 1793). Many more people were afraid of the past, particularly the Terror of the first French Revolution, which they expected to return. Such people were horrified by the February revolution of 1848, as well as by the establishment of the Paris Commune in 1871, and therefore supported politicians who acted to restore order. In 1848 they gave their support to Louis Napoleon (even though he had had nothing to do with the June Days), and in 1871 to the republic in abstract, but Adolphe Thiers in practice. 1871 showed what these various views of the past might mean for the present: military defeat and bloody civil war.

It should not be forgotten that this was the era when France had to adjust to the reality of mass democracy. In 1848 the vote was given to all adult males, and although the franchise was limited a little a year or two later (by the republicans) it was soon restored (by a president) and never again taken away. The French voter proved more conservative than radical, more concerned with order than with liberty. On the evidence of the elections and plebiscites that were held between 1848 and 1871 the form of the government mattered less to the voter than the substance of its policies. It took French politicians some time to come to terms with this new reality. They spoke for the people only occasionally during the Second Empire. Between 1869 and 1871 the people spoke for themselves and the politicians began to listen.

In 1875, in response to the new reality, the politicians thus agreed on a compromise that had many rough edges. Over the next 40 years the Third Republic narrowly avoided civil war. It did not, however, manage to restore France to its formerly glorious position in Europe. To do so would have required an industrial base that France never developed on a sufficient scale. There were further, harder lessons to be learned in the twentieth century.

Historical sources

The end of the Paris Commune, 1871

1 The report of a British journalist

The Parisians of civil life are wretched to the last drop of their thin, sour, white blood. Only yesterday they cried 'Vive la Commune!' Today they have rubbed their hands with livid joy to have it in their power to denounce a communist and reveal his hiding place. Very eager at this work are the dear creatures of women. They have found him, the scum. A tall, pale, hatless man. His lower lip is trembling but his eye has some pride and defiance in it. The crowd yells 'Shoot him! Shoot him!' An arm goes in the air and there is a stick in the fist. The stick falls on the head of the man. Ha, the infection has caught. Men club their rifles and bring them down on that head. A certain British impulse, stronger than consideration for self, prompts me to run forward. But it is useless. They are firing into the carcass now, thronging around it like flies on a piece of meat. His brains spurt on my foot and splash into the gutter where the carrion is bodily chucked, presently to be trodden on by the feet of the multitudes or rolled on by gun carriages.

Source: Archibald Forbes, writing in the *London Daily News*, 26 May 1871

2 The view of a French writer who lived in Paris during the Franco-Prussian War and Paris Commune, 31 May 1871

All is well. There has been neither compromise nor conciliation. The solution has been brutal, imposed by sheer force of arms. The solution has saved everyone from the dangers of cowardly compromise. The solution has restored self-confidence to the army, which has learnt in the blood of the communards that it is still capable of fighting. And finally, the bleeding has been done thoroughly and a bleeding like that, by killing the rebellious part of the population, postpones the next revolution. The old society has 20 years of peace before it, if the powers that be dare what they are free to dare at the moment.

Source: an extract from the private journal of Edmund de Goncourt, 31 May 1871

3 Karl Marx's judgement

The civilisation and justice of bourgeois order comes out in its lurid light whenever the slaves and drudges of that order rise against their masters. Then the civilisation and justice stand forth as undisguised savagery and lawless revenge. Each new crisis in the class struggle between the appropriator and the producer brings out this fact more glaringly. Even the atrocities of the bourgeoisie in June 1848 vanish before the infamy of 1871. The self-sacrificing heroism with which the population of Paris – men, women and children – fought for eight days after the entrance [of the government troops] reflects as much on the grandeur of their cause as the soldierly reflect the innate spirit of that civilisation of which they are the mercenary vindicators. A glorious civilisation, indeed, the great problem of which is how to get rid of the heaps of corpses it made after the battle was over!

Source: Karl Marx, *The civil war in France*, 1871

Historical-source questions

1. Study source 3. From this source and your own knowledge, explain what is meant by 'the atrocities of the bourgeoisie in June 1848'.
2. How reliable is source 3 as an account of the behaviour of the Paris communards in 1871?
3. Study sources 2 and 3. Compare and contrast the views of the end of the Paris Commune that are given in these sources.
4. Study all of the sources. Using your own knowledge and these sources, assess the consequences of the end of the Paris Commune for France between 1871 and 1875.

Summary questions

1. Identify and explain any *two* factors which resulted in the establishment of the French Second Empire in 1852.
2. How liberal was Napoleon III?
3. Identify and explain any *two* factors which explain why the Third Republic was established in 1875.

5 Having to change: Russia, 1825–81

Focus questions

- What were the main features of tsarist Russia in 1825?
- How successfully did Nicholas I govern Russia?
- How significant were the main forms of oppositional thought?
- How successfully did Alexander II govern Russia?
- How and how far did Russia change between 1825 and 1881?

Significant dates

1825	Death of Alexander I; Decembrist Revolt; Accession of Nicholas I
1828–29	Russo-Ottoman War over Greece
1831	Polish Revolt
1853–56	Russo-Ottoman War; Crimean War; Treaty of Paris
1855	Death of Nicholas I; accession of Alexander II
1861	Emancipation of the serfs
1863–64	Polish Revolt
1864	*Zemstva* established
1876	Land and Liberty established
1877–78	Russo-Ottoman War; Congress of Berlin
1881	Alexander II assassinated; Alexander III becomes tsar

Overview

'A riddle wrapped in a mystery inside an enigma' was how Winston Churchill famously described Russia in 1939. Apart from the special significance of Soviet communism in 1939, what was it about Russia that made it so puzzling? Was it a question of geography, of its being on the eastern edge of the European continent, making it hard to get to and therefore little known? This is part of the answer. It is important to realise that Russia was both European and Asian: although its base was European, the greater part of its territory was Asian, making its experiences far different from those of the wholly European states to the west. Indeed, Moscow was ruled by the Mongols (also known as Tatars or Golden Horde) of central Asia for some 200 years during the thirteenth, fourteenth and fifteenth centuries, a time when Russia was in effect separated from Europe, as well as from such European cultural developments as the Renaissance.

Difference was as important as distance. Both its way of life and its values set it apart from the rest of Europe, which is mainly why Russia perplexed Churchill. Taking the most obvious example, the Russian calendar was different from that of the rest of Europe (as well as that of the Western world). When Europe refined its calendar during the eighteenth century so that it more closely matched the movement of the sun and the moon, Russia did not. When it was 12 January in nineteenth-century Europe, it was 1 January in Russia. Only after the October Revolution of 1917 was Russia's calendar brought into line with that of the West. This difference in calendars can be regarded as a symbol of Russia's 'backwardness'. Indeed, to outsiders, Russia seemed more like a medieval state than a modern nation. All authority rested with just one person, the tsar (or emperor), on whom there were no formal restraints, while the idea of private property, so central to the development of Western Europe, simply did not exist for much of Russia's history. The Russian Orthodox version of Christianity had developed very different traditions from those of Roman Catholicism and Protestantism. A proper appreciation of the history of Russia therefore requires some understanding of such differences.

If Russia was so different from the rest of Europe, can it really be classed as being European? In fact, it has always been considered European, and perhaps for three main reasons. Firstly, it had been Christian since the tenth century, and Christianity was the faith that all of Europe shared, if in different versions. If anything, Russians considered 'Holy Russia' the only true defender of Christian values, with Moscow the 'third Rome' and Byzantium (or Constantinople, today's Istanbul) the second. Secondly, it began to open itself up to the rest of Europe from the sixteenth century, if only in limited ways, with the reign of Peter the Great, from 1682 to 1725, being the most significant period of Westernisation. As a result of visiting England incognito and seeing the latest shipbuilding methods Peter the Great founded the Russian navy. By the nineteenth century Russian culture, especially its music and literature, was definitely European. The tsarist court spoke French rather than Russian, while the poetry of Pushkin, the novels of **Tolstoy** and Dostoyevsky, as well as the music of Tchaikovsky, were all among the finest of the period. Although we shall concentrate on politics, diplomacy and economics, the contribution of these artists should not be forgotten. Thirdly, other European countries

Leo Tolstoy (1828–1910) was the author of the two great literary masterpieces *War and peace* (1869) and *Anna Karenina* (1878), as well as many other works. He came to believe in Christianity, the innate wisdom of the Russian peasantry and the benefits of sexual abstinence.

involved Russia in their affairs, most obviously when occasional attempts were made to invade Russia: those of Charles XII of Sweden in 1700 and Napoleon Bonaparte in 1812. The latter attempt resulted in Russian armies for the first time marching across Europe in order to defeat the French.

There were other ways in which Russia stood apart from the rest of Europe, too. Compared with the other European great powers – and Russia was definitely one of four or five great powers – it came either top or bottom of various orders of rank. It was the largest of all of the continental European states during the 1820s, both in terms of its area and population, as well as the most powerful, but it was also the poorest and the most unequal. Compared with the rest of Europe Russia always seemed 'backward'. This leads to perhaps the single most important theme of Russian (and Soviet) history: since the sixteenth century its leaders have always faced the problem of how far Russia should try to keep up with the West and, if so, how best to do so.

During the nineteenth century Russia seemed to 'fall behind' in two respects. The first was economic. As was eventually shown by the rise of Prussia, the basis of military might was now industrial power. The question was whether Russia would be able to modernise its economy in order to maintain its military power and, if it could, what the consequences of doing so would be. Could Russia achieve the material benefits of modernisation without suffering the social division and unrest that, on the evidence of Western Europe, seemed its inevitable consequences? The second was political. The French Revolution and the Napoleonic wars had seen Europe influenced by such ideas as freedom and democracy. Even in Russia, remote and isolated as it was, a few people were affected. They longed for such liberties. The question was whether Russia should give its people the same sort of freedom that was being granted to most others further west. Although some thought that it should, others disagreed, believing that their introduction would destroy the very features that made Russia so distinctive and special.

Grappling with these difficult and demanding questions made nineteenth-century Russia as lively and as turbulent as other European states. Before we start to consider this history in detail, however, we need to have a better idea of the state of Russia in 1825.

What were the main features of tsarist Russia in 1825?

The first feature of note of tsarist Russia in 1825 was the sheer size of the country. In 1820 a Scotsman, John Cochrane, set out to walk across Russia. Although it took him three months to walk from the French coast to **St Petersburg** (an average of 20 miles per day), it took him over two years to reach the Pacific coast, admittedly by means of a circuitous route. The more

> Identify three ways in which nineteenth-century Russia differed from other European states.

St Petersburg was the Russian capital city that was built during the early eighteenth century on the orders of Peter the Great to symbolise Russia's links with the West. It was constructed on a river estuary (at great human and financial cost) in a classical European architectural style.

direct route that he took to return to St Petersburg took 10 months, although he did not travel by foot for all of the way. Russia's population matched its size: at 40 million it was almost twice the size of that of the next largest country, France, in 1800. Its population growth furthermore outstripped that of all the other European countries: by 1900 Russia contained 130 million people, more than twice the number of Europe's second most populous country, Germany.

The second important feature of Russia in 1825 was that virtually all of its people lived in the country and worked on the land. The 1858 census showed that four in ten Russians were **state peasants**, while another four in ten were **serfs**. The remaining 20 per cent of the population consisted of industrial workers, members of the middle class and landowners. (At around the same time one in eight people worked on the land in Britain.) Not only was Russia's economy essentially agricultural, but its farming methods were very inefficient by Western standards. As a result, Russian society was the most unequal in Europe: the peasants and serfs lived lives of terrible poverty and hardship, while their landlords and owners enjoyed great wealth and luxury.

The third feature of note is that not all of the people of Russia were Russian. Not even half of them were. Russia was a multi-ethnic empire, with Ukrainians, Poles and Jews, as well as various Asiatic nationalities, making up most of the rest. The Russians were **Slavs** and Russia therefore claimed to be a Slav state. This became important later in the nineteenth century when some Russians began to regard Russia as the protector of other Slav peoples.

If the majority of the tsar's subjects were peasants or serfs, they worked for, or were the property of, landowners. The land-owning class – around 1 per cent of the population – also provided the officials who ran local, regional and central government. In the practice of governing Russia the landowners were a very important group. In theory, though, they were subordinate to the tsar or emperor, who shared his authority with no one. Russia was an **autocracy**. Those institutions that often acted as a check on the power of monarchs in Western Europe did not exist in Russia. The landowners had influence and wealth only thanks to the tsar. The Orthodox Church, too, was controlled by the tsar. The middle class, the other social group that often challenged Western governments, hardly existed in Russia, for the commerce and trade that had been the basis of its growth in Western Europe was a much smaller part of Russian economic life. For good or ill, the tsar had power to an extent undreamt of in the West. It is important to realise that this concentration of power was not simply a consequence of a succession of evil tsars having had their wicked way over many centuries. Indeed, Russia's experience had shown that the only way in which to bring order to a country of its size was for all groups to accept that one person had the God-given authority to rule it. A

Serfs were owned by private individuals and **state peasants** by the state; the material conditions of serfs were usually the worst of the two.

Slavs are the peoples of Eastern Europe who speak Slavonic languages (for example, Russian, Ukrainian, Polish and Czech), as opposed to such European languages as Germanic (which includes English). This definition became the basis of Slav nationalism, as well as of pan-Slavism, during the nineteenth century.

autocracy is the unconstrained rule of one person. Its meaning also embraces such terms as absolute (but not limited) monarchy, dictatorship and despotism, each of which have more specific meanings.

This photograph of Russian peasants was taken in the 1880s. What evidence does it provide of the group's standard of living? How useful is the photograph in explaining the situation of the ordinary Russian people in the 1820s?

great deal therefore rested on the shoulders of just one person, more than in any other European country.

At the beginning of 1825 Russia was ruled by Tsar Alexander I, a member of the Romanov dynasty that had ruled Russia since 1613. He had been tsar for 24 years, having come to the throne in 1801 following the murder of his father, Paul I, at the hands of court officials. In terms of the central theme of Russian history, its modernisation, Alexander I had raised the hopes of the reformers, only to dash them again. During his early years as tsar he had relaxed controls on the press and had even talked of introducing some kind of constitution. (It took almost exactly 100 years for this revolutionary idea to become reality, and then only in response to large-scale demonstrations by the people.) He backed off. During the second half of his reign, he became more concerned with the well-being of Europe. Because Russia had played an important part in the downfall of Napoleon, Alexander thought that it should have an equally prominent role in guiding the destiny of post-war Europe. By then his idealism had taken a religious form, and he put his energies into building some kind of Christian unity in support of the new order of 1815. If the new status quo had to be ensured in Europe, then the old status quo had to be preserved

Having to change: Russia, 1825–81

in Russia, which meant that any idea of introducing political reforms into Russia was soon forgotten.

A few of those who wanted to modernise Russia and were expecting Alexander to introduce political reforms could not forgive him for this. They started to take matters into their own hands. In an age when secret societies were common throughout Europe, these would-be reformers set up their own such societies, often modelled on the Freemasons' lodges. Even though the numbers involved were small – probably no more than 1,000 – members could not agree, with the result that during the early 1820s they split into two main groups: the Northern Society, which was based in St Petersburg, and the Southern Society, which was based in the Ukraine. By the mid-1820s these groups were talking either of assassinating the tsar or of overthrowing him. They became the basis of what became known as the Decembrist Revolt.

The Decembrist Revolt, 1825

Alexander I died suddenly, aged 48, in November 1825. A few years earlier he had changed the line of succession from his brother Constantine to another brother, Nicholas. Only one or two people knew of this at the time. When, on the death of Alexander I, the change became public knowledge both Constantine and Nicholas dithered. As a result, people were faced with the dilemma of having to choose to which of the brothers they should swear an oath of loyalty. In the confusion, the Northern Society tried to seize power in St Petersburg. Several thousand troops assembled in one of the city's main squares in a hasty attempt to challenge the tsarist system. After trying to avoid bloodshed, Nicholas sent troops loyal to him against the demonstrators, who then fled. The plotters were rounded up across Russia; of the 121 who were tried, 5 were sentenced to death, the remainder being sent either to Siberia or to prison. Although this improvised revolt had posed no threat to tsarist autocracy, it would have great significance for the later history of nineteenth-century Russia. So who were the Decembrists and why did they attempt to overthrow the tsarist state? More importantly, why were they so significant?

Who were the Decembrists?

Most of the Decembrist leaders were army officers. This is rather surprising because most army *coups d'état* have the aim of taking away freedoms instead of increasing them. These officers had been actively involved in the war against Napoleon from 1812 to 1814, and had therefore visited Western Europe. Having seen what Western European countries were like for themselves, they found that Russia suffered by comparison. Regarding themselves as true Russian patriots, they wanted to change Russia, to rid it of its worst features, such as serfdom, and to introduce such reforms as freedom of speech and a constitution. This was why they formed their secret societies. Not that their societies were all that secret. Their activities became known to Alexander I and yet he took no action against them. The reasons for this inactivity remain unclear. Perhaps he thought he could trust army officers not to challenge his rule.

The Decembrist officers came mainly from noble families, which shows that there were some aristocrats who were prepared to challenge the autocracy of the tsar. Although they were few in number and their revolt failed, their example would nevertheless inspire others. Yet because the conspirators were nobles and army officers the plot attracted no officials or merchants – in other words, members of the middle class – and no provincial landowners or peasants. The Decembrist Revolt can therefore be described as a row within the Russian ruling class.

Why did the Decembrists try to overthrow the tsarist state?

The main reason why the Decembrists tried to overthrow the tsarist state in December 1825 was that the confusion that followed the death of Alexander presented the conspirators with the brief opportunity of doing so. They seem to have been inspired by revolts in Greece, Spain and Italy a few years earlier. (Greece was a fellow Christian Orthodox state, while army officers had led the revolts in Spain and Italy.) They were also products of the Romantic age, the age of Byron and Pushkin, a time when the heart prevailed over the head and when sacrifice was regarded as noble. Although their cause was always a hopeless one, they dedicated themselves to it all the same. Five of their number died for the cause.

Why were the Decembrists so significant?

Some historians regard the Decembrist Revolt as the last of several military *coups d'état* of the eighteenth and early nineteenth centuries. Others argue that 1825 was the first in a series of challenges to autocracy, the climax of which was the February Revolution of 1917. Evidence can be provided to support both theories. In terms of the history of Russia up to 1881 there is plenty of evidence to show that the revolt of 1825, as well as the government's response to it, spurred others to question the tsar's authority and to challenge the state. The reign of the new tsar gave little warning of the upheavals that would follow his death in 1855, however.

> Identify (a) the immediate causes and (b) the longer-term factors which explain why the Decembrists revolted in 1825.

How successfully did Nicholas I govern Russia?

Historians have given Nicholas I an almost universally bad press. The usual view can be summarised thus: he was a narrow-minded, repressive autocrat who prevented necessary change, thereby making Russia's problems much worse. This negative tone was set by such writers as **Alexander Herzen**, who described the events following the Decembrist Revolt as follows:

> The day after receiving the terrible news [of the executions] there was a religious service in the Kremlin. After celebrating the execution Nicholas made his triumphal entry into Moscow. I saw him then for the first time. He was on horseback, riding beside a carriage in which the two empresses, his wife and Alexander's widow, were sitting. He was handsome, but there was a coldness about his looks. No face could have more mercilessly betrayed the character of the man than his. The sharply retreating forehead and the lower jaw developed at the expense of the skull were expressive of iron will and feeble intelligence rather [than] of cruelty and sensuality. But the chief point in the face were the eyes, which were entirely without warmth, without a trace of mercy, wintry eyes.

The man described by Herzen was 29 years old. Like the Decembrists, he had visited Western Europe between 1814 and 1815, but unlike them he had not been impressed. The only exception concerned Prussia. Having been brought up as a soldier he always remained a soldier, and he admired Prussia's military qualities, equating as he did the strength of a country with the size of its army. Although he had not expected to become tsar until a few years before he actually did so, he had a strong sense of duty, as is shown by his coronation manifesto, which also set out his approach to government:

> Not by daring and rash dreams, which are always destructive, but gradually and from above, laws will be issued, defects remedied and abuses corrected. In this manner all modest hopes for improvement, all hopes of strengthening the rule of law, for the expansion of true enlightenment and the development of industry will be gradually fulfilled. The legitimate path, open for all, will always be taken by Us with satisfaction. For We do not have, and cannot have, any other desire than to see Our motherland attain the very heights of happiness and glory preordained for her by Providence.

Before considering Nicholas I's reign there is one further primary source that is worth examining. In 1844 the tsar went to Britain, where he met Queen Victoria, who summarised her impressions of Nicholas in a letter to the king of the Belgians:

Alexander Herzen (1812–70) was the son of a Muscovite nobleman. A student radical, he was sent into internal exile from 1837 to 1842. He left Russia in 1847 and never returned. During the 1850s he edited the publications *The Pole Star* and *The Bell*, which highlighted abuses in Russia. He was a lifelong critic of tsardom.

> There is much about him which I cannot help liking. He is stern and severe – with fixed principles of *duty* which *nothing* on earth will make him change; very *clever* I do not think him and his mind is an uncivilised one; his education has been neglected; politics and military concerns are the only things he takes great interest in; the arts and all softer occupations he is insensible to but he is sincere, *sincere* in even his most despotic acts, from a sense that that is the only way to govern; he is not, I am sure, aware of the dreadful cases of individual misery which he so often causes for I can see by various instances that he is kept in utter ignorance of *many* things, which his people carry out in most corrupt ways, while he thinks that he is extremely just. He thinks of general measures but does not look to detail. And I am sure that *much* never reaches his ears and (as you observed) how can it?

This gives a very different account of the tsar from that of Herzen, so how much does Nicholas I deserve the judgement that history has given him? We need to study his reign. It is sensible to subdivide his rule as tsar into three periods: 1825–33, 1834–48 and 1848–55. Despite Nicholas's best efforts, his reign was not an unchanging era of order and stability.

Establishing order, 1825–33

The Decembrist Revolt, the first open challenge to tsarist rule, came as a great shock to Nicholas I. A few years later, in 1830, he received another shock when, following others that had occurred in Western Europe, there was a revolt in Poland, a country that was under Russian control. For the first few years of his reign Nicholas took what he regarded as necessary action in order to contain such revolutionary ideas as liberalism and democracy. Cholera had reappeared in Europe, killing many people in 1830. To autocratic rulers like Nicholas I revolutionary ideas had the same effect on the political body as cholera did on the human body. Like cholera, these ideas were perceived as coming from elsewhere, in this case Western Europe, and the Decembrists were evidence of this foreign infection. Nicholas therefore argued that such ideas had to be curbed, contained and kept at bay if their potentially fatal effects were to be avoided.

Where did people get these dangerous ideas from? Firstly, by reading newspapers and magazines. Thus press censorship was introduced. A very severe set of press laws was enacted in 1826 before a government department was made responsible for the slightly more relaxed laws of 1828. Throughout Nicholas's reign newspapers and magazines had to be extremely careful about what they published. Secondly, they listened to others, especially if they were teachers and professors in schools and universities. Because schools were often the source of radical ideas, government controls over them were increased and educational opportunities were limited, especially for peasant children. Universities, however, remained largely untouched, which would prove an oversight of some significance. Thirdly, they went abroad, so opportunities for education abroad were restricted. Some people managed to evade these various controls, however, so in 1826 Nicholas also established a new branch of his personal office, His Majesty's Own Chancery, to which he gave very great power. This new branch was given the rather unexciting title of the Third Section (or Department). It could watch anyone, Russian or foreigner. By the end of Nicholas's reign it was watching his second son. It could report on anything that it felt was a threat to the security of tsardom. The Third Section became a state within a state, able to do anything that it wanted in the name of autocracy. It developed into the tsarist secret police, a forerunner of the Soviet KGB.

In 1833 Nicholas appointed a new minister of education, Sergei Uvarov, who developed a doctrine that came to underpin Nicholas's autocracy. This doctrine was summed up in three words, which became a kind of slogan: orthodoxy, autocracy and nationality. Uvarov explained the idea in 1843, when looking back on the 10 years that he served as minister of education, as follows (the italics are the author's):

> A Russian, devoted to his fatherland, will agree as little to the loss of a single dogma of our *orthodoxy* as to the theft of a single pearl from the tsar's crown. *Autocracy* constitutes the main condition of the political existence of Russia. The Russian giant stands on it as on the cornerstone of its greatness. An innumerable majority of the subjects of *Your Majesty* feel this truth; they feel it in full measure though they are placed on different rungs of civil life and although they vary in education and in their relations to the government. The strong conviction that Russia lives and is protected by the spirit of a strong, humane and enlightened autocracy must permeate popular education and must develop with it. Together with these two national principles there is a third, no less important, no less powerful, *nationality*.

> Explain in your own words what was meant by 'orthodoxy, autocracy and nationality'.

Although Uvarov did not explain what he meant by nationality, it is clear that he did not mean ethnic Russian nationality as opposed to that of the Poles or the Jews. He meant the shared identity of all those who lived in Russia, who benefited from its orthodoxy and autocracy. In order to distinguish between the two concepts of nationality, Uvarov's doctrine is often called 'official nationality'. It gave Nicholas's government a more coherent philosophy than it would otherwise have had, although it did not mean a great deal in practice.

There was one major challenge to tsarist rule in these years and it came from the Poles. Many Poles felt that they benefited little from Nicholas's autocracy. In 1830 they rebelled. Nicholas took resolute action. Russian forces were sent to Poland to crush the rebels. As a result the previously semi-independent Poland lost its constitution and became fully integrated into Russia. It was to be another eighty years before Poland regained its freedom.

Nicholas I did consider reform as well as repression during these years. He set up several secret commissions to review aspects of Russian life, including the position of the serfs, which the tsar accepted needed to be improved. The main achievement of these commissions was the codification of much of Russia's law, which made it easier to understand. Apart from this there was little notable reform. Nicholas was too cautious (whether by nature or as a result of his experience) to promote change.

The tsar also worked to restore order in the realm of foreign affairs, as well as furthering Russian interests (which were one and the same in his eyes). In doing so the main problem that he faced was the **Eastern question**. When Nicholas became tsar the Greeks, who were fellow Orthodox Christians, were in revolt against Ottoman rule. Russia was drawn in, declaring war on the Ottoman Empire in support of the Greeks in 1828. With Nicholas I leading the Russian army, the Ottoman Empire was defeated in the same year. Greece eventually became independent, while Russia gained the right to protect the autonomy of the two Ottoman principalities, Moldavia and Wallachia at the mouth of the river Danube. Then, in 1832, Ottoman rule was threatened once more, this time by a challenge from Mehemet Ali, the ruler of Egypt. When it seemed that the complete collapse of the Ottoman Empire was imminent, Russia and the Ottoman Empire signed the Treaty of Unkiar-Skelessi in 1833, whereby Russia agreed to protect the Ottoman Empire, the Ottoman Empire agreeing in return that it would close **the Straits** to foreign warships if Russia asked it to.

To Nicholas, the Treaty of Unkiar-Skelessi was a sensible defensive move. To those suspicious of Russian intentions, such as the British, it was regarded as further evidence of Russian expansionism. They saw Russia as intent on expanding first into the Black Sea and then in two different directions. One, via the Straits, would lead into the eastern Mediterranean. This would threaten both British – and French – interests in what we now call the Middle East as well as trade routes to India. The other, via control of the Danubian principalities, led to the Balkans, which threatened Habsburg interests. These developments in Russo-Turkish relations in the early 1830s were the basis of strained relations between Russia and Western powers over the fate of the Ottoman Empire for the rest of the century. The two sides went to war in 1854 and nearly did so again in 1878. Russian aims in the region were rarely as

The **Eastern question** was concerned with the international problems caused by the decline of the Ottoman (or Turkish) Empire, a Muslim-ruled empire that included countries in the Balkans (in Europe), the Middle East and north Africa. The decline of the empire encouraged some subject peoples, often Christians, to revolt against Ottoman rule. All of the European great powers had some interest in the lands that comprised the Ottoman Empire, whether strategic, ethnic or religious.

The Straits were the narrow stretch of water that linked the Mediterranean and the Black Sea. They consisted of the Dardanelles (at their western end) and the Bosphorus (at their eastern end) and were controlled by the Ottoman Empire. The rights of warships to pass through the Straits became a major international issue during the nineteenth century.

ambitious as Western governments – and newspapers – believed them to be. Their anti-Russian stance was based more on misperception than on reality.

Following these upheavals in the Near East and the 1830 revolution in Poland, Nicholas signed the Münchengrätz Agreement with Austria and Prussia in 1833, the three powers agreeing to work together to maintain the Ottoman Empire, to suppress the Poles and to act against revolution whenever it occurred. This partnership was to be the linchpin of Russian foreign policy for almost 20 years.

By 1833 Nicholas had therefore established the systems and relationships, both at home and abroad, that he needed if he was to maintain order and contain the spread of dangerous radical ideas. He spent the rest of his life working to maintain these systems. For most of the time, he succeeded. From 1848 his systems started to crumble.

Upholding order: 1834–48

The 14 years between 1834 and 1848 were very uneventful ones in terms of Russian history. Although, as we shall see, important developments occurred within opposition circles, at the time they had no significant impact on either government policy or national events. This is not to say that there was no change, because slow and gradual change did occur in such areas of national life as education, literature and the economy. If events did have an effect on government during this period, the state lacked the energy to do much about them. Take, for example, the key issue of Russian life at the time, serfdom: the number of peasant revolts increased during each of the three decades that Nicholas ruled Russia, from 148 between 1826 and 1834, to 216 between 1835 and 1844, and to 348 between 1845 and 1854. The tsar even went as far as saying in 1842: 'There is no doubt that serfdom, in the form we have it now, is clearly and obviously bad for everyone.' Nicholas set up various commissions to examine serfdom, but nothing effective was done to address the problem. Although government reforms were occasionally introduced, as was the case for state peasants in 1836–37, when the departments responsible for the state peasantry were reorganised, they made little difference. Opposition groups that might have caused trouble were curbed by censorship and closely watched by the Third Section. Russia between 1833 and 1848 was a quiet place.

Abroad, the threats to Russian interests were never serious enough to require military action. Between 1834 and 1847 the Russian army took part in no wars. Admittedly it fought campaigns against rebel groups in the Caucasus, a remote, mountainous region between the Black and Caspian seas, but these had been going on for years. There were some setbacks for Russia, as in 1841, when the Treaty of Unkiar-Skelessi was replaced by the Straits Convention (by which all of the great powers agreed that the Ottoman Empire would not allow any foreign warships to pass through the Straits in times of peace). However, this setback was not great enough to require upsetting the peace and stability of Europe in order to reverse it.

With relative quiet at home and peace abroad it seemed that the autocracy of Nicholas I was working well during the late 1830s and the early 1840s. Nicholas himself was certainly working hard to ensure its success, travelling the country, walking the streets of St Petersburg and listening to the opinions of the people that he met. More than any other tsar since Peter the Great, he took interest in the details of government. He probably took too much interest, for he became overwhelmed by the finer details of administration, with the result that he neglected strategic issues and failed to appreciate the implications of technological change. For example, he did nothing to stimulate the growth of railways in Russia. The first Russian railway line, which was built in 1837, covered the few miles from St Petersburg to the tsar's summer palace. Construction of the first major line within Russia, linking St Petersburg and Moscow, was not begun until 1842 and was not completed until 1852. By 1855 Russia had 1000 kilometres of track, while at around the same time France had 3,000, the German states 8,000 and Britain 11,000 kilometres. Indeed, the problems that Russia experienced during its Crimean campaign were caused in part by the lack of railways, especially in southern Russia.

The relative stability of this period strengthened Nicholas's belief in the wisdom of his policies and in the superiority of Russian autocracy over Western democracy. As the tsar and his ministers became older – and Nicholas was loyal to the men whom he had appointed – an even greater conservatism became apparent. This tendency was reinforced when revolutions occurred in Europe in 1848, although not in Russia.

Containing disorder: 1848–55

The last seven years of Nicholas's reign began with news of the 1848 revolutions that were sweeping across the continent. Nicholas's response was defiant, and on 14 March 1848 he issued the following manifesto:

> After blessed peace of many years, the western part of Europe has been disturbed by the present troubles, threatening the overthrow of legitimate powers and the entire social order. At this very moment, this insolence, knowing no limits, threatens in its madness even Our Russia, entrusted to Us by God. But it will not succeed! Following the example of our Orthodox ancestors and invoking the help of Almighty God, We are ready to meet our enemies. We shall, in indissoluble union with Our Holy Russia, defend the honour of the Russian name and the inviolability of our frontiers. We are certain that every Russian, each of

> Our faithful subjects, will answer with joy the call of his [*sic*] Emperor and that our ancient cry 'For the Faith, the Tsar and the Motherland' will now show us the way to victory and we all as one will cry out 'God is with us! Take heed, O nations, and submit, for God is with us!'

At a time when his fellow monarchs in Austria and Prussia were making concessions to the revolutionaries, Nicholas thus stood firm, frightening the rest of Europe into expecting a Russian onslaught.

The government took a series of measures to halt the spread of revolution to Russia, tightening censorship, controlling the movement of people in and out of Russia and ordering home those Russians who were abroad. In 1849 the government found evidence of what it thought was a possible conspiracy, centring around Mikhail Petrashevsky, a disenchanted civil servant with an interest in French socialism, but it turned out to be little more than a discussion group and was easily crushed. Autocracy, that barrier against Western innovation, was holding firm. Abroad, Russian troops helped Austria to defeat the Hungarian Revolution in 1849, which showed not only that the alliance of conservative powers was still effective, but also that Russia remained the '*gendarme*' [policeman] of Europe'.

Despite these successes, the period between 1848 and 1849 was still a difficult time for the Russian government. Famine occurred on a large scale as poor harvests resulted in serious food shortages. In addition, cholera returned, killing people in greater numbers than ever before. The scale of the revolutions in Europe had come as a shock and Nicholas, who was said to have aged 10 years overnight, became even more cautious. The idea of reforms was completely forgotten as the increased repression of 1848–49 was sustained over the following years. During the early 1850s Nicholas isolated Russia from the rest of Europe as never before.

Russia's isolation increased as the Eastern question returned once more. Although Louis Napoleon started the crisis, Nicholas made one demand too many on the Ottoman Empire when he occupied the Danubian principalities and then refused all attempts at compromise, as a result of which the Ottoman Empire declared war on Russia. In November 1853 Russia sank the Ottoman fleet at Sinope, in the Black Sea, prompting Britain and France to declare war on Russia in March 1854. For the first time in 40 years Russia was at war with other European great powers. Although Nicholas had expected Russia's old ally, Austria, to support him, it did not, its interests being opposed to Russia's. At first Austria remained neutral, but then it began to side with Britain and France. After a bad start the allies slowly began to gain the upper hand in the Crimean War, aided by Russia's difficulties in supplying its forces in the Crimea.

The Crimean War. A portion of the fortified bastion at Sebastopol, with the abandoned Russian guns. 'Along the whole line of the Sebastopol bastions, which for so many months now had been seething with an unusually active life, had seen heroes released one by one into the arms of death, and had aroused the fear, hatred and, latterly, the admiration of the enemy forces, there was now not a soul to be seen. The whole place was dead, laid waste, uncanny – but not quiet; the destruction was continuing' (commentary from *The Sebastopol sketches* by Leo Tolstoy (1856)).

> Identify (a) the different incidents concerning the Eastern question during the reign of Nicholas I and (b) the policies followed by Russia with regard to each.

With the war less than a year old Nicholas died a sudden death after catching a cold. He left Russia just as Russia was facing its greatest challenge since his accession.

Assessing Nicholas I's rule

Russia under Nicholas I is among the best examples of an autocracy in modern history. Between 1825 and 1855 one man – Nicholas – took all of the major political decisions in Russia. Once the Decembrists had been dealt with no one challenged his power and his officials worked hard to carry out Nicholas's decisions. Nicholas I was in some respects the model autocrat. He took his responsibilities extremely seriously and worked very hard. He was not personally corrupt, dissolute or brutal. He regarded himself as being duty bound to work to defend tsarist Russia against its many opponents, both outside Russia and within. He also believed that he had a duty to Europe to use Russia's military power to curb and control the revolutionary forces that had so disturbed its peace during the Napoleonic era. He was convinced that he would succeed if his controls – both military and bureaucratic – were strong enough. It was an essentially defensive, negative approach, one that relied on the suppression of dangerous ideas.

In trying to keep such dangerous ideas – all of which came from Western Europe – out of Russia in order to keep it 'pure' and 'uncorrupt', Nicholas was acting as a kind of Slavophile (see page 115). He succeeded to a certain extent, for such Western ideas as liberalism meant little in the Russia of Nicholas I. Its ability to ride out the revolutionary storm of 1848 furthermore showed that Russia was managing to contain the dangers posed by Western influences.

The successful development of an autocracy depends upon the autocrat, however, and Nicholas failed to provide new policies in response to both old and new problems. Only he could provide Russia with a sense of direction. Orthodoxy, autocracy and nationality were not enough. Nicholas I's main fault was not that his regime was repressive and brutal but that he failed to provide the policies that were necessary to prepare Russia for future threats and challenges. The nature of his autocracy had been determined by his early experiences: his military upbringing, his visit to Europe and the Decembrist Revolt. He believed that the power of the Russian army and the Russian bureaucracy could contain the forces of liberalism and nationalism and, indeed, it did so for a while. But Nicholas I was trying to make Russia stand still while the world moved on. For a time he succeeded. His success simply created more problems for his successor.

> Taking your examples from the reign of Nicholas I, identify (a) three events which show that Russia was an autocracy and (b) three events which show that that autocracy had its limits.

How significant were the main forms of oppositional thought?

Not everyone in Russia bowed down before Nicholas I's autocracy and gave in to the Third Section during the 1830s and 1840s: a few individuals, probably no more than a couple of thousand at the most and almost all of them young noblemen, continued to debate and argue. Their discussions were abstract and theoretical, and although they achieved little in their own time their debates provided the basis for the expression of more political, more practical and more revolutionary ideas during the reign of Alexander II. Indeed, Alexander was eventually assassinated by two revolutionaries. The impact of a few intellectuals on Russian history was thus out of all proportion to their numbers.

That the tsarist autocracy did not allow opposition does not mean that there was none. So how did the opposition develop? How important were the ideas that challenged those of the state? Once more, the period needs to be subdivided, this time covering the reigns of both Nicholas I and Alexander II. The development of oppositional ideas is best seen in terms of five distinct periods. It is important to realise, however, that some of the ideas that were expressed early in this period persisted up to 1881 and even beyond.

Slavophiles and Westerners, 1836–47

There was no public intellectual debate during the 10 years that followed the Decembrist Revolt. Then, in 1836, the magazine *The Telescope* published an article on the history of Russia by Peter Chaadyev, a disillusioned army officer turned intellectual. In his article Chaadyev argued that Russia had had no history until the reign of Peter the Great and that all of Russia's best features came from its links with the West. Herzen described its impact as being like 'a shot that rang out in the dark night'. As a result of its publication the magazine was closed down and Chaadyev was declared insane. The argument had started, however.

Those who opposed Chaadyev's arguments became known as the Slavophiles. They regarded the reign of Peter the Great and his policy of developing links with the West as disastrous for Russia. They believed that the essence of Russia was to be found in the Orthodox faith, which they considered to be the purest form of Christianity, superior to Catholicism and Protestantism. They emphasised the virtues of the Russian way of life, as well as its unique features, like the village commune, or *mir*, a collective form of living that was in marked contrast to the more individualistic way of life that was emerging in the West. Such Slavophile writers as Alexei Khomyakov, the Aksakov brothers, Ivan and Konstantin, and Ivan Kireyevsky began to express a form of Russian nationalism.

The Westerners took the opposite point of view. Peter the Great was their hero. They regarded Russia as being less advanced than the West and therefore believed that Russia should take up and adapt the best features of the Western way of life. Although they refused to accept orthodoxy, autocracy and nationality, they disagreed about what they did want: some argued for a constitution and freedom of speech, others for the emancipation of the serfs. Although the treatment that had been meted out to the Decembrists inspired rather than deterred them, at this time none of them wanted the tsarist state to be overthrown or even challenged. This pro-Western group included Timofei Granovsky (a historian), Vissarion Belinsky (a literary critic), Alexander Herzen (an essayist) and Mikhail Bakunin (an intellectual and an eventual founder of anarchism).

It is important to remember that the Slavophiles and Westerners were not two distinct, organised groups that were at loggerheads with each other. On the contrary, they came from the same small social group and their disagreements were intellectual, not political. The ideas of such German Idealist thinkers as Hegel had a great effect on the two groups, and they argued about ideas and theories in university tutorials, learned journals and semi-formal discussion groups. The debate was mainly about philosophy, history and literature, subjects that often have a political dimension in an autocracy. The

> Summarise the main differences between the Slavophiles and the Westerners.

expression of their arguments was sometimes tolerated by the censors, perhaps because their ideas were so abstract. Freedom of thought did survive during the reign of Nicholas I.

'Seven dismal years', 1848–55

'Seven dismal years' was the phrase that Nicholas's opponents applied to the last years of his reign. They began badly enough. By 1848 Bakunin had been exiled, Herzen had left Russia and Belinsky was dead. The revolutions of 1848 had brought greater censorship and controls, and links with the West were now virtually non-existent. It was a bleak time for freethinkers in Russia. One example illustrates several aspects of the autocracy of Nicholas I. In 1852 Ivan Turgenev, at the time one of Russia's most famous novelists, sent a St Petersburg newspaper a letter in praise of Nikolai Gogol, another great Russian novelist, who had just died. The censor in St Petersburg refused to allow the letter to be printed, so Turgenev sent the letter to Moscow, where the censor passed it. When he heard of this, Nicholas ordered the sacking of the Moscow censor and the arrest of Turgenev. Turgenev, who was an observer of life and no political activist, was imprisoned for a month and then kept under police surveillance for several years.

In his essay *Russia and 1848* (1948), Isaiah Berlin argued that even these repressive years had a profound effect upon Russian oppositional thought: being cut off from the West, radical thinkers became less interested in the finer points of German Idealism and more concerned with conditions in Russia. This shift of emphasis was reinforced by the failure of the revolutions in Europe. If Western liberalism could not succeed in Western Europe, what chance did it stand in Russia's more hostile autocracy? Finally, these years distinguished the committed radicals from those who did not have the heart to continue the struggle in the face of increasing persecution. After the death of Nicholas I these radicals would pose a much greater challenge to his successor: his son, Alexander II.

Emancipation, 1855–61

The first six years of Alexander II's reign were a great contrast to the last seven years of his father's. It was a time of great debate and discussion, to which many great writers contributed. Censorship was relaxed (although not abolished). The debate about the emancipation of the serfs encouraged discussions about a wide range of social issues. In 1855 Herzen, who was now living in the West, published a new magazine, *The Pole Star*, followed in 1857 by *The Bell*, both of which highlighted the failings of the Russian system. The government was powerless to close down these magazines and Herzen's periodicals were smuggled into Russia – even Alexander II read them. New, more radical, thinkers emerged who were younger, more concerned with social issues and critical of their fathers' attitudes.

Turgenev's novel *Fathers and sons*, which was published in 1862, illustrates the change in the political climate. The fathers in Turgenev's novel are the 'men of the 1840s': writers such as Belinsky and Herzen, all of them romantics and idealists. The sons are the 'men of the 1860s': practical, realistic and, to use the word that was invented at the time, nihilistic. The sons criticised their fathers for their romanticism, for being concerned only with theories, while the sons themselves believed in no principles, hence the term 'nihilism' (which is derived from the Latin word *nihil*, meaning 'nothing'). Yet despite the word's origins they did not believe in nothing at all: they rejected abstract ideas and accepted only material facts. They regarded science as more important than history, surveys of the people's condition as more useful than philosophical debates. The younger generation was more practical than their fathers had been. They were also more openly critical of tsarist government.

It is almost impossible to discern the development of any clear trends of thought during these first few years of Alexander's reign, for many people were waiting to see how the government would act. Once they saw the reality of the emancipation of the serfs between 1861 and 1862, a new political approach did emerge.

Nihilism and socialism, 1862–69

The emancipation of the serfs dashed the hopes of many reformers. This new generation, which had been hardened by the 'dark seven-years-long night' (as Herzen described it) of the final years of repression under Nicholas I, now had to face the false dawn of the first years of 'liberalisation' under Alexander II. Nihilism now became fashionable, many young people regarding it as the only appropriate response to Russia's situation.

Other people were more active. There were student demonstrations in 1862. New revolutionary groups were formed, such as Young Russia in 1862. Turgenev's novel had caused such a sensation that in 1863 the leading radical of the time, Nikolai Chernyshevsky, wrote *What is to be done?* as a reply. A more positive account of what the 'sons' (and daughters) would achieve, Chernyshevsky's novel remained a continuing inspiration for many radicals (indeed, Lenin named one of his most important books after it). Originally a literary critic, Chernyshevsky became the prototypical revolutionary who was committed to the cause of equality and never wavered in the face of government persecution. Although such radicals were, in their way, as idealistic as their fathers had been, the difference was that their idealism took a political form, for they believed in political action. And the form of political action that was taken up by many such men – and women – during the 1860s was socialism. Influenced by the example of the socialist groups that were being formed in the West, and inspired by people like Bakunin (who was now a Western-based socialist revolutionary), they believed that they should work towards the removal of the great inequalities from which Russia and its people suffered.

During the 1860s the more abstract, Westerner–Slavophile debate therefore gave way to more practical arguments about political ends and means. And as more people protested so more were arrested; when, in 1866, a student tried to assassinate Alexander II, further repression followed. By the late 1860s two possible responses seemed open to government opponents: either bypassing the government to create a social revolution among the Russian people or creating a political revolution by undermining and even overthrowing the Russian state. The first approach was attempted during much of the 1870s, but when that seemed to fail a small group turned to the second.

Populism and terrorism, 1870–81

In reality there was no neat dividing line between the 1860s and 1870s. However, in around 1870 radicals focused increasingly on ideas that became known as **populism**. These socialists came to believe that the newly emancipated Russian peasantry (although its emancipation was only partial) could be encouraged to overthrow the existing social order. They also believed that the peasant commune, or *mir*, which was unique to Russia, could provide the basis of a socialist society. Developing the commune, they argued, would enable Russia to bypass the capitalist stage of economic development that the West was having to go through. Bakunin helped to articulate and stimulate such revolutionary views as he developed his ideas on **anarchism** during the years before his death in 1876. The Paris Commune of 1871 (see Chapter 4) was a further inspiration.

In 1874 'going to the people' occurred, when several thousand radical socialists went to the small towns and villages of European Russia in an attempt to win the support of the peasants. The peasants were bemused, however, and the radicals were arrested. The social revolution had to be postponed.

The radicals' initial response to the failure of 1874 was to develop a new form of political organisation: the establishment of the first revolutionary party in 1876. Its name, Land and Liberty, emphasised its links with a similar group of the early 1860s, for like its predecessor it was committed to both social revolution and public agitation. The big difference between the two parties was that the party membership of the second remained secret, its members being organised into cells – small, self-contained groups that were set up to prevent members from betraying others to the authorities if they were

Populism is the idea that the people are the source of wisdom and authority. It is different from democracy in that populism has an almost mystical belief in the superiority of the masses, however poor their education. Strongest in Russia, and now unknown elsewhere, populism never developed into an organised political force.

Anarchism is the belief that all forms of government act against the interests of the governed and that the only just form of government is self-government by committed responsible citizens. Several assassinations during the 1880s, including that of Alexander II, led to anarchism being associated with bomb-throwing terrorists.

This grim-looking bunch of Russian revolutionaries (members of the People's Will) is grouped around a small table covered with a lace tablecloth. Four wear hats, even though they are indoors. One is wearing a smart pair of boots.

arrested. When the government eventually tried, and then punished, some of those who had been involved in the 1874 protest, and some radicals consequently started to kill police officials, Land and Liberty faced some hard choices. Although some of its members stuck to their aim of social revolution, others opted for political revolution instead – including terrorism – forming a separate group called the People's Will in 1879. Alexander II became the prime target of the People's Will and a number of assassination attempts were made on him between 1879 and 1880 until, in March 1881, two of its members finally succeeded in killing him. (The tsar helped bring about his own death by getting out of his carriage to attend to those who had been wounded by the first bomb instead of driving away, giving a revolutionary 'suicide bomber' the chance to detonate a second bomb.) By 1881 oppositional ideas had clearly come a long way from the idealism of Herzen and Belinsky of the 1830s and 1840s.

Summary

This brief guide to the development of oppositional thought in Russia identifies the main changes that occurred over some 40 years, changes that were greatly influenced by developments in both Europe and at home. Even at the height of repression, during the last years of Nicholas's reign, Russia was never entirely cut off from news from the West, Herzen making sure of that. The events that occurred within Russia itself were even more important, however.

Four men and one woman were publicly hanged in April 1881 for their involvement in the murder of the tsar. Note the prominent place of the clergy of the Orthodox Church.

It is a paradox that there should have been more radical protest during the reign of Alexander II, the 'tsar liberator', than there was under the more oppressive Nicholas I. By the end of his reign there had evolved that classic Russian figure, one which looms large in contemporary Russian novels, the professional revolutionary. The link with the Bolsheviks of the next century was a close one. For plotting the assassination of Alexander III several members of the the People's Will were hanged in 1887. One of them was Alexander Ulyanov. His younger brother soon changed his name to Lenin.

So what had Alexander II done to turn moderate radicals into violent revolutionaries?

> Identify the contribution to Russian political thought of
> (a) Herzen,
> (b) Chernyshevsky and
> (c) Land and Liberty.

How successfully did Alexander II govern Russia?

The 37-year-old Alexander II became tsar when Russia was in the middle of the Crimean War. He had been groomed for the responsibility of office, Nicholas I having made sure that his son had a broader education (although not that broad) and more experience of all aspects of government than he had had. Although Alexander had thus been learning the tsar's trade for almost 20 years, nothing could have prepared him for the situation that he faced on becoming tsar in February 1855: Russia was losing the war, the government had no money and the peasants were revolting in ever-increasing numbers. Alexander did not consider ending the war straight away, however, even after the fall of Sebastopol in October 1855. It was only when the threat of Austrian intervention arose that he decided that continuing the war was pointless, the Treaty of Paris consequently ending the Crimean War in early 1856 (see Chapter 4).

With the war now over, how would Alexander II deal with Russia's domestic problems? The main issue that he faced was whether to free the serfs.

> Compare the situation of Russia on the accession of Alexander II in 1855 with that of Russia in 1825, when Nicholas I became tsar.

The emancipation of the serfs

Freeing the serfs from their owners' control was a massive task which would have profound implications for Russia. In 1858 there were some 22 million serfs, more than 1 in 3 of the population. Furthermore, because many features of Russian economic and social life were based on serfdom, ending it would create the need for many other reforms and thus much greater change. The main losers of emancipation would be the landowners, a very powerful elite whose opinions could not be ignored. Although there was therefore a case for doing nothing, there was nevertheless little opposition to emancipation. The impression usually given is that the tsar gave the lead with his statement of 1856 (see historical sources, page 132) and that from then on it was only a matter of working out the details of emancipation. However, the usual impression is misleading.

In reality, Alexander sought the views of the landowners. They indicated that although they wanted their serfs to receive personal freedom, they did not want them to be given land as well. In 1858, however, the government decided that the serfs should have land as well as freedom, fearing that if they did not receive it there would be peasant unrest. So what form did emancipation finally take? The edicts that freed the serfs, which were published in February 1861, were extremely complex. Their key points were as follows:

- Peasants were no longer the property of the landowners.
- The landlords retained ownership of agricultural land and the peasants had to fulfil certain obligations to their landlords.
- Details of land allocation and peasant obligations were to be agreed within two years.
- If two sides agreed on the sale of land the peasants had to pay 20 per cent of the total.
- The landowner received the remaining 80 per cent in the form of government securities.
- The peasants then had to pay the state the 80 per cent over the next 49 years at a rate of interest of 6 per cent, in what were called 'redemption payments'.
- Property ownership passed from the landowner to the village commune, or *mir*, which was also responsible for making redemption payments and distributing the land.

Reading the decree that emancipated the serfs, the Prozorov estate, Moscow Guberniya, in 1861. A fascinating picture, even though posed.

Although the peasants' response to the emancipation of the serfs is often hard to assess, many thought that they should not pay for land they believed was theirs. The government was forced to issue a statement saying that there would be no second emancipation edict that would be more favourable to the former serfs. As we have seen, students and radicals were angered by the terms of the serfs' emancipation and considered more extreme ideas and actions.

Neither the peasants nor the radicals had any power, however. The landowners had power, and although the tsar occasionally reprimanded them he had to listen to them. The landowners did well out of emancipation: although they no longer had direct control over the peasants they also ceased to have direct responsibility for them. Emancipation led to one of two likely outcomes. One was that the peasant still had to work for the landowner. The other was that the peasant worked on land that the landowner agreed to transfer to the peasant. However, the land transferred was often the less fertile parts of an estate. The peasant paid the landowner a lump sum for land which was almost always valued to the owner's benefit. The state paid the difference. The peasant then faced repaying the state over a period of up to 49 years.

What impact did the emancipation of the serfs have upon Russian life? Emancipation was introduced in order to avoid peasant unrest on the scale of the **Pugachev Rebellion** of 1773 to 1775, to enable the modernisation of the army and the economy, as well as to right a moral wrong. If there were peasant

The **Pugachev Rebellion** of 1773 was a large-scale revolt in eastern European Russia that was started by the Cossacks and involved peasants and serfs. Atrocities were committed by both sides before the rebellion was eventually crushed. Thereafter landowners became very fearful of a repetition of the events of 1773 to 1775.

122 *Having to change: Russia, 1825–81*

revolts in the short term they soon subsided; the army reforms are considered below. The key issue is the effect that emancipation had on the Russian economy.

Most historians believe that the emancipation of the serfs delayed the modernisation of the Russian economy. Before 1861 the serf had been restrained by his landowner, while after 1861 the peasant was constrained by the *mir*. If the peasant ever wanted to leave the commune the permission of the village elders was needed. A collective-based method of agriculture made the introduction of new farming methods very difficult. Furthermore, after 1861 the peasant had even greater financial obligations than before. On the other hand, the landowner received additional finance, much of which was used to pay off debts, little being invested in Russian industry.

Although the economy was modernised and did indeed grow, the way in which the serfs were freed slowed down the rate of modernisation over the next 40 years or so. This is not to say that the emancipation of the serfs was carried out in the 'wrong' way, for it was implemented with relatively little unrest over the longer term. Social stability had been achieved, but at the expense of more rapid economic growth. Had emancipation been intended to achieve greater economic growth — as would have happened, for example, if the peasants had been given freedom but no land, thereby increasing the mobility of labour — it would probably have been at the cost of greater social unrest.

> Identify and explain three ways in which the emancipation of the serfs was limited.

Other reforms

Serfdom was so central to the Russian existence that its abolition – however limited – forced other aspects of Russian life to change as well. Although reforms had started before 1861, they gradually increased in 1862–63, with 1864 being the year of the greatest change. Until 1863 the details of emancipation were still being worked out. In 1863 itself Alexander was largely preoccupied with a revolt in Poland, which he crushed with a severity similar to that of his father between 1830 and 1831, even if unlike his father, he also introduced reforms. By 1864 it had become possible to implement further reforms.

Army reforms, from 1862

The Crimean War had exposed the grave limitations of the Russian army. At the same time as Prussia, France and Britain were reforming their armies, Dmitri Milyutin, Russia's war minister from 1863 to 1881, also implemented a wide range of reforms. He improved training, expanded the army reserves and, in 1874, introduced universal conscription for all men when they became 21 years old. Noblemen could now serve as ordinary soldiers, even if they rarely did. The state only needed one in four of all those who were eligible to serve. By the end of Alexander's reign the army was larger, better trained and better organised than it had been in 1855.

Financial reforms, from 1862

The Crimean War had ruined the government's finances. In addition, there was a major financial crisis from 1857 to 1858 during which national banks collapsed. Russia's finances gradually improved, however, particularly under Count Mikhail Reutern, the minister of finance from 1862 to 1878. Better accounting and auditing procedures were introduced and the granting to other bodies of the right to collect taxes for the state (tax-farming) was replaced by a state-run tax on goods (the excise). Tariffs on foreign imports were reduced, although only for a few years. Reutern encouraged the development of the Russian economy, mainly by stimulating the growth of railways and commercial banks, both of which attracted foreign investment to Russia.

The gains were short-lived, though, for when Russia became involved in another war with the Ottoman Empire in 1877 its finances suffered and Reutern had to leave office.

The *zemstva*, 1864

Zemstva were district and provincial assemblies. Representatives were elected at the district level by landowners, townsmen and peasants voting separately, and district *zemstva* in turn chose delegates for the provincial assembly (*zemstvo*; *zemstva* is the plural noun).

The introduction of the *zemstva* in 1864 was the first time that democracy had been introduced into Russian government, however limited its form. The *zemstva* were given a range of responsibilities for providing public services, such as schools, hospitals and roads. In 1870 elected town councils were established, although only people who owned their houses could vote for the representatives. Despite their limited power, the *zemstva* and their urban equivalents did some useful work in improving public facilities over the next half a century. Russians were at last experiencing some kind of representative government.

Judicial reforms, 1864

In 1864 some of the features that are regarded in the West as being essential to the rule of law were introduced in Russia. Judges were appointed for life; they were well paid and better educated and trained. A hierarchy of courts was established, and justices of the peace (or magistrates) and trial by jury were introduced. The cross-examination of witnesses was now permitted in court. There were limits to these reforms, however, the ministry of the interior, for example, not always being subject to the law. Despite this, the reforms marked a considerable improvement in the administration of the law.

Education, 1863 and 1864

There were three elements to the reform of education in Russia: firstly, how much freedom universities would have to educate their students; secondly, what type of secondary education would be provided for a privileged few;

and, thirdly, how best to provide some form of elementary education for all.

The 1863 reform gave greater autonomy to universities, which, following two years of repression and student unrest, suggests that Alexander still had some liberal values. In 1864 both secondary and elementary schools were reformed, albeit in limited ways. Following the attempted assassination of the tsar, Count Dmitri Tolstoy (no relation of Leo Tolstoy, the author of *War and peace*), was appointed minister of education. Tolstoy, who was well known for his reactionary beliefs, was convinced that the study of science encouraged student radicalism and therefore changed the curriculum of the schools that prepared their students for university. Students now spent a large part of their time studying ancient Greek and Latin. (There is no evidence that student radicalism decreased over the next few decades, however.) The growth in elementary schooling, which was neither free nor compulsory, during this period seems to have been more the result of increased peasant demand than of the government deciding to build more schools. Despite its growth, its impact was limited: in 1897 the literacy rate for the whole of Russia was 21 per cent, and among women who lived in the country it was only 10 per cent.

The limitations of Alexander's reforms

From the 1860s many aspects of Russian public life under Alexander's direction thus experienced what might be called a 'quiet revolution'. But the reforms were usually limited and there were boundaries beyond which the tsar would not go. Perhaps the most significant reform that Alexander refused to countenance was the creation of a national assembly for all of Russia: although the nobles of Moscow requested such an assembly in 1865 their request was dismissed as an affront to autocracy. It would be another 40 years before another tsar, Nicholas II, granted a national assembly, and then only when faced with a national revolution. Some historians argue that had his grandfather done something similar in 1865 the course of Russian history would have been different, but as with all 'what ifs?' this cannot be proved.

Another change that Alexander tried to limit was greater freedom of speech. As increasingly radical ideas were being expressed in periodicals and magazines, so the government struggled to compose a set of regulations that would enable it to rein in the more extreme journals. Having been embarrassed in 1863, when, perhaps through ignorance, the censor had allowed the publication of Chernyshevsky's *What is to be done?*, new rules were issued in 1865. Editors had to submit their publications to the censor after they had been printed but before they had been published. In 1866 a leading radical magazine of the past 30 years, *The Contemporary*, was closed down. For the rest of Alexander's reign the state censors tried to prevent the publication of views that they regarded as being dangerous to the state. Their efforts met with only limited success, however, for the number of new books that were published continued to grow, if anything even more rapidly. Only after 1881, when Alexander III came to the throne, was effective censorship re-established.

From reform to repression?

The year 1866 is often seen as a turning point in Alexander II's reign. It was the year in which the liberal approach of the previous 11 years was replaced by the more reactionary regime of the following 15 years and it was also the year in which the first of several assassination attempts were made on Alexander. In 1866 a new head of the Third Section, Count Peter Shuvalov, was appointed. For the next seven years he would use his power to try to prevent further reforms and to appoint anti-reformers to key government posts.

Alexander's reign cannot be divided so simply, however. Institutional reforms that had already been agreed were implemented after 1866. Not only did the attempt to impose greater control after 1866 not succeed, but if anything it confirmed the arguments of the revolutionaries and helped to increase their support (although those who supported them represented only a minuscule proportion of the tsar's 80 million subjects). The 16 years of Alexander's reign were times of increasing unrest and greater attempts to control that unrest. The two seemed to feed off each other and by 1881 the situation seemed to be slipping out of the government's control. But before we consider the final act in the tragedy of Alexander II we should consider his economic and foreign policies.

Economic policy

One of Russia's weaknesses during the Crimean War had been its economy: despite its size it could not mobilise the resources needed to defeat the small Anglo-French force that occupied only a tiny part of Russia. It was clear that the economy had to be modernised. The development of the railways would lead the way. The relevant government decree was published in 1857. It stated:

> Railways, the need for which has been doubted by many over the past 10 years, have now been recognised by all strata as a necessity for the empire and have become a national need and a common and consistent desire.
>
> The network will link together three capitals, our main navigable rivers, our richest grain regions and two ports on the Black Sea and the Baltic that are open almost all the year round. Thus it will facilitate our exports abroad and will ensure the transportation and supply of food at home.

Note the date of the decree. Note the point made in the first line. And note the reasons for developing the railways.

The decree provided for the building of nearly 4,500 kilometres of track, four times the amount that existed at the time, and by 1876 almost 20,000 kilometres had been built. Raising the money to fund this railway-building programme was a problem, however, which was one of the reasons why Russia sold Alaska to the USA for $7 million in 1867. Much of the rest of the funding was borrowed from foreign investors, who usually required the Russian government to guarantee their loans.

Stimulated by the growth of the railways, Russian industry and trade grew during the 1860s and 1870s. The encouragement of industrialisation was not one of Alexander's goals, however (that had to wait until his son and grandson came to the throne), for on the evidence of Western Europe's experience, industrialisation would result in a class-based society that would threaten the existing social order. Alexander was instead aiming to modernise the economy of Russia in order to ensure that it was efficient enough to benefit from its huge natural resources, both of people and raw materials.

> 1 Put each of Alexander's main reforms under one of the following headings: political, social and economic.
>
> 2 Under each heading, list the reasons why the reform was introduced, its main features and its impact on Russia.

Foreign policy

When viewed from Western Europe, there were two main incidents in Russia's foreign policy under Alexander. One was the Crimean War (1854–56), which led to the Congress of Paris; the other was the Russo-Turkish War (1877–78), which led to the Congress of Berlin. One resulted in a military setback for Russia, the other in a diplomatic defeat. Both were to have profound consequences within Russia.

When viewed from St Petersburg, however, the most significant external development of Alexander II's reign was the emergence of a united and powerful Germany on its western borders. Russia did not oppose the unification of Germany under Prussia's leadership at the time (and Bismarck usually took great care to 'keep open the line to St Petersburg', as he put it). One reason for this was that Russia's attitudes had been affected by the Crimean War: it could not forgive Austria for turning against Russia (especially after Russia had helped Austria to defeat the Hungarian Revolution in 1849). Thus it did not intervene in the Austro-Prussian War of 1866. Russia also resented the Treaty of Paris (1856), and in 1871 renounced the terms of the treaty that prohibited a Russian fleet from entering the Black Sea. No one apart from the British prime minister, William Gladstone, took much notice of this at the time because the Franco-Prussian War (1870–71) had diverted attention from Russia. Although the growing strength of Germany after 1871 caused Russia some concern, it was intent on maintaining good relations with the newly unified country, in part because it benefited from the growing economic links between them. This is one of the reasons why the Russian tsar joined the *Dreikaiserbund*, the League of the Three Emperors (of Russia, Austria-Hungary and Germany), which was formed in 1872, broke down in 1878 and was re-formed during the 1880s.

When viewed from an Asian perspective, Russia's foreign policy under Alexander takes on a different aspect. Russia established complete control in the Caucasus, where its authority had previously been less than total. It gained Turkestan, in central Asia, and moved into territories that were close to Afghanistan and British India. In the Far East, Russia gained territory at the expense of China and Japan, too, including what would later become Vladivostok on the Pacific coast, as well as the island of Sakhalin. Taking these areas together, Russia absorbed huge amounts of territory into its empire during the reign of Alexander II. Its reasons for doing so were a mixture of the material and non-material: it would gain access to more resources and new markets and many Russians also believed that they had a responsibility to 'civilise' the more backward peoples of these regions. Although its expansion was the Russian equivalent of the overseas empires being developed at much the same time by such Western European states as France, Britain and Germany, these territorial advances convinced the British that Russia was an expansionist power that was either threatening India itself or the route to India.

It was fear of Russian expansionism at the expense of the Ottoman Empire that caused the Eastern question to become a major international crisis again in 1877–78, when Russia went to war with the Ottoman Empire. This time it was Russia that declared war on the Ottoman Empire. Its reason for doing so was the Ottomans' persecution of the Orthodox Christians in the Balkans and their refusal to respond to diplomatic pressure. Many Russians, especially the **Pan-Slavs**, pressed for stronger action, as a result of which the tsar (who was now in a weak domestic position) reluctantly went to war. The Ottomans were besieged in the fort of Plevna by the Russians, who took an embarrassingly long time to force them to surrender. Eventually the Ottomans were defeated and Russia imposed peace terms, the Treaty of San Stefano giving such Slav peoples as the Bulgarians greater freedom. The British and Austrian governments objected to the peace terms, Britain even threatening war to get them changed. In order to try to keep the peace, Bismarck called an international congress at Berlin in 1878. Although he tried to act as an 'honest broker' between the two sides he was trying to achieve the impossible and Russia, finding itself in a weak position, had to back down. The Treaty of Berlin radically revised the Treaty of San Stefano.

Pan-Slavs believed in the unity of all of the Slav peoples and, as the leading Slav state, in Russia's duty to protect all Slavs. Pan-Slavism was a form of greater-Russian nationalism.

This is often said to be a picture of the 'notorious Sophia Bluvshtein – the "Golden Hand", who was sentenced to three years' hard labour for escaping from Siberia. She is a small, thin, already greying woman, with a crumpled face. Looking at her, one finds it unbelievable that not so long ago she was beautiful and could charm her jailers, as she did in Smolensk, when a guard helped her escape.' From *The island of Sakhalin*, by Anton Chekhov (1895).

This final settlement of the latest episode of the Eastern question made the government even more unpopular in Russia. The period between 1877 and 1878 was also the time when the trials of the Land and Liberty conspirators were held, causing a sensation in St Petersburg. In 1877 Tolstoy wrote from his country estate, 'I think we're on the verge of a great revolution.' If a great revolution is defined as the assassination of the tsar, then Tolstoy was right.

> Identify (a) the different incidents concerning the Eastern question during the reign of Alexander II and (b) the policies followed by Russia with regard to each.

The last act

By the 1870s Alexander II was being criticised for both his government's policies and his private life. From 1866 he had a mistress, Princess Catherine Dolgorukaya, who was much younger than he was and with whom he soon lived openly. They had several children. After his wife died in 1880 the pair married as soon it as was legally possible to do so. This long-running personal scandal weakened the tsar's authority over his people. Some historians believe that Alexander's new wife played a political role as well as a personal one. Something of a liberal, she wanted Alexander to rebuild his relationship with the Russian people before it was too late. For from 1879, when the People's Will publicly condemned Alexander II to death, the attempts that this small group of revolutionaries made on his life became more frequent. One of the most destructive attempts was made in 1880, when the Winter Palace in St Petersburg was bombed and up to 40 soldiers were killed.

Alexander did indeed try to win over moderate opinion, appointing General Loris-Melikov to head an enquiry into the revolutionaries and the causes of their dissatisfaction. Although Loris-Melikov promised tough action against the revolutionaries he also made some relatively liberal moves, sacking conservative ministers like Tolstoy, the minister of education, for example, and abolishing the Third Section (while retaining its functions in a different department under his control). Censorship was relaxed and prisoners released. Plans were drawn up to call two assemblies (one elected) to approve further reforms. On the very day that Alexander approved these plans, however, he was blown up.

Assessing Alexander II's reign

Alexander II's reign can be assessed in one of two ways: positively or negatively. The positive assessment accentuates the many ways in which Russia was modernised under his leadership. It argues that the lives of most Russians improved during his 26 years as tsar. The negative assessment emphasises the limitations of the reforms that were introduced, the repressive policies that continued to be followed, as well as the growing unrest. The disagreement between the two views is over the motives for, and the impact of, the reforms, for it cannot be denied that Russia was modernised during the reign of Alexander II.

The tsar himself remains something of a shadowy figure. He lacked the stature of other modernisers, such as Peter the Great, and was not as consistent as his father, which makes him harder to understand. His inconsistency, or lack of clear purpose, is reinforced by the way in which he moved from liberalism to reaction and back again. He was bound to face great problems as he tried to modernise – which, during the mid-nineteenth century meant to liberalise – Russia after a period of repression. Indeed, the image of Pandora's box is hard to resist, as is the much-repeated assertion that the most dangerous time for an autocracy is when it starts to reform itself. In this respect Alexander II can be compared to two of his twentieth-century successors as rulers of Russia (by then the Soviet Union), Nikita Khrushchev and Mikhail Gorbachev, both of whom tried to reform the Soviet Union and came to grief in doing so. Although they all deserve some credit for recognising the need for reform, as well as for making it happen, Alexander II somehow suffers by comparison with the other two, for it seems that Alexander regarded the reforms of the 1860s as being necessary solely because of Russia's defeat in the Crimean War and not because they arose from his vision of a new Russia. In this respect he was the agent of change rather than its originator.

For the last words on Alexander II it is best to consider two contemporary views. Tolstoy (the novelist) and Kropotkin took opposite positions. In a letter to the new tsar, Alexander III, which he wrote a few days after the assassination, Tolstoy called Alexander II 'a kind old man who had accomplished much good and had always wished people well'. Kropotkin, by contrast, wrote the following assessment of Alexander II in his memoirs:

> People could not understand how it was possible that a tsar who had done so much for Russia should have met his death at the hands of revolutionists. To me, who had the chance of witnessing the first reactionary steps of Alexander II and his gradual deterioration, who had caught a glimpse of his complex personality, and had seen in him a born autocrat, whose violence was only partially mitigated by education, a man possessed of military gallantry but devoid of the courage of the statesman, a man of strong passions and weak will – it seemed that the tragedy developed with the unavoidable fatality of one of Shakespeare's dramas.

Which verdict is closest to the truth?

How and how far did Russia change between 1825 and 1881?

Russia changed a great deal during the 56 years between 1825 and 1881. The Russia of 1825 was still essentially an eighteenth-century state: agrarian, rural and dominated by the landowners. By 1881, however, Russia had developed features of the more advanced nineteenth-century society of Western Europe: parts of Russia were industrial and urban, and the middle class was growing in both numbers and influence. In this respect the Westerners of the 1840s had won the argument, albeit a generation later. If Russia was to retain its leading position in Europe it had to adopt Western methods. The Slavophile case was not completely redundant, however. Virtually every Russian regarded themselves as being different from, and superior to, the peoples of Western Europe. They believed that the form of the society that they were developing, particularly its collectivist, co-operative nature, was better than the individualistic, competitive societies that could be found in Britain and Germany. In an age of nationalism this sense of a separate, Slav identity strengthened, becoming the basis of a form of Russian nationalism that later made itself strongly felt, both within Russia and outside.

The Russian state did not adopt the Western system wholesale, however. It borrowed some Western administrative features, as well as some economic ones, while refusing to import features of its political systems. Some – just a few – Russians wanted aspects of a Western political system as well, and the impact that these few people made on Russia's history was out of all proportion to their numbers, whether during the 1840s or the 1880s. Although one tsar tried to contain them and the other to tolerate them, if their aim was thereby to control the growth of oppositional ideas neither approach worked.

If the history of nineteenth-century Russia shows how important ideas can be to the historical process, physical force played an equally important role. Russia was a violent society, and at both the start and the end of this period force was used against the tsar. The first attempt failed and brought greater repression; the second attempt succeeded and also brought greater repression. The state used force either against rebels (particularly the Polish ones) and radicals or against other states. Three wars were fought against the Ottoman Empire during these 56 years; several were fought in Asiatic Russia; and one – the Crimean War – was fought against European great powers. The Crimean War highlighted the weaknesses of the Russian state and made the reforms of the 1860s all but inevitable. Alexander II did not have a great deal of choice if Russia was to remain a great power. Although Russia reorganised itself in these years it still remained an autocracy.

Historical sources

The emancipation of the serfs

1 A statement of intent?

It is better to begin abolishing serfdom from above than to wait for it to begin to abolish itself from below.

Source: an extract from a speech given by Alexander II to the leaders of the Moscow gentry on 30 March 1856

2 Putting Alexander's statement into context

I have learned that rumours have spread among you of my intention to abolish serfdom. To refute any groundless gossip on so important a subject I consider it necessary to inform you that I have no intention of doing so immediately. But, of course, and you yourselves realise it, the existing system of serfdom cannot remain unchanged. It is better to abolish serfdom from above than to wait for it to begin to abolish itself from below. I ask you, gentlemen [members of the Muscovite nobility], to think of ways of doing this. Pass on my words to the nobles for consideration.

Source: the full version of the speech made by Alexander II on 30 March 1856 from which extract 1 is taken

3 Alexander berates the Moscow gentry

I find it pleasant, gentlemen, when I can thank the nobility, but I cannot say what I do not believe. I always speak the truth and, unfortunately, I cannot thank you now. You will remember that when I spoke to you in this very room two years ago I told you that sooner or later it would be better to change serfdom and that it would be better for this change to begin at the top than at the bottom. My words were misinterpreted. After that I thought about it for a long time and, having prayed to God, decided to set about the task. As a result of the appeals from the St Petersburg and Lithuanian governors my decrees [to give freedom to serfs in their regions] were issued. I laid down certain principles for you and will not deviate from them in any way.

Source: a speech given to the leaders of the Moscow gentry by Alexander II on 31 August 1858

4 Peasants petition Alexander

The most merciful manifesto of your Imperial Majesty from 19 February 1861 put a limit to the enslavement of the people in blessed Russia. But some former serf-owners – who desire not to improve the peasants' life but to oppress and ruin them – apportion land contrary to the laws, choose the best land for themselves and give the poor peasant the worst and least usable land. To this group must be counted our own, Anna Mikhailovna Raevskavia, during the division of fields and resources which the 600 peasants of the village of Podosinovaka have used since time immemorial.

The community refused to accept so ruinous an allotment.

The police chief informed the governor of [the province] of Voronezh of our refusal.

The provincial governor sent 1,200 soldiers to our village.

The provincial governor – without making any investigation and without interrogating a single person – ordered that the birch rods be brought and the punishment commence. They punished up to 200 men and women. The governor ordered the constable to punish the women; [he] cruelly punished innocent women with 100 blows each and struck them on the cheek with his fist so that [they] were left unconscious.

Merciful emperor, permit us to be called state peasants. Such monarchical mercy, your all-merciful father and liberator, will echo in our hearts with eternal gratitude and our prayers will profoundly rise to the heavenly creator for the health and long life of God's anointed and for all members of your imperial family.

Source: a petition to Alexander II from peasants in Podosinovaka, May 1863

5 The view of a nobly born populist and subsequent anarchist

Where were the uprisings which had been predicted by the champions of slavery? If anything could have provoked revolts it was precisely the perplexing vagueness of the conditions created by the new law. And yet – except in one or two places where there were insurrections and a very few other spots where small disturbances, entirely due to misunderstandings and immediately appeased, took place – Russia remained quiet, more quiet than ever. With their usual good sense, the peasants understood that serfdom was done away with, that 'freedom had come' and they accepted the conditions imposed on them, although these conditions were very heavy.

Source: Peter Kropotkin, *Memoirs of a revolutionist*, written during the 1890s

Historical-source questions

1 Study source 5. Using this source and your own knowledge, explain what is meant by 'Russia remained quiet, more quiet than ever'.
2 Study sources 1, 2 and 3. Compare Alexander's attitudes to emancipation that are found in these sources.
3 How useful is source 4 as an account of the emancipation of the serfs?
4 Study all of the sources. Using your own knowledge and these sources, consider how far 'freedom had come' (source 5) as a result of the emancipation of the serfs.

Summary questions

1 How autocratic was Nicholas I?
2 Compare the importance of at least *three* reasons for Alexander II's decision in 1861 to emancipate the serfs.
3 Identify and explain the consequences of any *three* features of the reign of Alexander II for the development of oppositional thought at the time.

6 Changing the face of Europe: Germany, 1862–90

Focus questions

- What different forms of German unification were being considered in 1862?
- What were the main forces working for and against the unification of Germany in 1862?
- Who or what was responsible for the creation of the German Empire in 1871?
- What problems did Germany face between 1871 and 1890, both at home and abroad, and how successfully were they overcome?
- How can Bismarck's leadership of Prussia and Germany be assessed?

Significant dates

1862	Bismarck appointed minister-president of Prussia (and chancellor of Germany in 1871)
1864	Prussia and Austria go to war against Denmark
1866	Austro-Prussian War
1867	North German Confederation established
1870–71	Franco-Prussian War
1871	German Empire established; Treaty of Frankfurt
1873–78	*Kulturkampf* against the Centre Party and the Roman Catholic Church
1878–90	Anti-socialist law passed and renewed
1878	Introduction of tariffs on some industrial and agricultural goods; Near Eastern Crisis; Congress of Berlin
1883–89	Social insurance policies introduced (sickness, 1883; accident, 1884, old age and invalidity, 1889)
1888	The 'Year of the Three Emperors': William I, Frederick III and William II
1890	Bismarck resigns as chancellor

Overview

The emergence of a united and powerful Germany in the centre of Europe was the single greatest change in the European states' system during the nineteenth century. The consequences of this change would be felt across Europe for many years to come: indeed, some historians believe there was a direct link between the German Empire (1871–1918) and Hitler's Third Reich (1933–45). How Germany's unification occurred, how it was governed and how it developed, as well as its place within the new Europe, are all issues of great significance, both for contemporaries and for historians.

The development of this powerful German force was associated with one man in particular: Otto von Bismarck, the Prussian prime minister and later the German chancellor. If an era can be identified with one person, then the Europe of the 1860s, 1870s and 1880s would have to be called the 'Age of Bismarck'. In the 1860s Bismarck led Prussia and worked towards the unification of Germany. For the next two decades he dominated both Germany and Europe. Historians usually regard the year in which Bismarck left office, 1890, as the end of an era in European history. His approach to public affairs, which is usually summed up in one word, ***Realpolitik***, came to influence a whole generation of politicians.

Bismarck's historical importance derives from his position in government, initially as Prussia's political leader. However, neither the later pre-eminence of Bismarck nor the predominance of Germany could have been predicted when he was appointed minister-president of Prussia in 1862. In European terms, Prussia was not one of the great powers. In 1850, for example, it had meekly allowed **Austria** to reassert Habsburg power over the German states. Nor did it take part in either the Crimean War or the campaigns in Italy. Prussia also lacked the cultural traditions of France, Austria and even Russia (although the same was not true of the wider Germany). Yet it was Prussia that would lead the process of unifying Germany and would complete the process within nine years of Bismarck's coming to power. Once unified, Germany continued to develop at such a rate that by 1890 its economy was close to equalling that of the hitherto unchallenged industrial power, Britain. The consequences of that economic parity would become manifest during the early years of the next century.

So how was the position of Prussia, and subsequently of Germany, transformed so radically and so quickly? And what problems did this transformation create for Germany? Trying to answer these, as well as related questions, provides the basis for this chapter. The rise of Germany may seem to have been inevitable in hindsight. It was not. It was based on the actions, thoughts and decisions of many tens of thousands of people, only one of whom was

---

The German word ***Realpolitik*** literally means 'realistic politics' – that is, the basing of decisions on the realities of power rather than on moral or ideological considerations. It is therefore often regarded as being amoral and cynical.

The more accurate title for **Austria** during this period is the Habsburg Empire (see also marginal note, p. 26). The Habsburgs were a German royal dynasty. Until the abolition of the Holy Roman Empire in 1806 the Habsburgs had provided the Holy Roman emperor and thus the leader of the 1,000 German states. Austria regained this leadership in 1815 when the German *Bund* was established. By then there were just 39 German states and most of the Habsburg lands were outside the *Bund*. It was a confusing situation, not least for the Habsburgs themselves.

Bismarck. However powerful he may have been, he could not have transformed Germany by himself.

What different forms of German unification were being considered in 1862?

German national identity was stronger than that of the Italians (see Chapter 3). There was already a German language, for example, while German nationalism can be said to have had an institutional expression in the form of the **Holy Roman Empire**. There was also an identifiable German culture, of which the dramatists and poets Goethe and Schiller, who both had an enduring European reputation, were the finest representatives during the late eighteenth and early nineteenth centuries. Before 1800 German nationhood was more cultural than political; it was only Napoleon's conquests that provoked some feeling of national unity in the desire to defeat the French enemy. The military efforts of the leading German states, Austria and Prussia, were not very effective against France, but in 1815, in Vienna, the allies replaced the Holy Roman Empire with a German confederation, or *Bund*. The *Bund* represented a form of German unity and was therefore an organisation that could provide a focus for the hopes of German nationalists.

The *Bund* had been Austria's idea. It included the 39 German states that had been created by the merger of many small princedoms over previous decades. These states now agreed to work together on matters of common interest, mainly security matters. The *Bund* had an assembly, or diet, consisting of representatives of those states, which met in Frankfurt. It had no government of its own, however, and the *Bund*'s decisions normally required the agreement of all of the states. Austria was the leader of the *Bund* and Prussia her junior partner in what was sometimes called a 'dual leadership'. The relationship between these two leaders would become a crucial factor in the unification of Germany.

The people who wanted a united German state as the political expression of German national identity were not themselves united. Although they agreed on their desire to create a single state which would include most, if not all, Germans (and few, if any, non-Germans), they disagreed over both how to achieve a united Germany and the form that the new Germany would take. During the early nineteenth century most nationalists were also liberals and democrats. They initially thought that unification would result from the will of the German people being freely and peacefully expressed in elections. The revolutions of 1848 to 1849 showed that view to be wrong. Although a national parliament (called the Frankfurt Parliament, after the city in which it was based) had been elected and had agreed a constitution for Germany, the

> The **Holy Roman Empire** was formed during the ninth century as a loose grouping of German and Italian states. Led by the Austrian Habsburgs, by the eighteenth century it roughly approximated to the German-speaking part of Europe and contained over 1,000 states, most of them very small. It was abolished by Napoleon in 1806.

states closed the parliament down once they had dealt with the political problems within their own borders. No state would be likely to agree to hand over its power to a new state that was based on the sovereignty of the people. The problems of the nationalists had been made worse in 1848–49 because they could not agree on the shape of a new Germany.

A closer examination of the *Bund* highlights these, as well as related, problems. Many non-Germans – for example, Italians and Czechs – lived within the *Bund*'s borders, while many Germans lived outside them. To complicate matters further, most of the lands that were governed by Austria that together comprised the Habsburg Empire were outside the frontiers of the *Bund*. Among the more significant non-German peoples who lived in these lands were the Magyars, Slavs and Italians.

There were three possible ways of overcoming these problems, although none of them was perfect:
- to unify Germany by including only the Austrian part of the Habsburg Empire;
- to unify Germany by including all of the Habsburg Empire;
- to unify Germany by excluding the Austrian part of the Habsburg Empire.

The 1815 *Bund* was a limited version of the first option. It was the main form of the *Grossdeutschland* (greater Germany) solution that was advocated by many nationalists. In order to satisfy their demands, however, a united Germany would have required two radical reforms of the *Bund*: an elected diet and a central German government. For Austria to have accepted this model would have required the Habsburgs to agree to their empire becoming two even more unequal halves. Redefining Austria in such a way was suggested only once by the Austrians.

The second model, a united Germany incorporating the whole of the Habsburg Empire, was a second version of the *Grossdeutschland* option. It was never considered seriously, however, at least in its political shape, and Austria suggested it briefly on only two occasions, without ever specifying the form that it would take. Because the creation of an economic union covering central and south-eastern Europe was a little more feasible, during the 1850s and early 1860s Austria made a more sustained attempt to establish such a union. However, the economic differences between the Habsburg Empire and the rest of Germany proved too great to be bridged.

Both versions of the *Grossdeutschland* concept proved too radical for most politicians, yet many German nationalists continued to hope that a greater Germany could be created. They had been disappointed between 1848 and 1849 and would be disappointed again between 1867 and 1871; it was not until 1938–45 that their wishes would be fulfilled.

The third possibility, known as *Kleindeutschland* (smaller Germany), already existed in an economic form in 1862: the *Zollverein* (customs union), which had been established in 1834 at Prussia's instigation. Because the Prussian lands in northern Germany were separated by a number of smaller states, and customs barriers were common, trade between the different parts of Prussia was difficult. Under pressure from Prussia, in 1834 18 central and southern German states consequently joined together in a limited form of economic union, with Prussia acting as the *Zollverein*'s leader. Austria was not a member of the *Zollverein*; the Austrian leader at the time, Metternich, had tried to stop the union from being formed. Most of his successors took the opposite line and tried to join the union. The issue of Austrian membership of the *Zollverein* became an additional complication during the 1850s and 1860s. In practice, the political form of *Kleindeutschland* would involve a German government led by Prussia. This does not mean that Prussia formed the *Zollverein* in 1834 with this goal in mind, however. The motives of the Prussian government of the time were financial and economic: the economic union of states would lead to an increase in trade and thus to increased tax revenue. Political benefits did not enter its calculations, especially in relation to a united German nation state.

> Explain the main differences between the *Zollverein* and the *Bund*.

Many people, including those who saw the eventual political benefits of the *Zollverein*, were uneasy at the thought of a Prussian-led Germany. Centred on the states of Prussia and Brandenburg in northern Germany, Prussia was an authoritarian state that had expanded rapidly during the eighteenth century, mainly as a result of its military conquests under **Frederick the Great**. Prussia had been given further lands in western Germany in 1815 to enable it to act as a barrier against French expansionism. The geographical separation of Prussia's lands in the east and west was the reason for establishing the *Zollverein*. Prussia's new lands around the Rhine also gave it large coalfields, which, although they were of little benefit at the time, would prove a great asset once Germany had started to industrialise itself.

> **Frederick the Great** (1712–86) was king of Prussia from 1740 to 1786. He expanded and consolidated Prussia, by force and diplomacy, and provided it with an enlightened government. He made Prussia a European great power and was something of a hero of Bismarck's.

There were other models of German unity, too. One possibility – which has largely been forgotten today, although it was much discussed at the time – was a united Germany jointly led by Austria and Prussia in a kind of dualist system. In one sense the *Bund* had a similar dual leadership, but the relationship between Austria and Prussia was a very unequal one.

There were thus at least three or four models to choose from and some tough decisions would therefore be required if Germany was to be united. The history of Germany from 1849 to 1862 gives some idea of the size of the obstacles involved.

In 1849 the Frankfurt Parliament had reluctantly accepted the idea of a *Kleindeutschland* and had offered the leadership of a united Germany to King

Changing the face of Europe: Germany, 1862–90

Frederick William IV of Prussia. Frederick William turned it down, however, commenting that a crown offered by an elected national assembly would be 'a diadem moulded out of the dirt and dregs of revolution, disloyalty and treason'. The chances of creating a *Kleindeutschland* now seemed very remote. Yet Austria was preoccupied with defeating the revolution in Hungary, which gave Frederick William the opportunity of expanding Prussian interests in Germany. This he did by supporting the introduction of the Erfurt Union, a version of the Frankfurt Parliament modified to ensure that states' interests predominated. Some 25 of the smaller states were involved, although not Austria. Once the Hungarian revolution had been crushed, Austria turned its attention to Germany and objected to the Erfurt Union. A German civil war seemed imminent until Prussia backed down, accepted Austrian terms and signed the Olmütz Convention in October 1850. The Erfurt Union was dissolved, the German *Bund* restored. Austria had reasserted its leadership of Germany and had put Prussia in its place. Many Prussians felt humiliated. Although the civil war was delayed for 16 years, in 1866 they got their revenge.

Although various forms of unity were debated during the 1840s and 1850s, only two existed in any practical form: the *Bund* and the *Zollverein*, neither of which satisfied the nationalists. Following the failures of 1849 to 1850, the goal of German unification seemed more distant than ever to supporters and opponents. The former were losing hope and the latter were gaining in confidence. Both camps would be surprised by the events of the 1860s.

> Distinguish between the different proposals for a united Germany put forward in the 1850s.

What were the main forces working for and against German unification in 1862?

Both the supporters and opponents of German unification could take some comfort from the situation in 1862.

Strengthening the cause of unity

The cause of unity was strengthened by the following factors.

The unification of Italy

Following Austria's defeat by France, a united Italy had been formed in 1861. Not only was Italian nationalism not as strong as its German counterpart, but Italy had had no national institutions like the *Bund* and the *Zollverein*. Although some German nationalists regretted Prussia's failure to support Austria in the 1859 war, many took heart from Italy's success in the face of such odds.

The rise of Napoleon III

Napoleon III's rise helped the cause of a united Germany in two contradictory ways. Firstly, France's success in Italy had given credence to Napoleon's claim to be the leader of Europe. Many Germans regarded him as another Napoleon I and feared that his next move would be against them, probably on the Rhine. Their fear therefore made them more willing to consider uniting against the Napoleonic danger. Secondly, Napoleon wanted to change the 1815 settlement in ways that were based on nationalism. His policies in Italy in 1859 and 1860 were evidence of this commitment. Napoleon III was not unsympathetic to the claims of German nationalism, as long as those claims did not weaken France.

Growing popular support for national unity

Various nationalist groups were formed during the late 1850s and early 1860s. Many members of the middle classes had turned away from politics following the setbacks of 1849–50 to concentrate on business. By the late 1850s, however, many were rediscovering their appetite for national politics. Nationalist groups could either be political in focus, as was the *Nationalverein* (National Society), which was modelled on the Italian National Society, or they could be cultural, as were such societies as the sharpshooters' league or the singers' league. Whatever their differences, they all emphasised their common German identity.

The development of the *Zollverein*

The *Zollverein* was renewed in 1841 and 1854, by which time it had expanded to cover a population of over 23 million people. This limited form of economic union brought material benefits to its member states, as well as being a successful form of co-operation within a German framework. It provided a model and a means for closer co-operation in the future, perhaps in areas other than trade relations. Whether that happened would depend on its member states, and on Prussia in particular.

For *Kleindeutschland*: the policies of the Prussian government

Since the disappointments of 1848–49 the Prussian government had acted in ways which had won it support from the liberal-national middle classes. In 1850 King Frederick William IV accepted a constitution which, although it was not very democratic, was at least seen as a step in the right direction. Prussia now had an elected assembly, even if the electorate was divided into three groups based on social status. When Frederick William's son, William, became regent in 1858 (and King William I three years later) he appointed liberal ministers, prompting talk of a new era. In 1861 Prussia signed a free-trade treaty with France, which both strengthened the economic basis of the *Zollverein* and widened the divide between the *Zollverein* and Austria.

to became the political leader of northern Germany, either with Austrian consent (in a more equal form of dualism) or without it (a less complete *Kleindeutschland*). William I was very uneasy about challenging Austria, a fellow German power. Having eventually persuaded the king that his goals were right, Bismarck then proceeded to put continuous pressure on Austria. Because there was always a danger that the other great powers might support Austria, he worked to gain their support, or at least their neutrality.

In August 1865, by the Treaty of Gastein, Bismarck eventually succeeded in persuading Austria to accept the division of Schleswig-Holstein, Austria receiving Holstein and Prussia Schleswig. The dualist system had apparently survived, although in practice it simply gave Bismarck an excuse to complain about Austrian rule in Holstein and thus to threaten the end of the Austro-Prussian partnership. In February 1866 the Prussian government agreed to prepare for a war with Austria, signing a treaty with the new state of Italy in April that agreed that Italy would go to war against Austria if Prussia attacked Austria within the next three months. Austria was thus faced with the probability of a two-front war within twelve weeks. Because it took Austria eight weeks to mobilise her armies, and Prussia only four, Austria had to move first. Austria's forces were accordingly mobilised in April 1866 and Prussia's in May. The war began in June and by the end of August the map of Germany had been redrawn.

The course of the war
The war that changed the face of Germany is known by several names. Calling it the Seven Weeks' War emphasises its brevity, although its more familiar label is the Austro-Prussian War. The latter title is in one sense accurate, in that the war was essentially a struggle for power between Austria and Prussia, but it is also misleading because no fewer than eight other states participated in the war: Italy fought against Austria. Seven German states fought for the Habsburgs. Bismarck had failed to win over any of the medium-sized states within the *Bund*. Some historians therefore call the conflict the German Civil War. Whatever its label, the war was Bismarck's greatest gamble of all.

It is important to realise that most contemporary commentators did not expect Prussia to win. Austria had the greater number of troops, as well as the most recently battle-hardened. By contrast, Prussia had not fought a campaign since the Napoleonic wars and had had problems mobilising its forces in 1859. These expectations made the speed and the scale of the Prussian victory even more surprising.

There was just one major battle, which goes under two names: Sadowa or Königgrätz, towns in Bohemia that was then part of Austria. Involving some 450,000 men, Königgrätz was the largest battle of the nineteenth century, yet it receives little coverage in most textbooks, perhaps because the Prussian victory is seen as having been inevitable. It was not. The battle was a close-run thing and the Austrian army was not annihilated. There were three main reasons why the Prussians won: the military leadership of the Prussian leader **Helmut von Moltke** (as compared with Austria's Ludwig Benedek); the effective use of new technology, especially railways and the telegraph; and the use of the breach-loading rifle by the Prussian infantry (instead of Austria's muzzle-loaders). Winning a battle is not the same as winning a war, because for one side to win a war the political leaders of both sides have to accept it. Bismarck was willing to end the war against Austria because Austria was prepared to give him all that he wanted. He was also afraid that France would intervene in the war. Austria gave in because it realised its leadership of Germany had ended and could not be restored.

The outcome of the war

The consequences of the short Austro-Prussian War were dramatic. Austria lost all of its power in Germany (and also in Italy) by the **Treaty of Prague** in August 1866 and concentrated thereafter on maintaining its multi-national empire in south-eastern Europe. In Germany, a form of political *Kleindeutschland* emerged alongside the *Zollverein*. A North German Confederation was quickly established and the *Zollverein* reformed. In Prussia, Bismarck's position was immeasurably strengthened as a result of Prussia's victory and he used his power not to attack the liberals in the *Landtag* further, but to ask deputies to pass an indemnity bill approving the government's unconstitutional expenditure of the past four years. When the majority of them did so the constitutional struggle was over. Most of the liberals became Bismarck's allies for the next 12 years, forming an unorthodox partnership that had considerable significance for the Second Empire. Bismarck's biggest gamble had paid off.

Bismarck's apparent restraint in 1866 has been much commented on. At the time some Prussians, William I among them, wanted to continue the war against Austria. They also believed that the Treaty of Prague had treated Austria too generously. Many found Bismarck's conciliatory approach to his previously bitter enemies in the *Landtag* impossible to understand. But Bismarck was aware of the political realities, both at home and abroad, and knew that he might need the support of both Austria and the liberals before long. For Prussia's success had created new problems. Within Germany, Bismarck would need all the Prussian support that he could muster in establishing the new North German Confederation. Within Europe, he did not want to antagonise Austria and thereby drive it into an alliance with other great powers which had been alarmed by Prussia's success in 1866.

Helmut von Moltke (1800–91) was the head of the Prussian general staff from 1857 to 1888. His key achievements were the development of the Prussian general staff, which resulted in the effective co-ordination of the Prussian armies; his appreciation of the benefits of new technology, especially the railways; and his development of a new military strategy that required armies to 'march separately, fight jointly'.

By the terms of the **Treaty of Prague**: (a) the 1815 *Bund* was abolished; (b) a Prussian-led North German Confederation was established; (c) the southern German states became a confederation with links with the North German Confederation; (d) Austria lost control of Venetia in Italy; and (e) Austria had to pay an indemnity to Prussia for the costs of the war. Following the Treaty of Prague Prussia annexed four-and-a-half north German states and Schleswig-Holstein, as well as signing military alliances with the four southern German states.

Identify and explain three reasons why Bismarck agreed to a 'moderate' peace settlement with Austria in 1866.

Hohenzollern candidature

In 1868 Spain was looking for a new king and therefore approached a junior Catholic member of the Prussian royal family, Leopold of Hohenzollern. Leopold accepted the throne on condition that Prussia supported him. Bismarck secretly gave that support (but later denied that he had done so). An error made by a telegraph clerk in Madrid meant that news of his candidature leaked out before Leopold was confirmed as king. France suspected that it was a Prussian attempt to encircle France by placing a Prussian on the throne of Spain.

Ems telegram

France demanded the withdrawal of Leopold of Hohenzollern's candidature to the throne of Spain, to which Prussia agreed. The French ambassador then demanded that William I guarantee that Prussia would never support the Hohenzollern candidature. William, who was at Ems, sent a telegram to Bismarck giving an account of his meeting with the ambassador. Bismarck altered the account to give the impression that William had snubbed the French ambassador and then published the telegram. For France, this was the final provocation, the last in a long line of insults.

Napoleon III of France, for example, who was especially aggrieved by Prussia's gains, was demanding territorial compensation for France, mainly because the French public wanted to counter the emergence of a more united, more powerful, German state to the east. Bismarck both encouraged and discouraged Napoleon during the Luxembourg crisis. Napoleon proposed that France should receive Luxembourg as compensation for Prussia's territorial gains of 1866. Bismarck privately supported the idea before making the matter public. But when in 1867 German nationalists objected to the proposal, Bismarck opposed it, causing French pride to receive another blow. Was Bismarck aiming to provoke France into war?

The Franco-Prussian War, 1870–71
Origins

If the causes of the Austro-Prussian War have provoked little debate among historians, those of the Franco-Prussian War have generated an immense amount of argument. This is rather surprising, given that the Franco-Prussian War seemed to have been inevitable: after 1866 many thought that it would only be a matter of time before France and the newly reorganised Germany fought each other. It was not inevitable that the war should have broken out when it did, however, and its outbreak in the summer of 1870 was the result of the words and actions of various individuals.

Since 1870 opinion about who was responsible for the war has shifted from one side to the other. At the time France was regarded as being largely to blame; since the 1890s, however, when he published his memoirs, many have held Bismarck responsible. So how far did Bismarck engineer the outbreak of war and, if he did, what were his motives for doing so?

The explanation that is favoured by those who blame Bismarck for the outbreak of the Franco-Prussian War is that he pushed France into declaring war in order to complete the unification of Germany. Fighting France would enable him to absorb the four southern German states into a new German empire. This interpretation regards Bismarck as being the manipulator of events in furtherance of his long-term plans. Supporters of this theory quote the **Hohenzollern candidature** and the **Ems telegram** as evidence for their case.

One revisionist view is that Bismarck did not want a war with France – at least not until the very last minute – and that he did not want to complete the unification of Germany. Although he may have wanted to put diplomatic pressure on France – hence the episode of the Hohenzollern candidature – there were no national interests at stake that required a war. This school of thought regards the Ems telegram as Bismarck's immediate response to the diplomatic defeat that Prussia had suffered when William I was forced to withdraw the Hohenzollern candidature. Although he was prepared to risk a war by then, the argument goes, his aim was to recover Prussia's lost prestige rather than to unify Germany. This view suggests that Bismarck did indeed manipulate events, but this time as much for personal reasons as for political. Indeed, with regard to unification, Bismarck often doubted whether southern Germany should be absorbed. The peoples of the four southern states were predominantly Roman Catholic and had little in common with the Protestant peoples of the northern German states. During the late 1860s they showed little enthusiasm for joining the new Germany. To include them in a German Empire in 1870 would create greater problems for Bismarck – which it did, even if they were largely self-inflicted.

The converse of this view regards France as having been more responsible for starting the war. The French press and people were vigorous in their demands that France should stand up to Prussia. Napoleon III, politically weak and physically ill, could not afford to back down, especially since he had failed to gain any compensation for France after the Austro-Prussian War of 1866. Not only did the honour of France demand war, but France lacked the strength of will and self-confidence to ignore Bismarck's provocations. (See also Chapter 4.)

Events

The Franco-Prussian War in 1870 was similar to the Austro-Prussian War of 1866 in that many 'experts' did not expect Prussia to win. Not only was France the greatest of the European great powers, but it also had the latest military equipment: a breech-loading rifle superior to Prussia's and an early form of machine gun. France also expected the support of the great powers. However, 1870 was different from 1866 in that most Germans supported Bismarck, including the southern German states, which joined the war on Prussia's side.

When Napoleon III had declared war on Prussia in July 1870, it had been anticipated that France would invade Germany. The war itself began when Prussia invaded France. Within months of the Prussian invasion one of the French armies was besieged at Metz and the other had been defeated at Sedan. Prussia won because its forces were more mobile than the French, which were soon surrounded, its artillery fire was more accurate and because the recently reorganised French army was at sixes and sevens. Napoleon III had become a prisoner of Germany and the Second Empire was no more. The key Prussian victory, at the Battle of Sedan, was just as sudden as that of the Battle of Königgrätz in 1866, but was more of a clear-cut triumph for Prussia.

The war dragged on for another four months, however, for two reasons. Firstly, following the fall of Napoleon III the French refused to submit: they replaced the Second Empire with the Third Republic. The newly formed French Government of National Defence raised three new armies. Even when

William I of Prussia is proclaimed German emperor at Versailles on 18 January 1871. Bismarck takes centre stage with von Moltke to his immediate left. In reality, most of the leading figures were arguing until the very last moment about the exact phrasing of William I's new title.

Prussian forces besieged Paris from September 1870 to January 1871 the French would not surrender. It was only when the Prussian artillery shelled Paris that they conceded defeat. Secondly, the Prussian demands were simply too great for the new French government to accept.

The Franco-Prussian War was different in nature from the Austro-Prussian War. 1866 had been a fight between German governments for limited, political aims, while 1870–71 was a conflict between two nation states for greater goals of national unity and identity. This was the first war in which civilians (in Paris) became the direct target of military fire. The modern era had begun.

Outcomes

There were three main consequences of the Franco-Prussian War. Firstly, Prussia imposed a far harsher peace on France in 1871 than it had on Austria in 1866. This was because there was no possibility of the remaining great powers, Russia and Britain, intervening, which enabled those in the Prussian government who wanted to punish France, such as Moltke, to have more influence. This hard line also matched the increasingly nationalistic mood of the German public. Although Bismarck opposed some of the more extreme demands that would be made on France by the **Treaty of Frankfurt** in 1871, he was unsuccessful. He was not all powerful.

Secondly, Prussia announced the formation of a new German empire. Northern and southern Germany were now united under the leadership of the new German emperor, William I, the Prussian king. A form of political

By the terms of the **Treaty of Frankfurt**, 1871, (a) Germany gained Alsace and the northern third of Lorraine; (b) France had to pay an indemnity of 5,000 million francs; (c) German forces were to occupy Paris until the indemnity had been paid; and (d) the German army was to march through Paris.

Kleindeutschland had been accomplished and the German people (apart from those in Austria) were now united within a German empire. So were some non-Germans, too, some of them for the first time. The Danes of Schleswig and the French of Alsace-Lorraine felt no identity with their new state.

Thirdly, a new European balance of power had been created: Germany had replaced France as the leading continental power. Germany's effective political and military leadership, as well as its increasing industrial wealth, made the other European powers wary of this rising nation.

The age of the nation state

The map of central Europe had been redrawn in 1871. Because the formation of a German nation state occurred soon after that of an Italian nation state the history of Europe seemed to be entering a new stage. Before 1871 central

> Identify and explain three reasons why Bismarck imposed a harsh peace settlement on France in 1871.
>
> Summarise the five wars in which either Prussia or Austria took part between 1854 and 1871 in terms of their consequences for the development of Germany.

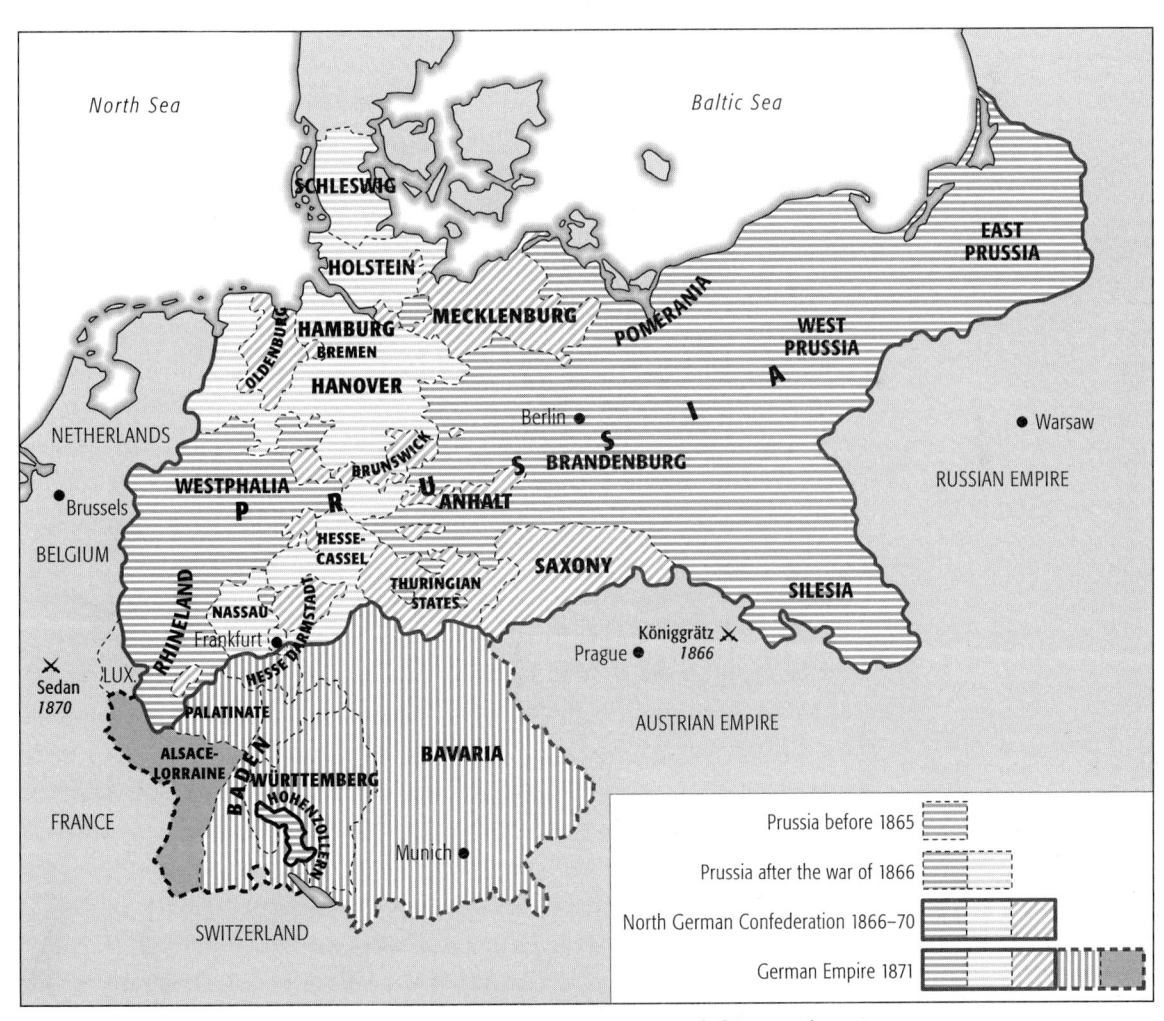

Germany in the nineteenth century. This map shows the main territorial changes of 1866–71. The *Bund* of 1815–66 also included a large part of the Austrian Empire.

Changing the face of Europe: Germany, 1862–90

Europe had consisted of small states, the basis of which had often been a matter of chance; kings and dukes had ruled over people whose primary identity was as their rulers' subjects. These small states had now been absorbed into larger states, the basis of which was national identity. Nationalism had proved a more powerful force than liberalism, one of its fellow ideologies of the early nineteenth century. It had popular appeal. It also appealed to governments as an instrument with which they could isolate a force for change that they feared – more democracy. Bismarck had shown the way during the 1860s. The age of the nation state had begun.

What problems did Germany face between 1871 and 1890, both at home and abroad, and how successfully were they overcome?

Bismarck became the first political leader of the German Empire in 1871. As Prussia's minister-president he had been a destroyer (or a creator, depending on your point of view), but as Germany's chancellor he became a defender. As Prussia's minister-president he had been determined to challenge the status quo in Germany and to build a new order to the benefit of Prussia. Having done this, in 1871 he sought no further territory and fought no further wars. Instead, he wanted to maintain the new order and to consolidate the new German state, which faced much domestic opposition and great suspicion from the rest of Europe. That Bismarck remained Germany's chancellor for 19 years was both a blessing and a curse. On the one hand he provided continuity and stability, but on the other his predominance meant that the politics of the new Germany in some ways reflected his own restless, suspicious nature. These new politics posed greater problems for Germany once Bismarck had gone.

The 19 years of Bismarck's chancellorship are usually divided into two periods: 1871 to 1879 and 1879 to 1890. At home, the contrast between the two periods was between the broadly liberal policies that were pursued between 1871 and 1879, especially in economic and social affairs, and the adoption of an approach that involved greater state intervention between 1879 and 1890. Over the same two periods Bismarck's style of diplomacy similarly changed from a cautious, flexible policy to the creation of a more complex and rigid alliance system within Europe. During the 1880s, for reasons which still remain obscure, Germany under Bismarck also acquired various colonies in Africa.

The whole period from 1871 to 1890 saw the continuing development of Germany as an industrial economy that was both urbanised and class-based. This mass society soon took *Kleindeutschland* for granted and expected greater rewards for Germany's growing ascendancy over continental Europe.

Bismarck could not ignore the demands of the new middle and working classes and therefore altered his policies to meet those demands as far as he could. At the start, in 1871, his immediate challenge was to establish the political structure of the new Germany.

The new state

New states need new rules to live by. Just as the USA's founding fathers had debated long and hard before deciding on the American constitution in 1787, so Bismarck thought long and hard before deciding on northern Germany's constitution in 1867. He saw little reason to change the constitution when the North German Confederation became the German Empire. Bismarck created a very complex system of government. Fritz Stern, in his book *Gold and iron* (1977), called the 1867 constitution 'a masterpiece of intricate obscurity'. The system put the Prussian state at the centre of government while giving most political groups some limited say. Although he tried to reconcile key political interests to the new Germany, if he thought that this could not be done he attacked them. He used this tactic against two important bodies: the Catholic Church, which remained a significant force in various parts of Germany, and the Social Democratic Party, which represented the new working class.

Bismarck hoped to accomplish the difficult task of achieving stability by balancing the various political interests within Germany as follows:

- Monarchy: hereditary rulers of smaller states kept their positions. As well as remaining king of Prussia, William I became emperor of Germany. This meant that he controlled foreign policy and the army, appointed the chancellor and could dissolve the *Reichstag*.
- Democracy: the new *Reichstag* was a national assembly that was elected by universal male suffrage, a radical idea at the time. Its power over the government was limited and it only approved federal policy, of which decisions relating to the army were the most important. Even then, the army budget was approved for seven years at a time. The *Reichstag* had no control over government ministers. Its deputies were unpaid.
- Nationalism: the new German empire marked the achievement of *Kleindeutschland* and gave most Germans a new feeling of self-respect. The democratic election of the *Reichstag* also meant that the German people (except for those in Austria) were represented by a national body.
- The states: the 25 German states kept their own governments and parliaments. In addition, state governments chose delegates for the *Bundesrat*, a national council which provided federal government and, with the *Reichstag*, made federal law. The delegates were paid state officials who were instructed by their governments as to how they should vote. The *Bundesrat* had the final say on the new constitution.

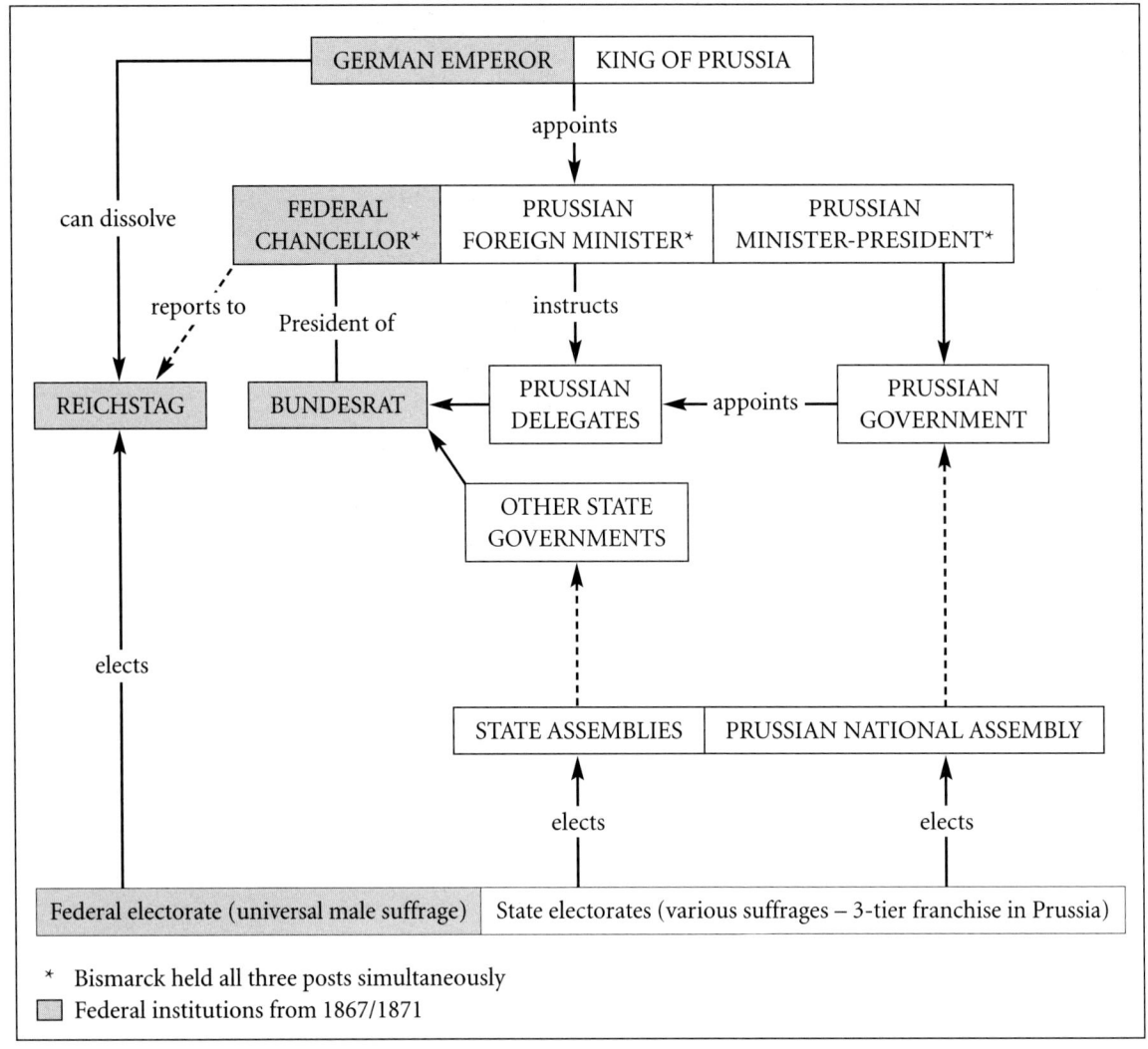

```
                    ┌─────────────────┬──────────────┐
                    │ GERMAN EMPEROR  │ KING OF PRUSSIA │
                    └─────────────────┴──────────────┘
                             │ appoints
              ┌──────────────┼──────────────────────┐
              │      ┌───────────────┬──────────────┴──┬─────────────────┐
              │      │   FEDERAL     │    PRUSSIAN     │    PRUSSIAN     │
 can dissolve │      │  CHANCELLOR*  │ FOREIGN MINISTER*│ MINISTER-PRESIDENT* │
              │      └───────┬───────┴──────┬──────────┴─────────┬───────┘
              │        reports to  President of   instructs      │
              │              │       │              │            │
              ▼              │       ▼              ▼            ▼
        ┌──────────┐         │  ┌──────────┐  ┌──────────┐  ┌──────────┐
        │ REICHSTAG│         └─▶│ BUNDESRAT│◀─│ PRUSSIAN │◀─│ PRUSSIAN │
        └──────────┘            └──────────┘  │DELEGATES │ appoints │GOVERNMENT│
                                              └──────────┘  └──────────┘
                                                    ▲             ▲
                                              ┌──────────┐        │
                                              │OTHER STATE│       │
                                              │GOVERNMENTS│       │
                                              └──────────┘        │
                                                    ▲             │
                                              ┌──────────┬─────────────────┐
                                              │  STATE   │ PRUSSIAN NATIONAL│
                                              │ASSEMBLIES│    ASSEMBLY      │
                                              └──────────┴─────────────────┘
                    ▲                               ▲             ▲
                 elects                          elects         elects
        ┌─────────────────────────┬───────────────────────────────────────┐
        │Federal electorate       │State electorates (various suffrages – │
        │(universal male suffrage)│ 3-tier franchise in Prussia)          │
        └─────────────────────────┴───────────────────────────────────────┘
```

* Bismarck held all three posts simultaneously
▓ Federal institutions from 1867/1871

The constitution of the German Second Empire. The arrows show how authority is given by one body to another, the direction of the arrows symbolising the direction of the transfer. A dotted line means a *less* formal relationship between two bodies, one influencing the other without having formal authority over the other.

- Prussia: Prussia provided most of the federal government and dominated the *Bundesrat*. It also kept its 1850 system of government, which was both more liberal (because it had a constitution) and less democratic (because it had a three-tier voting system for the Prussian assembly rather than universal suffrage) than that of many German states.
- Bismarck: as well as remaining Prussia's minister-president, Bismarck became the imperial chancellor, which was the only federal office to be created. There was no federal cabinet. Bismarck was accountable to the emperor alone and not the *Reichstag*. (See the diagram above for the relationship between the different parts of this complex system.)

Explain the roles in the new Germany of
(a) the *Reichstag* and
(b) the *Bundesrat*.

Bismarck and some of the deputies to the new Reichstag in 1871, Bismarck in military uniform, the deputies in civilian dress. Compare this picture with that in the photograph on page 147, taken seven years previously.

Rather than the German people it was the old states that were at the heart of the new empire. David Blackbourn, in his book *The Fontana history of Germany, 1780–1918* (1997), compares the German Empire with today's European Union (EU): 'The federal empire resembled more closely the present-day European Union than it did contemporary federal states such as the USA and Switzerland.' Indeed, there are both similarities and differences between the German Empire and the EU. One parallel that can be drawn between them is the limited nature of their democracies. Although Bismarck had introduced an element of democracy into the new empire by basing the election of the *Reichstag* on universal male suffrage, the *Reichstag* only had a very indirect influence over the government. In practice, however, Bismarck worked with the leading political groups in the *Reichstag*, believing that he could not afford to ignore them because they were forming themselves into organised and disciplined political parties that attracted popular support.

Unlike the EU, however, the German Empire was dominated by one power, Prussia. Had it not been for the victories of the Prussian armies Germany would not have been unified in 1871. There was also another, more basic, reason why Prussia dominated Germany: it contained around two in every three citizens of the new state. The main question was whether such a uniquely lopsided system of government would effectively provide for the many groups that had been brought together, sometimes against their will, within the new German Empire. Bismarck's problems were just beginning, both at home and abroad.

Bismarck's domestic policy, 1871–90

The era of national liberalism, 1871–78: the *Kulturkampf*

Bismarck worked with the National Liberals for the first eight years following the formation of the German Empire. They had been his main allies since 1866, when they had supported the passage of the Indemnity Bill through the Prussian *Landtag*. In 1871 they were the leading group in the *Reichstag*, holding 125 of the 397 seats. They supported the reforms that were needed to establish the new German state, like the creation of a national bank and currency (the mark was introduced in 1875). As well as supporting such unexciting, but important, reforms, the National Liberals also backed Bismarck in his most dramatic initiative of the 1870s: the so-called *Kulturkampf*.

Although the *Kulturkampf* (struggle of cultures) may appear to have been a throwback to the sixteenth-century struggle between the Reformation and Counter-Reformation, it demonstrates that religious attitudes and divisions were still significant during the nineteenth century. The conflict was between the German state and various Catholic organisations, including the Catholic Church itself. It was a kind of cultural Cold War. Why did it occur?

> **The course of the *Kulturkampf***
>
> *1872* The Society of Jesus (the Jesuits) is banned from Germany; the state takes control of Catholic schools
>
> *1873* The May Laws are passed (in Prussia only); the state takes control of the appointment of the clergy; the Catholic Church's legal powers over its members are limited and those of the state are increased
>
> *1874* The state assumes the power to expel members of the clergy if they refuse to conform; civil marriage is made compulsory
>
> *1875* Pius IX declares Germany's anti-Catholic laws illegal

Religious divisions

Germany was divided in terms of the religious loyalties of its population: about two-thirds were Protestant and one-third Catholic. The Catholic minority included people who lived in the states and provinces that had been taken over in 1871 – that is, the southern German states and Alsace-Lorraine. In addition, the Poles of East Prussia were Catholic and resented being ruled by Prussia, a traditionally Protestant state. Prussia's dominance of the German Empire caused Catholics throughout the empire to feel isolated and vulnerable, although they received some comfort and support from the Catholic Church.

The Catholic Church

Pius IX, who had been pope since 1846, had become strongly opposed to such modern ideas as liberalism and nationalism (see Chapter 3). In 1870, the year in which the pope lost control of all but a few square miles of Rome, a Church Council announced that he was infallible (incapable of error) in spiritual matters. Although most Catholics welcomed the announcement, many German liberals regarded it as a challenge to the freedom of the individual and to their new state.

The Centre Party

In 1870 German Catholics formed their own political party, the Centre Party, which was based on a Catholic party that had existed in Prussia. The Centre Party became a rallying point for those who opposed the new German Empire, and not just because they were Catholics. In the first elections to the new *Reichstag* the Centre Party gained 61 seats, this figure rising to 95 in the second election. Under its leader, Ludwig Windhorst, the Centre Party developed policies that were opposed to the liberal policies of the government and the National Liberals. It was not long before Bismarck was describing the supporters of the Centre Party as enemies of the empire.

The constitution

The German constitution of 1871 did not guarantee religious freedoms or the independence of the Catholic Church, as the Prussian constitution of 1850 had done to a great degree. Catholics regarded this omission as unfortunate and even suspicious. Their suspicions were reinforced when the government began to argue that it had a duty to those who chose to leave a church, as well as to those who remained within it.

Bismarck

Despite his success in unifying Germany, Bismarck doubted whether the empire was actually united. He believed that many interest groups were working against the empire and that they were often conspiring together to do so. Catholics within Germany were likely to co-operate with such Catholic states as France and Austria, both of which bore a grudge against Prussia/Germany, and were also supported by the Catholic Church. Because the loyalty of German Catholics to the German Empire could not be guaranteed, the government felt compelled to take action against the 'enemy within' and consequently passed some very illiberal laws.

A change of direction, 1878–79

Although the German government's anti-Catholic policy was popular with Protestants, it proved counterproductive: priests refused to accept the new laws, with the result that many parishes found themselves with no spiritual leaders. By 1877 Bismarck could see that the state was not winning the struggle for power. He faced political, economic and financial problems that would require policies that the National Liberals would oppose. He needed the support of the Centre Party. He had to change course. Why did he have to?

Why in 1878–79 did Bismarck abandon the *Kulturkampf*?

Political problems

In 1875 two socialist parties that had been formed during the previous 12 years decided to merge. The new party, which was known as the German Social Democratic Party (SPD), was committed to a form of Marxist socialism. Bismarck feared that the Social Democrats would work to undermine the German Empire and would also attract large-scale working-class support, especially in times of economic depression. The Social Democratic Party therefore became Bismarck's new 'enemy within' and he was determined to contain this new menace.

Economic problems

For the first two years following the formation of the German Empire the economy boomed. In 1873, however, the stock markets crashed and an economic depression followed that lasted longer and was more severe than anyone could remember. Prices and profits were particularly badly affected and both industry and agriculture suffered from foreign competition. Industrialists and landowners demanded action. The government found itself unable to resist this pressure.

Financial problems

The German taxation system was as complex as its constitution. The 25 states controlled direct taxation. The federal government was too dependent on state taxes. Bismarck wanted it to have its own independent sources of income. He believed that tariffs and indirect taxes would provide these revenues.

Bismarck's approach to all three problems was essentially the same: he wanted the federal state to take more control over national life. Realising that the National Liberals would not accept this policy, Bismarck decided that he had to break with them. This change of direction, which took 15 months to achieve, was greatly assisted by the death of Pius IX in 1878, which gave Bismarck the chance to bring the *Kulturkampf* to an end. When two attempts were made to kill William I later in 1878 Bismarck seized the opportunity to act. After the first assassination attempt he introduced an anti-socialist bill, even though the would-be assassin had no socialist connections. This was rejected by the *Reichstag*. After the second assassination attempt the *Reichstag* was dissolved, less than eighteen months into its three-year term, Bismarck using the subsequent election to attack the liberal parties. As a result, conservative parties made considerable gains at the expense of the liberals. Bismarck now relied on the conservative and Centre parties to see his programme through the *Reichstag*.

By July 1879 Bismarck had achieved most of what he wanted. Firstly, an anti-socialist law had been passed in October 1878. The law aimed to prevent associations of socialists that were committed to overthrowing the existing state and society. Specific political parties were not banned. They could still take part in elections. People could still vote socialist. What could be banned, however, were meetings, newspapers and processions that promoted socialist ideas, while the police could stop any fundraising activities on behalf of socialist parties. The law was to last for three years, until 1881, when it would have to be renewed. During the 1880s it was renewed four times.

Secondly, the *Reichstag* approved the imposition of tariffs in 1879. The duties were set at 10 or 15 per cent on industrial imports and 5 and 7 per cent on agricultural products. The tariffs achieved their broad economic purpose in that the level of imports into Germany was reduced and the balance of trade consequently improved. (The agricultural duties did not stop the flow of imported grain from Russia and the Americas, however.) The federal government's finances also improved, although not sufficiently to escape relying on contributions from the states. If the economic and financial consequences of the imposition of tariffs were not wholly positive, their political significance was great, for their passage through the *Reichstag* had formally ended Bismarck's collaboration with the National Liberal Party, which promptly split into two. A new era in German politics had begun.

The era of national conservatism, 1879–90

If there is a common theme to German politics during the 1880s it is Bismarck's continued attempts to increase the role of the state in public life and to attack liberalism. There is one clear exception to this theme: the abandonment of the *Kulturkampf* during the early 1880s, when a series of laws called the Peace Laws, which limited the power over the Catholic Church which the state had taken in the 1870s, were passed. Although the state did not give up all of its powers, in practice it could no longer use those powers, opposition being too strong. In that sense Bismarck had had to beat a retreat, thereby suffering a clear political defeat, a rare occurrence in a long political career.

In fact, Bismarck had to experience the bitter taste of more political defeats during the 1880s. He had wanted to increase indirect taxation, such as a state monopoly of the sale of tobacco, in order to give the federal government more revenue, thereby ending its dependence on the states' financial contributions. Between 1880 and 1882 he therefore made several such proposals, all of which were rejected by the *Reichstag*. The passage of the *Septennat*, the *Reichstag*'s seven-year approval of army expenditure, proved increasingly difficult during the 1880s, too, and between 1886 and 1887 Bismarck ensured its passage only by stimulating political crises at home and abroad.

Bismarck was finding it increasingly difficult to get his own way, mainly because the voters returned anti-government majorities to the *Reichstag* – this was certainly the case in 1881 and 1884. Bismarck continued to fight various political battles against these numerical odds. He could normally count on the support of the conservatives, but as they comprised only a quarter of the total number of deputies he had to work with at least one other large party. Until 1887 it was the Centre Party, but in 1887 Bismarck created a partnership of conservatives and National Liberals that became known as the *Kartel*. The co-operation between these parties on the second ballot resulted in their winning a comfortable majority. The *Septennat* was subsequently approved.

As Bismarck faced increasing opposition the negative features of his policies came to the fore. If the *Reichstag* would not support the government, he considered replacing it completely. Even though the growing number of socialist deputies in the *Reichstag* suggested that the anti-socialist legislation was not working, he nevertheless persisted in having it renewed. Indeed, Bismarck remained as manipulative, and as restless, as ever, as is best seen in his creation of crises, both at home and abroad, between 1886 and 1887 in order to create a pro-government majority in the 1887 election.

Yet Bismarck was never wholly negative, as is shown by two radical innovations that he made during the 1880s. One was the policy of social insurance, the compulsory payment of benefits to workers who were suffering from sickness (1883), from the effects of accidents (1884) and from old age and disabilities (1889). Employers made the greater contribution to accident insurance and employees to sickness payments, while employers, workers and the state all contributed towards old-age pensions. Germany was the first state to introduce such policies, policies that would become commonplace throughout Europe during the next century. In this respect Bismarck remained something of a radical, 'a man ahead of his time'. He introduced social insurance partly because it offered a positive way to weaken voters' support for the SPD (which indeed occurred, but only briefly) and partly because he believed that better-off people, as well as the state, had a responsibility to help the poorer members of German society. Here we might detect echoes of the Junkers' sense of duty towards those who lived on their estates. Had Bismarck had his way, however, the taxpayer would have contributed to all of the new insurance schemes. The second of Bismarck's radical innovations was the acquisition of an overseas empire between 1884 and 1886 (his motives for this brief flirtation with imperialism are considered more fully on pages 165–66).

> How did Bismarck deal with the challenge of the Social Democratic Party?

Compared with the early and mid 1880s 1887 was a successful year for Bismarck: the *Reichstag* elections had returned a pro-government majority for the first time in the decade, the *Septennat* had been approved and even the anti-socialist law seemed to be working, the number of SPD deputies having fallen from 24 to 11. Yet within two years of William I's death in March 1888 Bismarck would be out of office. Before his fall is explained, however, his foreign policy after 1871 must be considered.

Bismarck's foreign policy, 1871–90

Isolating France and brokering the Eastern question, 1871–78

Following Prussia's war with France and the formation of the German Empire Bismarck had only one aim in his foreign policy: to maintain the 1871 settlement. He had no further territorial ambitions and simply wanted to prevent any future challenge to the new European order. In Bismarck's view, the main threat to this order would come from France, which was embittered by its military defeat and the loss of Alsace-Lorraine. He was therefore determined to ensure that France remained weak and isolated. Although the punitive peace settlement imposed on France by the Treaty of Frankfurt, including the large war indemnity, was Bismarck's way of achieving the former objective, isolating France would be more difficult. Britain, which was more concerned with her empire than with Europe, and was also more pro-German than pro-French, would not present Bismarck with any problems. Austria, though, still remembered its defeat by Prussia in 1866, while the Eastern question was harming its relations with Russia. Bismarck, however, managed to bring Germany, Austria and Russia together to form the Three Emperors' League (or *Dreikaiserbund*) in 1873, by which the three empires confirmed their commitment to monarchical government (which excluded a republic such as France) and agreed to work together to maintain peace. (For details of all Bismarck's alliances, see Appendix D.) France was isolated. Bismarck had got what he wanted.

Yet Bismarck was still worried about a potential threat from France, especially when it paid its war indemnity more quickly than he had expected. When the *Kulturkampf* was at its height he came to fear French aggression as part of a Catholic conspiracy against Germany. He therefore started a major war scare in 1875 by encouraging German newspapers to discuss a preventive war against France, but this tactic only caused Russia, supported by Britain, to remind Germany of the need to maintain peace, forcing Bismarck to deny all knowledge of the war rumours. Germany had been put in its place – in marked contrast to the 1860s – and Bismarck had been given a sharp reminder of how little room for manoeuvre he now had. This lesson was reinforced by the next crisis, which occurred on the other side of Europe. So serious was the Near Eastern crisis of 1875 to 1878, which was a real crisis and not an invented one, that at one stage there was even talk of war between Britain and Russia.

The nineteenth-century equivalent of today's photo opportunity. Bismarck is shaking the hand of the Russian ambassador to Berlin at the meeting of European powers to resettle the Balkans after the Russo-Turkish War. On the far left, the Russian foreign minister reaches out to touch Disraeli, the British prime minister, on the forearm.

The **Treaty of Berlin** (1878) brought about major changes in the Balkans at Turkey's expense. Serbia, Montenegro and Romania became fully independent. Bulgaria was autonomous. Bosnia-Herzegovina was handed over to Austria. The large Bulgaria created at San Stefano was greatly reduced in size, against Russia's wishes.

In 1875 the problems created by the decline of the Ottoman Empire – the so-called Eastern question – re-emerged and came to dominate European affairs for the rest of the 1870s. Although Bismarck famously declared in 1876 that he saw 'no interest for Germany [in the problems of the Ottoman Empire] which would be worth the healthy bones of a single Pomeranian musketeer', Germany did have an interest in trying to prevent Austria and Russia from falling out. Indeed, Bismarck was worried that if they did so one of them might join France in an alliance that would have an anti-German dimension.

The Near Eastern crisis, 1875–78

- 1875 Bosnia-Herzegovina revolts against Ottoman rule
- 1876 Bulgarian atrocities take place
- 1877 Russo-Turkish War
- 1878 The Treaty of San Stefano: the Ottoman Empire gives up its territory in the Balkans; the Congress of Berlin: the Treaty of San Stefano is altered by the great powers in the **Treaty of Berlin**

The Eastern question often divided Austria and Russia: Russia was increasingly sympathetic to the cause of those Slav peoples who were subject to the rule of the Ottoman Empire, but Russian support for the Slavs in the Ottoman Empire might encourage the Slavs in Austria to try to win greater freedom as well. Because the interests of Bismarck's two allies were contradictory, the *Dreikaiserbund* collapsed in 1878. Austria sided with Britain in attempting to reverse the gains that Russian had made at the Ottoman Empire's expense by the Treaty of San Stefano in 1878. Bismarck tried to reconcile their conflicting interests by holding a congress in Berlin, claiming that he would be an 'honest broker' between Russia on one side and Austria and Britain on the other. Russia was forced to give way and blamed Bismarck for its humiliation. Bismarck's attempt to act as an honest broker had backfired. The demise of the *Dreikaiserbund* meant that he no

What were the three main consequences for German foreign policy of the Near Eastern crisis of 1875–78?

longer had the influence over Austria and Russia's foreign policies that he desired. What was he to do?

Choosing Austria, 1879

In the autumn of 1879 Bismarck took a step that would have great consequences for Europe: he signed the Dual Alliance with Austria. This was a secret, defensive, military alliance. Russia was the specified threat. It was secret. It would last for five years and could then be renewed (which it regularly was, up to 1914). Until then alliances had been short-term agreements that were signed either when a war was about to break out or during a war itself. The Dual Alliance, a long-term agreement signed when there was no threat of war, became the model for further alliances that were made during the 1880s. But what were Bismarck's reasons for signing such an unusual agreement with Austria?

From Bismarck's viewpoint in 1879 this new kind of alliance did not have the significance that it would later come to have: it was just another move in the series of diplomatic manoeuvres that were part and parcel of great-power relations. He signed it with Austria because Austria wanted an ally against Russia following the Near Eastern crisis. At the same time Germany's relations with Russia were poor, for two reasons: the Near Eastern crisis and the disruption of trade between the two countries following the introduction of tariffs by Germany. Bismarck's domestic and foreign policies were once again interrelated.

Building alliances and acquiring an empire, 1880–90

Bismarck developed an increasingly complex alliance system during the 1880s. In 1881 he managed to bring Austria and Russia together again in a second *Dreikaiserbund*. In 1882 he brought Italy into his alliance system with the Triple Alliance (of Germany, Austria and Italy). He made occasional efforts to create an alliance with Britain as well. France remained isolated. Bismarck therefore stood at the centre of his system, weaving a web of international commitments that would help to uphold the 1871 settlement. It was a fair-weather system, however: the fundamental national interests of Austria and Russia, for example, or of Austria and Italy, were not identical. Allies would fall out if they were forced to uphold those interests. This had happened between 1875 and 1878 over the Balkans and would happen again during the mid-1880s.

The **crises of 1885–87** created another minor revolution in Bismarck's diplomacy: the *Dreikaiserbund* collapsed again, although Germany's links with Russia were retained by means of the Reinsurance Treaty of 1887. Germany had a closer relationship with Austria, however, which Bismarck

crises of 1885–87
A series of interrelated problems occurred between 1885 and 1887 that tested Bismarck's system to the limit: (a) the Bulgarian crisis, (1885–87) resulted in conflict between the new Bulgarian king and Russia; (b) General Georges Boulanger, the French war minister (1886–87), talked of a war of revenge; and (c) the Triple Alliance was renewed in 1887.

encouraged to work with Italy and Britain against Russia. Germany's relations with France remained poor. In 1889 Bismarck asked Britain to join Germany in a defensive alliance, France being the common threat. Britain declined his invitation, preferring to rely on its navy. Bismarck might have maintained peace, but he never achieved security for Germany.

Bismarck's colonial policy

Another aspect of Bismarck's foreign policy during the 1880s that should be considered is his short-lived colonial policy. Between 1884 and 1885 Germany acquired colonies in Africa (German South West Africa, German East Africa and the Cameroons) and the Pacific (New Guinea). Before 1884 and after 1885 Bismarck expressed little interest in colonies, so why did he suddenly, and briefly, change his mind in 1884? A number of reasons have been proposed by historians.

Three reasons of domestic policy that may have contributed to Bismarck's colonial policy have been identified. Firstly, Bismarck needed to defeat the left-wing, anti-colonial Progressive Party in the 1884 elections. Secondly, he wanted to undermine support for the German crown prince, Frederick, who was married to a daughter of Queen Victoria: Frederick was bound to succeed to the throne before long and was very pro-British. Gaining colonies would upset the British and embarrass Frederick. Thirdly, he wanted to win the support of the various business groups that argued for the economic benefits of having colonies in times of economic depression.

In terms of foreign relations, two motives have been proposed for Bismarck's acquisition of colonies. The first is that Bismarck wanted to upset the British government of the time, which was led by the Liberal prime minister **William Gladstone**, whose moralistic approach he could not stand. The second is that he wanted to improve Germany's relations with the French government, which was then led by Jules Ferry, a moderate republican who was trying to turn the French people's preoccupation away from Germany and Europe and towards Africa and Asia, policies that Bismarck was prepared to support.

When the governments of Gladstone and Ferry fell from office in 1885 Bismarck abandoned his colonial policy. Was that merely a coincidence or did Bismarck just turn his attention away from the colonies towards the more urgent and more significant crisis in the Balkans? Whatever the reason, the acquisition of a colonial empire during the mid-1880s was an aberration in Bismarck's foreign policy.

William Gladstone (1809–98) was one of the great figures of nineteenth-century liberalism. He started public life as a Tory, but slowly became more liberal. Prime minister four times between 1868 and 1894, he maintained a very moralistic approach in domestic and foreign policy.

Why in 1884–85 did Germany acquire colonies?

Assessment

How successful was Bismarck's foreign policy between 1871 and 1890? Peace was maintained and the settlement of 1871 upheld. France remained isolated, while the other great powers looked to Germany as an important ally. Germany acquired a colonial empire, which made it a global, as well as a European, power.

Although these were considerable achievements, they had been gained using a form of diplomacy that involved increasingly complicated alliances and secret treaties. Bismarck also seemed to respond to short-term, often personal, factors, as is demonstrated by his colonial policy. Yet he possessed the necessary diplomatic skills and reputation to maintain the system that he had created. The methods that he used, however, aroused other states' suspicions of Germany and were too sophisticated to be maintained once Bismarck was gone. Was Bismarck's foreign policy therefore totally successful?

> Trace the changes in Bismarck's policies towards (a) Austria, (b) Russia and (c) France between 1862 and 1890.

The end of an era, 1888–90

The only person to whom Bismarck was accountable was the emperor: only he could dismiss the chancellor. As long as William I was emperor Bismarck's position was secure, for the relationship between the two men, which had been difficult for many years, had become easier during the 1870s and 1880s. In March 1888 the 90-year-old William I died. When his son, who became Frederick III on his accession, died three months later of cancer of the throat, Frederick's twenty-nine-year-old son became the new emperor: William II would be a key figure in European politics for the next 30 years.

William's left arm had been damaged during his birth in 1859, and some historians have argued that this injury had a great effect on William's personality and thus on European history – a claim that is impossible to prove. He certainly grew up into a conceited, arrogant young man, who soon fell out with his parents. Because William's mother, the daughter of Queen Victoria, and father, Crown Prince Frederick, wanted the German system of government to be more like the British, Bismarck had feared Frederick's accession and had done his best to influence William against his parents. William's narrowly nationalistic views meant that Bismarck felt more secure when William acceded to the throne. Eighteen months later, however, Bismarck was out of office, dismissed by the new emperor.

This dismissal was partly Bismarck's own fault. He had worked extremely hard on his relationship with William I, certainly during the early years, when Bismarck had seen the emperor several times a week at least. Yet when William II became emperor Bismarck did not seem to bother, spending most of the next 18 months on his country estates. Many people took advantage of his absence from Berlin to encourage the emperor to be his own man. It may, however, have been that Bismarck stayed out of the emperor's way because he did not get on with him. Bismarck was a bad-tempered old man and William an arrogant young one. Their different personalities and the generation gap

Bismarck and William II at Bismarck's country estate in October 1888, shortly after the emperor's accession. Rather than looking towards the camera, as the guards are doing, the two men are looking directly at each other, which is unusual.

meant that there was little chance of an effective relationship being developed between the two men. One of them would have to go and it would not be the new emperor.

The end came more quickly than Bismarck had anticipated, however, with William soon beginning to assert himself in ways that would have been alien to his grandfather. He disagreed with his chancellor's policies, and in particular with those that dealt with the working classes and Social Democrats. William wanted the government to do more for the poor, a policy that he believed would weaken popular support for the Social Democrats. Bismarck, on the other hand, wanted to strengthen the anti-socialist law, mainly by making it permanent. The elections of February 1890 made matters worse: the Social Democrats won 1,400,000 votes, more than any other party (even if the voting system only gave them 35 seats out of the total 375), while the Centre Party came second. Because most of the votes had gone to anti-government parties, Bismarck would lose control of the new *Reichstag*. There is evidence that Bismarck welcomed this defeat because it would have enabled him to take more drastic action against his enemies in order to save the German Empire. Where Bismarck wanted confrontation, William, after some hesitation, sought compromise.

By March 1890 William had had enough of Bismarck's manoeuvrings. The breaking point was a Prussian royal order of 1852, which said that government ministers could approach the king (now the emperor) only with the

168   *Changing the face of Europe: Germany, 1862–90*

consent of the prime minister (now the chancellor). Following a blazing row William ordered Bismarck to issue a decree repealing the order. When Bismarck refused he was forced to resign. The official version of events said that Bismarck had requested the emperor's permission to resign because of ill-health.

Bismarck lived for another eight years, resentful and perplexed. He insisted that his tombstone was inscribed with the following words: 'Here lies Prince Bismarck, faithful German servant of the Emperor William I.' What do those words tell us about the man?

How can Bismarck's leadership of Prussia and Germany be assessed?

How can one best try to assess the man who had done so much to influence the history of Germany and Europe? It is important to start by considering Germany, the country that he ruled over for so long. It is also vital to realise that he led two countries, Prussia and Germany, and that our assessment of Bismarck's leadership will therefore depend upon which country we are considering.

Bismarck is usually regarded in the context of Germany. Although Germany did not exist as a nation state in 1862, it had an economic and a

The apotheosis of Bismarck. On Bismarck's left-hand side is the goddess of victory. To his right is Germania and, below her, Clio, the muse of history, with the volume of history for 1870 to 1871. In front of Bismarck are various admiring and thankful German citizens. The picture was painted in 1890.

political form, the *Zollverein* and the *Bund*, which covered a number of different states, all of which were sovereign. By 1890 these economic and political forms of Germany had come together in a single state, the German Empire. In theory the member states shared their sovereignty in this new Germany. In practice, twenty-four of them lost power to the twenty-fifth state, Prussia. Because Germany had industrialised itself during these decades it was also a wealthy and powerful state that had become continental Europe's leading power and was furthermore starting to challenge Britain's pre-eminent position. The contrast between the Germanies of 1862 and 1890 was therefore great and clear for all to see. In this respect Germany was the success story of the second half of the nineteenth century.

Germany's transformation had been accomplished mainly through the economic and political leadership of Prussia. Between 1862 and 1890 Prussia both survived and strengthened its position within the smaller, united, but more powerful, Germany. Indeed, it dominated the new Germany: the Prussian government provided much of the German government, while its economy was the basis of German industrialisation. The old Prussian political order still remained largely intact: the landed *Junkers* may have shared their power with industrialists, but the propertied classes still ruled. Although the German *Reichstag* was based on universal male suffrage the Prussian Diet was not, and democracy was not a central feature of the new Germany, a point that is reinforced by the persecution of the Catholics and social democrats during the 1870s and 1880s.

But what of Bismarck himself? Bismarck was controversial at the time and has remained so ever since. Historians' views on Bismarck differ tremendously. Conservative historians have usually praised Bismarck for having created the German nation state. Liberal historians, such as Erich Eyck, however, have criticised him for having failed to encourage the development of liberal democracy (Eyck was writing during the 1940s, when the Third *Reich* was demonstrating just how shallow German democracy really was.) Two more recent studies of Bismarck are also worth mentioning. Lothar Gall, in his two-volume work *Bismarck, the white revolutionary* (1986), regards Bismarck as a 'white revolutionary', willing to overthrow old ideas and to accept new ones in order to preserve a greater social and political order. According to Gall, because the new ideas of democracy and liberalism grew stronger than Bismarck would have wished, he can be described as something of a 'sorcerer's apprentice', conjuring up forces that later he could not control. Otto Pflanze, in his three-volume study *Bismarck and the development of Germany* (1962 and 1990), sees Bismarck as a conservative (but not a reactionary) Prussian politician and the unification of Germany as an extension of Prussian power by which democracy lost out to nationalism. The new state institutions that

> Summarise the different views of Bismarck's place in the history of Germany.

had been improvised in 1867 were proving difficult to maintain 20 years later, and by 1890 Bismarck's system was close to collapse Much the same was true of his foreign policy. According to Pflanze, Bismarck left his successors a troubled legacy.

Finally, under Bismarck, Prussia became the political as well as economic leader of the new Germany and the new Germany became the leading economic power of continental Europe and a rival to Britain – both substantial achievements, if not Bismarck's alone. Yet Bismarck also stifled the development of democratic values within the new Germany, a policy that both reinforced the authoritarian elements that already existed within Prussia and applied them to the rest of Germany. In Europe, by 1890, many regarded Germany with suspicion. Bismarck's restless diplomacy had won few friends for the new Germany. Thus Bismarck left for his successors a mixed legacy of great achievements to live up to and major problems to deal with. Although they failed to meet both sets of challenges Bismarck cannot be blamed for their failure. Or can he? The debate continues.

> Using Appendix D and your own knowledge, how consistent were the commitments that Bismarck made to his various allies between 1879 and 1890? (Note that the 'benevolent neutrality' mentioned in Appendix D means supporting an ally that is involved in a war without joining in the fighting.)

Historical sources

Aspects of German unification, 1850–71

1 A comparison of the *Bund*'s and Austria's level of industrialisation between 1850 and 1869

Years	COAL (million tonnes, yearly average)		PIG IRON (thousand tonnes, yearly average)		RAILWAYS (kilometres in 1850, 1855, 1860 and 1865)	
	Bund	Austria	*Bund*	Austria	*Bund*	Austria
1850–54	9.2	1.2	245	173	5,856	1,579
1855–59	14.7	2.2	422	226	7,826	2,145
1860–64	20.8	3.6	613	216	11,084	4,543
1865–69	31.0	5.3	1,012	227	13,900	5,858

2 Bismarck's statement to Benjamin Disraeli, the leader of the British Conservative Party, 1862

The Russian ambassador gave a large dinner at which I was present. Among the guests was the Prussian minister in Paris, Bismarck, who had a long conversation with Disraeli after dinner. The following is part of this conversation which the leader of the Opposition [Disraeli] repeated to me on the same evening.

'I shall soon', said in effect the Prussian statesman, 'be compelled to undertake the conduct of the Prussian government. My first care will be to reorganise the army, with or without the help of the *Landtag* [the lower house of the Prussian parliament]. The king was right in undertaking this task but he cannot accomplish it with his present advisers. As soon as the army shall have been brought into such a condition as to inspire respect, I shall take the first best pretext to declare war against Austria, dissolve the German *Bund*, subdue the minor states and give national unity to Germany under Prussian leadership. I have come to say this to the Queen's ministers'.

Disraeli's commentary on this programme, which has since been carried out step by step, was, 'Take care of that man! He means what he says'.

Source: an extract from the memoirs of Count von Eckstadt, *St Petersburg and London in the years 1852–1864* (1886)

3 Bismarck's view on the future of the *Zollverein*

Should the *Zollverein* continue with its present scope, the creation of organic institutions, by means of which south Germany can participate in legislating on tariff questions, it is quite unavoidable.

It is difficult to believe that such a common legislative institution for tariffs – I do not wish to underrate it by simply calling it a Customs Parliament – I do not wish to underrate the importance of its being possible to create an economic community for the whole of Germany. It is difficult to believe that such a common legislative institution could avoid gradually taking on most of the things that come under the heading[s] of economic welfare and commercial procedure, or could avoid bringing into use regulations in these affairs common to the whole of Germany.

Source: Bismarck's speech to the North German Confederation, 11 March 1867

4 A historian's view of Prussia and the *Zollverein*

Even more doubtful than the extravagant claims for the *Zollverein*'s economic significance are allegations about its contribution to German national unification. The *Zollverein* was created by bureaucrats who were interested in fiscal reform rather than nation-building. Prussia's leading role in the [*Zollverein*] was part of its long-term efforts to extend its influence over neighbouring north German states. In retrospect, of course, the *Zollverein* seems to fit perfectly into the story of Prussia's 'national mission' to unify Germany. Actually [it] had little to do with the nation and a great deal to do with the German states.

Source: James Sheehan, a historian, *Germany, 1770–1866* (1989)

Historical-source questions

1. Identify the main changes in the production statistics given in source 1. Compare (a) the differences between the *Bund* and Austria and (b) the differences between products within the *Bund*.
2. How reliable is source 2 as an explanation of Bismarck's plans?
3. Which of the explanations of the significance of the *Zollverein* given in sources 3 and 4 do you find the more convincing and why?

Summary questions

1. Identify and explain any *two* factors which explain why Prussia became the leading economic power in Germany in the 1860s.
2. Compare the importance of any *three* consequences of the Austro-Prussian war of 1866 for Germany.
3. How successful was Bismarck's foreign policy in the period 1871–90?

7 Towards collectivism: Europe during the 1880s

History is usually subdivided by wars and revolutions. When none occur, making the necesssary division is hard. It is especially true of the period between 1870 and 1914, dates which themselves are based on the outbreak of wars. Should the 1880s be separated from the 1870s or from the 1890s? Was the late nineteenth century significantly different from the early twentieth century? These questions emphasise the difficulty of trying to find a term that summarises the key features of the 1880s. Norman Stone did not even attempt the task in his book *Europe transformed, 1878–1919* (1983), labelling the politics of the decade 'transformism', a term that could be applied to almost any decade. If a contrast were to be made with the 1820s it would be helpful to be able to call the 1880s the 'age of reform'. Unfortunately, however, some parts of Europe experienced reaction rather than reform during the 1880s, Russia being the most notable example.

Yet in a way Norman Stone is right: the 1880s were a decade when old societies were being transformed into new and different ones more rapidly than had ever happened before. Compared with just a few decades earlier the pace of change was accelerating. Although the extent of the change varied across Europe, and the west–east divide of the 1820s still existed, the nature of the change was much the same all over Europe. The emergence of a new society – an urban, industrial and class-based mass society – was common to all parts of Europe. This society had been evident during the 1820s, but was only found in one or two corners of the continent. By the 1880s Europeans of all nationalities were moving into towns and working in factories in far greater numbers than ever before. It is therefore possible to identify some themes that are common to the decade, even if deciding on a suitable label for the 1880s remains as difficult as ever.

Urban growth and rural decline

European towns grew rapidly during the 1880s (which in terms of the nineteenth century was not a new phenomenon). By 1890 the proportion of the European population that lived in towns had almost doubled in comparison

A romantic painting, by William Bell Scott (1861), which suggests that the industrial ironmaster was little different from the pre-industrial blacksmith. The newspaper gives details of Garibaldi's victory at the Volturno.

with the figure for 1850 – and this despite the rapid growth in population during the same period. If the whole of Europe is taken into consideration, more people still lived in the country than in towns. However, in the most industrialised countries, such as Germany and Britain, around half of the population were town-dwellers. A large number of industrial towns had also sprung up in addition to the few large cities of the 1820s, towns that were centred on the production of new industrial goods such as steel or raw materials like coal. The towns of Germany's Ruhr region were examples of these new towns, while old towns, like Lyons in France, or Milan in Italy, developed into mixed economies, combining traditional industries with new ones and creating different and complex societies as a result.

The new towns, which sprawled into the surrounding countryside, were more socially divided than their older counterparts: wealthy people lived in big houses on the edge of town while poor people inhabited overcrowded houses in the centre of town. Although the middle classes were usually able to make the best of the new opportunities that were offered by the industrial towns, the working classes always struggled to do so. The physical conditions in what are now called 'inner-city areas' could not be ignored: the lack of clean water, for instance, gave rise to such diseases as cholera, dysentery and diarrhoea. In contrast to the traditionally non-interventionist role of the state (generally called **laissez-faire**) of the early nineteenth century, governments were now forced to ensure that there was an adequate supply of clean water and to prevent the spread of disease as far as possible. Even so, life for the

Laissez-faire is a French phrase meaning 'allow [them] to do'. It means that the state allows individuals to do what they like in business matters. In other words, the free market prevails and the state plays a minimal role in economic and social matters.

Towards collectivism: Europe during the 1880s

majority of townspeople remained 'nasty, brutish and short'. Many people thought that the wealth of the middle classes should, and could, be redistributed. The middle classes in turn regarded such people as having been infected by a disease that was as dangerous in its own way as tuberculosis: socialism. The rapid growth of the towns therefore did nothing to reduce social divisions. Indeed, if anything, it made them worse.

This rapid urban growth contrasted with the stagnation and even decline of the countryside. During the last quarter of the nineteenth century European agriculture experienced a deep depression. Thanks to the revolution in transport – the introduction of railways and steamships – grain could now be imported from the USA, Canada and Australia in huge quantities and at a low cost that European producers could not match. Prices fell rapidly and farming incomes were hit hard. Agricultural labourers often left the neglected farms, either to move into the towns or to emigrate to new worlds. Indeed, emigration from Europe was at its height during the 40 years before 1914. The landowning classes, which had been a powerful social group during the 1820s, no longer had the wealth to sustain their position. The countryside, which until the 1880s had been at least equal to the town in terms of wealth and of status, was now its inferior. It had suffered from the technological changes that the towns had benefited from. This contrast was reflected in the economic conditions of the 1880s.

Technical innovation and economic depression

By the 1880s the pace of technological change was accelerating. Sixty years previously dedicated individuals had developed new machines by means of trial and error; great scientific knowledge was not essential. George Stephenson, for example, the inventor of the steam engine, could hardly read or write. By the second half of the century, however, technical change was increasingly the result of science-based research. The chemical and electrical industries – the two important new industries of the late nineteenth century – developed more rapidly as a result. The chemical industry benefited from the development of synthetic dyes, which were based on the chemical compound aniline. The growth of the electrical industry was based on the dynamo, a device which used knowledge of electro-magnetism to turn mechanical power into electrical energy. New production techniques furthermore enabled steel to be produced in large quantities using lower-grade iron ore. All of these breakthroughs occurred during the 1860s, but because it takes time to transform new ideas into large-scale and widespread production techniques their impact was only fully felt during the 1870s and 1880s. Innovations such as these cut production costs, which in turn resulted in lower prices and reduced profits. This may help to explain the so-called 'Great Depression' that lasted from 1873 to 1896. It may have been be coincidental, but few technical innovations can be dated to the 1880s and lower profits would have meant less investment in new techniques.

A key feature of the economy of the 1880s was therefore the slump in both industrial and agricultural prices. For those whose livelihoods were not directly affected, the falling prices resulted in higher living standards (always assuming that wages stayed at the same level). The 'Great Depression' did not take the form that is usually associated with the term, however, for there was only occasional large-scale unemployment during the 23 years from 1873, and even then it never affected all of Europe at the same time. The danger of widespread working-class unrest that was feared by the more pessimistic of the middle classes never became a reality. Although some social groups, such as the landed gentry and businessmen whose profits were cut, were hit hard by the Great Depression, they did not receive much popular sympathy.

In broad terms, during the 1880s Europe experienced the economic and social consequences of the sustained technical innovation that had occurred over the previous 10 or 20 years. This setback to the economic growth of the 1850s and 1860s caused concern, prompting people to demand action, to protect either the nation or the working classes.

Socialism and nationalism

The existence of feelings of national and class identity during the 1880s was one of the major contrasts with the 1820s. The new societies were mass societies, and individuals were increasingly being seen – and saw themselves – as belonging to a larger social group based on class, nation or gender. During this period a few women, almost all of them in Britain and France, began to join together to campaign for women's rights. Some of the rights demanded were general, such as the right to vote, to divorce husbands or to have a university education. Others were specific, such as the demand to end state regulation of prostitution, which criminalised prostitutes but not their clients. The number of women involved in such movements was very small, however, and the movements became significant only after 1890. Class awareness was much stronger than female solidarity.

People now belonged to the 'middle class' and 'working (or labouring) class', with the 'upper class' becoming a term that was applied to a very small elite. These terms were widely accepted by the 1880s. The working class in particular had developed a strong sense of common interest and had devised a range of organisations and beliefs with which to express those interests. Political parties and trade unions, co-operative and friendly societies, in which

An unusual photograph and for several reasons. It is of a group of Welsh women, probably agricultural labourers, in their place of work. They are taking a break, relaxing. The photograph, which dates from the 1860s, seems natural but must have been posed.

workers joined together to gain financial benefits and mutual support, flourished across Europe. As well as socialism, the ideas of syndicalism (a belief in direct industrial action by trade unions for political ends), anarchism and communism were developed.

With the creation of mass socialist parties that were committed to some form of Marxist idea, the working class became an important social and political force during the 1870s and 1880s. The German Social Democrats were among the most significant of these parties, and Bismarck's reaction to them (see Chapter 6) typified that of many members of the ruling class who feared what the disciplined power of the working class might achieve. If memories of the French Revolution – which was by then almost a century old – had faded, they had been replaced with the reality of the Paris Commune and of the assassination of Tsar Alexander II. Some socialists, communists and anarchists did indeed argue for the necessity of using violence against the state and its ruling class. Although few advocated revolution, they considered assassination and bombing to be legitimate political tactics. How best to deal with the threat of socialism would be a major concern of the upper and middle classes for many years to come. Their task was made much easier by the tendency of left-wing groups to argue amongst themselves.

If people did not identify with a social class, then they identified with their national group. Geography, history and language were used by a series of propagandists to develop a distinct national identity. The best-known and most significant of these propagandists was Mazzini, but there were many others. The successful unification of both Italy and Germany had served as an example for other nationalist groups. The Hungarians within the Habsburg Empire had been granted virtual self-government in 1867. During the 1870s and 1880s national groups within the Ottoman Empire were fighting for their freedom and gaining autonomy as a prelude to eventual independence.

Greater stress was being placed on national identity, even within 'old' nation states like Britain and France. Primary education (or elementary education, as it was then called) for all, was introduced to much of Europe from the 1860s as the ruling classes accepted the need to ensure that workers could at least read, write and recite key religious texts. This elementary schooling was organised by the state, which made sure that young people became aware of their national identity. The growth of overseas empires during the 1880s also encouraged people to regard themselves as belonging to a nation that had global, as well as European, interests. Nationalism soon became hard to differentiate from imperialism.

The negative side of national identity was its tendency to criticise other groups, usually, but not exclusively, different national or ethnic groups. One group of people, the Jews (a partly ethnic and partly religious group), was increasingly attacked from the 1880s. Although anti-Semitism had long been a feature of European life it was rejuvenated during the late nineteenth century. Jews were often blamed for the 'Great Depression': for example, they were regarded as having caused the collapse of a French bank in 1882. One of the reasons why the trial of Colonel Alfred Dreyfus, an officer in the French army, became so controversial from 1896 was because he was a Jew. In Russia Jews were subjected to a series of **pogroms** following the assassination of Alexander II, causing many of them to flee westwards, where they endured further persecution in the Habsburg Empire and Germany. Indeed, there were few, if any, European countries in which the Jews did not experience persecution towards the end of the nineteenth century. The anti-Semitism of the Third Reich was not invented by Adolf Hitler and the Nazis; it grew out of nineteenth-century European attitudes and beliefs.

Like socialism, nationalism therefore had a darker side. The new brotherhood of European nations that Mazzini had hoped for was turning out to be little different from the old brotherhood of European monarchs. In fact, the old monarchies were often exploiting nationalist feeling to enable them to remain in power: the sovereignty of the people could be exploited to support sovereign monarchs.

Pogrom is the old Russian word for a round-up or lynching. It was used to describe mob attacks upon Jews to which the local authorities turned a blind eye. Such pogroms became an occasional feature of Russian life from 1881 to 1918.

Conservatism and reform

By the 1880s the old political order was responding to the demands of the new society in a skilful way. Although it had initially feared the arrival of democracy, which it believed would soon become mob rule, Napoleon III had demonstrated how the masses could be guided (or manipulated) into supporting anti-democratic policies. Bismarck had taken Napoleon's lesson to heart and by the 1880s was developing a form of national conservatism (**Disraeli** had developed a milder version of it during the 1870s in Britain). There were three main features of Bismarck's modern form of national conservatism: firstly, the making of limited improvements to the social conditions of the working class; secondly, the protection of the national economy; and, thirdly, the placing of restrictions on the political freedoms of socialists. In other words, national conservatism combined a very diluted form of socialism, an incomplete form of economic nationalism and a partial form of authoritarianism. Although the third element was extremely controversial, and was soon abandoned by Bismarck's successor, the two remaining features provided a model for conservative parties in other countries.

By the 1880s the ruling classes had had to accept social reforms and the state's increasingly interventionist role. In the old agrarian society, local landowners had taken some responsibility for the welfare of the poorest in society. In the new industrial society, the role of the landowners was gradually being taken over by the state, both local and national. It was much harder to be a complete reactionary, as in the 1820s, for example, because change could be found in all areas of life. The question was no longer whether change would be accepted but what sort of change was acceptable. The change that was accepted by some governments was certainly minimal. This was true of the Russian governments of the 1880s following the murder of Alexander II in 1881. Although the new tsar, Alexander III, was as close to being a reactionary as it was possible to be, even he did not oppose all types of reform, as his grandfather, Nicholas I, had eventually done. Instead he tried to strengthen the unity of the Russian peoples through a policy of Russification, hoping that Russian nationalism would thereby develop at the expense of non-Russian nationalism. The policy failed, however, for attacking nationalist beliefs is almost always counterproductive.

By the 1880s most European governments had accepted that some kind of limited reform was necessary. Many reforms were uncontroversial, like army reforms and most public-health measures. The more controversial reforms often deepened the division between moderate and radical reformers, with the result that the latter often became isolated, thereby helping to preserve the existing distribution of power. By the 1870s the ruling classes of most

Benjamin Disraeli (1804–81) was a leading Conservative Party politician who did much to establish the ideas of modern Conservatism. A flamboyant figure in early life, he became prime minister in the 1870s. He was the opposite of Gladstone, taking a pragmatic and cynical view of life.

European countries had learned to accept democracy of a limited kind (which was a major change in itself). A new, more collectivist society was starting to form which would set new challenges for all European governments. Would the ruling classes continue to adapt and meet these challenges as successfully as they had done since 1848?

8 Revolutions and nationalities: Europe, 1825–90

Looking back over the history of nineteenth-century Europe, its key features become clear. Most of the dramatic changes of the nineteenth century occurred between 1848 and 1871, when political revolutions broke out and two new nation states – Italy and Germany – were created. Although the periods on either side of 1848 and 1871 seem relatively calm by comparison, a closer examination reveals the contrast to be less distinct than at first sight. Before 1848, revolutions broke out during the 1820s and 1830s; some failed, as in Italy and Germany, but some succeeded. Two new nation states were formed during the 1830s: Greece and Belgium. They may have been less important than Germany and Italy, their formation less dramatic, but they were revolutionary nation states all the same. And what of the period after 1871? If our definition of 'revolution' is purely political then there is certainly a marked contrast with the period from 1848 to 1871. It was not until 1905 that the next European revolution to follow that of the Paris Commune of 1871 broke out (in Russia). The process of forming new nation states continued after 1871, however, the main changes taking place in the Balkans as a result of the disintegration of the Ottoman Empire: the Slav peoples of Serbia and Romania broke away from Ottoman rule in 1878 when Bulgaria won its autonomy. (It finally won full independence from the Ottoman Empire in 1908.) Within the Habsburg Empire the Hungarians (or Magyars) were also given their autonomy, in 1867. Indeed, no less than six nationalities gained full independence between 1825 and 1890, with two more winning the right to self-government.

We should not forget the one nationality that lost its political freedoms during this period: the Polish people, who had had their own state until the eighteenth century. Granted autonomy under the rule of the Russian tsar by the Congress of Vienna in 1815, the Poles revolted and proclaimed their independence in 1830, only to be defeated by the Russians. In 1862, a generation later, they revolted again; this time the Russian government lost its patience with them and incorporated Poland into the Russian Empire. The Poles would have to wait until 1918 before they regained their independence.

A romantic portrayal by Arthur Grottger of the Polish revolt of 1863, setting the Poles last stand in a forest glade rather than the streets of the capital city, which was much more usual.

Nationalism and liberalism

The growth of nationalism was one of the key developments of the nineteenth century. Although few people in 1825 believed that a state should be composed of people of the same nationality, by 1890 this idea had become the basis of the European states' system. It had been an intellectual revolution of great significance, and if there was one person who had set Europe on the road to nation-statehood it was Mazzini. Although he did not achieve his specific goals for Italy during his lifetime, the idea of nationhood that he had developed, first for Italians and then for other nationalities, took root and flourished in nineteenth-century Europe.

Nationalism's revolutionary twin, liberalism, also flourished. In fact, liberal ideas became more readily accepted across much of Europe, especially when it came to economic matters: freedom of trade and freedom from state control resulted in economic growth and prosperity, if the evidence of Britain was anything to go by. The expansion of the railways gave practical opportunities for increased freedom of movement, and building the railways required capital to be moved from one country to another. These greater freedoms helped to stimulate the rapid economic growth of the 1850s and 1860s. Indeed, we should not forget that the middle decades of the nineteenth century saw massive economic changes, as well as great political upheavals. The case for economic liberalism was dented by the 'Great Depression' of the 1870s and 1880s, however, resulting in a return to protectionism. Yet by then people had had several decades to become accustomed to greater political freedoms, which no longer created the fears they once did.

Nationalism and liberalism eventually parted company: as liberalism was partly abandoned nationalism continued to flourish. Nationalism's success was in part due to its adoption and use by certain politicians, of whom the two most important were Napoleon III and Bismarck. Napoleon III was the first ruler to show that democracy was not the monster that many people believed it to be: his use of plebiscites with which to gain popular support for major political changes demonstrated that government by propertied elites could be reconciled with the sovereignty of the unpropertied people. Bismarck learnt from Napoleon III's experience and then implemented a more effective nationalist policy, achieving the unification of Germany at the same time as protecting the interests of the Prussian state. Tracing Bismarck's political path after 1862 is a revealing exercise. He began by opposing both the liberals and the nationalists, but then began working with the liberals in 1866, before breaking with them in 1879 in order to adopt the nationalist policies of economic protection and anti-socialism. Bismarck is perhaps best described as a radical conservative, someone who accepted that in times of rapid economic change the ruling class also had to accept radical political change in order to protect its interests. Where Bismarck led, others would later follow.

The absence of revolutions

The popular revolution – a common feature of European history from 1789 to 1848 and much hoped for by left-wing political factions thereafter – failed to materialise during the second half of the nineteenth century. Only in Russia (which was a special case) did it occur, and then not until 1917. It is important to explain why there were no more popular revolutions in western and central Europe after 1848. One major reason for their absence was the economic revolution that was experienced by much of Europe from the 1830s onwards. The changes that occurred in people's lives over the 50 years to 1890 were extraordinary. During the early part of the century most people had lived restricted lives, staying close to the farm or village in which they had grown up. Towards the end of the century they could move quickly and freely from one end of Europe to the other, and even to the other side of the world. Tens of millions of people travelled to the new industrial towns and millions more sailed the oceans in search of better opportunities; the movement of people on this scale had never been seen before. Although the conditions in the new towns were initially no better – and sometimes worse – than those in the villages that had been left behind, they slowly improved as technical innovations (mainly) and government action (partly) raised the standard of living. The capitalist revolution, for which Marx had expressed admiration at the start of the *Communist manifesto*, had defused the danger of a socialist revolution. When the working class organised itself during the 1880s, and an economic depression caused unemployment, popular support for the revolutionary overthrow of the old order was minimal.

Nationalism and revolutionary change

The Europe of 1890 differed greatly from the Europe of 1825. This may seem a statement of the obvious that could also be applied to any equivalent period of modern history: for example, the following 65 years, from 1890 to 1955. But, although 1890–1955 experienced two world wars and 1825–90 was a time of relative peace, the economies and societies of 1955 had not changed substantially in form and content since 1890. Both were mass industrial societies built around a common national identity. It was during the 'short nineteenth century', a time of nationalities and of revolutionary change, that Europe was transformed from an agrarian to an industrial society, and from a monarchical Europe to a Europe of nation states. The apparent calm of Europe in the period 1825–90 was deceptive. The impact of these great changes would last for many years, with immense consequences for the peoples of Europe. But that is another story.

Document study

Italian unification, 1848–71

> **Focus questions**
> - Why was Italy not united in 1848–49?
> - How important to the unification of Italy were foreign circumstances and assistance? In particular, what was the contribution of France under Napoleon III?
> - How important to the unification of Italy were the efforts of Italians? In particular, what were the roles of Mazzini, Garibaldi and the state of Piedmont, including Piedmont's main leaders, Victor Emmanuel II and Cavour?

This section concentrates on developing skills in using primary sources. There are three main skills that are needed when considering such sources:

1. interpreting them;
2. analysing and evaluating them; and
3. using them to test an argument or assertion.

The first skill involves the ability to explain the source, either in general or on a specific point, and in the context of the subject that is being studied. The general question that should be asked is 'What is this source telling us?'

The second skill requires the ability to consider how reliable or how useful a source may be. Both usually involve comparing the descriptions and arguments of a source with those of another source. Sometimes the source may contradict itself, which brings its reliability into question, but although it may be unreliable the source may still be useful. Whether a source is useful or not depends on the answer to the question 'Useful for what?' A contemporary account of an event could well be useful for conveying the view of the writer, or the mood of the time, even though it may turn out to be inaccurate in some way. Comparing sources also helps decide whether one is more useful – or reliable – than another. The attribution of the sources is often significant in this respect: when, for example, was an account of the 1848 revolutions written? Who wrote it? And why did he or (rarely) she write it?

The third skill, using the source to test an argument, requires the ability to select those elements from the sources that are relevant to the point being made. To continue the example, how far do the sources show that the 1848 revolutions failed because the Italians were divided?

The developments of the period have already been described and analysed in Chapter 3, which should be consulted for the wider context of these sources. Some of the original vocabulary and phrasing has been modernised in order to help the reader. These changes have been kept to a minimum.

Document study: Why was Italy not united in 1848–49?

1 The revolutions of 1848 to 1849

1.1 Palermo, Sicily, 12 January 1848: the first day of the first revolution of 1848

When the new day dawned, it was found that the armed militia were standing by. The streets were crowded with people, all waiting for the conspirators to appear, for the signal to be given, for the first shout to arise. A bold youth, truculent by nature and weary of delay, brandished a gun and shouted resolutely, 'To arms! To arms!' [A group of men] ran up, all of them armed. One of them tied a white handkerchief and a red one to the end of a stick with a green ribbon and began waving the Italian colours.

At the sight of weapons and the small number bearing them, the crowd thinned out and then entirely disappeared. The handful of intrepid spirits found themselves almost deserted. But no one lost heart. Little bands and squads of people began to form here and there; the more forceful took the lead and the rest followed their example, not their orders. There were no rules, ranks or plans. No one barricaded the streets or cordoned them off as might have happened elsewhere. People did not assemble in any one place. One band [of rebels] put a patrol to flight in one street; others were successful elsewhere. So the whole day went by. Two rebels were dead and so were ten soldiers; the wounded were more numerous. The rebels then returned to the square which ever since the morning had been the centre of their activities. Not more than fifty carried firearms. A single company of infantrymen would have been enough to disperse them; but the militiamen had not stirred from their posts; remembering the events of 1820, they would not venture into the densely populated parts of the city. Meanwhile every house was festively illuminated, balconies and windows crowded with people clapping their hands and shouting: 'Long Live Italy, the Sicilian Constitution and Pius IX!' This was a spontaneous, unexpected and universal assent of the people, which put the authorities in a quandary and took the heart out of the soldiers.

Source: Giuseppe La Farina, one of the leaders of the Sicilian revolution, *The story of Italy, 1815–60*, 1861

1.2 The proclamation of Charles Albert, king of Piedmont, 23 March 1848

The destinies of Italy are maturing, and a happier future is opening up for those of us who bravely stand up for their rights against the oppressor.

We, out of our love for our common race, understanding as we do what is now happening, and supported by public opinion, hasten to associate ourselves with the unanimous admiration which Italy bestows on you.

People of Lombardy and Venetia, our arms, which were concentrating on your frontier when you forestalled events by liberating your glorious Milan, are now coming to offer you in the latter phases of your fight the help which a brother expects from a brother, and a friend from a friend.

We will support you in your desires, confident as we are in the help of God, who is manifestly on our side; of the God who has given Pius IX to Italy; of God whose helpful hand has wonderfully enabled Italy to rely on her own strength.

In order to show more openly our feelings of Italian brotherhood, we have ordered our troops as they move into Lombardy and Venice to carry the cross of Savoy imposed on the tricolour flag of Italy.

Source: Denis Mack Smith, *The making of Italy, 1796–1866* (1988)

1.3 The Papal Allocution, 29 April 1848

Seeing that some at present desire that We too, along with the other princes of Italy and their subjects, should engage in war against the Austrians, We have thought it convenient to proclaim clearly and openly that such a measure is altogether alien from our counsels inasmuch as We reach to and embrace all peoples and nations with solemn affection.

We cannot refrain from repudiating, before the face of all nations, the treacherous advice of those who have the Roman Pontiff to be the head of and preside over the formation of some sort of novel republic of the whole Italian people. Rather, on this occasion, moved by the love We bear them, we do urgently warn and exhort the Italian people to abstain from the like counsels [advice], deceitful and ruinous to Italy herself, and to abide in close attachment to their respective sovereigns, of whose good will they have already had experience . . . For if they do otherwise, they . . . would run a risk of dividing Italy herself with fresh discords and intestine factions.

Source: Denis Mack Smith, *The making of Italy, 1796–1866* (1988)

1.4 Mazzini speaks to the constituent assembly in Rome, March 1849

There are not five Italies, or four Italies or three Italies. There is only one Italy. God, who in creating her, smiled upon her land, has awarded her the two most sublime frontiers in Europe, symbols of eternal strength and eternal motion – the Alps and the sea. Rome shall be the holy ark of your redemption, the temple of your nation. Rome, by the design of providence, and as the people have divined, is the *Eternal City* to which is entrusted the mission of disseminating the word that will unite the world. Just as to the *Rome of the Caesars*, which through action united a great part of Europe, there succeeded the *Rome of the Popes*, which united Europe and America in the realm of the spirit, so the *Rome of the People* will succeed them both, to unite Europe, America and every part of the terrestrial globe in a faith that will make action and thought one. The destiny of Rome and Italy is that of the world.

Source: Christopher Hibbert, *Garibaldi and his enemies* **(1987)**

Document-study questions

1 Explain the reference in 1.2 to the 'cross of Savoy imposed on the tricolour flag of Italy'.
2 How reliable is 1.1 as an account of the 1848 revolutions in Italy?
3 How useful is 1.4 as a description of Italian nationalism in 1849?
4 Using these sources and your own knowledge, consider the view that the revolutions of 1848 to 1849 showed that the Italians were too divided to establish an Italian state by themselves.

Document-study: How important to the unification of Italy were foreign circumstances and assistance?

2 The Plombières agreement and the war with Austria, 1858–59

2.1 Cavour's account of the meeting with Napoleon III, July 1858

As soon as I entered the Emperor's study, he raised the question which was the purpose of my journey. He began by saying that he had decided to support Piedmont with all his power in a war against Austria, provided that the war was undertaken for a non-revolutionary end which could be justified in the eyes of diplomatic circles – and still more in the eyes of French and European public opinion.

The Emperor readily agreed that it was necessary to drive the Austrians out of Italy once and for all and to leave them without an inch of territory south of the Alps . . . But how was Italy to be organised after that? After a long discussion . . . we agreed more or less to the following principles, recognising that they were subject to modification as the course of war might determine. The valley of the Po, the Romagna, and the Legations would form a kingdom of Upper Italy under the House of Savoy. Rome and its immediate surroundings would be left to the Pope. The rest of the Papal States, together with Tuscany would form a kingdom of central Italy. The Neopolitan frontier would be left unchanged. These four states would form a confederation on the pattern of the German *Bund*, the presidency of which would be given to the Pope to console him for losing the best part of his States.

After we had settled the fate of Italy, the Emperor asked what France would get and asked whether Your Majesty would cede Savoy and Nice. I answered that Your Majesty believed in the principle of nationalities and realised accordingly that Savoy should be ceded to France. The question of Nice was different because the people of Nice by origin, language and customs were closer to Piedmont than France. The Emperor stroked his moustache several times and merely remarked that these were for him quite secondary issues which we could discuss later.

Source: Denis Mack Smith, *The making of Italy, 1796–1866* (1988); Cavour sent this account to Victor Emmanuel I

2.2 The Franco-Piedmontese treaty, January 1859

Article 1 If aggression by Austria leads to war between the Piedmontese King and the Emperor of Austria, an offensive and defensive alliance will come into force between the Emperor of the French and the King of Piedmont-Sardinia.

Article 2 The aims of the alliance will be to liberate Italy from Austrian occupation, to satisfy the wishes of the people, and to end the complications which threaten war and keep Europe unsettled. The object would be, if the issue of war so permit, to create a Kingdom of Upper Italy with about eleven million inhabitants.

Article 3 The Duchy of Savoy and the Province of Nice will, by the same principle, be reunited with France.

Article 4 Whatever happens in the war, it is expressly stipulated that the interests of the Catholic Religion and the sovereignty of the Pope shall be maintained.

Article 5 The cost of the war will be born by the Kingdom of Upper Italy.

Article 6 The High Contracting Parties will accept no overtures for peace without previous agreement.

Source: Denis Mack Smith, *The making of Italy, 1796–1866* (1988)

2.3 The Truce of Villafranca, 11 July 1859

[1] The two sovereigns support the creation of an Italian confederation under the presidency of the Pope.

[2] The Emperor of Austria concedes to the Emperor of the French his rights over Lombardy except for the fortresses of Mantua and Peschiera . . . The Emperor of the French will then hand over these territories to King Victor Emmanuel.

[3] Venetia will become part of the Italian Confederation though still belonging to the Austrian crown.

[4] The Grand Duke of Tuscany and the Duke of Modena will return to their states.

[5] The two Emperors will ask the Holy Father to make certain indispensable reforms in his states.

Source: Denis Mack Smith, *The making of Italy, 1796–1866* (1988)

2.4 A report of the views of Victor Emmanuel II, 14 July 1859

As regard these preliminaries [of peace] the King informed me that he at first refused to sign them but, as the Emperor Napoleon insisted and he was therefore in a great measure helpless, he consented. His Majesty seemed to own that a great deal had been done but [he] was doubtful whether in its present shape the treaty would be a guarantee against another war. In point of fact His Majesty seemed to me personally quite contented with what had been done. H. M. said that, if left to his own choice, his life would be spent hunting, travelling or soldiering, that he hated 'his life as a king' and only followed it because it was his duty to do so.

After this H. M. talked of Count Cavour, who that day had tendered his resignation. 'He is a muddle head who is always pushing me into some wasps' nest or other. Cavour is mad. I have often told him he was off his head. He goes off playing follies, like this rising in the Romagna, and heaven knows what else. But he is finished now. He did a good job but he is finished.' His Majesty also gave an amusing description of his having put Cavour under arrest before the outbreak of the war for crying out at the top of his voice every accusation against France and the Emperor. Luckily, His Majesty added, 'that lucky ultimatum' came and Cavour reappeared rubbing his hands and quite contented.

His Majesty entered also into his differences with the Pope, who, he said, had threatened to excommunicate him, a proceeding at which he would snap his fingers (using a much blunter phrase). Finally, His Majesty expressed himself as quite taken aback by Napoleon's sudden peacemaking with all its attendant circumstances, but explains it by the only fact in this narration which may be considered important, if true, viz. that Napoleon is unable to continue the war for which he was in reality anything but prepared.

Source: the dispatch of the British military attaché in Milan to the British foreign secretary, 14 July 1859, quoted in Denis Mack Smith, *The making of Italy, 1796–1866* (1988)

Document-study questions

1 Explain what is meant in 2.3 by 'an Italian Confederation under the presidency of the Pope'.
2 Compare the terms of the treaty in 2.2 with the terms of the peace in 2.3.
3 How reliable is 2.1 as an account of the meeting at Plombières?
4 How useful are the sources in helping us to understand the role that Napoleon III played in the unification of Italy?

Document-study: How important to the unification of Italy were the efforts of Italians?

3 Garibaldi's expedition to Sicily, May 1860

3.1 Garibaldi lands at Marsala on 11 May 1860

Source: Lithograph from the Bertarelli Collection, Milan

3.2 Garibaldi's account of the landing at Marsala

My first idea was to land at Sciacca but as the day was advanced and we were afraid of meeting enemy cruisers we resolved to put into the nearest port – that of Marsala (May 11 1860).

As we approached the western coast of Sicily we began to discover sailing vessels and steamers. On the roadstead of Marsala two men-of-war were

Italian unification, 1848–71 193

anchored, which turned out to be English. Having decided to land at Marsala, we approached the port and reached it about noon. On reaching the harbour we found it full of merchant vessels of different nations.

Fortune indeed favoured us and so guided our expedition that we could not have arrived at a more propitious moment. The Bourbon cruisers had left the harbour of Marsala that morning, sailing eastward, while we were arriving from the west. Indeed they were still in sight as we entered – so that, by the time they came within cannon shot, we had already landed all of the men out of the *Piemonte* and were beginning to disembark those on board the *Lombardo*.

The presence of the two English men-at-war in some degree influenced the determination of the Bourbon commanders, who were naturally impatient to open fire on us, and this circumstance gave us time to get our whole force on shore. The noble English flag once more helped to prevent bloodshed and I, the Benjamin [i.e. the favourite son] of these lords of the ocean, was for the hundredth time protected by them.

The assertion, however, made by our enemies, that the English had directly favoured and assisted our landing at Marsala, was inaccurate. The British colours, flying from the two men-of-war and [from] the English consulate, made the Bourbon mercenaries hesitate and, I might even say, impressed them with a sense of shame at pouring the fire of their imposing batteries into a handful of men armed only with the kind of muskets usually supplied to Italian volunteers.

Notwithstanding this, three-fourths of the volunteers were still on the quay when the Bourbons began firing on them with shells and grapeshot – happily without injury to anyone. The *Piemonte*, abandoned by us, was carried off by the enemy, who left the *Lombardo*, which had grounded on a sandbank.

Source: Giuseppe Garibaldi, *The autobiography of Garibaldi*, vol. 2, published in English in 1889

3.3 A British account of the landing at Marsala

The Sardinians were putting ashore men, stores and ammunition as fast as possible. Presently a boat was seen to quit the Neopolitan steamer and pull towards the grounded Sardinian. She had not, however, reached more than halfway to the vessel, when a panic seized those in her, and a retreat was hastily made to their ship which now opened fire upon the breakwater with heavy guns. [The commanders of the British ships and the British Consul] proceeded on board the Neopolitan to tell her captain to direct his shot and shell clear of the British wine establishments. He seemed much impressed with the responsibility of his situation but promised not to injure British property. We now left him and were pulling for the *Intrepid* [one of the English ships] when the Neopolitan sailing frigate came bearing down on our boat and her officers waved us to pull faster. Hardly had they done so when a veritable storm of shot and missiles of all kinds, delivered from her broadside guns, passed over our heads but fell short of the breakwater. One of the shot, however, entered [the British] wine establishment and nearly killed the manager's wife.

The Sardinian steamers being completely deserted, the Neopolitans sent in armed boats to take possession of them. They succeeded in bringing out the one that had entered the inner harbour but scuttled the one that had grounded at its entrance.

The Neopolitan steamers continued, during this operation, to fire heavily at parties dragging guns and ammunition into the town but we saw only one man knocked over (he was wounded in the shoulder). The patriots stood fire splendidly and appeared altogether to be a fine body of men.

Source: Rear Admiral H. F. Winnington-Ingram, the captain of one of the English ships at Marsala in 1860, *Hearts of oak*, 1889

3.4 A speech made by Victor Hugo, 14 June 1860

Gentlemen, the earthquake in Sicily which we are witnessing is the work of God. Flaming on high above the scene you may behold Patriotism, Faith, Liberty, Honour, Heroism, an eruption to eclipse Etna.

All, be who we may, applaud Italy. Let us glorify her, the land of wonder-births. It is in such nations that certain abstract dogmas become real, for they are virgins in their honour and mothers by reason of their progress.

Italy a living entity, Italy now Italy! Where there was once a geographical term there is now a nation; where there was a corpse, there is now a living soul; where there was a ghost there is now an archangel, the mighty archangel of the peoples of the earth, Liberty, watching over her with wings outstretched.

Gentlemen, I tell you that there is but one reality: Right. If you would make comparisons between Right and Force, make trial by means of figures. On 11 May eight hundred [sic] men landed at Marsala. Twenty seven days later, on 7 June, eighteen thousand scared men quit Palermo. The eight hundred represent Right, the eighteen thousand represent Force.

Let all those who suffer be comforted, all those that are in servitude take heart. All that is happening at present is remorselessly logical.

My message to the four winds of heaven is: Hope! Let the mujik, the fellah, the proletarian, the negro that is bought and sold, the oppressed whites – let them all hope. Chains are like a net: they are perfect when intact but let one link or one mesh be broken and the whole is undone. Therein lies the solidarity of despotisms. The Pope is more akin to the Sultan than he imagines.

But I repeat: the end is at hand. Oh, how fine is the force of circumstances! There is something superhuman in the force of deliverance. Liberty is a divine abyss which bids us leap; revolutions are irresistible in their essence. Progress is as inevitable as the law of gravitation; who then shall put it into shackles? Once the impulsion is given, the uncontrollable is set in motion.

Despots! I defy you! Stop, if you can the falling stone, hold back the torrents, arrest the avalanche, put a period [halt] to '89, bring to a standstill the world launched by God into the light!

Source: a speech given by Victor Hugo to the Friends of Sicily in Jersey

Document-study questions

1 Explain the reference in 3.4 to 'Patriotism, Faith, Liberty, Honour, Heroism'.
2 How useful a depiction of the landing at Marsala is 3.1?
3 Which account of the landing at Marsala is the more reliable, 3.2 or 3.3?
4 Using these sources and any other evidence known to you, assess the importance of Garibaldi's invasion of Sicily in May 1860 to both Italy and Europe.

Appendix A

**European states, 1825 and 1890
(excluding Monaco, Liechtenstein and San Marino)**

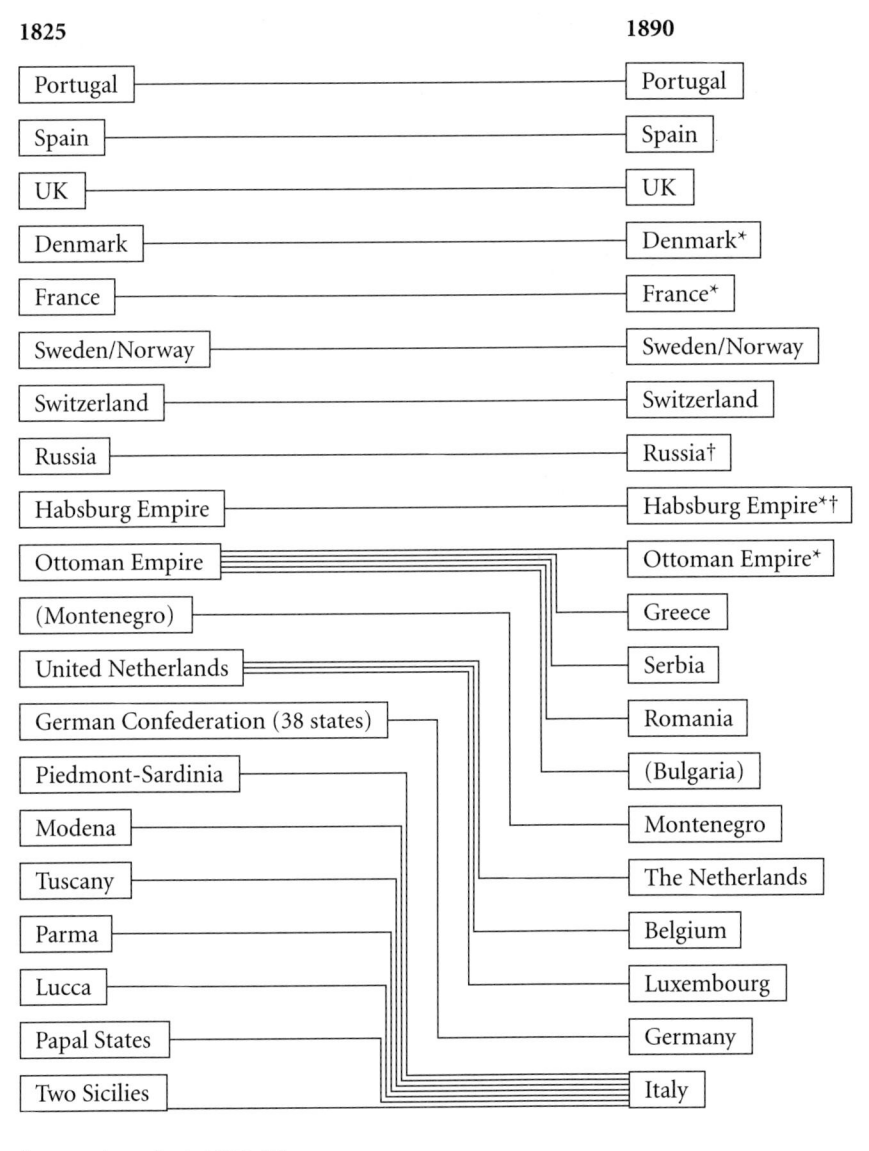

1825	1890
Portugal	Portugal
Spain	Spain
UK	UK
Denmark	Denmark*
France	France*
Sweden/Norway	Sweden/Norway
Switzerland	Switzerland
Russia	Russia†
Habsburg Empire	Habsburg Empire*†
Ottoman Empire	Ottoman Empire*
(Montenegro)	Greece
United Netherlands	Serbia
German Confederation (38 states)	Romania
Piedmont-Sardinia	(Bulgaria)
Modena	Montenegro
Tuscany	The Netherlands
Parma	Belgium
Lucca	Luxembourg
Papal States	Germany
Two Sicilies	Italy

* territory lost, 1825–90
† territory gained, 1825–90
( ) autonomous state

The new Italy did not include the Vatican City, but did include Lombardy-Venetia from the Habsburg Empire.

Appendix B
The use of military force by type, 1825–90

Dates	Between states	National revolts	Armed intervention	Outside Europe
1825–47	• Russia v Turkey over Greece, 1828–29	• Greece v Turkey, 1821–30 • Belgium v The Netherlands, 1830–39 • (Egypt v Turkey, 1830–41) • Poland v Russia, 1831–32 • Poland v Austria, 1847	• UK and France in Greece, 1827–28 • Russia in Moldavia, 1832 • Austria in Italy, 1832–38 • France in Belgium, 1832 • France in Italy, 1832–38 • Russia in Poland, 1832+ • UK and Austria in Syria, 1840 • Austria in Krakow, 1847+	• Russia v Persia, 1826–28 • UK v China, 1839–42 • France in Algeria, 1832–47 • Russia in Caucasus, 1832–64 • Russia in Central Asia, 1839+
1848–71	• Piedmont v Austria, 1848 and 1849 • Germany v Denmark, 1849 • CRIMEA, 1854–56 • France and Piedmont v Austria, 1859 • Austria and Prussia v Denmark, 1864 • Austria v Prussia, 1866 • France v Prussia, 1870–71	• Hungary v Austria, 1848–49 • Poland v Russia, 1863	• Russia in Moldavia, 1848 • Russia in Hungary, 1849 • France in Italy, 1849–66 and 1867–70	• Russia in Far East v China and Japan to 1860 and 1875 • Indian Mutiny v UK, 1857 • UK and France v China, 1858–60 • France in Indochina, 1859–60 • France in Syria/Lebanon, 1860 • France in Mexico, 1862–67
1871–90	• Russia v Turkey, 1878			• UK in Afghanistan, 1878–79, 1885 • UK v Transvaal, 1880–81 • France in Indochina, 1883–84 • UK in Sudan, 1884–85 • France in Ivory Coast, 1887–89

Appendix C
The use of military force by great powers, 1825–90

	Austria	Britain	France	Prussia/Germany	Russia
1825–47	• **Italy, 1832** • Syria, 1840 • **Poland (Krakow), 1847**	• Greece, 1827–28 • China, 1839–42 • Syria, 1840	• Greece, 1827–28 • **Belgium, 1831** • **Italy, 1832–38** • Algeria, 1832–37		• Persia, 1826–29 • Turkey, 1828–29 • **Poland, 1832** • **Moldavia, 1832** • Caucasus, 1829–64 • Central Asia, 1839+
1848–71	• **Piedmont, 1848 and 1849** • **Denmark, 1849** • **France, 1859** • **Denmark, 1864** • **Prussia, 1866**	• Russia, 1854 • China, 1857–60 • India, 1857	• **Italy, 1849–70** • **Russia, 1854** • China, 1858–60 • Lebanon/Syria, 1858 • **Austria, 1859** • Indochina, 1859–60 • Mexico, 1862–67 • **Prussia, 1870–71**	• **Denmark, 1849** • **Denmark, 1864** • **Austria, 1866** • **France, 1870–71**	• **Moldavia, 1848** • **Hungary, 1849** • **Ottoman Empire, 1853–56** • **France and UK, 1854–56** • Caucasus (continued) • Central Asia (continued) • Far East, to 1875
1871–90		• South Africa, 1880–81 • Afghanistan, 1878–79 and 1885 • Sudan, 1884–85	• Indochina, 1883–85 • Ivory Coast, 1887–89		• **Ottoman Empire, 1877–78**

Bold type refers to conflicts within Europe.

Appendix D
Bismarck's alliance system, 1879–90

Title	Signatories	Duration	Main terms	Renewed?
Dual Alliance (1879)	Germany, Austria	Five years	• Mutual military support if attacked by Russia • Neutrality if attacked by another power • If one attacked by Russia plus another power, then other to provide military support	Regularly
***Dreikaiserbund* (1881)**	Germany, Austria, Russia	Three years	• Neutrality if attacked by another power • Agreement to respect interests of Austria and Russia in the Near East • Secret agreement on claims in Near East	In 1884 but not in 1887
Triple Alliance (1882)	Germany, Austria, Italy	Five years	• If France attacked Italy, the other two signatories to support it with all of their forces • If France attacked Germany, Italy to provide support • If any attacked by two great powers, others to provide all support • If any attacked by one great power, others to observe benevolent neutrality	Regularly
Reinsurance Treaty (1887)	Germany, Russia	Three years	• If one attacked by another great power, the other to observe benevolent neutrality • Germany recognises Russian rights in the Balkans • Secret agreement by which Germany supports Russian claims in the Balkans	Not renewed by Germany in 1890

Appendix E

The British system of government in the nineteenth century

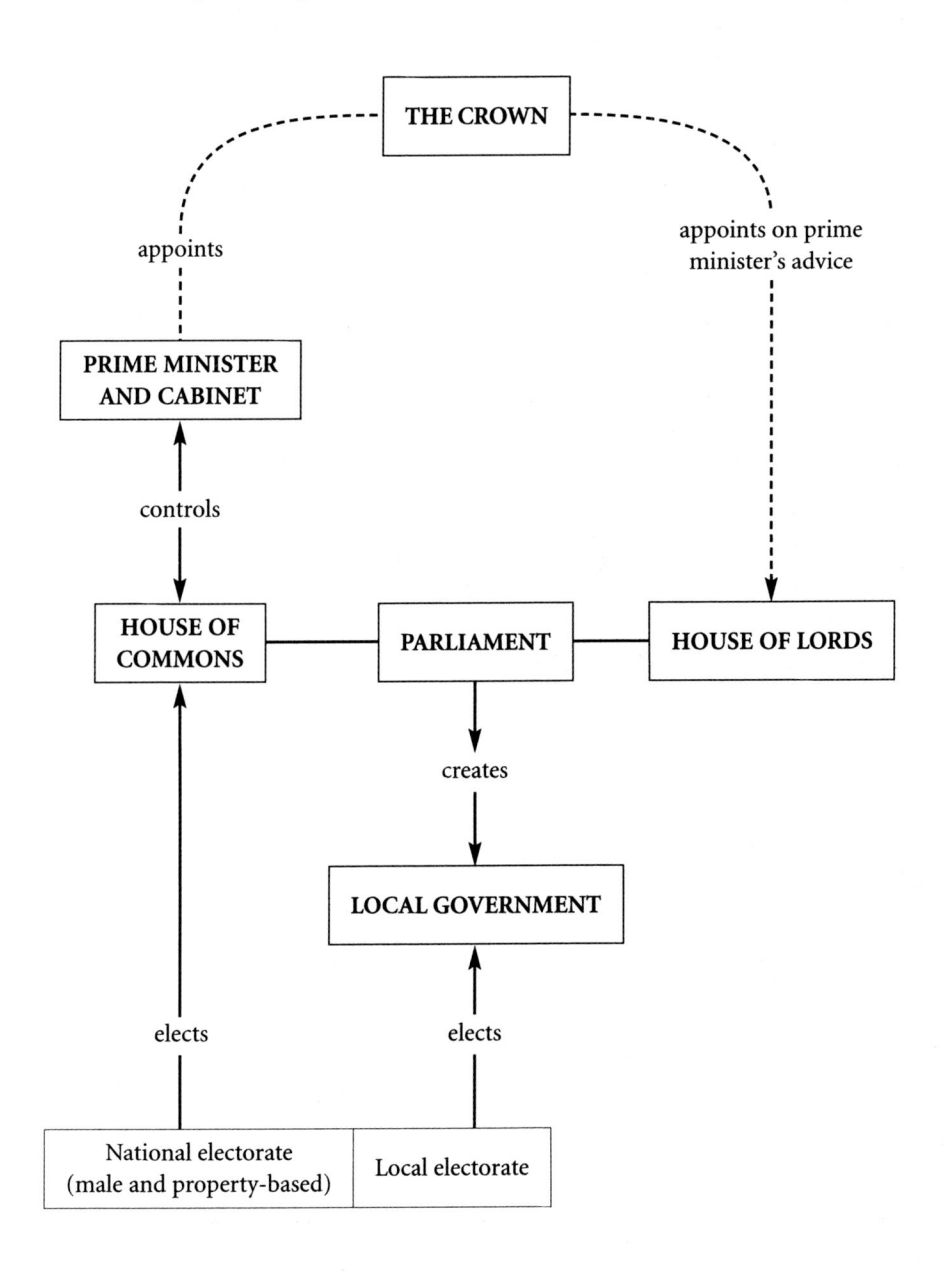

```
                    THE CROWN
         appoints                appoints on prime
                                 minister's advice

    PRIME MINISTER
    AND CABINET

         ↕ controls

    HOUSE OF      ―  PARLIAMENT  ―  HOUSE OF LORDS
    COMMONS
                        ↓ creates

                   LOCAL GOVERNMENT
                        ↑ elects
         ↑ elects
    National electorate      Local electorate
    (male and property-based)
```

This chart provides a useful model to compare with the French and German systems of government (pp. 95, 156). The arrows symbolise a power relationship, the arrow pointing towards the *less* powerful of the two. A dotted line symbolises a formal, but more limited, relationship.

Further reading

General surveys

There are two single-volume surveys of nineteenth-century Europe which provide useful information and some analysis: *The ascendancy of Europe 1815–1914* (Longman, 1985) by M. S. Anderson and *Barricades and borders: Europe 1800–1914* (Oxford UP, 1996) by Robert Gildea. The whole nineteenth century is covered in just one chapter of Norman Davies' controversial *Europe: a history* (Oxford UP, 1997). It provides both a very broad overview as well as some unusual perspectives on the period, the latter by means of what the author calls 'capsules'.

The short nineteenth century has been covered as part of two series of general textbooks. All three of the Longman series are still in print: *Europe 1780–1830* (1989) by Franklin Ford, *Europe in the nineteenth century 1830–80* (1988) by Harry Hearder and *Europe 1880–1945* (1988) by J. M. Roberts are thorough surveys. Two of the original Fontana histories of Europe were republished by Blackwell in 1999: *Europe reshaped 1848–78* by J. A. S. Grenville and Norman Stone's more idiosyncratic *Europe transformed 1878–1919*.

Eric Hobsbawm has written a trilogy on the history of the world since 1789 which includes a great deal on Europe: *The age of revolution 1789–1848* (Abacus, 1977), *The age of capital 1848–78* (Abacus, 1987) and the *Age of empire 1878–1914* (Abacus, 1994). Their focus is more economic, social and cultural than political. However, in providing insights into the world of the nineteenth century they are invaluable.

A useful work of reference which summarises the development of the various nationalities of Europe is *The Longman companion to European nationalism 1789–1920* (1994) by Raymond Pearson.

And there is one general book which does focus on Europe from 1830 to 1890, *Themes in modern European history 1830–90* (Routledge, 1990). Edited by Bruce Waller, it includes essays on each of the four countries which form the basis of this book as well on other aspects of the period.

Italy

The great name of historical writing on nineteenth-century Italy is Denis Mack Smith. Not only has he written a great deal on the subject but his studies of the *Risorgimento* have changed people's ideas about the subject. He has edited an excellent collection of documents on the period, *The making of Italy 1976–1866* (Macmillan, 1988). His more general history of Italy starts with unification in 1861. The first three chapters of

Modern Italy: a political history (Yale UP, 1997) covers only a part of the subject considered here but are worth reading. Mack Smith has also written biographies of the three main political figures of the *Risorgimento*, of which only *Mazzini* (Yale UP, 1994) remains in print. The most accessible account of the amazing life of Garibaldi is *Garibaldi and his enemies* (Penguin, 1987) by Christopher Hibbert. There is no brief biography of Cavour currently in print.

There are a number of books which provide a mixture of primary sources and secondary commentary. *The Risorgimento and the unification of Italy* (Addison Wesley Longman, 1982) by Derek Beales was the first. It took a predominately narrative approach, though only to 1861. With Vyvyen Brendon's *The making of modern Italy 1800–1871* (Hodder and Stoughton, 1998) the emphasis is more on the primary sources. Andrina Stiles' *The unification of Italy 1815–1870* (Hodder and Stoughton, 1989) has more commentary than sources plus some documentary exercises. *The Italian Risorgimento* by Martin Clark (Longman, 1998) has an analytical narrative followed by a selection of sources. All are useful. *The unification of Italy* (Routledge, 1986) by John Gooch is a brief introduction to the subject but without any primary sources.

Also available is *The origins of the Italian wars of independence* (Longman, 1992) by Frank J. Coppa, which is not as narrow as its title suggests. It is a detailed secondary narrative of the main diplomatic and military events which resulted in the unification of Italy.

And for a different perspective Lucy Riall's *The Italian Risorgimento: state, society and national unification* (Routledge, 1994) is well worth seeking out.

France

The best single volume on nineteenth-century France is *France 1814–1914* (Longman, 1996) by Robert Tombs. Organised thematically, it provides sound coverage of all aspects of France at the time. The same author's *The Paris Commune 1871* (Longman, 1999) is also worth reading as the most recent analysis of a very controversial event of the time.

With regard to the specific aspects of French history between 1848 and 1875, the first, the outbreak of the revolution of 1848, is placed in the context of the preceding period by Pamela Pilbeam in *The constitutional monarchy in France 1815–1848* (Longman, 2000). The 1848 revolution and its repercussions to 1851 are covered by reference to various primary sources in *Documents of the French Revolution of 1848* (Macmillan, 1996) by Roger Price. This author also provides the best introduction to Napoleon III in his *Napoleon III and the Second Empire* (Routledge, 1997), though this time without providing primary sources. A biographical approach to the French emperor is taken by James McMillan with *Napoleon III* (Longman, 1991).

Three books which combine secondary text and primary sources in varying proportions cover different aspects of the period. A more analytical approach is developed by W. H. B. Court in *Second Empire and Commune: France 1848–71* (Longman, 1996). Keith Randell in *France 1814–70: monarchy, republic and empire* (Hodder and Stoughton, 1991) provides commentary, sources and exercises. The best brief introduction to the final part of the period, 1870 to 1875, is the first part of *France 1870–1914* by Robert Gildea (Longman, 1996).

Russia

Of the four countries covered in this book, there are fewest accessible sources on Russia. Russia from 1825 to 1881 is placed in a broader context by J. N. Westwood in *Endurance and endeavour: Russian history 1812–1992* (Oxford UP, 1993). Despite the long period covered, the author provides plenty of detailed evidence and explanation. A more focused secondary text is *Russia in the age of reaction and reform 1801–81* (Longman, 1992) by David Saunders. Hugh Seton-Watson's *The Russian Empire 1801–1917* (Oxford UP, 1988) is still in print. Its painstaking approach demands much of the reader.

There are only two brief introductions which contain both primary sources and secondary comment. One is on central political themes and that is *Russia 1815–81* (Hodder and Stoughton, 1991) by Russell Sherman. The other, which focuses on the growth of opposition is *Nineteenth century Russia: opposition to autocracy* (Longman, 1999) by Derek Offord.

The Longman companion to imperial Russia 1689–1917 (available 2000) by David Longley should be a valuable reference source.

Germany

Germany is relatively well provided for. There are general textbooks within which Germany from 1862 to 1890 is covered. These include *A history of Germany 1815–1990* (Arnold, fourth edition, 1991) by William Carr, *German history since 1800* (Arnold, 1997) by Mary Fulbrook and *The history of Germany since 1789* (Pimlico, 1996) by Golo Mann. This last book is very well written, if now a little dated. A more recent general account of nineteenth-century Germany is *The Fontana history of Germany 1780–1918* (Fontana, 1997) by David Blackbourn. Those who persevere with the dense content of the book will eventually gain a very sound understanding of the period.

There are several more focused accounts of the Bismarck era which are suitable as an advanced introduction. Books which provide primary sources as well as secondary text include *The unification of Germany* (Cambridge UP, 1989) by Michael Gorman, *Bismarck and the unification of Germany* (Macmillan, 1991) by David Hargreaves, *Bismarck and Germany* (Longman, 1997) by D. G. Williamson and *The unification of Germany 1815–90* (Hodder and Stoughton, 1989) by Andrina Stiles. Each has its good points. There are two introductory books which link the second half of the Bismarck era with Germany to 1918. One is *Bismarck and the German Empire 1871–1918* (Routledge, 1995) by Lynn Abrams, the other *Imperial Germany 1871–1918* (Routledge, 1998) by Stephen Lee. Those who want more detail on Bismarck's Germany from 1866 would do best to consult the early chapters of *Germany 1866–1945* (Oxford UP, 1978) by Gordon Craig. There are three general biographies of Bismarck currently in print. The briefest is *Bismarck* (Blackwell, 1997) by Bruce Waller. The oldest is A. J. P. Taylor's *Bismarck: man and statesman*, first published in 1955 and republished by Penguin in 1995. The third, *Bismarck*, published by Papermac in 1992 is by Edward Crankshaw, a journalist turned historian.

For an account of the wars of 1862–71 the best source is *The wars of German unification* (Longman, 1991) by William Carr.

Other relevant texts

The main criteria for inclusion in this section are books which increase understanding of central themes. On political revolutions *Revolutions 1789–1917* (Cambridge UP, 1998) by Allan Todd, which includes some primary materials, is useful. On the main revolution of the period, 1848, *The revolutions of 1848* (Longman, 1991) by Peter Jones is the best introduction. On nationalities *Nationalism in Europe 1789–1945* (Cambridge UP, 1998) by Timothy Baycroft enables the growth of nationalism to be placed in a wider context. And a stimulating, readable perspective on the growth of nationalist ideas is *Holy madness: romantics, patriots and revolutionaries 1776–1871* (Weidenfeld & Nicolson, 1999) by Adam Zamoyski.

One issue throughout the period is the problem caused by the decline of the Ottoman Empire. A. L. MacFie's *The Eastern Question* (Longman, 1996) will provide an accessible introduction to a very complicated subject.

Index

agriculture, 3, 176; in Russia, 123
Aksakov, Ivan and Konstantin, 115
Alexander I, tsar of Russia, 103–4, 105
Alexander II, tsar of Russia, 82, 114, 120–31; and army reforms, 123–4; assassination of, 114, 119, 120, 129–30, 132, 178, 179, 180; assessment of the reign of, 130–1; character, 131; and the Crimean War, 120–1, 123, 124, 126, 127, 130, 132; economic policy, 126–7; and educational reform, 124–5; and the emancipation of the serfs, 117, 121–3, 132–4; and financial reforms, 124; foreign policy of, 127–9; and judicial reforms, 124; limitations of reforms, 125–6; and oppositional thought, 116–19, 120; and the *zemstva*, 124
Alexander III, tsar of Russia, 126, 131, 180
anarchism, 118, 178
ancien régime, 16
aristocracy, *see* nobility
Asia, Russian territorial gains in, 128
Austria: and the Crimean War (1855–57), 41, 42, 83, 112, 121; and the Dual Alliance (1879), 165; and the Eastern question, 164; economy, 144, 171; and France, 85–6; French war with (1859), 76, 81–2, 83–4, 143; and Germany, 136, 137, 138, 139, 140, 142; and Italy, 22, 26, 27, 31–2, 33–4, 35, 36, 40, 42, 44, 51–2, 54, 56–7, 144; and Metternich, 11, 22; Prussia and German unification, 139, 140, 141, 142; and Russia, 110, 127, 128; and Schleswig-Holstein, 146, 147; sovereign rule in, 3; and the Triple Alliance, 165; war with Prussia (1866), 8, 12, 147–50, 151, 152
autocracy, in Russia, 102–3, 108, 111, 112, 113–14
Azelgio, Massimo d', 38, 39, 40

Bakunin, Mikhail, 115, 116, 118
balance of power in 1871, 145, 153
banks: in France, 78–9; in Russia, 124
Belgium, 11, 182
Belinsky, Vissarion, 115, 116, 117, 119

Berlin, Treaty of (1878), 128, 164
Bismarck, Otto von, 1, 12, 56, 64, 85, 88, 178; appointment as Prussian first minister, 143, 144; assessment of his leadership, 169–71; and the Austro-Prussian war (1866), 147, 148, 149, 150; background and character, 143–4; 'blood and iron' speech, 145–6; chancellorship of the German Empire, 154–69; and conservatism, 161–3, 180, 184; dismissal from office, 163, 167–9; domestic policy (1871–90), 158–63; and the Ems telegram, 86, 150; foreign policy (1871–90), 163–7, 171; and the Franco-Prussian war, 150–1, 152; and the German constitution, 155–7; and the German occupation of France, 90, 92, 93; and German unification, 136, 150–1; and nationalism, 184; and Russia, 127; statement to Disraeli (1862), 171–2; style of diplomacy, 154
Bluvshtein, Sophia (the 'Golden Hand'), 129
Bonaparte, Louis Napoleon, *see* Napoleon III
Bonaparte, Napoleon, *see* Napoleon I
Boulanger, General Georges, 165
bourgeoisie, *see* middle class (bourgeoisie)
Britain: conservatism in, 180; and the Crimean War (1855–57), 41, 42, 82, 83; and the Franco-Prussian war, 152; and Germany, 136, 163, 165–6, 166; and the Greek War of Independence, 20; industrial growth in, 16–17; and Italian unification, 44, 52; and Napoleon III of France, 82, 84; and Russian territorial expansion, 128; urban growth in, 175
Bulgaria, 182
Bulgarian crisis (1885–87), 165
Byron, George Gordon, Lord, 18, 105

canals, 17–18
Carbonari, in Italy, 28, 29, 37
Catholic Church, 9, 10, 20–2; in Germany, 142, 151, 158–9, 161, 170; and Napoleon III of France, 77, 80, 82; *see also* papacy

Cavour, Count Camillo di, 1, 37, 38–40, 43, 45, 58, 84, 192; and the Crimean War, 41–2; death of, 54; and Garibaldi's conquest of Sicily, 45–6, 47–8; meeting with Napoleon III at Plombières, 42–3, 83, 190–1; and Piedmont's invasion of the Papal States, 48–9; and the unification of Italy, 50, 51, 52, 53
Chaadyev, Peter, 115
Chambord, Comte Henri de, 92–3
change, forces for, 4–9
Charles Albert, king of Piedmont, 29, 33, 34, 36, 189
Charles Felix, king of Piedmont, 26, 29
Charles X, king of France, 23, 28, 64
Charles XII, king of Sweden, 101
chemical industry, 176
Chernyshevsky, Nikolai, *What is to be done?*, 117, 125
Christian churches, 10, 20–2; *see also* Catholic Church; Orthodox Christianity; Protestantism
Christian IX, king of Denmark, 146
Churchill, Winston, 99, 100
cities, 3, 15, 28
Clausewitz, Karl von, *On war*, 147
Cobden, Richard, 80
Cochrane, John, 101–2
collectivist policies, 12–13, 181
colonialism, 13, 179; and the German Empire, 154, 162, 166, 167
communism, 7, 178
conscription, military, 9, 123
conservatism, 180; in the German Empire, 161–3, 180, 184
constitutional government, 6
consumer society, 13
continuity, forces for, 9–11
coups d'état: Decembrist Revolt in Russia (1825), 104–5; France (December 1851), 63, 71, 72–5
Crimean War (1855–57), 1, 41–2, 51, 82–3, 111, 112–13, 120–1, 123, 124, 126, 127, 130, 132, 145
customs barriers, 17

Darwin, Charles, 3
Delacroix, Eugène, *Liberty leading the people*, 18–19

democracy, 6, 181, 184; and the German Empire, 155, 157; and Napoleon III of France, 88; and the *zemstva* in Russia, 124
demographic change, 4
Denmark, war with Prussia (1864), 146–7
Disraeli, Benjamin, 164, 171–2, 180
Dolgorukaya, Princess Catherine, 129
Dreikaiserbund (Three Emperors' League), 163, 164

Eastern question: and the German Empire, 164; and Russia, 109–10, 112–13, 128–9, 164
economic change, 4–5, 184–5
economic depression: and the 1848 revolution in France, 65; in the German Empire, 160; Great Depression (1873–96), 12–13, 177, 179, 184
economic development, 13, 183–4; in the French Second Empire, 78–80; in Germany, 135, 144
economic liberalism, 12, 184; in the French Second Empire, 79–80
education: church schools, 22; and national identity, 179; in Russia, 107–8, 124–5
1815 settlement, 20, 21, 22, 42; and the German *Bund*, 137; and Napoleon III, 78, 82, 141, 145; and Russia, 103–4
emigration from Europe, 4, 15, 176
Ems telegram, 86, 150
Engels, Frederick, 3
Enlightenment, 18, 20
equality, concept of, 6, 10, 63
Eugénie, empress of France, 77, 83
European Union (EU), compared with the German Empire, 157

Ferry, Jules, 166
Fichte, Johann, *Address to the German nation*, 7
First World War, 1
Fourier, Charles, 7
France, 62–98; army, 8, 82–3, 86–7, 151; and the balance of power in 1871, 145; 'bloody week' (1871), 63; Bourbons and Orléanists, 64, 92–3; conscription in, 9; *coup d'état* of December 1851, 71, 72–5; and the Crimean War (1855–57), 41, 42, 82–3; and the elections of 1848, 68–9; and the German Empire, 64, 89, 163, 165, 166; Government of National Defence, 89, 151–2; and the Greek War of Independence, 20; and the Hohenzollern candidate to the throne of Spain, 150; industry in, 17; and Italy, 8, 25, 36, 43–4, 54, 55, 56–7, 83, 84–5, 190; July Revolution (1830), 11, 15, 18–19, 22–3, 28, 65; and the 'June Days' (1848), 63, 66–8, 73, 75, 90, 96; male literacy in, 15; Napoleonic legend in, 69, 71; and the Napoleonic wars, 9, 14; National Guard, 64, 67–8, 72, 89; Paris Commune, 63; revolution of 1848 (collapse of the July Monarchy), 11, 15, 62–3, 64–6, 67, 69, 74; Second Empire, 9, 12, 63, 74–88, 96; Second Republic, 63, 65–74, 75; Siege of Paris (1870–71), 73, 89, 151–2; socialism in, 13; Third Republic, 63, 89–95, 96–7, 151; and the Treaty of Frankfurt (1871), 92, 152; and the 'Walloon amendment' (1875), 93–4; war with Austria (1859), 76, 81–2, 83–4, 143; *see also* French Revolution; Napoleon I; Napoleon III; Paris
Franco-Prussian war (1870–71), 12, 63, 85–7, 89–90, 127, 150–3
Frankfurt, Treaty of (1871), 92, 152, 163
Franz Joseph, emperor of Austria, 44, 84
fraternity, concept of, 6–7, 10, 63
Frederick of Augustenberg, 146, 147
Frederick II, king of Prussia (the Great), 139
Frederick III, emperor of Germany (formerly crown prince), 166, 167
Frederick William IV, king of Prussia, 140, 141
free trade, 12, 17; treaties in Piedmont, 40; treaties in Second Empire France, 79–80
freemasons, in Italy, 28
French Revolution (1789), 1, 6, 15, 17; antireligious aspects of the, 20; memories of the, 9, 10–11, 96, 178; political consequences of the, 63

Gambetta, Léon, 89
Garibaldi, Giuseppe, 1, 34–5, 36, 37, 43, 45–6, 58; conquest of Sicily, 45–8, 51, 192–6; defeat at Aspromonte, 55–6; defeat at Mentana, 57; and the unification of Italy, 49, 51, 52, 53–4
Garibaldi biscuits, 58
Gastein, Treaty of (1865), 148
German Empire, 165–69, 170–1; and Britain, 136, 163, 165–6; Centre Party, 159, 162, 168; constitution, 155–7, 159; and the crises of 1885–87, 165–6; and the Dual Alliance (1879), 165; economy, 160; formation of the, 152–3; and France, 64, 89, 163, 165, 166; and the *Kulturkampf*, 158–61, 163; National Liberal Party, 158, 159, 161, 162; overseas colonies, 154, 162, 166, 167; Peace Laws, 161; *Reichstag*, 155, 156, 157, 158, 159, 160, 161–2, 170; Social Democratic Party (SPD) in, 13, 160, 162–3, 168, 178; social insurance policies, 9, 12, 162; and tariffs, 161, 165; and taxation, 160, 161; and the Triple Alliance, 165
German nationalism, 6–7, 20, 137–8, 140, 141, 142, 152, 155
Germany, 135–73; and the balance of power in 1871, 145; *Bund*, 25, 27, 137–8, 139, 140, 148, 149, 153, 170, 171; culture, 137; economic development in, 135, 144; forces working for and against unification, 140–5; Frankfurt Parliament, 137, 139–40; *Grossdeutschland* (greater Germany) concept, 138, 142, 145; and the Habsburg Empire, 22; *Kleindeutschland* (smaller Germany) concept, 139–40, 141, 148, 149, 152–3, 154; and Napoleon III of France, 85–6, 140–1; and the Napoleonic wars, 14; national identity, 137; North German Confederation, 149; and *Realpolitik*, 136; revolution of 1848, 11; and Russia, 127–8; Third Reich, 136, 179; trade barriers in, 17; and the Treaty of Frankfurt (1871), 92, 152, 163; unification of, 9, 12, 145–54, 171–3, 182, 184; urban growth in, 175; *Zollverein* (customs union), 22, 27, 40, 139, 140, 141, 144, 145, 149, 170, 172; *see also* German Empire; Prussia
Gioberti, Vincenzo, 7, 31
Gladstone, William, 166
Gogol, Nikolai, 116
Gorbachev, Mikhail, 130
Granovsky, Timofei, 115
Greece, 7, 182; War of Independence (1821–30), 19–20, 22, 109
Gregory XVI, Pope, 27, 31
guilds, 17
Guizot, François, 64

Habsburg Empire, *see* Austria
Haussmann, Baron, 79
Hegel, G. W. F., 115
Herzen, Alexander, 67–8, 106, 115, 116, 117, 119
Hitler, Adolf, 1, 136, 179
Holy Roman Empire, 137
Hugo, Victor, 18, 73, 75–6
Hungarian Revolution (1849), 112, 127, 140
Hungary, self-government for, 179, 182

industrial growth, 3, 5, 16–17, 18; and factory legislation, 9; in Prussia, 144, 170, 171; and the railways, 2, 12; and Russia, 127; and warfare, 8
Irish nationalism, 7
Italian nationalism, 31, 32, 36–7, 59, 140
Italy, 3, 24–61; abolition of feudalism in, 28, 29; and Austria, 22, 26, 27, 31–2, 33–4, 35, 36, 40, 42, 44, 51–2, 54, 56–7, 144; and the Austro-Prussian war

(1866), 148; and the balance of power in 1871, 145; 'brigands war', 54; censorship in, 31; constituent assemblies in, 52–3; customs union, 31–2; disunity of, 25; forces against unity in, 26–8; forces for unity in, 28; and France, 8, 25, 36, 43–4, 54, 55, 56–7, 83, 84–5, 190; and Germany, 137; languages in, 27; and the Napoleonic wars, 14; National Society, 42, 43, 51; neo-Guelph movement, 31, 33; revolt (1830) in, 11, 23, 60, 61; and the revolutions of 1848–49, 11, 32–7, 188–90; and the *Risorgimento*, 25, 26, 27, 29, 58–9; and the September Convention (1864), 56; society in, 27–8; states and regions in, 26–8; support for unification of, 35–6; system of government following unification of, 52–4; 'Third War of Italian Independence' (1859), 43–4; and the Triple Alliance, 165; unification of, 10, 12, 25, 37–52, 140, 141, 179, 182, 187–96; Young Italy, 29–30, 34, 59–60; *see also* Naples; papacy; Papal States; Piedmont-Sardinia; Sicily; Tuscany; Venice

Jesuits (Society of Jesus), 22, 158
Jews, and anti-Semitism, 179

Khomyakov, Alexei, 115
Khrushchev, Nikita, 130
Kireyevsky, Ivan, 115
Königgrätz, battle of (1866), 148–9, 151

laissez-faire, 175
Land and Liberty (Russian revolutionary group), 118–19, 129
landowners, 10, 15–16; and economic depression, 176, 177; and industrial society, 180; in Italy, 27; in Russia, 102, 121, 122, 123, 133
League of the Three Emperors, 128
Lenin, V. I., 1, 117, 120
Leopold of Hohenzollern, 150
liberalism, 183–4; and Bismarck, 146, 158, 160, 161, 184; economic, 12, 79–80, 184; and nationalism, 154; replaced by collectivist policies, 12–13
liberty, 10, 63; concept of, 6
life expectancy, change in, 15
literacy: in the 1820s, 15; in Russia, 125
Lombardy-Venetia, 26, 32, 33, 36, 42
'long nineteenth century', 7
Loris-Melikov, General, 130
Louis Napoleon, *see* Napoleon III, emperor of France
Louis-Philippe, king of the French, 28, 64–5
Luxembourg crisis (1867), 85–6, 150

MacMahon, General Patrice, 92, 94
Malthus, Thomas, 4
Manin, Danieli, 35, 42
Manzoni, Alessandro, *The betrothed*, 27
Marx, Karl, 1, 3–4, 6, 7, 72; *The civil war in France*, 90, 98; *The communist manifesto*, 3, 5, 185; *The eighteenth Brumaire of Louis Napoleon*, 75
Maximilian, emperor of Mexico, 84
Mazzini, Giuseppe, 1, 29–31, 34, 35, 36, 40–1, 42, 51, 52, 58, 179, 183; address to the Constituent Assembly in Rome, 189–90; and Aspromonte, 56; and Rome, 57; statement of principles (1831), 59–60; and the unification of Italy, 54, 55
Metternich, Prince Klemens von, 11, 22, 27, 33, 61, 139
Mexico, and Napoleon III, 76, 84, 88
middle class (bourgeoisie), 1, 6; in France, 65; in Germany, 141, 155; and nationalism, 7; and political reforms, 11; in Prussia, 143; in Russia, 102, 131; and socialism, 178; in towns, 175, 176
migration of people, 4, 15, 176, 184–5
military change, 7–9; army reforms, 8–9, 86, 123–4, 142, 143
Milyutin, Dmitri, 123
Moltke, Helmut von, 149, 152
Münchengrätz Agreement (1833), 110
Mussolini, Benito, 88

Naples, 27; 1820 revolution in, 28; Garibaldi's conquest of, 47, 49; and the revolutions of 1848–49, 32; and the unification of Italy, 52–3
Napoleon I, emperor of France, 1, 6, 9, 12, 14, 18, 63, 75, 96; 1815 settlement following the defeat of, 20, 78, 82; and Germany, 137; invasion of Russia, 101, 103, 104; and Italy, 25, 28; and Napoleon III's exercise of power, 77, 78
Napoleon III, emperor of France, 1, 9, 12, 63, 96; abdication, 76; and the battle of Sedan, 86–7; Bordeaux speech, 73; character, 70–1; and the *coup d'état* of December 1851, 63, 71, 72–5; election manifesto (1848), 69–70; in exile, 145; foreign policy, 81–6, 88, 112; and the French economy, 78–80, 88; and Germany, 140–1, 145; and Italy, 34, 37, 42–3, 44, 45, 51–2, 55, 56, 57, 83, 84–5, 141, 190–1; and the 'liberal empire', 80–1; marriage, 77; and nationalism, 184; as the 'people's emperor', 77; as president of the Second Republic, 68–73; and Prussia, 150, 151; Victor Hugo on, 75–6
Napoleonic wars, 9, 14

nation states, 3, 13; creation of, 9, 153–4, 182; formation of Germany, 153–4
nationalism, 6–7, 18–20, 23, 154, 178–9, 183, 184, 185; and conservatism, 180; German, 6–7, 20, 137–8, 140, 141, 142, 152, 155; Italian, 31, 32, 36–7, 59, 140; and Napoleon III of France, 78, 88; Slav, 102, 115, 118, 128, 131, 164
neo-Guelph movement, 31, 33
Nicholas I, tsar of Russia, 22, 82, 106–14, 120, 180; assessing the rule of, 113–14; and censorship, 107–8, 112, 116; character, 106–7; death of, 113; and the Decembrist Revolt (1825), 104, 105, 106, 107, 113, 114; foreign policy, 109–10, 112–13; and oppositional thought, 107–8, 113, 114–16; and the revolutions of 1848–49, 111–12; and the 'seven dismal years' (1848–55), 116, 117
Nicholas II, tsar of Russia, 125
nihilism, 117
nobility: as landowners, 10; Prussian *Junkers*, 143, 170; in Russia, 105

Ollivier, Emile, 80
Olmütz Convention (1850), 140
Orsini, Felice, 42–3, 83
Orthodox Christianity, 10, 20; in Greece, 19–20; in Russia, 100, 102, 115, 128
Ottoman Empire, 11, 18, 179; Balkan breakaway from the, 182; and the Crimean War, 82; and Germany, 164; and the Greek War of Independence (1821–30), 19–20, 22; and Russia, 109–10, 110–11, 112–13, 124, 128–9; and the Russo-Turkish War (1877–78), 127, 128, 164; and the Straits Convention, 110–11
Owen, Robert, 7

papacy: and Italian unification, 54, 56, 57, 60, 84–5, 189; in Italy, 10, 25, 26–7, 28, 31, 37, 38, 44; and *The syllabus of errors* (1864), 10; *see also* Pius IX, Pope
Papal Allocution, 33, 189
Papal States, 26–7, 31, 33, 34, 36, 44; and Napoleon III of France, 85; Piedmontese invasion of the, 48–9, 52
Paris: Commune (1871), 1, 89, 90–2, 96, 97–8, 178; redevelopment of in the Second Empire, 79–80; Siege of (1870–71), 73, 89, 151–2
Paul I, tsar of Russia, 103
peasants, 14–15; in Italy, 27–8; in Russia, 102, 103, 110, 122, 123, 133
People's Will (Russian revolutionary group), 119, 120, 129
Peter the Great, tsar of Russia, 11, 100, 115, 130
Petrashevsky, Mikhail, 112

Piedmont-Sardinia: 1821 revolutions in, 26; Charles Albert's accession to the throne of, 29, 189; constitution (*Statuto*), 37, 38, 53; and the Crimean War (1855–57), 41–2; and Garibaldi's conquest of Sicily, 45–8; invasion of the Papal States, 48–9; and Mazzini's attempted insurrection, 30; peace and reform in (1849–55), 38–41; plots, wars and revolts (1858–59), 42–5; and the unification of Italy, 10, 47–54, 49; wars with Austria, 32, 33–4

Pius IX, Pope, 10, 31, 33, 34, 36, 38, 57; and Catholicism in Germany, 158, 160

plebiscites: and the Second Empire in France, 45, 73, 74, 77, 81, 88, 184; and the unification of Italy, 53

Poland: nationalism in, 7, 84; revolt in (1830), 11, 23, 107, 109, 110, 132, 182, 183

political change, 6–7, 10–11
population growth in Europe, 4
populism, 118
poverty, 4, 14
Prague, Treaty of (1866), 149
presidency, in France, 68–9, 72, 94, 95
Protestantism, 10, 20, 22; in Germany, 142, 158

Prussia: army reform in, 8, 86, 142, 143; Austria and German unification, 139, 140, 141, 142; Austro-Prussian war (1866), 12, 147–50, 151, 152; conscription in, 9; constitution, 159; and the Crimean War, 83; Erfurt Union, 140; Franco-Prussian war (1870–71), 12, 63, 85–7, 89–90, 127, 150–3; and the German *Bund*, 137; and the German Empire, 157, 158, 170; and German unification, 9, 12, 136, 142; government and *Landtag*, 145–6; industrial growth in, 144, 170; *Junkers*, 143, 170; and the *Kleindeutschland* (smaller Germany) concept, 139–40, 141, 148; and Nicholas I of Russia, 106; political crisis in (1862), 142–3, 145; and Russia, 110; sovereign rule in, 3; trade barriers in, 17; war with Denmark (1864), 146–7; and the *Zollverein* (customs union), 22, 139, 140, 141, 145, 149, 172; *see also* Bismarck, Otto von; Germany

public-health reforms, 175–6, 180
Pushkin, Alexander, 18, 100, 105

railways, 18, 183; and economic change, 4–5; European railway system, 1, 2; in France, 79; and industrial growth, 12; in Russia, 111, 124, 126–7; and the transport of armies, 8, 43

Rattazzi, Urbano, 38, 42

Realpolitik, 136
reform, 174, 180–1
Reutern, Count Mikhail, 124
revolutions of 1848–49, 1, 4, 9, 11; in France, 11, 15, 62–3, 64–6, 67, 69, 74; and German unification, 137–8; in Italy, 11, 32–7, 188–90; and Russia, 111–12

rifles, breechloading, 8, 57, 149, 151
roads, 17
romanticism, 18–19, 105, 117
Rome: and the revolutions of 1848–49, 34–5, 35–6, 36–7; and the unification of Italy, 56, 57

Roon, General Albrecht von, 143
Rossi, Count Pellegrino, 34
rural areas, 3, 14–15, 176; in Italy, 27–8
Russia, 99–134, 174; attempted revolt in (1825), 22; autocracy in, 102–3, 108, 111, 112, 113–14; and the balance of power in 1871, 145; calendar, 100; censorship in, 107–8, 112, 116, 125–6, 130; change in (between 1825 and 1881), 131–2; and the Crimean War (1855–57), 41, 42, 81, 82, 83, 111, 112–13, 120–1, 123, 124, 126, 127, 132; Decembrist Revolt (1825), 104–5, 106, 107, 113, 114, 115; differences from the rest of Europe, 99–100; and the Eastern question, 109–10, 112–13, 128–9, 164; education in, 107–8, 124–5; European and Asian identities of, 99–100; and the German Empire, 165; and the Greek War of Independence, 20; judicial reforms in, 124; landowners in, 102, 121, 122, 123, 133; large size and population of, 101–2; middle class in, 102, 131; and modernisation, 101, 104, 123, 126–7, 130; multi-ethnic nature of, 102; nationality in, 108, 114; oppositional thought in, 114–20, 132; Orthodox Christianity in, 100, 102, 115, 128; peasants in, 102, 103, 110, 122, 133; pogroms against Jews in, 179; and Poland, 182; Pugachev Rebellion (1773–75), 122–3; railways in, 111, 124, 126–7; representative government in, 124; revolution (1917), 1, 182, 184; Russification policy of Alexander III, 180; St Petersburg, 101, 104; secret societies in, 104, 105; serfdom and the emancipation of the serfs in, 10, 14, 102, 105, 110, 117, 121–3, 132–4; Slavophiles and pan-Slavs in, 102, 115–16, 118, 128, 131, 164; sovereign rule in, 3; Third Section in, 108, 110, 114, 126, 130; Westerners in, 115–16, 118, 131–3; *see also* Alexander II; Nicholas I

Russo-Turkish War (1877–78), 127, 128

Saint-Simon, Comte de, 77–8
San Stefano, Treaty of (1878), 128, 164
Schleswig-Holstein question, 146–7, 148
secret societies: in Italy, 28, 29; in Russia, 104, 105
Sedan, battle of (1870), 86–7, 89, 151
senate, in France, 94, 95
serfdom in Russia, 14, 102, 105, 110; emancipation of the serfs, 10, 117, 121–3, 132–4

Shelley, Percy Bysshe, 18
'short nineteenth century', 1–4, 11–13, 185
Shuvalov, Count Peter, 126
Sicily: revolt and Garibaldi's invasion of (1860), 45–8, 51, 193–6; revolution of 1848 in, 32, 188
Slav nationalism, 102, 115, 118, 131, 164; pan-Slavs, 128
Smith, Adam, *The wealth of nations*, 17
social change, 5–6
social class, 5–6, 177–8; landowning class, 10, 15–16; and welfare reforms, 13; *see also* middle class (bourgeoisie); nobility; working classes
social control, attempts by the ruling class at, 16
social welfarism, 13; National Workshops in France, 66
socialism, 7, 13, 176, 177–8; in the German Empire, 13, 160, 160–1; and Russian oppositional thought, 117–18; and state governments, 9
sovereign rulers, 3
Spain, Hohenzollern candidature for the throne of, 86, 150
state governments, 9–10
state peasants, in Russia, 102, 110, 133
the Straits, and the Ottoman Empire, 109, 110–11
strikes, 13; right to strike in France, 80
Suez Canal, 79
The syllabus of errors (1864), 10
syndicalism, 178

tariffs, 12, 13, 54, 124, 161
taxation: in the German Empire, 160, 161; in Prussia, 146; in Russia, 124
technological innovations, 4, 13, 176–7, 185; military, 8, 149
terrorism, in Russia, 119
Thiers, Adolphe, 1, 73, 89, 90, 92, 93, 94, 96
Three Emperors' League (*Dreikaiserbund*), 163, 164
Tolstoy, Count Dmitri (minister of education), 125, 130
Tolstoy, Count Leo (novelist), 100, 129, 131
towns: growth of, 3, 15, 174–5; in Italy, 28; move from countryside to, 3, 5;

social divisions and living conditions in, 175–6, 185
trade: and customs barriers, 17; and the German *Zollverein* (customs union), 139, 141; obstacles to, 17; and tariffs, 12, 13, 54, 124, 161; *see also* free trade
trade unions, 178
transport, 17–18
Turgenev, Ivan, 116; *Fathers and sons*, 117
Turkey, *see* Ottoman Empire
Tuscany: Piedmont's absorption of, 45, 52, 53; and the revolutions of 1848–49, 33, 34

unemployment, and the 'Great Depression' (1873–96), 13, 177
universal male suffrage, 3; in France, 68, 72, 73, 75, 88, 96; in Germany, 155, 156, 170
universities, in Russia, 107–8, 125
Unkiar-Skelessi, Treaty of (1833), 109, 110

urban growth, 3, 15, 174–6
Utopian socialists, 7
Uvarov, Sergei, 108

Vatican City, 57
Venice (Venetia): and the revolutions of 1848–49, 35; and the unification of Italy, 54, 56–7
Verdi, Giuseppe, 31
Victor Emmanuel II, king of Piedmont (later Italy), 34, 38, 40–1, 41–2, 43, 44–5, 192; and Garibaldi, 55, 56, 57; and the unification of Italy, 49, 51, 53, 54
Victoria, Queen, on Nicholas I of Russia, 106–7
Villafranca, Treaty of (1859), 44, 190–1
voting: in French elections, 78, 80; rights, 3, 6, 72; *see also* plebiscites; universal male suffrage

wars, 1, 7–9; and Napoleon III of France, 12, 76, 81–4, 85–7; revolutions and wars (1848–71), 11–12; *see also individual wars*
William I, king of Prussia (later emperor of Germany), 141, 155; assassination attempts on, 160; and the Austro-Prussian war (1866), 148, 149; death of, 163, 167; and the Ems telegram, 150; and the political crisis (1862), 142–3; proclaimed German emperor, 152
William II, emperor of Germany, 167–9
Windhorst, Ludwig, 159
women: and literacy, 15, 125; rights of, 3, 177
working classes, 5; and the absence of revolution, 185; Parisian workers, 16, 63, 79, 90; and socialism, 13, 177–8; in towns, 175–6

Young Europe, 31
Young Italy, 29–30, 34, 59–60
Young Russia, 117

STRATTON
UPPER SCHOOL
LIBRARY